Teaching Mathematics
Foundations to Middle Years

Dianne Siemon

Kim Beswick

Kathy Brady

Julie Clark

Rhonda Faragher

Elizabeth Warren

OXFORD
UNIVERSITY PRESS
AUSTRALIA & NEW ZEALAND

Oxford University Press is a department of the University of Oxford.

It furthers the University's objective of excellence in research, scholarship, and education by publishing worldwide. Oxford is a registered trademark of Oxford University Press in the UK and in certain other countries.

Published in Australia by
Oxford University Press
253 Normanby Road, South Melbourne, Victoria 3205, Australia

© Dianne Siemon, Kim Beswick, Kathy Brady, Julie Clark, Rhonda Farragher and Elizabeth Warren 2011

The moral rights of the authors have been asserted
First published 2011

All rights reserved. No part of this publication may be reproduced, stored in a retrieval system, or transmitted, in any form or by any means, without the prior permission in writing of Oxford University Press, or as expressly permitted by law, by licence, or under terms agreed with the appropriate reprographics rights organisation. Enquiries concerning reproduction outside the scope of the above should be sent to the Rights Department, Oxford University Press, at the address above.

You must not circulate this work in any other form and you must impose this same condition on any acquirer.

National Library of Australia Cataloguing-in-Publication data

Dianne Siemon ... [et al.]
Teaching mathematics: Foundations to middle years.

ISBN 9780195568455 (pbk.)

1. Includes bibliographical references and index. 2. Mathematics–Study and teaching (Primary)
3. Mathematics–Study and teaching (Secondary)
I. Siemon, Dianne E. (Dianne Elizabeth), 1948–

372.7044

Reproduction and communication for educational purposes
The Australian *Copyright Act 1968* (the Act) allows a maximum of one chapter or 10% of the pages of this work, whichever is the greater, to be reproduced and/or communicated by any educational institution for its educational purposes provided that the educational institution (or the body that administers it) has given a remuneration notice to Copyright Agency Limited (CAL) under the Act.

For details of the CAL licence for educational institutions contact:

Copyright Agency Limited
Level 15, 233 Castlereagh Street
Sydney NSW 2000
Telephone: (02) 9394 7600
Facsimile: (02) 9394 7601
Email: info@copyright.com.au

Edited by Elaine Cochrane
Text design by Sarah Hazell
Typeset by Norma van Rees
Proofread by Carolyn Pike
Indexed by Russell Brooks
Printed by Sheck Wah Tong Printing Press Ltd

Links to third party websites are provided by Oxford in good faith and for information only. Oxford disclaims any responsibility for the materials contained in any third party website referenced in this work.

Brief Contents

List of Figures	xi
List of Tables	xvi
Dedication	xviii
Acknowledgments	xix
About the Authors	xx
Preface	xxii
Guided Tour	xxv

Part one: 2
Setting the Scene

1	Understanding School Mathematics	4
2	Learning Mathematics	24
3	Teaching Mathematics	46

Part two: 66
Understanding the Challenges and Opportunities

4	Thinking Mathematically	68
5	Communication: Making Connections in Mathematics	83
6	Representations: Materials, Language, and Recording	98
7	Assessing and Reporting	122
8	Diversity	142

Part three: 166
Exploring the Big Ideas in Mathematics

9	Numeracy in the Curriculum	168
10	Developing a Sense of Number	186
11	A Sense of Measurement and Geometry	210
12	Statistics and Probability	231

Part four: Laying the Basis for F-4 Mathematics — 246

13 Pattern and Structure — 248
14 Developing Early Number Ideas and Strategies — 265
15 Introducing Place Value — 290
16 Developing Additive Thinking in F–4 — 320
17 Developing Multiplicative Thinking in the Early Years — 350
18 Introducing Fractions and Decimal Fractions — 394
19 Developing Measurement Concepts and Strategies — 438
20 Developing Geometric Thinking and Concepts — 454
21 Early Chance and Data — 468

Part five: Extending Mathematics to the Middle Years — 490

22 Extending Number: Fractions, Decimals, and Reals — 492
23 Working with Addition, Subtraction, and Additive Thinking — 517
24 Working with Multiplication, Division, and Proportional Reasoning — 548
25 Algebraic Thinking, Pattern, and Order — 586
26 Consolidating Measurement Concepts — 604
27 Shape and Space: Geometric Thinking and Concepts in Years 5–9 — 627
28 Statistics and Probability in the Middle Years — 646
29 Becoming a Professional Teacher of Mathematics — 664

Glossary — 679
Bibliography — 689
Index — 716

Contents

List of Figures	xi
List of Tables	xvi
Dedication	xviii
Acknowledgments	xix
About the Authors	xx
Preface	xxii
Guided Tour	xxv

Part one: Setting the Scene — 2

1 Understanding School Mathematics — 4

Introduction	5
What is mathematics?	6
Goals of school mathematics	9
Affordances and constraints	12
Conclusion	20

2 Learning Mathematics — 24

What does it mean to learn mathematics?	26
Learning and understanding mathematics	38
Developing your own theory of mathematics learning	43

3 Teaching Mathematics — 46

What does it mean to teach mathematics?	48
Connections between beliefs	49
How can we know we are teaching?	50
Knowledge for teaching mathematics	54
Effective mathematics teaching	57

Part two: Understanding the Challenges and Opportunities — 66

4 Thinking Mathematically — 68

A chance to think in a different way	69
Making a start with mathematical thinking	69
Mathematical thinking in the curriculum	71
General processes for mathematical thinking tasks	72
Helping learners to think mathematically	78
Conclusion	81

5 Communication: Making Connections in Mathematics — 83

- Introduction — 84
- The language of mathematics — 84
- Language and culture — 86
- Communicating in the mathematics classroom — 89
- Conclusion — 96

6 Representations: Materials, Language, and Recording — 98

- How representations help us understand concepts — 99
- Building abstract thinking — 102
- Role of materials and models — 106
- Choosing materials and models — 107
- The role of mathematical language and recording — 111
- Traditional representations — 113
- Multi-representational learning environments — 117
- Conclusion — 119

7 Assessing and Reporting — 122

- Assessment is about testing, right? — 123
- Assessment *of* learning — 126
- Assessment *for* learning — 128
- Reporting — 138
- Conclusion — 139

8 Diversity — 142

- Who are diverse learners? — 143
- Language of diversity — 143
- Diversifying the curriculum — 145
- Supporting diverse learners — 153
- Working with teacher assistants — 163
- Conclusion — 163

Part three: — 166
Exploring the Big Ideas in Mathematics

9 Numeracy in the Curriculum — 168

- What is numeracy? — 169
- Numeracy across the curriculum — 176
- Critical numeracy — 179
- Conclusion — 183

10 Developing a Sense of Number — 186
- Understanding number sense — 182
- Number sense in practice — 188
- Developing a sense of number — 197
- Conclusion — 207

11 A Sense of Measurement and Geometry — 210
- Linking measurement and geometry — 211
- What is measurement? — 212
- Developing measurement sense — 214
- Geometry — 221
- Spatial sense — 223
- Conclusion — 228

12 Statistics and Probability — 231
- Introduction — 232
- Statistical literacy — 232
- What is statistics? — 234
- What is probability? — 241
- Conclusion — 244

Part four: — 246
Laying the Basis for F–4 Mathematics

13 Pattern and Structure — 248
- What is pattern and structure? — 249
- Why is pattern and structure important? — 251
- Early algebraic thinking — 256
- Functional thinking — 256
- Conclusion — 262

14 Developing Early Number Ideas and Strategies — 265
- The origins of number — 266
- Research on early number learning — 272
- Playing with number — 275
- The numbers 0 to 10 — 279
- A sense of numbers beyond 10 — 286
- Scaffolding solution strategies — 287
- Conclusion — 288

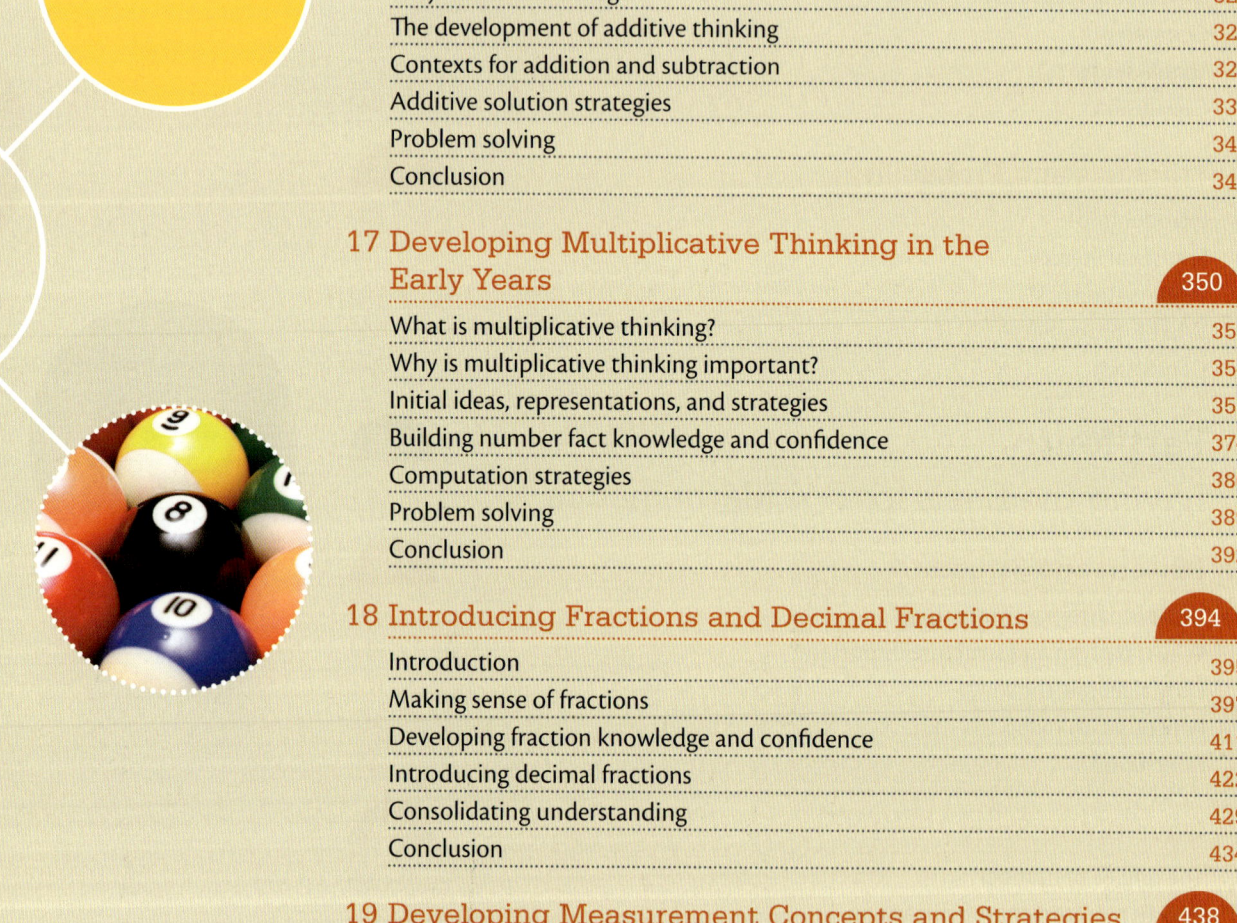

15 Introducing Place Value — 290

- Prerequisite ideas and strategies — 291
- Understanding tens and ones — 296
- Introducing three-digit numeration — 304
- Developing four-digit numeration — 307
- Extending to millions and beyond — 310
- Conclusion — 317

16 Developing Additive Thinking in F–4 — 320

- Why additive thinking? — 321
- The development of additive thinking — 324
- Contexts for addition and subtraction — 324
- Additive solution strategies — 330
- Problem solving — 345
- Conclusion — 347

17 Developing Multiplicative Thinking in the Early Years — 350

- What is multiplicative thinking? — 351
- Why is multiplicative thinking important? — 354
- Initial ideas, representations, and strategies — 355
- Building number fact knowledge and confidence — 374
- Computation strategies — 380
- Problem solving — 389
- Conclusion — 392

18 Introducing Fractions and Decimal Fractions — 394

- Introduction — 395
- Making sense of fractions — 397
- Developing fraction knowledge and confidence — 411
- Introducing decimal fractions — 422
- Consolidating understanding — 429
- Conclusion — 434

19 Developing Measurement Concepts and Strategies — 438

- Why is teaching measurement important? — 439
- Measurement concepts in the curriculum — 439
- Measurement learning sequence — 441
- Approaches to developing an understanding of length — 444
- Approaches to developing an understanding of time — 449
- Conclusion — 452

20 Developing Geometric Thinking and Concepts — 454
Classifying spatial objects — 455
Relationships between spatial objects — 461
Developing dynamic imagery — 464
Location — 465
Conclusion — 466

21 Early Chance and Data — 468
Grappling with uncertainty — 469
The development of students' thinking about probability — 473
Representing data — 476
Understanding distributions — 480

Part five: — 490
Extending Mathematics to the Middle Years

22 Extending Number: Fractions, Decimals, and Reals — 492
Building the number line — 493
Whole numbers — 494
Scientific notation — 502
The rationals — 504
The reals — 512
Conclusion — 515

23 Working with Addition, Subtraction, and Additive Thinking — 517
Ways of working with addition and subtraction — 518
Algorithms — 520
Fractions — 524
Decimals — 536
Integers — 540

24 Working with Multiplication, Division, and Proportional Reasoning — 548
Introduction — 549
Meanings for multiplication and division — 550
Working with an extended range of numbers — 557
What is proportional reasoning? — 576
Planning for diversity — 580
Conclusion — 582

Contents

25 Algebraic Thinking, Pattern, and Order — 586
- What is algebraic thinking? — 587
- Why is algebra important? — 588
- Arithmetic, algebraic thinking, and problem structure — 588
- Letters, unknowns, and variables — 589
- Functional thinking — 592
- Equivalence and equations — 598
- Model approach—using the length model — 599
- Conclusion — 602

26 Consolidating Measurement Concepts — 604
- Extending measurement concepts — 605
- Area — 605
- Developing area formulae — 610
- Volume and capacity — 617
- Mass — 622
- Money — 623
- Conclusion — 624

27 Shape and Space: Geometric Thinking and Concepts in Years 5–9 — 627
- Working with spatial objects — 628
- Transformational geometry — 632
- Non-Euclidean geometry — 639
- Location — 641
- Learning geometry in the middle years — 643
- Conclusion — 644

28 Statistics and Probability in the Middle Years — 646
- Data investigation — 647
- Data representations — 650
- Data measures — 654
- Variation — 655
- Describing chance events — 655
- Conclusion — 662

29 Becoming a Professional Teacher of Mathematics — 664
- Looking forward — 665
- Standards for mathematics teaching — 667
- Final words of advice — 676

Glossary — 679
Bibliography — 689
Index — 716

List of Figures

Figure 1.1:	Nick's response to a division problem	12
Figure 1.2:	Teaching response to decimal misconception	17
Figure 2.1:	Linking symbolic and iconic modes	31
Figure 2.2:	Work samples by Grade 1 and 2 children	36
Figure 2.3:	An unsuccessful attempt at solving $3 \div 0.5$ using flawed instrumental understanding	39
Figure 2.4:	A successful attempt at solving $3 \div 0.5$ illustrating relational understanding	39
Figure 3.1:	Clown in circus tent	51
Figure 3.2:	Self-portrait	51
Figure 3.4:	Examples of right-angled triangles	60
Figure 5.1:	Example page from a Primary Student Mathematics Dictionary	85
Figure 6.1:	Teaching and learning trajectory for building to abstraction	103
Figure 6.2:	Continuum for developing an understanding of Euler's formula, $V - E + F = 2$	105
Figure 6.3:	Sequence of representations used to explore the base 10 system	107
Figure 6.4:	Difficulties students experience with Cuisenaire rods and counting frames	108
Figure 6.5:	Students' different ways of describing rectangles	111
Figure 6.6:	Finding 63 on the three types of number lines	113
Figure 7.1:	An excerpt from a NAPLAN report to parents	127
Figure 7.2:	Feedback on fractions: Year 7 student workbook	129
Figure 7.3:	Year 6 student workbook	130
Figure 7.4:	What might this be a graph of?	131
Figure 9.1:	Three key factors in being numerate	174
Figure 9.2:	Daily temperature, showing a stable weather pattern	181
Figure 9.3:	Daily temperature, showing a varied weather pattern	181
Figure 10.1:	CD sales task and response	190
Figure 10.2:	Different interpretations of fraction addition	197
Figure 10.3:	Representations for multiplication	201
Figure 10.4:	Interpreting fraction diagrams: 'for each' idea	202
Figure 10.5:	Matchstick problem	205
Figure 11.1:	Deciding on the origin	216
Figure 11.2:	Partitioning the units	216
Figure 11.3:	Tiling using iteration of units without gaps or overlaps	216
Figure 13.1:	An example of a repeating pattern	252
Figure 13.2:	Repeating patterns are representations of repeated addition	254
Figure 13.3:	Young students engaging with functions	257
Figure 13.4:	Contexts for understanding the patterns for 10	260
Figure 14.1:	Greek system of numeration	268
Figure 14.2:	Early Chinese numeration system	269
Figure 14.3:	Later Chinese numeration system	269
Figure 14.4:	Babylonian numeration system	270

List of Figures

Figure 14.5:	Mayan numeration system	270
Figure 14.6:	Subitising card sets	281
Figure 14.7:	Establishing meaning for the number names and symbols to 10	282
Figure 14.8:	Number cards	283
Figure 14.9:	Coordinating the count	285
Figure 14.10:	Representations to support a sense of numbers beyond ten	287
Figure 15.1:	Richard's solution	290
Figure 15.2:	Developing a sense of numbers beyond ten	293
Figure 15.3:	Masked 0–99 number chart	296
Figure 15.4:	Make and count tens	297
Figure 15.5:	Number slides	300
Figure 15.6:	Line models	300
Figure 15.7:	Counting backwards to support subtraction	303
Figure 15.8:	Place-value game board	303
Figure 15.9:	Non-standard number chart	304
Figure 15.10:	An example of a quipu	306
Figure 15.11:	Making a four-digit number expander	309
Figure 15.12:	Place-value charts for five-digit numbers and beyond	311
Figure 15.13:	'Odometer' representation of numeration	313
Figure 16.1:	Two solutions to the frog problem	322
Figure 16.2:	Using data to support addition and subtraction	322
Figure 16.3:	The importance of part–part–whole and place-value knowledge	323
Figure 16.4:	Modelling addition situations	326
Figure 16.5:	Modelling subtraction situations	328
Figure 16.6:	Number walks	331
Figure 16.7:	Modelling counting on	332
Figure 16.8:	Scaffolding the make to 10 strategy	336
Figure 16.9:	Strategies for two-digit addition (e.g. 43 + 28)	339
Figure 16.10:	Strategies for two-digit subtraction (e.g. 83 – 47)	339
Figure 16.11:	Multiple addend format	340
Figure 16.12:	Using a number expander to support four-digit subtraction	343
Figure 16.13:	Counting unit fractions	344
Figure 16.14:	Adding and subtracting tenths	345
Figure 17.1:	Two solutions to the muffin recipe problem	352
Figure 17.2:	A composite of composite units	354
Figure 17.3:	Young children's solutions to the Baa-Baa Black Sheep problem	356
Figure 17.4:	Pathways to multiplicative thinking F–4	357
Figure 17.5:	Sharing 16 equally	359
Figure 17.6:	A composite of composite units for the toy car problem	359
Figure 17.7:	Tree diagram representation for book problem	360
Figure 17.8:	Folded paper model	361
Figure 17.9:	Partition division	362
Figure 17.10:	Equal groups representation of Sam's problem	363
Figure 17.11:	Quotition division	366
Figure 17.12:	Count-all-groups solution to 128 divided by 6	367
Figure 17.13:	Arrays and regions	368

List of Figures

Figure 17.14:	Arrays and regions (equal groups)	369
Figure 17.15:	Arrays and regions (times as many)	369
Figure 17.16:	Tree diagram representation for T-shirt problem	372
Figure 17.17:	Area representation for multiplication	372
Figure 17.18:	The language of measurement	373
Figure 17.19:	Demonstrating the commutative property	374
Figure 17.20:	Using Cuisenaire rods to explore array-based strategies	379
Figure 17.21:	Number chart	380
Figure 17.22:	Informal 'jottings' for multiplication	380
Figure 17.23:	Initial forms of recording for multiplication	381
Figure 17.24:	Initial forms of recording for division	381
Figure 17.25:	Bella's 'talking head' response to two problems	382
Figure 17.26:	Using base ten blocks to model two-digit by one-digit multiplication	384
Figure 17.27:	Language and recording for two-digit by one-digit multiplication	384
Figure 17.28:	Modelling partition and quotition division	386
Figure 17.29:	Alternative form of recording	387
Figure 17.30:	Playing with zeros	391
Figure 18.1:	Response to CD sales task (MYNRP)	396
Figure 18.2:	Tree problem	398
Figure 18.3:	Multiple interpretations	399
Figure 18.4:	Partitioning geometric shapes	400
Figure 18.5:	Different-looking halves	401
Figure 18.6:	Two responses to the 'locating half' task	401
Figure 18.7:	Stories for 4.6 + 5.3 = 9.9	402
Figure 18.8:	Four responses to a discrete fraction task	403
Figure 18.9:	Unequal area problem	403
Figure 18.10:	Fraction as measure	408
Figure 18.11:	Best buys	410
Figure 18.12:	Fraction posters	412
Figure 18.13:	Halving and halving again using paper models	415
Figure 18.14:	A poster for a fraction in the halving family	416
Figure 18.15:	Kieran's strategy for cutting the muesli slice	417
Figure 18.16:	The thirding strategy	418
Figure 18.17:	The fifthing strategy	419
Figure 18.18:	Making sense of fraction symbols	421
Figure 18.19:	Models for representing and naming tenths	424
Figure 18.20:	Modelling ones and tenths on a place-value chart	425
Figure 18.21:	Empty number charts for ones and tenths	425
Figure 18.22:	Number expanders	425
Figure 18.23:	Models for representing and naming hundredths	426
Figure 18.24:	Relating hundredths to percentages	427
Figure 18.25:	Closer to …	430
Figure 18.26:	Fraction cards	431
Figure 18.27:	Rope activity for fractions and decimals	431
Figure 18.28:	Using partitioning to rename fractions	432

Figure	Description	Page
Figure 18.29:	'Make a whole' game	433
Figure 21.1:	Spinners designed to make blue the least likely and most likely outcome	473
Figure 21.2:	Animals grouped in categories: Year 1	477
Figure 21.3:	Data cards arranged to explore bus travel and pet numbers	478
Figure 21.4:	Using a 3 × 2 table to organise a collection	479
Figure 21.5:	Student-generated data representation showing numbers of students and suburbs	481
Figure 21.6:	Student generated data representation showing the numbers of students at various post codes	482
Figure 21.7:	Student generated data representation showing numbers of students and their post codes	482
Figure 21.8:	Student generated data representation showing the post codes of students' addresses	483
Figure 21.9:	Grade 3 student's graph of a button collection	483
Figure 21.10:	Graph of the heights of Year 5/6 girls and boys	485
Figure 21.11:	Graph of a collection of 50 cent coins by mint date	486
Figure 21.12:	Graph of 50 cent coins minted by year	486
Figure 22.1:	Representation of a number	500
Figure 22.2:	Types of numbers	514
Figure 23.1:	An attempt to use the standard algorithm to calculate 17.72 − 16.9	521
Figure 23.2:	A successful response	521
Figure 23.3:	A number line representation of ¾ + ½	527
Figure 23.4:	Using rectangular arrays	528
Figure 23.5:	A common error in adding fractions	529
Figure 23.6:	Further evidence of problems adding fractions	529
Figure 23.7:	Evidence of meaningful addition of fractions	530
Figure 23.8:	Different 'wholes'	531
Figure 23.9:	Finding pairs of numbers that add to 1	536
Figure 23.10:	Number line representation of 1.2 + 0.75 = 1.95	537
Figure 23.11:	10 × 10 grid representation of 1.2 + 0.75 = 1.95	538
Figure 23.12:	Decimat	538
Figure 23.13:	Using a number line to solve integer problems	542
Figure 23.14:	Examples of number line representations of integer calculations	542
Figure 23.15:	Three possible counter representations of 3	543
Figure 24.1:	Applications of the region idea for multiplication	551
Figure 24.2:	Area representation for 32 by 23	552
Figure 24.3:	Lattice representation for 32 × 23 and 43 × 56	552
Figure 24.4:	Cross-hatch or 'sticks' method for multiplying 43 × 56	553
Figure 24.5:	Napier's bones	553
Figure 24.6:	Area representations for non-integer multiplication	554
Figure 24.7:	Area representations for decimal fraction multiplication	555
Figure 24.8:	Representations for the Cartesian product idea	555
Figure 24.9:	Mental strategies for the division of whole numbers	562
Figure 24.10:	Mental strategies for the multiplication and division of decimal fractions	563

Figure 24.11:	Year 7 student's response to medicine dose problem	564
Figure 24.12:	Long multiplication in 1863	566
Figure 24.13:	Fraction multiplication	570
Figure 24.14:	Using the distributive property	571
Figure 24.15:	Two approaches to fraction division	573
Figure 24.16:	Integer addition and subtraction	574
Figure 24.17	Two solutions to the beanie problem	578
Figure 24.18:	Year 7 student response to speedy snail problem	579
Figure 26.1:	Tessellating shapes that could be used as units of area	607
Figure 26.2:	The area of this figure is 6 square units	608
Figure 26.3:	Cover this figure we use 6 whole square units and 2 half square units. In total, the area is 7 square units.	608
Figure 26.4:	The area of this figure is approximately 9½ square units	608
Figure 26.5:	In this rectangle the bottom row has 6 squares, so there must be 6 squares in all of the other rows. There are 4 rows. So the area will be 6 × 4 = 24 square units	611
Figure 26.6:	Three groups of 4 square centimetres or 3 × 4 square centimetres or 12 square centimetres	611
Figure 26.7:	Rearranging a parallelogram to form a rectangle: $A = b \times h$	613
Figure 26.8:	Arranging two identical triangles to form a parallelogram or a rectangle	614
Figure 27.1:	Enlarging an object	636
Figure 27.2:	Polar coordinate grid	642
Figure 28.1:	Data collection and analysis cycle	648
Figure 28.2:	Comparison of training and finishing times	649
Figure 28.3:	Transportation survey	651
Figure 28.4:	Transportation survey	652
Figure 28.5:	Fraction tests scores	653
Figure 28.6:	Football scores	653
Figure 28.7:	Student engaged with a capture–recapture simulation	660
Figure 28.8:	Work from a student's notebook	661
Figure 28.9:	Calculation using all of the data from all seven samples	661

List of Tables

Table 1.1:	Structure of the *Australian Curriculum: Mathematics* (ACARA, 2010)	13
Table 2.1:	Piagetian stages of cognitive development	29
Table 3.1:	Relationships between beliefs. From Beswick (2005, p. 40)	50
Table 3.2:	Example of three-column planning	54
Table 3.3:	Shulman's (1987) seven knowledge types	55
Table 3.4:	Types of question (from Vale, 2003, p. 690)	62
Table 4.1:	Types of mathematical thinking	70
Table 6.1:	Representations used in mathematics	100
Table 6.2:	Students' responses to two questions probing understanding of fractions	109
Table 7.1:	Multiple purposes of assessment	125
Table 7.2:	Proportional NAPLAN achievement of 'Suburbia', by state, and national, by band	127
Table 7.3:	An example of an annotated checklist	137
Table 7.4:	Multiple forms and timing of reporting	138
Table 7.5:	Rating student achievement	139
Table 8.1:	Examples of words used in mathematics	154
Table 8.2:	Strategies for assisting boys and girls to learn mathematics	157
Table 10.1:	Recording mental strategies to highlight important mathematics	196
Table 11.1:	Conceptual foundations necessary to the development of measurement understandings (Lehrer, 2003; Lehrer, Jaslow & Curtis, 2003)	215
Table 11.2:	Common personal referents	220
Table 11.3:	Development of spatial aspects according to Clements (1999)	224
Table 11.4:	Amended van Hiele levels of geometric thought (adapted from Battista, 2007)	226
Table 12.1:	Probability content of the Australian curriculum	243
Table 13.1:	Examples of pattern and structure across the strands in mathematics	250
Table 14.1:	Examples of additive numeration systems	267
Table 15.1:	Language and recording for the numbers 20–99	299
Table 15.2:	Language and recording for the numbers 11–19	301
Table 15.3:	Language and recording for four-digit numbers	308
Table 16.1:	Addition contexts	327
Table 16.2:	Subtraction contexts	328
Table 16.3:	Materials, language, and recording to support two-digit subtraction	342
Table 16.4:	Materials, language, and recording to support four-digit addition	343
Table 17.1:	A region representation of the multiplication and division facts 1×1 to 9×9	376
Table 17.2:	Remaining facts	379
Table 17.3:	Using equivalent number sentences to solve multiplication problems	384
Table 17.4:	Thinking, language, and recording to support multiplication of a four-digit number by a one-digit multiplier	385

Table 17.5:	Materials, language, and recording to support division of a two-digit number by a one-digit divisor	387
Table 17.6:	Materials, language, and recording to support division of a four-digit number by a one-digit divisor	388
Table 18.1:	Two different ways of thinking about fractions	407
Table 18.2:	Relationship between partitioning acts and the total number of parts	429
Table 20.1:	Young children's understanding of shape labels	457
Table 22.1:	Common misconceptions about decimals	507
Table 24.1:	Language and recording for 2-digit by 2-digit multiplication	566
Table 24.2:	Contrasting the two forms of division	567
Table 24.3:	Materials, language, and recording to support decimal division	568
Table 24.4:	Base 10 system of numeration shown in exponent form	575
Table 28.1:	Transportation survey	651
Table 28.2:	Pie chart calculations	652
Table 29.1:	Features of unit of work based on curriculum	673

Dedication

We dedicate this book to our own teachers, from whom we have learnt much more than mathematics. We have learned a love for the discipline and for introducing that love to others. We continue to be inspired by all those who strive to be the very best teachers of mathematics they can be.

Acknowledgments

We are grateful for the support of our families and work colleagues throughout the development of this book. We would like to thank all those students past and present who have taught us so much. It has been a privilege to work with the staff at Oxford University Press, who never ceased to be supportive and encouraging. Finally, it has been an immense pleasure to work with all of the writers on the team who made this a professionally inspiring experience.

The authors and publisher would like to thank and acknowledge the many reviewers whose advice, criticism of and support for the book, from conception to final manuscript, has proven invaluable to its creation. We are especially grateful for the feedback we received from our mathematics educator colleagues:

Leischa Bragg, Deakin University
Robyn Brandenburg, University of Ballarat
Diane Itter, LaTrobe University
Claudia Johnstone, Research Assistant, RMIT University
Dona Martin, LaTrobe University
Ray Peck, Australian Council of Education Research
Sandy Schuck, University of Technology Sydney

We'd also like to thank Margarita Breed for her chapter on assessment and reporting and Jeanne Carroll for her work on the chapters on extending number and extending fraction knowledge.

Lastly, we are indebted to the team at OUP, who have shaped and developed the book so carefully throughout its many stages. In particular, we thank the Development Editors, Belinda Leon and Rachel Saffer, Senior Editor, Natalie Davall, our Editor, Elaine Cochrane and our Publisher, Debra James.

About the Authors

Di Siemon is Professor of Mathematics Education in the School of Education at RMIT University (Bundoora). She has directed a number of large scale research projects in mathematics education and is well known for her work with teachers, schools, and State and Territory Departments of Education on the 'big ideas' in; number, the development of multiplicative thinking, and the use of rich assessment tasks to inform teaching. Di is a past President of the Australian Association of Mathematics Teachers and the Mathematical Association of Victoria. Di wrote chapters 1, 10, 14, 15, 16, 17, 18 and co-wrote Chapter 24.

Kim Beswick taught secondary school mathematics for 13 years before joining the University of Tasmania where she is currently an Associate Professor in mathematics education and Associate Dean (Research). She was awarded an Australian Learning and Teaching Citation in 2008 and is currently co-leading a national ALTC project aimed at establishing a culture of evidence based continual improvement of mathematics teacher education. Kim is a past co-editor of *Australian Primary Mathematics Classroom* and will be President of the Australian Association of Mathematics Teachers 2012-2013. Kim wrote Chapters 2, 3, 21, 29, and co-wrote Chapter 23.

Kathy Brady is a mathematics and numeracy education Lecturer, in the School of Education at Flinders University. As a mathematics educator, Kathy's teaching priorities are to combine theory and practice in ways that are accessible to undergraduate students. Kathy's research interests include how paper-folding can be used to promote engagement in mathematics learning in the primary classroom, investigating the experiences of early career primary mathematics teachers, and exploring how teacher education courses can best prepare graduating teachers in the area of mathematics. Kathy wrote Chapters 9, 19, 26, and co-wrote Chapter 11.

Julie Clark has been in mathematics education for 30 years. Her career has spanned across primary, secondary and tertiary levels. She is passionate about mathematics and teaching and is currently the Associate Dean in Learning and Teaching in the School of Education at Flinders University, South Australia. Julie has worked and studied in both Australia and the USA. Her research interests centre on the effective teaching and learning of mathematics and have recently focused on rural schools and technology. Julie has received a University Teaching and Innovation grant and is currently part of an ALTC project. She has worked for a number of mathematics professional organisations and is the Vice President (Communications) for the Mathematics Education Research Group of Australasia (MERGA). Julie wrote Chapters 5, 12, and 28.

Rhonda Faragher has taught mathematics across all levels, early childhood to tertiary, and is now a Senior Lecturer in mathematics education at the Canberra Campus of the Australian Catholic University. Her research interests have centred on helping all learners experience success with mathematics. She is the project coordinator for the Leading Aligned Numeracy Development project supporting learners in low SES schools. She has received a Vice-Chancellor's award for Excellence in Teaching and in 2009 a Commonwealth of Australia Endeavour Executive Award. She is the current recipient of the Alderson Award for Services in the field of Down syndrome. Rhonda wrote Chapters 4, 8, 20, 27, and co-wrote Chapters 11, 22, and 24.

Elizabeth Warren is a Professor in Mathematics Education at ACU (Brisbane). Her particular interests in mathematics education lie in two main areas; patterns and algebra and Indigenous students' education. Her research in these areas is focused primarily in the early years of schooling, and has been recognised at both the national and international level. Over the last ten years her research has been substantially supported by competitive funding from the Australian Research Council and DEEWR. All of her research is grounded in the context of 'real' classrooms. Her focus on these two areas of mathematics eduation are underpinned by a strong belief that (a) mathematical thinking is accessible to all, and (b) the types of activities that occur in the classroom and the discussion that ensues are crucial to young students access to mathematics. Elizabeth wrote Chapters 6, 13, and 25.

Margarita Breed is a lecturer in literacy and numeracy at RMIT University. Her doctoral research focused on multiplicative thinking and meeting the needs of at-risk Middle Years students in numeracy. Prior to her appointment at RMIT, she was involved in the Scaffolding Numeracy in the Middle Years Research Project, an ARC Linkage project with the Victorian and the Tasmanian Departments of Education. Her background has been in primary teaching with a particular passion for students in the Middle Years and as a Middle Years Numeracy Leader for Eastern Metropolitan Region. Whilst completing her Master of Education (Research) she was Research Assistant for the Mathematics Teaching and Learning Centre at the Australian Catholic University. Margarita wrote Chapter 7.

Jeanne Carroll is a senior lecturer in Mathematics Education in the School of Education at Victoria University. She enjoys working with teachers and pre-service teachers both locally and overseas to foster their love of mathematics, a fascination for the structures, an eye for the beauty and a hunger for the challenge of discovering the patterns of mathematics. Jeanne is a past president of the Mathematical Association of Victoria, convened the annual conference for MAV for many years and has been elected vice- president of the Australian Association of Mathematics Teachers. Jeanne co-wrote Chapters 22 and 23.

Preface

The creation of a text book is a dynamic and changing process. *Mathematics: Foundations to Middle Year*s began with two alternative titles, 'Teaching K–8 mathematics in changing times: Developing mathematical knowledge and confidence' and 'Learning and teaching mathematics in the early, primary and middle years of schooling: Making connections'. In the end we chose a simpler and more straightforward title but the driving force for the book remained; to write a text for pre-service teachers that would help them build mathematical knowledge and become confident about teaching the subject to a range of age groups in a range of classrooms and learning environments.

From the start, our aim in writing this text was to reflect and critique mathematics education research and current theories relating to the teaching and learning of mathematics. We have emphasised conceptual understanding as well as computational fluency and flexibility in order to improve pre-service teachers' capacity to interpret, analyse and communicate mathematically.

We have addressed aspects of the Foundations–9 mathematics curriculum in terms of concepts such as 'big ideas', strategies, representations, major sequences and learning trajectories. We have focused on the 'big ideas' and the ways in which mathematics is used to solve everyday problems, with a resolve to facilitate communication and mathematical reasoning.

Our book views mathematics as a social practice, with historical roots, and different cultural applications. It acknowledges that there are different modes of learning such as visual and kinaesthetic, and endeavours to make connections between 'big ideas' in number, measurement, probability and statistics, space and algebra.

We have structured it to address developmental learning capabilities in key areas. As a result, the book focuses on planning, assessing for, of and as learning. It covers different organisations for learning and classroom interaction, and caters for diverse learning needs. It includes student work samples, practical exercises, problems, illustrative activities, investigations, and use of multi-media and current technologies.

Each of the five parts, though covering different learning levels and knowledge, combines to form a cohesive text book with the goal of providing pre-service teachers with the confidence to be creative with mathematics teaching whilst observing the assessment and reporting requirements of mathematics curricula in Australia.

- **Part One** introduces what we know about teaching and learning mathematics and why school mathematics is constantly changing.
- **Part Two** builds on the broad overview presented in Part 1, and examines each area in depth, using student work samples, examples of best practice (tasks, activities, questions, planning ...) to raise issues and emphasise opportunities.
- **Part Three** has two aims: to develop pre-service teacher's own understanding of mathematics, and best practice teaching approaches arising from research. Each chapter addresses the aims in Part 2 using work samples, models of best practice, tasks and activities, assessment ideas and strategies, and incorporates the aspects of teaching and learning from Part 1 with links to cultural and historical applications.

- **Parts Four and Five** also have two aims: to develop personal knowledge and confidence in key areas and specific Pedagogy Content Knowledge for teaching mathematics at this level. Each chapter reasserts the 'big ideas', and identifies the key strategies, materials, language and recording needed to develop in these areas.

Our stated intention of building confidence in teaching mathematics is realised through these essential features:

- A focus on problem solving, reasoning and communicating mathematically across all areas of the curriculum;
- Carefully chosen examples and illustrations for more difficult concepts;
- A framework for building on understanding from simple concepts to more complex ones;
- A focus on making connections;
- Progression towards developing number skills, with extensive coverage of fractions and decimals;
- Coverage of different ways of teaching, such as working in groups;
- Development of understanding of algebra, geometry, number, probability, measurement and statistics;
- Help for pre-service teachers in lesson planning;
- Relevance to real life; and,
- A plentiful array of sample questions, exercises and activities.

Adding depth and readability to the text are the design elements, which include:

- **Vignettes at start of each part and chapter:** Short stories with some exploratory questions to engage the pre-service teachers with the underlying themes and concepts of each chapter.
- **Big Ideas:** Introduce the main concepts of the chapter and encourage mathematical thinking.
- **Consider and Discuss:** Specific tasks, questions and activities that encourage participation in tutorials.
- **Making Connections:** Provide links to the big ideas in mathematics, to other disciplines, and relevant mathematical learning.
- **Did you know?:** Short historical and cultural facts that show mathematics in the broader context and illustrate why mathematics is viewed and taught in the way it is today.
- **Issues in Teaching:** Discussion of contentious topics and poor but commonly seen practice.
- **Integrating Technology/ICT:** Suggests uses of software, interactive whiteboards, social networking sites, mobile phones, and other digital technologies.
- **For the Classroom:** Activities students can pick up and take with them into the classroom. Quite specific and framed for the different school year levels.
- **Communicating Mathematically:** Develops student's communication skills in mathematics by illustrating conventions, uses of language, materials, symbols diagrams, interaction patterns. Includes material on questioning, and patterns of communication and classroom interaction.
- **Handy Hints:** Practical tips to help students prepare their lessons with confidence.

- **Think and link:** Helps students navigate their way throughout the book, drawing on information introduced in earlier chapters and then elaborated on in later chapters.
- **Chapter objectives, key terms, review questions:** Help students cement their learning.
- **Tasks/Activities:** To develop practical professional knowledge and support lesson planning.

For students, to help with examinations and other forms of assessment, Oxford University Press has created an Online Resource Centre at <http://oup.com.au/orc/teachingmaths>.

It contains:

- a Flashcard Glossary
- additional exercises and material from the text
- a bank of activities that you can take into your classroom
- a 'Big Ideas' matrix
- questions to challenge your knowledge of the maths

For lecturers who adopt the text, supplementary material is also available. There are activity banks, image banks and test banks available. There are also PowerPoint slides (ISBN: 9780195518535) prepared by Dona Martin and Diane Itter from La Trobe University. These slides look at the content in the text by using a thematic approach instead of by age, as this book does. They include activities and Instructors' Resources. Please contact your Sales Representative for more details.

We entrust our many years of combined knowledge of mathematics and teaching to those future teachers who are using this book as their text. If we have been able to transfer our joy of mathematics to you, then our efforts in writing the book will be rewarded. We welcome feedback from you to assist the continued development of the book. Please contact us at highered@oup.com.

Di
Kim
Kathy
Julie
Rhonda
Elizabeth

Guided Tour

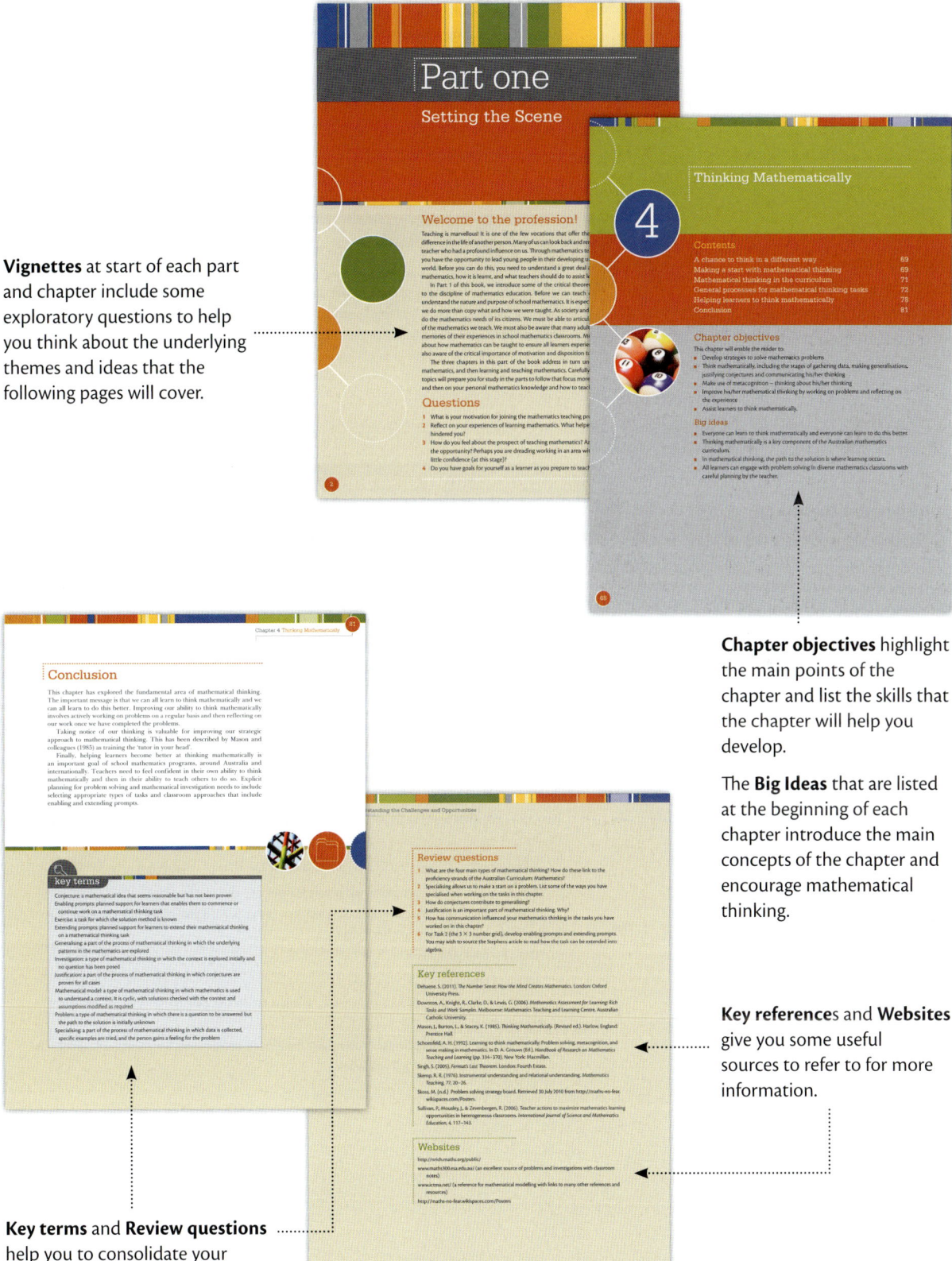

Vignettes at start of each part and chapter include some exploratory questions to help you think about the underlying themes and ideas that the following pages will cover.

Chapter objectives highlight the main points of the chapter and list the skills that the chapter will help you develop.

The **Big Ideas** that are listed at the beginning of each chapter introduce the main concepts of the chapter and encourage mathematical thinking.

Key references and **Websites** give you some useful sources to refer to for more information.

Key terms and **Review questions** help you to consolidate your learning.

To help you with **Communicating Mathematically**, these boxes help you pick up some of the tips, tricks and tools that you'll need to develop your communication skills.

communicating mathematically

Pape et al. (2003) stressed the importance to mathematical reasoning of 'argument and controversy', and listening to others critically. These activities are much more demanding than simply sharing solution strategies. Teaching children to use argument constructively in mathematics is an important way to raise the intellectual quality of classroom interaction and facilitate the development of mathematical reasoning and understanding.

Did you know? are small historical and cultural facts that help put mathematics into a broader context.

did you know?

The English language is unusual in having distinct words for 'teaching' and 'learning' that refer to distinct activities of the teacher and learner. Other languages, including Russian, Japanese, French, Dutch and many other northern European languages, combine the notions of teaching and learning in a single word.

Consider and Discuss are tasks, questions and activities that can be used in groups or alone to encourage deeper thinking about the content.

consider and discuss

1. Think about a mathematical big idea that you feel you really understand? Explain what you mean when you say you *understand* it. How do you know you understand it? How is this different from not understanding?
2. Discuss your thoughts with others and then write a definition of what it means to understand.

The **Integrating Technology/ICT** boxes suggest ways that you can use digital technologies in your classrooms.

integrating technology/ICT

The place of calculators

Here is a task to explore with your calculator. (Don't use the power key—that will spoil the fun.)

What number raised to the 5th power is 371 293? That is, what is n if $n^5 = 371\,293$?

As you work on the problem, what role/s does the calculator play?

A basic calculator cannot solve the problem for you. And yet, most of us would not bother with this problem without one.

Did you find you were:

- testing conjectures?
- using the calculator as a tool—that is, using it to do the calculations while you were doing the thinking?
- correcting misconceptions? (You might have tried dividing by 5—the calculator can be used to test whether this will work.)

handy hint
Act it out

To help students understand what is involved in a word problem, it is useful to explore how it might be acted out.

Handy Hints are practical tips to help students prepare their lessons with confidence.

making connections

The theoretical underpinnings of scaffolding lie in Vygotsky's notion of 'zone of proximal development' (ZPD). ZPD refers to the learner's potential development, just beyond what is currently possible alone but which is achievable with assistance that builds upon the learner's existing capabilities. You are likely to hear about ZPD in many aspects of your studies in education. Scaffolding cannot be fully understood without a sound understanding of ZPD (Verenikina, 2003).

Making Connections link the big ideas in mathematics to other disciplines.

issues in teaching

It can be a challenge to incorporate the proficiency strands—understanding, fluency, reasoning, and problem solving—appropriately throughout the mathematics topics being studied. The curriculum detail can be overwhelming, but it is important to make connections between mathematics topics and across learning areas to provide adequate opportunities for students to develop the skills associated with the proficiency strands.

The **Issues in Teaching** boxes discuss some of the contentious topics in maths education.

for the classroom

Ask students to write about the best maths lesson they can imagine. Ask them, 'What sorts of tasks or questions would you be working on?' 'What would you be doing?' 'What would the teacher be doing?' O'Shea (2009) described Grade 5 and 6 students' responses to a task like this.

Having young children draw themselves in maths time can provide insight into their thinking about what maths lessons are all about. Walls (2007) reports the implications for teaching of children's responses to this task and includes a number of student work samples.

For the Classroom boxes give you activities you can pick up and take into the classroom.

think + link

Chapter 4 considers what is involved in building mathematical proficiency and the confidence and competence to view the world mathematically.

The **Think + Link** feature helps you navigate your way through the book.

Further Resources

For further resources to help you with your study, please visit **www.oup.com.au/orc/teachingmaths**.

Part one

Setting the Scene

Welcome to the profession!

Teaching is marvellous! It is one of the few vocations that offer the chance to make a difference in the life of another person. Many of us can look back and remember at least one teacher who had a profound influence on us. Through mathematics teaching in particular, you have the opportunity to lead young people in their developing understanding of the world. Before you can do this, you need to understand a great deal about the nature of mathematics, how it is learnt, and what teachers should do to assist learners.

In Part 1 of this book, we introduce some of the critical theoretical underpinnings to the discipline of mathematics education. Before we can teach others, we need to understand the nature and purpose of school mathematics. It is especially important that we do more than copy what and how we were taught. As society and culture changes, so do the mathematics needs of its citizens. We must be able to articulate the importance of the mathematics we teach. We must also be aware that many adults do not have good memories of their experiences in school mathematics classrooms. Much has been learnt about how mathematics can be taught to ensure all learners experience success. We are also aware of the critical importance of motivation and disposition to learning.

The three chapters in this part of the book address in turn understanding school mathematics, and then learning and teaching mathematics. Carefully reflecting on these topics will prepare you for study in the parts to follow that focus more closely on learners, and then on your personal mathematics knowledge and how to teach that to others.

Questions

1. What is your motivation for joining the mathematics teaching profession?
2. Reflect on your experiences of learning mathematics. What helped you? What hindered you?
3. How do you feel about the prospect of teaching mathematics? Are you excited by the opportunity? Perhaps you are dreading working in an area with which you have little confidence (at this stage)?
4. Do you have goals for yourself as a learner as you prepare to teach others?

1

1 Understanding School Mathematics

Contents

Introduction	5
What is mathematics?	6
Goals of school mathematics	9
Affordances and constraints	12
Conclusion	20

Chapter objectives

This chapter will enable the reader to:
- Understand the contribution of mathematics to society and the role of school mathematics in a futures-oriented curriculum
- Develop a broad understanding of what is involved in the teaching and learning of mathematics in contemporary Foundation to Year 9 classrooms
- Appreciate the range of issues and challenges impacting on the provision of school mathematics at this level
- Recognise the important role of reflection and research in mathematics education.

Everyone can do maths

'I was never any good at maths ... I dropped it as soon as I could.' Most teachers of mathematics experience this reaction in a social context when they are asked their occupation. Such responses are amazing when you consider that the same people would probably not have made the same claims about their capacity to read or write. It seems that it is socially acceptable to admit to disliking or not being 'very good at' mathematics. It is a sad irony that those who profess such views frequently demonstrate sophisticated uses of mathematics in their everyday activities. For instance, I recall a taxi driver who, having confessed that he had 'failed mathematics in Year 9', expertly gauged the flow of the traffic, consulted a global positioning system, decided to take an alternative route to ensure we arrived in time, and at the end of the journey mentally added the airport tax to the fare and calculated the change.

>
> ### consider and discuss
> 1. When was the last time you truly, madly, deeply, really enjoyed doing some mathematics? What did you do and how did it make you feel?
> 2. Can you recall a teacher who made a significant impact on your learning of mathematics or an experience when you were 'turned off' mathematics? If so, describe the circumstances in terms of who, what, when, and where. How did it make you feel?
> 3. What lessons can be learnt from this?

Big ideas

- Sophisticated mathematical skills are inherent in many daily activities.
- School mathematics needs to change and is changing.
- Learning mathematics is both an individual and social enterprise.
- Teaching mathematics is a rewarding but complex and demanding task.

Introduction

We introduced this book by talking about teacher quality and what it means to be an effective teacher of mathematics. While it is relatively easy to list generic characteristics, what matters is what students experience, individually and collectively. Teacher quality is clearly related to teacher knowledge and confidence, but what actually happens in classrooms is also affected by what teachers feel they have to teach, how they go about teaching it, and the social contexts in which teaching takes place. Ultimately, teachers' decisions about content and pedagogy are very much related to why they do what they do (personal motivations), and what they know and believe about the nature of mathematics and the teaching and learning of mathematics (Brady, 2007; Fennema, Carpenter & Peterson, 1989; Thompson, 1984).

Teachers choose to teach for a variety of reasons—and it is rarely for the money! The most commonly cited reason for choosing to teach is 'to make a difference'. In *A Sense of Calling: Who teaches and why*, Farkas, Johnson and Foleno (2000) report that 96 per cent of new teachers surveyed reported that they chose teaching because it 'involves work they love doing' and gave them 'a sense of contributing to society and helping others' (p. 11). 'Understanding what matters to people, what motivates them and why they do what they do can make the difference between a conversation that moves forward and one that goes nowhere' (p. 8).

>
>
> **consider and discuss**
>
> **job, vocation or career?**
>
> *For me, in Year 12, teaching was the obvious choice. Where else do you get an opportunity to do all the things you like doing, such as learning mathematics, studying history, discussing literature, playing sport, singing, and performing. But most of all, I became a teacher because I somehow felt it was the right thing to do … helping others learn is not only very satisfying, it increases people's opportunities in life … education is the key to making the world a better, fairer, more environmentally responsible place.*
>
> 1 What were your reasons for choosing to become a teacher? Was it because of particular strengths and interests, role models, or opportunities?
> 2 What do you hope to achieve as a teacher of mathematics?
> 3 What do you see yourself doing in ten years' time?

Given that most teachers are motivated by a desire to support the learning and well-being of others, and given what we know about effective mathematics teaching, why is it that students' experiences of learning mathematics are not that much different from what they were in the past, particularly in the middle years of schooling (Bodin & Capponi, 1996; Yates, 2005)? It appears that what teachers know and believe about mathematics and the teaching and learning of mathematics is one of the most important reasons for the poor history of reform efforts in mathematics education (Handal & Herrington, 2003; Siemon, 1989; Yates, 2005). As there is evidence to suggest that teachers tend to teach mathematics in the way they were taught (e.g. Brady, 2007; Stigler & Hiebert, 1999), it is important to examine critically the assumptions that underpin school mathematics.

In what follows we will look at what we mean by mathematics, the goals of contemporary school mathematics, and the influences, including teacher knowledge and beliefs, that act to promote (or constrain) the teaching and learning of mathematics in the primary and middle years of schooling.

What is mathematics?

We all have views on what constitutes mathematics, and these views shape our decisions about how we teach and learn mathematics (Handal & Herrington, 2003; Thompson, 1984). For instance, if mathematics is viewed as a set of universal truths, teachers are more likely to see their task as transferring a given set of facts and skills to students and to view student learning as the capacity to reproduce these facts and skills as instructed. If, on the other hand, mathematics is viewed as a socio-cultural practice, a product of reflective human activity, then it is more likely that teachers will see their task as engaging students in meaningful mathematical practices and view student learning in terms of conceptual change.

Many views have been advanced to describe the nature of mathematics:

> Mathematics as an expression of the human mind reflects the active will, the contemplative reason, and the desire for aesthetic perfection. Its basic elements are logic and intuition, analysis and construction, generality and individuality. (Courant & Robbins, 1941, p. xv)

Mathematics reveals hidden patterns that help us understand the world around us … Mathematics is a science of pattern and order. (Mathematical Sciences Education Board, 1989, p. 31)

[A]ll cultural traditions … find connecting patterns and apparent symmetries throughout nature. Individually and collectively, we accept these patterns as part of the background of our lives: beyond question or doubt, all Australians agree we live in an orderly, knowable universe. Yet the patterns which organise, and the laws which govern, European knowledge and perception apparently have little in common with the patterns which make sense of the Aboriginal world … both kinds of patterning form complex and mathematically sophisticated systems, both have powerful ideological underpinnings, both are social constructions emerging from historically identifiable contexts, both attempt to account for natural as well as social phenomena, both are rational in principle and practical in application. (Watson, 1989, p. 31)

These views all propose that mathematics offers a way of understanding the world we live in. Mathematics provides a consistent framework, a symbolic technology, by which we can model 'reality', solve problems, and support predictions, but how this is described and communicated depends very much on our cultural values and traditions. For instance, our taken-for-granted view of mathematics—the mathematics of our schooling that Bishop (1991) refers to as 'Mathematics' with a capital 'M'—is governed by number patterns and relations. There are other cultures whose ways of understanding the world are not governed by 'how much and how many' but by complex kinship patterns that connect all things to each other without the need of numbers (e.g. Watson, 1989; Bishop, 1991). In other words, mathematics is a 'pan-cultural phenomenon: that is, it exists in all cultures', and 'Mathematics' is a 'particular variant of mathematics, developed through the ages by various societies' (Bishop, 1991, p. 19).

This is a difficult notion to grapple with, as we can scarcely imagine a world without Mathematics, and yet we happily accept that different languages are developed by different cultural groups in order to communicate. This prompted Bishop to ask: if language develops from the need for, and activity of, *communicating*, what are 'the activities and processes which lead to the development of mathematics?' (p. 22). According to Bishop, there are six fundamental mathematical activities that occur in some form across all cultures, which he describes as follows.

- *Counting*—the use of a systematic way to compare and order discrete phenomena. It may involve tallying, using objects or string to record, or special number words or names
- *Locating*—exploring one's spatial environment and conceptualising and symbolising that environment, with models, diagrams, drawings, words or other means
- *Measuring*—quantifying qualities for the purposes of comparison and ordering, using objects or tokens as measuring devices with associated units or 'measure-words'
- *Designing*—creating a shape or design for an object or for any part of one's spatial environment. It may involve making the object, as a 'mental template', or symbolising it in some conventional way
- *Playing*—devising, and engaging in, games and pastimes, with more or less formalised rules of play that all players abide by
- *Explaining*—finding ways to account for the existence of phenomena, be they religious, animistic or scientific (Bishop, 1988, pp. 182–183).

In looking at these activities and processes, we can see how it might be possible for there to be many mathematics underpinned by different cultural norms and values. For Bishop, mathematics can be viewed as a 'way of knowing'.

did you know?

An apocryphal story describes a group of tourists who were being escorted through the central Australian desert by a local Indigenous man. When they had been travelling for some time and were feeling overwhelmed by seemingly unchangeable landscape, one of the tourists asked the guide, 'What do you do when you get lost out here?' The man turned to the tourist somewhat bemused, and said, 'I go home.' In other words, for him, there was no notion of 'lost'. He knew the landscape intimately, and could discern its patterns and variations. By this means he knew exactly where he was and in which direction he needed to travel to return home, without the need of GPS, compass, or paper map.

Mathematics as we know it evolved from the earliest civilisations of Egypt, Greece, Mesopotamia, India, and China. These were established in river valleys where there was plenty of water, fertile soil, and a climate conducive to an agrarian economy. It is not too difficult to imagine a scenario where competition for land and resources to sustain rapidly growing populations led to a system of quantifying to settle disputes and support trade. Land could be identified by precise measures, permanent structures could be erected, goods could be exchanged on a comparable basis, taxes could be levied on produce, time could be measured by reference to the sun and the stars, and journeys could be described in terms of units of length, time and direction. When trade and travel expanded, systems of quantifying were used to transcend language barriers.

Mathematics was also pursued as an intellectual pursuit in its own right. For example, the Pythagoreans noticed that for right-angled triangles, the sum of the squares on the smaller sides was equal to the square on the longest side, the hypotenuse. At the time, the only numbers that were recognised were the natural numbers (1, 2, 3, 4, ...) and numbers that were ratios of these numbers (e.g. 1:2, 4/2, or 17/3). Subsequent explorations of right-angled triangles in which the two smaller sides were both one unit in length led to the proposition of a new type of number, in this case the square root of 2. Although resisted at first, this proposition eventually led to the recognition of the irrational numbers, which are numbers that cannot be expressed as ratios of natural numbers. The irrational numbers include pi (π) and non-terminating decimals. This example illustrates an interesting philosophical question: were the irrational numbers always there, 'waiting to be discovered', or were they the product of human reflective activity at a certain time in a certain cultural setting? This question is often characterised as a debate between *absolutist* and *fallibilist* views of mathematics, that is, between mathematics as a set of irrefutable truths, and mathematics as a socially constructed practice (e.g. Bishop, 1991; Ernest, 1991; Presmeg, 2007). While these views may co-exist to some extent, what teachers believe about the fundamental nature of mathematics has important implications for practice as we shall see below.

Goals of school mathematics

Niss (1996) suggests that there are three fundamental reasons for the existence of school mathematics as we know it today. They are that the study of mathematics contributes to:

> the technological and socio-economic development of society; the political, ideological and cultural maintenance and development of society; [and] the provision of individuals with prerequisites which may assist them in coping with private and social life, whether in education, occupation, or as citizens. (p. 22)

In ancient times, the study of mathematics was restricted to a select few, generally young men, who had the time to converse with more learned others. For some, this was simply an enjoyable pastime, an intellectual pursuit for its own sake, while for others such as the Pythagoreans, in Greece, this activity was shrouded in secrecy and mysticism. However, as production became more specialised and trade expanded, mathematical know-how was acquired as a matter of necessity. Merchants, builders, navigators, tax collectors, artisans, and religious leaders all needed some mathematics, and they inducted those that followed them into their particular mathematical practices.

Before the nineteenth century, there was little offered in the way of formal education beyond the opportunity to learn a trade. For the very few who did receive some sort of formal education, this was largely justified on the grounds that it contributed to 'the political, ideological and cultural maintenance of society' (Niss, 1996, p. 22). This situation changed with the advent of the industrial age and the introduction of compulsory schooling. Elementary mathematics was included as a core component of the curriculum, presumably 'to contribute to the technological and socio-economic development of society, while at the same time placing some emphasis on equipping individuals with tools for mastering their vocational and everyday private lives' (Niss, 1996, p. 23).

consider and discuss

From an 1875 school mathematics textbook

A wine merchant buys 3 hhds. of wine at Bordeaux, at £15 per hhd., pays duty 1 s. per gallon, and carriage £3. What must he sell the wine at per gallon, to clear £10 in the transaction? (Davis, 1875, p. 47)

1. What does this say about the assumptions underpinning the teaching and learning of mathematics at the time? How different are these from the assumptions underpinning your experience of school mathematics? Discuss in terms of the three fundamental reasons for studying mathematics described by Niss above.
2. What knowledge and skills are needed to solve this problem? (Hint: you may need to rewrite this in a more familiar form first.)

In the same book, a 'simple multiplication' was given as 856439082 × 7008001 (p. 13). These days, it is difficult to understand why this was regarded as 'simple' or why such a problem would be set. My first thought was that perhaps it was because the number of rows in the written algorithm could be reduced by recognising the role of the zeros in the second factor. But other 'simple' problems on the same page (e.g. 259136472 × 8837582) showed this was clearly not the case. It was not until I found the chapter on 'compound multiplication' that I understood—a compound problem involves measures (e.g. 4 leagues 2 miles 7 furlongs 2 poles 5 yards × 72, p. 39).

integrating technology/ICT

Is it possible?

What tools would you use to find the exact answer to one of these 'simple' multiplication problems, and how would you use them? If you attempted to do this using the long multiplication algorithm, what mistakes might you make? What do you think was the purpose of this type of task? Use your knowledge of the base-ten numeration system to estimate an answer to the first 'simple' problem. How long do you think it might have taken a Year 5 student at the time to solve the other 'simple' problem?

These examples nicely illustrate that school mathematics is a human construction reflecting societal values and priorities at particular points in time. The fact that all students, not just a select few, were expected to solve these problems is indicative of the goals of school mathematics at the time and the assumptions made about the teaching and learning of mathematics. Contrast this with how an Aboriginal child living in a remote part of Australia in 1875 might have been expected to learn to find his or her way home in the desert.

A shift in emphasis

Today, all three of Niss's reasons for including mathematics in school curricula can be found in contemporary curriculum documents, for example, the Principles and Standards for School Mathematics (National Council of Teachers of Mathematics [NCTM], 2000) and the Australian Mathematics Curriculum (Australian Curriculum Assessment & Reporting Authority [ACARA], 2010), which aims to ensure that students:

> are confident, creative users and communicators of mathematics, able to investigate, represent and interpret situations in their personal and work lives and as active citizens ... develop increasingly sophisticated understanding of mathematical concepts and fluency with processes, able to pose and solve problems and reason in number and algebra; measurement and geometry; and statistics and probability ... [and] recognise connections between the areas of mathematics and other disciplines and appreciate mathematics as an accessible and enjoyable discipline to study. (p. 1)

think + link

The chapters in Part 3 examine what we mean by numeracy and explore its relationship to school mathematics in Years F–9. In particular, these chapters focus on the 'big ideas' in mathematics and how these can be applied in everyday contexts to solve problems and inform decision making.

It is interesting to note the order in which these aims are stated. The first echoes Niss's (1996) third reason for studying mathematics, that is, the 'provision of individuals with prerequisites which may assist them in coping with private and social life, whether in education, occupation, or as citizens' (p. 22). This reason for studying mathematics has become much more prominent recently because of its association with *numeracy*, which is defined as the 'effective use of mathematics to meet the general demands of life at school and at home, in paid work, and for participation in community and civic life' (National Numeracy Benchmarks Taskforce, 1997, p. 30).

This shift in emphasis arose in response to concerns about the capacity of individuals to function effectively in a modern technological society, in particular to critically question public policy decisions and understand the ways in which mathematics is being used to monitor and shape our lives (Gellert & Jablonka, 2008).

We have never needed mathematics more

While it is true that technology has replaced many of the routine procedures traditionally taught in school mathematics, the advent of sophisticated information and communication technologies has also drastically changed the way we conduct our everyday lives. Mathematics underpins much of this technology, and mathematics is used in increasingly powerful and subtle ways to persuade voters and consumers to act in certain ways. This suggests that we have never needed mathematics more. But the mathematics we need is not the school mathematics of the past with its emphasis on isolated skills and rote learning.

for the classroom

Collect a range of newspapers, magazines, food containers, and screen dumps from a variety of websites. Ask students to identify where mathematics is being used and how. Encourage younger students to look beyond numbers to measures, and older students to look for instances of proportion and other, more subtle, uses of mathematics, such as location of visual displays and headings.

Today, individuals need to be able to make sense of vast amounts of quantitative and spatial information presented in increasingly sophisticated multimedia formats, make decisions on the basis of that understanding, and communicate their reasons for doing so if challenged. According to Becker and Selter (1996), the 'ultimate objective of student learning at all levels is the acquisition of a *mathematical disposition* rather than the absorption of a set of isolated concepts or skills' (p. 542). In their opinion, students should learn to:

be creative: to look for patterns, make conjectures, generate new problems ... to *reason*: to give arguments, uncover contradictions, distinguish between facts and assertions ... to *mathematize*: to collect data, process information, interpret data and solutions ... and to *communicate*: to express their own thoughts, accept the ideas of others, establish forms of cooperation. (p. 542)

This is consistent with Bishop's view of mathematics as 'a way of knowing' rather than 'a way of doing'. The values they represent are reflected in the *Australian Curriculum: Mathematics* (ACARA, 2010) in the form of proficiencies, specifically:

- conceptual understanding
- procedural **fluency**
- problem solving (or strategic competence), and
- adaptive **reasoning**.

think + link

Chapter 4 considers what is involved in building mathematical proficiency and the confidence and competence to view the world mathematically.

From the student's perspective

Student responses to mathematical tasks can reveal a lot about their perceptions of the goals of school mathematics. Nick was a Year 4 student who knew his number facts and was 'good at' 'doing division' by the traditional 'goes into' algorithm. For example, he could confidently divide 364 by 7 by saying '7 guzinta [goes into] 3? No, carry the 3. 7 guzinta 36 ... yes, 5 times and 1 left over [writes 5 underneath and 1 beside the 4], 7 guzinta 14, yes 2 times [writes 2]'. After some time in class exploring an alternative approach involving sharing and base 10 materials, which Nick clearly understood and could justify to his peers, he was given the problem 'Eight families shared a prize of $348. How much did each family receive?' Nick provided the following 'talking head' response. He drew a face to show how he felt about the task and wrote a brief explanation of what he had done.

Figure 1.1 Nick's response to a division problem

Source: Siemon (1993)

Despite his demonstrated understanding of both forms of division, Nick chose to create his own algorithm based on what he knew about subtraction and renaming. In this case, reading from the top down and starting with the ones he reasoned, '8 how many 8s? … 1 … 4 how many 8s? Can't do, so trade a hundred, 14 tens how many 8s? … 1 and 6 over', which he records over the 2 in the hundreds place. Realising '2 how many 8s?' is not going to work, he crosses the 6 out and rewrites the 2 and the 6 as 26 and proceeds, '26 how many 8s? … 3 and 2 remainder' which he records. His comments indicate his beliefs about what he sees school mathematics is about, that is, using 'sums' to get answers. When asked about his answer, Nick, said, 'Oh if it was real money I wouldn't do it like that'. Prompted to say how he would do it, Nick replied, 'Well 8 families, $40 each that'd be $320, $50 each would be $400, I reckon it's about $43'. Nick's problem was not with division, but with the values and beliefs he held about the nature and purpose of school mathematics. Asked why he did this, Nick said that, he knew his 'old way of doing it would work but Mrs … didn't like that' and he could do it the new way 'but that was too long'.

think + link

Chapter 2 examines the role of beliefs and values in learning school mathematics and stresses the importance of conceptual understanding as a basis for procedural fluency.

Affordances and constraints

Teaching mathematics is a complex, demanding, but rewarding task that requires a knowledge of students, of content, and of how that content might best be represented to engage and support learners. Referred to by Shulman (1986) as **pedagogical content knowledge** (PCK) and, more recently and with respect to mathematics teaching and learning, as **knowledge for teaching mathematics** or KTM (Ball, Thames & Phelps, 2008), it clearly involves much more than a knowledge of mathematics at the level taught.

> Teaching is about building relationships—between students and the teacher and among students themselves around mathematics—and engaging together in constructing mathematical meaning. Teaching involves orchestrating the content, the representation, and the people in relation to one another. It is about making decisions

in the moment that serve the individuals and collective. It is about understanding the students ... It is about working together to negotiate meaning. (Franke, Kazemi & Battey, 2007, p. 228)

Teachers need to have a deep understanding of what makes particular mathematics content difficult to learn (content knowledge), what representations and instructional strategies are best suited to the needs of individual students (pedagogy), and how to manage the relationships in which the teaching and learning takes place (social context). Although indistinguishable in practice, these three key aspects of teacher knowledge are briefly described below.

think + link

The characteristics of effective teachers are discussed in more detail in Chapter 3 and in Parts 4 and 5 of this book

Knowledge of content

In Australia, decisions about what mathematics to teach, and when, are largely guided by mandated curriculum documents developed by state and territory education authorities. These are variously organised in terms of broad **content** strands such as Number, Measurement, and Space, and a smaller number of process strands such as Working Mathematically. From 2011, all Australian states and territories will be expected to implement the Australian Curriculum. For mathematics this will be described by Year level (F–12) across three strands and four proficiencies, as shown in Table 1.1.

Table 1.1

Structure of the *Australian Curriculum: Mathematics* (ACARA, 2010)	
Content strand	Proficiencies
Number and Algebra	Conceptual Understanding
Measurement and Geometry	Procedural Fluency
Statistics and Probability	Mathematical Problem Solving
	Mathematical Reasoning

A major shift in the curriculum is the recognition of the importance of *big ideas*. A 'big idea' provides an organising framework that encompasses and connects a number of related ideas and strategies and supports further learning and generalisations. For example, *multiplicative thinking* not only encompasses the various meanings and representations of multiplication and division, together with a range of appropriate solution strategies, but also supports connections between these operations and the base 10 system of numeration, the rational numbers, and generalisations associated with proportional reasoning.

Modern curriculum also attempts to build on what is known about the progression of children's thinking towards the big ideas. Referred to as *learning trajectories* (Simon, 1995), teachers need to be aware of the developmental pathways, intermediate goals, and the instructional strategies, tasks, and representations by which student thinking is likely to be further enhanced.

think + link

The 'Consider and Discuss' and 'Issues in Teaching' sections throughout this book are designed to assist you to build your mathematical knowledge for teaching.

The language of mathematics teaching

Teachers need a vocabulary to reflect on their practice, share their thinking and decision making, and engage in further professional learning. In the chapters that follow we will endeavour to introduce the terms commonly used in relation to the teaching and learning of mathematics in a clear and consistent manner. A glossary of key terms is provided at the end of this book.

The many faces of curriculum

Curriculum comes in many different forms. The curriculum produced by education systems is often referred to as the intended curriculum. It sets the standard for what is valued and what will be assessed at a system or national level. However, schools and teachers need to interpret the intended curriculum in the light of their own knowledge and experience and what they know about their particular student population. This can lead to subtle and not-so-subtle variations in the curriculum that is actually translated into practice and assessed. These versions of the curriculum are often referred to as the implemented curriculum and the evaluated curriculum respectively.

These variations highlight the competing tensions faced by teachers as they try to balance the learning needs of the students with system and community expectations. This is a non-trivial task that can lead to underachievement or learners being left behind if it is not managed well. High but realistic expectations of student learning are associated with effective mathematics teaching (e.g. Hattie, 2003). This requires accurate information about what each student knows and is able to do, something that is rarely, if ever, identified by mandated testing.

The introduction of the *Australian Curriculum: Mathematics* (ACARA, 2010; National Curriculum Board [NCB], 2009) will present many challenges, but it also provides an important opportunity to critically examine assumptions about what should be taught at what levels of schooling and to engage with the 'big ideas' in mathematics.

Pedagogy

Although originally used to refer to the 'art and science' of teaching children, **pedagogy** is now more broadly understood as the 'knowledge and principles of teaching and learning' (Griffith & Kowalski, 2010, p. 111), the art and profession of teaching or, more particularly, instructional strategies or a style of instruction.

Research on teaching and learning and developments in technology have prompted considerable changes in how mathematics is taught. For instance, it is now recognised that:

> Learning mathematics is basically a constructive process … pupils gather, discover, create mathematical knowledge and skills mainly in the course of some social activity that has a purpose … Instead of being the main if not the only source of information, the teacher becomes a 'privileged' member of the knowledge building community of the classroom who creates an intellectually stimulating climate, models learning and problem-solving activities, asks provocative questions, provides support to students through coaching and guidance, and fosters students' responsibility for their own learning. (Verschaffel & De Corte, 1996, p. 102)

As a consequence, school mathematics now emphasises interaction, collaboration, and a variety of organisational styles (e.g. Boaler, 2002). Teachers are encouraged to focus on important mathematics through the use of challenging problems, extended investigations, **rich tasks**, **open-ended questions**, games, mental computation, the discussion of solution strategies, visualisation, and the appropriate use of materials and representations supported by appropriate information and communications technologies. In short, quality mathematics instruction involves a rich and varied supportive learning environment in which all learners feel they have a place and the capacity and desire to contribute to the collective enterprise.

We now know a lot more about how mathematics is learnt. Meaningless, mind-numbing, text-based drill and practice, and doing it one way, the teacher's way, does not work. Concepts need to be experienced, strategies, need to be scaffolded, and everything needs to be discussed.

Communication

From the student's perspective, the critical element in their learning is the quality of teacher explanations, in particular the capacity of teachers to connect with their level of understanding and communicate effectively. As Vincent, a Year 9 student identified as 'at risk' by his teachers, said so eloquently, 'change the way it's explained, they need to think about how you understand, not how they explain' (Siemon & Virgona, 2001, p. 49).

Teachers not only need to know the key concepts, skills and strategies that underpin the mathematics they are teaching, but also need a deep knowledge of the links between these ideas, what makes them difficult, and how they are best communicated. **Communication** patterns in mathematics classrooms are shaped by a number of factors, including the established or assumed social norms of the classroom, students' cognitive, cultural and/or linguistic background, and the beliefs and attitudes of both teachers and students. In the past, teachers typically asked relatively low-level, closed questions, students responded, and the teacher evaluated the response in some way. Known as the initiation-response-evaluation or IRE form of interaction, this is now regarded as fairly restricted in comparison to the more productive forms of interaction that have been recognised in recent years (see e.g. Wood, 1994; Siemon, Cathcart, Lasso, Parsons & Virgona, 2004).

Representations

Teachers draw on a range of materials (also referred to as manipulatives), models, and **representations** to support communication in mathematics classrooms. While these are valuable as tools to support the negotiation of meaning, they do not, and cannot, convey meaning. Indeed, many, such as fraction diagrams, presuppose the learning they are intended to support. Language plays an important role in mediating the use of such tools and negotiating learning. Teachers need to be critically aware of the assumptions underpinning the use of materials and representations, as well as of the language and questioning needed to scaffold their use. If these materials and representations are seen purely as an interesting game or as the only means of finding a solution, then their use needs to be questioned. There is the added trap that sometimes our taken-for-granted models can prevent us from 'seeing' or 'hearing' what it is that students are trying to tell us.

The lengths to which students will go in their attempts to make sense of mathematics are illustrated by the responses a number of pre-service teachers gave to a decimal task on a written mathematics competency test (Siemon, 1999). Although entry to teacher education programs at the time required Year 11 mathematics, approximately 35% of the first-year cohort had completed a Year 12 mathematics course. The task required the teacher education students to order the following decimal fractions from smallest to largest: 0.612, 0.6,

think + link

Chapters 2 and 3 consider what we know from research and practice about the learning and teaching of mathematics in Years F–9.

think + link

Chapter 5 examines communication in more detail, and Chapter 8 considers the challenges and affordances of mixed ability, diverse classrooms.

0.26, 0.621, and 0.62. In 1989, just on 10% of the sample of over 240 students ordered the decimals in the following way: 0.621, 0.62, 0.612, 0.6, and 0.26. My initial reaction to this was that it was simply an oversight. After all, the numbers were ordered correctly, albeit from largest to smallest: perhaps the students had misread the question. When approximately the same proportion of students provided the same response the following year, I thought it was worth investigating, so I set up a meeting where I invited all those who had responded in this way to come along, with a friend if they wished, to discuss their reasoning. The following is a slightly abbreviated version of the discussion that took place. (L stands for myself as the lecturer, S1, S2 … stands for different students.)

> L: Can you tell me why you did it this way? [pointing to the question and response which had been recorded on the whiteboard]
> S1: Because it asked for smallest to largest. [at least four other students nod in agreement]
> L: So, this is the smallest? [pointing to 0.621 on the left]
> S2: Because, it's the furthest away from zero. [at least two of the other students nod vigorously]
> L: That's interesting. I agree it's the furthest away from zero but I think it's the largest for the same reason.

At this point, I suggested we rename the decimal fractions as common fractions. The students had little difficulty with this initially, and when I asked, 'Do you still think these are ordered from smallest to largest?' they responded fairly quickly, 'Oh, you can't tell … the denominator needs to be the same.' At that point we proceeded to rename the common fractions as thousandths (see Figure 1.2). This proved a little more difficult but what was surprising was that when I repeated the question about the order of the common fractions, pointing to the row of thousandths, the response was, 'Oh, when it's like that, it's the other way around.' This was met with nods of agreement and the following discussion ensued.

> L: Does that mean that your answer up here [pointing to the decimal fractions at the top of the whiteboard] … the order … can that be reversed?
> S3: No … when it's like that [referring to the decimal fractions] that's right.
> L: But don't you agree we haven't changed anything here … we've just renamed the decimal fractions as common fractions? [long period of silence]
> S1: I'm not sure … it's just the way it is.

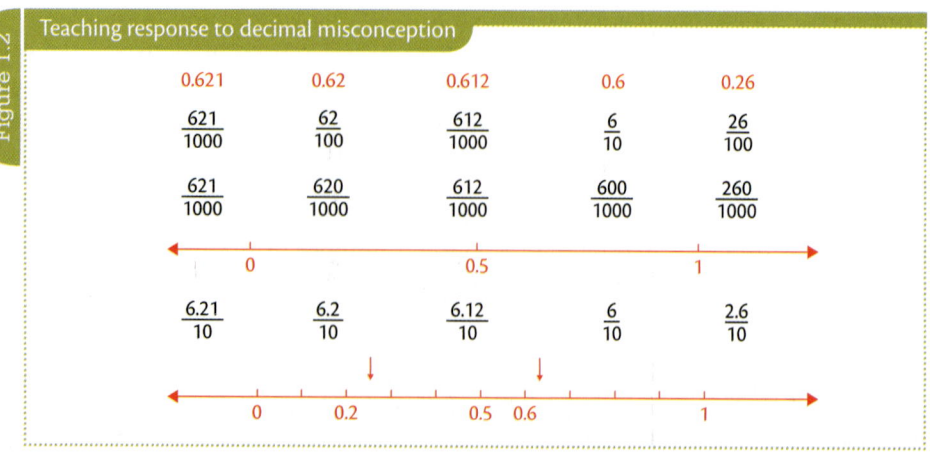

Figure 1.2 Teaching response to decimal misconception

Source: Siemon (1999)

Perplexed by this response, I drew a number line on the board, marked the points for 0 and 1 and asked the students to identify where 0.5 should be located. Most agreed that it should be placed half-way between 0 and 1 because 0.5 was a half. Having done that, I asked if this gave a clue as to where any of the decimal fractions might live, for example 0.6. With some uncertainty, it was agreed that 0.6 lived just a bit further to the right of 0.5, at which point I sketched in the remaining tenths. When it became clear that the students were uncertain where any of the other decimal fractions lived I suggested we rename them all as tenths. This proved extremely difficult but I persisted and used arrows to demonstrate that 6.21 tenths was a bit more than 6 tenths and 2.6 tenths was more than halfway between 2 tenths and 3 tenths. This was an unmitigated disaster. I had clearly lost them, and had no idea where to go to next. Nevertheless I asked:

L: Does that help? [very long pause]
S2: Sort of ... [another very long pause] ... you know, you said ... it goes thousands, hundreds, tens, ones, tenths and hundredths ...
L: Yes, the place-value parts [writing these on the board as Th H T O t h]
S2: Well, ... [coming out to the board and standing for a while in front of the 0 on the number line] ... if the ones, tens, hundreds, thousands and so on live down here [walking to the right and beyond 1 on the number line] ... then [returning to 0 and walking in the opposite direction] ... the tenths, hundredths, thousandths live down here.
L: Oh, now I see why you think 0.621 is the smallest, you think it lives down here. [points to the left of 0 on the number line, vigorous nods from at least four students]
S1: Yes, that's how I do it ... I never thought about it before, I just did it that way.
L: That's interesting. Can you tell me where you think the negative numbers live?
S1: Yes, you know ... [coming to the board and taking the pen] ... it goes like this [drawing two orthogonal number lines] ... they live down here [indicating the lower left hand quadrant].
L: That must have made learning secondary mathematics difficult ... Did you talk to your teacher about this?
S2: I tried, but he didn't understand ...

This indicates that a small but significant number of these primary pre-service teachers had independently constructed a shared view of the number line that was completely at odds with the conventional view. It is hard to conceive that they were ever taught or exposed to this view, so where has it come from? Having written the place-value headings on the board, I pointed to the 'O' (for Ones) and asked if this is what prompted them to marry the relative positions of the place-value parts to the number line. While two students said 'no' and a third offered, 'in my day it was "U" for units', I suspect that it was the appearance of a linear ordering that motivated their thinking, together with a view of the number line as a count of discrete junks rather than an infinite set of points.

I asked them how they managed to pass Year 11 maths, and the response was 'we learnt it off by heart'. It is hardly surprising that their mathematics teachers did not understand—they would be operating, as indeed I was, on the basis of an assumed model of the number line and would never have imagined that this other construction might exist. Indeed, it was entirely fortuitous that this conception came to light at all.

think + link

Chapter 2 discusses the importance of prior learning and understanding in the construction of shared mathematical meaning, and Chapter 6 examines the role of materials and representations in this process.

think + link

Chapter 7 discusses techniques for probing student understanding in more detail, in particular, it will describe the talking heads approach illustrated above to elicit Nick's strategies and beliefs.

From this experience I learnt never to underestimate the capacity of students to construct their own mathematical meanings—what might pass for learning on the surface may well be founded on misconceptions. In other words, it's wise to continue to probe student thinking and interrogate one's own understanding of mathematics.

Meaningful contexts

In 1985 Carraher, Carraher and Schliemann reported a study that involved school-aged children working as street vendors in Reciffe, Brazil. They had observed how efficiently the children had calculated the price of goods in the marketplace, and were interested to see if they could solve similar problems in a school context. The researchers identified the mathematics involved in the marketplace transactions, and created a comparable, context-free, symbolic problem and a related word problem. When these were presented in a school environment, it was evident that the children were not as successful as in the very specific context of the marketplace, although they were more likely to solve the related word problem correctly than the symbolic one. At the time, this research was used as an argument to include 'real-world' mathematics and multiple strategies in school pedagogy.

issues in teaching

Mathematics in the streets and schools

Asked how much 10 coconuts would cost, a 12-year-old street vendor in the third grade at school said, '3 will be 105 (cruzeiros), with 3 more that will be 210 ... I need 4 more, that is, ... 315 ... I think it is 350.'

However, when asked to add 105 and 105 and solve an equivalent word problem at school (Mary bought 35 bananas. Each banana cost 10 cruzeiros. How much did she pay altogether?), he attempted to solve the problems using school-taught strategies but was unsuccessful.

- What are the implications of this work for the teaching and learning of school mathematics?
- How might the students have learnt to carry out these calculations?
- There is an argument that these responses say more about the students' beliefs and expectations of schooling than about their capacity to solve problems. Do you agree?

for the classroom

Invite students to make a video and/or group poster of the contexts in which they or their friends use mathematics on a reasonably regular basis outside school. Compare and discuss examples and use the contexts to create a bank of similar problems.

Problem-solving is a one of the most important reasons for studying mathematics. But, as indicated above, the problems have changed significantly from the days of our great-great-grandparents. Today's problems can be found in popular culture more than in everyday calculations, and we need to be able to reason mathematically in order to interrogate the claims and counter-claims that are made in increasingly sophisticated ways. For example, mobile phone companies advertise their phone plans in ways that make it very difficult to decide which plan is the most appropriate. Solutions to these types of problems require a capacity to model and investigate complex situations, seek and process data, and communicate this effectively in a much wider range of ways than was the case in the past.

Assessment

Assessment plays a critical role in teaching and learning. There are two main purposes of assessment. The first, sometimes referred to as assessment of learning, is used for reporting purposes; it compares achievement against expected norms or standards. This information can be used to inform school-based decisions about curriculum offerings (e.g. the amount of time spent on geometry), education policy more generally, and system-wide initiatives such as additional professional development or targeted resourcing (e.g. Rowe, 2006). However, while this form of assessment is useful, it cannot be used to inform teachers about where to start teaching with individual students.

Scaffolding student learning is the primary task of teachers of mathematics, but this cannot be achieved without accurate information about what each student knows already and what might be within their grasp with some support from their teacher and/or peers. This second form of assessment, *assessment for learning*, requires assessment tasks and techniques that expose students' thinking in ways that it can be interpreted in terms of a recognised developmental progression of related ideas and strategies, ideally an evidence-based learning trajectory such as the *Learning Assessment Framework for Multiplicative Thinking* (Siemon, Breed, Dole, Izard & Virgona, 2006).

Social context

Teachers' decisions about what they do in classrooms are powerfully shaped by what they know and believe about the nature of mathematics and the teaching and learning of mathematics. They are also shaped by the behaviour of their students and the social context in which the teaching of mathematics is situated (Fennema et al., 1989). Poverty, racism, isolation, language background, and physical disability are among the many factors known to affect education outcomes. While schools alone cannot redress these inequities, there is much that schools and teachers can do to improve the education outcomes of students from disadvantaged backgrounds. For instance, we know from middle years research (e.g. Siemon & Virgona, 2001; Siemon et al., 2006) that the quality of teacher explanations, choice of instructional strategies, and capacity to recognise where to start teaching are crucial in meeting the needs of at-risk learners.

The social and physical arrangements of classrooms have changed since the days when it was assumed that the purpose of education was the transfer of knowledge into the 'empty heads' of children. Classrooms are now seen as collaborative communities of inquiry, with accepted ways of interacting (social norms), and negotiated ideas about what constitutes an explanation or what counts as a different solution, an efficient strategy, or a useful representation, all of which are examples of socio-mathematical norms (Yackel & Cobb, 1996).

think + link

Chapter 4 discusses problem solving and the importance of using real-world contexts, in considerably more detail.

think + link

Chapter 7 explores the purposes and forms of assessment in mathematics and discusses the important role of feedback in student learning.

think + link

Chapter 8 explores what we mean by diversity and the implications of this for the teaching and learning of mathematics.

> **consider and discuss**
>
> **role of affect in learning**
>
> STOP! Before you read the sentences below, cover them with a piece of paper. Slowly slide the paper down and read one sentence at a time, then stop and record your emotional reaction at the end of each sentence.
>
> The baby kicked the ball.
> The football player kicked the ball.
> The golfer kicked the ball.
>
> 1. What did you notice?
> 2. What are the implications of this for teaching and learning mathematics?
>
> Chances are that after the first sentence you experienced a warm feeling: 'Oh, how cute.' After the second sentence, you may have had a more neutral reaction, depending on your love or otherwise of football. But if you know anything at all about the rules of golf, you undoubtedly would have reacted with some indignation at the thought of a golfer kicking the ball.

The issues of agency (available means) and identity are often ignored in programs designed to improve school mathematics outcomes or attempts to understand why some students are indifferent or resistant to mathematics (Sfard & Prusak, 2005). Sagor and Cox (2004) have identified five essential feelings they believe are crucial to a young person's well-being and success at school: 'the need to feel competent, the need to feel they belong, the need to feel useful, the need to feel potent, and the need to feel optimistic' (p. 4). They explain why working only on the behaviours and attitudes of discouraged learners is insufficient, and suggest including an additional dimension, the need to feel they have a valued role to play in the social context.

> **handy hint**
>
> **Engage students as teachers**
>
> Establish a classroom culture that ensures all students have an opportunity to participate and share their strengths with their peers.

think + link

The issue of streaming will be considered in Chapter 8. Chapter 29 explores what is involved in becoming a reflective practitioner and what is involved in the broader work of a teacher of mathematics.

Teaching does not take place in isolation. Mandated curriculum, national testing, parent expectations, and public perceptions about the capacities of school leavers all exert pressure on education systems, schools, and teachers. This can lead to poor practices such as 'teaching to the test', over-scaffolding learning, and ability-based organisational structures (otherwise known as streaming or tracking), so teachers need to have the knowledge and confidence to withstand such pressures while meeting reasonable institutional requirements. Collaborative planning and a commitment to ongoing professional learning are key to maintaining quality in mathematics teaching and learning.

Conclusion

A deep understanding of mathematics is necessary for responsible citizenship in an increasingly globalised world. What we know and believe about the nature and purpose of school mathematics determines what we value and what we assess. It also has important implications for how we teach and what we expect of students as they engage with mathematics. The citizen of tomorrow will need to be able to mathematise, that is, to make sense of the world using mathematics through modelling and problem solving, rather than regurgitate a set of arid facts and procedures.

School mathematics is changing in response to research about the nature of children's learning of mathematics and studies of effective classroom practice, but it is also changing with advances in technology. If you were born before 1990, your school might have had one computer per classroom, but that computer would have had significantly less memory and processing capacity than a modern mobile phone, and it was far less user-friendly than an MP3 player. Digital technologies are changing how we learn and how we think about teaching. We now recognise that students need to have a deep understanding of how numbers work, access to a wide range of strategies that they can use confidently and flexibly to reason mathematically and solve problems, and the capacity to examine quantitative and spatial information critically.

Our collective knowledge of how mathematics is learnt has increased over the last 40 to 50 years. Before the 1950s, mathematics education was not recognised as a field of academic inquiry in English-speaking countries. The study of learning was very much the province of psychology, itself an emerging field, governed strictly by the rules of scientific experimentation, where rats in mazes and pigeons pecking levers were used as a basis for making claims about human learning. We now know that learning mathematics is a much more complex affair. While there is a place for perceptual learning—for instance, we need to recognise the number names and symbols—beyond this, most learning in mathematics needs to involve **conceptual understanding**; that is, it needs to build on meaningful ideas and multiple representations and be supported by collaborative discussion, rich and challenging tasks, and personal success.

As a consequence, what it means to be a teacher of mathematics has changed and is changing. We can no longer justify the 'sage on the stage' approach, where the teacher is seen as the font of all wisdom, where power differentials are routinely exercised and one voice, the teacher's voice, dominates the discourse. Teachers are now expected to be orchestrators of engaging, purposeful learning environments who have the knowledge and confidence to make connections between important mathematical ideas and strategies and between individual learners and mathematics in-the-moment. It is critically important for teachers to understand the students they teach and the social context in which teaching occurs.

key terms

Conceptual understanding: understanding indicated by the quality and quantity of connections that are made between new and existing ideas (e.g. a conceptual understanding of area enables students to solve unfamiliar problems such as determining the dimensions of a paddock given a certain length of fencing)

Content: subject matter (e.g. in mathematics this might refer to Pythagoras' Theorem or the formula for calculating the area of a rectangle)

Curriculum: document specifying content to be taught (often stated as outcomes), generally incorporating advice on how to teach (pedagogy) as well as assessment

Knowledge for teaching mathematics (KTM): synonymous with PCK but emphasises knowledge needed to teach particular content domain

Mathematical communication: any mode of expression that supports an exchange of mathematical ideas or strategies; generally, spoken or written language, visual representations such as diagrams and graphs, or symbolic expressions

Mathematical fluency: capacity to use mathematical knowledge and strategies in multiple ways (e.g. access to a variety of efficient ways to add 2 two-digit numbers mentally)

Mathematical problem solving: processes involved in making sense of a mathematical problem, situation, or task, exploring and implementing possible strategies, and checking the reasonableness of results

Mathematical reasoning: capacity to think through mathematical problems logically and systematically and apply what is known; often involves inferring, proving, formulating, and testing conjectures

Open-ended questions/activities: questions or activities that generally involve some higher-order thinking (e.g. analysis, synthesis), present opportunities for learning, and have several plausible solutions (e.g. 'How might I have paid for an item costing $5.35?'; 'The answer is 24. What is the question?')

Pedagogical content knowledge (PCK): accredited to Shulman (1986), PCK refers to the knowledge needed to teach a particular discipline; it involves content or subject-matter knowledge, pedagogical knowledge (how to teach in general), and knowledge about what makes the particular content easy/difficult to teach and learn (knowledge of students)

Pedagogy: the art and science of teaching; knowledge of the principles and practices of teaching and learning

Representations: forms of elaboration; a physical, visual, or symbolic model of a particular phenomenon (e.g. fractions can be represented using region diagrams or number lines, a set of ordered pairs can be represented in a table of values, as a graph, or a symbolic expression)

Rich tasks: tasks similar to open-ended questions but generally more complex, involving investigation, data collection, analysis, and reporting (e.g. How much rubbish does our classroom produce in one year?)

Review questions

1. Many people believe mathematics is an exact science where an answer is either right or wrong. Do you agree? Why? Can you find an instance where this is not the case?
2. What do you believe to be the principal goal of school mathematics? Consider this same question from the perspective of students, parents, employers, and politicians. What differences, if any, might you expect?
3. Who is likely to be advantaged and disadvantaged in learning school mathematics? Why?
4. Write a maths autobiography about your experience as a student of school mathematics. Which teacher stands out? Why? Share your observations and make a list of the attributes of effective teachers of mathematics. Describe the sort of mathematics teacher you aspire to be.
5. How students feel about mathematics affects the way they participate and learn. Find out about mathematics anxiety. What are the likely causes, and how might it be avoided?
6. At the outset, we asked you to consider when you last 'truly, deeply, madly' enjoyed doing some mathematics. Describe your experience to a friend and consider the implications of this for teaching mathematics.

Key references

Australian Curriculum Assessment and Reporting Authority [ACARA] 2011. *The Australian Curriculum: Mathematics*. Sydney: ACARA.

Ball, D., Thames, M., & Phelps, G. (2008). Content knowledge for teaching: What makes it special? *Journal of Teacher Education*, 59(5), 389–407.

Bishop, A. (Ed.) (1988). *Mathematics Education and Culture*. Dordrecht, Netherlands: Kluwer.

Boaler, J. (2002). *Experiencing School Mathematics* (rev. ed.). Mahwah, NJ: Erlbaum.

Carraher, T., Carraher, D., & Schliemann, A. (1985). Mathematics in the streets and in the school. *British Journal of Developmental Psychology*, 3, 21–29.

Ernest, P. (1991). *The Philosophy of Mathematics Education*. Basingstoke, UK: Falmer Press.

National Council of Teachers of Mathematics (2000). *Principles and Standards for School Mathematics*. Reston, VA: Author.

National Curriculum Board (NCB) (2009). *Shape of the Australian Curriculum: Mathematics*. Canberra: Commonwealth of Australia. Accessed 22 March 2010 from: www.acara.edu.au/verve/_resources/Australian_Curriculum_-_Maths.pdf.

Sagor, R., & Cox, J. (2004). *At-risk Students: Reaching and Teaching Them* (2nd ed.). New York: Eye on Education.

Sfard, A., & Prusak, A. (2005). Identity that makes a difference: Substantial learning as closing the gap between actual and designated identities. In H. Chick and J. Vincent (Eds.). *Proceedings of the 29th Conference of the International Group for the Psychology of Mathematics Education*, Vol. 1 (pp. 37–52). Melbourne: PME.

Shulman, L. S. (1986). Those who understand: Knowledge growth in teaching. *Educational Researcher*, 15(5), 4–14.

Siemon, D. (1989). Knowing and believing is seeing—A constructivist's perspective of change. In K. Clements & N. Ellerton (Eds.), *School Mathematics: The Challenge to Change* (pp. 250–268). Geelong, Vic: Deakin University Press.

Siemon, D., Breed, M., Dole, S., Izard, J., & Virgona, J. (2006). *The Final Report of the Scaffolding Numeracy in the Middle Years Project*. [CD-rom], Melbourne: RMIT University.

Thompson, A. (1984). The relationship of teachers' conceptions of mathematics and mathematics teaching to instructional practice. *Educational Studies in Mathematics*, 15(2), 105–127.

Watson, H. (1989). *Singing the Land, Signing the Land*. Geelong, Vic: Deakin University Press.

Wood, T. (1994). Patterns of interaction and the culture of mathematics classrooms. In S. Lerman (Ed.), *The Culture of the Mathematics Classroom* (pp.149–168). Dordrecht, Netherlands: Kluwer.

Yackel, E., & Cobb, P. (1996). Sociomathematical norms, argumentations, and autonomy in mathematics. *Journal for Research in Mathematics Education*, 27(4), 458–477.

Websites

http://research.acer.edu.au/timss_2007/3/
http://timss.bc.edu/timss2007/index.html
www.acara.edu.au/default.asp
www.aamt.edu.au/Standards
www.acer.edu.au/ozpisa/
www.education.vic.gov.au/studentlearning/teachingresources/maths/mynr.htm
www.education.vic.gov.au/studentlearning/teachingresources/maths/snmy/resourcelib.htm
www.nctm.org/
www.oecd.org/pages/0,3417,en_32252351_32235731_1_1_1_1_1,00.html

2 Learning Mathematics

Contents

What does it mean to learn mathematics? 26
Learning and understanding mathematics 38
Developing your own theory of mathematics learning 43

Chapter objectives

This chapter will enable the reader to:
- Be introduced to a range of learning theories as they apply to learning mathematics
- Develop an understanding of the relationship between theories of learning and the practical activity of learning and teaching mathematics in classrooms
- Develop an appreciation of the beliefs about mathematics and mathematics learners that underpin learning theories
- Consider beliefs about mathematics and mathematics learners and the ways in which they influence personal theories of mathematics learning
- Begin to articulate a personal theory of mathematics learning.

A story of learning

Once there was a toddler who liked to help his mother hang out the washing. He could pass her one clothes peg at a time as she asked for it. Later he could hand her one or two, depending on which number she asked for. He seemed to know exactly what 'one' and 'two' meant, and his mother was very proud. Then one day when they were driving in the country they passed a paddock in which a herd of dairy cows was grazing. 'Two! two!' the toddler exclaimed.

 **consider and discuss**

What had the toddler learnt about the numbers one and two? How might he have learnt this?

Big ideas

- Learning is about change: in behaviour, thinking, social participation, or brain structure.
- Theories of mathematics learning are based on beliefs about learners and mathematics.
- All teaching is based on a theory of learning.
- Learning is both an individual process and a social activity.
- Theories of human development can inform learning theories.

There are many theories about how learning happens, each with implications for how teachers can best help students to learn. Whether or not they can articulate it, all teachers have a theory of learning that informs their teaching (Bigge & Shermis, 1999, p. 3). The choices they make about the activities and materials they provide, how they interpret the curriculum, the ways in which they organise students for learning, the kinds of questions they ask, and the aspects of students' mathematical performances that they value are all informed by theory. Bigge and Shermis (1999, p. 5) observe that teachers who are not informed by a coherent theory as they make these choices 'are behaving blindly; little evidence of long term rationale, purpose or plan is evident in their teaching'. The education theorist Kurt Lewin argued 'There is nothing so practical as a good theory' (Lewin, 1951, p. 169). Having a carefully considered personal theory about how students learn mathematics will allow you to make teaching decisions based on principles rather than fads, to justify your choices, and, most importantly, to maximise the learning that happens in your classroom.

The following are quotes from teachers about how students learn mathematics. They reflect a range of views, some compatible with one another and others that are contradictory. These teachers had thought through their theoretical positions about mathematics learning to different extents, and there was evidence that their differing beliefs about learning contributed to differences in their classrooms (Beswick, 2005). As you read them, think about the implications that each might have for the classroom. How would you teach mathematics if this was your belief about learning?

> Give them an example; they can basically follow the pattern of the problem. (Paul)
>
> Practice makes perfect, I think. (Brian)
>
> People learn, by saying no, this either fits with what I already know or no it doesn't fit, and when it doesn't fit then you make progress. (Andrew)
>
> I guess they've got this handle in their head, and if they've got that then they can just grab that new idea and link it onto it. (Jennifer)

What does it mean to learn mathematics?

Before we can answer this question we need to think about what mathematics is and what it means to learn. As we found in Chapter 1 in relation to the **nature of mathematics**, simple questions don't always have simple answers.

What is mathematics?

In Chapter 1 we explored several definitions of mathematics and its integral relationship with culture. If you ask most people what they think mathematics is, their answers commonly express opinions about mathematics, e.g. maths is interesting, useful, or boring, or they comprise topics that are typically part of the mathematics curriculum, such as adding and subtracting, fractions, algebra. Sometimes answers will refer to processes or to experiences of learning mathematics at school. Even teachers of mathematics have trouble answering this question. The following are some examples of their responses to this question from Beswick (2003):

> Well, basically numbers I suppose, and problem solving.
>
> Maths was getting the right answer, as quickly as we could.
>
> It gives me a way of making sense of things.
>
> When I hear the word mathematics I think of, well, numbers obviously.
>
> Well, I suppose things one sees in a maths book for a start, and everyday things that you just solve all the time, like how much curtain material to get and that type of thing.

None of these descriptions of mathematics actually gets to heart of what mathematics is. The question continues to exercise the minds of mathematicians and philosophers, even after centuries of thought. Ernest (1989) described three views of mathematics that have implications for what teachers believe about how students learn mathematics and how it should be taught. These are *instrumentalist*, *Platonist*, and *problem-solving*. People with an **instrumentalist** view of mathematics see it as a useful kit of tools or techniques for use in everyday life. For them, learning mathematics is about acquiring practical facts and skills. **Platonists** are less interested in the uses of mathematics and instead emphasise the relationships between mathematical ideas and the hierarchical structure of the discipline. They regard mathematics as existing independently of humans and awaiting discovery. For Platonists, learning mathematics is about coming to understand the interconnectedness of mathematics and developing an appreciation of the discipline for its own sake. From a **problem-solving** view, mathematics is regarded as a dynamic and creative human invention, a process rather than a product. To learn mathematics is to engage in a creative process.

Most people do not have **beliefs** about mathematics that fall neatly into any one of Ernest's categories, but rather believe it has elements of more than one

think + link

Take a few minutes to write down and discuss what you think mathematics *is*. With which of Ernest's views is your own view most closely aligned? How do you think you came to see mathematics this way?

category. You may have felt that parts of each ring true, perhaps in different contexts. It is important that you know what you believe mathematics is, and that you think carefully through the implications for how you teach mathematics of what you believe about it. Even if you are not consciously aware of them, your views about the nature of mathematics will have a powerful influence on how you teach, and hence on how your students learn mathematics and come to view the discipline for themselves.

consider and discuss

1. How do you think that seeing mathematics in the way you do will influence how you teach it?
2. Why do you think so many people associate mathematics with numbers when school mathematics curricula include much more? (Look at the Contents page of this book, for example.)

did you know?

Plato set out his views on education in *The Republic* in approximately 375 BCE. He viewed the study of mathematics as of central importance and valued it as a means of training the mind rather than for its practical uses.

This view of the purpose of studying mathematics still affects the teaching of mathematics today and is evident in students' views about mathematics. For example, in a recent survey of 643 Australian students in Years 5–8, more than 75% agreed with the statement that 'maths helps to develop my mind and teaches me to think' (Beswick, Watson & Brown, 2006).

What is learning?

There are also many views about the processes involved in learning. Common to all is that **learning** is about lasting change that is not simply a consequence of maturation or development (Bigge & Shermis, 1999), but rather of experience (Schunk, 2004). Changes may relate to behaviour or the capacity for behaviour as a result of changes internal to the individual (Schunk, 2004).

Learning theories are coherent sets of principles that explain how learning occurs. The most influential learning theories of the past century can be broadly grouped according to their focus on change to behaviour or to thinking (Bigge & Shermis, 1999). More recently, advances in neuroscience have led to increasing interest in the relationship between learning and the structure and function of the brain (Bransford, Brown, & Cocking, 2000).

The remainder of this chapter considers developmental theories that have informed theories of learning, and then uses the object of change (behaviour, thinking, social participation, brain) to categorise learning theories. The theories mentioned are illustrative and vary in the degree to which they are embraced by mathematics educators, but the influences of all are to be found in present-day mathematics classrooms. Inherent in each are ideas about the nature of mathematics learners, learning, and mathematics itself.

for the classroom

Children's drawing of maths time

You can find out a lot about what children think about mathematics and learning mathematics by asking them to draw themselves during maths time at school. Older children might prefer to write about themselves in maths time or to produce a combination of drawing and writing. Asking younger children to talk about their drawings can provide particularly rich information about their thinking.

Once you have a set of students' drawings or writings, consider what they reveal about the students' beliefs about what mathematics is and what it means to learn mathematics. Consider how they might have arrived at these beliefs. What classroom experiences would have led to them? Are they the kinds of beliefs you would like your students to have? Why, or why not? How might you influence students' views of mathematics and mathematics learning?

(See Walls (2007) for examples of student responses to a task like this, and MacDonald (2010) for a discussion of the drawing/talking process with young children.)

Learning and development

Development relates to changes that occur as a result of maturation. Just as children develop physically, they also develop socally, emotionally, and cognitively. Theories of human development are not learning theories, but they are closely linked to, and underpin, most theories of learning. Children's stages of development have an impact on the ways in which they learn, and on the kinds of skills, knowledge, and understandings that they are able to acquire. This is what teachers mean when they talk about children's readiness to learn.

You may be aware of debates about nature versus nurture. These concern the extent to which we are born with certain capacities and tendencies that unfold and play themselves out as we grow (nature), compared with how much influence our environment, upbringing and indeed education has on the kinds of characteristics and capacities that we eventually develop (nurture). As we consider various developmental and learning theories you will notice aspects that suggest greater or lesser roles for nature and nurture. Although the debate makes for attention-grabbing headlines, the consensus is that both play a part, and there is increasing evidence that innate and environmental influences interact in surprising, subtle, and complex ways (e.g. Spencer, Blumberg, McMurray, Robinson, Samuelson & Tomblin, 2009).

issues in teaching

'Claims that innate intelligence can be measured scientifically and used to predict future academic success have condemned many children to a second-class education. By contrast, an education that sets no limits on a child's potential to understand, and appreciates that understandings are intensely personal, will encourage diversity and celebrate individual differences' (Sankey, 2007, p. 544).

Children are commonly grouped in terms of perceived ability, and many teachers would argue that teaching in any other way would be impossible. The practice tends to become more formalised in secondary school. However, the Australian mathematics curriculum is intended to be underpinned by a commitment to equity. The National Curriculum Board (2009) recommended heterogeneous groupings, and differentiating common tasks to cater for diversity. It explictly stated that 'All students can learn mathematics' and that 'all students should experience the full mathematics curriculum until the end of Year 10.'

- What do you think is meant by 'ability' in the context of teaching children in ability groups?
- How might teachers decide a child's ability? What problems might there be with this?
- Consider the advantages and disadvantages of teaching children in groups based on ability.
- How can the disadvantages of grouping students by ability be minimised while maximising the advantages?
- How can the disadvantages of mixed-ability groups be minimised while maximising the advantages?
- Write a paragraph explaining and justifying your view on ability grouping.

making connections

The following quote is from an article by Steven Pinker in *Time* magazine on 20 January 2003:

> The discovery that genes have something to do with behavior came as a shock in the second half of the 20th century, when most people still thought that the mind of a newborn was a blank slate and that anyone could do anything if only he or she strove hard enough. And the link continues to set off alarm bells about what it will lead to. Many people are worried about a Brave New World in which parents or governments will try to re-engineer human nature. Others see genes as a threat to free will and personal responsibility, citing headlines like MAN'S GENES MADE HIM KILL, HIS LAWYERS CLAIM.

How might stories such as this influence the controversy over the nature of intelligence and its implications for schooling? How should educators respond?

We will briefly consider the ideas of Piaget and Bruner, two developmental theorists who have been particularly influential in shaping current ideas about mathematics learning. We also consider recent understandings of the development of the human brain and the mechanisms involved in learning.

Piaget

Cobb (2007) describes Piaget as a genetic epistemologist. That is, he was interested in the origins (genesis) of knowledge (epistemology is the study of knowledge). Piaget saw learning as an individual process that occurs in **response** to environmental stimuli, and his work is foundational to **constructivist theories** of learning (Lerman, 1989).

Piaget described four distinct stages of an individual's cognitive development, with transitions between stages involving radical transformations in cognitive structures. In Table 2.1 the stages are described briefly, and the ages to which Piaget believed each typically applied are given.

Table 2.1 Piagetian stages of cognitive development

Stage	Typical age range (years)	Characteristics of the stage
Sensorimotor	0–2	Rapid cognitive development resulting from spontaneous physical actions; no clear distinction between self and the world
Preoperational	2–7	Inability to conserve, manifested in, for example, a tendency to see a spread-out collection of objects as larger than one in which the same number of objects are tightly grouped; self regarded as separate, and can conceive of others thinking and feeling diffferently from them but fantasy and reality not readily distinguished; beginning to use symbolic representations (e.g. drawing and graphics) and to develop the ability to imagine events without direct physical action
Concrete operational	7–11	Cognition increasingly separate from physical objects; can imagine actions and undoing actions, can classify and reclassify things and see relationships between classes of things; draws on experiences as well as immediate perceptions
Formal operational	11 to adult	Ability to hypothesise and consider multiple aspects of problems; abstract reasoning; construction of ideals

Piaget's stages have attracted a number of criticisms. One critique centres on the implied completion of cognitive development by adolescence. Smith and Reio (2006, p. 120) argue that the formal operational stage does not account fully for the abilities of adults to 'deal with ambiguity, subjectivity, contradictions and relativism'; nor does it deal adequately with the role of emotion in reasoning and decision making. It seems that cognitive abilities develop beyond Piaget's formal operational stage. Others have noted that primary school children are able to think in ways characteristic of the formal operational stage (Linn & Eylon, 2006); that children's cognitive development does not follow Piaget's stages consistently across domains (e.g. they can be at different stages in mathematics and history); and that adults do not think at the formal operational level in all circumstances (Schunk, 2004). It is valuable for teachers to be aware of Piaget's stages but they should not be applied rigidly, and certainly should not be used to justify denying young children opportunities to demonstrate and develop sophisticated ways of thinking.

Arguably of greater relevance to the development of learning theories are the processes by which Piaget envisioned an individual's cognitive structures develop (Cobb, 2007). His three processes are *assimilation*, *accommodation*, and *equilibration*; they are internal to the individual and occur as the individual responds to sensory input from the world.

- Assimilation is the process by which we interpret input from our senses in terms of our existing cognitive structures. It is the process that explains why different people can interpret the same information differently.
- Accommodation occurs when existing cognitive structures need to be changed to allow new input to be assimilated, such as when there is an apparent contradiction between what we believe and new information (Schunk, 2004). For example, many primary school children believe (perhaps because they have been incorrectly told) that a larger number cannot be subtracted from a smaller number. This idea causes no difficulty until they are introduced to negative numbers, and now are told that you can subtract any number from any other number! Making sense of negative numbers requires alteration of existing cognitive structures related to number.
- Both assimilation and accommodation are directed towards achieving a state of equilibrium, in which there is a match between the individual's cognitive structures and perceived reality. In the example of negative numbers, equilibration is the process driving the accommodation and subsequent assimilation that allows the learner to come to terms with the new and initially contradictory information (Schunk, 2004).

Bruner

Piaget's stages suggest that innate capacities unfold at particular ages. In contrast, Bruner emphasised the role of the child's culture in his/her cognitive development and regarded people as inseparable from their culture. According to Bigge and Shermis (1999), Bruner regarded learning as an active process by which people select, keep, and alter information, relating it to existing knowledge. Through this process they build up a mental model of the world and organise information so that patterns in their experiences can be recognised. In so doing the individual extends the information that was received. As they grow, people become increasingly able to think about things independently of actual objects and events, but Bruner did not regard this development as linked to particular ages.

Bruner described three different modes of representation that individuals develop, usually in order, and retain into adulthood (Bigge & Shermis, 1999).

- The *enactive* mode of representation is about knowing how to do things without using symbols or words to express that knowledge. Knowing how to use a spoon or ride a bicycle are good examples of the enactive mode.
- The *iconic* mode of representation involves using symbols to represent concepts. The symbol doesn't define the concept fully; rather it stands for it in the way that a stick figure can stand for a person.
- Language is increasingly important in the *symbolic* mode, and thought and symbol systems, such as those of a language or mathematical notation, encode knowledge and allow the development and consideration of abstract concepts (Schunk, 2004).

Knowing how to ride a bicycle illustrates how all three modes can exist together. When people say 'It's like riding a bike', they are referring to the enactive mode of representation—knowledge of how to ride a bicycle is not held in symbols or language; rather you know how to do it. At the same time, though, you may also have a sensory image of bicycle riding; perhaps you can remember how it feels to balance, how increasing speed makes balancing easier, and so on. These images of bicycle riding are examples of the iconic mode. You might also know about concepts like centre of gravity and momentum, and so can explain why it's easier to balance on a bicycle if the weight to be carried is lower (carrying books in paniers is less likely to make you fall off than carrying them in a back pack), and why increasing speed makes balancing easier. That is, you also have knowledge of bicycle riding represented in the symbolic mode.

Young children use multiple modes similarly. Figure 2.1 shows a Year 2 child's linking of symbolic and iconic representations of multiplication facts that make 12.

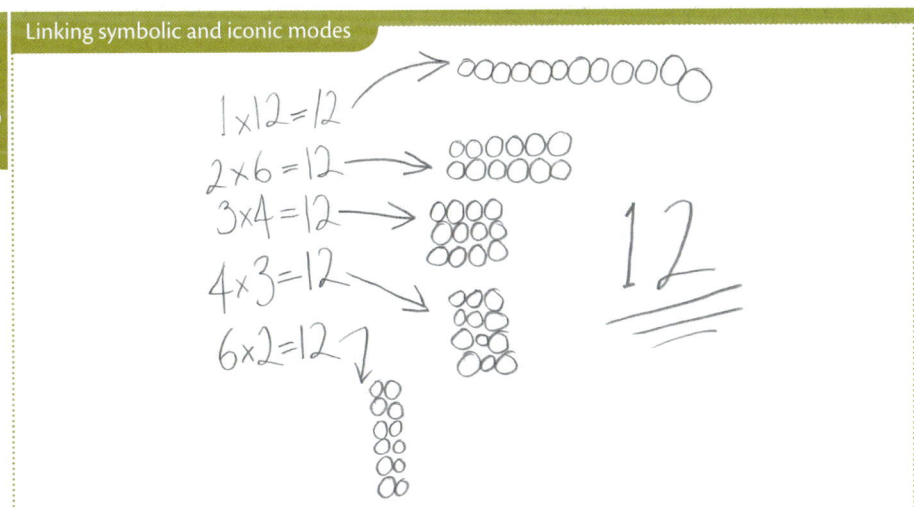

Figure 2.1 Linking symbolic and iconic modes

Brain development

It is clear that some aspects of learning are dependent upon the physical development of the brain. It is also possible to consider brain-based learning as a learning theory, albeit relatively underdeveloped, in that it provides an explanation of how at least some learning occurs. We revisit brain-based learning later in the chapter.

The brain is comprised of cells called neurons that connect with one another at synapses. At birth the human brain is approximately two-thirds of its adult size. It develops rapidly, and by age three has more synapses than the adult brain. Subsequent brain development proceeds by the selective loss of synapses, with those that are used being retained and those that are not used being lost. Bransford et al. (2000) emphasise that this process is not simply influenced by experience but is in fact driven by it, and different kinds of experience appear to be particularly potent at different stages of brain development. For example, initial synapse production is particularly rapid in the area of the brain governing vision, but is much slower in the region governing higher order cognitive functions. Experience is also crucial to the brain development that occurs following the selection and loss of synapses. In this phase, which continues throughout life, synapses are modified and new synapses created (Bransford et al., 2000).

Different areas of the brain control different functions, but the extent to which specific functions are confined to particular areas is not clear; there is evidence that multiple areas are involved in the performance of complex tasks. This evidence extends to the popular view of the brain's right hemisphere governing visual, auditory, and spatial perception and the left being the site of analytic thinking and language. Schunk (2004) warns against simplistic interpretations of these sorts of findings, pointing out that although the different hemispheres appear to process certain types of information more efficiently, both are involved in almost all tasks.

Learning as changing behaviour

Behaviourists regard learners essentially as stimulus–response systems. Rather than actively exploring the world, they are shaped by environmental influences (**stimuli**) upon them to which they respond. Behaviourist theories dominated education for most of the twentieth century, and although rarely advocated today their influence in classrooms remains powerful (Bigge & Shermis, 1999). Arguably the most influential of the behaviourists was B. F. Skinner (e.g. Skinner, 1974). Skinner's operant conditioning was based upon extensive experiments with animals in which it was demonstrated that desirable but initially random behaviours (e.g. a rat pushing a particular lever) could be made more likely to occur when followed by a reward (e.g. the release of food). Conversely, if a behaviour consistently results in an unpleasant consequence or the absence of a reward, then its likelihood is decreased (Bigge & Shermis, 1999). One version of **behaviourism** is operant conditioning.

Operant conditioning

Biggs and Telfer (1981) described **operant conditioning** as follows:

> If you want someone to do something you make it worth his while; if you want him to stop, you likewise make it worth his while, or more worth his while to do something else. Not a very noble message but an effective one. (p. 147)

Operant conditioning has been applied to behaviour management as well as to academic learning, and is still highly influential in relation to the former (e.g. Rogers & MacPherson, 2008). In academic learning, it was associated with considerable interest in motivation as a means of engaging students so that correct performance of a task could be rewarded. Behaviourists are particularly interested in the roles of extrinsic and intrinsic rewards in reinforcing desired behaviours that define learning (e.g. correctly performing a calculation algorithm) and hence make the desired behaviours more likely (Biggs & Telfer, 1981). Behaviourists regard extrinsic rewards as particularly important for motivating students to engage with a task initially, before it is possible for them to find any intrinsic value in performing it.

Teachers with a behaviourist view of learning tend to set learning objectives in terms of observable behaviours. For them it makes no sense to have lesson objectives phrased in terms of what students will understand. Even if the goal of teaching is understanding, this is an internal and hence unobservable state, and except by observing students' behaviour, the teacher has no way to know whether or not or to what extent it has been achieved. Objectives therefore must be framed in terms of observable behaviours, which can include things that students say or do.

Many aspects of learning, including of learning mathematics, can be readily observed. Students can either recall facts and demonstrate skills or they cannot. For a teacher who believes that mathematics is a set of facts and skills (i.e. Ernest's instrumental view), then behaviourist learning theories make perfect sense, and teaching that is consistent with a behaviourist view of learning is common in many Australian classrooms (Beswick, Swabey & Andrew, 2008).

More recently it has been argued that there is more to understanding than can be defined in terms of observable behaviours. We consider the nature of understanding later in this chapter.

Learning as changing thinking

The second major category of learning theories views learning as something that happens inside the learner: 'Learning is a process of gaining or changing insights, outlooks, expectations or thought patterns' (Bigge & Shermis, 1999, p. 11). These theories build upon and amend, rather than replace, earlier behaviourist theories. In particular they extend the idea of the individual learner responding or reacting to environmental stimuli to an interactionist view in which the learner also acts upon and influences the environment, and in which the notion of environment itself refers not simply to physical aspects but most importantly to the psychological environment of the individual (Schunk, 2004).

Social learning theory

Bandura (e.g. Bandura, 1977) developed social learning theory to address perceived shortcomings in behaviourism. Among the observations that drove the development of his theory was that people learn a great deal by imitating others. Operant conditioning explains this in terms of imitative behaviour happening essentially randomly and then being reinforced. For example, when a young child hears and then repeats the counting sequence 1, 2, 3, she receives praise and smiles that reinforce the behaviour, making it more likely to be repeated. Social learning theory argues that, rather than pleasant consequences simply providing reinforcement, they change the learner's thinking by providing information (e.g. about the sorts of responses that the behaviour elicits, and about what is socially acceptable and valued) and motivation. Bandura (1977) argued that it is the changed thinking, rather than the changed behaviour, that constitutes the learning. A further important distinction between social learning theory and behaviourism arises from this. According to social learning theory, behaviour need not change, either immediately or at all, as a result of learning. That is, the learner may think differently as a result of interacting with the environment, but this may not be evident in any observable behaviour. This clearly presents a dilemma for teachers committed to strictly behavioural objectives.

Social learning theory emphasises modelling as a means of teaching (Schunk, 2004). It underpins the common lesson pattern in which students attend to the teacher as he demonstrates a new skill (e.g. a mathematics algorithm), then practise that skill, and finally receive feedback on their performance. Schunk (2004) terms this observational learning, and makes the point that it is even more effective when it is accompanied by cognitive modelling or the modelling of thinking, for example by 'thinking aloud', and/or explanations. In recent years, mathematics educators have emphasised that it is process and strategy rather than particular procedures that should be modelled (e.g. Department of Education, Science and Training, 2004; Doig, McRae & Rowe, 2003). Such views stem from a belief in the importance of understanding in contrast to procedural efficiency based on meaningless mimicry (Beswick et al., 2008).

Bandura (1977) also emphasised the role of self-regulation and self-efficacy in learning. Self-regulation refers to the control that the learner exercises over his/her thinking, and self-efficacy refers to individuals' beliefs about their capacities to learn and their likelihood of success with a given task. These ideas are fundamentally related to problem-solving behaviour and motivation, and emphasise the three-way interactions between the individual, the individual's behaviour, and the environment (Schunk, 2004).

consider and discuss

1. Think about some of the mathematics you have learnt. Try to identify examples of skills or knowledge that you have acquired in ways that:
   - could be explained by operant conditioning
   - could be explained by social learning theory
   - could be explained by both theories
   - could be explained by social learning theory but not by operant conditioning
   - could be explained by operant conditioning but not by social learning theory
   - could not be explained by either theory.

   Discuss the kinds of learning that you placed in each category. What generalisations can you make about the applications of the two theories?

2. Classify examples of mathematics teaching that you have experienced or observed according to the same categories.

3. Which theory best describes the way that you are learning as you read sections of this text, and as you engaged with the classifying exercises in 1 and 2? Justify your choice.

Constructivism

The development of constructivism as a theory of learning can be traced to the work of Piaget (Lerman, 1989) and Bruner, and can be seen as a development of earlier interactionist theories of learning including Bandura's social learning theory. Constructivism envisages learners as actively interacting with their environments: physical, social, and psychological. Von Glasersfeld (1990) defined constructivism in terms of two essential tenets:

> Knowledge is not passively received either through the senses or by way of communication. Knowledge is actively built up by the cognising subject. (p. 22)

> The function of cognition is adaptive, in the biological sense of the term, tending towards fit or viability. Cognition serves the subject's organization of the experiential world, not the discovery of an objective ontological reality. (p. 23)

Implicit in these tenets is the importance of the learner's existing knowledge, constructed on the basis of past experiences. Each learner's experience is unique, and hence current knowledge means that each learner is likely to construct differing knowledge in response to a given experience. The second tenet emphasises the purposive nature of the individual's constructive activity in that it is directed to constructing knowledge that is powerful, that makes sense of the broadest possible range of experience. Learning therefore amounts to the process whereby an individual actively and purposefully modifies, or if necessary completely changes, their constructions in order to achieve an optimal fit with their experience.

As with other learning theories, there is a range of variations on this basic description, particularly in regard to the extent to which the second part of von Glasersfeld's second tenet is accepted. Von Glaserfeld (1990) defines a view of constructivism commonly termed 'radical'. Radical constructivists argue that because learners only access the external world by way of their senses, the knowledge they construct is based solely on their own experiences. Hence no individual can know either the extent to which his/her knowledge corresponds with (i) any external reality (assuming that there is such a thing) or to (ii) anyone else's knowledge. Both of these limitations have implications that need to be addressed.

In relation to the first, Lerman (1989) explained that radical constructivism's rejection of a knowable independent world external to the knower does not mean that we have no basis for valuing some knowledge more highly than other knowledge, or even for using words such as truth. Rather it necessitates a constant examination of evidence and comparison of the criteria by which such things as truth might be judged. He pointed to the notion of the Earth as the centre of universe as a proposition once ascribed the status of truth but now rejected to illustrate that this has ever been the case. In philosophical terms, radical constructivism requires a fallibilist rather than absolutist view of knowledge (Ernest, 1998). A fallibilist view of knowledge sees all theories as potentially refutable, but still 'allows us to ask how does one know this answer is better than that one, what might constitute a notion of "better", might they not both be possible' (Lerman, 1989, p. 217). In contrast, an absolutist view sees knowledge as definite and unchanging. You might think that mathematical truths are beyond dispute, but Ernest (1998) reports a widespread shift in the views of mathematicians and mathematical philosophers to the view that mathematical knowledge is as fallible as any other. For example, Kline (1980, p. 6, cited in Ernest, 1998) concluded:

> It is now apparent that the concept of a universally accepted, infallible body of reasoning—the majestic mathematics of 1800 and the pride of man—is a grand illusion. (p. 32)

And Hersh (1979, p. 43, cited in Ernest, 1998) suggested that;

> It is reasonable to propose a new task for mathematical philosophy: not to seek indubitable truth but to give an account of mathematical knowledge as it really is—fallible, corrigible, tentative and evolving, as is every other kind of human knowledge. (p. 34)

The second implication of von Glaserfeld's second tenet, that we have no way of knowing what anyone else knows, is important if we are to have the debates about criteria for truth or to communicate meaningfully at all. It is certainly of great importance to teachers and relates to the second dimension upon which versions of constructivism differ: the extent to which social interaction plays a role in knowledge construction (Schunk, 2004). Vygotsky stressed the critical role of language in social contexts in the development of children's thinking. **Social constructivists** argue that knowledge is socially constructed in a process that leads to the construction of negotiated shared meanings (Simon, 2000). Simon (2000, p. 220) described these shared meanings as 'usable by community members without explanation or justification' and hence able to be used in the construction of increasingly sophisticated ideas. In essence, shared meanings enable us to have sensible conversations. Social constructivists regard other people as parts of the context in which individuals construct knowledge and, through their interactions, 'are able to challenge one another's constructions in ways that facilitate the construction of increasingly shared and powerful knowledge' (Beswick, 2005, p. 5).

consider and discuss

1. Revisit the story at the start of the chapter of the toddler learning about numbers. How can constructivism account for his learning?
2. Think of a time when you told two people the same thing but they interpreted it in two completely different ways, or think of a time when you thought you understood something but later found out that what you understood was different from what was intended. How do incidents like these relate to constructivism? What messages for teachers might there be in this story?
3. Consider the work samples in Figure 2.2. In each case:
   a. What mathematics knowledge might have been constructed?
   b. What evidence is there of this?
   c. What beliefs about the nature of mathematics might the student be constructing?
   d. What evidence is there of this?
   e. What inferences can you make about the teacher's views of the nature of mathematics and of how children learn mathematics?

Figure 2.2 Work samples by Grade 1 and 2 children

$10 + 10 = 20$ ✓
$37 + 10 = 47$ ✓
$78 + 10 = 88$ ✓
$19 + 10 = 29$ ✓
$28 + 10 = 38$ ✓
$295 + 10 = 305$ ✓

6/6

Learning as changing social participation

Although social constructivists attempt to incorporate social interaction into their views of learning, they still ultimately regard knowledge as residing in the individual learner's mind, even if at least some of that knowledge is shared with others. That is, social interaction causes learning. In contrast, those who view learning from a socio-cultural perspective see social interaction as learning (Lerman, 2002). Learning is about becoming someone different through participation in social practices. As soon as students enter a classroom their participation in what happens there begins to shape who they are. As a result of interactions, individuals may be positioned as the class clown or the one who is really good at maths. Whether they are keen to join in the classroom activity or resist it, and even if they leave the context after only a short time, their participation means that they are not the same person that they were (Lerman, 2002). Vygotsky's emphasis on the inextricable link between thought and language (Bigge & Shermis, 1999) and the inherently social nature of language and the meanings attached to it are drawn upon in these theories.

Lerman (2002, p. 107) defines learning mathematics as 'learning to speak mathematically'. The speaking referred to is not only oral, but also includes written mathematical communication. Students learn the kinds of mathematical speaking that are approved of and gradually acquire more sophisticated mathematical language. In so doing they become mathematical (Lerman, 2002).

The teacher's role in establishing norms for interaction, validating or challenging the positions that individuals adopt or are placed in, and approving some mathematical communications and not others, is crucial to this process. The teacher is not just teaching mathematics but is shaping the identities of students.

Learning as changing brain structure

Schunk (2004) points to a historical disconnect between neuroscience and learning theory that is beginning to break down. Brain research can be considered the basis of a learning theory to the extent that it describes learning in terms of changed brain structure and function. Understanding the workings of the brain has the potential to shed light on biological bases of learning, but caution is needed (Bransford et al., 2000; Schunk, 2004). For example, some interpretations of brain research have been over-generalised in their application to education (Schunk, 2004), or led to faddish ideas lacking an evidential base (Bransford et al., 2000). Both Schunk (2004) and Bransford et al. (2000) pointed to important convergences between brain research and developmental and cognitive psychology. Importantly, these convergences underscore the complexity of learning and corroborate the more multifaceted learning theories (Schunk, 2004).

Bransford et al. (2000) summarised the relationship between learning and brain structure in three points:

1 Learning changes the physical structure of the brain.
2 These structural changes alter the functional organization of the brain; in other words, learning organizes and reorganizes the brain.
3 Different parts of the brain may be ready to learn at different times. (p. 115)

We have already seen that experience drives brain development, both in the initial phase of selection and loss of synapses and the ongoing modification and creation of new synapses (Bransford et al., 2000). It appears that learning is reflected in changes to the structure of the brain that 'make the nerve cells more efficient and powerful' (Bransford et al., 2000, p. 118).

The differential development of particular areas of the brain suggests that particular experiences may be of greater significance at different stages of life. In particular, brain research adds impetus to the findings from other disciplines about the importance of the quality as well as the quantity of early childhood experiences (Schunk, 2004).

Bransford et al. (2000) also describe how brain research has shed light on the nature of memory and on influences upon the formation and retention of memories. Rather than simply recording events, the brain actively organises inputs, linking them with existing memories and other information. The brain has a propensity to create false memories, for example in response to repeated rehearsal in the form of discussions of fictitious events. It seems that the brain does not distinguish external experience from experiences generated within it. Activities that require people to manipulate existing knowledge, for example by categorising or summarising it, or making conclusions from it, constitute experiences that lead to further learning (Bransford et al., 2000).

Learning and understanding mathematics

In this chapter we have considered learning as lasting change that is not simply a function of maturation. Most mathematics educators and teachers are interested in facilitating change in both students' behaviour (by developing their procedural fluency) and thinking (by developing their understanding of important mathematical ideas). We have seen that behaviourist theories of learning are readily applicable to teaching for procedural fluency. Learning theories that focus on the learner's thinking have more to say about the development of understanding, which proponents of these theories would argue is a more solid basis for procedural fluency as well. In this section we focus on what it means to understand, and what we know about the development of mathematical understanding.

Although we have been using the word *understanding* as if we all know what it means, defining it is not that simple. Before we consider what various writers have said on the matter, take some time to think about what you mean when you say you understand.

consider and discuss

1. Think about a mathematical big idea that you feel you really understand? Explain what you mean when you say you *understand* it. How do you know you understand it? How is this different from not understanding?
2. Discuss your thoughts with others and then write a definition of what it means to understand.

The Australian mathematics curriculum defines **understanding** as including 'building robust knowledge of adaptable and transferable mathematical concepts, the making of connections between related concepts, the confidence to use the familiar to develop new ideas, and the "why" as well as the "how" of mathematics' (National Curriculum Board, 2009, p. 6). This definition relates closely to constructivist learning theories, according to which understanding is something that occurs in the mind of the individual. It also draws on the pioneering work of Skemp (1978), who identified two distinct meanings that people have in mind when they say that somebody understands some aspect of mathematics. One meaning equates understanding with simply knowing a fact or being able to perform a procedure. He termed this form of understanding *instrumental*, and contrasted it with *relational* understanding, which involves knowing what and how and also knowing *why* a procedure works or a fact is true. Relational understanding includes links with other ideas, and provides a basis on which procedures can be reconstructed if they are forgotten. Instrumental understanding relies on an ability to remember isolated facts or steps. If any are forgotten or misremembered, the learner with an instrumental understanding has no way to retrieve them or even to judge whether or not a solution is reasonable.

Figures 2.3 and 2.4 show the responses of two middle-school students asked to calculate $3 \div 0.5$. Both students indicated that they could perform the calculation mentally. The student who produced Figure 2.3 seems to have partly remembered the standard procedure for dividing one number by another; she has set up the format but incorrectly placed the 3 and the 0.5 so that her calculation is instead 0.5 ÷ 3. In performing the division she has put a '*' (to indicate that 3 'won't go into' 0), and then a decimal point nicely lined up above the decimal point in 0.5. She also seems to have correctly found that 3 'goes into' 5 once with 2 remainder, and she has remembered the convention for naming remainders using 'r'. There is no indication that this student understands that the question was asking 'how many 0.5s are there in 3' or 'by what must I multiply 0.5 by to get 3'. She may or may not know what 'r2' means (i.e. what is a remainder of 2? 2 what?).

Figure 2.3 An unsuccessful attempt at solving 3 ÷ 0.5 using flawed instrumental understanding

First, can you work out 3 ÷ 0.5 in your head?   Yes ✓   No ☐

Write down your answer: *1 r2*

Now, show or explain how you worked out your answer: *3)0.5 with *.1r2 above*

The student who produced Figure 2.4 has not used a written procedure but was able to articulate how the answer was obtained mentally. The explanation suggests that this student has correctly understood what the question means. She also seems to have drawn on knowledge that 0.5 is the same as one-half; hence there are two 0.5s in 1 and so there are 6 0.5s in 3. Her understanding of the expression 3 ÷ 0.5 seems to be related to meaningful ways of understanding what working it out means, and her understanding of the decimal, 0.5, is related to her understanding of half. That is, in contrast to the student who produced Figure 2.3, this student has a degree of relational understanding of 3 ÷ 0.5. It is significant that we have said *a degree* of relational understanding, because there are other relationships of which she may or may not have been aware. For example, we don't know whether she is aware of the relationship between dividing by a fractional number, such as 0.5 or $\frac{1}{2}$, and multiplying by its reciprocal, 2, or that the approach she has used can be generalised to other fractions.

Figure 2.4 A successful attempt at solving 3 ÷ 0.5 illustrating relational understanding

First, can you work out 3 ÷ 0.5 in your head?   Yes ✓   No ☐

Write down your answer: *6*

Now, show or explain how you worked out your answer: *There are two 0.5's in number 1 and there are three one's in three so there are six.*

These observations illustrate two important points about understanding:

1 Relational understanding is never complete. There are always new connections/relations that can be made
2 Relational understanding provides a basis on which further understandng can be built by extending and/or adding to existing connections or relations.

for the classroom

Thinkboards

Encourage students to make connections between different ideas within mathematics and between mathematics by using a thinkboard. The idea for students to think about is written in the centre of the board. The categories provided for students can be varied to help students to focus on particular connections. The thinkboard is a useful tool for helping students to think about and make connections and also to show their (relational) understanding of an idea. The example below was completed by a Year 4 student.

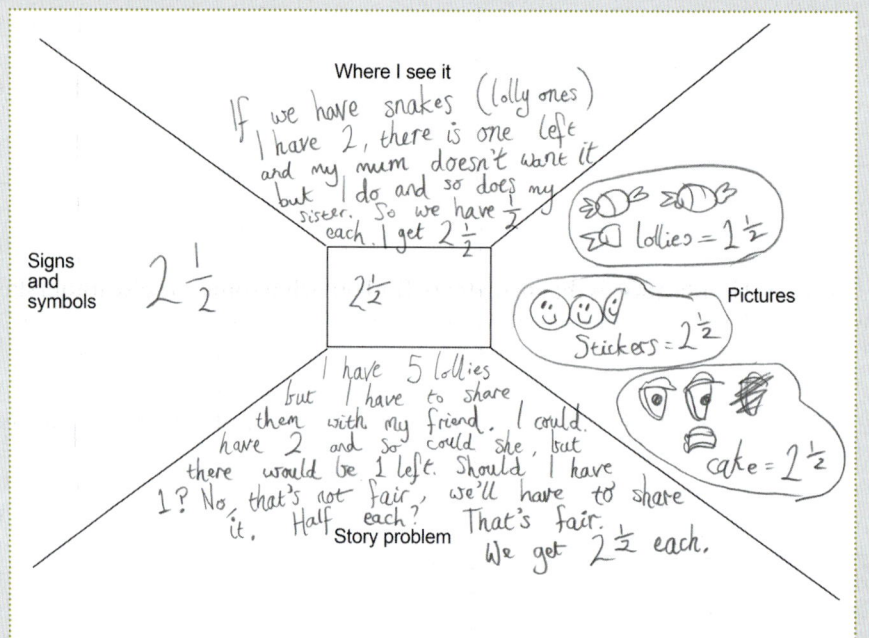

Alternative views of understanding have arisen from learning theories that emphasise the participation of individuals in social practices. These views locate understanding between, rather than within, individuals. The distinction between these views is not clear cut, and they can be regarded as complementary. Nevertheless, we will consider each in turn before considering how teachers might integrate the two.

Understanding as an individual activity

According to constructivist learning theories, individuals actively construct knowledge by incorporating experiences of the world derived from their senses into their existing knowledge. Hiebert and Carpenter (1992) described the knowledge that is formed as networks of representations. In the case of mathematical knowledge, the networks comprise connected representations of ideas, procedures, or facts. Understanding a mathematical idea, procedure, or fact means that it is part of a network of representations: the more or stronger the connections, the better the understanding (Hiebert & Carpenter, 1992). The representations involved can take many forms, including images, symbols, words and emotions (Barmby, Harries, Higgins & Suggate, 2009). The ways in which representations are linked include noticing similarities or differences between representations, or noticing that a particular representation is a special case of a broader category (Hiebert & Carpenter, 1992). More recently, Barmby et al. (2009) have described the links as resulting from mathematical reasoning, which could include noticing relationships. In the Australian mathematics curriculum, reasoning is, along with understanding, one of four proficiency strands. (We will consider all four strands in Chapter 4.) It is defined in terms of 'the capacity for logical thought and actions, such as analysing, proving, evaluating, explaining, inferring, justifying, and generalising' (National Curriculum Board, 2009, p. 6).

There are some important implications of regarding understanding as making connections among representations of facts, procedures, and ideas. The first is that understanding is not a state that is ever achieved. It is always possible to add more representations to a network or to make more or stronger links between existing representations in a network. As White and Gunstone (1992) state:

> Everyone understands to some degree anything that they know about. It follows that understanding is never complete: for we can always add more knowledge, another episode, say, or refine an image, or see new links between things we know already. (p. 6)

A second implication is that in order to find out what someone else understands about a mathematical idea, procedure or fact, we need to look at the connections that they make between that idea and others (Barmby et al., 2009). It is not enough simply for someone to state a fact or successfully carry out a procedure or define a concept: all of these can be done without any understanding at all as we have defined it. Rather, we need to infer the nature and extent of understanding from what the individual can explain or demonstrate about the connections he/she has formed with the knowledge of interest. Asking students to explain their reasoning or how different representations of an idea (e.g. the symbolic and diagrammatic representations of multiplication facts shown in Figure 2.1) are related, to justify their choice of strategy, or to analyse and evaluate alternative solutions, are all important ways in which insights into understanding can be gained. Observing that a student can choose and use appropriate mathematics in unrelated contexts or can adapt procedures according to the particular context are also important indicators of understanding.

making connections

One of the four proficiency strands of the Australian mathematics curriculum (National Curriculum Board, 2009) is understanding, which is defined as follows:

> Understanding, which includes building robust knowledge of adaptable and transferable mathematical concepts, the making of connections between related concepts, the confidence to use the familiar to develop new ideas, and the 'why' as well as the 'how' of mathematics. (p. 6)

Given that mathematical reasoning involves 'logical thought and actions, such as analysing, proving, evaluating, explaining, inferring, justifying, and generalising' (National Curriculum Board, 2009, p. 6), explain how reasoning mathematically can contribute to the development of mathematical understanding.

issues in teaching

Barmby et al. (2009) included emotions among the forms that representations of knowledge might take.

Is there a mathematics topic that conjures up a strong emotional reaction (positive or negative) in you? Why might this be? What was there about the way in which you learnt that mathematics that has caused it to be linked to that particular emotion? If the emotional response you have just considered was negative, try to think of a mathematics topic that evokes a positive emotional reaction.

What implications does this have for teaching?

Understanding as a social practice

Hiebert and Grouws (2007) adopt a very similar definition of understanding, but they place more emphasis on social participation. Rather than emphasising individual mental activity, understanding mathematics is seen as becoming an increasingly confident and adept participant in the social/cultural practice of doing mathematics, making sense of it, and coming to value it. This perspective emphasises the role of interactions with others. Voigt (1994) describes mathematical meaning (or understanding) as follows:

> Mathematical meaning is taken as a product of social processes, in particular as a product of social interactions. From this point of view, mathematical meanings are primarily studied as emerging between individuals, not as constructed inside or existing independently of individuals. (p. 276)

This perspective emphasises the ambiguity of mathematical meanings and the need for their ongoing negotiation (Voigt, 1994). Often we use words as if we all know what we mean and we all share the same meaning, but when we dig a little deeper it is common to find that our understandings are quite different. This is true even of very basic concepts. For example, the child in the story at the start of this chapter would correctly say 'two' if he was shown a pair of objects, but it was only by noticing that he also said 'two' when looking at a herd of cows that it became obvious that his understanding of what two meant was not the same as an adult's. Socio-culturalists like Voigt argue that it is in these interactions that meaning emerges between those involved in the conversation.

Socio-cultural views of mathematical understanding have important implications for classrooms. Not only is conversation and interaction of paramount importance, but also all of the participants in the classroom, teacher and students, can be seen as forming a community of practice (Pape, Bell & Yetkin, 2003). The teacher has a crucial role in establishing norms for interaction that encourage and facilitate both the participation of all students and mathematically productive interactions. The aim should be the formation of a community of practice that mirrors as closely as possible the kinds of activities in which mathematicians engage. These include justifying, analysing, and evaluating solutions; exploring different ways of approaching problems; and refining techniques. These activities are essentially those that were used in the previous section to describe the mathematical reasoning that forms the links in an individual's network of knowledge. Indeed, Pape et al. (2003, p. 181) stressed the important role of reasoning in worthwhile mathematical interactions:

> Argument and controversy, which rely on mathematical reasoning for validation, are naturally a part of mathematical discourse. Through critically examining others' reasoning and participating in the resolution of disagreements, students learn to monitor their thinking in the service of reasoning about important mathematical concepts.

Cobb (1994) described constructivist and socio-cultural views as complementary, and advocated using both where they are most usefully applied. For example, if we are interested in the mathematical development of an individual child, or perhaps a particular misconception that the child appears to have, then it may be sensible to think of that child's understanding separately from the social context, in terms of the connections among ideas that he/she appears to have made. At other times the social context of the classroom and beyond is very relevant, for example, when we consider why a student may or may not engage with certain activities, or the impact of the social tone of the classroom on affective aspects of students' learning. We do, however, need to be wary about deciding too quickly that two perspectives are compatible. As is always the case, the use of similar words can lead us too quickly to assume that we understand the same things by them!

communicating mathematically

Pape et al. (2003) stressed the importance to mathematical reasoning of 'argument and controversy', and listening to others critically. These activities are much more demanding than simply sharing solution strategies. Teaching children to use argument constructively in mathematics is an important way to raise the intellectual quality of classroom interaction and facilitate the development of mathematical reasoning and understanding.

Developing your own theory of mathematics learning

At the beginning of this chapter you were encouraged to consider what you believe mathematics is and how it is learnt, because what you believe will influence how you teach. The various theories considered have similarities and differences, and in reality very few teachers adopt any particular perspective completely. Rather, they draw on aspects that they find useful in a range of theories, and over time develop their own personal theory of mathematics learning. Such a theory forms the basis of their approach to teaching the subject. The most effective teachers are those who have a personal theory that is well thought through and internally consistent. These teachers can articulate why they are doing what they do, and they find the myriad decisions that must be made on a daily basis much easier because the appropriate action flows naturally from a clear, reasoned, and defensible perspective. You should have already begun the process of working through the issues for yourself and testing ideas so that you are on the way to your own personal theory of mathematics learning.

key terms

Behaviourism: a view of learning as a result of the learner's responses to stimuli in the environment

Constructivism: a theory of learning as arising from learners' active interaction with their physical, social, and psychological environment

Development: change resulting from maturation

Instrumentalist: a view of mathematics as a useful set of skills

Learning: Lasting change that is a result of experience and not simply a consequence of maturation or development

Learning theory: a coherent set of principles that explains how learning occurs

Nature of mathematics: what the discipline of mathematics actually is; what it concerns, and what distinguishes it from other disciplines

Operant conditioning: a behaviourist learning theory based on rewarding desired behaviours

Platonist: a view of mathematics as independently existing and comprised of interconnected and hierarchically structured ideas

Problem solving: a view of mathematics as a dynamic and creative human invention; a process rather than a product

Response: action resulting from a stimulus

Social constructivism: a constructivist theory of learning in which interactions with others play a crucial role in developing students' thinking

Stimulus: an environmental influence that provokes a response in a learner

Teacher beliefs: propositions that a teacher accepts as true, which may or may not be more widely accepted

Understanding: the extent and nature of connections between an idea and other ideas

Review questions

1. Think again about what you believe mathematics is. Which of the theories of learning, or which elements of the theories, are consistent with your beliefs? Are these learning theories ones that ring true for you? If not, how can the conflict be resolved?

2. Imagine your future classroom and describe it in as much detail as possible. What will you, as the teacher, be doing? What will the students be doing? Now imagine an observer in your classroom watching what is happening. What might they infer about your beliefs about the nature of mathematics? What evidence would they cite? What might they infer about your beliefs about how children learn mathematics? What evidence would they cite? Do these beliefs match what you really do believe? If this is a mismatch, why might this be? How can it be resolved?

Key references

Australian Curriculum, Assessment and Reporting Authority. (2011). *The Australian Curriculum: Mathematics*, Version 1.2. Sydney: ACARA.

Beswick, K., Swabey, K., & Andrew, R. (2008). Looking for attributes of powerful teaching for numeracy in Tasmanian K–7 classrooms. *Mathematics Education Research Journal*, 20(1), 3–31.

Bigge, M. L., & Shermis, S. S. (1999). *Learning Theories for Teachers* (6th ed.). New York: Longman.

Bransford, J. D., Brown, A. L., & Cocking, R. R. (Eds.). (2000). *How People Learn* (expanded ed.). Washington, DC: National Academy Press.

Cobb, P. (2007). Putting philosophy to work: Coping with multiple theoretical perspectives. In F. K. Lester Jr. (Ed.), *Second Handbook of Research on Mathematics Teaching and Learning* (Vol. 1, pp. 3–38). Charlotte, NC: Information Age Publishing.

Hiebert, J., & Carpenter, T. P. (1992). Learning and teaching with understanding. In D. A. Grouws (Ed.), *Handbook of Research on Mathematics Teaching and Learning* (pp. 65–97). New York: Macmillan.

Lerman, S. (1989). Constructivism, mathematics and mathematics education. *Educational Studies in Mathematics*, 20, 211–213.

Schunk, D. H. (2004). *Learning Theories: An Educational Perspective*. Upper Saddle River, NJ: Pearson.

Skemp, R. R. (1978). Relational understanding and instrumental understanding. *Arithmetic Teacher*, 26(3), 9–15.

von Glasersfeld, E. (1990). An exposition of constructivism: Why some like it radical. In R. B. Davis, C. A. Maher & N. Noddings (Eds.), *Constructivist Views on the Teaching and Learning of Mathematics* (pp. 19–29). Reston, VA: National Council of Teachers of Mathematics.

3 Teaching Mathematics

Contents

What does it mean to learn mathematics?	48
Connections between beliefs	49
How can we know we are teaching?	50
Knowledge for teaching mathematics	54
Effective mathematics teaching	57

Chapter objectives

This chapter will enable the reader to:
- Develop your understanding of what it means to teach mathematics
- Develop an appreciation of how beliefs about mathematics, mathematics learning, and mathematics learners underpin mathematics teaching
- Consider aspects of effective mathematics teaching
- Explore the role of planning and assessment in mathematics teaching
- Explore the role and nature of the knowledge required to teach mathematics effectively.

A conversation about mathematics teaching

The following exchange is based on an actual conversation with an experienced mathematics teacher. It raises many issues about teaching in general and mathematics teaching in particular.

A teacher once said, 'For those [students] who struggle and those who have an attitude, a big attitude problem … I don't expect them to remember from one lesson to the next lesson what to do.'

A colleague challenged him, saying, 'but if they don't remember anything then surely you haven't taught them anything.'

'Yes I have, I go through each task step by step, explaining everything clearly. When I ask them if they understand they nod. I get them to practise what I've taught them and they can do it—until next lesson.'

consider and discuss

1. Do you think that what the mathematics teacher described is 'teaching'? Why, or why not?
2. In what ways is his description of his mathematics teaching similar to and different from mathematics teaching that you have experienced?
3. How does the colleague define learning? Do you agree with this definition? Why, or why not?
4. What do you think the teacher in the conversation might believe about:
   - what mathematics is
   - how mathematics is learnt
   - mathematics learners
   - what it means to teach mathematics?
5. If you were the colleague in the conversation, what would you say next?

Big ideas

- Teaching has occurred only if someone has learnt.
- Planning and assessment are intrinsically related. Assessment tells us what has been learnt and hence what has actually been taught, and informs future planning.
- Your beliefs about the nature of mathematics and about mathematics teaching and learning affect your teaching.
- Knowledge for teaching mathematics is complex and encompasses much more than mathematical content and general pedagogy. Pedagogical content knowledge is crucial.
- Effective teaching is a function of teachers' knowledge and beliefs. When underpinned by sound knowledge and coherent beliefs certain broad principles have been associated with effective teaching of mathematics.
- Every teacher needs to be able to articulate a coherent, reasoned and defensible personal theory of learning, based on considered beliefs about what mathematics is. This can form the basis of a personal philosophy of mathematics teaching.

The theoretical perspectives on **learning** we considered in Chapter 2 all have implications for mathematics teaching, but none actually prescribes a particular approach to teaching. They do, however, offer some starting points and provide a basis on which to assess the consistency and reasonableness of various teaching approaches.

Teaching is much less theorised than learning, and is sometimes talked about as more of an art than a science. In this chapter we look at what it means to teach, and consider the implications for their teaching of teachers' beliefs about what mathematics is, how students learn mathematics, and the nature of mathematics itself. We will critique common teaching practices and examine research-based principles that underpin effective teaching of mathematics. Key considerations will be how teachers can monitor and continuously improve the quality of their teaching, and what teachers need to know in order to teach mathematics effectively. We will see that teaching mathematics is every bit as demanding and rewarding as learning it.

What does it mean to teach mathematics?

Teaching can be defined in terms of giving systematic information to someone about a subject or skill. In general conversation, teaching is often used to mean whatever it is that teachers do. But is everything that teachers do teaching?

In reality we can only know teaching has happened if somebody learns something. Even though everything that teachers do may be intended to be teaching, only the teacher behaviour that results in learning really is teaching. This judgment can be made only in hindsight. In addition, what is learnt may not be what was intended to be learnt. For example, the students referred to in the conversation above may not have learnt much mathematics, but they were almost certainly learning something about what mathematics is, what mathematics lessons in school involve, themselves as mathematics learners, and their mathematics teacher. What they learnt may or may not resemble what the teacher believed about these things.

Clarke (2005) discussed the dangers of seeing teaching and learning as distinct processes, arguing that the classroom activities of teachers and learners are complementary and cannot sensibly be analysed separately. Nevertheless, because we have different words for what teachers do and what learners do, it is often convenient to talk about teaching and learning as separate processes. It is vital, however, that we remember that teaching and learning really are inseparable, and so this chapter and Chapter 2 should be read and understood as whole. Everything that we know about teaching derives from understandings of learning, and you should actively try to relate your developing ideas about the best ways to teach mathematics to the theories of and beliefs about mathematics learning that they reflect.

did you know?

The English language is unusual in having distinct words for 'teaching' and 'learning' that refer to distinct activities of the teacher and learner. Other languages, including Russian, Japanese, French, Dutch and many other northern European languages, combine the notions of teaching and learning in a single word.

We have already considered several different views of what mathematics is. Which of these you believe, and your other beliefs about what it means to do and to learn mathematics, will obviously affect what you believe it means to teach mathematics. For example, if you hold an instrumentalist view of mathematics, that is that mathematics is a set of skills and procedures that are useful in everyday life, then **effective teaching** will be anything that enables students to acquire the relevant skills and to perform useful procedures efficiently and accurately. If, on the other hand, you see mathematics as a creative problem-solving enterprise, then teaching will be concerned with helping students to become effective and creative problem solvers. Approaches to teaching that work in one case will be unlikely to be optimally effective in the other, so you do need to continue to reflect on exactly what you believe it is that you are aiming to teach when you teach mathematics.

consider and discuss

The content descriptors of the *Australian Curriculum: Mathematics* describe content that is to be *taught* and *learnt*.

1. What does this imply about the relationship between teaching and learning?
2. What difference might there be to the way in which the content descriptors are interpreted if they were described only as content that students will *learn*?

Connections between beliefs

We have just seen that mathematics teaching and mathematics learning are intimately related. In this section we consider in more detail the relationships between beliefs about mathematics teaching and learning and the origins of both in beliefs about the nature of mathematics. Beswick (2005) summarised the connections in Table 3.1. Categories of beliefs in the same row are theoretically consistent with one another. The three categories of beliefs about mathematics, instrumentalist, Platonist and problem-solving, were described in Chapter 2. Essentially the table suggests that if you believe that mathematics is a set of skills and procedures (an instrumentalist view) then your teaching will emphasise covering content and helping students to perform skills accurately and efficiently. The learners' role is to take on board what he/she is told and master the skills, probably through a lot of practice. If, however, you regard mathematics as a pre-existing hierarchical structure (a Platonist view) then teaching will emphasise the logical relationships between mathematics topics and students will be expected to construct understanding of these connections. Teachers who regard mathematics as an evolving human creation (a problem-solving view) will be inclined to be guided in their teaching by what the student already understands and is interested in learning, seeing his/her role as facilitating the students' self-directed learning.

As noted in Chapter 2, it is unlikely that your beliefs will fit neatly into any of these categories. Nevertheless, it is important that you consider the logical implications of the beliefs you espouse in any of these areas. It is also important that you are aware that our own beliefs about mathematics learning are essentially constructivist, and this inevitably has shaped our views on mathematics teaching.

think + link

Look back at your notes from Chapter 2 about which of Ernest's views of mathematics most closely reflected your own, or take a few minutes to think about that now. To what extent are you comfortable with the views of teaching and learning that according to Table 3.1 are aligned with that view of mathematics? How might you reconcile any conflicts?

Take a few minutes to write down your own views about the nature of mathematics, mathematics learning, and mathematics teaching, remembering that they might draw on more than one of the categories listed in Table 3.1 or could differ from all of them. To what extent are your views consistent with one another?

Table 3.1 Relationships between beliefs. From Beswick (2005, p. 40)

Beliefs about the nature of mathematics (Ernest, 1989)	Beliefs about mathematics teaching (Van Zoest, Jones & Thornton, 1994)	Beliefs about mathematics learning (Ernest, 1989)
Instrumentalist	Content-focused, with an emphasis on performance	Skill mastery, passive reception of knowledge
Platonist	Content-focused, with an emphasis on understanding	Active construction of understanding
Problem-solving	Learner-focused	Autonomous exploration of own interests

How can we know we are teaching?

The simple answer, of course, is that we are teaching if someone is learning as a result of our actions. How we can know this is happening is rather more complex, and how we can know what is being learnt is more complex still. When we attempt to answer these questions we are making an **assessment** of our students' learning. This assessment is not simply, or even primarily, to assign a grade to the students' performance; arguably its most important purpose is to assess our own teaching so that we can adjust our activity and the tasks we provide to help students to learn the relevant mathematical ideas better.

In the following sections we consider some current ideas about assessment in mathematics and then consider how such assessment feeds into planning for teaching.

Assessing mathematics learning

Callingham (2008) described assessment as relating to both the quantity and quality of learning. Large-scale assessments such as the National Assessment Program—Literacy and Numeracy (NAPLAN) provide data for schools and school systems. More nuanced assessment that can directly and immediately inform teaching is best situated in classrooms. This kind of assessment is often referred to as formative, in that it is not an end in itself but rather shapes subsequent teaching and learning activity. At the classroom level all assessment should have a formative component; even if an assessment task is designed to assess whether or not a particular concept has been understood so that a level of achievement can be reported to an audience beyond the classroom (e.g. parents), it will also provide information about the effectiveness of teaching and the learning needs of students. Assessment in the classroom is essentially about setting up a dialogue between teacher and students (Callingham, 2008) in which the students provide evidence of what they can do and of the understandings they have constructed, and the teacher provides feedback that guides subsequent learning.

consider and discuss

Consider the work samples in Figures 3.1 and 3.2. The two drawings were produced by the same child when she was aged 4 years, 0 months (Figure 3.1) and 4 years, 11 months (Figure 3.2). What mathematical understandings are evident in each of the drawings? What evidence of learning do these drawings provide?

Assessing learning is, of course, related to the learning that was intended. It is impossible assess anything meaningfully if you are unsure of what you hoped would be learnt, or of precisely what might constitute evidence that such learning has occurred. It is not enough simply to say that you will assess students' understanding during a lesson by monitoring students' conversations and observing what they are doing. You must have a clear idea of exactly what sorts of things students might say or do that will indicate that they do or do not understand the mathematics that you intend them to learn. This leads us to the importance of planning and of deep understanding of the mathematics to be taught, the ways in which students typically learn it, and the kinds of tasks and questions that are likely to be effective in helping students to learn.

Figure 3.1 Clown in circus tent

Figure 3.2 Self-portrait

issues in teaching

When we assess students' work it is easy to make judgments about the student rather than the evidence they have presented, and to communicate our assessments of students' work as if they are assessments of the students themselves. Perhaps you can relate to feeling personally judged, either positively or negatively, by a teacher or even a university lecturer.

There is evidence that we need to help students to distinguish between themselves and their work, and to see their current achievement as a reflection of things that they can control—such as the amount of effort they put in— rather than some fixed quality of themselves as learners. This is not to say that we reward effort only and not achievement, but students need to know that their achievement is something they can influence, something that they can work on and improve. This applies equally to students who are performing well and those who are struggling.

Dweck (2002) recommends that teachers praise work and work habits, not the students themselves. For example, telling a student that he is an 'A' student can create anxiety about maintaining the impression of being smart, whereas saying 'I can see that you thought carefully about that explanation' reinforces a learning behaviour that will be beneficial into the future.

communicating mathematically

Valuing thinking

Black line masters, on which children write their answers, are common in mathematics lessons in some classrooms. These are convenient in terms of ensuring consistency in the way that students' work is set out, and they can relieve students of the tedium of writing out questions. However, a necessary part of learning to think mathematically is learning to structure and organise one's thoughts. When students are encouraged to record their thinking in whatever way is meaningful for them, the work they produce will not be uniform and may be more difficult to follow than neatly completed boxes, but it will also provide much richer insights into their thinking and is far more likely to contribute to meaningful learning. In addition, it can be a valuable prompt for discussion of alternative ways of approaching problems and recording thinking. Similarly, doing 'working out' on scrap paper that is discarded not only devalues the sometimes necessarily messy thinking that goes into solving a worthwhile and challenging problem, but also jettisons a rich source of information about the ongoing development of students' thinking.

In the following sections we briefly consider planning for mathematics teaching before taking a closer look at what teachers need to know in order to teach mathematics effectively.

Planning for mathematics learning

The first step in **planning** a teaching episode in mathematics is to know what you want students to learn (Kilpatrick, Swafford & Findell, 2001). This should be a statement of the important mathematical ideas with which you want students to grapple, and the specific understanding that you want them to develop. Whether objectives are stated in terms of observable behaviours or in terms of understandings will depend upon your theory of mathematics learning (see Chapter 2). In any case, without clear objectives (or aims or goals) it is unlikely that very much will be achieved, and impossible to make a sensible assessment of the extent to which teaching was successful.

handy hint

Questions to consider when planning for maths teaching

- What important idea(s)/concept(s) do you want students to engage with and develop an understanding of?
- What do we know about how these understandings develop?
- What understandings develop earlier?
- What common misconceptions are there?
- How can I find out about students' existing understanding?
- What specific questions can I ask?

- What activities might reveal particular understandings or misconceptions?
- How can I help students to develop their understanding?
- What activities or experiences will be of value?
- How can I adapt these to cater for diversity?
- How can I monitor students' developing understanding?
- What specifically will I look for that will indicate understanding or misunderstanding?
- What additional questions can I ask to explore students' thinking more deeply?
- How will I know they understand the concept?

Once you are clear about what you want students to learn, you need to decide how the lesson will be introduced, how you will uncover and build on existing understanding, what tasks and activities you will offer students, how you will adapt these to cater for the diverse needs of students in the class, how you will organise the students, what questions you will ask at various points, and how you will monitor the effectiveness of the lesson (in relation to your objectives). In addition, Panasuk, Stone and Todd (2002) recommend planning for a range of levels of intellectual activity, as identified by Bloom and colleagues (Bloom, Hastings & Madaus, 1971), ranging from recall of knowledge through to higher-order thinking such as analysis and evaluation. This is particularly important given that there is evidence that relatively little activity in typical primary and middle school mathematics lessons requires higher level intellectual engagement of students (Beswick, Swabey & Andrew, 2008).

Finally, you need to think carefully about how to bring the lesson to a close. Too often lessons simply end when the bell rings at the end of the session. Every lesson should end so that you and your students are clear about what has been achieved in terms of learning mathematics.

One commonly used structure for mathematics lessons is the three-part lesson. This begins with an introductory activity or starter that is done as a whole class. It could be a mental computation activity such those described by

McIntosh and Dole (2004) and McIntosh, DeNardi and Swan (1994). Following the introduction, the main teaching activity may be undertaken as a whole class, in small groups, individually, or in some combination of these. As always, decisions about the nature of the activity and classroom organisation must be informed by your objective: what will best help students to learn the intended mathematics. Finally, the lesson ends with a plenary session that focuses on the mathematics with which the students have been engaged. It is common to have students share their solution strategies and thinking in this time, but the purpose is not to have an enjoyable sharing experience but to draw students' attention to the mathematics and to consolidate their learning.

integrating technology/ICT

Using technology purposefully

Technology provides powerful teaching tools that can be used to develop understanding as well as to facilitate practice. As with any other teaching tool, technology is not inherently valuable; rather it is a tool that can enhance students' learning if used effectively.

Decisions about which technology to use, and how, should be driven by your purpose for the lesson and the extent to which the technology can contribute to achieving your objectives. It is worth considering what the technology can offer in relation to the lesson objectives that could not be done without it. If it offers a virtual version of a concrete experience, how are the two experiences different? Are both important? Consider also how your attitudes to technology might be influenced by your own experiences of learning mathematics: some teachers have resisted the use of calculators in the early years, claiming that they detract from learning to compute mentally. If your purpose in a particular lesson is for students to practise mental computation strategies, then perhaps calculators will not be appropriate, but if your purpose is for students to explore patterns in numbers and make generalisations about them, then calculators can be powerful tools.

Planning is intimately related to assessment. The content that is taught and the approaches used to teach it must be informed by assessments of the students' existing knowledge. These assessments can be part of the teacher's knowledge of the typical development of students in relation to the particular mathematical ideas, including the misconceptions they are most likely to have or could develop and the kinds of tasks that they are likely to find engaging and helpful for developing their understanding. Sound planning also builds in opportunities for assessing students' thinking and developing understanding throughout each lesson, including at the start. Importantly, planning needs to take account of how the information gained from ongoing assessment will be used to inform the teaching that follows. This is a difficult task that expert teachers can make appear effortless as they seamlessly redirect their teaching and adapt tasks as a lesson progresses. Very experienced teachers may not need to document this on-the-spot planning, but the best teachers, regardless of their experience, think through these matters carefully. In many ways a teaching plan is a thought experiment in which you imagine in as much detail as possible what you will do and anticipate the ways in which students might respond.

One useful technique for thinking through a lesson and planning for contingencies is the use of three columns for lesson planning, as shown in Table 3.2. This shows an excerpt from a teachers' planning for a lesson that aimed to develop understanding that:

1 all numbers can be represented on a number line
2 there are numbers between consecutive whole numbers
3 fractions are numbers.

Table 3.2 Example of three-column planning

Activity/Task	Potential student responses	Possible teacher responses
Write down as many numbers as you can that are between 2 and 6.	Can't get started	What comes between 2 and 4? Now think about the numbers between 2 and 6.
	Writes whole numbers 3, 4, 5, quickly	Is that all there are? What about fractions? Have you got them all? How do you know? How many numbers are there between 2 and 6?

Notice the specificity of the lesson objectives and the detail of planning associated with just the first question to be posed. Of course, no matter how well prepared we are, students will still surprise. In the lesson from which this example was actually taught, one of the students responded immediately by calling out 'Are fractions numbers?', a contingency that had not been planned for!

The following are quotes from experienced teachers about the role of planning in mathematics teaching. Note that they all regard planning as necessary, even though they acknowledge the need for flexibility.

> Obviously you need a plan to start with (Nick)

> You've got to gauge what's happening in your classroom. If the children aren't ready to go to step X, and you've got to go to Z and W before you can get to X, that's what you've got to do. (Andrew)

> Someone might ask a question that raises a problem. Well, if they're interested in that, it's better to have your lesson on that and deal with that rather than what you might have planned, so I think you have got to be flexible. (Anne)

Longer term planning, for example for a unit of work lasting a number of weeks, is also important. The process is similar, in that the objectives are the starting point. For longer time frames these may comprise a small number of overarching objectives that are broken down into more finely grained objectives. Sequencing of the main ideas to be taught is an additional aspect of longer term planning.

Knowledge for teaching mathematics

consider and discuss

Brainstorm what you think teachers need to know to teach mathematics effectively—make a list. Sort your list into things that teachers need to know to teach any subject and things that are specific to mathematics teaching.
- How are the demands of teaching mathematics similar to those of teaching any subject? How are they different? What implications does this have for you as you prepare to teach mathematics?

Teaching is neither simply common sense nor something that some people are born able to do; rather it is an extremely complex task that can be learnt (Kilpatrick et al., 2001).

The specific knowledge that is needed to teach mathematics has received increased attention in recent years. This has built on the seminal work of Shulman (1987), who outlined seven types of knowledge that teachers require. These are summarised in Table 3.3 in the context of mathematics teaching, even though Shulman's work concerned teaching generally. The table also introduces some common abbreviations for several of the knowledge types.

Shulman's key contribution was drawing attention to the fact that teaching a subject requires much more than simply **knowledge** of that subject. Knowing and deeply understanding the mathematics is crucial, but it is just the beginning. One of the most important aspects of Shulman's knowledge types is the distinction between **content knowledge** (CK) and **pedagogical content knowledge** (PCK). PCK is a mix of content and pedagogical knowledge that is uniquely needed by mathematics teachers. Rather than simply the addition of knowing the mathematics and knowing in general how to teach, it involves a blend of mathematical knowledge and pedagogical knowledge that only a mathematics teacher would need. For example, mathematically competent adults know how to divide one fraction by another, typically by inverting the second fraction and multiplying. To teach fraction division adequately, however, requires having an answer to the question of *why* the invert and multiply rule works. The teacher needs to know mathematical content about reciprocals, and the relationship between division and multiplication, that others don't need to know, as well as specific mathematical pedagogy about how these ideas can be explained in a number of ways (e.g. using diagrams, examples, and patterns), and which of these explanations particular students are likely to find most meaningful. Crucially, the teacher needs to understand how the mathematics pedagogy employed is mathematically sound and faithful to the nature of the discipline.

Table 3.3 Shulman's (1987) seven knowledge types

Knowledge types	Description/Example
Knowledge of the curriculum	Knowing about the structure of the Australian curriculum, the specific content to be taught at the relevant year, and how the mathematical proficiency strands are incorporated throughout that content.
Knowledge of students as mathematics learners (KSL)	Knowing about the typical development of student understanding and their likely responses to mathematical tasks, e.g. knowing that many students struggle to develop understanding of fractions as numbers, to compare and order them, and locate them on the number line.
Knowledge of mathematical content (KMC)	Knowing the key mathematical ideas to be taught, e.g. that fractions are rational numbers that can also be represented as decimals and percentages, and knowing how to use these various forms of rational numbers in solving problems.
General pedagogical knowledge (PK)	Knowing generally applicable strategies for managing and organising the classroom, e.g. how to get the attention of the class and organise transitions from one activity to the next.
Pedagogical content knowledge (PCK)	Knowing a variety of ways to present mathematical content and to assist students to develop their understanding of it, e.g. knowing that 10 × 10 grids can be useful models for helping students to understand decimals, and being aware of the limitations and affordances of this and other decimal representations.
Knowledge of the purposes and values of education	Knowing the overarching aims of the curriculum and the values that underpin it.
Knowledge of educational contexts	Knowing about the workings of a school and/or system and the wider educational community, their governance structures and cultures.

In the example of fraction division, Ball and colleagues (e.g. Ball, Thames & Phelps, 2008) distinguished two categories of CK: common content knowledge that any adult might reasonably be expected to have, and specialised content knowledge uniquely required for teaching. (Knowing how to divide fractions would be common content knowledge, whereas knowing the underpinning mathematics would be specialised content knowledge.) Ball et al. (2008) also identified a further category of CK that they called horizon content knowledge. They claimed that teachers also need to know how mathematical ideas are connected across the span of the curriculum; teachers of very young children need to know how the mathematics that they teach relates to and will underpin the development of concepts encountered much later. Ball and colleagues also offered a refinement of PCK. They identified three types of PCK that represent intersections of content knowledge with knowledge of students as learners, of the curriculum, and of pedagogy.

Your mathematics knowledge

Many pre-service primary teachers begin their courses with little confidence in their mathematical abilities and have negative attitudes to the subject (Beswick, 2006). If this sounds like you, then you need to resolve to grapple with the mathematics that you plan to teach and quite a bit beyond (mathematical horizon knowledge (Ball et al., 2008)) until you are comfortable with it. Some rationalise their lack of mathematical knowledge by arguing that it helps them to identify with struggling learners, and even claim that improving their mathematics knowledge might be detrimental to their teaching by reducing their ability to empathise with struggling students. Some also misconstrue constructivist theories of learning as meaning that knowing the content is unimportant. They argue that the teacher is a facilitator of the students' mathematical explorations who can learn alongside the students (Schuck, 1999). The response to this suggestion of Andrew, an experienced and expert mathematics teacher we have quoted elsewhere, is instructive. He said:

> You're not just a supporting role, you are a facilitator, but you're also more than that. You're someone who hopefully understands the clear path that might be needed and can also see different paths to get to the end point and send the kids off on appropriate paths, not just let them wander through the minefield.

Another teacher, who also described himself as a constructivist, likened the teacher to a ring master who knows 'where the whole thing is going' and can 'link [students'] ideas to some of the formal mathematics'.

making connections

Everything that a teacher does conveys a message. Negative messages about mathematics and particularly about students' abilities to learn it are particularly damaging. It's worth thinking about how a teacher might show that they are uncomfortable with mathematics as well as how they can communicate to certain students (boys and girls) that they are not good at mathematics.

However uncomfortable it might be, every teacher needs to understand deeply the mathematics that they teach. This is just the beginning of what you must know to teach the subject effectively, but mathematics teaching can be learnt. One of the most exciting things about teaching mathematics is the fact that you are always learning from your teaching.

> **consider and discuss**
>
> Have you ever heard an adult say that they are not very good at reading? Have you ever heard an adult say that they are not very good at maths?
>
> Most people have heard the second confession much more often than the first.
>
> **1** Why do you think it is socially acceptable to say that you're not good at maths but not that you can't read?
>
> **2** How do you think the view that mathematics is difficult and that it is okay not to be good at it might affect students' approaches to the subject at school?
>
> **3** How might a teacher communicate his or her own lack of confidence with mathematics to students? What impacts could this have?

Effective mathematics teaching

In 2002 the Australian Association of Mathematics Teachers (AAMT) released their Standards for Excellence in Teaching Mathematics in Australian Schools. These standards have been useful in guiding professional developments for teachers of mathematics, and influential in driving a national standards agenda for teachers generally. AMMT (2002) organised the standards into three broad categories: professional knowledge, professional attributes, and professional practice.

In the sections that follow we use these categories to consider what is known about effective mathematics teaching, but first we need to be clear about what we mean by 'effective'. The word effective suggests a goal. What are we trying to achieve when we teach mathematics? What do we want to do effectively?

In Table 3.1 we saw how beliefs about the nature of mathematics can be related to views about how it should be taught and what it means to learn the subject. How you define 'effectively' in relation to mathematics teaching will ultimately depend upon how you view the discipline. This will have a powerful influence on what your students come to believe mathematics is all about and how they see themselves in relation to it. These are long-term impacts and difficult to quantify, but there other shorter term measures of effectiveness that are also important, not least because they can have a profound influence on the life opportunities available to students.

Society, as represented by parents, schools, school systems, and government, has its own view of how effective mathematics teaching is defined. Essentially, teaching is regarded as effective if it improves students' achievement (as measured by standardised tests such as NAPLAN) by more than would happen if we did not teach them (progress must be more than can be accounted for by natural development). Although we might use broader measures of achievement than standardised tests, this is also a reasonable definition of **effective teaching** for teachers, because students should be better of in terms of their learning as a result of being in your class!

In the following sections we rely principally on three large-scale studies that employed rigorous, although different, assessments of students' achievement as a basis for recommending best practice. These studies are the Early Numeracy Research Project (EYNRP) (Clarke, Cheeseman, Gervasoni, Gronn, Horne, McDonough et al., 2002), the Middle Years Numeracy Research Project (MYNRP) (Siemon, Virgona & Cornielle, 2001), both conducted in Australia, and the UK Effective Teachers of Numeracy Study (Askew, Brown, Rhodes, Johnson & Wiliam, 1997).

think + link

Remind yourself of what you believe mathematics is. It might help to look back over the relevant section of Chapter 2 and at notes you made in that chapter and earlier in this one. If this is what mathematics is, what does it mean to do mathematics, know mathematics, and learn mathematics? What does your view of the nature of mathematics say that it means to be an effective teacher of mathematics?

issues in teaching

Standardised tests such as those in NAPLAN have been criticised for, among other things, testing only a small part of what students learn. Although there is much more to students' mathematics learning than can be captured by such a test, the results can provide some valuable insights into students' thinking and hence the teaching they have received. Consider the following example from the 2009 Year 5 NAPLAN numeracy test:

> Which one of these has the same value as 12×3?
>
> $10 + 3 + 2$ $10 \times 3 + 2$ $10 \times 3 + 3$ $10 \times 3 + 6$

The incorrect choices are designed to identify particular types of incorrect thinking; some do this better than others. The question can be answered in two ways: by calculating 12×3 and comparing that answer with each of the options, or by using the distributive law. This states that you can multiply a number by another by breaking the first number into parts, multiplying each part by the second number, and adding the results. In this case 12×3 is the same as $(10 + 2) \times 3$, which is $10 \times 3 + 2 \times 3$ or $10 \times 3 + 6$. Students will probably not encounter the distributive law formally until much later, but in terms of future mathematics, including algebra, this way of thinking is far more powerful than just calculating the value of each expression. The approach a teacher takes will depend upon what they believe mathematics is, and also on their own mathematical understanding—specifically, the extent to which he/she appreciates the current and future power of distributive law.

What do effective teachers know?

We have already considered the knowledge that is required to teach mathematics. The AAMT (2002) emphasised that teachers need to have sound mathematical knowledge as well as knowledge of their students and of how students learn mathematics. Clarke et al. (2002) noted that effective teachers were confident about their own mathematical knowledge, while Askew et al. (1997) pointed to effective teachers' awareness of the conceptual connections among the various mathematics topics that they taught.

What are effective mathematics teachers like?

Personal attributes of effective mathematics teachers include belief in the capacities of all students to learn mathematics and a commitment to providing learning opportunities that will engage and challenge all students and that help students to become autonomous, self-directed learners with positive attitudes to mathematics (AAMT, 2002). The importance of high yet realistic expectations of students was also mentioned by Clarke et al. (2002), and Askew et al. (1997) reported that effective teachers exhibited very positive attitudes to mathematics.

Effective teachers of mathematics also engage in ongoing mathematics-specific professional learning (Askew et al., 1997; AAMT, 2002). This contributes to continuing learning about mathematics and mathematics teaching, keeping up to date with current issues and developments in mathematics teaching, and constantly adding to a repertoire of teaching strategies (AAMT, 2002). Importantly, professional learning is not confined to attending organised events but can include personal professional reading, engaging in collegial discussions in a variety of forums, including online, and constantly trying out and reflecting on new approaches in one's own classroom. Many of these activities position teachers not only to improve their own practice constantly, but also to make a contribution to the profession more broadly (AAMT, 2002).

What do effective mathematics teachers do?

The things that teachers know and believe and their professional involvements beyond the classroom all affect what they do in their classrooms. However, there is a not a neat set of things that effective teachers do, and consequently one cannot become an effective teacher of mathematics simply by doing certain things and avoiding doing other things (Askew et al., 1997). Rather, it is the principles or beliefs that underlie particular practices that determine their effectiveness (Watson & De Geest, 2005). Nevertheless it is possible to identify broad features of teaching practice that, when accompanied by sound knowledge and coherent beliefs and used in the service of broader principles, have been associated with effective teaching of mathematics.

Muir (2008a) identified six principles prominent in the literature on effective teaching of numeracy and common to Askew et al. (1997) and Clarke et al. (2002). The six principles were:

- make connections
- challenge all students
- teach for conceptual understanding
- purposeful discussion
- focus on mathematics
- positive attitudes.

Based on these and detailed classroom observations, Muir (2008a) identified five observable teacher actions that contribute to effective teaching of numeracy (mathematics). She was also careful to point out that these actions cannot be interpreted or implemented in any simplistic way but that interactions between them and with the teachers' knowledge and beliefs influence their effectiveness. We will discuss each in turn.

for the classroom

Ask students to write about the best maths lesson they can imagine. Ask them, 'What sorts of tasks or questions would you be working on?' 'What would you be doing?' 'What would the teacher be doing?' O'Shea (2009) described Grade 5 and 6 students' responses to a task like this.

Having young children draw themselves in maths time can provide insight into their thinking about what maths lessons are all about. Walls (2007) reports the implications for teaching of children's responses to this task and includes a number of student work samples.

Choice of examples

Examples can be used to illustrate mathematical ideas, to highlight particular solutions strategies, or may constitute contexts intended to motivate learning about a particular topic. Huckstep, Rowland and Thwaites (2003) illustrated the need to select examples with care by describing a pre-service teacher who chose half past six as an example to illustrate 'half past' times on an analogue clock. Later a child showed half past seven by drawing both clock hands pointing to the seven. Half past six is arguably the least helpful possible example of half past. Huckstep et al.'s (2003) example illustrates well the link between skill in selecting examples and teacher knowledge. It is also important that children experience many different examples of the same idea in order for them to form a rich understanding of a concept. A student who has only ever seen right-angled triangles illustrated as in Figure 3.3a would be quite reasonable to think that the triangle in Figure 3.3b would be called a left-angled triangle. (This has really happened!)

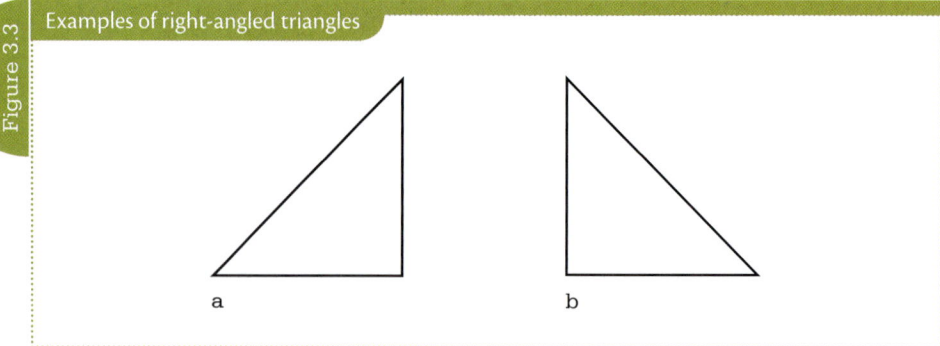

Figure 3.3 Examples of right-angled triangles

a   b

Choice of tasks

Tasks also need to be chosen to assist students to construct the intended mathematical understandings. They need to not only engage students in an activity, but engage them with important mathematical ideas. Siemon et al. (2001, p. 103) recommended that teachers use 'open-ended questions, games, authentic problems, and extended investigations' in a regular and systematic fashion. They argued that as well as helping students to learn mathematics, such tasks can provide opportunities for students to apply their knowledge. Open-ended tasks that enable students of a range of abilities to engage meaningfully with the mathematics are a key way in which to cater for the diversity of abilities in any classroom. Sullivan and Lilburn (1997) described how the closed questions or tasks that are commonly found in textbooks and used in classrooms can be changed to be open-ended. They suggest identifying the mathematics topic to be addressed, finding or making up a standard closed question, and then adapting that question. For example, if the topic is length measurement, standard closed questions could be 'Find the length of your desk'. This could be made open by changing it to 'Find an object that is three handspans long' (Sullivan & Lilburn, 1997, p. 6). Sullivan, Clarke and Clarke (2009) identified four distinct types of task and emphasised the vital role of the teachers' content and pedagogical content knowledge in converting tasks to effective lessons.

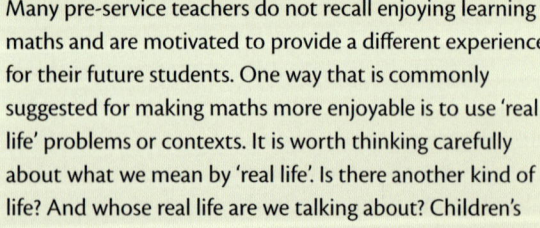

making connections

Many pre-service teachers do not recall enjoying learning maths and are motivated to provide a different experience for their future students. One way that is commonly suggested for making maths more enjoyable is to use 'real life' problems or contexts. It is worth thinking carefully about what we mean by 'real life'. Is there another kind of life? And whose real life are we talking about? Children's lives are not the same as those of adults, and school and learning play a very large part in their lives, along with stories and games and imaginative play. Things that we might consider to be 'real life', like shopping or designing a garden or driving cars, may have very little to do with the lives or interests of children. Perhaps what is really needed is teaching that makes mathematics accessible, understandable, and meaningful for students.

Henningsen and Stein (1997) observed that teachers are often too quick to reduce the intellectual demands of tasks when students begin to struggle. They argue that a careful balance must be maintained between students' engagement and intellectual challenge, because students can potentially learn most when they are challenged. Beswick et al. (2008) noted a similar lack of intellectual challenge in the vast majority of F–8 mathematics lessons that they observed, and Watson (2004) contrasted the focus on the complexities of the relevant mathematics that characterised Japanese and Hong Kong mathematics lessons with the teaching observed in other less successful countries, including Australia, that were part of the seven-nation Trends in International Mathematics and Science (TIMSS) video study. Judgments about engagement and sustained challenge require much knowledge of individual students and what will best facilitate their mathematics learning. It also has implications for the kind of mathematics classroom environment that the teacher seeks to create.

Teachable moments

Clarke et al. (2002) highlighted the importance of capitalising on opportunities to make connections between different parts of mathematics or between the mathematics of interest and the current thinking or interests of students. Teachers' abilities to capitalise on such **teachable moments** are dependent on their knowledge of the mathematics, and particularly on their ability to see potential connections. Muir (2008b) illustrated the potential of such moments to enhance students' understanding, but noted that teachers in her study often failed to notice or actively ignored them. One example that she gave involved a student who suggested zero might be a square number because zero times zero is zero. This caused some controversy, with another student claiming that zero is not even a number. The teacher Muir observed chose to ignore this moment.

Modelling

Modelling can be an effective means of showing students what mathematical thinking looks like in action. It can be used to demonstrate the required skills, knowledge, or attitude. It can assist students not only to learn strategies for solving problems but also to learn strategies for improving their learning, including strategies for making connections (Siemon et al., 2001). Siemon et al. (2001) stressed the importance of such metacognitive learning for students in the middle years of schooling in particular. Importantly, if modelling is to contribute to the development of conceptual understanding and assist students to make connections between various aspects of mathematics and between mathematics and other aspects of the curriculum and their own lives, then it must not amount to demonstrating a recipe for performance that is to be mindlessly mimicked.

Use of representations

The need for students to encounter a range of examples of particular mathematical ideas is related to the need for mathematical concepts to be represented in a variety of ways. Different **representations** highlight and obscure different aspects of a concept. Askew et al. (1997) explained how an over-emphasis on models of fractions as parts of wholes (e.g. pizzas) can inhibit the development of other understandings of fractions, and result later in difficulties such as relating fraction notation to the idea of ratio. In choosing representations, teachers need to be aware of exactly what mathematics each makes apparent and what it does not, as well as of potential ways in which the particular representation or material might give rise to misconceptions.

Questioning

Effective teachers require students to explain and justify their mathematical thinking (Askew et al., 1997; Clarke et al., 2002; Siemon, et al., 2001), and **questioning** is one important way of doing this. However, much questioning in mathematics lessons follows an 'initiation–response–feedback' pattern, and usually does not stimulate students to think more deeply (Tanner, Jones, Kennewell & Beauchamp, 2005). Vale (2003) identified seven types of questions used in primary mathematics classrooms. These are shown in Table 3.4 along with definitions and examples of each type.

Table 3.4 Types of question (from Vale, 2003, p. 690)

Type	Definition	Examples
Closed	Questions that have a definite answer	How many 7s in 21?
Open	Questions with more than one solution or that have no definite right or wrong answers	How many different ways can you arrange 5 counters to make different shapes? How would you measure the floor for new carpeting?
Probing	Questions that ask children to explain their thinking, methods, or solutions	How did you work that out?
Thinking	Questions that lead to further discussion and investigation or encourage thinking strategically or problem solving	What patterns do you see? How can we use this process or strategy in a real-life situation?
Sharing	Questions that ask children to share and explain alternative methods, of solution	Who worked that out a different way?
Caring	Questions that you use to find out about a student's understanding, progress, or attitude towards mathematics	Do you want me to explain that to you again? Who is happy with what they've mastered today? Why?
Managing	Questions that you use to monitor and manage a student's behaviour in maths lessons	Did you listen to instructions?

Although there have been attempts to classify questions according to the intellectual level of response that they seem intended or likely to elicit (e.g. Presseisen, 2001), it is really not possible to foresee the effectiveness of a question in isolation from the context in which it is used and the nature of student responses that it elicits. This depends not only on the question itself but also on its place in a teaching sequence or series of questions, and on the tacit understandings about the kinds of responses that are expected and acceptable in the class.

consider and discuss

Notice how the teacher in the following dialogue uses questions in a Year 7 lesson on ratio.

Teacher: Compare the numbers of students and teachers in the room. Write it up in mathematical language, using mathematical symbols.
Nick: 24 : 2
Teacher: Can you write it a different way?
Nick: 24/2
Teacher: You are right, but I don't want to go down that track … Can I just leave that for now?
Paul: A decimal, 24.2
Scott: 12 : 1
Teacher: How did you do it?
Scott: I divided both by two.

Ellie:	If you started with 12 : 1 you could multiply by 2 to get 24 : 2.	Teacher:	50 : 5, well that proves how much richer teachers are than students.
Teacher:	Yes, there are other ratios the same.	Susan:	That's wrong.
Kate:	48/4	Robert:	They have to be the same, 50 : 500
Teacher:	How did you get that?	Teacher:	As long as we're comparing the same things we don't need the units, but we must be careful that we are comparing the same things. How else can I write
Kate:	Multiplied by four.		
Teacher:	Where have you seen this sort of thing before?		
Brian:	Equivalent fractions.		
Teacher:	Yes, we'll find that ratios are very similar to equivalent fractions.		50 : 500?
		Claire:	0.5 : 5
		Paul:	5 : 50
		Teacher:	How else? I'll leave that with you for a while.

A few minutes later, when the students were working on examples from their textbook, the teacher stopped the class.

Teacher:	Scott was just comparing 1 mm to 5 mm, and asked, 'Do I have to write mm down?' Why was he worried about that?
Drew:	It could be cm or m.
Teacher:	Let's go back a step. Who's got some money in their pocket?

Several students indicated that they did. The teacher focused on one who had $5. He produced a 50 cent piece.

1 Classify each of the eight questions that the teacher asks according to Vale's types as shown in Table 3.4.
2 Which of the questions prompted students to do more than simply recall information?
3 What evidence is there that the teacher's questioning prompted students to make connections?
4 What types of teacher knowledge are evident from this exchange?
5 What evidence is there of other effective mathematics teaching practices?

The five observable features of effective mathematics teaching (Muir, 2008a) that we have just described can all be seen as aspects of an over-arching focus on establishing meaningful, mathematics-focused dialogue with and among students. This is one aspect of the AAMT's (2002) description of professional practice as exhibited by excellent teachers of mathematics.

AAMT (2002) also stressed the importance of the psychological, emotional, and physical learning environment that teachers create for their students. An appropriate environment fosters understanding and enjoyment of, and enthusiasm for, mathematics. Such environments are characterised by trust, engagement, and collaboration, and maximise the opportunities of all students to learn. Planning and assessment for learning are also important parts of effective mathematics teaching (AAMT, 2002).

consider and discuss

In Chapter 2 we considered two of the four proficiency strands of the Australian Curriculum: Mathematics; we will consider them all in Chapter 4. The four strands (understanding, fluency, reasoning, and problem solving) were derived from four of five strands of mathematical proficiency suggested by Kilpatrick et al. (2001). Kilpatrick et al.'s fifth strand, *productive disposition*, defined as a 'habitual inclination to see mathematics as sensible, useful, and worthwhile, coupled with a belief in diligence and one's own efficacy' (p. 116) is not included.

1 Why might this strand have been omitted?
2 In what ways is a productive disposition important?
3 How might you incorporate it in your teaching of mathematics?

Scaffolding

The metaphor of scaffolding applied to the teaching and learning process is intended to capture a particular kind of dialogic interaction between teacher (in this context referring to a more knowledgeable other) and learner. Each of the features of effective mathematics teaching described in the previous section has the potential to scaffold students' learning. Scaffolding is sometimes defined as actions of the teacher that enable a learner to complete a task successfully that would be beyond his/her ability working alone, but this is just part of what is intended (Verenikina, 2003). Verenikina (2003) explained that although there is a range of interpretations of scaffolding, it has been argued that to qualify as scaffolding the teacher's actions must be designed to increase the learner's competence so that he/she will eventually be able to complete the task unassisted, and there should be some evidence of improved learner competence following the exchange. It is, therefore, not the same as simply telling students the steps to follow, and it is certainly not an automatic result of conversation between teacher and learners or among learners.

In the context of describing unsuccessful attempts to scaffold mathematics learning in a Year 3 class, McCosker and Diezmann (2009) explain how consistently requiring students to explain their thinking, helping students to understand the requirements of a task (perhaps by restating or re-contextualising it), and providing tasks that require students to reason mathematically and that provide opportunities for them to explore multiple solution strategies and to justify their approaches, can all contribute to successful scaffolding.

making connections

The theoretical underpinnings of scaffolding lie in Vygotsky's notion of 'zone of proximal development' (ZPD). ZPD refers to the learner's potential development, just beyond what is currently possible alone but which is achievable with assistance that builds upon the learner's existing capabilities. You are likely to hear about ZPD in many aspects of your studies in education. Scaffolding cannot be fully understood without a sound understanding of ZPD (Verenikina, 2003).

Developing your own mathematics teaching philosophy

In Chapter 2 you were urged to begin work on developing a coherent, reasoned and defensible personal theory of learning, based on considered beliefs about what mathematics is. In this chapter we have extended these ideas to consider mathematics teaching. The material that we have presented has been influenced inevitably by our own essentially constructivist view of mathematics learning. If you subscribe to a different view of learning, then hopefully you have been weighing the material in this chapter in light of that view, and have been thinking through what can and cannot be reconciled. Even if you share a constructivist view of learning, you must still think through how the knowledge, attributes, and practices we have described relate to you. In either case there is much personal work to do in synthesising these various aspects into a coherent whole that will constitute your personal philosophy or integrated set of beliefs about mathematics teaching.

Chapter 3 Teaching Mathematics

key terms

Assessment: judgment about the quality or quantity of learning

Content knowledge: knowledge of mathematical processes and understanding of the concepts that underpin them

Effective teaching: teaching that is successful in achieving the intended learning objectives

Knowledge: propositions that are widely accepted as true in the relevant context

Learning: lasting change that is a result of experience and not simply a consequence of maturation or development

Modelling: demonstrating a skill, process, or strategy

Pedagogical content knowledge: an amalgam of content and general pedagogical knowledge that is more than the simple combination of the two

Planning: deciding on the learning you want to happen, designing activities likely to make it happen, and devising ways to know the extent to which the intended learning has occurred

Questioning: asking for information with a view to understanding another's thinking more clearly and/or to stimulate their thinking in a particular direction

Representations: models or images that assist with building understanding of mathematical ideas or communicating such understanding

Tasks: activities that students engage with in order to facilitate their learning

Teachable moments: unplanned opportunities to make connections between the maths at hand and other mathematics or contexts

Teaching: processes that result in another's learning

Review questions

1. If there was a single English word that meant both teaching and learning, how would you define it?
2. Create a diagram that shows how you see the connections between assessment, planning, and teaching.
3. How would you rate your knowledge for teaching mathematics? (Think about each of Shulman's knowledge types.) What steps can you take to build on this?
4. Re-write each of the following as open-ended questions:
   a. Calculate the area of this shape:

   6 cm
   4 cm

   b. What is the difference between 356 and 217?
   c. Find the missing number in this list: 97, 92, 87, __, 77, 72.
5. How would you respond if you were the teacher of the class in which a student suggested that zero was a square number? What factors would influence your decision?

Key references

Askew, M., Brown, M., Rhodes, V., Johnson, D., & Wiliam, D. (1997). *Effective Teachers of Numeracy*. London: School of Education, King's College.

Ball, D. L., Thames, M. H., & Phelps, G. (2008). Content knowledge for teaching: What makes it so special? *Journal of Teacher Education*, 59(5), 389–407.

Callingham, R. (2008). Dialogue and feedback: Assessment in primary school mathematics. *Australian Primary Mathematics Classroom*, 13(3), 18–21.

Dweck, C. S. (2002). Messages that motivate: How praise molds students' beliefs, motivation, and performance (in surprising ways). In J. Aronson (Ed.), *Improving Academic Achievement*. New York: Academic Press.

Kilpatrick, J., Swafford, J., & Findell, B. (Eds.). (2001). *Adding It Up: Helping Children Learn Mathematics*. Washington, DC: National Academy Press.

McIntosh, A., DeNardi, E. & Swan, P. (1994). *Think Mathematically!* Melbourne: Addison Wesley Longman.

Muir, T. (2008a). Principles of practice and teacher actions: Influences on effective teaching of numeracy. *Mathematics Education Research Journal*, 20(3), 78–101.

Shulman, L. S. (1987). Knowledge and teaching: Foundations of the new reform. *Harvard Educational Review*, 57(1), 1–22.

Sullivan, P., & Lilburn, P. (1997). *Open-ended Maths Activities* (2nd ed.). Melbourne: Oxford University Press.

Watson, A., & De Geest, E. (2005). Principled teaching for deep progress: Improving mathematical learning beyond methods and materials. *Educational Studies in Mathematics*, 58(2), 209–234.

Part two

Understanding the Challenges and Opportunities

It's about people!

In the first part of this book, we considered what was involved in learning and teaching mathematics. One of the most exciting aspects of teaching mathematics is the recognition that learning and teaching are fundamentally human activities that ultimately depend on the people doing the learning and teaching and the contexts in which they are doing this.

Part 2 explores the confluence of mathematics and people. We begin by learning about thinking mathematically. This is best done by watching yourself as you do mathematics. There is good news here: we can all learn to think mathematically and we can all learn to do this better!

Undertaking mathematical thinking relies on communication—to ourselves, and to others. It also involves the use of models and representations. Researchers involved with understanding the psychology of learning mathematics have discovered a great deal about how learners learn through communication and representing mathematics.

Chapters 7 and 8 consider learners in closer detail. In Chapter 7 we explore frameworks for assessing and reporting learning, and the challenges and opportunities involved in this critically important aspect of a teacher's work. Finally, in Chapter 8, we move to focus on the learner. We look at the diverse ways in which people engage with mathematics and suggest how teachers can harvest the rich rewards of working with the full range of learners.

Questions

1. Do you believe all people can learn to think mathematically?
2. Is it easier for you to speak about mathematics, draw diagrams, or use symbols?
3. If the choice was yours, how would you show another person what you know about mathematics?
4. At this point in your career, what do you see as the biggest opportunity for you as a teacher of mathematics? What is the biggest challenge?

4 Thinking Mathematically

Contents

A chance to think in a different way	69
Making a start with mathematical thinking	69
Mathematical thinking in the curriculum	71
General processes for mathematical thinking tasks	72
Helping learners to think mathematically	78
Conclusion	81

Chapter objectives

This chapter will enable the reader to:
- Develop strategies to solve mathematics problems
- Think mathematically, including the stages of gathering data, making generalisations, justifying conjectures and communicating his/her thinking
- Make use of metacognition – thinking about his/her thinking
- Improve his/her mathematical thinking by working on problems and reflecting on the experience
- Assist learners to think mathematically.

Big ideas

- Everyone can learn to think mathematically and everyone can learn to do this better.
- Thinking mathematically is a key component of the Australian mathematics curriculum.
- In mathematical thinking, the path to the solution is where learning occurs.
- All learners can engage with problem solving in diverse mathematics classrooms with careful planning by the teacher.

A chance to think in a different way

Until the mid-1980s, learning mathematics in Australian classrooms involved learning how to do exercises and techniques and to reproduce these techniques in tests or examinations. This was like an apprentice carpenter learning how to make timber joints and use the tools of the trade, but never getting the opportunity to make a piece of furniture or build a house. In mathematics, we learnt useful procedures but never had the opportunity to engage in the real work of mathematicians. With the advent of research on the nature of mathematical thinking, problem solving and investigations began to be included in school syllabuses.

Around this time I was teaching a Year 10 class. The class was given a problem to work on. It was the first time they had worked on a task where they did not know the way to find the solution. I clearly remember one girl who usually passed her maths tests, but not by much. She thought of herself as an 'average' learner of mathematics. This task was very different for her. She spent a long time working on the problem. She took the task home and spent more time on it. Days later, she brought her work back—six pages of mathematics where she grappled with her solution. Later she learnt a more efficient way to solve the problem, but this was a remarkable experience for her. For the first time, she had an opportunity to work on generating her own mathematics—and she found she loved it! She tended not to respond well to timed assessments as she needed time to mull over her work. But she did learn that there are other ways to do mathematics—and she could be good at it.

consider and discuss

About you

What styles of mathematical thinking have you undertaken? Have you had the opportunity to work on extended mathematical tasks? In what ways have you demonstrated your understanding of mathematics: tests? assignments? presentations? group projects? Do you believe you are good at mathematical thinking?

Making a start with mathematical thinking

Extensive research discounts the idea that some people are born with a mathematical brain and others aren't (e.g. Dehaene, 2011; Mighton, 2003). All of us can think mathematically and we can all learn to do this better. If you sometimes find mathematical thinking hard work, painfully slow with many wrong turns and times of complete stalemate, you may need to convince yourself that you have a mathematical brain by actually watching yourself think mathematically and then learning to do this better.

> **handy hint**
>
> In this chapter, we explore the nature of mathematical thinking. You will gain most from this if you *actively work through* the tasks as they are presented. Some may take considerable time. You may have to leave some while you allow your brain to work on them. However, if you make a serious attempt to work through the tasks and *reflect on your thinking* as you do so, you will learn most about thinking mathematically and gain in confidence in your ability to teach others to do so, too.

In Australia, problem solving became a part of mathematics syllabuses in the early 1980s, in response to at least two international influences: the Cockroft Report in the United Kingdom (Cockroft, 1982), and from the United States with the National Council of Teachers of Mathematics publishing *An Agenda for Action* (National Council of Teachers of Mathematics, 1980). In reviewing the development of problem solving as an approach to thinking mathematically, Schoenfeld (1992) notes a variety of meanings attributed to problem solving. Clarification of definitions is helpful for ensuring a shared understanding of the mathematical thinking types we are discussing. We adopt the definitions given in Table 4.1.

Table 4.1 Types of mathematical thinking

Type of mathematics activity	Description	
Exercise	Q ⟶ A	A question is posed to a person who has already solved a similar problem or has been taught a solution method. There is a known path to the solution. Exercises are also known as 'knowledge' or 'procedures', and can be thought of as learning for problem solving (Siemon & Booker, 1990).
Problem		A question is posed to a person who initially does not know what direction to take to solve the problem. There may be many possible paths to solution. There is a question to be answered. Once the problem has been solved, the solution path becomes known. If the same person is given the problem again, it will now be an exercise for that person.
Investigation	Task (arrows in four directions)	A situation or task is given to a person for exploration in any direction they choose.
Model		Questions arise from real contexts. Mathematics can be used to develop a model of the problem and find solutions, which are then reviewed in light of the context.

Each type of mathematical thinking has its place in a balanced mathematics program. Unfortunately, many people have only experienced **exercises**. In this chapter, we focus on problems and investigations. Mathematical modelling is beyond the scope of this book; however, modelling is of considerable importance in senior mathematics programs around Australia. For further information and references, visit the website of the International Community of Teachers of Modelling and Applications. The reference has been listed at the end of the chapter.

Mathematical thinking in the curriculum

The four proficiency strands in the *Australian Curriculum: Mathematics* (National Curriculum Board, 2008) are stated as:

- *Understanding*, which includes building robust knowledge of adaptable and transferable mathematical concepts, the making of connections between related concepts, the confidence to use the familiar to develop new ideas, and the 'why' as well as the 'how' of mathematics
- *Fluency*, which includes skill in choosing appropriate procedures, carrying out procedures flexibly, accurately, efficiently, and appropriately, and recalling factual knowledge and concepts readily
- *Problem solving*, which includes the ability to make choices, interpret, formulate, model and investigate problem situations, and communicate solutions effectively
- *Reasoning*, which includes the capacity for logical thought and actions, such as analysing, proving, evaluating, explaining, inferring, justifying, and generalising.

consider and discuss

Analyse the terms understanding, fluency, problem solving, and reasoning in the light of the discussion in this chapter and references.

Understanding and fluency

Understanding and fluency are important aspects that can be connected with the exercise category listed in Table 4.1. Being able to do mathematics involves learning the standard techniques of the discipline. Skemp (1976) distinguishes between 'instrumental' and 'relational' understanding. Instrumental understanding can be thought of as the 'how' of mathematics. That is, a learner may know how to follow a procedure to complete an exercise. For example, they may have learnt the formula for the area of a circle and be able to use it to calculate the area. Relational understanding is the 'why' of mathematics. A person with relational understanding would not only know how to follow a procedure, but also would understand why that procedure worked.

Once we have learnt a technique, it is important to consolidate our learning through practice. This is the basis of fluency. Therefore, as learners of mathematics, we need to have opportunities to:

- work with others to understand important techniques of mathematics. We need to understand why techniques work as well as how to perform them.
- once we have learnt techniques, we need to practise these until we reach a point of fluency. This allows us to use the techniques as required. The more techniques in which we have achieved fluency, the more we are able to use in working on new problems. *The more mathematics we learn, the easier mathematics becomes.* The more mathematics available at automatic recall, the less of a load on our working memory.

handy hint

To learn the techniques of mathematics:
- work with others (friends, fellow students, tutors) to understand the important techniques of mathematics
- understand why techniques work, as well as how they work
- practise specific examples
- communicate your understanding (journal, summarise, teach others).

Problem solving and reasoning

Problem solving, as identified in the *Australian Curriculum: Mathematics*, includes all problem situations—problems, open investigations, and **mathematical models**. Reasoning involves the processes for undertaking mathematical thinking. In this chapter you have opportunities to work through some problems and investigations and watch yourself thinking mathematically. In doing this, you have the opportunity for reasoning.

Many authors have described approaches for teaching problem solving (for a review, see Schoenfeld, 1992). In this chapter, we adapt an approach described by John Mason, Leone Burton and Kaye Stacey (1985).

General processes for mathematical thinking tasks

consider and discuss

Task 1

I wish to make a set of dot cards where each card has the numbers 1 to 10 shown in dots.

1. How many dots will I need to make the set?
2. What if I wanted to make other sets, such as 1 to 20?

Before you begin working on this task, rule your page into two columns: Working, and Thinking.

In your Thinking column, write down what you might do to make a start. Perhaps you need to check a maths dictionary to find out what some of the terms mean. Do this now and write down the problem in your thinking column in a clear way that makes sense to you.

List a few ideas of what you might try. Don't actually begin yet. Just list what you think you might do.

Try this now!

(Adapted from Downton, Knight, Clarke & Lewis, 2006, p. 34.)

Specialising

In the task above, did you find yourself wanting to try a few numbers just to see what happened? This is a very natural approach to mathematical thinking. Mason et al. have called this 'specialising'. It is a better term than the expressions 'guess and check' or 'trial and error', because 'guess' implies a degree of randomness or capriciousness; 'error' implies a mistake. 'Specialising', however, describes an important part of the problem-solving process in which we try specific examples to gain a sense of what we are trying to do to solve the problem. Specialising also allows us to gather data about the problem.

handy hint

Specialising is:
- the process of gathering data
- trying specific examples
- coming to understand what the problem requires us to find out
- an excellent place to start a problem
- an excellent place to return to if we become stuck.

Go back to Task 1. Work through the problem but as you do, record your thinking. This is not easy to do at all but if you persist, you will find yourself becoming much more aware of how your brain is guiding your thinking. In turn, you will train the voice in your head to give you better and better advice. Once you can help yourself, you are in a position to begin to help others to solve problems. Learning to focus on your thinking helps you become aware of the metacognition you are undertaking, described as 'thinking about thinking … and refers to our ability to monitor, control and organise our own mental activities' (Krause, Bochner, & Duchesne, 2003, p. 145).

Spend time working on the problem now.

consider and discuss

Task 2

1 Choose any 3 × 3 set of numbers in a hundreds chart, for example:

14	15	16	17	18
24	25	26	27	28
34	35	36	37	38
44	45	46	47	48
54	55	56	57	58

2 Investigate the sum of any three of those numbers.

In your Thinking column, plan what you *might* do to make a start. Think about possibilities for specialising. This task is an example of an investigation. You do not have a question to answer at this stage, so it may seem hard to make a start. Try a few possibilities, being careful to record your thinking. You will also need to be very clear about how you describe your choice of numbers.

Work on this now.

(Adapted from Stephens, 2003.)

Generalising

Once you have specialised for a while, you will start to gather a lot of data. What do you notice about your data? Look for patterns. Does anything surprise you? Write down patterns in words. Many people find this a difficult process. (Do it anyway! Your efforts will be rewarded.)

Once you begin to spot patterns, you are in the part of the mathematical thinking process called **generalising** by Mason and colleagues. Generalising begins when we start to notice patterns in the data and to spot aspects of the problem or investigation that stay the same when other things change. This is the place in mathematical thinking when we make **conjectures**. Conjectures are mathematical ideas that seem reasonable but have not been proven.

making connections

In 1742, the German mathematician Christian Goldbach made a claim, later revised, that all even counting numbers greater than two can be expressed as the sum of two primes. For example, 6 = 3 + 3; 18 = 11 + 7.

Try other examples.

This claim has become known as 'Goldbach's conjecture', and it is famous because, to this day, no one has been able to prove if the claim is true. A million dollar prize for a convincing proof has yet to be claimed.

As you work through Task 2, identify conjectures in your thinking column. Identify patterns. Many authors have suggested useful strategies for helping to generalise. These are variously known as heuristics, or problem-solving strategies. Decades ago, courses on problem solving gave explicit instruction on the use of particular strategies and provided problems where these techniques were to be used. Unfortunately, it was found that heuristics do not transfer to new domains or problem contexts, particularly when they are taught as algorithms or processes (Schoenfeld, 1992, pp. 352 and 354).

handy hint

Generalising is:
- the process of noting underlying patterns in data
- making conjectures
- exploring patterns.

It can be helped by:
- organising data
- specialising systematically
- trying other examples to see what stays the same (for example, in Task 2, try a different set of 3×3 numbers).

As you work through Task 2, note strategies you use to find patterns. What strategies have others used? Keep a list as you work through different tasks.

for the classroom

Matt Skoss suggests using a 'strategy board' in classrooms: <http://maths-no-fear.wikispaces.com/Posters>. Make a laminated poster of strategies such as:
- draw a diagram
- break the problem into manageable parts
- make a table
- test all combinations.

After a problem is complete, students can look back over their work and decide which strategies they used. They can put a peg against the strategy or write the name of the problem on a sticky label and put it on the poster.

This approach helps students identify strategies used while solving problems, rather than being taught the strategies in isolation.

consider and discuss

Task 3

Which numbers have an odd number of factors?

Again, use your working and thinking column. Begin by planning what you *might* do to make a start. What will you do to *specialise*? This might involve clarifying the task. What exactly does it mean to have an odd number of factors?

Work on the task now. As you begin to spot patterns and make conjectures, highlight these in your thinking column.

(Adapted from Mason et al., 1985, p. 184.)

In this chapter, we are making use of terms such as prime, factor, odd, even, etc. If you are unsure of the meaning of these words, consult your mathematics dictionary. Many of these terms come from the field of mathematics called number theory.

Task 3 is an example of a problem because there is a specific question to be answered. Have you convinced yourself of the types of numbers that have an odd number of factors? You might have tried looking at specific examples. Perhaps you tried 24. This number has the set of factors: {1, 2, 3, 4, 6, 8, 12, 24}. The number of factors is eight, which is even. Therefore, 24 is not an example of a number with an odd number of factors.

You might have noticed that each factor has a pair. For example, $1 \times 24 = 24$. To have an odd number of factors, we would need to find an example where there was not a pair. This seems unlikely until you try a number like 9. The factors of 9 are 1×9 and 3×3. As 3 is repeated, we do not need to write it twice in the set of factors: {1, 3, 9}, so 9 has an odd number of factors. Aha! 9 is an example of a square number.

We can now claim that any square number will have an odd number of factors. Because square numbers have one factor that is multiplied by itself, and therefore not counted twice, a square number will have an odd number of factors.

think + link

You will find more information about number theory in Chapter 22.

integrating technology/ICT

The place of calculators

Here is a task to explore with your calculator. (Don't use the power key—that will spoil the fun.)

What number raised to the 5th power is 371 293? That is, what is n if $n^5 = 371\,293$?

As you work on the problem, what role/s does the calculator play?

A basic calculator cannot solve the problem for you. And yet, most of us would not bother with this problem without one.

Did you find you were:

- testing conjectures?
- using the calculator as a tool—that is, using it to do the calculations while you were doing the thinking?
- correcting misconceptions? (You might have tried dividing by 5—the calculator can be used to test whether this will work.)

Justifying

We have got to the stage in Task 3 where not only do we have the answer to the original question, we are able to justify our response. We do not need to test every number, which of course would be impossible. Because we have identified and explained the underlying pattern, we can be certain our answer will hold in every case. **Justification** is an important part of mathematics, leading to the area of mathematical proof. Proof is one of the distinctive aspects of mathematics, and is the work of mathematicians. Learning how to do mathematical proof begins in the early years of school!

handy hint

Justifying:
- is the process of proving your conjecture for all cases
- involves:
  - convincing yourself
  - convincing a friend
  - convincing a sceptic
- is the basis of mathematical proof.

Justification is an important part of mathematical thinking. Sometimes students ask teachers, 'Is that right?'. If you need to ask, you are not yet convinced. Once you are convinced you will not need to ask anyone else—you will know. What is more, you will be able to argue your case to others.

making connections

One of the distinguishing features of the discipline of mathematics is the central idea of proof. In mathematics, we are interested in finding out what happens in the general case and proving beyond doubt what we know. Proof begins with justifying conjectures, and children begin this development in early childhood. As students move through school, their understanding of proof matures until in the senior secondary years students learn established proof techniques such as proof by induction, proof by contradiction, even proof by exhaustion! The book *Fermat's Last Theorem* (Singh, 2005), gives a very readable insight into the world of proof and the work of mathematicians in generating proof as it describes the path to Andrew Wiles' proof of Fermat's last theorem in 1994.

If you have the opportunity to try to convince others, you might find it is hard to do. You might find you can 'see' the solution, but that when you try to explain it, the words fail you and your ideas seem to evaporate. This is a very common experience and leads researchers to believe that mathematical thinking is not happening in our natural language. In a model of memory, Badderley and Hitch (1974) proposed a structure for working memory that included a 'phonological loop' and a 'visuo-spatial sketchpad' that supported a central executive system. It would appear that a great deal of mathematics is done in the 'visuo-spatial sketchpad'. When we come to describe the mathematics, we need to convert our thinking into language, and this involves a translation process. It is natural for this to be difficult. Once we have spoken or written our understandings, we then store them in memory in language. This would appear to be why explaining mathematics helps us understand.

Communicating mathematically

Once we have convinced ourselves we have a solution to our problem, a great deal of the motivation for the task disappears. It can be very challenging to force ourselves to communicate our mathematics. Convincing others helps, and in the classroom setting this should be a planned part of the problem-solving process, including whole-class discussion.

Two activities are necessary to improve our mathematical thinking:

1. engaging in mathematical thinking by solving problems and investigating mathematical situations
2. reflecting on the experience.

Reflecting on our mathematics may involve writing a reflection on where we got stuck, what we did to become unstuck, conjectures we tried, patterns we found, strategies we used. These can help us with strategies for the next problem we attempt.

for the classroom (and you!)

Reflection may also include writing up a solution to a problem. If you are required to do this, you may choose to use the following standard headings to organise your report:

- Statement of problem—a short statement explaining the problem.
- Methods—a description of the path you took to the solution. It is appropriate to include dead ends and conjectures that proved incorrect.
- Results—you may use tables, graphs, or diagrams to succinctly explain what you have found and how you came to be convinced.
- Conclusion—this final statement should answer the question posed in the statement of problem.

There are many sources of good problems. Most teachers have a collection of problems that they use again and again. The reference list at the end of this chapter contains sources of classroom-tested problems. Add to your collection throughout your career. Many teachers find it invaluable to have some 'ready to go' problems on a handout, card, overhead projection transparency, or interactive whiteboard file.

consider and discuss

Task 4
1. Choose a two-digit number with no repeated digit, e.g. 27
2. Reverse the digits to make a second number. 72
3. Subtract the smaller number from the larger. 72 – 27 = 45
4. Find the difference between your original two digits. 7 – 2 = 5
5. Divide your answer by this difference. 45 ÷ 5 = 9
6. Try different numbers.
7. Explain the pattern.

(Adapted from Swan, 1996, p. 20.)

Task 4 is a challenging problem. It is relatively straightforward to follow the instructions and to convince yourself that something similar happens no matter what digits you choose; it is much more challenging to explain why the pattern occurs.

Being stuck

You are likely to find that you are stuck on occasion when you are working on problems. In all tasks that are genuine **problems** or **investigations** for you, you will become stuck at some point. If you are able to work through to the solution without becoming stuck, it is likely that you are working on an exercise (albeit perhaps a complex one). Being stuck is a natural part of the process of mathematical thinking, and it is not a nice place to be! You may find that the tutor in your head has stopped being helpful and has starting saying things such as, 'This is hopeless. Give up'. Even experienced problem solvers sometimes have these unhelpful thoughts. Fortunately, there are techniques you can use to overcome this. Sports psychologists have found positive self-talk to be effective, and we can use the technique in mathematics as well. If you notice your thinking is becoming negative and unhelpful, deliberately stop the thoughts and replace them with thoughts such as, 'I have been stuck before. I have got unstuck. I will get unstuck this time, too'. Note in your thinking column that you are stuck. Then go back over previous problems and look for what helped last time.

handy hint

- Make a note in your thinking column so you can track back to find how you became unstuck when you are reflecting on your work.
- Try:
  - specialising. Often we get stuck because our brain is trying to generalise when it does not have enough data to find patterns.
  - organising your data. It is easier to spot patterns if you have organised your work in tables or sequence (such as ascending order).
  - simplifying the problem. For example, if the problem asks for 10 dot cards (see Task 1), change the problem to five cards.
  - explaining to someone else what you know and what you are trying to find out.
  - writing a paragraph summarising what you have learnt so far.
  - leaving the problem for a time. While you are doing something else, your brain will continue to work on the problem!
- Avoid 'looking in the back of the book'. It is very natural to want to be unstuck, and there is an almost overwhelming desire to be told the solution, by a friend or by looking on the internet. However, in order to learn how to think mathematically, you need to resist this. If you are told the solution, you will not have learnt how to get there. In mathematical thinking, the path to the solution is where learning occurs.

Helping learners to think mathematically

Students need to have problems and open-ended tasks to work on to develop their thinking. If the mathematics program consists only of learning how to complete exercises, then according to Schoenfeld (1992, p. 343) students learn 'that answers and methods to problems will be provided to them ... or may curtail their efforts after only a few minutes'. Therefore, the most important step for a teacher is to plan regular opportunities for students to engage in mathematical thinking. Many teachers find that initially they structure specific tasks. After they gain experience with this style of teaching, they continue to plan specific tasks but also find that their teaching style takes on a problem-solving approach in which even the demonstration of exercises proceeds with a mathematical thinking, questioning, and justification process.

Planning tasks is an involved process. First, a good task needs to be selected. The ability to identify a good task comes with experience, and with solving lots of problems yourself. The tasks may be connected to the content of the unit, but need not be directly related. For example, if the class is studying a unit on naming 2D shapes, it could be useful to include a task that encourages students to visualise. It does not have to be specifically about the properties of quadrilaterals. Research into problem solving has found that people will not use their most recent mathematics when working on problems; instead they will revert to well-practised techniques where they feel confident. Therefore, posing a problem to make use of the newly learned techniques is likely to fail.

issues in teaching

Puzzles, problems and learning to solve problems

When problem solving first started to be taught, it became fashionable to give students 'problems of the week'. Without explicit teaching of mathematical thinking, students were left to solve the problems by themselves. Those who could do them enjoyed them. Those who could not did not learn how. Also, work on one problem did not lead to improved performance on future problems.

It is more effective to:
- undertake explicit teaching of problem solving as described in this chapter
- provide opportunities for regular problem solving
- allow time for learners to mull over their work
- provide explicit opportunities for students to reflect on their solutions to a problem.

Having selected a task, teachers next have to plan how to present the task to the class. Sullivan, Mousley and Zevenbergen (2006) suggest that teachers explicitly plan **enabling prompts** and **extending prompts**. Enabling prompts are ways to make the task accessible so that all students may make a start. For example, in Task 1, a teacher might provide an example of a dot card so students are clear what is meant. A further prompt might be to reduce the task. The number of cards could be reduced. Actual cards and sticker dots could be provided. Sullivan et al. (2006) caution teachers against providing the enabling prompts to the whole class and against providing them before they are needed. Instead, they recommend posing the task and allowing students to grapple with it for a short time. Having allowed the students to work individually at first (to allow all to make a start and become committed to the problem), the teacher would then tour the room to check for understanding of the task. If students are encouraged to plan in their thinking column before starting, teachers can notice those unable to begin. Only when a student is clearly in need would a teacher provide an enabling prompt. The minimum prompt to make a start is what is required.

integrating technology/ICT

Interactive software

Many powerful problem-solving experiences can be enhanced by interactive computer software. Maths 300 is a website with a collection of exemplary lessons focusing on problem solving. There is companion software to accompany lessons and extend tasks. This is particularly helpful in the specialising stage, enabling students to explore many specific examples rapidly. It is essential, though, that students undertake the initial physical involvement in the task, such as with whole class modelling of the problem with resources.

As work progresses, students will become stuck. Teachers may be tempted to help the student by giving hints to the solution. The student will like this, but will not learn how to solve problems and will only learn to be dependent on the teacher. Instead, offer strategic help. Ask questions such as, 'What have you tried?' 'What do you know?' 'What are you trying to find out?'. These questions help the student to learn to ask the sorts of questions of themselves that help them clarify their thinking.

For learners who solve the problem easily, teachers need to prepare extending prompts. These may arise naturally in the problem, and learners can be encouraged to look for their own extensions to tasks. Extensions to Task 1, the dot cards problem, could include bigger numbers of cards or finding a general rule for any number of cards.

handy hint

Teaching mathematical thinking

- Include a balance of exercises, problems, and investigations in every unit.
- When students ask for help as soon as the task is given:
  - clarify they understand the task
  - offer enabling prompts only as required and the minimum to allow the student to make a start.
- When students ask for help after working on the problem:
  - ask: What have you tried? What do you know? What are you trying to find out?
  - offer suggestions for getting unstuck (see page 78).
- Encourage students to work together, but only after they have engaged with the task alone first.
- Prepare extending prompts for students who are looking for a further challenge. Make these prompts available to all learners at some stage (perhaps in the reporting back stage) so that all students learn how problems can be extended, even if they are not in a position to explore them at the time.
- Use whole-class reporting to allow students to learn to justify conjectures. Model the style of questioning where the work is probed for gaps. Allow other students to clarify arguments and explanations.
- Publish solutions. This might take the form of a formal written report for assessment. It might also be posters for display around the classroom, aural presentations at parent nights, or a paragraph in a learning journal read by the teacher.

Conclusion

This chapter has explored the fundamental area of mathematical thinking. The important message is that we can all learn to think mathematically and we can all learn to do this better. Improving our ability to think mathematically involves actively working on problems on a regular basis and then reflecting on our work once we have completed the problems.

Taking notice of our thinking is valuable for improving our strategic approach to mathematical thinking. This has been described by Mason and colleagues (1985) as training the 'tutor in your head'.

Finally, helping learners become better at thinking mathematically is an important goal of school mathematics programs, around Australia and internationally. Teachers need to feel confident in their own ability to think mathematically and then in their ability to teach others to do so. Explicit planning for problem solving and mathematical investigation needs to include selecting appropriate types of tasks and classroom approaches that include enabling and extending prompts.

key terms

Conjecture: a mathematical idea that seems reasonable but has not been proven

Enabling prompts: planned support for learners that enables them to commence or continue work on a mathematical thinking task

Exercise: a task for which the solution method is known

Extending prompts: planned support for learners to extend their mathematical thinking on a mathematical thinking task

Generalising: a part of the process of mathematical thinking in which the underlying patterns in the mathematics are explored

Investigation: a type of mathematical thinking in which the context is explored initially and no question has been posed

Justification: a part of the process of mathematical thinking in which conjectures are proven for all cases

Mathematical model: a type of mathematical thinking in which mathematics is used to understand a context. It is cyclic, with solutions checked with the context and assumptions modified as required

Problem: a type of mathematical thinking in which there is a question to be answered but the path to the solution is initially unknown

Specialising: a part of the process of mathematical thinking in which data is collected, specific examples are tried, and the person gains a feeling for the problem

Review questions

1. What are the four main types of mathematical thinking? How do these link to the proficiency strands of the Australian Curriculum: Mathematics?
2. Specialising allows us to make a start on a problem. List some of the ways you have specialised when working on the tasks in this chapter.
3. How do conjectures contribute to generalising?
4. Justification is an important part of mathematical thinking. Why?
5. How has communication influenced your mathematics thinking in the tasks you have worked on in this chapter?
6. For Task 2 (the 3 × 3 number grid), develop enabling prompts and extending prompts. You may wish to source the Stephens article to read how the task can be extended into algebra.

Key references

Dehaene, S. (2011). *The Number Sense: How the Mind Creates Mathematics*. London: Oxford University Press.

Downton, A., Knight, R., Clarke, D., & Lewis, G. (2006). *Mathematics Assessment for Learning: Rich Tasks and Work Samples*. Melbourne: Mathematics Teaching and Learning Centre, Australian Catholic University.

Mason, J., Burton, L., & Stacey, K. (1985). *Thinking Mathematically*. (Revised ed.). Harlow, England: Prentice Hall.

Schoenfeld, A. H. (1992). Learning to think mathematically: Problem solving, metacognition, and sense making in mathematics. In D. A. Grouws (Ed.), *Handbook of Research on Mathematics Teaching and Learning* (pp. 334–370). New York: Macmillan.

Singh, S. (2005). *Fermat's Last Theorem*. London: Fourth Estate.

Skemp, R. R. (1976). Instrumental understanding and relational understanding. *Mathematics Teaching, 77*, 20–26.

Skoss, M. (n.d.) Problem solving strategy board. Retrieved 30 July 2010 from http://maths-no-fear.wikispaces.com/Posters.

Sullivan, P., Mousley, J., & Zevenbergen, R. (2006). Teacher actions to maximize mathematics learning opportunities in heterogeneous classrooms. *International Journal of Science and Mathematics Education, 4*, 117–143.

Websites

http://nrich.maths.org/public/

www.maths300.esa.edu.au/ (an excellent source of problems and investigations with classroom notes)

www.ictma.net/ (a reference for mathematical modelling with links to many other references and resources)

http://maths-no-fear.wikispaces.com/Posters

Communication: Making Connections in Mathematics

5

Contents

Introduction	84
The language of mathematics	84
Language and culture	86
Communicating in the mathematics classroom	89
Conclusion	96

Chapter objectives

This chapter will enable the reader to:
- View mathematics as a universal language
- Appreciate the role mathematics has played historically in all cultures
- Develop an understanding of mathematics as a way of describing the world
- Understand the role communication plays in teaching and learning mathematics.

The story of Tom: Part one

Tom is an 11-year-old boy who lives in a remote rural town with a population of 235. He often helps on the family farm, and can accurately work out the amount of wool that will be produced from a flock of sheep. Last week, Tom was responsible for ordering enough fencing material to build a new paddock. At the end of term Tom took home his latest NAPLAN test results and was disappointed to be labelled as below the benchmark for measurement and data. His parents discussed the results with Tom and advised him to think about careers that did not involve mathematics.

Big ideas

- Mathematics is a powerful international language with its own vocabulary and structure.
- The genres of mathematics are explanation, arguments, proof, and written communication.
- Being able to interpret and effectively communicate mathematically are essential for students to develop good understanding.

consider and discuss

1. What information do you have about Tom's mathematics ability?
2. Discuss Tom's understanding and application of mathematics.
3. What is your response to Tom's NAPLAN results?
4. How could Tom's teacher support his mathematics learning?
5. What is your response to the above situation?

Introduction

In this chapter we explore the special nature of mathematics as a language and powerful form of communication. Like any language, users need to understand the vocabulary and structure in order to use and interpret it. Connections between culture and language and student learning are introduced, and are developed further in Chapter 8. The close links between genres of mathematics, including explanation, arguments, proof, and written communication, and student learning are demonstrated. In addition, we discuss effective communication practices in the mathematics classroom.

The language of mathematics

Mathematics is a unique form of communication and it is important to understand the way the world can be viewed and interpreted using mathematics. Mathematics is a language that requires knowledge of concepts and skills, and the ability to translate between general and specific situations. Symbols, words, diagrams, and graphs all carry significant information and meaning.

The story of Tom: Part two

One of the questions in the NAPLAN numeracy tests that Tom struggled with involved interpreting a timetable and calculating the length of a journey. Tom, unlike the majority of his city-based peers, has no experience with bus travel and timetables. Do all students have the same access to this kind of question?

consider and discuss

View Figure 3b: Achievement of Year 7 Students in Writing, by State and Territory, 2010. found on page 16 of the 2010 National Naplan report <www.naplan.edu.au/verve/_resources/NAPLAN_2010_Summary_Report.pdf>.

At a glance you can gain some useful knowledge from the graph of results. Indigenous students have scored significantly lower than non-Indigenous students throughout Australia. A visual image offers a summary of information but also allows readers to determine more detailed knowledge from a careful examination. The graph contains information that would require pages of text if mere words were to be used instead.

1. What information is available concerning the numeracy achievement of Indigenous students in Australia?
2. Are the results consistent across Year levels and states?
3. What questions does this data raise?
4. What is your response to this data?
5. What suggestions do you have to support the learning of mathematics by Indigenous students?

While mathematics is largely a symbolic language, oral and written languages are used to support and enrich it. Some terms, such as isosceles triangle, are used for specific mathematical purposes (a three-sided figure with two sides of equal length). Each term contains multiple pieces of information and often requires significant conceptual understanding on behalf of the student.

Other everyday words carry specific meaning within mathematics. For example, the word *expression* is usually associated with the act of clearly stating something or indicating feelings. In mathematics, *expression* is a string of numbers and symbols that are connected by operation signs, for example 45×3 or $3 \times n - 2$. Students for whom English is a second language face particular challenges in learning to interpret and use mathematical language.

for the classroom

Have students in your class make their own mathematics dictionary. They can add new terms and meanings as they encounter them.

Figure 5.1 Example page from a primary student mathematics dictionary

Factor
A factor is a number that divides into another number without any decimals.
eg. 2 is a factor of 10

Multiple
A number added to itself numerous times. eg.
100 is a multiple of 10

Prism
A 3D shape with top and bottom sides the same.
eg.

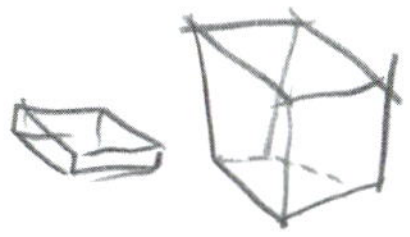

Language and culture

communicating mathematically

Communication systems such as Morse code, telegraph and semaphore use mathematics to code letters and words.

'When language is used in contexts of communication, it is bound up with culture in multiple and complex ways' (Kramsch, 2003, p.3). A discussion of culture is essential in any examination of language and mathematics. 'Ethnomathematics', a term coined by D'Ambroisio in the 1980s, is generally concerned with the mathematics of specific cultural groups. An associated area, historiography, the history of mathematical knowledge, examines non-traditional mathematics and highlights the Eurocentric nature of mathematics in most Western classrooms (Presmeg, 2007).

Although you won't be teaching this kind of theoretical framework for viewing mathematics to your students, for teachers to be able to communicate mathematically with students from a diverse range of backgrounds they need to recognise the significance of the important connections between culture and mathematics. Children's learning is highly influenced by background experiences of both their home and their culture. This can involve notions of what mathematics is, experiences of mathematics, and, most importantly, attitudes about mathematics.

for the classroom

Provide your students with examples of mathematics in a range of cultures. Display posters and discuss contributions made to mathematics by different cultures. Some examples include:

- Australian Aboriginal people used mathematics to develop complex kinship systems, used patterns like the Fibonacci sequence for weight systems, and used geometry to calculate time from the angles formed by the positions of the Sun, Moon, and stars.
- Sudanese mathematicians used magic squares (called *Ilm al-Awfaq*) and developed accurate solar calendars.
- Native Americans developed accurate geometrical systems and used probability in meteorology to make weather predictions.

Although most people value mathematics, it is also viewed through very narrow and specific lenses. Many people, and in particular some cultural groups, believe mathematics to be a procedurally bound discipline; one that requires students to rote learn and apply numerous rules. The dissonance created by conflicting understandings can interfere with students' approach to learning mathematics. It is important for you as a teacher to help mediate between the students' two worlds. This task is not simple, as you must respect the students' background and yet endeavour to provide the most effective learning experiences possible. Throughout this book, we will explore ways for you to provide positive learning environments for all students. In this discussion we emphasise the importance of understanding your students' cultural perspective on mathematics and learning.

The Indigenous Australian perspective is of particular significance. Policy supports all Indigenous Australian students having access to the same mathematics curriculum as non-Indigenous students. While this may be true, access alone does not ensure achievement of outcomes. According to Perso (2003), the reasons are complex but connected to background experiences of the students that are not always recognised by classroom teachers. 'If we are to teach the whole child we must first attempt to know the whole child and to try to "see" as the child sees, so that we can better respect and understand their "ways of knowing" and to use this in developing the teaching and learning programs' (Perso, 2003, p. 10). A note of caution, however: it is important to remember that all children are individuals and it is not possible to generalise understanding and knowing across all Indigenous Australians.

For many Indigenous Australians language can be a compounding issue for learning mathematics, as English may be the student's second, third, or fourth language. While mathematical needs will vary according to context and location, '(a)boriginal people in general want their children to have Western education, they also want their children to be numerate in a Western context' (Perso, 2003, p. 13). As a teacher you should teach mathematics using the most effective methods possible, regardless of the students' cultural background. In addition, it is important to gain an understanding of what Indigenous Australians have in terms of mathematical understanding and to try to create a learning environment that connects the classroom with the culture as much as possible. For example, Indigenous Australian students tend to rely on visual rather than auditory cues for learning. As a teacher you can use visual and hands-on learning tools such as charts, diagrams, models, and manipulatives to facilitate learning. Many Indigenous Australian students will need to be encouraged to take risks when learning mathematics; they are traditionally taught to observe and wait until they are confident that the skill has been mastered (Perso, 2003).

integrating technology

There are many resources available to support the teaching of mathematics to Indigenous students. Some examples include <http://ab-ed.boardofstudies.nsw.edu.au/go/maths-k-6/>: this site includes teaching units, assessment information, work samples, and video and audio examples. Another site, <www.blackdouglas.com.au/taskcentre/indigen.htm>, has mathematics kits with teacher-trialled activities.

Where possible, teachers need to make connections between mathematics and the contexts of the students. One example of a disparity between Indigenous Australian and Western viewpoints is seen in the concept of time. Western cultures view time as linear, divided up into units, and track the progress of events according to when they occurred. In contrast, Indigenous Australian culture views time as cyclic, and tracks time and events as they relate to nature, place, and people. For Indigenous Australians, mathematical concepts are intertwined with family, relationships, land, and nature. These ideas will be further explored throughout the textbook.

think + link

Read the discussion about second language learners in Chapter 8.

It is important to note that effective pedagogies for Indigenous Australians will generally be best practice for all students. Another group of students who require particular mention are new arrivals to Australia. In particular, refugee children may start school at any Year level according to their chronological age. In addition to issues with language and culture, many of these children have had little or no previous schooling. Such children will have different mathematical experiences to build on, and may not understand the unwritten rules of a school classroom. As a teacher you need to make an effort to connect with these newly arrived students, and as much as possible find ways to connect mathematics learning to familiar contexts.

Being aware of cultural learning preferences, such as visual, symbolic, and kinaesthetic, is important, but these should not be used exclusively. According to Bay-Williams (2007), focusing only on symbols may limit a student's access to the fullness of a concept and limit a student's understanding. Conceptual understanding is gained through multiple representations. In addition, 'symbols do not exist separate from language but are language-dependent' (Bay-Williams, 2007, p. 45). For a teacher with second-language learners, additional support may be required to assist students to learn language with mathematical concepts.

for the classroom

- Play 'What am I?'
- Provide some examples for the students: 'I have three sides. All of my angles are equal. What am I?'
- Ask students to develop their own 'What am I?' questions.

Describing the world with mathematics

Galileo stated:

> [The universe] cannot be read until we have learnt the language and become familiar with the characters in which it is written. It is written in mathematical language, and the letters are triangles, circles and other geometrical figures, without which means it is humanly impossible to comprehend a single word. (O'Conner & Robertson, 2010)

Mathematics describes and makes sense of patterns, and patterns are everywhere in the world. Often described as a universal language, mathematics uses **symbols** and vocabulary that are understood globally.

for the classroom

Create a class pattern photo-book. Divide your class into groups and ask the students to take digital photos of examples of different patterns around the school.
Have the students add text to describe the patterns.

Part of your role as a teacher is to empower students to use and interpret information mathematically. There are many situations for students to use mathematical knowledge in real contexts. Look for opportunities to engage your students in the power and use of mathematics in their world.

for the classroom

Your class is concerned about a new development that will close a local park. Have the students collect data on the use of the park and predict possible issues that may result from its closure. Encourage the students to write a letter using appropriate mathematical language, and include tables and graphs to provide visual support for the case.

In the park example, the students' first need is to understand mathematical concepts such as patterns and statistics. They must then apply mathematical skills to a new unknown situation. After interpreting the data, the students are required to communicate the information persuasively in a mathematically accurate manner.

integrating technology

Many resources connected to patterns are available on the internet. For example, <www.learner.org/teacherslab/math/patterns/> is a well-developed site that is part of the Annenberg mathematics and science project. Resources are available in the areas on number patterns, logic patterns, and word patterns. <www.google.com.au/images?q=patterns+in+mathematics> provides visual images of mathematical patterns.

Communicating in the mathematics classroom

Traditional and contemporary classroom communication

Traditional classroom discourse involves a series of direct questions that require brief precise responses from the teacher. The teacher does not join in a discussion, and usually knows what answer to expect before asking the question. This discourse shows a pattern of I-R-E—teacher *initiation*, student *response*, teacher *evaluation*. Too often this structure results in **closed questions** that do not allow students to explore effectively and develop concepts. There is a place for this form of closed questioning because it provides teachers with a snapshot of student knowledge, but it does little to promote learning and it should not be the main method of discourse.

Teacher: What is the difference between the two dice?
Student 1: 8
Teacher: Wrong. Anyone else?
Student 2: 9
Teacher: Wrong. Anyone else?
Student 3: 2
Teacher: Correct. Next question…

In this example, there was no opportunity for students to learn. Students 1 and 2 probably still don't know the meaning of the term *difference*. In addition, the teacher gained little insight into student understanding.

consider and discuss

1. What is the purpose of asking questions like those in the example?
2. What follow-up question(s) could the teacher have asked student 1 after the incorrect response of 8 was given?
3. How could the teacher support student learning through questioning?

Non-traditional discourse has been encouraged in mathematics lessons since the late 1980s. Teachers still pose questions, but the subsequent discussion/debate takes the discourse to a different level. In this discourse pattern, students listen to and respond to the teacher and each other, and try to convince themselves and others of the validity of a viewpoint, solution or conjecture. This process can be assisted by the teacher's revoicing of a student's comment to ensure it is heard and perhaps to assist with interpretation, but this should not be the sole method as it takes power back to the teacher.

Teacher:	What is the difference between the two dice?	
Student 1:	8	
Teacher:	How did you get that answer?	
Student 1:	I added the dots.	
Teacher:	Why did you add the dots?	
Student 1:	To get the difference.	
Teacher:	Can someone tell me what the difference means?	
Student 2:	When you take away.	
Teacher	What answer did you get?	
Student 2:	2	
Teacher:	How did you get that answer?	
Student 2:	I took away three from five. (Student shows using the dots to explain.)	
Teacher:	Is there another way to do this question?	

For student 1 the problem was a misunderstanding of the vocabulary. If the teacher had not probed, the student would not know why he/she was wrong. In addition, sharing strategies gives students an opportunity to develop deeper conceptual understanding and to broaden their knowledge of strategies.

Cazden and Beck (2003) also explore the right to speak. The teacher has an inherent right to speak to anyone at any time—students' right to speak has traditionally come from the teacher—but there are other models by which students select students to speak next. There is an important component of the teacher assisting students to listen carefully and respond to other students' comments—beyond talking at each other. This needs to be modelled and practised.

The term *wait time* was coined by Rowe (1986) to mean the time between a student's response and the teacher evaluation. Consider how much thinking time you are giving the students: some students do not think as fast as others, or may need to translate back and forth between their primary and second language. Teacher evaluation of a response usually cuts off further student thought and interaction.

think + link

Read Chapter 2 about effective classroom environments.

issues in teaching

It can be a challenge to incorporate the proficiency strands—understanding, fluency, reasoning, and problem solving—appropriately throughout the mathematics topics being studied. The curriculum detail can be overwhelming, but it is important to make connections between mathematics topics and across learning areas to provide adequate opportunities for students to develop the skills associated with the proficiency strands.

In contrast to the traditional simple questions, students are being encouraged to discuss and justify their ideas and to listen and learn from each other. This approach recognises the importance of the social component of learning. The language of classroom discourse is specialised, and often is unfamiliar to minority groups. It is important for the teacher to bridge the gap and empower all students to participate actively in classroom discussions. Accomplishing this involves setting up an appropriate classroom environment and modelling classroom discussions.

According to Franke, Webb, Chan, Ing, Freund and Battey (2009), teachers are good at asking initial clarifying questions but not as good at follow-up questions to help students develop a deeper conceptual understanding. Teachers gain insight into students' thinking and understanding by listening to student talk. Effective questioning techniques require teachers to listen carefully to student responses and use their knowledge of mathematical concepts to allow students to further justify and build on their knowledge.

By talking, students help develop understanding. In describing and explaining their thinking, students clarify concepts and may at times recognise an error in their logic (Chi, 2000). Students learn from listening to peers explain their reasoning, discover different perspectives, and develop new strategies.

Metacognitive questions such as 'what do you mean?', and 'why do you say that?' are important in providing a framework for students to think about their responses. These are usually referred to as **open-ended questions** (questions with no set answers). The approach/interaction summarised below gives examples of teacher prompts in a rich classroom environment (Siemon & Virgona, 2003).

- Requesting explanation
  - How did you do that?
  - How did you work it out?
  - What did you say to yourself?
  - Remind me.
- Sharing
  - Help me out. Can we do this?
  - As you tell the answer explain how you got the answer.
- Waiting—Use hand gestures to indicate 'wait time' without interrupting the lesson.
- Prompting/cueing
  - Do you want me to repeat it?
  - You need to put the hundred over there, don't you? (Student gets confused when giving a response, teacher assists to get them back on track.)
- Leading/directing—I would like you to choose one of these, one you would like to do.
- Focusing
  - What about 15 take away 9?
  - Let's remind ourselves.
- Linking—'Just reversed addition' (student response).
- Asking students to share strategies—'She used addition strategies to work it out.'
- Rephrasing—repeating an explanation from a student, rephrasing it for emphasis.
- Affirming/filtering positive feedback—'Did everyone understand how Emily worked it out?'
- Encouraging students if their answers are wrong.
- Modelling—'Why don't we set the blocks out this way?'
- Peer tutoring (students checking each other's work)—'Would you like to ask someone to help you?'
- Reviewing/reflecting
  - What have we learnt? Name one thing.
  - What would you like to learn more about?
  - What have you learnt from this session?

>  **consider and discuss**
>
> A student in your Year 5 class approaches you and says 'I need to know what 7 × 6 is to finish this question.' How would you respond, and why?

Moving to a different pattern of discourse is not simple and will involve a change in the classroom environment. Students should be *investigating, justifying, explaining, predicting, describing, representing,* and *constructing*. Peers are encouraged to assist each other with explanations: sometimes peers can communicate to assist understanding in ways that teachers may not be able to. Some scaffolding and modelling are needed to make this method as effective as possible. An example of a teacher facilitating students' learning of an important number concept follows (Siemon & Virgona, 2003).

A Prep teacher working with domino tiles helps students to notice the generalisation about the sum of even and even numbers.

Teacher:	Now, I want us to have a look at what we've got ... I want us to have a look at your sheet and I want you to find me one that's got even and even together, even and even, right? Now tell me what you have for even and even.
Student 1:	I had a 4 and a 4. [teacher records]
Teacher:	And what answer did you get?
Student 1:	8.
Teacher:	And they were all even weren't they?
Student 1:	Yep.
Teacher:	What did you have that was even even? ... Where they were all even ... [child points to domino] that's odd ... Who's got something where you've got two even numbers?
Student 2:	I've got 2 and 2. [teacher records]
Teacher:	Even, even, even!
Student 3:	2 and 4
Teacher:	So , what's that then?
Student 3:	6.
Teacher:	So that's even, even, even ... Have a look up here. Even, even, even! Even, even, even! Even, even, even! I'm going to think of an even number and put it in.
Student 4:	6 and 6.
Teacher:	Oh, that's a good one, so we've got 6 and 6, 12 [records] and that's even, even, even! So, when I have two even dominoes, what did I get? ... For the answer, what did I end up with?
Student 4:	Even.
Teacher:	Even. Hmmm ... Okay, let's try a different one, let's try an even and an odd.

The mathematics classroom needs to be a safe environment where students are willing to take risks, where it is considered necessary to make mistakes and false starts in solving problems. Students must be able to trust each other with their ideas. Developing this kind of classroom environment involves creating a healthy supportive community of learners and providing students with appropriate mathematical challenges: students need to explore concepts beyond simple procedurally based tasks.

How does a teacher communicate with students so as to encourage reflection? This partly involves listening and observing students as they work and interact with one another. Do not give the answer or method to solve a problem directly. Ask questions that build on students' knowledge, and encourage them to explore further. If they have become sidetracked or used incorrect reasoning, ask questions that will allow them to determine this for themselves. As a teacher, your role is often one of facilitator.

- How did you do that?
- Why did you multiply by 2 here?
- (in a class discussion) Is there another way that we could do this?

Most of the communication in the classroom should be student to student rather than teacher to student. Communication with others is an important part of the learning process. Engaging in explorations that involve sharing ideas, justification, and challenges to others encourages reflection by the students. Anthony and Walshaw (2008) used multiple research studies to conclude that: '(c)lassroom cultures that provide opportunities for mathematical argumentation on a regular basis, lead to enhanced students' mathematical understandings' (p. 202).

consider and discuss

Take a minute to think of some examples where students may be actively doing mathematics rather than passively observing.

1. How can students sharing ideas and justifying their answers support learning and understanding?
2. How can you, as a teacher, construct mathematics activities that encourage active student discussions?

Explanation and justification

While the concept of mathematical proof is generally reserved for secondary and tertiary students, it is important for primary-aged students to understand the concept of **proof** and **justification** of mathematical solutions and ideas.

Justification is important for two reasons: it assists students to clarify their knowledge and understanding, and it gives the teacher information about students' understanding. Proof and justification highlight the social nature of mathematics, as 'the concept of proof is social—in that what is offered as a convincing argument by one person must be accepted by others—one must take into account the social nature of the proving process' (Harel & Sowder, 2007, p. 808).

Justifying an answer helps students form more solid conceptual understanding. You have probably heard it said that you don't really understand something until you teach it. This applies to students—it is in explaining and justifying their work that they develop a deeper understanding of mathematical concepts. According to Yackel (1995), explaining to others helps students to sort out their own understanding. Even young children can justify their answer with an explanation.

An example of a teacher encouraging students to justify their answers in a Year 4/5 class follows (Siemon & Virgona, 2003):

A Year 4/5 teacher is working on consolidating place-value ideas and the role of zero.

Teacher: We'll have to have a really microscopic look at these numbers ... You have to be able to rationalise and explain why your number's bigger.
Student 1: Mine's bigger.
Teacher: Why is yours biggest?
Student 2: No, his is, he's got more tenths.
Student 3: Oh yeah ... he's got more tenths ... you won.
Teacher: You have to convince him now, because he's not too sure. Are you?
Student 1: Because if you look at the first numbers after it ... the first number is tenths. I've got five, you've got nine.
Student 2: I've got two.
Teacher: I haven't got any.
Student 1: You've only got one hundredth.
Teacher: I've got one thousandth, I've got the tiniest, tiniest bit. You've got nine hundred and nineteen thousandths. If you wanted to read it that way.
Student 2: And I've got two tenths.
Student 1: And I've got five tenths.
Teacher: OK. Do you agree with everybody? Did they convince you? So why do you get to win this round?
Student 3: Because I've got more tenths than anyone else.

issues in teaching

Despite the clear value of justification of answers, teachers can feel pressured to move through the curriculum quickly. It is impossible to ignore the imperative of teaching a full curriculum. Teachers must also take NAPLAN into account, as well as other school activities. Rich discussions do take time, but they are an important way to help students develop conceptual understanding.

Written communication

Written communication involves more reflection than an oral explanation and its value should not be underestimated. It is important to engage students through a variety of communication media—most problems will require some form of written and/or oral communication. Larger projects may also include communication in the form of posters and media such as PowerPoint. A written report will provide a permanent record of the development of their knowledge and give the teacher evidence of understanding. Both written and oral communications allow students to own the mathematical ideas—they become more personalised.

for the classroom

- Use mathematics journals.
- Have students write descriptions of key mathematics concepts.
- Journals can also be used to record questions students may have, and interesting information.
- Some teachers ask students to write about their feelings in response to mathematics.

Communicating mathematics through children's literature

Moyer (2000) emphasises the strong connections between learning mathematics and use of language, stating that 'the separation of language and mathematics instruction is very unnatural for children' (p. 253). Children's literature provides mathematical ideas in real contexts and gives opportunities for rich problem solving (Forbringer, 2004).

Mathematical discourse arising from children's literature provides opportunities for students to communicate mathematically and to justify their reasoning, and enables students to gain awareness of other perspectives (McDuffe & Young, 2003). Children's imagination and creativity are stimulated through reading interesting and exciting stories. Moyer (2000) states that the problems incorporated within stories allow children to understand that real world problems are often 'messy' and may have many legitimate solutions.

Sir Cumference and the Great Knight of Angleland, by Cindy Neuschwander, was read to a Year 5 class. This is one of a series of five books that begins with *Sir Cumference and the First Round Table*. Before reading, the students were asked to take note of any mathematics in the story. If you haven't read these books, I highly recommend them to you. Sure they are corny, but the students and teachers enjoy them! In the story, Radius, a young knight in training, sets out on a quest to find and rescue King Lell. Along the way he faces danger and solves puzzles using a mysterious medallion (a protractor). As a result of his success the kingdom is renamed Angleland (now known as England).

The story immediately captured the students' imaginations. The students shared their observations about mathematics concepts during pauses in the reading. This presented ideal opportunities to address concepts such as circumference that were unfamiliar to many students.

At one stage, a medallion that came with the book was passed around the class. The students gazed with wonder at the special medallion, which was in fact a decorated cardboard protractor! This is a great way to engage students' interest in using a protractor. Everyone laughed about *a cute* village with steep roofed houses, and the Mountains of *Obtuse*.

Later in the story, some students used mathematical knowledge to hypothesise about the ending. As Radius solves the riddle using his medallion, the students are able to see a protractor in action. Radius successfully completes his quest by rescuing King Lell and his pets (the Lell dragons). When the King shouted *Pair of Lells* the dragons would form a living drawbridge by lying side by side across the moat. 'They became so famous that today *parallel* means any straight lines side by side' (Neuschwander, 2001, p. 32).

for the classroom

- Ask students to write their own mathematical adventure stories.
- Ask the students to explain the mathematics connections in their stories.
- As an extension, students may be able to read their stories to a buddy class.

Students were asked to write reflections about the story for homework that night. Next time we were together, students shared their reflections as a group. The most memorable comment came from a capable but often disengaged student, who said that he learnt that 'maths saves the day'. He went on to explain that mathematics skills had enabled Radius to solve the riddle and complete his quest. This was then likened to the connection between mathematics and everyday life. Many students commented that the story was both funny and clever. One wrote, 'I think it is amazing how someone has made this book! It is great how it makes you remember hard things easy!' Another wrote, 'I liked the cute village and how they make a play on words to make the story maths.'

The teachers were excited to observe specific students engaged in a subject that they had often disdained. Following the success of the story, students began to explore angles and circles. They began with an angle scavenger hunt, and continued to build on the concepts found in the story with a variety of related activities. Students were tasked with finding examples of different types of angles in the classroom environment. The range of angles found by the students was impressive. Some students discovered ways of manipulating the environment to display a variety of angle types. For example, a pair of scissors can be opened to demonstrate different angles. Other students used the hands of the clock to show acute, obtuse, straight, and reflex angles (Clark, 2007).

Conclusion

Lampert and Cobb (2003, p. 237) describe communication and language 'as a primary means by which mathematics is taught and learned'. Students must have knowledge and understanding of the language of mathematics and develop skills in its application. Symbolic records allow students to represent their knowledge, while written and oral communication encourage clarification and justification of ideas.

As a teacher, you must acknowledge the important link between culture and background experiences in learning to communicate mathematically. Understanding students' background experiences should guide your planning and teaching. Modelling and facilitating rich classroom discourse will provide a classroom environment that encourages learning with understanding.

key terms

Closed questions: questions that can be answered with one word or a short phrase
Justification: use of evidence to support an argument
Mathematical symbol: a mathematical shorthand way of writing something e.g. %, =, π
Open-ended questions: questions that prompt a respondent to think, allow multiple responses, and usually require a long answer
Proof: a set of logical arguments to demonstrate that a statement is always true

Review questions

1. Explain what is meant by 'communicate mathematically'.
2. What factors influence students' ability to learn mathematics in school?
3. Compare and contrast the use of questions in traditional and contemporary mathematics classrooms.
4. How can you develop a classroom environment that encourages students to communicate mathematically?

Key references

Anthony, G., & Walshaw, M. (2008). Characteristics of effective pedagogy for mathematics education. In H. Forgasz, A. Barkatsas, A. Bishop, B. Clarke, S. Keast, W Seah, & P. Sullivan. *Research in Mathematics Education in Australasia 2004–2007.* (pp. 195–222). Rotterdam, The Netherlands: Sense Publishing.

Bay-Williams, J. (2007). Is 'just good teaching' enough to support the learning of English language learners? Insights from sociocultual learning theory. In W. Martin, M.Struchen & P. Elliot (Eds.), *The Learning of Mathematics Sixty-Ninth Yearbook.* Reston, VA: NCTM.

Cazden, C., & Beck, S. (2003). Classroom discourse. In A. Graesser, M. Gernsbacher, & S. Goldman (Eds.), *Handbook of Discourse Processes* (pp. 165–197). Mahwah, NJ: Erlbaum.

Clark, J. (2007). Maths saves the day. *Australian Primary Mathematics Classroom*, 12(2), 21–24.

Franke, M., Webb, N., Chan, A., Ing, M., Freund, D., & Battey, D. (2009). Teachers questioning to elicit students' mathematical thinking in elementary school classrooms. *Journal of Teacher Education*, 60(4), 380–392.

Lampert, M., & Cobb, P. (2003). Communication and language. In J. Kilpatrick, W. Martin, & D. Schifter (Eds.), *A Research Companion to Principles and Standards for School Mathematics* (pp. 237–249). Reston, VA: NCTM.

McDuffe, A., & Young, T. (2003). Promoting mathematical discourse through children's literature. *Teaching Children Mathematics*, 9(7), 385–392.

Presmeg, N. (2007). The role of culture in teaching and learning mathematics. In F. Lester (Ed.), *Second Handbook of Research on Mathematics Teaching and Learning* (pp. 435–458). Charlotte, NC: Information Age Publishing.

Siemon, D., & Virgona, J. (2003). Identifying effective scaffolding practices through structured peer observation and review. In L. Bragg, C. Campbell, G. Herbert & J Mousley (Eds.), *Mathematics Education Research: Innovation, Networking, Opportunity* (Proceedings of the 26th Annual Conference of the Mathematics Education Research Group of Australasia, pp. 618–625). Geelong, Vic: MERGA.

Yackel, E. (1995). Children's talk in inquiry mathematics classroom. In P. Cobb & H. Bauserfield (Eds.), *The Emergence of Mathematical Meaning: Interaction in Classroom Cultures* (pp. 131–161). Hillsdale, NJ: Erlbaum.

Websites

http://ab-ed.boardofstudies.nsw.edu.au/go/maths-k-6/

www.blackdouglas.com.au/taskcentre/indigen.htm

www.google.com.au/images?q=patterns+in+mathematics

www.learner.org/teacherslab/math/patterns

www.naplan.edu.au/verve/_resources/NAPLAN_2010_Summary_Report.pdf

6

Representations: Materials, Language, and Recording

Contents

How representations help us understand concepts	99
Building abstract thinking	102
Role of materials and models	106
Choosing materials and models	107
The role of mathematical language and recording	111
Traditional representations	113
Multi-representational learning environments	117
Conclusion	119

Chapter objectives

This chapter will enable the reader to:
- Recognise the role of representations, materials, language, and recording in learning and assessing mathematics
- Formulate frameworks for integrating representations into mathematics teaching and learning
- Appreciate the different modes of learning and the role research plays in understanding how students engage with representations.

Big ideas

- Mathematics concepts can be represented in a variety of ways.
- A deep understanding of the concept emerges from exploring a variety of representations with an ability to translate from one to the other.
- Students who use concrete materials and models develop more precise and more comprehensive understandings of concepts.
- These students are often more motivated to engage with mathematics, and better able to apply their understanding to real-life situations.

How representations help us understand concepts

Teacher: What do you think half is?
Student: When you divide something into 2.
Teacher: Here is a square piece of paper. Show me half. How do you know they are half?
Student: They are the same shape and size?
Teacher: Here is a parallelogram. Show me half.
Student: I can't. I can't fold it down any lines. It hasn't got lines of symmetry.
Teacher: Is half about symmetry?
Student: Yes.
Teacher: What if I cut it down the diagonal? Is this half?
Student: Yes, I suppose it is. (Flipping one of the shapes and checking.)
Teacher: So what is half?
Student: I get it. They are the same shape.
Teacher: Here are two rectangles. What if I cut them like this? Are they all halves?

Student: Yes I guess so.
Teacher: Are they all the same shape?
Student: No.
Teacher: So how do I know they are halves? What do you think half means? What if I had a piece of string? What would half mean?

What are mathematical representations?

Representations are increasingly seen as 'useful tools for building and communicating both information and understanding' (National Council of Teachers of Mathematics, 2000), and they play an important role in mathematical activity. Representations are classified as either internal or external, in our minds (**mental models** or mental images) or in the world around us. **Internal representations** include verbal/syntactic, imagistic, formal notational, visual images, and affective (Goldin, 2002). **External representations** refer to physical, embodied, observable configurations, and include the traditional representations (graphs, number lines, equations, and tables of values) (Goldin & Kaput, 1996), and other concrete materials used in the teaching of mathematics.

The two types of representations that affect students' understanding of, and solution to, mathematics problems can be classed as instructional representations (definitions, examples, and models) used by teachers to impart the knowledge to students, and cognitive representations constructed by the students themselves as they try to make sense of a mathematical concept or attempt to find a solution to a problem. Students create mental images of the mathematical relationships described by the teacher, and use representations (write a formula, draw a diagram) to communicate their mathematical ideas. This chapter focuses on the external representations, and in particular the instructional representations that support the instruction of mathematics.

The broad view of what we consider mathematical representations includes the traditional representational systems such as number lines, grids, and tables of values, in addition to models, materials, language, and symbols. Physical materials and models enable us to explore mathematical ideas in concrete ways. This is called **concrete thinking**. Language assists us to explain and share our understanding of mathematics. Symbols are mathematical characters used for the succinct representation of relations or operations. Thus, representations enable us to discuss mathematical relations and meanings, and they underpin our understanding of all mathematical tasks.

Table 6.1 lists the concrete representations commonly used in mathematics classrooms.

Table 6.1 Representations used in mathematics

Strand	Sub-strand	Representations Within strands	Across strands
Number & Algebra	Counting and operations	Buttons, stones, counters, straws, Unifix, hands, sorting frames, ten-frames, hundreds boards, dice, number lines, number tracks, pattern blocks, function boxes, balance scales, peg boards, counting frames	Language, symbols, graphs, tables of values, grids, pictures, virtual manipulatives
	Place value	Bundling sticks, ten-frames, MAB, abacus, hundreds boards, place value charts, number expanders, flip charts	
	Fractions	Shapes, lengths, volumes, number lines, fraction boards, fraction sticks, fraction circles, fraction rectangles	
	Algebra	Algebra blocks, patterning blocks, balance scales, function boxes	
Measurement & Geometry	Space	3D shapes, 2D shapes, maps, compasses, mirrors, attribute blocks, geo-boards, tangrams, nets, Pentominoes, straws, geo-strips	
	Measurement	Tape measures, rulers, scales, measuring cylinders, angle wheels, protractors, trundle wheels, measuring jugs, cups, spoons, sundials, clinometers, sand timers, clocks, stop watches, thermometers, weights	
Probability & Statistics		Spinners, dice, counters	

Chapter 6 Representations: Materials, Language, and Recording

did you know?

Mayan mathematics used a base number of 20, representing each number with a bar and dot when written, stones or cocoa beans and sticks as concrete representations. A dot stood for one, a bar stood for five, and a shell stood for zero.

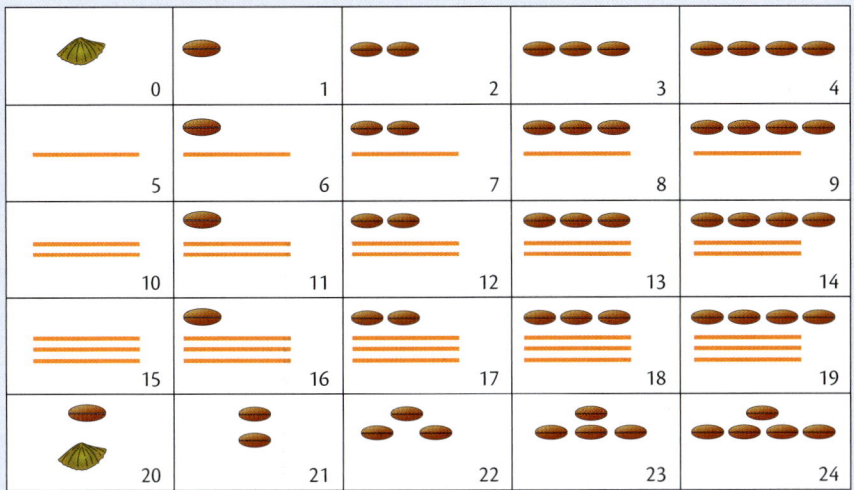

The numbers are written from bottom to top in rows. For example, for 20 the bean above the shell represents one group of 20. Thus a bean in the third row would be worth 400. An understanding of how Mayans represented numbers is important as it allows us to discuss the representations we use for our base 10 system and the importance of zero.

consider and discuss

The structure of number systems

How would the Mayans represent 40, 100, 142, 3721? How does this system differ from the way we represent numbers?

Try adding 1256 to 3478 in our system and the Mayan system. Discuss the strengths and weaknesses of each. How are they similar and how are they different?

Why are representations important?

Representations provide new layers to our understanding. They allow students to communicate mathematical ideas and understanding about concepts to themselves and to others. For example, for students to become deeply knowledgeable about number they need to see numbers represented in a variety of ways: as a set of objects, different lengths and areas, bars on graphs, distances on number lines, and symbols on a number chart. They are also required to communicate about number, utilising mathematical language and symbols.

The foundations of mathematics rest on the core representations that we have internalised (Dehaene, 1997). Linking of representations 'enables us to see complex ideas in a new way and apply them more effectively' (Kaput, 1998).

communicating mathematically

Representing the medal tally for the Olympics

How we should represent the medal tallies from each country is debated each time the Olympic Games are held. Consider the 2010 Winter Olympics medal count:

Country	Gold	Silver	Bronze	Population (millions)
USA	9	15	13	309
Canada	14	7	5	34
Germany	10	13	7	81
Norway	9	8	8	5
Austria	4	6	6	8
China	5	2	4	1336
Australia	2	1	0	22

Even though the Olympic games are officially competitions between athletes in individual and team events, we have moved towards ranking countries. Discuss the various methods we could use to rank the results for the 2010 Winter Olympics, and how you would represent the results.

Building abstract thinking

Learning and making generalisations requires **abstract thinking**. Building abstract thinking requires the careful planning and sequencing of materials and models (Figure 6.1). The role of the teacher is to ensure that students extract from the materials the target mathematical knowledge represented.

Each mathematical concept/skill is first modelled using concrete materials; students are provided with opportunities to demonstrate their mastery of the materials. Once mastery has occurred, the concepts are presented at the semi-concrete level (drawings and pictures) that represent the concrete objects. Finally, the concept is modelled at the abstract level, using only numbers and mathematical symbols. The role of the teacher is to ensure that students extract from the materials the target mathematical knowledge represented. For example, once students have had concrete experiences in counting concrete materials they move onto semi-concrete models, counting pictorial representations using language to describe what they see, then finally to abstract representations, using symbols to record the amount. Students experiencing difficulties may need to 'fold back' to less abstract materials in their explorations.

The sequence is spiral, with the abstraction from one level informing the choice of representations for the next. For example, writing the number 8 in symbolic form is only the beginning of the journey. We now spiral through a number of 'loops', each time exploring a deeper understanding of the concept and connecting it to other key concepts. As we do this we 'work through'

Chapter 6 Representations: Materials, Language, and Recording

an array of representations, often beginning again with the concrete, as shown. Thus abstract ideas can become concrete and the concrete assists the understanding of the abstract (Basson, Krantz & Thorton, 2006).

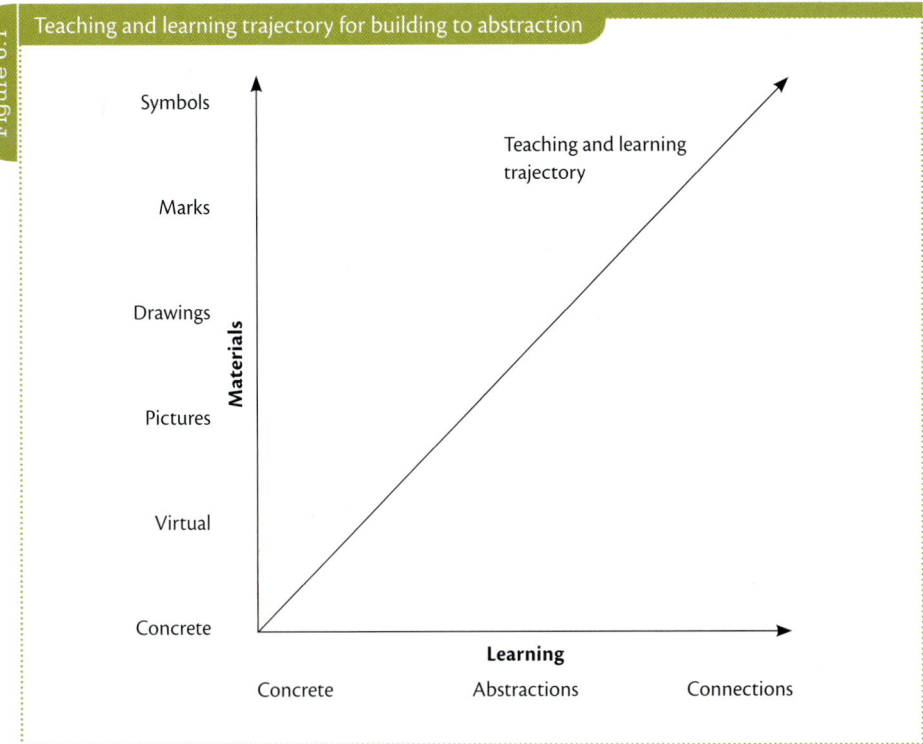

Figure 6.1 Teaching and learning trajectory for building to abstraction

for the classroom

The nearest 10

Give each child a ten-frame and eight counters, all the same colour. Ask them to place the counters on the ten-frame and describe all of the stories that they can see.

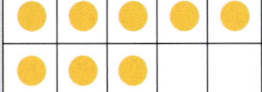  

- How many is 8?
- What stories can you see?
- Can you see the double stories?
- How many is 8 from 10?

Each time ask the child to show the representation that justifies their story. Continue for all numbers up to 10.

Once students understand how to find the nearest 10 and have a mental model of these relationships from their work with ten-frames, we move to making **connections**. Are these relationships applicable to other numbers in our number system? For example, what is the nearest 10 to 28? How far away from 28 is 30?

for the classroom

99 and 100 boards: the nearest 10

- Give each child a hundreds board. Ask them to place a counter on 38. Put 38 on the flip chart and ask them to count onto the nearest 10 (i.e. move counter two places, flip the chart through two numbers).

0	1	2	3	4	5	6	7	8	9
10	11	12	13	14	15	16	17	18	19
20	21	22	23	24	25	26	27	28	29
30	31	32	33	34	35	36	37	38	39
40	41	42	43	44	45	46	47	48	49
50	51	52	53	54	55	56	57	58	59
60	61	62	63	64	65	66	67	68	69
70	71	72	73	74	75	76	77	78	79
80	81	82	83	84	85	86	87	88	89
90	91	92	93	94	95	96	97	98	99

- Find the nearest 10 for all numbers. Discuss the patterns that emerge. For example, 7 is 3 away from 10, 17 is 3 away from 20, 27 is 3 away from 30. What is the nearest 10 to 457, and how far away is 457?
- Use this understanding to assist in mental computation. For example, 457 + 6 think 457 + 3 + 3 is 463. This thinking assists with mental computation.

Concrete activities are hands-on, and include visual and kinaesthetic learning. In the example above, encourage students to place a counter on numbers ending with 8 and count on to the nearest 10. Once the connections have been made students can then move to the abstraction that all numbers ending in 8 are two away from the nearest 10, or $b8 + 2 = (b + 1)0$, where b represents the number of tens. This is a new abstraction that spirals out from our first, namely that the symbol 8 represents eight objects. We now know what 8 represents, and how far all numbers ending in 8 are from the nearest 10. The next abstraction involves exploring where this generalisation applies across the number domain, exploring all numbers ending in 5, 6, 7, and 9. A further abstraction extends the concept to decimals. What about 1.8? What is the nearest whole number? How far is it away? To explore these questions we move back to using concrete materials or number lines to show the links between learning about whole numbers and learning about decimal numbers.

Thus learning is a continuum that begins with the concrete and culminates in the abstract. For example, 2 + 3 can be represented on a hand as two red finger puppets and three blue finger puppets. If we turn our hand around we now see 3 + 2, three blue finger puppets and 2 red finger puppets. This is a very concrete representation of the commutative law—the turn arounds. Exploring this idea within a variety of different representations and concrete situations gives understanding to the abstract expression of the law: $a + b = b + a$ (Warren, 2006).

handy hint

When exploring number properties ensure you use a variety of representations, for example set model, length model, area model, language and symbols, and review the various representations as you move across the number system. These examples represent:

- 4 add 6 is the same as 6 add 4, or
- 2 times 6 is the same as 6 times 2

Abstract and concrete are intertwined conceptual understandings. Abstract ideas can become concrete and the concrete assists the understanding of the abstract (Basson, Krantz & Thorton, 2006). Thus beginning an exploration of concepts with physical materials and models is vital to developing deep understanding and does not belong solely to the beginning years of school. It should impregnate all discussions as we continue our journey to abstraction.

This spiralling of activities applies to all strands of mathematics. In the space domain, for example, when exploring three-dimensional shapes the concrete stage could involve identifying the number of faces, edges, and vertices of real objects. Recording their findings in a table of values assists students to make connections. Encourage students to look across the rows of the tables and ask them what patterns they see. What is the generalisation? Then move to the formula. If students experience difficulties with the formula, our role as teachers is to assist them to fold back to the table of values, and if necessary fold back to the concrete materials.

Finally, challenge students to create concrete three-dimensional representations using 'building' materials and ascertain if Euler's formula (Figure 6.2) holds true. In this instance, revisiting the concrete is not about 'discovering' the concept but testing its generality.

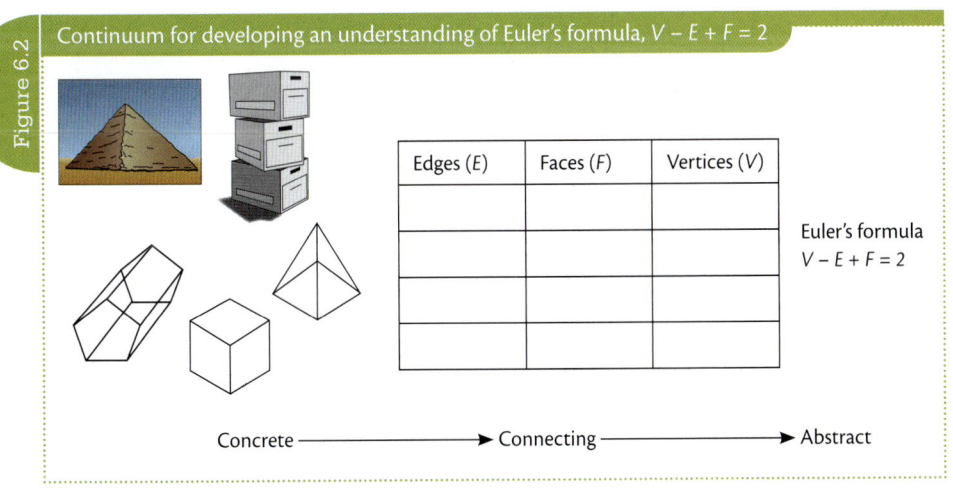

Figure 6.2 Continuum for developing an understanding of Euler's formula, $V - E + F = 2$

Euler's formula
$V - E + F = 2$

Concrete ⟶ Connecting ⟶ Abstract

communicating mathematically

As we explore mathematical concepts our questions are:
- How can we represent this idea with concrete materials?
- Which models best map the concrete to our target concept?
- How do we make connections to reach the generalisations?
- Do we need new models that will assist students' understanding to extend to the abstract?
- As a teacher, how can we help students 'see' the mathematics in the model, and represent this in either mathematical language or symbols?
- What do we fold back to when students are experiencing difficulties?

consider and discuss

Percentages and decimals

A common approach for changing decimals into percentages is to show students the trick of *moving the decimal point two places* (e.g. 0.2 is 20%, 0.20.). For many students this is a meaningless trick. How would you show students the relationship between decimals and percentages? What different representations would you use? How would you sequence them? What questions would you ask? What connections would you make?

Role of materials and models

The use of concrete materials in the classroom is often associated with the learning theories of Piaget. Piaget suggests that children in the concrete operational stage (7–11 years) are not ready for abstract thinking because they are cognitively immature. However, more recent research shows that young children are capable of thinking logically, abstractly, and engaging with representations that are not purely concrete (e.g. Clements & Sarama, 2007; Warren & DeVries, 2009b). Vygotsky (1978) states that 'children's [and teachers'] development is best guided by people who are experienced in using these tools (i.e. language, mathematical systems, and technologies)' (Hill, Stremmel & Fu, 2004, p. 15). That said, using materials increases students' engagement, development of internal representations, and ability to apply their understanding to real-life situations.

integrating technology/ICT

Interactive media

Technology such as interactive whiteboards allows teachers to use virtual manipulatives. These are dynamic representations of concrete materials that can be manipulated. Commonly they involve more than one representation (e.g. verbal and visual). Virtual manipulatives are considered to be one step away from the concrete. They can help students understand abstract concepts, and may lead to more complex and richer understandings of concepts, but students need guidance in understanding the concepts that manipulatives represent (Moyer-Packenham, Salkind, & Bolyard 2008).

When integrated into the curriculum they provide students with opportunities for guided exploration, helping them to build understanding of mathematical concepts and demonstrate learning.

When selecting activities for the interactive whiteboard, consider:

- Do they have levels of difficulties that can be adjusted for the diversity of students?
- Is feedback provided?
- Is this feedback supportive of learning?
- Will the teacher need to provide support to the students?
- Are the instructions clear?

Choosing materials and models

Ensure that students are not abstracting an unintentional property from the representations given.

MAB materials are often used in teaching students the structure of our number system. These materials closely map the bundling of 10 as we move from ones, to tens, to hundreds to thousands. The relationship between the size of the physical representations for ones, tens, hundreds and thousands mirrors the base 10 relationship that exists in our number system: 200 is physically ten times bigger than 20 and 20 is physically ten times bigger than 2. However, many students experience difficulties 'seeing' the key feature of MAB materials, the bundling of 10, that is, 10 consists of 10 ones and 100 consists of 10 tens. Experience with physically bundling concrete materials, such as bundling sticks and ten-frames, assists these students to 'concretise' the bundling of 10 in the MAB materials. Thus moving to MAB too quickly can cause confusion.

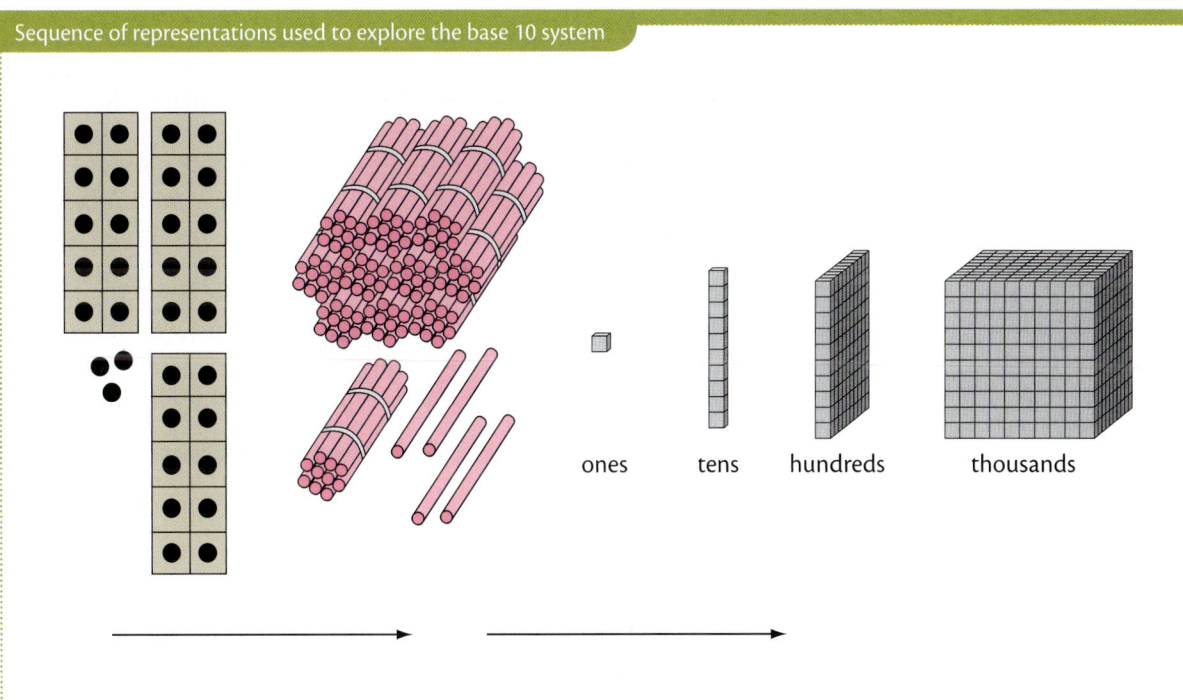

Figure 6.3 Sequence of representations used to explore the base 10 system

Difficulties also occur when teachers use MAB materials to explore the structure of the decimal number system. This entails reassigning different values to each MAB block, for example, assigning the unit block to 1 hundredth, the ten block to 1 tenth, and the hundred block to one. While the materials still physically mirror the structure of our number system, students tend to relate the physical features of the models to the whole number system. Thus when they 'see' the unit cube some students continue to see it as one whole rather than one hundredth. This demonstrates the confusion students may experience if we use the same concrete materials to explore different understandings.

Sometimes it is the materials themselves that cause difficulties for students (e.g. Cuisenaire rods and counting frames).

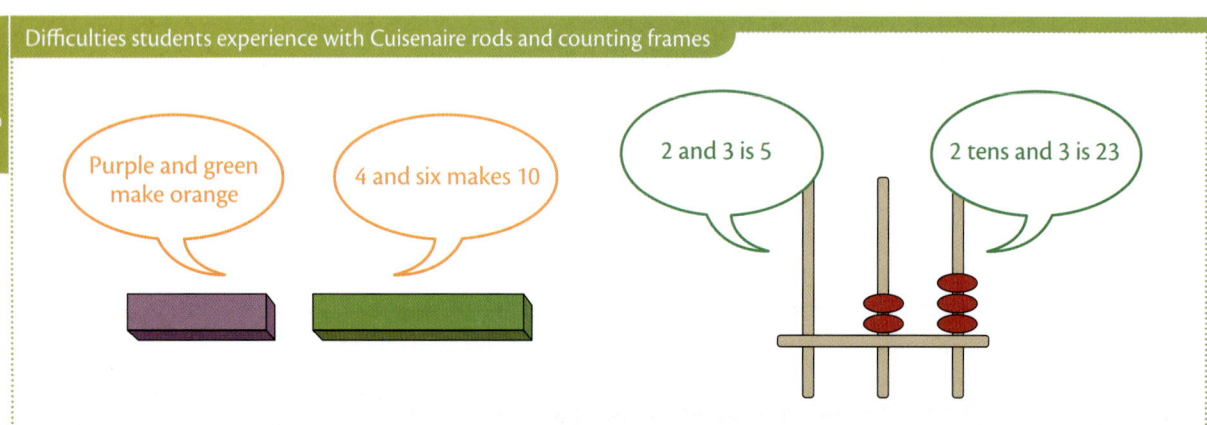

Figure 6.4 Difficulties students experience with Cuisenaire rods and counting frames

Therefore, when choosing materials we need to consider the epistemic fidelity of the material and its accessibility. *Epistemic fidelity* is a measure of the quality of the mapping between the material's features and the target knowledge domain. If this mapping is strong the model is often termed transparent, as it allows students to 'see through it' to the underlying mathematics, without being confused by features of the model itself (Stacey, Helme, Archer & Condon, 2001). For example, when exploring the notion of place value, the counting frame in Figure 6.4 has a lower epistemic fidelity than MAB materials, and the MAB has a lower epistemic fidelity than bundling sticks. The bundling sticks clearly show the groupings of ten and numbers composed of tens and ones. In contrast, the counting frame relies on where the counters are threaded as to whether they represent bundles of tens or not. Thus the counting frame is considered to be a more abstract representation of the concept of place value.

Accessibility refers to the ease with which students relate the concrete material to the mathematical concept. In the case of MAB representing the decimal system, epistemic fidelity is high but accessibility is low, as students already have a strong image of these materials representing the whole numbers.

handy hint

When choosing concrete materials, consider:
- how well the materials represent the target knowledge
- how engaging students find the materials
- the types of questions to pose to scaffold students to 'see' the key concept embedded in the materials.

Chapter 6 Representations: Materials, Language, and Recording

Strengths and weaknesses

All models and materials have strengths and weaknesses. Strengths lie in how well they map onto the mathematical concept. Weaknesses reflect how well the chosen model or materials provides a full understanding of the concept and which features 'interfere' with students reaching this understanding.

issues in teaching

Students often experience great difficulties with the concept of fractions. Many of these difficulties result from continually exploring diagrams of shapes with line symmetry that have already been partitioned. This is a common problem with many mathematical texts. The fact that fractions are parts of *equal area* is often missed. Table 6.2 presents the results from a segment of our rational number research project (Warren & DeVries, 2009a). The test was administered to 960 students whose average age was 10.5 years.

Many students believed that the trapezium in the first question was divided in halves, and in the second many tried to partition the hexagon by drawing horizontal lines through it. We suggest that these students had limited experience in physically partitioning fractions using concrete materials, and that what practice they did have tended to be with materials that were symmetrical, for example rectangles, squares, equilateral triangles, and circles. In addition, the focus did not seem to be on the kernel of the concept, that is, that the areas of each part must be equal. Their predominant explorations about the fraction concepts had been with drawings and pictures from textbooks (see Figure 6.1).

Table 6.2 Students' responses to two questions probing understanding of fractions

Model	Question	% correct	Typical response
	Tick the shapes that have been divided into halves	58	
	Colour this shape to show 2 sixths	49	

consider and discuss

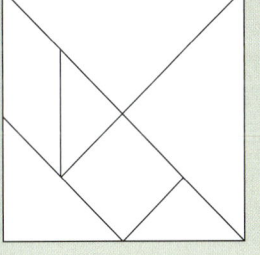

The meaning of fractions

1. Fold the parallelogram in half.
2. How many different ways can you show a quarter using the tangram pieces?

Why are these types of activities important for students?

Students are often introduced to fractions by watching adults cut up real-world models. Most classroom experiences involve identifying the number of parts from pictures that have already been partitioned, and colouring some of these parts to represent particular fractions. Partitioning fractions is not about colouring diagrams or folding down lines of symmetry; nor is it about the resulting parts having the same shape. For these models, it is about the resultant shapes having the same area. The lines of symmetry 'interfere' with the development of the fraction concept. Symmetrical shapes, while being accessible, lack epistemic fidelity: they do not give a full understanding of what fractions are.

The same difficulties occur in other areas of mathematics. For example, rectangles that are 'sitting on their base' are the ones that teachers commonly present in their classrooms. If students are always presented with rectangles like this, then they can erroneously conclude this is a property of the shape. The rectangles sitting on their base that they are shown become the students' prototype for identifying rectangles, and thus they will not recognise rectangles presented in different orientations as rectangles. This is often referred to as *prototypical thinking*. At a higher level, students can also refuse to recognise squares as rectangles and rectangles as parallelograms.

The following is an eight-year-old's response to the instruction to colour all the rectangles:

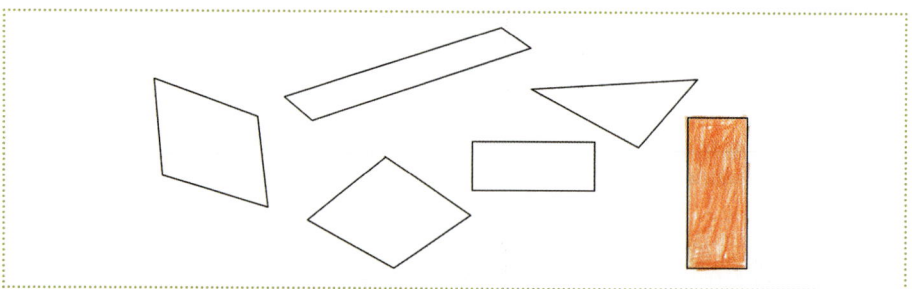

handy hint

Five key steps to addressing prototypical thinking

- Identify the concept.
- List its defining characteristics.
- Identify several different examples that contain the appropriate defining characteristics, and ensure that the examples do not all contain an inappropriate defining feature, such as symmetry, regularity, consistent orientation, same colour.
- Identify non-examples (ensure you can explain why they are non-examples).
- Have students sort the examples and non-examples according to the concept name.

making connections

The representational system of a culture depends on the types of mathematical knowledge that the culture has. For example, Pacific Island navigation is an organised knowledge system that has no writing, no calculation, and no compasses, but the Pacific was nonetheless colonised. Hawaiians relied on recognising stars and knowing where they 'come out of the ocean and go back into the ocean'. It is impossible to look *up* at the stars and find where you are, and navigation relied on remembering where you came from, constantly remembering speed, time, and direction.

Harris (1991) suggests that Australian Indigenous people from desert areas keep some kind of dynamic 'mental map' in their mind that is continually updated in terms of time, distance, and bearings, and realigned with changes in direction as the people move from place to place. In some Asian languages, such as Chinese, representation of number in language is closely related to the base 10 numeration system. This is believed to give speakers of those languages an advantage in acquiring number skills.

The role of mathematical language and recording

Representations cannot stand alone. While they assist in learning, the use of language [and writing] is integral to the construction of meaning (Vygotsky, 1978). Thus language itself can be viewed as either an internal or an external representation. Students' utterances give us insights into their internal thought processes, just as do their scribbles on pieces of paper. When we pose a problem in context, the language used to describe the context forms an external representation. In conjunction with this is the language of mathematics. In the early stages of arithmetic there is a close association between the words used to describe real contexts and the procedures used to solve problems associated with these contexts. Talking and writing are aspects of doing mathematics.

Revisiting the learning process illustrated in Figure 6.1, as students move through representations from concrete to abstraction, the developmental process also involves the development of language and mathematical 'words' that accompany the actions. Figure 6.5 illustrates the relationship between language and representations as students come to a deeper understanding of the concept of a rectangle.

Figure 6.5 Students' different ways of describing rectangles

Rectangles look like windows.
My front door is a rectangle.
Breeanna – Prep J

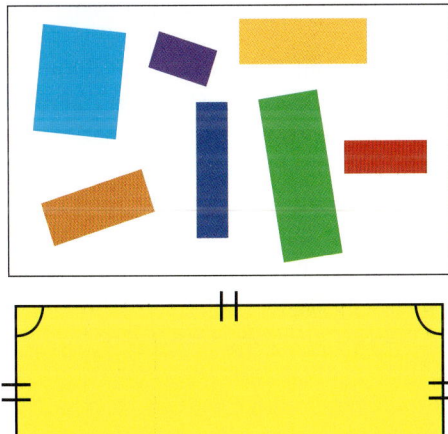

They are oblongs. Some sides are long and some are short. They have four right angles.

A quadrilateral, with opposite sides equal and parallel all angles are right angles.

The mathematical discourse students are to master is a specialised type or genre of speech that is commonly called the mathematical register (Halliday, 1978). This register is not learnt as a separate language but instead is intertwined with everyday speech in effective classroom discussions. The development of abstract mathematical concepts at even the most elementary level requires careful guidance in which talk and writing play a crucial role (Sfard, 2000). If students are struggling with the language it may at times be necessary to 'fold back' on the materials, and thus 'fold back' on the language. Folding back can play a vital role in enabling students to communicate their reasoning effectively, allowing them to describe their thinking in terms of a concrete situation rather than as an abstract thought.

communicating mathematically

ESL and Indigenous students

The importance of oral language as the foundation for learning is often not fully recognised in classrooms. Verbal communication, including instructions, explanations, and questions, dominates many of our mathematics classrooms. Many ESL students and Indigenous students are not able to make a strong start in the early years of schooling because the discourses of the family often do not match that of the school (Cairney, 2003). This mismatch of home and school language has been shown to disadvantage Indigenous students' achievements in numeracy in the long term (Dickinson, McCabe & Essex, 2006). It is well recognised that oral communication is dominant in the lives of many Indigenous students, and that their experiences with print and other literacies are often limited. Understanding and accepting Aboriginal English (AE) as a dialect of spoken English used by most Aboriginal and Torres Strait Islander people is vital, and knowing that there are variations across particular communities is important. While Standard Australian English (SAE) is the discourse of the school, teachers need to create a bridge for young Indigenous students between AE and SAE as they grapple with new language, new concepts and vocabulary presented for numeracy. For example, describing numbers in mathematics entails relating their position to other numbers. This involves a very specific understanding of words such as 'between', 'next to', 'how far', 'one more than', 'two less than'. Many of these students have little understanding of these types of words as they enter school (Warren & DeVries, 2009b).

The three words *more*, *less*, and *between* underpin many of our mathematical discussions but cause great difficulties for many students (Warren, 2006). In everyday situations we often use *more* and *less* to compare two situations; for example 'Jill has more Smarties than Jack has'. But in mathematics the use of *more* and *less* also occurs where the original amount has changed, for example 'If I gave you two more, how many would you have now?' and to compare two situations and quantify the difference, for example 'How many more does Sue have than Barry?' This type of language accompanies the introduction to addition and subtraction. In everyday language *between* is used commonly to indicate one thing between two things, for example 'Jill is between Sue and Barry', but in mathematics the use of *between* often entails many things between two things, for example 'What are the numbers between 26 and 35?'

Traditional representations

Number lines, tables of values, graphs and grids are the traditional representations used in mathematics. This section will briefly address some of the common difficulties students experience with these representations.

think + link

These issues will be explored in greater detail in Chapters 13 and 25.

Number lines

Number lines are classified as either structured or unstructured. Structured number lines have all the marks for the numbers. Semi-structured number lines have some of the marks for the numbers. The empty number line has none of the markings and allows students to draw marks for themselves. Figure 6.6 presents the types of number lines commonly used in the primary classroom.

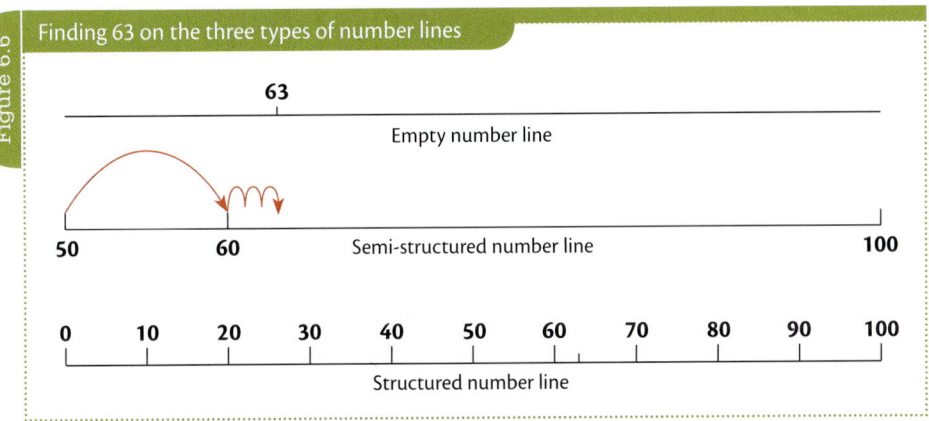

Figure 6.6 Finding 63 on the three types of number lines

It is suggested that use of structured number lines associated with a rigid ruler and pre-given distances resulted in counting along the line and passive reading of answers, lacked creativity and flexibility, and did not raise the level of strategies students used to solve problems. The empty number line's strength is that it provides the opportunity to raise the level of the students' activity, gives students freedom to develop their own solution procedures, and employs a model that fosters the development of more sophisticated strategies (Klein, Beishuizen & Treffers, 1998). Its weakness is that students need to know the structure of a number line, and in particular number as length, in order to use an empty number line effectively.

Students need to explore the structure of the number line before they can use the empty number line to help answer arithmetic problems. Young students are capable of placing numbers on 'unmarked' number lines (Warren & DeVries, 2009a). They may not initially 'see' numbers as length, but they do understand that the gaps between the numbers must be the same. Activities with empty number lines also assist students to develop an understanding of proportional reasoning. These activities can be adapted and used with older students as their number domain expands. The following activity illustrates how we assisted students to explore the structure of number lines across varying Year levels and number domains.

for the classroom

Creating number lines

Pegging 1 to 10
- Give young students a piece of rope and some pegs with the numbers 1 to 10 on them (or possums with tails that will hang on the rope).
- Ask them to take turns to put the pegs on the rope or take turns to hang the possums. Represent the numbers as dots initially, then move to symbols.
- As they hang their numbers, ask them to explain their decision.
- Finally use a measure like a duster to ensure the numbers are evenly spaced.

Ordering numbers to 30
- Give students cards with the numbers 3, 10, 13, and 21, and a piece of rope that is the same length as a number track for 0–30.
- Ask them to place the cards on the rope, explaining their decision as they place them.
- When they have completed the activity use the number track to check their accuracy.

Placing fractions on the number line
- Ask three students to place a peg where they think three-fifths of the rope is.
- The rest of the class are then asked to vote for the peg that they think is closest to three-fifths.
- Fold the rope to verify which one was closest.

issues in teaching

It is easy to get confused with the conventions of number lines and place value charts.

Number lines

The number track is a precursor to the number line. Number lines can be represented horizontally and vertically. The horizontal number line is a precursor for the *x* axis and the vertical number line is the precursor for the *y* axis. For the horizontal number line, numbers get larger as you move to the right. For the vertical number line, numbers get larger as you move up the number line. Both number lines can extend in either direction to form the Cartesian axes. Their point of symmetry is the number 0. It is important to adhere to these conventions in the primary classroom and to present situations where the number line and number track are in horizontal and vertical orientations. It is important to realise that the number line does not have to begin with the numbers 0 or 1. We often use sections of number lines and number tracks when working mathematically.

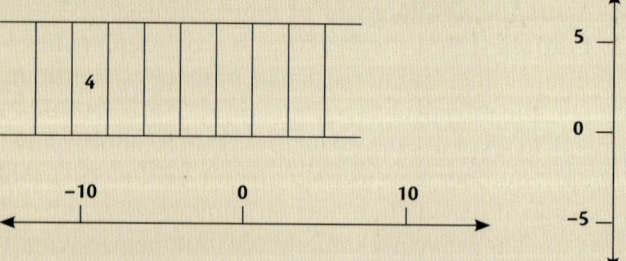

Place value charts

For place value charts the numbers get larger as we move to the left. This is the opposite of the convention for the number line, and can cause confusion when teaching. Place value charts can also be extended in both directions. The point of symmetry of place value charts is the ones.

Hundreds	Tens	Ones	Tenths	Hundredths
		↑		

Tables of values

Tables of values are commonly used to assist us organise information (see Figure 6.1). In problem solving they are used to organise two sets of numbers that are related in an ordered fashion. For example, in the problem 'How many different ways can 20 people shake hands with each other?' one column consists of the number of people shaking hands and the other column consists of the number of different handshakes for that set of people.

Number of people	Number of handshakes
2	1
3	3
4	6
5	10

Now consider the problem 'A racing car is travelling at 120 km/h. Draw a graph showing the distances travelled'. In this case, the first column of the table of values lists the numbers substituted for one of the variables in an equation, and the second column lists the value of the second variable after that substitution has occurred. In both instances placing values in the same row indicates that those two values are the corresponding members of the two sets. Once created students move to reflecting on the table and finding the relationship between the two sets.

Time (hours)	Distance travelled (km) at a speed of 120 km/h
1	120 km
2	240 km
3	360 km
4	480 km

Students tend to search for relationships in tables of values in three distinct ways.

1. Looking down each column. This most commonly occurs when the first variable is created as an indexing variable, for example, the number of people is increasing by 1 and the number of handshakes is increasing by 2, 3, 4, 5, and so on.
2. Trying to relate the two sets by using language. For example, as the number of people increases by one, the number of handshakes increases by the total number of people less 1; as the time increases by 1 hour the distance increases by 120 km.
3. Looking for relationships between the two sets of variables (across the two sets). For example, to find the number of handshakes we multiply the number of people by one less than the number of people then divide our answer by 2.

All of these ways are mathematically correct, but the third way is the most powerful mathematically. This is illustrated by asking how many handshakes

Part 2: Understanding the Challenges and Opportunities

think + link

Chapters 13 and 25 present other activities that assist students to reach generalisations from tables of values.

would there be if you had 321 people. Many students experience great difficulties moving from the first to the third way of thinking (i.e. from recursive to relational thinking). One strategy is to cover the table and reveal one row at a time, asking students what relationship they can see between the two numbers.

Graphs and grids

Older students may experience difficulties in drawing graphs, particularly in determining the scale for the x and y axes. This difficulty often results in middle-year students' inability to 'fill the page with their graph'.

consider and discuss

Difficulties with creating graphs

The graphs here were drawn by Year 6 students in response to the problem: 'Draw a graph. Plot all the points on the graph.'

Number of dogs	Number of legs
6	24
2	8
12	48
4	16

1 List the difficulties the students are experiencing.
2 Why you think they might be experiencing these difficulties, and how you would help these students?
3 What other representations would you use in these discussions?
4 What sequence of activities would you use?

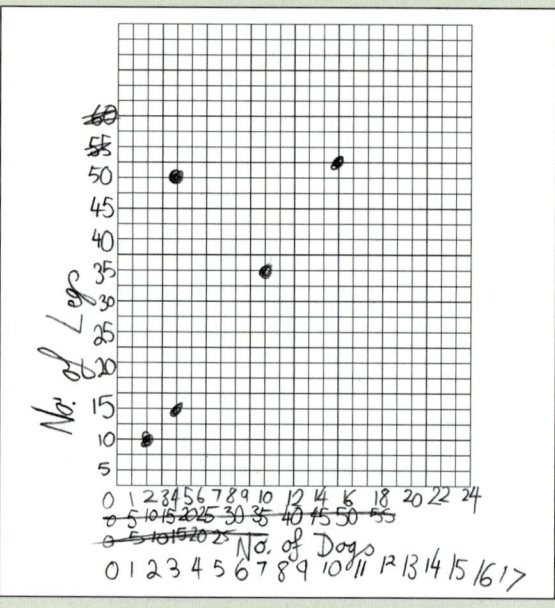

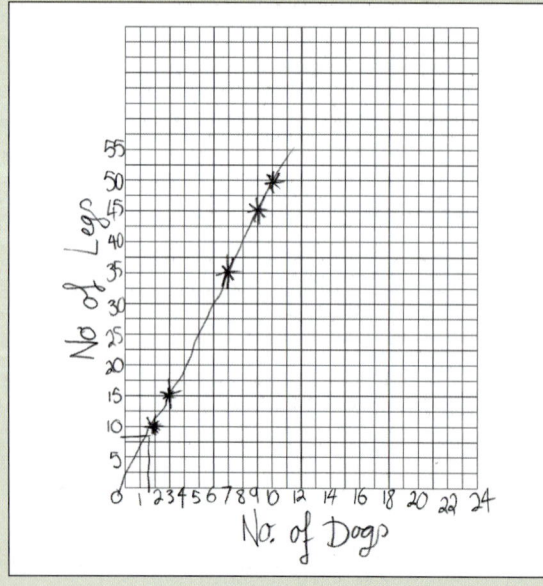

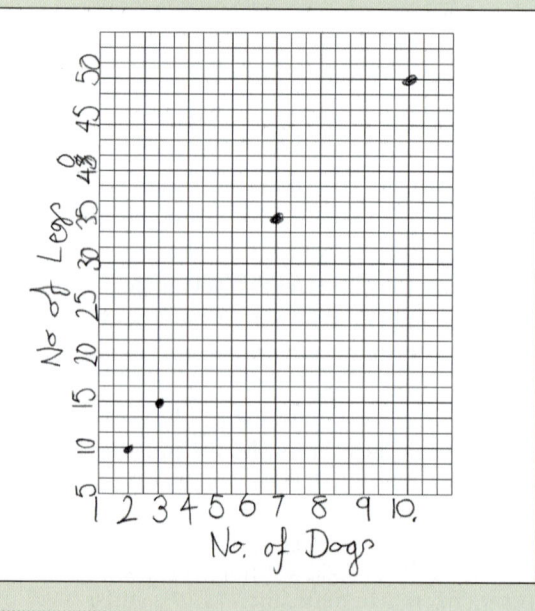

Multi-representational learning environments

Multi-representational learning environments are environments where a variety of different external representations are used simultaneously to provide the same information in more than one form. For example, rates of change can be represented as slopes of graphs in coordinate planes, differences in quotients, or as derivatives. Linear functions can be represented as straight-line graphs, tables of values, sets of ordered pairs, or equations. Kaput (1998) claimed that 'the cognitive linking of the representations creates a whole that is more than the sum of its parts … it enables us to see complex ideas in a new way and apply these ideas more effectively'.

issues in teaching

It is in the linking of representations that deep understanding of a concept development occurs.

When you are teaching it is important not to use the same representations continually to explore a concept, and to recognise that each representation gives you only limited access to the full understanding of the concept. One area of mathematics where students consistently experience difficulties is place value and the notion of renaming and regrouping. One representation that is often used in this context is the number expander.

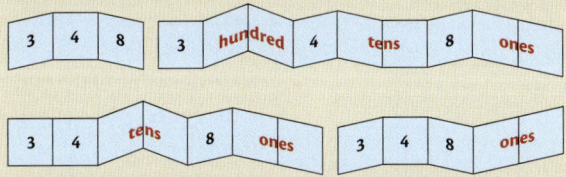

The number expander is useful for discussing the concept of renaming but this is only one aspect of place value. Students also need to know the regrouping structure of our number system. For example, they need to know that 348 is also 2 hundreds 14 tens and 8 ones; or 1 hundred 24 tens and 8 ones; 34 tens and 8 ones; 24 tens and 18 ones, and so on. An understanding of this structure is used for addition, subtraction, and mental computation. This understanding can be accomplished by using a place value chart and ten frames to represent the tens and hundreds.

In addition, the structure of our place value system is multiplicative. The use of appropriate language can assist in establishing this link. For example, 348 is 3 groups of one hundred, 4 groups of 10, and 8 ones ($3 \times 100 + 4 \times 10 + 8$). It is also 34 groups of 10 and 8 ones ($34 \times 10 + 8$), 1 group of 100, 24 groups of 10 and 8 ones ($1 \times 100 + 24 \times 10 + 8$), and so on. In a multi-representational learning environment these representations may be used simultaneously.

Hundreds	Tens	Ones
	34 tens	8 ones

Hundreds	Tens	Ones
	24 tens	8 ones

Hundreds	Tens	Ones
	14 tens	8 ones

Communicating mathematics often requires the simultaneous use of a variety of representations, including language, symbols, concrete materials, and place value charts.

When exploring mathematical concepts, using a variety of representations provides different perspectives of the concept. This approach also assists in addressing the weaknesses inherent in all models and representations. Seeing the concept in a variety of ways provides learners with the opportunity to obtain the mathematical essence of the abstraction (Dienes, 1973). The ability to construct and switch between multiple perspectives of a domain is fundamental to successful learning. Also, students gain better problem-solving skills when they are presented with both text and pictures. The disadvantage relates to the difficulty that many students experience in translation, the cognitive process of transferring from one representation to another. For example, when we move from a symbolic equation to a graph and vice versa we are translating between the two representations. Students who understand an idea are those who can recognise the idea in a number of representations, can flexibly manipulate the idea within given representations, and translate the idea between representations.

for the classroom

Interpreting points

Bird	Sparrow	Pigeon	Sandpiper	Goose	Owl	Eagle
Highest altitude (m)	600	4000	3500	1200	1000	1000
Wing span (cm)	25	46	37	89	112	250

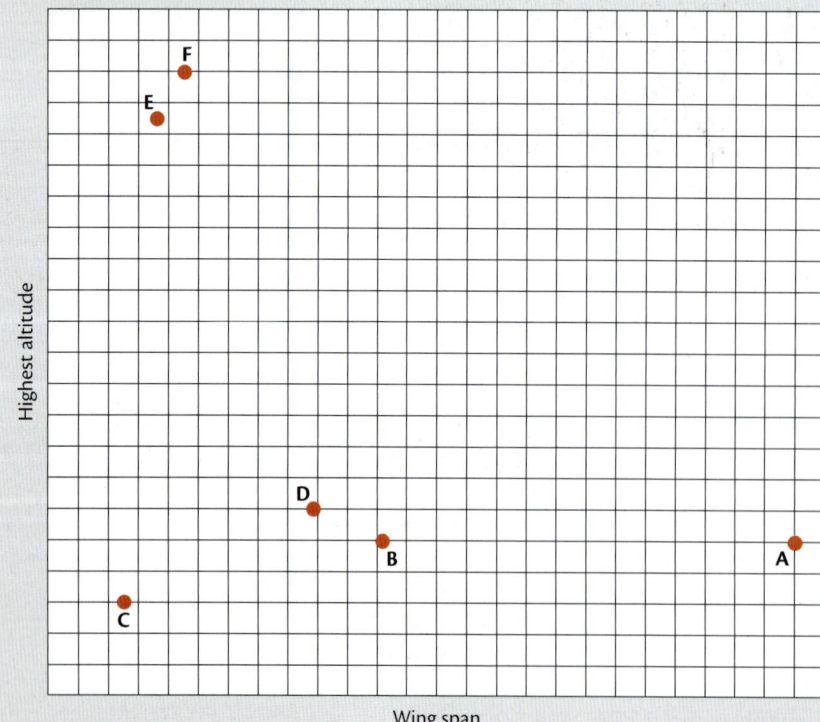

- Write the name of the bird at the correct point on the graph.
- What other variable may determine the altitude a bird may reach?
- How did you work out your answers?

issues in teaching

Designing tasks to meet learning objectives

The major challenge for teachers is designing activities that address well-formulated learning goals in advance of classroom interactions. The activities need to include a range of external representations. To account for the range of abilities:

- choose tasks that incorporate rich and varied representational systems that cater for a range of learning styles, for example visual, kinaesthetic, and auditory learners
- choose tasks that students can represent meaningfully but that also offer challenges
- integrate the use of virtual manipulatives into the curriculum
- plan for contingencies and use research to assist in identifying cognitive obstacles or common representation difficulties
- maximise students' interaction with the learning environment, encouraging a variety of representational modes
- incorporate means of assessing students' learning through their own representations of mathematical concepts
- develop a repertoire of proven successful activities.

Conclusion

Representations are fundamental to the teaching, learning, and communicating of mathematics. A wide array of representations, including verbal, formal notational, visual images, concrete materials, graphs, equations, and virtual manipulatives, all assist us to help our students understand mathematics and provide us as teachers with insights into student thinking. It is important to consider which representations best support students' access to the ideas. We commonly begin with the concrete and move to the symbolic, continually connecting and abstracting.

Teachers commonly choose to use the types of representations with which they themselves feel most comfortable. We must, however, remember that each new representation provides a new layer of understanding. Moving from one to another is an essential component of developing understanding. As teachers, we need to:

- choose the representations that best support student learning
- know how to fold back to other representations as we explore mathematical concepts
- be aware that folding back language may be necessary as we explain and justify our thinking to others
- assist students to discover the mathematics embedded in the representations
- assist students to use a variety of representations as they explore ways of solving problems.

key terms

Abstract thinking: thinking removed from the facts of the 'here and now', and from specific examples of the things or concepts being thought about

Concrete thinking: thinking characterised by a predominance of actual objects and events and the absence of concepts and generalisations

Connection: linking of signs and symbols that represent the same object or concept

External representation: an external sign or symbol that represents an object or concept

Internal representation: a presentation to the mind in the form of an idea or image

Mental model: an internal representation of a concept or ideas indicating the relationships between its various parts

Multi-representational learning environment: using a variety of external representations simultaneously to explore an idea or concept

Review questions

1. Describe the relationship between internal and external representations.
2. When planning for a series of lessons, what should teachers consider when choosing representations? Illustrate your discussion using a particular content area of mathematics.
3. Examine a mathematics text. List the representations used and discuss the type of learners it caters for.
4. Reflect on the representations you favour when teaching mathematics. Why do you favour them, and what type of learning do they support?
5. Select three virtual manipulative websites. Using the criteria listed above, evaluate each site, indicating its strengths and weaknesses.

Key references

Clements, D., & Sarama, J. (2007). Early childhood mathematics learning. In F. Lester (Ed.), *Second Handbook of Research on Mathematics Teaching and Learning* (Vol. 2, pp. 461–556). Charlotte, NC: NCTM/Information Age Publishing.

Dehaene, S. (1997). *The Number Sense: How the Mind Creates Mathematics*. Oxford: Oxford University Press.

Dienes, Z. P. (1973). *Mathematics Through the Senses, Games, Dance and Art*. Windsor, UK: The National Foundation for Educational Research.

Goldin, G. A. (2002). Representation in mathematical learning and problem solving. In L. D. English (Ed.), *Handbook of International Research in Mathematics Education* (pp. 197–218). Mahwah, NJ: Erlbaum.

Kaput, J. (1998). Representations, inscriptions, descriptions and learning: A kaleidoscope of windows. *Journal of Mathematical Behaviour, 17*(2), 265–281.

Klein, A.S., Beishuizen, M., & Treffers, A. (1998). The empty number line in Dutch second grades: Realistic versus gradual program design. *Journal for Research in Mathematics Education, 29*, 443–464.

Sfard, A. (2000). Symbolizing mathematical reality into being: how mathematical discourse and mathematical objects create each other. In P. Cobb, K. E. Yackel, & K. McClain (Eds), *Symbolizing and Communicating: Perspectives on Mathematical Discourse, Tools, and Instructional Design* (pp. 37–98). Mahwah, NJ: Erlbaum.

Warren E. (2006). Learning comparative mathematical language in the elementary school: A longitudinal study. *Education Studies in Mathematics*, 62(2), 169–189.

Websites

http://www.simerr.educ.utas.edu.au/numeracy/critical_numeracy/critical_numeracy.htm

www.thenetwork.sa.edu.au/teachingandlearning

http://activated.act.edu.au/ectl

7. Assessing and Reporting

Contents

Assessment is about testing, right?	123
Assessment of learning	126
Assessment for learning	128
Reporting	138
Conclusion	139

Chapter objectives

This chapter will enable the reader to:
- Understand the nature and purpose of assessment
- Understand the nature and purpose of reporting
- Engage with current research
- Explore best practice examples, especially in relation to enhancing student learning
- Appreciate the role and impact of standardised tests
- Make connections to planning for student learning.

A testing time

A group of Year 5 students are completing a maths test. The students are given an hour to complete all the questions and have been asked to work in silence. Adam is angry because the questions are too difficult for him and he is not allowed to ask the teacher for help. He completes about one-third of the tasks and says, 'I'm dumb at maths. I am too slow and I don't know my tables … I hate it'. Adam is just one of many students whose experience of assessment is painful. This type of experience clearly does not help him or anyone else learn mathematics. Indeed, it only serves to further diminish how he feels about himself as a learner. We know that poor self-esteem has a negative influence on learning. The challenge is to turn this situation around. Reconceiving assessment practices has the potential to achieve this.

Big ideas

- Assessment serves two primary goals: assessment of learning, and assessment for learning.
- Assessment of learning is used to inform parents, educational leaders and policy makers on a periodic basis.

- Assessment for learning is integral to teaching and learning and informs teaching decisions on a daily basis.
- Diverse assessment strategies are needed to identify and support the learning needs of all students.
- Reporting is about communication of student achievement, progress and improvement, to students, parents, teachers, and the education system.

Assessment is about testing, right?

Assessment has been conceived and implemented as a way of measuring achievement, frequently in the form of tests or examinations. Tests are marked and scored, and aggregated over time to constitute a grade, such as A, B, or C. The grades are then reported periodically to students and parents. The students with high grades would feel 'good' and be empowered to study more mathematics. But what of the student with a low or failing grade? What about the 'average' student? What does 'average' really mean? Does reporting grades or scores to students improve student learning? Adam, at the beginning of this chapter, is one example of a student whose performance on a test has resulted in negative feelings about himself and mathematics.

for the classroom

If you want to find out more about your students' views about how they feel about their learning, consider using Clarke's (1985) impact procedure:

- Write down the two most important things that you have learnt in maths during the last month.
- Write down at least one sort of problem which you have continued to find difficult.
- What would you like most help with?
- How do you feel in maths classes at the moment? (Circle the words that apply to you.)
  a Interested
  b Relaxed
  c Worried
  d Successful
  e Confused
  f Clever
  g Happy
  h Bored
  i Rushed
  j Write down one word of your own.
- What is your biggest worry affecting your work in maths at the moment?
- How could we improve maths classes?

The description above is of how assessment has been generally conceived and popularly recognised. Results from examinations at the end of secondary school have significant bearing on gaining a place at university. National tests such as the National Assessment Program—Literacy and Numeracy (NAPLAN) (Ministerial Council on Education, Employment, Training, and Youth Affairs, MCEETYA, 2008) provide information about the standard of literacy and numeracy achievement in Australia. Results can influence policy as well as assist schools and teachers to plan for both school and student improvement. To determine trends globally, there are international tests such as Trends in International and Science Study (TIMSS) (see http://timss.bc.edu/) and Program for International Student Assessment (PISA) (see www.pisa.oecd.org) that assess knowledge and application extensively across countries.

It is important to recognise that measuring student achievement is only one aspect of why we assess. The other, much more common but less public, aspect of assessment, is the practices teachers use to identify student learning needs, evaluate their own teaching, and provide constructive feedback to students. So, how is assessment defined?

According to Griffith & Kowalski (2010, p. 10), 'Assessment is the process of evaluation through the use of a range of recording instruments.' Given this, there are two essential purposes of assessment: assessment *for* learning and assessment *of* learning.

Assessment *of* learning is when teachers or school systems gather evidence about student learning to make judgments against goals and standards. This evidence often comes in the form of tests or examinations at the local school level as well as at the national and international levels. Assessment *of* learning is summative in nature. This aspect of assessment is perhaps the one that we are most familiar with.

Assessment *for* learning is when teachers and students gather evidence about student understanding to inform future learning. Assessment *for* learning is formative, and this evidence is collected in diverse ways. Reporting is integral to the assessment process as a whole.

did you know?

The origin of the word *assess* dates back to the Latin *assere*, meaning 'to sit with'. Historically, a judge, with the aid of an assistant (sitting beside the judge), would determine the amount of tax requiring payment. Today, the action of 'sitting with' is an important part of the assessment process. Working closely with students reduces the distance between the teacher (teaching) and the learner (learning).

Assessment today

Contemporary views of learning recognise that learning is both personally constructed and shaped by social practices. Current views of assessment reflect this; for example, we are more inclined to have students construct a response and work with others, as opposed to only relying on recall or remembering some fact or procedure (Clarke, 1996). Not only do we assess student progress and achievement in mathematics, but also students' beliefs and attitudes. It is commonly accepted that there is a close link to beliefs and attitudes, and student learning.

Assessment opportunity is drawn from a range of instructional activities and *looks* more like 'teaching' than like 'testing'. 'What effective teachers do' is characterised by phrases like 'exemplary teaching' or 'exemplary practice'. We make the same demand of assessment. Assessment provides answers to the questions we ask about teaching, student learning, and schooling in general. How can I improve my teaching? Exactly what do I need to teach my students? What is the most effective way to communicate to them? Do my students understand key concepts and ideas? How do they feel about learning mathematics? What are their specific learning needs? What resources will best support student learning? As we endeavour to answer these and other questions, assessment becomes reflective in nature.

The purpose of assessment is to model, monitor, and inform (Clarke, 1996). This is consistent with assessment *of* learning and assessment *for* learning. Table 7.1 brings these ideas together.

Table 7.1 Multiple purposes of assessment

Assessment	Model	Monitor	Inform
Assessment *of* learning	Curriculum Valued performance	Achievement: against goals and standards	Policy School systems Parents and students
Assessment *for* learning	Exemplary practice	Learning: determine starting points for teaching	Teachers and students Parents

Clarke (1996) identifies four principles of assessment that underpin these multiple purposes:

- Assessment is an exchange of information.
- Assessment must optimise students' expression of their learning.
- Assessment must have instructional value.
- Assessment must anticipate action.

It is timely to be reminded of the *Standards for Excellence in Teaching Mathematics in Australian Schools* (Australian Association of Mathematics Teachers, AAMT, 2006) (see chapters 1 and 29). In relation to assessment, the *Standards* state that:

> Excellent teachers of mathematics regularly assess and report student learning outcomes, both cognitive and affective, with respect to skills, content, processes and attitudes. They use a range of assessment strategies that are fair, inclusive and appropriate to both the students and the learning context. They maintain on-going, informative records of student learning outcomes that are used to map student progress and to plan appropriate future learning experiences. The excellent teacher of mathematics provides constructive, purposeful and timely feedback to students and their parents, and the school authorities, as required'. (p. 4)

Insights from research

Views about assessment have been transformed as behavourist views of student learning have changed to social constructivism.

Assessment *of* learning continues to be a legitimate purpose of assessment, but this needs to be well defined and used only for that purpose. In general, test results can indicate levels of student achievement overall, assist in adjusting the curriculum and help teachers evaluate the effectiveness of their teaching (Leahy, Lyon, Thompson & Wiliam, 2005). In any given community where school mathematics is valued, assessment *of* learning serves as a mechanism for accountability. Assessing competence in school mathematics ensures teachers are accountable for their teaching, schools are accountable to government, and government is accountable to the community (Clarke, 1996).

How well students participate in school mathematics determines entry into further education and employment. Clarke (1996) recognises that:

> It is through assessment that society provides or withholds its rewards ... assessment, which has been used as a competency measure by many professions and education systems. Where statewide competency testing has been employed, a mathematics component is standard. (p. 329)

What is assessed then will determine what is taught. This is a top-down approach to learning. Stiggins (2002) argues for balance between assessment *of* and assessment *for* learning. Assessment *of* learning on its own will not make the same gains for student learning that assessment *for* learning and assessment *of* learning can achieve together. There has been a general tension between *quality control* (assessment *of* learning) and *quality assurance* (assessment *for* learning), with a shift in focus from teaching to learning (Leahy et al., 2005). The Australian Association of Mathematics Teachers (AAMT) (2006, 2008) also positions student learning upfront. Assessment *for* learning starts at the micro-level, that of the student and/or the school.

Where assessment is used to advance student learning, student achievement improves. Black and Wiliam (1999) summarise key research in this area and identify five key conditions for this to occur:

- provision of effective feedback to students
- active involvement of students in their own learning and assessment
- adjustment of teaching based on what assessments reveal
- recognition that assessment influences student motivation and self-esteem, and
- the need for students to understand for themselves how to improve.

Reporting test scores to students does not lead to student learning (Wiliam, 2005). In particular, there is significant negative impact on low-achieving students, who are led to believe that they lack ability and therefore are not able to learn (Black & Wiliam, 1998). Teacher comments are critical to student learning when framed in such a way that they enable students to move forward. However, if both scores and comments are communicated to students, the mention of scores negates the benefit afforded by the comments (Wiliam, 2005).

Assessment strategies *for* learning will look different in different classrooms. However, what is most likely to be consistent is that:

> Students will be thinking more than they will be trying to remember something, they will believe that by working hard, they get cleverer, they will understand what they are working towards and will know how they are progressing. (Wiliam, 2005, p. 34)

Assessment *of* learning

The global education community is interested in trends in achievement across a range of school systems and instructional approaches. For instance, the Trends in Mathematics and Science Study (TIMSS) has assessed mathematics and science achievement every four years since 1995. The goal of TIMSS is to provide comparative data about achievement in these areas across countries, as well as track the relative progress of the cohort assessed in Year 4 as they become the Year 8 cohort in the next iteration.

In Australia, the National Assessment Program—Literacy and Numeracy (NAPLAN) tests are administered to determine the standard of literacy and numeracy achievement of students in Years, 3, 5, 7, and 9. Before NAPLAN, similar tests were administered on a state-by-state basis. The tests focus on four aspects: language conventions, reading, writing, and numeracy. Results are reported against 10 bands that represent increasing levels of skill and understanding. At the system level, results can inform policy and decisions on resourcing. At the school level, information derived from the tests enables schools and teachers to plan for whole-school and student improvement. Thornton (2009) shares NAPLAN results for Year 9 students attending a secondary school referred to by the pseudonym 'Suburbia'. The minimum standard for Year 9 is Band 6. It is possible to view an individual school's performance in relation to the state and national average, as shown in Table 7.2.

Table 7.2 Proportional NAPLAN achievement of 'Suburbia', by state, and national, by band

Band	'Suburbia' %	Queensland %	National %
Band 10	1.2	4.3	8
Band 9	0	12.3	14
Band 8	17.6	25.2	25
Band 7	25.9	30.2	28
Band 6	35.3	20.2	18
Band 5 or less	20	6.6	5

Source: Thornton, 2009, p. 30.

NAPLAN results are also communicated to parents. The report below (Figure 7.1) allows this parent to compare their child's achievement in relation to the national Year 7 average as well as the middle 60% of all Year 7 students Australia-wide. The student's acheivement is set against a scale of 10 bands, of which Band 5 is the national minimum standard for this Year level.

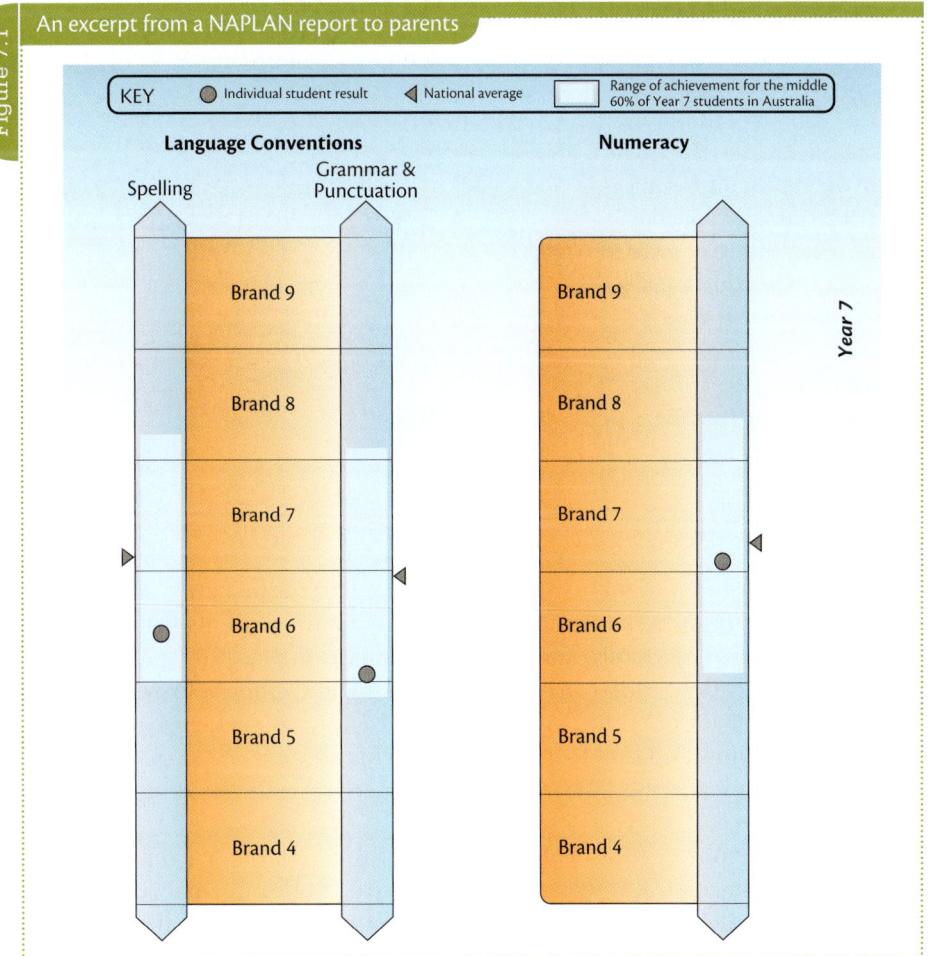

Figure 7.1 An excerpt from a NAPLAN report to parents

Source: Student Report 2008 NAPLAN—Year 7

Part 2: Understanding the Challenges and Opportunities

did you know?

Summative assessments are those practices that locate and/or describe students' achievement in relation to defined goals and standards (norm-referenced). The excerpt of the NAPLAN report presented in Figure 7.1 is an example of summative assessment. The student's achievement for numeracy is located just below the national average.

Individual schools and teachers cannot control the content or the timing of NAPLAN tests. However, they can elect to implement tests that have been trialled widely and distributed by reputable organisations such as the Australian Council of Educational Research (ACER, 1998). The Developmental Assessment Resource for Teachers (DART) Mathematics, and Progressive Achievement Test in Mathematics (PAT-M) are examples. These are suited for use in both primary and secondary schools. PAT-M provides norm-referenced information about students' skills and understanding in mathematics. The DART Mathematics uses a developmental approach based on national benchmarks. Consistent with NAPLAN, schools can assess their students' performance in relation to a large sample of other students, as well as have access to more diagnostic information at the level of the individual student.

Assessment *for* learning

communicating mathematically

Students have a say

Giving students the opportunity to write about their learning can reveal important information. The illustration opposite from a student's journal is the result of students being asked to draw a face to show how they felt about their maths learning (Siemon, 1988), and complete the sentence starter 'I feel … because …' (Smith, 2003)

Knowing how students feel is an important part of assessment. This student's teacher is aware that a positive change in attitude has resulted from specifically teaching efficient mental computation strategies.

think + link

If an aspect of assessment requires making recommendations for future learning, then assessment must be closely tied to teaching mathematics (see Chapter 3).

As teachers, we want students to make progress, to like mathematics, and to enjoy engaging in meaningful mathematical activity. We want students to understand key concepts, learn new skills, and utilise efficient or purposeful strategies. The focus is on the student rather than the curriculum, and student learning rather than teaching. Assessment for learning is about gathering evidence to find out what students know and can do, to determine what students need to know next, and how best to teach this. What follows are specific strategies designed to do just that.

Terms and phrases associated with assessment for learning include constructive, alternative, formative, informative, and informal assessment. Essentially they all mean an approach based on the following guiding ideas:

- The exchange of ideas provides students with the opportunity to demonstrate their thinking.
- Student learning needs are met by identifying what students can do as a starting point for teaching.
- Assessment is a regular and ongoing part of classroom activity.

consider and discuss

A teacher gave a test to a Year 8 mathematics class. The students are anxious to find out how well they did in the test. The teacher communicates the students' scores as percentages by reading the students' names and their scores out loud in class. A few students have done well, but most students have fallen below 50%. The students are told that they would now be moving onto the next topic.

What do you think the consequences of this approach might be? How else might the teacher have handled this?

Feedback

Feedback is information, written or oral, provided by the teacher to the student in relation to student progress and achievement. The nature of feedback given to students has changed as we have come to understand its role in assessment for learning. Reporting scores to students does not lead to student learning. What does make a difference are teacher comments, both written and oral. Such comments are framed in a way that fosters thinking that then enables students to take action.

There is no single recipe for effective feedback. Essentially, feedback becomes effective when it is about the future and informs the student about what they need to do to improve, as opposed to feedback about the past that informs the student about what they've done well or not so well. Figure 7.2 is an example from a Year 7 student's workbook. Written feedback from the teacher appeared in the margin stating 'Heading? Neat ticks please'.

Feedback on fractions: Year 7 student workbook

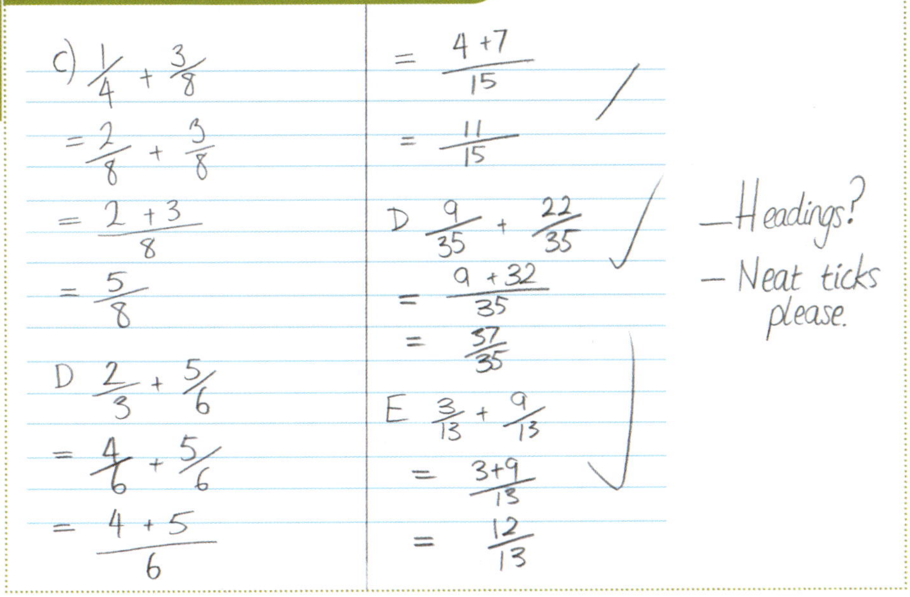

Figure 7.2

Thinking about the feedback provided in Figure 7.2, we can ask: Do these comments improve student understanding? Is the student in a position to understand the concepts and ideas more deeply in the future? The comments provided to this student relate closely to compliance on organisational matters rather than to the student's approach to the mathematics. In contrast, Figure 7.3, from a Year 6 student's workbook, shows how teacher feedback contributed to student improvement.

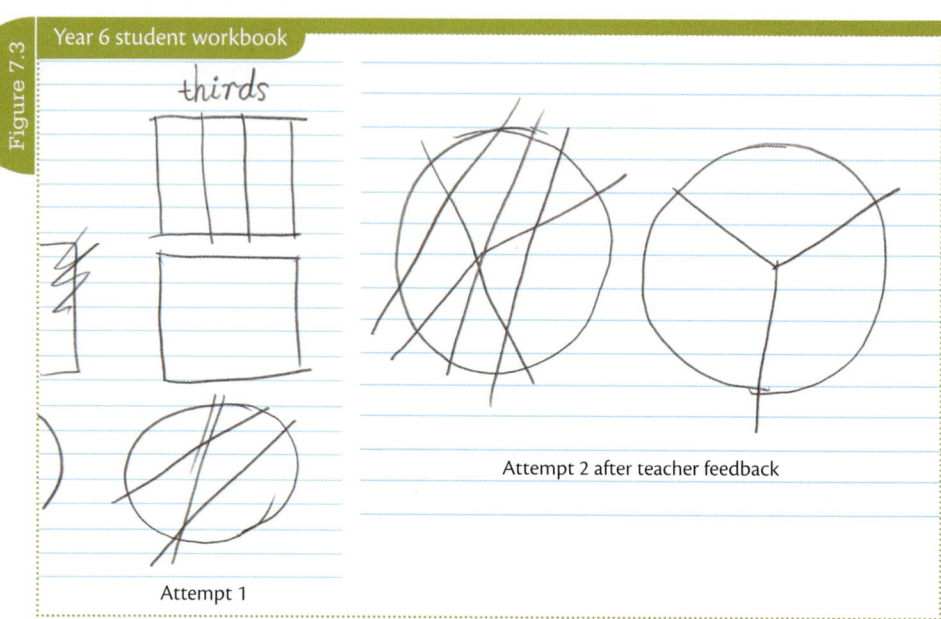

Figure 7.3 Year 6 student workbook
Attempt 1
Attempt 2 after teacher feedback

The first image shows a Year 6 student's attempt to construct their own fraction diagram for thirds. It is clear that the student understands the need for three equal parts when partitioning, but has difficulty when partitioning the circle. This attempt has been crossed out. The teacher provides the following feedback to the student: 'Try thinking back to the strategies you used when folding the paper circles to show thirds'. The student's second attempt is successful.

Questioning

think + link

The nature of questions and questioning is a critical aspect of teaching and learning (Chapters 3 and 29).

The posing of questions is a regular classroom activity and is an important aspect of assessment. Questioning should not used for managing classroom behaviour by redirecting an inattentive student's focus back to the issue at hand. Nor should questioning feature only an initiation–response–evaluation (IRE) discourse pattern. This widely recognised form of questioning is characterised by a teacher-initiated routine, or closed, question, followed by a one- or two-word student response, which is then evaluated as either right or wrong. It is generally understood that this approach inhibits rather than enhances student learning.

Questioning should, instead, encourage meaningful extended conversation with the purpose of improving student learning. This provides a strong link to assessment. Often, questions and their answers help to determine what students know and do not know. If we see questioning as strategic classroom conversation between teacher and students that includes a variety of strategies, then improved student learning will result.

Asking open questions is a useful starting point. Open questions (Sullivan & Lilburn, 1997) differ markedly from closed questions and have the following features:

- They require more than remembering a fact or reproducing a skill.
- They have a range of acceptable answers.
- They enable students to learn by answering the question.
- They enable the teacher to learn about each student from their response.
- They engage students of different abilities.

Joshua (2001), in advocating the use of open questions with students in Years 7 to 10, states that they are important as the same question can be presented to a group of students of varying ability. The variety of responses generated can be the stimulus for discussion about those responses that indicate deep thinking with the potential for making generalisations. Re-framing closed questions as open questions is a useful way to encourage student learning as opposed to routine recall of facts.

Consider the question 'I have four sides. What shape might I be?' This question clearly has more than one suitable answer, and has the potential to stimulate a sustained conversation between teacher and students.

Open questions can be presented to students orally and become the basis of a stimulating conversation, or they can be written (on whiteboard or worksheet), encouraging students to offer more than 'answer'. Questions like the one below provide rich information for assessment purposes.

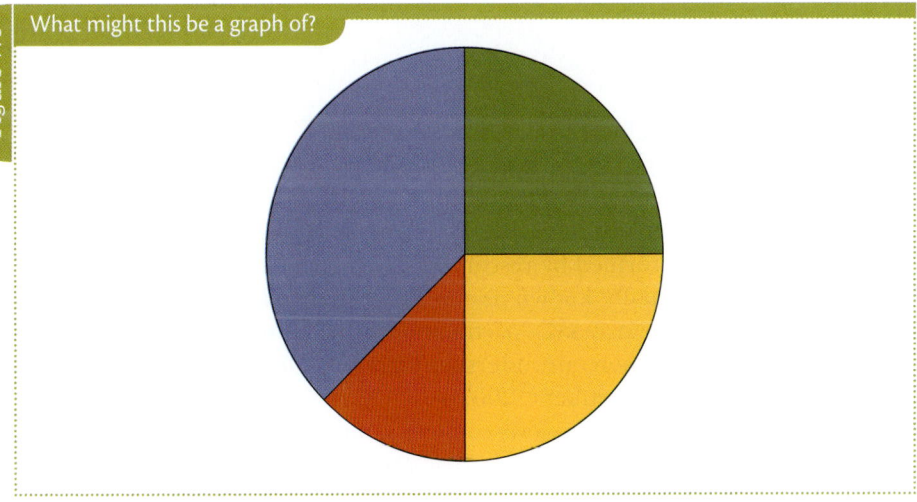

Figure 7.4 What might this be a graph of?

Source: Adapted from the Name the graph task, Beesey, Clarke, Clarke, Stephen & Sullivan (1998), p. 104.

For instance, a student whose response to the task shown is 'This can't be a graph because there are no bars on it' reveals a limited understanding of representing data visually. This would prompt the teacher to provide opportunity to broaden and deepen the student's understanding in this area.

did you know?

Teacher questioning is an important part of student learning. Increasing wait time (the time between the teacher's question and student answers) can improve the quality of students' responses.

Wiliam (2005) advocates including statements in regular classroom dialogue. The question 'Do squares have four sides?' can be turned into a statement, for example 'Only squares have four sides'. The potential here is for students to take a position as to whether they agree or disagree with the statement and to justify their reasoning for doing so. Throughout the dialogue or debate that ensues, the teacher learns about the students' conceptions and misconceptions, and the students learn from each other. The students are no longer passive recipients of information, facts and procedures, but active participants by expressing their thinking and listening to and respecting the views of others.

integrating technology/ICT

A plethora of resources and opportunities

We have a range of technological hardware, software, and online options for student learning.

In terms of assessment, this is a potentially resource-rich environment. However, user caution is required! Recently a teacher found an online activity that asked students to respond to an addition problem by pressing an arrow key that changed the number from 1 to … by ones until the correct answer was reached. It is therefore vital that teachers look carefully and critically at what is on offer to ensure that it is pedagogically sound.

A good example to explore is maths300 (Curriculum Corporation), a web-based site that provides teachers with an expansive lesson library suitable for implementation in F–12 schools. Site licences are required, but you can log in as a guest to find out more. A number of their lessons, for example Number Charts, include software that allows students to practise mental computation strategies by completing grids of various sizes and level of difficulty. There is opportunity for students to monitor their own learning by trying to improve their 'personal best'.

Interviews

Interviews are purposeful conversations that have the potential to assess mathematical knowledge, skills, strategies, and understandings. By listening to children in a one-to-one situation, interviews reveal more than is possible through observation and testing alone. The interview task or suite of tasks can be teacher-designed or informed by research, for example Victoria's Mathematics Online Interview (formally known as the Early Numeracy Interview), Count me in too, in New South Wales (Department of Education and Training, 2009), and Assessment for common misunderstandings (e.g. Department of Education and Early Childhood Department, 2007).

Teachers who conduct interviews come to know their students more deeply than if they do not implement this approach. In particular, as students engage with the interview tasks, the teacher is informed not only about the student's beliefs, but also about the strategies they use and their reasoning. The students themselves feel valued by having their teacher take the time to meet with them on an individual basis. Interviews allow teachers to:

- understand students' learning needs
- find out more about how students think and feel while doing mathematical tasks
- gain insight into students' thought processes in action
- generate detailed profiles showing students' achievements in relation to growth points or developmental stages
- track student learning over time
- inform planning for focused teaching at the point of need.

The following example illustrates the need to probe into student thinking, rather than accept students' answers at face value. Two interviews revealed significant differences between the students who had both written the correct answer.

communicating mathematically

Interviews reveal student thinking

Some children are making patterns with square tiles in an art class. To make the pattern shown you need 5 black tiles, 3 grey tiles and 1 white tile. It looks like this.

To repeat the pattern you need 5 black tiles for every 3 grey tiles. How many black tiles would you need if you had 12 grey tiles?

Two Year 5 students gave '20' as their answer. Their teacher wanted to do more than correct their responses, and conducted an interview to find out more.

The teacher asked the students individually to explain how they had arrived at the answer of 20. The first student explained that 'I added the 3, 5 and 12 and got 20.' The teacher was alarmed by the inappropriateness of this strategy. The second student explained, 'Well, I know that 3 grey tiles make one pattern, 6 grey makes two patterns … so 3, 6, 9, 12. So you could make the pattern 4 times with 12 grey tiles and you would need 4 times the number of black tiles. 5, 10, 15, 20. You need 20 black tiles'.

This example demonstrates why we cannot assume that a student who gives the correct answer understands the mathematics.

Rich assessment tasks

'When are we goin' to hafta use this?' This is the catch-cry of the student who does not understand the purpose of completing numerous procedural exercises presented on a worksheet or contained in a textbook.

Rich assessment tasks, also referred to as *authentic* assessment tasks, have the potential to challenge this view. They are designed to add to the range of evidence about student progress. Rich assessment tasks are problems or investigations that are contextualised in some way and integrate assessment into routine learning experiences. Through completing the task, there is opportunity for learning to occur. Consider the following example from the Scaffolding Numeracy in the Middle Years (SNMY) Project.

Adventure camp

Camp Reefton offers four activities. Everyone has a go at each activity early in the week. On Thursday afternoon students can choose the activity that they would like to do again.

The table shows how many students chose each activity at the Year 5 camp and how many chose each activity at the Year 7 camp a week later.

	Rock wall	Canoeing	Archery	Ropes course
Year 5	15	18	24	18
Year 7	19	21	38	22

1. What can you say about the choices of Year 5 and Year 7 students?
2. The Camp Director said that canoeing was more popular with the Year 5 students than the Year 7 students. Do you agree with the Director's statement? Use as much mathematics as you can to support your answer.

Rich assessment tasks such as this provide students with the opportunity to apply mathematics in a real-world situation. Typically they feature the following characteristics:

- All students can make a start, so they support diversity in the classroom.
- They encourage students to share their thinking, which in turn discloses their understanding.
- They are time-efficient in that a task that may take 15–20 minutes for students to complete can reveal a wealth of information and, as learning is central to this strategy, assessment is achieved at the same time.
- They provide a measure of choice and/or 'openness', in that there may be more than one way to approach the task or more than one solution.
- They involve multiple areas of mathematics and multiple disciplines.
- They give a sense of purpose and authenticity that in turn increases student engagement.

A **rubric** or scoring framework provides students and teachers with established criteria for success, and clarifies and shares the intentions of the given task. The rubric for the Adventure Camp task is given below. You will notice that different scores are allocated according to different levels of student response.

Adventure Camp		
Task	Response	Score
1	No response or incorrect statement	0
	One or two relatively simple observations based on numbers alone, e.g. 'Archery was the most popular activity for both Year 5 and Year 7 students', 'More Year 7 students liked the rock wall than Year 5 students'	1
	At least one observation that recognises the difference in total numbers, e.g. 'Although more Year 7s actually chose the ropes course than Year 5s, there were fewer Year 5 students, so it is hard to say'	2
2	No response	0
	Incorrect (No); argument based on numbers alone, e.g. 'There were 21 Year 7s and only 18 Year 5s'	1
	Correct (Yes), but little/no working or explanation to support conclusion	2
	Correct (Yes), working and/or explanation indicates that numbers need to be considered in relation to respective totals, e.g. '18 out of 75 is more than 21 out of 100', but no formal use of fractions or percentage or further argument to justify conclusion	3
	Correct (Yes), working and/or explanation uses comparable fractions or percentages to justify conclusion, e.g. 'For Year 7s it is 21%. For Year 5s, it is 24% because 18/75 = 6/25 = 24/100 = 24%'	4

Peer and self-assessment

The implementation of rich assessment tasks and associated rubrics helps to communicate the learning intentions explicitly to the student. Peer- and self-assessment strategies provide this opportunity. Students can be invited to assess their own responses, as well as the responses of others, with a predetermined rubric or criterion for success, or students can be directly involved in the creation of a rubric for later use.

Peer assessment takes place when students assess each other's or a group's response against given criteria. Self-assessment is similar and involves the student assessing their own responses. Students have the opportunity to reflect on and share with others what they have learnt and what they need to learn next. The benefits of building this approach into regular classroom assessment activity are that:

- students take an increased responsibility for and ownership of their own learning and the learning of others
- students become more reflective on their role and the role of others in the learning process
- the feedback itself is more tightly focused and relevant
- the assessment process is demystified.

issues in teaching

When students use inefficient and inappropriate strategies

The Butterfly House task (Siemon, Breed, Dole, Izard & Virgona, 2006) presented the following:

Some children visited the Butterfly House at the zoo. They learnt that a butterfly is made up of four wings, one body, and two feelers. While they were there, they made models and answered some questions.

One of the tasks was to determine how many wings, bodies and feelers would be required to make 98 model butterflies.

The Year 5 student's response below indicates an attempt to model all the components for 98 butterflies, then count the parts. This suggests that this student conceives numbers as a 'collection of ones' and is still reliant on a 'model all, count all' strategy. This is a strategy you would expect a student in the first year of school to use.

At this point, the student became involved in a period of targeted teaching that in part focused on the strategic development of efficent mental strategies (see Chapter 14) and conceptual understanding of multiplication (see Chapter 17). At the conclusion of this period of learning, the student completed the same task.

This new response is presented below.

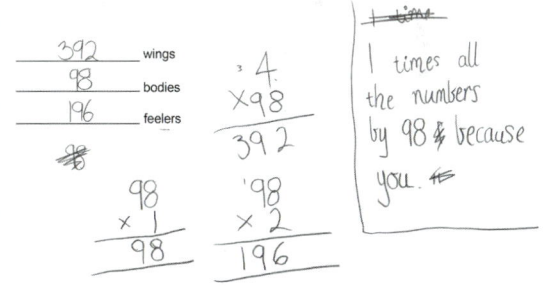

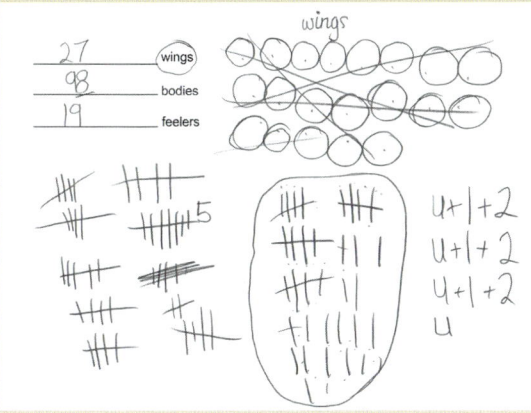

> **handy hint**
>
> The greater the diversity and frequency of assessment strategies used, the richer the portrayal of student learning.

Observation

Teachers work closely with their students, and when given the opportunity can speak at length about individual students' personality, disposition, understandings, and skills in relation to key areas of mathematics. Teachers know their students, and this is in part a result of the frequent observations teachers make as part of their day-to-day interactions. Observing students is an important part of the core business of teaching, and critical to effective assessment practice. Small-group teaching provides the teacher with rich opportunities for close observation of students at work.

Talking to students and watching what they do can uncover misconceptions. These misconceptions can potentially go unnoticed if observation is not seen as a valid strategy. Consider the following two scenarios.

Scenario 1

A teacher of Year 6 students, in wanting to know more about students' understanding of written procedures, prepared a worksheet with four written algorithms. These equations required solutions to the four processes of addition, subtraction, multiplication, and division. The students were required to solve the equations using written methods, but also to describe what they did and why. The teacher's premise was that if the student could solve one sum of each type, then they could also solve more than one. Also the teacher was particularly interested in the students' reasoning about what they did and why. This proved a useful task. Some student responses revealed a lack of understanding of place value. One student, when referring to the numbers regrouped to the tens place, said that 'these numbers were decimal numbers, because they were really small.' This suggests that this student may view decimal numbers as those numbers that live between zero and one.

Scenario 2

A teacher of Year 3 and 4 students had wanted his students to work mentally with multiplication, and had found a game using playing cards that might be suitable. Students sat with a partner on the floor and each pair had a deck of playing cards. The students took turns at dealing out three playing cards, arranged in the form of a 2 digit by 1 digit multiplication. For instance, if a two, eight and three card had been dealt, then this could represent '3 twenty-eights'. The students were then required to solve this mentally as quickly as possible. The teacher noticed that one particular student's strategy was to scribe an imaginary sum on the carpet with their finger (as one might when using a pen and paper method). This alerted the teacher to the suitablity of the task for this student, the inability of the student to use appropriate mental strategies, for example place-value based or 'doubles and one more group' (see Chapter 17), and that perhaps there were other students like this one. The teacher resolved to teach efficient mental strategies more explicitly.

It is all very well to notice things while working with students, but these 'noticings' need to be documented easily and effectively. It would be impossible to carry this information in one's mind for recall at a later date. A sensible way to manage this would be to decide on a small number of students to focus on at a time. Checklists and anecdotal records are useful tools. These can be both open-ended or more tightly focused, as the example shows in Table 7.3.

Chapter 7 Assessing and Reporting

Table 7.3 An example of an annotated checklist

Addition strategies	Count on from larger	Doubles and near doubles	Make to ten	Notes
Ben	✓			Reliant on counting by ones?
Jessica	✓	✓	✓	Check strategies for subtraction
Anita	✓	✓		
Jacqui	✓	✓	✓	Check strategies for subtraction
Rylie	✓			
Luke	✓	✓		

did you know?

Formative assessment is when teachers use an ongoing range of assessment strategies to identify specific learning needs and target teaching accordingly (criterion referenced).

consider and discuss

Assessment is measurement?

Imagine that each week a pot plant is measured to determine how well it is growing. The results suggest that the plant has grown because the plant has become taller. However, there are other indicators of the plant's well-being, for example, the colour of the leaves, condition of the stem, and whether it is in bloom or not. To be able to assess the plant further we need to do more than measure its height. We need to know more about this particular variety, its optimum environmental conditions and nutritional needs, and what it looks like when in peak condition.

Measuring the plant to determine growth is similar to conducting weekly quick maths tests or quizzes and looking for improvement in scores. If you wanted to improve students' mental computation skills, what would you do in addition to periodic testing? Like the plant, other knowledge and strategies need to be in place. Apply the knowledge and understanding you have gained so far in this and other chapters.

consider and discuss

Reporting student achievement

In the late 1970s and early 1980s it was common for school reports to communicate student achievement in the form of a grade or score and a sentence or two about the student. For example:

'Lee has worked hard to achieve this mark. Well done.' (December 1976)

'A very keen conscientious student. Lee is always interested and works consistently well.' (July 1979)

'Lee has continued working very well but needs to revise work more strongly with plenty of revision exercises.' (July 1980)

These comments are from actual school mathematics reports. What are your thoughts about the value of these?

Reporting

Integral to the assessment process, **reporting** is about communication. In particular, it is about communicating:

- student progress, achievement, and success (academically, socially, and in terms of general well-being)
- specific learning needs and where to next.

Reporting is the process by which assessment information is communicated in ways that assist students, parents, teachers and the system in making decisions by providing information about what students know and can do, along with recommendations for future learning. (DEECD, 2009, Assessment and reporting, para. 2)

This feedback to students, parents, teachers, and the education system is derived from the diverse range of assessment for and assessment of learning strategies. Ultimately, assessment information is used to guide decisions when planning for future learning. Reporting therefore is strategic and timely, a regular feature of any given academic year.

Student progress and achievement are reported in a variety of ways, which can be written and oral, informal and formal, as Table 7.4 indicates. When these are likely to occur is also given in parentheses.

Table 7.4: Multiple forms and timing of reporting

Reporting	Oral/verbal	Written
Informal	Incidental discussion (ongoing, as required)	Annotations and comments in student diaries and/or journals (ongoing, as required)
		Letter and email (ongoing, as required)
Formal	Information night (early in the school year, mid-year)	School report: written report to parent/guardian (mid- and end of year)
	Interview: parent–teacher (two-way) conferences and parent–teacher–student (three-way) conferences (early, mid- and/or end of year, often following the delivery of formal written reports)	School progress report: less detailed written report to parent/guardian (before mid- and end-of-year report)

Written reports are often structured by an organising framework or template designed to give a clear picture of student progress. School progress reports and the more detailed descriptive school report may feature any number of the following aspects:

- details of attendance or absence from school
- attributes of attitude, behaviour, and effort
- comprehensive descriptions in plain language about the nature of progress; this should include plans for future learning and how the school will support the student, as well as an indication of what can be done at home
- teacher judgment against given goals or standards; this may use a rating system or achievement descriptors, such as the one in Table 7.5.

Chapter 7 Assessing and Reporting

Table 7.5 Rating student achievement

Reporting	Rating of student progress
A	Excellent, or Well above the expected standard
B	Good, or Above the expected standard
C	Satisfactory, or At the expected standard
D	Limited, or Below the expected standard
D	Very low, or Well below the expected standard

Conclusion

Assessment and reporting are integral to teaching and learning. The diverse nature of assessment practices in schools today attempts to address the need for coordinated efforts in relation to assessment of and assessment for learning. It is timely to be reminded that a focus on summative assessment practices alone will continue to ecourage rote learning based on applying rules and procedures. This focus does not necessarily enhance student learning. In particular, over-emphasis on grades and scores has negative effects. Formative assessment, on the other hand, results in particular positive effects on students' learning, in particular on those students who are at risk of falling behind. Reporting is about communicating student achievement, progress, and improvement to students, parents, teachers, and the education system.

consider and discuss

A drawing task

A student completed the Draw This task (Beesey et al., 1998). The task was to draw lines of given lengths using millimetres and centimetres and to create 2D shapes of given areas or perimeters. In particular, item 4 required the student to draw two different shapes that have a perimeter of 12 cm, and item 5 required the drawing of two different shapes with an area of 12 cm.

The student completed this task first when in Year 4 and again one year later.

Compare the two responses. What do you notice about what the student knows and understands in the first response and how this differs from the second response?

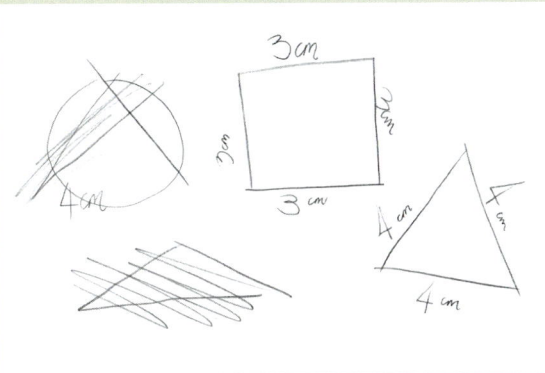

Student's Year 4 response to item 4 and 5

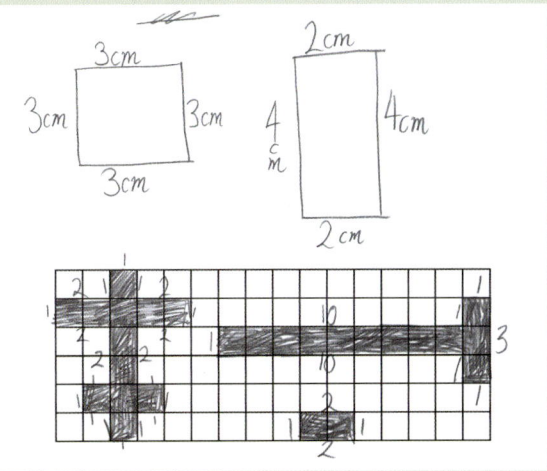

Student's Year 5 response to item 4 and 5

key terms

Assessment *for* learning: teachers and students gather evidence about student understanding to inform future learning; assessment for learning is formative in nature and this evidence is collected in diverse ways

Assessment *of* learning: teachers or school systems gather evidence about student learning to make judgments against goals and standards; this evidence often comes in the form of tests or examinations at the local school level as well as at the national and international levels, and is summative in nature

Feedback: information, written or oral, provided by the teacher to the student in relation to student progress and achievement; constructive feedback is comments framed in a way that allows for thinking to take place, which then enables students to take action to improve learning

Formative assessment: teachers use a range of assessment strategies in an ongoing manner to identify specific learning needs and target teaching accordingly

Peer assessment: students assess each other's or a group's response against given criteria; self-assessment is similar and involves the student assessing their own responses

Reporting: the communication of student achievement, progress, and improvement to students, parents, teachers, and the education system

Rubric: a scoring framework that provides teachers and students with established criteria for success, and clarifies and shares intentions of the given task; often different scores are allocated according to the varying levels of student response

Summative assessment: those practices that locate and/or describe students' achievement in relation to defined goals and standards

Review questions

1. Think about a particular student you have worked with recently. What mathematics does the student know? What strategies does the student use? How does the student feel about learning mathematics?
2. Describe and illustrate the difference between assessment *of* learning and assessment *for* learning.
3. Find a standard closed mathematics question. Re-form or re-frame this question into:
   a. an open question that invites more than one acceptable response,
   b. a statement that invites students to discuss and justify their thinking.

   Reflect on the potential information gained from having students answer questions like these.
4. Look at the responses the student gave to the 'Draw This' assessment task one year apart (p. 143). For each response, identify what the student knows and understands, as well as what the student does not yet know or understand. If you were the student's teacher, what would you like to find out more about?

Key references

Australian Association of Mathematics Teachers, Inc. (2006). *Standards for Excellence in Teaching Mathematics in Australian Schools.* Adelaide: AAMT Inc.

Australian Association of Mathematics Teachers, Inc. (2008). *Position Paper on the Practice of Assessing Mathematics Learning.* Adelaide: AAMT Inc.

Australian Council for Educational Research (1998). *Developmental Assessment Resource for Teachers—Mathematics.* Melbourne: ACER.

Beesey, C., Clarke, B., Clarke, D., Stephen, M., & Sullivan, P. (1998). *Effective Assessment for Mathematics.* Melbourne: Board of Studies.

Black, P., & Wiliam, D. (1998). Inside the black box. *Phi Delta Kappan,* 80(2), 139–148.

Black, P., & Wiliam, D. (1999). Assessment for learning: Beyond the black box. *Assessment Reform Group,* 1–12. Assessment Reform Group. Retrieved 11 December 2009 from www.mendeley.com/research/assessment-for-learning-beyond-the-black-box-1/.

Clarke, D. (1996). Assessment. In A. J. Bishop, K. Clements, C. Keitel, J. Kilpatrick & C. Laborde (Eds.), *International Handbook of Mathematics Education* (pp. 327–370). Dordrecht: Kluawer Academic Publishers.

Clarke, D. J. (1985). *The IMPACT Project: A User's Guide.* Melbourne: Monash University Mathematics Education Centre.

Department of Education and Early Childhood Development (2007). Assessment for common misunderstandings. www.education.vic.gov.au/studentlearning/teachingresources/maths/common/.

Stiggins, R. (2002). Assessment crisis: The absence of assessment FOR learning. *Phi Delta Kappan,* 83(10), 758–765.

Websites

Department of Education and Early Childhood Development (DEECD)—Assessment: www.education.vic.gov.au/studentlearning/assessment/default.htm

maths300: www.curriculum.edu.au/maths300/

NAPLAN: www.naplan.edu.au/

TIMSS: www.timss.bc.edu/

PISA: www.pisa.oecd.org/

8 Diversity

Contents

Who are diverse learners?	143
Language of diversity	143
Diversifying the curriculum	145
Supporting diverse learners	153
Working with teacher assistants	163
Conclusion	163

Chapter objectives

This chapter will enable the reader to:
- Appreciate the diverse approaches learners take to engaging with mathematics
- Explore approaches to challenge all learners
- Consider implications for planning, specifically extending and modifying tasks.

The chance to make a difference

Professor Michael Barnsley is a geometer of international repute, making major contributions to the development of the field of fractal geometry (the fractal image known as the Barnsley fern is named after him). In his keynote address to the 2007 annual conference of the Canberra Mathematical Association, Professor Barnsley credited his primary school teachers for noticing and encouraging his flair with geometry, even though he claimed not to be particularly good at number or algebra.

consider and discuss

Many successful people give credit to particular teachers for inspiring them. Teaching is one of the rare professions that allows us to make a difference in the life of a child.

1. What was significant about Professor Barnsley's teachers?
2. Would you expect learners to have variable success with different aspects of mathematics?
3. Which teachers have inspired you?
4. What does each student need to improve their learning of mathematics?

Big ideas

- Diverse learners are any students who learn in a different way from the standard classrooom approach of a particular teacher.
- Meeting the needs of diverse learners requires attention to the learning needs of all students.
- Mathematics achievement can be expected for all learners with good teaching and the right support.
- Teaching diverse learners is about good teaching for all.
- Teaching diverse learners is not an add-on extra: it is part of the core business of every teacher.
- Ability grouping is a practice that has little positive benefit and causes harm to students in low streams.

Who are diverse learners?

consider and discuss

Who do we mean when we talk about diverse learners of mathematics? Stop and list all the characteristics of learners that might classify them as diverse.

Perhaps you might have included gifted and talented learners, those who speak English as a second or other language, Indigenous students, students with learning difficulties, those with hearing impairments, girls, boys …

Many categories of learners could be encompassed in the term 'diverse learners of mathematics'. Really, though, a diverse learner is someone who learns in a different way from the teacher. Do you agree with this statement?

A powerful influence on the way we teach is the way we learn ourselves. This in turn is influenced by how we were taught. Learners who respond to a different way of teaching will present as diverse learners in a classroom. *It is the job of a teacher to recognise that we are responsible for the learning of all students in our class.*

Language of diversity

The way we refer to concepts has a bearing on the impression we give. Concepts are labelled in our mind using words, and words convey meaning. It is for this reason that we need to take care in our choice of language when referring to diverse learners. In this section, we offer suggestions for thoughtful use of language. Initially, some of the suggestions may seem clumsy. However, with practice, you will find the terminology becomes second nature. While you are learning, if you are unsure of how to refer to a disability or circumstance, ask!

The myth of ability

Describing learners in terms of ability has been a longstanding practice in mathematics. Terms such as 'low ability group', 'smart' and 'slow' abound in mathematics, and until recently have been largely unchallenged. There is now considerable evidence that all of us can learn mathematics. There is no such thing as 'a mathematical brain' where you either have it or not (see, for example, Dehaene, 2011). As a result, there are now a number of authors challenging the discourse of 'ability' in terms of mathematics. These include Jorgensen (Zevenbergen) and Niesche (2008) and Mighton (2003).

Some learners do appear to acquire mathematics concepts and skills more easily than other students. In the past, it has been believed that this observation could be explained by ability. It is now known that a great many factors can influence school performance. These include:

- beliefs learners hold about themselves as learners and beliefs teachers hold about learners (Rosenthal & Jacobsen, 1969)
- socio-economic status (Dowling, 1998; Emerson, Graham, McCulloch, Blacher, Hatton & Llewellyn, 2008) and power relations (Diversity in Mathematics Education Center for Learning and Teaching, 2007)
- type of mathematics activity (particularly influencing gender differences) (Boaler, 1997; Burton, 1995; Vale, 2002)
- school structures and groupings, for example streaming (Linchevski & Kutscher, 1998; Zevenbergen, 2005).

consider and discuss

Is it possible to describe learners without referring to ability? When would this be difficult? What other qualities could be described?

Success in mathematics can be attributed to opportunity and application. For learners and their teachers, this is good news! Achievement in mathematics is not dependent on some immutable quality of a person, such as 'ability'. Rather, mathematics achievement can be expected for all learners with good teaching and the right support. Learners of mathematics need to understand that achievement is within their power to influence (Wiliam, 2003). As Harries notes, 'ability is not fixed but all pupils possess the potential to develop their mathematics' (2001, p. 23).

Person-first language

Sometimes, those who are new to the field of disability feel unsure about the language to use. Fortunately, correct terminology when referring to disability is straightforward.

- Refer to the disability or condition only if it is relevant.
- Use person-first language, for example, 'the student with autism', not 'the autistic student'. This is important because a person is always much more than their disability.
- Avoid phrases such as 'suffers from'. It is not for us to say if a person suffers or not. Rather than 'suffers from cerebral palsy', say 'the student has cerebral palsy'.

- If you are unsure, ask the person or their carer for the appropriate way to refer to their disability.

Learning difficulty, learning disability, or learned difficulties?

Many terms have been used to describe learners who need more assistance than others to be successful at mathematics. Consistency around the world is a long way off. Even in Australia there have been different definitions in use (Louden, 2000). However, some consensus is starting to emerge and we will use the following definitions.

Description	Definition	Source
Mathematics Learning Difficulties	Those problems experienced by a large group of children who need extra assistance to learn mathematics	van Kraayenoord & Elkins (2004)
Mathematics Learning Disabilities (MLD)	Experienced by a subset of students with mathematics learning difficulties who achieve at lower than the 25th percentile on mathematics achievement tests, often with low to average IQ results. Between 5% and 8% of children have some form of MLD and both genetic and environmental factors may contribute.	Geary (2004)
Dyscalculia	An inability to calculate as a result of brain injury. This term seems more commonly used in the United Kingdom. Because mathematics is far more than calculation, this is not a particularly helpful term for general mathematics learning difficulties.	Geary (2004)

For many students with difficulties learning mathematics, it may be that their problems are 'learned difficulties'. That is, for some reason or other, they have developed problems with learning mathematics during schooling. It could be that they were absent from school for substantial periods, developed misconceptions with respect to key concepts, believe themselves to be unable to learn mathematics, or they might live in poverty without access to necessary equipment and support.

Diversifying the curriculum

At the beginning of this chapter, we suggested that a diverse learner could be thought of as any student who has a different learning style from the teacher's. Certainly, each class will comprise students with a range of needs and strengths. It is impractical to plan individual programs for each learner, or to attempt to individualise each lesson for each student. Indeed, such an approach would not be of advantage to learners (Sullivan, Mousley & Zevenbergen, 2006a). Instead, we consider approaches to planning that enable all learners to engage in mathematics lessons, experiencing the same tasks and joining in the mathematics conversation of the classroom.

>
> ### for the classroom
>
> #### Cubes and hoops
> I have some cubes in my pocket. I noticed that when I shared the cubes into two equal groups there was one left over. When I shared them into three equal groups, there were two left over. How many cubes might I have in my pocket?
>
> - Do the task. Record your working and your thinking as you go.
> - Now that you have worked on the task, consider how you might plan to use this in the classroom. (You can use hoops to arrange the groups.)
> - What introduction would you use to ensure students understood the task?
>
> (Adapted from Downton, Knight, Clarke & Lewis, 2006, pp. 41-43)

Working with students

When students begin to work on problems or investigations, they will reach a point where they become stuck. When these students ask for help it is tempting to tell them the next step. As discussed in Chapter 4, a teacher needs to support a learner to learn how to work their way out of being stuck. For students with learning difficulties, we need to provide support that enables them to learn strategies for solving not just the present problem but also the ones to follow. A useful strategy is to ask two questions: What have you tried? What are you trying to find out? These questions allow students to summarise what they have done, often clarifying their approach to themselves, and also to look to what they need to find out. This sometimes gets forgotten in the midst of working. These questions also allow the teacher time to understand the approach the learner is taking.

When students have a chance to explain their work and where they are stuck, the teacher has to decide how they are going to assist the learner without telling them what to do. Sullivan, Mousley and Zevenbergen (2006b) describe the use of **enabling prompts** as an approach to support learners, particularly those with difficulties. Enabling prompts are the provision of strategic assistance that takes learners from where they are to a point where they are able to proceed. This might involve clarifying the task, teaching prerequisite knowledge, offering suggestions for organising results, or reducing the task complexity.

> This complexity might be a result of the number of steps involved, the modes of communicating responses, the degree of abstraction or visualisation required, or even just the size of the numbers to be manipulated. It may not be clear which aspects may be contributing to a particular student's difficulty, but by anticipating some of the factors … the teacher can explore ways to give the student access to the task without the students being directed towards a particular solution strategy for the original task. (Sullivan et al., 2006b, p. 124)

handy hint

Enabling prompts for reducing task complexity

- Reduce the number of steps required by breaking the problem into smaller stages.
- Make the task more concrete, for example acting out the situation, using manipulative materials, drawing diagrams.
- Reduce the size of the numbers involved, for example trying specific examples using smaller numbers
- Support learners to organise results so they can see patterns.

Adapted from Mason, Burton & Stacey, 1985; Sullivan et al., 2006b.

Some enabling prompts need to be prepared by the teacher before the lesson. It is important not to offer the prompts unless required, but the teacher needs to be ready to support learners. With experience, teachers also find they are able to provide some enabling prompts 'on the spot' as required by particular circumstances. However, even experienced teachers find it useful to prepare enabling prompts before the lesson, as resources are then available as needed.

for the classroom

Return to the Cubes and Hoops task on page 146.

- What enabling prompts might you prepare to assist learners who become stuck?
- What resources would you provide?

Here are some suggestions:

- Have paper plates and small blocks or counters for students to use as they wish.
- Ensure students understand the concepts of sharing and remainders. Ask a student to take a handful of cubes and share them evenly with a few friends. Discuss with children how to record the results.
- The task has two conditions—one where the sharing is with two groups, and the other where the sharing is with three groups. Break the task into small steps by suggesting learners focus on one of these conditions first.

Specialising is the process of gathering data. Encourage learners who are stuck to gather more data—to try some specific examples.

Learners who are mathematically promising are not always the high achievers in class. Open-ended tasks are one of the places where talented students are likely to be noticed. In these contexts, learners are able to make use of strategies and approaches of their own choosing. Students who approach problems in novel ways, use visualisation, or describe their thinking in different ways can find that open-ended tasks allow them freedom to explore mathematics in ways that suit them. Many of these students will need opportunities to extend the tasks given. Confident learners who have had previous opportunities to engage in mathematical thinking will often extend problems themselves as conjectures present themselves. Teachers can support this process by planning **extending prompts**, defined as supplementary tasks or questions that extend their thinking and activity (Sullivan, 2007, p. 378).

handy hint

Extending prompts for providing challenge and further development of thinking

- Mathematicians are interested in knowing how many solutions for a particular problem are possible. They are also interested in being convinced they have them all. Ask students, 'How many solutions are there?', 'How do you know?'.
- Add complexity to the task. For example, with the Cubes and Hoops task, we could ask students to consider sharing with other numbers and other remainders. We could invite them to explore a general rule for any number of cubes and any remainders.

Teachers need to prepare extending prompts as part of their lesson planning. For students who solve the set task early, it is important to provide challenges to extend learning. Early finishers who are rewarded with more of the same work quickly learn to slow down. If they are rewarded by being taught next year's work, they are likely to experience boredom next year. Instead, extending prompts extend the set task into greater mathematical challenge and depth of understanding.

A broad rich curriculum

Research confirms that it is possible to accommodate all learners in a classroom program (see e.g. Boaler, 1997; Linchevski & Kutscher, 1998; Sullivan et al., 2006b). The material covered remains the same but the learning outcomes may be modified.

issues in teaching

Age-appropriate curriculum

The Australian Curriculum: Mathematics requires all learners to be taught an age-appropriate curriculum. That means, if a student is in Year 6, for example, they are to be taught the curriculum for Year 6. Every student—without exception! Indigenous students in remote communities; learners with intellectual impairments; learners who speak English as a second or other language. Consider the implications of this for your teaching.

At first thought, this might seem impossible. Surely we need to find out where learners are and work from there? Certainly, this has been the advice given to beginning teachers for many years. However, this view has been challenged in recent times. The traditional approach has led to students revisiting material year after year with little progress, while missing out on the opportunity to access new and necessary mathematics.

making connections

Mathematics is a constantly expanding field of human endeavour. Occasionally, completely new areas of mathematics open up. For example, queuing theory has evolved into a large area of mathematics and is part of the field of operations research. Queuing theory helps organisations such as theme parks improve customer satisfaction. On popular days, crowd numbers may mean visitors spend a long time in queues for rides, rather than on the rides themselves. In such cases, visitors can be very unsatisfied. Through queuing theory, parks can estimate how long customers will have to wait, based on numbers lining up and other variables.

New areas of mathematics can become part of the school curriculum. These topics can provide opportunities for learners to engage with new mathematics, perhaps experiencing success where they have not done so in the past.

for the classroom

Students with intellectual impairments can engage with age-appropriate curriculum content with modifications. For example, if a Year 9 class is studying trigonometry, a student with an intellectual impairment can study the same topic with modified outcomes. The student could learn to identify right angles and label the sides. They can use prompt cards (step-by-step instruction cards) to follow procedures. Number work and use of a calculator can be revised through the new topic.

handy hint

Working with students with learning difficulties in diverse classrooms

- Do *not* begin where the learner is. This statement seems to go against common sense. However, learners can become trapped in a cycle of being assessed, not doing well, and going over old ground again and again, without progress.
- *Do* begin with the specified curriculum, appropriate to the age of the student.
- Ensure topics from across the mathematics curriculum are included (following the Australian Curriculum: Mathematics is an excellent approach to ensuring broad coverage). Many learners have difficulties with aspects of number and thrive on other topics. Unfortunately, some never get the chance as they are constantly going over number work.
- The following strategies are effective (and reflect good teaching):
  - aim for over-learning; that is, provide opportunities for consolidation and practice after the concept has been acquired
  - focus on the key ideas
  - use the 'little bit often' rule for reinforcing key ideas
  - make the key ideas retrievable through posters, journals or photographs.

Being in the conversation

Throughout this book, you will read of the importance of communication in mathematics classrooms. It is particularly critical that opportunities are given each lesson for students to discuss what they have learnt. All learners need to be engaged in the tasks of the classroom in order to be able to contribute to the conversation about what has been learnt. If learners are withdrawn from mathematics lessons to work on other tasks, they miss the opportunities to learn by listening to peers and sharing their own understandings. Clarke and Faragher (2004) provided an example where children at various stages of learning to count were involved in a class discussion and learnt from each other. Similarly, Faragher (2006) documented a case of a student with Down syndrome in Year 9 learning trigonometry. This student's teachers, parents, and the boy himself had been unhappy with his mathematics program, where he was mostly doing 'dot to dot' worksheets when not in the special education unit. For the boy, it was obviously babyish. In replacement, the teaching team and the researcher worked to develop a more age-appropriate program. The student was then able to engage in the conversation of the classroom, receiving assistance from time to time from peers.

for the classroom

The conclusion to a lesson is critical, especially following group work where students may have been involved in different activities or taken their work in different directions. Whole-class discussion at the end of a lesson allows the teacher to ensure learners have got the point of the lesson and that what the teacher intended for them to learn has indeed been understood.

A lesson conclusion should include:
- a summary of the main points
- a final check for understanding
- a reminder of why the topic is important
- where the topic leads to.

issues in teaching

The students left behind

As students move through school, some become left behind their peers. This may be a result of extended absences, frequent moving between schools, or other factors. Perhaps the students have attended a school where insufficient time was allocated to mathematics.

It is critical—and a moral imperative—to find ways to re-engage these learners in the work of the classroom. Particularly at transition points, such as the start of secondary school, there is an opportunity for a fresh start. Teachers need to communicate to all students their belief in the student's ability to learn. Lessons that provide opportunities for learners to engage with the content at their own level, such as open investigations, have proved effective.

communicating mathematically

Questioning

In a diverse classroom, questioning becomes a particularly important teaching strategy.

Teachers who know their students well can target questions to particular students, pushing them to extend their understanding.

Open questions, such as, 'How do you know?', 'What have you tried?', 'What are you trying to find out?' encourage thinking.

The way teachers ask questions is also important. The most effective format is: question—pause—name a student. With the student not named until after the question has been asked, all students will be preparing an answer if they can. If the name of the student is given first, only that student is likely to be thinking about the answer—the rest are probably relieved!

Finally, the length of the pause gives a clue to how much thinking students are expected to do. A pause of three seconds (time this—it seems much longer when in front of a class) is ideal.

Why not stream?

A common approach to teaching learners of varying levels of achievement has been to place students in classes according to their achievement level. This practice has many names, including streaming, setting, tracking, and ability grouping. On first consideration this seems a helpful approach, but research has shown the opposite is the case. John Hattie (1992) has undertaken meta-analyses of research studies to investigate the effect size of innovations in education. Meta-analyses are studies where researchers look at the results of other studies and analyse the combined findings. Hattie's work indicates that almost any innovation in education will have some positive effect, and from analysis of 134 studies, the mean effect size was 0.4. That is, innovations on average have a positive effect—improving results by 0.4 standard deviations (the average person in the experimental group is 0.4 standard deviations above the average person in the control group). When Hattie (2003) analysed 'ability grouping' he found the effect size was only 0.18—well below the average benefit of any innovation. *Streaming has very little positive effect on learning.*

Apart from being of little benefit for student achievement, streaming has some very serious consequences for learners, particularly those placed in bottom groups. These factors have been studied by a number of researchers and summarised by Zevenbergen (2005). Learners in bottom level groups may experience slower paced lessons, reduced content, poorer teaching, poorly managed classes, and detrimental effects on their personal beliefs about themselves as learners. These usually combine to ensure students are unable to move out of bottom stream classes once they are assigned there.

It is known that streaming increases the gap between learners in the top stream and learners in the bottom stream, but streaming does not advantage high-attaining students either. Linchevski and Kutscher undertook an important study to investigate whether the gap widens because the students in the top stream improve relative to the others—that is, they studied if streaming enhanced the learning outcomes of those in the top stream. They found this was not the case. They concluded, 'the increase in the gap due to learning in the same-ability classes emanates mainly from the loss for the students in the lower ability levels instead of from gain for the stronger ones' (Linchevski & Kutscher, 1998, p. 550).

It is clear streaming can cause considerable harm to students. As an influence on educational outcomes, the benefits as measured by effect size are minimal. Fortunately, as we have seen earlier, there are more effective approaches for working with diverse learners.

issues in teaching

What about 'the basics'?

When faced with a full curriculum, some teachers feel they should just focus on 'the basics' for low-attaining students. There are problems with such an approach.

First, what constitutes 'the basics'? What would you include?

Many writers (see for example, contributions in Steen, 1997; Willis, 1990) have attempted to specify what really is the basic mathematical knowledge required for all, with little lasting success. The world is changing, and with it what is needed to function mathematically. Unfortunately, when the assertion to 'just teach the basics' is followed, students end up with a very impoverished mathematics curriculum, rarely including any of the proficiencies necessary to engage with mathematics in a productive way.

Affective aspects of mathematics

Many authors in general mathematics education literature write of the importance of the affective aspects of learning—the emotional contribution (McLeod, 1992). This may be especially critical for children who find learning mathematics difficult, catching students in a cycle from which it is hard to recover.

Parmar and Cawley (1991) describe a cycle producing passive learners, in which students who lack the necessary understanding of a concept are required to rely on teacher assistance to complete practice exercises. Without experiences of learning how to learn and create mathematics, these learners increasingly come to rely on the teacher for explanations and feedback ('Is this right, Miss?'), and become passive learners. Unfortunately, some authors (e.g. Ellis, 2005; Westwood, 2000) promote an approach for learners with difficulties that emphasises direct instruction rather than using teaching approaches that encourage students to develop strategies for learning how to think mathematically. As noted in Chapter 4, there is a place in the mathematics curriculum for learning and practising techniques. However, the teaching, consolidation, and revision of exercises must be balanced with approaches that encourage learners to learn how to think mathematically. All too often, students with difficulties learning end up receiving a very restricted mathematical diet focused on learning and practising how to do mathematics that others have generated, without ever having the opportunity for enjoying generating mathematics themselves.

consider and discuss

Think of a critical incident in your mathematics learning. This might be a good or poor experience, but it should have been significant in your memory of mathematics. Write a summary of this incident.

Discuss your reflections with your study group. What common features are there? What effects on learning were there?

Sometimes adults are astonished to find they are not alone in having less than ideal experiences of mathematics in school. Mathematics anxiety is an acknowledged specific learning difficulty (Dossel, 1993). Sue Wilson and Steven Thornton (2006) have described a process to assist learners with maths anxiety to overcome their negative affective response to mathematics, enabling them to eventually come to view themselves as successful learners of mathematics. Their approach can be followed in detail by those with particular difficulties with support from an experienced mathematics educator or counsellor.

handy hint

Affective aspects of learners

Students must view themselves as effective learners of mathematics.

- Provide opportunities for all learners to experience the richness of mathematics through open-ended tasks, investigations, problem solving, real problems with social significance, etc. These tasks should arise from all aspects of mathematics, including number, geometry, statistics, and algebra.
- Give learners targeted feedback. Targeted feedback means that comments are given on the work, and clear direction is provided to indicate how the mathematics can be developed.
- Feedback should be immediate. Delayed feedback has limited effect on performance (Sousa, 2008).
- Believe and make clear to your students that everyone can learn to think mathematically, and everyone can learn to do this better.
- Never give up on a student, and tell them you will never give up on them.
- Focus class time on mathematics. Inappropriate classroom behaviour (such as incomplete homework, lateness, attention seeking) can be redirected with a comment such as, 'You are missing the opportunity to learn mathematics. Don't waste another second! What help do you need to make a start? Which student can help you?'

Supporting diverse learners

Meeting the mathematics learning needs of diverse learners involves providing a rich learning environment focused on accommodating and planning around difficulties. Note that strategies that are useful for learners with diverse needs will be helpful for other learners in the class. Teaching for diverse learners is just good teaching!

Learning styles

When we receive information, we mostly use our senses such as sight, hearing, touch, taste, smell, and balance. Studies in the field of educational psychology have produced many models of learning or cognitive styles. These include visual/auditory/kinaesthetic learners, competitive/collaborative/avoidant/participant/dependent/independent learning styles, and field dependent/independent cognitive styles (Krause, Bochner & Duchesne, 2003). Many of these learning styles are helpful in considering learners of mathematics. However, they are not categories of individuals. Unless we have a sensory impairment, we are able to use all our senses. We might favour visual stimuli, but this does not mean we will not make use of auditory stimuli. Therefore, when planning for teaching, we do not attempt to identify the 'visual learners' and separate them from the 'auditory learners' and teach them differently. Instead, we attempt to provide a range of approaches to any topic that would support learning through as many senses and cognitive styles as possible.

Learners who speak English as a second or other language

Mathematics is sometimes mistakenly viewed as being 'the universal language', with the implication that the spoken language of students is irrelevant to learning mathematics.

consider and discuss

Use the Arabic numerals shown to complete the following calculations. Give your answer in Arabic. Time yourself while you do these.

٠	١	٢	٣	٤	٥	٦	٧	٨	٩
0	1	2	3	4	5	6	7	8	9

٧ + ٢ =   ٨ − ٥ =   ٦ ÷ ٢ =   ٢ × ٤ =   ٠ ÷ ١ =

٢ × ٥ =   ٦ − ٣ =   ٩ + ١ =   ٨ − ٧ =   ٤ × ٠ =

1   How easy was it to do these calculations?
2   What did you feel as you were working?
3   What factors added to the complexity of the task?

If Arabic is not a familiar language for you, you might have found that you were involved in complex translation processes while doing the previous task. Even though the task has very low mathematical demands, the task becomes much more difficult when different symbols are used. Perhaps you noticed the immense cognitive load, the frustration of taking a long time to complete an obviously simple task, and the challenge of not having sufficient information provided (e.g. how to write two-digit numbers in Arabic).

Learners who speak English as a second or other language may experience these same difficulties.

handy hint

For supporting learners who speak English as a second or other language:
- allow more time to complete tasks
- allow time to rest
- allow students to work in their natural language as required
- keep in mind that students may be more accomplished than they appear
- avoid being trapped by cultural stereotypes, for example, students from Asian backgrounds do not automatically excel at mathematics.

think + link

See Chapter 5 for further discussion of the role of language in learning and doing mathematics

Considerable research has now been undertaken on the language load of mathematics. Aspects of mathematics that need to be considered here are the structure of mathematics tasks and the language used in mathematics. There are some words that have the same meaning in mathematics as in common language, some that have different meanings, and some that are unique to mathematics (Table 8.1).

Table 8.1 Examples of words used in mathematics

Same meaning	Different meaning	Unique meaning
Graph	Sum (in mathematics means 'addition')	Trapezium
Calculate	General case (in mathematics means 'in every situation')	Hypotenuse
Circle		

Indigenous Australian learners

issues in teaching

In a remote Indigenous Australian community, there is a primary school with just over 100 students. The Year 3 NAPLAN scores are a cause of considerable concern—not one student has reached the national benchmarks in numeracy. Why might this be?

To understand this situation, we need to know more of the context. This school educates children from one skin group with an intact Indigenous language. When children begin school, they rarely speak any English. Instruction at school begins in the Indigenous language and gradually more and more English is used. Teachers (who mostly speak only English) are supported in their work by bilingual teaching assistants. By Year 4, instruction is in English alone and reading and writing in English has commenced (the year after the first NAPLAN test).

NAPLAN is a nationally administered test, presented in written English. Two possibilities exist: translate the test into the local language, or read the test to the children in the local language. Neither of these is feasible. The Indigenous language is an aural language without a written form. (This implies the children commence school being unfamiliar with written text.) More fascinating is the differences between available words. There are some words used in mathematics that do not have meaning in this Indigenous language. For example, the teaching assistant was asked to find a word for an enclosed solid. After considerable thought she was unable to do so, and explained that as these were desert people they did not have enclosed spaces—even their original dwellings were open-ended to allow breezes through. (It is also likely there are words in this Indigenous language that have no English language equivalent.)

This example reminds us that there are many factors involved in achievement in mathematics. Once again, we need to be mindful of the myth of ability. For all learners, we need to consider their experiences and their opportunities. Teaching children in remote Indigenous communities is complex and requires sensitive conversations with community elders to ascertain desired outcomes from schooling. One response is to recognise that children do not need Western schooling to prepare them for adulthood in a traditional setting—this is best taught by community elders. However, a Western education alongside teaching of traditional knowledge can offer access to opportunities outside the community.

for the classroom

Amy Carty is a teacher in an Indigenous community school in north-western Australia. She describes using a large painted number grid:

These number grids are a great interactive tool for any school. The numbers are nice and big so that all students can read them. There are so many activities involving these large number grids that teachers can use with students from pre-primary to secondary. Students love running around and finding out new things. Some example activities are students using the grids for addition and subtraction. They can kangaroo-jump to the answer. I use them for number recognition as my students seem to have trouble recognising numbers over 20. I ask them to go and stand on a number with 4 or 7 in it. Once they have decided on a number we as a whole class work out what number the child is standing on. The students really enjoy being outside and being active. It has also been fantastic to see that the students use the grids during recess and after school and develop their own games.

The features of this resource that make it successful for her learners include:

- kinaesthetic: it allows children to move
- cooperative: children can work in groups, learning from and helping each other
- tasks are repeatable: children have opportunities to return to the task throughout the year
- tasks can be extended to increase the intellectual challenge
- all children can make a start and achieve learning success
- tasks are retrievable: after an activity is complete, there is lasting evidence of what had been done (Zevenbergen & Flavel, 2007)
- it is focused on an important concept of mathematics—children have fun, but there is a mathematical purpose to the lesson.

making connections

Australian researchers Kevin Jones, Lorraine Kershaw and Len Sparrow (Jones, Kershaw & Sparrow, 1995) describe the very different way some Australian Indigenous groups classify objects compared with Western constructions. Western cognition emphasises a hierarchical structure of concepts, increasing in abstraction. For example, a collection of red objects → red → colour → attribute. We become so used to this way of thinking that it is almost impossible to imagine that others do not do this. Jones et al. quote the work of Christie with people from north-east Arnhem Land. Christie noted: 'there are very few names at all which divide the world up into the sorts of macro categories which English speakers imagine are really real' (Christie, 1994, p. 26 cited in Jones et al., 1995, p. 11). How would this affect teaching and learning?

Gender differences

A strongly held community view has been that boys are better at mathematics than girls. Certainly, up until the 1990s, the proportion of boys was higher than girls in advanced levels of mathematics in the senior years. Research had focused on the question 'What is wrong with the girls?'. There was a perceived need to 'fix up girls' to make them able to study mathematics. Towards the end of the 1980s, researchers began to recognise that the way the mathematics curriculum was being taught was affecting the performance of girls, and that the curriculum and how it was delivered could be adapted to accommodate girls. These approaches have been described as 'deficit' and 'assimilationist' models (Forgasz, Leder & Vale, 2000). More recent theory ('post-modern') has argued that girls and boys may be shaped by the contexts they are in. Vale and Bartholomew (2008, p. 273) argue, 'According to this theory, paying attention to the relationships within the classroom, the different identities, and hence the different needs of students in the mathematics classroom, are central to equity'.

In more recent times, the problem of underperformance of adolescent boys has received attention. The most successful boys continue to do well, but increasingly others are not succeeding at school. In 2002, the Australian House of Representatives Standing Committee on Education and Training initiated an inquiry into the education of boys and noted in the final report:

> While it is dangerous to generalise, boys and girls do tend to prefer different learning styles. Boys tend to respond better to structured activity, clearly defined objectives and instructions, short-term challenging tasks and visual, logical and analytical approaches to learning. They tend not to respond as well as girls to verbal, linguistic approaches. Good teachers respond to the different learning styles of their students and utilise students' preferred learning styles while also aiming to develop the full range of capacities in each student. (House of Representatives Standing Committee on Education and Training, 2002, p. xviii)

From the early 1980s, as researchers and teachers had become more aware of gender issues affecting performance, a number of approaches have become standard practice and have been credited with contributing to greater equality of performance. These include an emphasis on collaborative learning, discussion in small and whole-class groups, using applications of mathematics to social contexts, making contexts clear (for example, descriptions of sporting contexts made overt, rather than assuming all learners have played particular sports), and including contexts that would appeal to girls and boys.

In summarising current Australasian research, Vale and Bartholomew conclude:

> The salient lesson from these studies is that it is important not to dichotomise girls and boys or to think that all girls will be interested or disinterested in mathematics and particular contexts and processes within mathematics lessons. (Vale & Bartholomew, 2008, p. 286)

Teachers will always be concerned with meeting the educational needs of all the students they teach. We have seen in this section that at times girls' performance has been a concern; and now it is boys'. However, it is clear from Table 8.2 that approaches useful for boys and girls represent good teaching and can be incorporated in all lessons to benefit all learners.

Table 8.2 Strategies for assisting boys and girls to learn mathematics

Girls	Boys
Include group work. Include opportunities for discussion in both small groups and whole-class settings. Include contexts of interest to girls. Provide assessment opportunities that allow for a variety of responses (e.g. open-ended investigations). Avoid multiple choice questions as the only assessment approach.	Structure activities. Assist learners to break tasks into achievable steps, particularly extended tasks such as investigations. Structure assignments with long deadlines (e.g. over several weeks) to include regular class work and milestones that are achievable. (This also assists a teacher to be aware of ownership of the work.) If homework is set, ensure it is checked regularly.
Ensure contexts are understood (e.g. if football is used as a context, ensure all students are familiar with the context).	Employ clearly defined objectives and instructions. Ensure all students in the class are clear about what they are required to do. Put tasks on the whiteboard so they are *retrievable*. If a student has not heard the instructions, or joined the class after the task was set, the student will be able to catch up if the task has been recorded clearly. Use the 'tour to be sure' strategy: when a task has been set, wait for a few minutes for students to begin and then move around all the students to check for understanding of the task.
Use contextual tasks. Include tasks that show the value of mathematics to the solution of social problems. These can include looking at environmental and social justice issues.	Set short-term challenging tasks. Include tasks with a focus on mathematical thinking for all learners in the class. Open-ended tasks allow challenge for all learners (see Chapter 4).
Use verbal and linguistic approaches. Communication is an important part of mathematics and needs to be taught explicitly and emphasised for all learners. Girls may particularly enjoy opportunities to communicate mathematics in linguistic forms. Engage learners with problems set in real contexts.	Use visual, logical, and analytical approaches. A great deal of mathematics can be accessed using visual representations. See Chapter 6 for more information. Allow students opportunities to explain their thinking and to record it in a variety of ways.

making connections

Gender bias in textbooks for schools was once a serious concern. Secondary mathematics textbooks from the 1970s and 1980s were renowned for stereotyping men and women through use of images and contexts of examples. These problems have largely been overcome and reputable publishers now go to considerable efforts to check material for bias before publication.

However, television and advertising is still an area of concern. Consider, for example, the television program *Beauty and the Geeks*. Intellectual accomplishment, particularly in mathematics, is seen as both undesirable, and a male characteristic. Young women are portrayed as attractive, and unintelligent. Lack of education is not seen as a detriment. Popular culture for young girls is once again encouraging many to think that being attractive is more important than being educated.

Talented learners

Popular culture depicts talented learners of mathematics as high achieving geniuses tending towards the eccentric. Similar images are also conveyed by television programs that feature individuals with prodigious calculating abilities. Such portrayals of individuals with mathematical talent are unhelpful. Teachers can mistakenly believe that talented learners of mathematics will be easily identified and will be high achievers. Sometimes this is the case, but unfortunately many others are overlooked.

Characteristics of gifted learners of mathematics have been described by Diezmann and Watters (2002) to include:

- exceptional reasoning ability
- exceptional memory and concentration span
- preference for working abstractly and self-directed
- ability to solve problems in unexpected ways
- ability to identify patterns and relationships
- preference for mathematical activities and puzzles, including enjoyment in posing problems.

Spatial ability has also been identified as a characteristic of gifted students (Diezmann, Faragher, Lowrie, Bicknell, & Putt, 2004).

Perhaps it is surprising that not all talented learners of mathematics are high achievers. Unfortunately, some learners have experienced classrooms where creative thinking and divergent approaches have not been encouraged. For others, living up to a label of 'gifted' can be challenging in itself. There are many reasons why potentially talented learners of mathematics are not necessarily the high achieving students in the class.

handy hint

Supporting learners with talent

- Encourage risk taking and provide opportunities for mistakes to be made and learning to follow. Learners need to understand mathematics is not about having the correct answer all the time.
- Provide rich tasks that allow students to use creative, divergent and visual thinking.

- Ensure learners are provided with challenging extensions to tasks. Boredom can lead to inappropriate classroom behaviour.
- Avoid teaching work from higher grade levels. This will only lead to boredom in years to come.
- Avoid providing more practice and consolidation than is necessary. Again this will lead to boredom.

integrating technology/ICT

Hunting for stars

Maths300 (www.maths300.esa.edu.au) includes a lesson called 'Hunting for Stars'. This lesson begins with a practical activity with a group of students (perhaps 12) standing shoulder to shoulder in a circle. A rope is passed from the first person to every nth person. For example, you might begin passing the rope to every third person.

Can you predict what will happen? If you pass the rope to every fourth person, what will happen? If you choose to pass the rope to every fifth person, and keep going once you get back to the start, you will find the rope makes a star.

Participants are invited to explore what numbers will produce a star. This lesson is accessible to learners at many levels. Young children can learn a great deal about factors and multiples. It is a very successful activity for use in the middle school years as the activity can be extended. For talented learners of mathematics, it allows extension to astonishly sophisticated mathematics—including modular arithmetic and advanced geometry (see for example, http://mathworld.wolfram.com/StarPolygon.html).

Hearing, vision, and other sensory impairments

The World Health Organization has made a distinction between the terms, handicap, disability, and impairment (Foreman, 1996).

- **Impairment** is an abnormality in the way organs or systems function, usually of medical origin, for example, short-sightedness, heart problems, cerebral palsy, Down syndrome, or deafness.
- **Disability** is the functional consequence of an impairment. For example, because of the impairment of short-sightedness, the disability may be that a person is unable to see clearly.
- **Handicap** is the social or environmental consequences of a disability, for example, inability to follow television news because of short-sightedness.

This is an important distinction for teachers. By providing support in the learning environment, it may be possible to completely or partially eliminate the social or environmental consequences of the disability. For example, a person with short-sightedness who wears glasses may have no consequences as a result of the disability arising from the impairment. For sensory impairments, there are many advances in technology that can support learners. In Australia, organisations such as Australian Hearing and Vision Australia can provide guidance on the latest equipment available to support learners. It is very important for teachers to ensure students access the adaptive equipment available to support their learning, as research from the United States has shown that many students are not receiving full benefits of the latest advances in technology (Kelly, 2009).

Education provision in Australia for learners with disabilities is subject to legislation, in particular the federal *Disability Discrimination Act 1992*, known as the DDA. You can find out more about the DDA and the requirements of teachers from the website of the Human Rights and Equal Opportunity Commission: <www.hreoc.gov.au/disability_rights/dda_guide/getting_/getting_.html>. It is particularly important for teachers to ensure they read and action the Individual Education Plans of any student they are teaching.

integrating technology/ICT

All Australian universities provide support to learners with disabilities. Visit a campus library and ask the access librarian to show you the resources available for people with vision, hearing, and other impairments.

There are implications of sensory deficits for the teaching of mathematics. Sometimes, loss of sensory function has a direct effect on the learning of mathematics concepts.

In a study on the effect of hearing impairment on the learning of mathematics, Nunes and Moreno (2002) stated that being deaf could not be considered a *cause* of difficulties with learning mathematics but was a *risk factor* for at least two reasons. Children with profound hearing loss had fewer opportunities for incidental learning and would need to be explicitly taught some concepts, for example additive composition (understanding that any number can be seen as the sum of other numbers). The second factor concerned the concept of time: 'deaf children may need support when communicating and reasoning about time, particularly if they need to consider a gap in a story sequence' (Nunes & Moreno, 2002, p. 121).

Mathematics relies heavily on visualisation (Zimmermann & Cunningham, 1991). Therefore, it is to be anticipated that vision impairment may affect learning of mathematics. A number of researchers have investigated the effect of vision impairment on the development of mental imagery (see, for example, Arditi, Holtzman & Kosslyn, 1988; Cornoldi & Vecchi, 2003). While there are differences, Dulin (2007) concluded, 'It seems therefore that the blind can create and manipulate spatial representations just as the sighted do, but that visual experience allows a faster generation and treatment of images' (p. 342). Dulin's research investigated the use of line drawings. In mathematics these are particularly important as they encompass graphical representation of information. Dulin cautions that while students can learn to interpret raised images, the process is not innate and needs to be specifically taught. Specialist teachers, experienced in vision impairment, would be able to assist with this aspect of teaching mathematics.

communicating mathematically

Language effects on learning

Language is inextricably linked with mathematics. It is bound up with perceiving the context and communicating the findings of problem solving. In communicating mathematics, we provide further stimulus for our own brains to work on. The connection of language with mathematics is not limited to 'word problems' where questions are posed as problems in a paragraph of text. Communication affects all aspects of mathematics. Arvedson (2002) studied the effects of specific language impairment on numerical cognition and noted differences when the children concerned were compared with age-matched (AM) children without language impairment.

> The AM group consistently used verbal counting to facilitate numerical problem solving. Conversely prompting the children with SLI [speech language impairment] to use verbal counting while completing any of the numerical tasks resulted in a 50% decline in accuracy. Children need opportunities to strengthen numerical constructs, such as those enhanced through verbal counting. However, children with SLI also need opportunities to fortify their nonverbal enumeration and numerical reasoning without requiring the use of their deficit area. (Arvedson, 2002, p. 970)

Learning disabilities

A paradigm shift has occurred in the conceptualisation of disability similar to that noted in gender differences. Once there was a view of disability as one of deficit—identification of deficiencies in students was of prime importance, with the goal of 'fixing them up'. More recently, conceptions of disability regard the deficit not with the learner but with how the curriculum matches the needs of the student: 'the emphasis in the last decade has been less of one seeking to define, diagnose and remediate learning difficulties in individual students to one of identifying ways to make the curriculum more accessible to all learners' (Diezmann et al., 2004, p. 176). Even so, the literature abounds with specific areas of difficulties learners may encounter. These include:

- memory (Geary, 2004; Miller & Mercer, 1997)
- basic fact recall (Robinson, Menchetti & Torgesen, 2002)
- counting difficulties (Houssart, 2001)
- affective aspects of learning (Bottge, 2001; Parmar & Cawley, 1991)
- language (Carnine, 1997; van Kraayenoord & Elkins, 2004).

Assisting learners with learning disabilities in mathematics

As we turn our focus to assisting learners with learning disabilities in mathematics, keep in mind one of the big ideas of this chapter: that all learners, with good teaching and the right support, are able to learn mathematics.

Good teaching involves making decisions about planning and what to teach. From the early years, learners should engage with the full mathematics curriculum, ensuring students access topics from across the discipline. Work in the area of number is important, but care must be taken to give learners opportunities to study other areas, such as geometry and measurement. Sometimes students' difficulties might be in number alone, and relative

think + link

See Chapter 4 for discussion of memory.

See Chapter 14 for discussion of basic facts.

In Chapter 16, you can read about how counting is learnt as well as noting activities for use in the classroom. If you are teaching the upper primary grades, or even in lower secondary, you may need to revisit these ideas with students on a regular basis, particularly if you have students with learning difficulties, learning disabilities, or difficulties learning mathematics.

See Chapter 5 for discussion of the effects of language.

strengths in other branches of mathematics may be missed through lack of exposure to these topics.

As learners move through the school years and reach secondary school, teachers can become anxious that they must help students with intellectual disabilities prepare for life after school. However, rarely can teachers or even parents know what post-school experiences await any student. It is impossible to determine what work and leisure contexts a learner will encounter, and therefore it is very difficult for teachers to prepare them for the future. Fortunately, this is not what parents and students request of teachers. In a research study (Faragher, 2006), parents of adults with intellectual disabilities expressed concern that secondary school had not focused sufficiently on teaching mathematics. Parents felt confident with teaching life skills as they arose in adult contexts where skills were needed, but they did not feel they were able to teach mathematics adequately.

In summary:

- Learners with intellectual impairments *can* learn mathematics—even algebra (Monari Martinez, 1998).
- Students *should* learn mathematics, from across the discipline, as this is necessary for an adulthood with good quality of life (Faragher & Brown, 2005).
- Students should learn age-appropriate mathematics. The *Australian Curriculum: Mathematics* requires all learners to study the curriculum set for their Year level.
- Strategies for teaching that help learners with intellectual disabilities are just good teaching strategies that help all learners.

handy hint

Assist students with learning disabilities by:
- reading and actioning current Individual Education Plans (IEPs)
- actively contributing to the development of IEPs
- seeking advice from relevant professionals such as educational psychologists
- working closely with parents. Parents often carry the role of 'case manager'. They know the educational history of their child and often know a great deal about any underlying conditions leading to the intellectual disability
- including the student in discussions and meetings about their progress, where appropriate.

for the classroom

Index notation

In the middle years of mathematics, students are taught the potential of index notation to simplify numbers. Students from around Year 7 learn to move between index and expanded forms, for example $2^3 = 2 \times 2 \times 2 = 8$.

Learners with intellectual disabilities can also learn this.

- Begin with square numbers. Use blocks to emphasise the square shape and the pattern in the numbers.

- Ensure the student records the patterns in their notebook or augmentative communication device. This should include both diagrams and symbols. Photographs can be taken and included with the record.

- Similarly, cubes can be made and the pattern built up. Emphasise the evolving pattern—draw the student's attention to the power notation, the number of repeats of the number being multiplied, and how the final answer connects with the model.
- Remember to teach, not test. Try statements such as, 'I am going to make 4^3. Make it with me. It will be four blocks long [make it], four blocks wide [add the new rows], and four high [finish the cube].' Invite the student to join in when they are ready.
- Count the number of blocks and record the result.
- Show the student how to enter this on their calculator: 4 y^x 3 =. Note that you will need to teach all learners how to use their calculator correctly.
- Provide opportunities for practice and consolidation, aiming for over-learning. That is, continue to provide opportunities for consolidation and practice after the concept appears to have been learnt. When learning is unstable and easily forgotten, over-learning is essential. In an inclusive classroom, learners with intellectual disabilities can be consolidating key ideas such as index notation while others extend the concept.

Working with teacher assistants

Teachers are responsible for the learning of *all* the students in their class, even if a teaching assistant (TA) is available to support individual learners. In most jurisdictions, teacher assistants are allocated to the teacher, not to the student. This means that teachers are able to make decisions about the best use of adult classroom assistance. Sometimes this might mean that the TA works with a group of students, including a child with support needs. Sometimes the TA might assist students in the whole class, freeing the teacher to work with individuals. TAs have also been used effectively to work with students requiring extra challenge. Additional classroom support is often very helpful; however, it remains the responsibility of the qualified teacher to prepare learning programs and maintain responsibility for all learners. Inappropriate use of learning assistance has a detrimental effect on learners, particularly through development of dependency by learners and removal of responsibility by teachers (Giangreco, Edelman, Luiselli & MacFarland, 1997).

Conclusion

In this chapter, we have explored the area of working with diverse learners. All classrooms are places of diversity and it may seem a daunting prospect for you if you are preparing to enter the teaching profession. However, it is also one of the factors that makes teaching a stimulating and rewarding profession. We really do have the opportunity to make a difference in the life of another person—a precious task, indeed.

key terms

Disability: the functional consequence of an impairment; for example, because of the impairment of short-sightedness, the disability may be that a person is unable to see clearly

Dyscalculia: an inability to calculate as a result of brain injury

Enabling prompts: provision of strategic assistance taking learners from where they are to a point from which they are able to proceed

Extending prompts: supplementary tasks or questions that extend students' thinking and activity

Handicap: the social or environmental consequences of a disability, for example inability to follow television news because of short-sightedness

Impairment: an abnormality in the way organs or systems function, usually of medical origin, for example short-sightedness, heart problems, cerebral palsy, Down syndrome, or deafness

Mathematics learning difficulties: those problems experienced by a large group of children who need extra assistance to learn mathematics

Mathematics learning disabilities (MLD): are experienced by a subset of students with mathematics learning difficulties who achieve at lower than the 25th percentile on mathematics achievement tests, often with low to average IQ results; between 5% and 8% of children have some form of MLD and both genetic and environmental factors may contribute

Review questions

1. Write a statement encapsulating your personal philosophy on the teaching of mathematics to all learners in your class.
2. Explain the role of enabling prompts and extending prompts in mathematics lessons.
3. Describe some approaches teachers can use to diversify the curriculum.
4. Take a lesson topic for a Year level of relevance to you. Plan the lesson assuming you will have access to a teaching assistant (TA). Plan for the following different scenarios:
   a. the TA works with a small group of high achieving students
   b. the TA supports learners with intellectual disabilities to engage with whole-class teaching.
5. What remains the greatest concern for you in meeting the needs of all learners of mathematics in your class? What support can you access to assist you?

Key references

Boaler, J. (1997). *Experiencing School Mathematics: Teaching Styles, Sex and Setting*. Buckingham: Open University Press.

Carnine, D. (1997). Instructional design in mathematics for students with learning disabilities. *Journal of Learning Disabilities*, 30(2), 130–141.

Diezmann, C., Faragher, R., Lowrie, T., Bicknell, B., & Putt, I. (2004). Exceptional students in mathematics. In R. Perry, G. Anthony & C. Diezmann (Eds.), *Research in Mathematics Education in Australasia 2000–2003*. Flaxton: Post Pressed.

Diversity in Mathematics Education Center for Learning and Teaching (2007). Culture, race, power, and mathematics education. In F. K. Lester (Ed.), *Second Handbook of Research on Mathematics Teaching and Learning: A Project of the National Council of Teachers of Mathematics*. Charlotte, NC: Information Age Publishing.

Forgasz, H., Leder, G. C., & Vale, C. (2000). Gender and mathematics: Changing perspectives. In K. Owens & J. Mousley (Eds.), *Mathematics Education Research in Australasia: 1996-1999* (pp. 305–340). Sydney: MERGA.

House of Representatives Standing Committee on Education and Training (2002). Boys: Getting it right. Report on the inquiry into the education of boys. [Electronic Version]. Retrieved 13 October 2009 from www.aph.gov.au/house/committee/edt/eofb/report/front.pdf.

Linchevski, L., & Kutscher, B. (1998). Tell me with whom you're learning, and I'll tell you how much you've learned: Mixed-ability versus same-ability grouping in mathematics. *Journal for Research in Mathematics Education, 29*(5), 533–554.

Louden, W. (2000). Mapping the territory: Overview. In W. Louden, L. Chan, J. Elkins, D. Greaves, H. House, M. Milton, S. Nichols, J. Rivalland, M. Rohl & C. E. van Kraayenoord (Eds.), *Mapping the Territory*. (Vol. 1, pp. 1–27). Canberra: Department of Education, Training and Youth Affairs, Commonwealth of Australia.

McLeod, D. B. (1992). Research on affect in mathematics education: A reconceptualization. In D. A. Grouws (Ed.), *Handbook of Research on Mathematics Teaching and Learning* (pp. 575–596). New York: Macmillan.

Sullivan, P., Mousley, J., & Zevenbergen, R. (2006b). Teacher actions to maximize mathematics learning opportunities in heterogeneous classrooms. *International Journal of Science and Mathematics Education, 4*, 117–143.

Wiliam, D. (2003). Keeping learning on track: Formative assessment and the regulation of learning. In M. Goos & T. Spencer (Eds.), *Making Mathematics Vital: Proceedings of the 20th Biennial Conference of the Australian Association of Mathematics Teachers* (pp. 20–34). Brisbane: AAMT.

Websites

http://mathworld.wolfram.com/StarPolygon.html

www.maths300.esa.edu.au

www.hreoc.gov.au/disability_rights/dda_guide/getting_/getting_.html

Part three

Exploring the Big Ideas in Mathematics

Numeracy is the new literacy of our age. As the printing press gave the power of letters to the masses, so the computer gives the power of numbers to ordinary citizens (Steen, 1997, p. xv)

It is hard to imagine a society without technology as we know it—it has spawned a vast new vocabulary and an internationally recognised system of signs and symbols, and invested existing words with new meanings. The advent of digital devices means we now interact with tools differently, we use 'menus' and change 'modes', we read complex visual displays, and we are more likely to communicate using 'keypads' or 'keyboards' than pen and paper.

Numeracy is indeed the literacy of our age as Steen suggests, but just as literacy involves reading, writing, speaking, and listening, numeracy involves much more than working with numbers. In the chapters that follow, we will explore what we mean by numeracy, how numeracy relates to school mathematics and the curriculum more generally, and how the three key fields of Number, Measurement and Geometry, and Statistics and Probability collectively contribute to the development of a numerate citizenry in the twenty-first century.

Questions

1 Make a list of all the texts that someone in your household engages with over the course of a year (e.g. newspapers, magazines, web pages, illustrations, digital screen displays, accounts from energy agencies or telecommunications companies, do-it-yourself instructions, knitting patterrns, building plans, maps, superannuation statements, tax forms …). What percentage of these texts requires little or no appreciation of mathematics? What mathematics knowledge, skills, and understandings do these texts assume?
2 Consider what is involved in answering the following everyday questions.
    - Is it more expensive to travel from Sydney to Brisbane by car or plane?
    - How could Australia's carbon emissions be reduced by 25% by 2020?
    - Is it better to pay HECS fees up front or defer?
    - When do I need to start cooking the roast for a family dinner?
    - When is it least likely to rain, the last week of October or the middle week of April?
    - Can you tell me how to get to …?

9 Numeracy in the Curriculum

Contents

What is numeracy	169
Numeracy across the curriculum	176
Critical numeracy	179
Conclusion	183

Chapter objectives

This chapter will enable the reader to:
- Understand the relationship between mathematics and numeracy
- Explore the key aspects of numeracy and critical numeracy
- Appreciate the opportunities and challenges that arise from connecting mathematics and numeracy to all learning areas
- Consider the planning implications for incorporating an understanding of critical numeracy across all learning areas.

The essence of numeracy

The essence of numeracy is being prepared to use mathematics to understand a particular situation or issue better. Hogan and Thornton (2003) provide the following anecdote as an example of how this disposition might transpire in a classroom.

Julie is a Year 7 science teacher. The class was watching a DVD about how blood circulates around the body. The narrator described the number of red blood cells in the body, their purpose, and how they travelled around the body. After the DVD was finished, Julie asked the students if they had any questions. Immediately David asked: 'What does 250 million look like? That's a lot of blood cells! How can all those cells fit into our body?' It soon became clear to Julie that many of the students did not know how to represent 250 million using numbers. Additionally, most of the students were not able to visualise 250 million as a quantity of cells, or a quantity of anything.

When David asked his questions he was behaving numerately—by asking the questions. He was using his limited knowledge of mathematics to try and make sense of something new. We can suppose that he was imagining that 250 million cells was a lot of cells, and how do you fit that many 'things' inside a body? The mathematics and the context (the science) were interacting to confuse him. However, having the nerve to ask the questions is something we would want to encourage in all students.

Big ideas

- Numeracy involves choosing and using mathematics in a broad range of contexts.
- The ability to meet the numeracy demands of daily life can determine who is able to participate and contribute most effectively in home life, at work, and in community life.
- Being numerate involves having fluency in mathematical skills and knowledge; a clear understanding of the contextual requirements; the disposition to choose and use mathematics confidently; and a critical appreciation of how mathematics can be used.
- Critical numeracy is the ability to make discerning decisions about how mathematics is used to describe and explain our world.

What is numeracy?

Numeracy is a term that has become widely used in discussions about education in both the media and academic literature. There are many interpretations of what exactly is meant by numeracy, as the definition has evolved and expanded over time. Some working definitions of numeracy that have been developed in more recent years include:

> Numeracy involves using some mathematics to achieve some purpose in a particular context. (Australian Association of Mathematics Teachers, 1997)

> Being numerate, at the very least, is about having the competence and disposition to meet the general demands of life at home, in paid work, and for participation in community and civic life. (Willis, 1998)

> [Numeracy] implies recognising where mathematics can be used, choosing the appropriate mathematical tools and being able to interpret the results. (Hughes-Hallet, 2001)

Using these definitions as exemplars it would seem that crafting a definition of numeracy ought to be reasonably straightforward: that is, it involves the ability to apply number and computational skills to everyday purposes, together with the ability to interpret the quantitative information that pervades everyday life (Westwood, 2008). However, Coben (2003, p. 9) warns us that numeracy is a 'notoriously slippery concept'. This is because it is difficult to determine which specific mathematical skills and knowledge constitute numeracy. According to Turner (2007, p. 28), 'Numeracy has become a personal attribute very much dependent on the context in which the numerate individual is operating … [and] numeracy will mean different things to different people according to their interests and lifestyles'.

So, in combining the straightforward and the 'slippery' we could say that **numeracy** involves choosing and using mathematics in a broad range of authentic and practical contexts, and that the skills and knowledge involved will vary according to the context and purpose for which they are used.

did you know?

The term 'numeracy' was first used over 50 years ago in the United Kingdom. In 1959 the authors of the Crowther Report on education suggested that 'numeracy' should 'represent the mirror image of literacy', indicating that this should imply 'on the one hand ... an understanding of the scientific approach to the study of the phenomena' and 'on the other hand ... the need in the modern world to think quantitatively' (Central Advisory Council for Education, 1959). However, their definition does not add much to our contemporary understanding of the term.

By 1982 the British Cockcroft Report, *Mathematics Counts* (Committee of Inquiry into the Teaching of Mathematics in Schools, 1982), proposed a definition that begins to approach our current understandings. To be 'numerate', according to the authors, should imply the possession of two attributes: first, an 'at-homeness' with mathematics that enables a person to cope with the practical demands of everyday life; and second, the ability to understand information presented in mathematical terms.

The 1989 education report *Everybody Counts* (Board on Mathematical Sciences [and] Mathematical Sciences Education Board, National Research Council, 1989) produced in the United States, further advanced the definition of numeracy: 'Numeracy requires more than just a familiarity with numbers. To cope confidently with the demands of today's society, one must be able to grasp the implications of many mathematical concepts ... that permeate daily news and routine decisions'.

Why is numeracy important?

If the fundamental purpose of school education is to prepare young people to participate in a satisfying personal, social, and working life, this must include developing young people as numerate individuals who will be able to manage the requirements of everyday life efficiently, in a range of situations that involve the use of mathematics.

Numerate behaviour is required in many aspects of daily life, including shopping, budgeting, preparing food, administering medicine, and reading and interpreting information. Students use their numeracy skills in a range of contexts outside school, such as managing a mobile phone account or their timesheet for a part-time job.

School leavers entering the workforce need to be proficient in choosing and using mathematics, and not just in occupations with obvious mathematical demands. Workers need to understand their employment conditions and entitlements, such as rates of pay, superannuation, and taxation scales, and this requires an understanding of mathematical relationships and applications. Additionally, school leavers no longer expect to remain in the same occupation for their whole life. Young people need to be able to adapt to the demands of changing employment, and numeracy requirements will vary in specific occupational contexts.

Students moving into post-school education and training also need to be numerate. Post-school education encompasses a wide range of numeracy demands on students, in contexts that are not specifically the study of mathematics. Examples are interpreting tables of information in sociology studies, determining trends and rates of population growth in geographical and demographic studies, and calculating maximal oxygen uptake in sports sciences.

consider and discuss

Which numeracy demands are represented in these pictures? What do they tell you about why numeracy is so important?

Numerate individuals are also able to participate more effectively and successfully in wider community and social spheres. For example, political initiatives and public policy decisions are frequently explained, and justified, through the use of quantitative information presented in tables and graphs that use mathematical relationships and arguments. Hence, there is a need to be able to view and interpret quantitative data critically.

Finally, the growth of a socially just society depends upon individuals gaining appropriate levels of numeracy. Although innumeracy is not treated with the same level of social concern as illiteracy, it can have dire consequences. For example, Parsons and Bynner (2005) found that poor numeracy, rather than poor literacy, was associated with low economic well-being in adults at age 30 years, and that for women in particular low numeracy had a greater negative effect regardless of their literacy levels. Hence, the demands of the tasks and activities of daily life mean that numeracy can determine who is able to participate and contribute most effectively in home life, at work, and in the community.

issues in teaching

Numeracy and socio-cultural contexts

For many students, the numeracy and mathematical experiences provided at school are not socially or culturally consistent with their home lives. Therefore, teachers need to consider socio-cultural contexts in planning for numeracy learning. Numeracy is practised in socio-cultural contexts and so classroom teaching ought to be sensitive to these contexts. For example, there is nothing 'real life' about investigating mortage rates for students from economically disadvantaged backgrounds who have little comprehension of mortgages because their families have generationally lived in rental accommodation. If numeracy learning in the classroom fails to take account of social or cultural contexts, there is little chance that students will make long-term connections to other areas of their lives.

Two different approaches could be taken when considering the differing social or cultural backgrounds of students in planning for numeracy learning. First, a culturally responsive approach to numeracy adopts teaching strategies and curriculum content that are adjusted so that students can build upon their familiar, existing skills and knowledge. Alternatively, a culturally relevant approach to numeracy uses the students' social and/or cultural skills and knowledge to create new understandings.

How are mathematics and numeracy different?

Numeracy was described above as choosing and using mathematics in a broad range of contexts. While numeracy and mathematics draw upon the same body of skills, numeracy is not the same as mathematics; nor is it an alternative to mathematics. Consider these definitions of mathematics:

> [Mathematics is] the science of space, number, quantity, and arrangement, whose methods involve logical reasoning and usually the use of symbolic notation, and which includes geometry, arithmetic, algebra, and analysis; mathematical operations or calculations. (Soanes et al., Concise Oxford English Dictionary, 2008)

> Mathematics by definition and tradition is abstract, dealing with universal truths and relations among ideal objects. (Steen, 2001)

These definitions emphasise the abstract nature of mathematics, and it is the study of mathematics as an abstract construct that has traditionally been most highly valued in secondary school mathematics. Steen (2007) observes that 'unfortunately numeracy is often characterised as watered-down mathematics—minor-league curriculum that schools offer to those unable to compete in the major league of algebra, trigonometry and calculus'. The characterisation of numeracy as a second-class form of school mathematics is neither accurate nor valid, because mathematics and numeracy cannot be formed into a hierarchical relationship. Rather:

- mathematics conveys the power of conceptualising and abstracting; numeracy conveys the power of context and practicality
- mathematics does not need to consider the real world as it can focus purely on abstract constructs and ideas regardless of their potential applications; numeracy is the application of mathematics in authentic contexts
- mathematics is organised using categories from the past; numeracy focuses on the way quantitative knowledge is used in the information age
- mathematics is most encountered in educational institutions; numeracy mostly in the world around us.

While numeracy and mathematics have distinct differences, many of the competencies implied in numeracy are to be found in school mathematics curricula. These skills and understandings include an understanding of our number system and a repertoire of computational skills. However, an individual's level of numeracy does not necessarily reflect how much mathematics they know, because more than mathematical skills and knowledge is required to be an effectively numerate individual (Martin, 2007).

Numeracy comprises not only mathematics skills, but also the *way* in which they are used. This involves marrying the mathematical meaning of the symbols and operations to their contextual application, and thinking simultaneously about both. This is considerably more difficult than the ability to perform the underlying mathematical operations stripped of their context. Hence, numeracy is not a set of low-level basic mathematical skills; it includes the disposition to think mathematically where mathematical skills and knowledge are integral to the thinking processes employed in specific contexts.

> **did you know?**
>
> The terms numeracy and literacy have been linked by various sources in a number of ways since the 1959 Crowther report (Central Advisory Council for Education, 1959). For example, official documentation for the International Year of Literacy (1990) stated that literacy included numeracy. Terms such as 'quantitative literacy' (Hughes-Hallet, 2003) or 'mathematical literacy' (de Lange, 2003) have been used to refer to numeracy. Others have explicitly linked literacy and numeracy by drawing upon literacy frameworks such as that of Freebody and Luke (1990) to describe numerate behaviour. This blurring of terminology has resulted in the tendency for numeracy to be subsumed under literacy. However, by the end of the 1990s the Australian Association of Mathematics Teachers (AAMT) was strongly expressing the view that literacy and numeracy were separate domains of competence. In its policy document on numeracy teaching the AAMT (1997) emphasises that literacy and numeracy are fundamentally different areas of student learning, and that each merits separate and distinct consideration. The adoption of the term numeracy, in its own right, has since been reflected in further policy documents (DETYA, 2000; DEST 2004) and in the inclusion of numeracy in national benchmark testing.

Being numerate

Australian researchers have offered a range of descriptions of what being numerate encompasses. Forrest (1997) has described the four roles of a numerate person. Hogan (2000) and Willis (1998) propose that a blend of three 'know-hows' with the capacity to take up three distinct roles is required to be numerate. Scott (1999) describes three key factors that need to coalesce in order to become and be numerate. Each of these frameworks is worthy of a little further consideration.

Forrest's four roles of a numerate person (1997) are an adaptation of Freebody and Luke's four roles of a literate person (1990). Being numerate, according to Forrest, requires adopting the roles of numeracy technician, numeracy participant, numeracy user, and numeracy analyst. The role of numeracy technician foregrounds mathematical knowledge and understandings. The emphasis of the numeracy participant role is the ability to work mathematically and transfer knowledge to new situations. The numeracy user's role focuses on the ability to select, integrate, and represent the mathematical ideas and relationships involved in a particular situation. Finally, in the numeracy analyst role, being numerate involves appreciating that mathematics is value-laden and can be challenged.

Hogan (2000) and Willis (1998) propose that being numerate within a context involves a blend of three types of know-how: mathematical, contextual, and strategic. Mathematical know-how involves knowing, understanding, and using mathematical ideas that typically comprise the school mathematics curriculum. Contextual know-how requires an understanding of how the mathematics is shaped by the **context**. Strategic know-how involves approaches to problem solving used in routine or non-routine situations. Hogan extended this framework by proposing that the blend of the three types of know-how is also influenced by an individual's capacity to take up three corresponding roles: fluent operator, learner, and critic. This means that individuals who are numerate will be able to use mathematical skills and knowledge fluently in context. This role calls for a comfortable, quick, and intuitive use of mathematics. The numerate individual also uses mathematics to make sense of an unfamiliar task or new situation; that is, to learn. Finally, to be numerate calls upon using mathematics sensibly and critically, knowing what mathematics is and is not, and what it can and cannot do, in order to judge and question the appropriateness of its use.

Scott (1999) proposes three key factors that are necessary to become and be numerate: confidence, context, and content. However, Scott argues that while each of these factors is fundamental to numeracy, they do not exist independently, and an interaction between the three is essential to being numerate. Indeed, all three factors need to be present in any situation that involves being numerate. Absence of any one will result in behaviours that fall short of effective numeracy, as evident in Figure 9.1.

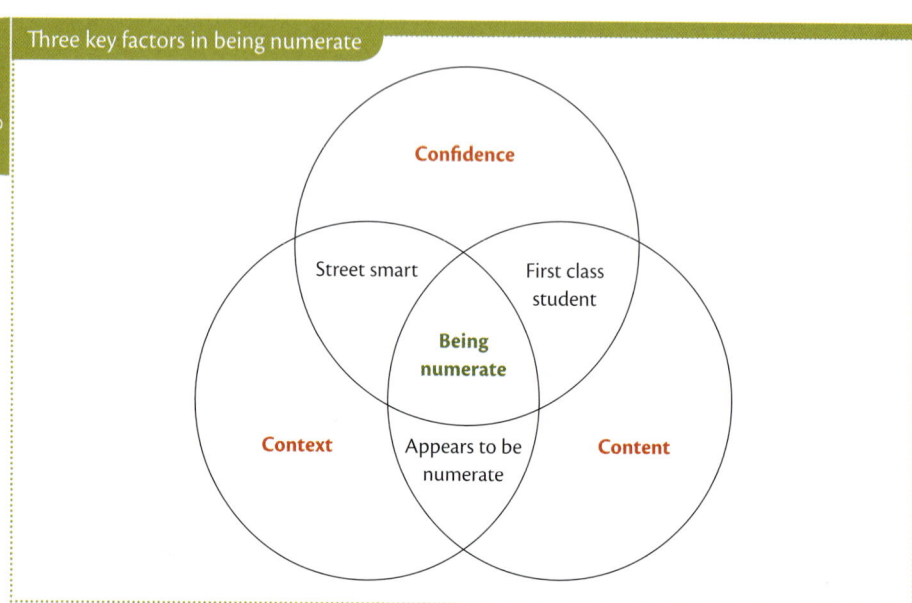

Figure 9.1 Three key factors in being numerate

To summarise, while there are some differences between each of the frameworks in the behaviours and roles they propose are involved in being numerate, they agree that to be numerate involves having:

- a fluency in mathematical skills and requisite knowledge
- a clear understanding of the contextual requirements
- the disposition to choose and use the mathematics appropriate to the context with confidence
- a critical appreciation of how mathematics can be used, and misused, in order to question or judge the appropriateness of its use.

making connections

Grocery label unit pricing

Doing the weekly shopping demands numeracy. Unit pricing, recently introduced to some supermarkets, allows shoppers to determine the best value between similar products more readily. As well as the actual price, grocery shelf labels also show a price per unit, typically unit volume or unit mass.

Suppose an item weighing 1 kg costs $5.00 to buy. Its unit price is $3.00 per kg, or $0.50 per 100 g. Another brand of the same type of item is $4.80 for 800 g. Its unit price is $0.60 per 100 g. How was this unit price determined?

On a cost per unit basis, the 1 kg item at $5.00 is better value ($0.50 rather than $0.60).

Unit pricing can also be used to compare different size packages for the same product.

Suppose a 900 g box of Sunny cornflakes is priced at $2.70. The unit price is $0.27 per 100 g (the price divided by the mass). The 100 g provides the basis for comparison.

Sunny also produces a 1.6 kg box of cornflakes. In general, the more you buy of an item the cheaper the unit cost. The shelf label shows that the unit price for this size packaging is $0.25, which is 5 cents per 100 g cheaper than the 900 g box.

Note that all we have shown here is that buying a bigger size is cheaper by volume. The additional cost of buying this size ($1.30) may not be possible in a shopper's budget.

A numerate shopper would appreciate that unit pricing is most beneficial when items of similar volume that are within their budget are compared. For instance, compare the 900 g box of Sunny cornflakes with an 800 g box of Crunchy cornflakes. The 800 g box is $2.56, or $0.32 per 100 g, and the Sunny box has a unit price of $0.30 per 100 g. This means that Sunny is better value by 2 cents per 100 g.

While unit pricing assists the shopper to identify the best valued item based upon a common unit of measurement, purchasing decisions may be based on factors other than price. For example, a shopper may be prepared to pay the extra 2 cents per 100 g if they prefer the taste of one brand over another.

for the classroom

Get the students to practise calculating the unit prices of various size packages of the same item and to gather data about the numeracy skills of a range of shoppers by using this investigation.

- Working in pairs or small groups, the students visit a supermarket to gather information about the price of the same product that is available in three different size packages. Using this information, the students will practise determining the unit price of each size and explain their reasons for deciding which size represents the best value.
- The students then create a display of the items, or a poster illustrating the items as either photographs or drawings. Each of the items or illustrations should be labelled separately with the actual item price. For example, if the item were Sunny cornflakes, the labels would be 1.6 kg $4.00, 900 g $2.70, 500 g $2.00.
- Arrange for the students to survey a range of adults of various ages using the following questions:
  - Which package, 1.6 kg, 900 g or 500 g, is the best value for money?
  - Why did you choose this package? Unit value? Largest? Cheapest? Other?
  - Which package is the worst value for money?
- Students should record information about the gender and age group of the survey participants. They then evaluate their results to determine the percentage of people who correctly identified the best value item, recording also whether any particular age group is better at determining the best value without unit pricing, or whether there are any differences in the male and female ability to determine best value.
- Finally, the students write a report, which includes graphs, to present and support their conclusions from the survey.

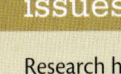

issues in teaching

Research has found a serious mismatch between the mathematics taught in secondary schools and the types of mathematics required to function effectively in the world outside. This means that most secondary mathematics content does not contribute to developing student numeracy. Some students, because secondary mathematics becomes increasingly abstract, lose their confidence and motivation as mathematics learners.

Secondary schools often structure their mathematics classes by student ability, and the students with limited mathematical ability or diminished interest are placed together in the lower ranked classes. Often these classes are given supposedly appealing titles, such as Life Maths or Maths at Work (though many students will, sadly, refer to it as Veggie Maths). The curriculum content in such classes is modified to suit the learning needs of the students, and normally there is heavy emphasis on practising routine arithmetic processes. Ideally, classes such as these could become far more relevant to lower ability students and make a significant contribution to developing their numeracy skills, if a better balance could be established between strengthing computational skills and applying these skills in authentic and realistic ways.

integrating technology/ICT

Calculators and numeracy

The hand-held calculator is an effective teaching and learning resource to be used in developing numeracy skills across the curriculum. Australian research has shown that providing primary students with access to calculators makes a significant and profound contribution to their developing numeracy skills.

To build numeracy skills involving the use of calculators, first guide students to decide when calculator use is most appropriate. Additionally, they need to acquire skills in using a calculator, especially with entering numbers and operations accurately. Students also need to be able to interpret whether the results displayed are feasible or reasonable. Finally, they should be able to discern the level of accuracy required for a particular context and round the displayed result accordingly.

Numeracy across the curriculum

Being numerate is about having the disposition and the competence to use mathematics to meet the general demands of home life, the workplace, learning environments, and community participation. Therefore, in the school context, numeracy is more than knowing and doing the mathematics involved in mathematics lessons. This view was emphasised in the National Numeracy Review (COAG Human Capital Working Group, 2008) recommendation that the development of numeracy requires experience in the use of mathematics across the curriculum beyond the mathematics classroom.

Numeracy demands are made on students in all learning areas when students are presented with ideas to understand, tasks to complete, problems to solve, and objects to make that require the thoughtful and practical use of mathematics. This creates a two-way relationship between the mathematics that students learn at school and the numeracy they use at school. In mathematics lessons students acquire numeracy skills by developing mathematical skills and knowledge. This is learning for numeracy. In other learning areas students use and enhance their numeracy skills in contexts other than in mathematics classes. This is numeracy for learning. This means that for every student every lesson is potentially a numeracy lesson, and hence all teachers are numeracy teachers responsible for engaging their students in numeracy learning.

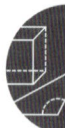

for the classroom

Always be alert to the possibilities for building numeracy demands into tasks and activities in all learning areas. For example:

- Science: A documentary states that the triceratops was 9 metres long. Get the students to lay out a measuring tape on the floor to assist in visualising the size of the creature. Comparisons could be made with the height of humans or the size of other familiar animals.
- English: If the class is watching DVD of a popular and exciting book that they are reading, get the students to note the sequence of events. After discussing the film, they should record the events on an accurate timeline.

- Society and environment: When the students are researching a country, have them locate it in an atlas and describe its position. This will lead to an investigation of latitude and longitude as a way of accurately identifying a location on a map, and the use of scale to determine distances.
- Art and design: If students are painting a mural, this will involve the use of scale and proportion to enlarge their paper image accurately, and measurement, approximation and costing to organise the materials required to complete the job.

Opportunities and the challenges across the curriculum

Managing the numeracy demands in all learning areas can provide teachers with a range of opportunities and challenges. Teachers need to develop an understanding of how students use their mathematical skills and knowledge in a range of differing contexts.

Hogan, Van Wyke and Murcia (2004) identify four key factors associated with successfully teaching for numeracy across the curriculum:

- planning for possible numeracy moments in the learning area
- paying attention to and understanding the students' numeracy issues
- giving time to numeracy opportunites in all learning areas
- reflecting on the way that mathematics is taught.

consider and discuss

Imagine you have given your Year 5 or 6 students the task of using a map of Australia to plan a long-term trip. What are all the possible numeracy demands that might be associated with this activity?

In relation to the first three of these factors, they suggest a range of teaching strategies for engaging students with numeracy across the curriculum.

First, they emphasise the significance of *being aware of the possible numeracy demands* of each learning area when planning in order to consider the range of student strategies and approaches that might be used in managing the learning experience. Next, they highlight how *capturing the numeracy in the moment* asks teachers to be flexible and open to following the students' numeracy interests and learning needs as they arise incidentally in class. Bringing the mathematical demands of the context to the students' attention is recommended, as this contributes to raising the students' awareness of the numeracy that is embedded across the curriculum. Additionally, they advise that students require the opportunity to *work things out for themselves* and to use *collaborative group* sharing of skills, knowledge, and strategies, and that *students ought to be given time* to do this. For the teacher, this can require constraining the urge to rush in and complete it for the students. Rather, teachers need to take a patient and flexible approach, providing the time necessary for the students to engage in the numeracy themselves, to ask questions, and to gain confidence as numeracy learners.

for the classroom

A variety of generic numeracy tools can be incorporated readily into a range of learning areas across the curriculum.

Generic numeracy tool 1: tables

Being numerate beyond school will include reading and interpreting tabulated information. If students encounter a variety of tables in their numeracy learning they will become familiar with the common features of tables and hone their interpretation skills, particularly in recognising the relationship between the values presented in the table.

Generic numeracy tool 2: flow charts

Flow charts are a useful way of illustrating the various components of a complex situation. Designing flow charts develops students' skills in logical thinking, as they are required to break the more complex situation into a series of component parts, and to recognise the sequence of the parts.

Generic numeracy tool 3: maps

Students will encounter a variety of maps in contexts and out of school. The ability to read and interpret maps is an essential aspect of being numerate. When students use maps they are developing the numeracy skills associated with the use of scale, coordinate grid references, and reading and interpreting keys and legends.

The fourth key factor associated with successful teaching for numeracy across the curriculum is reflecting upon the way that mathematics is taught. Thornton and Hogan (2005) argue that the learning in the mathematics classroom could engage and support students in their numeracy learning across the curriculum if:

- their experiences in the mathematics classroom build upon their confidence, and their disposition, to see themselves as competent users of mathematics
- they are provided with an appreciation that all areas of mathematics are richly connected
- they have the chance to act numerately in the mathematics classroom by engaging with tasks that are mathematically rich and contextually authentic.

issues in teaching

Why some students have difficulty with numeracy demands

Students having difficulty handling the numeracy demands of tasks or activities in any learning area across the curriculum may:

- have limited strategies for problem solving
- rely on procedures that have been acquired through rote learning without any real understanding
- have gaps in their mathematical understanding or be required to use mathematical skills they have not yet been taught in mathematics classes
- have limited contextual understanding of textual or graphical material
- avoid using mathematics when working in contexts outside the mathematics classroom
- lack the confidence, or the disposition, to deal with the numeracy in the task
- lack the cultural skills and knowledge to create new understandings.

for the classroom

Generic numeracy tool 4: graphs

Graphs represent information diagrammatically. The ability to read and interpret graphical information is an important aspect of being numerate. It is also important to develop the understanding that different kinds of graphs are used for different purposes.

Generic numeracy tool 5: timelines

Timelines can take various forms and are used to summarise and represent information in chronological order. When students design timelines they are developing their numeracy skills in sequencing of events, and in plotting events accurately to scale.

Generic numeracy tool 6: diagrams

Diagrams are useful for presenting information and showing relationships. Tree diagrams, Venn diagrams and mind maps are some examples of the types of diagrams that could be useful for numeracy learning across the curriculum. When students construct and use diagrams they are developing their logical and analytical thinking skills.

Critical numeracy

consider and discuss

Why are motor vehicles so frequently advertised at $14 990, $19 990 or $29 990?
The retailer uses number in this way for some very good reasons that are not necessarily in the interests of the consumer. What could these reasons be?

The component of numeracy associated with a critical appreciation of how mathematics is used to describe and explain our world is commonly referred to as critical numeracy. Hogan (2000) refers to being numerate in this way as adopting the role of 'critic', while Forrest (1997) refers to this as the 'numeracy analyst' role.

Critical numeracy is the ability to make discerning decisions about everyday issues that involve the use of mathematics (Watson, Stack & Neal, 2009). A critical numeracy perspective encourages students to go deeper into mathematical ideas and the context, to challenge the usefulness of the mathematics used in relationship to the context. Additionally, students come to appreciate that numeracy can involve questionable social and cultural practices, and to understand the consequences of these practices for themselves and others. Hence, critical numeracy is about critique and it is about being empowered.

The critical numeracy perspective challenges students to consider the following questions:

- Whose view is being promoted and to whose advantage?
- What arguments are being promoted? Is there a bias?
- Who is empowered and who is disempowered?
- What mathematics is being used, and is the mathematics being used appropriately?

consider and discuss

Some retailers are so confident of their competitive pricing that they make claims in their advertisements that they will match or better competitors' prices. Consider the following two claims made by leading retailers:

- Retailer A. Find an identical stocked item at a cheaper price and we will beat it by 10%.
- Retailer B. Find an identical stocked item at a cheaper price and we will refund 110% of the difference.

1. What is the key difference between the claims made by Retailer A and Retailer B? (Hint: think about the word 'refund'.)
2. If an item were on Retailer A's shelf for $100 and you found it at a competitor for $90, how much would Retailer A sell you the item for?
3. If you had purchased an item at Retailer B for $100 and then found it at a competitor for $90, how much would be the refund?
4. Which is the better claim?
5. What is the power in the numbers being quoted by Retailer A and Retailer B in attracting customers?
6. What assumption does Retailer B make with regard to their price guarantee?

making connections

The Body Mass Index (BMI) is a good example of how a particular value can acquire a persuasive numerical authority, despite its limitations.

Originally, the BMI provided a simple numeric measure of a person's 'fatness' or 'thinness', allowing health professionals to discuss problems of being either over or under weight with their patients. The formula for calculating the BMI is given by:

$$BMI = \frac{mass}{height^2}$$ where mass is in kilograms and height in metres

A common application of the BMI is to assess how much a person's body weight departs from what is desirable for their height. The value settings that have been defined to interpret the BMI value are: 18.5 to 25 indicates optimal weight; lower than 18.5 suggests the person is underweight; above 25 indicates the person is overweight; and above 30 suggests the person is obese. These ranges of BMI values are only valid as statistical categories when applied to adults, and do not predict health.

The BMI has become controversial, however, because many people rely on its apparent numerical authority as an indicator of health, which was never its intended purpose. It is crucial that those adopting the BMI as a indication of lifestyle also consider the limitations of the value. These include:

- BMI value settings vary according to age, sex and body type
- BMI does not differentiate between muscle and fat and will therefore underestimate body fat in some and overestimate for others
- BMI does not identify where body fat is distributed, and since fat around the waist is more dangerous than that around the hips this will not be picked up by BMI.

According to Stoessiger (2002), there are four main aspects to being critically numerate. These are being able to critique mathematical information; being able to unpack, interpret, or decode mathematical situations; using mathematics in a self-reflective way; and using mathematics to operate more powerfully in the world. Similarly, Watson et al. (2009) proposed a four resource model for critical numeracy that has affinities to Freebody and Luke's (1990) literacy model. This model is designed to build student capacities to ask questions about the meaning, validity, and usefulness of texts that contain mathematical concepts or information.

communicating mathematically

In this four resource model for critical numeracy (Watson et al., 2009) each quadrant contains examples of the types of questions teachers may ask to assist their students become more familiar with mathematical ideas and contexts (De-coding and Meaning-making) before applying a more critical lens (Using and Analysing).

De-coding
- What terminology is being used and what does it mean?
- What are the key mathematical concepts, processes, and procedures being used?

Using
- In what way are the mathematical concepts in this context significant or useful?
- How does the text promote particular points of view?
- What are the possible applications or likely implications?

Meaning-making
- How can I use what I already know?
- How do the mathematical concepts make sense in this context and help me to understand the context?
- What is confusing or misleading?

Analysing
- Is it true?
- Is it fair?
- How does it position me?
- Do I believe it?

The Chance and Data strand in mathematics curricula is a key area that can be used to promote and develop critical numeracy skills. Students need to develop awareness of how statistical information can be manipulated to reflect a particular point of view. In this way they will acquire the type of analytical skills necessary to interpret, analyse, and critique such information, especially when it is presented in the media. For example, the daily temperatures recorded over a week (21, 16, 23, 18, 25, 17, 15) can be graphed to show a reasonably stable weather pattern for the week (Figure 9.2) or a widely varied pattern (Figure 9.3), depending upon how the axes are drawn.

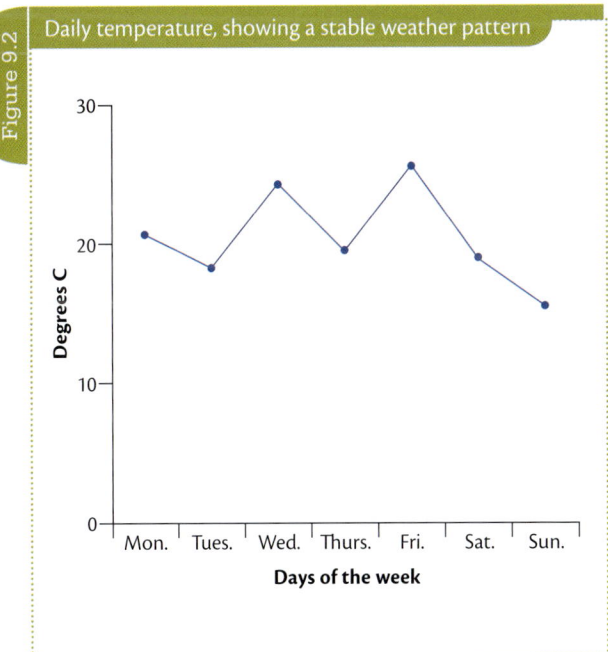

Figure 9.2 Daily temperature, showing a stable weather pattern

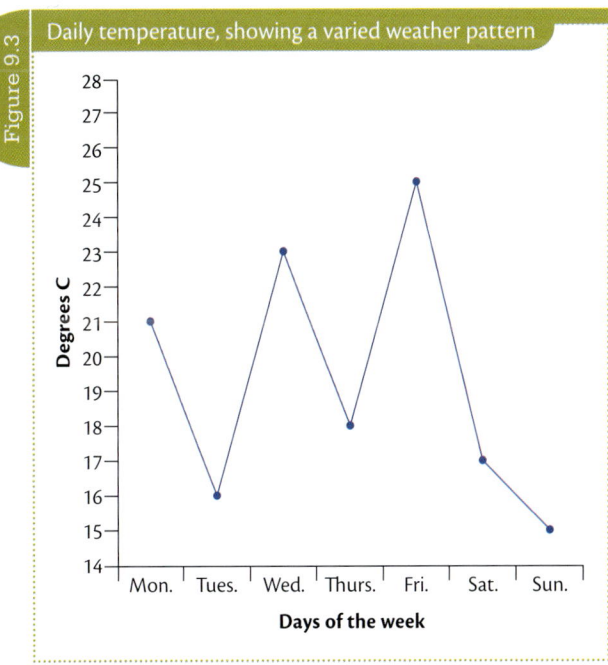

Figure 9.3 Daily temperature, showing a varied weather pattern

Part 3: Exploring the Big Ideas in Mathematics

for the classroom

Get the students to collect examples of poorly constructed or misleading graphs that appear in the newspapers. This should not be difficult.

Ask the students to analyse and record why the graph is misleading and why it may have been presented in this way. Whose point of view or interests are being served? Have the students redraw the graph in a more accurate way if appropriate, either by hand or using a spreadsheet. Have them compare and analyse the two graphs and draw conclusions about the differences between the information presented in each graph.

Incorporating critical numeracy across the learning areas

Critical numeracy can be integrated across learning areas as a means for students to explore both their local and the global physical, social, cultural, and political environments. This approach provides students with the opportunity to consider real issues, such as equity or resource sustainability, and use aspects of mathematics in authentic ways to engage with these issues. The critical numeracy perspective encourages students to use mathematics as a 'lens' to critique both their own plans, actions, and views, and those presented by others.

Watson et al. (2009) examine how teachers bring critical numeracy perspectives into their classrooms. Arising from this study a number of strategies are suggested for incorporating critical numeracy across the learning areas.

First, teachers need to help the students make connections between the context and the mathematical ideas and tools being used. One way is to allow for more group work so that students can develop deeper conceptual and contextual understandings through discussion. The study (Watson et al., 2009) found that many teachers are not well versed in bringing critical numeracy thinking into their teaching. Hence, they suggest that teachers will often need to practice using the four-resources model for critical numeracy so it becomes a natural part of their thinking processes. They will then be able to model its use to their students. Finally, choosing and designing appropriate learning activities is vital. A range of contexts are applicable to building critical numeracy skills, but these need to be contexts that teachers are able to assume comfortably, and ones that the students will relate to.

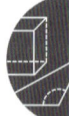

for the classroom

Using newspaper articles to develop critical numeracy skills

Newspaper articles are an excellent classroom resource for developing critical numeracy skills in students. They provide an everyday context where the mathematical ideas presented can encompass all learning areas.

When choosing an article from the newspaper for classroom use, teachers need to consider:

- the opportunities for exploring particular mathematical concepts through the article
- whether the context will be understood by the students and if it will interest them
- the extent to which the article lends itself to the different aspects of critical numeracy
- the links that can be made to particular learning areas
- the pre-existing understandings that the students will require and how much teacher scaffolding will be needed.

consider and discuss

Walking school bus

A walking school bus is a school bus powered by legs, not an engine. Children walk in a group to school, with an adult 'driver' in the front and an adult 'conductor' at the rear. The 'bus' travels along a set route to or from school, picking up or dropping off children along the way at designated 'bus stops'. Bus stops can be meeting points along the route, or each child's front gate. For more information, see www.vichealth.vic.gov.au/wsb, www.travelsmart.gov.au/schools/schools2.html or www.curriculumsupport.education.nsw.gov.au/policies/road/travel/walkingbus1.htm.

Use a critical numeracy perspective to consider:

1. How can primary students become involved in exploring, critiquing, and acting upon the social, environmental, and economic impact of travelling to school by car?
2. What mathematical tools will help them do this?
3. What will be the impact of their investigations on their physical and social environments, and how will they know there has been an impact?

Conclusion

Numeracy involves choosing and using mathematics in a broad range of authentic and practical contexts. While numeracy and mathematics draw upon the same skills, numeracy comprises not only mathematical skills, but also the way that the skills are used. Thus, being numerate involves:

- fluency with the required mathematics skills
- an understanding of contextual requirements
- the disposition to choose and use mathematics appropriate to the context
- a critical appreciation of the appropriateness of the mathematics being used.

This creates a two-way relationship between the mathematics that students learn at school and the numeracy they use at school. In mathematics lessons students acquire numeracy skills by developing their mathematical skills and knowledge. This is learning for numeracy. In other learning areas, students use and develop their numeracy skills to learn in contexts other than mathematics.

Limiting students' numeracy to mathematical skills alone, together with the capacity to choose and use mathematics specific to the context, is to ignore the need to develop a critical appreciation of how mathematics is used to describe and explain our world. Critical numeracy is the ability to make discerning decisions about everyday issues that involve the use of mathematics. As students' critical numeracy perspectives develop they come to appreciate that numeracy involves social and cultural practices, and to understand the consequences of these practices for themselves and others. Hence, critical numeracy is about critique and empowerment.

Critical numeracy perspectives can be integrated across learning areas to provide students with the opportunity to consider real issues, using aspects of mathematics in authentic ways to engage with those issues.

key terms

Context: the circumstances or situation that requires the application of numeracy skills

Critical numeracy: the component of numeracy associated with a critical appreciation of how mathematics is used to describe and explain our world

Numeracy: the application of mathematical skills and knowledge to a broad range of authentic and practical contexts

Numerate behaviour: the disposition to choose and use mathematics, with confidence, as appropriate to the context

Review questions

1. How would you describe the relationship between mathematics and numeracy?
2. List five reasons for why good numeracy skills are important.
3. What are the key behaviours that are essential to being numerate?
4. What factors do teachers need to consider when planning for the numeracy opportunities that arise across the curriculum?
5. What does the term 'critical numeracy' mean to you?
6. How can a teacher encourage their students to take a critical numeracy perspective across the learning areas?

Key references

Australian Association of Mathematics Teachers (1997). *Numeracy = Everyone's Business*. Adelaide: Australian Association of Mathematics Teachers.

DETYA (Commonwealth Department of Education and Youth Affairs). (2000). *Numeracy: A Priority for All*. Canberra: Commonwealth of Australia.

Forrest, M. (1997). *Four Roles of a Numerate Person*. Adelaide: Department of Education and Children's Services.

Hogan, J., Van Wyke, J., & Murcia, K. (2004). *Numeracy Across the Curriculum*. Canberra: Commonwealth of Australia.

Stoessiger, R. (2002). An introduction to critical numeracy. *The Australian Mathematics Teacher*, 58(4), 17–20.

Thornton, S., & Hogan, J. (2005). Numeracy across the curriculum: Demands and opportunities. *Curriculum Leadership*, 3(16), n.p.

Watson, J., Stack, S., & Neal, D. (2009). *Developing Critical Numeracy Across the Curriculum*. Retrieved August 30, 2010 from www.simerr.educ.utas.edu.au/numeracy/default.html.

Westwood, P. (2008). *What Teachers Need to Know about Numeracy*. Melbourne: ACER.

Websites

http://www.simerr.educ.utas.edu.au/numeracy/critical_numeracy/critical_numeracy.htm

http://www.thenetwork.sa.edu.au/pages/educators/my_lit_num/?reFlag=1

http://activated.act.edu.au/ectl

http://www.vichealth.vic.gov.au/wsb

http://www.travelsmart.gov.au/schools/schools2.html

http://www.curriculumsupport.education.nsw.gov.au/policies/road/travel/walkingbus1.htm

Developing a Sense of Number

Contents

Understanding number sense	187
Number sense in practice	188
Developing a sense of number	197
Conclusion	207

Chapter objectives

This chapter will enable the reader to:
- Understand the critical role of number sense in everyday problem solving and reasoning
- Appreciate what is involved in having a well-developed sense of number
- Recognise that conceptual understanding is needed to interrogate numerically based claims and support efficient computation and/or estimation
- Develop an awareness of the key ideas and strategies needed to work flexibly and confidently with numbers in a variety of forms.

An advertisement for household linen was emblazoned with the statement 'Half-price or 50% off, whichever is the cheapest'. In the last days of the Sri Lankan civil war, a newsreader announced that the Tamil Tiger resistance had been confined to an area of 800 square metres. A nurse about to insert a drug into a drip insisted that a 1% solution meant 10 millilitres in 100 millilitres. An experienced Airbus pilot might be expected to know that a fully laden jet about to take off on a long distance flight would be more likely to weigh 362 tonnes than 262 tonnes, but an apparent keystroke error nearly cost 257 people their lives when the tail of the jet hit the runway. What were they thinking? How could this happen?

Big ideas

- Number sense enables people to read, interpret, and evaluate numbers in everyday contexts.
- Number sense requires a deep understanding of numbers and operations.
- Procedural fluency is a necessary but not sufficient requirement for number sense.
- Number sense is used across the curriculum to solve problems and reason mathematically.

Understanding number sense

Number sense has been referred to as:

> a person's general understanding of number and operations along with the ability and inclination to use this understanding in flexible ways to make mathematical judgements and to develop useful and efficient strategies for managing numerical situations ... It results in a view of numbers as meaningful entities and the expectation mathematical manipulations and outcomes should make sense ... Those who use mathematics in this way continually utilise a variety of internal 'checks and balances' to judge the reasonableness of numerical outcomes. (McIntosh, Reys, Reys, Bana & Farrell, 1997, p. 3)

Together with a sense of measurement, chance and data, and space, number sense is a critical component of numeracy (Australian Association of Mathematics Teachers, 1997).

The origins of number sense

did you know?

According to Dehaene (1997), the term 'number sense' was first used by Dantzig in 1954 to describe a faculty observed in laboratory animals and infants that permits the animal or the young child to recognise that something has changed in a small collection without any direct knowledge that an object had been added or removed. This facility was recognised as a 'new dimension of sensory perception through which the cardinal of a set of objects can be perceived just as easily as their colour, shape or position'.

In humans, the capacity to create complex symbolic systems, including oral and written language, allows this numerical intuition to evolve into something much more powerful that enables us to see immediately that, for example, 20 is greater than 10, without counting or computing. However, our memory works by association of ideas, which possibly accounts for the fact that many of us have 'such a hard time remembering the small number of equations that make up the multiplication table' (Dehaene, 1997, p. 7). As a consequence, this more evolved form of number sense needs to be based on meaningful relationships between numbers and between numbers and operations, as these are variously represented in different contexts. Although this is not easy to define or measure, as noted by Sowder and Schappelle (1989):

> Number sense is not a body of knowledge; rather it is a way of thinking, and so teaching and assessing number sense cannot be thought of in the same manner as we think about such topics as operations on whole numbers ... an individual must be disposed towards making sense of mathematics for number sense to develop. (p. 4)

The critical importance of number sense was recognised with the emergence of problem solving as a goal of school mathematics in the early 1980s. In 1991, Greeno suggested that number sense 'refers to several important but elusive capabilities including flexible mental computation, numerical estimation, and quantitative judgement' (p. 170). McIntosh, Reys and Reys (1992) added an 'ability and inclination to communicate, process, and interpret information'

(p. 2), while Sowder (1992) listed a range of competencies that included a disposition to make sense of numbers and a capacity to compose and decompose numbers, recognise and deal with the relative and absolute magnitude of numbers, use benchmarks, estimate, make connections between different representations, understand the effects of arithmetic operations, and invent strategies.

More recent references to number sense have tended to restate or re-affirm these views (e.g. Beswick, 2004; Bishop & Forgasz, 2007; Clements & Sarama, 2007), which suggests that the focus has shifted from describing number sense to what it looks like in practice and how it can be developed (e.g. Steen, 1997).

Access to a well-developed sense of number that builds on the intuitive number sense is associated with more positive views about one's own mathematical capacity, and the likelihood of future study in mathematics (Beswick, 2004; Howden, 1989).

Number sense in practice

While the street vendors in Brazil (Chapter 1 p. 18) were able to use well-established mental computation strategies to calculate the cost of coconuts in the market place, where they had a deep appreciation of context and were familiar with the likely range of numbers, it was evident that their sense of number did not extend beyond this to deal with the decontextualised problems presented at school. A well-developed sense of number goes beyond 'knowing what to do when' in very specific contexts. It requires a deep knowledge of numbers and operations that can be used confidently and flexibly in multiple contexts.

Clements and Sarama argue that number and operations are highly interrelated in practice, and that 'operations' should not be limited to the 'standard arithmetic operations of adding, subtracting, multiplying, and dividing but include counting, comparing, unitizing, grouping, partitioning, and composing' (2007, p. 466). These areas are dealt with separately in subsequent chapters.

making connections

Imagine you are running late for a country wedding. In deciding whether or not to turn off the highway to get petrol or continue to your destination 137 kilometres away, you might reason as follows: 10 kilometres to the litre, approximately a quarter of a tank left, that's about 15 litres, average speed 90 kilometres/hour, it will take about an hour and a half, that's about 15 minutes before the wedding—I'll chance it.

List the mathematical knowledge and skills that underpin this reasoning to illustrate the importance of recognising and using the connections between different aspects of mathematics.

Number sense also entails a critical capacity to question the ways in which numbers are used to support quantitative reasoning.

for the classroom

Choose issues of concern to students, such as the real cost of running a mobile phone, why concert tickets cost so much, or the cost of school uniforms versus 'casual clothes' and use these to review what is needed (e.g. planning, reliable data, estimation) and to demonstrate the usefulness of having a well-developed sense of number.

A disposition to make sense of numbers

The news item on page 186 that stated the Tamil Tiger resistance had been confined to an area of 800 square metres could have been a typographical error or a misreading of the text, but the chances are that this 'sounded like' a big enough number to be plausible; what it actually represented on the ground (an area equivalent to 40 metres by 20 metres) was not questioned. A disposition to make sense of numbers, in particular, a capacity *to deal with the relative and absolute magnitude of numbers*, would have prompted the subeditor or newsreader concerned to stop and think about what this meant then check or query the information source.

Pre-school children up to the age of four or so demonstrate an awareness of the **relative magnitude** of numbers when they spontaneously recognise that there are more birds by the park bench than on the path, or that their share of the apple is less than someone else's share. They may also recognise the **absolute magnitude** of some numbers, for example three peas on a plate. They are demonstrating an intuitive, age-appropriate sense of number that precedes, and involves much more than, rote counting. As they grow older, children develop deeper insights into the ways in which numbers work and how they can be interpreted, communicated and manipulated to solve problems.

communicating mathematically

Making sense of decimals

It appears that when children are unsure of the meaning of a decimal, 'they try to change the unfamiliar into the familiar ... Many seem to ignore the decimal point altogether or treat the number as if it were two independent natural numbers separated by a dot' (Swan, 1990, p. 47). Asked to write a word problem for 4.6 + 5.3 = 9.9, one 12-year-old responded as follows.

> Mr Brown had 4 and a half dozen sausage rolls (4.6) and Mrs Brown brought 5 and a quarter dozens sausage rolls (5.3) so for tea they now have 9 and three-quarter dozen rolls (9.9) for their tea. (p.50)

What do you think contributed to this construction? What does it suggest about the student's understanding of fractions and decimals?

Interpreting and communicating quantitative information

The nurse who believed that a 1% solution meant 10 millilitres in 100 millilitres illustrates the critical importance of having a *capacity to interpret and communicate quantitative information* (McIntosh et al., 1992). The CD sales task in Figure 10.1 illustrates the importance of recognising the *relative magnitude* of numbers. The task required students to decide whether or not the manager of a music shop was correct in claiming that there had been a big increase in CD sales.

Figure 10.1 CD sales task and response

The manager of a music shop showed this graph and said 'There's been a big increase in the number of CD sales this month'.

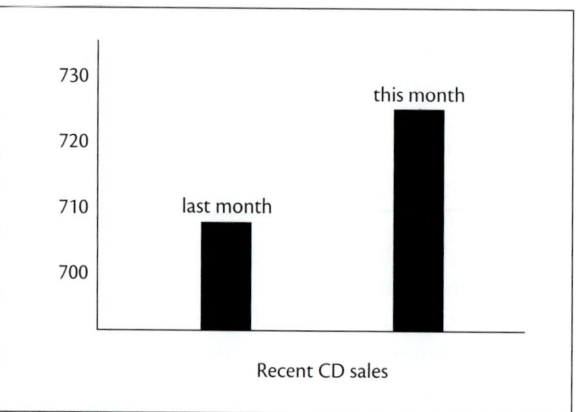

Do you consider the manager's statement to be a reasonable interpretation of the graph? Explain your reasoning.

Response: No because the increase has been exagerated. If you were to go from zero you would see that the increase isn't very large. The graph above only shows the tip of the graph making it look bigger.

Source: Middle Years Numeracy Research Project 5–9 (Siemon, Virgona & Corneille, 2001)

While this response, from a Year 8 student, indicates a solid sense of number, it was scored as a 3 on a scale of 0 to 4 because the explanation did not include a fraction, ratio, or percentage. This was a requirement for a score of 4 on the grounds that to be numerate, students needed to be able to support their argument using conventional mathematical texts and symbols. (Students were made aware of what it meant to 'explain your reasoning' before testing.) It is interesting to note that of the 4227 students in Years 7 to 9 that attempted this task as part of the *Middle Years Numeracy Research Project* (MYNRP), fewer than 1% received a score of 4 from their teachers (Siemon, Virgona & Corneille, 2001). This outcome points to another important aspect of number sense, which is the ability to work with multiple forms of representation.

consider and discuss

What sense?

A well-developed sense of number is needed to make sense of the following excerpt from an editorial in a major US newspaper in 1996 written in the context of a presidential election campaign.

> One-ninth of the population holds seven-tenths of the nation's wealth. The ultra-rich one-tenth of this group holds three-tenths of the nation's wealth.

1. Assuming this information was accurate, what does 'one-tenth' in this statement refer to? What does 'three-tenths' refer to?
2. What fraction of the upper one-ninth's wealth is held by the 'ultra-rich'?
3. What proportion of the nation's population is described as 'ultra-rich'?
4. What do you think the writer's objectives were?
5. If the population of America was approximately 270 million at the time, how many people could be described as ultra-rich?

Making connections between different forms of representation

The many ways in which numbers are represented, recorded, and used require a deep understanding of the context and purpose for which they are used. Moving flexibly between different number sets and representations is a complex task that requires more than a knowledge of the context-specific units and forms of recording involved; it also requires a disposition to make sense of numbers in whatever context they occur.

Before one and two cent coins were withdrawn from use in Australia, I interviewed a number of Year 4 students using the Mars Bites Task below.

> Sophie bought 2 Mars Bites and a jelly snake which cost 38c. Altogether she paid $1.32. What was the cost of one Mars Bite? ... If Sophie gave the shop-assistant $1.50, how much change did she get back? ... What coins might she have received?

All of the students were able to work out the cost of one Mars Bite mentally. There were various strategies for doing this, but the most common was to subtract the cost of the jelly snake from the total by subtracting 32 cents from $1.32 to get to $1, recognising $1 as 100 cents and subtracting the remaining 6 cents, then halving 94 cents by a variety of means (e.g. 'half of 80 is 40, and half of 14 is 7, so 47 cents'). The follow-up questions were used to probe students' understanding further. Again, the students had no difficulty mentally calculating the change (most by using an efficient form of counting such as '8 cents to $1.40 and 10 more cents, 18 cents', but some by less sophisticated methods), and most were able to specify at least one and usually two or more ways to receive the change. After a brief discussion about what they were doing in maths at the time (two-dimensional shapes and nets), the following problems were presented on separate sheets of paper, one after the other. In each instance, the child was asked if they had seen anything like this today, to which all but one child responded, 'no'. They were then asked to say what they thought the problem was asking them to do.

$$\begin{array}{r} 150 \\ -132 \\ \hline \end{array}$$

$$2 \times \square + 38 = 132$$

For the subtraction problem, all of the students said something like subtract or take-away to find the answer. For the equation, most said 'find what goes in the box'. One or two said something like, 'you have to times what's in the box by 2 and add 38 and that will give you 132'. The one boy who recognised that it was 'the same as' the Mars Bites task simply said 'it's 47, we did that before'.

When asked to solve the problems, all except one of the students reached for a pencil and attempted to solve the subtraction algorithm by decomposition (i.e. by renaming the 5 tens to 4 tens and 10 ones). It was obvious that for many of the students this was what they thought they had to do in the circumstances, and quite a few experienced difficulty without ever making the link to the efficient strategies that they had demonstrated earlier. For the equation, most students reverted to trial and error, with some wildly inaccurate guesses to start with that suggested that their sense of number was constrained by the formal algorithmic context.

issues in teaching

Working with symbolic representations

As illustrated by the street vendors in Brazil and the responses to the Mars Bites task above, there is a well-documented disconnect between children's capacity to solve problems in meaningful, familiar contexts and their ability to solve problems presented in a decontextualised, symbolic form. The Realistic Mathematics Education movement in Holland (e.g. Van den Heuvel-Panhuizen, 2001) advocates that learners should begin with realistic problems that with the teacher's help can lead to an exploration of relevant and increasingly powerful mathematical ideas and procedures, including symbolic representations. Earlier Soviet researchers (see e.g. Kilpatrick & Wirszup, 1975) advocated a more direct approach:

- Problem information should be given in words as well as symbols to encourage conversations about what is required and why.
- Alternative representations should be actively invited and explored.
- The number and nature of operations required should be discussed.
- Students should be encouraged to simplify problems by breaking down complex problems into smaller parts, substituting simpler numbers, or by changing the context into something more familiar.

Given that classroom norms and values play a big part in student's strategy choices, creating a classroom culture that openly values and explores multiple representations and solution strategies would appear to be a necessary first step in building students' capacity to deal with symbolic representation.

Using benchmarks

Another example of number sense in practice is provided by Amanda, a Year 5 student who mentally computed percentages *using known benchmarks*. For instance, asked to calculate $12\frac{1}{2}$ per cent of $560, she first determined 50% ($280), halved that to get 25% ($140), then halved that again to get $12\frac{1}{2}$% ($70). To find 70% of 35 000, Amanda found 50% (17 500), then 10% (3500), which she doubled to get 20% (7000) and added to the 17 500 to get 24 500.

for the classroom

Use structured mental quizzes in Years 4 through 9 to draw students' attention to the value of using benchmarks such as 50%, 10%, and 33⅓%. An example of an eight-item quiz is: 50% of 40, 50% of 380, 50% of 5600, 25% of 80, 25% of 4000, 10% of 90, 10% of 650, and 5% of 320.

Some further examples are provided in Dole and McIntosh (2004)

In doing these calculations mentally, Amanda also exhibited a strong sense of the relationships between numbers, in particular, a capacity to **compose and decompose numbers**, and a willingness to create her own solution pathways, that is, *to invent strategies*.

Numbers are also used to count, compare, order, measure, calculate, and *estimate*. While we can calculate with measures in much the same way as we do with numbers more generally, comparing, ordering, and estimating measures can be problematic where different units are involved. For example, recognising the difference between 345 grams and 3.2 kilograms requires more than an appreciation of the attribute of mass. When comparing these quantities, students need to recognise the relationship between the different units and take that into account when interpreting the *relative magnitude* of the two amounts.

making connections

A sophisticated sense of number is needed to be able to integrate the understandings and capacities required by some tasks. For example, while a decision whether to buy a 2.5 litre bottle of fruit juice for $5.75 or a 1 litre carton for $2.25 might well be made on the basis of considerations such as fridge storage space or likely consumption rate, a comparison based on price alone requires a capacity to recognise and manipulate proportional relationships.

Comparing or calculating with time also presents problems. For example, if you left home at 8:43 am for a walk and returned at 9:34 am, how long was your walk? What do you need to know and be able to do?

To compare the feral cat problem in two national parks, given the area of both parks (146 and 103 hectares) and an estimate of the number of cats in each park (35 and 27 respectively), students need to be mindful that the 'problem' refers to the number of cats per unit of area.

Tasks of this type require a capacity and inclination to *make connections between representations* and/or to *unitise* (rename measures to common unit or find the amount for one unit).

think + link

The components and particular requirements for a well-developed sense of measurement and space will be discussed and illustrated in Chapter 11.

Understanding the effects of arithmetic operations

Most young children come to school with a beginning appreciation of three of the four operations. They know what it means to 'get more', have something 'taken away', and not have as much as someone else. They also generally know what it means to 'share equally', as evidenced by the cheeky grin of a four-year old who, when asked to cut a fairy cake to share equally with his younger brother, knowingly cut the cake into two unequal parts, the larger of which he gleefully claimed as his share.

There are many reported instances of students using inappropriate procedural approaches to solving word problems. Often these approaches rely on key words to indicate what is needed, but children will also make decisions on the basis of less obvious 'clues'. Consider the monkeys problem: 'The monkeys at the zoo ate 45 bananas in the morning and 37 bananas in the afternoon. How many banana skins were left on the floor of their enclosure?' When this was presented to two classes of Year 4 students, just under 35% (17 students) subtracted to find the answer. When asked to explain their reasoning, 12 students said that they subtracted because the word 'left' was included in the question. Of those remaining, three indicated that they subtracted because something had been eaten, and two indicated that they subtracted because the larger number appeared first (Siemon, 1993). By contrast, many of the students who added were able to explain their reasoning by paraphrasing the problem in their own words, for example, 'the banana skins would pile up on the ground'. This illustrates the importance of being able to connect the meaning of operations to the context rather than rely on procedural clues.

handy hint

Act it out

To help students understand what is involved in a word problem, it is useful to explore how it might be acted out.

Another example is provided by Julia, a Year 4 student, who saw herself as 'doing as well as most' in mathematics. While she excelled in most areas of the curriculum and her performance on class tests of mathematics was generally average to above average, she viewed mathematics as a painful (but necessary) interruption to the things she liked doing.

> I don't like it anyway, because it disturbs what you are doing … you're just sitting down and you've just got into something and you have to have maths … it interrupts, it always happens when you are doing something good.

Julia demonstrated a remarkable capacity for retaining very detailed knowledge about what 'Mr H did' in class, which she used purposefully to solve whatever problems were presented immediately after the teaching session. Her behaviour seemed to be based on the belief that mathematics was about 'doing something with numbers to get an answer', that problems presented on the same day were of the same type, and that to be good at mathematics amounted to remembering and reproducing exactly what the teacher did. These beliefs had served Julia reasonably well as she knew her number facts by heart, could follow procedures accurately to solve algorithms, and most word problems conformed to what she expected. That is, they contained no redundant or missing information and could be solved by applying the operation being considered in class at the time.

Consider this more complicated problem (Siemon, 1993): 'Each 7 metre length of fencing timber costs $9 and each fence post costs $6. How much would it cost to fence a rectangular paddock using 12 lengths of timber?'

Interviewer:	Can you tell me how you solved that problem?
Julia:	It's 84 ... Twelve sevens.
Interviewer:	Why did you do that?
Julia:	Because ... it's seven metres ... (mmm) ... and then you've got twelve lengths of timber.
Interviewer:	Then what would the eighty-four tell you?
Julia:	Well, it's ... that it's eighty-four dollars.
Interviewer:	Dollars? ... can you tell me again why you chose 7 and 12?
Julia:	Because they were the first and last numbers ...

Julia's apparent disregard for meaning and her reliance on unrelated cues are more likely to be a reflection of her prior experiences and beliefs and the prevailing classroom norms rather than her capacity to learn mathematics, but we cannot be sure. What this example points to is the critical importance of conceptual understanding to a sense of number. Automatic recall of basic number facts and being able to perform algorithms is helpful, but it is not necessary or sufficient for a well-developed sense of number. A positive *disposition towards making sense of numbers* is needed for students to engage meaningfully and purposefully with school mathematics.

think + link

The meanings for addition and subtraction and for multiplication and division will be discussed and illustrated in Chapters 16 and 17 respectively.

This example also illustrates the importance of being able to record one's thinking in a way that exposes it to examination and is meaningful to others.

Flexible mental strategies

As part of a professional learning experience, primary and secondary teachers of mathematics were asked to mentally calculate 48 sixes then describe the strategy they used in writing. In the report-back session that followed, the strategies were re-presented in symbolic form on the whiteboard. A sample of these is shown in Table 10.1.

Once this exercise was completed, we went back over the recorded strategies and annotated them according to the principle and/or properties used. For example, 'renaming', 'place value', and 'distributivity' were used to annotate the first strategy. Other labels included, 'associativity', 'commutativity', 'doubling', 'rounding'. What this example illustrates is the importance of procedural fluency, flexibility, and a knowledge of the relationships between numbers to a well-developed sense of number.

for the classroom

Ask students to mentally calculate something that is within their grasp (e.g. at Year 2 or 3 this might be to add 27 and 36, at Year 5 or 6 it might be to calculate 48 sixes). Then ask them to describe their solution strategies, taking care to record what was done in symbolic form. An example of what this might look like is given in Table 10.1.

Table 10.1 Recording mental strategies to highlight important mathematics

Mental strategy used to calculate 48 sixes	As recorded on the whiteboard
I multiplied 40 by 6 then added 6 eights.	$48 \times 6 = (40 + 8) \times 6$ $= (40 \times 6) + (8 \times 6)$ $= 240 + 48$ $= 288$
I did it a different way. 48 is 24 by 2, so it's 24 by 12, but 24 is 2 twelves, so that makes it 2 by 144, 288.	$48 \times 6 = 24 \times 2 \times 6$ $= 24 \times 12$ $= 2 \times 12 \times 12$ $= 2 \times 144$ $= 288$
I turned it around to 6 forty-eights, 2 forty-eights are 96, so I doubled that, 192, then added another 96 by adding 100 and taking away 4.	$48 \times 6 = 6 \times 48$ $= 96 \times 2 + 96$ $= 192 + 100 - 4$ $= 292 - 4$ $= 288$
I did something like that but I rounded 48 to 50 and said 6 fifties are 300 and then I took away 12.	$48 \times 6 = 6 \times 48$ $= 6 \times (50 - 2)$ $= (6 \times 50) - (6 \times 2)$ $= 300 - 12$ $= 288$

did you know?

Enrico Fermi (1901–1954) was an Italian physicist who acquired a reputation for 'solving' what seemed to be impossible problems in his head, such as, 'How many piano tuners are there in New York?' Fermi came up with what turned out to be a reasonable approximation of the actual number by means of a process we refer to as *mathematical modelling*. That is, he made some reasonable assumptions based on an assessment of the number of pianos in his immediate vicinity, how often they might need tuning, how long it took a piano tuner to tune a piano, and so on, then scaled up his findings to make a prediction. Problems of this type are referred to as Fermi problems. They are easy to imagine and well worth exploring as an example of what it means to have and use a sense of number.

integrating technology/ICT

Critical numeracy

The internet offers a vast array of easily accessible information with little or no guarantee as to its accuracy or reliability. Ensuring students develop a critical mindset in dealing with this data is an important function of schooling, and one that mathematics can and should contribute to explicitly. Quality websites such as the Australian Bureau of Statistics (www.abs.gov.au/) or the UNICEF site which reports on the State of the World's Children (www.unicef.org/sowc06/) can be used to initiate discussions about reliability, investigate particular issues such as the proportion of children attending school in different countries, or to prepare a case for changing a particular policy or practice.

Developing a sense of number

> Number sense can be described as good intuition about numbers and their relationships. It develops gradually as a result of exploring numbers, visualising them in a variety of contexts and relating them in ways that are not limited by traditional algorithms … No substitute exists for a skilful teacher and an environment that fosters curiosity and exploration at all grade levels. (Howden, 1989, p. 11)

A well-developed sense of number requires a deep and flexible understanding of numeration, that is, a knowledge of different number sets and how they are written, represented, and related, together with an understanding of the ways in which the operations on number might be represented in different contexts. For example, addition is often understood as aggregation (getting more), and subtraction as disaggregation (losing some or all). While this applies to addition and subtraction involving positive integers, it does not generalise to all number sets. For instance, if you are $350 in debt, depositing $100 will result in less debt but no more money (i.e. –350 + 100 = –250). There are also situations where collections can be combined but interpreted in different ways. For instance, in Figure 10.2, combining collections A and B could be interpreted as 3 counters and 4 counters is 7 counters (aggregation), or we could consider the proportion of counters that are yellow prior to combining the two collections, one-third in the case of collection A and three-quarters in the case of collection B. When the two collections are combined, four-sevenths are yellow. In this case, it makes sense to 'add' the denominators and numerators ($\frac{1}{3} + \frac{3}{4} = \frac{4}{7}$) but the 'total' ($\frac{4}{7}$) is considerably less than one of the parts ($\frac{3}{4}$).

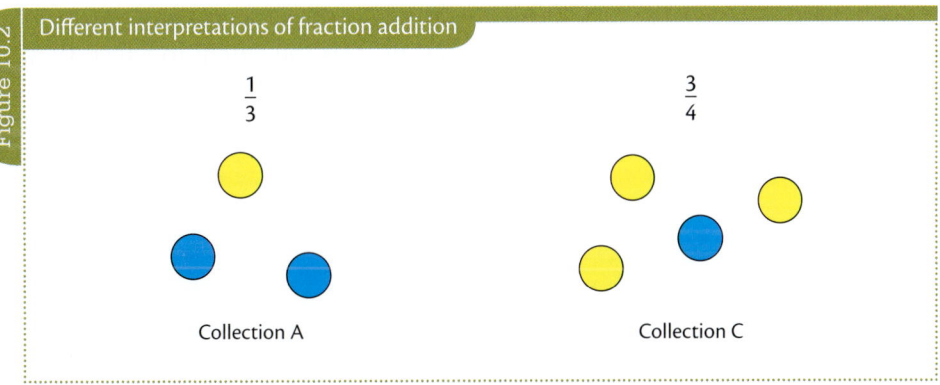

Figure 10.2 Different interpretations of fraction addition

Scaffolding student learning is the primary task of teachers of mathematics. This is particularly important in relation to a relatively small number of big ideas and strategies in Number, without which students' progress in mathematics will suffer (Siemon, 2006). These big ideas are crucial to a well-developed sense of numeracy, and are elaborated in subsequent chapters.

Trusting the count

The term **trusting the count** was originally proposed by Willis (2002) to refer to the fact that children may not believe that if they counted the same collection again they would arrive at the same amount. I have appropriated this term to incorporate not only this initial and literal interpretation but also to refer to a child's capacity to access flexible **mental objects** for the numbers 0 to 10.

think + link

The notion of mental objects for the numbers to 10 is elaborated in Chapter 14.

Many students are able to recite the number naming sequence to 20 and beyond, recognise, read, and write number words and numerals to 10, and count and model small collections (less than 20), but will guess when asked 'how many' in a particular collection or which of two single-digit numbers presented orally or in written form is the larger/smaller. A considerable number will also experience difficulty in counting larger collections (40 or more) accurately. This could be because of or associated with a:

- failure to understand that counting is a strategy to determine 'how many' and/or that the last number counted says how many
- mismatch between the oral words and the objects counted (e.g. matches objects to syllables, omits certain number names)
- failure to organise the count to avoid counting objects already counted
- superficial understanding of numbers 0 to 10 (i.e. limited to simple counts and recognising, reading and writing number names and numerals).

By the end of their first year in school, children need a deep understanding of the numbers to 10, in terms of both what they represent and how they might be reconfigured or viewed in relation to other numbers. In particular, they need to have developed flexible mental objects for each of the numbers going beyond the recognition of number names and numerals to include rich *part–part–whole knowledge* based on visual imagery. This supports trusting the count in the sense that when students read, write, or hear 'seven', they can imagine what that collection might look like and how it relates to other numbers. For example, they can see a 7 in their mind's eye as 1 more than 6, as 1 less than 8, as 3 and 4, or as 5 and 2. This is not about addition or subtraction. It is about deeply understanding what each number means and the various ways in which 7 might be represented. A key indicator of the extent to which students have developed mental objects for the numbers 0 to 10 is the extent to which they can recognise collections of these numbers without counting, that is, they can **subitise**.

think + link

The role of subitisation in building part–part–whole knowledge will be considered further in Chapter 14.

issues in teaching

The role of counting

A well-known task requires young children to say how many counters there are altogether when five are shown and four more are hidden (Steffe, von Glasersfeld, Richards & Cobb, 1983). This task continues to be used in some form to examine children's counting strategies (e.g. Early Numeracy Interview and Count Me in Too). However, the original task was devised before educators in the English-speaking world were aware of research in other parts of the world (e.g. Hatano, 1982) on how children's perception-based capacity to enumerate small collections without counting (subitising) was being recognised and used to build a sense of number.

With the translation of key mathematics education research papers from the Soviet Union during the 1970s (e.g. Kilpatrick & Wirszup, 1975), further research (e.g. Clements & Sarama, 2007; Labinowicz, 1985), and increased use of subitising activities in schools (e.g. Bobis, 2008), it has become apparent that children's capacity to identify 9 as the total number of counters may be a consequence of their part–part–whole knowledge of 9 rather than their use of a particular counting strategy.

Evidence for this comes from responses that are immediate; when asked to explain children will say 'I just know' or 'it's 9 because 9 is 4 and 5' or 'it has to be 9 because if you said 5 there and 5 under, it would have been 10'. Part–part–whole knowledge is a particular form of additive partitioning. It refers to a knowledge of each whole number to 10, not only in terms of its parts (part–part) but also as it relates to those numbers of which it is a part (part–whole). For example, 9 is 1 less than 10 or half of 18. For other numbers such as 6, this can include the knowledge that 6 is 1 less than 7, 2 less than 8, 3 less than 9, 4 less than 10, or half of 12.

Place value

Many students are able to identify place-value parts (e.g. they can say that there are 4 hundreds 6 tens and 8 ones in 468) and count orally to 100 and beyond, but still think about or imagine two- and/or three-digit numbers in terms of ones (i.e. 468 is actually understood as a collection 468 objects). This could be because of or associated with:

- inadequate part–part–whole knowledge for the numbers 0 to 10 and/or an inability to trust the count
- an inability to recognise 2, 5, and 10 as composite or countable units (often indicated by an inability to count large collections efficiently by 2s, 5s, or 10s)
- little or no sense of numbers beyond 10 (e.g. 14 is 10 and 4 more)
- a failure to recognise the structural basis for recording two-digit numbers (e.g. sees and reads 64 as 'sixty-four', but thinks of this as 60 and 4 without recognising the significance of the 6 as a count of tens); this is exacerbated by the use of extended notation such as 468 = 400 + 60 + 8, which effectively represents each component in terms of ones).

By the end of their third year in school (generally Year 2), students need a deep understanding of the place-value pattern, '10 of these is 1 of those', to support efficient ways of working with two-digit numbers and beyond.

Place value is difficult to teach and learn, as it is often masked by successful performance on superficial tasks such as counting by ones on a 0–99 or 1–100 number chart. The structure of the base 10 number system is essentially multiplicative, as it involves counts of different sized groups that are powers of 10. Unfortunately, place value is often introduced before students have demonstrated an understanding that the numbers 2 to 10 can be used as countable units. As a consequence, many students develop misconceptions that serve to undermine their capacity to develop meaningful, efficient strategies for mental and written computation and their later understanding of larger whole numbers and decimal fractions. These ideas are considered further in Part 5.

A key indicator of the extent to which students have developed a sound basis for place value is the extent to which they can count large collections efficiently and make, name, record, compare, order, sequence, count forwards and backwards in place-value units confidently, and rename two- and three-digit numbers in terms of their parts.

think + link

The prerequisites and key steps involved in developing a deep understanding of place value will be discussed in Chapter 15.

making connections

Comparing, ordering, and renaming measures provide a valuable context to review numeration. For example, a length of 280 centimetres can be given in metres by renaming 280 in terms of hundreds and ones (2 hundreds and 80 ones), using a number expander if necessary (see Chapter 15). This can then be written as 2 metres and 80 centimetres or 2.8 metres, depending on the Year level concerned.

The relationships between different metric units also reinforces the notion of units based on 10, in particular '10 of these is 1 of those' (10 millimetres is 1 centimetre), '100 of these is 1 of those' (100 centimetres is 1 metre) and '1000 of these is 1 of those' (1000 metres is 1 kilometre).

Additive thinking is not regarded as a big idea in its own right as it builds upon the two ideas of trusting the count and place value. It is evident when children work with numbers as mental objects and rename numbers as necessary to facilitate calculations. For example, asked to calculate 36 and 27, an accomplished additive thinker might draw on her knowledge of place value to recognise this sum as 5 tens and 13 ones and therefore 63. Alternatively, she might add 2 tens to 36 to get 56 then, recognising 7 as 4 and 3, add 4 to 60 then 3 more to arrive at 63.

Multiplicative thinking

Most students come to school with the conceptual underpinnings to support addition and subtraction but this is not the case for multiplication, although sharing and elementary forms of grouping are used intuitively to support the child's interaction with their environment. By the end of primary school most students have some knowledge of the multiplication facts to 100 and can perform simple multiplication and division procedures correctly. However, many rely on rote learning and/or a naive, 'groups of', understanding for multiplication based on repeated addition (often counting equal groups by ones). With little or no access to a broader range of ideas for multiplication they find it difficult to develop efficient mental strategies, and as a consequence tend to rely on memorised procedures for multiplying and dividing larger whole numbers and decimals. This could be because of or associated with:

- an inability to trust the count and see numbers as countable units in their own right, that is, view 6 items as 1 six ('a six') rather than 6 ones
- poorly developed or non-existent mental strategies for addition and subtraction
- an over-reliance on physical models to solve simple multiplication problems
- little or no exposure to alternative models of multiplication.

consider and discuss

Meanings for fraction division

Many students in the middle years of schooling have difficulty making sense of fraction division. This is often a result of their over-reliance on the 'groups of' idea for multiplication. One way to assess this is to ask students to write and solve meaningful word problems for expressions such as the following:

$$\frac{3}{4} \div \frac{3}{5} \qquad \frac{7}{8} \div \frac{11}{3} \qquad \frac{22}{5} \div \frac{1}{9}$$

Try this for yourself and discuss how you might estimate, then calculate, a solution without appealing to a rule.

By the end of Year 4 students need to be able to think about multiplication in a number of different ways so they can recognise when multiplication is required and how it relates to division, to support efficient mental and written computation, and to solve a wider range of problems involving equal groups, simple proportion, combinations, and rate. To do this they need to recognise the numbers 2 to 10 as countable units and count large collections efficiently. In particular they need to appreciate the advantages of representing multiplicative situations in terms of arrays and regions on the basis that these representations:

- represent all aspects of the multiplicative situation more neutrally, that is, the number of groups, the equal number in each group, and the product (last two not as evident in groups of models)
- can be used to relate the two ideas for division—partition (or sharing) and quotition (or how many groups in)—to multiplication
- support commutativity (e.g. 3 fours can be rotated to show that it is the same as 4 threes), so halving the amount of learning required for the multiplication facts
- support more efficient, generalisable mental strategies for multiplication
- provide a basis for moving from a count of equal groups (e.g. 1 six, 2 sixes, 3 sixes, 4 sixes, and so on) to a constant number of groups (e.g. 6 ones, 6 twos, 6 threes, 6 fours, 6 fives, and so on), which supports more efficient mental strategies (e.g. 6 groups of anything is double 3 groups, or is 5 groups and 1 more group).

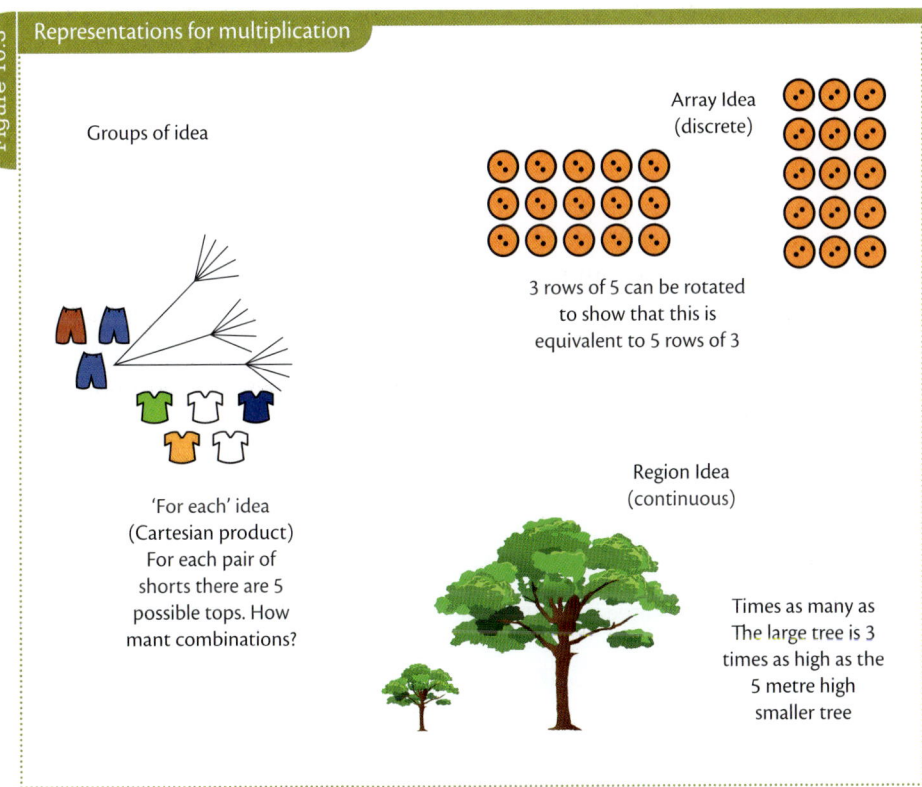

Figure 10.3 Representations for multiplication

More importantly, arrays and regions support the shift from an additive, 'groups of' model to a 'factor–factor–product' model. This is needed to support fraction representation, the multiplication and division of larger whole numbers, fractions and decimals, and algebra. An awareness of the 'for each' idea or Cartesian product is also needed at this level of schooling to support work in statistics and probability (e.g. problems involving data or the likelihood of particular events), measurement (problems involving measures and/or rates), and further work in proportional reasoning. This idea, together with the region idea, is needed to make sense of fraction diagrams. For example, a diagram showing thirds that is subsequently halved and halved again to show twelfths (see Figure 10.4) can only be understood if students are able to interpret the initial diagram as one whole divided into three equal parts that, when halved

Figure 10.4 Interpreting fraction diagrams: 'for each' idea

By halving and halving and halving again (a 2-split), each third has been partitioned into 4 smaller parts.

For each third there are 3 parts so 12 parts altogether.

3 parts by 4 parts (region idea) give 12 parts.

and halved again, generates four smaller parts 'for each' third (hence 3 × 4 parts or thirds by quarters are twelfths). This understanding is not supported by the 'groups of' idea for multiplication or division.

A key indicator of the extent to which students have developed a broad range of ideas to support **multiplicative thinking** is the extent to which they manipulate both the size of the group and the number of groups to meet specific needs (e.g. instead of committing 6 eights to memory in a meaningless or rote way, recognise that this can be thought of as 5 eights and 1 more eight, or 3 eights doubled).

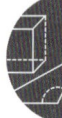

for the classroom

Invite different groups of students to work on one of the following Fermi problems, then present their results and strategies to the rest of the class.

- How many pallets of bottled water (500 mL) were consumed by firefighters in the fires of 2009?
- How much water is lost by uncovered swimming pools in Adelaide on Boxing Day?
- How many deer are there in the Dandenong Ranges?
- How much money is spent by 15-year-olds per week?
- How many people will go without a meal tonight?

Partitioning

The idea that a collection or a quantity can be expressed in terms of its parts is fundamental to developing a strong sense of number. However, a sizeable proportion of students in Years 5 to 9 experience difficulty with fractions, decimals, and percentages (e.g. Lamon, 1999; Siemon et al., 2001; Siemon, Breed, Dole, Izard & Virgona, 2006). A major contributing factor is that many students misinterpret the meaning of the denominator. Also, while students may exhibit an intuitive understanding of proportionality in terms of the 'out of' idea, this is limited to familiar contexts and proper fractions (e.g. three-quarters of a pizza or the fraction of Smarties that are red in a packet of Smarties). Few students at this level see fractions as numbers that can be arrived at by partitive division (e.g. three pizzas shared among four) and that 'live' uniquely on the number line as measures. This could be because of or associated with:

- viewing the denominator in the same way as the numerator (i.e. as a count or 'how many' number, rather than an indication of 'how much')
- a limited exposure to practical experiences that show what happens as the number of parts is increased and how fractional parts are named
- only a 'groups of' idea for multiplication and division
- little or no access to strategies that support the construction of appropriate fraction representations.

> ### communicating mathematically
>
> #### Fraction diagrams
>
> One of the most misunderstood forms of mathematical representation is fraction diagrams. For example, while most would interpret the following diagram as three-fifths, it is possible to interpret this in a number of other ways, such as one and a half, one, one and two-thirds, and two-thirds of three-fifths. It all depends on what we choose to see as the unit.
>
>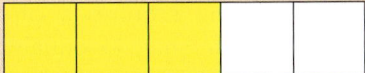
>
> In my view, shading in parts of someone else's diagram is next to useless, as it requires little more than a capacity to count (usually to less than 10) and to colour between the lines. Such activities are highly unlikely to support the construction of robust, generalisable models of fractions and decimals. Students need to be able to construct their own rational number representations based on an understanding of unit parts and **partitioning**.

By the end of primary school and the beginning of secondary school, students need to be able to work meaningfully with a wider range of numbers. In particular, they need to have established a meaningful basis for thinking about rational numbers in whatever form they appear (e.g. proper fractions, mixed fractions, decimal fractions, and percentages). This requires the recognition that:

- equal parts are required
- the number of parts is related to the name of the part (i.e. fifths for 5 parts, sixteenths for 16 parts)
- as the number of parts increases, each part becomes smaller
- fraction representations are created by partitioning discrete or continuous quantities into equal parts.

Understanding the relationship between fractions and partitive division is essential for fraction renaming (equivalent fractions) and, as referred to above, students need to recognise how the 'region idea' for multiplication is related to fraction diagrams.

A key indicator of the extent to which students have developed an understanding of fractions and decimals is the extent to which they can construct their own fraction models and diagrams, and name, record, compare, order, sequence, and rename common and decimal fractions, moving fluidly between representations appropriate to context.

> **consider and discuss**
>
> 1 What is the difference between one hundred and one thousandth and one hundred and one thousandths?
> 2 Can you find at least three different ways in which this question might be interpreted?
> 3 Some languages do not have a phoneme for 'th'. What problems might students from these language backgrounds having in learning the English names for decimal fractions?

Proportional reasoning

One of the reasons many junior secondary students experience difficulty interpreting and using ratios, rates and percentages is that they have not yet acquired a capacity for **proportional reasoning**. This is a complex form of reasoning that depends on many interconnected ideas and strategies that develop over a long period of time. Lamon (1999) described proportional reasoning as 'the ability to recognise, to explain, to think about, to make conjectures about, to graph, to transform, to compare, to make judgements about, to represent, or to symbolize relationships of two simple types … direct … and inverse proportion' (p. 8).

At its core, proportional reasoning requires a capacity to identify and describe what is being compared with what. Essentially, there are two types of proportional reasoning problems, both of which require some form of comparison. The first typically involves a comparison of two rates, for example, which car had a faster average speed, Car A, which travelled 217 km in $1\frac{3}{4}$ hours, or Car B, which travelled 204 km in $1\frac{1}{2}$ hours? The second type is referred to as missing-value problems. These problems typically provide three quantities with a fourth quantity missing, for example if a supermarket worker can unpack 24 boxes in 1 hour, how many boxes could she unpack in 10 minutes?

Recognising what is being compared with what is not always straightforward. It can be confounded by the types of quantities used, how they are represented, and the number of variables involved. Also, not all problems in which three quantities are given and a fourth is missing require proportional reasoning. As Lamon (1999) notes, there are 'no shortcuts available here! Thought, common sense, and experience must be used to determine whether a situation is proportional or not. You must always bring into play your knowledge about how things work in the real world' (p. 225).

> **for the classroom**
>
> Using the feral cat problem below, explore the issue of determining what to compare with what in problems involving proportional reasoning.
>
> Trap reports and sightings suggested that there were 35 feral cats in the Rocky Ranges National Park (146 hectares) and 27 in the Gorges National Park (103 hectares). Which park had the worse feral cat problem?

Proportional reasoning also requires a capacity to work flexibly and confidently with the quantities involved (i.e. measures, rates, and/or ratios expressed in terms of natural numbers, rational numbers, and/or integers), and an ability to recognise multiplicative relationships in a range of problem contexts, including the idea of rational numbers as operators (e.g. understanding

$\frac{2}{3} \times \$24$ as $\frac{2}{3}$ of 24, or 3.5×68 as three and a half times 68). Neither of these abilities can be assumed to be in place for all students in the middle years of schooling (e.g. Siemon et al., 2006).

Generalising

While considerably more is expected of students in Years 9 and 10 in relation to their understanding and use of number than is expected at earlier levels, most students are able to work with rational numbers to some extent and have an emerging appreciation of the real numbers. However, this is not necessarily the case when these numbers are represented by pronumerals or used in expressions containing pronumerals. For many, the very power and density of algebraic text can be the feature that renders it impenetrable.

An extensive body of research has examined the difficulties students experience with algebraic text (e.g. Booth, 1988; Carraher & Schliemann, 2007; Filloy & Sutherland, 1996; Warren, 2003). These range from misunderstanding the equals sign, assigning literal meanings to letters (e.g. $3a$ interpreted as 3 apples), to viewing expressions as instructions to operate, rather than as objects that can be operated on in their own right (e.g. that $4x - 7$ is an object that can be multiplied by any other number or pronumeral). Some students may also have problems with the fact that the multiplication sign is omitted (e.g. $a \times b$ is written as ab), and division is invariably written as a fraction (e.g. $(a + b)$ divided by c is written as $\frac{(a + b)}{c}$).

consider and discuss

Algebra

Algebra has been described as **generalised** arithmetic. It is used to capture important number properties that are true regardless of the number chosen, for example $a + b = b + a$ or $a(b - c) = ab - ac$ are true for all real values of a, b, and c. It is used to represent a missing value in equations (e.g. $x + 7 = 16 - 2x$). But algebra can also be used to represent variables in general relationships, such as the GST component of any purchase price (GST = purchase price ÷ 11) or the cost of car hire (e.g. daily charge = base hire charge + an amount per km over 200 km + insurance).

A class of Year 5 and 6 students were asked to describe how they counted the number of matchsticks needed to make the arrangement shown in Figure 10.5. They came up with four different strategies: $11 \times 2 + 9$, $4 \times 10 - 9$, $10 \times 3 + 1$, and $4 + 9 \times 3$.

Explain how each strategy relates to the count and how you might use each strategy to determine the number of matches needed to make 23 squares in a row. Write each strategy as a generalised rule using n for the number of squares.

Matchstick problem

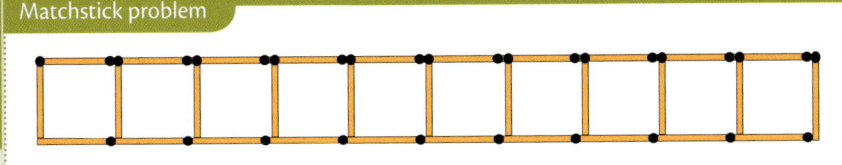

Figure 10.5

Brainstorm some similar activities and discuss how you would use these to develop students' capacity to recognise and record patterns and relationships.

Constructing algebraic text to describe relationships is another area of difficulty for many students. A range of external representations (e.g. balances, concrete materials, graphs, diagrams, and tables of values) are typically used to explore patterns and relationships in school mathematics. Referred to as intermediate sign systems by Filloy and Sutherland (1996), they variously serve to facilitate the construction of meaning for the conventional mathematical sign system, in this case, the 'algebra code' (p. 143). One of the difficulties here is that different conceptions arise from different representations, and these may inhibit students' capacity to make connections between representations, to generalise, or to recognise when a representation learnt earlier is inappropriate. For example, while it is meaningful to interpret $5 \times \square = 20$ as 'find the number that 5 must be multiplied by to equal 20', this interpretation (or intermediate sign system) cannot usefully replace x in the equation $5x + 9 = 3x$. Nor is it appropriate to expect that strategies such as 'back-tracking' that work for the first equation will work with equations like the second, where the unknown appears on both sides.

The difficulties experienced in making the transition from arithmetic to algebra may be caused by or associated with:

- naive understanding of the equals sign in terms of 'makes' or the 'answer is'
- different interpretations of letters (Booth, 1988) and/or a lack of knowledge about the conventions used to record generalised expressions (e.g. that multiplication is recorded as $3a$ not $a3$ or $3 \times a$)
- limited understanding of the properties of numbers and operations (e.g. multiplication only understood in terms of groups of; division not seen as the inverse of multiplication)
- an inadequate understanding of arithmetic and/or an over-reliance on procedural solution strategies aimed at getting numerical answers
- little or no experience in communicating mathematical relationships in words and/or translating relationships described in words into symbolic expressions, for example, 's is 8 more than t' or 'the Niger is three times as long as the Rhine' (MacGregor, 1991, pp. 95–97)
- limited access to multiplicative thinking and proportional reasoning more generally, which restricts students' capacity to recognise and describe relationships in terms of factors.

By the end of Year 10 students are expected to be able to work meaningfully with a wide range of numbers and mathematical relationships in whatever form they appear, including equations, identities, inequalities, functions, and relations. A key indicator of the extent to which students are ready to engage with these curriculum expectations is their capacity to deal with equivalent forms of expressions, recognise and describe number properties and patterns, and work with the complexities of algebraic text.

Conclusion

In this chapter we have described what is meant by number sense and illustrated what this looks like in practice. In particular, we have emphasised the critical importance of a deep understanding of numbers and operations which can be used confidently and flexibly in multiple contexts. Number sense is a way of thinking rather than a particular body of knowledge. It develops over time as a result of challenging experiences and a focus on the 'big ideas'.

key terms

Absolute magnitude (numbers): cardinality of a set (e.g. 5 eggs, 23 people)

Additive thinking: capacity to work with the ideas of aggregation and disaggregation with a range of number sets

Composing and decomposing numbers: numbers can be constructed in many different ways using a combination of operations, or numbers can be broken down into their constituent parts in many different ways

Generalising: capacity to devise general statements, symbolic expressions from patterns, form conclusions

Mental object: images, words, and metaphors to describe or represent a particular experientially-based phenomena (e.g. yellowness, square)

Multiplicative thinking: capacity to work with an extended range of concepts, meanings, and representations for multiplication and division in a variety of contexts

Partitioning: physically separating or renaming a collection in terms of its parts; this can be additive (as in 8 is 5 and 3, or 2 and 1 and 5), or multiplicative, where parts are equal (as in 8 is double 4 or 2 fours)

Place value: system of assigning values to digits based on their position (e.g. in a base 10 system of numeration, positions represent successive powers of 10)

Proportional reasoning: capacity to recognise and work with relationships between relationships

Relative magnitude (numbers): measure (e.g. 8 centimetres versus 8 metres, 150 in 3000 compared to 150 in 300 chances)

Subitise: recognise the numerosity of a small collection without counting

Trusting the count: access mental objects for numbers to 10 without having to make, model, or record the number

Review questions

1. List and illustrate the key characteristics of a well-developed sense of number.
2. Describe a recent situation or experience where you used or needed a sense of number. What knowledge, skills and/or strategies were involved? When and where did you learn to do this?
3. At the outset of this chapter we said that procedural fluency was a necessary but not sufficient requirement for number sense. Do you agree? If so, why?
4. Work through the problems presented in the chapter, share your strategies with a friend, and discuss what you needed to know and be able to do to make sense of the situation and answer the problem.
5. Devise some Fermi problems of your own that connect to other aspects of the curriculum at different levels of schooling (e.g. health, geography, or science)

Key references

Australian Association of Mathematics Teachers, (AAMT) (1997). *Numeracy = Everyone's Business*. Report of the Numeracy Education Strategy Development Conference. Adelaide: AAMT/DETYA.

Bobis, J. (2008). Early spatial thinking and the development of number sense. *Australian Primary Mathematics Classroom*, 13(3), 4–9.

Clements, D. & Sarama, J. (2007). Early childhood mathematics learning. In F. Lester (Ed.), *Second Handbook of Research on Mathematics Teaching and Learning* (pp. 461–556). Charlotte, NC: Information Age Publishing, NCTM.

Dehaene, S. (1997). *The Number Sense: How the Mind Creates Mathematics*. New York: Oxford University Press.

Dole, S., & McIntosh, A. (2004). *Mental Computation: A Strategies Approach*. Hobart: Department of Education Tasmania.

Howden, H. (1989). Teaching number sense. *Arithmetic Teacher*, 36(6), 12–16.

Lamon, S. (1999). *Teaching Fractions and Ratios for Understanding: Essential Content Knowledge and Instructional Strategies for Teachers*. Mahwah, NJ: Erlbaum.

MacGregor, M. (1991). *Making Sense of Algebra: Cognitive Processes Influencing Comprehension*. Geelong, Vic: Deakin University Press.

McIntosh, A., Reys, B., & Reys, J. (1992). A proposed framework for examining basic number sense. *For the Learning of Mathematics*, 12(3), 2–8.

Siemon, D. (1993). The role of metacognition in children's mathematical problem solving: An exploratory study. Unpublished PhD thesis, Monash University.

Siemon, D. (2006). Assessment for common misunderstandings. Materials prepared for and published electronically by the Victorian Department of Education and Early Childhood Development. Available from www.education.vic.gov.au/studentlearning/teachingresources/maths/common/default.htm.

Swan, M. (1990). Becoming numerate: developing conceptual structures. In S. Willis (Ed.), *Being Numerate: What Counts?* Melbourne: ACER.

Warren, E. (2003). The role of arithmetical structure in the transition from arithmetic to algebra. *Mathematics Education Research Journal of Australasia*, 15(2), 122–137.

Willis, S. (2002). Crossing borders: learning to count. *The Australian Education Researcher*, 29(2), 115–129.

Websites

www.eduweb.vic.gov.au/edulibrary/public/teachlearn/student/snmy.ppt

www.education.vic.gov.au/studentlearning/teachingresources/maths/common/default.htm

www.eduweb.vic.gov.au/edulibrary/public/curricman/middleyear/MYNumeracyResearchFullReport.pdf

www.simerr.educ.utas.edu.au/numeracy/critical_numeracy/critical_numeracy.htm

www.thenetwork.sa.edu.au/teachingandlearning

A Sense of Measurement and Geometry

11

Contents

Linking measurement and geometry	211
What is measurement?	212
Developing measurement sense	214
Geometry	221
Spatial sense	223
Conclusion	228

Chapter objectives

This chapter will enable the reader to:
- Understand the scope of two major areas of mathematics: measurement and geometry
- Appreciate how we develop a sense of measurement and geometry
- Explore the conceptual foundations associated with the process of measurement
- Appreciate how the use of standard and non-standard units, and estimation, are key to developing measurement sense
- Understand the nature of geometry and aspects of geometrical thinking
- Be aware of current models for understanding how geometry is learnt.

The importance of understanding measurement

A colleague was teaching an introductory mathematics course in adult education. A recent school leaver was in the class. When she was asked what she had done on the weekend, the student replied that she had been to Melbourne. Our colleague asked her how far away that was in terms of distance. While the student did not really know how far, she was confident that it was closer by car than by walking. Thinking that the student was referring to time, not distance, the teacher took the chance to discuss with the class the student's understandings, but the student remained convinced that Melbourne was physically closer if you went by car. With this in mind, our colleague set about planning some activities to explore this concept further in the following week. But at the beginning of the next lesson, the student arrived with a newspaper article about the opening of a new section of freeway with a headline that was something like 'Car travel—Melbourne now closer that ever before'!

- What measurement concepts did the student have difficulty in grasping?
- What was the meaning of the headline used for the article?
- How might you have responded when the student produced the newspaper headline?

Big ideas

- Measurement and geometry are important areas of mathematics.
- The process of measurement involves comparing an attribute of an object with a unit of measurement that has the same attribute.
- Units of measurement enable us to measure and compare quantities that are separated by time or space and to give a numerical value to such quantities. Making meaningful measurements, and estimating measurements, both depend upon a personal fluency with the unit of measurement being used.
- In order to develop a sense of measurement, it is necessary to understand the relationship between the attribute that is being measured and the unit of measurement, and the properties of units of measurement.
- Measuring skills are essential to successful numerate behaviour in managing day-to-day situations.
- Geometry is a major area of mathematics and new topics continue to be explored. How students develop geometrical understanding is not fully understood and is still an area of research.
- Spatial sense includes two main abilities: spatial orientation, and visualisation and imagery. It is an important aspect of numeracy.
- Geometric reasoning and mathematical visualisation are fundamental to spatial sense. Mathematical visualisation is a process of thinking leading to understanding. It is based on uses of images and is used in all areas of mathematics, including geometry.
- We can all develop our spatial and geometric reasoning ability.

Linking measurement and geometry

In common with some other curricula from around the world, such as in New Zealand, the *Australian Curriculum: Mathematics* (ACARA, 2010) combines the areas of measurement and geometry. Other curriculum organisations are possible; for example Singapore includes measurement in mathematical skills, and places geometry with mathematical concepts. Measurement and geometry are important aspects of mathematics that have strong links with each other, but they also link with other areas of mathematics. For example, measurement involves estimation and use of number; geometry links with patterns and algebra.

In this chapter, we consider the areas of measurement and geometry, in particular how learners come to develop proficiency in these areas. In later chapters we look in greater depth at teaching these areas of mathematics to students in schools.

making connections

An understanding of measuring and measuring systems is essential in many aspects of everyday life. For instance, a sound grasp of lengths and weights is needed to interpret the following Australia Post chart of postage charges. This not only requires a knowledge of the measures themselves (millimetres, grams), but also an understanding of the relationships that need to exist between them.

Envelope size (mm)	Maximum Weight (g)	Maximum Thickness (mm)	Charge per article	Charge per pack of 10 Single pack	Charge per pack of 10 5+ packs
DL (110 × 220)	250	5	65c	$6.34	$6.18
C6 (114 × 162)	250	5	65c	$6.34	$6.18
C5 (162 × 229)	500	20	$1.30	$12.68	$12.35
C4 (324 × 229)	500	20	$2.50	$24.38	$23.75
B4 (353 × 250)	500	20	$2.90	$28.28	$27.55

Find an envelope of one of the sizes and investigate possible postage charges.

What is measurement?

communicating mathematically

What does it mean to measure?

Some Year 5 students were asked to explain what measurement meant to them. Here is how they responded:

Sam: Measurement is seeing how many things can fill up a box exactly.
Max: Measuring is what you do when you want to decide if something will fit in, or not.
Lelia: You need to measure when you want to know if someone is taller than you.
Alex: You can measure things in lots of different ways with lots of different things. You will need a ruler if you are going to measure how long something is.

All four students understand measurement as something that they 'do' to find the size of an object. Lelia is focusing on comparing two objects, and Sam wants to count how many things will fill his box exactly. Max is probably thinking about a time that he needed to know whether there was enough room for an object, and Alex thinks about measurement more generally, but then gives us an example: that measuring length requires the use of a ruler.

Chapter 11 A Sense of Measurement and Geometry

The National Council of Teachers of Mathematics (2000) defines **measurement** as 'the assignment of a numerical value to an attribute of an object' (p. 44). In order to assign a numerical value to a measurement, it is necessary first to identify the **attribute** to be measured, and then to select a unit against which to compare the attribute.

consider and discuss

Think further about Sam's definition of measurement above. He thought of measuring a box in terms of filling it exactly with things. In this case, Sam was describing the capacity of the box as an attribute that could be measured. That is not the only attribute of the box that Sam could have measured. He could have also measured its weight, its height or circumference, or its surface area.

What kinds of units of measurement could Sam have used to measure each of these attributes?

Units of measurement enable us to measure and compare quantities that are separated by time or space, and to give a numerical value to such quantities. For measurement to be meaningful it is essential that units of measurement possess the same attribute as the attribute of the object being measured. For example, the length of an object is measured using units that have length.

The process of measurement involves three basic steps:

- decide on the attribute to be measured
- select an appropriate unit of measurement with the same attribute
- compare the unit of measurement with the attribute of the object being measured. The number of units required to match the object is the measure.

If the unit of measurement is smaller than the attribute being measured, then the numerical value of the measurement is described in terms of multiples of the unit. If the unit is larger than the attribute in question, then the measurement would be provided in terms of parts of the unit.

Measurements commonly include a quantity of whole units together with parts of the units. The level of **precision** in a measurement is reflected in the fractional part that is given. Greater precision results from small divisions of the unit. Measurement therefore represents a location on a continuous scale. Sharp and Hoiberg (2005) suggest that this concept of continuity can be thought of as the idea that a unit 'goes from here to there'. They continue that awareness of this concept means realising that a unit has a specific beginning and an ending.

Units of measurement that are used are often **standard units**. This means they are universally employed and are the same size regardless of who uses them. **Non-standard units** can also be used. These may be created for a particular purpose, or have some cultural significance that is not relevant outside of a local context.

Measuring devices that supply the standard or non-standard units of measurement can facilitate the process of measurement.

making connections

A carat (abbreviation ct) is a unit of measurement that is specifically associated with measuring gold and precious gems. It is used to measure two different attributes, the proportion of gold in alloys, and the mass of gemstones.

A measure of purity

Pure gold is defined as 24 carat. The proportion of gold in an alloy is measured as parts in 24, as given by the following formula:

$$X = 24 \frac{M_g}{M_m}$$

where

X is the carat rating of alloy

M_g is the mass of pure gold in the alloy

M_m is the total mass of the alloy

For example, if a gold bracelet has a total mass of 40 grams, which includes 30 grams of pure gold, then the carat rating of this bracelet would be:

$$X = 24\left(\frac{30}{40}\right)$$
$$= 18 \text{ carats}$$

A measure of mass

A carat is also used for measuring the mass of gemstones, where one carat is a unit of mass equal to 200 mg. A flawless diamond of 100 carats, or 20 g, is known as a paragon.

think + link

In Chapter 9, you considered the connection between mathematics and numeracy. Measurement involves understanding of context and therefore is strongly linked with the development of numeracy. Reflect back over the major ideas of numeracy as you work through this chapter.

consider and discuss

1. In what ways have you used measurement in the last week?
2. What did you measure?
3. What units of measurement did you use?
4. Why did you need to measure?
5. Did you physically measure using a measuring instrument, or did you estimate a measurement?
6. Did you use measurement without even realising that you did so?

Developing measurement sense

Effective measurement sense involves being able to:

- understand and identify the attribute to be measured
- determine an appropriate unit for measuring the attribute
- estimate the number of units required to measure the attribute
- understand the requirements of the context to determine the level of precision required in the measurement.

To appreciate how primary students develop their measurement sense, it is essential to consider three key aspects:

- the conceptual foundations of measurement
- the use of non-standard and standard units
- the use of estimation.

issues in teaching

Traditionally, teaching of measurement involved rote memorisation and application of formulae to complete pen-and-paper exercises. This approach often resulted in students who rarely understood what they were doing and why. The key focus in teaching measurement effectively is that students should be frequently and actively involved in measuring activities rather than completing abstract textbook tasks. In this way students will be provided with an appreciation of why we measure and why it is important to measure.

Conceptual foundations

According to Lehrer (2003), the development of children's sense of measurement arises from a gradual consolidation of the conceptual foundations associated with the nature and properties of units and scale. These are summarised in Table 11.1.

Table 11.1 Conceptual foundations necessary to the development of measurement understandings (Lehrer, 2003; Lehrer, Jaslow & Curtis, 2003)

	Conceptual foundation	Description
Conceptions of units	Unit–attribute relationship	Correspondence must be established between unit of measurement and the attribute being measured.
	Iteration	This understanding is based on the subdivision of the object being measured and the translation of the unit of measurement. For example, measuring an object with length 8 units is achieved by translating a single unit successively 8 times from the starting point to the end point. Iterating a unit implies an infinitely repeatable process with an identical unit.
	Tiling	When the same unit is iterated, the end of each unit is immediately adjacent to the next without gaps or overlaps. This can occur when units are end-to-end as in measuring length, or side-to-side as square tiles may be in measuring area, or face-to-face to measure volume.
	Partitioning	Single units can be partitioned into fractional parts to measure a portion of an object that remains after as many whole units as possible have been used.
	Proportionality	Measurements using different sized units imply that different quantities can represent the same measure. For example, a metre long rod has a measure of 100 centimetres, or 1000 millimetres.
	Additivity	Measurements are additive. This means, for example, that the length of a line is equal to the sum of the lengths of any two segments that subdivide the line.
Conceptions of scale	Origin	This conception implies that any location on a measurement scale can serve as the origin. For example, in measuring a line with length 10 units, the measure can be made over any interval (0–10, or 30–40, or 72–82, etc.).
	Precision	The choice of units in relation to the object being measured determines the relative precision of the measure. This implies that all measurement is inherently approximate.

Part 3: Exploring the Big Ideas in Mathematics

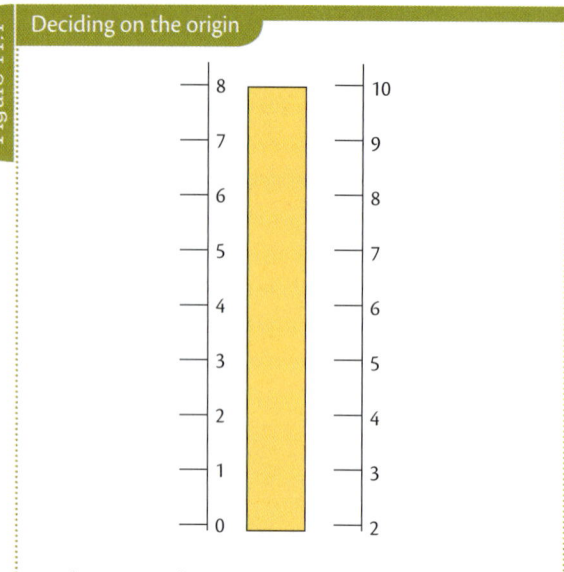

Figure 11.1 | Deciding on the origin

Any location on the measurement scale can serve as the origin. In this figure the length of 8 units can be made over the interval 0–8 or 2–10.

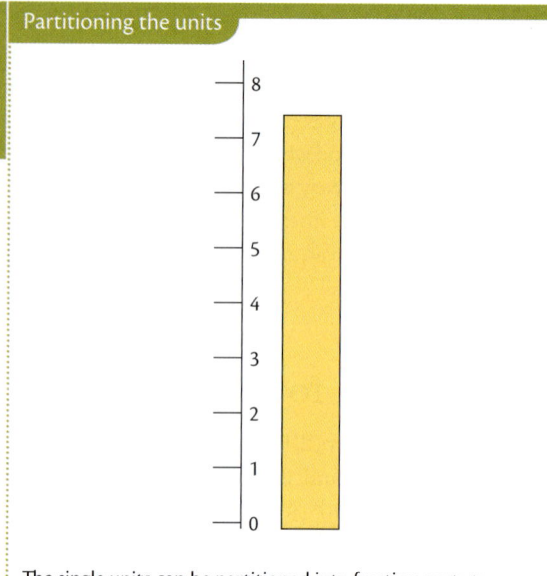

Figure 11.2 | Partitioning the units

The single units can be partitioned into fraction parts to measure the portion that remains after whole units have been used. In this figure the unit between 7 and 8 can be partitioned into halves to record the measurement more accurately.

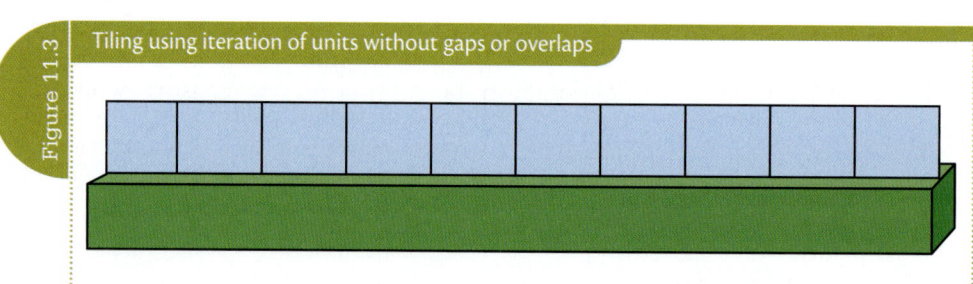

Figure 11.3 | Tiling using iteration of units without gaps or overlaps

issues in teaching

Is measurement a better starting point than number to teach mathematics?

Russian psychologist and educator Vasily Davydov (1930–1988) proposed an entire mathematics curriculum that started not with number and counting, but with measurement. This curriculum begins by guiding students through a series of measurement activities designed to develop non-numerical understandings of length, volume, and mass. The earliest years begin with students comparing and measuring common classroom objects. They learn what can be compared, such as two pencils, and how, for example by measuring length. Students also develop an understanding of greater than and less than as basic concepts. In addition to this students begin to learn about area by, for example, comparing two pieces of paper with differing shapes, as well as volume by comparing containers holding different quantities of water.

Students are quickly encouraged to explain what they are comparing by writing pictorial or symbolic sentences to represent the comparative relationships. It might be difficult to perceive that very young students would be able to do this, as almost all students begin their mathematics learning with number and counting. However, Dougherty (2007) has shown that the early learners are not fazed by the use of symbols rather than number as it is directly related to representing physical situations.

The benefits to young students of beginning their mathematics learning through measurement through this approach are:

- the experience of exploring and comparing quantities such as length, area, and volume lays the foundation for algebraic thinking

- there is an emphasis on communicating mathematical ideas in writing
- the physical experience of measuring means that students start to make links between the mathematical concepts being investigated.

This approach has been successfully adopted in Hawaii through the Measure Up program. More information about this program can be found at the following websites:
- http://hawaii.edu/crdg/sections/math/documents/Measure-Up.pdf
- www.hawaii.edu/crdg/news/documents/TCM2007-05.pdf

Non-standard and standard units

The use of non-standard units in the primary years is integral to developing measurement sense. There are a number of reasons why teachers in primary mathematics classrooms include the use of non-standard units:

- Non-standard units make it easier to focus on the attribute being measured. For example, in measuring the length of an object, units such as paper clips, crayons or toothpicks could be used and each would give a different measurement. The discussion would focus on what it means to measure length rather than the actual length of the object.
- In the early primary years, careful selection of the non-standard unit of measurement means large numerical values can be avoided when students make measurements.
- The use of non-standard units demonstrates the concept that measurements need to be communicated, and so standard units of measurement are required to avoid confusion. Thus, the use of non-standard measurements provides a sound rationale for the use of standard measurements.
- The use of non-standard measurement is generally fun, and therefore an engaging way to develop measurement understandings.

consider and discuss

When thinking about teaching primary mathematics, which of these reasons for the use of non-standard units seems most important to you? Explain how and why you made your selection.

did you know?

In the absence of calibrated measuring devices, many historical units of measurement originally referenced characteristics of the human body. Perhaps the most obvious illustration is the foot as a measure of length. The basic Egyptian unit of measurement, a cubit, represented the length of a man's forearm from the elbow to the tip of the middle finger. The measure of a mile can be traced back to Roman times. As Roman armies marched they kept count of their paces: a distance of 1000 paces was referred to as *mille passus*, and it is from this phrase that the word mile is derived. As a final example, the English King Henry I (1100–1135) decreed that the measure of a yard would be the distance from his nose to his thumb when his arm was outstretched. But what would happen to that measure when he died?

The use of standard units is, however, essential to developing measurement sense in the primary years. The standard system of measurement in Australia is metric units. Students need to understand the use of standard units in order to make sense of the process of measurement, including being able to estimate in standard units and interpret measurements made using standard units. There are three key goals that primary teachers need to keep in mind that are relevant to the use of standard units. The first is familiarity with the unit, that students develop a basic idea of the size of commonly used standard units. Related to unit familiarity is the student's ability to select an appropriate unit; this involves knowing what would be a reasonable unit of measure in a particular situation for a required level of precision. Finally, students need to develop an understanding of the relationships between commonly used standard units.

for the classroom

For each standard unit of measurement you want to focus on, give the students a model of one standard unit. For example, to develop a familiarity with a metre, give students a piece of rope 1 metre long. Get them to measure and list various items and features around the classroom and school yard that are about 1 metre long. Ensure that students also make measurements that are curved to emphasise that the measurement of a length does not necessarily mean a straight measurement. The same activity could be adopted for other length units.

communicating mathematically

Whole class and small group discussions are an essential aspect of teaching and learning measurement. Verbal interactions contribute to developing students' understanding of the measurement process and the development of an appropriate measurement vocabulary. However, discussing measurement concepts might be difficult for some students if the ideas communicated by other students are contrary to their own understandings, or if shared ideas are expressed using unfamiliar language or reasoning. When conducting whole class discussions or facilitating small group work teachers must be aware that students' vague or inconsistent verbal descriptions (which are inevitable) can affect the learning and participation of other students. Teachers should take care to model correct use of language, prompt their students to use accurate language, and encourage students to seek further clarification if they are having difficulty interpreting the explanations made by others.

making connections

People who drink alcohol sensibly try to monitor how much they are drinking. This can be difficult, as the concentration of alcohol can vary between beverages. A *standard unit of measure* has been developed to allow comparisons between alcoholic drinks. A common unit of 'standard drink' makes it possible to compare the alcoholic content of various beverages and to regulate the amount of alcohol consumed. Many restaurants, clubs, and hotels now use wine glasses with a 150 mL volume mark. This provides an approximate measure of a 'standard drink' unit for wine. However, the concentration of alcohol in wine can vary significantly, so the mark is really only a guide.

A standard drink contains 10 grams of alcohol. Alcohol is a liquid, and so we need to convert 10 grams of alcohol into a liquid measure. One gram of water has a volume of 1 mL. Alcohol is close to this, but we can find a more accurate value by finding the specific gravity of alcohol.

Specific gravity is a measure that compares the density of a liquid with the density of water. The specific gravity of the type of alcohol that is contained in alcoholic beverages is 0.782. This means that alcohol is less dense than water. Density is the ratio of mass to volume. So this specific gravity tells us that 1 mL of alcohol has a mass of 0.782 grams.

Returning to the 'standard drink' measure, we need to find the volume of 10 grams of alcohol.

$$1 \text{ mL} \rightarrow 0.782 \text{ g}$$
$$? \text{ mL} \rightarrow 10 \text{ g}$$
$$\frac{1}{x} = \frac{0.782}{10}$$
$$x = \frac{10}{0.782}$$
$$x = 12.67 \text{ mL}$$

This calculation tells us that the 10 grams of alcohol in a standard drink has a volume of 12.67 mL. Alcoholic beverages vary in their concentration of alcohol, with stronger drinks containing a higher percentage of alcohol. This percentage is required by law to be listed on the label.

Full strength beer is about 5% alcohol by volume. This means that in 100 mL of beer there would be 5 mL of alcohol. Red wine can be as high as 14% alcohol by volume. So if you were to drink red wine, you would drink less volume to consume the same amount of alcohol.

Let's think about a stubby of beer (375 mL) with 5% alcohol.

5% of 375 is alcohol
$$= 0.05 \times 375$$
$$= 18.75 \text{ mL}$$

That means that a stubby has 18.75 mL of alcohol. Since a 'standard drink' is 12.67 mL of alcohol, a stubby has more than one standard drink. We can calculate how many standard drinks there are in a stubby in this way:

$$\frac{18.75}{12.67} = 1.47$$

or approximately 1.5 standard drinks.

Our calculations use a stubby of beer as an example. It is possible to generalise the calculations if we know:

- the percentage of alcohol in the beverage
- the volume of the beverage consumed.

Looking back at the previous example, we calculated the percentage of alcohol in the beer by finding 5% of 375 mL. We then divided this by the volume of 10 grams of alcohol (which will always be 12.67).

You can find out more about standard drinks at the Australian Commonwealth Department of Health and Ageing website: www.alcohol.gov.au/internet/alcohol/publishing.nsf/content/standard.

consider and discuss

1. Look back over the calculations and develop a general rule for calculating the number of standard drinks in a given volume when you know the percentage alcohol.
2. Use your rule to calculate the number of standard drinks in a 750 mL bottle of red wine with 14% alcohol. Find a label on a bottle to check.
3. You might have generated a rule similar to the following. Justify to yourself or your study group why the rule works.

$$\text{Number of standard drinks} = \frac{(\% \text{ of alcohol expressed as a decimal}) \times (\text{Volume of beverage in mL})}{12.67}$$

Estimation

The notion that measurement of continuous attributes is always an estimate is essential to understanding the concept of measurement. Between any two partitions we can, theoretically, always create a new partition that will provide a more precise measurement, and this theoretical partitioning will ultimately extend into the realm of infinity. Clearly, this theoretical understanding of measurement will be beyond the practical needs of most primary students. However, that all measurement is an estimate is a 'big idea' that primary mathematics teachers need to consider.

Schwartz (2008) claims that half of the time we use mathematics in daily life, an estimate is all that is needed. If this is the case, then plenty of time should be spent building and developing **estimation** skills in a variety of contexts, including measurement.

think + link

Link to points made about estimation in the number chapters.

consider and discuss

Keep a log of when and how you used estimation over the course of a day. Share your list with the lists that others have made. What observations can you make about the significance of estimation in daily life and about how adults estimate?

In the early primary years, when students make an estimate they are initially doing nothing more than making a guess. However, the guess establishes a commitment to the measurement activity, and measurements that are made provide useful feedback on the accuracy of the guess. Estimation of measurements is a skill that can be learnt through trial and error. Each time an estimate is made and feedback is received about the accuracy of the measurement, the learnt skill of estimation in a particular context is developed. The more estimates that are made, the more feedback that is received, the more the skill develops.

for the classroom

Select and display a common object in the classroom, for example a watermelon. Each day, select a different attribute to estimate. For a watermelon, the students could estimate its height, circumference, mass, volume, and surface area. When the estimation activities are concluded the watermelon will then become a healthy classroom treat!

Estimating measurements is the process of using mental and visual information to measure or make comparisons without the use of measuring devices. Effective estimation is underpinned by the development of robust **personal referents** for a range of units. Students who have mental reference points for measurement and have practised using them in measurement activities become much better estimators (Joram, 2003).

Referents should be things that are easily envisioned or enacted. For example, if you have run a 100 m sprint on a school oval, you will have some idea of the distance involved. Here are some common units of measurement for which a personal referent may be useful. A possible referent is suggested, but you can add your own personal referent to the list.

Table 11.2 Common personal referents

Measurement	Possible referent	Personal referent
100 m	Sprint distance	
50 m	Length of full-sized swimming pool	
1 kg	Bag of onions	
2 L	Container of milk	
1 g	Mass of 1 Smartie	
5 mL	Volume of a teaspoon	
250 mL	Volume of a standard measuring cup	
1 m	Distance from nose to tip of fingers of an extended arm	
1 s	Time taken to say 'one elephant'	
30 min	Time taken to watch an episode of *The Simpsons*	
50 000 L or 50 kL	Volume of a backyard swimming pool	
1 tonne	Mass of a large family car	

Chapter 11 A Sense of Measurement and Geometry

for the classroom

Estimation scavenger hunt

Give teams of students a list of measurements, and direct them to find items that are close to having those measurements. The use of formal measuring devices is not permitted. A list might include:

- a length of 2.5 m
- something that weighs more than 1 kg but less than 2 kg
- a container that holds 400 mL
- an item with an area of 1 square metre.

Discuss with the students how to determine the suitability of the items collected in terms of the accuracy of their estimation.

integrating technology/ICT

Computer tools both complement and supplement the use of physical manipulatives and materials for measurement investigations. Programs that allow students to manipulate blocks on the screen or an interactive whiteboard are commonly available and can provide students with a broad variety of exploratory activities. For students that have poor fine-motor skills or a disability that makes physical block manipulation difficult, computer versions of blocks especially provide genuine benefits. In addition, students can generate colourful printouts that can be displayed and discussed. These types of programs allow students to:

- enlarge or reduce the size of the blocks
- join blocks together to create new composite figures
- measure area, perimeter, or volume
- rotate blocks or figures to explore attributes from a variety of perspectives.

Check the possibilities at these websites:

http://illuminations.nctm.org/ActivityDetail.aspx?ID=6
http://nlvm.usu.edu/en/nav/frames_asid_170_g_2_t_4.html?open=activities&from=category_g_2_t_4.html
http://nlvm.usu.edu/en/nav/frames_asid_129_g_2_t_3.html?open=activities&from=category_g_2_t_3.html
http://nlvm.usu.edu/en/nav/frames_asid_195_g_2_t_3.html?open=activities&from=category_g_2_t_3.html

Geometry

Geometry is a major field of mathematics that forms a significant part of the school curriculum. Through geometry, students learn to understand their world, to develop visualisation and **geometric reasoning**, and learn that mathematics is constantly changing and growing. Best of all, though, geometry takes us into an area of mathematics that is truly beautiful!

did you know?

Geometry began as a practical study to understand the world. Geometry was closely linked with measurement. In addition to dealing with practical problems such as land measurements, early geometry was used to explore astronomy. Hipparchus (around 120 BCE), for example, calculated the mean distance of the Earth to the Moon by taking accurate measurements and using geometry.

Branches of geometry

From its beginnings as a practical subject, geometry became formalised through the work of Greek mathematicians who transferred ideas from the practical world into the 'pure' theoretical world of abstract thought. Euclid, a Greek mathematician living around 300 BCE, wrote what has been described as the most successful textbook of all times—*The Elements*—which led to the emergence of Euclidean geometry. This work was based on a series of postulates or principles that were assumed to be true, and it remained the accepted view of geometry until mathematicians in the nineteenth century started exploring geometries based on different postulates. From that time, geometry rapidly developed into new fields (described collectively as non-Euclidean geometries). Some of these non-Euclidean geometries have become important in modern physics, including Einstein's theory of relativity.

think + link

In Chapter 27, you can read how Euclid's fifth postulate led to the emergence of new types of geometry.

When determining mathematics school syllabuses, educators have needed to take account of emerging areas of geometry. In addition, studying and appreciating the mathematics of non-Western peoples, such as Pacific Islanders and peoples from African cultures (ethnomathematics), has led to the valuing of **transformational geometry**, the study of the effects of various processes in transforming geometrical objects. This will be introduced in more detail in Chapter 20 and further developed in Chapter 27.

Euclidean geometry remains important and provides students with necessary concepts and ways of understanding the field. In upper primary, students are able to extend their thinking to the study of *Earth geometry*, where they can learn how geometry is used to map a solid earth and give locations. Towards the end of the middle years of schooling, students need to become aware of other geometries, as well as the continuing importance of **coordinate geometry**, the field linking geometry with algebra.

We now turn our attention to how we develop geometric thinking.

 **consider and discuss**

Painted tyres

Once while riding a bicycle along a path I crossed a strip of wet paint about 15 cm wide. After riding a short time in a straight line, I looked back at the marks on the footpath left by the wet paint on my tyres.

What did I see? Remember to record your thinking.

After you have worked on this for a bit, discuss with your study group. What extra information do you want to know? Do you really need it?

When you get stuck, you might think of finding a real bike to try this out. Avoid doing this! That would be like looking in the back of the book! Instead, remember your strategies for getting unstuck. Some of these are in Chapter 4. For example, try simplifying the problem. What if I were riding a unicycle? What if two riders were using unicycles?

Adapted from Mason, Burton & Stacey, 1985, p. 65.

Spatial sense

When you worked on the painted tyre activity above you might have wanted to find a bike to try it out. It can be difficult to work on visual problems in your head or with diagrams and yet this is an important mathematical process—the process of visualisation. Zimmerman and Cunningham (1991) have defined mathematical visualisation as 'the process of forming images (mentally, or with pencil and paper or with the aid of technology) and using such images effectively for mathematical discovery and understanding' (p. 3). This is different from the common usage, in which visualising is about forming a mental image. Gutiérrez (1996, p. 6), explains the distinction as follows:

> [M]ental image is a mental representation of a mathematical concept or property containing information based upon pictorial, graphical or diagrammatic elements. [V]isualisation or visual thinking is a kind of reasoning based on the use of mental images.

Therefore, **mathematical visualisation** is a means to understanding—not just in geometry but in all areas of mathematics. In the specific area of geometry, other terms are important to define. Battista (2007) has described *geometric reasoning* as 'the invention and use of formal conceptual systems to investigate shape and space' (p. 843).

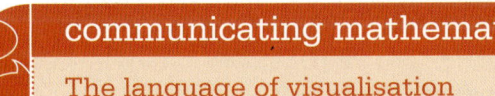

communicating mathematically

The language of visualisation

Not all communication in mathematics occurs in natural language. When we are involved in visualisation, we are forming images, either mentally or externally through diagrams. Diagrams can be on paper or in dynamic geometry environments provided by computer software. Being able to reason using visualisation is an important aspect of mathematics, and you and your students need opportunities to practise this. When you are working with students, encourage them to draw what they are thinking. Allow them to see you drawing diagrams and thinking using visualisation.

think + link

In Chapters 20 and 27 you will have the opportunity to develop further your geometric reasoning when we explore conceptual systems such as using properties of shapes to understand general principles.

Underlying geometric reasoning is *spatial reasoning*. This has been defined as 'the ability to "see", inspect, and reflect on spatial objects, images, relationships and transformations' (Battista, 2007, p. 843). We can all develop our spatial and geometric reasoning, that is, we can develop our spatial sense.

According to Clements (1999), **spatial sense** includes two main spatial abilities: spatial orientation, and spatial visualisation and imagery. Spatial visualisation and imagery have been discussed above. **Spatial orientation** involves knowing where you are and how to get around. For example, if you are looking at a map in a shopping centre to find a particular shop, you need to know where you are and then how to get to the new location. In addition, spatial sense involves (Clements, 1999):

- the ability to manipulate dynamic images
- developing our store of images for shapes and other objects
- connecting spatial knowledge to verbal/analytical knowledge.

Spatial sense is an important aspect of numeracy, being inherently mathematical and also essential for living and interacting in our world. Clements (1999) has reviewed the research available on how children develop these components; this is summarised Table 11.3.

Table 11.3: Development of spatial aspects according to Clements (1999)

Age	Development of mental maps (building relations among objects in space)	Development of physical maps	Linking primary and secondary uses
Birth to 3 years old	Babies: • associate objects as being near a person • cannot associate to distant landmarks. Toddlers: • can place objects in pre-specified locations. Children may be able to form simple frameworks, including their own location.	3-year-olds can build simple maps. Can learn from maps.	
4–7 years old	Without landmarks children will make mistakes with location. Build local frameworks that are less dependent on own position. Rely on relational cues such as boundaries.	Children learn layouts better from maps than from navigation alone. Children know maps represent space. Preschoolers have trouble knowing where they are in space.	Form primary, direct relations to spaces on maps.
From 8 years old	Can use larger, encompassing frameworks including the observer of the situation.	Children can draw from memory simple sketch maps of areas around their home. Can recognise features on aerial maps.	Children develop their abilty to take a secondary view of maps (i.e. the perspective of an abstract frame of reference). This continues to adulthood.

making connections

Map reading is a good application of geometry, and the sport of orienteering can be used to teach and enhance skills. Orienteers run around a course finding markers along the way. The location of the markers is shown on topographic maps. Topographic maps use contour lines to convey the three dimensions of the Earth's surface on a two-dimensional map. They also show other natural and constructed features. Many orienteering clubs offer courses for schools.

How geometry is learnt

For many people, memories of learning geometry include completing pages of textbook exercises and memorising theorems, rules, and properties. Ian Lowe (1991), an influential Australian educator, argues for an alternative approach:

> Geometry is mainly about ideas. The nature of the ideas is that they are practical, and deal with relationships between real things. It follows that geometry should mostly be learned by performing two kinds of activities:
> - doing things, such as making, designing, constructing, drawing, measuring,
> - and at the same time thinking about what is being done, such as visualising, analysing, explaining, justifying (that is, informal proof), describing, modelling, finding applications. (p. iv)

for the classroom

One of the major applications of geometry is in the field of graphic design, particularly in the area of packaging. Cleverly designed boxes can be a selling feature for products such as chocolates. Packaging also has to be made from flat cardboard that is folded up. Fast-food packaging is especially well constructed to lie flat for transport and storage and then fold up quickly at point of sale.

Invite students to find examples of boxes. Unfold them and study how they are made.

Students can make their own packaging for a specified product. This activity can be of value to students in a range of year levels. Encourage students to focus on the thinking they are doing as they design their packaging.

Theories of learning geometry

A number of researchers in the field of mathematics education have studied how learners develop proficiency with geometry. More research is required, and as you continue your career, engaging in professional learning will help you keep abreast of changes in this field.

Piaget and Inhelder

Piaget and Inhelder (1967) wrote extensively on children's development of geometrical concepts. They noted that the level of sophistication of children's thinking developed with age. Initially, young preschool children could distinguish between open and closed shapes and older children between shapes with straight versus curved sides, but it was not until later that children could distinguish between shapes such as squares and rhombuses. Piaget and Inhelder argued that young children are unable to relate two perceptions mentally. To create ideas about shapes, children need physical interaction with objects and to be able to connect their actions. That is, children's 'representations of space are constructed through the progressive organization of the child's motor and internalized actions' (Clements, Swaminathan, Hannibal & Sarama, 1999, p. 193).

think + link

In the later chapters on teaching geometry, the emphasis is on allowing students at all levels of schooling to actively engage in tasks with the purpose of constructing their own understandings of properties.

Clements (1999) summarised the findings of Piaget and Inhelder's research as:

The main point is that children's ideas about shapes do not come from passive looking. Instead, they come as children's bodies, hands, eyes ... and minds ... engage in action. In addition, the experiment illustrates that children need to explore shapes extensively to understand them fully. Merely seeing and naming pictures is insufficient. Finally, they have to explore the parts and attributes of shapes. (p. 67)

van Hiele

The research of Pierre and Dina van Hiele (van Hiele-Geldof, 1984; van Hiele, 1986) took an educational perspective to the development of the concepts of geometry. They claimed that children developed their geometric thinking by moving through discrete stages of reasoning when supported with appropriate instruction. The original theory and much subsequent work have focused on students in the middle years of schooling (Clements et al., 1999). Subsequent research by others investigating the cognition of young children has led to amendments of the original model proposed by the van Hieles. The **van Hiele levels** are summarised in Table 11.4.

Table 11.4 Amended van Hiele levels of geometric thought (adapted from Battista, 2007)

Level 0	Pre-recognition	• Children attend to only some of a shape's characteristics. • Children are unable to identify many common shapes.
Level 1	Visual	• Children identify and operate on geometric shapes according to their appearance. • Children recognise shapes as whole structures and rely heavily on memorised examples. For example, children may be able to name a square when it is positioned with horizontal sides but not be able to name a square that has been rotated.
Level 2	Descriptive/analytic	• Students recognise and can classify shapes by their properties.
Level 3	Abstract/relational	• Students can form definitions, distinguish between necessary and sufficient sets of conditions, and understand logical arguments. • Some students may be able to construct logical arguments.
Level 4	Formal deduction	• Students establish theorems within an axiomatic system.
Level 5	Rigour/metamathematical	• Students reason formally about mathematical systems.

for the classroom

A geoboard is a useful manipulative device invented by the Egyptian mathematician Caleb Gattegno in the 1950s for teaching geometry in primary schools. Geoboards are fascinating and can be useful throughout the school years—through to university level mathematics!

Children in the early years, perhaps in the van Hiele levels 0 and 1, can experiment with making shapes such as triangles in different orientations. Many children at this age find it difficult to draw triangles, but they are easily made with rubber bands. As children become more accomplished, they should be encouraged to record their diagrams on dot paper. Note in the picture the sheet of dot paper has been drawn to match the pegs on the geoboard. Later, children can learn to use standard square dot paper where the scale is different.

Children in upper primary years, perhaps working in levels 2 and 3, can explore perimeter and area relationships. They could be challenged to make different shapes with a perimeter of 16 units, keeping a record on their dot paper. They can then calculate the area of the shapes. They should also estimate the value of the area by looking at the squares enclosed. There are computer applications that allow virtual exploration of geoboards; this task is adapted from www.mathplayground.com/geoboard.html. Note it is very important for children to work with the physical objects and dot paper representations before exploring in the computer environment.

Geoboards can allow students in the middle years of schooling and beyond to work at the very top of the van Hiele levels. In the photograph, the yellow triangle touches four pegs and has no internal pegs. The red triangle touches six pegs and has one internal peg. Students can be introduced to Pick's formula for finding the area of a polygon with T points touching and I internal points:

$$\text{Area} = \frac{T}{2} + (I - 1)$$

Test this rule on the red triangle. You should find it gives an area of 3.

This rule can be investigated. A related problem is to investigate which combinations of touching and interior points can occur in polygons. This leads to sophisticated mathematics, including formal proofs (Weaver, 1977).

Considerable research has been undertaken to attempt to verify the levels proposed by the van Hiele model. An Australian researcher, John Pegg, has argued that the levels are not as discrete as the original model would claim. The levels appear distinct at first, but considerable disagreement occurs when researchers try to place learners at a particular level. Pegg and colleagues (Pegg, 1997; Pegg & Davey, 1998) have attempted to elaborate the levels and to understand the path learners take through the levels.

Another criticism of the van Hiele model is that it is difficult to apply beyond two-dimensional shapes (Battista, 2007). It may seem discouraging to read that the major theories of learning geometry have faced criticism and revision. As you prepare to teach, you will find that there is much to gain from considering the ideas inherent in models of learning. These will be developed in subsequent chapters. You must also understand that your personal approach to teaching geometry will develop throughout your career, and will be influenced by future research in the field.

issues in teaching

Other ways of seeing the world

As we have seen, much school geometry is derived from the work of the ancient Greeks. This has led to a particular style of thinking. For example, in Western mathematics location is characterised by a Cartesian system that uses two axes perpendicular (orthogonal) to each other. This is not the case for all cultures, however. Owens (2010) describes a Yolngu (Indigenous group in the Northern Territory) perspective as a topological mapping rather than a Cartesian mapping. Topological maps are simplified to show main features and to eliminate unnecessary cluttering of information.

Indigenous groups in tribal settings do not use left and right for specifying location because these are dependent on the orientation of the person. Instead, a global system (similar to compass points) is used (Harris, 1980). Should all learners be taught this method? How might Indigenous learners who are used to a topological system be disadvantaged if taught by a teacher who was not aware such a system exists?

integrating technology/ICT

Turtle geometry

LOGO is a programming language originally developed to teach computing to young children. LOGO was used to program a robot, nicknamed a turtle. On desktop computers the turtle became a computer graphic, and young children could program its movement on the screen to make shapes and designs. Seymour Papert, one of the creators of LOGO, published the first edition of the influential book *Mindstorms* in 1980, giving teachers an insight into possible uses of computers in classrooms, particularly for the teaching of geometry (Papert, 1993).

Recent developments in LOGO include programming with robots (LegoLogo), used in many Australian schools. New products, such as BeeBots, are also available for use in primary classrooms. These are more than toys, and there are many applications to geometry. For example, children can

program the robot to make a square by moving forward and specifying turns.

Free downloads of LOGO software are available (www.softronix.com/logo.html), as well as materials for assisting teachers to use the programs.

Conclusion

In this chapter we have provided an overview of measurement and geometry, two fundamental and closely linked areas of mathematics. These strands of mathematics are linked through their practical applications, as well as through the conceptual areas that focus on visualisation.

To appreciate how primary students develop their measurement sense it is essential to consider three key aspects: the conceptual foundations of measurement, the use of non-standard and standard units, and the use of estimation. In developing their spatial and geometric sense students will acquire a deeper understanding of their world, develop visualisation and geometrical reasoning, and learn that mathematics is constantly changing and growing.

Measurement and spatial sense are both best developed by involving the students in practical activities such as making, designing, constructing, and drawing. Simultaneously, students need to be thinking about what they are doing by, for example, visualising, explaining, describing, or modelling.

key terms

Attribute: the characteristic of an object that is to be measured, for example length or volume

Coordinate geometry: the field of mathematics linking geometry with algebra

Estimation: the process of using mental and visual information to measure or make comparisons without the use of measuring devices

Geometric reasoning: the type of thinking involved in the investigation of shape and space

Mathematical visualisation: a process of thinking leading to understanding based on use of images

Measurement: the assignment of a numerical value to an attribute of an object

Non-standard units: units of measurement that are created for a particular purpose that have no relevance outside the context in which they are used

Personal referents: easily envisioned or enacted mental reference points used for estimating measurements

Precision: the degree of accuracy required when making a measurement; greater precision results from small divisions of the unit of measurement

Spatial orientation: knowing where you are and how to move to another place

Spatial sense: the ability to 'see', inspect, and reflect on spatial objects, images, relationships, and transformations

Standard units: universally employed units of measurement that are the same size regardless of who uses them

Transformational geometry: the study of the effects of various processes in transforming geometric objects

Units of measurement: units that give a numerical value to an attribute that enable the measurement and comparison of quantities that are separated by time or space

van Hiele levels: a model for the development of geometric thinking

Review questions

1. Describe the three basic steps in the measuring process.
2. Why is the use of non-standard units important in developing a sense of measurement?
3. How might the use of non-standard units hinder the development of measurement sense?
4. Explain what is meant when we say that measurement is always an estimate.
5. What connections can be made between measurement and other mathematics strands?
6. Why is measurement sense an important aspect of numerate behaviour?
7. Explain what is meant by spatial sense. How does it relate to visualisation, imagery and geometry?
8. Describe the van Hiele theory of the development of geometric thinking. Discuss criticisms of the model and some possible amendments.

References

Battista, M. T. (2007). The development of geometric and spatial thinking. In F. K. Lester (Ed.), *Second Handbook of Research on Mathematics Teaching and Learning* (pp. 843–908). Reston, VA: NCTM.

Clements, D. H., Swaminathan, S., Hannibal, M. A. Z., & Sarama, J. (1999). Young children's concepts of shape. *Journal for Research in Mathematics Education, 30*(2), 192–212.

Gutiérrez, A. (1996). Visualization in 3-dimensional geometry: In search of a framework. In L. Puig & A. Guttiérez (Eds.), *Proceedings of the 20th conference of the International Group for the Psychology of Mathematics Education* (Vol. 1, pp. 3–19). Valencia: Universidad de Valencia.

Lehrer, R. (2003). Developing understanding of measurement. In J. Kilpatrick, W. Martin, & D. Schifter (Eds.), *A Research Companion to Principles and Standards for School Mathematics*. Reston, VA: NCTM.

Lehrer, R., Jaslow, L., & Curtis, C. (2003). Developing an understanding of measurement in the elementary grades. In D. Clements (Ed.), *Learning and Teaching Measurement: 2003 Yearbook*. Reston, VA: NCTM.

van Hiele, P.M. (1986). *Structure and Insight: A Theory of Mathematics Education*. Orlando, FL: Academic Press.

Zimmermann, W., & Cunningham, S. (1991). Editors' introduction: What is mathematical visualization? In W. Zimmermann & S. Cunningham (Eds.), *Visualization in Teaching and Learning Mathematics* (Vol. MAA Notes Number 19, pp. 1–8). Washington, DC: Mathematical Association of America.

Websites

www.alcohol.gov.au/internet/alcohol/publishing.nsf/content/standard

http://hawaii.edu/crdg/sections/math/documents/Measure-Up.pdf

www.hawaii.edu/crdg/news/documents/TCM2007-05.pdf

http://nlvm.usu.edu/en/nav/vlibrary.html

http://illuminations.nctm.org

www.softronix.com/logo.html

www.mathplayground.com/geoboard.html

http://nrich.maths.org

Statistics and Probability

12

Contents

Introduction	232
Statistical literacy	232
What is statistics?	234
What is probability?	241
Conclusion	244

Chapter objectives

This chapter will enable the reader to:
- Demonstrate an understanding of statistical literacy
- Critically analyse everyday statistical examples
- Describe the concepts of statistics and probability
- Identify key steps to teach statistics and probability.

I don't have to teach statistics and probability!

I had a conversation with a preservice primary teacher who plans to teach children in F–2. She stated that she did not need to learn about data and probability because it isn't important for young children. When I asked her what the areas of data and probability are, she replied 'using formulae to calculate problems about dice and cards and working out averages.' It is true that cards and dice and averages are part of data and probability, but there is a lot more to it than that. The foundations of these areas are introduced from the first year of schooling.

Big ideas

- Statistics and probability are embedded in our everyday lives.
- Statistical literacy is important for all people.
- Statistics provides a numerical method to describe and analyse the world.
- Probability involves understanding chance and can provide the information needed to assess risk.

Introduction

The study of statistics and probability has become an accepted part of the curriculum from Foundation to Year 12, although, depending on when you attended primary school, you may not have formally encountered statistics or probability in those years. We are continually presented with statistics in our everyday experiences, and statistics and probability is acknowledged as important knowledge for all people.

Imagine a typical day. While eating breakfast, you read the newspaper and are informed of the latest alarming statistics about global warming. You turn on the radio and listen to the weather report: 'there is an 80% chance of rain on the weekend'. The NAPLAN results for your class have arrived, and you must interpret the graphical and tabular information about your students' numeracy and literacy achievement. After school, you have an appointment with an insurance broker so that you can choose insurance for your newly purchased house. After eating dinner, you turn on the TV to watch the latest news, and you are concerned about the story on teenage road accidents—can the statistics really be that bad?

This scenario illustrates the level of knowledge needed to be numerate as an adult in the areas of statistics and probability. As a teacher, you must therefore be prepared to lay down solid foundations of knowledge in the strand of statistics and probability. You may be surprised to find out that you already have some understanding of this field.

In this chapter the big ideas associated with statistics and probability are presented, with some foundational concepts important for primary school students. Chapters 21 and 28 will provide specific teaching tips and sequences for working with students in both the early and middle years.

did you know?

Children with bigger feet spell better!

Wow! On first reading, this appears to be a significant finding. This was stated in a newspaper report of a study that found that children with larger feet have better spelling skills. Yes, it is true! Take a minute to consider this finding. As children grow and develop, their feet grow larger. So this finding simply indicates that older children (who also happen to have larger feet) have better spelling skills.

Statistical literacy

Statistics is the application of mathematics to answer real-world problems, and the study of statistics is most effective when it is done is a real context. It remains important for people long after they finish school—all school graduates should attain a basic level of statistical literacy.

Statitistical literacy is the meeting point of the data and chance curriculum and the everyday world, where encounters involve unrehearsed contexts and spontaneous decision-making based on the ability to apply statistical tools, general contextual knowledge, and critical literacy skills (Watson, 2006, p. 11).

The purpose of teaching statistics extends to the critical interpretation of the use of statistics in real-world situations. Adults must be able to effectively decode statistical information in order to evaluate data-related arguments.

Too often the analysis of data is accepted as factual because it involves numbers and impressive statistics. It is important to read the information critically. In fact, the first question I ask myself is *does this make sense?* Where did the information come from, does the source have interest in the outcome, is it accurate, is the analysis fair, and is the conclusion reasonable?

An article that appeared in *The Times* in 2006 (Nugent, 2006) featured reporting that is fairly typical of the kind of articles we read everyday. The 2006 UK headline 'Germans are brainiest (but at least we're smarter than the French)' resulted in spin-off stories worldwide. The story was inspired by the release of a new European league table of IQs in which England was eighth and France nineteenth. The British were beaten by Germany, Netherlands, Poland, Sweden, Austria, and Switzerland. Researcher Professor Lynn explained that people living in colder climates have larger brains than those living in warmer climates. He hypothesised that the protein, minerals, and vitamins in the people living in colder climates may have stimulated larger brain development. He further surmises that migrants from these cold climates moved to London.

The article ranked countries according to average IQ scores. However, there is no information given as to the source of the IQ scores. Was the same method used in each country to determine the average IQ score? In addition, I would question the validity of the IQ test. Read the article summary and see what conclusion you come to.

The media is a ready source of statistics that you may be able to use in your classroom. Note that you may need to simplify some information to ensure that the content is age-appropriate and that your students have the necessary reading level to access the information.

Whitin (2006) describes a critical orientation towards statistics and details seven dimensions as follows (p. 32):

- motive—what was the reason for collecting data?
- question—the way a question is asked influences the answers
- categories—how were the categories decided?
- definitions—how and why were terms defined in this way?
- sample—who was asked?; is the sample representative?
- conclusions—what was not shown, and how did the motive influence the conclusions?
- visual representation—how has the representation chosen influenced the interpretation?

Begin with the questioning of the students' own data and results. Having students delve into data is important—what is not shown?; is the sample actually representative of the population? This can be explored by doing surveys with different sample compositions. For example, should only girls, or only Year 5 students, be used to represent the whole school? This basic process of questioning data is important for all people.

consider and discuss

Consider the newspaper headline 'Children receiving free breakfast at school score lower in NAPLAN tests'.

How do you interpret this statement?

Statements like this are based on statistical links or correlations. Does this mean that receiving free breakfast *causes* students to score lower than their peers in NAPLAN tests?

Statements such as that about free breakfasts and NAPLAN results occur all too frequently in the media. It is a trap to believe that correlation is equivalent to causation. If providing students with free breakfast causes low test scores, then the obvious solution would be to stop the free breakfast program. Clearly that is a nonsensical response. Because the two factors are statistically linked does not mean that one directly causes the other. Other causal factors may be possible, or the results may just be coincidence.

Both mathematical and literacy skills are important foundational skills for statistical literacy. In addition, an individual must decode the statistics used—this includes evaluating the analysis and conclusion. Developing a critical approach to statistics requires an informed logical approach to examining the data and analysis. These dispositions clearly link to the school mathematics proficiency strands as detailed in the Australian curriculum.

While mathematics has the responsibility for teaching the concepts and skills of statistics, it is important for the applications of statistics and statistical literacy to be integrated into all learning areas (Watson, 2006). Elements that are core to statistical literacy are:

- knowledge and understanding of variation
- understanding of the importance of using empirical data to explore processes
- understanding of the use of randomisation in data collection.

Developing the knowledge and skills of statistical literacy requires not only the knowledge of calculations but also the development of dispositions described within the proficiency strands. It is important to be aware of students' ability to explore and question data beyond a surface level description. Given that knowledge and conceptual understanding of both statistics and probability are key to statistical literacy, this is the focus of the remainder of the chapter and is further explored in Chapters 21 and 28.

What is statistics?

Statistics involves the collection and analysis of data to describe the world. According to Patilla (2008), **data** is information or facts you find out or are given. Data can be words or numbers or a mixture of both.

Freil and Bright (1998) describe four stages in data analysis:

- ask a question
- collect data
- analyse data
- form and communicate conclusions.

Although this process appears to be linear, as data is collected and analysed researchers may discover unexpected results and change questions:

> In these respects, data analysis is like a give-and-take conversation between the hunches researchers have about phenomena and what the data have to say about those hunches. What researchers find in their initial understanding changes how they look at the data, which changes their understanding and so forth. (Freil & Bright, 1998, p. 194)

for the classroom

An excellent children's book entitled *If the World Were a Village* (Smith, 2002) carefully integrates statistics and demographic information of countries all around the world.

The premise used by Smith is to reduce the population of the world to a representative global village of 100 people. Readers are then led through a series of data about population, ages, schooling and literacy, food, and air and water. Teaching suggestions and a website resource (www.mapping.com/village.html) are provided in the book. For example, in the village there are 6000 languages but more than half speak just eight languages: 21 people speak a Chinese dialect and 16 Mandarin, nine speak English, nine speak Hindi, seven Spanish, four Arabic, four Bengali, three Portuguese, and three Russian.

As a first step, students must ask a question that can be answered through the collection of data. What data can be collected, and from where? Students need to understand the importance of carefully worded questions when collecting data via surveys. How will the questions be interpreted, and will the answers provide the data needed to answer the research question?

think + link

A more in-depth discussion about randomness is found in Chapter 21.

There is also the issue of sampling a representative group. This often can be best achieved by using a random sample. Students often have difficulty grasping the concept of randomness (Konold & Higgins, 2003) and tend to think you must question everyone for the results to be valid.

Provide opportunities for students to collect data and to gain an understanding of the importance of appropriate sampling. Discuss the issue of selecting a group that will adequately represent the population being investigated. For example, suppose your school has received a donation to benefit students. The Principal has some ideas for projects that include playground equipment, laptops, sports equipment, and digital microscopes. The Principal would like to include the primary school community of 700 students and 45 staff in the decision-making process. Discuss with your class who and how many people should be asked to give an opinion about the school project.

making connections

Use fields such as sports to engage students' interest in statistics. There are countless examples of the use of statistics in all sporting activities.

The Australian Sports Commission website <www.ausport.gov.au/> is an excellent source for all kinds of sports statistics.

Be aware that some students are not interested in sport and be prepared to provide examples from a range of fields.

Children's experiences

When young students are presented with pictographs they are more likely to respond to the images than to the data unless they are prompted. The following scenario in a Year 1 class has been adapted from Russell (2006).

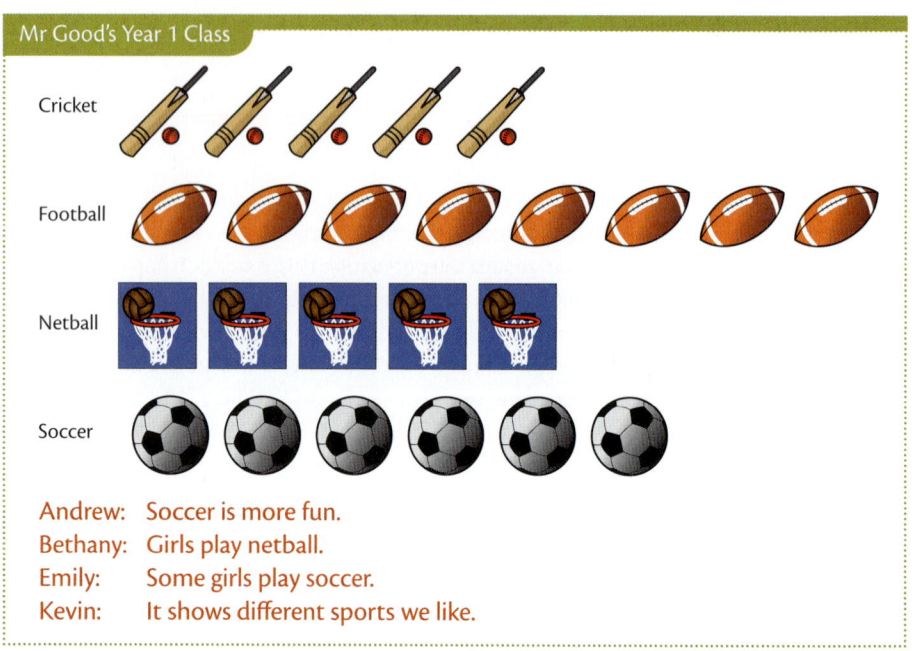

Mr Good's Year 1 Class

Andrew: Soccer is more fun.
Bethany: Girls play netball.
Emily: Some girls play soccer.
Kevin: It shows different sports we like.

The students have responded about the pictures of the sports rather than about the actual data. When prompted about how many students like soccer and which sport was most liked by students they could answer correctly, but they did not initiate this kind of description themselves. As a next step the students asked students in another class about their favourite sports. Below are the results of the survey.

Mrs Bell's Year 3 Class

Bethany: More students in Year 3 like netball.
Andrew: Soccer is the last sport in Mrs Bell's class.

It is important to frame questions and data collection carefully. Comparisons of two data sets may encourage students to think more about the meaning of the results. When confronted with a set of data by which a comparison could be made, students are able to speak more about the meaning of the data.

Data

'Data are not the same as events in the real world, but they help us understand phenomena in the real world' (Russell, 2006, p. 17). Part of your role as a teacher is to help students understand that the data collected must reasonably represent the event being investigated. There are many types of data, and your students have encountered a range of data formats. You need to build on this experience to assist students in representing and interpreting data appropriately.

Surveys are only one source of data. You can use data from almost any area of the curriculum. For example, your class may be growing and recording the growth of bean plants in science. Personalising the data allows the students to feel a connection and can assist in engagement with the concept.

Variation

'The reason data are collected, graphs drawn, and averages calculated is to manage variation and draw conclusions in relation to questions based on phenomena' (Watson, 2006, p. 21). Students need to experience variation in different formats. Variation involves situations in context, such as clothing sizes, as well as random variation like that in games of chance. Although variation is at the core of statistics and probability, it is often given little emphasis in the curriculum. Watson (2006) posits that this may be because it seems obvious, but in reality the concept requires explicit scaffolding for children in the early years.

Given that variation is contextual, Watson (2006) argues that it doesn't make sense to teach it separately from other elements of statistics and probability: the concept should be addressed in association with specific investigations. In general, students associate mathematics with absolutes and certainty, so the concept of variation and uncertainty may cause discomfort. As a teacher, you must provide opportunities for students to grapple with these fundamental components of statistics and probability.

A question of average

'Average' is probably the best known concept in statistics. It is however often misunderstood and over-simplified. As a term in everyday life, we often use it to mean ordinary, or typical. Students have preconceived ideas as to its meaning; for example, when asked about a movie they have just seen, a person might say that it was just average, meaning that it wasn't very good. It is in fact a statistical tool used for data reduction. According to Patilla (2008), the '**average** is a number that best represents a set of numbers'.

There are three traditional types of averages: mean, median, and mode. Consider the five numbers 3, 3, 4, 6, 9.

- The **mean** is 5 because $\frac{3 + 3 + 4 + 6 + 9}{5}$ equals 5.
- The **median** is 4 because it is the middle value when the numbers are placed in order: 3, 3, ④, 6, 9.
- The **mode** is 3 because it occurs most often.

While mean is the typical average used, students do not have a good concept of mean as average. Being able to calculate the mean does not necessarily indicate understanding of the concept. We should avoid introducing the formal algorithm too early!

The mean, median, and mode are all valid descriptions of data and have different functions with specific kinds of data. Unfortunately, results of data analysis are frequently reported in the popular media using the generic term of average. According to Konold and Higgins (2003), students tend to think of the most common value (mode) as the average. Mode is most useful for describing qualitative data, such as favourite food.

You often read about the 'average Australian income', but the mean is usually not the best representation of typical incomes. A few very large incomes (or outliers) may cause the mean to appear much higher than the median, and hence *artificially* raise the average.

Examine the following data to illustrate how a single piece of data can affect the mean. A group of students in a Teacher Education tutorial are asked about their yearly income. The data are presented below.

$11 000 $7000 $22 000 $16 000 $5000 $10 000 $12 000 $19 000 $23 000 $84 000 $15 000

Both the mean and the median represent an average and can be used to describe the data. However, the data is better represented by the median because one value, the income of $84 000, has raised the mean. Such a piece of data is referred to as an outlier. It may be interesting to remove the outlier and recalculate the averages.

$$\text{Mean} = \frac{\$140\,000}{10} = \$14\,000$$

Median: $5000, $7000, $10 000, $11 000, ($12 000, $15 000,) $16 000, $19 000, $22 000, $23 000

$$\text{Median} = \frac{\$(12\,000 + 15\,000)}{2} = \$13\,500$$

Removing the outlier has changed the mean more significantly than the median. This supports the original premise that the average income for the above data was best represented by the median.

consider and discuss

1. What everyday examples of averages can you use for Year 6–7 students?
2. Why is it important for students not only to know how to calculate averages but to also understand how averages can be used?

introducing technology

Australian CensusAtSchool is an online program supported by the Australian Bureau of Statistics (ABS) that can be accessed from www.abs.gov.au/websitedbs/cashome.nsf/home/home. The program coordinates Years 5 to 12 students from all over Australia to collect real data about themselves by completing an online questionnaire similar to the population census. The project is part of a larger international project designed to improve statistical literacy. CensusAtSchool actively engages students in collecting and critically analysing relevant data. Over 44 000 students from 3500 schools across Australia participated in the 2008 CensusAtSchool Questionnaire, and tables of data can be accessed on nine topics. These include average weekly income of students, hours spent on different activities per week, and food eaten for breakfast. Support materials are available for teachers, including lesson ideas in learning areas such as mathematics, science, and SOSE.

Representations

Organising and communicating data is also important. Representations are particularly important in the area of data as they are an effective way to communicate the results of data analysis. Students need to use a range of **representations**, including line graphs, bar graphs, pictographs, and tables. The choice of representation is influenced by the purpose and audience. While many representations are valid some require more abstract understanding.

Patilla (2008) describes a range of representations, such as pictographs, pie charts, and bar charts:

- In a pictograph, pictures can stand for one thing or a number of things. Pictographs are used for categorical data.
- In a pie chart, information is shown as a circle and the different sized slices of the pie stand for the quantities. Pie charts show proportions of a whole, and are used for categorical data.
- A bar chart is a graph that uses horizontal or vertical bars to show information. Bar charts are used for either categorical or grouped numerical data. The width of the bars is usually the same but width can vary if the area of the bars is used for purposes of comparison instead of height.

think + link

As indicated in Chapter 6, representations assist students in making sense of concepts and give the teacher insight into students' understanding.

introducing technology

Spreadsheets allow students to create high-quality graphs to illustrate data. Online tutorials and lesson materials are readily available. Students can readily explore the appropriateness of different representations.

Tinkerplots is a special data analysis program designed for students in Years 4–8. The process used to make graphs with Tinkerplots helps to scaffold student learning.

In addition to providing opportunities for students to select and represent the data accurately, students need to be taught how to interpret graphs. Reading graphs and developing the ability to answer questions about the data is an essential skill for all students to have.

communicating mathematically

As explained in Chapter 5, students should always be encouraged to justify their analysis and conclusions. For example, upper primary students can discuss which average is the most representative in specific situations. The data should not always be tidy, as a lot of data in real life are messy!

for the classroom

Have students in your class collect data to answer real questions they are interested in. For example, suppose the local council plans to sell land currently used for a park and playground. The students could design a simple questionnaire and collect and analyse the data. Perhaps you could encourage the students to write a letter to the local council and use the survey results to support their position.

consider and discuss

An article in the *Mercury* newspaper reported that two million children die of diarrhoea each year. This situation is all the more tragic, given that there are very simple and effective treatments available. While deaths of children from diarrhoea have declined over the past 30 years, the current treatment involves taking a mixture of zinc tablets and oral rehydration salts. This treatment costs approximately 48c a child, and it is estimated that 50 million children's lives have been saved so far. Money is also required to find out further information and to develop even more effective treatments.

1. Consider how the figure of 50 million children saved might have been arrived at.
2. How might the World Health Organization have found that diarrhoea accounts for 20% of all child deaths?
3. Find a current article in the newspaper that uses statistics and summarise the main points. Examine the use of statistics.
    a. How is the data represented?
    b. Is enough information provided for you to critique the use of statistics?
    c. What questions are you left with?
    d. What is your overall opinion of the use of statistics in the article?

What is probability?

did you know?

Ancient Egyptians played games of chance more than 4000 years ago. A games board found in the tomb of Tutankhamun was used to play a game called 20-squares. The object of this game was to move five cone-shaped pieces diagonally down a central row of squares from one side of the board to another. Casting sticks were used like dice are in games today.

The concept of risk and chance is often challenging for students, but we encounter risk and uncertainty in all aspects of our life. Developing an understanding of probability concepts assists students to develop the ability to make decisions that are associated with risk. For example, people who smoke are at increased risk of developing specific diseases.

According to Patilla (2008), **probability** is the chance of something happening. You often write the probability of something happening as a fraction. Words you might use when talking about probability include chance, likelihood, and odds.

consider and discuss

A story in the *Mercury* newspaper on 1 November 2008 included the following claim:

> Dr Taylor said pregnant women who smoked had twice the risk of a low birthweight baby, which was a threat to the short and long-term health of the child.

If we take low birth weight to mean less than 2500 g, and this is the birth weight range of approximately 6% of Australian babies, what is the risk of a low birth weight baby for women who smoke?

Express this risk using fractions or ratios rather than percentages.

The language of probability is part of everyday life, and as such students will have preconceived ideas about the topic. Even young children are familiar with the concept of chance in games such as snakes and ladders. This background experience is clearly positive, in that it provides scaffolding for you as a teacher to build on. There are, however, some misconceptions that come from the common understanding of probability. For example, when playing dice games, many players wrongly believe that dice results are influenced by previous throws.

issues in teaching

Alice, Peter, Julia, and Geoff are playing snakes and ladders. No player has thrown a 6 for many rounds. Alice needs a 6 to win the game and confidently states that surely she will roll a 6 because it is time for one!

- What is your response to this statement?
- Should Alice expect to roll a 6?

This is a great teachable moment! Good teachers recognise and use unplanned opportunities to provide real examples of mathematics concepts.

- How can you, as a teacher, use this situation to teach about chance?

The ability to understand and use probability has become essential for all adults. Shaughnessey (1998) explains that '(p)eople will be required to make more and more decisions in lives under conditions of uncertainty' (p. 223). Students must gain an understanding of chance and risk and be prepared to contribute to community situations that involve data and chance.

> ### communicating mathematically
>
> Consider some of the following words: certain, uncertain, likely, unlikely, possible, and impossible. What understanding of these terms do you think your students may have? How can you use students' background experiences in your teaching?

Important terms are further defined in Chapters 21 and 28.

The big ideas of probability are gradually developed through the primary and middle years. Although formal understanding and use of more complex mathematical terms is not introduced in the early years, it is important for all teachers to have knowledge of the main concepts and terminology.

Teaching probability

The Australian curriculum emphasises statistics concepts in the early years, and most educators (e.g. Shaughnessey, 1998) suggest teaching about data before introducing chance.

> ### issues in teaching
>
> Students have many preconceived ideas about what is fair, and this influences their perception of probability. Teachers need to create activities that challenge students' misconceptions.

Teaching methods and appropriate activities for learning probability concepts are explored in Chapters 21 and 28.

Broad ideas about basic chance are introduced in Year 1 and knowledge is gradually developed more formally through the primary and middle years. Table 12.1 provides an overview of the development of probability concepts given in the Australian curriculum. The use of ratios and fractions to describe probability is not introduced until Year 4. It is important for students to have some understanding of the concepts of chance before formalising the information. Students do not have the prerequisite background knowledge until Year 4.

Teachers should use students' background experiences to introduce chance concepts. Young children are capable of distinguishing between random and predetermined events. Shaughnessey (1998) discusses research that indicates students have a tendency to believe that all events are equally likely. This idea is no doubt connected to the belief that everything should be fair. It is therefore important for teachers to expose students to activities that challenge this belief. In the middle years students begin to explore odds in situations such as gambling and insurance. The calculation of probability in these situations is subjective—based on estimations only. This brings in a different dimension from previous probability examples that were based on clearly defined rules. This area is conceptually more complicated and an area that requires careful handling.

Table 12.1 **Probability content of the Australian curriculum**

Year level	Content
1	Identify outcomes arising from familiar chance events and describe using everyday language such as yes, no, or maybe
2	Experiment with chance devices and describe outcomes as likely or unlikely and identify some events as certain or impossible
3	Conduct chance experiments and recognise that there will be variation in results as well as having expected outcomes
4	Predict the outcomes of chance experiments involving equally likely events, and compare and contrast the predictability of outcomes of experiments with small numbers of trials to those with large numbers, including using ICT to generate the trials Justify representations of simple situations with unequal outcomes such as constructing spinners using technology
5	Quantify chance with fractions, and apply this to investigate complementary events
6	List all outcomes for chance events and quantify probabilities using simple fractions, decimals, and percentages
7	Construct sample spaces for single-step experiments with equally likely outcomes and use them to assign probabilities Calculate relative frequencies, and recognise variation between results of chance experiments
8	Identify complementary events and use the facts that probabilities range between 0 and 1 and sum to 1 over the sample space to check probabilities Use Venn diagrams or two-way tables to illustrate 'and', 'or', 'given', and 'not' criteria, and to calculate simple probabilities
9	Calculate probabilities for two- and three-step experiments with equally likely outcomes which involve 'with replacement' and 'without replacement' Compare theoretical and experimental probabilities for two- and three-step experiments Evaluate non-random and random sampling techniques

Source: ACARA <www.acara.edu.au/default.asp>

issues in teaching

While gambling provides a natural link to the real world, it can be a sensitive issue for many people. Studying this field requires a certain amount of maturity. Students may have gambling issues in their own family. Other families may object to gambling being part of the school curriculum. Consider these issues when developing any content that includes gambling. Speak to experienced teachers and find out how they teach this area.

Conclusion

An understanding of statistics and probability is essential, as we are all bombarded with data on a daily basis. As teachers, we must prepare students to have a critical approach to the use and interpretation of data. Students have preconceived ideas about data that can be used to begin teaching foundational concepts. It is important, however, to be aware that some of their ideas are inaccurate and will need to be challenged through carefully chosen learning activities.

The use of real data actively engages students in the learning process. The language of chance is familiar to students and provides a useful entry point for you to build on. Chance concepts are best taught through students' understanding of statistics. These areas of the curriculum have become increasingly important and should be valued.

key terms

Average: a number that best represents a set of data. This can be calculated as a mean, median, or mode

Data: information or facts you find out or are given. Data can be words, numbers, or a mixture of both

Mean: a kind of average determined by dividing the total of the quantities by the number of quantities

Median: a kind of average that is the middle value in a set of numerically ordered data.

Mode: a kind of average that is the quantity or number that occurs most often

Probability: the chance of something happening; can be written as a fraction or percentage

Representations: ways of organising and communicating data

Statistics: the collection and analysis of data to describe the world

Review questions

1. What experiences with statistics and probability do children have in their daily lives?
2. Select a newspaper article with statistics and describe how you may be able to use it in teaching.
3. What is meant by statistical literacy?
4. What are some common misunderstandings that students have about the concept of chance?
5. Why is knowledge of statistics and probability considered important?

Key references

Freil, S., & Bright, G. (1998). Teach-Stat: A model professional development in data analysis and statistics teachers K–6. In S. P. Lajoie (Ed.), *Reflections on Statistics Learning, Teaching and Assessment in Grades K–12* (pp. 89–117). Mahwah, NJ: Erlbaum.

Konold, C., & Higgins, T. (2003). Reasoning about data. In J. Kilpatrick, W. Martin & D. Schifter (Eds.), *A Research Companion to Principles and Standards for School Mathematics* (pp. 193–214). Reston, VA: NCTM.

Nugent, H. (2006) Germans are brainiest (but at least we're smarter than the French). Retrieved 1 November 2007 from www.timesonline.co.uk/tol/news/uk/article697134.ece.

Patilla, P. (2008). *Oxford Primary Maths Dictionary* (revised ed.). Oxford, UK: Oxford University Press.

Russell, S. (2006). What does it mean that '5' has a lot? From the world to data and back. In G. Burrill & P. Elliott (Eds.), *Thinking and Reasoning with Data and Chance: Sixty-eighth Yearbook* (pp. 17–29). Reston, VA: NCTM.

Shaughnessey, M. (1998). Research on students' understandings of probability. In S. P. Lajoie (Ed.), *Reflections on Statistics Learning, Teaching and Assessment in Grades K–12.* (pp. 216–226). Mahwah, NJ: Erlbaum.

Smith, D. (2002). *If the World were a Village*. New York: Kids Can Press.

Watson, J. (2006). *Statistical Literacy at School: Growth and Goals*. Mahwah, NJ: Erlbaum.

Whitin, D. (2006). Learning to talk back to a statistic. In G. Burrill & P. Elliott (Eds.), *Thinking and Reasoning with Data and Chance: Sixty-eighth Yearbook* (pp. 31–39). Reston, VA: NCTM.

Websites

ACARA www.acara.edu.au/default.asp

CensusAtSchool Australia www.abs.gov.au/websitedbs/cashome.nsf/home/home

Australian Sports Commission www.ausport.gov.au/

Part four

Laying the Basis for F–4 Mathematics

Young children possess an informal knowledge of mathematics that is surprisingly broad, complex, and sophisticated … They explore patterns, shapes, and spatial relations; compare magnitudes; and count objects … They engage in mathematical thinking and reasoning in many contexts, especially if they have sufficient knowledge about the materials they are using (e.g., toys), if the task is understandable and motivating, and if the context is familiar and comfortable. (Clements & Sarama, 2007, p. 462)

Proud Grandmothers

Having discovered while waiting for a flight from Darwin to Katherine that they both had three-year-old granddaughters, two women struck up a conversation about what each child could do. One, an Indigenous woman who was returning to a community outside Katherine, spoke of her granddaughter's ability to name her relationship with each member of her extended family and visit her aunts on the other side of the community. The non-Indigenous woman spoke about her granddaughter's knowledge of the alphabet and her ability to count to 10, but acknowledged that there was no way her granddaughter could, or would be allowed to, find her own way home from the park even though it was just around the corner from the family home in Casuarina.

This story illustrates that young children come to school with a vast repertoire of knowledge, skills and experience that is culturaly bound and variously valued. Young children also learn more in their first five years than they ever will again (e.g. Macmillan, 2009), and they largely learn this in ways that are different from how we expect them to learn at school.

The chapters in Part 4 explore what is involved in developing young children's intuitive sense of pattern, number, measurement, space, and chance more formally. Although we deal with the various strands of mathematics separately and number is considered in terms of numeration and operations, in practice effective teachers draw on the rich connections between these to ensure students develop firm foundations for future mathematics learning.

Questions

1. What abilities do you expect young children to have when they come to school? How might this vary with home background and location? Which of these might be regarded as mathematical abilities?
2. How would you answer these challenging questions from young children:
   - Is 0 an even number?
   - How big is the Moon?
   - Will it rain on my birthday tomorrow?
   - What happens to the knot when you untie your shoe?

13 Pattern and Structure

Contents

What is pattern and structure?	249
Why is pattern and structure important?	251
Early algebraic thinking	256
Functional thinking	256
Conclusion	262

Chapter objectives

This chapter will enable the reader to:

- Recognise the role of patterns in learning and how all patterns can be extended and generalised
- Develop a broad understanding of the structure of mathematics and the impact this has on early mathematics learning and teaching
- Recognise the pedagogical practices that support the exploration of patterns and structure in classroom learning.

Structure of the number system

Peter is an 8-year-old student in our early algebra research project.

Interviewer:	Does 2 + 3 = 3 + 2?
Peter:	Yes it does ... Because 3 and 2 is 5 and 2 and 3 is 5. They are the same number.
Interviewer:	Does 3 − 2 = 2 − 3?
Peter:	No.
Interviewer:	How do you know?
Peter:	Because 3 − 2 is 1 but 2 − 3 isn't 1. You can't take 3 from 2.
Interviewer:	Why can't you take 3 from 2?
Peter:	Because my teacher said you can't. You can only take small numbers from big numbers ... [after a very long pause] ... But you can. He doesn't know what he is talking about.
Interviewer:	Can you? What is the answer?
Peter:	Negative 1.

Interviewer: How do you know that?
Peter: I went home and asked my brother.
Interviewer: Can you show me?

Peter then drew the following diagram.

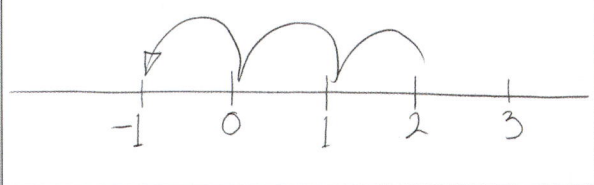

Big ideas

- Generalising patterns is seen as a key to developing mathematical thinking and algebraic understanding.
- Paying attention to similarities and differences is a powerful way to teach mathematics and it assists in unveiling its structure.
- Understanding the structure of arithmetic is not only a key factor for effectively understanding algebra, but also assists students' ability to compute.

What is pattern and structure?

Mathematics is often defined as the science of **patterns**. Applications of mathematics use these patterns to 'explain' and predict natural phenomena (Australian Education Council, 1991).

Much of mathematics is about patterns, and mathematics teaching is about searching for, describing, **generalising**, and justifying these patterns (Steen, 1988). This transforms mathematics in the primary classroom from a focus on finding one numerical answer to arithmetic problems to providing opportunities for pattern-building, conjecturing, and generalising mathematical facts and relationships.

The structure of mathematics refers to its architectural features and its characteristics. Mathematics as a discipline is essentially comprised of definitions, procedures, theorems, and proofs. Thus its structure is both defined and discovered (Lakoff & Nùnez, 1997). For example, addition can be defined as the process of adding one number to another. When exploring the process of adding two numbers we discover that it does not matter what order we add them: this is an example of the commutative law. Thus mathematical theories explain the relations among patterns.

Discovering pattern and structure in mathematics is a powerful way of thinking about mathematical learning. Table 13.1 lists examples of pattern and structure from all strands of mathematics.

Table 13.1: Examples of pattern and structure across the strands in mathematics

Strand	Sub-strand	Patterns and structure within strands
Number	Counting and operations	Adding 3 to 23 involves the same pattern as adding 3 and 373. It does not matter in what order we multiply numbers, the answer is the same.
	Place value	MAB blocks reveal the place value structure of our number system: the hundreds are 10 times larger than the tens, the tens are 10 times larger than the units, and so on.
	Fractions	If we share one pizza among 2 we each get a ½. If we share one pizza among 3 we each get ⅓. If we share one pizza among 6 we each get a ⅙. The more people we share with, the less we get. The fraction we get is related to the number we share with.
Space		The volume of a cone is a third of the volume of a cylinder with the same base and height.
		The volume of a square-based pyramid is a third of the volume of cuboid with the same base and height.
		The volume of a triangular-based pyramid is a third of the volume of a triangular prism with the same base and height. This is true for all pairs of shapes with the same base and height.
Measurement		There are 100 mm^2 in 1 cm^2
		There are 100 cm^2 in 1 dm^2
		There are 100 dm^2 in 1 m^2
		As we increase the unit of measure by 10 the area increases a hundredfold.
Chance & data		The more times we repeat an experiment the more the outcomes mirror theoretical probability.
Patterns & Algebra		If you add 0 to a number the number remains the same ($a + 0 = a$)
		If you multiply a number by 1, the number remains the same ($a \times 1 = a$)
		Addition and subtraction are inverse operations.

did you know?

The mathematician Leonardo of Pisa is better known by his family name of Fibonacci. In his book *Liber abaci* he described the Hindu-Arabic numerals and the place-valued decimal system for expressing numbers that we use today, and gave detailed instructions on how to compute with them (a process that became known as algorism, which subsequently led to the modern word *algorithm*). He also introduced the Western world to the pattern 1, 1, 2, 3, 5, 8, 13, 21, 34 … commonly known as the Fibonacci sequence. This pattern turns up in some surprising places, including music and poetry. As the sequence extends, the ratio of the last two numbers approaches the value of the golden ratio.

Why is pattern and structure important?

Searching for patterns is a natural process. For most of us as we look at examples we wonder what binds them together. As students learn mathematics it is natural for them to search for patterns as they build up images of mathematical concepts, but these images may conflict with the mathematical concept. Examples are statements such as 'When you multiply two numbers together the answer is always bigger', 'When you divide two numbers the answer gets smaller'. These misconceptions are difficult to redress when students are introduced to negative numbers and fractions. While these patterns hold for whole numbers, they are in conflict with the structure of mathematics, and with the concept definition for addition. Our role as teachers is to help students find patterns and ensure that these patterns are aligned with the structure of mathematics.

Understanding the structure of arithmetic forms the basis of algebraic understanding and assists students with computation. For example, if we know that 2 and 3 makes 5 then we also know that 20 and 30 is 50, 200 and 300 makes 500, and 0.2 and 0.3 makes 0.5. This is the way our number system is structured, how it has been built. Early development of one's ability to recognise pattern and structure has a positive influence on mathematical achievement overall and enables a stronger foundation for algebraic thinking (Mulligan, Mitchelmore & Prescott, 2006).

> ### making connections
>
> **String art**
>
> The different ways in which we join dots in string art creates different patterns. The structure dictates which dots we join to which, and the pattern is the outcome.
>
> The first pattern represents all of the ways we can make 11 (10 and 1, 9 and 2, 8 and 3 …) The second pattern represents all the ways we can make 12. Different structures give different patterns.

Repeating patterns

Repeating patterns are patterns that occur in many classrooms in the early years. Often young students are asked to copy, create and extend repeating patterns. They may use a large variety of materials including informal materials such as leaves, buttons, paper clips, straws, and more formal materials including geometric blocks and counters to do this. When we have asked their teachers why they teach repeating patterns they often cannot answer, or they give reasons such as that they help students to learn to read as they go from left to right.

The kernel of the mathematics in repeating patterns is the part that repeats (Papic, 2007), yet many of the students we talk to in classrooms cannot show us what part repeats. We believe that this is because many teachers in the early years understand that patterning is important but do not understand why the pattern structure is so important. Their focus tends to be on rhythmic chants with more and more complex repeating patterns, rather than the structure of the pattern itself (Threlfall, 1999). 'Jump clap jump clap jump clap jump clap' is an example of a simple repeating pattern; so is Figure 13.1

Figure 13.1 An example of a repeating pattern

handy hint

When selecting materials for creating patterns, select only two different kinds initially. The more visually different they are, the easier it is for students to see the pattern. Pattern structure is best seen in simple patterns.

Many students need intervention to assist them to continue the pattern both ways. They tend to extend the pattern only to the right and find extending to the left is more difficult.

for the classroom

Making pattern strips

Give the students a selection of simple materials, such as blocks, buttons, straws, shapes. Select two of the materials and use them to create a repeating pattern. Encourage students to first copy the pattern shown, and then extend the pattern as far as they can. The challenge is for them to extend it in both directions. Cover part of the pattern. Ask them to make the part that is missing on top of the cover. Repeat this activity using more and more complex repeating patterns.

Same pattern, different material

Have students make repeating patterns with one set of materials. Ask another student to make the same pattern using another set of materials. Encourage students to 'act out the pattern'; for example 'sit jump jump jump sit jump jump jump'.

handy hint

The ability to translate patterns to different modes of representations is a key understanding in all areas of mathematics.

issues in teaching

Identifying the repeating part

Students may need intervention to assist them to identify the repeating component (Warren & Cooper, 2008a). Ask the students 'What do you think is repeating? What is happening over and over again?' As they construct a pattern, encourage them to stop after each unit/repeat is made and tell you what the next part would be. Often students can identify part of the repeat but not the whole repeat. For example, they will tell you that 'three butterflies are repeating over and over again' or 'the spider is repeating over and over again' but not necessarily that the block or unit of a spider and three butterflies is repeating.

It is important to encourage students to stop each time they make a repeat, identify it by placing a loose band around it, and then continue to make the next repeat. You could also use a series of paper plates and encourage students to place each repeat on a separate plate.

Repeating patterns are a powerful representation of repeated addition and can serve as a first introduction to this concept. The ability to identify the repeating component can form the foundation to discussion about this concept.

for the classroom

Predicting unknown positions

This activity is the precursor for discussions about multiplicative thinking.

The elements in a repeating pattern can be numbered 1, 2, 3, 4 and so on. Before students extend the pattern, ask them what they think number 10 will be (or the tenth item). They should be encouraged to explain how they worked out which item it was. Students up to Year 2 will find this task difficult.

- What is shape number 10?
- What is shape number 21?
- Is it the first star, the second star or the heart?
- How do you know?

for the classroom

Multiplicative structure

- Have students make a repeating pattern.

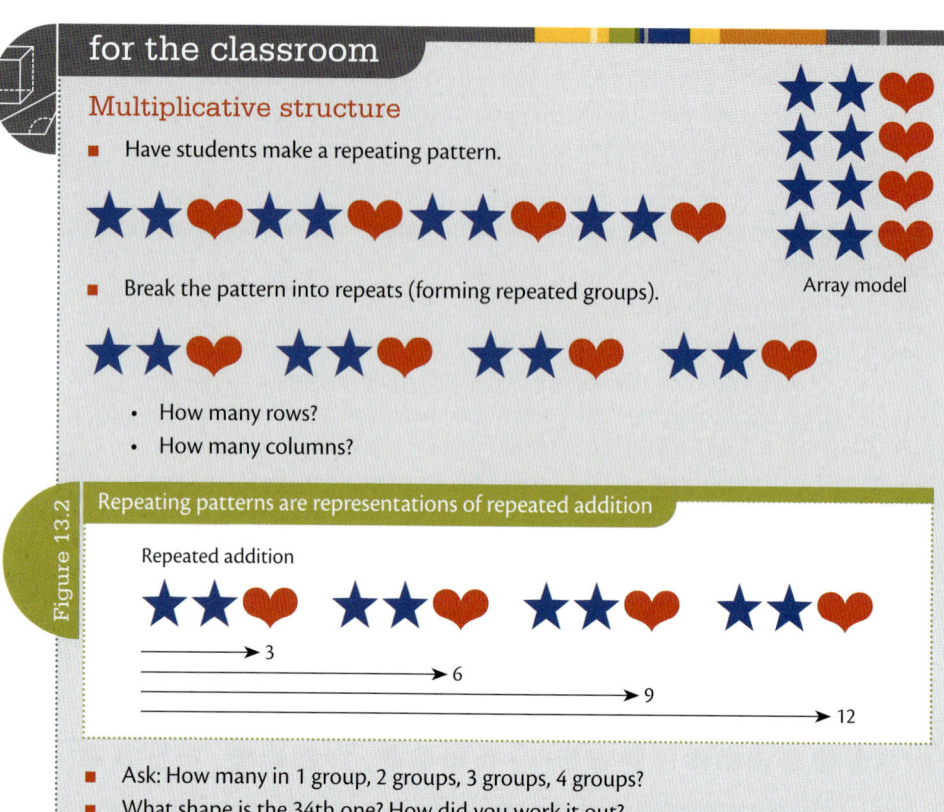

Array model

- Break the pattern into repeats (forming repeated groups).

  - How many rows?
  - How many columns?

Figure 13.2 Repeating patterns are representations of repeated addition

Repeated addition

→ 3
→ 6
→ 9
→ 12

- Ask: How many in 1 group, 2 groups, 3 groups, 4 groups?
- What shape is the 34th one? How did you work it out?
- Rearrange the pattern to show your answer in another way.

making connections

Multiplicative thinking underpins the development of our number system.

consider and discuss

Exploring patterns on the hundreds board

A common classroom activity is to colour number patterns on the hundreds board. A much more powerful activity is to place the above repeating pattern on the hundreds board. Once the board is covered, ask students to remove the stars.

1. What patterns can they see down the diagonals?
2. Add the digits that make each number. What pattern do you see?
3. How can you check if a number is divisible by 3?
4. Prove that this rule is true for all numbers divisible by 3.
5. Extend this thinking to find the rule for checking if a number is divisible by 9.
6. If we change the width of our board to 5 rather than 10, which numbers will make diagonal patterns?
7. How are the column patterns and diagonal patterns related to the width of the board?

1	2	3	4	5	6	7	8	9	10
11	12	13	14	15	16	17	18	19	20
21	22	23	24	25	26	27	28	29	30
31	32	33	34	35	36	37	38	39	40
41	42	43	44	45	46	47	48	49	50
51	52	53	54	55	56	57	58	59	60

Growing patterns

Growing patterns are patterns in which each section experiences consistent growth. Growing patterns are also the visual link to number patterns (Warren & Cooper, 2008a). It is important for young students to understand differences between repeating patterns and growing patterns, as each leads to different mathematical thinking. Repeating patterns lead to multiplicative thinking, including proportional reasoning and ratios. Growing patterns lead to functional thinking. This distinction will be discussed in greater depth in Chapter 21.

for the classroom

Introducing growing patterns

This activity assists students to 'see' the structural differences between a repeating pattern and a growing pattern.

- Ask students to make the following repeating pattern and separate the pattern into its repeats.

- Ask students to grow the blue by two.

Many students (and teachers) end up generating a new repeating pattern. They fail to make the blue grow by two each time, but simply add two blue tiles to each repeat. It is important for the students to physically 'experience' the growth.

- Strip the pink from the pattern and rearrange the units vertically.

- Discuss the growing pattern as a visual for the number pattern 1, 3, 5, 7.

All number patterns involve some form of progression (e.g. +2, +3, –2, ×2) and can be concretely represented as growing patterns. Growing number patterns can be either increasing or decreasing patterns (e.g. 3, 6, 9, 12, or 28, 25, 21, 18). Activities consist of continuing the pattern, finding missing terms in the pattern, or predicting numbers further along the pattern. The challenge with growing patterns is not to extend them but to predict down the line to find the missing term. This is an approach commonly used in the introduction of **algebra**, and one in which many students experience difficulties. Research suggests that students' difficulties stem from lack of experience with concrete materials and meaningful patterning experiences that focus on abstracting the pattern structure (Warren & Cooper 2008b). In the later years these patterns are used as an introduction to functional thinking and an understanding of the concept of a variable (see Chapter 25).

handy hint

When teaching, make instruction as language-rich as possible. We often limit students' experiences when we view language and mathematics as separate endeavours. A strategy to support language learning is to pair language with a gesture or visual images.

integrating technology

Number patterns on the calculator: skip counting

Students press the [2] and then [+] [2] [=] [=] [=] [=] and continue pressing the [=]. Ask them to describe the pattern they see. What numbers are always in the ones place? Repeat for the patterns of 3s, 5s, and 6s. Encourage them to stop and predict what number will come next. What is the largest number in the pattern? How do you know that a number is in the pattern?

Encourage students to also pattern backwards. For example, enter 256 then [−] [2] [=] [=] [=].

Early algebraic thinking

Many students experience difficulties with algebraic thinking. Some of these difficulties stem from students' lack of understanding of the structure of arithmetic (Warren, 2003). There has been a move internationally to reconsider the focus of arithmetic in the primary school, and to ensure that classroom experiences reach beyond introducing arithmetic as simply a computation tool. Classroom experiences also need to involve experiences that assist students to generalise the structure of arithmetic, a change in focus from procedural to conceptual understanding (Malara & Navarra, 2003).

In classrooms in the early years algebraic thinking entails:

- making explicit the mathematics of pattern (particularly repeating and growing patterns), and extending these patterns to our number system
- studying early functional thinking with a focus on the relationships between the operations, such as the inverse relationship between addition and subtraction, commutative law for addition, and the identities
- studying the structure of the number system and operations, for example the meaning of equals and the meaningful use of unknowns.
It does not entail the use or the manipulation of symbols.

Functional thinking

Functional thinking focuses on the relationship between two (or more) varying quantities. In the early years functions often involve following rules for consistent changes, and reversing this change. The rule uniquely associates elements from one set with elements from another. For example, if the rule was 'multiply by 2', then this rule uniquely associates 2 with 4, 8 with 16, 20 with 40.

This type of activity can occur in the beginning years of school, and is a very powerful approach to explicitly demonstrating the **inverse** relationship between addition and subtraction, and multiplication and division. These activities are enhanced with the use of representations such as function machines, and physically acting out the change and reversing processes (Warren, Benson & Green, 2007).

Functions involve consistent change. When focusing on the structure of mathematical concepts, numbers often get in the way (Davydov, 1975). Students focus on the computational aspects rather than the underlying concept.

Teachers of Year 1 were challenged to create a series of activities that did not involve number (Warren, Benson & Green, 2007).

for the classroom

Functions in the early years

Figure 13.3 Young students engaging with functions

- Assign one student to be the function machine.
- Give other students a series of objects or cards with pictures on them (the input). As students place their object or card in the machine, encourage them to predict the object card that would come out of the output slot.
- Students then walk past the machine, place the card or object through the input slot and collect the object or card that is passed through the output slot by the person operating the function machine.
- Complete the activity by asking the same students to walk backwards past the machine and predict what might happen to the output card if they place it back in the output slot to reverse the process. This sequence assists students to understand the notion of following rules, reversing rules, and the relationship between the rule and its inverse.

Our research has shown that acting out the input and output and the reverse function in this way is crucial to learning and understanding functional thinking. Ask questions such as: What happens when you walk forwards past the machine? What happens when you walk backwards?

The kinaesthetic movement of acting out the functions is crucial to developing young students' understanding of the concept of a function.

communicating mathematics

Encouraging students to predict and justify their predications supports students' mathematical thinking and their ability to communicate this thinking to others.

for the classroom

Linking representations

Once students have a clear understanding of the concept of functional thinking, move to applying this thinking to number situations.

- Repeat the above sequences using number.
- Try subtraction. For example: 'My rule is take 3. What is my rule if I go in the opposite direction?'
- Encourage students to also act out the change on number tracks.
- Discuss all the relevant relationships. For example, if we know 8 − 3 = 5 we also know 5 + 3 = 8, and that adding 3 is the opposite of subtracting 3.
- Link the 'change' to movement on the number track. For example, if I put 7 in the machine then the output would be 4. I would stand on 7 and walk back 3. To reverse the change I would stand on 4 and walk forwards 3.

If you allow students to select their own input cards you can guarantee that 2 and 1 will be some of their first choices. Interestingly, Australia is one of the few countries that does not explore negative numbers in the early years.

handy hint

'What's my rule' games can be used with young students to introduce them to algebraic thinking by encouraging them to express their generalisations in words.

consider and discuss

Exploring equivalent expressions

'What's my rule' games can be very challenging, especially if the change involves two or more rules. A two-rule change means that the output number has been changed by two different operations applied consecutively. Different orders for the operations result in different rules. Discuss what the rules are for the following changes. Find at least two different rules and express each as an algebraic expression. Discuss why these rules produce the same outputs.

In	Out
3	14
8	36
10	44

Two rule changes

In	Out
3	0.5
8	3
10	4

Two rule changes

What are some real world contexts for these rules?

The meaning of equals and equivalence

The equals sign is one of the most important symbols used in all areas of mathematics, but it is also one of the most poorly understood.

issues in teaching

Meaning of equals

In our study on early algebraic thinking, 878 students (average age 8 years and 6 months) were given the following sets of cards. The students were asked if the statements on the cards were true or false and asked to explain how they knew.

2 + 3 = 3 + 2	31 + 16 = 16 + 31
2 − 3 = 3 − 2	31 − 16 = 16 − 32

Twenty-three (27%) students stated that the first set was true and the second set was false.

Thirty-four students stated that both sets of cards were true. (False generalisation: commonly caused by a failure to explore similarities and differences between these two types of equations.)

Thirty-one students interpreted the = sign as a marker to put in the answer. A typical response was '2 and 3 makes 5 not 3' or 'the answer should be 7 as 2 and 3 makes 5 and 5 and 2 makes 7' (Warren, 2002). Carpenter, Franke and Levi (2003) reported similar patterns of responses in a study they conducted in the United States.

Many teachers use the term the 'is the same as' when comparing expressions on both sides of the equations, but the typical examples they are using in the primary classroom have the problem on one side and the answer on the other (e.g. 7 + 8 = 10; 29 − 16 = ☐; 3 × ☐ = 21). In these instances students experience equals as indicating a place to put the answer, like pushing the equals sign on the calculator. This is a very common misconception and occurs in the early years of school. Once students have this misunderstanding of the meaning of equals it is very difficult to address. Take care to examine the types of examples you are using closely. Remember, the equals sign means having the same quantity or value as something else, and thus it is imperative to pose problems such as 2 + 3 = 4 + ☐ to assist students to gain an understanding of its meaning.

handy hint

Reinforce through your own language that the equals sign means 'is the same as' even when you are recording results to computational problems.

When we focus on pattern and structure in our classroom, we are searching for relationships rather than answers. For example, if we ask students to find all of the ways they can make 10, then we are generating a range of expressions that represent 10, and the relationship between all of these expressions is that they are **equal** (e.g. 12 − 2 = 5 + 2 + 3, or 1 + 9 = 2 + 8, 2 + 8 = 3 + 7, 3 + 7 = 4 + 6). The pattern for relating all facts for 10 is that: Starting with 10 + 0, as we increase the first number by 1 we decrease the second number by 1. Figure 13.4 presents this pattern visually. It can also be stated in a problem context, for example: 'I had two bird cages that were joined and my 10 birds (all the same variety) could move freely between them. Show all of the ways the birds could be in the two cages.'

Figure 13.4 Contexts for understanding the patterns for 10

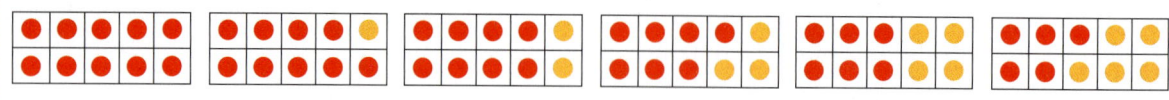

Students' misconceptions about the equals sign are also an obstacle when they begin to engage with algebraic expressions. Even a simple equation such as $23 = 3x - 4$ is problematic, as students are required to understand that the values on both sides are the same in order to find the solution. It is not possible to compute the right-hand side.

for the classroom

Equals as balance

Explore equations using a variety of representations including balance scales and lengths to represent different numbers.

When creating the equations with the balance scales, flip them around so students can see that equations such as $7 + 6 = 9 + 4$ is the same equation as $9 + 4 = 7 + 6$. It is also important to explore expressions that are not equal, asking questions such as: 'Is $9 + 12$ the same as $5 + 13$? Which one is larger and which one is smaller?'

Further generalisations of the number system

Conjecturing about mathematics is important in assisting students to make their implicit knowledge about the properties of operations explicit (Carpenter et al., 2003). Our role as teachers is to assist students to articulate, edit, and refine their conjectures, and to identify important mathematical ideas about which students can make conjectures. True/false sentences support these explorations. While some of the properties of the operations may seem trivial in an arithmetic context, an explicit understanding is important for later algebraic engagement. An example of this is the identities for the four operations.

for the classroom

The properties of 0

- Are these true or false? $23 + 0 = 23$; $23 + 11 = 23$ (Why is it false?)
- What can you tell me about 0? What is your conjecture? What about $12\,234 + 0 = 12\,234$?
- What is the rule?

As a teacher our role is to keep refining responses until the conjecture is mathematically correct (e.g. When you add zero to a number you get the number you started with). We also need to extend this thinking to other related cases.

- Are these true or false? $58 - 0 = 58$; $58 \times 0 = 58$. What is the rule? Justify your answer.
- Are these true or false? $76 - 76 = 0$; $12\,800 - 12\,800 = 0$. What is the rule?

Justifying solutions and reaching generalisations are key components of mathematical thinking—and remember, young students are capable of such thinking.

issues in teaching

The identities and negative numbers

Many Australian curricula do not introduce negative numbers until the middle primary years. This is at odds with many international curricula. When we asked students for all of the possible solutions for 13 − ☐ = 0, a number of students believed there was a range of possible answers, including all numbers that were greater than 13. 'If you take away 14 you have taken them all away so there is none left.' The classroom discussion continued until all were convinced that the only solution was 13. The use of a **number line** and negative numbers assists, but the introduction of negative numbers needs to occur in real contexts (e.g. a thermometer as the number line, and discussions about the weather in cold climates). Many young students have had 'out of school' experiences with negative numbers, especially if they have been on a holiday to the snow or a cold country.

The above conversations need to also occur with regard to the number 1. What operations is 1 the identity for? If we divide a number by itself, what answer do we get? An understanding of these properties is crucial as we often use the identity and inverses to solve algebraic problems in later years. They also underpin our understanding of some of our exploration into the number sense domain.

As indicated at the commencement of this chapter, many teachers fall into the trap of making statements that are imathematically incorrect. Some examples of these are 'you can't take a larger number from a smaller number', 'when you add numbers the answer is always bigger', 'when you divide a number the answer is always smaller'. These statements are true only if we are considering the natural numbers. Unfortunately, many of these statements become entrenched in students' thinking and are difficult to 'undo' in the latter years of school.

consider and discuss

Using the identities to assist mental computation

The compensation strategy for addition involves changing one of the numbers in an addition problem to a number that it is easier to compute mentally and then compensating for that change.

Bree wrote: 27 + 38; 30 + 38 is 68 … now subtract 3; that is 65. She added 3 to 27 then subtracted 3 from the answer.

1 How could you describe this strategy as a general rule?
2 Using the compensation strategy, try calculating 1000 − 458 mentally. What is the rule of subtraction, and why does it work?

An understanding of the identities assists students to 'make sense' of many of the rules we use in mathematics. For example, it is not uncommon for students to tell you that you generate equivalent fractions by multiplying the top and bottom by the same number. There are many students who misunderstand this rule and believe that a fraction remains the same as long as you do the same to the top and bottom. They wrongly believe this includes adding the same number to the top and bottom. Understanding the identity for multiplication assists students to see that if you multiply something by 1 it remains the same. Thus multiplying by $\frac{2}{2}$ is the same is multiplying by 1.

$$\frac{7}{8} \times \frac{2}{2} = \frac{7 \times 2}{8 \times 2}$$

integrating technology

The calculator can be used to explore the identities.

Wipe-out

Work in pairs. Ask one student to enter the number 476 in their calculator. The other student uses the operations to first wipe out the 7 and then the 4.

The other student then uses the operations to reinstate the 7 and then the 4.

(This activity requires an understanding of place value, the inverse relationship between addition and subtraction, and the properties of 0.)

The Golden Ratio

Exploring the ratios of consecutive Fibonacci numbers to demonstrate the Golden Ratio is more effective when a calculator is used for the computations.

Ratio of consecutive Fibonacci numbers	Result after dividing first number by second number
1 : 1	
1 : 2	
2 : 3	
3 : 5	
5 : 8	
8 : 13	
13 : 21	
21 :	

1. What did you notice happened each time you divided?
2. What do you think will happen if you keep dividing in the sequence?
3. The number that the Fibonacci sequence is 'getting close to' is called the Golden Ratio. It is considered to be the ideal ratio. Measure some rectangular (or nearly rectangular) objects in your classroom. Record them in a table like the one below, and write a ratio that compares the shorter dimension to the longer dimension. Then divide to compare the two numbers to see if they are near the golden ratio.

Object and dimensions	Ratio	Division comparison
Large table		
Smaller table		
Door		

communicating mathematically

Mathematical games can foster mathematical communication as students explain and justify their moves to one another.

Conclusion

Identifying pattern and structure in mathematics is at the heart of learning and teaching mathematics. It changes not only the way we think about mathematics but also the way we teach it. Our role as teachers is to understand the key ideas in mathematics and to choose materials and pedagogical approaches that allow students to explore patterns in all strands of mathematics, patterns that illuminate its structure. This approach is highly motivating as it allows students to 'discover' the beauty of mathematics and to act as mathematicians.

Each pattern leads to a generalisation. At this stage the focus should be on encouraging students to express their generalisation verbally, ensuring that the description is mathematically correct and justified. As we explore examples our attention is on 'What is the same? What is different? Does it work for all cases? Will it work for all numbers and for all operations?' The act of generalising is fundamental to learning mathematics (e.g. Cooper & Warren, 2008; Kaput, 1999) and has been described in the literature as the ability to see the general in the particular (Kruteskii, 1976). This involves looking across a number of cases and identifying the common structure, perceiving the commonalities in all cases. Kruteskii (1976) and Mason (1996) suggest that there is a duality in this process. One not only needs to see the general in the particular, but to also use the general to identify other particulars. It involves 'awaking and sharpening' both students' and teachers' sensitivity to the structure of mathematics and to ways of exploiting situations that have the potential for algebraic thinking to occur (Mason, 1996). This is a process that Kaput and Blanton (2001) refer to as algebrafying the curriculum.

key terms

Algebra: the branch of mathematics concerning the study of the rules of operations and relations, and the constructions and concepts arising from them

Equal: having the same quantity, value, or measure of another

Function: a mathematical relation such that each element of a given set (the domain of the function) is associated with an element of another set (the range of the function)

Generalising: a principle, statement, or idea having general application

Growing patterns: a pattern that grows or increases (or decreases) by a constant difference.

Identity: an equality that remains true regardless of any of the values for the variables that appear within it (e.g. $a \times 1 = a$; 1 is the identity)

Inverse: opposite in nature or effect or relation to another quantity

Number line: line marked with numbers

Pattern: a pattern constitutes a set of numbers or objects in which all the members are related with each other by a specific rule

Repeating patterns: a pattern of a group of items that repeats over and over

Review questions

1. Describe the pedagogical issues related to teaching from a pattern and structure perspective.
2. Describe your understanding of what algebraic thinking means for primary school students. Illustrate your discussion using a particular content area of mathematics.
3. Describe why equality, change, and generalisation are important ideas in algebraic thinking.
4. Review some current resource books for using ideas and patterns in the primary context. Describe one idea in detail, listing the resources you would use and the particular mathematical structure the idea focuses on.

Key references

Carpenter, P., Franke, M., & Levi, L. (2003). *Thinking Mathematically: Integrating Arithmetic and Algebra in the Elementary School*. Portsmouth, NH: Heinemann.

Davydov, V. V. (1975). The psychological characteristics of the 'prenumeral' period of mathematics instruction. In L. P. Steffe (Ed.), *Children's Capacity for Learning Mathematics* (Vol VII, pp. 109–205). Chicago: University of Chicago Press.

Kaput, J. (1999). Teaching and learning a new algebra. In E. Fennema & T. Romberg (Eds.), *Mathematics Classrooms that Promote Understanding* (pp. 133–155). Mahwah, NJ: Erlbaum.

Mason, J. (1996). Expressing generality and roots of algebra. In N. Bednarz, C. Kieran & L. Lee (Eds.), *Approaches to Algebra: Perspectives for Research and Teaching*. Utrech: Kluwer.

Warren, E., & Cooper T. J. (2008a). Patterns that support early algebraic thinking in the elementary school. In C. Greenes & R. Rubenstien (Eds.), *Algebra and Algebraic Thinking in School Mathematics. Seventieth Yearbook National Council of Teachers of Mathematics*. Reston, VA: NCTM.

Developing Early Number Ideas and Strategies

14

Contents

The origins of number	266
Research on early number learning	272
Playing with number	276
The numbers 0 to 10	279
A sense of numbers beyond 10	286
Scaffolding solution strategies	287
Conclusion	288

Chapter objectives

This chapter will enable the reader to:
- Appreciate the rich history of numbers
- Understand what mathematical knowledge, skills, and strategies young children bring with them to school
- Understand what is involved in learning the numbers 0 to 9
- Recognise the role of counting and subitising in the development of initial number ideas and strategies
- Understand what is meant by trusting the count and why it is so important in building a strong sense of number
- Recognise the value of counting large collections more efficiently and developing a sense of numbers beyond 10.

But can she count?

Emma was in her first year of teaching. She had found out in December the previous year that she would be teaching a Foundation class, and since then had spent some time planning and preparing for her first few weeks of teaching. Three weeks into Term 1, Jenny's mother made an appointment to see Emma after school. Emma collected her folder of work samples for Jenny. She need not have worried, Jenny's mother was effusive: 'The children are all loving school, we are very happy with what you are doing … but, did you know that Jenny can count to 100? We think she needs to be extended in maths.' Emma was aware of this and knew exactly what to say in reply – would you?

Big ideas

- Counting involves much more than a knowledge of the number naming sequence.
- Subitising holds the key to developing a rich understanding of the numbers to 10 and beyond.
- Part–part–whole knowledge of the numbers to 10 is essential in building a sense of number.
- Trusting the count is a prerequisite for understanding all further work in number.

The origins of number

Since the earliest of times, human beings have developed systematic ways for storing and/or recording useful information and passing it on to future generations. A considerable amount of this information was and is embedded in stories about the origins of the group's existence, where and at what times particular food sources were available, and how best to live (social norms). But a large proportion of this information was also concerned with forms and quantities (Gundlach, 1989) as evidenced by early cave drawings and the hieroglyphics found in ancient Egyptian tombs.

making connections

Ethnographic studies suggest that the ordered use of body parts to keep track of quantities such as the number of sheep in a flock, or to negotiate the number of items to be exchanged in trade, were widely used across different cultural groups before specific number words or symbols were developed. Referred to as **enumeration** by Gundlach, this amounted to matching each item with a well-known, ordered sequence of body parts, with the last body part pointed to or touched indicating the total number of items. **Enumerating** systems such as this have served the needs of hunter–gatherer and/or nomadic societies for tens of thousands of years, and can still be found today (e.g. Bishop, 1991; Saxe, 1995).

By using names to denote each body part, it was not necessary to point to all of the body parts in sequence: it was sufficient to use the words in the same sequence. Eventually these words became de facto number words, but this does not mean that their use constituted a generalised understanding of number.

This type of matching procedure might be thought of as qualitative rather than quantitative. Indeed, in this primitive form, numeration seems to reside entirely in the things enumerated rather than in the human mind ... The use of number words, however, does not in itself imply the concept of cardinal number, though it undoubtedly did lead to it. (Gundlach, 1989, pp. 20–21)

No one really knows when unique number names for given quantities (e.g. 'six') first appeared, although it would seem that various versions of these existed in different parts of the ancient world at much the same time, most notably in China, Egypt, and India. Referred to as **cardinal numbers**, they uniquely name the number of elements in a set, independently of the elements themselves and the order in which they are arranged. In general, the answer to any question that asks 'how many' is best given by a cardinal number. For example, 26 is the answer to the question, 'How many letters are there in the English alphabet?'.

A necessary precursor for the development of cardinal numbers is the abstract notion of a collection as an entity, that is, as a 'set', although it was not referred to as such until much later. When the Yolngu people of North-East Arnhem Land refer to *lurrkun' rulu*, effectively 3 fives, they are recognising *rulu* (the name of an arrangement of five turtle eggs with four on the bottom and one on top) as a name for a set of five objects, that is, as a cardinal number.

In societies that value quantitative over qualitative world views, number words and ultimately number symbols and **numeration systems** emerged as the size of collections outnumbered body parts and as agriculture, trade, and construction called for more efficient ways of communicating and recording quantitative information.

Historical number systems

The earliest number systems were based on five or 10, presumably because of the connection to fingers and hands. Initially, these systems relied on repetition, with single lines or dashes to indicate ones and symbols or pictographs for quantities such as five, 10, 100, and so on. These symbols and/or pictographs were used as many times as necessary to indicate the total amount required, as shown in Table 14.1. As a consequence, such systems are referred to as *additive* systems of numeration. It is believed the subtractive principle, illustrated by writing IV (literally 'one before five') for four instead of the additive IIII, was not used by the Romans and rather was introduced into the Roman numeration system many hundreds of years later when mechanical forms of printing became more common (Gundlach, 1989).

Table 14.1 Examples of additive numeration systems

Roman system of numeration		Egyptian system of numeration
I = one V = five X = ten L = fifty C = hundred D = five hundred M = thousand	For example, 1964 would be written as MDCCCCLXIIII With the subtractive principle it would be written as MCMLXIV	(hieroglyphic examples showing = 3244 and = 21237; symbols for 1–9, 10, 100, 1000, 10000, 100000, 1000000)

Source: Hardegree, 2001, p. 12

consider and discuss

Roman numerals today

Roman numerals are often used to indicate the year that a movie was made or that a signficant building was erected. Find examples, and discuss. Write the year of your birth in Roman numerals. The film *Gone With The Wind* was made in MDCCCCXXXIX. What year was this?

Using Roman numerals, try adding 456 and 1208 or subtracting 678 from 923. What do you notice?

The ancient Greeks had at least two systems of **numeration**, the Attic (Athenian) and the Ionic, both of which were additive. The Attic system, which was similar to the Roman system, used a multiplicative principle to a limited extent in that 50 and 500, for example, were written by incorporating the symbol for 10 (Δ) or 100 (H) under the 'arm' of the symbol for 5 (Γ) respectively. By contrast, the Ionic system used all the letters of the Greek alphabet plus three additional letters that had fallen out of common usage to refer to each of the numbers to 10 and each multiple of 10 and 100 thereafter, 27 symbols in total (see Figure 14.1). To write 862 for instance, the symbols for 800 (ω), 60 (ξ) and 2 (β) were used but as addition is commutative, these could be written in any order as the sum of the values indicated the number represented. Thousands were indicated by a stroke before the symbols for the ones, for example, 4000 was indicated by /δ and 8000 by /η. Tens of thousands were represented by writing the symbol for 10 000 (M for myriad) below the number of ten thousands required, for example, 43 000 would be written by writing the symbols for 43 (μγ) above M. Although essentially an additive system, the Ionic system was also referred to as a *ciphered system* because of its use of the ordinal alphabet system.

Figure 14.1

Greek system of numeration

	Units	Tens	Hundreds	Thousands
1	α alpha	ι iota	ρ rho	/α
2	β beta	κ kappa	σ sigma	/β
3	γ gamma	λ lambda	τ tau	/γ
4	δ delta	μ mu	υ upsilon	/δ
5	ε epsilon	ν nu	φ phi	/ε
6	ϝ digamma	ξ xi	χ chi	/ϝ
7	ζ zeta	ο omicron	ψ psi	/ζ
8	η eta	π pi	ω omega	/η
9	θ theta	ϙ koppa	ϡ sampi	/θ

ωξβ = 800 + 60 + 2 = 862

for the classroom

Invite middle year students to write their age and year of birth using Greek numerals, then solve the following problems using these symbols.

- 34 + 52
- 348 + 271
- 56 × 3
- 78 − 45
- 82 − 47
- 61 × 10

The Greeks used tables of basic facts to calculate. What might these have looked like? How difficult would they be to learn and use?

The earlier rod-based, and the more recent character-based Chinese systems of numeration both made some use of multiplication and/or position to indicate the value of the symbols used. For example, the early Chinese numeration system used two sets of symbols for the numbers 0 to 9 as shown in Figure 14.2. The first set was used for ones, hundreds, and tens of thousands, and the second set was used for tens, thousands, and hundreds of thousands. This necessitated a symbol for zero as the relative location or position of the symbols now became important. This system is regarded as an early *positional* numeration system.

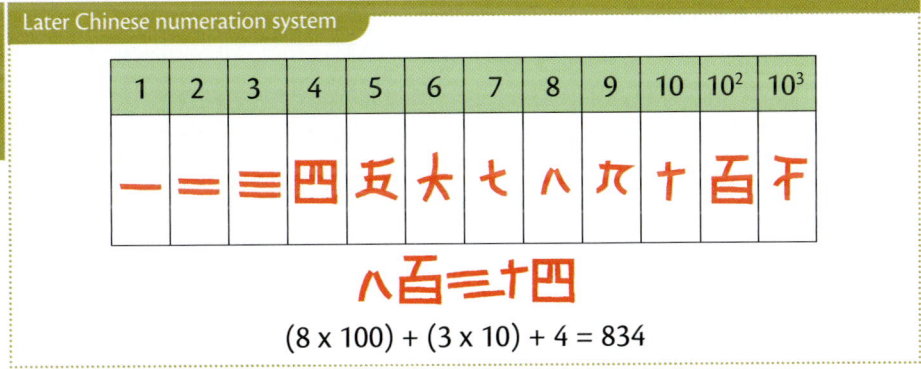

Figure 14.2 Early Chinese numeration system

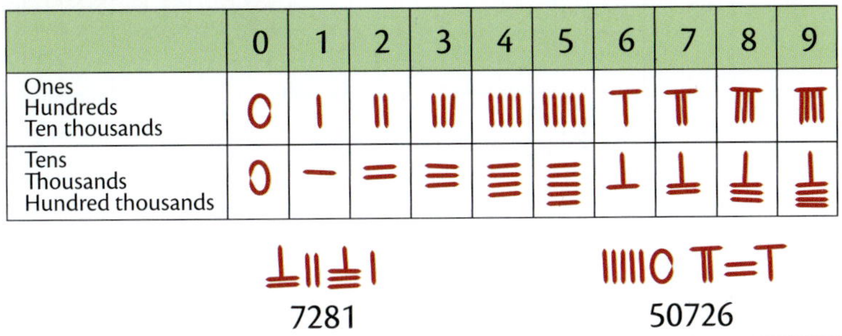

The later Chinese numeration system used nine symbols for the ones and additional symbols for each power of 10. This did not require a symbol for zero, but it did require that the symbols were written and read in an ordered fashion from left to right, starting with multiples of the largest power of 10 as shown in Figure 14.3.

Figure 14.3 Later Chinese numeration system

1	2	3	4	5	6	7	8	9	10	10^2	10^3
一	二	三	四	五	六	七	八	九	十	百	千

八百三十四

(8 x 100) + (3 x 10) + 4 = 834

This sytem, which is still used in some parts of China today, is regarded as a *multiplicative* numeration system.

The Babylonian system of numeration was probably the first place-based or *positional* numeration system although there was no symbol for zero; instead spaces were used to indicate the absence of a particular place-value part. This system used two symbols, formed by pushing different cross-sections of river reed into soft clay tablets. The base of the river reed was used to make the symbol for one, and the upper part of the reed was used to make the symbol for 10. These symbols were used additively to represent all of the numbers to 59, then repeated as needed in columns representing successive powers of 60 as shown in Figure 14.4. This allowed the Babylonians to represent large numbers relatively efficiently.

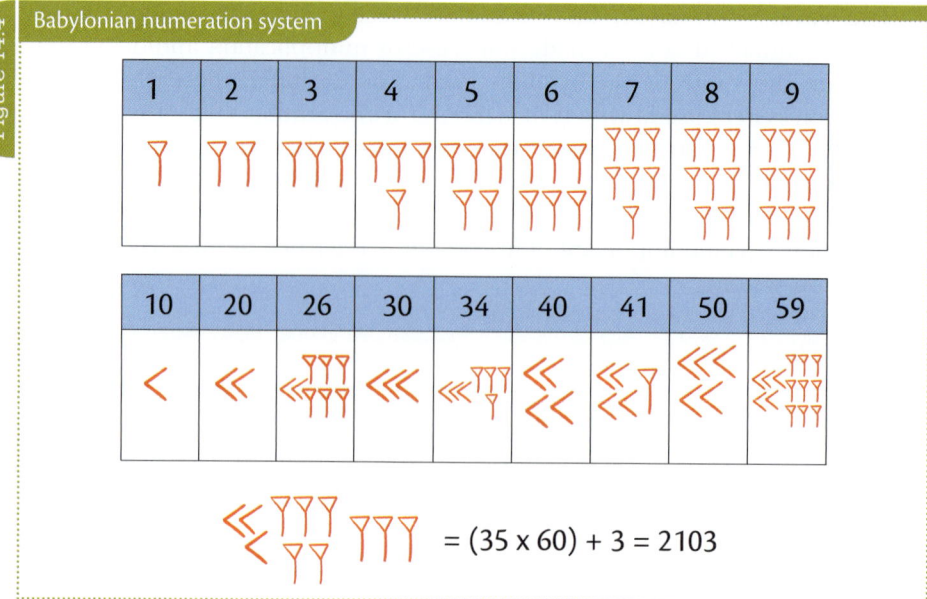

Figure 14.4 Babylonian numeration system

From about the fourth century CE, the Mayans developed a more systematic place-value system based on 20 with the exception of the third place-value part; instead of being 20^3 this was 20×18 (possibly to align with the Mayan calendar). Symbols were written vertically and read from the bottom up, so 20 was written by recording the symbol for 1 in the second place (1×20) over the symbol for zero in the first place (0×1), which is analogous to the way we write 10 from left to right meaning 1×10 (1 ten) and 0×1 (no ones).

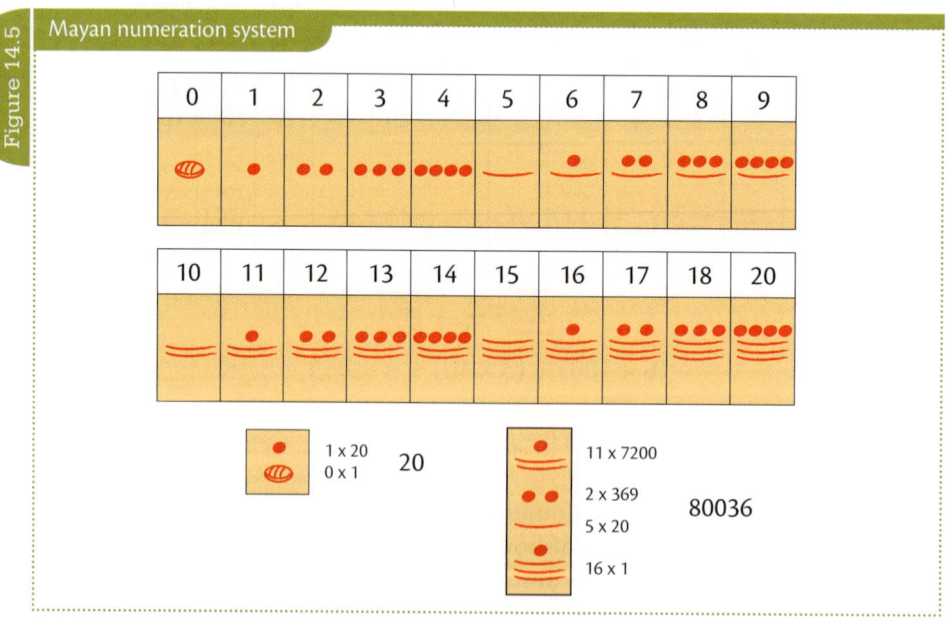

Figure 14.5 Mayan numeration system

No one really knows how our present system of numeration, referred to as the Hindu-Arabic system, emerged to become the dominant numeration system, although it is generally understood that this occurred in India in the time between the fourth and the seventh century CE and had its origins in the symbols and place-value based system used in India at the time. Its widespread adoption throughout the Middle Ages is attributed to the movement of the Arabs from about 800 CE with the development of decimal fractions emerging much later as an extension (Gundlach, 1989).

Initially, what set numeration systems apart from methods of enumeration was that they were not dependent on the objects being counted or a process of matching each and every element of a set with a gesture, marker, or number word. As numeration systems evolved over time to include a symbol for 0 and a consistent, place-based recording system, they offered a powerful means of codifying the world that transcended language barriers, supported trade and navigation, and facilitated the development and dissemination of new knowledge in mathematics, physics, astronomy, and many other fields, leading ultimately to the digital age in which we live and largely take for granted today.

communicating mathematically

Binary numbers

Digital technologies rely on the binary numeration system. This has two digits only, 0 and 1. The numbers are used to represent the two states of an electronic circuit, where off = 0 and on = 1. Numbers such as 9, 67, or 249 can be written in binary form as a sequence of 1s and 0s and are manipulated at extremely high speeds to perform various functions.

Just as the base 10 numeration system is made up of multiples (0 to 9) of powers of 10 (e.g. $249 = 2 \times 10^2 + 4 \times 10^1 + 9 \times 10^0$), the binary number system uses multiples (in this case 0 or 1 only) of powers of 2 (e.g. $9 = 1 \times 2^3 + 0 \times 2^2 + 0 \times 2^1 + 1 \times 2^0 = 1001_{two}$).

1. Write the base 10 numerals 24 and 35 in binary form then try adding them together.
2. What do you need to do to subtract the smallest from the largest? What do you notice?

We should not forget that numbers are only one way of codifying the world. While there is evidence that children and animals are born with an intuitive sense of quantity, the notion that numbers have names and can be represented by symbols which can be combined together in particular ways is something that is learnt over time through shared forms of communication and supportive social practices (Macmillan, 2009; Perry & Dockett, 2008). This has important implications for how number is taught and learnt.

consider and discuss

Numbers are everywhere

Work in groups to collect as many digital images as possible of numbers used in everyday contexts. Sort these according to some criteria (e.g. measures, quantities, comparisons, labels) and make a PowerPoint presentation or electronic whiteboard activity to demonstrate the influence that numbers have on our lives.

Reflect on your own initiation into the world of numbers. Discuss your experiences with others. What implications does this have for the teaching and learning of number in the early years of schooling?

Research on early number learning

More has been written about and more classroom time is devoted to the teaching and learning of number than any other domain of school mathematics (for reviews see Clements & Sarama, 2007; Verschaffel & De Corte, 1996). This is not surprising when we consider the abstract nature of numbers and what is involved in coming to understand and use numbers. Nor is it surprising that this area of research dominates theorising about the mechanisms and processes involved in learning mathematics.

Theoretical perspectives

One of the most important influences on the teaching and learning of number in English-speaking countries was the work of Jean Piaget. The translation of Piaget's work on the development of number (Piaget, 1952) generated a significant amount of research on the role of logical operations such as conservation, classification, and **ordering** in the development of number. Subsequent research concentrated on the role of **counting** in the development of number ideas and strategies, building on the ideas of Piaget in terms of the mechanisms of learning (*assimilation* and *accommodation*); the building blocks of learning (*schemas*); and the principles of *equilibration* and *reflective abstraction* (e.g. Steffe, Cobb & von Glasersfeld, 1988). Referred to as *constructivism*, the focus was on the individual as an active agent in the construction of mathematical meaning on the basis of his/her prior knowledge and experience.

In the mid 1990s, researchers recognised the importance of both the individual's construction of meaning and the *social context* in which this takes place (e.g. Cobb, 1995; Cobb & Yackel, 1996). From this perspective, individual 'students are seen as actively contributing to the development of both classroom mathematical practices and the encompassing microculture, and these both enable and constrain their individual mathematical activities' (Cobb & Bauersfeld, 1995, p. 9). This shift in emphasis prompted a reassessment of how young children come to learn number and the recognition that while counting is important, so too is the child's lived experiences with number in all its manifestations.

The emergence of quantitative reasoning

Humans and animals share an innate capacity to discriminate quantities from an early age (see Chapter 10). Initially, this is based on the *relative magnitude* of the quantities rather than *absolute magnitude*, although it is evident that young children can recognise the absolute magnitudes of small collections up to four without counting (Buys, 2001; Perry & Dockett, 2008). Relative judgments are often made on the basis of perceptual cues related to 'how much' (continuous quantity) rather than 'how many' (discrete quantity), as demonstrated in the conservation experiments conducted by Piaget. While this innate capacity to judge relative magnitude does not extend to larger numbers or operate entirely consistently, it is now viewed as an important precursor of number sense (Clements & Sarama, 2007; Schmittau & Morris, 2004).

This was not always the case. Piaget believed that the child's concept of number was underpinned by the logical operations of classifying, ordering, and conservation. That is, it was based on the ability to discriminate and sort collections on the basis of attributes such as size, shape, colour, or texture; the ability to sequence an ordered set of objects such as six drinking straws of different lengths; and the ability to recognise that the numerosity of two matching collections remained the same irrespective of changes made to one, such as moving the objects further apart. Subsequent research (see for example, Bryant, 1974; Clements & Callahan, 1982; Clements & Sarama, 2007; Nunes & Bryant, 1996; Verscaffel & De Corte, 1996) has largely discounted these as necessary and sufficient skills, but acknowledges that they are important capabilities that serve mathematics well more generally, for example in recognising attributes and making inferences about size, shape, and orientation.

According to Clements and Sarama's (2007) analysis of the literature:

> early numerical knowledge includes four interrelated aspects (as well as others): recognizing and naming how many items are in a small configuration (small number recognition, and when done quickly, subitizing), learning the names and eventually the ordered list of number words to ten and beyond, enumerating objects (i.e., saying the number words in correspondence with objects), and understanding that the last number word said when counting refers to how many items have been counted . (p. 478)

Two of these (subitising and recognising and naming how many) involve the construction of **mental objects for each of the numbers to 10**, and includes the notions of more than/less than and part–part–whole. The remaining aspects can be seen as social practices (e.g. reciting the number names, matching objects to number names, and counting to find how many). While both are acquired as a result of activity, there is a tendency to over-emphasise counting and matching number words and symbols to discrete collections at the expense of constructing mental objects for each of the numbers to 10, with the result that a significant proportion of students in the middle years of schooling develop an over-reliance on some form of counting and/or additive thinking to solve problems that involve multiplication or division (Siemon, Breed, Dole, Izard & Virgona, 2006).

issues in teaching

Counting not the only way 'in' to number

As we saw in Chapter 11, an alternative approach to teaching number and arithmetic starts out with measurement (e.g. Davydov, Gorbov, Mikulina & Saveleva, 1999). This approach is based on the claim that working with continuous, quantitative relationships such as 'longer than', 'shorter than', and 'is the same as' before working with discrete counts provides a better introduction to the real numbers and the use of symbols than counting.

This has important implications for how number is taught and learnt in the early years of schooling. To find out more, visit <www.maa.org/devlin/devlin_01_09.html> and investigate the impact of the *Measure Up* curriculum in Hawaii (e.g. Schmittau, 2003; Schmittau & Morris, 2004)

In this context, it is interesting to note that the developmental frameworks offered by two of Australia's most respected and widely used programs to support early mathematics learning, *Count Me In Too* (CMIT, e.g. Wright, Stanger,

Stafford & Martlkand, 2006) and the *Early Years Numeracy Project* (ENRP, e.g. Clarke & Clarke, 2004), are both framed in terms of counting. The fact that students in Singapore and Japan outperform students from other countries in assessments of international mathematics achievement suggests that counting-based curricula can work. However, both Singapore and Japan place a greater emphasis on the development of proportionality, something that the Davydov curriculum also emphasises, than countries like Australia and the United States.

This implies that there might be some advantage in approaching the teaching and learning of number from both measurement and counting perspectives, each grounded in structured, real-world experience. Developing mental objects for each of the numbers to 10 and beyond (numeration) and participating in a range of social practices that use and apply numbers in context (operations) are both needed to ensure children develop a deep sense of number, so it makes sense to consider what each of these approaches can offer.

The important role of experience

Knowledge is constructed through activity, interaction, and reflection on experience. In the early years, this is most powerfully realised through play and interaction with more learned others. (Perry & Dockett, 2008)

We would like to suggest children learn about numbers in much the same way we all learn about 'yellow'. Initially, the young child is exposed to the notion of yellow by more learned others who 'point to' yellow in various ways, for example, 'Look at the yellow duck' or 'That flower is yellow'. Through this means and by testing their use of the word 'yellow', children build a mental object for 'yellowness' that includes a whole range of 'yellows' from lime-yellow to brown-yellow, to which they can attach the word 'yellow'. In a similar way, young children come to recognise the word and symbol for each of the numbers to 10 but they need to be exposed to many different embodiments of each number to build a mental object for that number. For example, they need to 'see' 8 as 1 more than 7, 6 and 2 more, 2 less than 10 and so on, to build a mental object for 8.

Young children are constantly exposed to the language of comparisons: 'My, haven't you grown? You are nearly as tall as the table', 'There is the same amount of milk in your glass as in your brother's', 'The elephant is enormous, the mouse is tiny' and so on. These relative judgments are based on the continuous dimensions of length, capacity, and volume. While absolute quantities are also 'pointed to' by adults, for example, 'There are three peas left on the plate', or 'Let's set four places for dinner', such instances are often followed by a count, for example, 'Three bears, see … one, two, three'. Children also meet other representations and uses of numbers through 'pointing', for example, 'We live at 5 Jackson Street' (nominal use), or 'Jeremy came second in the race' (ordinal use).

To summarise, we learn about cardinal numbers (e.g. 'threeness') in much the same way that we learn about any other concept, by being exposed to many examples and non-examples and by learning to attach words and ultimately symbols to instances which exemplify the concept. But we also learn by imitating valued practices, such as **comparing** and counting.

Trusting the count

The big idea of **trusting the count** in developing a sense of number was introduced in Chapter 10. The term was originally used by Willis (2002) to refer to the fact that children may not believe that they will arrive at the same amount if they count the same collection again or if it is re-arranged. This use refers not only to the physical act of counting (enumeration), but also to the result of the count.

Given that 'how many' can also be arrived at by recognising collections up to four or five without counting (subitising) and that the remaining numbers to 10 can be perceived and ultimately understood in terms of their parts (part–part–whole knowledge), it seems reasonable to suggest that the notion of trusting the count be extended to include the capacity to recognise the **numerosity** of numbers to 10 without having to model and/or count. In this sense, children trust the count for a given number not only when they believe that counting will produce an invariant result (literal interpretation), but also when they have access to a mental object for that number that renders counting unnecessary in most dealings with that number (Freudenthal, 1991; Siemon, 2006). For example, a child trusts the count for 8 when he or she can access a repertoire of knowledge items and images for 'eightness' that obviates the need to make and count a collection of 8 in order to decide what is 3 more than 8. In this case, the child might access his/her knowledge of 8 in relation to 10, that is, 8 is 2 less than 10, so 8 and 3 is '8, 10 and 1 more, 11'.

In short, *trusting the count* has been appropriated to incorporate not only its initial and literal interpretation but also to refer to a child's capacity to access flexible mental objects for the numbers 0 to 10 based on their experiences with these as cardinal numbers. Trusting the count in that sense is demonstrated when children are able to reason with these numbers in flexible and efficient ways without having to physically represent or manipulate the numbers in any way.

think + link

A more detailed account of the theories and perspectives that underpin the learning and teaching of mathematics can be found in Chapters 2 and 3.

Playing with number

Young children's exposure to the language of comparative relationships and counting may involve hearing/making statements about relative size of two objects, or, in the case of number, listening to the numbers in word order as a parent assists a toddler to walk up a flight of stairs, learning to say the numbers in word order as hands are clapped at a child's birthday party, or collaboratively counting the images in a children's counting picture book or the number of peas left on a plate. Children are encouraged to notice numbers in the environment, to recognise the numbers on remote control devices, on car number plates or signs, and they generally know how to write their own age in numerals by the time they are three. These practical experiences with number, while informal and often spontaneous, play an important role in enculturating young children to the world of numbers.

making connections

Social practices such as story telling, playing games and enacting nursery rhymes provide rich opportunities for learning about number.

> Imagine a mother with a young child sitting on her knee reciting and actioning the nursery rhyme, 'This little piggy went to market'. The child—and maybe the adult—may not realise that the mathematical principle of one-to-one correspondence is being enacted. Nevertheless, the child is being introduced to the concept in a social and cultural context—the context's social dimension has language being expressed, and there is perceptual and physical communication between people; the cultural dimension is the traditional nursery rhyme. (Macmillan, 2009, p. 20)

The role of language

The further development of mathematical ideas and competencies depends to a large extent on the development of language appropriate to the task in hand (e.g. Ellerton, Clarkson & Clements, 2000; Macmillan, 2009; Perry & Dockett, 2008). This starts with simple words of comparison such as 'bigger/smaller', 'longer/shorter', 'same', 'more', 'less', names for known small collections such as 'two' and 'three', and simple relations such as 'one more/one less', and requires the development of more sophisticated forms of language that enable children to communicate their ideas with their peers and teachers and to elaborate and defend those ideas when necessary (Perry & Dockett, 2008).

> Teachers who are effective in promoting their children's learning through play often adopt the role of provocateur ... through which they observe and assess the understandings demonstrated by individual children and then generate situations which challenge these. This may involve asking questions, introducing elements of surprise, requiring the children to explain their position to others and working with children to consider the logical consequences of the positions they adopt ... For this to occur, the children need to feel comfortable in their classroom (Perry & Dockett, 2008, p. 90).

The comparative language related to quantities and collections needs to be explicitly developed through structured, purposeful play using physical materials, pictures, story books, and the children themselves.

- 'Bigger than/smaller than/the same size as' can be explored by comparing the items in a collection of stuffed toys.
- 'More/less/same as' can be considered by comparing different sized packs of cards or collections of marbles or by using beam balances to compare quantities of unifix blocks.
- 'Before/after' ordinal relationships can be explored by placing toys and/or play equipment in a row and discussing which toy is after the red truck, which toy is before the soccer ball, and so on. This can ultimately extend to a discussion of which number comes before four and which number comes after six.

Chapter 14 Developing Early Number Ideas and Strategies

for the classroom

Devise a simple treasure hunt, giving different groups different objects to find. For instance, each group could be given two lengths of string and asked to find an 'in-between' object, that is, one longer than the shorter piece of string but shorter than the longer piece. Objects could be compared and ordered from shortest to longest and discussed in terms of what comes before/after a given object.

Attention to language can help young children become aware of the distinction between 'how much' (referring to continuous quantity such as length, area, volume, or capacity) and 'how many' (referring to the number of discrete objects). While continuous quantities are more strongly connected with children's early experiences of the world than are discrete quantities both need to be explored in developing a deep sense of number.

issues in teaching

English language learners (ELLs)

Access to the language of instruction is a challenge for the many students for whom English is not the first language (see e.g. Chapter 8). For many it may be a third or fourth language, so referring to these students as 'second language' learners underestimates the challenges they face as well as the richness of their cultural–linguistic background. English as a Second Language (ESL) strategies may be appropriate for all these students. Borgioli (2008) makes the following suggestions.

- Connect student backgrounds and prior knowledge to new learning rather than dilute the curriculum.
- Choose tasks that are 'potentially rich in learning opportunities not only for mathematics but also in language' (p. 187).
- Encourage tool usage (manipulatives and representations) as a means of communication, not only as 'answer-getting devices'.
- Take time to listen and understand the speaker.
- Facilitate participatory dialogue through all four language modes—listening, speaking, reading, and writing—and by supporting use of home languages wherever possible.
- Keep a visual, written, or pictorial record of key ideas presented by students and teachers.

Nursery rhymes, number poems, and counting books also offer a powerful means of alerting young children to numbers and how they are used. For example, the number naming sequence can be introduced and rehearsed through activities and songs that involve alliteration and picture cards (e.g. one whale, two turtles, three thistles, four frogs, five fish, six snakes), engaging stories and illustrations in counting story books such as *The Very Hungry Caterpillar* (Carle, 1974) and *One is a Snail, Ten is a Crab* (Sayre & Sayre, 2003), and through physical activity in nursery rhymes such as:

One, two, three four, five	Why did you let it go?
Once I caught a fish alive.	Because it bit my finger so.
Six, seven, eight, nine, ten	Which finger did it bite?
But I let it go again.	This little finger on my right.

for the classroom

Involve older children in devising number rhymes and actions for younger students based on 'One, two, buckle my shoe, Three, four, knock on the door, Five, six, pick up sticks, Seven, eight, shut the gate, Nine, ten, a big fat hen'.

Older children could also be involved in writing and illustrating counting books in collaboration with younger children. The products of these activities can then be shared, presented, displayed, and discussed.

Experiences with symbols

Symbols also need to be considered as an important aspect of number-related language learning (see Chapter 6 for further discussion of this issue). In a classic research study, Hughes (1986) encouraged three- and four-year-olds to explore a number of buttons in each of four identical tins, containing 0, 1, 2, and 3 respectively. After some time, he asked if the children could mark the top of the tins in some way to show how many buttons were in that tin. The children showed that they had an early appreciation of the role of symbols in denoting a numerical amount. However, as Perry and Dockett (2008) warn, children eventually need to engage with conventional symbols of mathematics:

> it is unnecessary, and even counterproductive, to expect this level of symbol use among many young children who often have developed their own system of symbols and use these consistently until another, more standardised system, can be taken on board. (p. 93)

consider and discuss

Twice five plus the wings of a bird

It is worth trying to access this well-known and engaging video from the BBC about young children's spontaneous use of symbols (Hughes, 1986). Although the production values are not high, there is much that we can learn from the children's activity and responses. For instance, what are the teaching and learning implications of children inventing and using their own symbols for numbers?

In the Davydov curriculum (see above), 'the concept of number and actions on numbers ... are developed from relationships between quantities' (Schmittau & Morris, 2004, p. 61). Young children exposed to the systematically ordered problems have no difficulty generating and using symbols (capital letters) for abstracted quantities such as length or area and the signs for equality and inequality ($=$, $\neq$, $<$, $>$) to describe physical situations. For example, they compare the lengths of two boards, name the lengths A and B, and represent the relationship between them as $A = B$, $A \neq B$, $A > B$, or $A < B$. There is no reference to numbers during this work: A represents the unmeasured length of the board.

While these examples suggest that we should not underestimate children's capacity to deal with symbols, the conditions of both situations need to be taken into account. For instance, it may be that the property of length is more accessible to perception and thereby a better candidate for abstraction than is number stripped of its instantiation.

The numbers 0 to 10

The whole numbers 0 to 9 are the only numbers most of us ever need to know, as every other number we routinely come across is made up of some combination of these numbers in accordance with accepted patterns such as place value (e.g. 5308) or conventions (e.g. fraction symbols, indices, repeating or terminating decimals, and surds). While there are some numbers that cannot be expressed neatly in this way (e.g. irrational numbers such as $\sqrt{2}$, π, and e), and the square root of -1 (i), most, apart from π, are not seriously considered until the senior years of secondary school, if at all. Given the importance of 10 in our number system and the fact that the vast majority of the numbers we deal with are made up of the digits 0 to 9, it is essential to establish mental objects for each of the numbers to 10 (trusting the count). This big idea underpins all further work with numbers, in particular an acceptance and understanding of how numbers are organised and represented in place-value parts and how numbers can be variously composed and decomposed to support mental computation and problem solving more generally.

It seems that an approach that gives due regard to the roles of both measuring and counting is appropriate. Comparing continuous quantities (early measuring) can be used to establish a sense of, and language for, *relative quantity*. Matching number words to discrete collections in a systematic and ordered way (counting) can be used to develop a sense of *absolute quantity* or cardinal number. However, according to Clements and Sarama (2007), **subitising**, that is the capacity to recognise small collections without counting, was recognised as early as 1912 as an underpinning for number ideas, on the grounds that 'whereas measurement focused on the whole and counting focused on the unit item, only subitizing focused on both the whole and the unit' (p. 469).

did you know?

The word **digit** is used to refer to the written number symbols for the numbers 0 to 9. This term is most often used to refer to the magnitude of particular number sets; for example 3829 is a four-digit number, as is any number from 1000 to 9999. As letters are to words, so digits are to numbers.

By contrast, the term **numeral** refers to any symbol or word used to denote a number. For example, π is a numeral, and we refer to the Roman numerals.

Most pre-schoolers will have some knowledge of the number names and symbols to 10, but it is highly likely that students will vary considerably both in the amount that is known and the consistency and accuracy with which it can be demonstrated in practice. This might range from a tenuous grasp of the first few number names to the confident and accurate recitation of the number naming sequence to 20 or more. While the latter feat is impressive, it does not necessarily indicate that the child understands what numbers mean or is capable of accurately counting a collection to say how many. Much more is needed to work confidently with numbers to 10 and beyond. In particular, young children need to be able to:

- identify which of two quantities (collections) is bigger or smaller (more or less)
- recognise small collections to five without counting (subitise)

- match collections to number names and symbols (and vice versa)
- demonstrate a knowledge of the number naming sequence
- identify one more, one less, what comes after, what comes before a given number
- recognise that counting words and objects need to be in one-to-one correspondence, the last number says 'how many', and that the count remains the same even if the objects are rearranged
- recognise numbers as composite units and name the numbers to 10 in terms of their parts
- demonstrate a sense of numbers beyond 10 in terms of '1 ten and so many more'.

While many young children come to school with some of these skills, this is not necessarily the case, particularly for children in remote Indigenous communities, where the language of more and less may need to be taught explicitly. However, it seems that many of these children have an exceptionally well-developed capacity to subitise (e.g. Willis, 2002), which suggests that this might be a more appropriate starting point than rote recitation of the number naming sequence or counting.

Some activities that might be used to develop these capacities were listed above. We will now consider what is needed more formally to develop a deep sense of the numbers to 10 and beyond in terms of the four interrelated aspects identified by Clements and Sarama (2007).

Subitising and part–part–whole ideas

The early research on subitising was conducted by experimental psychologists interested in the mean response times of adults and children. The people in their study were asked to identify the numerosity of small collections shown for 200 milliseconds or so. While this established that most children can 'instantly' recognise collections up to 3 and adults can do this up to 4, the implications for teaching and learning number were not widely recognised at the time. What is of interest is what individuals can do with more time and greater exposure to visual representations that utilise and build on the capacity to recognise small collections without counting.

The immediate recognition of numbers up to 4 is referred to by Clements (1999) as *perceptual subitising*. With practice, this can be built up to 5, and the remaining numbers to 10 can be recognised in terms of their subitised parts (e.g. 8 is 'seen' as 1 more than 7, as 5 and 3 more, as double 4, or as 2 more than 6). Clements refers to this secondary capacity as *conceptual subitising* and both capacities are regarded as fundamental to the development of a sense of number. The numbers to 10 and the relationships between them can be represented using number frames, initially five-frames then ten-frames (see Figure 14.6), which can be used to construct different representations or as flash cards for the purposes of subitising. The numbers to 10 should be dealt with systematically starting with the numbers 1 to 5, then 0 as a number in its own right. The numbers 6 to 10 can be modelled by counting on from 5 (e.g. 6 is 1 more than 5), recognising 6 in terms of its subitisable parts (6 is 3 and 3, or 4 and 2 more), and by recognising 6 in relation to 10 (6 is 4 less than 10).

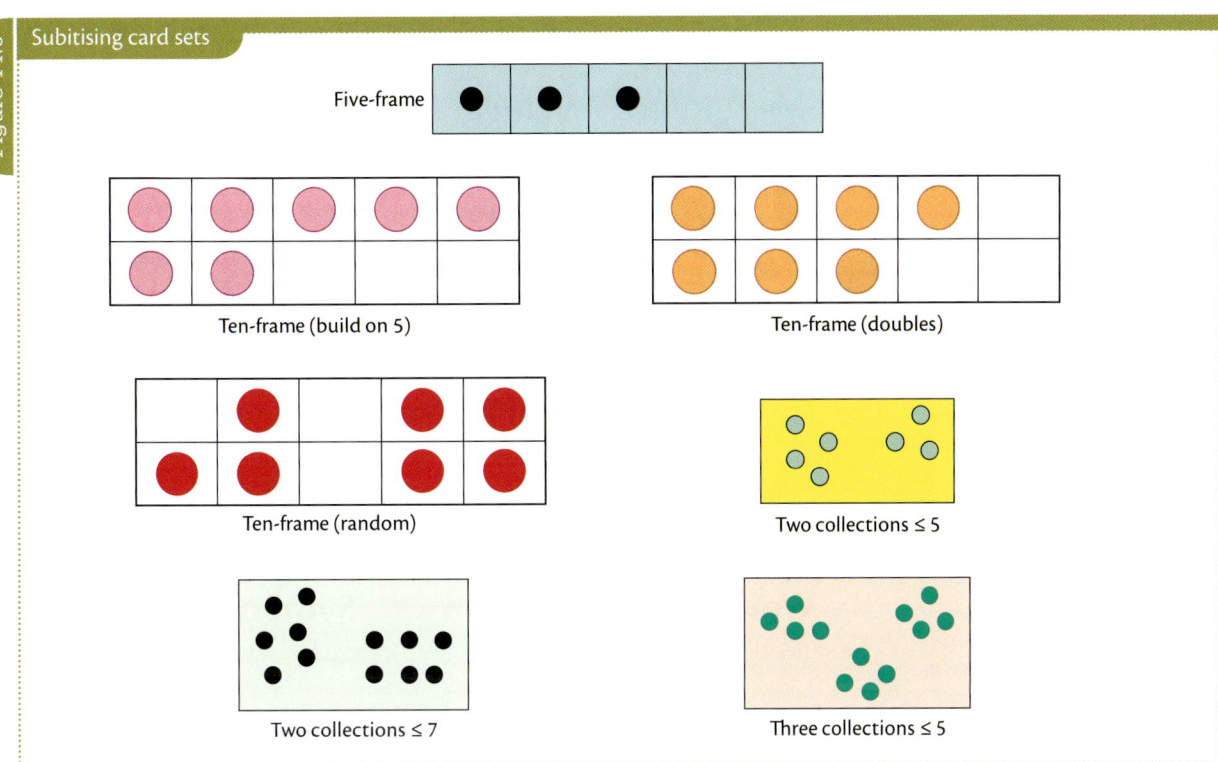

Figure 14.6 Subitising card sets

Source: Siemon (2006)

The different representations can be made up as subitising card sets and used on a regular basis to build number recognition and part–part–whole knowledge for each of the numbers to 10. Cards should be shown for about 2 seconds and discussed in terms of 'what did you see', 'how do you know' and so on. This can be combined with physical activities that partition a given collection into two or more parts (e.g. 'How many different ways can 9 cows be placed in 2 paddocks?'), although it is important in this case to 'capture' the results in a poster for future reference.

The ability to rename numbers in terms of their parts is an essential prerequisite for mental strategies and further work with place value. For example, to add 6 and 8, it is helpful to start from the larger number and recognise that 8 is 2 less than 10 and that 6 is 2 and 4, then, 'combining' that, generate the thinking: 8, 10, 14.

Part–part–whole knowledge is also recognised as a key factor in determining later computational sense (Steffe, Cobb & von Glasersfeld, 1988; Steinke, 2001). For instance, one way of adding 28 and 57 mentally is to start with 57, add 2 tens to get 77, then add 3 more by making 80 and 5 more, 85.

think + link

Mental strategies and the importance of part–part–whole knowledge for addition and subtraction more generally are explored in Chapter 16.

Number names and symbols

Even though some elements of the number naming sequence may be known, number names need to be connected to collections and the symbols that represent them more formally, as represented in the triad shown in Figure 14.7.

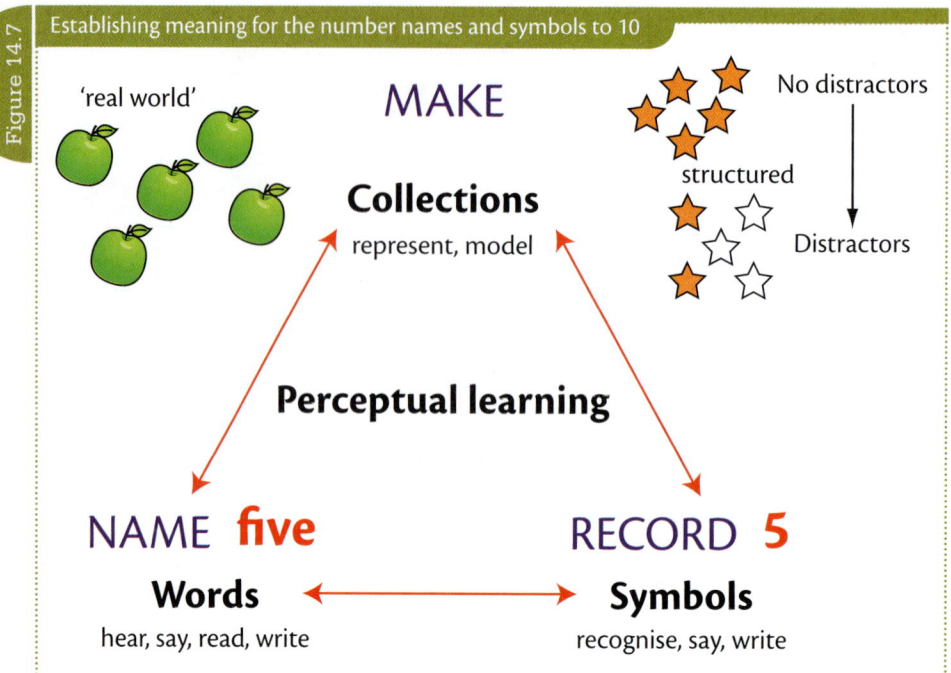

Figure 14.7 Establishing meaning for the number names and symbols to 10

There are six possible connections to be made:

1. a collection can be presented (physically or in picture form) and children asked to say, write, or match the number word to the collection (collection to words)
2. a collection can be presented and children asked to write or match the relevant symbol to the collection (collection to symbol)
3. a number word (oral, written) can be presented and children asked to make or draw a collection to match the number word (word to collection)
4. a number word (oral, written) can be presented and children asked to write or match a symbol to the number word (word to symbol)
5. a symbol (written) can be presented and children asked to make or draw a collection to match the symbol (symbol to collection)
6. a symbol can be presented and children asked to say, write, or match the number word to the symbol (symbol to word).

There are multiple ways of referring to the three important elements in this triad and a number of different modes by which they might be demonstrated. For instance, 'collections' could be referred to as *sets*, or more pragmatically as *materials*, which might be 'real-world' (e.g. buttons, farm animals, toy cars, jelly beans, or the children themselves), or structured, that is, materials designed more or less exclusively for the purposes of teaching number. Structured materials can be *discrete* (e.g. counters, tiles, blocks, bead frames, and bundling material such as straws and icy-pole sticks), *continuous* (e.g. Cuisenaire rods and knotted ropes), or both (e.g. bead strings and stacking materials such as unifix), and *representations* (e.g. number cards and dice). 'Words' can be referred to as *language* and 'symbols' as *recording* to recognise that numbers may be recorded in multiple ways (e.g. tallies). Number words and symbols need to be recognised and responded to in all language modes, that is, listening, speaking, reading, and writing, through the use of flash cards, posters, visual models, oral exchanges or presentations, and drawing or writing tasks.

Chapter 14 Developing Early Number Ideas and Strategies

communicating mathematically

Writing the numbers to 10

Although many children come to school with some capacity to write numerals, it is a good idea to teach this formally. One way to do this is to use the following anonymous rhyme, which students enact by tracing over sandpaper numerals. A small star sticker can be placed on the numerals on permanent display in the classroom to show where to start recording (top left for most numbers, top right for 8 and 9).

1. Number one starts at the top. Straight down we go until we stop.
2. Around, down, across we go. Number two is made just so.
3. Around, around like a little bee. Sniffing the flowers in number three.
4. Straight down to near the line. Turn right and cross so four is fine.
5. Number five's head is first, his body's fat. Don't forget on top—his hat.
6. Straight little back and big round tummy. Number six looks oh so funny.
7. Left to right and down we zoom. Seven is standing in the room.
8. Make an 'S' for number eight and do not stop till you reach the top.
9. Along and around, up and down. Number nine is a real clown.

While many children will have heard and can say the number words to 10, most will not be able to read or write these words. Their capacity to say and hear these names needs to be connected to the written words using appropriate experiences and early literacy strategies (e.g. Fellowes & Oakley, 2010). In a booklet designed to support the teaching and learning of mathematics in Indigenous schools (Northern Territory Department of Education, 1987) this triad is referred to in terms of concrete experiences (*do*), language (*talk*), and creative recording (*record*). This focus on activity, which is similar to *make*, *name*, and *record* in Figure 14.7, will be used more generally when introducing larger whole numbers, fractions, and decimals in later chapters.

for the classroom

Involve children in making sets of number cards for each of the numbers to 10, using a simple draw program and/or stickers. Use as flash cards and for memory and matching games as appropriate.

Bead strings can also be made to talk about the numbers in terms of their parts and how they relate to 10.

Figure 14.8

Number cards

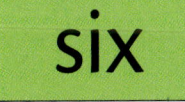

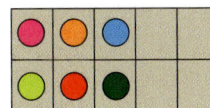

Number-naming sequence

The development of a stable ordered sequence of number names, referred to here as the number naming sequence, is crucial to the activity of counting and the structure of the whole number system. Although this can be learnt by rote, children need to know the name order and patterns inherent in the sequence well enough to be able to identify what number comes before or after a given number and, ultimately, to count on or back from any given number by ones (Steffe, Cobb & von Glasersfeld, 1988). For instance, when Jenny's mother at the start of the chapter says that Jenny can count to 100, she probably means that Jenny can recite the number names to 100, rather than accurately count a collection to say 'how many', identify one more or one less than a given number in the sequence, or start counting from any two-digit number. Even if Jenny could do this, it would be extremely unlikely that she could count backwards from a given number in this range or recognise the numbers to 10 in terms of their parts. In other words, the language associated with one more and one less (e.g. 'the number before', 'the number after', 'what number comes next' and so on) needs to be developed explicitly, as does the use of the number-naming sequence in the actual task of counting.

The number-naming sequence can be introduced and rehearsed though counting rhymes and story books, and through oral counting. Collaborative object counting can be used to demonstrate the physical act of counting. Continuous representations such as a numbered pathway or number cards pegged on a rope can also be used to connect children's understanding of relative quantity to numbers and establish the idea that numbers live in relation to one another, for example, '5 is halfway between 0 and 10'.

for the classroom

Have the class work in groups to make a large number frieze that can be displayed in the classroom. Routinely refer to this and use it to practise pointing to and counting to each of the numbers in turn. Progress to starting at any number, and ultimately to counting backwards. Periodically cover one or more of the numbers and ask the children to identify what number is missing. The frieze can also be used to identify numbers before/after, or one more/one less than a given number.

Cardinal and ordinal numbers

Number can be used to indicate a quantity (e.g. 4 is the name for a collection of four objects), in which case they are referred to as cardinal numbers. They can also be used for ordering, as in first, second, third, fourth, fifth and so on, in which case they are referred to as ordinal **numbers.**

consider and discuss

What is involved in learning number names?

To explore what is involved in learning the number names, it can be useful to invent number names and symbols for the numbers we know as 0 to 9.

1. Work in groups to create a set of number names and symbols, then consider how you might teach these to another group.

2. Derive ordinal names from your cardinal number names and design some questions for other groups to consider, for example 'how would you ask what the third number is after 2?'.

3. Reflect on your experience and discuss the implications of this for teaching the cardinal and ordinal number names for the base 10 system.

Counting

> Children all over the world, schooled and unschooled, learn to count … and, like reading, once you can do it, it may not seem like much of an achievement. But this does not mean that the achievement is insignificant, that the task is easy, or that every child is well positioned to learn to count and, importantly, to learn beyond counting. (Willis, 2002, p. 116)

The verb 'to count' can mean many different things (e.g. see Willis, 2002), from reciting the number names without reference to a collection, to the physical act of enumerating a collection, to recognising that the last number says 'how many'. To count effectively, children need to:

- know the number naming sequence
- match number words to objects in a one-to-one correspondence
- recognise invariance of cardinality (e.g. that three means three no matter what it looks like)
- understand that the last number counted says how many.

We have already referred to the first of these, but physically coordinating the match of objects to words (e.g. by pointing or touching) and recognising that the count has a beginning and an end can be tricky for young children, particularly those who have learnt to say the number naming sequence relatively quickly with little or no reference to objects or the act of counting. In their haste, children can often leave out a number word, mismatch objects to parts of a number word as shown in Figure 14.9, or fail to recognise that they have already counted some of the objects.

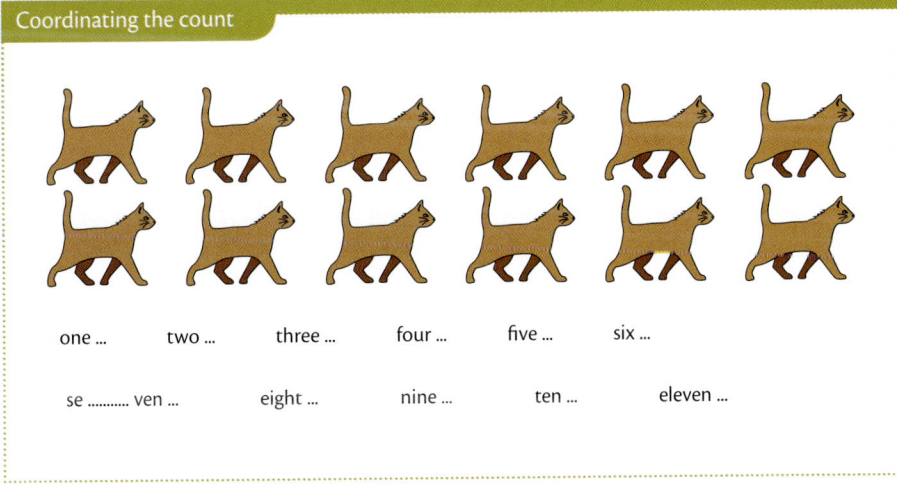

Figure 14.9 Coordinating the count

In planning mathematics activities, it is important not to waste children's time. Hegland (1991) describes activities that 'combine an easier mathematics concept or skill with a motor response that is sufficiently challenging' (p. 36) as 'control' activities.

> If students have to concentrate on the directions, the type of representation, the motor response, or the perceptual array, they may be distracted from the mathematics task involved … colouring, cutting, pasting, and drawing were judged to be challenging motor responses capable of distracting students from mathematics concepts. (Hegland, 1991, p. 36)

integrating technology/ICT

Avoiding 'control' activities

Technology can be used to reduce the type of motor challenges referred to by Hegland (1991). There are many commercial programs designed to provide practice in counting, number recognition, ordering, and comparing quantities and so on that do not require complex forms of sensorimotor coordination and instead build on children's facility with technological interfaces. Images can be downloaded and reproduced to create number stories, digital photographs can be used to record what was done physically with materials, and small portable video players can be used to record student explanations.

Numbers as composite units

Before children can be expected to appreciate why numbers are written as they are, they need to understand each number as a *composite unit*. That is, as a unit made up of units. The feet counting book, *One is a Snail, Ten is a Crab* (Sayre & Sayre, 2003), demonstrates what this means for even numbers by attaching numbers to animals according to their number of feet. That is, 'two is a person … four is a dog … six is an insect … eight is a spider' and 'ten is a crab'. This provides a many-to-one representation of each number that allows children to think of each of these numbers as units; for example, it is possible to think of 5 spiders or 7 insects. Counting large collections more efficiently demands a capacity for working with composite units and demonstrates the value in counting by larger 'units', for example 5s and 10s, as well as the advantages of systematically arranging the count to ensure that items are not double counted and that the whole can be counted efficiently.

for the classroom

Chicken Scramble is an activity that encourages more efficient counting strategies. A group of six to eight children sit in a circle or U shape with their legs crossed and their hands under their armpits to resemble wings. The 'chickens' food' is a large tub of 350 to 450 counters, preferably stackable. These are tipped out on to the floor in front of the chickens, and when the teacher says 'go, chickens, go', the children gather up some of the counters. To ensure roughly equal shares, the teacher says, 'There are some greedy chickens here who need to share'. Once the relative size of the collections is more or less the same, the children are asked to determine who has the most food: 'Who is the greedy chicken?' Observe counting strategies—some will count by ones and lose the count, others will count by twos or fives, and some may count by tens, organising their 'stacks' systematically. Discuss counting strategies and follow up with a range of other counting tasks, such as placing a specified number of counters into a plastic bag and labelling the bags.

Being able to count by twos, fives and tens is a necessary precursor to recognising 10 as a composite unit, that is, that 10 ones is 1 ten.

A sense of numbers beyond 10

Although children will have seen 10 written in symbolic form (e.g. a 10 cent coin, a $10 note, or as a date on a calendar, as in 10 March) this does not mean that they understand the basis of this as 1 ten and 0 ones. This understanding generally develops some time later, and only after children have had extensive experience counting collections more efficiently by twos, fives, and ultimately tens, and that each of the numbers to 10 can be thought of as an entity in its own right.

The whole numbers beyond 10 are represented in terms of place-value parts. Once the ones are known it is possible to understand the numbers beyond 10 in terms of a count of tens and a count of ones. While children may well be able to accurately and reliably count collections beyond 10 and read and write the numerals for the numbers beyond 10, this does not mean that they understand the structure of the number system and the reason why the numbers are written in the way that they are. This is particularly problematic for the teen numbers, which are not written in the way they are heard. For example, many children will write 61 for 'sixteen'.

Two ten-frames, arithmetic racks (Gravemeijer, Cobb, Bowers & Whitenack, 2000), and 20-bead strings can be used to model the numbers to 20, using 5 and 10 as benchmarks. Working with these models helps establish the doubles facts to 20 and builds a sense of numbers beyond 10.

think + link

Chapter 15 will consider the issues associated with the teaching and learning of place value in more detail.

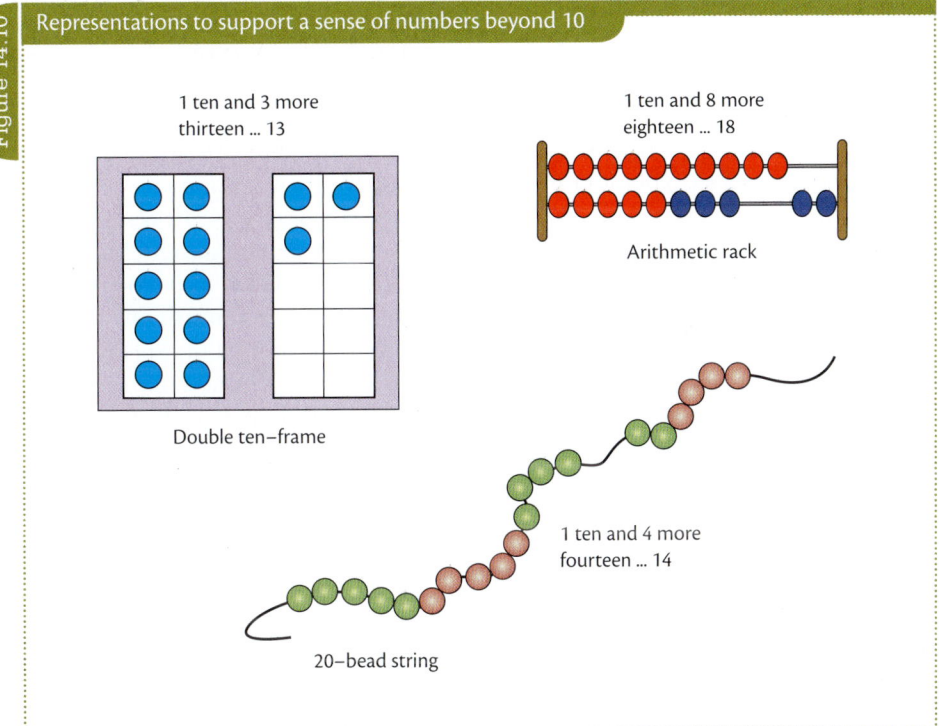

Figure 14.10 Representations to support a sense of numbers beyond 10

Scaffolding solution strategies

In the first year or two of schooling, most numerical problems are solved by making all and counting all, the 'make-all count-all' strategy. However, as children come to trust the count for numbers such as 1, 2, or 3, these numbers should be hidden and children encouraged to *count on* from these as appropriate to find a solution. Problems can be represented using materials, dot dice, playing cards (to 10), or ten-frames initially, replacing these materials by numeral cards as children come to trust the count for those numbers. In a similar vein, but only to the extent that doubles facts are known, doubles can be pointed to or covered to determine the sum, for example, for two dot dice showing a 4 and a 6, the two fours could be covered to generate the thinking '8 and 2 more, 10'.

think + link

Mental strategies for addition and subtraction and a more detailed description of how these might be scaffolded will be considered in Chapter 16.

> ### making connections
>
> Representing or connecting problem situations to the part–part–whole structure is a powerful way to link what children know about numbers to problem solving. It makes little sense to use a make-all count-all strategy to solve a problem like '5 ducks were on the pond and 2 more joined them' when children can subitise the 5 and the 2 and count on, or can recognise 7 without counting as a result of their experience with subitising and part–part–whole constructions.

Conclusion

Our base 10 numeration system has a long and rich history. A brief discussion of historical number systems was included to illustrate that this took a long time to develop, and we should not expect young children to understand the complexity and richness inherent in our number system immediately. A knowledge of what is needed in terms of the possibilities of measuring and counting, and skill in recognising the difficulties young children experience in learning about number and number relations, are necessary to ensure that all students are presented with learning opportunities that build on their strengths not their ignorance.

Children's number learning has long been a major focus of research in mathematics education. This research has not always been uncontested, but there is now a loose consensus around the key ideas presented here, in particular the role of subitising in the development of mental objects for the numbers to 10, and the important role played by experience, language, and interaction in coming to understand what numbers mean and how they are used. Young children need to be exposed to meaningful, purposeful activities that challenge their existing views about the mathematics in supportive and constructive ways that do not waste their time or squander their efforts.

key terms

Cardinal number: specific number name for how many in a given collection of objects

Comparing: determining whether objects, quantities, or measures are the same or different

Counting: ordered matching of number names to objects

Digit: any of the 10 Hindu-Arabic numerals from 0 to 9

Enumerating: the process of determining how many in a given collection or set; this could be arrived at by matching (enumeration), counting (numeration), or visual recognition (subitising)

Enumeration: keeping track of the objects in a collection by a one-to-one matching of the objects with other objects used as checks or counters (Gundlach, 1989); this could include an ordered sequence of body parts or a collection of pebbles

Mental objects for each of the numbers to 10: demonstrated by an ability to work flexibly with the numbers without having to make or represent the number

Numeral: symbol or group of symbols used to express a number (e.g. 3, 527, VI)

Numeration: the use of an ordered sequence of number words to keep track of the number of objects

Numeration systems: the systematic use of number names and symbols to count independently of the nature of the objects or quantities being counted

Numerosity: the number in a given collection or set, equivalent to cardinal number

Ordering: arranging objects, quantities, or measures according to some pattern or numerical sequence

Ordinal number: a number word used to indicate position (e.g. first, second, third, …)

Subitising: recognising the number in small collections without counting

Trusting the count: accessing mental objects for numbers to 10 without having to make, model, or record the number

Review questions

1. Why is the ability to recite the number names in order an insufficient guide to a child's understanding of number? How would you reply to Jenny's mother at the start of this chapter?
2. If a child has access to a 'mental object' for the number 6, what might you expect him or her to be able to do? Why is this understanding so important?
3. Describe in your own words and illustrate what you think is meant by part–part–whole knowledge, and explain why this might also be described in terms of structuring numbers, partitioning, decomposing, or composing numbers.
4. What is meant by 'trusting the count' and how would you recognise this critical capacity? What would you do for a child who did not trust the count for the number 7?
5. Use an example to illustrate the difference between ordinal and cardinal numbers. Create an invitation to a child's birthday party which uses as many different forms of the number 8 as possible.
6. Identify and share some rich mathematical tasks that have the potential to be rich learning opportunities both for mathematics and English.
7. Work in groups to construct alternative number names and symbols for 0 to 9. Then plan a lesson on how you might begin to teach these names and symbols to young children. Share your ideas with another group. What do you notice? What approaches are the same? What assumptions have been made?

Key references

Clements, D. (1999). Subitising: What is it? Why teach it? *Teaching Children Mathematics*, 5(7), 400–405.

Clements, D., & Sarama, J. (2007). Early childhood mathematics learning. In F. Lester (Ed.), *Second Handbook of Research on Mathematics Teaching and Learning* (pp. 461–556). Charlotte, NC: Information Age.

Fellowes, G., & Oakley, G. (2010). *Language, Literacy, and Early Childhood Development*. Melbourne: Oxford University Press.

Hegland, S. (1991). Kindergarten mathematics: Teaching or controlling. *Arithmetic Teacher*, 39(2), 34–37.

Hughes, M. (1986). *Children and Number: Difficulties in Learning Mathematics*. Oxford, UK: Blackwell.

Macmillan, A. (2009). *Numeracy in Early Childhood: Shared Contexts for Teaching and Learning*. Melbourne: Oxford University Press.

Nunes, T., & Bryant, P. (1996). *Children Doing Mathematics*. Oxford, UK: Blackwell.

Perry, R., & Dockett, S. (2008). Young children's access to powerful mathematical ideas. In L. English & M. Bussi (Eds.), *Handbook of International Research in Mathematics Education* (2nd ed.) (pp. 75–108). New York: Routledge, Taylor & Francis.

Schmittau, J., & Morris, A. (2004). The development of algebra in the elementary mathematics curriculum of V. V. Davydov. *The Mathematics Educator*, 8(1), 60–87.

Steffe, L., Cobb, P., & von Glasersfeld, E. (1988). *Construction of Arithmetical Meanings and Strategies*. New York: Springer-Verlag.

Willis, S. (2002). Crossing borders: Learning to count. *Australian Educational Researcher*, 29(2), 115–130.

Wright, R., Stanger, G., Stafford, A., & Martlkand, J. (2006). *Teaching Number in the Classroom with 4 to 8 Year Olds*. London: Paul Chapman Publishing.

Websites

www.simerr.educ.utas.edu.au/numeracy/critical_numeracy/critical_numeracy.htm

www.thenetwork.sa.edu.au/teachingandlearning

http://activated.act.edu.au/ectl

15 Introducing Place Value

Contents

Prerequisite ideas and strategies	291
Understanding tens and ones	296
Introducing three-digit numeration	304
Developing four-digit numeration	307
Extending to millions and beyond	310
Conclusion	317

Chapter objectives

This chapter will enable the reader to:
- Appreciate the power of the base 10 numeration system and the significance of the 'big ideas', that is, '10 of these is 1 of those', and '1000 of these is 1 of those'
- Understand the role of materials, language, and recording in developing a deep understanding of place value
- Recognise the potential sources of student difficulty in coming to understand the structure of the number system
- Appreciate what is involved in consolidating place-value knowledge and working fluently with number to thousands and beyond.

An unusual strategy

While Richard was generally able to add and subtract two-digit numbers and knew his shapes, he found the rest of Year 5 maths difficult. His strategy for solving '19 and 27' was identified by his teacher, who knew that Richard was an avid Australian Rules football fan. Unable, or lacking the necessary confidence, to work fluently with the base 10 number system, Richard applied what he did know by rewriting the numbers in terms of football scores: 19 points is 3 goals and 1 behind, 27 points is 4 goals and 3 behinds. Adding goals, he then recorded 42, on the grounds that 7 goals is 42 points, and 4 as the sum of the behinds. Consistent with AFL scoring he then added the 42 points and the 4 behinds to arrive at his answer of 46. Place value is a difficult idea to teach and learn and involves much more than recognising place-value parts.

Figure 15.1 Richard's solution

$$\begin{array}{r} 19 \\ +27 \\ \hline 31 \\ 43 \\ \hline 42\ 4 \end{array}$$

Big ideas

- Whole numbers can be recognised as cardinal numbers as well as composite units, that is, as numbers that tell how many in a set (e.g. 8 ones) or as units in their own right (e.g. 1 eight).
- A sense of numbers beyond 10 as 'a ten and some more' is necessary to appreciate the two-digit place-value pattern.
- Two patterns underpin place-value understanding at this level of schooling: '10 of these is 1 of those' and '1000 of these is 1 of those'.
- Place-value knowledge is developed by making (i.e. representing) numbers in terms of their place-value parts, naming and recording.
- Place-value knowledge is consolidated by comparing, ordering, counting forwards and backwards in place-value parts, and renaming.

Prerequisite ideas and strategies

Before they are ready to meet the 'big ideas' of place value, children need to be able to:

- count fluently by ones using the number naming sequence to 20 and beyond
- model, read, and write the numbers to 10 using materials, diagrams, words, and symbols
- recognise collections to 10 without counting
- trust the count (i.e. draw on a range of mental models including part–part–whole relationships) for each of the numbers to 10 without having to model or count by ones
- demonstrate a sense of numbers beyond 10 in terms of 1 ten and some more (e.g. 'see' 14 as 1 ten and 4 ones)
- count larger collections by twos, fives, and tens (i.e. recognise 2, 5, and 10 as countable units).

think + link

See Chapter 14 for a more detailed account of these important ideas and strategies and how they can be scaffolded.

Developing mental objects for each of the numbers to 10 is not straightforward. While young children may well recognise collections up to 4 immediately, they are less likely to be able to justify this in terms of 'it's a 2 and 2' or '3 and 1 more' and so on. Part–part–whole relationships need to be modelled, reinforced through subitising activities, and informally recorded on a regular basis, as this encourages children to build a range of visual models for each of the numbers to 10. Particular attention should be paid to the language involved, for example, 'It's 7 because it's a 5 and 2 more'.

Building part–part–whole knowledge and confidence should not be confused with the operation of addition, although it is related. It is about ensuring children have a deep knowledge of each of the numbers to 10 in terms of their parts, independently of having to make or model these collections. It is important to record these relationships initially as, for example, '8 is 1 more than 7' or '8 is 2 and 6', that is, by using key words and digits rather than symbolic expressions. Equations should only be introduced once children have been exposed to the equals sign as 'equivalence', are well acquainted with the numbers to 10 in terms of their parts, and recognise the '+' sign as 'and'.

handy hint

Introducing the '=' sign

Use a pan or beam balance and different coloured unifix blocks (or similar materials that are of equal mass) to construct and describe equivalent numerical relationships. For example, 3 red and 4 blue on one side is equivalent to 4 red and 3 blue, or 6 red and 1 blue. Use these relationships and part–part–whole knowledge to introduce the equals sign in terms of well-known equivalents—in this case, to record 3 + 4 = 4 + 3 and 3 + 4 = 6 + 1. The beam balance is an important metaphor for the = sign, which is often misunderstood at this level.

think + link

Chapters 6 and 13 deal with the use of the equals sign and the importance of working systematically. Chapter 16 deals with the ideas and strategies involved in addition and subtraction.

Recording that begins with the whole (e.g. 8 = 7 + 1 or 8 = 2 + 6, rather than 7 + 1 = 8) is important as it directly connects to the ways in which part–part–whole knowledge is represented and emphasises the point that the '=' sign does not mean 'makes'. Ultimately, children should be able to use equivalence statements in systematic ways to represent multiple expressions of 8 in terms of its parts or as a part of a larger whole, for example:

$$8 = 1 + 7 = 2 + 6 = 3 + 5 = 4 + 4 = 5 + 3 = 6 + 2 = 7 + 1$$
$$8 = 9 - 1 = 10 - 2 = 11 - 3 \ldots$$

As suggested in Chapter 14, a good way of demonstrating the importance of developing a sound understanding of each of the numbers to 10 is to establish posters for each of the numbers and leave these on permanent display, adding to them as needed. The activity 'Tell me all you know…' (described below) can be used as a warm-up activity with the whole class or a small group. Ask children to close their eyes (sit on their hands if need be) and encourage them to 'picture it in your heads', that is, to draw on their visual memories. Doing this regularly conveys the message that this knowledge is important and expected.

for the classroom

Tell me all you know

Check that children trust the count for the numbers to 10 by regularly asking them to close their eyes and tell you everything they know about a particular number. For example, 'What can you tell me about 6?', '6 is 1 more than 5 … it's 4 and 2 … 2 and 4 … double 3 … 1 less than 7 … or 4 less than 10', and so on. Responses can be added to number posters and reviewed regularly.

did you know?

According to Nunes and Bryant (1996), 'it is unlikely that children come to understand the numeration system from more and more practice on one-to-one correspondence counting' (p. 57). They suggest children's understanding of the additive composition of number (i.e. their ability to recognise and work with numbers in terms of their parts) is much more likely to 'provide a basis for understanding the properties of a number system with a base' (p. 57) than routine counting.

Trusting the count is evident when children are able to invoke a range of mental models for each of the numbers to 10 and work flexibly with those models without having to make or count the number. This involves more than being able to count on (or back) from a given number, a task that can be accomplished by 'locking' into the number-naming sequence. It involves working with numbers in terms of their parts (part–whole knowledge), particularly in relation to benchmark numbers such as 5 and 10.

Sense of numbers beyond 10

Many children experience difficulty with what is sometimes referred to as 'bridging ten'. Although by this stage virtually all students can count beyond 10, they may not appreciate the pattern involved because of the inconsistencies in the English number-naming sequence and 'because the numerals can be thought of as designating whole numerical quantities' (Boulton-Lewis & Halford, 1992, p. 9). That is, children can correctly make a collection of 16 objects and write 16 without necessarily recognising the part–whole relationship of the 10 and the 6 in the way that 16 is written.

These difficulties can be avoided by ensuring that children develop a sense of numbers beyond 10 before formally introducing recording for two-digit numbers. This requires part–part–whole knowledge for the numbers to 10, a working knowledge of the number naming sequence to 20 and beyond, and regular engagement in situations that require children to recognise the number of tens and how many more. For example, developing the doubles facts for the numbers 6 to 10 can be modelled on an arithmetic rack (see Figure 15.2) in a way that encourages children to see '8 and 8' as '1 ten and 6 more'. Extended subitising activities involving multiple ten-frames that require children to recognise the number of tens and how many more without counting can also be used effectively to build a sense of what happens after each decade. For example, shown the ten-frames in Figure 15.2, children would be expected to recognise '1 ten and 6 more … sixteen'.

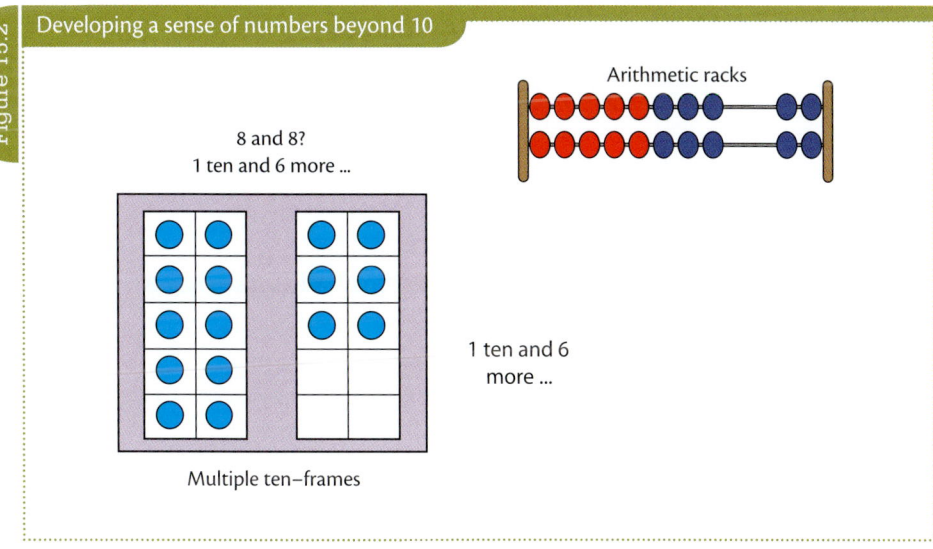

Figure 15.2 Developing a sense of numbers beyond 10

Counting large collections

Physically counting collections not only practises the number-naming sequence, it also demonstrates that counting by ones can be very tiresome once the collections go beyond 40 or so.

One of the keys to developing a deep understanding of the base 10 numeration system is the capacity to recognise numbers less than 10 as **composite units**. In part, this is achieved when children understand the numbers to 10 as cardinals (e.g. 8 ones is understood as 1 eight, or a set of 8) and they trust the count (e.g. when children know 8 in terms of its parts and in relation to 10). However, recognising 8 as a composite unit for the purposes of counting larger collections requires the essentially multiplicative notion that it is possible to have many eights.

Observing the strategies young children use to count large collections is a useful way of exploring the extent to which they are able to use numbers such as 2, 5, and 10 as countable units—as is asking children to tell you everything they know about a particular number (as described above).

Establishing the cardinal numbers to 10 as composite units (e.g. that 6 ones is 1 six and that it is possible to speak of a number of 'sixes') is not straightforward. The feet counting book by Sayre and Sayre (2003) offers a particularly valuable way of doing this. By assigning 1 to a snail on the basis that a snail has one foot and the even numbers to 10 to other animals, not only does it emphasise each of these as composite units (e.g. ' 8 is a spider' allows children to think of one spider or many spiders, 1 eight or many eights), but it also reinforces the notion that numbers can be represented in terms of their parts and demonstrates the successor relationship that applies to all numbers (i.e. for each number there is a number that is 1 more, as in '7 is an insect and a snail'). Opportunities for algebraic thinking emerge with the prospect that objects can be used to stand for numbers; this may prompt some children to invent symbols to reduce the task of writing (e.g. instead of '18 is 2 spiders and a person', they may write '18 = 2S + 1P'), which can be shared with the class and discussed.

think + link

Chicken Scramble, which was described in Chapter 14, is one way to encourage children to count larger collections more efficiently by twos, fives or tens.

for the classroom

The beautifully illlustrated counting-by-feet book, *One is a Snail, Ten is a Crab* (Sayre & Sayre, 2003) can be used to demonstrate the idea of composite units for even numbers (e.g. '6 is an insect') and that numbers can be represented in equivalent ways (e.g. '5 is a dog and a snail … 20 is 2 crabs or 10 people'). After reading the book, invite students to explore and/or draw the different ways a particular number within their counting range may be represented.

handy hint

Use an interactive whiteboard to facilitate the construction of different representations for numbers. Children could 'drag and drop' images of the animals they wanted to make up their number. They should then be asked to record what this in words (e.g. 28 is 7 dogs, or 2 crabs, an insect and a snail).

The idea that the numbers to 10 can be conceptualised as units in their own right is fundamental to establishing 10 as a countable unit (the notion of numbers as composite units is also fundamental to multiplicative thinking, but more about that later). Cobb (1995) makes an important distinction between children's understanding of 10 as a *numerical composite unit*, that is, where children count on in tens by ones, and 10 as an *abstract composite unit*, where children count on by 1 ten.

We have already seen how subitising cards featuring multiple ten-frames can be used to support a sense of numbers beyond 10, but they can also be used to draw attention to the count of tens and the fact that larger numbers can be represented in terms of their tens part and ones.

Tasks to assess readiness

The task described above by Cobb (1995) provides a good indication of children's readiness for more structured place-value experiences. Building or stacking materials can be used instead of or as well as the strips to observe the children's counting strategies. Children who appear to be relying on a count of 10 ones (sometimes indicated by the use of the names for the multiples of 10) rather than counts of 1 ten need further opportunities to develop the idea of 10 as an abstract composite unit.

communicating mathematically

Representations of two-digit numbers

Number charts (1 to 100 or 0 to 99) and bead frames (1 to 100) are commonly used to support two-digit numeration. However, neither of these directly supports the central idea, which is that 10 ones is 1 ten. Instead, both present images of the numbers to 100 as a count or collection of ones organised in rows of 10. Unless children already have a well-developed sense of 10 as a composite unit, these representations can be overwhelming. For example, 86 beads is exactly that, 86 single beads (ones). The ability to 'see' this as 8 tens and 6 ones is really only available to those who appreciate the 'oneness' of 10, which allows them to focus on the number of rows not the elements in the row.

How might this be avoided? What could these representations be used for?

The use of number charts and bead frames to develop students' understanding of the structure of the two-digit numeration system is a classic example of the learning paradox (Tzur & Simon, 2004), in which the materials being used to develop the idea require the idea to be well developed for the student to 'see it' in the materials. Just because children can count large collections fluently by tens as in 'ten, twenty, thirty, forty, …', or count by tens on a number chart, it does not mean that they have any sense of 10 as an abstract composite unit (Clements & Sarama, 2007; Cobb, 1995).

issues in teaching

The role of perception

It can be very revealing to mask a part of the 0–99 number chart and ask children to continue the count (forwards or backwards from a given point, by ones or by tens) without being able to see the numbers. I once masked the numbers from 23 to 57 with a rectangular card and asked a group of Year 1 and 2 students to count down the column that started at 4. The teacher was very surprised when they experienced difficulties, but when I removed the card, indicated the column, and asked the children to say what we were counting by, she was even more suprised as the students, in unison, said 'fours'.

- Why do you think the students responded in this way?
- What does this suggest about their understanding of the 0–99 number chart?
- What might you do to ensure students develop a capacity for counting by tens and ones?

Figure 15.3 Masked 0–99 number chart

0	1	2	3	4	5	6	7	8	9
10	11	12	13	14	15	16	17	18	19
20	21	22						28	29
30	31	32						38	39
40	41	42						48	49
50	51	52						58	59
60	61	62	63	64	65	66	67	68	69
70	71	72	73	74	75	76	77	78	79
80	81	82	83	84	85	86	87	88	89
90	91	92	93	94	95	96	97	98	99

Nevertheless, number charts can be effective when they are used to focus attention on 'what stays the same, what is different' as the class counts forwards or backwards across a row by ones, or down a column by tens. This is particularly the case for 0–99 number charts that show one decade per row (as opposed to a 1–100 number chart, which has the next multiple of ten at the end of the row). 0–99 number charts also have the advantage of being symmetrical about the axis between 4 ones and 5 ones, which supports rounding to the nearest ten.

Understanding tens and ones

Establishing the 'big idea': 10 ones as 1 ten

Bundling and stacking materials provide a useful means of demonstrating the 'oneness' of ten, but bundling and stacking on their own will not necessarily develop the idea that 10 ones is 1 ten. Children need to appreciate why counting by tens is a sensible thing to do. Counting large collections is one way of establishing a rationale for this, as is being able to 'read' a number organised in tens and ones (see Handy Hint below).

handy hint

Noticing table

To orient children's attention to a new topic or a concept of interest, set up a noticing table or shelf in the classroom. After a day or two, ask children what they noticed. For example, arrange 5 bundles/stacks of 10 and 4 single straws/unifix on one side of the table, and 54 straws/unifix on the other. Cover the materials with a cloth, allow the children one peep or glimpse, and ask them to say how many in each collection.

Modelling two-digit numbers using finger displays (Tickle, 2003) can also be used to model the oneness of 10 because each child serves as a marker of the count of 10: 10 fingers is 1 child. This can be emphasised by placing unifix cubes on each finger and asking the child concerned to make their unifix cubes into a rod of 1 ten.

One of the traps in bundling or stacking is the language that accompanies it. It is very tempting to count bundles using the language from the number naming sequence. That is, 'ten, twenty, thirty, forty, fifty, sixty, …'. However, it is preferable, from a pedagogical point of view, to count bundles or stacks of ten in terms of a count of tens, that is, '1 ten, 2 tens, 3 tens, 4 tens, 5 tens', and so on. It is important here to emphasise the count of tens.

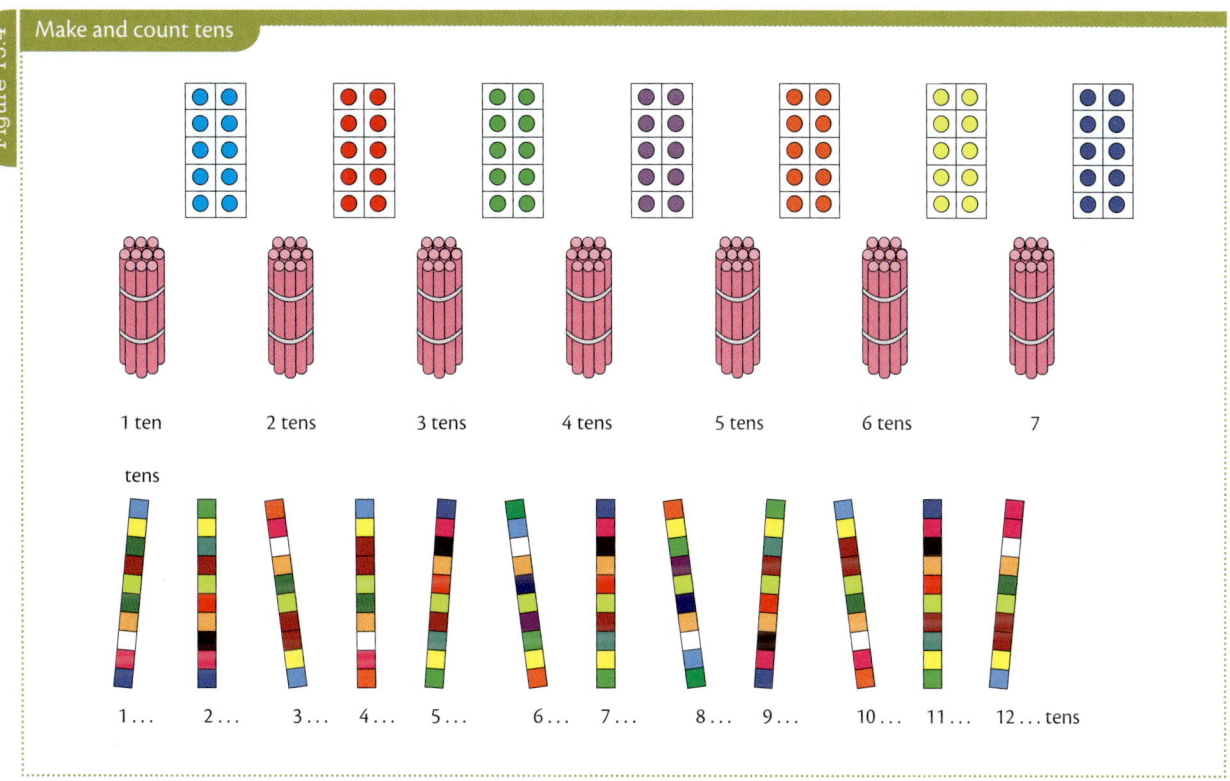

Figure 15.4 Make and count tens

Developing the names for the multiples of 10

The English names for the multiples of 10 are problematic (Boulton-Lewis & Halford, 1992; Nunes & Bryant, 1996; Verschaffel & De Corte, 1996), and should be dealt with as words before being introduced in symbolic form. In many languages the number-naming sequence is more consistent with the concept of a count of tens and a count of ones. For example, in the Vietnamese number-naming sequence the number name for 11 translates as 'ten one', for 12 it is 'ten two, for 27 it is 'two ten seven', and for 43 it is 'four ten three', and so on (Bell, 1990). This is clearly supportive of the multiplicative structure of the base 10 numeration system in that it refers explicitly to multiples of 10.

Although the English number-naming sequence counts hundreds and thousands in a way that is consistent with the concept of place value (i.e. 1 hundred, 2 hundreds, 3 hundreds, … 1 thousand, 2 thousands, 3 thousands, 4 thousands), this is not the case for the tens. The use of different names for the multiples of 10 masks the place-value pattern at the very point where children are meeting it for the first time. Many children who know the number-naming sequence may consider 'twenty' as the name and '20' as the numeral for a collection of 20 objects. While they may know that it is double 10, they are not necessarily connecting the '2' in '20' with a count of tens.

To avoid these difficulties, it is wise to focus on the names for the multiples of 10 that are most supportive of the pattern before focusing on those that are least consistent. For example, 'sixty', 'seventy', 'eighty' and 'ninety' are based on the cardinal numbers, and at least sound like an abbreviation for a count of tens (i.e. six-T, seven-T, eight-T, and nine-T). By contrast, 'thirty' and 'fifty' are drawn from the associated ordinal number names—for consistency they should be 'threety' and 'fivety'. 'Forty sounds like 'four-T' but is not spelt that way, 'twenty' should be 'twoty', and we don't have a 'onety'.

for the classroom

Incongruity can be a powerful learning device, particularly where it draws attention to an anomoly as is the case with the English number-naming sequence.

To emphasise that two-digit numbers represent a count of tens and a count of ones, it is a good idea to count in a manner that is consistent with this structure. Count 'one, two, three, …, nine, onety, onety-one, onety-two, onety-three, …, onety-nine, twoty, twoty-one, twoty-two, twoty-three, … twoty-nine, threety, threety-one, threety-two, … threety-nine, forty (sounds correct, spelt inconsistently), forty-one, … forty-nine, fivety, fivety-one, fivety-two, … fivety-nine, sixty …' From here on the numbers are consistent.

The incongruity of this is appealing to children and it prompts a discussion of the 'problems' caused by the English number names. If there are students from non English-speaking backgrounds in the class, find out if their number-naming sequence is more supportive of place value and, if so, consider inviting a parent to help the class prepare a chart of the number names in that language. This will further make the point that two-digit numbers are about a count of tens and a count of ones.

Further difficulties arise with the teen numbers, which are complicated by the so-called 'reversal error'. That is, 'six' is what is heard first in 'sixteen', and this leads many children to write the digits in the order they hear them rather than as a count of tens followed by a count of ones. This is not so much an 'error' as an attempt on the part of the child to deal with the world in an ordered and predictable way. It can be offset by stressing the structure of the teen numbers when building a sense of numbers beyond 10 and making and recording teen numbers, for example 'Make me 1 ten and 7 ones … it should be called onety-seven. Record 1 in the tens place and 7 in the ones place.'

issues in teaching

Writing what is heard

In the early years of schooling, children will often write numbers as they hear them. For example, 'sixteen' may be written as 61 on the basis that 'six' is heard first. Similarly, children may write '205' for 'twenty-five' if they know the number-naming sequence well and have seen twenty recorded as 20 before they have had a chance to appreciate the significance of the two digits.

- What do these responses tell you about the child's understanding of place value?
- What would be an appropriate teaching response?

Use of number charts and bead frames needs to be carefully scaffolded. For instance, number charts can be built up from 'tens families' (e.g. children can work in groups using bundling or stacking materials to record the numbers in a particular decade on a strip of paper—these can be collated and used to make a class chart or prepared and put together on an interactive whiteboard), with the digits in the tens place recorded in bold to highlight the count of tens.

Masking a part of the bead frame or number chart is also a very useful pedagogical tool. Bead frames can be masked using a piece of fabric and systematically revealed as children's counting progresses (starting with two rows only, then five rows, then one row at a time to 10 rows).

Making, naming, and recording the numbers 20–99

To develop a deep understanding of place value, it makes sense to start with those numbers that are generally supportive of the pattern (e.g. 67 and 93, which sound and look more like a count of tens and ones), before those that do not support the pattern. It is recommended that children make/model, name, and record numbers in the range 20 to 99 before dealing with the teens more formally, even though children have seen these numbers recorded in the course of everyday events such as writing the date on the board.

The conventional way in which whole numbers are represented at this level is through *discrete group models* such as ten-frames, bundling or stacking materials, and ten-strips. While continuous models such as number lines can be introduced at the same time as group models (van den Heuval-Panhuizen, 1999), it is generally acknowledged that *structured continuous models* such as MAB should only be introduced after children have had plenty of experience with composing and decomposing tens using discrete materials.

It is a good idea to have children create a large number of bundles of 10. These can be stored in a container and regularly counted as objects in their own right to make the point that the count of tens continues well beyond 10 tens. Bundled sticks can also be used with ones and place-value charts to model and record two-digit numbers.

The 'make' language helps emphasise the count of tens and ones and links the model to the number name and the symbolic representation (Table 15.1).

Table 15.1 Language and recording for the numbers 20–99

'Make me', model	Read, write, name	Read, write Tens	Ones
6 tens and 7 ones	sixty-seven 6 in the tens place and 7 in the ones place	6	7
3 tens and 4 ones	thirty-four (should be threety-four) 3 in the tens place and 4 in the ones place	3	4
4 tens and 0 ones	forty (should be fourty) 4 in the tens place and 0 in the ones place	4	0

Multiple representations

One way of building on children's experiences of counting larger collections by twos, fives, and tens is to use bead strings with successive groups of 10 in alternating colours. Bead strings can be used to support the construction and use of 'complete' number lines (number lines marked in equal intervals and numbered in ones), 'partial' number lines (marked in fives or tens) or 'empty' or 'open' number lines (lines with no numbers other than the beginning and end number).

A 4 to 5 m length of rope can be used in conjunction with number cards and pegs to build an awareness of where numbers live in relation to other numbers. For example, on a line with 0 and 100 as end-points, 50 could be located in the middle as 'it is half-way', '26 will be about half of that again', and so on. Number slides are another useful way of doing this, as they can be flipped to provide immediate feedback on the accuracy of the estimate (Figure 15.5). Models of this type are referred to as *line models* (Figure 15.6).

think + link

Bead strings and open number lines are also useful in building addition strategies to 20 and beyond. These will be discussed further in Chapter 16.

Figure 15.5 Number slides

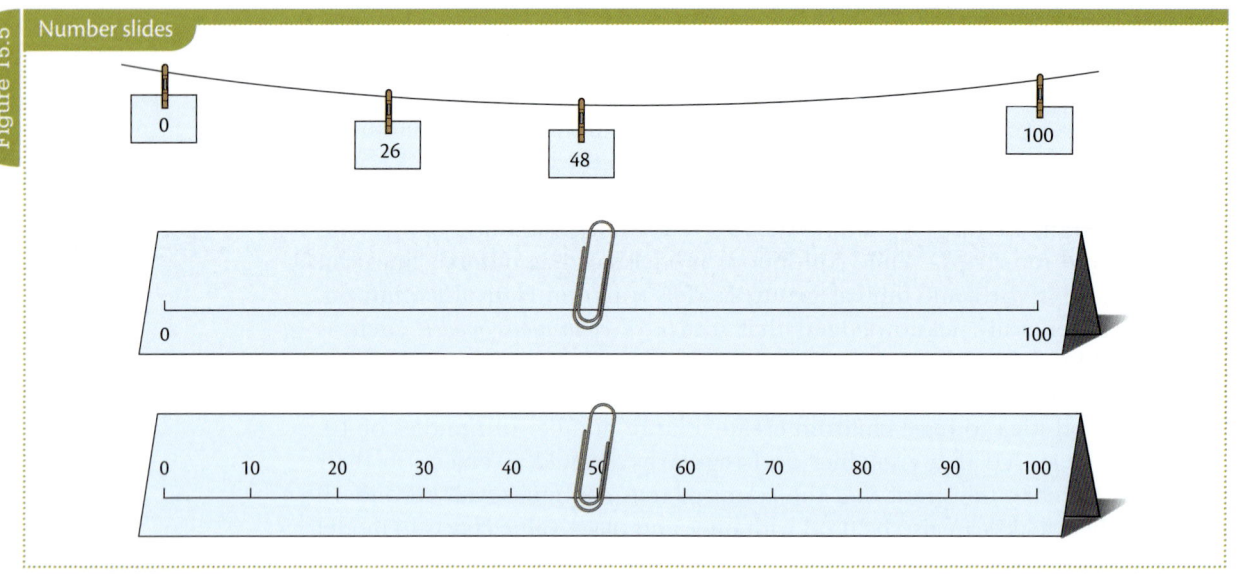

Figure 15.6 Line models

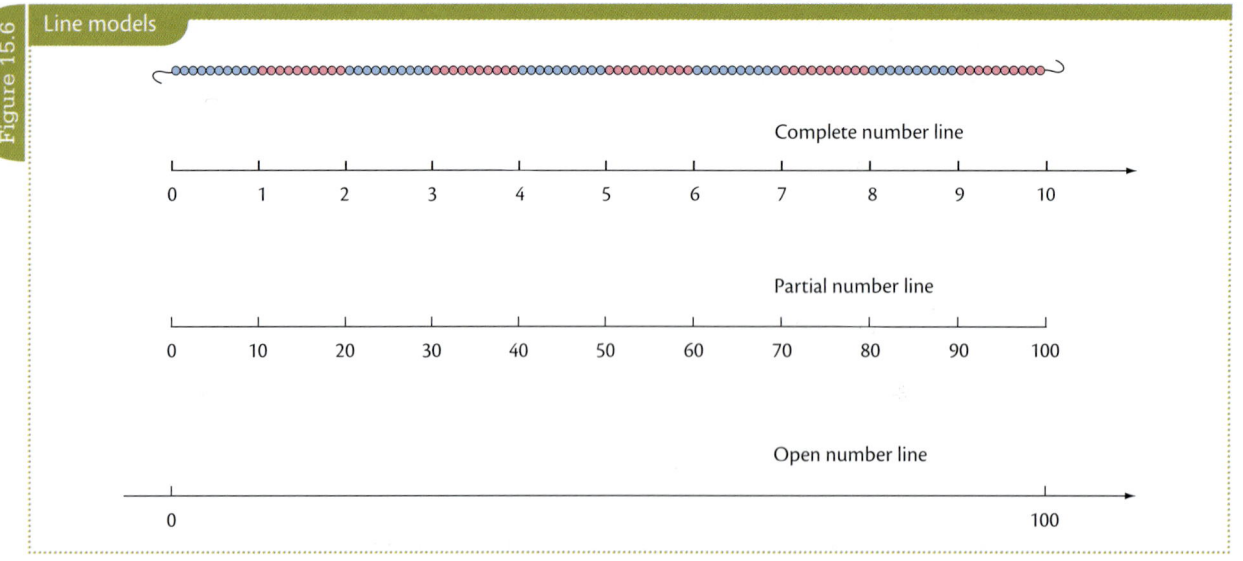

Making, naming, and recording the teens

The teen numbers present a particular problem because of their familiarity and their inconsistent number names. The teen number names have been routinely used when counting collections of ones. In the absence of a strong auditory pattern to the contrary, for example the 'ten one', 'ten two', 'ten three', 'ten four' and so on of the Vietnamese number-naming sequence, the use of the teen names in counting reinforces the notion that these names and numerals describe a collection of ones, not a 10 and some ones. This can be offset by ensuring children develop a sense of numbers beyond 10 (see above) before they are expected to work with place value more formally. Using the 'makes' language alongside what these numbers should be called if they were to support the pattern helps draw attention to the inconsistencies in the naming pattern (Table 15.2).

Table 15.2 Language and recording for the numbers 11–19

'Make me', model	Read, write, name	Read, write Tens	Ones
1 ten and 8 ones	eighteen (should be onety-eight)	1	8
	1 in the tens place and 8 in the ones place		
1 ten and 5 ones	fifteen (should be 'onety-five')	1	5
	1 in the tens place and 5 in the ones place		
1 ten and 2 ones	twelve (should be onety-two)	1	2
	1 in the tens place and 2 in the ones place		

Place value is a difficult idea to teach and to learn

In a classic sudy of children's understanding of place value, Ross (1989) asked 60 children in Years 2 to 5 to count a collection of 25 sticks and record the total. Once this was done, the interviewer circled the '5' and asked, 'Does this part of your twenty-five have anything to do with how many sticks you have?' This was repeated for the '2' in 25. Of the 60 students, 26 successfully identified that the 5 in 25 represented five sticks and the 2 in 25 represented the remaining 20 sticks. However, 12 students thought the individual digits had nothing to do with the number of sticks, 14 attributed irrelevant meanings to the digits (e.g. the 5 meant 'half of 10', or that the groups contained five sticks, or that the '2 meant count by twos'), and eight students thought that the 2 meant two sticks and that the 5 either had nothing to do with it or represented five sticks (p. 48). However, when two-digit numbers were represented by base 10 materials (e.g. 5 ten rods and 2 ones for 52), 44 of the 60 students were successful. This number was more than halved when non-standard representations were used (e.g. 4 ten rods and 12 ones).

This research suggests that while children may well read and write '25' for a collection of 25 objects, this does not mean that they understand the significance of the digits involved, that 2 refers to the count of tens and 5 refers to the count of ones. In a follow-up study, Ross (1989) individually interviewed 30 Year 3 students. The students were asked to count a collection of 26 objects and 'write down how many'. They were then asked to sort the objects into groups of four (generating 6 groups of four and 2 left over). Once this had been done, the interviewer circled the individual digits in turn and asked, 'Does this part of your 26 have anything to do with how many you have?' Nearly 50 per cent of the Year 3 students said that the 2 stood for the 2 left over, and the 6 for the number of groups.

While some might not think that this a fair test of place-value understanding, it does test the robustness of children's understanding of how two-digit numbers are written. This task is included in the *Assessment for Common Misunderstanding* materials available from the Victorian Department of Education website (URL included at the end of this chapter).

> **consider and discuss**
>
> ### Bridging 100
>
> While many children can say the number-naming sequence by the end of Year 1, some will experience difficulty with the counting sequence beyond 100. One of the most common errrors is to jump to the two hundreds, for example, '98, 99, 100, 101, 102, 103, 104, 105, 106, 107, 108, 109, 200, 201, 202'.
>
> Asked to say how many sticks there were in 13 bundles of 10 sticks and 16 loose sticks, one Year 2 child counted 10 of the bundles by tens to 100, the remaining three bundles as '200, 300, 400', then the single sticks as '401, 402, 403, 404, 405, 406, 407, 408, 409, 500, 501, 502, 503, 504, 505', miscounting one of the sticks.
>
> 1. What do you think contributed to this?
> 2. What would be an appropriate teaching response?

Working with number charts alone will not necessarily address these issues (e.g. Cobb, 1995). Children need regular opportunities to make, name, and record tens and ones using a variety of materials, and to participate in activities such as trading games to consolidate the big idea that '10 of these is 1 of those'. Initially, the trading game will involve place-value mats with only two columns ('tens' and 'ones'). Children take it in turns to toss a six-sided die and add the requisite number of sticks or straws to their mat. When a player has 10 ones, these are bundled to make 1 ten and transferred to the 'tens' column. The game proceeds until the number made exactly equals a designated number (e.g. 78). Structured materials such as base 10 blocks (MAB) can also be introduced once children have demonstrated that they have robust understanding of 10 as a countable unit, that is, once they can work with tens as units in their own right and can move freely between the count of tens language and multiples of 10 language.

Consolidating two-digit numeration

As children become familiar with matching the number names and numerals to collections and representing the count of tens and ones in place-value charts, flexibility and confidence can be built by applying this knowledge to practical, everyday problems. There are four basic ways to consolidate numeration:

- comparing (e.g. comparing two measures to determine which is longer or heavier)
- ordering a set of numbers (e.g. age of family members from youngest to oldest)
- counting forwards and backwards in place-value parts (supports calculation)
- renaming numbers in terms of their parts (supports calculation and estimation).

making connections

Counting forwards and backwards in place-value parts can be used to scaffold addition and subtraction on open number lines. For example, to subtract 37 from 71, we can count back 3 tens from 71 to 41, 1 more to 40, then 6 more to 34. Alternatively, we could take 4 tens from 71 to get to 31 and count 3 forwards to get to 34. These and other strategies for addition and subtraction will be explored further in Chapter 16.

Figure 15.7 | Counting backwards to support subtraction

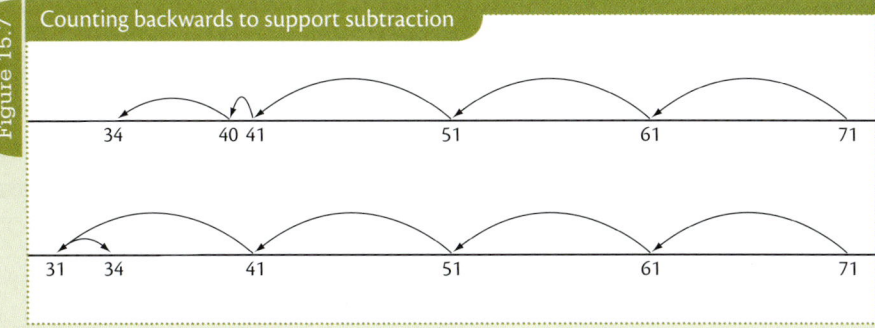

for the classroom

The place-value game

The place-value game provides an opportunity to make, record, compare, and order two-digit numbers.

Each player has a game board with 15 'stepping stones' or blank squares between 0 and 100. Players take turns to toss two 10-sided (0–9) dice. The two numbers are used to 'make' a two-digit number (e.g. a 5 and a 2 could be 25 or 52), which is recorded on one of the stepping stones. The object of the game is to record all the numbers thrown without missing a turn.

Figure 15.8 | Place-value game board

Introducing three-digit numeration

Extending the 'big idea': 10 tens is 1 hundred

Before working with hundreds as a new place-value part, it is important that children develop a sense of numbers beyond 100. Pattern work involving number charts that emphasise the continuing count of tens beyond 100 is useful, as are trading games of the type described below. It is best to ensure that two-digit numeration is deeply understood before proceeding to three-digit numeration too quickly.

for the classroom

Use non-standard number charts such as 50 to 149 to count forwards and backwards by 10, drawing attention to the continuing count of tens. Semi-masked charts like the one shown in Figure 15.3 can also be used to practise counting backwards and forwards in place-value parts and to emphasise the count of tens beyond 100 tens.

To cater for different learning needs, the 'star' symbol could be designated by the teacher or by chance (e.g. a two-digit number derived from the digits displayed on two 10-sided dice).

Figure 15.9 Non-standard number chart

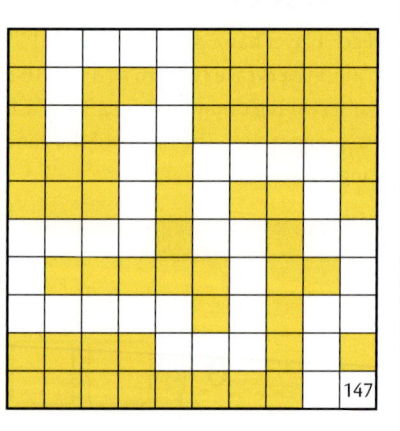

Making, naming, and recording three-digit numbers

Bundling or stacking materials can be used to establish and apply the big idea that '10 of these is one of those' and build a sense of numbers beyond 100, particularly in relation to the continuing count of tens, but these models quickly become cumbersome for larger numbers of hundreds. At this point, more use can be made of structured materials such as MAB or dot cards (e.g. Ellemor-Collins & Wright, 2008).

In introducing the new unit, it is essential that children understand that the relationship: '10 of these is 1 of those' continues to apply; in this case, that

10 tens is 1 hundred. To this end, it is useful, at least initially, to make and count hundreds using bundles of bundles (10 tens) and 'rafts' of ten-sticks (made from connectables such as unifix blocks) to ensure that hundreds are understood as a new, countable unit.

communicating mathematically

'They're hundreds, tens and ones!'

When MAB was introduced by Zoltan Dienes in the 1970s, the components were individually referred to as 'minis', 'longs', 'flats', and 'cubes' to support the 'new maths'. While the original intent was that these materials could take on multiple values, subsequent experience has demonstrated that children do not see these as anything other than ones, tens, hundreds, and thousands respectively. Given that the primary goal in using these materials is to establish each of these place-value parts as countable units, it seems sensible to use the language that supports this idea and is recognised by children.

Likely difficulties

Making and counting hundreds is nowhere near as problematic as it was for the tens, because the number-naming sequence is now fully supportive of the count. That is, three-digit numbers are named as a count of hundreds followed by a two-digit number name. Teen numbers (e.g. 513, 617, 311) and internal zeros (e.g. 708, 402, 600) can prove problematic for some children, so children still need to have plenty of opportunities to make, name, and record hundreds, tens and ones using structured materials and place-value charts, paying special attention to the language involved. In this case, it is wise to focus on the 'makes' language, which emphasises the count of place-value parts, for example 'make me five hundreds, zero tens and six ones'.

Expanded notation refers to the way in which a whole number can be written as the sum of each digit multiplied by its matching place-value part (e.g. 462 = 400 + 60 + 2). This use of expanded notation is misleading because it masks the multiplicative nature of the base 10 numeration system and increases **cognitive load** by suggesting 462 objects rather than 4 of one thing, 6 of another and 2 of a third. A more appropriate way to emphasise the value of each digit in a number is to represent it as a count of corresponding place-value units, in this case, 4 hundreds, 6 tens and 2 ones (note the plural form).

for the classroom

Trading games

Trading games can be played in teams or individually and provide a useful way of modelling the idea that '10 of these is 1 of those'.

You will need bundling materials (for two-digit numbers) or base 10 materials (for three- and four-digit numbers), a place-value mat for each person or team, and one or more dice. Initially a single 6-sided die might be used, then a 10-sided die (0–9), and finally two or more dice.

The game is played by each team/person taking turns to roll the die (dice), with the number thrown indicating how many ones are to be collected and placed on the mat. As the game proceeds, 10 ones is 'traded' for 1 ten and placed in the tens column, 10 tens for 1 hundred, and so on. The winner is determined by the team/individual who is the first to make a given number exactly (e.g. 60, 150, 483).

A variation on this is to start by modelling a given amount, say 354, and the winner is the first back to 0 exactly. This can be made more difficult by starting with a multiple of hundred or a thousand (e.g. 300 or 2000).

did you know?

From about 1400 to 1540 CE, the Incas controlled a large area between the Andes and the west coast of South America. They used a simple but very effective device known as a *quipu* (pronounced KEE-poo) for recording important data such as regional populations, the size of the harvest, or the amount of produce to be paid in taxes. Knots were tied in the string to indicate the number of each place-value part required. Different knots were sometimes used for the ones to avoid confusion, and a space was left if a particular place-value part was not required. This quipu shows how the sum of three numbers was recorded.

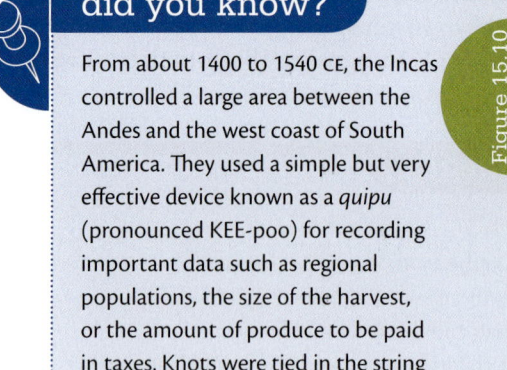

Figure 15.10 An example of a quipu

626

453 71 102

communicating mathematically

Writing multiples of 10

It is often said that to multiply a number by 10 'you add a zero'. What is meant by this is 'you write a 0 at the end of the number'. The language is unfortunate, as 'adding zero' makes no difference. A more appropriate way to emphasise the role of 0 is to emphasise the language and structure of place value. The reason we write a 0 when a number is multiplied by 10 is because this results in no ones; that is, when 56 is multiplied by 10, it becomes 56 tens; there are no ones, so it is written as 560.

Consolidating three-digit numeration

To develop fluency and confidence with three-digit numeration, children need to apply what they know in meaningful contexts. Realistic opportunities to compare and order three-digit numbers and/or measures can be generated from newspaper articles, magazines, and advertising brochures. Opportunities to rename numbers are less ubiquitous, but can arise with measurement. For example, builders' measuring tapes are generally marked in millimetres. If one of these is used to measure the height of a table, determining the height in centimetres becomes a renaming task as it is essentially asking 'how many tens in the number'. If the table measures 760 mm, there are 76 tens, so the table is 76 cm high.

Comparing and ordering can be accomplished more or less on the basis of 'face value' (e.g. there are more hundreds so it is bigger). Renaming is a relatively more sophisticated skill that needs to be modelled and explored. For example, 367 can be modelled in different ways using MAB as 3 hundreds, 6 tens and 0 ones, or as 36 tens and 7 ones, or even 367 ones. The different representations need to be named and discussed in terms of which is easiest to count, and why. Eventually, materials can be replaced with number expanders, and children's attention can be drawn to the fact that renaming simply involves 'reading' to the relevant place-value part (i.e. 367 can be read as '36 tens 7 ones').

Locating or representing numbers on a number line is also more sophisticated as it involves proportional reasoning. As with two-digit numbers, ropes, number cards, and pegs can be used to explore where three-digit numbers live. End-points can be varied as needed (e.g. a 0 to 500 range might be used before 0 to 1000).

integrating technology/ICT

Counting forwards and backwards in place-value parts

Use the constant function key on a hand-held or computer calculator to demonstrate forwards and backwards counting in place-value parts. For example, key in a starting number, say 23, then press [+], then enter 10 and press [=]: 33 will be displayed. Pressing [=] multiple times will generate a count of tens, that is, 43, 53, 63, 73, 83, 93, 103, 113, 123 … This helps children see the continuing count of tens beyond 100.

Counting backwards follows a similar process. For example, key in 928, then the subtraction key [−], and enter 100, then press [=]: 828 will be displayed. Continuously pressing [=] will generate a backwards count in the hundreds, that is, 728, 628, 528, 428 … Children's attention can be drawn to 'what stays the same, what is different' to describe the count in their own words and predict the numbers that will come next.

Developing four-digit numeration

Representing, naming, and recording four-digit numbers

While MAB extends to thousands and so can be used to demonstrate that 10 hundreds is 1 thousand, it is important to make this connection using as wide a range of other representations as possible. The metric measurement system is particularly useful; for example 1000 metres is 1 kilometre, 1000 grams is 1 kilogram, 1000 millilitres is a litre, and so on. The '10 of these is 1 of those' idea can be modelled using play money (e.g. ten $1 coins is one $10 note, and ten $10 notes is one $100 note), and, while there is no $1000 note, children will be able to appreciate that ten $100 notes is $1000.

Initially it is wise to use the 'makes' language to model, name, and record to ensure that the connection between the count and the place-value units is understood (Table 15.3)

Table 15.3 Language and recording for four-digit numbers

'Make me', model	Read, write, name	Read, write Thousands	Hundreds	Tens	Ones
4 thousands, 3 hundreds, 6 tens and 7 ones	four thousand three hundred and sixty-seven	4	3	6	7
6 thousands, 8 hundreds, 1 ten and 4 ones	six thousand eight hundred and fourteen	6	8	1	4
5 thousands, 0 hundreds, 0 tens and 7 ones	five thousand and seven	5	0	0	7

for the classroom

What's my number?

Write different four-digit numbers on paper party hats and place these on the children's heads without them seeing the number. Children move around the classroom asking questions that can only be answered by a 'yes' or a 'no', such as, 'Is my number odd?', 'Is it between 1000 and 2000?', 'Is there a 6 in the hundreds place?' A discussion of which questions were the most useful can follow.

Likely difficulties

Once again, some children may experience difficulty with four-digit numbers ending in teens and/or containing zeros. Careful attention to language and models is needed as well as renaming activities to ensure children appreciate the significance of the digits in each place-value location.

Another problem may arise in counting forwards and backwards in place-value parts. Questions such as 'what number comes before 6000?', 'what number is 10 less than 4502?', 'what number is 100 more than 3904?' can be very revealing of children's understanding of place value and how the number-naming system works. Extensive experience with structured models, number lines, place-value charts, and non-standard number charts is needed to ensure children develop a sound understanding of the base 10 numeration system.

issues in teaching

Catering for diversity

By Years 3 and 4, it is highly likely that children's understanding of place value will range from a very limited knowledge of two-digit numeration to a flexible and fluid understanding of thousands and beyond. Planning appropriate learning experiences for all can present a significant challenge. Games and investigations that involve children working in mixed ability teams or groups can be useful, as well as games that can be adapted to provide meaningful practice, such as the place-value game.

- Brainstorm and/or research some other ways of catering for diverse learning needs in relation to numeration.
- Under what circumstances might it be appropriate to group by ability, and how might this be managed in the social context of the classroom?

Consolidating four-digit numeration

Regular opportunities need to be provided to compare, order, count forwards and backwards in place-value parts, and rename numbers to ensure that the relative magnitude and structure of four-digit numeration is understood. A sense of the relative magnitude of four-digit numbers can be built up by comparing shorter, known distances (e.g. distance between the school and the nearest shopping centre, town, or city) to the distances between Australian capital cities. Locating four-digit numbers on a 0–10 000 rope model can be used to establish where the numbers live. Number lines can be used to demonstrate counting forwards and backwards, particularly in relation to examples such as 'what number comes before 6000?' or 'what is 2 tens more than 4692?' Number expanders are a particularly useful tool for renaming larger whole numbers.

for the classroom

Make a number expander and use it to practise renaming four-digit numbers, particularly those involving teen numbers and internal zeros.

Number expanders are made by taking a long strip of card and partitioning it so that there are three parts for each place-value part required (e.g. to make a four-digit number expander, you will need to partition the strip into 12 parts). The first of the three parts is used to record the digit. The remaining two are used to record the name of the place value unit in words. These are then folded concertina fashion to sit behind the first rectangle.

Figure 15.11 Making a four-digit number expander

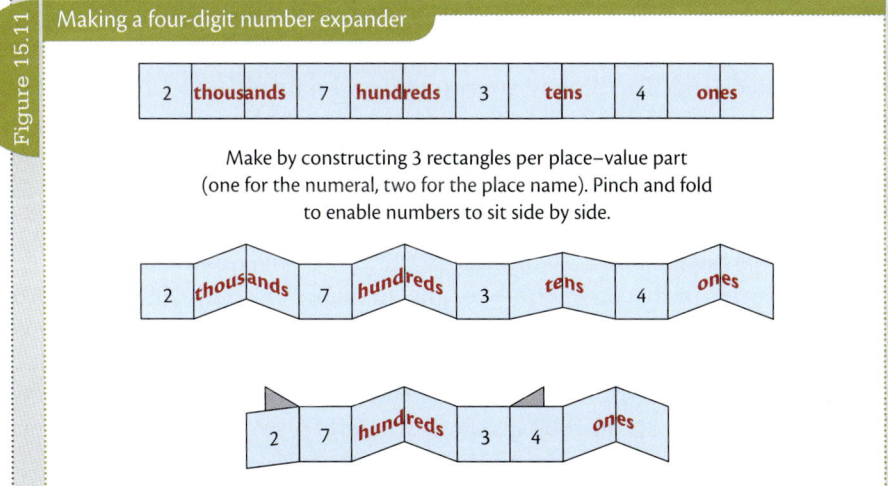

consider and discuss

Renaming

Renaming numbers is a powerful tool that can be used to support estimation, rounding, and more efficient forms of written and mental computation. It is also useful in converting measures. For example, long-distance athletic events are typically described in terms of metres (with the exception of marathons), but we tend to describe how far we walk in kilometres. On a golf course that is 6754 metres long, how many kilometres might you expect a professional golfer to walk? How many kilometres might a novice golfer walk? How could renaming be used to answer these questions?

Brainstorm and share some other situations that require changing one metric unit to another.

Extending to millions and beyond

There is very little research on students' understanding of place value and numeration beyond two- and three-digit numbers, but what there is suggests that many students in the middle years of schooling do not understand the multiplicative structure of the number system (e.g. Thomas, 2004). This observation is supported by our work on multiplicative thinking, where we found that fewer than 10 per cent of students in Years 4 to 8 were able to work flexibly with larger whole numbers and decimal fractions (Siemon, Breed, Dole, Izard & Virgona, 2006). This is not particularly surprising, given that larger whole numbers were not considered until the final years of primary school and computation, particularly multiplication and division, was generally restricted to two- and three-digit numbers. It may seem strange that the *Australian Curriculum: Mathematics* (Australian Curriculum Asessment & Reporting Authority [ACARA], 2010) includes the ability to read, write, and order numbers to 1 million at Year 4. However, in our view this is justified, as it encourages teachers to deal with the multiplicative patterns and relationships involved (e.g. 1000 of these is 1 of those) at the very point where there is an increased likelihood that children will develop misconceptions because of the apparent anomalies in the number-naming sequence. For example, although the '10 of these is 1 of those' pattern still applies, the number-naming sequence no longer supports the count of the unit in the ten thousands place (e.g. 30 000 is read as 'thirty thousand' not '3 ten thousands'). Introducing students to the big idea that '1000 of these is 1 of those' supports the simultaneous development of five- and six-digit numeration, as it suggests that thousands are not just counted from 1 to 9, they are counted and named from 1 to 999. This pattern is explored more fully below.

Another 'big idea': 1000 of these is 1 of those

While the initial big idea that '10 of these is 1 of those' still applies, larger whole numbers become particularly cumbersome to name beyond 9999. A more efficient number-naming sequence is needed for larger whole numbers. This is achieved by overlaying another place-value pattern, '1000 of these is 1 of those'. This involves the re-use of hundreds, tens, and ones to count thousands, then millions, billions, and so on. For instance, for 56 835 we do not say 'five ten thousands six thousands eight hundred and thirty-five', nor do we say 'three hundred thousands five ten thousands six thousands eight hundred and thirty-five' for 356 835. This pattern will be referred to here as the HTO pattern, although it can also be referred to as the second place-value pattern.

Representing and recording larger whole numbers

While MAB thousand blocks can be used to build a ten thousand unit tower to demonstrate that '10 of these is 1 of those', this becomes increasingly cumbersome (and potentially dangerous) for five-digit numbers and beyond. Nevertheless, it is important to find ways to help students appreciate the relative magnitude of these larger units, and that thousands, like millions, are a special type of new unit that we count from 1 to 999. One excellent way of doing this is to consider the different ways in which a million might be made or represented. For example, make a 3D model based on centimetre cubes (paper/card), use millimetre graph paper to represent a million, consider how long a coin trail would need to be to make a million dollars, or how many sell-out crowds at the MCG would be needed to make a million. Such activities necessarily deal with tens and hundreds of thousands in the process, and provide opportunities for talking about the relationships between these units.

A model of the number line in the form of a 5 m length of rope, pegs, and number cards can be used to locate large whole numbers relative to one another. The rope can be used to represent intervals of a thousand, tens of thousands, or even millions. Students can be asked to locate a number such as 45 358 on a 0–100 000 rope and to justify their thinking in terms of 'it's a bit less than half-way as it is nearly 50 000'. Place-value charts are useful only to the extent that they emphasise the HTO pattern. They need to be used in conjunction with the number-naming sequence to emphasise the count of thousands to 999 (e.g. see Figure 15.12).

Figure 15.12 Place-value charts for five-digit numbers and beyond

Millions	Thousands			(Ones)		
Ones	Hundred thousands	Ten thousands	(Ones) thousands	Hundreds	Tens	Ones
		3	4	5	8	1
	6	7	0	8	2	9
2	4	5	2	6	7	3

34 thousand 581

670 thousand 829

2 million 452 thousand 673

consider and discuss

Use of commas as a separator

In Australia, commas are commonly used to break up numbers of five digits or more to make them easier to read in terms of the HTO pattern. However, this is not a universal practice: commas are used in many countries to indicate the **decimal marker** (i.e. where the ones begin). For whole numbers with more than four digits, the International System of Units (SI) recommends that the groups of three digits be separated by a thin space rather than dots or commas. Find out more about the SI system. What are the implications of this for recording larger whole numbers in Year 4 and beyond?

think + link

Larger whole numbers can be represented in other ways. For example, a number such as 35 217 800 can be written as 3.521 78 × 10^7. This will be explored further in Chapter 22.

Likely difficulties

Apart from building a sense of relative magnitude and an understanding of how larger numbers are counted (i.e. that thousands are counted to 999), reading and writing larger whole numbers can be problematic if these patterns are not well understood. This can be offset by recording larger whole numbers as a mix of numerals that can be read (e.g. a three-digit number) and words for the new countable units (thousands, millions, etc.). For example, record 34 581 as '34 thousand 581' and 670 829 as '670 thousand 829'. It is important to provide regular practice in writing numbers given an oral stimulus or saying numbers given a symbolic representation, as well as in reading larger numbers in context, such as house prices, lottery prizes, and population statistics.

for the classroom

Ask children to take turns tossing a 0–9 die. As each number is read out, write these from right to left on the whiteboard and have the class read the resulting number in unison (e.g. 8, 48, 948, 1948 …). This can extend to the numbers in the millions and billions, and serves to illustrate the re-use of hundreds, tens and ones to name larger place-value units and the pattern '1000 of these is 1 of those'.

This activity can be made a little more challenging by recording the numbers from left to right. In this case, the numbers change their place-value position and more attention to the HTO pattern is needed. This activity also stimulates discussion about the use of commas as separators (see above).

A potential of difficulty arises from the premature use of 'spike abacus' or similar devices to represent the base 10 numeration system. Like place-value charts, these have their limitations as well as their strengths. While both illustrate the use of digits to count place-value units, unless children understand the relationship between place-value parts in terms of '10 of these is 1 of those' they can convey the impression that the base 10 system of numeration is additive rather than multiplicative. For example, a five-spike abacus that shows three discs on the first spike, two on the next, seven on the third, eight on the fourth and four on the fifth may be understood as '32 thousand 784', but it is more likely to be seen as the sum of the different parts, that is 3 ten thousands, 2 thousands, 7 hundreds, 8 tens and 4 ones. Another disadvantage of both place-value charts and abacus is that they do not convey any sense of the relative magnitude of different place-value units, and they are not supported by the number-naming sequence beyond thousands. In other words, they are *after-the-event* representations that require an understanding of the patterns and relationships involved. They cannot be expected to teach these relationships. Having said that, there are ways in which these representations can be used to support the notion that '10 of these is 1 of those'. For instance, for two- to four-digit numbers, place-value mats can be used with bundling, stacking, or structured materials to play trading games to emphasise this pattern. Revolving odometer representations (see Figure 15.13) can also be helpful in showing that as the count in one place-value part reaches 9 the next number produces a 0 in that column and the value of the digit in the next place increases by one.

Chapter 15 Introducing Place Value

Figure 15.13 'Odometer' representation of numeration

integrating technology/ICT

Make a digital collation of real-world uses of large whole numbers

Ask students and students' families to collect digital images of interesting ways in which whole numbers are used in the real world. For example, download statistics related to natural disasters to focus attention on the magnitude and impact of these events and to make connections to geography and science. UNICEF publishes a report on the state of the world's children which is an excellent source of comparative, accessible data, such as the number of children in the various countries who are able to attend school. In 2010, a special 20th anniversary edition was published. It is available from www.unicef.org/publications/files/SOWC_Spec._Ed._CRC_Main_Report_EN_090409.pdf

Consolidating whole number

While it becomes increasingly cumbersome to represent larger numbers, it is important to give students opportunities to practise naming and reading large numbers (see For the Classroom below), compare and order large numbers, count forwards and backwards in place-value parts, and rename numbers in multiple ways.

for the classroom

Dice numbers

In table groups, have children roll at least three 10-sided dice. (The number of dice can vary depending on the focus of the activity.) Give table points for different tasks, for example the highest (lowest) number using all of the digits, the smallest three-digit number, the largest even number (if not possible, why not?), the smallest six-digit number, and so on.

Comparing and ordering

It is often assumed that we primarily use numbers to calculate. While this is important, comparing and ordering on the basis of which is largest/longest/tallest, or ordering numbers from smallest to largest, is a necessary and inescapable part of what most of us do everyday.

making connections

Opportunities to compare and/or order numbers arise everyday in just about every discipline. Consider the following possibilities and work in groups to collate some more of your own.

- Compare and order thousands, for example, attendances at sporting matches, international flight distances, populations of Australian regional cities.
- Make a collection of large whole numbers found in the daily press and news bulletins—data associated with natural disasters such as the number of earthquake victims, hectares destroyed by bushfire, area covered by an oil spill.
- Organise a can recycle collection—aim to get some target number such as 500 000, and decide on an appropriate way to keep track of the number of cans and how much might be earnt as a result.
- Use a packaging situation such as 10 sweets per roll, 10 rolls per tray, 10 trays per carton, 10 cartons per box to demonstrate the multiplicative nature of the numeration system (in particular, the notion that '10 of these is 1 of those').

Counting forwards and backwards in place-value parts

Counting forwards and backwards in place-value parts as a strategy for solving addition or subtraction problems quickly becomes clumsy for whole numbers with more than two or three digits. Nevertheless, identifying, describing, and continuing patterns serves a useful purpose by focusing attention on the structure of the numeration system.

for the classroom

Invite students to construct and exchange counting patterns such as the following. Students should be asked to identify, describe, fill in missing elements, and/or continue.

56 149, ___, 56 327, 56 416, 56 505, ___

Think about the way in which this pattern might be described. Which would be the most beneficial from a place-value point of view?

Renaming

Regular practice in renaming larger whole numbers in terms of their place-value parts is vitally important, as this is recognised as a key to being able to work confidently and flexibly with numbers in further school mathematics (Seah & Booker, 2005; Siemon et al., 2006).

Renaming provides an efficient and meaningful way of working with metric units (e.g. to see at a glance that 2137 grams is 2.137 kilograms), scientific notation, and estimation. The latter skill is particularly important in making sense of numbers in the real world. It also helps to reinforce the multiplicative structure of the base 10 numeration system.

Chapter 15 Introducing Place Value

handy hint

Construct a table in Word or Excel with seven columns, one each for the key activities used to support and consolidate numeration (make/model/represent, name, record, compare, order, count forwards and backwards in place-value parts, rename) and six rows, one for each place-value part from ones to millions. Briefly describe at least one real-world example or context that could be used to illustrate each cell in the table (e.g. for the three-digit compare cell, you might record: 'Jeremy is 127 cm tall; Maria is 131 cm tall. Who is taller?').

Rounding

It is often easier to work with close approximations of numbers rather than the numbers themselves (e.g. 22/7 as often used is an approximation for π). Replacing a number by another number that is a close approximation of the original number is called rounding. The legitimacy of this very much depends on the purpose for which the numbers are being used; for example, it is reasonable to round crowd numbers at a grand slam tennis match to the nearest thousand, but inappropriate in most circumstances to round a medicine dose in milligrams to the nearest gram. Context also plays a part in how numbers are rounded. For instance, it is generally accepted practice to round a restaurant bill not just to the next cent or the next dollar, but often to the next multiple of 10 dollars. In this case the amount cannot be rounded to an amount less than the total value, but in the supermarket this is possible (e.g. $4.12 will be rounded to $4.10). Rounding is used to make it easier to comprehend or work with numbers and to estimate.

did you know?

There is an urban myth about a bank clerk in Europe who programmed the bank's computers to transfer 0.1 eurocents from each transaction to an account in Switzerland. The story goes that this rarely, if ever, changed what the bank's customers saw on their bank statements, or if it did, it was assumed to be as a result of 'rounding'.

Estimating how much money such a scam might generate is an example of a Fermi problem (see Chapter 10), solutions to which involve assumptions and working with rounded numbers.

Rounding numbers to the nearest specified place-value part can be difficult for children if they rely on remembering a rule or procedure, particularly where this is couched in terms of 'up' and 'down'. While it is true that rounding is governed by convention, a perceptual basis for this can be established early on through the use of 0–99 number charts as opposed to 1 to 100 number charts, and more generally by renaming numbers in terms of place-value parts. One important reason for starting with 0–99 charts before proceeding to a wider range of number charts is that the vertical line of symmetry on the 0–99 chart is between the numbers ending in 4 ones and the numbers ending in 5 ones, whereas on the 1 to 100 chart it is between numbers ending in 5 ones and numbers ending in 6 ones. Although this is not a mathematical rationale, it supports an intuitive notion of 'closer to' and ultimately the recognition that in rounding to the nearest 10, a two-digit number can round to either the 10 that it is or the next 10.

Rounding is a sophisticated skill that builds on a solid understanding of place value and a capacity to rename any number in terms of its place-value parts. As a general principle, children should be encouraged to consider the two possibilities when rounding a number to a nominated place. For example, to round 34 562 to the nearest 10, it makes sense to consider what the two possibilities are, namely, 3456 tens or 3457 tens, before worrying about which of these it is closest to. In this case, simply recalling the number chart arrangement for the digit in the next or *determining place* is sufficient to see that 34 562 is closest to the 10 that it is rather than the next 10—in this case, 3456 tens.

0	1	2	3	4	5	6	7	8	9

Number expanders can also be used to support rounding. For example, in rounding 68 573 to the nearest ten thousand, a number expander can be used to demonstrate that the two possibilities are 6 ten thousands or 7 ten thousands. Thinking about the number of thousands in terms of the number chart row above, it can be 'seen to be closer' to the next ten thousand. So, the nearest ten thousand to 68 573 is 70 000.

Difficulties arise where students have been taught rules based on 'up' and 'down' in relation to 5 on a number line. Because 5 is directly located in the middle of the two possibilities there is ambiguity about which it is 'closest to'. This can be offset by reference to the number chart row when considering the digit in the determining place. Some children experience difficulty in rounding to an internal place other than the ones. It appears to be 'easier' to round numbers to the place immediately to the left of the smallest place-value part, (as in the example involving tens), or to the highest place value part (as in the example involving ten thousands) than it is to round a number like 68 573 to an internal place such as thousands or hundreds. Again, this can be offset by close attention to renaming numbers in terms of all their place-value parts, using number expanders where necessary to reinforce the two-step process described above;that is, to identify the two possibilities and then decide which of the two possibilities is 'closest' on the basis of the value of the digit in the determining place.

Money

Rounding money amounts conforms to a different convention in that cents are rounded to the nearest 5 cents rather than the nearest 10 cents (e.g. $3.28 rounds to $3.30, but $3.27 rounds to $3.25). While dollars are rounded to the nearest dollar, there is potential for confusion in the language used. For example, when rounding $4.68 to the nearest dollar, we hear/read 'four' dollars and 'sixty-eight' cents; that is, the language of ones is followed by the language of tens and ones. In this case, the determining 'place' is the tens place in the count of cents. But as cents are not thought about in this way it is more sensible to consider the whole number of cents, that is, 68 cents, when deciding. As this is closer to 100 cents than 0 cents, $4.68 to the nearest dollar is $5.

Money is generally not an appropriate model of the base 10 numeration system because it involves the simultaneous use of two units, dollars and cents, which are counted separately as whole numbers (dollars from 0, and cents from 0 to 99). Other issues arise in relation to the value and sizes of different coins and notes (e.g. one coin for 5 cents, and the 10 cent coin is larger than $2). As a consequence, money is more appropriately considered in relation to measurement, although links can be made to number where dollars and cents are understood.

consider and discuss

Numbers in other bases

Working in other number bases is an effective way to draw attention to the structure of the base 10 numeration system as it takes us out of our 'comfort zone'.

In base 10, 23 = (2 × 10) + 3.

For numbers in other bases, a subscript is used to distinguish them from base 10 numbers, for example, $23_{five} = (2 \times 5) + 3 = 13_{ten}$.

1. What digits are needed for a base 5 numeration system? Write your age in base 5.
2. What would the following numbers be in base 10?
   a. 231_{five}
   b. 1033_{five}
   c. $420\,132_{five}$
3. In base 2, 769 is $1\,100\,011\,001_{two}$. What would your age be in base 2?
4. Discuss the advantages and disadvantages of base 2.
5. If 10^2 represents hundreds and 10^3 represents thousands, how might indices be used to represent place-value parts more generally?
6. How might you justify the fact that $10^0 = 1$?

Conclusion

Place value is one of the 'big ideas' needed to develop a deep sense of number. It is typically introduced too early, before young children have fully developed the prerequisite understandings (e.g. trusting the count and a capacity to recognise numbers as composite units). Considerable care must be taken in working with materials that children make the connection between how many (value) and how much (place). Language and initial forms of recording play a key role in helping children make this distinction (e.g. emphasise '3 tens' instead of 'thirty', '6 hundreds' instead of '600', and work with examples that support place value before dealing with zeros and teen numbers).

Two big ideas underpin the development of a deep understanding of whole number numeration, initially that '10 of these is 1 of those', and ultimately that '1000 of these is 1 of those', which is recognised in the repeated use of hundreds, tens, and ones to count thousands, millions, billions and so on. The key steps in developing any place-value part are listed below. (These steps also apply to decimal fractions, as we shall see in Chapter 22.)

1. Introduce the new unit: 10 of these is 1 of those … 1000 of these is 1 of those (and for decimal fractions the inverse of these patterns, that is, 1 tenth of this is 1 of those etc.).
2. Deal with any language issues or likely problem areas (e.g. for two-digit numbers the names for the multiples of 10 and teen numbers, and for five-digit numbers the re-use of the names for the multiples of 10 as the shift is made to count thousands in hundreds, tens and ones).
3. Make/model/represent numbers, name and record 'regular' examples (i.e. examples supported by language, such as 67, 456, 7238, or 237 726).
4. Make/model/represent numbers, name and record 'irregular' examples (i.e. examples not supported by language, such as 14, 604, 518, 4007, or 56 027).
5. Consolidate by comparing, ordering, counting forwards and backwards in place-value parts, renaming numbers in terms of their place-value parts, and recognising complements to 100, 1000 (e.g. 34 and 66 are complements to 100 because ones need to add to 1 ten and tens need to add to 9 tens).

key terms

Cognitive load: features of the learning situation or task that can affect attention and/or capacity to retain the information needed to undertake complex tasks

Composite unit: a unit made up of other units (e.g. when children understand 8 as 1 eight not as a collection of 8 ones)

Decimal marker: the symbol used to show where the ones begin; in Australia we use a point as the decimal marker, hence the term 'decimal point'

Expanded notation: the expression of a whole number in terms of the sum of its place-value parts written in symbolic form as ones (e.g. 456 = 400 + 50 + 6)

Renaming: writing a number in an equivalent form, usually in terms of its place-value parts (e.g. 4567 can be renamed in terms of 4 thousands, 5 hundreds, 6 tens and 7 ones, and can also be renamed in terms of 456 tens and 7 ones, or 45 hundreds and 67 ones, and so on)

Review questions

1. List the prerequisite knowledge and skills that children need to be able to demonstrate before being introduced to place value more formally.
2. Describe and illustrate the steps involved in developing an understanding of two-digit numbers. What numbers are likely to be difficult for young children, and why?
3. What would you do to assist a child who writes 2467 as 2000467? What might have contributed to this misunderstanding?
4. Use real-world problems or contexts to illustrate how three-digit place-value knowledge can be consolidated.
5. What is meant by the HTO pattern or second place-value pattern? Describe how and why it used to support the naming of larger whole numbers.
6. Describe and justify the procedure for rounding numbers. Generate some realistic examples that you might use with children in different Year levels to practise rounding to different place-value parts.

Key references

Australian Curriculum Assessment & Reporting Authority (ACARA, 2010). *Australian Curriculum: Mathematics*. Sydney: ACARA. Available from http://acara.edu.au/.

Cobb, P. (1995). Cultural tools and mathematical learning: A case study. *Journal for Research in Mathematics Education*, 26(4), 362–385.

Ellemor-Collins, D., & Wright, R. (2008). Developing conceptual place value: Instructional design for intensive intervention. In R. Hunter, B. Bicknell & T. Burgess (Eds.), *Crossing Divides* (Proceedings of the 32nd annual conference of the Mathematics Education Research Group of Australasia, Vol. 1 pp. 169–176). Palmerston, NZ: MERGA.

Nunes, T., & Bryant, P. (1996). *Children doing Mathematics*. Oxford, UK: Blackwell.

Ross, S. (1989). Parts, wholes and place-value: A developmental view. *Arithmetic Teacher*, 36(3), 47–51.

Siemon, D., Breed, M., Dole, S., Izard, J., & Virgona, J. (2006). *Scaffolding Numeracy in the Middle Years – Project Findings, Materials, and Resources*. Final report submitted to Victorian Department of Education and Training and the Tasmanian Department of Education, October. CD-rom subsequently published electronically: www.eduweb.vic.gov.au/edulibrary/public/teachlearn/student/snmy.ppt.

Thomas, N. (2004). The development of structure in the number system. In M. Johnsen Joines & A. Fuglestad (Eds.) *Proceedings of the 28th Conference of the International Group for the Psychology of Mathematics Education* (pp. 305–312). Bergen, Norway: PME.

Verschaffel, L., & De Corte, E. (1996). Number and arithmetic. In A. Bishop, K. Clements, C. Keitel, J. Kilpatrick & C. Laborde (Eds.), *International Handbook of Mathematics Education* (pp. 99–138). Dordrecht, The Netherlands: Kluwer.

Websites

www.bipm.org/utils/common/pdf/si_brochure_8_en.pdf

www.curriculumsupport.education.nsw.gov.au

www.education.vic.gov.au/studentlearning/teachingresources/maths/common/default.htm

16 Developing Additive Thinking in F–4

Contents

Why additive thinking?	321
The development of additive thinking	324
Contexts for addition and subtraction	324
Additive solution strategies	330
Problem solving	345
Conclusion	347

Chapter objectives

This chapter will enable the reader to:
- Understand what is involved in additive thinking
- Recognise the different ways in which addition and subtraction problems can be represented
- Appreciate the role of materials, language, and recording in scaffolding children's understanding and solution strategies
- Understand the importance of mental strategies and how these can be developed
- Recognise and address children's learning needs in relation to additive thinking
- Plan effective problem-solving experiences involving written and mental computation.

Frog in a well

A class of Year 4 students was working in groups on a problem that required them to determine how many days it would take Freddie Frog to climb out of a 12-metre deep well if each day he climbed up 4 metres but each night he slipped back 2 metres. Two solutions emerged, both of which were energetically defended. About half the class argued that it would take Freddie 6 days to get out of the well because he climbed up 2 metres each day. The rest of the class argued that it took Freddie 5 days on the basis of their modelling of the situation (Siemon, 1993). These responses illustrate the critical importance of being able to represent problems in more than one way, a capacity that comes with a deep understanding of the operations involved and how they interact.

Big ideas

- Additive thinking is inherently related to the construction and representation of number, in particular to part–part–whole ideas and place value.
- Knowing when to add or subtract and choosing a strategy appropriate to the task requires a deep understanding of the operations themselves and a well-developed sense of number.

- Strategies for adding and subtracting need to be modelled, scaffolded, and discussed to ensure all students have access to a range of efficient, flexible strategies that they can use with confidence.
- Estimation is a highly developed capacity requiring the integration of a number of subordinate skills and understandings.

Why additive thinking?

Additive thinking refers to the thought processes underpinning the aggregation or disaggregation of collections or quantities in a wide variety of contexts. In its most primitive form, it views numerical quantities as collections of ones that need to be put together or broken apart. In particular, additive thinking connects **part–part–whole** and place-value ideas with counting.

The capacity to distinguish the whole from its parts is a fundamental component of additive thinking. However, additive thinking is not fully developed until both the whole and its parts can be thought of simultaneously and the situation can be interpreted in terms of what is known and what is unknown (Fuson, 2009; Steffe, Cobb & von Glasersfeld, 1988). For instance, in the monkeys problem (Chapter 10, p. 200), it is necessary to recognise that the number of bananas eaten in the morning and the number of bananas eaten in the afternoon are both known parts of an unknown whole (the total number of bananas) to decide that addition is the relevant operation. By contrast, the children who relied on cue words (such as 'left' or the fact that something had been eaten) to conclude that subtraction was needed were not able to construct and coordinate the parts in relation to the whole.

consider and discuss

What is required?

Marika and Ted had $32 between them. They bought a capricciosa pizza and a soft drink. How much money did they have left?

1. What is involved in answering this question? Why is it important to include problems of this type in school mathematics? How would you describe the strategy or strategies you used?
2. Brainstorm some other situations like this which might generate similar opportunities for problem solving.

Additive thinking requires more than a capacity to execute a particular procedure or strategy. This is illustrated in the two solution strategies to the frog problem described above, where the students who explored what the actions meant in practice by modelling the frog's progress (see Figure 16.1) were able to see that it took five days to emerge from the well. Those who relied on a decontextualised interpretation of addition and subtraction ('he went up 2 metres each day') and assumed the answer would be given by the count of twos in 12 arrived at an incorrect solution, although their calculations were accurate and appeared to be relevant.

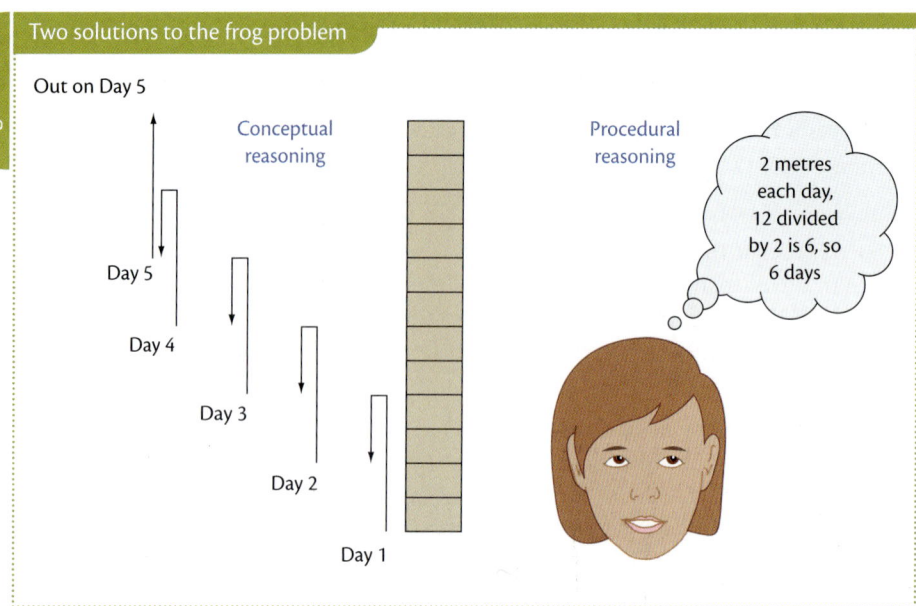

Figure 16.1 Two solutions to the frog problem

Historically, addition and subtraction were taught separately because the focus was on the introduction and use of formal *algorithms* (written methods or procedures used to calculate) rather than on an understanding of addition and subtraction and the acquisition of meaningful mental strategies. Today, while procedural fluency remains a key outcome of school mathematics, conceptual understanding and an appreciation of the internal connectedness of mathematics are more highly valued (e.g. Boaler, 2002; Kilpatrick, Swafford & Findell, 2001; Fuson, 2009). As a consequence, the teaching focus has shifted to the development of meaningful links between addition and subtraction, and the use of additive thinking more generally to solve problems using a broader range of more flexible strategies.

making connections

One example of the ways in which these links can be made is to pose and answer questions relating to data such as that shown in Figure 16.2. For example, questions might include 'How many four-legged animals are there?', 'How many more chickens are there than dogs?'

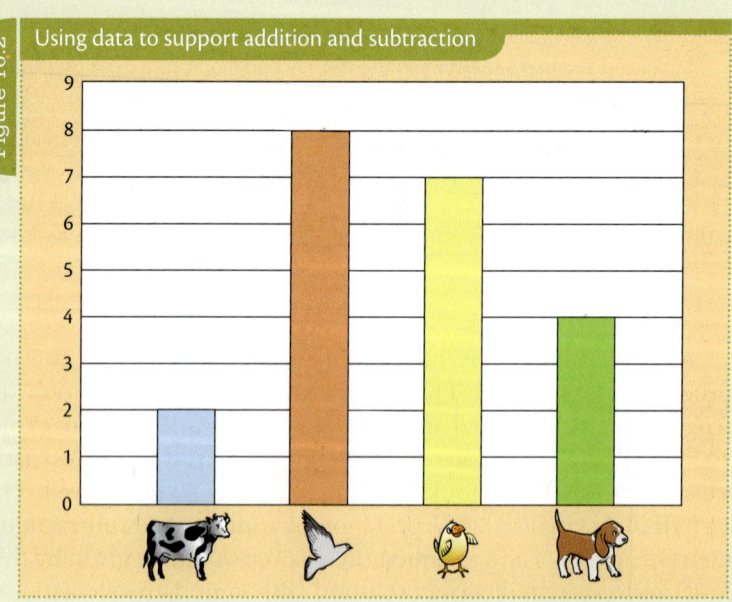

Figure 16.2 Using data to support addition and subtraction

Source: Selva, Falcao and Nunes (2005)

Additive thinking and numeration

Additive thinking is inherently related to the construction of number. Initially this is seen in the use of the number-naming sequence. The ideas of 1 more and 1 less can be applied iteratively to add and subtract by counting forwards and backwards respectively. Ultimately, this count-all strategy is replaced by a deeper understanding of the structure of the number system and the recognition that numbers can be **renamed** in many ways. For example, 56 can be renamed in terms of its place-value parts as 5 tens and 6 ones, or as 4 less than 60, as 44 less than 100, or in many other ways.

Additive thinking is served by two big ideas: *trusting the count* and *place value*. Part–part–whole knowledge of the numbers to 10 is needed to reconfigure numbers in different ways to suit specific task requirements (e.g. when adding 6 and 8, it is helpful to recognise that 8 is 2 less than 10, and 6 is 2 and 4). Place-value knowledge is needed to locate numbers within a counting sequence and to support more sophisticated counting-based strategies. For example, while a simple count-on strategy might be used to add 3 and 56 (i.e. 57, 58, 59), to subtract 8 from 56 it is useful to show 56 on a number line and jump back 6 to 50 then 2 more to 48. More generally, the capacity to rename numbers in terms of their place-value parts is a powerful tool that can be used to support calculations involving larger whole numbers and decimals. For instance, in subtracting 2586 from 4003 it is helpful to recognise that there are 400 tens in 4003 that can be renamed as 399 tens and 13 ones to facilitate a more straightforward subtraction.

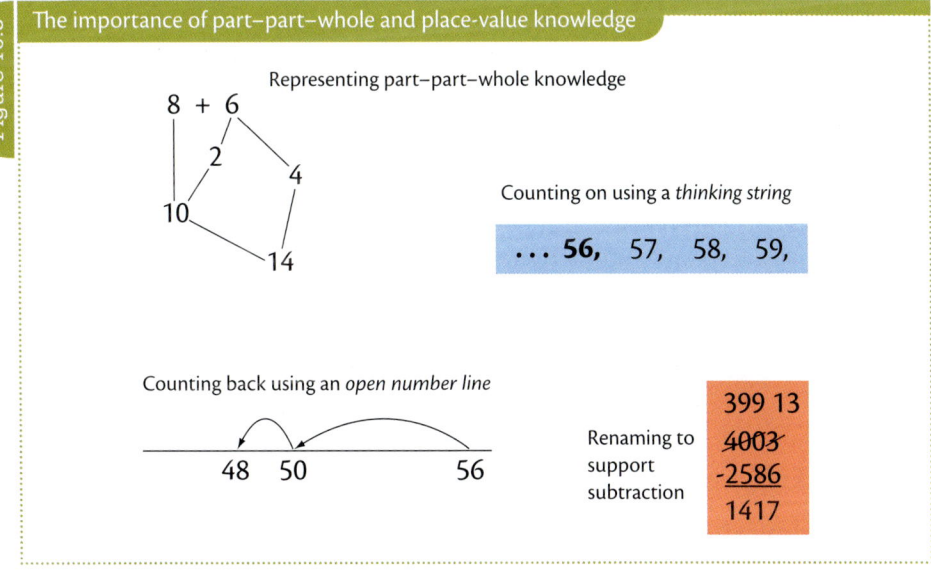

Figure 16.3 The importance of part–part–whole and place-value knowledge

did you know?

The capacity to rename numbers and work with place-value parts underpins the earliest of calculating devices: the abacus. It is believed the abacus originated in Greece, but it was popularised in Roman times as travel and trade expanded. Slightly different versions were also used in China (suan pan) and Japan (soroban) from the 6th century CE. These are still in use today. In the hands of skilled practitioners, they have proved faster and more reliable than modern calculators for addition and subtraction (see Zaslavsky, 1996).

The development of additive thinking

Children's early play experiences contribute to their understanding of the relative magnitude of different collections and/or quantities (e.g. bigger/smaller, more/less, same as) and the activities of joining or separating collections and amounts. These experiences are unlikely to involve quantification, and it may take some time before children are able to deal with the whole and its parts simultaneously. Activities that attach numerical values to recognised collections and quantities and use these as a basis for comparing and ordering can be helpful in establishing the idea of absolute magnitude of numbers (e.g. for a collection of three blue blocks and five red blocks, recognise not only that there are more red blocks than blue blocks but that there are two more red blocks). It is not until children develop a sound understanding of the numbers to 10 in terms of their parts and place value that they are ready to work more formally with addition and subtraction.

think + link

See Chapter 14 for a more detailed discussion of the development of part–part–whole ideas.

Key steps in the development of additive thinking in F–4 include:

- an appreciation of what it means to add and subtract in different contexts
- an ability to count fluently and accurately to 20 and beyond and recognise 1 more and 1 less than any given number
- recognition that adding or subtracting 0 leaves the number unchanged
- a knowledge of each of the numbers to 10 in terms of their parts (part–part–whole knowledge) and how this might be used to support addition and subtraction
- an appreciation of 10 as a composite unit and a sense of numbers beyond 10 (e.g. 1 ten and 4 more is 14)
- access to efficient, meaningful strategies for the addition and related subtraction facts to 20
- an understanding of the place-value structure of the number system for two-digit numbers and beyond and how these numbers might be represented to support addition and subtraction
- access to a broad range of meaningful, efficient strategies to support addition and subtraction involving larger whole numbers, decimals (to tenths), and like or related fractions.

think + link

Chapter 23 will consider addition and subtraction with decimals beyond tenths, fractions, and integers.

Contexts for addition and subtraction

We add and subtract to solve problems. We add to find how many altogether, and we subtract to find what remains, a missing part, or a difference. Most children come to school with a well-developed sense of what it means to 'want more', 'get more', have something taken away from them, or not have as much as somebody else. Collections or amounts that have some value, such as a treasured set of plastic animals or a plate of ice-cream, are seen as entities that can be increased (added to), decreased (reduced), or rearranged without changing the overall quantity (Smith, 2009). For instance, they recognise that the collection of animals remains the same if they are placed in a number of 'paddocks', or that the amount of ice-cream remains the same if it is partitioned into two smaller portions on the plate.

As a consequence of these early experiences, young children have a sense of addition in terms of putting two or more parts together (join), and a sense of subtraction in terms of a part being removed or missing (separate). They also appreciate when two collections or quantities are the same; that is, they have an intuitive sense of equivalence and thereby difference, as evidenced by statements such as, 'It's not fair. I haven't got as much as Tim'.

communicating mathematically

The language of addition and subtraction

Schooling introduces children to addition and subtraction more formally and often in ways that are disconnected from their early experiences. Examples are the use of words such as plus and minus, which have little meaning outside school (Anghileri, 2006), and the premature use of symbolic recording, both of which can be interpreted simply as an instruction to carry out a particular, decontextualised procedure, thereby depriving students of the opportunity to think additively. It is important to introduce and use meaningful terms such as 'and', 'more than', 'less than' before introducing symbolic recording, and to provide opportunities for children to discern problems on the basis of whether or not they require addition or subtraction. A commonly misused term is 'sum'—this should only be used to refer to the addition or two or more numbers, not to algorithms or operations in general.

Addition and subtraction situations presented to young children commonly involve two parts and a whole, one of which is unknown. In principle, this binary form generates two distinct possibilities: either both parts are known, in which case the task is to find the whole (addition), or the whole and one of the parts is known, in which case the task is to find the remaining part (subtraction). In practice these two possibilities are compounded by complex discourse patterns that mask both the operation required and its representation. Consider the following problems:

1. Jo has some marbles. She gave 3 away. Now she has 8 marbles. How many marbles did Jo have to start with?
2. Jack has 5 marbles. Kate gave him some more. Now Jack has 8 marbles. How many marbles did Kate give him?
3. Geri has 9 marbles. Tom has 3 more than Geri. How many marbles does Tom have?
4. Megan has 13 marbles. If she loses 8 marbles, she will have the same number of marbles as Mike. How many marbles does Mike have?
5. Jack had some marbles. Jill gave him 4 more marbles. Now Jack has 9 marbles. How many marbles did he have to start with?

Each of these problem structures is dicussed below.

While a number of attempts have been made to categorise the range of situations involving addition and subtraction (e.g. Carpenter & Moser, 1983, 1984; Fuson, 1992), these have tended to focus on semantic structure, in particular, the actions implicit in the problem and the order in which they occurred, rather than the meanings children might ascribe to the problem or the solution strategies they employ. Although these distinctions are useful in illustrating the complexities involved and there is some evidence to suggest that children's solution strategies reflect the semantic structure of the problem, this evidence is far from conclusive and the likelihood of these situations arising naturally is fairly small. A more useful way to understand the various **contexts**

for addition and subtraction might be to consider a classification system based primarily on mathematical structure rather than the semantic features or type of action or order implied in the problem.

The parts–whole model generates two possibilities: either the two parts are known and the task is to find the whole (*parts known*), or the whole and one of the parts is known and the task is to find the missing part (*whole–part known*). This makes the distinction between addition and subtraction more transparent and helps clarify the sequence of instruction by focusing on what makes problems easier or more difficult. A consequence is a reduction in the number of categories and a more generalisable way of determining which operation is required. For example, although Carpenter and Moser (1983) would classify problem 1 above as a 'separate-start unknown' problem ($\square - 3 = 8$), it can equally be viewed as a 'parts known' problem where the task is to find the whole ($3 + 8 = \square$). Similarly, although problem 2 would be classified as a 'join-change unknown' problem ($5 + \square = 8$), it could be interpreted as a 'whole–part known' problem where the task is to find the missing part ($5 + \square = 8$ or $8 - 5 = \square$).

Meanings for addition (parts known)

Addition can be generically represented as the sum of two known parts where the order does not matter (**commutative property**). That is, it has a 'parts known' structure and can be represented as part + part = $\square$ (or $\square$ = part + part). However, it is useful to distinguish between the notions of joining and combining, which is generally more difficult. Join problems, where 'like' is literally joined with 'like', as in 3 apples and 4 more apples (7 apples altogether), are clearly more accessible than combine situations, which involve the construction of an overarching set, as in 3 apples and 4 oranges, which requires the construction of '7 pieces of fruit' (see Figure 16.4).

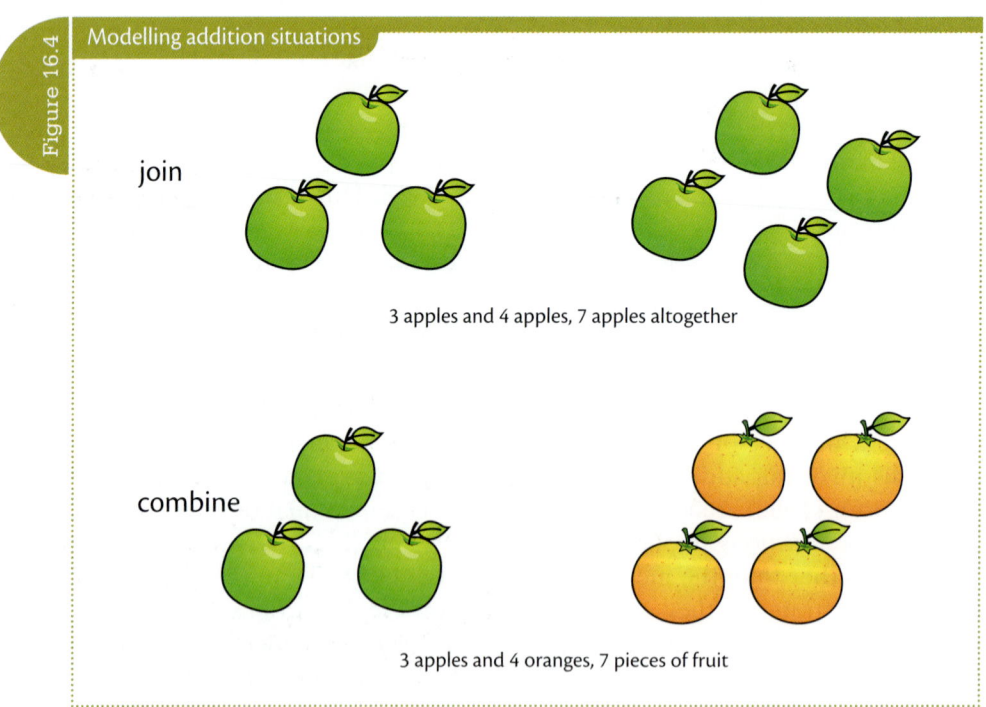

Figure 16.4 Modelling addition situations

join — 3 apples and 4 apples, 7 apples altogether

combine — 3 apples and 4 oranges, 7 pieces of fruit

Another source of difficulty arises when the activities of joining and combining are masked by language and context. For example, in problem 1 above, students need to recognise that it is still Jo's collection of marbles that need to be 'joined', even though she 'gave 3 away'. Problem 3 is more difficult again as it requires the recognition that Geri's marbles can be numerically 'combined' with Tom's on the grounds that he has the same number of marbles as Geri (9) and 3 more. The two meanings for addition are illustrated in Table 16.1 for situations that are transparent and masked.

Table 16.1

Addition contexts

Parts known	Example	Visibility of the operation
Join	Megan had 5 football cards. She was given 4 more. How many football cards does she have altogether?	Transparent
	Jan had some cards. She gave 3 away. Now she has 6 cards. How many cards did Jan have to begin with?	Masked
Combine	Max has 5 football cards and 7 basketball cards. How many cards does Max have altogether?	Transparent
	Megan has 3 cards. Jake has 4 more than Megan. How many cards does Jake have?	Masked

Meanings for subtraction (whole − part known)

Subtraction can generically be represented as the difference between the whole and one of its parts. The 'whole − part known' structure for subtraction can be represented in two ways, either as whole − part = ☐ (order matters), or as part + ☐ = whole (part order does not matter). The first typically represents situations where one part is removed or given away. These situations are typically described as *take-away* or separate problems (e.g. problem 4 above). The second representation is more commonly associated with a focus on what needs to be added to one part in order to arrive at the whole. Such situations are generally referred to as *missing* **addend** problems (e.g. problem 5). However, problem context, the relative magnitude of the numbers involved, and students' prior experience may result in alternative representations. For example, problem 5 could be represented as 9 − 4 = ☐, where undoing the action is seen as a means of identifying the original amount.

Take-away situations, where one part is removed in some way from a whole (as in '7 apples, 3 are eaten, how many left?'), are clearly more accessible than thinking about how many more might be needed to make a whole (as in 'I have 3 apples, I need 7, how many more do I need?'), that is, missing addend problems. A third idea, the *difference* idea, generally involves a comparison of two sets (see Figure 16.5). These situations, and those where the operation required is masked, are considerably more difficult than situations that essentially involve acting on one set. Difference situations can be represented in either form (i.e. as whole − part = ☐ or part + ☐ = whole) depending on the sense that is made of the particular problem context and/or situation.

Figure 16.5 Modelling subtraction situations

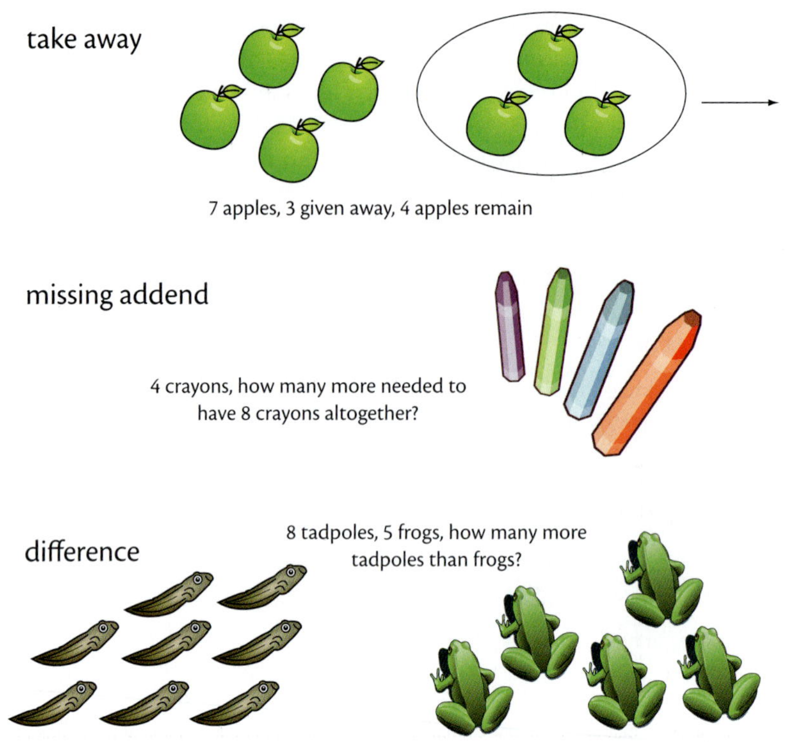

take away

7 apples, 3 given away, 4 apples remain

missing addend

4 crayons, how many more needed to have 8 crayons altogether?

difference

8 tadpoles, 5 frogs, how many more tadpoles than frogs?

The three meanings for subtraction are illustrated in Table 16.2 together with an indication of the transparency of the operation.

Table 16.2 Subtraction contexts

Whole – part known	Example	Visibility of the operation
Take away (separate)	Megan had 7 cards. She gave 2 to Sam. How many cards does she have left?	Transparent
	Kate has 14 cards. If Jake is given 6 more cards he will have the same number of cards as Kate. How many cards does Jake have?	Masked
Missing addend	Jeremy has 3 basketball cards. He wants the full set of 8. How many more cards does he need?	Transparent
	Jake had some cards. Kate gave him 3 more. Jake now has 7 cards. How many cards did Jake have to start with?	Masked
Difference (compare)	Kim has 6 cards. Sam has 4 cards. How many more cards does Kim have?	Transparent
	Jan has 9 cards. She has 3 more than Tom. How many cards does Tom have?	Masked

Order of introduction

It is clearly better to deal with situations where the operation is transparent before those where the operation is masked. In all cases it is important to model the situation using concrete materials or diagrams and discuss what is known and what needs to be found before deciding on a solution strategy. In general, children might be expected to meet simple, transparent join, take-away, combine and missing addend problems in their first year of school, while problems involving the idea of difference are probably better left until Year 1 or 2. Problems where the operation is masked in some way (by form of presentation, language, and/or context) need to be considered routinely at all levels of schooling once these initial forms have been introduced. This helps to develop students' capacity to analyse problems and make decisions about the operation(s) required.

for the classroom

Have children work in groups to create and illustrate or act out their own addition or subtraction problems. This problem posing can be used to gauge children's understanding of different problem situations (join, combine, take away, missing addend, and difference). The children's efforts can be classified as parts known or whole – part known, and made up into class books for future reference.

Non-binary forms

Situations involving the addition of lists of numbers is common in school mathematics (e.g. finding the total cost of a number of items or adding student heights to find the average height for the class), but this is not the case for subtraction. Rather, successive acts of subtraction generally result in binary situations. For example, to determine how much change there would be from $50 after purchasing three items costing $12, $17 and $9, it is likely that these amounts would first be summed then subtracted from $50.

One context involving repeated acts of either adding or subtracting is the trading game described in Chapter 15 in which students take turns to throw one or more (0–9) 10-sided dice to model the successive addition or subtraction of numbers to reach a given target number (p. 321). The trading game is particularly valuable as it demonstrates both the possibility and the result of adding 0. It is important that, from about Year 2 on, children are given opportunities to explore multiple acts of addition and/or subtraction in meaningful contexts using a variety of invented strategies before proceeding to more formal written procedures.

think + link

The repeated addition or subtraction of equal amounts is related to the 'groups of' idea for multiplication and division. These essentially additive activities form a basis for the more generalisable ideas for multiplication and division that will be considered in the next chapter.

Additive solution strategies

Left to their own devices, young children will represent and solve action story problems in a variety of ways. Initially, these solution strategies involve direct modelling and counting, but with the support of teachers and more learned peers, these eventually make way for more efficient counting-based strategies and, ultimately, strategies based on the recall of known facts. These three generic levels of strategy acquisition have been recognised for some time and are widely accepted (e.g. see Verschaffel, Greer & De Corte, 2007). However, the relevance of strategies such as counting on, counting-up-to, and counting-down-to by ones (e.g. Fuson, 1992; Steffe, Cobb & von Glasersfeld, 1988) is open to question given the increased emphasis on subitisation and the development of part–part–whole knowledge based on visual imagery (Clements & Sarama, 2007; Fuson, 2009). For instance, it is conceivable that as children develop mental objects for each of the numbers to 10 they will not need to solve addition and subtraction problems such as 6 and 8 by counting on, or 12 take away 7 by counting-down-to or up-from 5. Instead, they might recognise that as 8 is 2 less than 10 and 6 is a 2 and 4, 8 and 6 is 10 and 4 more, 14.

consider and discuss

Use of mental objects

Grace and her classmates have been exposed to subitisation on a daily basis since the beginning of the school year. Now in the third term of their first year of school, Grace and some of her classmates were asked to solve the the following problem:

> Yesterday, we gave the guinea pigs 3 celery sticks; today we gave them 5. How many celery sticks have they had altogether?

'Well', said Grace, 'that's easy ... it's 8 because 8 is 5 and 3, I know it from the cards [meaning ten-frames].'

With her knowledge of 8 as a mental object, Grace was able to utilise her knowledge of 8 in terms of its parts. Her friend Amy said '5 ... 6, 7, 8' but did not use her fingers to keep track of the count, suggesting that she was well on the way to developing mental objects for 5 and 3 but perhaps not 8 at this stage.

1. What do you think is involved in having a mental object for each of the numbers to 10?
2. While Amy's strategy is useful for combinations such as 3 and 16 or 24 and 2, counting on (or back) is not an effective strategy for combinations such as 7 and 9 or 3 and 8. Why not? What strategy would you suggest instead?

think + link

The development of part–part–whole knowledge and doubles is considered in Chapter 14 as an essential component of building mental objects for each of the numbers 0 to 10.

Teachers have a critical role to play in scaffolding students' solution strategies from their initial make-all-count-all approaches to adaptive, mental strategies based on a strong sense of number and number relationships. Part–part–whole knowledge for each of the numbers to 10 and a knowledge of *doubles* is essential in this process.

In Dutch schools, considerable care is taken to introduce addition and subtraction via realistic problems (e.g. van den Heuval-Panhuizen, 2001b). Actual or imaginary situations are modelled using a variety of materials and representations on the grounds that students benefit from exposure to multiple representations and solution strategies simultaneously, rather than waiting until one is well developed before considering other strategies (Heinze, Star & Verschaffel, 2009; Selva, Falcao & Nunes, 2005). In view of this, it is important that teachers are aware of the range of strategies that children might use apart from part–part–whole and doubles, as these tend to indicate not only their understanding of addition and subtraction but also their knowledge of the numbers themselves.

Initial counting strategies

The following strategies represent an approximate developmental ordering in that they proceed from a reliance on observable materials and sequence counting (counting by ones) to a more refined capacity to deal with some numbers as mental objects. In recognising and responding to the use of these strategies, the teacher plays a vital role in encouraging children to use what they know wherever possible to avoid counting by ones. Depending on the context, this may mean recognising a number without counting and counting on, or recognising a known double fact (e.g. for 3 and 4, recognising this as 3 and 3 and 1 more). Problems at this stage need to be presented as action stories (word problems) rather than symbolic expressions. Informal recording of some form will inevitably arise, but care should be taken not to introduce the equals sign before children are comfortable with the idea that numbers can be renamed in many different ways in terms of their parts.

think + link

The introduction of the equals sign is discussed in Chapter 15.

Make-all-count-all

Children's first attempts to deal with situations involving addition or subtraction invariably involve some sort of physical modelling and one-to-one counting despite the fact that they may know some of the numbers to 10 in terms of their parts as a result of subitising. This is because children need to experience the processes of physically adding and subtracting in relation to the number-naming sequence before they can make the connection between their part–part–whole knowledge and the outcome of the situation.

Asked to say how many blocks there would be if 5 blocks were added to their collection of 4 blocks, it is sensible and appropriate for a young child to collect the 5 additional blocks, physically count each set of blocks to check that they have the right number, and then count all the blocks to arrive at a solution of 9 blocks.

It is important to use a variety of materials and representations to model addition and subtraction, including fingers (e.g. Tickle, 2003), structured materials such as counters or blocks, collections such as farm animals or teddies, arithmetic racks, bead strings to 20, drawings, graphs (e.g. see Figure 16.2 above), dice, playing cards, and number charts or number walks (see Figure 16.6).

Figure 16.6 Number walks

If Jodie takes 4 more steps where will she end up?

Cover and count on, count on from larger displayed

Once children trust the count for numbers such as 1, 2, and 3, these collections can be covered and children can be encouraged to count on from known. For example, Rhonda, a Prep (F) teacher who participated in the Primary Numeracy Research Project (Siemon & Virgona, 2003) wanted the small group of students she was working with to count on from a known number to solve the addition problem '5 and 4'. Using large dice, she drew their attention to the fact that they knew the pattern for 5 and that they could start from there. Rhonda covered the 5 with her hand and said, 'Remember when we had the flash cards and you could all tell me there was five—you didn't have to make 5 or count it, you know what 5 is … picture it in your heads. What comes next when we count?' Rhonda tossed the dice again and invited the children to cover and count on (in this case, 4 and 3). The children immediately responded by covering the 4 and counting on 3 more to arrive at 7.

Figure 16.7 Modelling counting on

Source: Siemon and Virgona (2003)

Playing cards (ace to 10) can also be used to model the counting on process for single digit combinations up to 20. Recognising that it is easier and more efficient to *count on from larger* is only possible when children trust the count for the larger numbers. For example, if a 4 of hearts and an 8 of spades are dealt, children who do not recognise 8 immediately may feel more comfortable covering the 4 and counting on by ones pointing to each spade symbol in turn, whereas children who recognise 8 without counting might suggest covering 8 and counting on 4. The advantages of *counting on from larger* should be explored explicitly and practised on a regular basis, extending to combinations such as 25 and 4 or 5 and 37 on a 0 to 99 number chart to emphasise the point.

for the classroom

The process of covering and counting on can be introduced and modelled using six-sided dot dice like the ones shown in Figure 16.7. Once children trust the count for 1, 2, and 3, use a spinner or a six-sided die and ten-frames to practise reading the number names and recognising the number symbols, then covering the larger number (in this case 6) and counting on. Counts can be emphasised by physical movements such as clapping or jumping.

Difficulties with counting on arise when materials/representations are no longer available and children have to use some means of keeping track of the count beyond 3. This tends to occur where students have no mental models for working with the numbers concerned, so their only recourse is to use their fingers or some other means such as rhythmic tapping to manage the count of ones. While this may indicate that more work is needed to ensure children trust the count for the numbers concerned, it also points to the need to develop more efficient strategies for dealing with addends greater than 3. In this case, ten-frames and 20-bead strings can be used to model the use of part–part–whole knowledge to break up the counting on process into something that is more manageable. For example, to add 7 and 9, children who have demonstrated a sense of numbers beyond 10 can be supported to see the value in starting from 9, adding/counting on 1 to arrive at 10, and reasoning '6 more, 16'.

Counting back from, counting up to

Initial modelling of counting back from using materials has value in that it reinforces the backward number-naming sequence (important in recognising the number that comes before a given number), and it ultimately supports the use of more sophisticated models, such as the open number line and the use of place-value parts. It is a relatively inefficient strategy for solving subtraction problems more generally (Fuson, 2009), particularly in the absence of physical materials and when the number being subtracted is greater than 3.

Counting back from was identified by researchers in the 1980s (e.g. Fuson, 1992; Steffe, Cobb & von Glasersfeld, 1988) as a strategy children used for solving subtraction problems where a part was removed from a whole (take away). The evidence came from tasks where first graders were told that there was a particular number of counters hidden under a cloth, watched as some were removed, and then were asked to say how many counters remained (e.g. 'There are 13 counters under here. I have taken 7 away. How many are left?'). Counting backwards by ones matched by finger movements was one of the strategies they used to solve this problem. However, this strategy does not mean that counting back from in the absence of materials is a necessary or even desirable stage in the acquisition of more efficient strategies. The children's responses need to be seen in the context of the instructional practices of the time. Little was known about the role of subitisation in the development of meaningful mental objects for each of the numbers to 10 and the possibilities afforded by knowing the numbers to 10 in terms of their parts (part–part–whole knowledge). Without these learning opportunities, counting backwards may have been the children's only recourse. When a similar task was presented to a group of Year 1 and 2 students who had been exposed to subitising for some time and were able to demonstrate a knowledge of the numbers to 10 in terms of their parts, their responses were more likely to involve a decomposition, for example, for 13 take away 7, one child said, 'take 3 would be 10 … [take] 4 more leaves 6'.

Difficulties with counting back arise when the starting number is counted as part of the set to be removed (Fuson, 2009). For instance, in taking 3 away from 8 by counting back, some children will decide 6 is the solution because their count back was '8, 7, 6' as opposed to '7, 6, 5'. *Counting up to*, which tends to be prompted by missing addends (e.g. Peter had 3 cards, and he wanted 8. How many more did he need to collect?) is much less prone to error but, in the absence of materials and the relevant part–part–whole knowledge it also requires keeping track of the count. Counting up from 3 to 8 requires that the count of '4, 5, 6, 7, 8' is recognised as a 5-count, where 4 is 1, 5 is 2, 6 is 3, 7 is 4 and 8 is 5. Once again, where finger counting is the only means of keeping track of the count, it is better not to persist with these activities in the absence of materials or representations such as a number line or a Ten Frame, as this response indicates that more work is needed on understanding the numbers to 10 in terms of their parts. In this case, the required knowledge of 8 as a 3 and a 5 can be modelled on a Ten Frame showing 8 dots by covering 3 and inspecting what remains. Ultimately, *counting up to* is a useful strategy where it is based on counts in place-value parts. For example, to find the difference between 28 and 54, 27 can be marked on an open number line and a jump strategy used to count on by tens (38, 48, 2 tens) then by 2 (to 50) and 4 more to arrive at 54 (6 ones), so the difference is 26.

issues in teaching

Automatic recall of basic addition and subtraction facts

Often you will hear parents and community members complain that the standards of school mathematics are slipping, 'the children of today don't even know their basic number facts. When I was at school …' and they usually go on to describe how they had to learn these 'off by heart'. While there are some advocates for learning the facts through repetition and a focus on patterns, most mathematics educators today do not believe that rote or extremely repetitive forms of learning the basic number facts are appropriate.

- Investigate what is meant by automatic recall and its role in school mathematics.
- Observe the ways in which this is done in schools and compare this to what you have researched.
- How do children deal with 'number fact races' or games that publicly reveal what they know (or don't know)?
- How important is automatic recall? Is it sufficient to have an efficient way of working it out rather than commit every number fact to memory?

Mental strategies for addition and subtraction to 20

As children become confident in both recognising additive situations and utilising their knowledge of numbers to 10 in terms of their parts, **mental strategies for addition** can be scaffolded more directly using ten-frames, arithmetic racks, and partial or open number lines. However, mental strategies are just that, mental. Materials and models should be withdrawn once students trust the count and can exercise their part–part–whole knowledge.

Mental strategies should be named, practised regularly, and reviewed periodically. While there are minor variations in how the mental strategies are named, three distinct strategies are generally recognised for addition: count on 1, 2, or 3; doubles and near doubles; and make to 10, as described below. To reduce the cognitive demand and maximise attention on the strategies themselves, problems can be presented orally in a given context (e.g. birds in/around a bird bath, other birds arriving).

Count on 1, 2, or 3

This strategy applies for any combination involving a 1, 2, or 3. It is generally the first of the mental strategies to be acquired as it utilises the number-naming sequence, but particular attention needs to be given initially to identifying the larger number and recognising that the order of the numbers does not matter. For example:

- for 5 and 2, think: larger is 5 … and 2 more … 5, 6, 7
- for 3 and 6, think: larger is 6 … and 3 more … 6, 7, 8, 9.

The initial problem might be presented as 3 birds at the birdbath, 6 more arrive, how many birds altogether? Thereafter, the problem context can be assumed and the questions can be reduced to 5 and 3 birds? What about 2 and 7 birds?, 3 and 8 birds? This is a good context to explore the impact of adding 0 (e.g. no birds and 5 birds, 4 birds and 0 birds). The efficacy of this strategy can be emphasised through the use of large numbers that would be time consuming to model and count (e.g. 41 and 3, 2 and 75). It is also important to pose these problems in as many different ways as possible (e.g. what number is 3 more than 41?).

for the classroom

The count on 1, 2, or 3 mental strategy

Set up an additive situation such as a bus picking up passengers to model and rehearse the strategy. For example, 'The bus left the depot and it picked up 2 people at the first stop. At the next stop it picked up 7 passengers. How many passengers are there on the bus now?' Initially children could be used to model the numbers at each bus stop and to mark the counting on process. To develop the mental strategy it is important that children are given auditory cues alone, although numbers might be recorded. As they hear the numbers (in this case 2 and 7), ask them to 'grab' the larger number in their hand and raise it above their head. Explore, 'What number do you have in your hand?' '7' And what number do we need to add on?' '2' 'Let's do it'. At this point introduce some action such as pumping the air with the closed fist while saying '8, 9 … there are now 9 people on the bus'. Continue in this way, but only to add on 1, 2, or 3.

The model of a bus picking up passengers can be extended to explore other addition strategies and to include dropping off passengers as a means of exploring related subtraction strategies.

Symbolic recording can be introduced for these combinations once students are familiar with the use of the strategy and no longer rely on any form of modelling. At this level, recording should be a record of what is known or can be worked out mentally. If this is not the case, it indicates that more attention should be given to trusting the count for the numbers to 10 and physically scaffolding the strategy. Recording can be informal, 'vertical' (early form of written algorithm) or 'horizontal' (equations). Children's informal methods can be explored and justified to establish that these are legitimate provided we all understand what is meant by the representations used. Vertical forms are useful as they avoid the use of the equals sign and support renaming in place-value parts. It is important to establish that these should be read consistently from top to bottom to minimise the likelihood of later difficulties with subtraction. Equations should only be used if the equals sign has been introduced previously via well-known equivalences with at least two numbers on both sides of the equation (e.g. $5 + 3 = 6 + 2$) to offset the common misconception that the equals sign means 'makes' or 'the answer comes next' (see Chapter 15). This form of recording can be introduced as a way of recording part–part–whole knowledge (e.g. 7 is 3 and 4 translates fairly naturally to $7 = 3 + 4$).

Doubles, near doubles

A knowledge of doubles facts to 20 is a prerequisite for mental computation and can be developed using ten-frames and two-row bead frames (arithmetic racks). This strategy is also referred to as tied facts (e.g. van den Heuval-Panhuizen, 2001a)

The near doubles facts can be built on the basis of 1 more or 1 less than the nearest double. For example:

- for 7 and 8, think: double 7, 14 … and 1 more, 15
- for 9 and 8, think: double 9, 18 … 1 less, 17 (or double 8 and 1 more).

Recording can be introduced once students have access to doubling strategies and no longer need to rely on materials or representations. Doubling strategies more generally can be supported as children develop an understanding of 10 as a composite unit. For example, explore ways to double numbers such as 23 (e.g. double the tens and double the ones, 46) and move on to examples such as double 17. In this case, doubling the tens and doubling the ones results in 2 tens and 14 ones, which requires the further step of regrouping the ones as 1 ten and 4 ones, so 34. Practising doubling and rehearsing part–part–whole knowledge are useful activities for parents to engage in with children, as these provide an important basis for the development of meaningful mental strategies for the multiplication facts to 100.

Make to 10 and name

Sometimes referred to as bridging 10, this strategy is typically the last to be acquired as it requires a sound knowledge of the numbers to 10 in terms of their parts (part–part–whole knowledge) and a well-developed sense of numbers beyond 10. This involves recognising each of the numbers to 10 as abstract composite units. That is, 16 is recognised as 1 ten and 6 more, not 10 ones and a count of 6 more (11, 12, 13, 14, 15, 16). The make to 10 strategy can be developed using ten-frames, 20-bead strings and number lines as shown in Figure 16.8. For example:

- for 8 and 6, think: 8 … 2 to 10 and 4 more, 14
- for 5 and 7, think: 5 … 5 to 10 and 2 more, 12 (or 7, 10, and 2 more, 12).

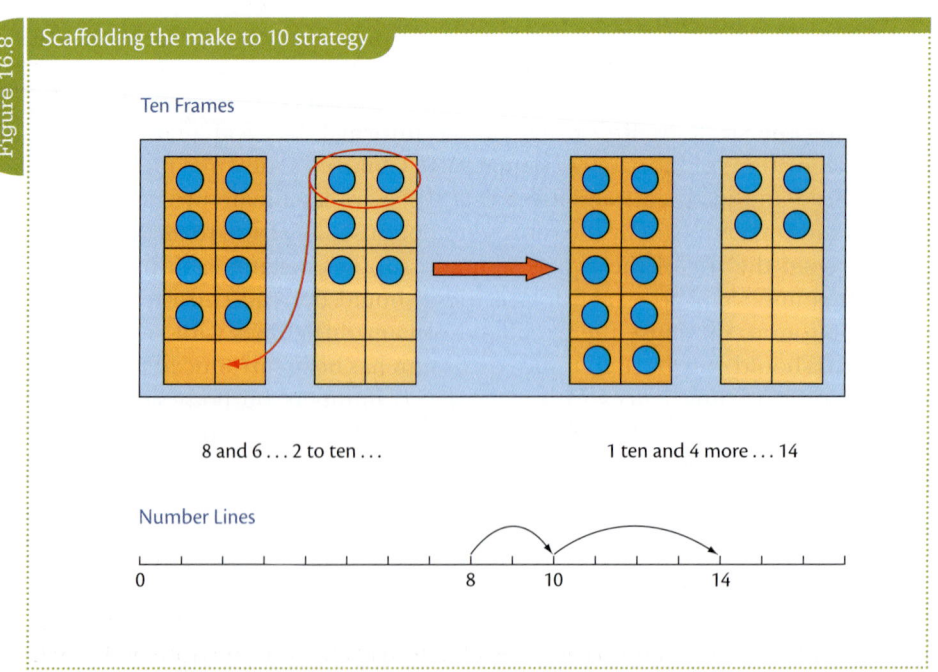

Figure 16.8 Scaffolding the make to 10 strategy

Recording can be introduced once students no longer need to rely on materials or representations. This strategy can be applied more generally as children gain confidence in using open number lines. For example, to add 26 and 7, 26 can be marked on an open number line, and on the basis that 7 is a 3 and 4 a '3-jump' can be made to 30, then a further '4-jump' can be made to arrive at 34.

Multiple strategies for subtraction

As the addition strategies are developed, the corresponding **mental strategies for subtraction** can also be modelled and explored using ten-frames, arithmetic racks, 20-bead strings, and open number lines. For example, for problems involving the subtraction of 1, 2, or 3 a **count back** strategy might be used (although this can lead to errors as described above), and halving or make back to 10 can be used for situations such as 14 take away 6. The most efficient strategy for subtraction problems, particularly those involving a relatively large **subtrahend** (the number being taken away), is to think of addition (Fuson, 2009). For example, for 15 take away 8, think: 8 and what is 15? Children should be encouraged to explore multiple strategies as relevant. For example, for 16 take away 9, the following strategies are possible.

- make back to 10: 16 … 10 … take 3 more …7
- halving: 16 … 8 … take 1 more … 7
- take 10 and compensate: 16 … 6 … and 1 more … 7
- think of addition: 9 … 1 more to 10 … 6 more to 16 … so 7.

Once again, various forms of recording can be shared and discussed as children demonstrate access to meaningful mental strategies. The strategies can be explored more generally using open number lines and the make back to 10 strategy. For example, for 35 take away 8, 35 can be marked on the right of an open number line, and on the basis that 8 is a 5 and 3 a '5-jump' backwards can be made to 30 then a further '3-jump' backwards can be made to 27. When recording, children should be encouraged to recognise when the order of reading and operating is important (subtraction) and when it is not (addition).

integrating technology/ICT

Number Charts

This excellent activity from maths300 has already been described in Chapter 7. It encourages mental computation and reinforces the relationships between addition and subtraction by providing a grid-based system of presentation. It also has the added advantage that degree of difficulty can be selected by children on the basis of grid size (4 by 4 to 10 by 10), operation (addition or multiplication), and types of numbers involved (0–20, 0–100 or fractions). It also provides feedback that allows children to correct any errors and indicates the time taken to complete the grid accurately. These features are particularly useful in catering for mixed ability learners.

Strategies for two-digit numbers

Informal computation strategies

The strategies used for the initial number facts can be extended to addition and subtraction problems involving a single-digit number and a two-digit number. For example, to add 3 and 91 it is sensible to use a count-on strategy (92, 93,

94); to add 57 and 8, it is sensible to use the make-to-10 strategy, which can be scaffolded using an open number line or as a thinking string (e.g. 57, 60, 65).

These strategies are not always the most appropriate or efficient for working with two-digit numbers. For instance, adding 34 and 57 is not as straightforward as adding 23 and 64, which simply involves joining tens with tens and ones with ones in any order.

While it is tempting to use the 0–99 or 1 to 100 number chart as a tool to scaffold mental strategies for adding and subtracting two-digit numbers, Cobb (1995) reported that there was little evidence to suggest that children's use of the hundreds board supported 'the construction of increasingly sophisticated concepts of ten' (p. 362), which he argued was necessary for the development of mental computation strategies based on counting by tens and ones. This suggests that open number lines as described in Chapter 15 and developed by Beishuizen (1999) offer a more powerful means of modelling addition and subtraction strategies based on counting forwards or backwards in place-value units, as these provide a stronger representation of 10 as an abstract composite unit.

> There are many studies which show that children's mental methods operate very differently from standard written algorithms in several respects ... and when children use written methods to support their calculation they prefer to set the numbers down horizontally rather than vertically ... Consequently, it seems unrealistic to expect that there will be a smooth transition from mental methods to the standard written algorithms for the four basic operations. (Thompson, 1999, p. 170)

Given this, and evidence to suggest that children's successful use of standard written algorithms does not necessarily indicate conceptual understanding (Clark, 2008), there is an argument for exploring the low-stress or user-friendly algorithms that build on the strategies used by children who have not been taught formal algorithms (Thompson, 1999). There has been a significant amount of work on the strategies used by children to add and subtract two-digit numbers to 100 (e.g. Beishuizen, 1999; Clark, 2008; Fuson, 2009; Heirdsfeld, 2003; Heirdsfeld, Dole & Beswick, 2007; Torbeyns, Vanderveken, Verschaffel & Ghesquière, 2006). According to an analysis of the literature by Torbeyns et al. (2006), children tend to use three different types of strategies:

- the *split* strategy, which involves dealing with the place-value parts separately (e.g. for 43 + 28 add tens with tens (60), ones with ones (11), then add 60 and 11). Cobb (1999), citing Beishuizen, refers to this as the '1010' strategy, while elsewhere it is referred to as 'structuring' (e.g. Treffers & Buys, 2001)
- the *jump* strategy, which involves counting on/back from one of the given numbers (e.g. for 43 + 28, add 4 tens to 28 (68) then add 3 more to get 71). Treffers and Buys (2001) refer to this as 'positioning', while Cobb (1999), again citing Beishuizen, refers to it as the 'N10' strategy
- a *compensation* strategy (described but not named) in which the numbers are reconfigured in a way that maintains equivalence but makes the calculation easier (e.g. 43 + 28 is renamed as 43 + 30 − 2).

According to Fuson (1992), the first two strategies, which we will refer to as the *by parts* and *jump* strategies respectively, are associated with different interpretations of two-digit numbers: collections-based and sequence-based. While the second strategy tends to be associated with higher achievement on mental computation tasks, it is suggested that this is an 'all-or-nothing' capacity 'made possible by the construction of abstract composite units of ten in an image-independent manner' (Cobb, 1999, p. 377). This points once again to the critical importance of abstracting the big idea that 10 of these is 1 of those (see Chapter 15) in developing procedural fluency.

These strategies tend to be associated with different representations as shown in Figures 16.9 and 16.10. They should be modelled, named, and discussed explicitly together with any others that children might invent to emphasise the value of working in place-value units rather than counts of ones.

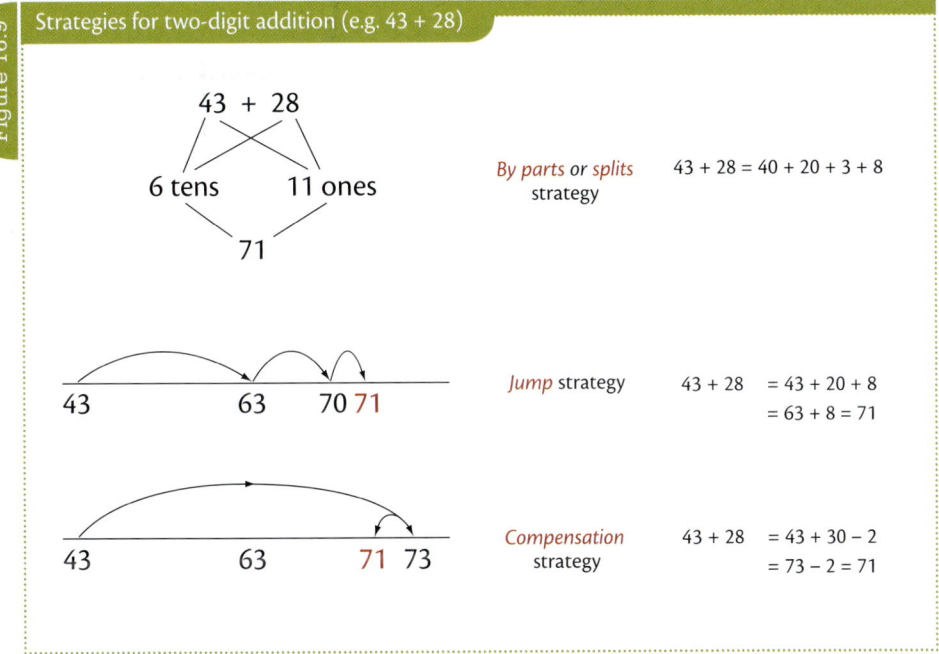

Figure 16.9 Strategies for two-digit addition (e.g. 43 + 28)

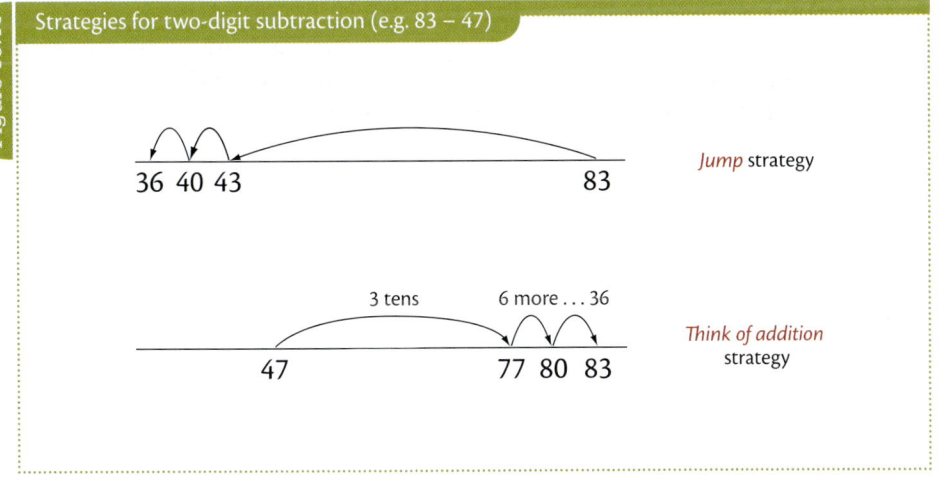

Figure 16.10 Strategies for two-digit subtraction (e.g. 83 − 47)

for the classroom

Non-binary addition and subtraction problems can be presented in a 2 × 2 grid to encourage multiple ways of working mentally with numbers. This format can be introduced using single-digit numbers to show that the sum is written in the shaded cell before introducing two-digit examples. One possible strategy is to add tens (5 and 3 tens, 8 tens and another 8 tens, 16 tens), add the 7 and 3 ones that make a 10 (17 tens) then combine the remaining ones with the count of tens (176).

The advantage of this is that children can choose where to start, which numbers they work with, and the order in which they work with them. The format can also be used for subtraction by including the sum and omitting one of the addends.

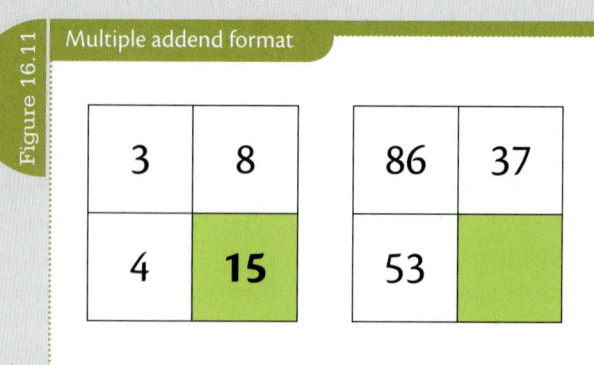

Figure 16.11 Multiple addend format

Wherever appropriate (and when students are able to use and describe these strategies fluently), opportunities should be taken to model what Thompson (1999) refers to as *formal non-standard* forms of recording. For example, where a jump strategy was used to solve 83 – 47 this could be modelled as follows to emphasise the importance of maintaining equivalence.

$$83 - 47 = 83 - 40 - 7$$
$$= 43 - 7$$
$$= 43 - 3 - 4$$
$$= 40 - 4$$
$$= 36$$

While this looks cumbersome, it serves two purposes: it sets the scene for algebraic forms of recording more generally, and it serves to justify the more efficient and formal forms of recording that involve decomposition (see below). More importantly, this form of recording provides an opportunity to reflect formally on what was done and how it might be represented in an equivalent manner. Annotating open number line diagrams is another useful way to make these strategies explicit.

consider and discuss

Multiple strategies

How many different ways can you think of to calculate the following mentally? Describe and name as many strategies as you can. What models might you use to scaffold student's understanding of these strategies?

1. 16 take away 9
2. 27 and 8
3. 36 + 58 + 74 = ☐
4. 23 + ☐ + 54 = 93
5. 267 – 178 = ☐

Construct and discuss how these solutions might be recorded to demonstrate the thinking involved.

Introducing formal recording

Standard algorithms are used more generally to support the addition and subtraction of large numbers and ultimately decimal fractions and common fractions. Their development is not problematic if it is delayed until students have had the opportunity to explore a wide range of solution strategies using materials (e.g. bundling straws, stacking cubes, and base 10 blocks), develop the language needed to convey and justify their solution strategies to others, and create and interpret written or diagrammatic representations such as the ones described above.

In introducing formal recording, most school mathematics curricula distinguish between additive problems where there is no requirement to rename numbers (e.g. 23 + 45 and 76 – 34) and problems that do require **regrouping** or **trading** (e.g. 56 + 38 and 63 – 27). Delaying the introduction of formal recording for these problems is justified on the grounds that this is difficult for many children in English-speaking countries. However, comparative research involving US and Korean students (Fuson & Kwon, 1992) suggests these difficulties may be a consequence of introducing formal procedures before children have developed a deep understanding of place-value units as composite units.

issues in teaching

Is there a place for written algorithms?

Many argue that technology means there is no longer a place for written algorithms in modern school mathematics curricula. Do you agree or disagree? What evidence is there for and against?

- When, if ever, is it appropriate to introduce formal recording (standard, written algorithms for multi-digit addition and subtraction)?
- What is the role of written recording?
- There is a saying that if you expect something to be difficult, it will be. Discuss in terms of the issues raised above about regrouping and trading.

Delayed introduction of recording of additive problems that require regrouping or trading provides little or no justification for starting with the ones in column addition and subtraction. A perception that these problems are much more difficult can be avoided if careful attention is given to prerequisites such as a capacity to count forwards and backwards fluently in place-value units.

As a precursor to introducing column addition or subtraction, children need to explore regrouping and trading situations with bundling and stacking materials, not as a means of calculating *per se* but to demonstrate the regrouping and trading processes. For example, asked to model and find the sum of 46 and 37, most Year 2 or 3 children will have no difficulty manipulating the materials to arrive at 83, but, left to their own devices, most will work with the tens first and then the ones (Fuson, 1992; Thompson, 1999). This suggests that it might be appropriate to work first with formal non-standard algorithms before proceeding to the standard form in which materials used with a place-value mat model the regrouping process and provide a basis for starting with the ones (the tens only have to be considered once). Fuson (2009) makes a strong case for progressing from the use of materials to the use of diagrams, for the *write-all-totals* non-standard algorithm before or as well as the standard algorithm, and for writing the regrouped 10 at the bottom rather than at the top of the standard algorithm on the grounds that 'each number is in its own horizontal space … children can write the teen total in the order in which they usually write it … it is easier to add the three numbers because you add the two that you see [from the original presentation] then increase that total by 1' (p. 352).

Asked to model 74 and find a strategy to take away 26, children will either remove 2 tens then realise that they have to trade 1 ten for 10 ones, or they will realise this at the outset and trade before they remove the tens. While the former approach can be modelled on a number line using the jump strategy, the 'tens first' strategy becomes cumbersome beyond two- and three-digit numbers and does not lead to a standard algorithm that can be applied more generally. By starting with situations that require trading, children can come to see for themselves why it is important to start with the ones rather than be told that this is the place to start. Given this, it is important to model the decomposition process using materials and place-value mats until children are confident with the related recording.

Where children have had numerous opportunities to use a place-value mat to play forms of the trading game that involve regrouping and trading, that is, first to reach a given target or first to return to zero from a set amount (see Chapter 14), they are less likely to experience difficulty with formal recording.

Table 16.3 Materials, language, and recording to support two-digit subtraction

Materials	Language	Recording
	4 ones take away 6 ones; physically impossible Trade 1 ten for 10 ones	Tens | Ones 7 | 4 − 2 | 6

	Rename 74 as 6 tens and 14 ones
	
	14 ones take away 6 ones is 8 ones; record with the ones
	
	6 tens take away 2 tens is 4 tens; record with the tens
		Tens | Ones
		  7⁶ | 4¹⁴
		− 2 | 6
		  4 | 8

Strategies for adding and subtracting multi-digit numbers

Problems such as the following lend themselves to the use of written algorithms or calculating devices as the numbers are simply too difficult to keep in one's head.

1. The distance from Adelaide to Brisbane by road is 2100 km. The distance from Adelaide to Darwin by road is 3042 km. How much further is it to drive from Adelaide to Darwin?

2 Crowd attendances for the five days of the cricket Test match at the MCG were 77 690, 34 783, 31 507, 28 364, and 53 173. How many people attended in total?
3 The population of Townsville in June 2010 was 185 768. The population of Cairns was 168 251. How many more people live in Townsville than in Cairns?

In these situations, it makes sense to work in place-value parts starting with the ones to manage the regrouping of place-value units where required. MAB materials can be used initially to model four-digit addition and subtraction and to demonstrate the value of working in place-value columns, particularly where regrouping or trading is required (see Table 16.4). MAB soon becomes cumbersome for larger whole numbers or for situations such as 4003 take away 2587, but number expanders (see Chapter 15) are a useful tool that can be used to support renaming as appropriate in these situations.

Table 16.4 Materials, language, and recording to support four-digit addition

Materials	Language	Recording
(MAB blocks showing 3854 and 5548)	4 ones and 8 ones is 12 ones Record as 12, 1 ten and 2 ones	3 8 5 4 + 5 5 4₁8 _____ 2
	5 tens and 4 tens is 9 tens and 1 more ten is 10 tens Record as 1 hundred and 0 tens	3 8 5 4 + 5 5₁4₁8 _____ 0 2
(MAB blocks)	8 hundreds and 5 hundreds is 13 hundreds and 1 more hundred is 14 hundreds Record as 1 thousand and 4 hundreds 3 thousands and 5 thousands is 8 thousand and 1 more thousand is 9 thousand	3 8 5 4 + 5₁5₁4₁8 _____ 9 4 0 2

Figure 16.12 Using a number expander to support four-digit subtraction

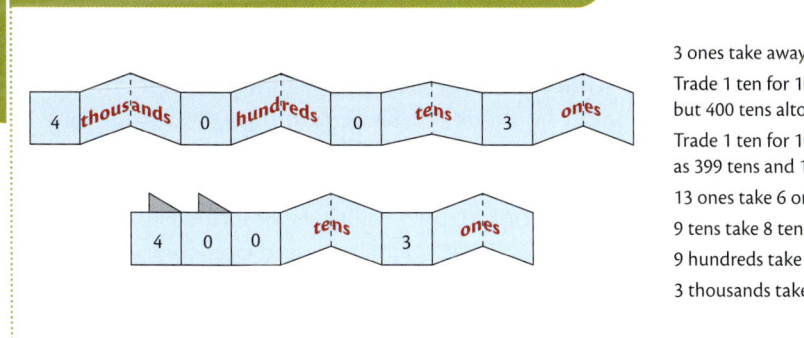

3 ones take away 7 ones not physically possible
Trade 1 ten for 10 ones . . . 0 tens in the tens place, but 400 tens altogether
Trade 1 ten for 10 ones, rename and record 4003 as 399 tens and 13 ones
13 ones take 6 ones is 7 ones
9 tens take 8 tens is 1 ten
9 hundreds take 5 hundreds is 4 hundreds
3 thousands take 2 thousands is 1 thousand

      3 9 9 13
      4̶ 0̶ 0̶ 3̶
    − 2 5 8 7
      _____
      1 4 1 6

Adding and subtracting fractions and decimals

There is little justification for dealing with the addition and subtraction of fractions formally at this level of schooling. However, the informal addition or subtraction of like (same denominator) or related fractions (e.g. halves and quarters) might arise, for example 'Jamie ate 3 eighths of the pizza. Lisa ate 1 eighth of the pizza. How much of the pizza remained?' Modelling the situation and recognising eighths as units in this context means that the 3 and the 1 can be added together to establish that 4 eighths of the pizza has been eaten so 4 eighths or 1 half of the pizza remains. Problematising this situation (e.g. Jamie ate 3 eighths but Lisa ate 1 quarter of the pizza) reinforces the importance of the units being the same. In this case, children might suggest that 1 quarter of the pizza is the same as 2 eighths and the addition can proceed. If Lisa ate 1 sixth of the pizza this is not so straightforward, further emphasising the point that the denominators (units) need to be the same.

making connections

Modelling the addition and/or subtraction of like fractions on a number line can be used to make the connection to whole number addition and subtraction and to stress that they both involve counts of like or related units. For example, in the pizza problem above, the units are eighths and the problem can be represented on a number line as shown.

The addition and subtraction of like fractions greater than 1 (e.g. 9 quarters of orange and 13 quarters of orange, how many quarters of orange altogether?) can be used to emphasise that the count of fractional units extends beyond 1.

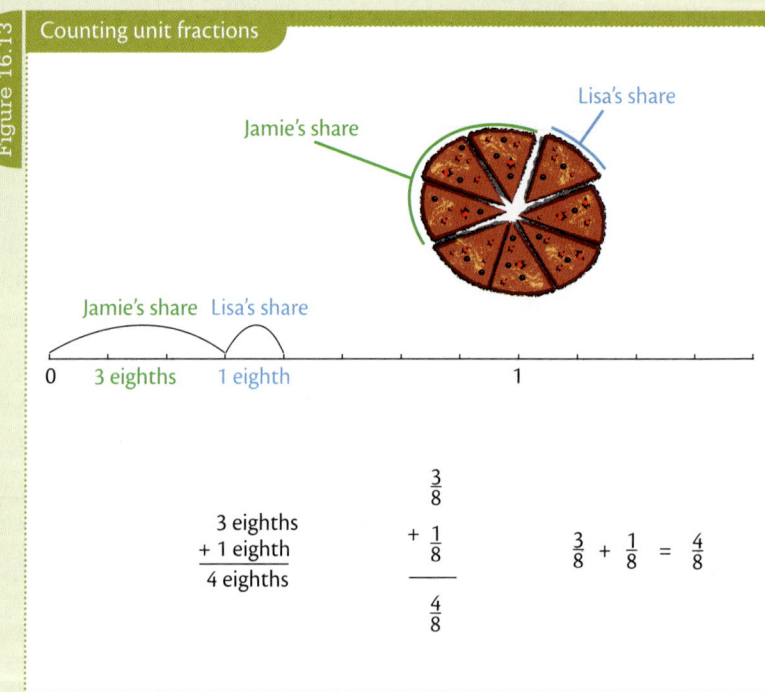

Figure 16.13 Counting unit fractions

Adding and subtracting decimal fractions (to tenths) can be considered as a logical extension of the strategies used to add and subtract whole numbers. Initially these situations might be modelled using bundling straws cut into 10 equal parts to model tenths or represented on a number line. (MAB is not appropriate for the reasons explained in Chapter 18.) The addition and subtraction of tenths can be recorded informally as described above. Once children understand tenths as a new place-value part and can work confidently to solve addition and subtraction problems involving larger whole numbers, they can be introduced to more formal, place-based forms of recording the addition and subtraction of ones and tenths as shown in Figure 16.14.

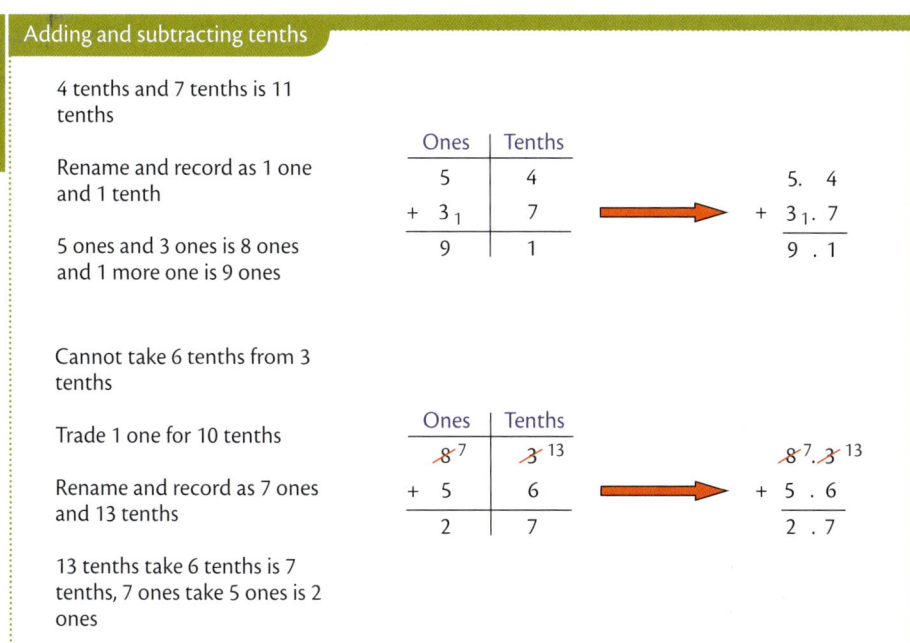

Figure 16.14 Adding and subtracting tenths

Problem solving

The primary purpose of adding and subtracting is to solve problems. This requires the problem to be analysed and interpreted relative to context, a strategy to be chosen and applied, and the outcome to be reviewed and justified. Where this does not deliver a satisfactory outcome, the process is repeated to clarify understanding and/or choose a more effective strategy.

Some years back, I described this cyclical process as 'ask–think–do' for the purposes of supporting problem-solving instruction (see Barry, Booker, Perry & Siemon, 1983–91; Siemon & Booker, 1990) and researching the role of metacognition in children's mathematical problem solving (Siemon, 1993).

The year-long teaching experiment in a Year 4 classroom found that an explicit focus on problem structure, strategies, and the problem-solving process increased children's awareness of what they knew and what they could do. While this had a positive impact on the children's problem-solving capacity, this was mediated by their beliefs about the nature and purpose of school mathematics and their role in learning mathematics. Children who believed that their task was to understand mathematics (divers) tended to set conceptual goals and monitor their understanding, but used relatively inefficient strategies that they understood rather than apply a procedure or algorithm that they did not feel confident about using. Children who believed that mathematics was about 'doing sums to get answers' (players) tended to set procedural goals and focus much more on monitoring their use of algorithms (e.g. 'you put that there and carry that'). By the end of the year, divers recognised that they needed to develop more efficient strategies to solve problems, and players recognised that they needed to monitor their understanding of the situation better before they rushed in to use whatever algorithm came to mind. This work points to the importance of scaffolding and valuing both conceptual understanding and procedural efficiency and maintaining a balance between the two.

for the classroom

Photograph the list of prices at an ice-cream booth (ask permission first) and use this to encourage children to pose and solve their own problems, amending prices and ice-cream descriptions as necessary. For example:

- Kerry had $9. He bought a double-scoop chocolate cone. How much change did he receive?
- Shay ordered a banana and mango single-scoop in a tub and a double-scoop vanilla ice-cream cone. How much did this cost altogether?

Using this context (and assuming there are multiple options available), pose some problems with not enough or too little information to stimulate a discussion about what is needed to solve problems of this type. For example:

- Alice bought a strawberry-flavoured ice-cream. How much change did she receive from $10?

Difficulties can arise at each point in the problem-solving process. Interpreting a situation can be compounded by the complexity of the language involved and the order and nature of the activity. The operation(s) required can be masked by problem structure and context. Choice and use of a particular strategy can be affected by the number of steps involved, the amount of information (too little, too much), and the magnitude or type of numbers involved. The process of review and evaluation may not be valued or used routinely to consider the sense that was made of the situation.

communicating mathematically

Develop a language to talk about thinking and problem solving

Teachers need to be aware of the multiple sources of problem-solving difficulty discussed above and regularly choose problems and tasks that provoke metacognitive discussions about problem type, the operation(s) required, why, what strategies can be used, whether we can do it more efficiently, whether it makes sense, and so on. See Siemon and Booker (1990) for more suggestions.

Other sources of difficulty

Children are typically introduced to addition and subtraction in the form of abbreviated 'action stories'. These have a particular discourse structure consisting of two or more statements followed by a question. For example:

- The children had 7 balloons. (Statement A)
- They were given 4 more balloons. (Statement B)
- How many balloons did the children have altogether? (Question)

When presented in written form accompanied by pictures or drawn representations, these 'stories' can present problems for young readers who have to decode this rather unusual grammatical form in conjunction with whatever sense they make of the pictures (Exley & Abel, 2008). This suggests that the particular literacy demands of such problems need to be considered alongside the construction of relevant solution strategies and direct instruction in the interpretation, construction, and use of diagrams (Shigematsu & Sowder, 1994; Smith, 2009). One way of reducing these difficulties is to use multiple representations of additive problems from the outset to broaden children's experience of the ways in which quantitative information can be presented

(Selva, Falcao & Nunes, 2005; van den Heuval-Panhuizen, 2001b). Data sources such as picture graphs can be used to stimulate problem posing (see e.g. Figure 16.2) and to draw attention to the language associated with strategy usage. These difficulties can also be offset if the situations are interpreted in terms of what is known and what is unknown, and addition is linked to parts known situations and subtraction to whole–part known situations, as asking 'is it a part or is it a whole?' legitimates decontextualisation of the problem and offers a relatively straightforward heuristic to decode additive word problems (Siemon, 1993). This supports a problem-solving approach more generally as it values and develops a metacognitive language to talk about different types of problem or task.

Difficulty also arises with the use of compensation strategies to solve addition and subtraction problems. For example, in adding 29 and 36, children may rename 29 as 30 because 30 is 'easier to add than 29', then either 'take 1' from 36 and add, or add then 'take 1' to compensate for the 1 they 'added' initially. While this will work as long as children remember to keep track of what was added and what needs to be subtracted, it can lead to difficulties if it is learnt as a procedural rule with little or no conceptual basis (additive equivalence) and/or it is over-generalised and applied to subtraction. For example, when subtracting 19 from 31, children might well rename 19 as 20 to make the calculation easier but then 'take 1' from the result (11) to 'compensate for adding 1'. To offset this, it is a good idea to explore the principles underpinning compensation explicitly. One very effective way of doing this is to engage children in simple relational thinking exercises. Stephens (2006, p. 479) describes relational thinking as the 'capacity to see and use possibilities of variation between numbers in number sentences'. For example, relational thinkers are able to work with uncalculated pairs in equations such as 17 + 25 = 19 + ☐ because they recognise the relationship between 17 and 19 and adjust the relationship between 25 and the missing number (23) accordingly.

For the classroom

Use simple number sentences such as 8 + 5 = ☐, 13 + ☐ = 15 + 7, and 22 − ☐ = 20 − 7 to engage children in a discussion about how the missing number might be found without calculating, that is by reason alone, and what is needed to maintain equivalence and why. Record observations and examples for future reference and as an aid to support the use of compensation strategies more generally.

Conclusion

To become confident additive thinkers, children need a well-developed sense of number and a deep understanding of the contexts in which addition and subtraction can arise. While children need to model unfamiliar additive situations, it is the teacher's role to recognise what children already know, understand where they need to go to next, and scaffold learning. The transition from **make-all-count-all** strategies cannot occur without a corresponding focus on the development of mental objects for each of the numbers to 10, a knowledge of doubles, and a deepening understanding of place value in terms of a count of tens and a count of ones.

Interpreting additive situations in terms of the part–part–whole model, where addition could be recognised as parts known and subtraction as whole–part known, can alleviate some of the difficulties associated with language and the type and order of actions implicit in the problem, which otherwise children might construe differently according to their background knowledge and experience.

An important goal of mathematics education is to ensure that all students acquire a range of efficient strategies that can be applied flexibly and efficiently to solve problems. Additive strategies come in many different forms, from make-all-count-all, where parts are modelled physically using manipulatives or fingers, through to efficient strategies based on strong place-value knowledge and an understanding of equivalence. The teacher has an important role in scaffolding and exploring an extended range of strategies to ensure that children have a repertoire of strategies that they can use with confidence and justify relative to context. Games that provide practice in the use of strategies play an important role in developing procedural fluency, but this cannot be expected without a corresponding emphasis on conceptual understanding.

key terms

Addend: one of the numbers being added

Additive thinking: capacity to work with the ideas of aggregation and disaggregation with a range of number sets

Commutative property: the order in two numbers are added or multiplied does not matter (e.g. 3 + 4 = 4 + 3 and 3 × 4 = 4 × 3)

Contexts for addition (parts known): join—items in the two sets are the same (e.g. 3 oranges and 4 more oranges is 7 oranges); combine—items in the two sets are different (e.g. 3 bananas and 4 oranges is 7 pieces of fruit)

Contexts for subtraction (whole − part known): take away—part of a single set is physically removed; missing addend—single set is increased to a given size; difference—comparison between two sets (e.g. Jake has 8 cards, Bill has 5: how many more cards does Jake have than Bill?)

Make-all-count-all: counting strategies for addition—solution found by physically modelling and counting all by ones; count on—solution found by counting on from one of the two numbers; count on from larger—solution found by count on from larger of the two numbers; use known relationships—solution derived from known facts

Count back: counting strategies for subtraction—solution found by counting backwards by ones; think of addition—solution found by counting up from subtrahend; count up from

Mental strategies for addition: count on 1, 2, or 3 (e.g. for 2 + 7, think: 7, 8, 9); doubles and near doubles (e.g. for 7 + 8, think: double 7 is 14 and 1 more, 15), make to 10 (e.g. for 6 + 8, think: 8, 10 and 4 more, 14)

Mental strategies for subtraction: think of addition (e.g. for 16 − 9, think: 9 and how many more to 16? 1 to 10, then 6 more, so 7); halving (e.g. for 16 − 9, think, half of 16 is 8, need to take 1 more, 7); make back to 10 (e.g. for 16 − 9, think: 16 back to 10 is 6, need to take 3 more, 7); use known relationships or place value (e.g. for 16 − 9, think: 16 take 10 is 6, need to add 1 back, 7)

Part–part–whole: recognising numbers to 10 in terms of their parts (e.g. 8 is 5 and 3, 6 and 2, double 4) and their relationship to larger numbers and 10 (e.g. 8 is 1 less than 9, 2 less than 10)

Regrouping, Trading: ways of describing renaming when adding/multiplying or subtracting/dividing respectively (e.g. 5 tens and 8 tens is 13 tens, it is regrouped for recording purposes as 1 hundred and 3 tens, but when subtracting 28 from 45, the 8 ones can only be taken if 1 of the 4 tens is traded for 10 ones)

Renaming: naming numbers in other ways (e.g. 365 is 3 hundreds 6 tens and 5 ones, but it can be renamed as 36 tens and 5 ones, or 3 hundreds and 65 ones)

Subtrahend: number being subtracted

Review questions

1. Describe and illustrate the different ways in which addition might be presented to children in their first year of school.
2. Why is the difference idea for subtraction so much more difficult than the take-away or missing addend idea for subtraction? Which would you introduce first, and why?
3. Part–part–whole knowledge and an understanding of doubles are now recognised as prerequisites for building procedural fluency. Describe what is meant by these important ideas and what materials, representations, and language you might use to ensure that these are supported effectively in the early years.
4. Describe and illustrate the three mental strategies for addition. What would you do to develop doubles facts to 20?
5. Use examples to show how you would use open number lines and thinking strings to support efficient, place-value based strategies for two-digit mental computation.
6. Describe the materials, representations, language, and recording you might use in developing an understanding of written algorithms for addition and subtraction to thousands.

Key references

Anghilheri, J. (2006). *Teaching Number Sense* (2nd ed.). London: Continuum.

Beishuizen, M. (1999). The empty number line as a new model. In I. Thompson (Ed.), *Issues in Teaching Numeracy in Primary Schools* (p. 1). Buckingham, UK: Open University Press.

Boaler, J. (2002). *Experiencing School Mathematics: Traditional and Reform Approaches to Teaching and their Impact on Student Learning Outcomes*. Mahwah, NJ: Erlbaum.

Carpenter, T., & Moser, J. (1984). The acquisition of addition and subtraction concepts in grades one through three. *Journal for Research in Mathematics Education, 15*(3), 179–202.

Cobb, P. (1999). Where is the mind? In P. Murphy (Ed.), *Learners, Learning and Assessment*. London: Paul Chapman.

Exley, B., & Abel, K. (2008). Ah! Now I see: The literacy demands of mathematics problems in the early years. *Curriculum Leadership, 6*(33). Retrieved from www.curriculum.edu.au/leader/vol6_no33,25023.html?issueID=11616.

Shigematsu, K., & Sowder, J. (1994). Drawings for story problems: Practices in Japan and the United States. *Arithmetic Teacher, 41*(9), 544–547.

Siemon, D., & Booker, G. (1990). Teaching and learning FOR, ABOUT and THROUGH problem solving. *Vinculum, 27*(2), 4–12.

Smith, S. (2009). *Early Childhood Mathematics*. Boston, MA: Pearson.

Thompson, I. (1999). Written methods of computation. In I. Thompson (Ed.), *Issues in Teaching Numeracy in Primary Schools* (pp. 169–183). Buckingham, UK: Open University Press.

van den Heuval-Panhuizen, M. (2001a). *Children Learn Mathematics – A Learning-teaching Trajectory with Intermediate Attainment Targets for Calculation with Whole Numbers in Primary School*. Utrecht, The Netherlands: Freudenthal Institute.

Websites

www.simerr.educ.utas.edu.au/numeracy/critical_numeracy/critical_numeracy.htm

www.thenetwork.sa.edu.au/teachingandlearning

http://activated.act.edu.au/ectl

17 Developing Multiplicative Thinking in the Early Years

Contents

What is multiplicative thinking?	351
Why is multiplicative thinking important?	354
Initial ideas, representations, and strategies	355
Building number fact knowledge and confidence	374
Computation strategies	380
Problem solving	389
Conclusion	392

Chapter objectives

This chapter will enable the reader to:
- Understand what is involved in multiplicative thinking
- Recognise the different ways in which multiplication and division problems can be represented
- Understand the importance of mental strategies and how these can be developed
- Appreciate the role of materials, language, and recording in scaffolding children's understanding and solution strategies
- Recognise and address children's learning needs in relation to multiplicative thinking
- Plan effective problem-solving experiences involving written and mental computation.

Introducing multiplicative thinking

Baa-baa black sheep, have you any wool?
Yes sir, yes sir, three bags full.

Nursery rhymes can be a useful source of mathematics problems. In this case, having explored nursery rhymes in literacy with her class of 5–6-year-olds, a teacher revisited the 'Baa-Baa Black Sheep' rhyme and posed the following question: 'I wonder how many bags of wool would there be if there were 5 sheep?'

The children set about the task of answering enthusiastically, some with materials and others with pen and paper. While most decided that there would be 15 bags of wool, what was interesting was the number of children who constructed abstract representations, in particular representations that connected the three bags of wool with each sheep. More about this later, but this suggests that we should not delay playing with multiplicative situations and ideas until children have 'mastered' addition and subtraction.

Big ideas

- Multiplicative thinking involves a capacity to work with numbers as composite units in a variety of contexts. It is inherently related to equal sharing (partitioning), more efficient counting strategies, doubling, and place-value.
- Knowing when to multiply or divide and choosing a strategy appropriate to the task requires a deep understanding of the operations themselves and a well-developed sense of number.
- Strategies for multiplying and dividing need to be modelled, scaffolded, and discussed to ensure all students have access to a range of efficient, flexible strategies that they can use with confidence.
- Estimation is a highly developed capacity requiring the integration of a number of subordinate skills and understandings.

In previous chapters we have made the point that concepts need to be experienced, strategies need to be scaffolded, and everything needs to be discussed. In this chapter we will explore the meanings for the operations of multiplication and division, and the experiences needed to ensure that these are understood. We will also consider the range of strategies that can be used to solve problems involving multiplication and division, how these strategies develop over time, and how they might be supported.

What is multiplicative thinking?

For the purposes of the Scaffolding Numeracy in the Middle Years research project [SNMY] (Siemon, Breed, Dole, Izard & Virgona, 2006) we characterised **multiplicative thinking** as:

- a capacity to work flexibly and efficiently with an extended range of numbers (e.g. larger whole numbers, decimals, common fractions, ratio, and per cent)
- an ability to recognise and solve a range of problems involving multiplication or division including direct and indirect proportion, and
- the means to communicate this effectively in a variety of ways (e.g. words, models, diagrams, symbolic expressions, and written algorithms).

In short, multiplicative thinking involves recognising and working with relationships between quantities. It is indicated by a capacity to work flexibly with the concepts, strategies, and representations of multiplication (and division) as they occur in a wide range of contexts (Siemon & Breed, 2005). Although some aspects of multiplicative thinking are available to young children, multiplicative thinking is substantially more complex than additive thinking and may take many years to achieve.

consider and discuss

What is involved in these everyday calculations?

1. You are planning a school excursion to the zoo for 26 children. The cost per child is $37. What is the total cost of the excursion?
2. You are at the supermarket. A particular brand of coffee is available in small, medium, and large jars. Which size represents the best buy if the 300 gram jar costs $13.99, the 150 gram jar costs $8.55 and the 50 gram jar costs $2.85?
3. You are at a restaurant with six others. The bill comes to $736.55. How much would you expect each person to pay?

Multiplicative thinking requires more than a capacity to execute a particular procedure or strategy where word problems are involved. Re-arranging the number of groups to facilitate a solution (e.g. renaming 6 eights as 5 eights and 1 eight, or as double 3 eights) is one indicator of multiplicative thinking (try this for problem 1 above), as is the ability to use simple proportional reasoning (problem 2), and to think about division in terms of 'what do I have to multiply by?'. For example, for problem 3, you might recognise that 7 by $105 is $735, so each person would probably pay $110.

The two solutions to the muffin problem shown in Figure 17.1 nicely illustrate the distinction between additive and multiplicative thinking. The students were asked how many muffins could be made with 6 cups of milk if 2/3 cup of milk produced 12 muffins.

The first response uses repeated addition to determine how many two-third cups are in 6 cups, and then counting to find the total number of muffins. The second solution recognises the proportional relationship between the quantity of milk and the number of muffins. Both strategies produce the correct answer, but the first is additive whereas the second is multiplicative.

Figure 17.1 Two solutions to the muffin recipe problem

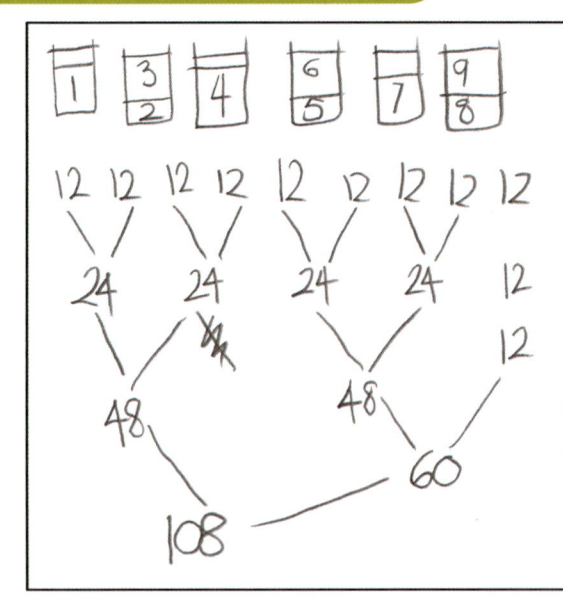

communicating mathematically

The language of multiplication and division

There are many ways that we can talk about multiplication and division. One way is that, for multiplication, the number of groups and the number in each group are known, and the problem relates to finding the total amount.

For division, the total is known and either the number of groups is known and the problem becomes one of finding the number in each group (referred to as *partition division*), or the total and size of each group are known and the problem becomes one of finding the number of groups (*quotition division*).

More formally, for multiplication, we refer to the number of groups as the *multiplier*, the number in each group as the *multiplicand*, and the total as the *product*.

Division involves the same three aspects but the total is referred to as the *dividend*, the number of groups as the *divisor*, and the number in each group as the *quotient*.

Ultimately, both multiplication and division are understood in terms of the *factor-factor-product* idea (see Chapter 24), where for multiplication we know the factors and have to find the total, and for division we know the product and one of the factors and have to find the other factor.

Multiplicative problems can be compounded by complex discourse patterns that mask the operation required and, for multiplication in particular, further compounded by the many different ways in which multiplication can be represented.

The essential difference between additive and multiplicative thinking relates to the nature of the units under consideration. For addition and subtraction, 'all the number meanings … are directly related to set size and to the actions of joining or separating objects and sets' (Nunes & Bryant, 1996, p. 144). In these situations it is possible to work with the numbers involved as collections that can be aggregated or disaggregated and renamed as needed to facilitate computation (e.g. counting on or back in place-value parts, renaming numbers in terms of their parts, and/or using known facts).

for the classroom

Pose the following problem (using real data if appropriate), and have students work in mixed ability groups to explore, document, and share as many different strategies as possible for finding the total number of Year 4 students.

At a large primary school, there are six Year 4 classes. There are 24 students in Mrs Blackwell's class, 26 in Ms Henderson's class, 23 in Mr Lee's class, 25 in Mrs Mathews' class, 27 in Mr Mancini's class, and 25 in Mrs Agathi's class. How many Year 4 students are there altogether?

Use the responses to this problem to illustrate how numbers can be rearranged to support calculation. Identify and justify 'efficient' strategies such as working with place value or known parts rather than ones.

While it is possible to use repeated addition to solve multiplication problems and repeated subtraction to solve division problems, these are essentially additive processes—the only difference is that the sets being added or subtracted are the same size. Multiplicative thinking involves much more than this and 'it would be wrong to treat multiplication as just another, rather complicated, form of addition, or division as just another form of subtraction' (Nunes & Bryant, 1996, p. 144).

For multiplication, it is necessary to simultaneously recognise and coordinate the number of groups (multiplier) and the number in each group (multiplicand) (Jacob & Willis, 2001; Nunes & Bryant, 1996; Vergnaud, 1983). According to Steffe (1992), for a 'situation to be established as multiplicative, it is always necessary at least to coordinate two composite units in such a way that one composite unit is distributed over the elements of the other composite unit' (p. 264), resulting in a composite unit of composite units as shown in Figure 17.2.

Figure 17.2 A composite of composite units

Recognising and working with composite units introduces the distinction between *how many* and *how much*. For example, from the young child's perspective, three bags of four marbles is different from four bags of three marbles, not in terms of how many marbles there are altogether, but in terms of how many (the number of bags) and how much (the number in each bag). In the first instance there are 3 four-units; in the second there are 4 three-units. This distinction between the count (how many) and the unit (how much) is often overlooked in the rush to symbolise, with the result that many children interpret 3 fours as 3 counts of 4 ones rather than 3 four-units. This has important implications for the development of multiplicative thinking and children's capacity to understand fractions, and it is why we advocate recording that distinguishes between how many and how much both for multiplication (e.g. 3 fours, 6 nines) and for fractions (e.g. 3 quarters, 5 thirds).

Language and representations play a critical role in shaping how we think (e.g. Nunes & Bryant, 1996). By distinguishing between the count (numeral) and the unit (word), children are more likely to recognise the relative magnitude of different units (e.g. that 3 quarters is larger than 3 eighths) and the inverse relationship between how many and how much. That is, they recognise that in partitioning a whole or re-unitising a given collection, the smaller the part/unit the greater the number of parts/units needed (e.g. a whole can be partitioned as 4 quarters or 15 fifteenths; a collection of 12 can be re-unitised as 2 six-units or 6 two-units).

think + link

Chapter 24 will consider multiplication and division with decimals, fractions, and integers.

In most cultural groups, young children's pre-school experience exposes them to the notions of fair shares and sharing equally. While this does not mean that they understand these processes as 'division', the notion of splitting quantities up into smaller and smaller equal parts and the equal groups generated by sharing provide a firm foundation for multiplicative thinking.

Why is multiplicative thinking important?

Some years back, I invited a large group of relatively senior public servants in Canberra to make a list of commonly encountered texts. This generated a very large and diverse list which included newspaper articles, computer screen graphics, 'do-it-yourself' instruction manuals, sales brochures, insurance policies, supermarket receipts, and so on. Of these, it was agreed that approximately 90 per cent necessitated some degree of quantitative and/or spatial reasoning to comprehend the text and that the mathematical knowledge most commonly required was some understanding of rational number and proportional reasoning; that is, fractions, decimals, percentages, ratio, and proportion. Multiplicative thinking is a pre-requisite for working with these powerful and necessary ideas. Students cannot be expected to understand rational number ideas and representations if their understanding of multiplication and division is restricted to an *equal groups* idea, as this is really useful only for small whole numbers (e.g. 3 groups of 8, how many sixes in 24?).

Multiplicative thinking is a 'big idea' in number that integrates a number of other key ideas and strategies (Vergnaud, 1983). For example, recognising the *many-to-one* relationship '10 of these is 1 of those', and the *one-to-many* relationship 'for each one there are 10 tenths', is fundamental to understanding the multiplicative structure of the base 10 system of numeration. Recognising the inverse relationship between the *divisor* and the *dividend* (e.g. the larger the divisor the smaller the dividend) is fundamental to developing a sense of rational numbers. Recognising that division is the inverse of multiplication is fundamental to computational fluency and ultimately algebraic thinking, while the related processes of *partitioning* and *unitising* underpin the capacity to work with fractions, percentages, and proportional reasoning (Confrey, 1994; Lamon, 1996). Here, partitioning refers to the act of dividing quantities into equal parts, referred to as **equipartitioning** by Confrey, Maloney, Nguyen, Mojica and Myers (2009) to distinguish this process from additive partitioning, and unitising refers the act of recognising different quantities as units. For example, 24 cans of soft drink can be partitioned as 1 pack of 24 cans (1 twenty-four unit), 2 twelve-packs (2 twelve-units) or 4 six-packs (4 six-units). In its most elementary form, unitising results in the construction of countable, **composite units** (e.g. 1 six, 2 sixes, 3 sixes, etc.), introducing the distinction between how many and how much.

Variation in the acquisition of multiplicative thinking skills is the single, most important reason for the eight-year range in mathematics achievement in Years 5 to 9 (Siemon, Virgona & Corneille, 2001; Siemon et al., 2006).

Initial ideas, representations, and strategies

In most English-speaking countries, multiplication and division are introduced separately, with multiplication typically considered before division. However, given young children's experience with sharing and evidence to suggest that simple proportion problems can be solved earlier than generally expected (e.g. Siemon et al., 2006), it is time to reconsider when and how we introduce these important ideas. This is supported by the work of Confrey and her colleagues (e.g. Confrey, 1994; Confrey et al., 2009) who point to an alternative approach to multiplication based on splitting and replication rather than repeated addition.

Young children's capacity to share equally is recognised in the *Australian Curriculum: Mathematics* (ACARA, 2010) as an outcome that can be realistically expected by the end of a child's first year at school (Foundation). Sharing discrete collections (e.g. 12 teddies among 3, 4, or 6 children) can be used to initiate discussions about equal groups and what happens when the number of shares increases. Exploring how a jug of fruit juice might be shared equally among family members can be used to initiate discussions about equal parts and what happens when the number of shares increases or decreases. These experiences are important as they simultaneously connect all three aspects of the situation: the amount to be shared, the number of shares, and the resulting amount per share. They also introduce, at least implicitly, the inverse relationship between how many and how much. This is not the case when children are asked to find the total number of counters arranged in 3 groups of 4. In this case, children only need to attend to two aspects of the situation, the number of equal groups and the number in each group, which they can find by counting-all in a rhythmic manner (e.g. 1, 2, 3, 4 ... 5, 6, 7, 8 ... 9, 10, 11, 12), or by skip counting (e.g. 4, 8, 12). While this makes an implicit distinction between the how many (3) and the how much (4), it does not draw attention to the relationship between the two and the total, which is a key aspect of multiplicative thinking.

As mentioned at the beginning of the chapter, many of the children's responses to the Baa-Baa Black Sheep problem were abstract (see Figure 17.3). In these responses, each sheep was clearly connected in some way with three bags of wool, suggesting that the children understood the situation in terms of *for each* sheep there are 3 bags of wool. This is essentially a *ratio* or *times as many* idea (e.g. 3 times as many bags of wool as sheep) and is quite distinct from the *equal groups* idea, even though the children invariably counted by ones to arrive at the solution of 15 bags of wool altogether.

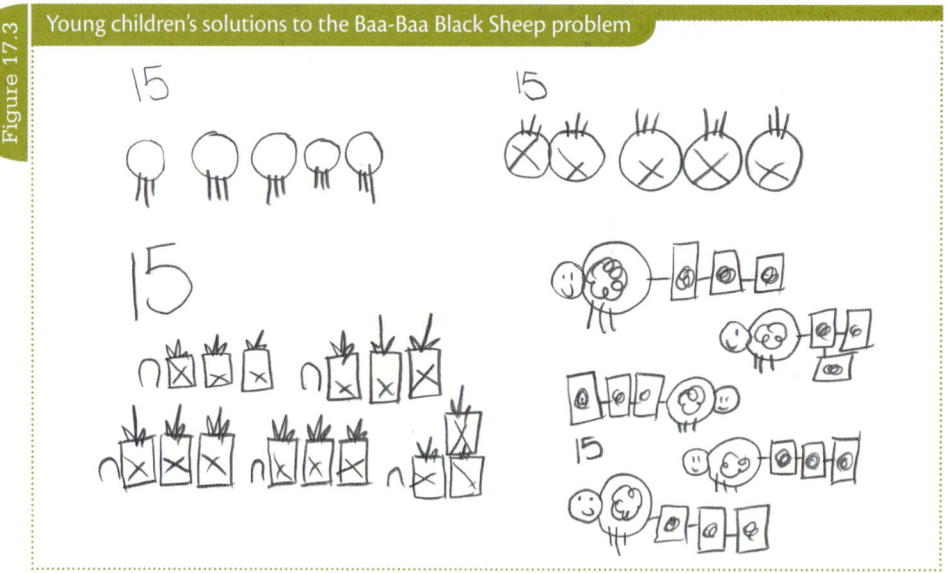

Figure 17.3 Young children's solutions to the Baa-Baa Black Sheep problem

These representations suggest that, in addition to being able to share equally from an early age, young children also appear to have a capacity to think relationally. This is supported by evidence from the SNMY research project (Siemon et al., 2006) which found that children could solve simple proportional reasoning problems before they could use multiplicative strategies to solve an equal groups problem involving a two-digit by single digit number.

Nearly all of the research-based developmental frameworks for multiplication are framed in terms of counting-based strategies that ultimately terminate with a reference to the use of number fact knowledge (e.g. Department of Education & Early Childhood Development, 2010; Department of Education & Training,

2007). This is not surprising given the almost exclusive focus on equal groups and repeated addition in the early years. However, an increasing number of researchers (e.g. Confrey et al., 2009; Nunes & Bryant, 1996; Schmittau & Morris, 2004) suggest that there is a parallel path to the development of multiplicative thinking based on young children's capacity to share equally and work with one-to-many relationships (as in the Baa-Baa Black Sheep problem).

In a teaching experiment designed to examine the impact of exposing children to a range of semantic structures for multiplication prior to instruction in division, Downton (2008) found that the equal groups and the times as many ideas were equally available to Year 3 students, and that experience with both 'provides a solid basis for children's developing understanding of division' (p. 177). She also concluded that emphasis should be placed on 'the relationship between multiplication and division and the language associated with both operations before any use of symbols or formal recording' (p. 177).

There are a number of different ways in which multiplicative situations may be understood and represented. These semantic structures have been variously described in the literature (e.g. Anghileri, 1989; Greer, 1992; Mulligan & Mitchelmore, 1997); most include the equal groups idea (for multiplication and division), partition, multiplicative comparison (times as many), rectangular arrays, and the Cartesian product. We draw on these but also take note of the parallel pathway suggested by children's capacity to share equally and work with many-to-many correspondences. That is, a pathway based on splitting rather than counting on the grounds that counting is inherently tied to the multiplicative operations of replicating (as in the reproduction of living cells), magnifying, and shrinking (Confrey, 1994), while counting is inherently tied to the additive operations of aggregation and disaggregation. Figure 17.4 shows how these pathways develop over time from the two primitives, counting and splitting, through to the confident use of known facts and relationships. Ideas underpinned by counting are shown in orange, ideas derived from or related to the splitting notion are shown in pale green, and strategies are highlighted in yellow.

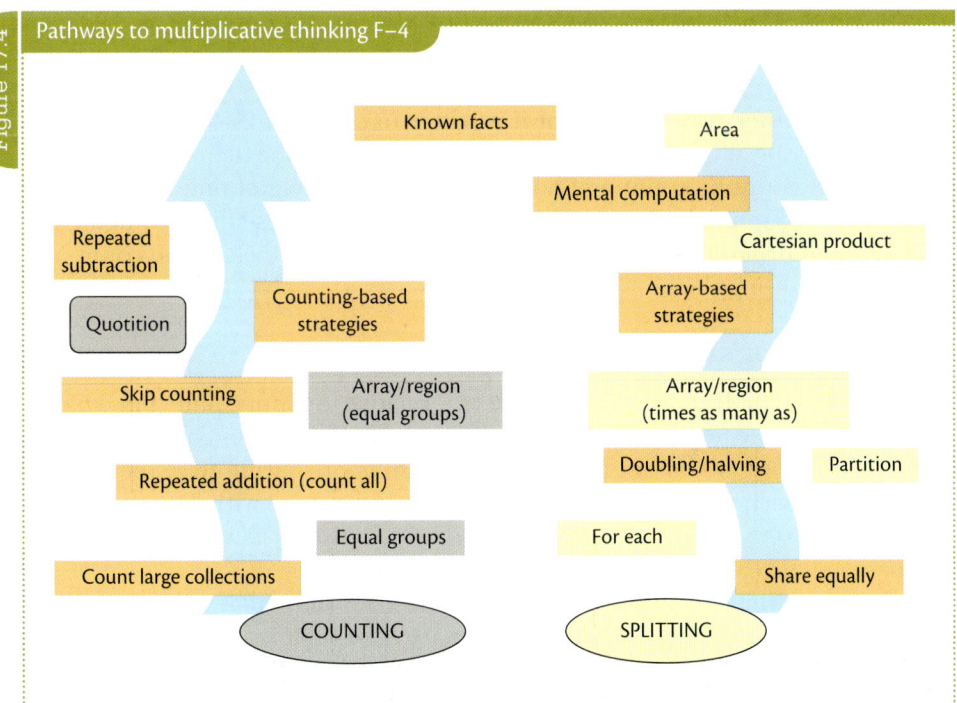

Figure 17.4 Pathways to multiplicative thinking F–4

A description of the respective ideas and the initial strategies they afford is given below. Where these relate to both multiplication and division and/or other ideas such as *rate* and *ratio*, we will consider them jointly, but the two ideas for division, *quotition* and *partition*, will be considered separately as these are widely recognised in the literature and powerfully illustrate the affordances and constraints of the counting/splitting dichotomy.

Counting and splitting

As indicated in Chapter 16, most children have had a range of lived experiences relating to addition, subtraction, and sharing division. However, it is highly unlikely that they have ever felt the need to make or count equal groups. While young children are capable of making and counting equal groups to find a total when instructed to do so, this activity is essentially additive and it may take some time before they can work with the numbers involved as composite units.

Counting large collections more efficiently and equal sharing have proved effective in introducing children to multiplicative thinking (Siemon & Breed, 2005). The first draws attention to the benefits of using small collections as countable units (e.g. count a collection of 62 items by 2s, 5s, or 10s). The second, based on **splitting**, draws attention to fair shares and many-to-many counts (e.g. 3 bags of wool per sheep). Both create a need for equal groups and an opportunity to recognise and record composite units (i.e. 31 twos; 5 threes).

The initial ideas and strategies are presented below in more or less developmental order.

Strategies for counting large collections

A critical step in the development of multiplicative thinking is the recognition of numbers to 10 and beyond as composite units (e.g. the capacity to see and work with 1 eight as opposed to 8 ones). This can be achieved through regular subitising activities and opportunities to physically count large collections. For example, the Chicken Scramble activity described in Chapter 14 (p. 292) can be used to encourage Year 1 and 2 children to count large collections more efficiently. Careful observation reveals that many will miscount and have to start again; others will realise that it is better to count by 2s or even 5s. Once counts are done, it is a good idea to ask children to describe their strategies then check their count by counting another way. Eventually, not only will children realise that counting by 5s and 10s is useful, they will realise that arranging the stacks in an ordered way is a useful means of keeping track of the count and avoiding counting the same pile twice.

think + link

Further information regarding subitising, composite units, and the Chicken Scramble activity can be found in Chapter 14.

Strategies for sharing equally

Most young children acquire a sense of relative quantity and 'fair shares' before they come to school. Sharing collections and quantities equally provides opportunities to talk about and name the results of sharing (e.g. there are 6 shares, 4 in each share, 6 fours) and what might be done with 'left overs' (e.g. 3 custard tarts shared between two children, 1 custard tart and half of the remaining tart each).

These informal language experiences should be followed by more structured activities in Years 1 and 2 where children are asked to explore the number of different ways in which a given collection might be shared equally. For example, the situation illustrated in Figure 17.5 could be prompted by a story about a teddy-bears' picnic where the problem was finding out how many different ways the teddies might arrange themselves so that there was an equal number on each picnic rug—small squares of tartan fabric can be used as 'rugs'. This gives rise to naming the outcomes in ways that distinguish between how many and how much (e.g. 2 eights, 4 fours, 8 twos) and the possibility of noticing that the more rugs there are, the fewer teddies can sit on each rug. Different groups could be given different collections to explore and the results could be shared and discussed with the class.

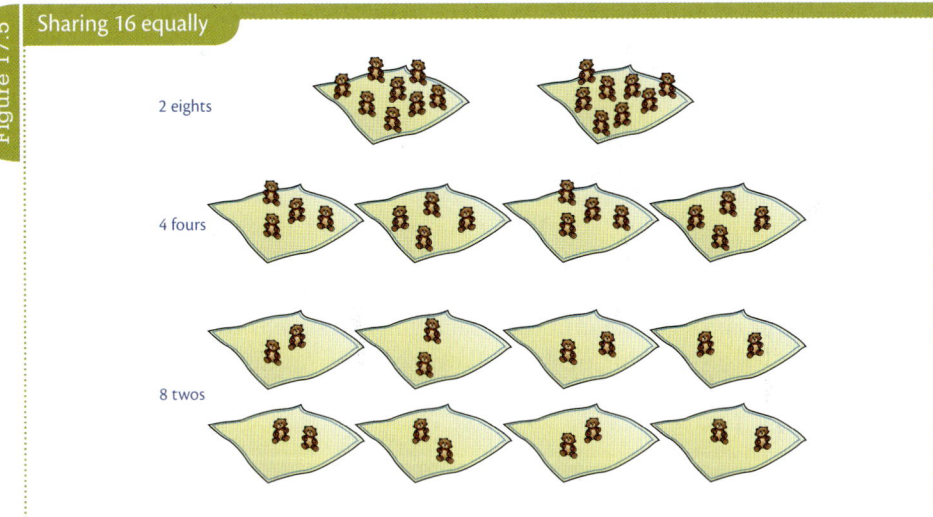

Figure 17.5 Sharing 16 equally

The 'for each' idea

As we have seen, young children have some capacity to think relationally; that is, they can comprehend and represent problems such as Baa-Baa Black Sheep in terms of a one-to-many count. While this and problems such as '3 cars, how many wheels?' and '6 children, how many feet?' can also be considered as *equal group* problems (see below), they have the potential to generate multiplicative thinking. For instance, having found how many wheels on 3 cars, the children can be asked, 'how many wheels on 6 cars?'. If this prompts the use of a *doubling* strategy rather than a *make-all-count-all* response, it suggests that the children have constructed a composite of composite units as shown in Figure 17.6. The use of doubling in this instance is indicative of emergent multiplicative thinking.

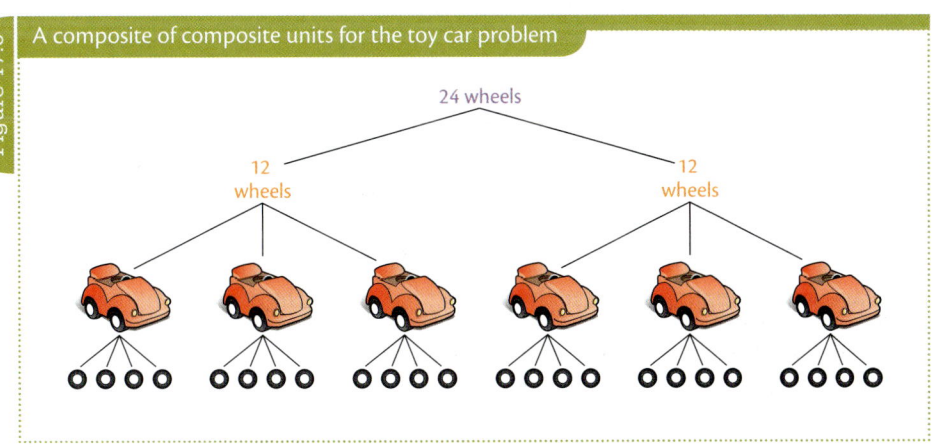

Figure 17.6 A composite of composite units for the toy car problem

The *for each* idea extends well beyond the early years to underpin later ideas such as *times as many*, *rate*, the *Cartesian product*, *ratio*, and proportional reasoning. For example, consider the following problems.

1. In the school Readathon, Kate read 3 times as many books as her friend Rachel. Rachel read 4 books. How many did Kate read?
2. On a country trip, Jodie travelled at a steady speed of 70 kilometres per hour (km/h). How far had she travelled after one and a half hours?
3. Two six-sided dice are rolled. If one die is red and the other is blue, how many different combinations are possible?
4. If 2 soccer tops can be made from 5 metres of fabric, how many tops can be made from 15 metres of fabric?

The first problem is not an equal groups problem although it may be solved by counting all (1, 2, 3, 4 … 5, 6, 7, 8 … 9, 10, 11, 12), repeated addition (4 and 4 more is 8 and 4 more is 12), or skip counting (4, 8, 12). Problems of this type are sometimes referred to as *comparison* problems in that one set is being compared to another set. When considered in this way it is clear the idea of *ratio* is involved, and where ratio is involved so too is the idea of 'for each'. Problems like this draw attention to the role of units. In this case, 4 books is the unit, and *for each* unit that Rachel has, Kate has three. Rather than representing this as a count of 3 unrelated groups (additive structure), this problem is better represented by a tree diagram (multiplicative structure) as shown in Figure 17.7.

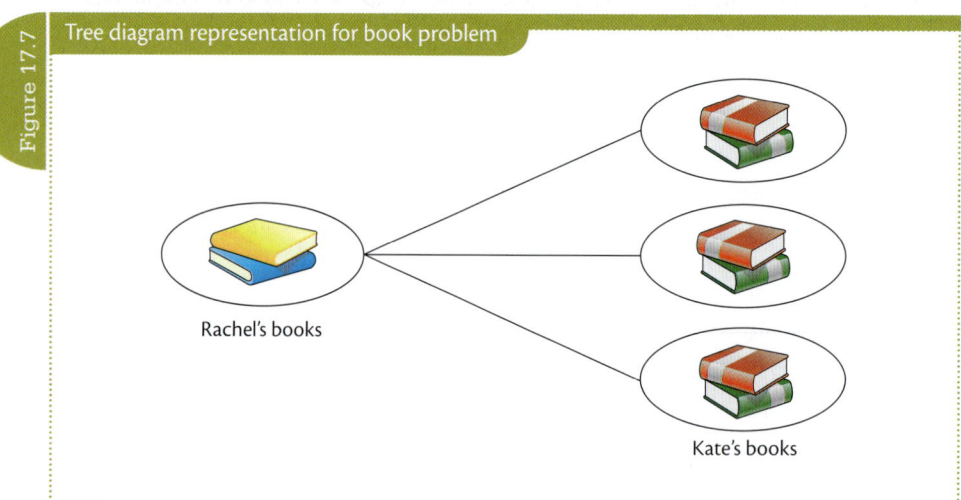

Figure 17.7 Tree diagram representation for book problem

As we shall see in Chapter 18, the *region* and *for each* ideas support the interpretation and construction of fraction representations in the middle primary years and beyond. For example, if a sheet of A4 paper is folded in half vertically then folded in half and half again horizontally, the resulting model should look like the one shown in Figure 17.8. This can be interpreted in terms of the *region* idea for multiplication (i.e. 4 parts by 2 parts gives 8 parts, or quarters by halves gives eighths), as well as the *for each* idea (i.e. for each half there are now 4 smaller parts; as there are 2 halves, so there are 8 smaller parts altogether.

The capacity to think relationally lies at the heart of multiplicative thinking. The *for each* idea provides a basis for thinking relationally in a range of contexts – as such it is a critical component in the development of multiplicative thinking.

Figure 17.8 | Folded paper model

```
                2 Parts (halves)

    ┌───────────────┬───────────────┐
    │               │               │
    ├───────────────┼───────────────┤
    │               │               │
4 Parts ├───────────────┼───────────────┤
(quarters) │            │               │
    ├───────────────┼───────────────┤
    │               │               │
    └───────────────┴───────────────┘

  For each half, 4 smaller parts, so 8 smaller parts altogether
```

consider and discuss

Explore the *for each* idea

Match the ideas listed above to problems 2, 3, and 4 on page 360. Consider and discuss how these relate to the *for each* idea and how you might represent and solve these in ways that support multiplicative thinking. Contrast this to how these types of problems are represented in school textbooks or worksheets.

Doubling and halving

Doubling and halving are extremely intuitive strategies. Most young children know what is meant by these terms and are able to double or halve a given collection or amount. Regular subitising activities support the development of the doubles to 10, and arithmetic racks (two-row bead frames) can be used to support the doubles to 20. Once these are known, place-value strategies can be used from Year 1 to develop efficient doubling strategies for two-digit numbers. The concept of doubling can also be explored in the early years through mirror printing activities (e.g. a number of dots are painted onto one half of an A3 sheet, the paper is folded, pressed and carefully unfolded to reveal a mirror image of the original dots).

think + link

Teaching ideas to support the development of doubling were discussed in Chapter 14. Arithmetic racks are illustrated in Figure 14.10.

Partition

The **partition** concept of division involves dividing a collection or quantity into a given number of equal parts. In partition division, the total or whole (*dividend*) and the number of groups, shares, or parts are known (*divisor*), and the question becomes 'how many in each group?' or 'how much in each share or part?'. Sometimes referred to as *partitive* or *sharing division*, this idea evolves from the informal experiences of sharing equally.

Partition division is inherently related to splitting in that it literally 'splits' the set or unit into a given number of equal parts (e.g. sharing 18 sweets among 6 children or 2 pizzas among 3 children). To solve the sweets problem, children might use six paper plates to mark each share, then deal the sweets out one or two at a time until all 18 sweets are distributed to conclude that there would be three sweets in each share. With more experience of multiplication, the indication of 6 shares might prompt a consideration of '6 whats are 18?' This in turn might prompt the response, '6 twos are 12, that leaves 6, that's 1 more each, so it must be 6 threes … they would get 3 sweets each.'

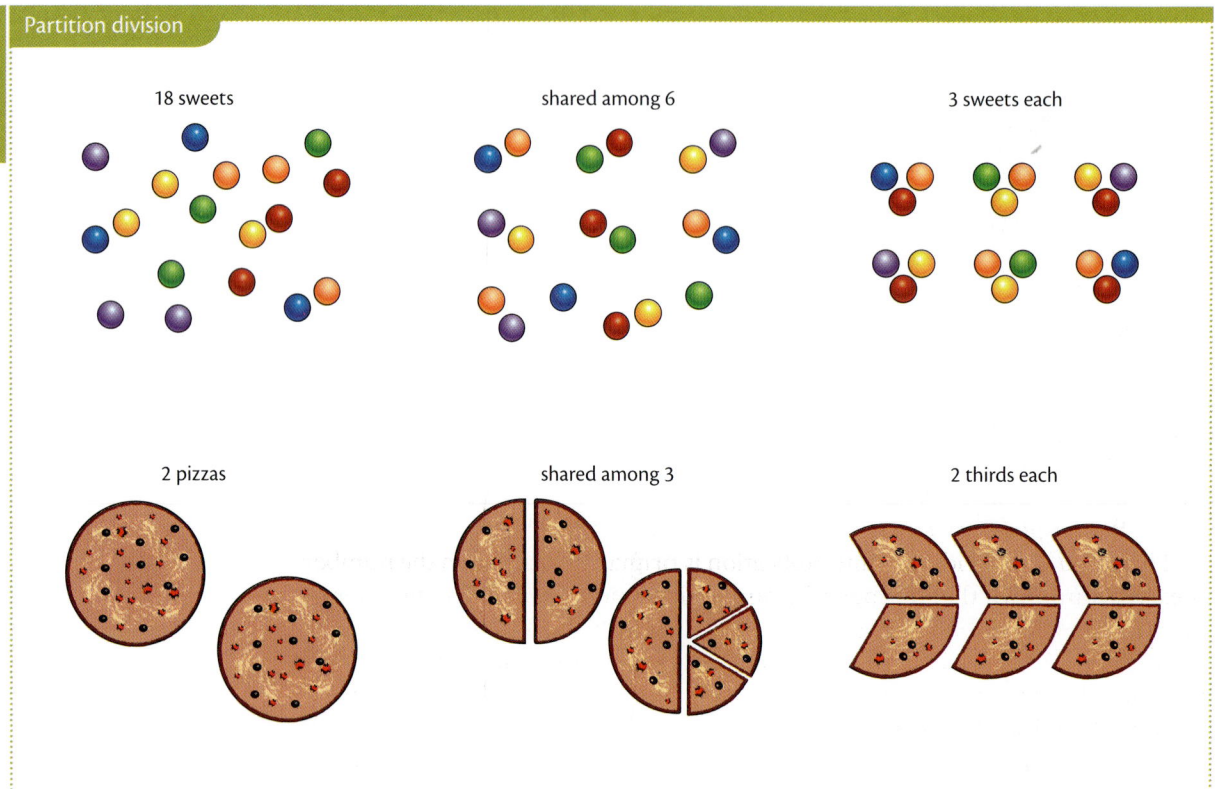

Figure 17.9 Partition division

By inviting the question, 'what do I have to multiply by?' (as in the sweets example above), partition division can be seen to be related to the *for each* (how many sweets per share), *times as many* (6 times what), and *array* and *region* (6 by what) ideas for multiplication.

The partition idea can also be applied to continuous quantities (e.g. 2 pizzas shared among 3, or a length of string cut into 4 equal pieces). For instance, in exploring the pizza problem, young children might make plasticine models of the pizzas and use icy-pole sticks to mark each share. While they may attempt to cut each pizza into 3 equal parts by trial and error, they are more likely to halve both pizzas, recognise that each person would get half a pizza each, then use trial and error to partition the remaining half into three roughly equal pieces. What is important at this level is not the answer (although students in Years 5 or 6 might be expected to recognise and name each share as 2 thirds of a pizza) but the process of partitioning, which ultimately extends to and supports the construction of multiplicative representations of common fractions and decimals. For instance, while children have little difficulty using repeated acts of halving to generate representations for fractions in the halving family (halves, quarters, eighths, etc.), a significant number of children in Year 3 and beyond will use guess work and/or additive strategies when asked to divide a given rectangular region into five or more equal parts.

think + link

Partitioning strategies for constructing common and decimal fraction representations will be considered in Chapter 18.

consider and discuss

Explore the partition idea

1. Share 59 icy-pole sticks among 4. Describe the language and strategy used, then repeat the task using 5 bundles of 10 and 9 ones. What did you notice?
2. When sharing materials, expressing the result as '14 each and 3 left over' is appropriate. Write two word problems for 59 shared among 4 that justify recording the remainder as (a) a fraction, and (b) a decimal.
3. Use the base 10 MAB to share (a) 392 among 7, (b) 3668 among 9. In each case, take photographs of the various stages involved and use these to illustrate a description of what you did and why.
4. How might you use the strategy, '6 whats are 438?' to mentally arrive at a solution for 438 shared among 6?

Equal groups

In their first year of school, children are often asked to help with the distribution of materials. For example, they might be asked to put 4 sheets of drawing paper or 2 pairs of scissors on each table. While this might look like sharing, the children are unlikely to view it as such as there is no necessity to attend to the whole (i.e. the pile of paper or the box of scissors) or the number of iterations (number of groups). The sole focus of attention is on the number of items per table, that is, the number *in* each group. While activities such as this help to establish the idea of equal groups, they are not multiplicative until at least two of the three aspects are coordinated simultaneously.

The **equal groups** idea for multiplication is primarily focused on the number *in* each group, with the number *of* groups being understood as the number of iterations of each group. As such it is related to addition, the only differences being that the sets being aggregated or counted are the same size and there are generally more than two of them. It is a counting-based idea that prompts counting-based strategies (see below).

In its most transparent form, the equal groups idea is devoid of context, for example, 'Make 5 groups of 7 counters. How many counters are there altogether?'. As word problems, however, these look more like *for each* problems, for example 'Sam has three bags of marbles. If there are five marbles in each bag, how many marbles does he have altogether?'. Despite this association with the *for each* idea, children are typically encouraged to solve word problems of this type by making three groups of 5 counters as shown in Figure 17.10, with the groups separated in space but not necessarily 'marked' in any way to emphasise the composite units involved.

Figure 17.10 Equal groups representation of Sam's problem

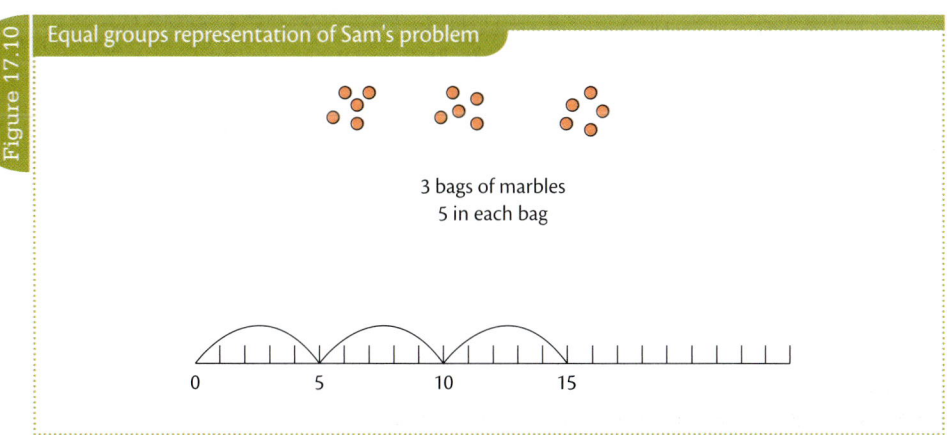

3 bags of marbles
5 in each bag

It is generally assumed that the *equal groups* idea is the starting point for teaching multiplication because of its close relationship to counting and additive processes. However, this brings with it a number of limitations, namely:

- the representation of equal groups as discrete groups of ones may inhibit children from seeing the group as a composite unit and prevent them from developing more efficient strategies
- it is difficult to appreciate all three aspects of the multiplicative situation at once. With the focus primarily on the number in each group and the number of groups, the total is often ignored until the model is constructed and the counting begins
- the equal groups of idea is only suitable for small, positive integer values (e.g. 6 groups of 8 or 23 groups of 4); it is not helpful to think about 57 groups of 81, $4\frac{5}{8}$ groups of $3\frac{2}{3}$, or 67.34 groups of 17.8, and it does not apply to negative numbers
- the physical representation of equal groups (e.g. 3 fours does not look like 4 threes) may inhibit recognition of the *commutative property* of multiplication, that is, that the product of a and b is the same as the product of b and a.

Repeated addition

Repeated addition is a counting-based strategy that, in its simplest form, is equivalent to the *make-all-count-all* strategy for addition discussed in Chapter 16. It is typically associated with the idea of equal groups and underpins the structure of the times tables (see Issues in teaching opposite). Initially repeated addition strategies are supported by physical models that are counted by ones in a serial, often rhythmic fashion until the number of groups counted is exhausted (e.g. for Sam's problem above: 1, 2, 3, 4, 5 … 6, 7, 8, 9, 10 … 11, 12, 13, 14, 15) or replaced by intermediary models such as number lines as shown in Figure 17.10). Some means of keeping track of the count is needed when physical models are unavailable. Some children will use their fingers both to model the count and to keep track of the count. For example, they will typically use one hand to model the count of the number in each group (1, 2, 3, 4, 5) and the other hand to keep track of how many groups they have counted (1, 2, 3). If this is the child's only strategy in these circumstances, it suggests that he/she does not trust the count (see Chapter 14) and that subsequent teaching would be better directed at building mental objects for the numbers to 10, as continued use of this type of strategy is unlikely to contribute to either conceptual understanding or procedural fluency.

Children who trust the count for the numbers to 10 are generally able to use repeated addition without the aid of materials. This may be achieved by skip counting, where the relevant number-naming sequence is known (see below), or the application of known facts and/or additive mental strategies. For example, for 17 multiplied by 3, a child might add 17 to 17 by adding 20 and taking off 3 to get to 34, then repeat this procedure to arrive at 51. However, this approach is limited unless some sort of record is kept of the number of groups counted.

Skip counting

Skip counting is a more sophisticated form of repeated addition that relies on known number-naming sequences (e.g. 2, 4, 6, 8, 10, 12 … or 5, 10, 15, 20, 25 …) that can be established from experiences with oral counting patterns and number chart activities. Initially, children will need to point to physical models of equal groups to support a skip count. In this case there is no need to keep track of the number of groups as the activity of pointing and counting proceeds until every group has been counted. Eventually the situation will not need to be modelled, but children will need to employ some sort of strategy to keep track of the count, such as fingers, tally marks, or rhythmic counting (e.g. 4, 8, 12 … 16, 20, 24 for 6 fours).

The other limitation with skip counting is that it really only works for a small number of groups and a group size generally less than 10 (e.g. 4 sixes, 7 eights, 9 threes) and it encourages a *count all groups* strategy to determine the 'harder to learn' facts such as 7 nines. Although children have little difficulty learning the number-naming sequences for counts of 2, 3, 5, and 10, and can generally count forwards or backwards by 3s from any starting point by the end of Year 2, skip counting by 6, 7, or 8 is much more problematic, particularly for students who do not trust the count or have little or no access to efficient mental strategies for addition. Also, although it is widely assumed, we know of no evidence that directly links skip counting to the efficient learning of multiplication facts. Indeed, it could be argued that attempting to learn the number facts by remembering the number-naming sequence and counting-all groups reinforces an additive, counting-based approach to multiplication that delays the transition from additive to multiplicative thinking in later years.

Having said this, there is considerable value in drawing children's attention to the patterns involved in different counts, as this supports number sense more generally and properties of divisibility in particular. For instance, recognising that multiples of 10 end with a zero, or that the digits in multiples of 3 less than 100 sum to 3, 6, or 9. Also, it is useful to encourage children to *build up from known* (e.g. for 7 nines, think: 5 nines are 45, 54, 63) rather than *count all groups*, as this extends to mental computation more generally (see array-based strategies below).

issues in teaching

Times tables

There is probably no issue in school mathematics of greater concern to parents, students, and teachers alike than the issue of learning the multiplication and division facts to 100, often referred to as the 'times tables'. However, we know from interviews with at-risk students (Siemon et al., 2001) that approximately 40 per cent of students leave primary school without a confident knowledge of all these facts and with little or no strategies to support mental computation beyond this (e.g. to calculate 23 nines mentally).

Access to meaningful, efficient strategies to determine the multiplication facts to 100 and beyond is non-negotiable. Automatic recall is a bonus. It should not be the focus of the endeavour.

The traditional 'times tables' are not really tables at all but lists of equations that effectively count equal groups in an additive fashion (e.g. 1 three, 2 threes, 3 threes, 4 threes, etc.).

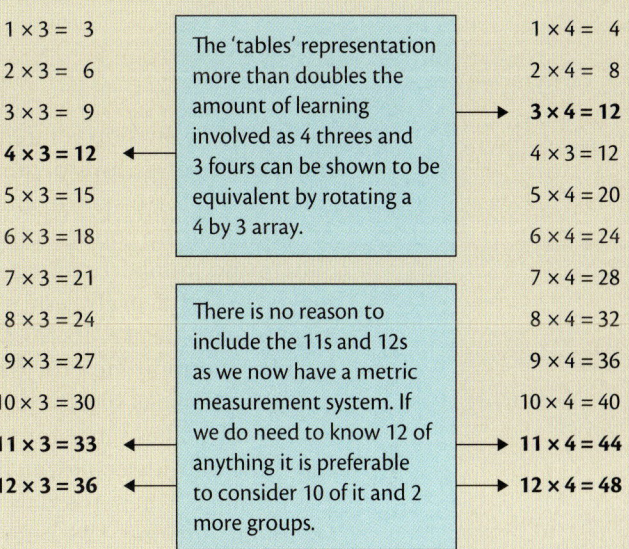

1 × 3 = 3	1 × 4 = 4
2 × 3 = 6	2 × 4 = 8
3 × 3 = 9	3 × 4 = 12
4 × 3 = 12	4 × 3 = 12
5 × 3 = 15	5 × 4 = 20
6 × 3 = 18	6 × 4 = 24
7 × 3 = 21	7 × 4 = 28
8 × 3 = 24	8 × 4 = 32
9 × 3 = 27	9 × 4 = 36
10 × 3 = 30	10 × 4 = 40
11 × 3 = 33	11 × 4 = 44
12 × 3 = 36	12 × 4 = 48

The 'tables' representation more than doubles the amount of learning involved as 4 threes and 3 fours can be shown to be equivalent by rotating a 4 by 3 array.

There is no reason to include the 11s and 12s as we now have a metric measurement system. If we do need to know 12 of anything it is preferable to consider 10 of it and 2 more groups.

This is an incredibly dense text that is confounded by the use of the word 'times'. What does '7 times 4' mean? Children know what 7 means and what 4 means, but how does this relate to '7 times 4'?

It has been claimed that oral skip counting (e.g. counting by 4s, 6s, 7s etc.) supports table facts. Do you agree/disagree? Why?

Rote learning has also been advocated as a means of learning the number facts. Find out what this means and why rote learning is no longer advocated.

Quotition

The **quotition** concept of division involves finding how many equal groups of a particular size are in a given amount (e.g. how many fours in 24?, how many halves in 3?). In quotition division, the total or whole (*dividend*) and the size of each group are known (*quotient*), and the question becomes 'how many groups *in* the total or whole?'. Sometimes referred to as *quotitive* or *measurement division*, this idea evolves from experiences with counting and measurement (e.g. how many paper clips will it take to measure the length of your desk?).

Figure 17.11 Quotition division

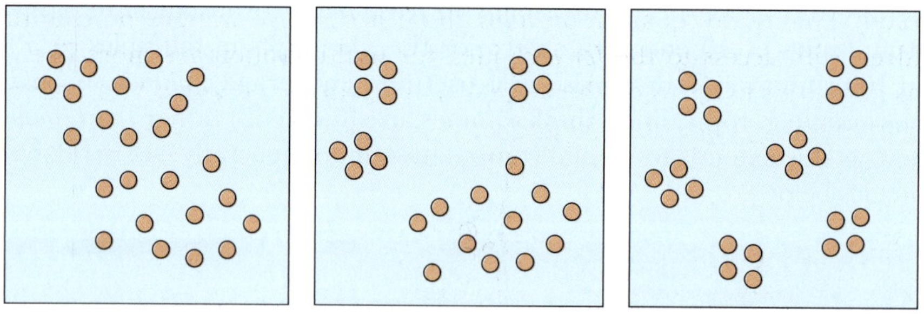

24 counters | Make fours | 6 fours in 24
How many fours in 24?

Quotition division is inherently related to counting in that it literally counts the number of groups or units in a given total or amount. To find how many fours in 24, for instance, children might count out 24 counters, make groups of 4 until all the counters have been used, then count the number of groups. Where the number-naming sequence for a count of fours is known, children may skip count orally and use their fingers to keep track of the number of groups (e.g. 4, 8, 12, 16, 20, 24 (six fingers showing) … there are 6 fours in 24).

The quotition idea for division is the inverse of the equal groups idea for multiplication. As such, it has many of the same limitations, in particular that it really only makes sense for relatively small whole number totals and groups. If this is the only idea children have for division it can lead to inefficient strategies. For example, when asked to solve the problem '128 divided by 6', a Year 7 girl set about drawing 128 ungrouped tally marks. When she had finished, she counted them all to check that she had 128, then proceeded to circle groups of 6. When this was no longer possible, she then counted the number of groups to conclude that there were 21 sixes in 128 (see Figure 17.12). Restricted to this

Figure 17.12 Count-all-groups solution to 128 divided by 6

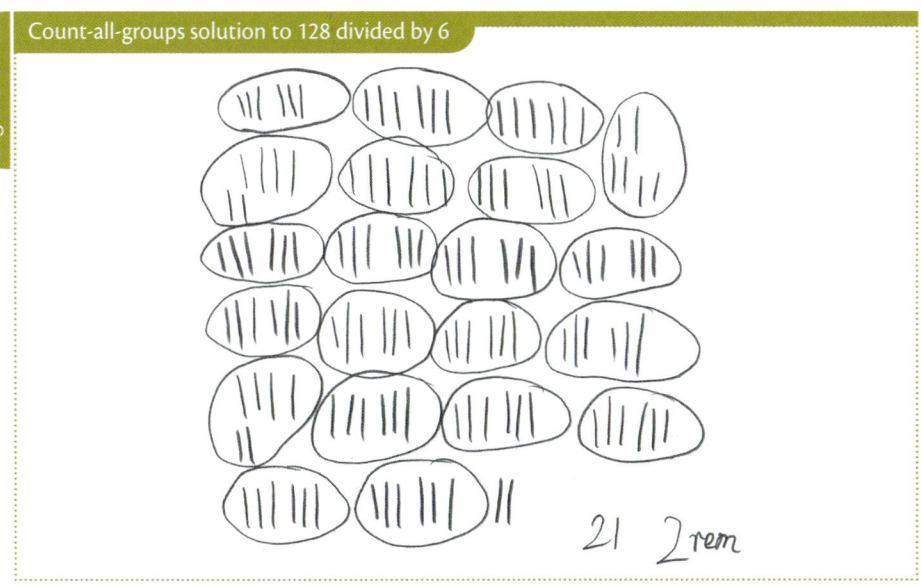

Source: Siemon et al. (2001)

notion of division, it is highly likely that she would experience considerable difficulty with division problems involving larger whole numbers, fractions, decimals, or proportional reasoning. For example, although it is possible to consider how many quarter oranges there are in 13 oranges by counting, children with access to the *for each* idea for multiplication are more likely to think about this in terms of 'there are 4 quarters in each orange; 13 oranges; so 13 multiplied by 4 quarters altogether'.

Repeated subtraction

Repeated subtraction is a counting-based strategy that is typically associated with quotition division and therefore with the equal groups idea for multiplication. While many quotition problems are solved by some form of repeated addition, they can also be solved by repeated subtraction. For example, consider the problem, 'Kate is making gift bags for her party. She wants to put 3 jelly snakes into each bag. If she has 36 jelly snakes, how many bags will have three jelly snakes?'. In its most elementary form, repeated subtraction is similar to repeated addition in that it involves physically representing the 36 snakes, counting 3 at a time, removing these from the collection as a group, then counting the number of groups. Without materials, repeated subtraction is really only possible where children know the backward naming sequence for 3s (36, 33, 30, 27, 24, 21, 18, 15, 12, 9, 6, 3, 0) and have some means of keeping track of the count as they go.

Counting backwards by ones and attempting to keep track of the counts of three in some way is grossly inefficient and prone to error. If this is the child's only strategy, it suggests that he/she does not trust the count (see Chapter 14) and that subsequent teaching would be better directed at building mental objects for the numbers to 10 rather than attempting to deal with division in this way.

As a strategy, repeated subtraction is clearly questionable given the modern emphasis on conceptual understanding and procedural fluency. Like the counting backwards strategy for subtraction, it is prone to error, and does not support the shift to multiplicative thinking that is better served by thinking about 'what do I have to multiply by?'.

The array/region idea

For our purposes here, an **array** is a rectangular arrangement of *discrete* objects in rows and columns (e.g. 4 rows of 6 counters) A **region** can also take this form (e.g. 4 rows of 6 square centimetres as shown in Figure 17.13) but, as a *continuous* representation, it can also be used to model the multiplication of multi-digit numbers in terms of their place-value parts (e.g. tens and ones by tens and ones), common fractions (e.g. $1\frac{2}{3} \times \frac{3}{4}$), and ultimately, algebraic expressions (e.g. $2x + 3$ by $x + 4$). In these contexts, the region idea is better known as the **area** idea for multiplication. While we will touch on the area idea below, the extended applications of the *region/area* model are considered in more detail in Chapter 24.

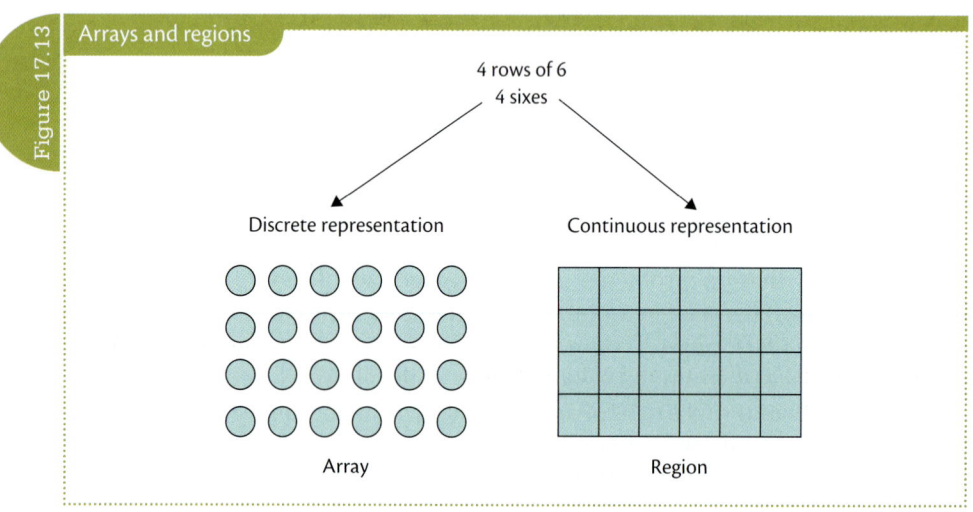

Figure 17.13 Arrays and regions

As both counting and splitting interpretations can be applied to these representations they will be considered separately here to illustrate the affordances and/or constraints offered by each.

Arrays/regions (equal groups)

From a counting perspective, arrays and regions can be interpreted as a count of equal groups where the array/region grows by adding groups of the same size to the bottom of the array. In this case, what stays the same is the size of each group, and what changes is the number of groups. The focus is on the size of the group (the *multiplicand*) and the strategies this interpretation affords are the same as those for equal groups; that is, some form of repeated addition or skip counting and/or number fact knowledge based on the 'times tables'. The limitations of this interpretation of the array model are the same as those for the equal groups idea (Figure 17.14).

Arrays/regions (times as many)

From a splitting perspective, arrays and regions can be interpreted in terms of the *times as many* or *for each* ideas, where the array/region grows by increasing the size of each group. For example, if 4 rows of one (4 ones) is duplicated it becomes 4 rows of two (4 twos), if 4 ones is tripled it becomes 4 threes (3 times as many), if 4 ones is increased by a *factor* of 5 it becomes 4 fives (5 times as many), and so on. In this case, what stays the same is the number of groups and

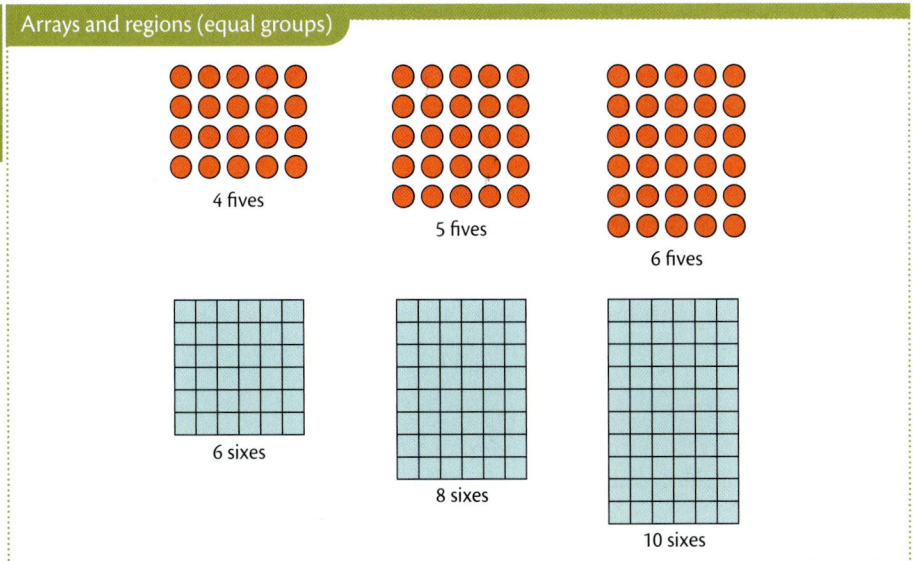

Figure 17.14 Arrays and regions (equal groups)

what changes is the size of each group (see Figure 17.15). Here, the focus is on the number of groups (the *multiplier*) and the strategies that this affords are based on the number of groups (referred to as *array-based strategies*) rather than the size of each group. For instance, '4 of anything' can be thought about in terms of doubling (e.g. for 4 nines, think double 9, 18, double again, 36). These strategies are described in more detail below.

The splitting-based interpretation of arrays and regions can be used to support a critical shift in thinking from counting-based interpretations and strategies to a more encompassing set of interpretations and strategies that support multiplicative thinking more generally. As such, the *array/region (times as many)* idea has a number of advantages over the equal groups idea. Specifically, it affords the following.

- All three aspects of the multiplicative situation can be observed at once; that is, the number of groups (rows), the equal size of each group (columns) and the total.

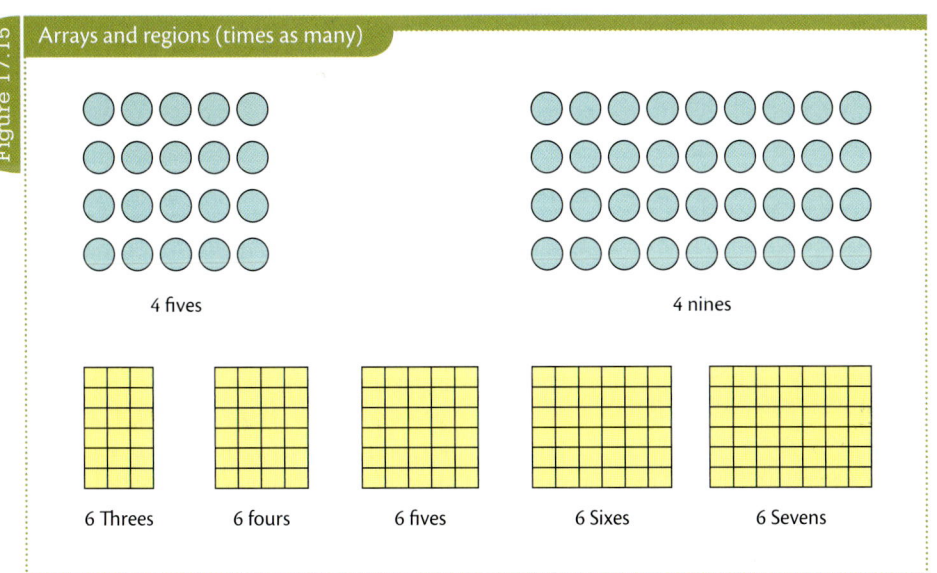

Figure 17.15 Arrays and regions (times as many)

- The focus on the number of groups increases the likelihood that children will see the group as a composite unit.
- It supports the development and use of more efficient mental strategies for the multiplication facts to 100 and beyond.
- The *commutative property* of multiplication can be demonstrated by rotating the array/region to show that the number in a rows of b is equivalent to the number in b rows of a. This can be used to reduce the amount of effort involved in building meaningful strategies for the multiplication facts to 100.
- Region representations interpreted from this perspective are particularly useful in helping children interpret and construct fraction diagrams and line models.
- Region representations underpin the *area* idea (see below), which can also be used to support the multiplication of multi-digit numbers (including decimal fractions), common fractions, and, ultimately, algebraic expressions.

think + link

The role of the *region* and *for each* ideas in the interpretation and construction of fraction diagrams and line models is explored in Chapter 18.

Given the critical importance of the *array/region (times as many)* idea in the shift from additive to multiplicative thinking and the importance of this in relation to meaningful participation in further school mathematics, teachers are strongly advised to explore children's thinking in this regard. One way of doing this is to use the array and region tool (Siemon, 2006; DEECD, 2010). This is a one-on-one interview that examines the strategies children use to determine the total number of partially hidden items. It provides an important indicator of the child's capacity to work with composite units and his/her readiness to work with more efficient, array-based mental strategies for the multiplication facts to 100. The interview generally takes less than 10 minutes and is supported by detailed teaching advice in the form of interpretations and starting points for teaching for four, increasingly sophisticated response categories (see Department of Education & Early Childhood Development, 2007).

for the classroom

Array and regions tool

Materials:
- 2 cards: Card 1 showing 4 rows of 6 dots; Card 2 blank and large enough to cover Card 1
- an A3 sheet of paper and 3 blank 'name-tags' (or business cards) measuring 9.5 cm by 5.5 cm (this needs to be accurate)

Instructions
1. Put Card 2 on top of Card 1 so that it is completely covered. Place it in front of the student, and say, 'I'm going to show you what is underneath this card very quickly and I want you to tell me what you notice'.
2. Remove Card 2 and replace it as quickly as possible. Note the student's response (e.g. 'there are dots in rows').
3. Say 'I'm going to show you some of the dots and hide the others'. As you say this, slide Card 2 over Card 1 so that only part of the array is shown, as in the diagram opposite. Ask, 'Can you tell me how many dots there are altogether?'.
4. Note the student's response. If correct (24 dots), remove the cards and place the A3 sheet of paper in front of the student together with the 3 blank name-tags and say, 'Can you tell me how many name-tags the same size as these could be made from this sheet of paper?'.
5. Note the student's strategy and response. Stop if the student appears unsure about how to proceed (e.g. guesses, or shows no signs of manipulating cards to determine how many might fit).

Source: Siemon (2006)

Array-based strategies

Array-based strategies build on the splitting-based interpretation of the array and region ideas for whole number multiplication where the focus of attention is on the number of groups (e.g. 4 of anything) rather than a count of groups (e.g. 1 four, 2 fours, 3 fours, etc.), which stems from the counting-based interpretation of arrays and regions and the traditional 'times tables'. Array-based strategies represent a fundamental shift in thinking from what is essentially an additive process (i.e. repeated addition of equal groups) to a multiplicative process that lays the foundation for multiplication more generally. Given their importance, these are dealt with on page 374 under the heading 'Building number fact knowledge and confidence'.

Cartesian product

The **Cartesian product** is based on splitting and is related to the *for each* idea for multiplication. It is typically associated with combination problems, such as 'How many different T-shirts are possible if they come in 4 different sizes, 5 colours, and 3 designs?'.

The Cartesian product idea supports the shift to a more generalised understanding of multiplication in terms of *factors* (or the '*by*' idea), and it accommodates repeated acts of multiplication. However, combination problems are more difficult than equal groups problems, as the numbers cannot be differentiated in terms of a *multiplier* and a *multiplicand*. Indeed, all the numbers invovled can be interpreted as multiplicands as they each represent the size of a particular group (4 sizes, 5 colours, 3 designs) and the question relates to the number of possible T-shirts, a fourth set constructed from all possible combinations of the elements of the other three sets.

While trial and error is a useful strategy to explore combination problems, it does not necessarily generate all possible outcomes. A helpful way to prompt a systematic consideration of all options is to reframe the situation in terms of the *for each* idea. In this case, how many outfits are possible *for each* size? This gives rise to the recognition that for each size (4) there are 5 different colours, and for each of these combinations (20) there are 3 possible designs, giving a total of 60 different T-shirts.

The capacity to recognise and represent problems of this type takes time and explicit attention. There are a number of ways in which Cartesian product problems can be represented to ensure that all combinations are recognised. For example, for problems involving two variables it is useful to construct a table. For problems involving a larger numbers of variables, a tree diagram is useful (Figure 17.16). However, both representations quickly become cumbersome once the size of the sets and/or the number of variables increases.

Area idea

The *area* idea for multiplication is an extension of the *region* idea. In measurement it represents the distribution of a length over a width. It is a continuous model that supports the multiplication of multi-digit numbers in terms of their place-value parts (e.g. hundreds, tens and ones by tens and ones), fractions, and ultimately algebra. At this level of schooling, its value lies in helping children come to understand how multiplication works across different place-value parts

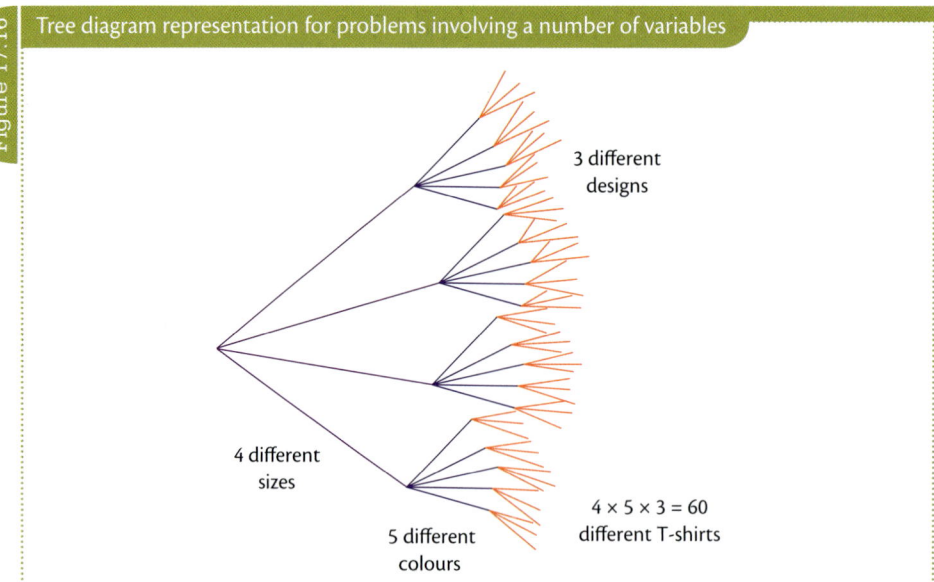

Figure 17.16 Tree diagram representation for problems involving a number of variables

and the efficiencies derived from being able to work in this way. For example, rather than physically representing or thinking about 4 seventeens in terms of 4 groups or rows of 17 ones, it is much easier to model this with base 10 blocks (MAB) as shown in Figure 17.17 and work with place-value parts.

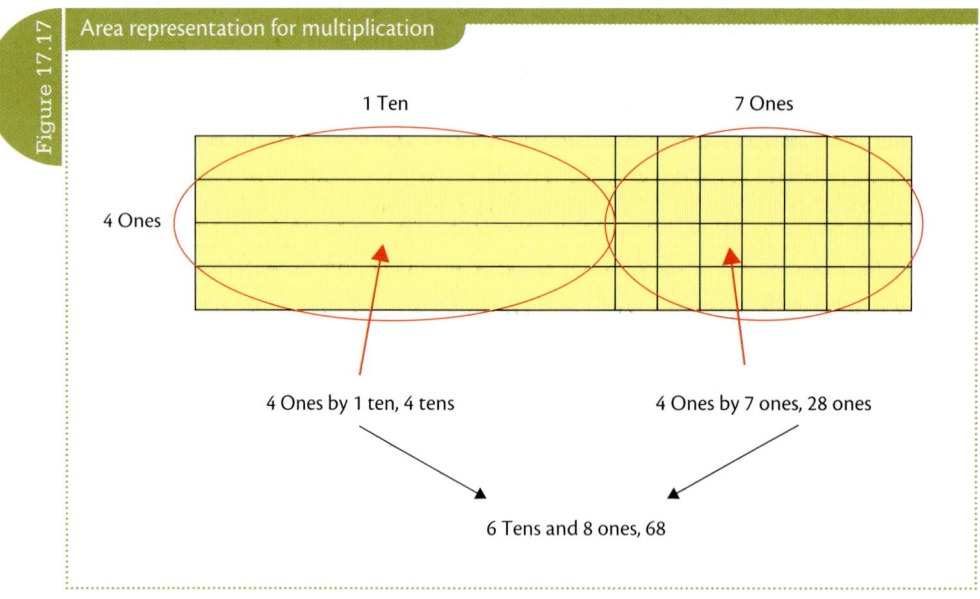

Figure 17.17 Area representation for multiplication

The area idea also provides a basis for the development of *extended fact knowledge* (e.g. 7 nines are 63, so 7 by 9 tens is 63 tens). If this is not understood it can lead to errors in written computation, particularly where children are encouraged to ignore place-value parts and use inappropriate language such as 'put down ... and carry ...'.

Problems involving the measurement of area can also lead to difficulties because of the language used to describe the units involved.

communicating mathematically

The language of measurement

There is a difference between 3 square metres and 3 metres squared. The first refers to 3 square metres, that is, 3 units of 1 square metre or an area of 1 metre by 3 metres. The second refers to an area 3 metres by 3 metres, that is, 9 square metres. The difference is a factor of 3.

This situation is not helped by the fact that the standard abbreviation for square metres is m², leading to the further complication that 3 m² could be read as '3 metres squared'.

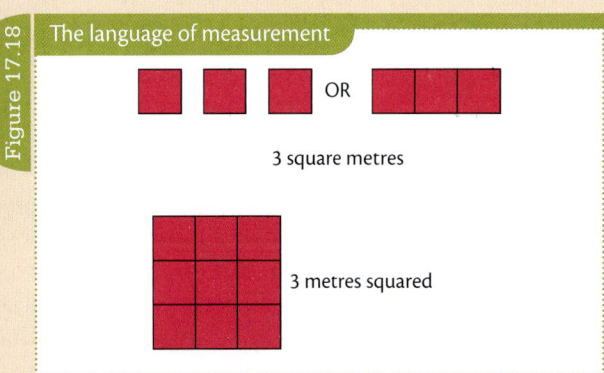

Figure 17.18 The language of measurement

Like other representations of multiplication, the area model quickly becomes cumbersome as the numbers involved increase. As a consequence, it is essential that children develop meaningful, efficient strategies for the multiplication facts to 100 and related division facts well before they leave primary school.

consider and discuss

Multiple representations

1. Consider and discuss how each of the following problems might be represented (e.g. physically, pictorially, symbolically). In particular, decide how each might be described in terms of the ideas presented above and what strategies might be used to solve each problem.
    a. In a card game each player is dealt 6 cards. There are 4 players. How many cards have been dealt in total?
    b. Jay rode his bike 2 kilometres to school. Kara had to ride 3 times as far. How far did Kara have to ride to school?
    c. A gardener has 9 rows of strawberry plants. There are 16 plants in each row. How many plants are there altogether?
    d. A 6-sided die and a coin are tossed to produce an ordered pair (e.g. a 5 and a head). How many different outcomes or ordered pairs are possible?
    e. Seven families shared an inheritance of $5680. How much did each family receive?
    f. My laundry is 3.4 metres long and 1.8 metres wide. What is the area of the floor to be tiled?
    g. How many 1 dozen egg cartons will be needed to package 3694 eggs?
    h. Mia travelled at an average speed of 75 kilometres/hour for 2 and a half hours. How far did she travel?
    i. What are your chances of winning Tattslotto?
    j. Mena travelled for 2 and a half hours at an average speed of 70 kilometres per hour. How far had she travelled after 1 and a half hours?
    k. If it takes 3 men 24 hours to paint the floor of a basketball stadium, how long will it take 8 men to paint the same sized floor?
2. Order the problems according to level of difficulty. Discuss your reasons.
3. These closed problems have been written in the style of most school mathematics texts (e.g. statement-statement-question). Write an open-ended problem for each category.

Building number fact knowledge and confidence

Developing a sound knowledge of the multiplication facts to 100 that can be used confidently and flexibly by the time students move to secondary school is non-negotiable. While most students will develop a degree of automaticity by this time as a consequence of familiar use, the most important outcome is that children have access to a range of efficient, meaningful strategies that they can apply not only to these facts but to mental computation in general. We believe this can be accomplished with less pain through the use of array-based strategies rather than the traditional 'times tables', but this requires a critical shift in thinking from a count of groups to a consideration of the same number of groups of any size, that is, from a counting-based to splitting-based interpretation of multiplication. For example, rather than thinking of the 4s facts as a count of fours (1 four, 2 fours, 3 fours, 4 fours, 5 fours, etc.), we advocate that the 4s facts be thought about in terms of 4 groups of anything (i.e. 4 ones, 4 twos, 4 threes, 4 fours, 4 fives, etc.). This shift in focus supports the development of multiplicative thinking more generally (e.g. the *factor* idea) and reduces the reliance on repeated addition and additive thinking.

The *array/region (times as many)* idea supports recognition of the *commutative property* of multiplication, that is, that $a \times b = b \times a$. This property can be used to significantly reduce the amount of time and effort involved in building array-based mental strategies for the multiplication facts to 100. For example, if 4 sevens are known, rotating the array through 90 degrees shows that this is equivalent to 7 fours (see Figure 17.19).

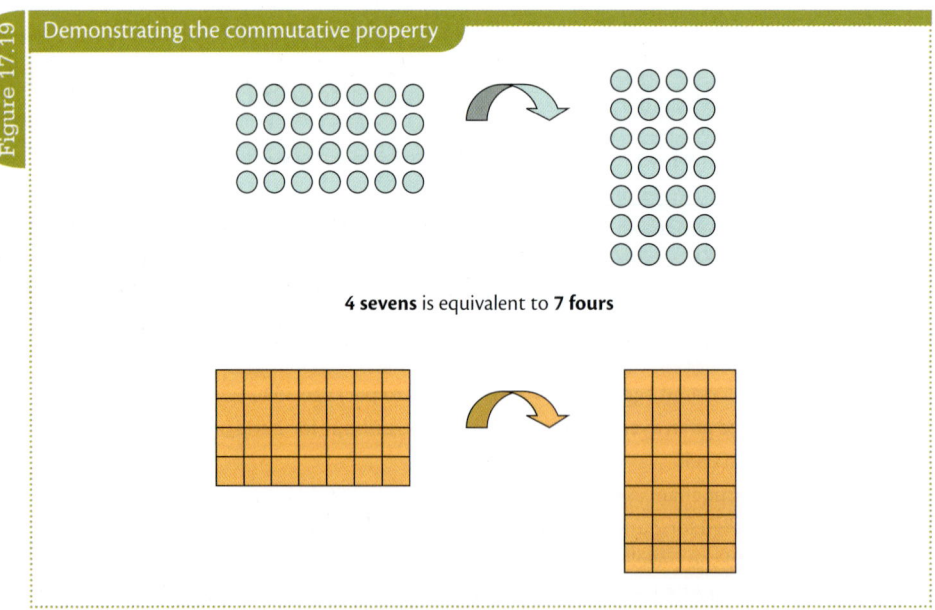

Figure 17.19 Demonstrating the commutative property

4 sevens is equivalent to **7 fours**

While this sounds straightforward, children need a considerable amount of experience with making, naming, rotating, and renaming arrays and regions to fully appreciate the significance of this property. This can be achieved through the use of interactive technologies (e.g. Barmby, Harries, Higgins & Suggate, 2009) and games such as Multiplication Toss.

for the classroom

Multiplication Toss

Equipment:
- 2 ten-sided dice (six-sided dice could be used initially)
- an A4 sheet of centimetre grid paper for each player or team (dot paper could be used initially)

Rules:
1. Two or more players/teams take turns to toss the two dice and use the resulting numbers to construct a region on the grid paper (arrays on the dot paper). For example, a 6 and 4 could be recorded as a 6 rows of 4 (6 fours) or as 4 rows of 6 (4 sixes).
2. The winner is the player/team who has covered the greatest area—no overlaps allowed.

This game can be played at various levels. Initially, 2 six-sided dice and dot paper could be used to make and name small arrays (e.g. 3 twos, 4 ones). This activity can be repeated with the 2 ten-sided dice and centimetre grid paper, and where certain number facts are known, the total can be recorded in the region.

A third level of the game allows children to rename the number of groups to produce 2 smaller regions. For example, if 8 and 6 are thrown and a player/team decide to take this as 8 sixes, they could rename and record this as 3 sixes and 5 sixes to strategically fill gaps that have arisen.

A fourth level of the game allows renaming and rotating. In this case, the 8 sixes might be renamed as 3 sixes and 5 sixes but the 5 sixes might be rotated and recorded as 6 fives.

When children are working at the fourth level of the Multiplication Toss game, they are implicitly recognising/using commutativity and distibutivity, for example:

$$8 \times 6 = (3 + 5) \times 6 = (3 \times 6) + (5 \times 6) = (3 \times 6) + (6 \times 5)$$

although they may not be able to record this formally.

Interestingly, commutativity is not something that appears to be constructed independently of schooling. For example, Schliemann, Araujo, Cassunde, Macedo and Niceas (1998) found that Brazilian street vendors with little or no schooling solved multiplication problems by repeated addition, whereas regular school attendees in Years 1 to 3 were more inclined to use multiplicative commutativity. They say this suggests that 'contrary to what was found in other studies … school instruction seems to play an important role in the emergence of use of multiplicative commutativity in the solution of multiplication problems' (p. 433).

To support the development of array-based mental strategies, a region representation of the number facts from 1×1 to 9×9 is used (see Table 17.1). The 10s facts should be known from place value but these can be included if desired. It is not possible to show the 0 facts, but experience with the Multiplication Toss game quickly establishes this knowledge as a 0 on any turn results in a loss of turn. There is, of course, no need to include the 11s and 12s as it is possible, from this array-based perspective, to think about this as '10 of it and 1 (or 2) more groups' if it is ever needed.

It is suggested that each child has a copy of this table, preferably printed with square 'cells' to demonstrate the commutative property by rotating (e.g. that 4 sevens is the same as 7 fours). As strategies are developed and named (e.g. doubles for the 2s facts), children can be encouraged to use a highlighter pen to shade in the 2s row. Once they become comfortable and accomplished with the 'turn arounds' as some children refer to renaming for example 7 twos as 2 sevens, the column that shows the count of twos can be shaded using the same highlighter pen. The strategies are presented in the most likely teaching sequence below. However, there are some important prerequisites that need to be established before children are ready to proceed.

Table 17.1 A region representation of the multiplication and division facts 1 × 1 to 9 × 9

×	1	2	3	4	5	6	7	8	9
1	1 one 1	1 two 2	1 three 3	1 four 4	1 five 5	1 six 6	1 seven 7	1 eight 8	1 nine 9
2	2 ones 2	2 twos 4	2 threes 6	2 fours 8	2 fives 10	2 sixes 12	2 sevens 14	2 eights 16	2 nines 18
3	3 ones 3	3 twos 6	3 threes 9	3 fours 12	3 fives 15	3 sixes 18	3 sevens 21	3 eights 24	3 nines 27
4	4 ones 4	4 twos 8	4 threes 12	4 fours 16	4 fives 20	4 sixes 24	4 sevens 28	4 eights 32	4 nines 36
5	5 ones 5	5 twos 10	5 threes 15	5 fours 20	5 fives 25	5 sixes 30	5 sevens 35	5 eights 40	5 nines 45
6	6 ones 6	6 twos 12	6 threes 18	6 fours 24	6 fives 30	6 sixes 36	6 sevens 42	6 eights 48	6 nines 54
7	7 ones 7	7 twos 14	7 threes 21	7 fours 28	7 fives 35	7 sixes 42	7 sevens 49	7 eights 56	7 nines 63
8	8 ones 8	8 twos 16	8 threes 24	8 fours 32	8 fives 40	8 sixes 48	8 sevens 56	8 eights 64	8 nines 72
9	9 ones 9	9 twos 18	9 threes 27	9 fours 36	9 fives 45	9 sixes 54	9 sevens 63	9 eights 72	9 nines 81

Prerequisite knowledge, skills and understandings

To be in a position to engage with array-based mental strategies for multiplication beyond the initial idea of doubling, children need to be able to demonstrate that they:

- *trust the count* (see Chapter 14); in particular, they need to recognise the numbers to 10 in terms of their parts
- recognise numbers to 10 and beyond as *composite units* (i.e. recognise and work with 1 eight instead of 8 ones)
- have a sound knowledge of two-digit *place value* and can rename two-digit numbers in terms of their parts (see Chapter 15)
- know their *doubles facts* to 20 and are developing effective strategies for doubling two-digit numbers
- have access to meaningful, efficient *additive strategies*, particularly the *make to 10* strategy (see Chapter 16)
- are comfortable with the *array/region (times as many)* idea for multiplication, the making and renaming of arrays/regions, and the commutative property for multiplication.

This does not mean that experiences with the different ideas for multiplication should be delayed until this knowledge is acquired. It is important that children have the opportunity to experience the ideas associated with both pathways to multiplicative thinking to broaden their concept of multiplication beyond a count of groups. However, a major reason why approximately 40 per cent of children currently leave primary school without a confident knowledge of the number facts to 100 is that they do not trust the count, and this makes it difficult for them to engage with the *for each* and *times as many* ideas and representations for multiplication. As a consequence, these children have little option other than to rely on inefficient counting-based strategies.

The multiplication facts to 100 can be referred to either as a count of groups (traditional 'times tables') or as the same number of groups of any size (array-based approach); this has important implications for how the table is read. For instance, the 7s facts can be read and represented as a count of sevens (reading down the 7s column) or as 7 of anything (reading across the 7s row). For array-based strategies, the facts are read and represented across the row. For example, we use '3s facts' to refer to 3 of anything (i.e. 3 ones, 3 twos, 3 threes, 3 fours, and so on). A major advantage of this approach is that it supports mental computation more generally.

Doubles strategy for 2s facts (2 ones, 2 twos, 2 threes, 2 fours …)

Doubling (and halving) appear to be intuitive strategies that develop early. Given that children generally know their doubles facts to 20 (i.e. 2 ones, 2 twos, 2 threes, 2 fours, etc.) by the end of Year 1 and are mostly capable of doubling any two-digit number by the end of Year 2, it seems a backward step to insist that children learn the 2s facts as the count of twos (i.e., 1 two, 2 twos, 3 twos, 4 twos, etc.), which is what is expected in the traditional times tables. The doubles strategy for 2 of anything is literally doubles, for example for 2 sevens, think: double 7 … 14.

The next step is to establish the 'turn arounds' or related facts, for example for 6 twos, think: same as 2 sixes, double 6 … 12.

Ultimately, if not already established, this strategy can be extended to larger numbers: 2 of anything—*doubles*.

'Double and one more' group strategy for 3s facts (3 ones, 3 twos …)

The double and one more group strategy for the 3s facts builds on the knowledge of doubles and additive strategies, for example for 3 fours, think: double 4 … 8, and 1 more four, 12.

The next step is to establish the 'turn arounds' or related facts, for example for 5 threes, think: same as 3 fives, double 5 … 10, 1 more five, 15.

This strategy can also be extended to larger numbers: 3 of anything—*double and 1 more group*.

'Double doubles' strategy for 4s facts (4 ones, 4 twos, 4 threes …)

The 4s facts also build on doubles and additive strategies, for example for 4 sevens, think: double 7 … 14, double again, 28.

The next step is to establish the 'turn arounds' or related facts, for example for 6 fours, think: same as 4 sixes, double 6 ... 12, double again, 24.

This strategy can also be extended to larger numbers: 4 of anything—*double doubles*.

'Same as' strategy for 0s and 1s facts

The 0s and 1s facts can be difficult for children if they have not had a lot of experience making and naming arrays/regions. Some children, for instance, will recognise that 0 eights means no eights, but think that 8 zeros sounds like there should be 8. With the 1s facts, some children, particularly those that do not trust the count or do not see 8 as a composite unit, will not be able to work with the notion of 1 group of 8, as to them it is only seen as 8 ones.

The *same as* strategy can be applied to the 0s, for example for 0 sixes, think: no sixes, 0.

The same strategy can also be used to make sense of the 1s, for example for 1 eight, think: same as 8.

0 or 1 of anything—*same as*.

'Relate to tens' strategy for 5s and 9s facts

This strategy builds on a solid understanding of place value, commutativity (e.g. 10 fours is the same as 4 tens), and halving strategies. It is particularly useful for the 9s (see below), but it also applies to the 5s. For example, for 5 eights, think: half of 10 eights, 80 ... so 40.

The related facts for 5s may already be known from children's experiences with learning to read an analogue clock, for example for 8 fives, think: 8 on a clock means 40 minutes, so 8 fives are 40. More importantly, it is not necessary to think about 'turn arounds' as they can be related to the 10s directly, for example for 7 fives, think: half of 7 tens, 70 ... so 35.

The *relate to tens* strategy can also be used to support the multiplication of larger numbers by 5, for example for 23 fives, think: half of 23 tens, 230 ... so 115.

For the 9s facts, the *relate to tens* strategy can also be used irrespective of the order of presentation, for example for 8 nines, think: less than 8 tens, 1 group of 8 less—although why it is 8 less may not be obvious unless this is linked to an array/region representation to show that 8 tens involves an additional column.

The relate to tens strategy can also be used to support the multiplication of larger numbers by 9, for example for 9×36, think: less than 10×36, 360 ... 1 group less, 330, 324.

Remaining fact strategies

Considered in this way, there are very few remaining facts to deal with (see Table 17.2). These can be tackled in a number of ways; for instance 6 of anything can be thought about in terms of '3 of it and 3 of it', or as '5 of it and 1 more group'. And, of course, 8 of anything can be thought about in terms of 'double, double, doubles'.

It is a good idea to invite students to invent and describe strategies more generally as other array-based strategies that might be used where children can build on known facts. For instance, 9 fives could be thought about as 8 fives (known fact) and 1 more 5, or 7 eights might be thought about as 3 eights and 4 eights, 24 and 32, 56.

Table 17.2 Remaining facts

×	1	2	3	4	5	6	7	8	9	10
1	✓	✓	✓	✓	✓	✓	✓	✓	✓	✓
2	✓	✓	✓	✓	✓	✓	✓	✓	✓	✓
3	✓	✓	✓	✓	✓	✓	✓	✓	✓	✓
4	✓	✓	✓	✓	✓	✓	✓	✓	✓	✓
5	✓	✓	✓	✓	✓	✓	✓	✓	✓	✓
6	✓	✓	✓	✓	✓				✓	✓
7	✓	✓	✓	✓	✓				✓	✓
8	✓	✓	✓	✓	✓				✓	✓
9	✓	✓	✓	✓	✓	✓	✓	✓	✓	✓
10	✓	✓	✓	✓	✓	✓	✓	✓	✓	✓

Think of multiplication for division facts

While division facts can be considered in terms of *quotition division* and thereby counting-based strategies (e.g. for 12 divided by 3, think, how many threes in 12), this approach is only suitable for small whole numbers. Ultimately, it leads to grossly inefficient and time-consuming strategies (see Figure 17.12).

A far better approach is to *think of multiplication*; in other words, 'what do I have to multiply by?'. This relates to the array-based strategies discussed above and ultimately supports a factor–factor–product approach to multiplication and division. For example, for 72 divided by 8, think: 8 whats are 72, 8 eights are 64, so it must be 9.

As an example of the power of this strategy, consider 128 divided by 6. This would be interpreted in terms of '6 whats are 128?', leading to a consideration of how many in each share, that is, *partition division*, and 'what do I have to multiply by?'. In this example, 6 by 2 tens is 12 tens (120), 8 left to share, so one more each, so 21.

for the classroom

A useful means of consolidating these strategies and building number fact knowledge to speed and accuracy is to use 2 ten-sided dice and Cuisenaire rods to generate Cuisenaire models that can be manipulated to support the use of known facts. For example, if an 8 and a 6 is thrown, this could be represented as 8 six-rods or 6 eight-rods. Children will almost invariably choose the smaller number of rods, and these can then be manipulated in a number of different ways (Figure 17.20). In this case, 6 eights could be arranged as 3 eights and 3 eights (24, 24, 48), or as 5 eights and 1 more eights (40, 48).

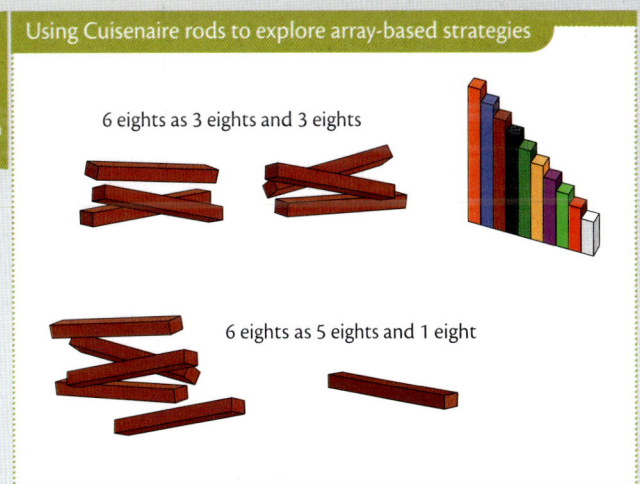

Figure 17.20 Using Cuisenaire rods to explore array-based strategies

6 eights as 3 eights and 3 eights

6 eights as 5 eights and 1 eight

integrating technology/ICT

Number Charts

The Number Charts activity from maths300 (Education Services Australia, 2010) has been described in Chapters 7 and 16. It is an excellent activity that encourages mental computation and reinforces the relationships between multiplication and division by providing a table in which two of the three relevant components are known or can be deduced; the object is to find the missing value (see Figure 17.21). The Number Charts environment provides different degrees of difficulty and provides a feedback mechanism that allows children to correct any errors before indicating the time taken to accurately complete the grid. These features are particularly useful in catering for the needs of mixed ability learners.

Figure 17.21 Number Chart

X	5	8		2
		32		
6			18	
				2
	45			

Computation strategies

As we have seen, multiplicative problems can be solved in a variety of ways, ranging from the use of *make-all-count-all* strategies to the confident use of known facts and relationships. Along the way, children will invent a number of informal written strategies to support their thinking. Some of these might look like the 'thinking strings' used above to illustrate the array-based mental strategies. Others will involve 'jottings' such as the two shown in Figure 17.22. The first of these uses place-value parts; the second uses repeat addition. In some instances (e.g. where answers and neat books are valued over thinking), such jottings are simply thrown away and all that is recorded is the equation and the answer. This is unfortunate, as such jottings provide valuable information for the teacher about what is known and where to start teaching.

Figure 17.22 Informal 'jottings' for multiplication

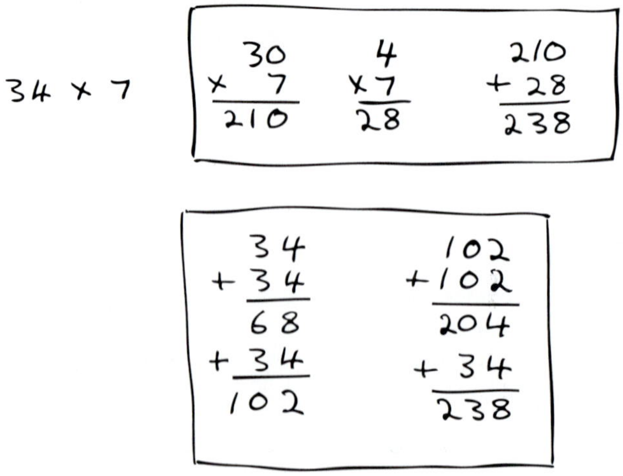

34×7

$$\begin{array}{r} 30 \\ \times\ 7 \\ \hline 210 \end{array} \quad \begin{array}{r} 4 \\ \times 7 \\ \hline 28 \end{array} \quad \begin{array}{r} 210 \\ +\ 28 \\ \hline 238 \end{array}$$

$$\begin{array}{r} 34 \\ +\ 34 \\ \hline 68 \\ +\ 34 \\ \hline 102 \end{array} \quad \begin{array}{r} 102 \\ +102 \\ \hline 204 \\ +\ 34 \\ \hline 238 \end{array}$$

Initial recording

Initial number fact knowledge for multiplication can be recorded in the same way as for addition and subtraction, that is 'horizontally' in the form of equations, or vertically to support regrouping (renaming) and subsequent work with multi-digit multiplication as shown in Figure 17.23.

Figure 17.23 Initial forms of recording for multiplication

$7 \times 4 = 28$

'Horizontal' equation form

This might be read as 7 times 4, 7 fours, or 7 multiplied by 4

$$\begin{array}{r} 4 \\ \times 7 \\ \hline 28 \end{array}$$

'Vertical' algorithmic form

Note, this is read as 7 fours (i.e. from bottom up) to support regrouping and multi-digit multiplication

Recording the initial number fact knowledge for division as an equation requires the use of the '÷' sign. This is read by many children who have only had equal group experiences of multiplication and division as 'how many' (e.g. see Bella's response on page 382 in Issues for Teaching). Given that this sign is only used for about two or three years at most and only in school contexts, it seems to us that it would be better ignored and referred to only in the context of calculator usage. Instead, there is an argument for using the vinculum (the horizontal bar introduced by the Arabs many years ago to separate the numerator from the denominator in fraction notation) or the forward slash (introduced at the time of the first printing presses and used in digital tools) to indicate division. Given the prevalence of all three signs for division, it is probably a good idea to introduce children to them all in the contexts in which they occur. Having said this, there is also a case for introducing the algorithmic form for division that supports trading (renaming) as it links to partition and the array-based strategy 'think of multiplication' (see Figure 17.24).

think + link

While children at this level understand that it is not always possible to share equally and that some items or amounts might be 'left over' or 'remain' at the end of sharing, it is not recommended that division with remainders be considered formally until the later years of primary school. Division with remainders will be considered in Chapter 24.

Figure 17.24 Initial forms of recording for division

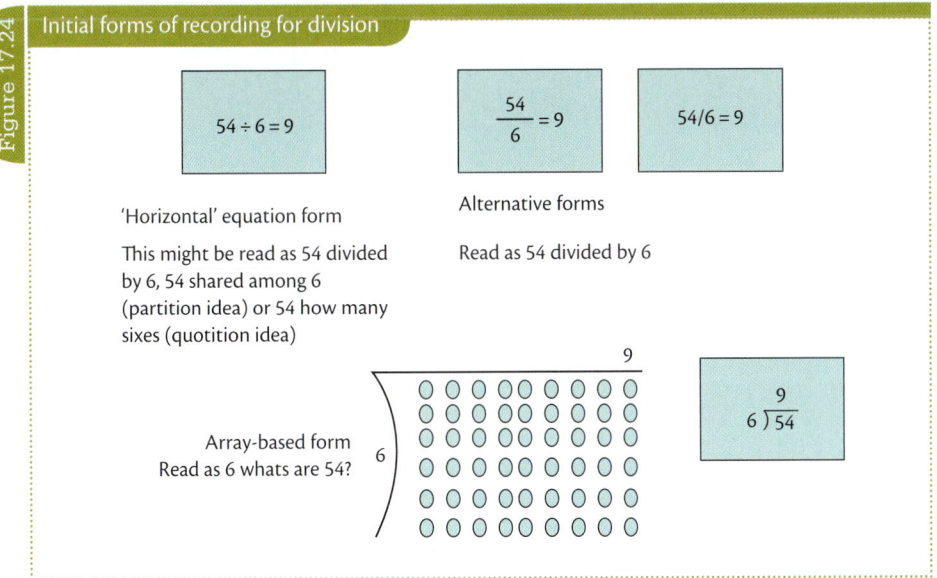

$54 \div 6 = 9$

'Horizontal' equation form

This might be read as 54 divided by 6, 54 shared among 6 (partition idea) or 54 how many sixes (quotition idea)

$\dfrac{54}{6} = 9$ $54/6 = 9$

Alternative forms

Read as 54 divided by 6

Array-based form
Read as 6 whats are 54?

$6 \overline{)54}$ with 9 on top

Difficulties with recording

Where children experience difficulty solving multiplication and division problems more formally, in particular, with the use of equations and/or written algorithms, it is generally because they are missing one or more of the above prerequisites for working with array-based strategies. Symbolic recording is very dense. Unless the meanings for the operations themselves are well understood and children have a well-developed sense of the numbers involved, many children will simply flounder.

issues in teaching

Symbolic recording

When to introduce 'formal recording' or algorithms is a vexed question for most teachers in the early to middle years of primary school. In a study on problem solving involving fourth graders (Siemon, 1993), a 'talking head' response format was used to elicit children's feelings and explanations about word problems in mathematics. These responses showed the considerable difficulty many children have at this level with the use of symbolic recording and algorithms.

In the first of the two responses, Bella (not her real name) shows that she is happy with her response to the algorithm vertically presented. However, her explanation shows that her recording was influenced by what she saw, heard, and wrote first in the more familiar, horizontal form of the multiplication fact, 7 × 6 = 42.

In the second response, Bella is clearly unhappy. She is possibly attempting to reproduce actions she has observed in relation to quotition division, but her response reveals much more.

Work with a friend to analyse Bella's response. What does it suggest is needed before children can be expected to engage with more formal types of recording?

Figure 17.25 Bella's 'talking head' response to two problems

This example suggests that teachers need to consider carefully when and how to introduce symbolic forms of recording. In particular, it suggests that once a fact is known, multiple forms of recording should be introduced at the same time, not sequentially as in the past. Number facts should not be written as unknown instructions to do something, but as a record of what has been arrived at as a result of working with materials in a way that supports the ideas involved or as the result of using a mental strategy. Until then, it is suggested that students use a numeral to indicate how many and a word to indicate how much, as in 6 eights, 7 threes and so on, and a sentence to indicate equality as in '4 nines is 36'.

Mental computation

Once children have access to meaningful, efficient strategies for the multiplication facts to 100 and the related division facts, they can be asked to solve relatively simple problems mentally, such as 37 sixes and 336 divided by 8. At this level, examples should be chosen carefully to promote the use of array-based strategies and known facts and avoid remainders. Children should be encouraged to share their strategies with each other and the class and, where appropriate, teachers can record these explanations in a written form (as in Table 17.3) to draw attention to the use of properties and strategies and model the use of equivalent number sentences.

Written solution strategies for multiplication

Initially, young children will record their solutions to tasks involving multiplication by drawing and recording the numerical result as in the Baa-Baa Black Sheep problem shown in Figure 17.3. Video snippets or photographs of children's work can be used to stimulate discussion and model written recording. For example, in the Baa-Baa Black Sheep problem, the teacher might do this by recording '5 threes is 15'. Eventually, phrases such as, '6 groups of 3 is 18' and '6 times 3 is 18' (once, twice, three times as many) can be used to introduce children to the counting and splitting-based interpretations of multiplication and the fact that we use the sign × for both. They can be encouraged to record their results in a variety of ways (see Figure 17.23).

As children move to problems involving two-digit by one-digit multipliers, it is important to work with the place-value ideas (regrouping/renaming) and the *array/region (times as many)* idea for multiplication, as the equal groups idea encourages repeated addition (see Figure 17.26).

The array/region idea encourages the use of extended facts and the *times as many* or *by* language. This can be supported by the use of number expanders as shown in Figure 17.27.

By the end of Year 5, children are expected to be able to 'use equivalent number sentences involving multiplication and division to find unknown quantities' (ACARA, 2010). Given that there will inevitably be some children who are able to deal with this a little earlier, it is worth considering some of the options for the example given in Figure 17.27 shown in Table 17.3.

Figure 17.26 Using base 10 blocks to model two-digit by one-digit multiplication

Equal groups representation for 6 x 45

Array/region representation for 6 x 45

Figure 17.27 Language and recording for two-digit by one-digit multiplication

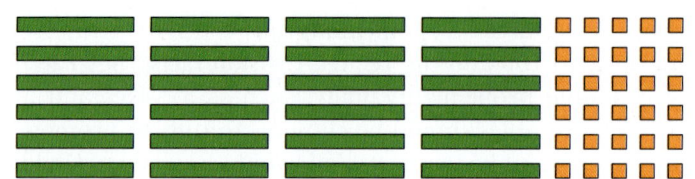

7 ones by 6 ones is 42

Record the ones with ones and the 4 tens to regroup

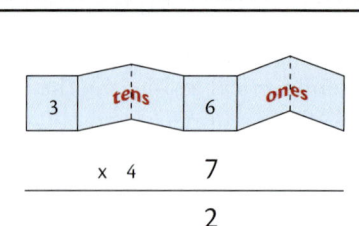

7 ones by 3 tens is 21 tens

And 4 more tens is 25 tens

Record the ones with the ones and the tens with the tens

25 tens and 2 ones or 252

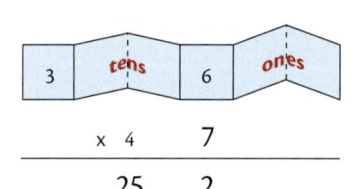

Table 17.3 Using equivalent number sentences to solve multiplication problems

Distributive property Relate to 10s and doubles strategies	Distributive property Place value, extended and known facts	Associative property Relate to 10s strategy

7 × 36 = (5 + 2) × 36
  = (5 × 36) + (2 × 36)
  = 180 + 72
  = 252
	7 × 36 = (7 × 30) + (7 × 6)
	  = 210 + 42
	  = 252
		7 × 36 = 7 × 4 × 9
		  = 28 × 9
		  = 280 − 28
		  = 252

While base 10 materials such as MAB can be used initially to model two- and three-digit multiplication by a single digit multiplier and to demonstrate the process of regrouping, this becomes cumbersome for larger whole number multiplication. Number expanders can be used to support renaming as appropriate in these situations, but there is a strong argument that children should not be expected to solve such problems without a confident understanding of the numbers they were working with. This suggests that it is worthwhile making the thinking explicit when working with larger numbers (see Table 17.4).

Table 17.4 Thinking, language, and recording to support multiplication of a four-digit number by a one-digit multiplier

Thinking	Language	Recording
7 times as many ones, 7 threes, 21	6783 multiplied by 7 7 by 3 ones, 21 Record the ones with the ones and the 2 tens to be regrouped	6 7 8 3 × ₂7 ――――― 1
7 times as many tens, 7 by 8 tens, 56 tens	7 by 8 tens, 56 tens And 2 more tens (cross out 2), 58 tens Record the tens with the tens and the hundreds to be regrouped	6 7 8 3 × 5₂7 ――――― 8 1
7 times as many hundreds, 7 by 6 hundreds, 42 hundreds	7 by 7 hundreds, 49 hundreds And 5 more hundreds (cross out 5), 54 hundreds Record the hundreds with the hundreds and the thousands to be regrouped	6 7 8 3 × 5₅₂7 ――――― 4 8 1
7 times as many thousands, 7 by 6 thousands, 42 thousands	7 by 6 thousands, 42 thousands And 5 more thousands (cross out 5), 47 thousands Record the thousands 47 481	6 7 8 3 × ₅₅₂7 ――――― 4 7 4 8 1

integrating technology/ICT

Recognising the limitations

Calculators are an important and valuable tool for performing calculations when the object of the exercise is mathematical problem solving and where the numbers or measures and/or the number of steps involved are simply too difficult to keep in one's head. However, it is important to be aware of their limitations. Calculators are of little use in discerning what the problem is asking, recognising what is meant by the numbers involved, or choosing the appropriate operation(s). While they can be used to keep track of the steps involved if the calculator has a memory function, different calculators have different ways of doing this and this may or may not create additional problems.

Solving multi-step problems on a calculator can lead to errors in recording. For example, finding the total cost of 8 items at $4.35 and one item costing $9.50 involves the following sequence of buttons. This arrives at 44.30, which is interpreted as $44.30.

$$8 \times 4.35 = + 9.50$$

However, when asked to record the solution in writing, a Year 4 child wrote:

$$8 \times 4.35 = 34.80 + \$9.50 = \$44.30$$

While this reflects the sequence of events on the calculator, it completely ignores the use of the equals key. This suggests that teachers need to attend to the conventions of written recording and the meaning and use of the equals sign alongside calculator usage.

Written solution strategies for division

Initially young children will record their solutions to division tasks by drawing and recording the numerical results. If the context is partition (e.g. 24 counters shared among 3), this might be written as '8 in each share'. If the context is quotition (e.g. 'how many threes in 24'), the result might be written as '8 threes'. Eventually, both situations can be described as '24 divided by 3 is 8' and the various ways of recording division can be introduced, that is, $2\frac{4}{8} = 3$ and $24 \div 8 = 3$, noting that the use of the fraction form only applies for partition division (i.e. 24 divided into 8 equal parts).

As children develop confidence in the use of mental, array-based strategies for the multiplication facts to 100 and the related division facts, they can be encouraged to record their results in a variety of ways (as in Figure 17.24). As they move to problems involving two-digit numbers divided by one-digit divisors, it is important to work with place-value ideas (trading/renaming) and the *partition* idea for division, as the quotition (equal groups) idea encourages inefficient additive strategies (see Figure 17.28 and Table 17.5).

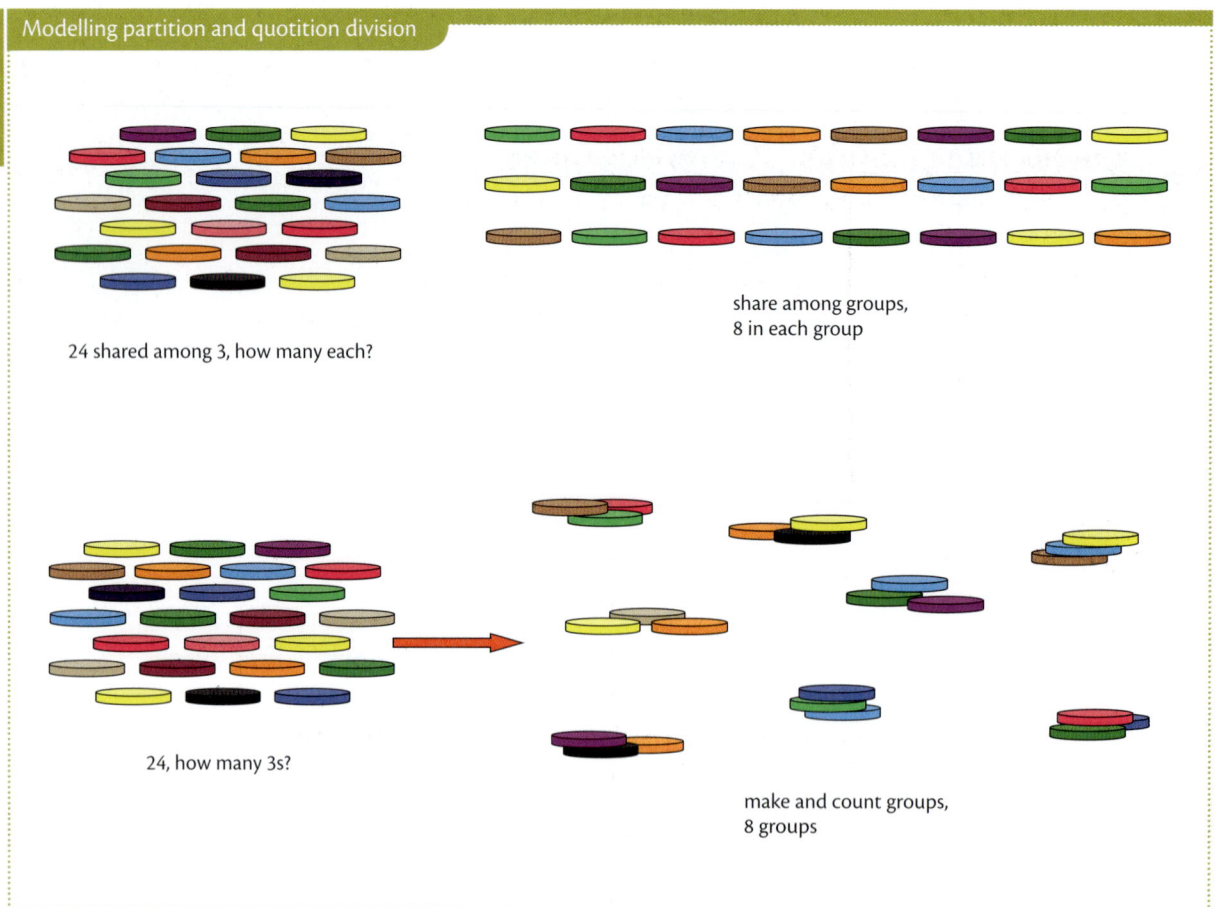

Figure 17.28 Modelling partition and quotition division

Table 17.5 Materials, language, and recording to support division of a two-digit number by a one-digit divisor

Materials	Language	Recording
	54 divided by 3	$3\overline{)54}$
	Can we share 5 tens among 3?	
	Yes, 1 ten each, record with the tens.	
	How many have we shared? 3 tens.	
	How many left to share?	$\begin{array}{r}1\\3\overline{)54}\\30\\\hline 24\text{ ones}\end{array}$
	2 tens and 4 ones.	
	Can't share tens, trade for ones, 24 ones to share	
	Can I share 24 ones among 3?	$\begin{array}{r}18\\3\overline{)54}\\30\\\hline 24\text{ ones}\\24\\\hline 0\end{array}$
	Think: 3 whats are 24?	
	3 eights are 24, so 8 ones each.	
	Record with the ones.	
	How many have we shared? 24.	
	Any left to share? No.	

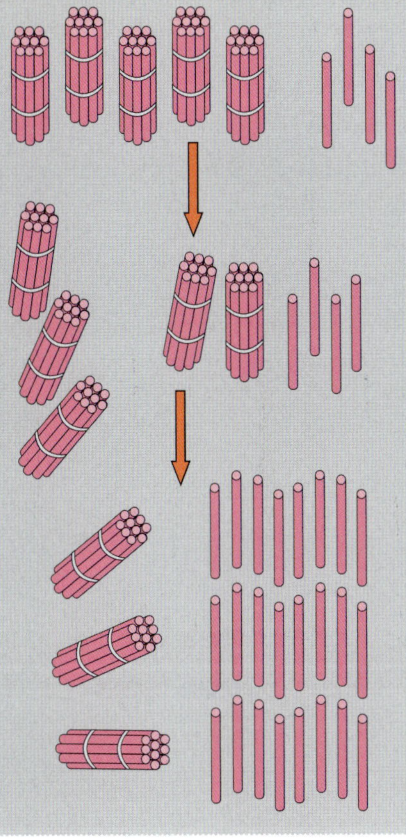

Children can be introduced to an alternative form of recording (see Figure 17.29) once they are comfortable with the trading and renaming processes involved in partitive division.

Figure 17.29 Alternative form of recording

$3\overline{)54^{24}}$ with 18 above

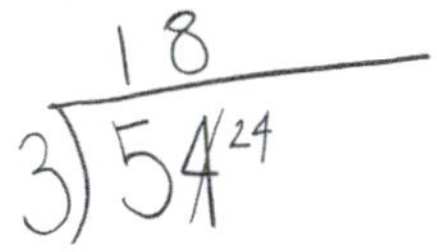

Base 10 materials (e.g. MAB) should be used to model three- and four-digit numbers divided by a single-digit divisor with trading until children are comfortable with the process. This is particularly important for problems that involve an internal zero, such as 1236 divided by 9, as this can be a source of difficulty for many children if it is not linked to materials first. Eventually, students should be encouraged to think about 'what do I have to multiply by' as shown in the example in Table 17.6.

Table 17.6 Materials, language, and recording to support division of a four-digit number by a one-digit divisor

Materials	Language	Recording
	4856 divided by 8 Can we share thousands? No. Rename as 48 hundreds. Think: 8 whats are 48? 8 sixes are 48, so 6 hundreds each, record in the hundreds place.	$8\overline{)4856}$ $\phantom{8\overline{)}}6$ $8\overline{)4856}$
	Can we share tens? No. Record 0 in the tens place and trade the tens for ones. 56 ones to share.	$\phantom{8\overline{)}}60$ $8\overline{)485\cancel{6}\,^{56}}$
	Can we share ones? Yes. Think: 8 whats are 56? 8 sevens are 56, so 7 ones each, record in the ones place.	$\phantom{8\overline{)}}607$ $8\overline{)485\cancel{6}\,^{56}}$

consider and discuss

Division recording

Consider and discuss all the ways in which the following problems might be solved (e.g. materials, drawings, written strategies, calculators). Compare and contrast the strengths and weaknesses of each. What methods/strategies support the development of multiplicative thinking?

1. A bike shop sold 9 bikes over the weekend for a total price of $5283. What was the average price of each bike?
2. A chocolate manufacturer packages chocolates in heart-shaped boxes. Each box contains 7 chocolates. He has 47 607 chocolates. How many boxes will this produce?

Estimation

The ability to estimate requires a well-developed sense of number, a knowledge of number facts and relationships, and an understanding of the meanings of the operations. In the past, teachers encouraged children to estimate before they had access to these capacities, with the result that they had no other option but to guess. Estimation is a complex skill that requires the integration of a number of ideas and strategies. For instance, consider how you would estimate the number of counters in a jar? What do you need to know?

Children need plenty of opportunities to explore how estimates might be arrived at for problems such as 356 multiplied by 6 or 549 divided by 9. For example, it might make sense to consider 356 as halfway between 3 hundred and 4 hundred, so, multiplying each by 6, it will be halfway between 1800 and 2400, that is, 2100 hundred. Alternatively, 356 might be thought about as 3.5 hundreds, double that is 7 hundreds, triple that is 2100.

did you know?

A method of multiplication reputedly used by Russian peasants until the early part of the nineteenth century involved doubling and halving. For example, to multiply 27 by 29, the number on the left was repeatedly halved, ignoring remainders, while the number on the right was repeatedly doubled until the number on the left was reduced to 1 (shown in the first box). Then the numbers in the right-hand column that corresponded to odd numbers in the left-hand column were recorded and summed (second box), the result, 783, is the product of 27 and 29.

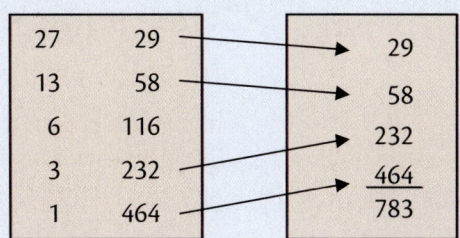

Why does this work? Hint: Write 27 in binary (base 2) notation.

Problem solving

Solving problems requires that the problem is analysed and interpreted relative to context, a strategy is chosen and applied, and the outcome reviewed and justified. Interpreting multiplicative situations can be compounded by the different ways in which multiplication and division can be represented in word problems. Other factors, such as the number of steps involved, the amount of information (too little, too much), the visibility of the operation(s) involved (transparent, masked), and the nature of the numbers involved can also have an impact on problem difficulty. For example, consider the following problems.

1. A nursery had 14 varieties of native grass and 6 different sized pots. How many pots would be needed to plant each variety of grass in each size pot?
2. A 4 metre fencing rail costs $27 and each fence post costs $16. How much will it cost to fence a triangular enclosure using 12 fencing rails?
3. An outdoor education camp provides archery, abseiling, a ropes course, badminton, kayaking, and orienteering. If there are 59 children at the camp and all activities are offered at the same time, how many children are at each activity?
4. The tennis championship organisers expect to use 4 new balls per match. There will be 53 matches. If tennis balls are packaged in cans of 3, how many cans of balls will need to be purchased?

The first is compounded by the fact that it is not clear how the problem might be represented. The result is that the operation required is not immediately obvious; that is, the problem is *masked* to some extent by the context and language involved (see Chapter 16 for similar examples of masked additive problems). The second problem requires the solver to recognise that there is not enough information. This may prompt the realisation that there is more than one possibility and an exploration of the possibilities through drawings and/or a table. The third problem requires some assumptions to be made as it is not clear what has to be done (if equal numbers are not assumed it is an open-ended additive task, but if equal groups are assumed it involves division and a decision about how to deal with the 'remainder'). The fourth problem is relatively straightforward but involves two steps.

Other sources of difficulty

Difficulties with representations

> the system of signs that is available to pupils when they solve multiplicative reasoning problems has a significant effect on their thinking … This means that, when we propose problems to children, we need to consider what systems of signs we are asking them to use. Their problem-solving capacity is not fixed, but can be enhanced or constrained by the representational environment in which they are solving the problem. (Nunes & Bryant, 1996, p. 194)

It is important to expose children to a wide range of different problem types so that they are in a position to recognise what is required and how the problem situation might be represented. Signs, symbols, and different ways of recording can be problematic for children who do not understand the different meanings for multiplication and division.

Discourse patterns and problem structures can be a source of difficulty. For instance, children are typically introduced to multiplication and division in the form of abbreviated 'action stories' that have a particular discourse structure consisting of two or more statements followed by a question. For example:

Statement A   The children were given 6 bags of marbles.
Statement B   Each bag contained 8 marbles.
Question   How many marbles did the children have altogether?

In this case the problem is straightforward, but when word problems are presented with extraneous information, information in associated images or tables, or in an unfamiliar context, these 'stories' can present problems for young readers. It is worth talking about problem 'genres' in the same way as is done in literacy to draw attention to the information sources and assumptions involved.

The problem with zero

Multiplication by powers of 10 introduces a problem that often leads to inappropriate 'rules', such 'when you multiply by 10, add a 0'. This is clearly not a rule in the conventional sense, as it is not true. Adding a 0 will leave the number unchanged. Of course, that is not what is meant by 'adding' here—what it means is 'write a 0 after the last digit'. While this might 'work' in the short term (e.g. see the child-invented algorithm in Figure 17.30), like the related 'rule' that the decimal point 'moves' when numbers are multiplied or divided by powers of 10 it is ultimately unhelpful, as it diverts attention from the numeration ideas involved and frequently leads to error. For example, students who are not sure how many zeros to 'add' or how many place to 'move' when multiplying or dividing by powers of 10 will often miscount places and 'be out' one or more powers of 10. Errors such as this can have catastrophic effects, as we shall see in Chapter 18.

Figure 17.30 Playing with zeros

Single and double ice creams available
Single – 150 millilitres (mL)
Double – 250 millilitres (mL)

A milk bar owner sold 40 single and 20 double ice creams.
If a single is 150 mL and a double is 250 mL, how much ice cream has he sold?

Show or explain your working in as much detail as possible.

$$\begin{array}{r} \overset{2}{1}5 \\ \times\ 4 \\ \hline 60 \\ +\ \infty \\ \hline 6000\ mL \end{array} \qquad \begin{array}{r} \overset{1}{2}5 \\ \times\ 2 \\ \hline 50 \\ +\ \infty \\ \hline 5000\ mL \end{array}$$

$$\begin{array}{r} 6000 \\ +\ 5000 \\ \hline 11000\ mL \end{array}$$

handy hint

Multiplying by powers of 10

When children are first introduced to the idea of multiplying a multiple of 10 by a single digit number, it is best to deal with this situation in words (e.g. 2 by 4 tens) as this appeals directly to extended fact knowledge, place-value knowledge and renaming. In this case, 2 by 4 tens is 8 tens, which is necessarily recorded as 8 tens and 0 ones—the 0 is not 'added'; it is warranted because there are 0 ones.

Difficulty arises in division problems where there are internal zeros in the number to be divided or where there is one or more internal zeros in the quotient. These situations can be avoided if they are adequately addressed in conjunction with base 10 materials before proceeding to written algorithms (see discussion above).

Conclusion

Multiplicative thinking involves recognising and working with relationships between numbers, whereas additive thinking only requires a capacity to work with the numbers themselves. Multiplicative thinking develops from the two fundamental activities of counting and splitting. Counting-based ideas and strategies build on young children's experiences with addition and subtraction and can be used to represent and solve a range of multiplicative problems that involve relatively small whole numbers. However, a counting basis does not support the thinking required to represent and solve problems involving common fractions and decimals. Ideas and strategies based on splitting appear to emerge, at least in their elementary forms, alongside the emergence of counting. As the splitting notion involves operations such as enlarging, shrinking, and replicating (as opposed to aggregating and disaggregating), it supports work with a wider range of numbers, particularly fractions and decimals, and ultimately with non-linear, functional relationships.

To become confident multiplicative thinkers, children need a well-developed sense of number and a deep understanding of the many different contexts in which multiplication and division can arise. The transition from additive strategies to meaningful, mental strategies that support multiplicative reasoning more generally requires a significant shift in thinking from a count of equal groups and repeated addition to the *for each* and *times as many* ideas for multiplication. While the array and region ideas for multiplication can be used to support a count of equal groups, their power lies in the fact that they can be used to underpin this important shift in thinking and, ultimately the factor–factor–product idea. The region and for each ideas are also critically important in the interpretation and construction of fraction representations.

key terms

Array: situations where the number in each group and number of equal groups are aligned as discrete elements in rows and columns (e.g. strawberry patch with 6 rows and 9 plants in each row)

Cartesian product or 'for each' idea: situations involving combinations (e.g. 4 pants, 3 tops, how many combinations) or rates (e.g. $1.75/kilogram, how much for 3.5 kg?)

Composite units: units that are themselves composed of units (i.e. recognising 6 as 1 six not 6 ones)

Equipartitioning: process of dividing (usually physically) a quantity or collection into equal parts with no remainder

Groups of: situations where the number of equal groups (multiplier) and the size of each group (multiplicand) is known and the task involves finding the total number (product); generally involves integer values for the number in each group and the number of groups (e.g. 3 groups of 4)

Multiplicative thinking: capacity to work with an extended range of concepts, meanings, and representations for multiplication and division in a variety of contexts

Partition (sharing) idea: situations where the total (dividend) and the number of groups or shares (divisor) is known, and the task involves finding the number in each group or share (quotient)

Quotition (how many groups in): where the total and the size of the group is known and task involves finding the number of groups

Region/Area: as for arrays, but continuous rather than discrete, this accommodates ones by ones (regions) and multiplication by place-value parts (e.g. 4 tens 2 ones by 3 tens 5 ones) and non-integral measures (e.g. 3.5 by 2.7 or fraction multiplication)	Splitting: action of simultaneously creating multiple versions of a collection or whole or the fair sharing of collections or wholes to produce equal parts

Review questions

1. What prerequisite knowledge and skills are needed to support multiplicative thinking?
2. What marks the shift from additive to multiplicative thinking and why is this important?
3. Name and illustrate the different ideas for multiplication.
4. Name and illustrate the two key ideas for division. Discuss the strengths and limitations of each.
5. What advantages do the 'array' and 'region' ideas have over the 'groups of' idea?
6. Describe and write at least two word problems to illustrate the 'for each' or 'Cartesian product' idea for children in Years 3 and 4.
7. What is the problem with the oft-cited strategy of 'adding a zero' for multiplying by 10?
8. The quotition language (this goes into that) for division is not recommended. Why?
9. Solve the problems listed in the problem-solving section, identify the multiplicative idea represented by each, and discuss your solution strategies with at least two people. What did you notice?
10. How might you solve the problem shown in Figure 17.30 in a way that makes effective use of place-value knowledge? What would your response be to the child whose working appears in Figure 17.30?

Key references

Anghileri, J. (1989). An investigation of young children's understanding of multiplication. *Educational Studies in Mathematics, 20*(3), 367–385.

Confrey, J., Maloney, A., Nguyen, K., Mojica, G. & Myers, M. (2009). Equipartitioning/splitting as a foundation for rational number reasoning using learning trajectories. In M. Tzekaki, M. Kaldrimidrou & C. Sakondis (Eds.), *Proceedings of the 33rd Conference of the International Group for the Psychology of Mathematics Education*, Vol. 2, pp. 345–352. Thessalonika, Greece: IGPME.

Greer, B. (1992). Multiplication and division as models of situations. In D. Grouws (Ed.), *Handbook of Research on Mathematics Teaching and Learning* (pp. 276–295). Reston, VA: NCTM and Academic Press.

Jacob, L., & Willis, S. (2001). Recognising the difference between additive and multiplicative thinking in young children. In J. Bobis, B. Perry & M. Mitchelmore (Eds.), *Numeracy and Beyond (Proceedings of the 24th Annual Conference of the Mathematical Education Research Groups of Australasia* pp. 306–313). Sydney: MERGA.

Lamon, S. (1996). The development of unitising: Its role in children's partitioning strategies. *Journal for Research in Mathematics Education, 27*(2), 170–193.

Mulligan, J., & Mitchelmore, M. (1997). Young children's intuitive models of multiplication and division. *Journal for Research in Mathematics Education, 28*(3), 309–330.

Nunes, T., & Bryant, P. (1996). *Children doing Mathematics*. Oxford: Blackwell.

Siemon, D., & Breed, M. (2005). From additive to multiplicative thinking: The big challenge in the middle years. In J. Mousley, L. Bragg, & Campbell, C. (Eds.), *Mathematics: Celebrating Achievement. Proceedings of the annual conference of the Mathematical Association of Victoria*. Melbourne: MAV.

Steffe, L. (1992). Schemes of action and operation involving composite units. *Learning and Individual Differences, 4*(3), 259–309.

Websites

www.simerr.educ.utas.edu.au/numeracy/critical_numeracy/critical_numeracy.htm

www.thenetwork.sa.edu.au/teachingandlearning

http://activated.act.edu.au/ectl

www.maths300.esa.edu.au

18 Introducing Fractions and Decimal Fractions

Contents

Introduction	395
Making sense of fractions	397
Developing fraction knowledge and confidence	411
Introducing decimal fractions	422
Consolidating understanding	429
Conclusion	434

Chapter objectives

This chapter will enable the reader to:
- Appreciate the different meanings and representations of fractions
- Become aware of the key generalisations needed to work more formally with fraction ideas and representations
- Use partitioning strategies to construct fraction diagrams and line models
- Recognise the important connections between fraction representations and the array/region (times as many), for each, and partition ideas for multiplication and division
- Understand decimal fractions, both as fractions and as an extension of the base 10 numeration system, and the 'big idea' that '1 tenth of this is 1 of those'
- Appreciate the role of representations, language, and recording in developing a deep understanding of decimal place value
- Appreciate what is involved in consolidating decimal fraction place-value knowledge
- Recognise the sources of student difficulty in relation to fractions and decimal fractions.

Early understandings of fractions

How often have we heard young children say, 'that's not fair, you've got more than me!'. Our earliest understanding of fractions is based on our notions of fair shares, that is, equal parts of a recognised whole such as a bar of chocolate or a packet of sweets. However, a fair share does not always mean equal parts. Indeed, in remote Aboriginal communities where hunting for fish and sea turtles is still widely practised, a fair share is determined by the role and status of the hunters, not by the amount or weight of their catch.

Fractions were used in ancient Egypt to decide what proportion of a farmer's land should be taxed after an unusual flood, and the Babylonians used a base 60 system for representing fractions as early as 2000 BC (Davis, 1989).

While fractions can be used to measure, they can also be used to indicate ratios and the results of division—they are inherently relative as opposed to absolute, although they can be represented uniquely on the number line. Fractions are, indeed, a most wondrous invention.

Big ideas

- Fractions can be interpreted and applied in different ways in different contexts.
- Apart from halves, the ordinal number associated with the number of equal parts names the part (e.g. 6 parts—sixths, 10 parts—tenths and 16 parts—sixteenths).
- Decimal fractions extend the base 10 system of numeration on the basis that '1 tenth of these is 1 of those'.
- For any given unit, there is an inverse relationship between the number of equal parts and the size of each part.
- Fractions need to be compared relative to the same referent unit (e.g. to compare $\frac{3}{5}$ and $\frac{3}{4}$ both fractions must relate to the same unit).
- For any given fraction, if the total number of parts (denominator) is increased/decreased by a certain factor, then the number of parts (numerator) increases/decreases by the same factor.

Introduction

What is the approximate value, to the nearest whole number, of the sum of $\frac{19}{20}$ and $\frac{23}{25}$? Given the choices of 1, 2, 42, or 45 on an international test, more than half of U.S. 8th graders chose 42 or 45. These responses are akin to decoding and pronouncing the word *elephant* but having no idea what animal the word represents. (Steen, 2007, p. 9)

These Year 8 students are not atypical. In their report of Australian data from the same study, Thomson and Buckley (2009) refer to the following problem:

A bowl contains 36 coloured beads all of the same size, some blue, some green, some red, and the rest yellow. A bead is drawn from the bowl without looking. The probability that it is blue is $\frac{4}{9}$. How many blue beads are there in the bowl? (p. 24)

In this case, the options were 4, 8, 16, 18, and 20. However, only '45% of Australian students identified 16 as the correct answer, compared with 50% of US students and 83% of students from Chinese-Taipei' (p. 25). While these results may reflect differences in curriculum focus and instructional strategies (e.g. only 35% of the Australian Year 8 teachers surveyed reported that they had considered fractions in this context), they illustrate the fact that many students find fractions difficult despite five or more years of instruction.

The Middle Years Numeracy Research Project (MYNRP) used relatively open-ended 'rich assessment' tasks to measure the numeracy performance (i.e. number sense, measurement and data sense, and space sense) of approximately 7000 Victorian students in Years 5 to 9 (Siemon, Virgona & Corneille, 2001). The tasks valued mathematical content knowledge as well as strategic and contextual knowledge, and generally allowed all learners to make a start. Scoring rubrics were used to evaluate student performance as shown in Figure 18.1.

Part 4: Laying the Basis for F–4 Mathematics

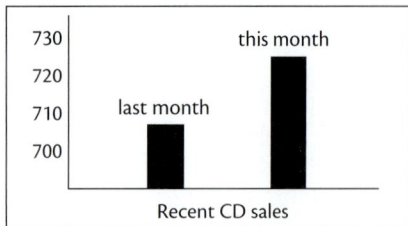

Figure 18.1 Response to CD sales task (MYNRP)

The manager of a music shop showed this graph and said, 'There has been a big increase in the number of CD sales this month'.

Do you consider the manager's statement to be a reasonable interpretation of the graph? Explain your reasoning.

Score	Description
0	No response or 'yes' or 'no' without a reason.
1	Reasoning based on numbers alone. No recognition that 'big' is relative.
2	Reasoning shows some recognition that 'big' is relative to total sales, but unsupported conclusion. Little/no explanation, e.g., 'it depends …'.
3	Reasoning concludes that increase is not 'big' relative to total sales. Some attempt to relate this to proportion, e.g., '15 out of 725 is not very big'.
4	Correct conclusion, 'not big'. %, fractions, ratio used correctly to support well-reasoned explanation.

Source: Siemon et al. (2001)

The project found that the major factor responsible for the eight-year range in performance at all Year levels was the differential performance on tasks involving multiplicative thinking (see Chapter 17). In particular, it was evident that a considerable number of students had difficulty with:

- reading, renaming, ordering, interpreting, and applying common fractions, particularly those greater than 1
- reading, renaming, ordering, interpreting, and applying decimal fractions in context
- recognising the applicability of ratio and proportion and justifying this mathematically in terms of fractions, percentage, or written ratios.

think + link

The importance of understanding common fractions and decimals to a well-developed sense of number was explored in Chapter 10.

For example, in the CD sales problem shown in Figure 18.1, less than 1% of the Year 7 to 9 students achieved a score of 4, while approximately 17% achieved a score of 3. These findings have important implications for the teaching and learning of fractions and related number ideas in the early and middle years of schooling.

think + link

The nature and importance of proportional reasoning and its connection to a sound understanding of fractions is explored in Chapter 24.

With the introduction of the metric measurement system, many regarded fractions as unnecessary apart from further mathematics study. However, a rich, connected understanding of fractions is now recognised as an important aspect of what it means to be numerate in a modern, digital economy. For example, to compare complex mobile phone plans, investigate the impact of an interest rate rise, or understand important health statistics such as the risk of contracting skin cancer, individuals need to be able to recognise and work with proportional relationships (e.g. Empson, Junk, Dominguez & Turner, 2006; Lamon, 1999, 2007; Smith, 2002). While a capacity for proportional reasoning draws on an extended range of ideas for multiplication, it also draws on a deep understanding of fractions, in particular on what fractions mean in different contexts, how they are represented and renamed, and how they can be used to solve problems.

Consider and discuss

What were they thinking?

The following statement was made in an editorial in a mainstream newspaper in the United States in 1996.

> One-ninth of the population holds seven-tenths of the Nation's wealth.
>
> The ultra-rich one-tenth of this group holds three-tenths of the Nation's wealth.

1. Assuming this information is accurate, what sense do you make of these statements?
2. What proportion of the population hold 30% of the nation's wealth?
3. Why was this information written in this way?
4. Does it help you to know that this was written at the time of Clinton's bid for re-election as President of the United States?
5. What implications does this have for numeracy education in Australia?

Making sense of fractions

Even before they come to school, many young children exhibit an awareness of such fraction names as half and quarter. During the first years of schooling, most will be able to halve a piece of paper, identify 3 quarters of an orange, and talk about parts of recognised wholes (e.g. half the class, 2 thirds of the netball court). While this conveys the impression that children understand the relationships inherent in fraction language and representations, most are simply using these terms as names for familiar objects and are unaware of the key ideas involved. That is, that:

- equal parts are necessary
- the number of parts names the parts (e.g. 8 parts—eighths)
- there is an inverse relationship between the number of parts and the size of each part (e.g. the larger the number of parts, the smaller each part)
- the size of each part depends on the size of the whole (i.e. fraction models are relative—an eighth of an A3 sheet of paper is not the same as an eighth of an A4 sheet of paper, $\frac{1}{8}$ of 24 is not the same as $\frac{1}{8}$ of 42).

for the classroom

Provide plenty of experiences for young children to share realistic collections and quantities equally (e.g. coloured pencils among a table group, a given collection of counters among a different number of sharers, 3 'pizzas' among 4 people, and so on). Contrast this to situations where the parts are not equal (e.g. by cutting up a plasticine 'sausage' or 'pizza' into 5 unequal parts). Make sure children recognise and apply the term 'fraction' to equal shares/parts.

Take photographs of equal and unequal sharing situations and use these to make a set of cards or interactive whiteboard objects that children can sort on the basis of 'fractions' (fair shares) and 'not fractions' (unequal shares). In each case, make sure that it is possible to 'see' the parts in relation to the whole.

These cards can also be used to introduce the relationship between the number of equal parts and the names of the parts (e.g. 6 parts—sixths; 8 parts—eighths). Invite children to suggest an alternative name for quarters based on this pattern.

Use these experiences to tease out and record key ideas/generalisations in a prominent place in the classroom.

to the area of the whole, which is the attribute relevant to fractions. This is particularly problematic where the shape of the part looks very different from the shape of the whole or other parts, as in Figure 18.4.

The use of concrete materials such as fraction blocks or pattern shapes to represent fractions can also present problems for young children, as the parts are not necessarily seen in relation to each other or the whole. Indeed, in this instance, unless the parts are directly compared to the whole and the referent unit is clearly indicated, it is highly likely that young children will simply attend to the number of different shapes and the patterns they create rather than to the relationships between them. Paper folding keeps the whole and the parts in touch with one another, but only when the paper is unfolded and the parts formed by the fold lines can be seen in relation to the whole. Figure 18.5 illustrates the difficulties experienced by children in appreciating the equivalence of different-looking halves (Nunes & Bryant, 1996). In this case it is important to recognise what is different (shape) and what is the same (they are both half of the same-sized whole), and how this might be demonstrated by further partitioning as shown in Figure 18.5.

Children will inevitably draw on what they know about whole numbers in their efforts to make sense of fractions. However, this can often lead them to construct different meanings for fractions written in symbolic form. This is illustrated in the two responses provided by Wong and Evans (2008) to a written task that required 646 Year 3 to 6 children to 'put a cross (X) to show where the $\frac{1}{2}$ would be on the number line' (p. 600) given a 0 to 3 number line marked in integer values (see Figure 18.6). They found that only 18% of students 'completed the question correctly with 57% placing a cross half-way between 1 and 2' (p. 601). In their follow-up interviews, however, the reasons given for placing the cross in that location were not always because it was half of the line. Student 1 reported using the numerator and denominator as a cue for placing the cross between 1 and 2. To test this thinking, the student was asked to identify a cross placed half-way between 2 and 3 and then half-way between

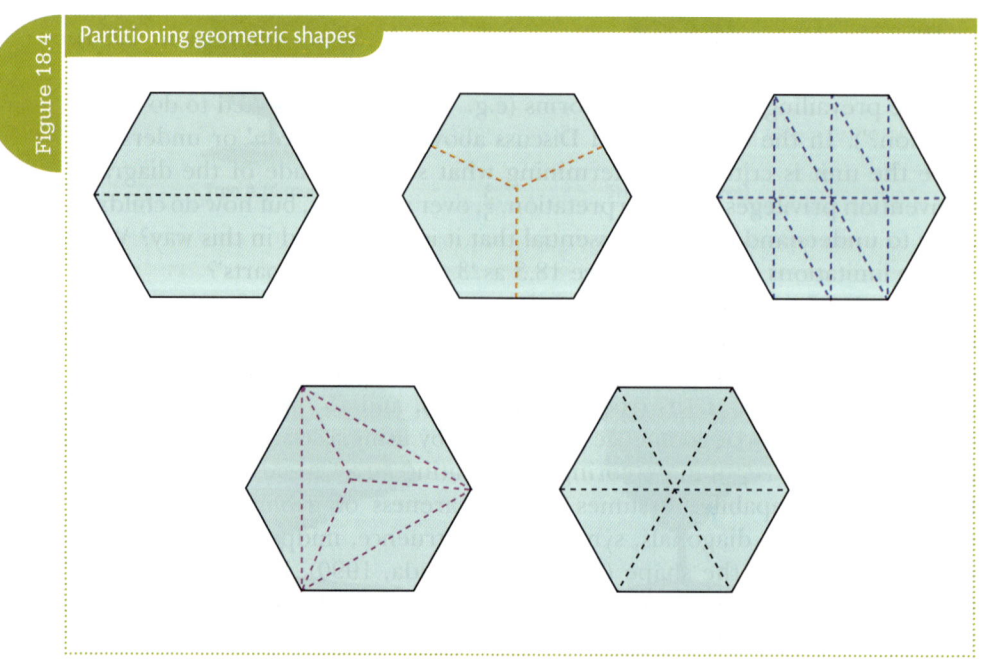

Figure 18.4 Partitioning geometric shapes

Source: Adapted from Pothier and Sawada (1990)

Figure 18.5 Different-looking halves

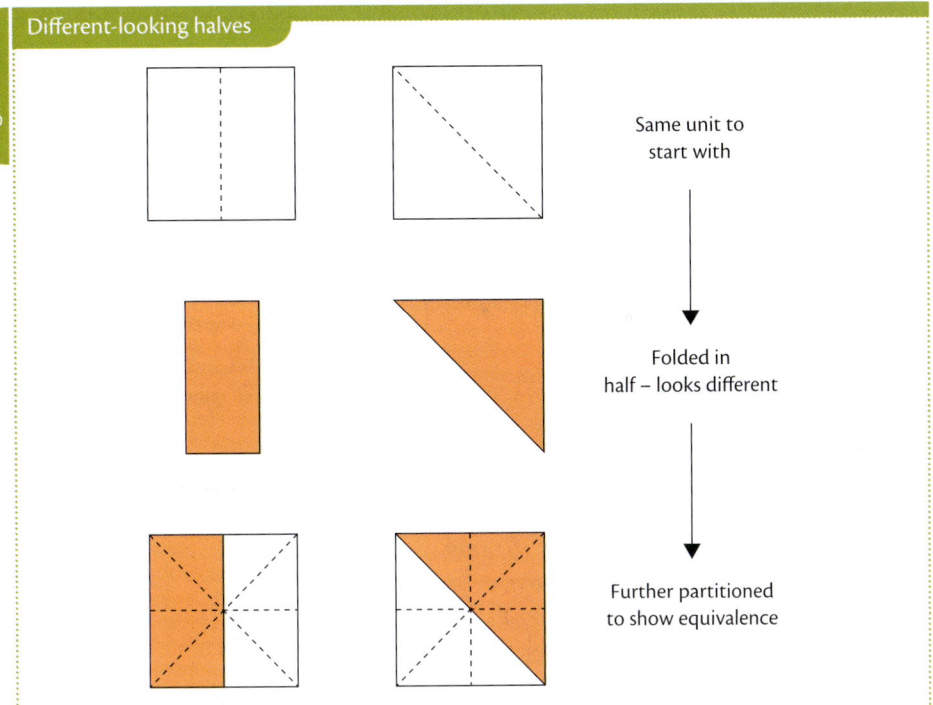

Same unit to start with

Folded in half – looks different

Further partitioned to show equivalence

Figure 18.6 Two responses to the 'locating half' task

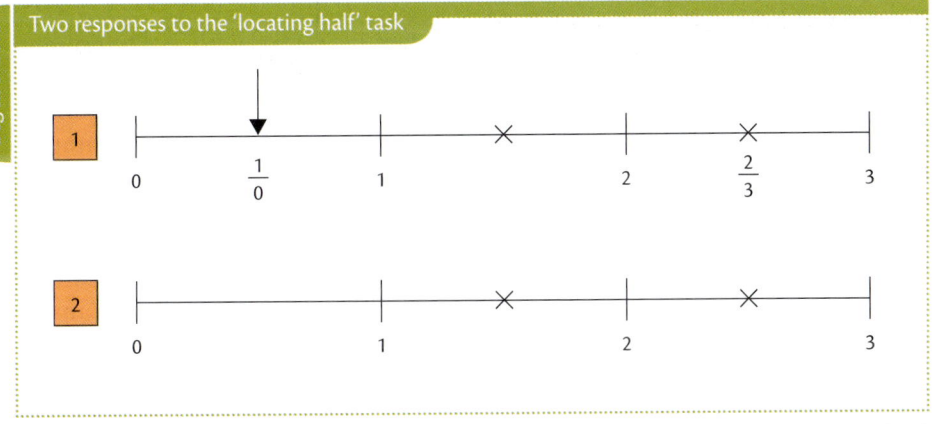

Source: Wong and Evans (2008)

0 and 1. The responses shown are indicative that this thinking was applied consistently. Student 2 used a similar strategy but when asked to place a cross to show where 2 thirds would be on the number line, she was able to use her knowledge of half to locate $\frac{2}{3}$ a little more to the right.

Students will also draw on their everyday knowledge to attach meaning to symbols. For example, Swan (1990) reported on a task that required children to create a realistic context for decimal addition. The children were shown the number sentence 5 + 2 = 7 and told 'A story which goes with this is: John has 5 records. His father gave him 2 more for his birthday. So now he has 7 records'. They were then asked to write their own story for 4.6 + 5.3 = 9.9. Figure 18.7 shows three of the responses, which illustrate the extent to which children draw on whole number or familiar fraction contexts to make sense of decimal numeration. These constructions have important implications for the teaching and learning of decimal numeration as well as fractions.

Figure 18.7 Stories for 4.6 + 5.3 = 9.9

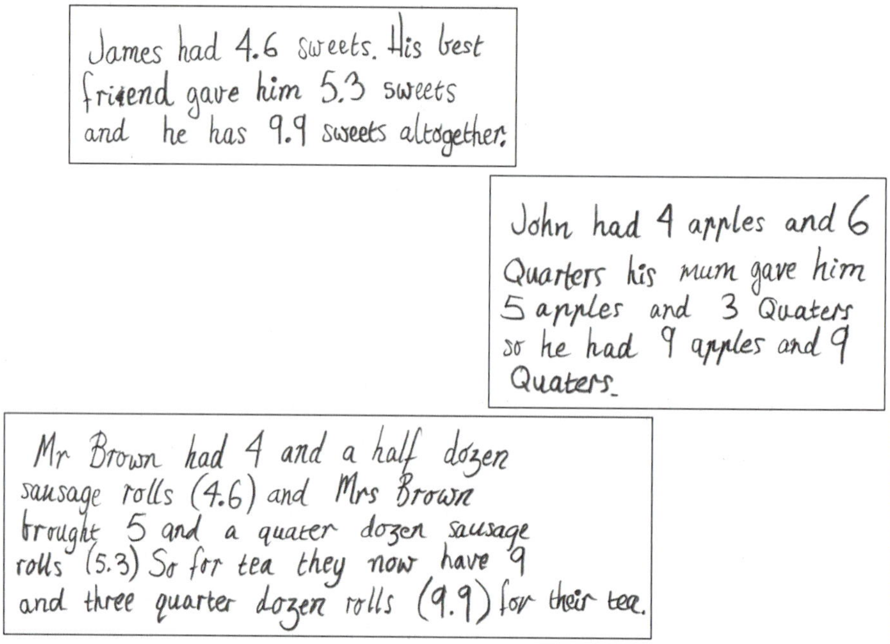

> James had 4.6 sweets. His best friend gave him 5.3 sweets and he has 9.9 sweets altogether.

> John had 4 apples and 6 Quarters his mum gave him 5 apples and 3 Quaters so he had 9 apples and 9 Quaters.

> Mr Brown had 4 and a half dozen sausage rolls (4.6) and Mrs Brown brought 5 and a quater dozen sausage rolls (5.3) So for tea they now have 9 and three quarter dozen rolls (9.9) for their tea.

Source: Swan (1990)

So far we have considered what are generally referred to as **continuous fraction models**, that is, area diagrams and number line models. Continuous fraction models are based on attributes that are, in principle, infinitely divisible (e.g. length, area, volume, capacity, mass). Commonly used examples include pizzas, chocolate bars, cordial mixes, plasticine, newspaper, and paper streamers. **Discrete fraction models** are collections that are not intended to be partitioned further than the items in the collection (e.g. a packet of Smarties, a dozen eggs). In this case, unless the collection is clearly defined as the unit or whole, children's natural inclination is to look at the individual items in the collection as ones. This can lead to problems of interpretation as illustrated by the talking-head responses to the discrete fraction task shown in Figure 18.8. The task, to shade in 2 fifths of the apples, was used with Year 4 students as part of a larger study on children's mathematical problem solving (Siemon, 1993). The first response indicates a confusion between the fraction word 'fifth' and the ordinal word 'fifth'. We can't know what motivated the child to shade 2 apples, but the chances are that the confusion prompted him/her to ignore the problematic word 'fifth' and use the '2' as a guide to the number required. The second response reflects a deep understanding of what is required ('I counted every two as one') but when it came to drawing 2 of her 'ones', she is distracted by the individual apples. The third response reflects some understanding of what is required but, in this case, the child has interpreted each row of 5 apples as the whole to be partitioned and shaded in 1 fifth of each row (conveniently 1 apple) to produce 2 fifths altogether. This is an additive response that reflects the ways in which whole number sets might be aggregated. From a teaching perspective, what is crucially important in these three responses is that, while all three students shaded in 2 apples, their reasons for doing so are entirely different. This makes a strong case for the use of assessment tools such as the 'talking-heads' response format that reveal student thinking.

Figure 18.8 Four responses to a discrete fraction task

Source: Siemon (1993)

Although there is a line of research that links the development of fraction understanding to children's counting schemes (e.g. Olive, 2001; Olive & Steffe, 2002), many researchers (e.g. Kieren, 1980; Lamon, 1999, 2007; Nunes & Bryant, 1996; Stafylidou & Vosniadou, 2004) caution against the use of representations or procedures that may prompt children to draw on their whole number knowledge in inappropriate or restrictive ways. In particular, they are concerned with the over-use of the *part–whole* interpretation and representation of fractions and the use of a procedure that Nunes and Bryant (1996) refer to as *double-counting*, that is, where children count the total number of parts shown in a diagram then count the shaded parts to name the fraction, without necessarily attending to the relationships involved between parts and between the parts and the whole. This leads to a focus on the number of parts as a count (e.g. 5 pieces of pizza) rather than the number of parts in relation to the whole (e.g. 5 eighths of the pizza), and the related *count-and-match* misconception (e.g. Mitchell & Horne, 2009; Saxe, Taylor, McIntosh & Gearhart, 2005) in which children count the parts without regard for the size of the parts. For example, Saxe et al. (2005) reported that of 384 Year 4, 5, and 6 students, 9% correctly identified the shaded region shown in Figure 18.9 as $\frac{1}{8}$, while 25% identified the shaded fraction as $\frac{1}{5}$.

Figure 18.9 Unequal area problem

Source: Saxe et al. (2005)

Viewing the denominator as a counting or 'how many' number can also lead to misconceptions related to order and equivalence. For example, '$\frac{3}{12}$ is bigger than $\frac{3}{8}$ because 12 is bigger than 8' and that fractions can be added by adding the numerators and the denominators (e.g. $\frac{4}{5} + \frac{2}{7} = \frac{6}{12}$).

Given the significant difference between fractions and whole numbers, the inherent difficulties associated with the language, contexts, and ways in which fractions are represented (e.g. materials, diagrams, number lines, symbols), and the misconceptions that can arise from an over-reliance on counting-based approaches, there is a strong argument for starting instruction with what children already know and can do in relation to partitive division (Lamon, 1999, 2007; Nunes & Bryant, 1996; Smith, 2002: Stafylidou & Vosniadou, 2004), in particular, to connecting children's understanding of what happens to each share as the number sharing is increased. There is also a considerable body of evidence to suggest that the formalisation of fractions should be delayed until children have had extensive practical experiences with the different contexts in which fractions are used and represented (e.g. Hart, 1981; Moseley, 2005; Nunes & Bryant, 1996; Thompson, 1994; Wong & Evans, 2008). But before we consider how this might be achieved in practice we shall clarify some terminology.

Conventional wisdom

A **fraction** is most commonly described as a part of a whole or as the result of dividing a collection or quantity into a given number of equal parts or shares. For example, it is possible to talk about 2 thirds as 2 parts out of 3 equal parts of a netball court, or as the result of sharing 2 pizzas among three people. Both can be recorded as $\frac{2}{3}$. As fractions were historically derived from the comparison of two whole numbers they are generally regarded as positive (e.g. ACARA, 2011; Lamon, 2007). However, fractions can also be thought about as measures, in which case it is possible to contemplate the possibility of negative fractions, although these are generally expressed as decimal fractions (e.g. –6.5 degrees Celsius).

Decimal fractions are fractions with denominators that are powers of 10 (e.g. tenths, hundredths, thousandths). As a consequence, decimal fractions can also be represented in place-value form, that is, as *decimal numbers* with a fractional part (e.g. $4\frac{1}{5}$ can be written as 4.2 and $\frac{2}{3}$ can be written as 0.6666...).

While fractions can be described literally as one number 'over' another number with a horizontal bar (*vinculum*) in between, this is unhelpful as it focuses attention on the two numbers and how they are written rather than on the relationship between them. At the outset it is more helpful to describe fractions in terms of their components, for example, the 'bottom' number (the **denominator**) tells you how many parts the whole is divided into and the 'top' number (the **numerator**) tells you how many parts you have, but this only represents the *part–whole* representation of fractions. Ultimately, students need to understand all of the different ways in which fractions can be interpreted and represented in order to solve problems involving proportional reasoning and work with mathematical symbolism more generally (Lamon, 1999, 2007; Nunes & Bryant, 1996, Smith, 2002).

From a mathematical perspective, fractions are **rational numbers** that are not integers (Groza, 1968), where rational numbers are numbers that can be represented as $\frac{p}{q}$, where p and q are integers and $q \neq 0$. The rational numbers include the integers, since any integer can be represented in the form $\frac{p}{q}$ (e.g. $4 = \frac{8}{2}$), as well as terminating or repeating decimal fractions such as 2.375 and 0.3333, as these can be represented as $2\frac{3}{8}$ (or $\frac{19}{8}$) and $\frac{1}{3}$ respectively.

Although the set of rational numbers includes both positive and negative fractions and decimal fractions (e.g. $\frac{2}{7}$, $-3\frac{3}{4}$, 5.666…, –0.8), because children's early experiences of fractions do not involve negative values of p or q we will restrict ourselves here to what is generally referred to as *simple common fractions*, that is, rational numbers where p and q are whole numbers and $\frac{p}{q}$ is not an integer (e.g. fractions such as $\frac{2}{7}$, $\frac{8}{5}$, $3\frac{4}{5}$, and $\frac{1}{100}$). *Like fractions* are fractions with the same denominator (e.g. $\frac{4}{5}$ and $\frac{7}{5}$), *related fractions* are fractions with denominators in the same family (e.g. $\frac{3}{8}$ and $\frac{5}{16}$), and *unlike fractions* have denominators with no common integer divisors (e.g. $\frac{4}{9}$ and $\frac{2}{5}$). *Proper fractions* are fractions with a value less than 1 (e.g. $\frac{2}{7}$), whereas **mixed fractions** comprise a whole number and a fractional part (e.g. $3\frac{4}{5}$). Mixed fractions can also be represented as *improper fractions* when the whole number part is expressed in terms of the fractional part (e.g. $3\frac{4}{5} = \frac{19}{5}$).

think + link

The defining features of all number sets included within the set of real numbers are described in Chapter 22.

communicating mathematically

Everyday meanings for fraction

One of the many difficulties with fractions is that the term is used in different ways. Apart from the different mathematical meanings for fraction, it can also be used to refer to:

1. the form in which two numbers are written, that is, as two numbers, *a* and *b*, 'one written over the other' (e.g. $\frac{a}{b}$) with little or no regard for what this means (although it is often recognised that *b* cannot be equal to 0); interpreted in this way, $\frac{\pi}{2}$ would be regarded as a 'fraction' although it is not a rational number

2. a small piece or part (as in, 'I'll just have a fraction' or 'taking the freeway took a fraction of the time'); interpreted in this way, there is no sense that the part is one (or more) of a number of equal parts or that there is a relationship between the part and the whole beyond the fact that it is smaller or less than the whole (i.e. an additive relationship).

Clarifying terms is essential if shared meanings are to be negotiated, but so is reconciling the many ways in which fractions can be represented and recorded—more about this below.

The ambiguous role of instruction

> As a whole, the studies in which young children were interviewed before they had had substantial fraction instruction show that powerful, intuitive strategies are available to children at an early age … On the other hand, research with older children who have had 5 or more years of traditional mathematics instruction … suggests that rules and algorithms replace reasoning strategies, and that these often fail the student when integral ratios do not exist … Researchers must begin to suspect that instruction plays a role in the poor performance of older children. (Lamon, 2007, p. 645)

Nunes and Bryant (1996) found that sixth grade children were able to solve fraction comparison problems presented in a real-life situation far more successfully than when the same problems were presented in symbolic form. The example they cite is where two pizzas of the same size were cut into six and eight parts respectively and the children were asked 'which pizza would they get more from' if they could have one piece of each pizza. While the students had little difficulty with this problem, a significant proportion made errors when the same fraction comparison task was presented symbolically (i.e. which fraction is bigger, $\frac{1}{6}$ or $\frac{1}{8}$?). Their conclusion was that:

> this gap is a consequence of the pupil's learning of fractional language in school through the double counting procedure ... The disconnection between pupil's understanding of division ... developed out of school and their learning of fractions might come about exactly because pupils do not think of fractions as having anything to do with division, and only relate fractions with part–whole language. (p. 228)

This is just a small sample of the research evidence that suggests schooling may be getting in the way of children making sense of fractions. In the next section we consider the many faces of fractions and the importance of moving beyond part–whole models to connect children's informal, intuitive, out-of-school knowledge and experience with what they need to learn about fractions at school.

issues in teaching

When is it appropriate to introduce the fraction symbol?

This vexed question has plagued curriculum developers for a long time. In the past fraction symbols were introduced and expected to be used by children in Years 1 and 2. These days, the difficulties inherent in decoding and making sense of fraction representations, language, and recording are more generally recognised, but there is little agreement as to when it is most appropriate to introduce symbolic recording. Explore this issue.

- Try some of the tasks described above with primary children and discuss your findings with teachers and peers. What do you notice? How might you describe the thinking involved?
- The *Australian Curriculum: Mathematics* (ACARA, 2010) appears to suggest that fraction symbols are introduced/used in Year 3. Do you agree?
- What prerequisite knowledge is needed before children can be expected to make sense of fraction symbols?
- Investigate the extent to which this is reflected in schools and/or commonly used texts or interactive whiteboard teaching materials. Describe how the symbol is introduced (i.e. what models and contexts are typically used).

The many faces of fractions

Fractions can be thought about in two related but different ways that loosely reflect the distinctions between the *counting*- and *splitting*-based approaches to multiplicative thinking referred to in Chapter 17 (e.g. see Table 18.1). This is helpful to keep in mind as it parallels the distinction between additive and multiplicative thinking and helps explain where and why children might experience difficulty (Siemon & Breed, 2005). However, given that 'the meaning of fractions derives from the contexts in which they are used' (Lamon, 1999, p. 41), we will focus on those contexts that children in Years F to 4 or 5 might be expected to come across in their out-of-school and school experience. In doing this it is important to recognise that although these contexts are named and referred to as if they are discrete categories, they are not. Different learners may well make completely different sense of the same situation as we shall see below. As Thompson (1994) observed, 'Mathematics, like beauty, is in the eye of the beholder—and the eye sees what the mind conceives' (p. 557).

Chapter 18 Introducing Fractions and Decimal Fractions

Table 18.1 Two different ways of thinking about fractions

Counting-based interpretations	Splitting-based interpretations
Numerator counts, denominator indicates what is being counted	Numerator is a multiplier, denominator is a divisor (operator)
$\frac{4}{5}$ viewed as a count of 5 things called fifths	$\frac{4}{5}$ viewed as division (i.e. 4 objects shared among 5)
Instructional emphasis on unit fractions, unitising, measuring	Instructional emphasis on fraction as a number, partitioning, and proportion (ratio)

Fractions occur in a wide range of contexts, some more obvious than others. For example, consider the following situations.

- Jan opened up the carton of eggs and found that 2 were cracked.
- Grace had 24 marbles, 3 quarters of which were glass.
- The muffin recipe called for $\frac{2}{3}$ of a cup of milk.
- Will had 36 cards of Australian and international soccer players. He had twice as many Australian ones as international ones.
- It takes Emma $3\frac{1}{4}$ hours to travel to her parent's home in the country by train.
- At the end of their cooking class, Kate was asked to share 20 pancakes equally between herself and her 7 'table mates'.
- In making up cordial for the school camp, Elly used 2 cups of concentrate to 5 cups of water.
- Three friends shared 2 pizzas equally.
- By the end of summer, the city's water storage was $\frac{2}{5}$ of what it had been at the end of winter.
- There are 10 toy cars in the set. Joe had collected 8.
- Alex wondered how much he would pay for a $50 pair of shoes marked '20% off'.
- Four of the 28 tiles were replaced.
- The ranger estimated that the cane toad population had increased by 350%.

While the fraction symbol is 'devoid of any physical meaning and context, … it has many interpretations including part–whole, quotient, measure, ratio and operator' (Wong & Evans, 2008, p. 597). Referred to by many authors as sub-constructs of rational number (e.g. Lamon, 1999, 2007; Mitchell & Horne, 2009), at this level it is better to think about these as possibilities for sense making and be on the alert for explanations that reflect different interpretations, than to assume a particular situation is indicative of a particular interpretation.

think + link

The different interpretations of fractions are explored further in Chapter 22.

Fraction as part–whole

It is generally acknowledged that children's initial, intuitive experiences of fractions are derived from fair sharing. But it is only when children are aware of the relationship between the individual shares and the original quantity that a sense of fractions is evident. In the first situation described above, the unit is undefined. If the carton contains a dozen eggs, then the fraction that is cracked is 2 *out of* 12 or $\frac{2}{12}$. However, if the carton contains 6 eggs, then the fraction cracked is 2 out of 6. Ambiguity is useful here as it draws attention to the unit. In this context it does not make sense to talk about equivalence in numerical terms as the number of cracked eggs is a given. But it is possible to *express the relationship* in an equivalent way. For example, for a carton of 12 eggs, the relationship of cracked eggs to the total number of eggs could also be expressed as 1 in 6 eggs are cracked. This is a ratio idea and demonstrates the claim made above that it is possible to interpret the same situation in different ways.

As we have already seen, the part–whole interpretation has limitations, not least of which is that the 'out of' relationship only applies to proper fractions. For example, 4 out of 28 tiles makes sense, but it would be meaningless to say '44 out of 28 tiles'). But part–whole interpretations can be applied to other situations if the 'out of' term is avoided. For example, the marbles, muffin, pancakes, pizza, water storage, and toy cars situations described above can all be interpreted in terms of part–whole.

Fraction as measure

Fractions were originally devised to provide more accurate measures of time and the area of land to be taxed. The muffin and travel situations described above invoke the interpretation of fractions as measure. In both cases, the referent unit (cup and hour respectively) is insufficient to convey the degree of accuracy required, so sub-units (equal parts) of the referent units need to be constructed to indicate the amount of flour or time more precisely. The eggs and tiles situations can also be interpreted in terms of fraction as measure. For example, 2 twelfths is the measure of the proportion of cracked eggs in a dozen carton. Many of the other situations can also be interpreted as measures (e.g. the water storage situation).

The measure interpretation is regarded as a more useful basis for understanding the addition and subtraction of fractions than part–whole because it provides a stronger, perceptual basis for renaming the parts in the same way. For example, if two fractions with unlike denominators are interpreted as measures (i.e. as distances from 0 on the same scale), then they can be added (or subtracted) as measures only of they have the same units (e.g. see Figure 18.10).

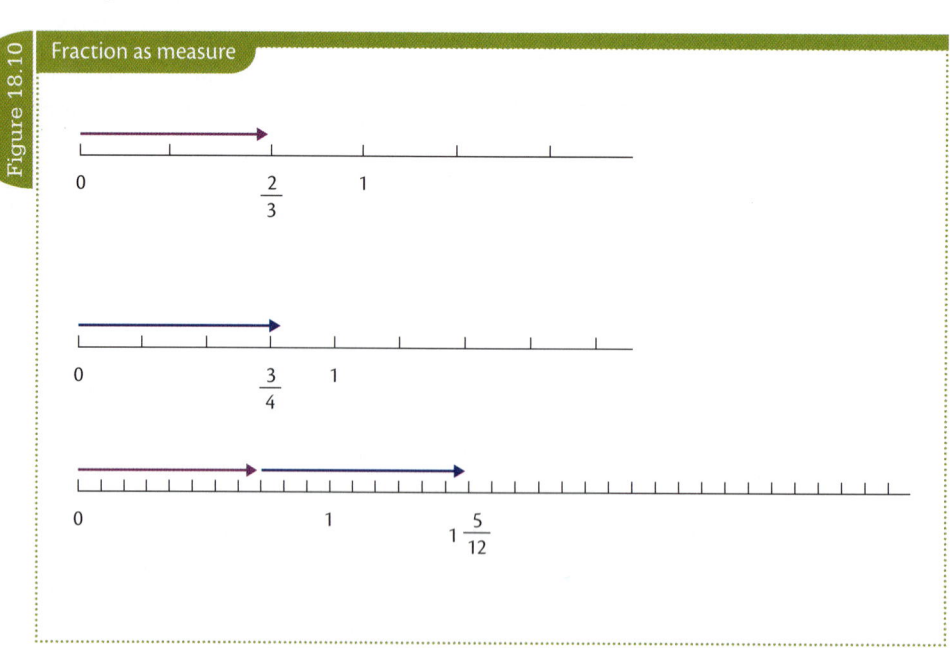

Figure 18.10 Fraction as measure

Fraction as operator

Situations such as the water storage and cane toad population scenarios described above use fractions to indicate a change from one state to another. In this case, the fraction symbol refers to the operations that need to be carried out to find the extent of the change. For example, to find the amount of water left in the water storages at the end of summer, it would be necessary to divide the number of megalitres of water in the storage at the end of winter by 5 and multiply by 2 (or vice versa). To find the increase in the cane toad population, it would be necessary to multiply the original population by 3.5 (on the grounds that $350\% = \frac{350}{100} = 3.5$). Used in this way, fractions can also be interpreted as measures of change.

The operator interpretation can also be applied to discrete amounts, as in the marbles situation described above where the number of glass marbles can be found by multiplying 24 by 3 and then dividing by 4 or by dividing 24 by 4 to find 1 quarter then multiplying by 3 (a part–whole interpretation). The operative word here is 'of', which is indicative of multiplication. Whenever a fraction is used in this context it is generally used as an operator. The discounted shoes situation is a good example of this. In this case, the cost of the shoes will be reduced by 20% or $\frac{1}{5}$ *of* the original cost.

Fraction as quotient (number)

This interpretation is also referred to as the fraction as number interpretation because *quotient* refers to the single rational number derived from dividing the numerator by the denominator (e.g. for $\frac{1}{4}$ dividing 1 by 4 results in 0.25, for $\frac{8}{5}$ dividing 8 by 5 produces 1.6). This interpretation provides a firm foundation for renaming and comparing fractions as decimals and making the connections between fractions, decimals, and percentages. It also provides an opportunity for children to recognise that although a fraction may have an infinite number of equivalent forms, they all correspond to the one rational number that exists uniquely on the number line. For example, $\frac{10}{4}, \frac{15}{6}, \frac{25}{10}$, and $\frac{85}{38}$ are all equivalent forms of the same rational number $\frac{5}{2}$, or 2.5 on the number line. However, as Stafylidou and Vosniadou (2004) found in their study of 10- to 16-year-olds, many students find this interpretation of fractions difficult, particularly where instruction has focused almost exclusively on part–whole language and models for fractions.

The fraction as division idea can be interpreted in two ways that parallel the two ideas for division—partition and quotition—discussed in Chapter 17. Partition division is clearly related to fractions as it connects to fair shares (Charles & Nason, 2000; Kieren, 1980; Lamon, 1996; Pothier & Sawada, 1990); the physical act of partitioning can be seen in the pizza and pancakes situations above where each share can be represented as $\frac{2}{3}$ and $\frac{20}{8}$ respectively. The toy cars situation illustrates the point made earlier about the role of language in making sense of fractions. In this case, the situation could be interpreted as 'how many more cars does Joe need to have a full set', or 'how much of the whole set has Joe collected to date'. That is, this situation could be responded to either additively (i.e. 2 more cars needed) or multiplicatively (i.e. he has $\frac{8}{10}$ or 80% of a full set). When interpreted in this way, this situation involves quotition division as it is effectively asking 'how many tens in 8'. Dividing 8 by 10 to obtain 0.8 indicates what proportion he has of the full set.

Fraction as ratio

think + link

A more detailed discussion of fractions as ratios can be found in Chapter 24.

The soccer cards and cordial situations are examples in which the fraction relationships involved can be interpreted as **ratios**. In both cases the comparison involved is part-to-part, that is, the ratio of Australian football players to international football players (2:1) and the ratio of concentrate to water respectively (2:5). The other form of ratio is part-to-whole. This interpretation can be applied to the marbles situation, where 3:4 represents the ratio of glass marbles to the full set of marbles.

consider and discuss

Best buys

Without using a calculating device, how might you determine which jar of coffee shown in Figure 18.11 offers the best value for money?

    What prior knowledge and skills did you draw on to solve this problem?

    Share your strategy with your peers and discuss the implications for the teaching and learning of fractions.

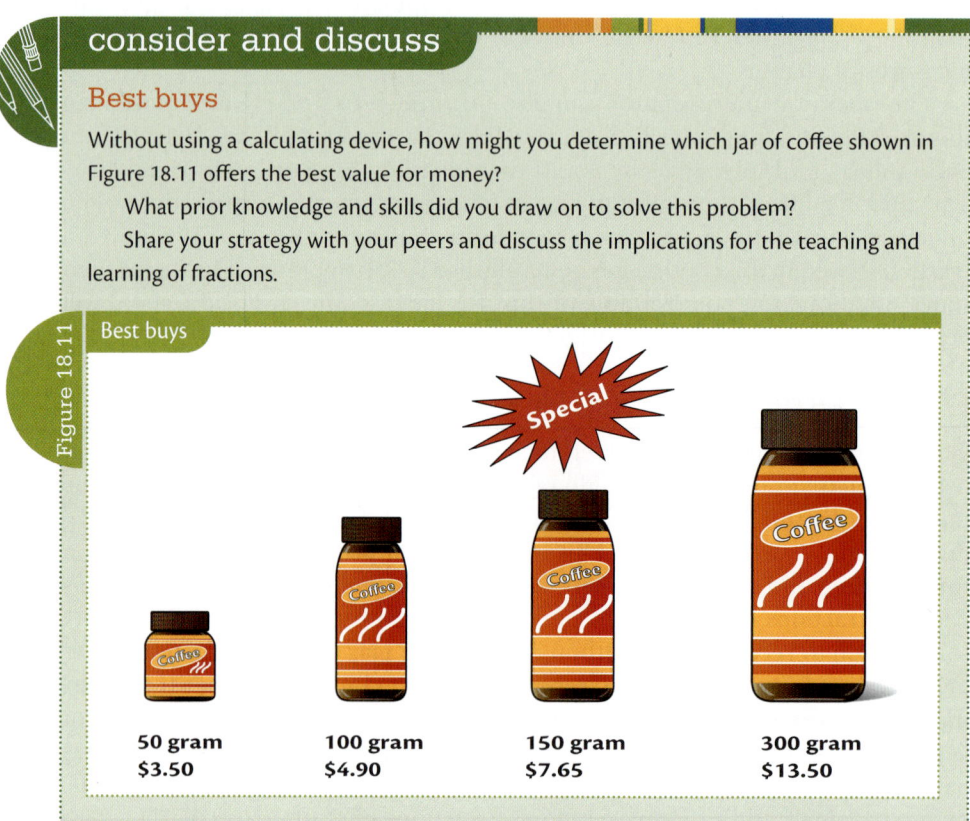

Figure 18.11

Best buys

| 50 gram | 100 gram | 150 gram | 300 gram |
| $3.50 | $4.90 | $7.65 | $13.50 |

The different interpretations discussed above illustrate the many faces and multiple interpretations of fractions but also their deep interconnectedness. According to Lamon (2007), children need a starting point in one of the interpretations and sufficient time and experience to develop a sense of fractions, a capacity for partitioning, and an understanding of the role of the unit in comparing fractions. But no one interpretation is sufficient on its own, and different children may well have a propensity for starting with different interpretations. The important thing is to ensure that children are exposed to a range of situations and contexts to provide opportunities to tease out the 'central multiplicative structures' (p. 658) of each interpretation.

The special case of decimal fractions

Decimal fractions, that is, fractions with denominators that are powers of 10, are a relatively recent invention arising from the need to approximate the roots of irrational numbers such as $\sqrt{2}$ in the fifteenth century. However it took another 300 years or so before any sort of agreement was reached as to how to differentiate the integral and fractional parts of numbers written in base 10. And even today in our digital, globalised world, there is no universally accepted form of writing the separator or decimal point as we know it. Note that the term **decimal(s)** is used colloquially to refer to decimal fractions but that any number expressed in base 10 is can be referred to as a decimal number.

Many of the same issues with respect to language and representation that apply to fractions also apply to decimal fractions. Decimal fractions are commonly used to indicate measures, but they can also be used as operators. This is most evident in the use of percentages (e.g. the discounted shoes and cane toad situations described above). Decimal fractions sit more comfortably with the whole numbers than with fractions, but this can mean that they are also more prone to whole-number induced errors. These are discussed in more detail in Chapter 22.

Developing fraction knowledge and confidence

> The ultimate goal of instruction is to help students to understand fractions as numbers in their own right ... as objects that can be manipulated with arithmetic ... An early step towards the goal is acquiring the ability to understand relative comparisons and to abstract a single common notion across a wide range of representations. (Lamon, 2001, p. 149)

Although the broad steps seem clear enough—that is, start with the knowledge and skills children bring to school from their everyday experience, expose them to carefully sequenced, related experiences that promote meaningful engagement with the different interpretations of fractions, regularly monitor children's thinking, and adjust planning as appropriate—this is easier said than done. Children's experience differs widely, there is a lack of agreement about what interpretations should be considered and when, and there are relatively few evidence-based learning trajectories to inform curriculum planning (Lamon, 2007). However, there is little doubt that children's early experiences with fair sharing and partitioning play a crucial role in the development of a sense of fractions (e.g. Charles & Nason, 2000; Empson et al., 2006; Lamon, 1999, 2001, 2007; Nunes & Bryant, 1996; Pothier & Sawada, 1990; Smith, 2002), and it is this premise that forms the basis of the key steps outlined below.

Building on what children bring to school

As we have already seen, young children come to school with a capacity to share collections and quantities more or less equally, and they can generally recognise whether or not two parts of a whole are equal or one is greater/larger than the other. That is, they are capable of recognising and using the *half boundary* (Nunes & Bryant, 1996) in a relational sense to make judgments about quantities. They also understand what it means to 'cut' objects into smaller, but roughly equal, parts by successively halving (e.g. cutting oranges or apples into quarters or pizzas into 8 equal parts). This suggests that children's earliest school experiences of fractions should be informal, play-based experiences that focus on sharing familiar quantities, for example, 'cutting' plasticine 'sausages' and 'pies' into a given number of roughly equal parts and discussing questions such as:

- are the parts the same or different? are they 'fair shares'?
- what happens to the size of each part/share as the number of 'sharers' increases?
- is this part more than, less than, or the same as a half? how do you know?

This is important as it serves to emphasise the relationship between sharing, division, and fractions.

Fraction words such as *half* and *quarter* can be introduced or consolidated using well-known relationships such as 'half of the apple', 'half of the class went to the art room', a 'quarter of the orange', or 'quarter-time at the football'. Note that in all these examples the referent unit is either explicitly or implicitly present (i.e. the apple, class, orange, or the duration of a football match). This is important as it serves to emphasise the relationship between the part and the whole in a more natural way than '1 out of 4 equal parts' (part–whole interpretation) and opens up possibilities for considering any number of fractional parts as measures (e.g. 9 oranges, 36 quarters).

Informal comparisons can be made between the same parts of different sized units (e.g. the respective halves of a small and large pizza) to emphasise the *relative* nature of fractions; in particular, that the size of the parts depends upon the whole, and the parts need to be equal to be 'fair shares'. Include non-examples to make the point (e.g. see For the Classroom below). Same-sized shapes could be partitioned in different ways to talk about how we know they are halves (e.g. they have the same amount of …). Again, it is important that the parts are seen in relation to the referent unit to avoid the tendency to view individual parts as objects in their own right.

for the classroom

Provide newspapers, magazines, paper streamers, string, felt-tip pens, etc. Have children work in groups to produce different models for a half to make a 'These show halves—these do not' poster, as shown in Figure 18.12. Note that the halves are shown in relation to their respective wholes to emphasise that it is the relationship, not the amount, that is important. Display and discuss the posters and record key generalisations or observations as they arise.

While continuous models should be used initially, later on sticky dots in different colours and/or photos of different collections could be used to make a similar poster showing halves (and not halves) of collections (discrete fraction models).

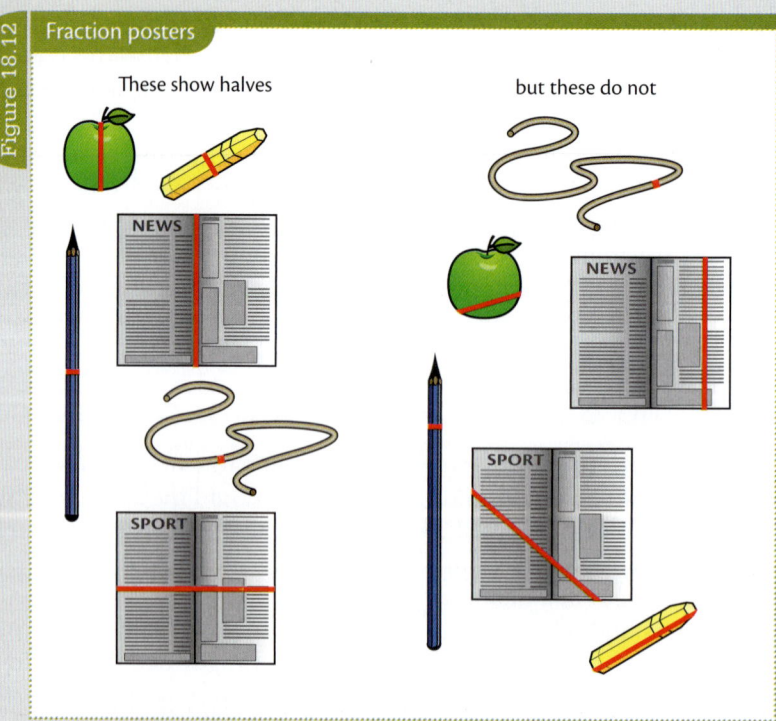

Figure 18.12 Fraction posters

Distinguishing between 'how many' and 'how much'

Fractions are different from whole numbers in a number of important ways, but one of the most important ways is that the 'unit' cannot be assumed: it varies from one context to another and can be continuous or discrete. From a measurement perspective, partitioning wholes into equal parts creates a multiplicity of different 'units' that are named using the ordinal number word associated with the number of equal parts (e.g. 6 parts, sixths; 8 parts, eighths). These different uses of whole numbers can be problematic for children if the fraction symbol is introduced before they have had sufficient experience to recognise and appreciate the distinction between 'how many' and 'how much'.

for the classroom

Construct a classroom Fraction Names chart to record the number of parts alongside the name of the parts. Include all the numbers to 32 for the number of parts as this provides a visual image of how the number of parts increases with successive acts of halving. Other fraction names and the strategies used to construct them could be added progressively as children become aware of the relationship and develop confidence with applying partitioning strategies.

This distinction can be supported in the same way that it was for multiplication, that is, by distinguishing between the count of groups and the size of the group by using numerals to indicate 'how many' and words to indicate 'how much' (e.g. 3 fours, 6 nines). For fractions, the same distinction can be made between the number of parts (how many) and the size of the parts (how much) when practical fraction examples are first encountered. For example, the Goal Shooter can play in *1 third* of the netball court, Jason ate *3 quarters* of the pizza. Ultimately, as we have seen above, students need to understand that 3 fifths means not only 3 'out of' 5 equal parts (part–whole) and 3 units of 1 fifth (measure), but 3 divided by 5, and that this is a number that exists uniquely on the number line irrespective of how it is named (e.g. $\frac{3}{5}$, 0.6, 60%, or $\frac{15}{25}$). However, before this can be realised, students first need to understand how parts are formed, named and renamed in order to develop a sense of fractions as relative quantities.

In the past, this step has been omitted. Teachers and mathematics programs have tended to assume that once students can identify fractions from a given diagram, shade a given diagram to show a particular fraction (nearly always a proper fraction), or find a simple part of a given whole (e.g. $\frac{1}{2}$, 25%, or $\frac{1}{3}$ of 24), they are familiar with fractions and ready to proceed to renaming fractions (equivalent fractions) and performing more complex operations on fractions. But recent research suggests that this is not so. If we are to prevent students adopting narrow, rule-based approaches to fraction manipulation in later years we must revisit how fractions are formalised in the middle primary years, paying careful attention to what might be regarded as the missing link in building fraction knowledge and confidence, that is, the connection between fractions and partitive division and thereby multiplicative thinking more generally (Siemon, 2003). As suggested above, this begins with a deeper understanding of how fractions are made, named, and renamed—in other words, partitioning.

Partitioning: the key to learning with understanding

This section describes and justifies **partitioning** as the missing link between the intuitive fraction ideas displayed in early childhood and the more generalised ideas needed to work with rational number more formally in the middle years of schooling. While children have little difficulty sharing familiar wholes such as pizzas, chocolate bars, and sweets, there is considerable evidence to suggest that they have difficulty making sense of fraction diagrams and line models (e.g. Empson et al, 2006; Lamon, 2007; Nunes & Bryant, 1996; Stafylidou & Vosniadou, 2004; Wong & Evans, 2008). The earlier activity and discussion in relation to Figure 18.3 highlighted some of the issues involved in counting and colouring/shading someone's pre-partitioned diagram. Such tasks either exercise what is already known, or they encourage children to apply whole number-based strategies such as double counting or count-and-match (e.g. Mitchell & Horne, 2009; Siemon, 1993).

To understand the point of tasks such as this, students need to understand how fraction diagrams are constructed and read, and attend to all aspects of the situation simultaneously, that is, the unit/whole, the number of parts in the whole, the size of each part, and the number of parts required. All too often children are focusing on only one of these aspects, the number to shade in or colour. Examples and non-examples of fraction representations need to be explored to ensure that students recognise that equal parts/equal shares are necessary. There are many ways to do this, for instance marking plasticine rolls into equal and unequal parts, sharing the packet of sweets equally and unequally to distinguish quarters from 4 parts, and talking about the implications of a netball court divided into 3 unequal parts.

By partitioning, we mean not just the experience of physically dividing continuous and discrete wholes into equal parts but generalising that experience to enable students to create their own fraction diagrams and number lines. Students learn by applying a range of well-known partitioning strategies based on reasoning about the relative size of particular fractions in relation to fractions in the halving family. Three strategies, applied singly or in combination, appear to be sufficient to achieve this, namely, **halving**, **thirding**, and **fifthing** (Siemon, 2003).

The halving strategy

Students do not need to be taught how to halve. This is an intuitive process that most students are familiar with from an early age through informal experiences with cutting and folding. Successive halving yields all of the fractions in the halving family (i.e. halves, quarters, eighths, sixteenths etc.), and illustrates the multiplicative nature of partitioning (Confrey et al., 2009). That is, each successive act of partitioning applies to each of the previously created parts to result in a doubling of the number of parts.

Initially, paper folding is used to explore fractions in the halving family. Because folding a piece of paper can produce an isosceles triangle or a rectangle it is important to acknowledge how these parts are different but also how they are the same, and how we could 'prove it' (see Figure 18.5). While halving triangles will produce fractions in the halving family as shown in Figure 18.13, this quickly becomes cumbersome as the number of folds increases. As

Figure 18.13 Halving and halving again using paper models

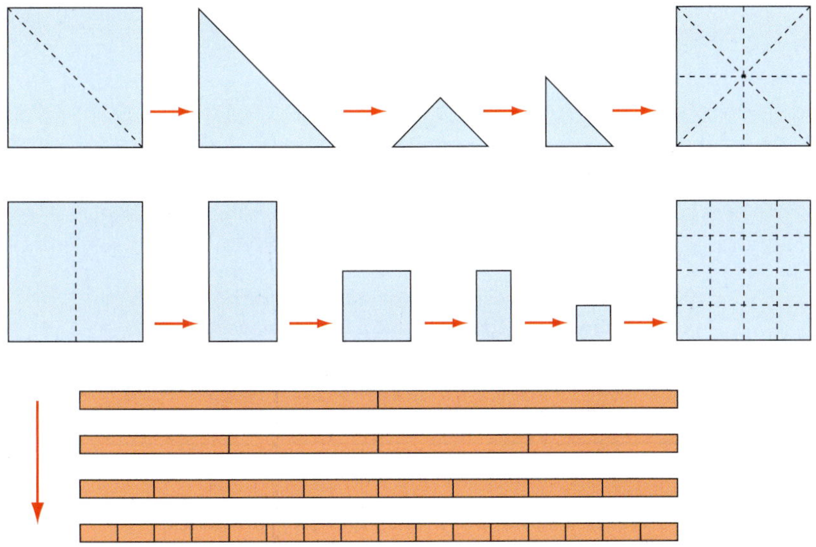

Rectangular area models and linear models make a stronger connection to the region and for each idea for multiplication

a consequence, rectangular models and line models are advocated as these more clearly illustrate the connection between fraction representations and the *region/area* and *for each* ideas for multiplication. Paper streamers can be used to construct linear fraction models.

Students should be encouraged to explore halving with different wholes (e.g. coloured paper squares, newspaper, paper streamers, plasticine, rope, and paper tablecloths), noting similarities and differences and recording observations and generalisations, such as:

- the parts are equal
- as the number of parts increase they get smaller
- the number of parts names the part.

Generating a very large number of parts is useful for demonstrating the inverse relationship between the number of partitions and the size of the parts, but it is also useful to observe how children determine the number of parts and thereby their readiness to work with fraction models more generally. For example, a paper tablecloth can be repeatedly halved to produce 256 parts (16 rows by 16 columns); if children are relying on a count-all approach, it suggests that they do not have access to the region idea for multiplication, and so are unable to use this to facilitate the count in regions (e.g. 10 by 10, 6 by 10, 10 by 6 and 6 by 6).

Mixed fractions in the halving family should also be explored at this time to emphasise that fractions can be made up of a whole number and fraction component and that this can be represented and expressed in a variety of ways. One way of doing this is to assign a different mixed fraction in the halving family to different groups of children and have them construct a poster or PowerPoint display (using photographs) to record everything they know or can find out about their fraction (e.g. see Figure 18.14).

Figure 18.14 A poster for a fraction in the halving family

From paper models to fraction diagrams

Although children are capable of generating drawings to show successive halving, this is not the case for odd partitions. Even when children engage in halving they do not necessarily attend to the process of partitioning beyond the act of 'cutting' or drawing lines. As halving is so fundamental to children's appreciation of relative amount it can be used as a reference for other partitioning strategies, but first attention needs to be drawn to how the lines are constructed. This can be done by scaffolding the construction of diagrams and line models to the paper models that children have constructed (e.g. Siemon, 2003). This came to my attention when I was working in a Year 4 class. We had been working on factors and composite numbers for some time and I was keen to see how they might make use of this knowledge in an unfamiliar problem context (Siemon, 1993). I brought along a muesli slice in a Swiss roll tin and said that we would have a piece each for play lunch if we could decide how to cut it up into 32 equal parts. The teacher suggested a plasticine model, which is just as well because it soon became evident that the students had no idea how to do this beyond what they knew from cutting pizzas or slicing bread, despite their facility with shading fractional parts on pre-partitioned fraction diagrams. We agreed to think about the problem overnight, but some time later, after the students had returned to their tables, one of the boys started halving a piece of A4 paper. Having realised that he could produce 32 parts by successively halving, we all returned to the mat to reconsider the problem. These are Kieran's words which should be read in conjunction with Figure 18.15 below.

Well the first fold [referring to his paper model] cut the top and bottom edge in half [he marked the top and bottom edge of the plasticine then drew a line to show the 'cut'].

The next fold cut the sides in half [repeated marking and cutting for sides then refolded the A4 paper to decide what the next fold did].

Then I halved the top and bottom again but it halved them both [meaning the original halves] so I do it here ... and here ... [repeated marking and cutting for both halves and refolded paper again to see what happened next].

Then I halved the sides again and that was the same [meaning it cut both side halves in half, he then repeated the marking and cutting procedure for a fourth time].

Then I have to cut the top and bottom ones again [he did this without referring to his paper model, systematically halving each quarter].

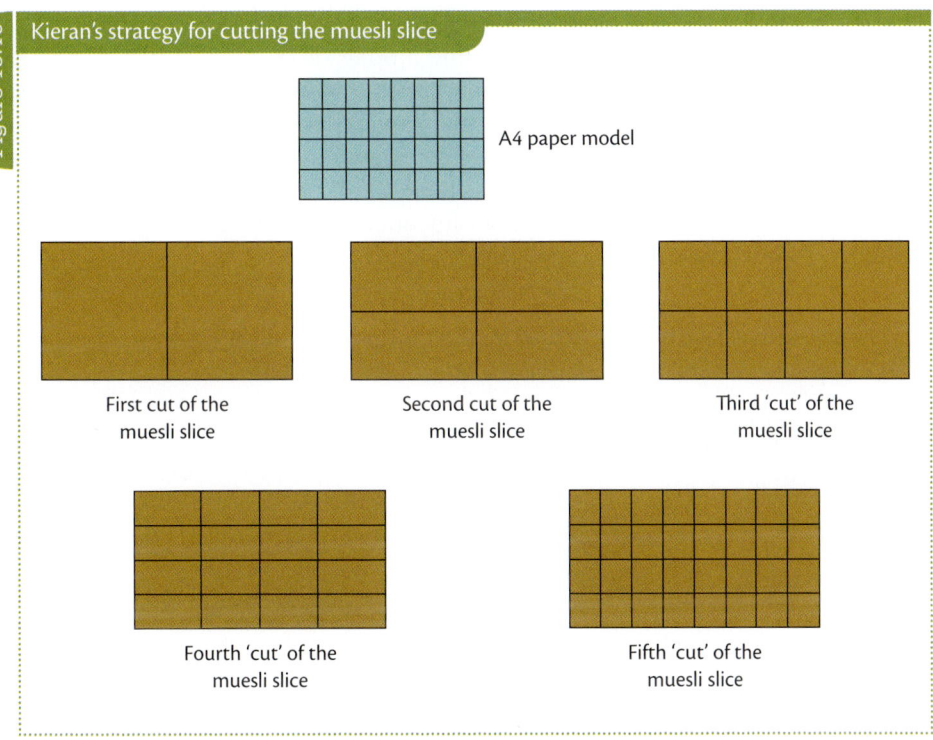

Figure 18.15 Kieran's strategy for cutting the muesli slice

The valuable lesson I learnt from this experience was that although children could partition physical objects by halving and halving again, they were looking at sides and lines not area. Their capacity to partition was intuitive and entirely disconnected from anything else they knew about numbers, particularly multiplication and the relevance of factors. Since then we have developed an explicit focus on teaching halving as a partitioning strategy and linking it to multiplication by drawing attention to the *region* and *for each* idea for multiplication (e.g. in this case, 4 parts by 8 parts is 32 parts, and for each quarter there are now 8 smaller parts, 4 quarters so 4×8, 32 parts altogether). This has proved to be very successful in enabling students to create their own fraction models for a range of fractions (e.g. Breed, 2011; Siemon et al., 2006).

Children should be offered extensive experience in applying their halving strategy to represent and name fractions in the halving family, including mixed fractions, and in a range of contexts (e.g. locate where three-digit numbers such as 497, 259, 751 live on a 0 to 1000 rope).

The thirding strategy

The *thirding strategy* builds on the halving strategy and quantitative reasoning. The notion of *thirding* should be experienced via paper folding using different sized sheets of paper, paper streamers, and rope. Children can be invited to explore what happens with successive acts of thirding (i.e. thirds, ninths, twenty-sevenths etc.) and what happens when thirding is combined with halving (e.g. sixths, twelfths). Once again, it is important to draw attention to the key generalisations listed above (i.e. equal parts, number of parts names the parts, and as the number of parts increases the size of each part decreases) and the link to the *region* and *for each* ideas for multiplication. For example, having 'thirded' a piece of paper and 'thirded' again to produce 9 parts, attention could be drawn to the fact that for each third there are now 3 smaller parts. There are 3 thirds so 9 smaller parts altogether.

To construct fraction diagrams and line models of fractions in the thirding family is significantly more difficult than halving, which can use the fold lines directly and children's intuitive perceptual capacity. Odd partitions are prone to guesswork, but they can be supported by using children's intuitive sense of halving and a quantitative reasoning strategy. For example, to third a blank rectangular region and an open number line interval showing 2 and 3 as shown in Figure 18.16, the reasoning is as follows:

- Think: Thirds are smaller than halves ... Estimate half.
- Then, estimate a third as something less than this, leaving room for two more parts.

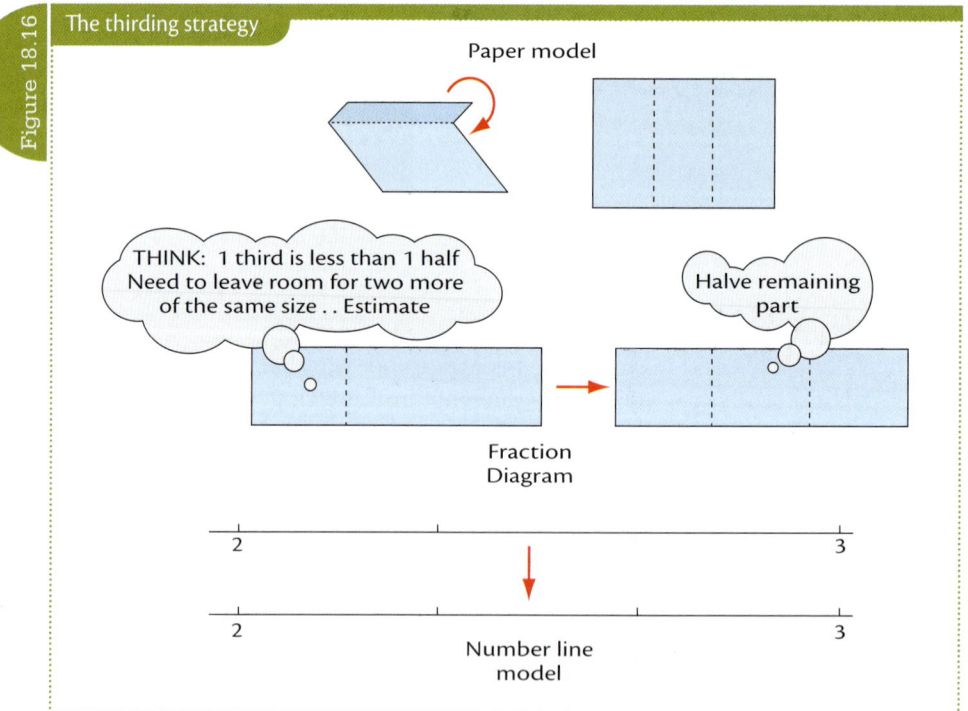

Figure 18.16 The thirding strategy

Children should be given plenty of opportunity to explore and apply the thirding strategy to partition a variety of rectangular regions and open number lines to represent and name fractions in the thirding family. Posters like the ones described above for fractions in the halving family could be used to explore mixed fractions and to connect these to real-world objects through photographs or digital images.

The fifthing strategy

The *fifthing strategy* also builds on the halving strategy and quantitative reasoning. Fifthing can be explored via paper folding using different sized sheets of paper, paper streamers and rope, and children can be invited to explore what happens with successive acts of fifthing (i.e. fifths, twenty-fifths etc.) and what happens when fifthing is combined with the other strategies. For example, fifthing and halving produces tenths, twentieths, and hundredths. Fifthing and thirding produces fifteenths. Once again, it is important to draw attention to the key generalisations listed above (i.e. equal parts, number of parts names the parts, and as the number of parts increases the size of each part decreases) and the connections to the *region* and *for each* ideas for multiplication. For example, having 'fifthed' a piece of paper and 'halved' it again to produce 10 parts (tenths), attention could be drawn to the fact that 5 parts by 2 parts (fifths by halves) gives 10 parts (tenths), or that for each fifth there are now 2 tenths; there are 5 fifths so 10 tenths altogether.

The fifthing strategy can also be used to construct fraction diagrams and line models by building on children's intuitive sense of halving and a quantitative reasoning strategy. For example, to fifth a blank rectangular region and an open number line interval showing 1 and 2 as shown in Figure 18.17, the reasoning is as follows:

- Think: Fifths are smaller than quarters … Estimate half, estimate 1 quarter.
- Then estimate a fifth as something slightly less than 1 quarter.
- As 4 more parts needed … halve and halve again the remaining part.

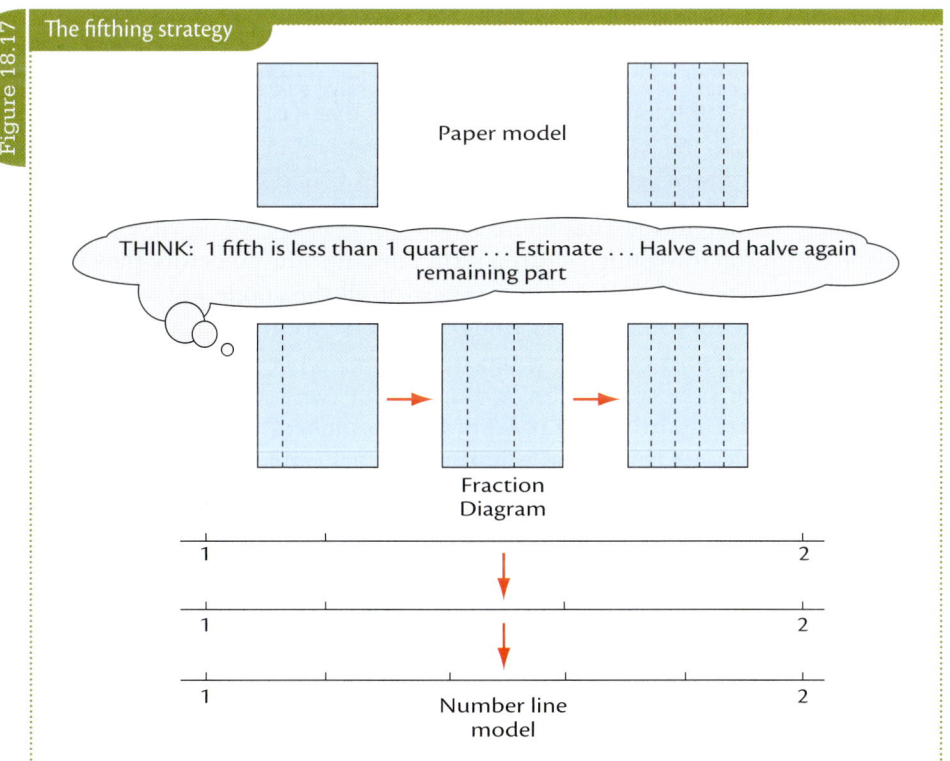

Figure 18.17 The fifthing strategy

Children should be given plenty of opportunity to explore and apply the fifthing strategy in combination with other strategies to partition a variety of rectangular regions and open number lines. Of particular interest are the fifthing and halving strategies as they can be used to construct representations of tenths and hundredths, that is, decimal fraction diagrams and line models (see section on decimals on page 422).

Having control over the representation of fractions provides children with a powerful means of making sense of fractions. Partitioning in this sense is a multiplicative process that invites a consideration of 'what do I have to multiply to get …?'. To return to the example of the muesli slice, children who understand and have had extensive experiences with partitioning as a quantitative reasoning process have little difficulty deciding how to generate 32 equal parts. They recognise the applicability of factors and have access to an explicitly known, as opposed to intuitive, strategy to produce 32 parts. They are also able to recognise that to compare fractions they need to relate to the same referent unit (see section on equivalence on page 432).

Once children are familiar with these strategies they can be encouraged to think about how they might construct other partitions by utilising what they know (e.g. sevenths by thinking 1 seventh is smaller than a sixth … I can estimate a sixth by halving and thirding).

Ultimately, being in charge of the partitioning process enables children to make connections between fractions and the *region/area* and *for each* ideas of multiplication, and recognise how equivalent fractions might be renamed as a consequence of **unitising** (e.g. Lamon, 1996), a process that will be described in more detail in Chapter 24.

Introducing fraction symbols

> [T]he key to the development of symbolic representations in close connection with the children's understanding of division situations and fractions is to work clearly with situations that involve two variables and offer the children the means of representing both of them. Instead of simply depicting one pizza that is cut into pieces and then teaching the pupils the fractional language, it is necessary to pose problems where two variables are concerned and must be represented. (Nunes & Bryant, 1996, p. 229)

As illustrated earlier in the chapter, fraction symbols are a known source of error and confusion for young children if they are introduced before they have had an opportunity to develop an awareness of all the subtle but substantial ways in which fractions differ from whole numbers. We have argued that the initial recording should emphasise the distinction between 'how many' and 'how much' in the same way as for multiplication (see Chapter 17) to make the point that fractions are different from whole numbers. This interpretation aligns with the fraction as a measure interpretation (3 quarter units), which is recognised as one of the entry points for understanding fractions (Confrey, Maloney, Nguyen, Mojica & Myers, 2009; Lamon, 2007). Recording fractional amounts in this way builds on students' appreciation of relative quantity and accommodates both proper and improper fractions (e.g. 3 quarters, 14 fifths). For proper fractions this form of recording also supports the part–whole interpretation. For instance, 3 quarters can be interpreted as 3 out of 4 equal parts. For an improper fraction such as 14 fifths, the 'out of' language only makes sense if the whole number and fractional parts are separated (e.g. 14 fifths is recognised as 10 fifths and 4 fifths, which leads to 2 and 4 out of 5 equal parts or $2\frac{4}{5}$). Thought about in this way, both the measure and part–whole interpretation provide a meaningful pathway to the fraction symbol as suggested in Figure 18.18.

Figure 18.18 Making sense of fraction symbols

Interpretation	Representation	Meaning for symbol
Part–whole	[three-quarters bar shaded]	3 out of 4 → $\frac{3}{4}$
Measure	[number line 0 to 1 with arrow]	3 quarters → $\frac{3}{4}$; 3 × (1/4)
Quotient	[3 pizzas shared among 4 people]	3 divided by 4 → $\frac{3}{4}$ → 0.75
Operator	3 quarters of …	3 × (1/4) → $\frac{3}{4}$ → 75%
Ratio	[3 blue and 4 orange circles]	3 : 4 → $\frac{3}{4}$

Where fractions are interpreted as division (either partitive or quotititive) the fraction symbol is supported more directly. Indeed, Empson et al. (2006) make a strong case for focusing 'on children's conceptualisations of multiplication, division, and ratios of quantities in the context of sharing multiple units among multiple sharers' (p. 5), suggesting that the most powerful and generalisable way to introduce the fraction symbol is through 'the coordination of two essentially composite quantities (items and sharers)' (p. 26). This view is echoed in the quote from Nunes and Bryant above; these authors also stress the importance of children working with two variables in division situations (e.g. 3 pizzas shared among 4 girls or 20 pancakes shared among 8 children). While the focus is on sharing (i.e. partition division) in the early years as this corresponds to children's intuitive capacities and understandings, the fraction as division idea also accommodates quotitive division and provides a basis for attaching meaning to fraction symbols. For example, consider the problem: 'A cardboard coffee cup tray holds 4 cups. How many trays are needed to carry 15 cups of coffee?' One way of responding to this is to say 4 trays, as 3 of the 4 'holes' on the fourth tray will be needed. But this could also be expressed as $3\frac{3}{4}$ trays, where each tray is regarded as a 4-unit.

The fraction-as-operator interpretation draws on the interpretation of fraction as division in making sense of fraction symbols. In this case the fraction refers literally to two operations, either division to find 1 part and then multiplication, or vice versa. This sense of the fraction symbol is important in later uses of fractions and fractional relationships in algebra and problem solving. The ratio interpretation is much more difficult to connect to the fraction symbol directly, although it too involves multiplicative comparisons of parts to parts as in the example shown in Figure 18.18, or parts to whole (in this case, 4 : 7 or $\frac{4}{7}$).

think + link

The connection between fractions, ratio, and multiplicative thinking is considered in more detail in Chapter 24.

Summary

According to Smith (2002), 'children's knowledge of fractions moves through two broad phases of development: (1) making meaning for fractions by linking quotients to divided quantities and (2) exploring the mathematical properties of fractions as numbers' (p. 7); that is, through a rich range of sharing experiences that connect what is being shared to the number of sharers and by exploring fractions as division and as measures. The part–whole interpretation is valuable up to a point but it should not be the only type of situation offered to young children as they endeavour to make sense of fractions. The following summarises the key steps involved in building fraction knowledge and confidence.

- Provide plenty of experiences in sharing recognised quantities (e.g. pizzas, chocolate bars, pancakes) and collections (e.g. sweets, pencils) in ways that emphasise the two variables involved (i.e. the amount to be shared and the number of shares).
- Consider examples and non-examples of fractions and discuss the fact that ordinal number names are used to indicate fractional parts.
- Investigate what happens as the number of sharers increases or decreases (i.e. explore relationship between 'how many' and 'how much').
- Record key generalisations, such as that equal parts are necessary (i.e. equal parts are necessary, the number of parts names the parts, and as the number of parts/sharers increases the size of each part/share decreases).
- Explore partitioning strategies and the ways they can be used to construct fraction diagrams and line models to represent and name proper and mixed fractions.
- Introduce fraction language and symbols to emphasis the distinction between how many (numerator) and how much (denominator) and link to different interpretations, particularly fraction as measure and fraction as quotient.
- Informally compare and order fractions in relation to known benchmarks (e.g. half, quarter, close to 1, proximity to whole number) and explore the use of diagrams and line models in this process.

Introducing decimal fractions

Children's strong intuitive basis for fractions suggests that decimal fractions need to be understood as fractions before children can be expected to appreciate these new numbers as an extension of the base 10 number system. Where children have a well-developed capacity to partition region and line models using the *fifthing* and *halving* strategies and are comfortable with naming fractions in a variety of ways (e.g. 7 tenths, $\frac{7}{10}$, 12 tenths, $1\frac{2}{10}$), they are likely to be ready to appreciate the link between fractions involving tenths and the base 10 number system.

While some have suggested an alternative approach to decimal fractions based on children's intuitive understanding of percentages (e.g. Moss & Case, 1999), there is a risk that the inherent place-value patterns (i.e. '1 tenth of these is 1 of those' and the inverse, '10 of these is 1 of those') might be overlooked. Also, the contexts associated with percentages tend to privilege fraction as operator interpretations (e.g. '25% off the original price'), which means that *per cent* may not be understood as another name for hundredths (e.g. '25 per cent' 'sounds' different from '25 hundredths). Percentages are useful in establishing and broadening the names for key fraction benchmarks such as half, a quarter, a third, a fifth, and 1, but the opportunities for making these connections should arise from children's language and experience and not be imposed.

A cautionary note: some curriculum documents suggest that hundredths can be introduced at Year 4 (e.g. ACARA, 2010), presumably on the grounds that children are familiar with money. While many children can solve problems involving money amounts at an early age, this does not mean that they are attending to those amounts as decimal fractions. Indeed, the language of money treats dollars and cents as two whole number systems side by side. Cents are counted in whole numbers to 99, and dollars are counted in whole numbers. This can be heard in how we read '$35.35' and how we read '35.35' metres. Also, in a digital age, children are no longer exposed to money in the same way that their parents were. We no longer have 1 cent coins, and the coins we do have tend to be treated as 'units' in their own right. That is, they have no physical relationship to the 'whole', and they are referred to using whole-number language.

Introducing decimal place value follows the same steps as whole number place value but there is a new pattern to be explored that is the inverse of the original pattern (i.e. '10 of these is 1 of those'), namely *1 tenth of these is 1 of those*.

Establishing tenths as a new place-value part

Tenths are introduced as a new place-value unit in much the same way that tens and hundreds were introduced. That is, by 'making', naming, and recording these new numbers in relation to what is already known. For example, in introducing two-digit place value, bundling and stacking materials are used to connect the known (ones) to the new unit (tens), explore the big idea that '10 of these is 1 of those', and connect number names to recording. In this instance, it is necessary to connect fractions to decimals by exploring the different ways in which the *halving* and *fifthing* partitioning strategies might be applied to region models and number lines to create tenths. These steps are briefly summarised here.

1. Introduce the new unit

Review tenths via fraction diagrams and number line representations that children have created using their halving and fifthing partitioning strategies. Collect as many different representations as possible and use them to make a classroom display. Discuss the 'specialness' of tenths (e.g. used in rulers, a millimetre is 1 tenth of a centimetre) and link to the place-value idea, 10 of these (indicating tenths) is 1 of those (indicating ones) on a number line. The *for each* idea for multiplication and a *tenthing* strategy (i.e. fifthing then halving or vice versa) can be used to demonstrate that tenths 'live' between whole numbers on a number line (i.e. for each one there are 10 tenths).

2. Make and name ones and tenths

Make, name, and record ones and tenths by *tenthing*, keeping in mind that 0 ones is just one example of ones and tenths. Tenths mats and open number lines (e.g. see Figure 18.19) can be used to explore models for ones and tenths more systematically as can drinking straws (see below).

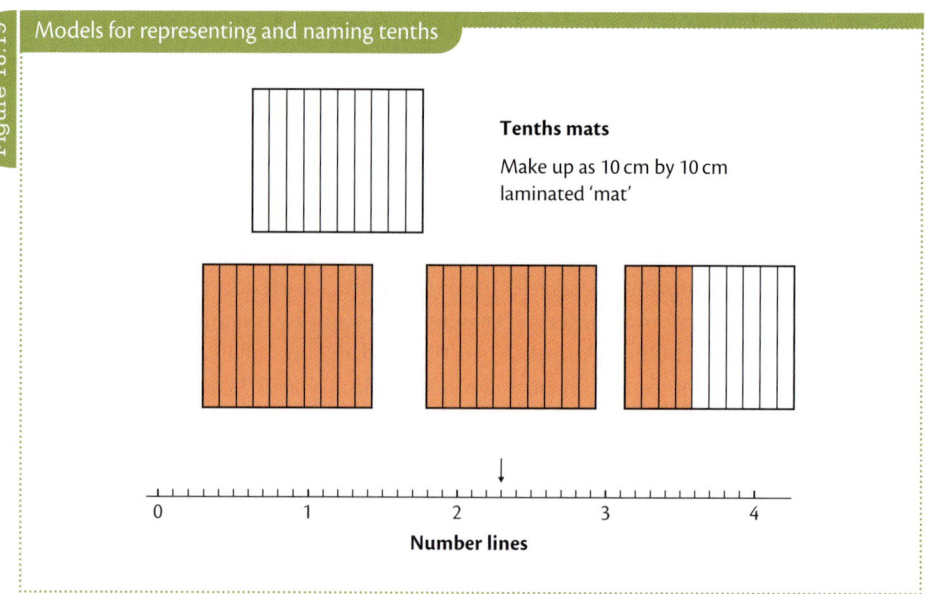

Figure 18.19 Models for representing and naming tenths

3. Introduce decimal recording

Review the structure of the base 10 number system using base 10 blocks and a place-value chart. Point out that 1 tenth of a thousand block is 1 hundred, 1 tenth of the hundred is 1 ten and 1 tenth of that is 1—some teachers have found it useful to 'slice' the unit cube into 10 parts to show the continuing pattern, but this requires considerable care.

Another word of caution: while the base 10 materials can be used for the purpose described, these do not work as models of decimal fractions. Children see these, understandably, as ones, tens, hundreds, and thousands, and many find it difficult to 'pretend' that they can take on other values. The same applies to stacking materials that have been used to model ones and tens.

Tenths mats, number lines, and drinking straws offer more appropriate concrete models as they can be partitioned into 10 equal parts more easily and mounted on poster displays as permanent records. These models can be used to represent, name, and record ones and tenths on a place-value chart as shown in Figure 18.20. Note that a separator is not needed on a place-value chart as there is no ambiguity about the value of the count. However, when the models and place-value chart are removed and only the numerals remain, a separator, in this case the decimal point, is needed to show where the ones begin. For this reason, 0 should always be included in the ones place for decimal fractions less than 1.

4. Consolidate understanding

Activities involving comparing, ordering, counting forwards and backwards in place-value parts, and renaming can be used to consolidate tenths as a new place-value part. For example, children can be given six different lengths of string, asked to measure these as accurately as they can, record their lengths in centimetres, then compare and order the lengths from smallest to largest (e.g. 4.6 cm, 7.8 cm, 11.7 cm, 15.2 cm, 21.7 cm, and 25.6 cm). Empty number charts like the ones shown in Figure 18.21 can be used to count forwards and backwards in ones and tenths.

Chapter 18 Introducing Fractions and Decimal Fractions

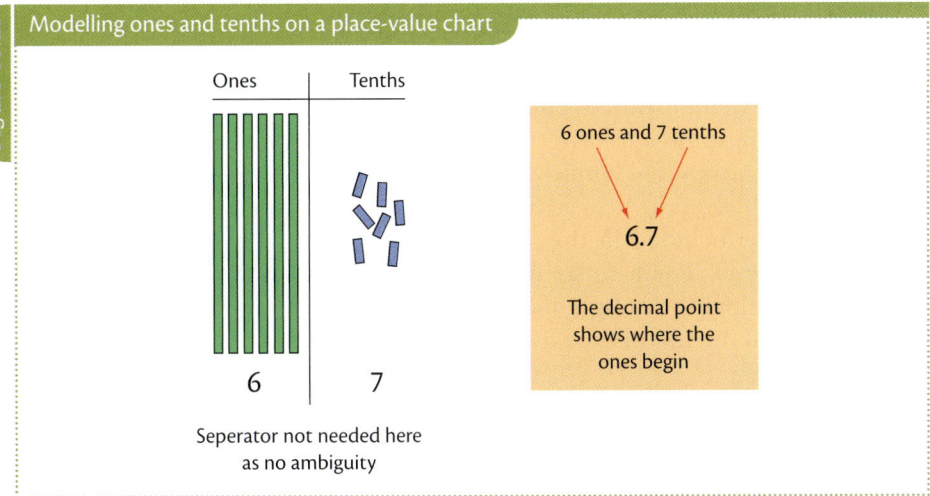

Figure 18.20 Modelling ones and tenths on a place-value chart

Figure 18.21 Empty number charts for ones and tenths

Renaming can be explored by measuring the same length in centimetres and millimetres, for example a length of 12.8 cm is 128 millimetres. Number expanders can also be used as shown in Figure 18.22 to rename tens and ones and tenths in as many different ways as possible.

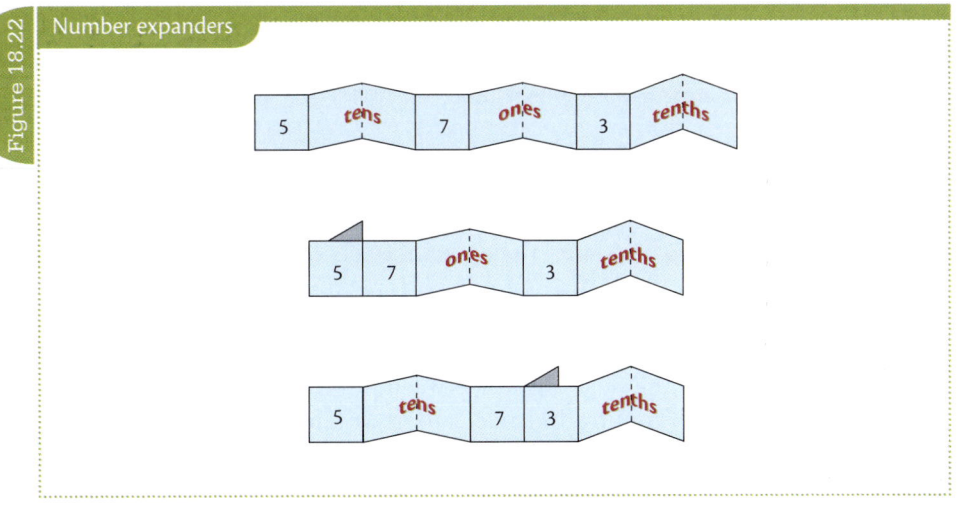

Figure 18.22 Number expanders

Extending decimal place value

Children are only ready to move on to hundredths as a new place-value part once they have demonstrated a deep understanding of tenths as a place-value part and recognise how *tenthing* can be applied to represent hundredths on diagrams and line models. Hundredths are briefly considered here as there may well be some children in Year 4 who are ready to proceed to hundredths and hundredths are included in the *Australian Curriculum: Mathematics* (ACARA, 2010) at this level. For a fuller discussion see Chapter 22. Hundredths can be explored initially through measurement activities involving metres and centimetres and the use of tape measures and/or rulers.

1. Introduce the new unit

Hundredths need to be closely tied to tenths in terms of the 'big idea' that '10 of these is 1 of those' through partitioning activities that demonstrate this relationship on fraction diagrams and number lines. For instance, while hundredths can be represented in a number of different ways on a fraction diagram (e.g. 5 parts by 20 parts, 25 parts by 4 parts, or 2 parts by 50 parts), it is important that the fraction models used to support hundredths as a decimal fraction show that *for each* tenth there are 10 hundredths. This can be accomplished by fraction diagrams that show that tenths by tenths are hundredths and by number lines, as shown in Figure 18.23.

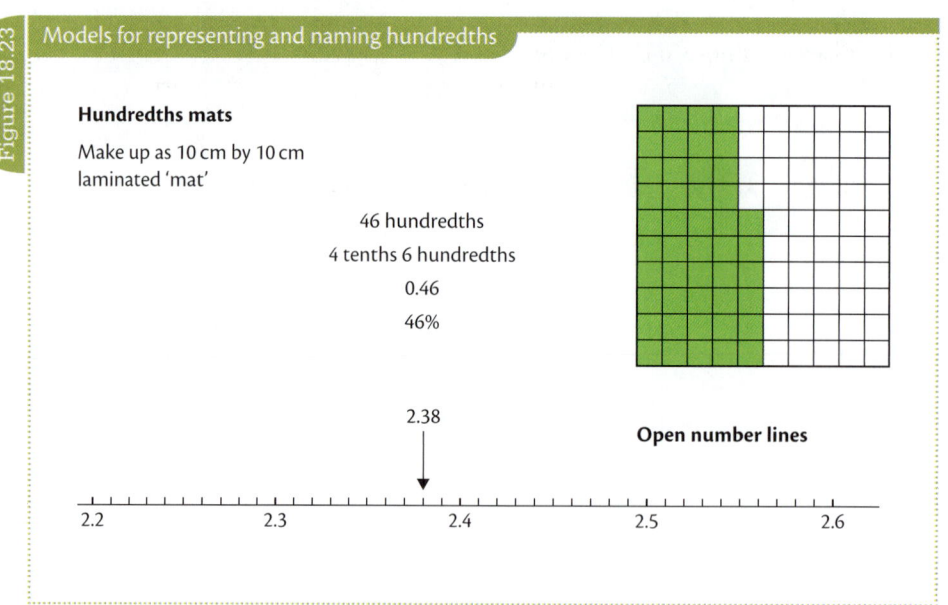

Figure 18.23 Models for representing and naming hundredths

2. 'Make', name, and record ones, tenths, and hundredths

Initially, children should construct their own models of hundredths to realise that there are many ways in which this might be done. But as this quickly becomes tedious, drawn representations can be replaced by hundredths mats and open number lines as shown in Figure 18.23. The important feature of both models is that they clearly show the relationship between hundredths and tenths.

Decimal recording of hundredths needs to be developed in a similar way to tenths, that is, by using hundredths mats and number lines to represent, name, and record ones, tenths, and hundredths on a place-value chart.

3. Consolidate

Hundredths can be consolidated as a new place-value part in much the same way as this was done for tenths. For example, a hop-skip-and-jump activity where jumps are measured in metres as 3.45, 2.98 etc. could be used to compare and order ones and hundredths. Number lines could be partitioned as shown in Figure 18.23 and empty number charts like the ones shown in Figure 18.21 can be adapted and used to count forwards and backwards in ones, tenths, and hundredths (e.g. a start number might be 5.34).

The place-value game described in Chapter 15 (p. 311) can also be adapted to locate hundredths between any unit interval (e.g. start and end numbers could be 2 and 3 respectively and the two 10-sided dice used to 'make' and locate hundredths between 2 and 3). A long length of rope can also be used with cards and pegs and different end-points to locate hundredths.

Number expanders can be used to rename decimal fractions in as many ways as possible, and renaming can also be explored in relation to length measures (e.g. 267 centimetres is 2.67 metres).

Link to percentage and proportion

Thinking about any collection or quantity in terms of 100 parts provides a powerful means of describing and comparing different quantities. For example, it is possible to compare the incidence of a particular disease in different populations by comparing the relative proportions of those affected with the disease in terms of how many hundredths of each population is affected by the disease. These measures are known as percentages. Per cent literally means per hundred, and percentages express a relative proportion of the whole, irrespective of its size. At this level, it is appropriate to focus on known benchmarks such as 50% (half), 25%, and 10%. These links can be made by re-unitising hundredths diagrams as shown in Figure 18.24.

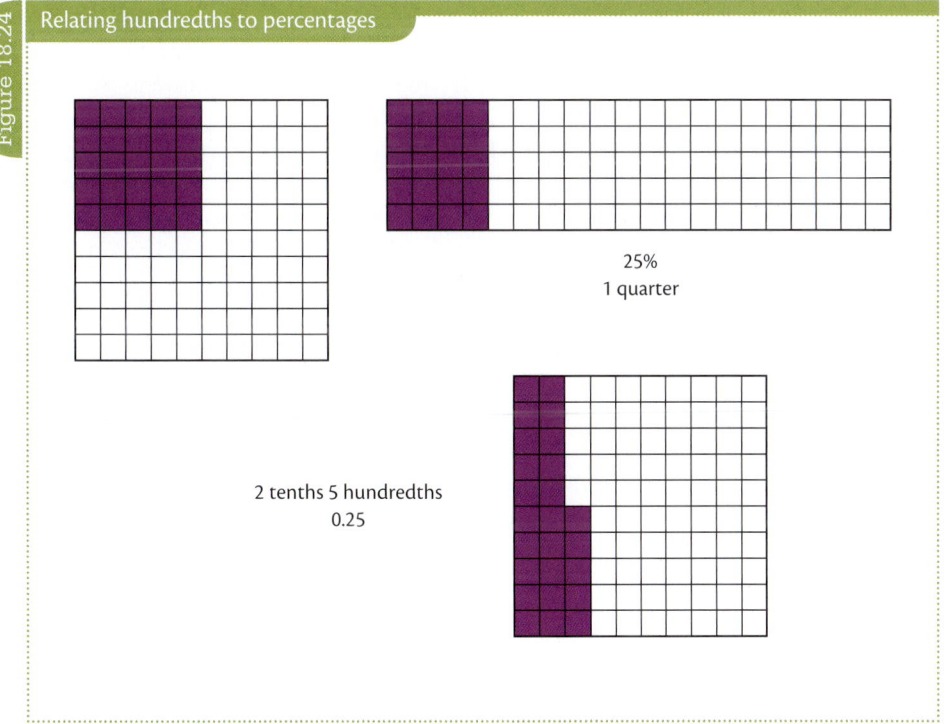

Figure 18.24 Relating hundredths to percentages

25%
1 quarter

2 tenths 5 hundredths
0.25

think + link

Percentages are a special type of ratio. They are considered in more detail in Chapter 22.

It is also important that children understand what is meant by percentages that are larger than 100% (e.g. 400%) and, later on, when calculating percentagess it is important that students see the relationship between percentages and hundredths as this obviates the need for the % key on a calculator.

did you know?

The base 10 (decimal) number system is symmetrical about the ones, not the decimal point. Many commercial materials include a decimal point in place-value charts; this is inappropriate, particularly if it is placed on the 'border' between the ones and the tenths.

Thousands	Hundreds	Tens	Ones	tenths	hundredths	Thousandths
4	3	0	7	8	1	9

4307.819

Decimal points are needed only when it is necessary to show where the ones begin. The main reason for this is that when the decimal point is shown on a place-value chart or number expander it can interfere with the renaming process. For example, 'reading' to the hundredths position on the place-value chart above without a decimal point facilitates the renaming of 4307.819 as hundredths and thousandths, that is, 430781 hundredths and 9 thousandths.

think + link

Addition and subtraction with decimal fractions is considered in Chapter 16.

Note that, when adding and subtracting decimal fractions involving ones and tenths or multiplying a decimal fraction by a whole number, it is important to read and refer to these in place-value parts, for example for 4.6 + 2.7 it is important to read this as 'four and 6 tenths and 2 and 7 tenths … 6 tenths and 7 tenths are 13 tenths, that is 1 one and 3 tenths' etc.

Sources of difficulty

The difficulties experienced by students and adults with decimal fractions have been well documented (e.g. Hart, 1981; Irwin, 2001; Stacey, Helme & Steinle, 2001). Internal zeros can be problematic in numbers such as 4.07 and language can be an issue, particularly where the fractional components are read as single digit numbers as in 'four point o seven' (with 'o' read as the letter 'o') or 'twenty-three point five six'. In both instances, children need to be supported in their efforts to make sense of what they are hearing by naming decimal fractions in terms of their place-value parts, that is, 'four and 7 hundredths' and 'twenty-three and fifty-six hundredths' respectively.

The materials and models used to support the teaching and learning of fractions and decimal fractions can also be problematic. For example, although place-value charts help explain why decimals are written the way they are, they do not teach decimals. Children need to understand the relationship of tenths to ones in the same way that they understand the relationship of ones to tens, tens to hundreds and so on before a place-value chart makes much sense. The potential problems involved in using base 10 blocks and money as models of decimal fractions have already been referred to.

One of the less obvious difficulties with decimal fractions is that the relative size of adjacent place-value parts is hard to comprehend. Children can imagine a unit being divided into 2, 4, and 8 parts relatively easily, but the number of parts created as a result of successive acts of *tenthing* become unimaginable very quickly. The result is that many older children are unable to conceive where hundredths 'live' in relation to other numbers, or how they might be represented on a number line.

consider and discuss

Exploring partitioning

Copy and complete the table below and use these values to construct a graph that shows the effect of successive acts of halving, thirding, and fifthing on the number of parts for the first three acts of partitioning. What do you notice?

What implications does this have for the teaching and learning of decimals? (Hint: Investigate what happens with successive acts of tenthing.)

Table 18.2

Relationship between partitioning acts and the total number of parts					
Number of partitioning acts	1	2	3	4	5
Halving	2	4	8	16	32
Thirding	3	9	27		
Fifthing	5	25			

Consolidating understanding

Children's understanding of fractions and decimal fractions at this level can be consolidated through activities and games that reinforce the key generalisations and help build knowledge and confidence of fractions as relative quantities through partitioning, comparing, ordering, and renaming.

Partitioning strategies can be evaluated through activities that require children to partition:

- unpartitioned shapes (e.g. partition to show $\frac{1}{6}$ of different sized rectangles, circles)
- line segments (e.g. on a number line marked in unit intervals from 3 to 7, show $3\frac{3}{4}$, 4.8, $5\frac{2}{3}$ and 6.2)
- discrete collections (e.g. partition to show $\frac{3}{8}$ of 24 eggs)
- to show mixed fractions (e.g. $3\frac{2}{3}$).

Recognising and naming parts in recognised wholes such as tangrams helps to consolidate fraction naming and build a sense of relative quantity. However, appreciating the relative quantities conveyed by fraction symbols can be problematic so children need plenty of opportunities to make sense of fractions in terms of known benchmarks. Initially, this involves deciding whether fractions are closer to 0, a half, or 1, but this can be extended to include mixed fractions, decimals, and percentages, as shown below.

integrating technology/ICT

Closer to …

Construct a table and a set of fraction 'cards' like the ones shown in Figure 18.25 for an interactive whiteboard. Invite children to locate the fractions according to whether or not they are closer to 0, 1, or 2. Simpler fractions could be chosen initially, but it is important to include fractions in multiple symbolic forms (i.e. proper, improper, mixed, and decimal fractions). Use the cards to discuss the meanings of the symbols and justify reasons for selecting locations.

Later on, the table could be replaced by a number line from 0 to 2 and children could be asked to locate the fractions on the number line. In this case, it is useful to have numbers like $\frac{3}{4}$ and 1.5 to test whether or not children are interpreting $\frac{3}{4}$ as a number or as a proportion of the line, and percentages such as 25% and 150% to test whether or not children are interpreting per cent as an operator or as a number.

Figure 18.25 Closer to …

Renaming fractions at this level should be based on perceptual recognition rather than an algorithmic procedure. Fraction models can be used to establish the connections between common and decimal fractions and percentages. Calculators can be used together with division to reinforce the meaning of fractions as quotient (division) and to demonstrate how fractions can be renamed as decimals (e.g. by dividing 1 by 2, 3 by 4). Where children have had plenty of experience with division of whole numbers and partition they may be able to carry out the division for fractions such as $\frac{4}{5}$ by recognising that 4 ones cannot be shared among 5, but by renaming 4 ones as 40 tenths it can be shared equally so that each share is 8 tenths or 0.8. Fraction models can be used to show the equivalence of 8 tenths to 80 hundredths and thereby 80%.

for the classroom

Make up fraction cards for at least 10 different fractions like the ones shown in Figure 18.26. Include at least two fractions larger than 1 and as many different representations as appropriate.

Cards can be selected according to children's learning needs and used for sorting or matching games such as patience and snap, or collection games such as concentration.

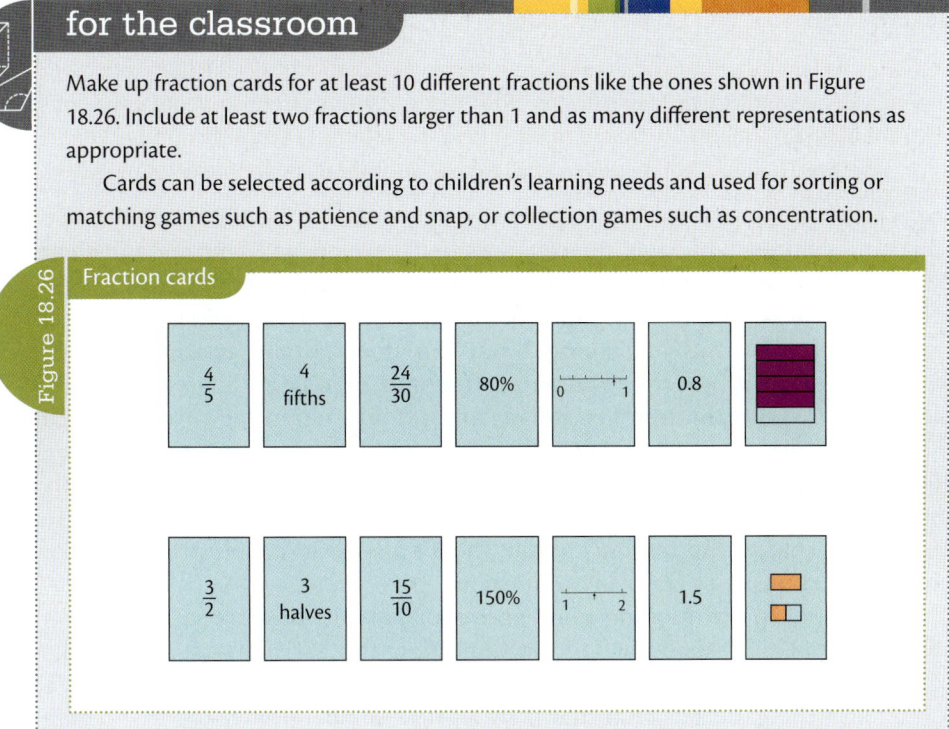

Figure 18.26 Fraction cards

Locating fractions and decimals on a 0 to 2 number line given multiple names for the same fraction as shown in Figure 18.27 can be revealing. In this case, cards can be attached to one another to demonstrate that they 'live' at the same place on the number line.

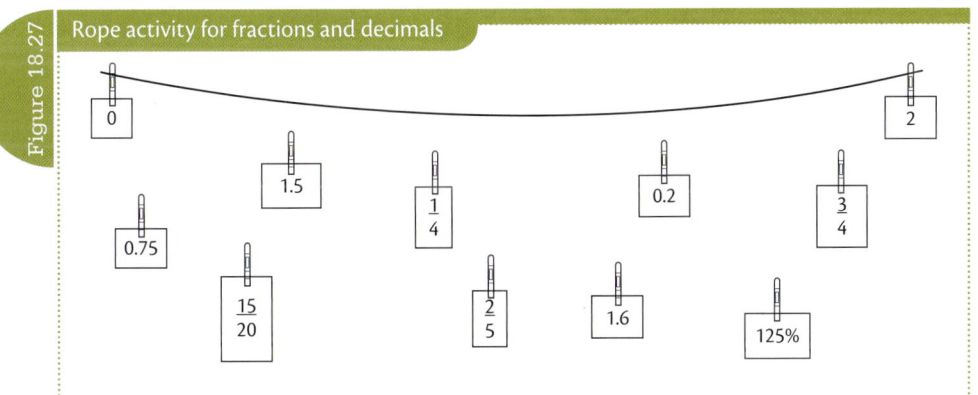

Figure 18.27 Rope activity for fractions and decimals

Counting forwards and backwards in fractional amounts is not really all that appropriate as a consolidating activity, as it can lead to the overuse of whole-number thinking more generally. However, as this is an essentially additive process, it can be used to model fraction addition and subtraction and, from a fraction as measure perspective, prompt the need to rename fractions in terms of common units. On the other hand, counting backwards and forwards is a useful consolidating activity for decimal fractions as we have seen above.

A sense of equivalence

> Two challenging, important, and often fascinating aspects of fractions are their equivalence and order properties. In both cases, fractions defy students' intuitions from natural numbers: There are many different fractions (an infinite number) equal to any given fraction, and between any two fractions there are infinitely many others. (Smith, 2002, p. 9)

Children will inevitably 'see' the relationships between well-known equivalent fractions such as $\frac{1}{2}$, 2/4 and $\frac{3}{6}$ from their many experiences with cutting and folding physical objects and using their partitioning strategies to construct fraction diagrams and line models, but this does not necessarily translate to a generalised process for renaming fractions or recognising equivalence, particularly where children are relying on a double-counting procedure. In the past, simple examples such as these were used to justify rules for finding equivalent fractions in the upper primary grades. For example, 'you multiply the top and the bottom number by the same number', or 'what you do to the top, you do to the bottom'. While these rules 'work', they are devoid of meaning and prone to error in application.

In later years, partitioning plays an important role in connecting fraction meanings and representations to multiplication and division and, ultimately, proportional reasoning (Lamon, 2007). In particular, partitioning can be used to establish the generalisation that *if the number of parts is increased by a certain factor, the number of shaded/marked parts increases by the same factor*. For instance, in the area model for $\frac{3}{5}$ shown in Figure 18.28, it is possible to appeal to the *region* idea for multiplication (i.e. 5 parts by 3 parts is 15 parts) to show that fifths by thirds are fifteenths and that, correspondingly, 3 fifths by 3 thirds is 9 fifteenths.

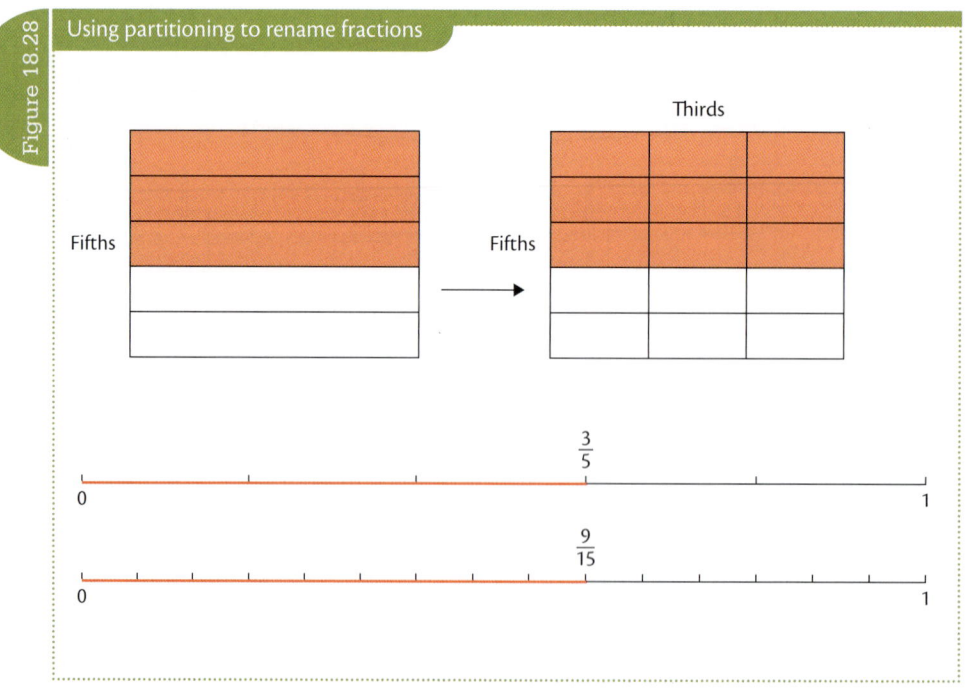

Figure 18.28 Using partitioning to rename fractions

For both models, it is also possible to make a connection to the *for each* idea for multiplication in that for each shaded fifth there are now three smaller parts (fifteenths), that is, 9 fifteenths shaded. While the first of these two connections might be seen as a more sophisticated form of double-counting, the second links more directly to proportional reasoning and the *factor–factor–product* idea for multiplication and division.

for the classroom

The 'make a whole' game

You will need a game sheet for each player or team as shown in Figure 18.29 and a set of numerator and denominator cards as listed below (40 blank playing cards can be used for this purpose).

- Numerator cards: 4 sets of numeral cards from 1 to 5 (20 cards in all)
- Denominator cards: 2 each of: 'wild', 'halves', 'fifths', 'sixths', 'eighths', and 'ninths'; 3 each of 'thirds', 'fourths'; and 1 each of 'tenths' and 'sevenths'.

Players take it in turns to take a card from each set, which has been shuffled and placed face downwards in the middle of the table. For a draw of '6' and 'eighths' a border would be placed around 6 eighths. If this is not possible, players may still be able to use their turn if they convince the others of an equivalent placement (e.g. 3 quarters). The wildcards can be used to indicate a denominator as the player chooses. The winner of the game is the person/team who completes the most rows (wholes).

Figure 18.29 'Make a whole' game

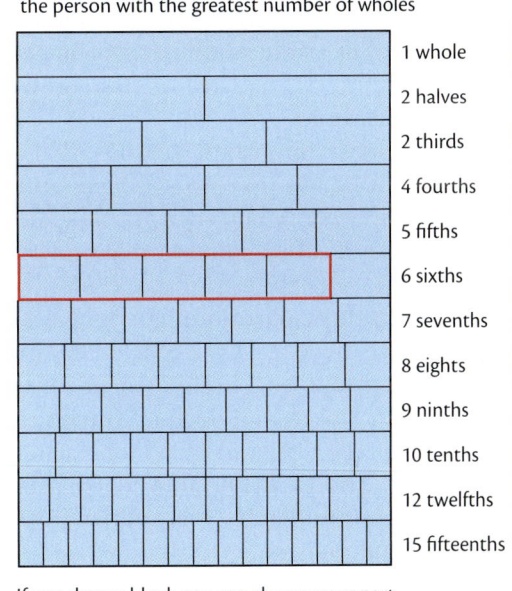

How many wholes can you make?

Choose a card that says 'how many' and a card that says 'how much'. Colour the amount. The winner is the person with the greatest number of wholes

1 whole
2 halves
2 thirds
4 fourths
5 fifths
6 sixths
7 sevenths
8 eights
9 ninths
10 tenths
12 twelfths
15 fifteenths

If you draw a blank you can choose your part

In general, it is inappropriate to pursue fraction equivalence and order properties formally at this level. However, it is appropriate to make connections to the *region* and *for each* ideas for multiplication informally and to draw children's attention to the relationships involved. Where appropriate, carefully selected fraction pairs or groups of fractions can be used to explore relationships between like and related fractions by asking the question 'Which of the following two (or more) fractions is greater, or are they equal?' As Smith (2002) notes, the phrasing here is important as 'it leaves it completely open whether fractions that "look different" really are or just seem to be' (p. 9).

Lamon (1996, 1999) suggests working with packaging as a basis for building a more general understanding of fraction equivalence. This process involves *unitising*. For example, soft drink cans can be bought in many different ways: as a 'slab' of 24 cans, a '6-pack', or a '12-pack'. This allows a relationship such as 18 cans out of 48 cans to be renamed in terms of the same-sized packs, that is, as $1\frac{1}{2}$ (12-packs)/4 (12-packs) or 3 (6-packs)/8 (6-packs), thereby exposing the ratio or proportion in its simplest form but also providing opportunities to play with number relationships and a motivation for looking for 'simpler' fractions.

Conclusion

In this chapter we have seen that young children have an important intuitive sense of fractions based on their notions of fair shares. While this can be useful in building fraction language and a sense of fractions as equal parts of a whole, it is important that children are also exposed to a range of experiences that go beyond the 'out of' idea, in particular that they experience fractions as the result of division, as numbers that exist uniquely on the number line irrespective of how they are named, as measures, as ratios, and as operators.

One of the most important reasons that children find fractions and decimals difficult is that they do not have access to a range of meaningful models to support and extend their understanding of fractions and decimal fractions. As a result, they come to rely on rules and procedures with little or no appreciation of the significance of the numbers involved. To this end, we explored three partitioning strategies, *halving*, *thirding*, and *fifthing*, which we believe need to be explicitly taught, regularly exercised, and thoroughly explored to enable children to construct their own diagrams and line models for fractions and decimal fractions. While these techniques will ultimately need to be replaced by a more generalised process for renaming and ordering fractions, being able to partition (mentally and physically) provides a firm foundation for connecting fraction representations to multiplication and division.

key terms

Continuous fraction models: models based on attributes that, in principle, are infinitely divisible (e.g. length, area, volume, capacity, mass)

Decimal: a numeral in the decimal (base 10) number system. Decimal numbers comprise an integer part and a fractional part; digits in the integer part indicate a multiple of a positive power of 10, digits in the fractional part indicate a multiple of a negative power of 10

Denominator: in the fraction $\frac{a}{b}$, b is the denominator. 'It is the number of equal parts into which the whole is divided in order to obtain fractional parts' (ACARA, 2011)

Discrete fraction models: collections that are not intended to be partitioned further than the items themselves (e.g. a packet of Smarties, a dozen eggs, a class of children)

Fifthing: the process of partitioning a continuous quantity into five equal parts using halving as a guide (i.e. by recognising that fifths are smaller than quarters, and in choosing where to locate 1 fifth, it needs to be possible to halve and halve again to create 2 more parts of the same size)

Fraction: a number written as $\frac{a}{b}$ (written alternatively as a/b) where a is a non-negative integer and b is a positive integer (i.e. $b \neq 0$), a is referred to as the numerator, and b is referred to as the denominator (ACARA, 2011); a fraction is said to be *proper* if it is less than 1 (as in $\frac{2}{7}$) and *improper* when it is greater than 1 (as in $\frac{8}{5}$)

Halving: the process of continually partitioning a continuous quantity into two equal parts to produce fractions in the halving family (i.e. halves, quarters or fourths, eighths, sixteenths)

Mixed fraction: a number made up of a positive integer and a proper fraction (e.g. $4\frac{5}{6}$)

Numerator: in the fraction $\frac{a}{b}$, a is the numerator; 'If an object is divided into b equal parts, then the fraction $\frac{a}{b}$ represents a of those parts taken together.' (ACARA, 2011)

Partitioning: the process of dividing (usually physically) a quantity or collection into equal parts with no remainder

Ratio: a quotient or proportion of two numbers; a way of comparing one quantity with another quantity, ratios can be expressed as $m:n$ or as $\frac{m}{n}$ ($n \neq 0$)

Rational number: any number that can be expressed as $\frac{p}{q}$, where p and q are integers, and $q \neq 0$

Thirding: the process of partitioning a continuous quantity into three equal parts using halving as a guide (i.e. by recognising that thirds are smaller than halves and that in choosing where to locate 1 third it needs to be possible to halve the remaining part to create 2 more parts of the same size)

Unitising: a cognitive process that involves 'thinking about a quantity in terms of different sized chunks' (Lamon, 1999, p. 83); for example, 24 can be thought about in terms of 3 eight-units, 4 six-units, or 8 three-units

Review questions

1. Describe the key generalisations that children need to be aware of before they are ready to work more formally with fraction ideas and symbolic representations.
2. Why is it important to initially record fractional amounts in terms of a numeral and a word, for example, 3 quarters, 5 eighths, 10 thirds?
3. Use diagrams and problem contexts as appropriate to illustrate at least four different ways in which $\frac{2}{3}$ might be represented and/or interpreted.
4. Describe and illustrate each of the partitioning strategies (i.e. halving, thirding, and fifthing). Use examples to show how you might use these strategies to help build a deep understanding of:
   a. decimal fractions
   b. the processes underpinning the renaming of common fractions.
5. Give 'real-world' examples of:
   a. a comparison activity involving related fractions
   b. an ordering activity involving ones, tenths, and hundredths.
6. A group of Year 4 children consistently claims that fractions are bigger or smaller on the basis of the size of the denominator. What would you do to explore their thinking and deepen their understanding of fractions?
7. Renaming is an important activity to consolidate place-value understanding, Construct a number expander and use this to rename 56.3 in as many different ways as possible.

Key references

Charles, K., & Nason, R. (2000). Young children's partitioning strategies. *Educational Studies in Mathematics, 43*(2), 191–221.

Empson, S., Junk, D., Dominguez, H., & Turner, E. (2006). Fractions as the coordination of multiplicatively related quantities: A cross-sectional study of children's thinking. *Educational Studies in Mathematics, 63*(1), 1–28.

Hart, K. (Ed.) (1981). *Children's Understanding of Mathematics: 11–16.* London: John Murray.

Irwin, K. (2001). Using everyday knowledge of decimals to enhance understanding. *Journal for Research in Mathematics Education, 32*(4), 399–421.

Lamon, S. (2007). Rational numbers and proportional reasoning: Towards a theoretical framework for research. In F. Lester (Ed.), *Second Handbook of Research on Mathematics Teaching and Learning. A Project of the National Council of Teachers of Mathematics* (pp. 629–667). Charlotte, NC: Information Age.

Nunes, T., & Bryant, P. (1996). *Children doing Mathematics.* Oxford, UK: Blackwell.

Olive, J., & Steffe, L. (2002). The construction of an iterative fractional scheme: The case of Jo. *Journal of Mathematical Behaviour, 20*, 413–437.

Pothier, Y., & Sawada, D. (1990). Partitioning: An approach to fractions. *The Arithmetic Teacher, 38*(4), 12–16.

Siemon, D. (2003). Partitioning the missing link in building fraction knowledge and confidence. *Australian Mathematics Teacher, 59*(2), 22–24.

Steen, L. A. (2007). How mathematics counts. *Educational Leadership*, November, pp. 9–14.

Swan, M. (1990). Becoming numerate: Developing conceptual structures. In S. Willis (Ed.), *Being Numerate—What Counts?* Melbourne: Australian Council for Educational Research.

Thompson, P. (1994). Concrete materials and teaching for mathematical understanding. *Arithmetic Teacher, 41*(9), 556–558.

Thomson, S., & Buckley, S. (2009). Informing mathematics pedagogy: TIMSS 2007 Australia and the world. Melbourne: ACER.

Wong, M., & Evans, D. (2008). Fractions as measure. In M. Goos, R. Brown & K. Makar (Eds.), *Proceedings of the 31st Annual Conference of the Mathematics Education Research Group of Australasia* (pp. 597–603). Brisbane: MERGA.

Websites

www.simerr.educ.utas.edu.au/numeracy/critical_numeracy/critical_numeracy.htm

www.thenetwork.sa.edu.au/teachingandlearning

http://activated.act.edu.au/ectl

www.education.monash.edu.au/research/projects/ttml/classroom-activities.html

http://extranet.edfac.unimelb.edu.au/DSME/decimals/SLIMversion/sources/devteam.shtml

Developing Measurement Concepts and Strategies

19

Contents

Why is teaching measurement important?	439
Measurement concepts in the curriculum	439
Measurement learning sequence	441
Approaches to developing an understanding of length	444
Approaches to developing an understanding of time	449
Conclusion	452

Chapter objectives

This chapter will enable the reader to:
- Explore how children develop their understandings of measurement through the use of a coherent measurement learning sequence
- Investigate approaches to developing an understanding of the concepts of length and time.

How important is 1 mm?

A carpenter and his apprentice were called upon to give a quote to repair some floor boards in a timber house. Termites had eaten through five of the vertical joint floor boards in the bedroom, leaving nothing but the paint behind! The young apprentice, who was in her first year on the job, was given the task of measuring the width of one of the floor boards. '100', she announced.

- What unit of measurement was she using?
- Why would she use that unit of measurement?
- What aspects of making a measurement was she able to perform?

When he heard the number, the carpenter replied, 'That's funny. It's usually 99 or 101. Measure it again.'

Big ideas

- Students will be able to manage the relatively complex process of accurately measuring an attribute effectively if they have had the opportunity to develop a sense of measuring processes through a coherent sequence of learning experiences.
- The measurement of length takes a central position in early learning experiences because it is foundational to building other measurement concepts.
- Measuring skills are essential to successful numerate behaviour in managing day-to-day situations.

>
> ### consider and discuss
>
> When considering the scenario described above:
> 1. Why would a difference of 1 mm be important?
> 2. What might the implications of this inaccuracy be?
> 3. What aspects of making a measurement does it seem that the apprentice is unable to perform effectively?
> 4. What does this scenario say about numeracy in context?

Why is teaching measurement important?

Measuring skills are essential to successful numerate behaviour. Therefore, there is a convincing justification for including a measurement strand in the primary mathematics curriculum.

Measurement also makes strong links with other mathematics strands, particularly with number and geometry. Measurement involves assigning a numerical value to the spatial qualities of an object or an event. Therefore, geometric, numerical, and measurement concepts need to necessary develop simultaneously. Consider the links between number, geometry, and measurement involved in investigating the value of π (pi) as the ratio of the diameter of a circle to the circumference of the circle, or the application of Pythagoras' theorem in calculating the lengths of sides in a right-angled triangle.

For primary teachers, measurement provides an excellent opportunity to link mathematics with other curriculum areas. Measurement skills are essential for all aspects of the school science curriculum, and they have a range of applications in humanities and social sciences, such as mapping, scale models, time lines, and time zones. Measurements of distance, weights, height, and time are integral to physical education. Another benefit is the prospect of engaging students through the practical activities that arise naturally in this mathematical strand. The teaching and learning of measurement provides students with the chance to apply their understandings and skills in meaningful and relevant contexts.

Measurement concepts in the curriculum

The *Australian Curriculum: Mathematics* (ACARA, 2010) includes the measurement of attributes that are either located in spatial or geometric contexts, such as length, area, and volume, or relate to physical properties, such as mass or time. Additionally, the Australian curriculum also includes money as an additional attribute for measurement.

Geometric or spatial measures

Length

Length is an attribute related to the geometric construct of lines, and refers to how long something is. It is the most easily understood of the geometric measures. Length refers to the attribute, while other terms that may be also be used, such as height, width, or depth, are specific to particular contexts.

Area

Area, the two-dimensional measure that describes the region enclosed by a plane figure, is expressed in square units that are derived from units of length. In the past, students were taught to calculate area through the rote application of various formulae without any real understanding of the concept of area. It is now recognised that primary students need to develop an awareness of the concept through investigative activities that involve either 'covering' the figure with non-standard or standard units, or subdividing the figure into an array of equal units (Outhred, Mitchelmore, McPhail & Gould, 2003).

Volume and capacity

Volume refers to the space occupied by a three-dimensional figure, and is expressed in cubic units that are derived from units of length. **Capacity** refers to the same three-dimensional attribute but specifically to measures of how much will fit in a volume of space. Volume could be considered to be a solid measure, and capacity the measure of the quantity that a three-dimensional figure can hold.

Physical attributes

Mass and weight

The terms mass and weight are often confused. The process of 'weighing' something is, in fact, measuring its mass. **Mass** is a measure of the amount of matter in an object. The metric units for mass are grams or kilograms. **Weight** is the force that gravity exerts on an object, and is measured in newtons (N).

> ### communicating mathematically
>
> Strictly speaking, it is incorrect to say 'an object weighs 5 kg' because weight is a force and is not measured in kilograms. The correct expression would be, 'an object has a mass of 5 kg'. Use of precise language by teachers helps students distinguish mass from weight.

> ### making connections
>
> On Earth, objects are attracted towards the centre of Earth with an acceleration of approximately 9.8 metres/second/second. This is pretty close to 10 m/s/s. We can use the equation Force = mass × acceleration to see the connection between mass and weight. To calculate the weight of an object with a mass of 55 kg:
>
> F = mass × acceleration
> F = 55 × 10
> F = 550 N
>
> Therefore, a mass of 55 kg has a weight on Earth of approximately 550 N.

Time

Time is unique as it cannot be measured using tangible experiences in the way that it is possible to measure other types of attributes. The effects of the passage of time can only be perceived through changes in natural occurrences, such as day and night and the passing of the seasons, or the visible movement of clock hands or changing numerals on a digital clock. Time, therefore, is one of the most difficult measurement concepts for children to understand.

Money

Money embodies the units that measure the value of an item. While classroom activities involving money rely heavily on number skills, children also need to develop the the ability to recognise coins and handle money. The development of concepts such as exchanging and equivalence of value are also developed when teaching measurement through the use of money.

> **consider and discuss**
>
> The *Australian Curriculum: Mathematics* (ACARA, 2010) includes time and money in the measurement framework. Could these attributes have been alternatively included in other mathematics content areas or curriculum learning areas? Explain your rationale.
>
> Check the *Australian Curriculum: Mathematics* to investigate whether any other attributes for measurement have not been included in the mathematics framework. Have these attributes been included in other curriculum areas? Which one or ones? What reasons might there be for locating other measurements in different curriculum learning areas?

Measurement learning sequence

Students will be able to effectively manage the relatively complex process of accurately measuring an attribute, stating this measurement in formal terms and recording it using conventional notation, if they have had the opportunity to develop a sense of measuring processes through a coherent sequence of learning experiences. The following measurement learning sequence is based on Outhred et al. (2003). It progresses through the primary years, providing teachers with an idea of what should happen in the earlier years and what is involved in the later years. A sound perception of where concepts have come from and what they are leading to allows teachers to focus on their role in developing measurement understandings. However, the learning sequence should not be considered in terms of a linear developmental process; rather it should be thought of as a continuum as there are overlaps between the various stages.

Identify and understand the attribute

The first and most important stage is that students identify, and are able to understand, the attribute they are going to measure. This involves developing an awareness of the attribute and adopting any new language that is associated with the attribute.

Compare and order different instances of the attribute

Students should next be given opportunities to **compare** and **order** different instances of the **attribute**. Activities that involve comparing two examples of the attribute should lead into those that involve ordering three or more examples. Many attributes can be compared directly, such as comparing length by lying objects directly in line with each other. Sometimes indirect measurement is more effective for making comparisons, as when comparing volumes by pouring sand from one container to another. These experiences reinforce the development of concepts associated with the attribute being used as the unit of measurement.

Make measurements using non-standard units

The next step is to learn to use units of measurement. The development of formal measurement skills proceeds from initial measurement activities that use units found in everyday experiences. Hence, students should be provided with many opportunities to measure using informal, non-standard units in order to prepare for measuring with formal, standard units.

Measuring activities that involve the use of, for example, hand spans or paces as the unit of measurement are considered to be natural and to relate to everyday experiences. Non-standard units provide a numerical value that describes the measurement outcome without the complications and difficulties associated with formal units of measurement and their associated notations. The use of non-standard units also provides opportunities to estimate the quantity of the attribute before the measurement is made, to make choices about the most appropriate unit to use, and to judge the degree of accuracy appropriate for a particular situation.

Conversely, through the use of non-standard units students can begin to discover that they are not appropriate for effectively communicating measurement information. For example, students could measure a length of 6 paces, and then get an older or younger group to do the same in order to discover discrepancies in the use of that non-standard unit. Ultimately, the use of non-standard units leads to establishing the need to standardise units in order to eliminate ambiguities and miscommunication and enhance precision. Conventional units should not be introduced until students have become well accustomed to measurement processes using non-standard units.

Make and use measuring devices

The jump from measuring with non-standard units to measuring in standard units using **measuring devices** is challenging. An ideal way to assist students in managing this transition is to provide them with the opportunity to create their own measuring tools using non-standard units. If students make a simple measuring instrument using a non-standard unit of measurement with which they are familiar, it is more likely that they will understand how such an instrument makes measurements.

Make measurements using standard units

The standard system of measurement incorporated in the primary mathematics curriculum in Australian schools is metric units. Through appropriate learning experiences all students need to be become familiar with the characteristics of, and quantities involved in, each unit, the correct language for naming the units, and the correct conventions for writing measures using recognised notations. This stage should include providing practical experiences in the use of formal measuring devices, estimating quantities in real-world applications, and mastering proportionality between the units.

consider and discuss

When teaching about the measurement of length using standard units, which of the metric units would you introduce first? Explain your rationale for this decision.

Apply measurements

Once students are comfortable with making accurate and meaningful measurements using appropriate standard units, learning experiences ought to be directed towards a wide range of authentic measurement applications and to the power that comes from the use of measurement formulae.

making connections

Measurement is essential to ensure that the Olympic facilities such as pools, courts, tracks, and fields comply with official Olympic regulations.

Olympic pools

An Olympic pool is the venue for swimming, diving, water polo, and synchronised swimming during the Olympic Games. The dimensions of a competition pool (50 × 25 metres) comply with standards set down in the handbook of the international body for swimming, which specifies details such as pool length, width, and depth. Usually some variation is permitted, provided it falls within a certain range (called the allowed tolerance). The competition pool must be 50.0 metres long with a tolerance of +0.03 metres and −0.00 metres. This means that the pool can be up to 3 centimetres longer than 50 metres, but cannot be even a millimetre shorter. A qualified surveyor must certify that all measurements are within the regulations.

Olympic stadiums

An Olympic stadium usually seats over 100 000 spectators and is used for events including track and field athletics and the opening ceremony. A standard athletics track has an inside running distance of 400 metres. Most tracks have straight sides, each 85 metres in length, with curves at either end with a radius of 36.41 metres. There are usually eight lanes, each 1.22–1.25 metres wide. Tracks must have two independent measurements made of their length, using either a steel tape or a laser-based surveying instrument. The two measurements may not differ from each other by more than the allowed tolerances or the track will not be certified for national and international competition.

The dimensions of Olympic facilities may vary within certain practical specified limits without significantly affecting their functioning. This is known as a tolerance. Tolerances allow reasonable leeway for imperfections and inherent variability without compromising performance.

> **did you know?**
>
> Much of the history of measurement is associated with the standardisation of units of measurement because of the discrepancies that arise from using non-standard units such as the length of a man's forearm or foot. The metric system that is used in Australia developed in France at the time of the French Revolution, when the scientists of the day recognised the flaws in a measuring system based on characteristics of the human body. The standard unit of length adopted in the metric system was the metre, the length of which is equal to the distance between the North Pole and the equator divided by 10 million. The metric system is named from the Greek word metron, to measure.

Approaches to developing an understanding of length

The physical measurement of length takes a central position within the measurement learning sequence (Buys & de Moor, 2005). Because an understanding of length is foundational to building the concepts of area and volume, it is the first of the measurement attributes to be introduced in Year 1.

Identifying the length attribute

The earliest learning experiences relating to length ought to be designed to develop awareness of the attribute. Activities that focus on length as a characteristic of either similarity or difference are useful. For example, students could compare a diverse range of materials that are all the same length, such as a juice box, a pencil, and a soft toy, and they could compare materials of the same type and different lengths, such as a collection of toys or a collection of boxes. Teacher-directed discussion about these two sets of objects would focus the students' attention to the length attribute and to the similarities and differences between the objects in each group with regard to length.

Building an awareness of length also involves introducing to students in the early primary years the wide variety of terms that are used to describe length. Activities to help students develop an awareness of length and to use appropriate length vocabulary could include:

- 'draw a tall boy and a short girl', 'draw some thin lines and some thick lines'
- discussing the length of items and objects around the classroom and the school yard using appropriate language, such as 'the window is wide', 'the cupboard is narrow', 'the whiteboard is long', 'Susan is tall but Jamie is short', 'the tree is tall'.

This naturally leads to making comparisons and the use of the language of comparison, reinforces awareness of the length attribute, and prepares students for measurement activities involving the use of units.

communicating mathematically

The language of length

In the early primary years students often use measurement language such as big, small, little, tiny, or huge, but these terms do not convey any sense of how big, or how small. When students have the opportunity to participate in measurement activities their language becomes more precise. Early learning experiences in length need to develop an awareness of the wide variety of terms that can be used when discussing length. The following list illustrates the extensiveness of this vocabulary:

| long | short | wide | narrow | high | low | thick |
| thin | deep | shallow | tall | | broad | near | far |

These terms should be used in class discussion whenever appropriate. This will gradually extend the early learners' vocabulary to become more precise.

Comparing and ordering lengths

Comparing and ordering lengths are the natural second phase in building and developing perceptions of the length attribute. This commences in Year 2. Activities designed to build an awareness of the length attribute often result in comparisons of length. Hence, a vocabulary of comparison develops simultaneously with an understanding of the attribute.

In daily life, people often compare lengths without using units. Direct or indirect comparisons often provide enough measurement information to address an immediate need, for example to determine whether an item of furniture will fit into a desired location.

It is essential that young students have the opportunity to participate in activities associated with the direct and indirect comparison of length. Developmentally, making direct comparisons precedes making indirect comparisons. **Direct comparisons** are made when two, or more, objects are compared directly against each other side-by-side to determine, for example, which is shorter, thinner, or wider.

for the classroom

Length scavenger hunt

Give pairs of students a strip of card of a particular length. Ask them to find five objects around the classroom that are longer than the length of card. On other occasions they could find objects that are shorter or the same length as the card.

An **indirect comparison** is made when an intermediary measuring device is used. This may be because it is not possible to compare the length of two objects side-by-side. Making indirect comparisons is a precursor to the use of non-standard and standard units, and the use formal measuring devices.

for the classroom

Indirect comparison is particularly useful when students are comparing lengths that are not straight.

Have the students investigate which is longer, the height of a can, or the distance around the circumference. Use a range of can sizes to explore this relationship.

Use chalk to draw curving lines in the playground. The comparison activity is to determine which of two lines is longer. Make string or rope available for the students but do not guide them into how they might use it in the activity. Discuss with the students how they made their comparisons.

What other readily available classroom objects could students use to carry out measurements using non-standard units?

Once students are able to compare and order two lengths accurately using appropriate language, they can begin to order the lengths of three or more objects. Early ordering activities use direct and indirect comparisons. Eventually, students begin to use transitive thinking to order the length of objects. This requires students to recognise that if object 1 is longer than object 2, and object 2 is longer than object 3, then object 1 must be longer than object 3.

Ordering activities that involve students' personal characteristics are always engaging, for example marking the heights of a group of students on the whiteboard, writing their names against the markings and the ordering the heights. An activity such as this could also involve the use of ordinal language, such as 'Who is the second tallest?'.

Measuring length using non-standard units

The use of non-standard units gets younger students (Years 2 and 3) started on measuring length quickly and easily because their focus is on the measuring process using units that are common and familiar to them, rather than using imposed formal units.

Students can use a wide variety of non-standard units. Encouraging students to use their own body parts as units provides experience in selecting a unit appropriate to the item being measured. Students could opt to use, for instance, the width or length of their finger, hand span, foot length, paces, or arm length.

for the classroom

When beginning to use non-standard units, ask each student to measure the length of a common classroom item, for instance their desk. Provide a range of choices of non-standard units that the students can select to use. Students could use non-standard units such as their hand span, the length of their finger, straws, or paper clips. Avoid making any detailed explanations of how to use the units; rather allow them to develop their own approach.

This will generate a range of measures and promotes discussion questions such as:

- How did you make your measurement?
- Did the students who measured using the same unit get the same length? Why not?

Focus on the importance of lining up non-standard units so there are no gaps or overlaps, and lining up the first unit level with the start of the item that is being measured. Blocks that link together, such as Unifix cubes, are ideal for early measuring experiences using non-standard units, as it is not possible to leave gaps or make overlaps.

issues in teaching

Building skills in estimating measurements should be incorporated into activities involving the use of non-standard units. Students should be encouraged to think and estimate, and then measure. Initially estimates will be nothing more than a guess, but resulting measurements provide feedback on the guess-timates. As students' familiarity with the unit size increases, the accuracy of their estimates will improve.

for the classroom

Make your own ruler

The transition from measuring length using non-standard units to making length measurements using a ruler and standard units can be challenging. An ideal way to assist students to understand the use of a ruler is to have them make their own personal ruler.

1. Pre-cut narrow strips of coloured paper into 5 cm lengths. Use two different colours.
2. Discuss with the students how the strips of paper can be used to measure by laying them down end-to-end.
3. Get the students to paste the strips of paper, alternating colours, onto a strip of card that is a little wider than the strips. Make sure that the students do not start at the end of the card, as many standard rulers are not made in such a way. If the first unit on their personal ruler does not coincide with the end of the ruler, then the student is forced to align the units on the ruler with the object being measured.
4. Students then use their personal rulers to measure a range of objects.
5. After some practice with using their ruler, have the students write numbers in the centre of each unit as a way of pre-counting the units.
6. A final step that needs to be taken slowly is to write the numbers on the ruler using a standard format. This will involve a careful discussion about how the ruler becomes a number line.

Using student-made rulers means that connections can be made between their own ruler and a standard ruler. Discussion points could include how their own ruler is similar to, and different from, a standard ruler. Would it be possible to make a ruler that is the same as a standard ruler? What do the numbers mean on a standard ruler? What units are being used on the standard ruler? Where do the units begin on a standard ruler? What do the other markings on a standard ruler mean?

Standard units

When students can measure efficiently and accurately using non-standard units they are ready to progress to the use of standard units (from Year 2 into Years 3 and 4). This can be a natural progression as students become aware of the discrepancies that can occur when differing non-standard units of measurements are used to measure the same length. It is important to establish that it was the need to communicate a consistency in measurements that led to the use of standard units.

The usual sequence when introducing standard length units is to commence with the centimetre and then move on to the metre. These two units are appropriate to almost all classroom or school yard measuring activities. The centimetre is introduced first as it is appropriate to measuring small items such as books, desks, or pens and produces a manageably small number. It is also a small enough unit for students not to be concerned, initially, with partitioning.

for the classroom

It is important that students begin to recognise the relative size of a centimetre unit.

Cut 1 cm pieces of drinking straws for the students to use as a measuring device to discover items in the classroom that are about 1 cm long or 1 cm wide. Have the students use this experience to identify other items that may be 2 cm or 3 cm long, and then to check these using the drinking straw unit. Give the students a chance to think about and discuss why measures of the same object may differ.

Metres, and ultimately millimetres, can be introduced using a similar sequence of learning activities designed to allow students to become very familiar with the relative size of the unit and then consolidate this understanding in appropriate measuring activities.

for the classroom

Get the students to work in small groups to build a tower that is 1 m high using classroom building materials and objects. When the students estimate that their tower has reached 1 m, have them check the height and make adjustments if necessary. Get the students to record how they made their estimate, how high their tower was when the measurement was made, and any differences between their estimate and the actual measurement.

handy hint

Children's picture books provide a rich resource on which to build student activities or to stimulate class discussions. In the area of measurement there are many excellent books that can be accessed, including the following. For each book, an indication of the aspect of measurement that is addressed in the book has been provided.

- *Too Tall Tina* (Pitino, 2005): language of comparison
- *Super Sandcastle Saturday* (Murphy, 1999a): comparing, ordering, use of non-standard and standard units of measurement
- *Inchworm and A Half* (Pinczes, 2001): partitioning units
- *How Big is a Foot?* (Myller, 1990): discrepancies in using, and miscommunication of, non-standard units
- *Room for Ripley* (Murphy, 1999b): capacity
- *Counting on Frank* (Clement, 1995): capacity
- *The Very Hungry Caterpillar* (Carle, 1974): time (days of the week)
- *A Day on the Avenue* (Roennfeldt, 1984): time (sequencing of hours in a day)

Approaches to developing an understanding of time

Time differs somewhat from the other measurement attributes because it cannot be seen or experienced in a tactile way. Hence it can be difficult for younger students to comprehend units of time. Nevertheless, the concept of time is something that young students face daily, for example hurrying to get to school or getting to stay up late. The measures of time should be included in classroom measurement explorations for younger primary students.

Developing an understanding of time involves three key aspects:

- understanding the concept of time duration
- appreciating the passing and sequencing of time
- determining a given point in time through reading a clock face.

While all three aspects are essential to developing time sense, Buys & Veltman (2005) observe that determining a given point in time through reading a clock face still receives the most attention in the early primary years.

Duration of time

Time can be considered as the duration of an event from its beginning to its end, and comparisons can be made of events with differing durations, but if the events compared commence at the same time, the focus becomes the end of the duration, rather than the duration itself. To develop an understanding of time as an attribute that can be measured, students should be encouraged to compare the duration of events that do not commence at the same time. In order to do this in the initial stages, non-standard units of measurement such as hand claps could be used. Students can also be encouraged to order the duration of everyday events in their lives, for example brushing my teeth is shorter than eating my breakfast, which is shorter than walking to school.

As with other attributes, early learning experiences in time using non-standard units of measurement ultimately leads to an appreciation for the use of standard units to be able to interpret and communicate the passage of time consistently. Additionally, to develop their understanding of time further, students need to appreciate that people use clocks to keep track of the passing of time. Schwartz (2008) argues that this is the most fundamental understanding a student needs to develop.

Passing and sequencing of time

Initial learning experiences associated with the passing and sequencing of time involve the division of days and weeks. Broad daily partitions, such as morning, afternoon, and night, are introduced, and the relationship between successive days, that is yesterday, today, and tomorrow, are also included in the earlier primary years. The ordering of the days of the week is also encompassed in early learning activities designed to appreciate the passing and sequencing of time.

for the classroom

Students with minimal reading skills can categorise pictures of common daily events according to the broad time of day—morning, afternoon, and night.

Use a classroom poster to illustrate school-based activities that occur on regular days of the week, for example, Monday is library day, Tuesday is sports day, and Wednesday is music lesson day.

Have the students use illustrations or magazine cut-outs to create their own poster of activities they undertake on regular days of the week, for example, Sunday I visit Grandma, Tuesday I have football practice, Thursday I have dancing lessons.

The next phase is to investigate the idea of a month. This could occur by taking a look at the current month in the calendar. Gradually, students will begin noticing the vertical patterns that link particular days of the week. The next step is extending from one calendar month to a full calendar year. Highlight the birthdays of the students in the class, school vacation periods, other important occasions such as Australia Day and Anzac Day, and decorate the full year calendar to illustrate the passing of the seasons.

Clock face reading

When the three broad divisions of morning, afternoon, and night have been grasped, the idea that the day can be divided further can be introduced. Students will need to investigate the standard units of second, minute, and hour to develop some understanding of how long these units are. The commonly used device for measuring time is the clock, either digital or analogue. Students need to learn to read a variety of clock faces. However, learning to read a clock face can be a challenge.

for the classroom

Get the students, with assistance from a carer or sibling, to time the length of common daily events such as cleaning their teeth, eating dinner, or walking to school. Students could bring this data to school and make comparisons with their class mates.

issues in teaching

Reading digital clocks

Most children now have ready access to a digital clock, but this does not necessarily result in the ability to tell the time in a meaningful way. Young students who are able to read the digits, such as 6:58, will often not know that this time comes between 6:00 and 7:00. A meaningful digital reading of time requires a child to understand that there are 60 minutes in an hour and that 58 is close to 60; hence this time is very close to 7:00.

The hour and minute hands

The hour and minute hands perform distinctly different actions and functions. The small hand indicates approximate time (to the nearest hour), and the big hand indicates the time (in minutes) before or after the hour. When adults look at the hour hand, we focus on where it is pointing. Looking at the minute hand, the focus is on the distance it has traversed around the clock, or how far it has to go to get back to the top. Because the minute hand is constantly changing position, some children have difficulty in observing the time that has elapsed as indicated by the hour hand.

To simplify the task of learning to read a clock face, begin with a one-handed clock that indicates just the hour of day. Move the hour hand to either a little past the hour or just before so that students can identify that 'It is nearly 5 o'clock', or 'It is just after 11 o'clock'. When students are managing the hour hand successfully, introduce the minute hand, beginning with hour and half-hour times. Encourage the students to find the shorter hour hand and read the hour, then to look at the longer minute hand. Students will be ready to tell the time to the nearest five minutes when they can count by fives to 60. Plenty of practice in counting by fives around the clock face as each numeral is touched will assist.

integrating technology/ICT

Measurement activities using interactive whiteboards are both engaging and effective. The following websites offer a range of useful interactive activities.

Lecky compares

Comparing and ordering different objects and using measurement vocabulary, such as longest, shortest, widest, biggest, and smallest:
www.crickweb.co.uk/assets/resources/flash.php?&file=compare-order7

Ordering height

Move the sports players to order from tallest to shortest:
www.abc.net.au/countusin/games/game14.htm

Analogue and digital clocks

Interactively set the time on digital and analogue clocks:
http://nlvm.usu.edu/en/nav/frames_asid_316_g_1_t_4.html?from=category_g_1_t_4.html

Match clocks

Show a given time on a digital and an analogue clock:
http://nlvm.usu.edu/en/nav/frames_asid_317_g_1_t_4.html?from=category_g_1_t_4.html

What time will it be?

Indicate what time it will be before or after a given time period:
http://nlvm.usu.edu/en/nav/frames_asid_318_g_1_t_4.html?from=category_g_1_t_4.html

Conclusion

The measurement of length and time are foundational components of measurement learning in the early years. Students who have had the opportunity to develop a sense of measuring processes through a coherent sequence of learning experiences will be able to manage the complex process of accurately measuring an attribute, stating this measurement in formal terms, and recording it using conventional notation. In the early primary years, students first begin to develop measurement understandings by identifying and perceiving the attribute to be measured, then comparing and ordering examples of the attribute. Measuring with non-standard units assists younger students to understand the principles of the measuring process. Students eventually notice that measurements made using non-standard units result in discrepancies and are not easily communicated, and this leads to an appreciation of the need for formal measurement using appropriate standard metric units. Ultimately the measurement process can be applied to a broad range of authentic situations.

The measurement of length takes a central position in the primary measurement curriculum because an understanding of length is essential to building other measurement concepts. Learning about length should be underpinned by the measurement learning sequence and involve extensive hand-on experiences, with a focus on developing estimation skills and practical applications. Time measurement needs to be included in the earlier primary years, as the concept of time is something that younger students face daily. Developing an understanding of measurement of time can be difficult as time cannot be seen, or experienced in a tactile way.

key terms

Area: the measure that describes the extent or coverage of a two-dimensional figure

Capacity: the measure of the quantity that a three-dimensional shape can hold

Comparing attributes: determining the relationship between two objects with regard to a particular measurement attribute by comparing the extent of the attribute in each object

Direct comparison: physically comparing the objects being measured with each other

Indirect comparison: using another item as a measurement referent to compare measurement attributes

Length: the measure that describes the extent of one dimension

Mass: a measure of the amount of matter in an object

Measuring device: an item that is used to make indirect measurements of the extent or amount of a particular measurement attribute in terms of a consistent unit of measurement

Money: the unit used to measure the attribute known as value

Ordering attributes: describing the relationship between three or more objects with regard to a particular measurement attribute by ordering the objects in various ways, for example from longest to shortest

Time: the duration of an event from its beginning to its end

Volume: the space occupied by a three-dimensional figure

Weight: the force that gravity exerts on an object

Review questions

1 Describe the six stages in the measurement learning sequence.
2 Why is the measurement of length foundational to developing measurement understandings?
3 What challenges might learners face when they are learning to measure length?
4 Explain the three aspects that need to be included when developing understandings of measuring time.
5 What challenges might learners face when they are learning to measure time?

Key references

Buys, K., & Veltman, A. (2005). Measurement in kindergarten 1 and 2. In M. van den Heuvel-Panhuizen & K. Buys (Eds.), *Young Children Learn Measurement and Geometry: A Learning-teaching Trajectory with Intermediate Attainment Targets for the Lower Grades in Primary School.* Utrecht, The Netherlands: Freudenthal Institute.

Outhred, L., Mitchelmore, M., McPhail, D., & Gould, P. (2003). Count me into measurement: A program for the early elementary school. In D. Clements (Ed.), *Learning and Teaching Measurement: 2003 Yearbook.* Reston, VA: NCTM.

Websites

http://nlvm.usu.edu/en/nav/vlibrary.html
www.abc.net.au/countusin/default.htm
http://illuminations.nctm.org/ActivitySearch.aspx?grade=2

20 Developing Geometric Thinking and Concepts

Contents

Classifying spatial objects	455
Relationships between spatial objects	461
Developing dynamic imagery	464
Location	465
Conclusion	466

Chapter objectives

This chapter will enable the reader to:
- Develop their personal knowledge and understanding of geometric concepts relevant for teaching years F–4
- Learn effective methods for teaching geometric thinking and concepts in F–4, as identified from research.

Learning about geometry

Look at the photograph below. What do you notice?

The child was photographed while playing. Play is an important part of early childhood learning. In this case, the play was completely self-directed by the child. She was playing with off-cuts from a building project. Notice how she is arranging the blocks? Even very young children observe geometrical patterns. Opportunities to explore shapes are important to encourage this development, particularly in the years before formal schooling begins.

Big ideas

- Learning geometry involves learning about our world and then extending ideas to abstract relationships and concepts.
- In the early years, children need considerable experience with geometric activities to develop the concepts of:
  - spatial objects, including geometric classification and language
  - relationships between spatial objects, including seeing the parts and the whole
  - developing dynamic imagery, including transformations
  - location.
- Spatial reasoning develops by building and manipulating mental representations of geometric concepts.

Classifying spatial objects

In geometry, we begin with some definitions and then build on from there. This is a common approach in mathematics and can lead to some interesting results—even completely new fields of geometry, particularly if we begin with different starting points. We will look at this further in Chapter 27.

We will define the following spatial objects (diagrams on next page):

point
A point is a location in space. It has no size at all! Points are labelled with a dot and a capital letter, for example A .

line
In Euclidean geometry, a line is the collection of points extending towards infinity in both directions. Lines are straight, so in geometry the term 'wavy line' does not make sense. Lines are labelled as a lower case italic letter, for example the line l, or by two points the line passes through with a bar with arrows over them, for example $\overleftrightarrow{AB}$. The arrows remind us that the line extends to infinity in each direction.

line segment
A line segment is a part of a line. (Remember a line extends to infinity in each direction.) A line segment is the collection of all the points between and including two end points. Lines are labelled with the two end points and a bar over the top of them to remind us that the segment stops at the points, for example $\overline{CD}$.

ray
A ray is half a line. Think about this for a moment. A ray starts at a specified point and extends through another point to infinity. Convince yourself that this means a ray is half a line. Rays are labelled showing the starting point on the left and another point the ray passes through on the right. The arrowhead shows the direction of the ray, for example $\overrightarrow{EF}$ would be a ray starting at E, and extending through F to infinity.

circle
A circle is a collection of points that are the same distance (radius) from another point (the centre).

These five objects will get us started with a considerable amount of geometry.

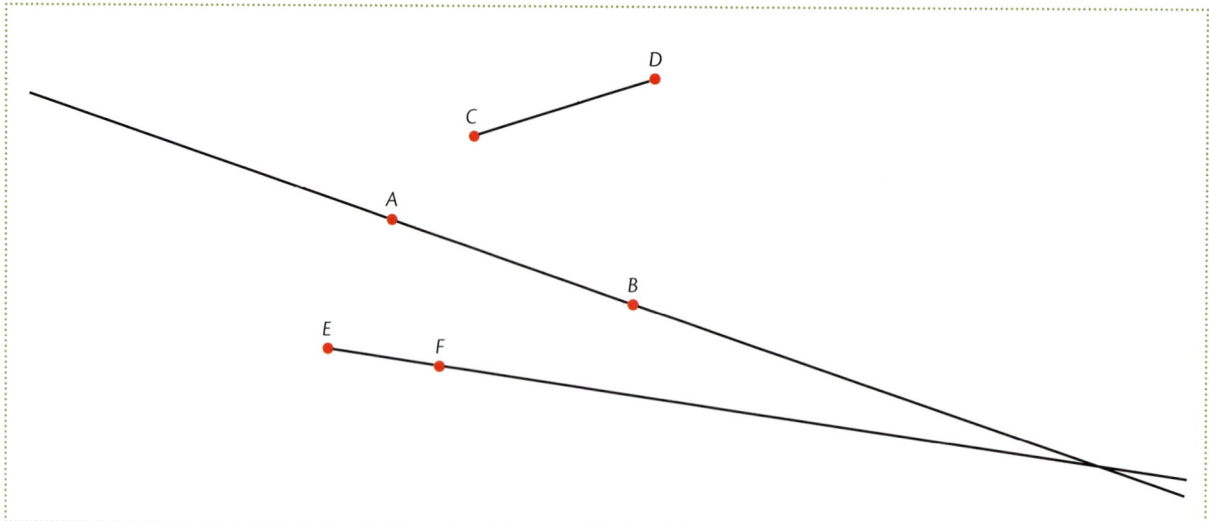

did you know?

Imagine the smallest dot you can. Now cut it in half. Now cut it in half again. Keep going. A point is smaller than that. This is moving into the idea of infinity—a point is infinitely small.

Mathematicians have grappled with notions of infinity over centuries, and it is a fascinating area that combines mathematics and philosophy. When we talk of a point, we are also talking of a *mathematical object* rather than a real one. Mathematical objects are abstractions, and some argue they are the pure, simplified versions of a complex, messy real world.

integrating technology/ICT

Dynamic geometry environments (DGE)

Computer software applications known as dynamic geometry environments (DGE) provide an invaluable resource for learning geometry. Two commonly used products are Cabri Géomètre and Geometer Sketchpad. Free software packages such as Geogebra are also readily available.

These packages begin with the simple objects we have already defined and then build from there. Ensure you have access to a geometry package as you work through the geometry chapters in this textbook, and undertake the constructions using the software.

Try this now.

1. Open your DGE. Draw lines and circles. Find out how to label the objects.
2. Use the DGE to construct a square using only the equivalent of a compass and a straight edge. What properties of a square did you use?

think + link

While you are working on the constructions, record your thinking as suggested in Chapter 4.

3. Now construct a square in a different way. The figure below shows a construction. What properties were used to make the square *ABED*? Experiment to copy the construction. The points are labelled in order of construction.

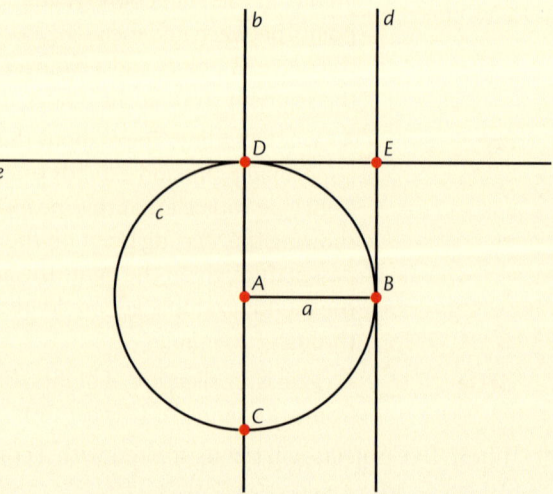

Classification and language

As we discussed in Chapter 11, an important aspect of the development of geometry, as described by the van Hiele model, is the notion of classification. Classification enables us to isolate a concept. Initially, children have prototypes that they learn to recognise and label. For example, they may regard ▲ as a triangle (described as the 'prototypical' triangle) but ◣ as 'half a triangle'. Similarly, initially, children seem to recognise squares only when they are placed with horizontal sides. When a square is rotated, young children are likely to label the object as a diamond. Peter Gould (2003, p. 5) argues this:

> highlights the importance of the link between the label ('square') and the category of squares. The language that we use to describe shapes in geometry is not dependent upon orientation. We do not have 'upside-down triangles' in mathematics because there is no absolute direction system in space.

communicating mathematically

The term 'diamond' is the only shape name that links orientation with a shape. That is, a shape is only described as a diamond if it is placed with diagonals horizontally and vertically. The other features of a diamond are that it has four congruent (equal) sides but does not necessarily have any right angles. In mathematics, the classification of a shape does not depend on orientation, and therefore 'diamond' is a term best avoided in a mathematics classroom. The correct term for a shape with four congruent sides and no right angles is a *rhombus*.

Children need many opportunities to play with shapes in all orientations and in many different forms. They need to have their attention drawn to the features of shapes that lead to their membership of particular categories. For example, children need to learn that shapes with three sides and three angles are called triangles.

It is important for teachers not to underestimate the prior knowledge of children in the early years of schooling. Many children enter formal schooling with a wide knowledge of shape names, and teachers need to develop the children's understanding, not just affirm what they already know. Horne (2003) summarises the research of Clements (2000) from the United States and adds research results for children in Australia (Table 20.1).

Table 20.1 Young children's understanding of shape labels

Clements (2000)	90% 3–6 year olds	Identify circles, differentiating these from ellipses and other shapes
	Over 80% 4–6 year olds	Identify squares (including non-prototypic* squares) from other shapes
	About 60% 4–6 year olds	Identify triangles (including non-prototypic triangles) from other shapes
Horne (2003)	Over 25% at start of school	Identify squares, circles, rectangles, and triangles (including non-prototypes)
	Over 60% at end of prep year	Identify squares, circles, rectangles, and triangles (including non-prototypes)
	48% of Year 1 children in research project schools	Use properties to sort shapes into classes Show some characteristics of van Hiele level 2 (see Chapter 11)
	Over 68% of Year 2 children in research project schools 32% of children in reference schools (typical of Victorian schools generally)	Regard squares as in a different class to rectangles (even though squares are a type of rectangle)

* A prototypic shape is a standard view. For example, a prototypic square would be drawn with horizontal and vertical sides. A prototypic triangle is described above.

consider and discuss

Shapes children see

Find as many examples as you can of shapes represented in children's literature, puzzles, games, and so forth. What types are most commonly found? What labels are given? Can you find shapes that have been incorrectly labelled? Are there examples where non-prototypic shapes are shown?

issues in teaching

Extending young children's geometrical understanding

Many curriculum documents from the late 1970s were influenced by Piaget's work, which is now shown to have underestimated the abilities of young children in the area of spatial development, as noted in the literature in both Australia (Perry, Young-Loveridge, Docket & Doig, 2008) and in the United States (Clements & Sarama, 2007, p. 510). It is important for early childhood teachers to elicit and verify prior knowledge, but also to extend this knowledge. Teachers should draw children's attention to properties of shapes, as well as the label. Extending children's geometrical understanding requires teachers to be confident in their own geometrical knowledge in order to identify what their students know and in what direction that knowledge could be extended.

Labels for shapes

Two-dimensional (2D) shapes are those that lie on a plane. The two dimensions are length and width. 2D shapes with straight sides are known as *polygons*. Solid, or 3D, shapes occupy space. The three dimensions are length, width, and depth. Solids with flat faces are known as *polyhedrons* (or *polyhedra*). Lines where the faces of a polyhedron meet are called *edges*. Points where the faces meet are called *vertices*. In the *Oxford Primary Mathematics Dictionary*, you can find the names for polygons and polyhedra. For example, a 10-sided polygon is a decagon, while a 20-faced polyhedron is called an icosahedron.

did you know?

There are exactly five polyhedrons that have faces made up of regular polygons that all meet at the same angle. A regular polygon has congruent angles and sides.

These five are called the *Platonic solids*. They are the tetrahedron (four equilateral triangular faces), cube (six square faces), octahedron (eight equilateral triangular faces), dodecahedron (12 pentagonal faces) and the icosahedron (20 equilateral triangular faces). There are many websites where you can find teaching resources on Platonic solids, such as the National Library of Virtual Manipulatives. The website references at the end of the chapter has the general address. Here is the page for Platonic solids <http://enlvm.usu.edu/ma/nav/activity.jsp?sid=nlvm&cid=3_3&lid=128>.

Chapter 20 Developing Geometric Thinking and Concepts

Classifying shapes by their properties

An important part of developing our geometric understanding is to investigate the properties that are common to all shapes in a particular class. Initially, children name shapes by what they look like, rather than their properties. In the early years, young children need to learn to recognise and attend to features of shapes.

consider and discuss

Properties of shapes

Two-dimensional shapes and three-dimensional solids have many properties.
   Make a list of of attributes that could be properties of two-dimensional or three-dimensional objects.

You may have listed the number of angles, the number of sides, and the relationship between sides (parallel, perpendicular, etc.). Shapes and solids may also have symmetry. There are two important types: line symmetry, and rotational symmetry. An object without symmetry is described as *asymetric*.

for the classroom

Mira mirrors are handy devices that help children see lines of symmetry as well as reflections. They are made of special plastic that allows a student to look through the mirror and see an image of the object. Children can study reflection and find lines of symmetry easily.

   Young children can be introduced to the devices, experimenting and gaining practice in drawing lines of reflection.

   Older children can undertake a range of activities, such as:

- Draw a large triangle.
- Use the Mira to bisect each angle. To do this, line up the Mira so that the reflection of one side of an angle sits on top of the other side of the angle. When it does, rule a line along the Mira. What do you notice about the bisectors? Try other triangles.

Line symmetry occurs when every point of an object on one side of a line can be matched to another point the same distance from the line on the other side. In other words, if the shape were folded along the line, the two sides would match exactly. Young children begin to spot symmetry from a very young age. Babies as young as four months old have been shown to detect vertical symmetry (Clements & Sarama, 2007, p. 508).

handy hint

When choosing shapes to demonstrate lines of symmetry, ensure that you include horizontal and oblique lines as well as vertical lines.

Rotational symmetry often causes challenges for children (Clements & Sarama, 2007, p. 499). Imagine an equilateral triangle oriented with the bottom side horizontal (the prototypical triangle). Now imagine that I am going to turn the triangle. If I turn the triangle a third of the way around a full turn (120°), the triangle will look the same as when I started. If I continue to turn another 120°, the same thing will happen. It takes three turns of 120° before I am back where I started. An equilateral triangle has 'three-fold rotational symmetry', or 'rotational symmetry of order three'.

for the classroom

Have students make a shape with six wooden cubes. Place the shape on paper and trace around the outline. Tell children that you are only interested in the shape of the bottom. Mark the top right corner of the object and the top right corner of the tracing. This records the starting position. Turn the object and have the children clap once when the shape again fits into the traced outline. For example, for a rectangular-based solid, there will be two claps—one half-way round, and the second when the shape has rotated back to the starting position. This shape, therefore, is said to have rotational symmetry of order two. This can also be called 'half-turn' rotational symmetry.

Invite children to investigate other arrangements of the blocks. Investigate other objects. Wooden jigsaw pieces with knobs can be found in preschool rooms and can help young children rotate the objects.

Note:
- Cubes with side length of at least 2 cm are better than centicubes for young children.
- Flat shapes can be used but these are often more difficult for young children to turn.

making connections

Chirality is a property of some molecules and is an application of reflection to chemistry. Molecules are made up of atoms, and in some molecules it is possible to arrange the atoms in different ways. Another name for chirality is 'handedness'. No matter how you turn your left hand, you can't make it sit directly on top of your right hand, and like your left and right hands, some molecules with the same atoms are reflections of each other. The handedness, or chirality, of a molecule can affect the way it reacts: one form of a molecule can be an effective drug and the other form can be completely different. An example is methorphan. The 'left-hand' version of the molecule, levomethorphan, is used as a pain killer, while the 'right-hand' version, dextromethorphan, is a cough suppressant.

Relationships between spatial objects

Naming and identifying individual objects is a part of our developing sense of the world. However, it is the relationship between spatial objects that gives us a powerful appreciation of our world and how we relate to it. There is evidence that infants have some abilities to distinguish objects in their world, and this develops and moves to a more sophisticated system as a child grows (Clements & Sarama, 2007).

did you know?

Some spatial abilities are present from birth! Even babies show skills in spatial orientation. For example, newborn babies can focus on objects, and while breastfeeding they show most interest in their mother's face, which is at just the right distance for the focus of their eyes.

Developing visualisation

As we noted in Chapter 11, visualisation is an important aspect of geometry and mathematics in general. It is more that just 'seeing images in the mind'. Rather, 'spatial visualisation is the ability to generate and manipulate images' (Clements & Sarama, 2007, p. 499).

Gutiérrez (1996) proposed a framework for visualisation that identified six main abilities:

- figure–ground perception
- mental rotation
- perception of spacial relationships
- perceptual constancy
- perception of spatial positions
- visual discrimination.

We will consider each of these in turn.

Shapes within shapes: figure–ground perception

It is important to be able to see parts and wholes in shapes. This is **figure–ground perception**, defined by Gutiérrez as 'the ability to identify and "isolate" a specific figure out of a complex background polygon' (1996, p. 10).

consider and discuss

The logo shown is from a business, HSBC. It is a simple design and yet it is possible to see many shapes within the overall shape.

How many pentagons do you see? You will need to be systematic to ensure you have found them all. Will you count different

colours as different shapes? Can you find a concave pentagon (one where at least one interior angle is greater than 180°)? For more information on concave and convex pentagons, see Chapter 27.

What thinking did you notice yourself undertaking as you completed this investigation? How easy was it for you to see the different pentagons?

Adapted from Johnston-Wilder & Mason 2005, p. 5.

for the classroom

Other logos

Young children are very attuned to logos. Many parents have noticed that very young children, even those barely talking, are able to identify fast food restaurants and other products from logos. Invite children to make a collection of different designs and use them to identify different shapes within them. Children can also take photographs of interesting designs and use them to identify and name various shapes. Children can trace around the outline of the shapes they have spotted.

Perceptual constancy

Perceptual constancy is the ability to recognise that some characteristics of an object are independent of 'size, colour, texture, or position' (Gutiérrez, p. 10). That is, a blue cup and a red cup are both cups. Also, a cup upside down is still a cup. (Reflect on the challenge young learners experience when we tell them 'b' is different from the letters 'd', 'p', and 'q', as this conflicts with their growing sense of perceptual constancy.) When we have labels for classes of objects, we are able to discuss and describe examples and non-examples.

consider and discuss

Perceptual constancy requires decisions about shapes that are on the border of a concept. For example, look at the shape below:

1 How would you label it?
2 What are its features?

Many will commonly, though incorrectly, identify the object shown as a rectangle, even though it has rounded corners and does not have vertices.

for the classroom

Odd one out

Using games can help young children to develop perceptual constancy. One such game asks children to select the object in a collection that is different from the others. Attribute blocks are useful for this. Children can select all the triangles, regardless of colour or thickness.

Mental rotation

Mental rotation, defined by Gutiérrez as 'the ability to produce dynamic mental images and to visualize a configuration in movement' (1996, p. 10), provides considerable challenge even to adults. Note that the movement does not specifically have to be rotation. It can be any movement of a mental image.

The following question was included in the 2010 NAPLAN test for Year 5.

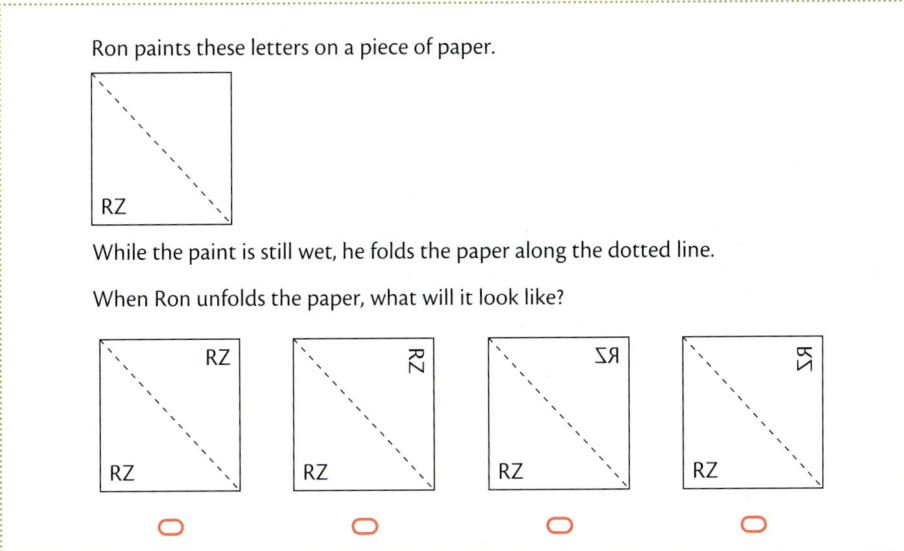

Which is the correct solution?

What mental processes are required to complete this question?

Before internalising the processes, many learners require opportunities to complete the movement physically, allowing them to 'replay the video' later mentally. However, it is also important for children to develop their ability to see the dynamic movement 'in their mind's eye'.

for the classroom

Tetris

Older students (and you) may enjoy playing Tetris. This potentially addictive computer game became popular in the late 1990s and involves rotating arrangements of four squares to fill rows. As rows are filled, they are removed. The game encourages the development of mental rotation as you make the blocks pack as efficiently as possible.

Perception of spatial positions and spatial relationships

The two abilities involving perception of spatial positions and spatial relationships are very closely related. **Perception of spatial position** is the ability of a person to relate objects (or pictures or mental images) to themselves, whereas **perception of spatial relationships** involves relating several objects to each other and to the person concerned.

It is easier for children to think of an object relative to their own position than it is to compare the position of two separate objects. For example, children will be able to understand the term 'under' with respect to themselves before they can follow an instruction to place an object under another.

These perceptions are the basis of location.

Visual discrimination

Visual discrimination is the ability to compare several figures and to determine how they are similar and how they are different.

making connections

Bill Bryson, in his book *A Short History of Nearly Everything*, introduced his readers to Bob Evans, an individual with an extraordinary gift for visual discrimination. An amateur astronomer, Evans lives in the Blue Mountains and is able to spot supernovae by recognising changes in the night sky. Bryson writes: 'To understand what a feat this is, imagine a standard dining room table covered in a black tablecloth and someone throwing a handful of salt across it. The scattered grains can be thought of as a galaxy. Now imagine fifteen hundred more tables like the first one—enough to … make a single line two miles long—each with a random array of salt across it. Now add one grain of salt to any table and let Bob Evans walk among them. At a glance he will spot it. That grain of salt is the supernova.' (Bryson, 2003, p. 30)

for the classroom

Children's activity books often include two similar drawings where the game is to find all the differences between the pictures. These puzzles are also popular in newspapers and can be collected for use in classrooms.

The television program *Sesame Street* has featured a segment with a song 'One of these things is not like the other' that focuses on visual discrimination. Teachers can copy this idea by making flashcards for young children to practise matching pictures of objects that are the same. Initially, particularly for children with developmental delay, it is a good idea to start with only one picture to match. This ensures success. Once the child understands the game, you can introduce a distractor—another card that is very different from the target match. Gradually you can increase the challenge by introducing more choices and making the objects more and more similar.

Developing dynamic imagery

Dynamic imagery is our ability to visualise changes to shapes as processes act on them. It is an important aspect of geometric thinking. Geometry software provides teachers and their students with considerable support for the development of dynamic imagery.

Transformations are processes that happen to shapes. If the process leaves the shape unchanged, but its orientation or location changed, the process is described as a *rigid transformation*. There are four types of rigid transformations:

1. translation (also known as a slide)
2. reflection (also known as a flip)
3. rotation (also known as a turn)
4. glide reflection (a combination of a translation and a reflection).

You will notice that rotation has already been mentioned in this chapter. Rotational symmetry is a property of a shape. Rotation can also be a *process* that happens to a shape.

 This shape does not have rotational symmetry. If I rotate it, it will not look the same until I have turned it a full revolution. However, I can use a rigid transformation of this shape to make a design.

I can rotate it about a point, making use of rotational transformation:

integrating technology/ICT

Computer drawing programs

Word processing programs such as Word include simple drawing tools that offer transformations to alter shapes. Find these aspects of the programs. Draw a simple object, such as an arrow. Find ways to translate, rotate, and reflect the shape.

issues in teaching

Number and geometry are related, but the connection is complex and not yet fully understood (Clements & Sarama, 2007, p. 489). Verbal reasoning and spatial reasoning occur in different parts of the brain. Clements and Battista (1992) reviewed the literature available at the time and note:

- Mathematics achievement, in general, is related to spatial abilities.
- Some research indicated children with specific spatial abilities have higher achievement in mathematics.
- Other research found students who favoured verbal processing out-performed those who processed visually.

More research is needed, and you can expect new developments in understanding the connection between number and geometry to be made throughout your career. Teachers need to be active followers of new research; this is often best achieved through reading professional journals, such as *Australian Primary Mathematics Classroom*, and attending conferences, such as those hosted by the Australian Association of Mathematics Teachers.

Current understanding suggests it is important not to focus on teaching number to the detriment of geometry. Also, it should not be assumed that a student having difficulty with number will also struggle with geometry.

Location

Understanding location of self and other objects is closely related to spatial perception, discussed earlier in this chapter. Concepts of location, such as *beside*, *in front*, *under*, *over*, *behind* are important ideas. Children first learn these concepts in relation to themselves (perception of spatial position). For example, a child learns to recognise an object that is in front of them. It is a later stage of development for a child to be able to place an object beside another (perception of spatial relationships). Learning the words that label the concepts is an important part of early childhood geometry, especially for children who speak English as a second or other language.

for the classroom

A number of children's books focus on the language of location. A perennial favourite is *We're Going on a Bear Hunt* (Rosen, 1997), available in 'big book' format.

Find another example of such a book and identify all the words of location. Analyse the accompanying artwork for its contribution to the understanding of the concepts. Plan how you could make use of the children's book for learning the mathematics of location.

Many parents are keen to support their children with mathematics. Write a paragraph you could include in a school newsletter to provide ideas for parents on using reading books at home to reinforce concepts of geometry.

handy hint

Point of view

It is harder for children to describe the position of other objects than it is to describe the position of themselves. If a child is having difficulty following instructions to place a teddy beside, behind, or in front of another teddy, check if the child can move him or herself beside, behind, or in front of another person.

The use of models and maps is one aspect of location. The type of model or map developed depends on the socio-cultural environment in which it is used. Clements and Sarama (2007, p. 500) note that children are unlikely, on their own, to represent their environment using models and maps. Explicit teaching is therefore important, and should begin in the early childhood years. Young children may be helped to understand a map by telling them to imagine the room shrunk to a very small size (DeLoache, Miller, Rosengren & Bryant, 1997).

integrating technology/ICT

Mapping

Google Maps can be used to give children a bird's-eye view of familiar locations, for example their own school. Moving between satellite, hybrid, and map views can help children make the connection between different representations. This can then be extended to other maps, such as maps of classrooms, fire escape routes in the school, and town maps showing tourist information. Provide many opportunities for children to explore different representations on maps.

Conclusion

The foundations of geometry are laid in the early childhood years through play-based activities such as jigsaws and shape sorting. Increasing interactions with the physical world allow children to extend these ideas into the abstract world of geometrical relationships and concepts.

The study of geometry in the early years involves developing concepts of spatial objects. When young children learn labels for concepts, they are able to use language to connect ideas. In turn, these connections of ideas become linked as concepts. Therefore, correct geometric classification and language is critically important. Throughout the early years of schooling, children need to develop their language of geometry and continually refine the associated concepts. Children learn that a shape is not defined by what it looks like; rather, the category of a shape is determined by features of the shape, such as symmetry, number of sides, and number of angles.

Relationships between spatial objects extend thinking into the area of visualisation. Seeing parts and wholes of shapes and exploring dynamic imagery are important facets of visualisation. Transformations of shapes rely on dynamic imagery and lead to spatial reasoning. Spatial reasoning is a critical feature of thinking in geometry. Without spatial reasoning, geometry is reduced to a series of facts, concepts, and properties to be learnt, with little of the fascinating, creative mathematics it should be.

key terms

Dynamic imagery: the ability to visualise changes to shapes as processes act on them

Figure–ground perception: the ability to identify and 'isolate' a specific figure out of a complex background polygon

Mental rotation: the ability to produce dynamic mental images and to visualise a configuration in movement

Perception of spatial positions: the ability to relate figures (object, picture, or mental image) to oneself

Perception of spatial relationships: the ability to relate several figures (as above) to each other, or simultaneously to oneself

Perceptual constancy: the ability to realise that some characteristics of an object are independent of size, colour, texture, or position

Visual discrimination: the ability to compare several figures and to determine how they are similar and how they are different

Review questions

1. The development of correct labels for shapes is an important part of early learning of geometry. Explain why a square is a special type of rectangle. Why is a diamond not a geometric term?
2. What is the difference between rotational symmetry and rotational transformation?
3. Use a dynamic geometry environment to construct a hexagon. Transform the shape using the four rigid transformations.
4. Define mathematical visualisation. How could a teacher understand the visualising of a child?
5. What are six of the abilities involved in spatial thinking? How can these be developed in young children?

Key references

Clements, D. H., & Battista, M. T. (1992). Geometry and spatial reasoning. In D. A. Grouws (Ed.), *Handbook of Research on Mathematics Teaching and Learning* (pp. 420–494). New York: Macmillan.

Clements, D. H., & Sarama, J. (2007). Early childhood mathematics learning. In F. K. Lester (Ed.), *Second Handbook of Research on Mathematics Teaching and Learning* (pp. 461–555). Charlotte, NC: Information Age.

Gould, P. (2003). Grasping space. *Australian Primary Mathematics Classroom, 8*(2), pp. 4–7.

Gutiérrez, A. (1996). Visualization in 3-dimensional geometry: In search of a framework. In L. Puig & A. Guttiérez (Eds.), *Proceedings of the 20th Conference of the International Group for the Psychology of Mathematics Education* (Vol. 1, pp. 3–19). Valencia: Universidad de Valencia.

Horne, M. (2003). Properties of shape. *Australian Primary Mathematics Classroom, 8*(2), 8–13.

Perry, B., Young-Loveridge, J., Docket, S., & Doig, B. (2008). The development of young children's mathematical understanding. In H. Forgasz, A. Barkatsas, A. Bishop, B. Clarke, S. Keast, W-T. Seah and P. Sullivan (Eds.), *Research in Mathematics Education in Australasia 2004–2007* (pp. 17–40). Rotterdam: Sense Publishers.

Websites

www.geogebra.org
    Free download of a dynamic geometry environment is available here.

http://mathworld.wolfram.com
    More geometry than convex and concave polygons here!

www.fi.uu.nl/rekenweb/en
    Many geometry activities are available here.

http://enlvm.usu.edu/ma/nav/browse_by.jsp
    This site is the National Library of Virtual Manipulatives and has many applets for use in mathematics classrooms—not just geometry.

21 Early Chance and Data

Contents

Grappling with uncertainty	469
The development of students' thinking about probability	472
Representing data	476
Understanding distributions	480

Chapter objectives

This chapter will enable the reader to:
- Enhance personal understandings of chance phenomena and the use of statistical methods to make conclusions about them
- Develop understanding of the development of children's understanding of chance processes and data representation
- Develop understanding of pedagogies that support the development of children's statistical reasoning
- Recognise links between probability and statistics and other areas of the mathematics curriculum.

Who does the thinking?

I recently asked an 8-year-old to sort a collection of buttons and record what she had done in any way she wanted. The openness of the task was a bit daunting, but eventually she decided to sort the buttons according to their size. Then she considered the question of how to record what she had done. Repeated reassurances that any way was fine were eventually met with the question 'Can I make a graph?'

'Yes, a graph would be fine.'

'But, I'm not sure how, the teacher always does them for us.'

consider and discuss

1. Where would you have taken the conversation next?
2. I suspect that when the student said, 'the teacher always does them for us' she was referring to the teacher modelling how to construct axes and use them to order the data. Discuss the pros and cons of modelling in this context. When is modelling useful? What might the pitfalls be, and how can they be avoided?

Big ideas

- The outcomes of many processes are unpredictable and this uncertainty is the basis of probability and statistics.
- Probability is concerned with quantifying and describing the outcomes of random events.
- Statistical reasoning allows us to make inferences about events whose outcomes are characterised by random variation.
- Data can be collected, organised, and displayed to answer questions and convey particular messages.

According to Jones, Langrall and Mooney (2007), probability involves describing, quantifying and modelling random processes, whereas statistics is concerned with making inferences about such processes. In this chapter we explore ideas related to probability and statistics as they apply to F–4 mathematics classrooms.

Statistics and probability are relatively recent inclusions in school curricula (since the late 1980s and early 1990s) and hence have not been researched as thoroughly as some other areas. Nevertheless, there are clear corroborated findings about the development of students' understandings of key ideas that can guide our teaching, and considerable consensus that students benefit from early teaching about these ideas that build upon and where necessary challenge their intuitive understandings. If we are to educate children to be statistically literate citizens then it is crucial that teaching emphasises thinking from the very beginning.

issues in teaching

Teaching sensitive issues

FitzSimmons, Seah, Bishop and Clarkson (2000) reported that Australian primary school teachers were in favour of using current social issues, such as gambling, in their mathematics teaching, but they recognised the sensitivity of such issues. They mentioned the importance of enlisting parental support and avoiding the unnecessary introduction of controversy.

- Why might gambling be a sensitive issue?
- Would you include gambling in your teaching about probability? Why, or why not?
- How could potential pitfalls be avoided?

Grappling with uncertainty

There is considerable confusion even among adults as to the meaning of 'random', and it is often used to mean haphazard or unexpected. In fact, although random processes are unpredictable in the short term, in the long term they have outcomes that are predictable and stable (Jones et al., 2007). This is counter-intuitive, and is at the heart of the difficulty students have with learning about probability and statistics since the long-term predictability of random events is the foundation of these disciplines. Jones et al. (2007) cite evidence that children as young as 4 years of age can show some understanding of uncertainty by recognising that the outcomes of some events cannot be predicted, but there is also a strong tendency for people of all ages to attribute events to spurious causes (Metz, 1998). You may be able to identify with experiences of trying to *will* a die to produce a particular outcome in a board game, and there are recurrent examples in the media of natural disasters being attributed to 'Mother Nature' or the misdeeds of people. We also struggle to appreciate the implications of the fact that unlikely things are not impossible (Watson, 1995). For example, several disasters, all unlikely, and even less likely in combination, can befall an individual in one day, purely by **chance**. People have an innate desire to explain the world in terms of **causes** and effects, and this has driven both science and religion for centuries. Probabilistic reasoning requires that such notions are revised.

making connections

Lambos and Delfabbo (2010) found no difference between problem gamblers and other adults in terms of their understanding of the gambling odds. In spite of this, problem gamblers were more likely to hold irrational beliefs about gambling, such as that:

- they could control outcomes, for example, by concentrating or following superstitious rituals
- an event that hasn't occurred for some time is more likely to happen next, or that avoiding a machine that has recently paid out increases the chance of winning
- outcomes are personal and can be influenced by talking to the machine or treating it nicely.

A possible explanation for this contradiction between mathematical understanding and rationality relates to the mental state that problem gamblers enter when they become personally involved with the activity. In this state rational thought is overridden. Lambos and Delfabbo suggested that educating gamblers about statistics and gambling odds is likely to be effective only if it occurs before they become emotionally and/or financially involved in the activity.

Konold (1989) pointed to the difficulty of teaching concepts, such as those central to probability and statistics, that conflict with students' existing beliefs and intuitions. He also warned that the ease with which other skills, for example counting up and tabulating outcomes, can be acquired can be misinterpreted as evidence that the underlying counterintuitive ideas are understood when this is not the case. Because of this, it is crucial that the development of conceptual understanding is the central focus of teaching in probability and statistics. Being able to construct tables and graphs and compute various numbers is not sufficient evidence that anything important has been understood.

did you know?

Williams, Francis and Robbins (2007) found that 41 per cent of the 279 Welsh 13–16-year-olds that they surveyed claimed to believe their horoscopes. Eve and Dunn (1990) cited evidence of extensive belief in pseudoscientific ideas, such as the existence of ghosts, astrology, and rocket launches influencing the weather, in the general population of the United States, and even among secondary teachers of biology!

Jones et al. (2007) cited early work by Piaget and colleagues on the development of understanding of the idea of randomness. Piaget concluded that 4–7-year-olds in the pre-operational stage had little understanding of randomness, often predicting that objects in a random mixture would return to their original positions, and that raindrops falling on a pavement would form a regular pattern. In the concrete operational stage (ages 8–11 years), children were better able to understand such phenomena, and increasingly reasoned about quantities when asked to predict the results of random selection from a mixture.

The language of uncertainty

Developing the language of probability is a central focus of the mathematics curriculum in the early to middle primary school years. Initially students can classify events as likely or unlikely, or as impossible, possible, or certain. Sets of cards depicting events with words and/or pictures can be placed on charts according to the category to which they belong, or students can come up with their own lists of events that fall within each category. The subjective nature of these words is a source of interesting debate that can help to deepen students' understanding of their meanings.

> **think + link**
>
> Piaget's stages of development are described in Chapter 2, along with some of the criticisms that they have attracted. It is important to remember that although many studies have confirmed Piaget's findings about children's understandings of randomness, some have not. Piaget's stages provide a useful guide to how children's understandings of randomness typically develop, but they should not be applied rigidly.

for the classroom

Impossible, possible, certain

Have students classify events like the following as impossible, possible, or certain:

- My aunty will visit on the weekend.
- My cat will talk.
- It will rain this afternoon.
- Things fall if you drop them.
- My bedroom will tidy itself.
- I'll get 6 if I roll a die.
- I'll get 7 if I roll a die.
- Everyone in our class owns a dog.
- Children will grow.
- It will snow at the beach.
- I'll eat Brussels sprouts.
- Grass is green.
- My budgie will learn to talk.
- The sun will rise tomorrow.
- A female kangaroo has a pouch.
- My mum is older than I am.
- I'll walk to school tomorrow.
- My football team will win.

Have students work in groups to make up their own lists of events that fall into each of the three categories.

It is worthwhile to order lists of words and phrases that students have heard used to describe the **likelihood** of events. A brainstorming session can generate a list that can then be ordered according to the degree of likelihood the terms express. Appropriate words and phrases will depend upon the ages and experiences of the students, and might include: sure thing, no chance, 50–50, Buckley's or none, lost cause, never, likely, could go either way, not in my wildest dreams, in the bag, maybe, equally likely, and not likely. Ordering events from least to most likely also helps to build understanding. Later students can add a numerical scale from 0 (impossible) to 1 (certain) to their ordering of language or the likelihood of events. This helps to establish connections between words and numerical probability.

for the classroom

What's possible now?

Place three to five cubes or other small objects of different colours into a bag so they cannot be seen. The children can watch the cubes being placed in the bag one by one.

Draw out one cube and ask the children what colour they think the next cube will be. For example, if the first cube selected is blue, we know the next one can't be blue, but it could be any of the other colours that we know are in the bag.

Take out further cubes one by one, each time encouraging children to articulate what the next cube could be. Encourage reasoning rather than guessing by asking them for reasons for their predictions.

Guide them in the use of appropriate language, moving from initial statements such as 'it could be red or could be yellow' or 'it is possible that the next one will be yellow' to 'it must be yellow' or 'the next one certainly will be yellow', if that is the only cube that has not been drawn out.

(adapted from Sangster & Cantrell, 2009)

It is important to be aware that students can think differently in different contexts. A wide variety of experiences and plenty of class discussion and questioning is important to elicit the reasoning behind students' responses, and can uncover misconceptions that may not be evident, and hence not available for challenge, from a single activity. We know that many students have idiosyncratic understandings of many of the words associated with chance and often misuse the language. For example, Fischbein, Nello and Marino (1991, cited in Jones et al., 2007) related how students aged 9 years and older described getting a particular number using a random number generator for numbers 1–90 as impossible, equating impossible with low probability.

communicating mathematically

Words that have particular meanings in probability are sometimes used with different meanings in everyday contexts. Children can develop their own idiosyncratic understandings of the meanings of these words. For example, some children use the word 'chance' to describe something that 'just happens' or an unusual event (Jones et al., 2007). Even more common is the use of 50–50 to describe an outcome that is possible but uncertain, rather than a situation in which two possible outcomes are equally likely (Watson, 2005, cited in Jones et al., 2007). So children could use 50–50 to describe the chance of getting either of two numbers on a die because each of the two numbers is equally likely, whereas each in fact has a $\frac{1}{6}$ chance, not 50% or $\frac{1}{2}$. Teachers need to pay careful attention to the meanings that students attach to words and not mistake the use of the words for understanding.

did you know?

The origins of probability can be traced to the middle of the seventeenth century, arising from considerations of the outcomes of games of chance and the study of mortality data (Aldrich, 2005). The word 'probability' is derived from the Latin word *probabilis*, meaning 'what may be proved' (Weekley, 1921). Probability models and probabilistic reasoning are now used in almost every area of science and business, from insurance and economics to epidemiology, traffic flows, physics, and even education.

The realisation that we live in a largely indeterministic world, in which many events are not attributable to direct causes, has resulted in renewed philosophical interest in nature of causation, although considerations of the issue date back to Aristotle. Recent thinking on causation accounts for the indeterministic nature of our world by conceptualising causation in terms of chance-raising. That is, an event *E* can be said to be caused by *C* if *C* occurs before *E* and the occurrence of *C* increases the chance that *E* will happen (Dowe & Noordhof, 2004). The nature of causation is an active area in philosophy and there are others who claim that chance-raising is either not a necessary condition for establishing a causal link between two events, or that it is not sufficient (Schaffer, 2000).

The tension between **deterministic** and indeterministic thinking about cause and effect is evident in debates about such things as the dangers of cigarette smoking. In the face of mounting evidence that smoking raises the chances of developing lung cancer (and a range of other health problems), tobacco companies tried to insist that only a deterministic definition of causation was adequate. That is, they argued that unless it could be shown that smoking leads directly and certainly to lung cancer it could not be said to cause it.

The development of students' thinking about probability

In the preceding discussion we have commonly referred to dice and assumed that they are understood as 'fair', in the sense that all possible outcomes are recognised as equally likely. However, students may not be convinced of this. Watson and Moritz (2003) documented the beliefs of 108 students from Grades 3–9 about the fairness of dice. They found that approximately 40% (including nearly 60% of Grade 3 students) did not believe that dice were fair, with many basing their opinions on recollections of experiences with dice. It is important to be aware that such thinking can exist even if students know that 'officially' the probability of each outcome is $\frac{1}{6}$. This has implications for other chance devices as well.

consider and discuss

Consider the work sample shown in Figure 21.1. It was produced by a student aged 9 years.

1. What understandings of the 'most likely', and 'least likely' are evident?
2. What evidence suggests this, and what further evidence would you look for to confirm your conclusions? What tasks might you provide? What questions might you ask?

Figure 21.1 Spinners designed to make blue the least likely and most likely outcome

Understanding of distributions—the frequencies of particular outcomes of multiple instances of an event—also takes time to develop. Students need experiences and explicit questioning and discussion aimed at helping them to appreciate that individual chance events are unpredictable, but that the long-term pattern of outcomes is highly predictable. This sophisticated understanding is unlikely to develop before the middle years but it is central to the nature of random or chance processes. Experiments with chance devices such as dice and spinners, in which the distribution of outcomes of many trials (maybe 20) by individuals in a class are pooled to create a much larger number of trials (several hundred), can be used with young students as a basis for comparison of the distributions of relatively small numbers of outcomes with those of larger numbers of trials. These experiences build the foundations for deeper and more formal understanding of the random processes in later years of schooling.

integrating technology

Random number generators such as the function provided by Excel and any number of freely available applications that can be found on the internet (just type 'random number generator' or 'virtual spinner' or 'virtual dice' into a search engine) can be used simulate random processes, including those concerning dice and spinners. **Simulations** like these can very quickly provide the large numbers of trials that are needed to demonstrate the long-term predictability of random processes.

It is, however, essential that young students work with real devices first so that they understand the process by which the data are generated (Watson, 2006). Watson (2006) also describes how very careful explanation must accompany the transition from real chance devices to computer simulations, and recommends that students are constantly questioned about what is happening in order to ensure that appropriate links are being made between the real situation and the simulation.

think + link

Look back at Chapters 17 and 18 and consider the connections between the development of students' thinking about probability and the development of **proportional reasoning**. How might experiences with probability contribute to students' understanding of fraction concepts and vice versa?

Ordering tasks require intuitive comparisons of probabilities that are often based on personal experiences. Teaching needs to help students to move from subjective bases for comparisons towards quantitative reasoning about relative likelihoods. Young students asked the probability of randomly selecting a particular coloured jelly bean or marble from a collection containing known numbers of two or more colours tend to focus only on the number of items of the desired colour, ignoring both the number of items that are not the desired colour and the relative proportions of desired and other items. Other students use idiosyncratic reasoning, such as believing that their favourite colour is most likely to be selected. By mid-primary, more students rely on comparing the numbers, but not the relative proportions of colours, and it is only in the middle school years that students begin to use comparisons of the proportions of each colour (Jones et al., 2007).

making connections

Statements and phrases like the following are commonly found in weather forecasts:

Fine apart from the chance of a late shower or two.

Cloud increasing later, with the risk of a late thunderstorm.

Possibly thundery.

In each case, how would you explain the meaning of the chance language that is used?
Which of the three examples suggests that the event referred to is most/least likely? How do you know?

How can examples like these be used to develop children's understanding of probability?

Understanding samples

A **sample** is a smaller set chosen from a population. This means the development of students' understanding of samples is linked to their understanding of the variability of outcomes of small numbers of trials. A key understanding is that there will be greater **variation** among successive small samples drawn from a given population than among larger samples. For young children, a crucial first step is simply understanding what a sample is. Watson and Moritz (2000) reported that almost half of 864 Year 3 students in their study showed little understanding at all of the meaning of sample, whereas approximately one-third understood samples in terms of their own experiences of trying a small bit of something, such as samples of food handed out in supermarkets. One in five displayed more sophisticated understandings that included recognition that a sample is part of a whole and **representative** of that whole. Overall, understanding of the meaning of sample appears to progress from an inability to distinguish a sample from a population, to recognising the difference between a sample and a population but without appreciating that a sample can represent a population, to eventually understanding that a sample can be representative of a population and used to estimate various characteristics of that population (Watson & Moritz, 2000).

did you know?

The word 'statistics' has its origins in the Italian word for state, *statista*. Its modern sense derives from the German word *statistik*, originally meaning the study of the resources of the state (Weekley, 1921). **Statistics** was initially concerned with demographic and economic data required by governments, but since the nineteenth century the word has been more broadly applied to **data** collection and analysis in general.

The first statistical publication is thought to be John Graunt's *Natural and political observations made upon the Bills of Mortality*, published in 1662. The Bills of Mortality were the records of births, christenings, and deaths and their causes, published in weekly church bulletins in England, and designed to detect outbreaks of plague at the time. Graunt tabulated and analysed these data.

Applications of statistics cover every area of the social and physical sciences.

Shaughnessy (2007) described many studies that examined students' abilities to predict an appropriate amount of variation in samples of 10 lollies drawn from collections of 100 composed of differing numbers of lollies of different colours. The progression in thinking observed in such tasks mirrors that described in the development of understanding of the probability of selecting a particular element from a collection. Some students, particularly younger ones (Years 3 and 4), are inclined to respond idiosyncratically, based on their personal experience. More sophisticated thinking emerges from the later primary years, and relies on considering the numbers of each colour but not their proportions. This is followed by consideration of proportions, and ultimately thinking that Shaughnessy, Ciancetta and Canada (2004) described as distributional, in that there is explicit linking of the sample proportions and the population proportions.

Young students' reliance on experience is an important reason to ensure that they have many experiences of selecting samples and comparing the variation in and among small and large samples with that of the population.

for the classroom

Sampling a small collection

Place five cubes of different colours in a bag so that they cannot be seen. Tell the students that this is what the bag contains. Have a child draw out one cube and record its colour. Ask the students what they now know about the colours of the cubes in the bag. For example, if the selected cube was red, 'we know that there is a red cube'. Replace the cube and repeat the process of selecting a cube, noting its colour, and prompting the students to articulate what they now know about the contents of the bag.

You might like to ask the students at the start how many times they think it will be necessary to pull out and replace a cube to be sure about the contents of the bag. Many will be surprised that more than 5 'samples' are required.

Other variations that can be used to increase the complexity of the task include:

- including two or more cubes of the same colour
- selecting two (or more) cubes at a time.

think + link

In Chapter 3 we talked about teachers' 'horizon' knowledge of mathematics. Why is it important that teachers of very young students have sophisticated understandings of concepts such as representativeness of samples? How might such knowledge affect teaching of young students?

With regard to the greater variability of small samples, Watson and Moritz (2000) cautioned against teaching that simply instils in students the belief that larger samples are better. Rather, the adequacy of a sample depends upon the extent to which it represents the population—that is, a sample should be a scaled-down replica of the population with respect to all aspects that might affect the answers to the questions under investigation. The idea that random samples of adequate size can be representative takes some time to develop, and would not be expected in the early or middle primary years. Nevertheless, it is underpinned by understanding of chance, randomness, variation, and early ideas about samples that should be developed from the earliest years.

Representing data

The purpose for which data have been collected should drive the ways in which it is summarised and represented. Representations of data are encountered every day in the media, and are designed to convey certain information about the data or to support particular conclusions. They are intended to be meaningful. Students should learn about data representations by working with data that they have collected to answer questions that interest them.

Shaughnessy (2007) refers to extensive research that has revealed students' difficulties with understanding the range of graphs commonly encountered in primary school and beyond. Rather than emphasising the prescriptive construction of neat tables and graphs, teaching should focus on more critical elements (Shaughnessy, 2007). Extensive class discussion about what such representations show and the relative benefits of alternative representations can help students gradually to create more sophisticated and conventional representations. Discussions of the meanings of graphical representations and using them to make **predictions** can help students to develop the understandings that will underpin their ability to understand the ways in which graphs are used in society, as well as providing a basis on which later teaching can be built (Pereira-Mendoza, 1995). Specifically, Pereira-Mendoza (1995) recommended that young students should:

- explore the assumptions underlying the classification of data and interpretation of the meaning of data (p. 3)
- discuss and explore the possibility of alternative representations (p. 4)
- predict from the data (p. 6).

Summarising data relies upon being able to distinguish attributes of the objects of interest. Initial activities can involve sorting collections according to criteria of the students' own choosing, as well as teacher-chosen criteria. Figure 21.2 shows a Year 1 student's categorisation of a collection of animals according to criteria that she chose for herself. Students of this age and younger can successfully divide collections according to multiple criteria and can understand representations that show overlapping categories. Large hoops or loops of string can be used to organise data in separate or overlapping categories, and can provide a structure to assist students to think about these ideas. Two-way tables or even 2×3 tables can be used by young children to answer relatively sophisticated questions about collections or data sets.

Figure 21.2 Animals grouped in categories: Year 1

Figure 21.3 shows the use of overlapping loops to explore the question, 'Are people with lots of pets more likely to come to school on a bus?'. A focus of teaching in probability and statistics from the earliest years should be to encourage children to ask and to investigate questions that can be answered by collecting data. Displayed as in Figure 21.3, the data can be used as the basis of a class discussion in which students are encouraged to refer to the data and to quantify the claims they make in answer to the initial question. For example, they might observe that only three students come to school by bus *and* have more than two pets, and that six students who have more than two pets do not travel to school on a bus. In the lower primary years, a key emphasis needs to be helping students to consider the data and make conclusions based on them. For some young students, the move from a focus on themselves and their own experiences (e.g. 'People with lots of pets come to school by bus because I live on a farm and we have lots of animals and I catch a bus') to relying

Figure 21.3 Data cards arranged to explore bus travel and pet numbers

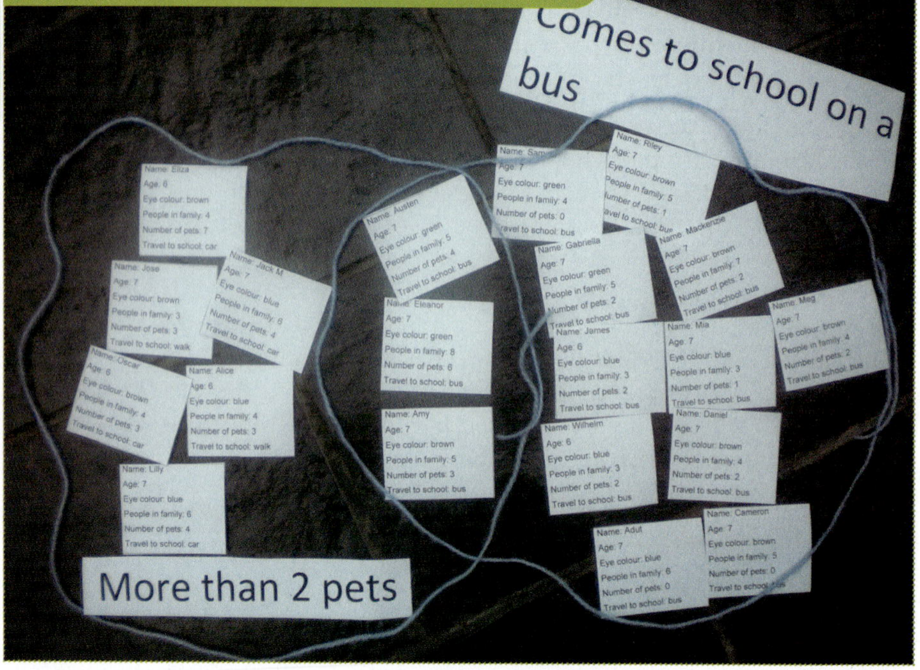

on data, particularly when it contradicts their experience, is a major step. In later primary school years, some children might refer to the proportions of bus travellers or owners of more than two pets that also fall in the overlapping category to make their case. This question could also be examined using a two-way table.

Figure 21.4 shows a 3 × 2 table used to classify a collection of bears and dolls. The table is made from tarpaulin (cheap ones work well) and electrical tape. In tables like this, including numbers labelling each category can help to focus on the meaning of the data rather than on repeated counting, and provides a convenient way to record the data when the collection needs to be packed away. Explicit discussion of the information that is kept and lost by using a table showing just the numbers and labels but not the actual toys can be the beginning of students' realisation that in any data summary some information is retained and other information is lost. Choices about how data are displayed need to take into account what is important about the data, and hence must be preserved, for the purposes for which they were collected.

As always, the focus of activities like these needs to be on students' thinking about what the data, displayed in this way, can tell us about questions of interest. Attractive displays are nice, but displays should always be a means to an end rather than ends in themselves. Shaughnessy (2007) cited earlier work by Curcio (1989, cited in Shaughnessy, 2007) who used the terms *reading the graph* (or representation), reading *within*, and reading *beyond* in relation to graphs, but these are also useful considerations for data representations that are not graphs in the formal sense. It is important to challenge young students to explain the reasons for the choices they make when they categorise data and to explain what their representations show about the data (reading the data/representation), to use representations to answer questions that involve interpretation (reading within the data), and to answer questions that involve

Figure 21.4 Using a 3 × 2 table to organise a collection

making predictions based on the data (reading beyond the data). Particularly when considering a representation that a classmate, the teacher, or someone else has produced, it is important to ask questions that draw students' attention to the possible purposes of the representation or factors in the context that might be relevant to understanding and interpreting the data. Shaughnessy (2007) called this reading *behind* the graph. For the arrangement shown in Figure 21.3, questions such as 'Why are these cards in this loop?' and 'Why are some cards in the area where the two loops overlap?' could help students to read the data. Questions like, 'Are students who have more than two pets likely to come to school by bus?' focus on reading within the data, and reading beyond the data is required by questions about the number of pets that a class member who is absent or a hypothetical new student might have if we know how they travel to school. Pereira-Mendoza (1995) argues that, although challenging, questions involving prediction should be asked of very young children so that they have opportunities to develop the required thinking.

consider and discuss

Consider the work sample shown in Figure 21.4. What questions could you ask that would help students to read:

1. the data?
2. within the data?
3. beyond the data?
4. behind the data?

for the classroom

Our class in a two-way table

Use chalk to draw a large 2 × 2 grid on concrete or asphalt or use masking tape on an indoor surface. Have students suggest two ways in which their class could be divided into two groups (e.g. boys and girls; brown eyes and not brown eyes; own a dog and don't own a dog; have tried skiing, have not tried skiing). Label the rows of the table with one pair of categories and the columns with the other, and have the students place themselves in the appropriate square. Ask several students to justify their choice.

If a safe vantage point is available, take a photograph of the class in the two-way table and have the class translate the information into a table containing numbers. Have students write about what the number in each cell tells about the class.

The activity can be extended to a 2 × 3 grid by including an attribute that divides the class into three groups.

Understanding distributions

Distributions refer to overall patterns in data and, as we have seen, helping students to take this broader focus is a key task of teaching statistics in the primary years. Examples like those shown in Figures 21.3 and 21.4 could and should be used to help students to focus on the data as a whole rather than on individual values.

Graphs are representations that help us to interpret data and to identify patterns and trends in them, to read a story from the data, or to use data to tell a story. Learning to read and interpret graphs is central to understanding distributions.

communicating mathematically

The purpose of all data **representations**, including graphs, is to communicate a message: to 'tell a story'. Representations need to be chosen with the story you want to tell and an audience in mind. They should be meaningful to both the creator and audience. Their effectiveness should not be judged in terms of how well formal conventions are followed, but in how effectively they communicate their message. Reading graphs is about reading the story of the data. It involves thinking about what story the person who made the graph wanted to tell.

for the classroom

Describing distributions

Collect data from a class and display it as a stacked plot such as the one shown opposite. This plot shows the number of pets belonging to each member of the class.

Ask students to describe the overall shape of the data. It might be helpful to provide a list of words from which students can choose. The list could include words like: peak, dip, skewed to the left, flat, and gap. What does the graph tell us about pet ownership in our class?

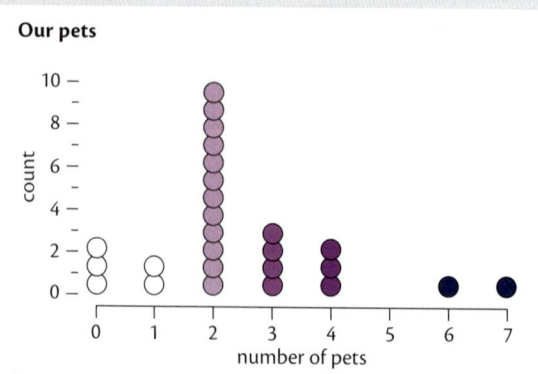

Figures 21.5 to 21.8 show a range of ways that students in an urban Prep class chose to represent postcode data to explore the suburbs in which they lived. These work samples illustrate well the capacities of young students to generate their own sophisticated data representations. They are invaluable as teaching tools to be used as the basis of class discussion. They also illustrate initial stages in students' abilities to construct graphs and their appreciation of the features of data representations that help to tell a story.

Figure 21.5 shows a representation involving circles labelled with the suburb name and the number of students who live in each (frequencies). The numbers of students could form the basis of a worthwhile discussion of ways to collect data systematically: how to be sure that everyone is asked once and only once. Other students used representations that included features of conventional graphs, even though they had had no formal teaching about graphs. For example, in Figure 21.6 each envelope represents one student and colour has been used 'to show which had the most. If they were all yellow, you couldn't see each one.' (kindergarten student). In Figure 21.7 the different postcodes have been written in columns that also share some important features of conventional graphs, that is, that the heights of columns relate to the frequencies of the various categories, and the use of the bottom of the sheet of paper as a baseline. The pair of boys who produced the representation shown in Figure 21.8 were able to explain that they had run out of space for the leftmost column and so had to make another column (the two envelopes drawn on the right side of the picture) for that postcode. This illustrates how even young students can find solutions to dilemmas that they encounter in such tasks that are meaningful to them.

Figure 21.5 Student-generated data representation showing numbers of students and suburbs

Figures 21.6 to 21.8 are pictographs because pictures (envelopes or postcodes) are used to represent data points. The work samples illustrate some of the four levels of response that Watson (2006) documented. She described how when students were presented with small cards on which pictures of books were drawn and asked to use the cards to show the numbers of books that several children had read, their responses could be described as:

1. simply making piles of cards in groups without an apparent appreciation of the need to be able to see all of the cards
2. spreading the groups of cards out so that all could be seen but without a systematic arrangement
3. making lines of columns of cards with a baseline but without consideration of the order of the columns
4. using an ordered baseline to place the columns, for example, from highest to lowest frequency.

Watson (2006) argued that these response types represent increasing complexity in students' thinking in terms of creating a graph to tell a story.

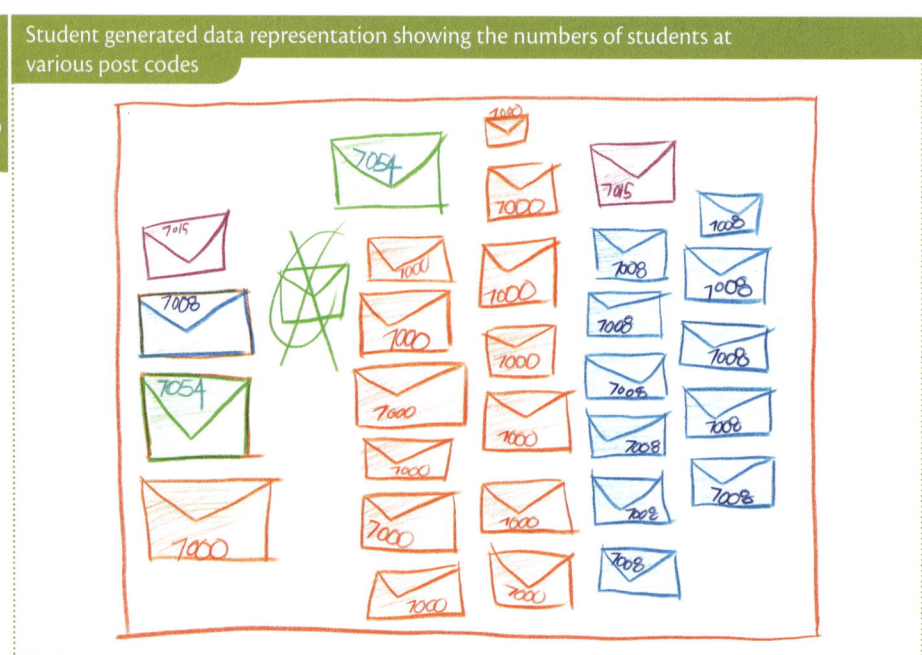

Figure 21.6 Student generated data representation showing the numbers of students at various post codes

Figure 21.7 Student generated data representation showing numbers of students and their post codes

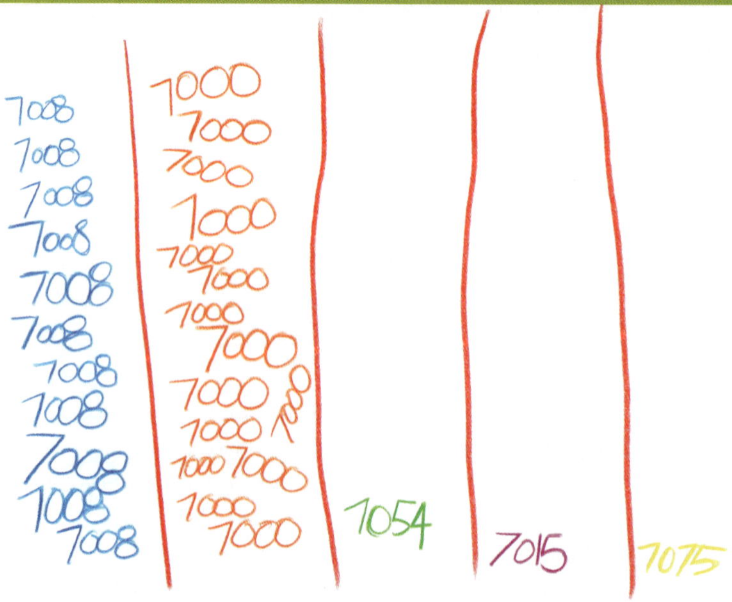

The collection of representations produced by a class can provide a rich context in which to introduce important ideas about graphs. Having students consider what the various alternatives show and the features that make this clearer can be used gradually to encourage students to adopt conventional features of graphs. The students in the class that produced the work samples shown in Figure 21.6 wrote their names and addresses on envelopes and together used these to make a class graph.

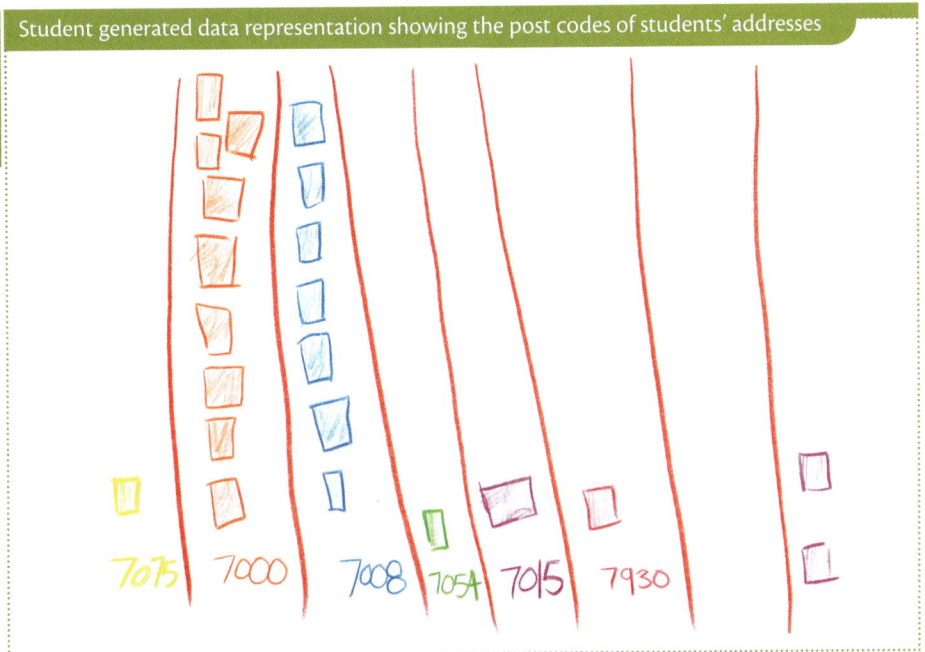

Figure 21.8 Student generated data representation showing the post codes of students' addresses

consider and discuss

Re-read the anecdote at the start of the chapter.

1. Why do you think the student initially claimed not to know how to draw a graph even though she clearly knew that graphs could be used to display data?
2. How might her experiences of learning about graphs have influenced this?
3. How would you help her to think about graphs in terms of telling a story? What specific tasks could you offer?

What conventions of graph drawing are evident in her work (Figure 21.9), and which seem not to be appreciated yet? How would you help her to progress in this regard?

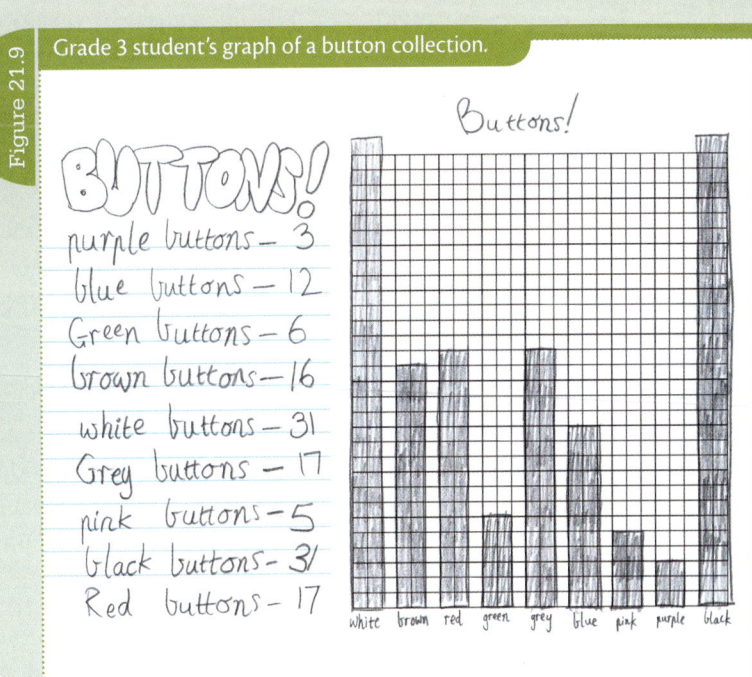

Figure 21.9 Grade 3 student's graph of a button collection.

Shaughnessy (2007) described the development of students' thinking about bar graphs and the difficulties that they pose. At their simplest, bar graphs represent frequencies of categorical data. Dealing with bar graphs in which the exact frequencies are not readily visible is a challenge for many students (Shaughnessy, 2007). A further transition is from vertical axes with integer scales to scales that are not integral, and from column heights representing frequencies to columns representing relative frequencies or proportions of the data. Later, the need to represent continuous data rather than categorical data leads to the need to divide the horizontal axis into continuous intervals of equal width, and hence to the use of histograms rather than bar graphs. Shaugnessy (2007) pointed out how these transitions mirror those from additive to proportional to distributional thinking as described in relation to understanding of samples.

Shaughnessy (2007) listed eight student behaviours that he claimed were evidence of *graph sense* or the ability to reason about graphs, and which he linked to Curcio's three levels and his additional level (Curcio, 1989, cited in Shaughnessy, 2007). Many of these aspects of graph sense will not be developed until the middle years and beyond, but the beginnings of all of them should be in students' earliest encounters with representing data. They were:

- recognising components of graphs (*reading* the data)
- speaking the language of graphs (*reading* the data)
- understanding relationships among tables, graphs, and data (reading *within* the data)
- making sense of a graph, but avoiding personalisation and maintaining an objective stance while talking about graphs (reading *within* the data)
- interpreting information in a graph and answering questions about it (reading *beyond* the graph)
- recognising appropriate graphs for a given data set and its context (reading *beyond* the graph)
- looking for possible causes of variation (reading *behind* the data)
- looking for relationships among variables (reading *behind* the data) (p. 991).

handy hint

Using a data-handling software package such as TinkerPlots or Excel to construct graphs can help to move the focus of activity from the technical skills required to construct graphs to the interpretation of the data.

Comparing distributions

Comparing data distributions can be a powerful way to focus students' attention on the overall shape of a data set. Considering and describing the spread of data and any clustering that might be evident in it builds students' intuitions about variation in data sets and about what might be expected if new data were added to the set. These fundamental ideas (variation and expectation) form the basis of later understanding of measures of spread and measures of central tendency (mean, mode, and median) (Watson, 2005). Shaughnessy (2007) recommends that comparison of data sets be included from the very beginning of teaching about probability and statistics.

handy hint

Help students to describe distributions by providing a word bank, in the form of a list to which words can be added, displayed on the classroom wall. Brodesky, Doherty and Stoddard (2008, p. 46) suggest the following words, but a class could come up with their own.

- spread out
- centre
- gap
- bunched up on one side
- valley
- stairs
- skewed
- clump
- flat
- mirror image
- hill
- symmetrical
- peak
- bunched together
- cluster
- hole

Comparisons of data about students in different classes or Years, or of boys and girls, are always of interest to students. As well as the individual data points, students might observe from a distribution of heights, for example (in Figure 21.10), that the shortest and tallest students are both boys and that the heights of the boys tend to clump in the middle, whereas the girls' heights tend to fall in two clusters and are less spread out than the boys' heights. Of course, when data are about the students in the class all students will be vitally interested in their own data points, so encouraging students to avoid personalisation and maintain an objective stance (point 4 in Shaughnessy's list of indicators of graph sense) can be a challenge. For older children a worthwhile discussion would be about why we might want to compare an attribute like height or test scores for boys and girls and whether any differences we find are important.

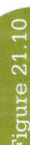

Figure 21.10 Graph of the heights of Year 5/6 girls and boys

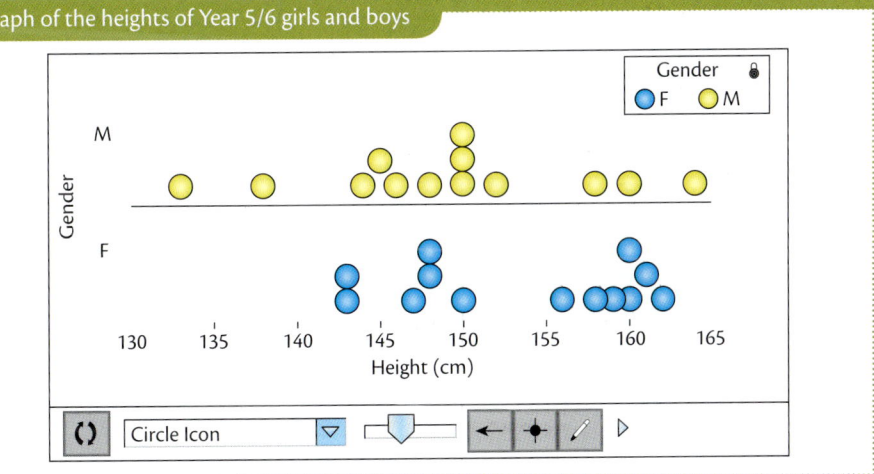

issues in teaching

Using personal data

Children enjoy considering data about themselves and it is often easier for them to relate to and understand than data from unfamiliar contexts. Teachers need to be aware of potential sensitivities when choosing data to be collected and/or considered. Whereas most children will be happy to share data about such things as their heights, handspans, reaction times, and birthdays, data about weight is much more likely to be sensitive for some students and is best avoided.

Consider the graphs shown in Figures 21.11 and 21.12. Figure 21.11 shows the number of coins in a 50 cent coin collection that were minted in each year from 1969 to 2008. How would you describe the distribution of coins in the collection? Students might notice the two clumps in the data, the gap in the middle, the fact that the tallest columns in both clumps are towards the right of the clump. The student who owned these coins wondered about the gap, and it was suggested that maybe it had something to do with the numbers of coins produced each year. Figure 21.12 shows a graph of the numbers of coins (in millions) produced in each year from 1966, when 50 cent coins were first minted, to 2008. The data were found on the Royal Australian Mint website at www.ramint.gov.au/designs/ram-designs/50c.cfm. There are obvious similarities between the shapes of the two distributions, including the dip between 1984 and 1994 and the spike at 2001. Students could also discuss possible reasons why most of the coins in the collection have mint dates after 1994 rather than before 1984, even though more 50 cent coins were minted in the earlier period.

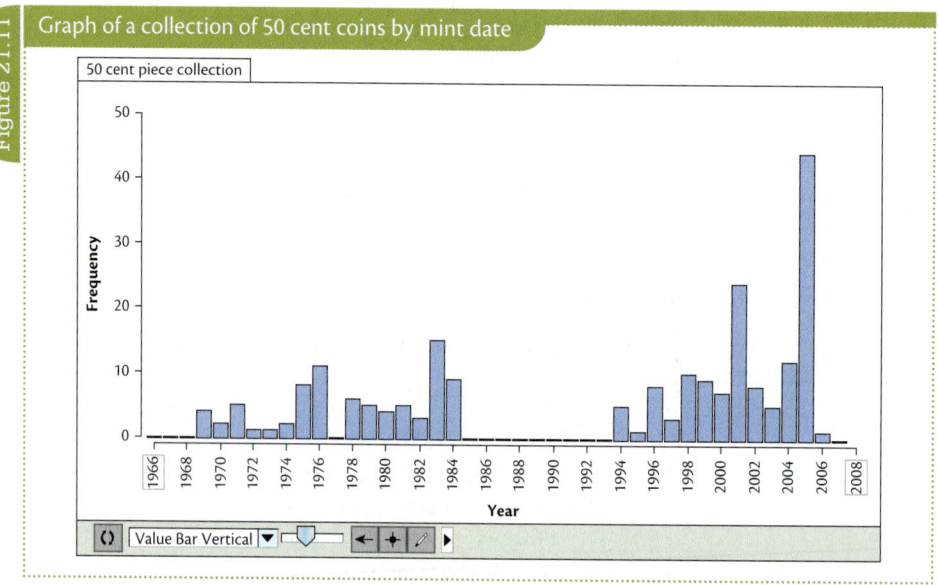

Figure 21.11 Graph of a collection of 50 cent coins by mint date

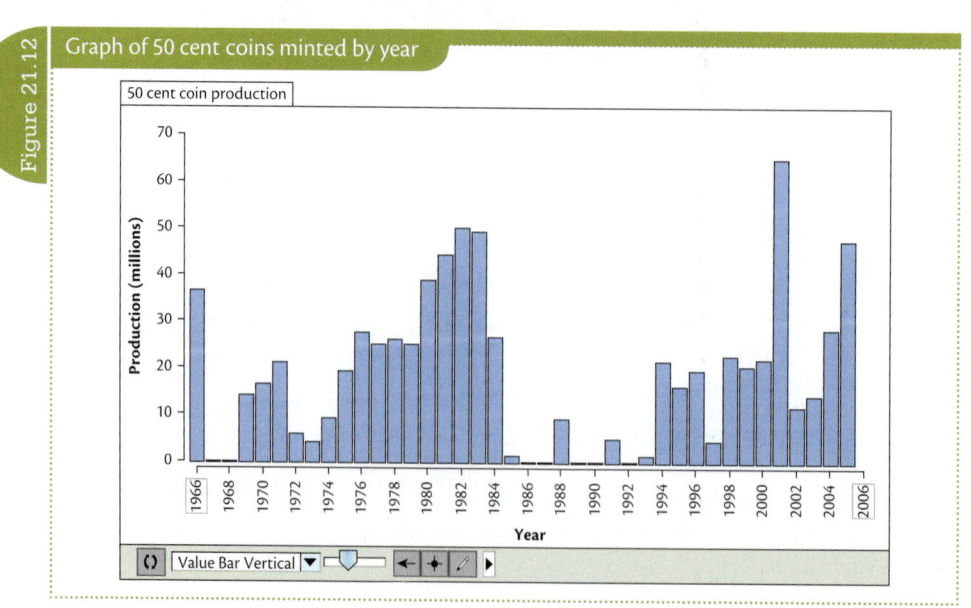

Figure 21.12 Graph of 50 cent coins minted by year

These graphs are less accessible to young students than are graphs of personal data, especially because the vertical scales on the graphs in Figures 21.11 and 21.12 do not show each number in the count. In addition, the vertical scales are different, with the numbers on the scale in Figure 21.12 more closely spaced than in Figure 21.11, and representing millions of coins rather than simply the number of coins. Students could try to imagine what the graph in Figure 21.12 would look like if it used the same vertical scale as Figure 21.11! Discussions of this sort alert students to the need to attend to such things as the scales on axes when they are reading and interpreting graphs. Despite the difficulties, if the context arises from students in the class, then relatively complex data can be explored meaningfully. Be guided by the students and their interests.

consider and discuss

Consider the distributions shown in Figures 21.11 and 21.12. How would you describe the two distributions? How might primary school students describe them?

integrating technology

The following attributes of technological environments that can support students' learning about data handling were listed by Garfield (1990, cited by Shaughnessy, 2007, p. 992). They are worth considering when evaluating software:

- direct access, which allows students to view and explore data in different forms, including subsets of data and different visual representations
- flexibility, which allows students to experiment with and alter displays of data, change intervals on a graph, and explore different models that fit the data
- connectedness, so that students are able to access resources from the internet, as well as to obtain software or data used in the study of other disciplines
- representations, including dynamic ones from which students may choose among different graphs in order to select the best way to interpret and display a data set.

think + link

In Chapter 12 we considered the concept of statistical literacy. Consider how the understandings of chance processes and data representation and interpretation discussed in this chapter contribute to the development of statistical literacy.

key terms

Cause: that which gives rise to an event

Chance: the likelihood of a particular outcome

Data: observations or measurements collected as part of an investigation

Deterministic: a view that all events have direct causes, in contrast to a probabilistic view that considers causation in terms of chance-raising or making an event more likely to occur

Distribution: the overall 'shape' of a set of data

Likelihood: the chance that a particular outcome will occur

Prediction: an expectation of the outcome of an experiment

Probability: a number between 0 (impossible) and 1 (certain) that indicates the likelihood or chance that a particular outcome will occur

Proportional reasoning: thinking that involves accounting for the relative sizes of two or more multiplicatively related quantities

Representative: used to describe a sample that is the same as the population from which it is drawn in relation to attributes that are relevant to an investigation

Sample: a smaller set chosen from a population

Simulation: a chance process, the outcome of which mirrors that of a process of interest

Statistics: the discipline concerned with making inferences about chance processes; a single number that summarises a characteristic of a population

Variation: the extent to which the outcomes of a chance process differ from one another

Review questions

1. In what ways is the thinking required to understand probability and statistics different from that required for other areas of the mathematics curriculum?
2. Find an example from the media or a recall an example from your own experience in which something unlikely happened. What evidence is/was there of a tendency to use deterministic rather than probabilistic reasoning in relation to the event? Why do you think this was the case?
3. Why is it important that young students have opportunities to represent data in ways that make sense to them?
4. In Chapter 2 we considered theories of learning. In what ways is the teaching approach advocated in this chapter consistent with a constructivist view of learning?

Key references

Jones, G. A., Langrall, C. W., & Mooney, E. S. (2007). Research in probability: Responding to classroom realities. In F. K. Lester Jr. (Ed.), *Second Handbook of Research on Mathematics Teaching and Learning* (Vol. 2, pp. 909–956). Charlotte, NC: Information Age.

Konold, C. (1989). Informal conceptions of probability. *Cognition and Instruction*, 6, 59–98.

Lambos, C., & Delfabbro, P. (2010). Numerical reasoning ability and irrational beliefs in problem gambling. *International Gambling Studies*, 7(2), 157–171.

Metz, K. E. (1998). Emergent ideas of chance and probability in primary-grade children. In S. P. Lajoie (Ed.), *Reflections on Statistics Learning, Teaching and Assessment in Grades K–12* (pp. 149–173). Mahwah, NJ: Erlbaum.

Pereira-Mendoza, L. (1995). Graphing in the primary school: Algorithm versus comprehension. *Teaching Statistics*, 17, 2–6.

Shaughnessy, J. M. (2007). Research on statistics learning and reasoning. In F. K. Lester Jr. (Ed.), *Second Handbook of Research on Mathematics Teaching and Learning* (Vol. 2, pp. 957–1010). Charlotte, NC: Information Age.

Watson, J. M. (2005). Variation and expectation as foundations for the chance and data curriculum. In P. C. Clarkson, A. Downton, D. Gronn, M. Horne, A. McDonough, R. Pierce, U. Roche & A. Roche (Eds.), *Building connections: Research, theory and practice (Procceedings of the 28th Annual Conference of the Mathematics Education Research Group of Australasia* Vol. 1, pp. 35–42). Adelaide: MERGA.

Watson, J. M. (2006). *Statistical Literacy at School: Growth and Goals*. Mahwah, NJ: Erlbaum.

Watson, J. M., & Moritz, J. B. (2000). Development of understanding of sampling for statistical literacy. *Journal of Mathematical Behavior*, 19, 109–136.

Watson, J. M., & Moritz, J. B. (2003). Fairness of dice: A longitudinal study of students' beliefs and strategies for making judgments. *Journal for Research in Mathematics Education*, 34(4), 270–304.

Websites

www.ramint.gov.au/designs/ram-designs/50c.cfm

Part five

Extending Mathematics to the Middle Years

Moving on

In Part 4 we explored the mathematics typically taught in the early years, both in terms of understanding the mathematics itself as well as how to teach the concepts to young learners. In this part, we will extend these ideas into the middle years of schooling. Many people entering the mathematics teaching profession select a year range such as primary or secondary teaching. For all mathematics teachers, it is important to understand the mathematics curriculum their students have already accessed as well as the direction in which they are headed. Teachers in the middle school need to understand the work of their colleagues in the early years.

A critical issue in middle school mathematics education is the retention of students. In this stage of schooling, students face the transition from primary to secondary schooling. Sometimes learning difficulties and misconceptions in learning become apparent. For other students they seem to drift further and further behind their age peers. The middle years also present some students with the choice to opt out of mathematics, to their serious detriment.

Therefore, middle school mathematics teachers have a vital role in maintaining or developing student enjoyment and accomplishment in mathematics. The *Australian Curriculum: Mathematics* is an *age-appropriate* curriculum, specifying what all students should be taught in the year level of their schooling. As was noted in Chapter 8, with good teaching and the right support, all learners should experience success in mathematics.

Teaching mathematics in the middle years is a rewarding undertaking. We introduce learners to new areas of mathematics and deepen their understanding of previous work. It is a stimulating field with significant opportunities teachers to show students the beauty and richness of mathematics.

Questions

1. 'Excellent teachers of mathematics have a sound, coherent knowledge of the mathematics appropriate to the student level they teach' (Standards for Excellence in Teaching Mathematics in Australian Schools, 2006). As you commence your work in Part 5, which aspects of mathematics at this level do you feel confident with, and which will require development?
2. Australia is facing a serious shortage of school leavers who are accomplished at mathematics. What role could middle school mathematics teachers play in addressing this problem?

5

22

Extending Number: Fractions, Decimals, and Reals

Contents

Building the number line	493
Whole numbers	494
Scientific notation	502
The rationals	504
The reals	512
Conclusion	515

Chapter objectives

This chapter will enable the reader to:

- Understand the difference between a number and a numeral and why this matters
- Develop an integrated mental number line
- Understand sets of numbers that make up the real numbers
- Explore useful properties of whole numbers in an introduction to number theory
- Develop conceptual understanding of rational numbers—fractions, decimals, percentages—and how to convert between them
- Recognise numbers that are not rational—the irrationals and complex numbers.

consider and discuss

Playing with digits

Make a set of cards with the numbers 0 to 10.

Arrange the cards to make the largest number you can. If you have enough people (perhaps in your tutorial group), you can wear the numbers. Convince another person that you have made the biggest number possible.

1. What method did you use to name the number? Did you find yourself grouping the digits in groups of three? If so, at which end did you start the grouping?
2. Now add a new card with a dot representing a decimal point. You can place the decimal anywhere. When is it necessary to rearrange the groupings of the columns? What is the effect of the decimal point?

Big ideas

- The number line is made up of different types of numbers:
  - counting numbers
  - whole numbers
  - integers

- rationals
- irrationals
- reals.
■ Any real number can be placed on the number line. Only complex numbers do not have a place on the number line.
■ The development of a single mental number line encompassing all types of numbers is an important aspect of numeracy development that continues into middle schooling and beyond.

Building the number line

Our numeration system

consider and discuss

What is a number?
Think of all the aspects that are encompassed in the term 'number'. Draw a concept map to show how the aspects link together for you.

A **number** is an idea about quantity. On our mental number line, each number has an individual place. If we wish to be pedantic, when we use symbols to give a label to a number, we are writing a numeral. A **numeral** is a symbol that represents a number. Each individual number or place on a mental numberline can be written using many different forms, ranging from tallies to complex numeration systems.

for the classroom

Numeration systems
Invite children to find different numeration systems. Many will be familiar with Roman numerals. They can find other ancient systems, such as Mayan and Egyptian, as well as systems still common today, such as Chinese and Arabic numerals.
  Children can record many different ways of writing different numbers.
  This activity is not just a quirky time filler. It offers students the opportunity to appreciate that the way we record the location of quantity on an imaginary number line is culturally based and many possible ways exist.

One very important aspect of a numeration system is whether it has position value, place value, or neither. One Egyptian numeration system used ∩ to represent 10 and I to represent 1. For example, the number 23 could be represented as ∩∩III. However, order was not important and it could equally have been written as ∩III∩. This system had neither position value nor place value. Roman numeration has position value. IX stands for 9. The I has the value of 1 and its position in IX indicates one less than 10 (the value of X). However, XI stands for 11. Here the I still has the value 1, but its position indicates the number is 11, one more than 10. By contrast, our Hindu-Arabic number system has place value. In our system, the value that a symbol takes depends on its place. For example, in 23, the 2 is worth 20, its place meaning 2×10. This is different from 32 where the 2 is now only worth 2×1. This is a very compact system and makes calculation relatively simple (once you have developed a method). This is not the case for other systems (try multiplying in Roman numerals if you need convincing!).

did you know?

The earliest evidence yet found of humans writing numerals dates from 35 000 BCE. A series of tally marks has been found on the fibula bone of a baboon.

Our numeration system has developed over human history as social, political, and cultural influences presented problems to be solved. From tallies on a bone to transcendental numbers, types of numbers have emerged as needed. The fascinating story of this development can be read in *The Story of Mathematics* (Mankiewicz, 2000).

Whole numbers

The development of our number system began with enumerating objects. A bone dating from 20 000 BCE appears to have tallies linked to phases of the Moon. Linking words to numbers and then symbols to the words is fundamental to our developing concept of number, and follows an ancient pattern of development. The set of numbers {1, 2, 3, 4 …} is known as the counting or natural numbers, and mathematicians give this set the label *N*.

Surprisingly, the idea of zero is fairly recent. There were two aspects to the idea of zero: the discovery that the number existed, and the invention of a symbol to denote it. The symbol came first, and took forms such as an empty column on an abacus, a dot, and 0. Understanding that nothing was actually something, and was a number with very special properties, took many centuries. You can read about zero in *From Zero to Infinity* by Constance Reid (1992).

When zero is included with the natural numbers, we have the set called the whole numbers, given the symbol *W*.

integrating technology/ICT

Playing with zero

Zero is an intriguing number. It is the only number that when you multiply it by any other number, your answer is always zero. When you add or subtract zero, the number you started with is unchanged. The most surprising, though, is the effect of division.

What happens when you start with zero and you try dividing by other numbers (not zero)? $0/n = ?$

Try with a variety of numbers. Try decimals, negatives … what happens?

As with multiplication, whatever number you choose as the divisor, the answer will always be zero.

Write a word problem around this context.

What happens when zero is the divisor? Try $n/0$ on your calculator. You are likely to have already experienced the result in your previous mathematics work. The 'I give up' message the calculator gives you indicates something unusual is going on. Because we can't use the calculator directly, we need to investigate what happens as we try to divide by numbers close to zero.

Chapter 22 Extending Number: Fractions, Decimals, and Reals

1. To investigate what is happening, start with 1. Now divide this number by a number close to 0, say 0.1. Record the result.
2. 0.1 is close to 0 but we can do better. Divide 1 by 0.01. Record the result.
3. Continue dividing by smaller and smaller numbers, recording the result.

Spreadsheets are perfect for performing many calculations quickly, recording the result, and then graphing the result later.

1. Set up columns:

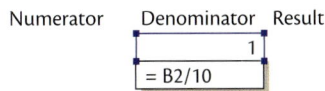

The Denominator column begins with 1, but row 2 now has =. In Excel, this tells the spreadsheet that you are entering a formula. When you enter it, it will calculate the value: 0.1. Now move the cursor to the bottom right-hand corner of the cell. Notice it change shape. Drag down and you will see that the results change. Each cell is a tenth of the cell above. Click on any cell and you will see the formula that has been used.

2. Now we need to use the spreadsheet to calculate for us. Click on the cell where you want the result. Enter =, click on the numerator (cell A2), enter / for division, and then click on B2.

Numerator	Denominator	Result
1	1	= A2/B2
	0.1	
	0.01	
	0.001	
	0.0001	
	0.00001	
	0.000001	

Press Enter and then fill down.

3. What do you notice about the results?

It appears that as we get closer to dividing by zero, the result is becoming huge. Could it be the answer is infinity? Not so fast.

4. What happens if the numerator is −1? Use the spreadsheet to check.
5. Use the spreadsheet to graph your results. Plot the value for the denominator on the horizontal axis and the result on the vertical axis.

We can also get a picture of this by drawing the graph of $y = \frac{1}{x}$ on a graphics calculator or a graphing package such as Geogebra:

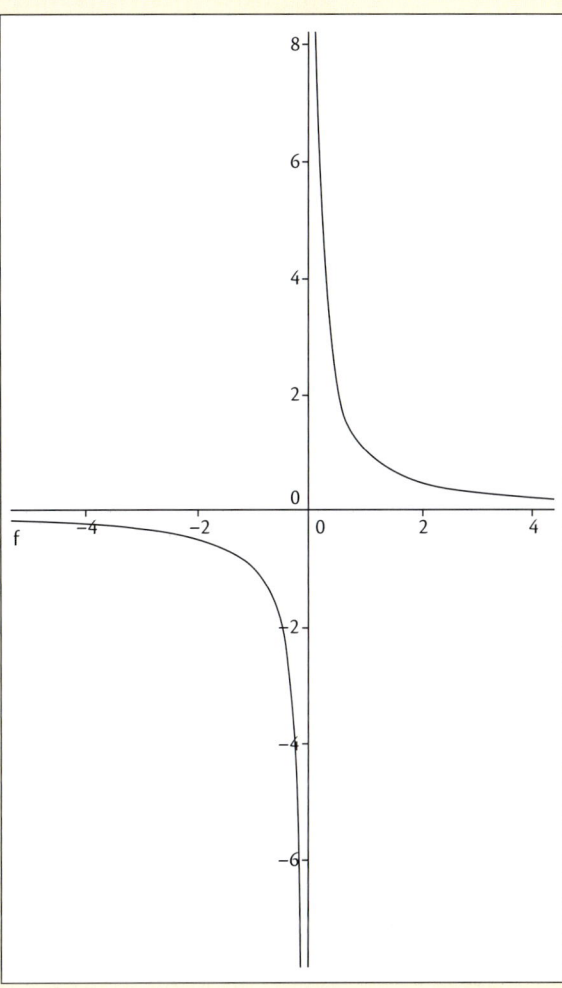

When we approach zero from the positive side, the result of $\frac{1}{n}$ approaches positive infinity.

When we approach zero from the negative side, the result of $\frac{1}{n}$ approaches negative infinity. Right at zero, there is a discontinuity in the graph. It would appear it is trying to have two answers at the same time: positive and negative infinity. This is not possible, and so $1 \div 0$ is *undefined*. Because the values are not the same, the answer is undefined.

$\frac{1}{0}$ is *undefined*. There is no answer—it is not just that you have not done enough mathematics.

Looking for a challenge?

If you've exhausted your investigation of $\frac{1}{0}$, investigate $\frac{0}{0}$.

What happens when you make both the numerator and denominator approach zero? Try different approach paths—make one approach from the negative side, the other from the positive side.

Because the result varies depending on the approach you take (sometimes defined, other times not) the result of $\frac{0}{0}$ is considered *indeterminate*.

communicating mathematically

Division by zero

With children in upper primary school, it is very important that correct language is used to avoid confusion in later years.

Division by zero is *undefined*. This does not mean 'nothing'. Children can mistakenly interpret undefined to mean zero.

Number patterns and properties

think + link

See Chapter 9 for further discussion about numeracy development.

The study of number patterns and properties is a fascinating branch of mathematics known as *number theory*. It has its beginnings in early childhood mathematics and continues into professional mathematics domains. Playing with numbers and becoming familiar with them is an important part of developing an 'at-homeness with number', described by Cockroft (1982) as an important aspect of numeracy.

A fundamental property of whole numbers concerns factors. **Factors** can be defined as pairs of counting numbers that multiply to give another counting number. This is one of the terms in mathematics that is more difficult to define in words than it is to understand in usage or through diagrams. Rather than having students learn or reproduce definitions for concepts like these, provide assessment opportunities that enable you to see if they understand and can use the term. In the following activity, children develop a visual and lasting image of factors. Later on, students are able to generate visual images without the need for blocks, and many children find these helpful for remembering multiplication facts.

for the classroom

Finding factors

A useful way for finding all the factors in a number is to look at the possible arrangements of blocks to make a rectangle. If we wish to find the factors of 12, we could start with a rectangle 12 × 1.

The only possible factors of 12 are the sides of the rectangles. Because factors are whole numbers, we don't have to worry about possibilities such as 1.5 × 8. Factors are listed as elements of a set.

communicating mathematically

Set notation

We show sets using braces with elements separated by commas. Factors of 12 would be listed as {1, 2, 3, 4, 6, 12}.

Notice that the factors are written in ascending order. Repeated factors (should they exist) are written only once.

A number that has *exactly* two factors, itself and 1, is called a **prime number**. This is an important definition. Notice that 1 is not prime as it does not have two factors—its only factor is 1. **Composite numbers** are counting numbers (other than one) that are not prime.

for the classroom

Finding primes—The Sieve of Eratosthenes

Eratosthenes was a mathematician living in Alexandria around 250 BCE. He is credited with a method for finding primes.

1. Begin with a hundreds chart. Put a star around 1, as it is neither prime nor composite. Circle the next number. Two is the first prime. Now cross off multiples of two. These multiples cannot be prime. (Why?) Where are these on the chart? Complete the following statement: Multiples of 2 end in …
2. Move to the next number after two and circle it. Three is the next prime. Cross off multiples of three. Where are these on the chart? What do the digits that you have crossed out add to? Did you notice the numbers in the diagonal under 3 have digits that add to 3? What do you notice about the digit sum of numbers in the diagonal under 6? Under 9? How can you tell if a number is a multiple of 3?
3. Move to the next number after 3 that has not been crossed out. Five is the next prime number. Where are the multiples of 5?
4. Continue until you have found all the primes to 100.

Notice how difficult it is to find some multiples. There is no pattern for multiples of 7, for example. This is why the seven times table is difficult to learn.

Notice where the multiples of 11 are. Why do they appear on the diagonal?

handy hint

Divisibility tests

In the classroom activity above, you observed ways to determine multiples of numbers. These are also known as divisibility tests. For example, you can tell if a number is divisible by 5 if it ends in either 0 or 5.

Make a table of results for divisibility tests based on your results. These tables are also available in mathematics dictionaries and are useful properties of numbers to remember.

think + link

Look back at the investigation of multiples of 3 and 9 in Chapter 13. In what ways is it similar to this activity?

making connections

The set of primes is infinite, and finding increasingly large prime numbers is a valuable search. Digital security, such as for electronic banking, internet transactions, and databases, relies on prime numbers underlying data encryption. Programs have been developed to search for primes whenever a computer is idle. Even so, it may be years before a new prime number is found.

consider and discuss

Is my number prime?

Finding all the factors of a number can be a time-consuming task. For example, is 149 prime?

Looking at our divisibility tests, we can tell at a glance that it does not have the factors 2, 3, 4, 5, 6, 9, 10, 11 but what about the others? How far up do we have to go to check?

> Remember back to the rectangles of blocks where the side lengths are the factors. If I had 149 blocks, how many rectangles would I have to make before I was sure I had found all the factors?
>
> A useful problem-solving strategy is to simplify the problem. Go back to thinking about 12 blocks. How many rectangles did you need to make before you had made them all?
>
> What if you had 16 blocks? How many rectangles then?

Prime factorisation and other techniques with factors

Composite numbers are built up from prime factors—primes are the building blocks of composite numbers. If we decompose composites into their prime factors, some interesting and important results emerge.

First, let us develop a technique for prime factorisation. A tree diagram is useful:

Break into factors.

Keep going until the factors are prime.

$60 = 3 \times 2 \times 2 \times 5$

What about a different start?

$60 = 5 \times 3 \times 2 \times 2$

Therefore, 60 has prime factors 2, 2, 3, 5. It does not matter which way I start, I will always get the same prime factors. This important result is known as the **Fundamental Theorem of Arithmetic**.

Find the prime factors of 192. Because there are so many prime factors of 192 that are the same, mathematicians find it convenient to use index or power notation: $192 = 2^6 \times 3^1$.

consider and discuss

Cutting squares

Suppose you have to cut squares from a rectangular sheet of cardboard and you wish to minimise waste. The sheet measures 420 cm × 378 cm. What dimensions of squares are possible?

Be sure to record your working and thinking.

Discuss your solutions strategies with your peers. What is the largest square you can cut?

Adapted from Bassarear (1997, p. 189).

A number of approaches to this problem are possible. You are looking for a number that is both a factor of 420 and 378. Prime factorisation can be used to find solutions:

$378 = 2 \times 3^3 \times 7$ and $420 = 2^2 \times 3 \times 5 \times 7$.

2 is a factor of both, so squares of side length 2 will leave no waste (and a lot of little squares). 2 and 3 are factors of both, so 6 also is a factor. If we try various combinations, the largest factor that is common to both is found by $2 \times 3 \times 7$, or 42. The need to find the highest common factor (often abbreviated to HCF) arises in many problem-solving situations and is often referred to as finding the HCF.

A related property of two numbers is the lowest common multiple, often abbreviated to LCM.

for the classroom

Finding the LCM

Ask the children in your class to stand in a line, wearing counting numbers in order (or ask them to count along the line and remember their number). Begin with 2. Ask the children to put out one foot if their number is a multiple of 2. Comment on what happens.

Now ask children whose number is a multiple of 3 to put out the other foot. Who has both feet out (and has therefore taken a step forward)? Which is the LCM? Is it possible to have a highest common multiple?

Number shapes

As you have seen, when making rectangles for some numbers of blocks it is possible to make squares. These are the square numbers. For example, 9 is a square number. We can arrange 9 blocks in a square 3×3. If we want to know what the length of the side of the square is, mathematically, we are asking 'What is the square root of 9?', or '$\sqrt{9} = ?$'. In the Consider and Discuss problem on page 497, we asked how many possible factors of 149 you would have to check before you could be sure you had found them all. The square root of our number is the side length of the square made from that number of blocks. For 12, this is not a whole number; it is between 3 and 4. Once we have made a rectangle with one side 3, we can be sure we have tested as far as we need to because after that, the rectangles are the same, just rotated.

Similarly, cubes are numbers that can be arranged in a cubic form. 8 is a cubic number from which a cube with side length 2 can be made. This can be written: $2 \times 2 \times 2 = 2^3 = 8$. What number is formed by a cube of side length 10? If I have 64 blocks, what would be the side length if I made a square? That is, $\sqrt{64} = ?$ These 64 blocks can also be made into a cube. What would be the side length? Or $\sqrt[3]{64} = ?$

integrating technology/ICT

Power keys

Scientific and graphics calculators have keys that can be used to calculate powers and find square, cube, and other roots. Different calculators use different symbols to show these. Consult your manual to find out which keys are the power keys on your calculator.

Triangular numbers are formed from triangular patterns (you guessed!). Notice the pattern of how the numbers are increasing:

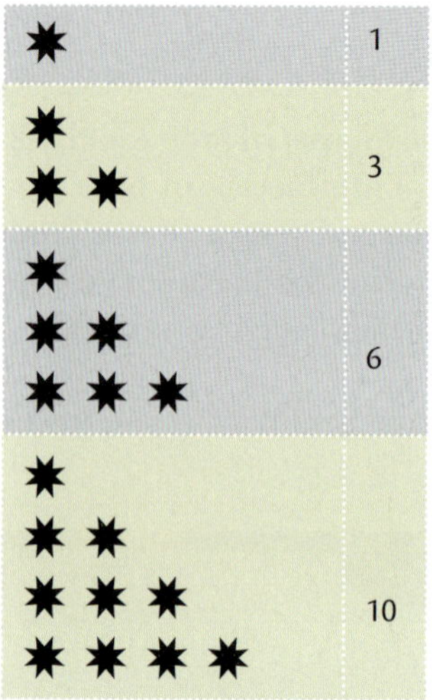

✸	1
✸ ✸ ✸	3
✸ ✸ ✸ ✸ ✸ ✸	6
✸ ✸ ✸ ✸ ✸ ✸ ✸ ✸ ✸ ✸	10

Triangular numbers arise in many number problems and are useful to recognise. With mathematics, the more you do, the easier mathematics becomes. If you are able to recognise the square numbers, cubic numbers, and triangular numbers, when the patterns arise in problem solving you will know what you are seeing.

There are many other number sequences based on shapes, including pentagonal numbers, tetrahedral numbers and even rhombic dodecahedral numbers! You can read more about these in *The Book of Numbers* (Conway & Guy, 1998).

Representing large numbers

Learning the arrangements of the columns is important for the understanding of large numbers. Each column works in exactly the same way. Each can have 0–9. As each column looks identical, we need a way to identify the units column. An abacus shows this with a bar of a different colour or with a dot on a column. In written notation, we use a decimal point.

Figure 22.1

Representation of a number													
Billions			Millions			Thousands			Units				
Hundred billions	Ten billions	Billions	Hundred millions	Ten millions	Millions	Hundred thousands	Ten thousands	Thousands	Hundreds	Tens	Ones •	Tenths	Hundredths	Thousandths	Ten thousandths

Notice the patterns in the labelling. Groups of three follow the pattern of hundred, ten, unit. Notice also that the mirror is around the ones column, not the decimal point.

> **did you know?**
>
> A 'googol' is a very large number! It is the number with 1 followed by 100 zeros. If you look at the columns above, that would mean a lot of paper. It is more compactly written as 1×10^{100}. This number has no particular mathematical significance but it is interesting!

Integers

Extending the number line

The set of integers introduces the idea of negative numbers. Mathematicians have been aware of the need for negative numbers for over 2000 years. The idea of negative numbers has been referred to in documents from ancient China, Egypt, and India. European mathematicians realised the need for negative numbers but avoided using them until the seventeenth century. In mathematics the need for negative integers arises from situations involving the difference between two whole numbers. Sometimes the solution in subtraction is not a positive integer, for example, $3 - 5 = ?$

> **handy hint**
>
> Young children can come across situations where negative numbers are needed, such as $3 - 5$. Even though the concept may be beyond their present work, never say it can't be done. Physically we can't take away more than we have, but clearly it is possible in other contexts. Instead, invite a curious child to think about what the result might be.

In real life there are a number of contexts involving the ideas of negative numbers that can be drawn upon in introducing negative integers. The measurement of temperature using a thermometer calibrated in degrees Celsius shows temperatures below freezing point as being below zero. Elevations above and below sea level are sometimes presented using negative numbers.

> **making connections**
>
> In banking and accounting the term 'in the red' means that you have spent more than you earned and your bank balance will be negative. Negative numbers are often printed in red, positive in black.

The use of real-life examples for negative numbers sets the scene for further study of the integers. Parallels can be drawn between the real-life situations and the number line representation of negative numbers.

> **handy hint**
>
> Make sure children don't just see horizontal number lines. They need to see other orientations, especially vertical, to prepare them for later work, in particular Cartesian coordinates.

Scientific notation

Once numbers become very large, for example the number of molecules in a spoonful of sugar, or very small, such as the distance between atoms in a molecule, a more efficient notation system is required. The system we use is called **scientific notation**.

integrating technology/ICT

Scientific notation on a calculator

Scientific and graphics calculators display numbers in either standard or scientific form. Consult your calculator's manual (or find it on the internet) to understand the way to enter scientific notation and toggle between scientific and standard form. You should also learn how to enter negative powers as well as negative numbers. For many calculators, if you wish to enter the number -3×10^{-5}, the keystrokes would be: 3 +/– EXP 5 +/– = .

consider and discuss

Converting to scientific notation

Look at the following examples written in standard form and the equivalent number written in scientific notation.

Standard form	Scientific notation
350 000	3.5×10^5
40 670 001	$4.067\,000\,1 \times 10^7$
0.000 000 78	7.8×10^{-7}
0.000 000 000 9	9×10^{-10}

Describe the patterns. If the scientific form has a negative power, it is a very small number. Be careful here. The number 9×10^{-10} is a positive number. If you were to place it on a number line, it would be to the right of the zero.

Try this one: $-0.000\,003$. Where would this number be placed on the number line? Make up some other examples and check on your scientific calculator.

for the classroom

Naming large numbers

You will need:
- a 10-sided die or a pack of 0–9 digit cards
- paper and pencil for recording.

1. Take turns to toss the die. Two packs of small cards marked with the numbers 0 to 9 can be used instead of a 10-sided die. Shuffle the cards, place the pile face down and draw a card instead of tossing the die.
2. Record the digit on the right-hand side of the page. Say the number.
3. The next person tosses the die and records the digit to the left of the last one, and says the number.
4. Keep taking turns to toss the die, record the digit to the left of the last one, and say the number.

Challenge: Use the 10-sided die or 0–9 digit cards and record the digits from left to right, saying each number as you go.

Chapter 22 Extending Number: Fractions, Decimals, and Reals

communicating mathematically

Naming convention

A source of confusion in the naming of large numbers arises from the fact that there are two conventions for naming large numbers: the American system and the European system. In the American system 1 billion is 10^9 = 1 000 000 000 while the European 1 billion is 10^{12} = 1 000 000 000 000 and 1 thousand million is represented by 10^9 = 1 000 000 000. Over recent years the American system has been taken up more widely than the European system and has been adopted in Australia (see <www.measurement.gov.au/Pages/MetricConversion.aspx>).

The use of scientific notation and standard form goes some way to addressing any ambiguity that may arise.

for the classroom

Make a collection of large numbers cut from newspapers and magazines. Name the numbers and put them in order. Select numbers from the collection to write using expanded form or scientific notation.

Operations with indices

Our symbol system is powerful because of the concise way ideas can be conveyed using a few symbols. Use of indices (also called powers) is an example.

communicating mathematically

Index notation

$a^n = a.a.a.a \ldots n$ times.

Notice how a dot has been used. The dot is another symbol for multiplication and is very useful to avoid confusion in algebra with the variable label x. The dot sits on the line. A decimal point often sits above the line, so we can tell them apart.

In the example, a is the base and n is the power or index. The plural form of index is 'indices'.

It is easy to make sense of expressions such as 7^3. This would be $7 \times 7 \times 7$. It is more challenging to explain 7^0 or 7^{-3}.

consider and discuss

Complete the following table. Make up other examples to test patterns you notice.

Index form	Expansion	Comments
10^3	$10 \times 10 \times 10$	
10^2	10×10	This is one-tenth of the row above
10^1	10	Each row is one-tenth of the row above
10^0	$\frac{10}{10} = 1$	
10^{-1}		Continue the pattern. Each row is one-tenth of the row above.
10^{-2}		

1. Study the patterns in the powers. Study the pattern of the results. What would happen if you changed the base? Try other numbers and check results on your calculator.
2. What is the general rule for any non-zero number raised to the power 0? You might like to explore what happens if zero is raised to the power 0. It is very interesting and leads to some fascinating results.
3. What did you notice about negative powers? It is important to distinguish between negative powers and negative numbers. For example, if you were to place -10^{-2} on a number line, it would be in the same place as -0.01. Therefore, it would be to the left of zero, with the negatives, one-hundredth of a unit from zero.

consider and discuss

The following index laws are useful in many contexts in middle school mathematics. Explore both, expanding them out to convince yourself why they are true.

$$a^m . a^n = a^{(m+n)}$$

$$\frac{a^m}{a^n} = a^{(m-n)}$$

did you know?

Multiplication and division are more difficult to do without a calculator than addition and subtraction. John Napier, a Scottish mathematician of the late sixteenth century, invented logarithms; these converted multiplication into addition problems and division into subtraction problems using the index laws you have just looked at.

Apart from being a very efficient method of writing very large or very small numbers, scientific notation allows easy methods of computation using index laws.

Suppose we want to calculate $6 \times 10^{-23} \times 8 \times 10^3$. This calculation can be done on a calculator, if we want to use the slow way! Instead, we can look at this and note that $6 \times 8 = 48$ and, using our index laws, $10^{-23} \times 10^3 = 10^{(-23+3)} = 10^{-20}$. The answer is 48×10^{-20} or 4.8×10^{-19}.

The rationals

When we add, subtract, or multiply integers, our answer will always be an integer. However, this is not always the case for division. The answer to $2 \div 4$ is not an integer. We need more numbers! These are the rational numbers. A **rational number** is defined as any number of the form a/b where a and b are integers and $b \neq 0$. We saw earlier why the denominator cannot be zero—division by zero is undefined.

The rationals comprise common fractions and their decimal equivalents, including fractions with denominators of 100—percentages. Understanding how learners develop the concepts of rational numbers is the province of mathematics education research, and students in pre-service primary and middle school courses gain particular expertise in this area. For many students, this is a very challenging area of mathematics. For researchers, it is as well. As Lamon (2007) notes,

> Of all the topics in the school curriculum, fractions, ratios, and proportions arguably hold the distinction of being the most protracted in terms of development, the most difficult to teach, the most mathematically complex, the most cognitively challenging, the most essential to success in higher mathematics and science, and one of the most compelling research sites. In the last decade or more, researchers have made little progress in unraveling the complexities of teaching and learning these topics. (p. 629)

communicating mathematically

Language of fractions

In common usage, 'fraction' often means a part of a whole. For example, you might hear people talking about 'a fraction of the students'. However, fractions can also be more than a whole.

In symbols, anything written in the form of a $\frac{number}{number}$ may be called a fraction. A number such as $\frac{\pi}{2}$ could be called a fraction, but because π is not a rational number $\frac{\pi}{2}$ is not rational. It is better to say this is written 'in fractional form' rather than that it is a fraction.

Sometimes a distinction is made between common fractions and decimal fractions. A common fraction is a rational number written in fractional form. For example, $\frac{1}{4}$ is written as a common fraction and its equivalent decimal form is 0.25. In this book, if not stated otherwise, we will call common fractions *fractions* and decimal fractions *decimals*.

Decimals

Decimals extend our numeration system to accommodate numbers between integers (although integers are forms of decimals as well; e.g. 3 can be written as 3.00000…). As we saw in Figure 22.1, all the columns in our numbers work in exactly the same way. We use the decimal point to indicate where the units column is—otherwise we would have no way of telling. There are many models people can use to understand decimals, such as an odometer, and these are included in other chapters in this book.

think + link

See Chapter 18 for a discussion about how to teach decimal fractions.

consider and discuss

I can tell if a fraction will convert to a terminating or recurring decimal—just by looking at the denominator!

What's more, after investigation, you will too!!

Let's make a start by specialising. Keep the numerator at 1 to begin with. Once you know what is going on, you will be able to determine what happens when the numerator takes other values.

Convert the following fractions to decimals:

1 $\frac{1}{2} =$

2 $\frac{1}{3} =$

Notice how, $\frac{1}{2}$ terminates and $\frac{1}{3}$ recurs.

Explore! You might need to convert some of the decimals by hand if your calculator runs out of display before you have seen a repeating pattern. This is a good opportunity to practise your skills at doing division by hand! Another approach is to use a spreadsheet.

communicating mathematically

Notation for recurring decimals

Recurring decimals can be indicated in a number of ways. Some common approaches are:

- $0.\dot{7}\dot{8}$ would indicate 0.787878... Notice how the dots are over both the repeating numbers. If I wanted to show 0.788888... I would show this by $0.7\dot{8}$.
- Another approach is to put a bar across the repeating pattern, e.g. $0.\overline{78}$.
- Sometimes you will see a dot on top of the bar.

There are only two options for fractions converted to decimals: they either terminate or they recur. If you find a decimal that does not terminate and has no recurring pattern, it can never be written as a fraction (i.e it cannot be written as an integer divided by an integer). Decimals that are non-terminating and non-recurring are *irrational*. We will discuss the irrationals in the section on real numbers later in this chapter.

Decimal misconceptions

Misconceptions in the notation and use of decimals are very common and surprisingly resistant to revision. Many adults (and many pre-service primary school teachers) retain misunderstandings of decimals (Stacey et al., 2001), leading to a significant impediment to using mathematics. Table 22.1 contains definitions from Steinle and Stacey (1998).

handy hint

To avoid reinforcing truncation or rounding errors, do not routinely ask students to give answers correct to two decimal places (as you will find in many textbooks). Instead, consider the context carefully and encourage students to provide answers that reflect the degree of precision of the problem.

Fractions

Many dictionaries written for primary students define fractions as part of a whole. Indeed that is one aspect of the concept; however, there is more to fractions than that.

There are at least five different interpretations of fractions (Bassarear, 1997; Kieren, 1988; Lamon, 2007). In representing $\frac{3}{4}$, many children will draw part of a whole. As you read through the different interpretations of fractions, identify:

1. part of a whole
2. part of a set; also described as 'fraction as operator', for example $\frac{3}{4}$ of something.
3. a quotient (or a model for division), for example 3 ÷ 4
4. a measure (or place on a number line)
5. as a ratio.

Table 22.1 Common misconceptions about decimals

Misconception type	Description	Example of error
Longer-is-larger misconceptions		
String length	Decimal point is ignored or decimal part treated as a whole number. The longer the string, the larger the number.	4.63 would be thought larger than 4.8 4.03 thought larger than 4.3
Numerator focused	Zeros after decimal point are disregarded.	6.3 would be seen as the same number as 6.03
Reverse	Decimal columns represent more whole numbers but written in reverse order (may occur from students not hearing the distinction between tens and tenths, for example).	0.163 would be thought of as one ten, six hundreds and three thousands
Zero makes small	Decimal with a zero or zeros in the first column(s) after the point is 'small'. Otherwise, they choose the longer decimal as larger.	would correctly select 4.08 as smaller than 4.5 but would incorrectly say 4.18 is larger than 4.5
Right-hand overflow	Incorrect extension of whole number understandings.	120 can be thought of as 12 tens so incorrectly 0.12 is thought of as 12 tenths rather than 12 hundredths
Shorter-is-larger misconceptions		
Denominator focused	Place value column names are used to decide on the size of the decimals. For example, knowing that tenths are larger than hundredths, this is incorrectly generalised to any number of tenths is greater than any number of hundredths.	0.2 would be thought larger than 0.54
Reciprocal thinking	Decimals are seen as the number of parts in a fraction.	0.3 interpreted as $\frac{1}{3}$, that is three parts of the whole rather than the correct interpretation of $\frac{3}{10}$
Negative thinking	Decimals are confused with negative numbers. Misconception may arise from thinking a decimal is smaller than something, so think smaller than zero.	0.35 would be thought smaller than 0.24 because −35 is smaller than −24
Apparent expert behaviour		
Truncation (to two decimal places)	Focus is on the first two decimal places and rest of the decimal number is ignored. May arise from using contexts of money or measurement (cm) to make sense of decimals.	15.348 seen as $15.34 with 8 as an error or ignored choosing the larger of 4.4502 and 4.45 would be difficult.
Rounding (to two decimal places)	Digits after the hundredths column are discarded but the discarded digits are taken into account.	15.348 would be seen as 15.35

consider and discuss

Three friends decide to share two pizzas (not yet cut). Using diagrams show how much each person gets.

Compare diagrams with your study group. Are some models clearer than others? If you weren't told the pizzas were uncut, would that make a difference to your solution?

handy hint

Using pizzas as a model can bring some confusing contextual knowledge. Fast food chains tend to cut their pizzas in set ways, often into eight pieces. Children may assume pizzas are always cut into eighths.

The pizza problem you have discussed raises some interesting features about fractions. Here we have an example of the second view of fractions from our list—fractions as operator. Each person gets to eat $\frac{2}{3}$ of a pizza. So, $\frac{2}{3}$ is the *operation* (2 divided by 3) and the *result*!

There are two possible interpretations of the following diagram: as $\frac{2}{6}$ or $\frac{2}{3}$:

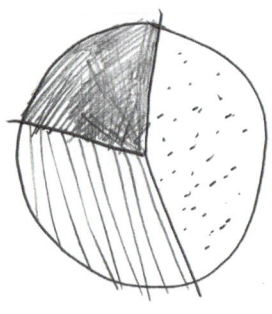 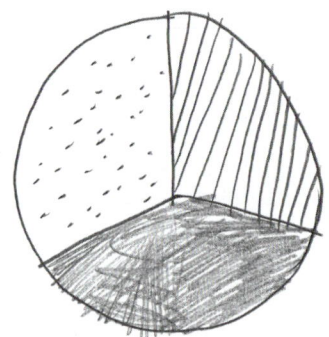

How do we reconcile these? One appears to indicate a person eats $\frac{1}{3}$, the other $\frac{2}{3}$. Here we need to be very sure what the *whole* is. The person eats $\frac{2}{3}$ of one pizza, or $\frac{1}{3}$ of the two pizzas. If only the fraction is stated, we assume we mean 'of one' so an answer of $\frac{2}{3}$ would mean '$\frac{2}{3}$ of one'. This corresponds with the location $\frac{2}{3}$ on a number line:

Fraction as ratio is an important interpretation. Suppose we have the following situation:

I have 2 squares and 3 circles. The ratio of squares to circles is $2:3$ or $\frac{2}{3}$.

But I also have 5 shapes. The ratio of squares to shapes is $2:5$ or $\frac{2}{5}$.

It is important to understand that two equally correct fractions can be represented by the same situation. Many secondary school textbooks only have one interpretation in exercises, leading to confusion when students need to solve problems.

communicating mathematically

Language of ratio

2 : 3 can be read as either '2 is to 3' or 'the ratio 2 to 3'. Note the order is important. If we were to mix cordial with water in the ratio 1 : 4, we know 1 part is cordial, 4 parts are water. The other way around would taste ghastly!

making connections

The diagram below is taken from a brochure for a bakery showing how to cut a cake for large numbers of guests. Convince yourself that each piece is a fair share. What properties of circles did you use?

issues in teaching

Counting in fractions

Many adults are unaware that fractions can be represented on a number line. For many, their school experiences of fraction work concerned learning procedures for adding, subtracting, mulitplying, or dividing fractions. Students need to be given opportunities to represent fractions in the various interpretations (Lamon, 2007). In particular, they must become accustomed to extending their view of the number line to include fractional quantities.

How would you represent $\frac{2}{3}$ on a number line? How could you show $\frac{2}{3} + \frac{1}{2}$?

Students who incorrectly generalise operations with fractions from whole numbers sometimes believe $\frac{2}{3} + \frac{1}{2}$ is the same as $\frac{3}{5}$. How could you show on a number line this could not be the case? What other diagrams could you use?

think + link

See Chapter 23 for further work on operations with fractions.

handy hint

Fractions can be represented in different types of diagrams.

Circles
- Commonly used
- Clearly show the whole and if a part is missing
- Once piece sizes become smaller than $\frac{1}{8}$, they are very difficult to distinguish

Rectangles
- Don't show if a part is missing
- Are very good for distinguishing different sizes
- Can be cut in two dimensions (length and width)
- Are a useful model for operations

Line segment or number line
- Reinforces fraction as a number
- Allows modelling of operations.

Percentages

In our base 10, or decimal, number system, tenths and hundredths are very useful fractions. Percentages are another representation of hundredths. 'Think per cent, think hundredths.' There is no need to learn complicated rules about percentage; indeed, these rules can be more confusing than the concept itself.

Number	How many hundredths?	Percentage?
0.06	6	6%
0.25	25	25%
0.125	12.5	12.5%
9	900	900%

consider and discuss

1. Is it possible to have more than 100%?
2. 100% means 100 hundredths or one whole. Can you have more than one whole?
3. In what contexts would it make sense to have more than 100%?
4. Does it make sense for a sports coach to ask players to 'give 110% effort'?

for the classroom

Most students are familiar with download bars that indicate the percentage of a file that has downloaded. These diagrams are very useful to use in classrooms.

Show various percentages on a bar, for example, 20%.

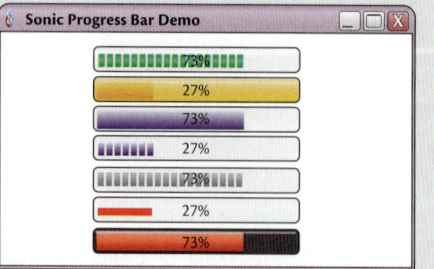

Uses of percentage

There are three common ways percentages are used in social contexts: to represent fractions, to compare numbers, and to show percentage increase or decrease.

Representing fractions

If we read 25% of the students are studying part-time, we are being told a quarter are part-timers. If we know there are 180 students altogether, we could work out how many 25% represents.

Example: Find 45% of $639.

Before doing any calculation, we should estimate what the answer is likely to be. In doing so, we may be able to obtain an exact answer mentally. If not, we then need to choose the method we will use. In this case, we could note that 45% is a bit less than 50%, and $639 is almost $640. Our answer is going to be less than $320.

We need to encourage students to draw a diagram. Diagrams are powerful for reminding us what we are calculating and also can show teachers that students understand what they are doing.

Finally, to obtain an exact calculation, we return to 'think per cent, think hundredths'.

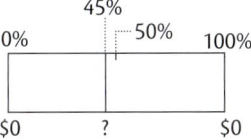

45% is 0.45.

45% of $639 = 0.45 × 639 = $287.55

Comparing quantities

If I got 24 out of 30 marks on one test and 65 out of 80 on another, which result is better?

To compare these results, we need them to be out of the same amount. Any denominator will do, but it is much easier to use a denominator of 100. Think per cent, think hundredths! We convert to percentages for a convenient common denominator.

Estimate the result first.
Draw a diagram next.
Now calculate.

$\frac{22}{30}$ (calculator 24 ÷ 30) = 0.8. As there are 80 hundredths, this is 80%.

$\frac{65}{80}$ = 0.8125. That is, 81.25 hundredths or 81.25%.

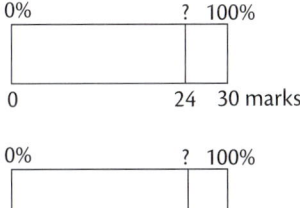

Percentage increase or decrease.

By definition, percentage increase or decrease is calculated by finding the fraction $\frac{\text{change}}{\text{original}}$ value.

If an annual salary is increased from $56 000 to $58 125, what is the percentage increase?

The change in salary is $2125. We need to find the fraction this is of the original salary, so $2125 out of $56 000.

Estimate.
Draw a diagram.
Calculate.

$\frac{2125}{56\,000}$ = 0.037 946 or 3.7946 hundredths or a percentage increase of 3.79%.

integrating technology/ICT

Percentage keys on calculators

In our calculations, we used calculators to do the division calculations. We have not made use of the % key. *These keys should be avoided in classroom use.* They are unnecessary for students who understand what they are calculating. Furthermore, the order of keystrokes required varies from calculator to calculator and is often not in the order of mathematics. They can cause considerable confusion.

communicating mathematically

Language of percentage

Percentage is a noun or adjective. Per cent is an adverb.

As for fractions in general, it is very important we are aware of what the whole is. We must always be thinking 'percentage of what', particularly if we are using critical thinking to interpret meaning in text.

Consider the newspaper headline that reads: 'Muslim numbers to rise 80pc in 20 years' [*Australian*, 29–30 January 2011]. Later in the article, it notes this would still be a very small number in total. In this case, if we ask '80% of what?', we find we are talking about a small number to start with.

The reals

Irrationals

We have defined a rational number as an integer divided by an integer (as long as the denominator is not zero). We have seen these fractions can be expressed as ratios ($\frac{2}{5}$ can be written as $2:5$). However, not all ratios are rationals.

Pi (π) is a famous irrational number. You can read more than you might ever have thought was possible about π in Petr Beckmann's (1971) fascinating book. π is defined as the ratio between the circumference of a circle and its diameter.

for the classroom

Accurately draw a large circle on paper. Use a piece of cord to measure the length of the diameter. Mark this or cut it.

Now mark diameter lengths around the circle. You should find the diameter goes around the circle a little bit more than three times.

What fraction of the diameter is the little bit left?

With another piece of cord, carefully measure the little bit left. Use this to step across the diameter. You should find it goes 7 times with a little bit more. Therefore, the fraction is between $\frac{1}{8}$ of the diameter and $\frac{1}{7}$. (Which is the bigger number?)

Our ratio lies between $3\frac{1}{8}$ and $3\frac{1}{7}$. We can do better. What fraction is the little bit left? Measure again and see.

No matter how many times you do this (you will need very good fine motor skills after a short while!) there will always be a little bit left over. π is not a rational number.

π is not rational, but how do we reconcile this with the definition that $\pi = \frac{C}{D}$? Our definition of a rational number is an integer divided by a non-zero integer. For π, if the circumference is an integer, the diameter will not be. Similarly, if the diameter is an integer, the circumference will not be.

making connections

The following was a slogan on a bumper sticker:

Mathematics is number $-e^{i\pi}$**!**

This is a bit of an in-joke: $-e^{i\pi} = 1$. This is Euler's identity, more often written: $e^{i\pi} + 1 = 0$. (Convince yourself that these expressions are equivalent.) It is a rather lovely formula, combining addition/subtraction, multiplication, and exponents. It also combines five central numbers in mathematics: 1 the multiplicative identity; 0 the additive identity; as well as *e*, and π, important irrational numbers, and *i*, a complex number.

Although π is perhaps the most well-known irrational number, there are others, including $\sqrt{2}$ and *e*. *e* is called 'Euler's constant', named after Euler (pronounced 'Oiler'), one of the most significant mathematicians ever, living 1707–1783. You can read more about *e* in Eli Maor's (1994) book.

integrating technology/ICT

Euler's constant

Like π, *e* is stored as a constant on scientific and graphics calculators. You can find the approximate value by entering e^1. It is about 2.71828…

e arises in many situations. For example, if you invest $1 for 1 year at 100% interest and compound that interest to be paid annually, then monthly, then fortnightly, then weekly, then daily, then every minute, then every second … you will find the amount earned approaches the value for *e*. Use a spreadsheet to try this.

There are two types of irrational numbers: algebraic and transcendental. *Algebraic irrationals* arise from solving algebraic equations. For example, the algebraic equation $x^2 - 5 = 0$ has two solutions: either $x = \sqrt{5}$ or $x = -\sqrt{5}$. Expressions containing algebraic irrational numbers, such as $(6 + \sqrt{3})$ or $(\sqrt{2} - 1)$, are known as surds. Algebra of surds was particularly useful before the advent of calculators and remains important in middle school mathematics. We will look in more detail at specific algebra related to surds in the next section.

Irrational numbers that are not solutions to algebraic equations are known as *transcendental* numbers. These include π and *e*.

Surds

As for other numbers, we can perform the four operations on surds. We need to remember, though, that the radical sign ($\sqrt{}$) acts as a bracket. The numbers underneath are 'protected'. So, for example, if we have $3 + \sqrt{a + 2}$, we can't add the 3 and the 2. It may help to remember that when we have a radical sign, it is asking us to work out the length of the side of a square, in our example that has $a + 2$ objects. The 3 is separate.

issues in teaching

Surds and exact form in the age of calulators

A commonly used triangle in secondary school trigonometry textbooks is the following:

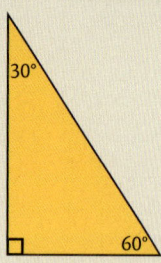

From Pythagoras' Theorem, we know that the sides are $1:\sqrt{3}:2$.

sin 60° can be found exactly as the ratio of the opposite side to the hypotenuse or $\frac{\sqrt{3}}{2}$. Because this is irrational, when we use a calculator the result will be a non-terminating or recurring decimal. It is more convenient to record the exact value. In addition, we can also do operations on the surd and retain the exact value rather than increasing the error in our result because of initial rounding. Small differences in decimal places can make a big difference, for example when building from a plan.

Therefore, even though we have access to calculators, there is still value in ensuring students in middle school mathematics learn how to work with surds in exact form.

Density of the number line

We have now introduced all the types of numbers making up the real numbers (we will call them the 'reals'). All of these can be placed on a number line. As mathematicians expanded their operations with numbers, they became aware that other numbers were needed. For example, if you are working with the natural numbers (or counting numbers), you can add all you like and there will always be enough numbers. However, if you begin to subtract, you may require zero and negative numbers. If you try to divide, you will find the need for numbers between whole numbers, for example when dividing 15 by 4. Our number system has grown to allow all calculations. The different types can be thought of as an expanding set as in Figure 22.3. For example, a group such as the integers includes all numbers inside the encompassed groups. Therefore, the integers includes the natural numbers, the whole numbers, and negative integers.

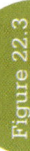

Types of numbers

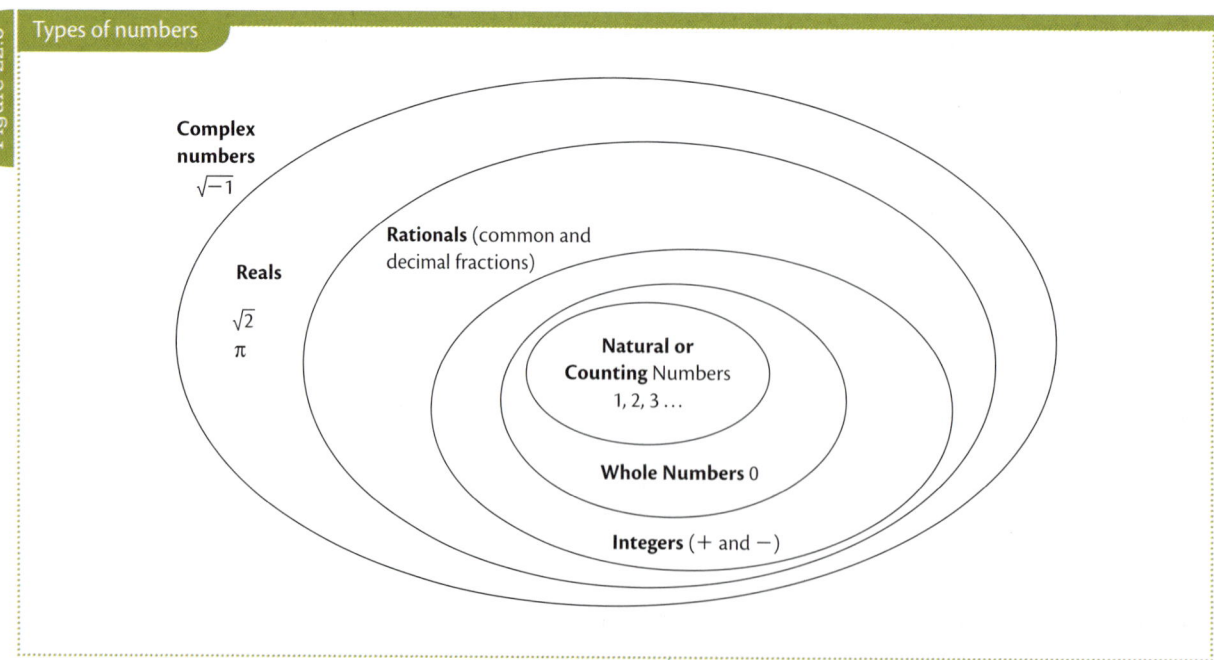

Chapter 22 Extending Number: Fractions, Decimals, and Reals

did you know?

Complex numbers cannot be placed on the number line and were once thought to be 'imaginary'. $\sqrt{-1}$ is known as *i*. Far from being imaginary, complex numbers have applications in many fields including electronics and fractal art.

The development of a single mental number line encompassing all types of real numbers is an important aspect of numeracy. This development continues across the schooling levels into senior schooling and adulthood.

for the classroom

Numbers on a number line

For this activity, you will need a long piece of clothesline, pegs, and number cards. On separate cards write examples of numerals (see suggestions below).

Have two students hold the line or tie it to sides of the classroom. One at a time, give students the following cards and ask them to peg them on the number line. Tell the students they can ask for assistance from the others in the class.

- **Counting numbers**: 1, 2, 3. (Don't worry where they place the numbers, but ensure they are evenly spaced.)
- **Whole number**: 0. (At this point draw attention to the set of whole numbers.)
- **Negative integers**: −1, −2, −3. This may force rearrangement of the numerals as particularly younger students often begin with 0 on the far left—rearrangement emphasises the expanding number line. (Again, note that we are now displaying the integers.)
- **Some rationals**: Include a variety of rationals in alternative forms. For example, include $\frac{1}{2}$, 0.5, 50% etc. Students will recognise that these are in the same place and will need to peg the numbers together.
Include $\frac{1}{3}$ and 0.3. Some students may be tempted to put these in the same place. This provides an opportunity to challenge a misconception.
Include negative fractions as well, e.g. −0.5, −0.125.
- Some irrationals: include π, −π, $\sqrt{2}$ etc.

Have some blank cards and invite students to pick numbers to place on the number line.

Conclusion

In this chapter, we have explored our expanding number line. Development of the concepts of number is one of the startling accomplishments of human thought and has taken thousands of years. A feature of number (an idea) is how we record it (the numeral). The Hindu-Arabic notation system is a complex yet succinct system. It takes each of us many years to come to a deep understanding of this system. It is the role of primary and secondary mathematics teachers to assist learners in this process.

key terms

Factors: pair of counting numbers that multiply to give another counting number
Number: an idea about quantity
Numeral: a symbol representing a number
Prime: a number that has *exactly* two factors: itself and one.

Composite: a counting number that is not prime
Fundamental Theorem of Arithmetic: any integer greater than one can be written as a unique product of prime factors
Scientific notation: system of notation used for very large or small numbers

Review questions

1. Explain the difference beween a number and a numeral. Which concept would a young child be expected to develop first?
2. Write everything you know about 64. Be creative. Include reference to prime, composite, factors, multiples, number shapes (e.g. square, cube, …)
3. Complete the following table. Add other rows including numbers of importance to you.

Fraction	Decimal	Percentage
	0.125	
$\frac{1}{8}$		
		50%

4. Write a word problem for each of the five interpretations of fraction for the fraction $\frac{1}{4}$.
5. $\frac{1}{2}$ and $\frac{2}{4}$ are different names for the same number. Can any fraction have more than one name?
6. Make a collection of the use of percentage from newspapers and magazines. Sort them into categories. Develop a problem you could use in your classroom for different types.

Key references

Bassarear, T. (1997). *Mathematics for Elementary School Teachers*. Boston: Houghton Mifflin.

Clements, D. H., & Battista, M. T. (1992). Geometry and spatial reasoning. In D. A. Grouws (Ed.), *Handbook of Research on Mathematics Teaching and Learning* (pp. 420–494). New York: Macmillan.

Clements, D. H., & Sarama, J. (2007). Early childhood mathematics learning. In F. K. Lester (Ed.), *Second Handbook of Research on Mathematics Teaching and Learning* (pp. 461–555). Charlotte, NC: Information Age.

Cockroft, W.H.C. (1982). *Mathematics Counts: Report of the Committee of Inquiry into the Teaching of Mathematics in Schools*. London, UK: HMSO.

Gould, P. (2003). Grasping space. *Australian Primary Mathematics Classroom*. 8(2), pp. 4–7.

Gutiérrez, A. (1996). Visualization in 3-dimensional geometry: In search of a framework. In L. Puig & A.Guttiérez (Eds.), *Proceedings of the 20th Conference of the International Group for the Psychology of Mathematics Education* (Vol. 1, pp. 3–19). Valencia: Universidad de Valencia.

Horne, M. (2003). Properties of shape. *Australian Primary Mathematics Classroom*, 8(2), 8–13.

Johnston-Wilder, S., & Mason, J. (2005). *Developing Thinking in Geometry*. London: Open University Press.

Kieren, T. E. (1988). Personal knowledge of rational numbers: Its intuitive and formal development. In J. Herbert & M. Behr (Eds.), *Number Concepts and Operations in the Middle Grades* (Vol. 2, pp. 162–181). Reston, VA: NCTM.

Lamon, S. J. (2007). Rational numbers and proportional reasoning: Towards a theoretical framework for research. In F.K. Lester (Ed.), *Second Handbook of Research on Mathematics Teaching and Learning*. (pp. 629–667). Reston VA: NCTM.

Perry, B., Young-Loveridge, J., Docket, S. & Doig, B. (2008). The development of young children's mathematical understanding. In H. Forgasz, A. Barkatsas, A. Bishop, B. Clarke, S. Keast, W-T. Seah, and P. Sullivan (Eds.), *Research in Mathematics Education in Australasia 2004–2007* (pp. 17–40). Rotterdam: Sense Publishers.

Stacey, K., Helme, S., Steinle, V., Baturo, A., Irwin, K. C., & Bana, J. (2001). Preservice teachers' knowledge of difficulties in decimal numeration. *Journal of Mathematics Teacher Education*, 4, 205–225.

Steinle, V., & Stacey, K. (1998). The incidence of misconceptions of decimal notation amongst students in Grades 5 to 10. In C. Kanes, M. Goos & E. Warren (Eds.), *Teaching Mathematics in New Times (Proceedings of the 21st Annual Conference of the Mathematics Education Research Group of Australasia. Gold Coast* pp. 548–555). Sydney: MERGA.

Websites

www.maths300.esa.edu.au

This website includes lessons, such as Hunting for Stars (HCF); First Principles Percent (%); Walk the plank (operations with negatives); Fraction Estimation and many others.

http://www.measurement.gov.au/Pages/MetricConversion.aspx

Working with Addition, Subtraction, and Additive Thinking

23

Contents

Ways of working with addition and subtraction	518
Algorithms	520
Fractions	524
Decimals	536
Integers	540

Chapter objectives

This chapter will enable the reader to:
- Understand what is involved in additive thinking with large whole numbers, integers, and rational numbers
- Recognise the different ways in which addition and subtraction problems with large whole numbers, integers, and rationals can be represented
- Appreciate the role of materials, language, and recording in scaffolding children's understanding and solution strategies
- Extend mental strategies for whole numbers to rationals
- Appreciate the importance and uses of approximation and estimation
- Critique written algorithms for addition and subtraction of whole numbers, integers, and rationals and understand how they can be developed meaningfully
- Recognise and address children's learning needs in relation to additive thinking in the contexts of whole numbers, integers, and rationals
- Plan effective problem-solving experiences involving written and mental computation.

Fractious fractions

A class who had just finished a unit on simple fraction equivalence and addition were asked to reflect on what they had learnt about fractions, what they had enjoyed, and what they were still confused about. Here are three responses to the question about what they found confusing:

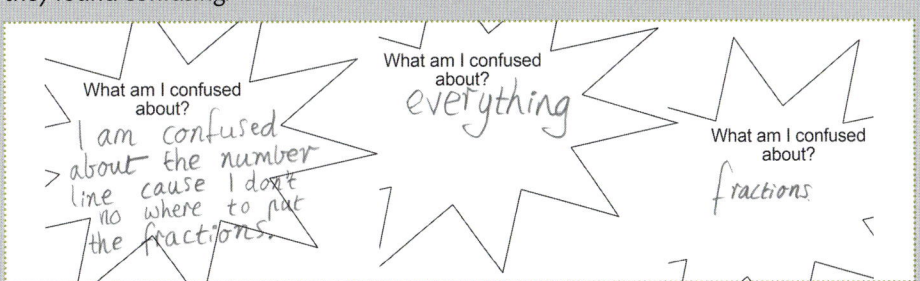

Although these were not typical responses, they illustrate that fractions present difficulties for many children. Many adults also nominate fractions as the point at which they stopped understanding and enjoying mathematics.

consider and discuss

1. Why do you believe that operating on fractions (including when they are represented as decimals) is the point at which many people 'part company' with learning mathematics meaningfully?
2. In what ways and to what extent is it true of your own experience or of others you know?
3. What role might the teaching of these topics play?

Big ideas

- The number line is a key representation for understanding and modelling addition and subtraction of integers and rationals.
- Strategies for adding and subtracting need to be modelled, scaffolded, and discussed to ensure all students have access to a range of efficient, flexible strategies that they can use with confidence.
- Estimation is a powerful strategy for adding and subtracting whole numbers, integers and rationals.
- Algorithms for adding and subtracting whole numbers, integers, and rationals must be developed meaningfully to be of lasting value.

Ways of working with addition and subtraction

Rational numbers were defined in Chapter 22 as numbers that can be represented in the form $\frac{a}{b}$ where a and b are integers and $b \neq 0$. This means that the rationals include whole number **integers** (e.g. $\frac{24}{6}, \frac{3}{3}, -\frac{5}{1}$) and fractions. **Fractions** may be represented as either common fractions (e.g. $\frac{2}{5}, \frac{8}{3}$) or **decimals** (e.g. 0.73, 9.4). In Chapter 16 we considered mental computation strategies for the addition and subtraction of whole numbers. These strategies can also be applied to integers.

Although all fractions can be written as decimals and all recurring or terminating decimals can be written as fractions, the specific ways of representing addition and subtraction depend on the form of the number. Similarly, there are specific techniques for estimating the results of addition and subtraction and for representing these operations, and the written algorithms for performing them depend on the form of rational number. For this reason these ideas are discussed separately according to the form of the number.

First, we discuss some properties of addition and subtraction that apply to all numbers and that underpin the techniques used to perform these operations on specific forms of rational numbers.

Chapter 23 Working with Addition, Subtraction and Additive Thinking

communicating mathematically

It is vital that teachers model mathematically correct language. 'Sum' is a word that is commonly misused. The word **sum** refers to the result of adding two or more numbers (Patilla, 2003). It does not refer to any operation other than addition, and so it is incorrect and unhelpful to use it to refer to calculations involving subtraction, multiplication, or division. A **difference** is the amount by which one number is greater than another. A difference is calculated by subtracting the smaller number from the larger (Patilla, 2003).

did you know?

According to Heinke (1989), the + sign, written with a not quite vertical downward line, was used as an abbreviation for 'et' (Latin for 'and') as early as 1417. Both + and − were reportedly used in manuscripts dating back to 1486 and were first used in print by Johann Widmann in 1498.

Useful properties

The commutative and associative properties of addition apply to all real numbers regardless of the form in which they are written. They are relevant and provide powerful tools from the moment that children begin calculating (as described in Chapter 16) all the way through to sophisticated algebra that is beyond the scope of this book. It is vital that students explore their application to each new group of numbers, or form of representation, as it is encountered.

The three properties that are discussed below illustrate the point that in all our teaching of mathematics from the earliest years we want students to develop an alertness to regularities and an inclination to generalise, but we must also insist that students test their conjectures and build support for them by actively trying to find examples that do *not* fit. In this case the generalisation about being able to add numbers in any order that they formed in their first years of schooling can be extended to rational numbers. Similarly, its inapplicability to subtraction also extends the rationals. Evidence gathering by careful trialling is not proof, but it is the beginnings of the kind of thinking that can lead to appreciation of mathematical proof.

Commutativity

A **commutative** operation is one in which the order in which steps are performed makes no difference to the outcome. When two numbers are added, the result is exactly the same regardless of the order in which the addition is performed. Subtraction, however, is not commutative. That is, the order of the numbers does matter. For example, $3.7 - 2.5 \neq 2.5 - 3.7$.

Associativity

An operation is **associative** if a calculation involving two or more instances of the same operation can be performed by combining pairs of the numbers involved in any order without affecting the result. For example, $3\frac{1}{4} + \frac{1}{4} + \frac{1}{2}$ can be calculated by first adding $3\frac{1}{4}$ and $\frac{1}{4}$ and then adding $\frac{1}{2}$ (written as $(3\frac{1}{4} + \frac{1}{4}) + \frac{1}{2}$), or by first adding $\frac{1}{4}$ and $\frac{1}{2}$ and then adding this to $3\frac{1}{4}$ (written as $3\frac{1}{4} + (\frac{1}{4} + \frac{1}{2})$). The commutativity of addition also means that we can re-order the numbers and therefore find the solution by adding $3\frac{1}{4}$ and $\frac{1}{2}$ and then adding $\frac{1}{4}$ (i.e. $(3\frac{1}{4} + \frac{1}{2}) + \frac{1}{4}$).

Subtraction, however, is not associative because the order affects the result. Consider, for example:

$$(6.1 - 2.0) - 0.6 \qquad\qquad 6.1 - (2.0 - 0.6)$$
$$= 4.1 - 0.6 \quad \text{and} \quad = 6.1 - (1.4)$$
$$= 3.5 \qquad\qquad\qquad\quad = 4.7$$

Additive identity

The **additive identity element** for a set of numbers is a number in the set that can be added to any number in the set without changing it. For rational numbers, and indeed for real numbers, zero is the additive identity. If we use n to represent any rational number, then we can say that $n + 0 = n$. This may seem trivial, but it is part of the special role of zero in our number system and may not be obvious to young children or even to older students whose attention has not been drawn to it. In particular it is important that students know that adding zero has no effect on numbers written as a fractions or decimals or on negative numbers.

Estimation and approximation

Estimation and approximation are important but subtly different processes that are important in working with rational numbers in their various forms.

An **estimate** is an inexact result arrived at on the basis of general considerations of the numbers and operations involved rather than as a consequence of a precise mathematical procedure. **Approximation** also results in an inexact result, but in this case an exact calculation has been performed but the precise result is not recorded. Approximate answers are commonly used in measurement contexts, in which the digits in places beyond tenths or hundredths are often not important. For example, if three stages of a bicycle tour were 50.1 km, 59.8 km, and 89.6 km, you might arrive at an estimate of 200 km for the total distance by adding 50, 60, and 90. If you added the exact numbers to find that the total length is in fact 199.6 km it would be reasonable for a journalist to report the event as covering an approximate total distance of 200 km. In this case the result is the same but the first is an estimate and the second an approximation because of the different processes used. It should be noted that the distances provided for each of the stages are almost certainly approximations as well—it would be possible, theoretically at least, to measure the distances to the nearest cm or even mm, but in the context amounts of less than 0.1 of a km are of no consequence.

Algorithms

An **algorithm** is simply a procedure that, if followed, will result in a desired outcome. Recipes are essentially algorithms, as is the set of steps that need to be followed to withdraw cash from an automatic teller machine. In each case, if you follow the procedure accurately (and you have sufficient funds in your bank account!) you will achieve the desired result.

Chapter 23 Working with Addition, Subtraction and Additive Thinking

Algorithms for operations with whole numbers and later for fraction and decimal operations are commonly taught in primary and secondary schools. Clarke (2005, p. 93) listed the following as reasons for this:

- algorithms have been traditional primary mathematics content around the world for many years
- algorithms are powerful in solving classes of problems, particularly where the computation involves many numbers, where memory may be overloaded
- algorithms are contracted, summarising several lines of equations involving distributivity and associativity
- algorithms are automatic, being able to be taught to, and carried out by, someone without having to analyse the underlying basis of the algorithm
- algorithms are fast, with a direct route to the answer
- algorithms provide a written record of computation, enabling teachers and students to locate any errors in the algorithm
- algorithms can be instructive
- for the teacher, algorithms are easy to manage and assess.

Nevertheless, Clarke (2005) argued, on the basis of existing literature and his own research with young children, that no conventional algorithms (even for whole-number calculations) should be introduced until at least Year 5. This leaves unanswered the question of whether algorithms have a place in the later primary years and in secondary school—the years in which algorithms for rational number operations are commonly taught.

Many of the arguments against teaching algorithms for whole-number operations also apply to operations with rational numbers. These include that when students learn an algorithm they tend to rely on the procedure and to stop thinking about the meaning of the numbers involved. They become concerned about doing calculations the 'right' way and are reluctant to use a more intuitive method even when this would be much easier. The work sample shown in Figure 23.1 illustrates an unsuccessful attempt to find the difference between 17.72 and 16.9.

Figure 23.1 An attempt to use the standard algorithm to calculate 17.72 – 16.9

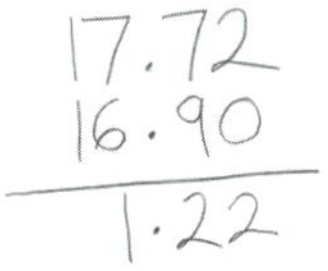

$$\begin{array}{r} 17.72 \\ 16.90 \\ \hline 1.22 \end{array}$$

Students are more likely to be successful if they use more intuitive approaches that focus on the meaning of the question and the numbers involved. A successful solution is shown in Figure 23.2. Notice that rather than attempting to use the standard algorithm, this student has counted on from 16.90, first by adding 0.1 to make 17.00 and then 0.72 to make 17.72.

Figure 23.2 A successful response

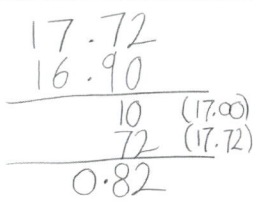

consider and discuss

1. Ask several people of any age to calculate $100 – $99.95. Present the problem in written form and make sure that you have a pen and paper available for them to use if they wish. Let them know that they can perform the calculation in any way they like, including mentally. Ask your participants to write down how they performed the calculation. Compare and categorise the responses you and your colleagues receive.

2. Hope (1986, cited in Clarke, 2005) used this problem of an example of applying a pen and paper algorithm when a more intuitive response is far easier and more likely to be accurate. Did any of your participants attempt to solve the problem using a pen and paper algorithm? If so, why do you think they might have done this?

A related argument against the formal teaching of algorithms is that they can lead to unthinking acceptance of the results even when an error in executing the procedure has led to a result that is clearly unreasonable (Usiskin, 1998). Usiskin (1998) points out that a reliance on pen and paper algorithms can also lead to helplessness when pen and paper are not available. This is the same as the dilemma faced by people who have become reliant on calculators when a calculator is not available. Usiskin argued in 1998 that pen and paper are sometimes less available than calculators, and nowadays this is far more likely to be the case. According to Northcote and McIntosh (1999) it is increasingly the case that using standard written algorithms is an activity that is confined to mathematics classrooms, with almost 85% of everyday calculations involving mental computation.

issues in teaching

To teach or not to teach algorithms

In recent years there has been considerable controversy around the issue of teaching algorithms, with some mathematics educators (e.g. Burns, 1994) arguing that students should develop their own as part of an ongoing process of gradually refining the ways in which they represent and solve problems. It is argued that the algorithms that result have a firm conceptual grounding and hence are far more likely to be remembered and applied appropriately than algorithms that are imposed. Others argue that the traditional algorithms have become standard because they are extremely efficient and generalisable. They express concern for students who may never develop algorithms for themselves that are comparable in terms of these criteria and hence will be hampered in their ability to perform routine calculations.

- Make a list of arguments for and against the teaching of standard algorithms.
- Do some further reading on this issue and organise a class debate of the topic: 'That no student should ever have to memorise an algorithm.'

Criteria for evaluating algorithms

Regardless of your stance on the role of formal teaching of algorithms, it is important that you can distinguish an algorithm that might be worth encouraging students to use from one that is of little value. Campbell, Rowan and Suarez (1998) described three criteria for assessing the value of student-generated algorithms. These are:

1. Efficiency: relates to the time taken to perform the procedure and the chances of errors being made in its execution. Algorithms that involve many steps or much counting are generally not efficient.

2 Mathematical validity: sometimes a procedure might result in the correct answer by chance rather than on the basis of a mathematically valid procedure.
3 Generalisability: relates the extent to which an algorithm can be applied to other problems of the same kind. A procedure that works for subtraction problems including those involving decimals is more useful than one that will work only for whole numbers.

When considering algorithms that might be taught to students we would add a fourth criterion:

4 Meaningfulness: By this we mean, does the algorithm reinforce conceptual understanding and assist students to link the procedure with the meanings of the numbers and operations involved.

In the sections that follow we not only consider the standard algorithms for adding and subtracting rational numbers in their various forms, but also some algorithms that are less routinely taught. In each case we encourage you to consider the extent to which the algorithm meets the criteria just described. In this way you will be able to make informed decisions about the particular algorithms that you choose to teach. We also consider mental computation strategies, including their role in estimating the results of calculations.

did you know?

The word 'algorithm' derives from the name al-Khowarizmi. Al-Khowarizmi was a Persian mathematician who wrote in the ninth century about processes for calculating with Hindu-Arabic numerals. In the twelfth century the Latin translation of his work, entitled *Liber Algorismi* (Book of al-Khowarizmi), brought the Hindu-Arabic number system and associated algorithms to the Western world (Gundlach, 1989).

issues in teaching

Who decides which algorithm is *the* standard?

At various times at least two different subtraction algorithms have been standard in various Australian educational jurisdictions. These are illustrated below for the calculation 463 − 278.

The one with which you are most likely to be familiar is as follows:

Starting with the ones, we would typically say, 'we can't take 8 from 3' so we borrow a 10 from the 6 to make the 3 into 13, leaving 5 tens	$\quad 4 \quad 6 \quad 3$ $- \: 2 \quad 7 \quad 8$
13 take 8 is 5. Now we observe that 'we can't take 7 from 5' so we borrow a hundred from the 4 to make the 5 into 15 (in fact the 5 tens are now 15 tens).	$\quad 4 \quad 6^5 \quad {}^{13}$ $- \: 2 \quad 7 \quad 8$ $\qquad\qquad\quad 5$
15 take 7 is 8, and finally 3 take 2 is 1, so our answer is 185.	$\quad 4^3 \quad 6^{15} \quad {}^{13}$ $- \: 2 \quad 7 \quad 8$ $\quad 1 \quad 8 \quad 5$

An alternative standard algorithm is as follows:

Starting with the ones, as before we say, 'we can't take 8 from 3' so we make the 3 into 13, and adjust the tens column by increasing the 7 by 1.		4 6 ¹3 − 2 7¹ 8
13 take 8 is 5. Now we observe that 'we can't take 8 from 6' so we make the 6 into 16 (in fact we are making 60 into 160) and adjust the hundreds column by adding one to the 2.		4 ¹6 ¹3 − 2¹ 7¹ 8 5
16 take 8 is 8, and 4 take 3 is 1, and so our answer is 185.		4 ¹6 ¹3 − 2¹ 7¹ 8 1 8 5

- Try several other subtractions using both algorithms and ensure that you understand how each works.
- Assess each of these algorithms according to their efficiency, mathematical validity, generalisability, and meaningfulness.
- Which would you recommend as the 'standard subtraction algorithm' and why?

Fractions

Anghileri (2007) described how although it is usual to begin teaching rational numbers with fractions and then to extend this to decimals and percentages, this is not the only possibility. She cited research by Moss and Case (1999, cited in Anghileri, 2007) that suggested there could be merit in beginning with percentages because such an approach could build on students' existing understanding of whole numbers and delay the need for them to work with ratios as is required for fractions. The important message is that we should be clear about why we approach any topic in the way that we do and be particularly aware of how we can build upon understanding that students already have.

Mental strategies

Mental strategies for adding and subtracting fractions rely on sound conceptual understanding of the various meanings of fractions and their representations. From a survey of 34 middle school (Years 5–8) teachers and 172 of their students, Caney (2004) found that most teachers (about 89%) reported working to develop students' mental computation with fractions at least sometimes. Their students, however, were more likely to indicate that they did not use mental strategies with fractions. Caney suggested that this could mean that teachers could be more explicit about mental computation as it arises in classroom activity, for example in the context of estimation, and that this might help students to be more conscious of their decisions to use or not to use mental strategies. There are also powerful arguments in favour of a greater focus on mental computation with fractions in terms of developing deep and lasting understanding of fraction algorithms. Lappan and Bouck

(1998) recommended allowing efficient computation methods to emerge from problem-solving activity that involves reasoning, including mental, about the meanings of fractions and relationships between them.

Addition and subtraction of fractions often requires renaming one or more of the fractions involved so that all have the same denominator. Doing this meaningfully relies on a deep understanding of fraction equivalence. Adding (and subtracting) fractions was traditionally taught using procedures that involved finding the lowest common multiple of the denominators involved (the common denominator) and then considering what each denominator must be multiplied by to get the common denominator, multiplying each numerator by that factor, and then adding (or subtracting) the numerators. Many adults, including pre-service teachers, struggle to recall the procedure and are at a complete loss to explain why it works. We now know that teaching algorithms for calculating with fractions before fraction equivalence is well understood rarely leads to robust or transferable understanding. In fact it is likely to be damaging. Kamii and Dominick (1998), in discussing the addition and subtraction of whole numbers in Years 1–4, described algorithms as harmful because they dissuade children from relying on their own reasoning and they undo work already done on developing place value concepts. In relation to fractions, introducing algorithms before equivalence is well understood removes the need for students to continue to grapple with the meanings of symbols, the nature of equivalence, and the meaning of fraction addition and subtraction.

consider and discuss

1. Ask colleagues to calculate $\frac{2}{3} + \frac{3}{5}$. Have pen and paper available for them to use if they choose. Ask them to explain their thinking and why their method worked.
2. Ask several people not involved with education to calculate $\frac{2}{3} + \frac{3}{5}$. Have pen and paper available for them to use if they choose. Ask them to explain their thinking and why their method worked.
3. Discuss the responses you obtained. What evidence of conceptual understanding of fractions was evident from the responses you obtained? Were there any differences in success rates between two groups of people? Why might this be? Were some kinds of methods more or less successful than others? Why? What role did mental computation play in successful and unsuccessful efforts?

It is reasonable to expect that students should be able to add and subtract fractions with like and related denominators mentally. Like denominators are the same for both fractions. Dole (2004) described a teaching sequence for mental computation with fractions that begins with finding pairs of fractions that total 1. She suggested working on problems such as $1 - \frac{1}{4}$ and $\frac{4}{5} + ? = 1$. Note that the fraction to be subtracted and the fraction to be found are unit fractions; that is, they have numerators of 1. Dole suggests progress by way of non-unit fractions and then adding fractions whose total is greater than 1, for example, $\frac{2}{7} + \frac{4}{7}$ and $\frac{3}{5} + \frac{4}{5}$. When the total is greater than 1, students need to think of the number of parts that there are in addition to a whole. Dole (2004) stresses the need to work with linear (including number lines) and area models for fractions throughout the development of mental strategies. This assists students to build the mental imagery that is the basis of performing mental addition and subtraction involving like denominators.

Related denominators are those in which one is a multiple of the other, for example, $\frac{2}{3}$ and $\frac{5}{6}$ have related denominators because 6 is a multiple of 3. Renaming thirds as sixths requires understanding that doubling the size of the denominator means that the size of the parts is halved and that this means there must be twice as many of them for the fractions to be equivalent. Similarly, renaming fourths (or quarters) as twelfths relies on understanding that each fourth is equivalent to 3 twelfths. Plenty of practice with partitioning areas and lengths (as described by Siemon, 2002) is a necessary basis for this work. It allows students to build up the necessary mental imagery on which mental computation can be developed.

Estimation

Just as mental imagery and conceptual understanding of fraction meanings and representations is crucial to meaningful calculation of sums and differences of fractions, it is also crucial to estimation. Estimation is a central part of adding and subtracting fractions, whether we require an approximate answer or an exact one. When computing with any numbers it is vital to have in mind an idea of the approximate size of the result so that the reasonableness of the outcome can be assessed.

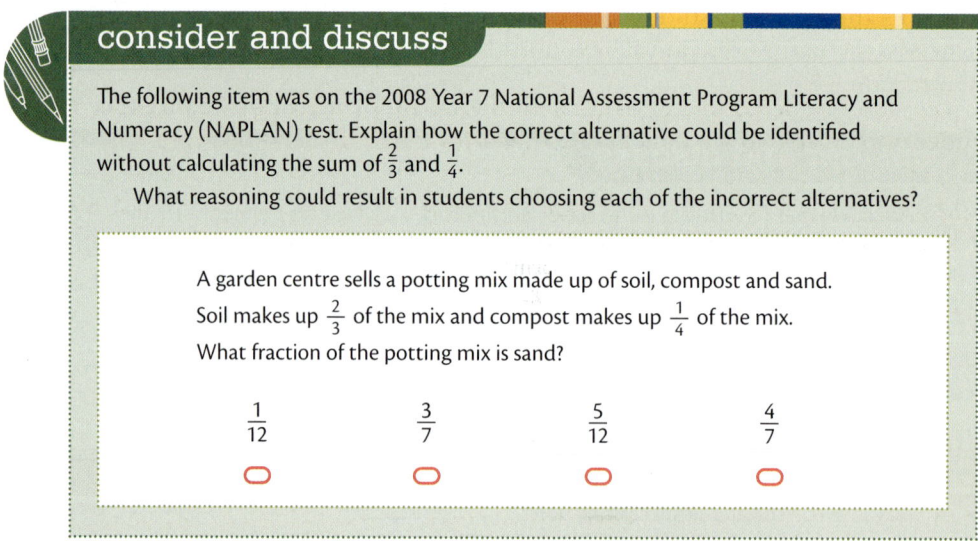

consider and discuss

The following item was on the 2008 Year 7 National Assessment Program Literacy and Numeracy (NAPLAN) test. Explain how the correct alternative could be identified without calculating the sum of $\frac{2}{3}$ and $\frac{1}{4}$.

What reasoning could result in students choosing each of the incorrect alternatives?

A garden centre sells a potting mix made up of soil, compost and sand. Soil makes up $\frac{2}{3}$ of the mix and compost makes up $\frac{1}{4}$ of the mix. What fraction of the potting mix is sand?

$\frac{1}{12}$ $\frac{3}{7}$ $\frac{5}{12}$ $\frac{4}{7}$

Sometimes we are not interested in the exact sum or difference of a pair of fractions but perhaps which is bigger or approximately what the sum would be. In these situations the ability to relate fractions to benchmarks such as $\frac{1}{2}$ and 1 is extremely useful. Fundamental understandings such that a larger denominator means smaller pieces are also vital. For example, in deciding which is the greater of $\frac{7}{8}$ and $\frac{11}{12}$ it is useful to realise that both fractions are one part less than 1, but that the 'missing' part is smaller for $\frac{11}{12}$ than for $\frac{7}{8}$ because twelfths are smaller than eighths. Similar strategies are useful in deciding whether the result of adding fractions will be greater or less than 1 or nearer to 2 or another whole number.

> **consider and discuss**
>
> In each of the following assume you know nothing about equivalent fractions or common denominators. Think conceptually about each of the following pairs and decide which is larger. Give one or more reasons in each case.
>
> 1 $\frac{4}{5}$ or $\frac{4}{9}$
> 2 $\frac{4}{7}$ or $\frac{5}{7}$
> 3 $\frac{3}{8}$ or $\frac{4}{10}$
> 4 $\frac{5}{3}$ or $\frac{5}{8}$
> 5 $\frac{3}{8}$ or $\frac{4}{7}$
>
> What strategies do you think students or other adults would use? Why? Test your predictions and discuss the results.

Representing fraction addition and subtraction

Using a number line to model fraction addition and subtraction requires an appreciation that numbers, including fractions, have particular positions on the number line in relation to other numbers, and also that their position on the number line represents a distance along the number line. When we ask students to place fractions on a number line they identify a specific point at which that number belongs, but the distance meaning is also involved because that point is located in relation to 0 or other numbers.

Consider the problem $\frac{3}{4} + \frac{1}{2}$. Ultimately this is a problem that we would expect students to be able to solve mentally. Initially, though, it could be represented on a number line by first locating $\frac{3}{4}$ and then 'stepping' along the number line a distance corresponding to $\frac{1}{2}$, as shown in Figure 23.3. Notice that implicit in this representation is the recognition that $\frac{1}{2}$ is equivalent to $\frac{2}{4}$.

Figure 23.3 A number line representation of 3/4 + 1/2

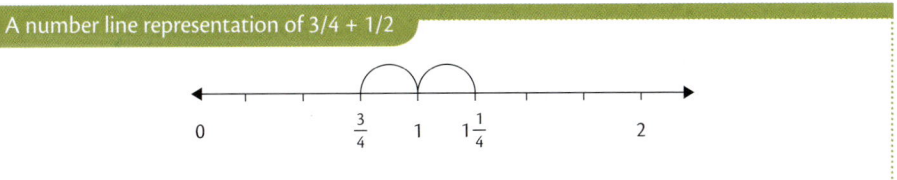

Paper strips or long rectangles constitute models that can be useful for solving such problems. For example, students can use a fraction wall to visualise relationships among fractions and to construct number sentences involving addition and subtraction of fractions. Open tasks such as using fractions to write 1 in at least 10 different ways can allow students to set their own level of challenge and assist with catering for the diversity of understanding that is present in every classroom. Additional constraints can be added as appropriate for particular students; for example, use fractions with at least two different denominators, include both subtraction and addition, or write sentences that make 2 or $\frac{3}{4}$. Clarke and Roche (2010) described the use of a game centred on the fraction wall that was effective in developing understanding of equivalence and fraction addition.

for the classroom

Have students fold paper strips of equal length into halves, thirds, fourths, fifths … and glue these onto a page to create a fraction wall as shown. Students are likely to need practice at folding, particularly for thirds and fifths.

Challenge students to write as many number sentences involving addition and/or subtraction as they can.

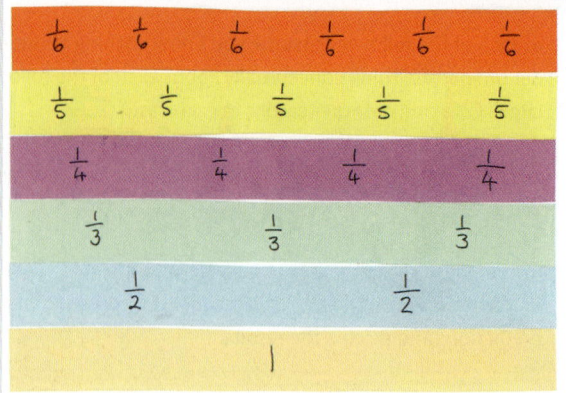

Addition and subtraction of fractions can also be usefully represented using **rectangular arrays**. The dimensions of the array need to be chosen to facilitate one fraction being represented by the rows and the other by the columns. For example, to add $\frac{1}{4}$ and $\frac{1}{2}$ we would use a 2 × 3 array because this involves 2 rows (each of which is $\frac{1}{2}$ of the array) and 3 columns (each of which is $\frac{1}{3}$ of the array. In total the array comprises six parts so each is $\frac{1}{6}$ of the array. As shown in Figure 23. 4, $\frac{2}{3}$ is equivalent to $\frac{4}{6}$, and $\frac{1}{2}$ is equivalent to $\frac{3}{6}$. The sum is, therefore, $\frac{4}{6} + \frac{3}{6} = \frac{7}{6}$. It can be seen from the diagram that this is $1\frac{1}{6}$ (one whole array, $\frac{6}{6}$, and one more sixth). It may be helpful for some students to use two identical arrays: one to show one fraction and one to show the other. If this approach is used it is important that students understand that the whole in relation to which the total number of parts is considered is a single array. This issue concerning the whole is discussed in more detail in the next section.

Figure 23.4 **Uisng rectangular arrays**

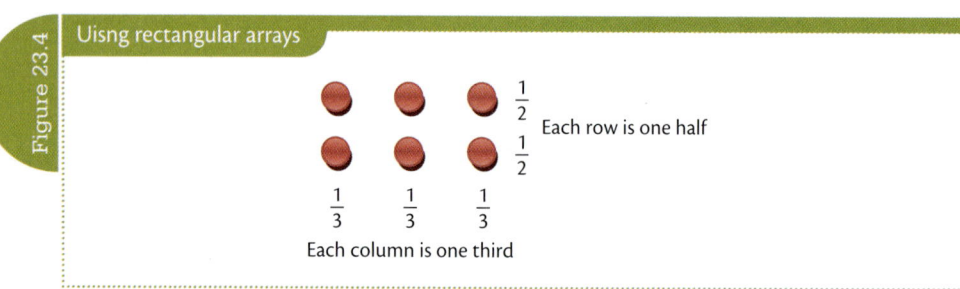

The difficulty of connecting the various representations of fractions with each other and with operations on them should not be underestimated. It is crucial that students work with multiple representations and have opportunities to link these representations with operations through games and tasks such as those just described. The work samples shown in Figures 23.5 and 23.6 were produced by a student in Year 7. In both cases the students can illustrate their chosen fraction using a circular area model but are unable to write a meaningful story or to produce a correct calculation. Both students fall into the very common error of adding both the numerators and the denominators. This suggests that the fractions are not understood as single numbers, and that there is no appreciation of the size of that number and hence of the expected size of the sum. Rather, the students seem to have attempted to apply what they know of whole addition.

communicating mathematically

In this text we have used both 'fourths' and 'quarters' to refer to $\frac{1}{4}$. Fourths relates more directly to the meaning of the fraction and is analogous to the naming of other fractions (beyond halves and thirds, which we don't call twoths and threeths!). Others would argue that quarters is the word that students will encounter in most non-school contexts and hence they should become familiar with it at school.

Whichever word we use in this case it is important to provide students with opportunities to connect the words and symbols and various representations of fractions. Fraction walls labelled as shown here or perhaps with words and symbols on the same wall provide one way to link fraction words and symbols and a linear model.

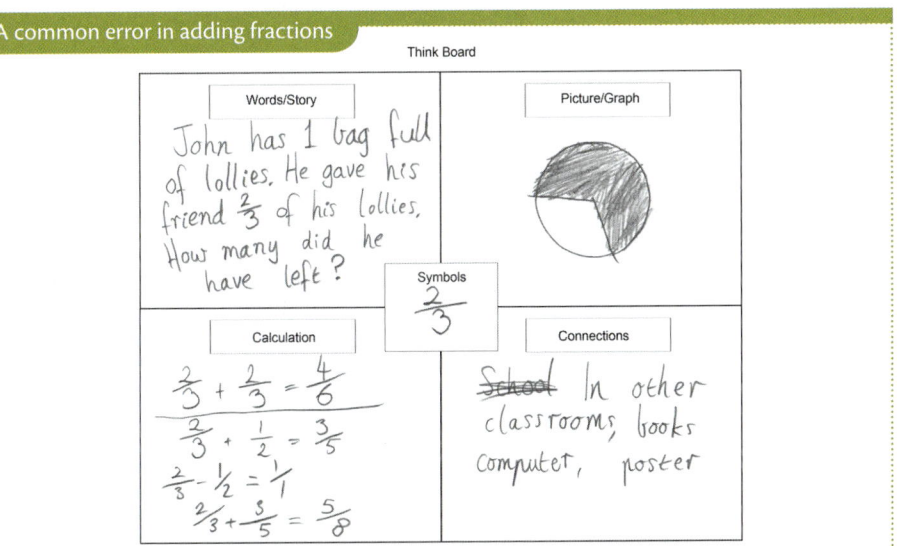

Figure 23.5 A common error in adding fractions

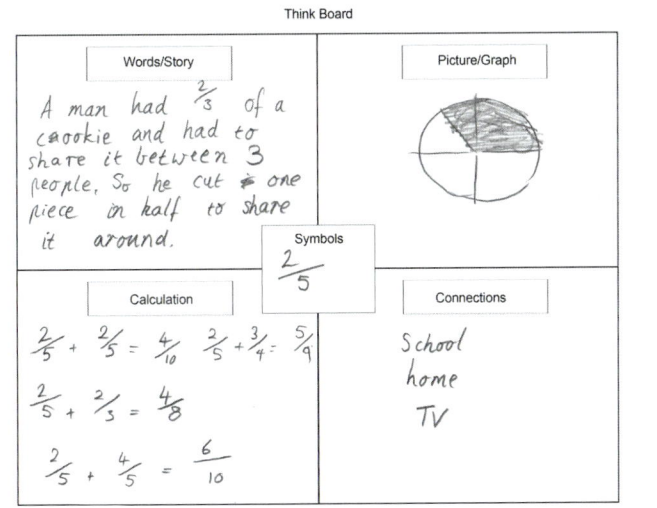

Figure 23.6 Further evidence of problems adding fractions

In contrast to Figures 23.5 and 23.6, the student whose work is shown in Figure 23.7 was able not only to draw a 'pizza' to show his fraction but also to write a story that indicated understanding of the equivalence of $\frac{3}{8}$ and $\frac{6}{16}$ and to write an accurate number sentence. His addition of the observation that $\frac{8}{8} = 1$ whole is further evidence of reliance on reasoning rather than procedural knowledge.

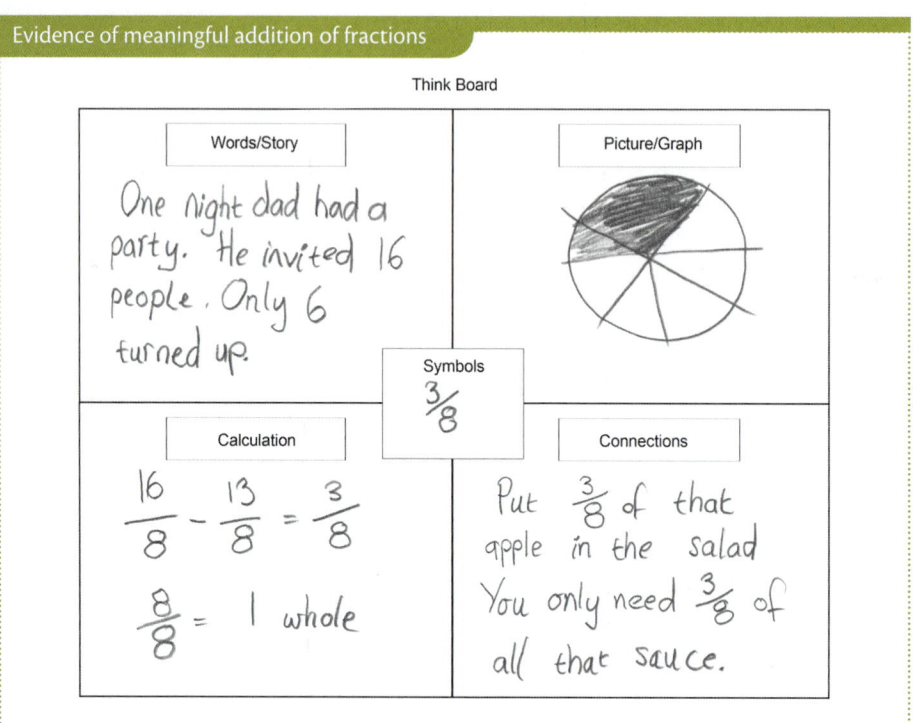

Figure 23.7 Evidence of meaningful addition of fractions

consider and discuss

Imagine that a student in your class believes that $\frac{1}{3} + \frac{1}{3} = \frac{2}{6}$. When asked to explain why he thinks so, he arranges 2 groups of 3 counters on his page, circles 1 counter in each group to represent the thirds, and then points out that 2 of the total of 6 counters are circled and that is 2 sixths. What is wrong with the student's *thinking*? How could you help the student first to understand why his thinking is wrong, and then to change his thinking about such problems?

Consider the advantages and disadvantages of various possible representations of the problem in terms of their likely usefulness in helping the student to move from his current thinking to thinking that is mathematically sound.

How might the misconception that fractions can be added or subtracted by adding or subtracting the numerators and denominators separately be avoided?

Having students develop the habit of estimating the results of the calculations before they perform them is also helpful in avoiding the kinds of errors shown in Figures 23.5 and 23.6. Estimating, as described earlier in this chapter, relies on an appreciation of the magnitude of the fractions involved and hence requires students to think about them as numbers in their own right. If students appreciate that $\frac{2}{3}$ is more than $\frac{1}{2}$ they will expect to get a result greater than 1 when $\frac{2}{3}$ and $\frac{2}{3}$ are added, and hence noticing that $\frac{4}{5}$ is not greater than 1 is likely to prompt them to rethink their reasoning.

for the classroom

Show students a solution to a fraction problem and ask them to discuss the thinking that could have led to it. The solution could be correct or incorrect, and may have been produced by someone in the class or be from somewhere else.

The role of the 'whole'

In our discussion so far we have made an important assumption: we have been considering fractions as numbers separate from any particular context, and assuming that each fraction relates to the same whole—the number one. If fractions do not relate to the same whole then adding or subtracting them, or even comparing them, is meaningless. In reality, the whole or unit is not always the same. For example, provided both relate to the same whole then $\frac{1}{2}$ is greater than $\frac{1}{4}$, but if the wholes are not the same then this might not be the case. For example, if a recipe called for $\frac{1}{2}$ a can of tomatoes, it would matter which of the cans shown in Figure 23.8 you had. In fact, given sufficiently differently sized 'wholes', any fraction could be greater than any other fraction. Watson, Beswick and Brown (2006) discussed the responses of middle school students and their teachers to an item that was aimed at assessing understanding of this concept. Of the 650 students who answered, just under one-third provided responses that indicated that they understood that the size of a fraction is dependent on the whole to which it relates. Misunderstanding of the whole is also at the root of the argument that $\frac{1}{3} + \frac{1}{3} = \frac{2}{6}$ because I can show one-third of each of two groups of three and so two-sixths of the total represents the sum. In this reasoning the whole has shifted from being a group of three counters to being a group of six counters but, unless the context of the problem specifically indicates that the whole to consider in the answer is different from the wholes in the question, we need to assume that they are same.

Figure 23.8 Different 'wholes'

consider and discuss

Solve the following problems:

1. Find the sum of $\frac{14}{26}$ and $\frac{15}{27}$. Before you begin the calculation, estimate the answer.
2. Two Year 6 classes were sharing a bus for an excursion. One class of 26 students comprised 14 boys and 12 girls, while the other class of 27 students was made up of 15 boys and 12 girls. What fraction of students on the bus were boys?

Discuss your answers to the problems. Explain why the answers are different. How do these problems relate to the scenario described in the previous Consider and discuss?

Algorithms

Huinker (1998) illustrates how Grade 5 students were able to arrive at their own algorithms for all four operations with fractions through solving carefully chosen problems. The algorithms that they 'invented' were very similar to the standard algorithms, but Huinker argued that allowing the students to invent their own algorithms has the following advantages:

- students developed an interest in solving and posing word problems with fractions
- students became flexible in their choice of strategy for solving fraction word problems and computation exercises
- students became more proficient in translating among real-world, concrete, pictorial, oral language, and symbolic representations
- students became accustomed to communicating and justifying their thinking and reasoning (p. 181).

These are all desirable outcomes. At the very least students should be given plenty of opportunities over an extended time to develop the standard algorithm meaningfully. If students have a sound understanding of equivalence, and have had sufficient time working with a range of representations of fraction addition and subtraction along with opportunities to make connections among them, developing the standard algorithm is a small step. Many students will arrive at the algorithm from working with the array representation because this shows how the common denominator relates to the different denominators of the fractions to be combined. There is much to be said for encouraging students to work with this model until they notice and exploit the shortcuts that can be achieved simply by visualising an appropriate array and renaming each of the fractions so that both have this denominator. Middle school students typically need little encouragement to exploit efficiencies when they spot them! Although the standard algorithm is efficient, generalisable, and mathematically valid, it will be meaningful only if students are able to connect it to its basis in equivalence and renaming. We would argue that continuing with a less efficient but more meaningful method (such as drawing arrays) is of greater long-term value than memorising an efficient procedure that is not understood.

The following examples illustrate how the standard algorithm relates to the array model.

Example 1: $\frac{2}{5} + \frac{3}{7}$

It is good to get into the habit, and encourage students also to develop the habit, of estimating the approximate result of calculations before they are performed. This provides a useful reference against which to check the reasonableness of your answer. In this case both fractions are close to but less than one half, so we should expect their sum to be close to but less than 1.

A 5 × 7 array allows the fifths and sevenths to be represented by the rows and columns. Each individual element of the array is one thirty-fifth, $\frac{1}{35}$.

Each row is one fifth

Each column is one seventh

Two-fifths is two rows:

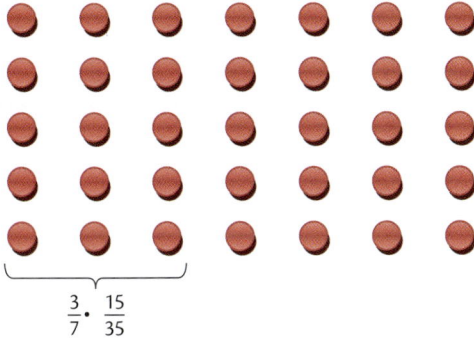

So we can see that $\frac{2}{5} = \frac{14}{35}$.

Three-sevenths is three columns:

$\frac{3}{7} \cdot \frac{15}{35}$

So we can see that $\frac{3}{7} = \frac{15}{35}$.

In terms of the standard algorithm, in these steps we have identified that the lowest common denominator is 35 (the smallest number of which both 5 and 7 are factors), and renamed both fractions so that both have the same denominator. We have used the array and the visual imagery that it provides instead of saying '5 into 35 goes 7, 7 × 2 is 14 and 7 into 35 goes 5, 5 × 3 is 15'.

So the problem is now $\frac{14}{35} + \frac{15}{35}$, which is $\frac{29}{35}$.

Subtraction works in the same way, as shown in Example 2.

Example 2: $1\frac{1}{3} - \frac{3}{4}$

We would expect the result to be a little more than one half because $1\frac{1}{4} - \frac{3}{4}$ would be $\frac{1}{2}$, and $1\frac{1}{3}$ is greater than $1\frac{1}{4}$ (because thirds are larger than quarters).

A 3 × 4 array allows thirds and fourths (quarters) to be shown. Each element of the array is one-twelfth, $\frac{1}{12}$.

Each row is $\frac{1}{3}$

Each colum is $\frac{1}{4}$

Representing $1\frac{1}{3}$ requires two identical arrays. It is important to remind students that the whole is still a single 3 × 4 array.

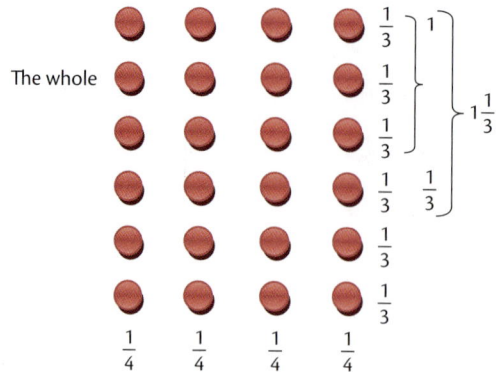

We can see that $1\frac{1}{3}$ is equivalent to $\frac{16}{12}$.

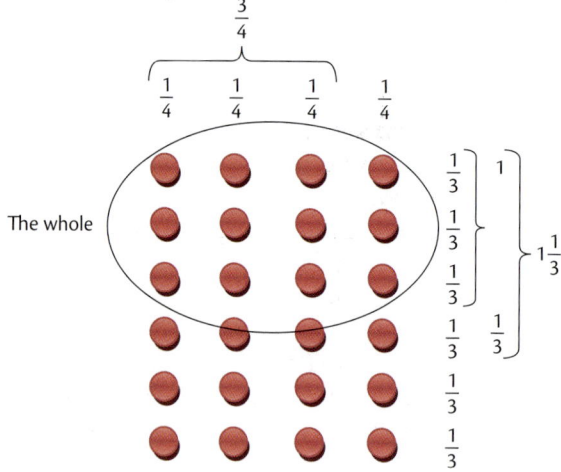

Three-fourths (quarters) is three columns.
We can see that $\frac{3}{4} = \frac{9}{12}$.
So the problem is now $\frac{16}{12} - \frac{9}{12}$, which is $\frac{7}{12}$.

As in Example 1, all but the last step in this sequence amounts to, in terms of the standard algorithm, identifying that the lowest common denominator is 12 (the smallest number with both 3 and 4 are factors), and renaming both fractions so that both have the same denominator, 12. We have used the array and the visual imagery that it provides instead of saying '3 into 12 goes 4, 4 × 4 is 16, and 4 into 12 goes 3, 3 × 3 is 9'. Notice also that using the arrays eliminates the need for another process that is often taught and learnt devoid of meaning, that is renaming $1\frac{1}{3}$ as $\frac{4}{3}$. It is inherent in the representations and is likely to seem quite obvious to students who work with these representations.

Variations on the standard algorithm for adding and subtracting fractions

Once students are comfortable using the standard algorithm or something like it there are at least two slightly different ways that it can be performed. Traditionally a calculation like $7\frac{1}{3} - 3\frac{3}{4}$ would be set out and completed as follows:

I expect an answer that is less than 4 because 7 − 3 is 4, and $\frac{3}{4}$ is greater than $\frac{1}{3}$.	$7\frac{1}{3} - 3\frac{3}{4}$
Write the mixed numbers as improper fractions.	$= \frac{22}{3} - \frac{15}{3}$
Identify the lowest common denominator, 12, and rename both fractions as twelfths.	$= \frac{88}{12} - \frac{45}{12}$ $= \frac{43}{12}$
Change the improper fraction to a mixed number.	$= 3\frac{7}{12}$

An alternative approach involves setting out the problem vertically and avoids the need to convert between improper fractions and mixed numbers.

I expect an answer that is less than 4 because 7 − 3 is 4, and $\frac{3}{4}$ is greater than $\frac{1}{3}$.	$7\frac{1}{3}$ $-3\frac{3}{4}$
Subtracting the whole numbers gives us 4 and we still have the fractions to subtract.	$= 4\left(\frac{1}{3} - \frac{3}{4}\right)$
Identify the lowest common denominator, 12, and rename both fractions as twelfths.	$= 4\left(\frac{4}{12} - \frac{9}{12}\right)$
$\frac{4}{12} - \frac{9}{12}$ is $-\frac{5}{12}$	$= 4 - \frac{5}{12}$
	$= 3\frac{7}{12}$

In the example above we needed to use negative numbers and subtract a fraction from a whole number. Middle school students who are ready to work with fraction algorithms are likely to have met negative numbers, and if sufficient attention has been paid to mental computation the subtraction will be unproblematic.

for the classroom

Have students fill in a 'think board' like the one opposite in relation to an addition or subtraction calculation that involves fractions. Adjust the difficulty of the calculation as appropriate or have students choose their own calculation to work on. You can find out a lot about students' understanding and also their confidence from the choices that they make.

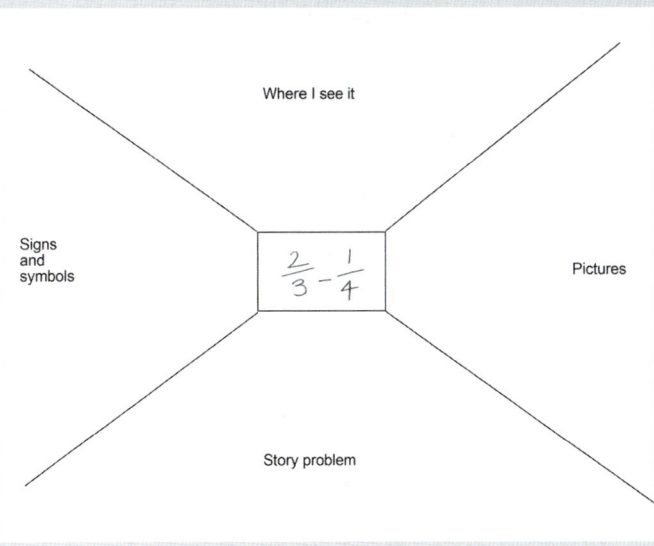

Decimals

As discussed in Chapter 22, understanding decimal notation involves extending place value concepts that were initially developed in the context of whole numbers. Addition and subtraction of decimals similarly involves the extension of strategies used for whole numbers.

Mental strategies

Dole (2004) proposed a sequence for developing mental addition and subtraction of decimals that begins with using number lines marked in tenths to build familiarity with pairs of decimals that sum to 1. For example, students should recognise that 0.2 + 0.8 = 1, as do 0.7 and 0.3, 0.6 and 0.4, 0.5 and 0.5, and so on. The corresponding subtraction statements, 1 − 0.8 = 0.2, 1 − 0.7 = 0.3 and so on should be learnt at the same time as the addition combinations (Dole, 2004). It is important that students make links between these facts and the corresponding whole number facts. At the same time it is vital that students do not simply treat the digits to the right of the decimal point as whole numbers. This is also the case when mental computation with decimals is extended to hundredths and thousandths. Sound understanding of place value and a sense of the meaning and size of the numbers involved will allow students to avoid common errors such as saying that 0.5 + 0.6 is 0.11. Students who make this error typically say 'point 5 and point 6 make point 11', indicating a lack of appreciation of place value.

When the task shown in Figure 23.9 was presented to students in Years 5–8, more than 55 per cent could not offer even a partially correct response. The response shown in Figure 23.9 includes mainly correct pairs, but the inclusion of 0.07 and 0.03, which total 0.1, suggests that the students could be looking at the digits involved rather than considering the size of the numbers involved as indicated by place value. Being able to make connections between decimal and fraction representations of numbers is also useful. A student who understood that 0.07 is another way of writing $\frac{7}{100}$ and that 0.03 is $\frac{3}{100}$, and who had an appreciation of the size of these fractions, would be unlikely to suggest that their sum could be 1.

Figure 23.9 Finding pairs of numbers that add to 1

0.5	0.25	0.07	0.1
0.2	0.01	0.75	0.03
0.3	0.007	0.6	0.4
0.13	0.8	0.013	0.99

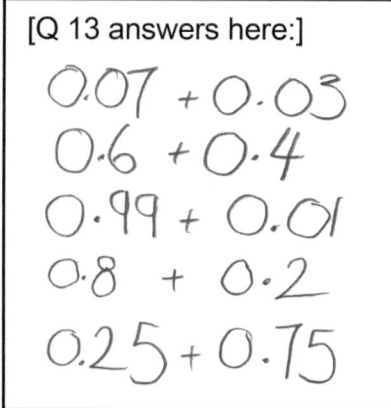

[Q 13 answers here:]

0.07 + 0.03
0.6 + 0.4
0.99 + 0.01
0.8 + 0.2
0.25 + 0.75

Estimation

Developing the habit of estimating the results of adding and subtracting decimals is crucial. Estimation strategies rely on an appreciation of the size and meaning of numbers based on place value, and hence the understandings that underpin it are crucial to meaningful computation with decimals. If students struggle to estimate the sums and differences of decimal numbers it is likely that their understanding of these numbers requires attention.

As with fractions, strong visual images play an important role in helping students to appreciate the sizes of the numbers with which they are working. Plenty of experience with a range of representations of decimal numbers, including number lines and 10×10 grids is crucial.

Approximation

Ideas related to approximating decimals, such as rounding, were discussed in Chapter 22. Decimals are, of course, a particular way of representing tenths, hundredths, thousandths, and so on. Any number can be approximated by a series of these fractions, but not all can be represented exactly in this form. When we are working with decimals we commonly deal with approximations that are sufficiently accurate for the context. For example, $\frac{1}{3}$ is approximately $\frac{3}{10}$ or 0.3. A closer approximation is 0.33, which is $\frac{3}{10} + \frac{3}{100}$. An even closer approximation is 0.333, which is $\frac{3}{10} + \frac{3}{100} + \frac{3}{1000}$. This is still not quite $\frac{1}{3}$. We could go on adding increasingly small fractions that would get us ever closer to $\frac{1}{3}$ but we would never arrive at a decimal representation that was exactly $\frac{1}{3}$. The best we can do is adopt a convention for writing decimals like this (recurring decimals) that indicates that the digit 3 repeats infinitely. Using this notation we can say that $\frac{1}{3} = 0.\dot{3}$. In most contexts using an approximate decimal representation of a rational number to an appropriate number of places is adequate, but we need to use fractions if we want to avoid errors that result from rounding and that can accumulate if rounding occurs at several stages in a calculation.

Representing decimal addition and subtraction

Two important representations of addition and subtraction of decimals are number lines and 10×10 grids. Number lines initially marked in tenths can be used to represent addition and subtraction. Figure 23.10 shows a number line marked in intervals of 0.05 and used to represent the sum of 1.2 and 0.75. Before we begin we would expect a result close to but less than 2 because 1.2 is less than $1\frac{1}{3}$ and 0.75 is $\frac{3}{4}$.

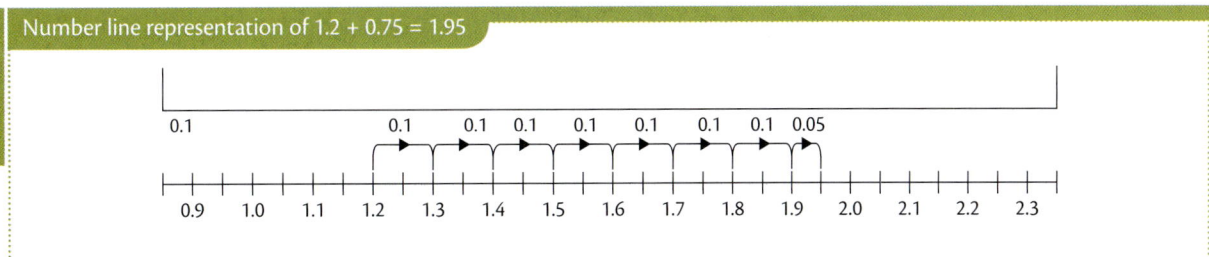

Figure 23.10 Number line representation of 1.2 + 0.75 = 1.95

Area models, such as 10 × 10 grids, have the advantage of reinforcing place value relationships between the digits in decimal numbers. Using 10 × 10 grids the same problem can be represented as shown in Figure 23.11. A 10 × 10 grid represents 1, the whole. It comprises 100 squares and so each individual square represents $\frac{1}{100}$ or 0.01 of the grid. The first number, 1.2, is shown in green, and 0.75 is shown in grey. We can see that the total shaded area is 1.95.

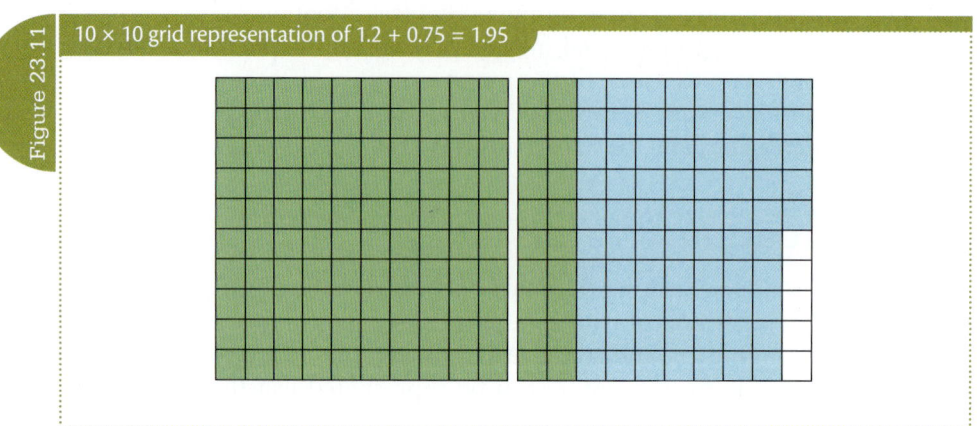

Figure 23.11 10 × 10 grid representation of 1.2 + 0.75 = 1.95

Roche (2010) described the use of a related area model that she called a decimat; this is shown in Figure 23.12. Roche described a game using the decimat that involves students in representing decimal numbers, relating their decimal and fraction representations, and calculating the cumulative total of decimal numbers.

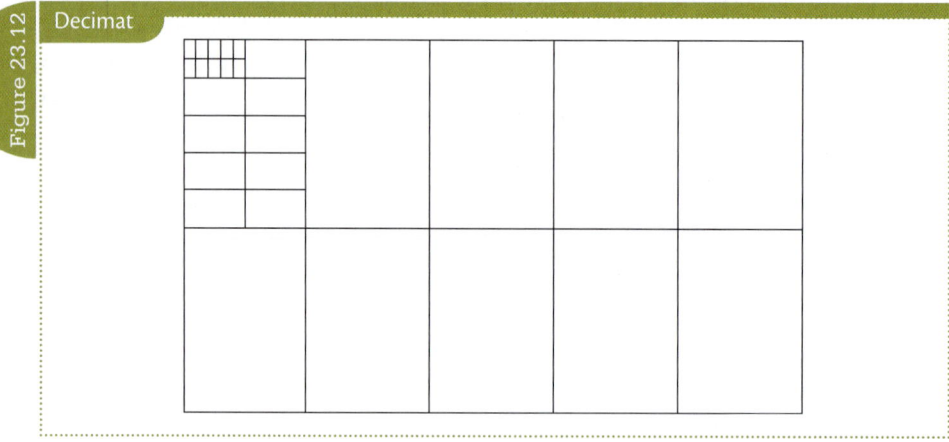

Figure 23.12 Decimat

Multi-base arithmetic blocks (MAB) have been used to represent decimals and their addition and subtraction. There is, however, a compelling case against their use for this purpose that centres on the difficulty that students have in reinterpreting the value of blocks that they have become accustomed to seeing as representing whole numbers (Stacey, Helme, Archer & Condon, 2001). Stacey et al. (2001) recommend the use of an alternative model, linear arithmetic blocks (LAB), that provide a length model for decimals and lend themselves particularly well to comparing the sizes of decimal numbers. LAB can be constructed from electrical conduit or similar. The longest block represents 1, blocks that are exactly one-tenth as long as the 1 represent 0.1, blocks exactly one-tenth length of the 0.1 block represent 0.001, and washers whose thickness is one-tenth the length of the 0.01 block represent 0.001. In practice it is wise to find the washers to be used first, and work upwards from there through the hundredths and tenths to the whole.

for the classroom

The following game provides a fun context in which students can practise adding and subtracting decimal numbers. Try it with the targets suggested or use a blank sheet and have students decide on their own target numbers—a great way to cater for diversity in the classroom.

Target practice

You need:
3 ten-sided dice (different colours are useful but not essential) and a copy of the game sheet for each student.

To play:
1. Take turns to throw the dice.
2. Choose two of the numbers thrown to make a number as close to the target number as possible.
3. Mentally calculate 'how close' and record in the space provided.
4. The winner is the player closest to the target.

Numbers thrown	Target	Number made	How close?
	74		
	3.5		
	1.9		
	5.7		
	3.5		
	4.7		
	9.3		
	0.8		

Algorithms

The standard algorithms for addition and subtraction that are used with whole numbers can be extended to decimal numbers. This can seem like a deceptively simple step, but applying the algorithms meaningfully depends on solid understanding of place value and so should not be rushed. As with all computation, estimation is a critical step that provides a check and, more importantly, requires understanding of the numbers involved and their magnitudes. Common errors include misplacing the decimal point and thereby obtaining answers that are out by a factor of 10 or more. When students make such errors it is not sufficient simply to emphasise the importance of lining up the decimal points. Rather, the focus should be on encouraging students to think about the sizes of the numbers involved and hence the size of the result to be expected. If students can do this they are unlikely to accept without question answers that are 10 times or one-tenth of the size that they should be. If they can't make such estimates it is likely that the conceptual underpinnings of the algorithm are not yet developed, and it is wise to spend the time necessary for these to be developed before proceeding with the algorithm. Allowing students to work with representations that are meaningful for them for as long and as often as they feel the need is generally the best approach.

for the classroom

Today's number is …

Play 'today's number is' using a rational number represented as a decimal or fraction.

Write your chosen number on the board and ask students to offer other ways of writing it. For example, if today's number is 0.6, suggestions could include:

0.3 + 0.3	6 tenths	$\frac{6}{10}$
0.7 − 0.1	0.8 − 0.2	$\frac{3}{5}$
$\frac{12}{20}$	0.5 + 0.1	$\frac{1}{2} + \frac{1}{10}$

Try to arrange the responses in groups to draw attention to patterns. Encourage students to use both decimals and fractions in their suggestions and to include sums and differences of decimals and/or fractions

Integers

'Integers' is the collective name for the positive whole numbers, zero, and negative whole numbers. Although computation with integers is not introduced until the middle years, students may already be aware of numbers that are less than zero. Contexts in which they arise include temperatures, sea levels, debt, and mine depths. Depending on where they live, students are likely to be able to relate to one of more of these contexts. It is sensible to use students' informal knowledge of integers and intuitions about them as the basis of teaching.

making connections

Even though most students will be able to relate to the existence of negative numbers it is still the case that negative numbers do not relate to concrete quantities or measures. This was the problem that they presented for the ancient Greeks. Greek mathematics was based in geometry, and hence dealt with lengths, areas, and volumes, which cannot be negative. The Greek influence on the development of Western mathematics meant that negative numbers were still regarded with suspicion and avoided where possible as recently as the eighteenth century in Europe.

In other cultures, such as China and India, systems for working with negative numbers were documented in the seventh century and earlier. For example, the Indian mathematician Brahmagupta stated rules for calculating with fortunes (positive numbers) and debts (negative numbers) in 620. In relation to addition and subtraction these were (Rogers, nd):

- A debt minus zero is a debt.
- A fortune minus zero is a fortune.
- Zero minus zero is a zero.
- A debt subtracted from zero is a fortune.
- A fortune subtracted from zero is a debt.

The key difference from the thinking of the Greeks that allowed Brahmagupta to deal with negative numbers (and zero) was that he thought of all numbers as abstract entities.

One source of difficulty for students in working with integers is that the symbol for negative numbers is the same as that used for the operation of subtraction (Anghileri, 2007). It is usual to attempt to distinguish the two by writing the sign to denote a negative as a superscript, for example $^{-}2$ is negative 2, whereas – 2 means subtract two. Confusion of the sign and the operator can be exacerbated if teachers use the same word for both. For example, – $^{-}2$ should be read as 'minus (or subtract) negative two' and not as 'minus minus two'.

Representing integer addition and subtraction

Representations of integer addition and subtraction generally fall into one of two categories:

- number line models
- models involving discrete objects such as counters.

A third approach to developing integer computation is based on extending patterns in the outcomes of operations on positive numbers to negative numbers.

An important consideration when deciding on whether to use either number line or discrete object models is that the steps that define the working of the model can be learnt without understanding and hence can be no more conceptually meaningful than simply memorising rules without any conceptual basis at all. It is important that students have plenty of time to play with the chosen models to explore how they might be used to represent calculations and to gradually document these for themselves.

Number lines

The number line is the model most widely used to represent addition and subtraction of integers, and represents a natural extension of a model with which students should be familiar. It is conventional to draw number lines horizontally with negative numbers to the left of zero and positive numbers to the right, but there is no reason why vertical number lines could not be used (Anghileri, 2007). Figure 23.13 shows how a Year 8 student used number lines to make simple representations of context-based problems involving integers. The problems were part of a task used to introduce integers with a view to determining how students could relate their intuitive understandings of negative numbers and the number line, as they had worked extensively with the number line in the context of decimals and fractions. Further details of this activity and the ensuing teaching sequence are provided in Beswick (submitted).

The problems were:

- I had 5 bracelets until I lost 2. How many do I have now?
- The water level in the dam was 5 cm lower than its normal level (normal level is 0). As a result of warm weather it dropped another 2 cm. What was the water level then?

Figure 23.13 Using a number line to solve integer problems

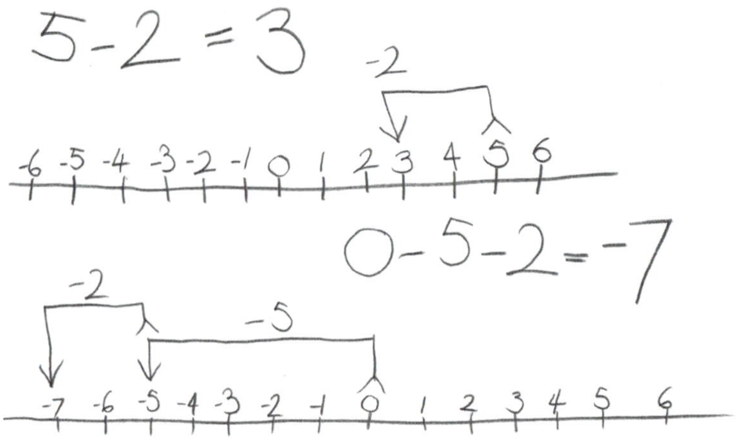

$5 - 2 = 3$

$0 - 5 - 2 = -7$

The number line model can be developed and formalised so that positive numbers are represented by distances to the right, and negative numbers by distances to the left. Addition is moving forward and subtraction is moving backwards. The result of a calculation is the distance between the beginning of the first number and end of the second, with the sign being the direction of this move (negative for left and positive for right). Figure 23.14 shows how a range of calculations are represented in this way. Students should draw much less elaborate diagrams and there is much to be said for minimising the emphasis on neatness and ruler use and encouraging students to focus on the meaning of their diagrams. Beswick (submitted) described how the Year 8 students with whom she worked rarely produced diagrams at all, preferring to step out their solutions physically along a number line marked on a whiteboard or the floor. They moved quickly from this to visualising moves along the number line without the need to step them out every time.

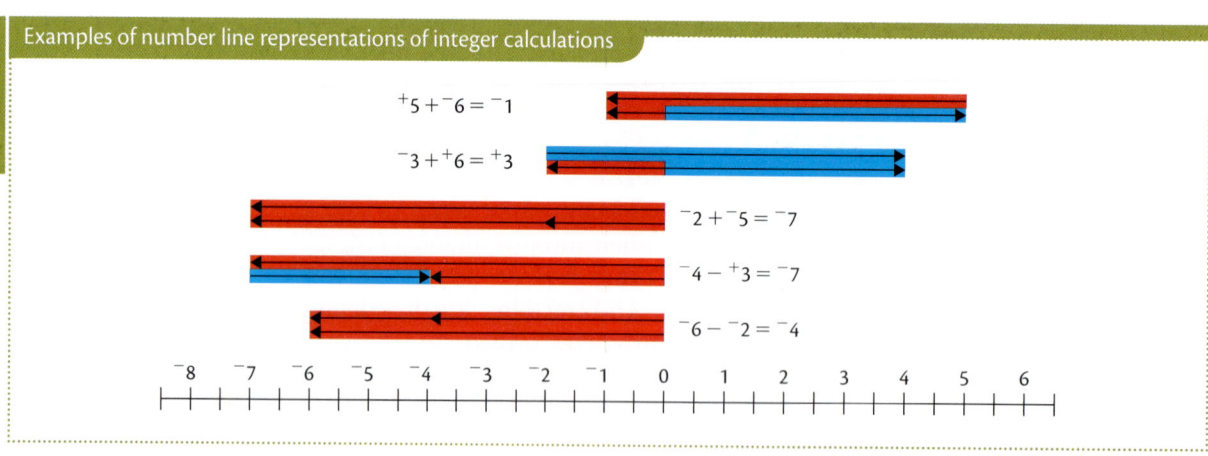

Figure 23.14 Examples of number line representations of integer calculations

$^{+}5 + {}^{-}6 = {}^{-}1$
$^{-}3 + {}^{+}6 = {}^{+}3$
$^{-}2 + {}^{-}5 = {}^{-}7$
$^{-}4 - {}^{+}3 = {}^{-}7$
$^{-}6 - {}^{-}2 = {}^{-}4$

Discrete objects

Discrete objects as models typically use small objects such as counters, with one colour used to denote negative numbers and another to denote positive numbers. Opposite coloured objects cancel each other out. A key understanding that should not be rushed in developing integer addition and subtraction with these models is that any number can be represented in infinitely many ways. For example, if blue counters are positive and red counters are negative, the number 3 can be represented in any of the ways shown in Figure 23.15, in fact it can be represented by any combination of red and blue counters that includes three more blue than red.

Figure 23.15 Three possible counter representations of 3

Using counters, addition is adding counters and subtraction is taking them away. The examples shown in Figure 23.15 can be represented using counters as shown below.

5 reds and 5 blues will cancel out leaving one red, so the result is ⁻1.

3 reds and 3 blues will cancel out leaving three blues, so the result is ⁺3.

All of the counters are red so the result is ⁻7.
⁻4 – ⁺3 = ⁻7: Negative 4 is represented by 4 red counters. To subtract ⁺3 we need to remove 3 blue counters, so we need a representation of ⁻4 that includes at least 3 blue counters such as the following:

When ⁺3 is taken away (subtracted) we are left with ⁻7
⁻6 – ⁻2 = ⁻4: In this case we need to remove 2 red counters (subtract negative 2), so representing ⁻6 with 6 red counters is fine.
Subtracting ⁻2 (taking away 2 red counters) leaves ⁻4

Linchevski and Williams (1999) described in detail two teaching experiments in which they used concrete situations (people entering and leaving a disco, and a card game) to facilitate students' construction of negative numbers and operations with them. In a manner analogous to the approach using counters described above, they used a double abacus to keep track of the total number of people in the venue (with one colour for people entering the disco and another colour for people leaving), and to keep score in the card game.

A pattern and structure approach

Freudenthal (1987, cited in Linchevski & Williams, 1999) concluded that neither number line nor discrete object models are completely satisfactory for developing conceptual understanding of operations on integers. He recommended delaying teaching integers until students are able to follow and believe arguments based on mathematical structure. This reasoning is consistent with the historical development of negative numbers, where acceptance of their validity necessitated a preparedness to think about numbers as abstract entities that were not necessarily related to concrete quantities and measures. Using a pattern and structure approach to integer addition and subtraction could involve creating and extending patterns such as:

$$^+3 + {}^+2 = {}^+5$$
$$^+3 + {}^+1 = {}^+4$$
$$^+3 + 0 = {}^+3$$
$$^+3 + {}^-1 = {}^+2$$
$$^+3 + {}^-2 = {}^+1$$
$$^+3 + {}^-3 = 0$$
$$^+3 + {}^-4 = {}^-1$$

Notice that the number added to $^+3$ decreases by 1 each time, necessitating moving through 0 to numbers beyond. At the same time the sum also decreases by 1 at each step, becoming 0 when the magnitudes of the negative and positive numbers are equal, and then negative as the magnitude of the second number exceeds 3. Students should be encouraged to create and extend similar lists and to describe and explain the patterns that are evident.

for the classroom

Magic squares

Magic squares are puzzles that many students enjoy. Most will find this one quite challenging.

Fill in each of the numbers $^-15$, $^-12$, $^-9$, $^-6$, $^-3$, 0, 3, 6, and 9 so that every row, column and diagonal has the same sum.

Encourage students to think about strategies that might be more efficient than just guessing. Have students share successful or helpful strategies. Have students design their own magic square using a different set of negative and positive numbers or even a square with different dimensions. Encourage them to generalise about what is possible and what is not.

Establishing generalisations

Generalisation is at the heart of what it means to do mathematics, and hence developing students' ability and inclination to generalise should be central to all mathematics teaching. It is included in the Reasoning proficiency strand of the *Australian Curriculum: Mathematics* (Australian Curriculum, Assessment and Reporting Authority [ACARA], 2010).

Rather than requiring students to memorise rules for adding and subtracting integers or even for working with number lines or counters, students need opportunities to notice patterns, hypothesise about the extent to which a particular pattern might apply to other numbers or contexts, and to test such conjectures. Whatever representation or approach is used, students should be encouraged to look for regularities in their answers. They will readily notice patterns that amount to the rules that are too often simply presented without explanation. If these 'rules' are discovered by students for themselves, they are far more likely to remember them and to apply them correctly. Some teachers might argue that there is insufficient time to allow students to discover such things for themselves, but most of these teachers would agree that a major point of the large numbers of repetitive exercises that students are traditionally required to complete are aimed mainly at memorising the rules. If the rules are meaningful then far less practice is required.

More importantly, providing opportunities for students to generalise, and requiring them to exercise this and other aspects of mathematical thinking as described by the proficiency strands of the *Australian Curriculum: Mathematics* (ACARA, 2010), contributes to students developing an appreciation of mathematics as a discipline.

key terms

Additive identity element: the additive identity element for a set of numbers is a number in the set that can be added to any number in the set without changing it; for rational numbers, and for real numbers, zero is the additive identity.

Algorithm: a set of clear steps that will lead to a solution

Approximation: an inexact result, sufficiently precise for the context and recorded as the outcome of an exact calculation

Associativity: a property of an operation on a set of numbers (e.g. addition and multiplication of real numbers) that means that when three or more numbers are combined the result is the same no matter which two numbers are combined first

Commutativity: a property of an operation on a set of numbers (e.g. addition and multiplication of real numbers) that means that the order in which numbers are combined does not affect the result

Decimal: a number written using the base ten numeration system

Difference: the result of subtracting the smaller of a pair of quantities from the larger

> Estimation: the process of arriving at an inexact result on the basis of general considerations of the numbers and operations involved rather than as a consequence of a precise mathematical procedure
> Fractions: the ratio of two numbers, usually a part to a whole, expressed with on number above a line and the other below
> Integers: the collective name for the positive whole numbers, zero, and negative whole numbers
> Rational numbers: numbers that can be written in the form $\frac{a}{b}$ where a and b are integers and $b \neq 0$; rational numbers can be expressed as fractions, decimals or percentages.
> Rectangular array: an arrangement or rows and columns in the shape of a rectangle.
> Related denominators: the denominators of two fractions are related if one is a multiple of the other
> Sum: the result of an addition

Review questions

1. Explain how the commutative and associative properties of addition can assist with addition calculations.
2. How is making an estimate different from providing an approximate solution?
3. How important do you believe the standard algorithms are? Why? List arguments for and against teaching them.
4. Estimate the answers to each of the following: $\frac{2}{3} + \frac{5}{7}$ and $2\frac{1}{4} - \frac{3}{5}$. Explain how you arrived at your estimates. Model each calculation using rectangular arrays. Now solve them using the algorithm. Explain how each step of the algorithm relates to the array model.
5. Estimate the answers to each of the following: 1.07 + 0.855 and 1.24 − 0.6. Explain how you arrived at your estimates. Model each calculation using a 10 × 10 grid. Now solve each using the algorithm. Explain how each step of the algorithm relates to the 10 × 10 grid.
6. What are the advantages and disadvantages of number line and discrete object models for teaching addition and subtraction of integers? What merit might there be in a pattern-based approach?
7. Why is it important for students to develop meaningful methods for working with addition and subtraction? What are the dangers of learning rules and algorithms without understanding?

Key references

Anghileri, J. (2007). *Developing Number Sense: Progression in the Middle Years*. London: Continuum International Publishing Group.

Beswick, K. (2011). Positive experiences with negative numbers: Building on students in and out of school experiences. *Australian Mathematics Teacher*, 67(2), 31-40.

Campbell, P. F., Rowan, T. E., & Suarez, A. R. (1998). What criteria for student-invented algorithms. In L. J. Morrow (Ed.), *The Teaching and Learning of Algorithms in School Mathematics* (pp. 49-55). Reston, VA: National Council of Teachers of Mathematics.

Clarke, D. M. (2005). Written algorithms in the primary years: Undoing the 'good work'? In M. Coupland, J. Anderson & T. Spencer (Eds.), *Making Mathematics Vital: Proceedings of the Twentieth Biennial Conference of the Australian Association of Mathematics Teachers* (pp. 93-98). Adelaide: AAMT.

Clarke, D. M., & Roche, A. (2010). The power of a single game to address a range of important ideas in fraction learning. *Australian Primary Mathematics Classroom*, 15(3), 18-23.

Huinker, D. (1998). Letting fraction algorithms emerge through problem solving. In L. J. Morrow (Ed.), *The Teaching and Learning of Algorithms in School Mathematics* (pp. 170-182). Reston, VA: National Council of Teachers of Mathematics.

Kamii, C., & Dominick, A. (1998). The harmful effects of algorithms in grades 1-4. In L. J. Morrow (Ed.), *The Teaching and Learning of Algorithms in School Mathematics* (pp. 130-140). Reston, VA: National Council of Teachers of Mathematics.

Lappan, G., & Bouck, M. K. (1998). Developing algorithms for adding and subtracting fractions. In L. J. Morrow (Ed.), *The Teaching and Learning of Algorithms in School Mathematics* (pp. 183-197). Reston, VA: National Council of Teachers of Mathematics.

Moody, G. (2011). Decipipes: helping students to "Get the point". *Australian Primary Mathematics Classroom*, 16(1), 10-15.

Siemon, D., (2002). Partitioning: The missing link in building fraction knowledge and confidence. Department of Education, Victoria. Retrieved 10 March 2010 from www.eduweb.vic.gov.au/edulibrary/public/teachlearn/student/pppartitioning.pdf.

24 Working with Multiplication, Division, and Proportional Reasoning

Contents

Introduction	549
Meanings for multiplication and division	550
Working with an extended range of numbers	557
What is proportional reasoning?	576
Planning for diversity	580
Conclusion	582

Chapter objectives

This chapter will enable the reader to:
- Understand what is involved in proportional reasoning
- Recognise the different ways in which multiplication and division problems can be represented at this level
- Understand the importance of mental strategies and how these can be developed
- Appreciate the role of materials, models, language, and recording in scaffolding students' understanding and solution strategies
- Recognise and address children's learning needs in relation to multiplicative thinking and proportional reasoning
- Plan effective problem-solving experiences involving written and mental computation.

Making use of structure

Many years ago I found myself teaching a Year 9 class of girls who were intent on leaving school as early as possible. Financial mathematics was a core component of their program but the available text treated these topics in a particularly procedural way. I decided to try a different approach. I asked the students to pinch the pages of the respective chapters between their forefinger and thumb (it amounted to about half a centimetre) and said, 'I'm going to let you in on a secret. All of the problems in these pages are of the type $n\%$ of $m = p$'. Over the course of two weeks we selected and solved problems according to type, that is, (i) n and m known, (ii) n and p known, or (iii) m and p known, with little regard for context (i.e. profit and loss, simple interest, discount, etc.). This might seem counterintuitive, but it worked. At the end of the two weeks not only were they happy to sit the test, they all passed with flying colours. This taught me a valuable lesson about the clarifying power of mathematical structure, and that context can sometimes get in the way of learning mathematics.

Chapter 24 Working with Multiplication, Division, and Proportional Reasoning

Big ideas

- Multiplicative thinking involves a capacity to work with an extended range of numbers in a variety of ways and to discern and reason about relationships between numbers and quantities in different contexts.
- Knowing when to multiply or divide and choosing a strategy appropriate to the task requires a deep understanding of the operations themselves and how they are represented.
- Strategies for multiplying and dividing an extended range of numbers need to be modelled, scaffolded, and discussed to ensure all students have access to a range of efficient, flexible strategies that they can use with confidence.
- Estimation is a highly developed capacity requiring the integration of a number of subordinate skills and understandings.
- Proportional reasoning involves recognising and working with relationships between quantities and/or variables.

Introduction

The capacity to think multiplicatively is crucial to success in further school mathematics. It underpins nearly all of the topics considered in Years 5 through 9 and beyond, and is the single most important reason for the eight year range in mathematics achievement in Years 5 to 9 (Siemon, Virgona & Corneille, 2001; Siemon et al., 2006). **Multiplicative thinking** involves recognising and working with relationships between quantities. In particular, it supports efficient solutions to more difficult problems involving multiplication and division, fractions, decimal fractions, **ratio**, **rates**, and percentage. Although some aspects of multiplicative thinking are available to young children, multiplicative thinking is substantially more complex than additive thinking and may take many years to achieve (Vergnaud, 1983; Lamon, 2007). This is because multiplicative thinking is concerned with processes such as shrinking, enlarging, and exponentiating that are fundamentally more complex, rather than the more obvious processes of aggregation and disaggregation associated with additive thinking and the use of whole numbers.

In this chapter we consider an extended range of meanings for multiplication and division and explore the type of experiences needed to ensure that these are understood. We also consider what is involved in proportional reasoning and the strategies that can be used to solve problems involving multiplication and division of integers, fractions, decimal fractions, and percentage, how these develop over time, and how they might be scaffolded.

think + link

Many of the important elements of multiplicative thinking were examined in Chapter 17, in particular the shift in thinking from a reliance on repeated addition (*equal groups* idea) to array-based strategies (*times as many* or *for each* idea). Some of these elements will be reviewed briefly here as a basis for supporting a more general view of both operations in terms of *factor–factor–product*.

Meanings for multiplication and division

In Chapter 17 we examined two different approaches to multiplication and division—counting and splitting (Confrey, 1994). The first represents multiplication as repeated addition and division as repeated subtraction (quotitive division), and is the approach most commonly adopted in the early years of schooling as this builds on students' understandings of whole numbers and counting. However, young children also have a capacity to share equally and work with the *for each* or *times as many* idea, as we saw in the solutions to the Baa-Baa Black Sheep problem in Chapter 17. These ideas and capacities underpin the second approach, which supports array-based mental strategies, partitive division and, ultimately, a more generalised conception of multiplication and division in terms of *factor–factor–product*.

While the *equal groups* idea is helpful initially in building an appreciation of all three aspects of a multiplicative situation, that is, the number of groups, the size of each group, and the total, this idea is really only useful for situations involving relatively small whole numbers. For instance, the *equal groups* idea and repeated addition do not support multiplication and division involving larger whole numbers (e.g. it is difficult to think about 46 groups of 83 or how many groups of 23 in 904). Although it is possible to think about how many halves in 3 or how many $\frac{2}{3}$ cups of milk in 6 cups of milk (quotitive division), the equal groups idea does not support the multiplication and division of fractions and decimal fractions more generally (e.g. 4.2×7.06 or $\frac{2}{3}$ divided by $2\frac{4}{5}$).

The use of *arrays* and *regions* as models or representations of multiplication was discussed in Chapter 17. In particular, we noted the critical shift in thinking afforded by arrays and regions from a focus on the *number in each group* and an emphasis on a count of equal groups (traditional times tables) to the *number of groups* or the notion of a constant **multiplier** (e.g. 4 of anything is double double). Array-based strategies support a much more efficient approach to number fact learning and mental computation more generally. For example, 3 thirty-sevens can be thought about as double thirty plus double seven (e.g. 60, 74) and 1 more thirty plus seven (e.g. 74, 104, 111), and 5 forty-threes can be thought about as half of 10 forty-threes (i.e. 430, 215).

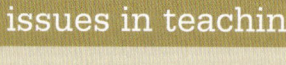

Rote learning versus meaningful learning

Approximately 40% of students leave primary school not fully confident that they can 'automatically recall all of the multiplication and division facts to 100' (Siemon et al., 2006). This is largely because the facts have been taught using the traditional times tables. The tables represent the facts as a count of equal groups and multiplication as repeated addition. In Chapter 17, a case was made for representing the facts differently. For example, instead of 1 four, 2 fours, 3 fours, 4 fours, 5 fours, etc., the 4s facts are listed as 4 of anything: 4 ones, 4 twos, 4 threes, 4 fours, 4 fives, etc. This facilitates the use of known strategies such as doubling and supports generalisation (e.g. 4 thirty-fours is double double 34, 68, 136).

Automaticity is greatly over-rated—it is better that students have access to efficient strategies that they can apply with confidence to an extended range of situations, rather than spend countless hours committing facts to memory by rote learning. Frequent use will ensure many become 'known facts', and the ability to deal with a larger range of numbers will bring its own reward in increased self-confidence.

- Do you agree or disagree? Why? Refer back to Chapter 17 for a detailed description of the strategies if needed.
- Is there a role for the use of number patterns and/or skip counting in learning the number facts?

The *region* idea also supports the construction and interpretation of fraction diagrams (e.g. Figure 24.1) and the extension to the *area* idea for multiplication (Barmby, Harries, Higgins & Suggate, 2009). This can be used to support multiplication of larger whole numbers, decimal fractions, fractions, and ultimately algebraic expressions.

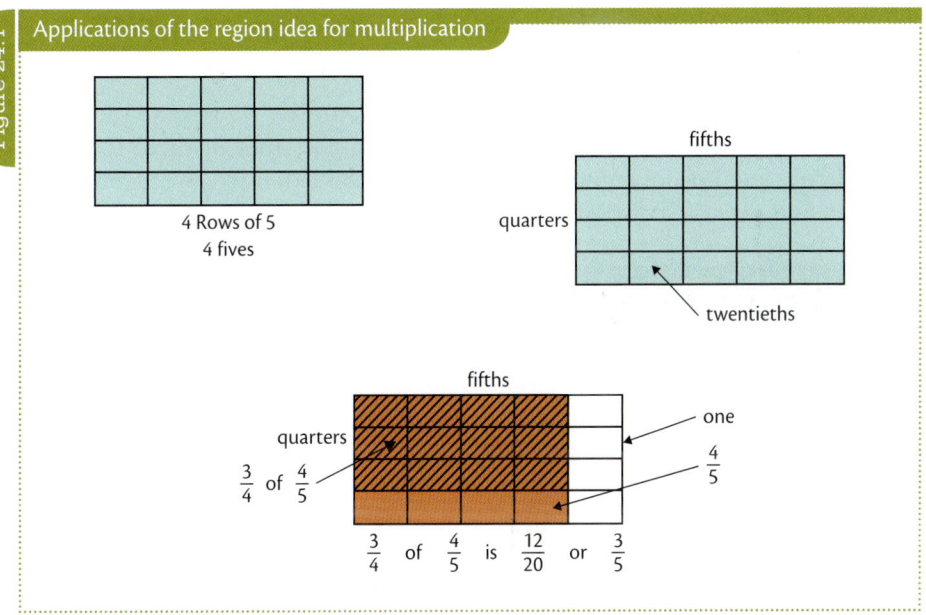

Figure 24.1 Applications of the region idea for multiplication

Area idea for multiplication

As discussed in Chapter 17, the **area idea for multiplication** is an extension of the *region* idea. The name derives from the same concept in measurement, as it also represents the distribution of a length over a width. It is a continuous model that supports the multiplication of multi-digit numbers in terms of their place-value parts (e.g. hundreds, tens, and ones by tens and ones), fractions, and ultimately algebraic factors. Although digital tools can be used to solve problems involving multiplication and division and an extended range of numbers, the value of exploring the area idea is that it provides a basis for understanding how multiplication works across different place-value parts and supports the use of 'by' as a more general term for describing multiplication (e.g. 3 tens by 4 ones); that is, for two-digit numbers, ones by ones, ones by tens, tens by ones and tens by tens. For example, 32 × 23 can be represented as an area using base 10 blocks (MAB) as shown in Figure 24.2 to demonstrate how each place-value part multiplies by each other place-value part to produce four *partial products*, which are then summed.

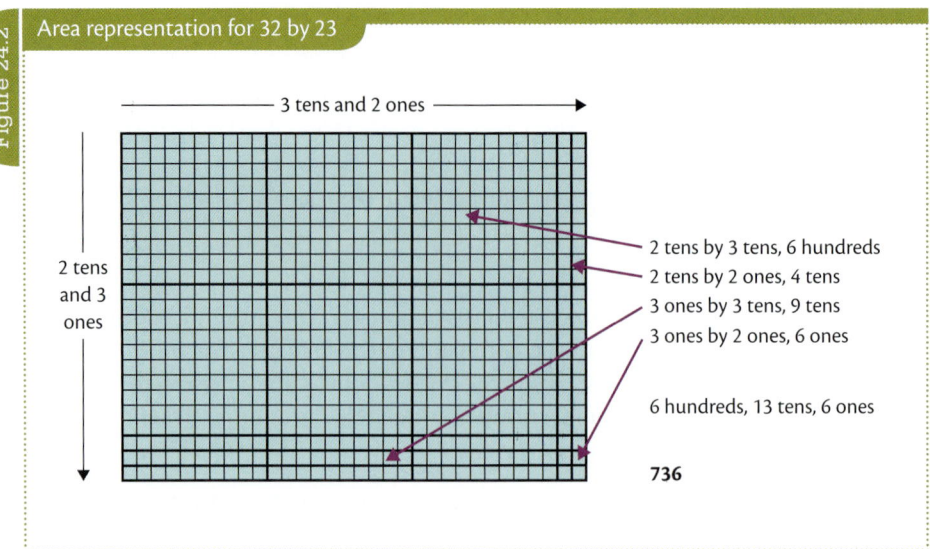

Figure 24.2 Area representation for 32 by 23

Once these ideas are understood, the process can be represented in more abstract ways as shown in Figures 24.3 and 24.4. The first of these is known as the lattice method of multiplication and can be extended to larger whole numbers and decimal fractions.

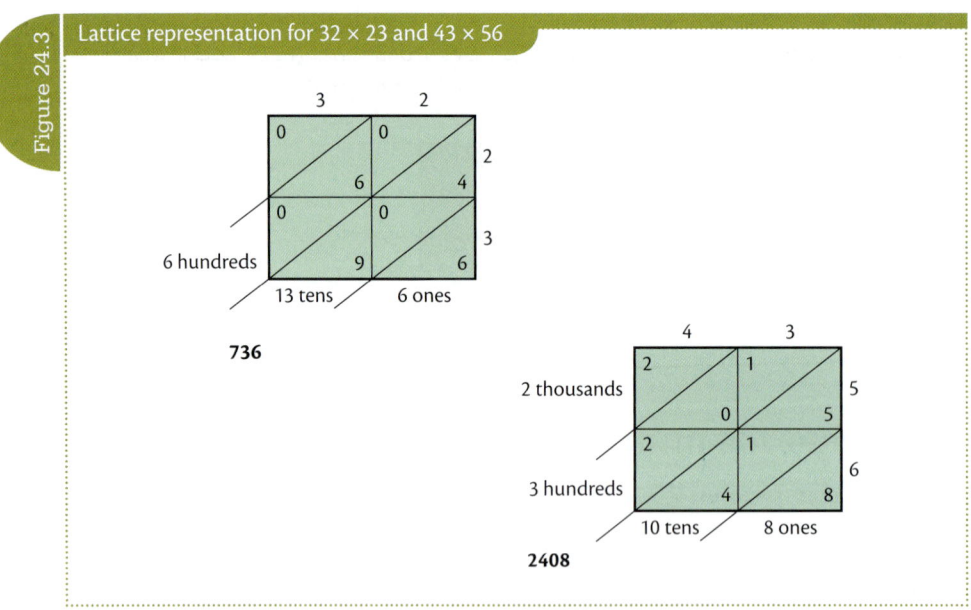

Figure 24.3 Lattice representation for 32 × 23 and 43 × 56

The second of the more abstract ways for multiplying is shown in Figure 24.4; it is referred to as the cross-hatch or 'sticks' method of multiplying. It can also be used to explore larger whole number and decimal fraction multiplication, although some care needs to be taken when labelling parts. A modified version of both can be created using a region diagram, where the number of rows and columns is determined by the number of digits in the respective multiplicands (e.g. a three-digit by two-digit multiplication can be represented on a 2 by 3 grid).

Chapter 24 Working with Multiplication, Division, and Proportional Reasoning

Figure 24.4 Cross-hatch or 'sticks' method for multiplying 43 × 56

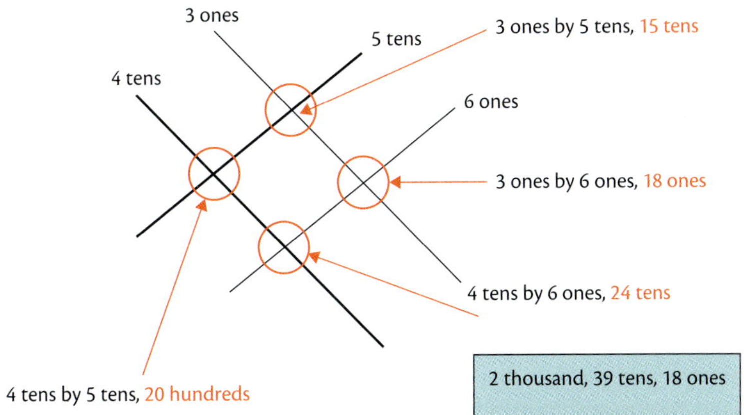

- 3 ones
- 5 tens
- 4 tens
- 6 ones
- 3 ones by 5 tens, 15 tens
- 3 ones by 6 ones, 18 ones
- 4 tens by 6 ones, 24 tens
- 4 tens by 5 tens, 20 hundreds

2 thousand, 39 tens, 18 ones
2 thousand, 40 tens, 8 ones
2408

consider and discuss

Alternative methods of multiplying

Use the lattice method of multiplication to solve the following problems. Include the names of the place-value parts as shown in Figure 24.3 in both cases. (HINT: Decide what place-value part belongs under the bottom right-hand corner first. Why?)

1. 742 × 395
2. 5.7 × 2.8

Use the cross-hatch or sticks method to multiply 456 × 21.

Consider and discuss what students need to know before using either of these methods.

How might these solutions be generalised?

did you know?

John Napier (1550–1617) is noted for promoting the use of logarithms. But he is also known for the ingenious set of rods he devised to support multi-digit multiplication. Napier's rods (sometimes referred to as Napier's bones) are regarded as the second calculating machine—the first being the abacus. These work in a similar way to the lattice method described above. Can you see why?

Figure 24.5 Napier's bones

The *area* idea, in which each part is multiplied by every other part, can be extended to support non-integer multiplication as shown in Figures 24.6 and 24.7. Fraction multiplication is inherently tied to proportion. As a consequence, for proper fractions it makes more sense to talk about 'of' rather than 'by' (e.g. $\frac{2}{3}$ of $\frac{3}{4}$). While common fraction representations can become problematic when mixed fractions are involved, this can be overcome by ensuring that the unit is clearly represented and that the language involved is generalised to 'by' rather than 'of' (e.g. $2\frac{3}{4}$ by $1\frac{4}{5}$). It is wise to pursue these models until students understand why multiplying numerators and multiplying denominators 'works' for fraction multiplication (e.g. fifths by halves give tenths, so 6 fifths by 5 halves give 30 tenths), as generalisation introduced too early or as a rule disconnected from a sense of what is happening to the total number of parts can lead to errors with fraction addition and subtraction.

For decimal fraction multiplication (e.g. 1.4 by 2.6), millimetre graph paper can be used to show that every part must multiply by every other part (in this case, ones by ones, tenths by ones and ones by tenths, and tenths by tenths). While the multiplication of decimal fractions clearly follows the same process as the multiplication of whole numbers, it is advisable to continue to work with models that show the effect of each part multiplying by every other part. In doing this careful attention should be paid to the language involved before considering the use of the more abstract models such as the one shown in Figure 24.7. After all, the idea here is to provide experiences to illustrate the *area* idea of multiplication and the notion of *this by that*.

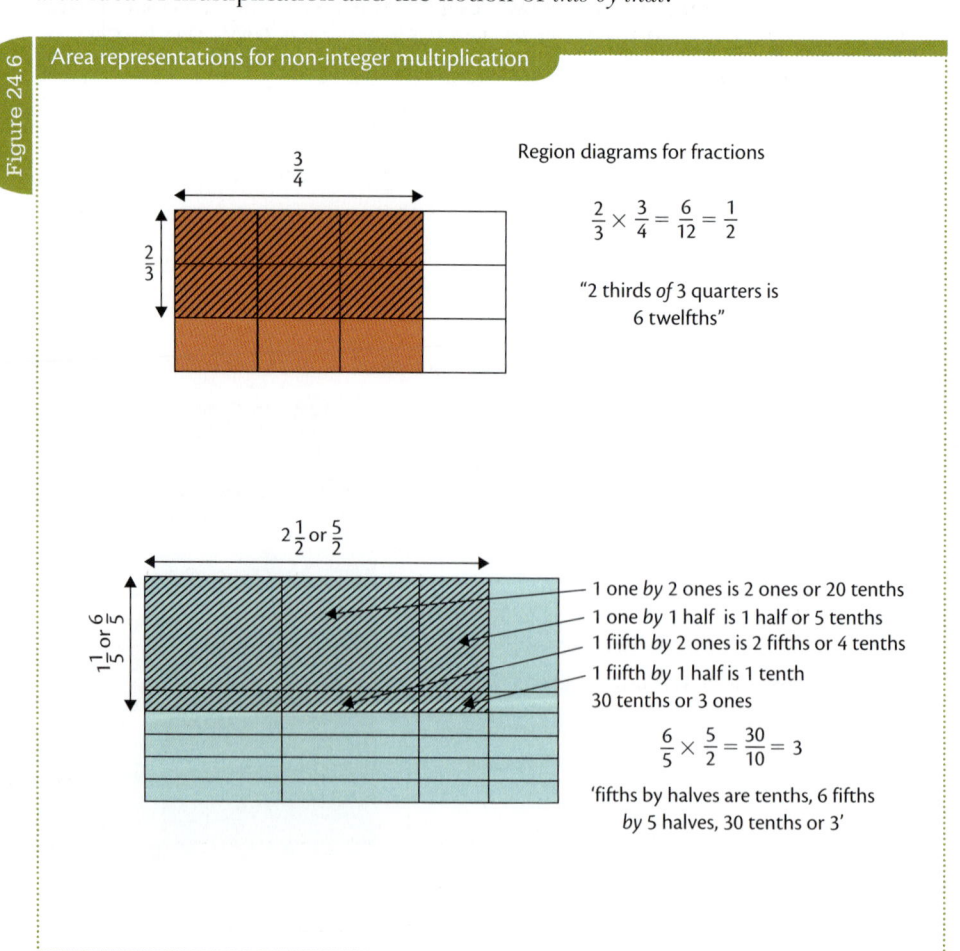

Figure 24.6 Area representations for non-integer multiplication

Region diagrams for fractions

$$\frac{2}{3} \times \frac{3}{4} = \frac{6}{12} = \frac{1}{2}$$

"2 thirds *of* 3 quarters is 6 twelfths"

1 one *by* 2 ones is 2 ones or 20 tenths
1 one *by* 1 half is 1 half or 5 tenths
1 fiifth *by* 2 ones is 2 fifths or 4 tenths
1 fiifth *by* 1 half is 1 tenth
30 tenths or 3 ones

$$\frac{6}{5} \times \frac{5}{2} = \frac{30}{10} = 3$$

'fifths by halves are tenths, 6 fifths *by* 5 halves, 30 tenths or 3'

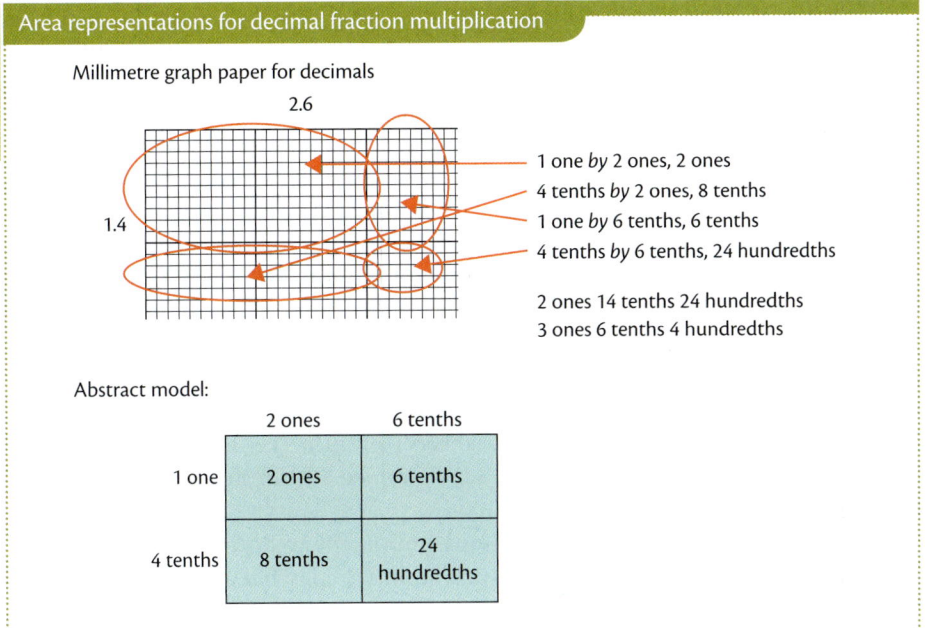

Figure 24.7 Area representations for decimal fraction multiplication

Cartesian product or *for each* idea

The **Cartesian product or 'for each' idea** is most generally associated with problems involving combinations, such as how many different outfits are possible given 4 pairs of pants, 3 tops and 2 jackets, or how many different lunch orders can be made up from 3 different types of bread, 5 different fillings, 4 choices of fruit and 5 choices of fruit juice. What distinguishes these products from other multiplicative situations is that the unit associated with the product (e.g. outfits) is different from any of the units that created it (e.g. pants, tops, jackets). This idea is connected to splitting (see Chapter 17) and is most commonly represented using a tree diagram or tables as shown in Figure 24.8.

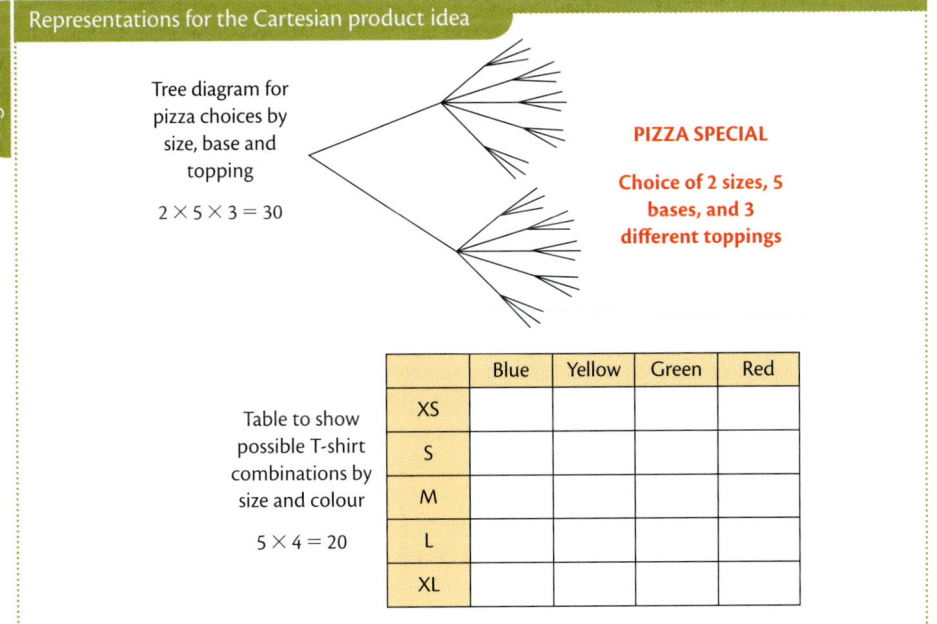

Figure 24.8 Representations for the Cartesian product idea

Tree diagrams and tables quickly become cumbersome as both the numbers involved and the number of variables increase. For instance, to determine how many different combinations are possible for numberplates involving 3 letters and 3 digits, it is necessary to reason using the *for each* idea. That is, as repetition is allowed, for each option of the first letter (26), there are 26 options for the second, and for each combination of first two letters, there are 26 options for the third. Furthermore, for each letter combination there are 10 options for the first digit, for each of these there are 10 options for the second digit, and finally, for each combination of 3 letters and 2 digits there are 10 options for the third digit, giving $26 \times 26 \times 26 \times 10 \times 10 \times 10$ possible numberplates.

The Cartesian product or *for each* idea is also useful, as we saw in Chapter 18, in helping students construct and understand fraction diagrams and line models. For example, to show where 4.27 'lives' on a number line, it is necessary to recognise that between 4 and 5 there are 10 tenths (i.e. for each 1 there are 10 tenths), and that between 4.2 and 4.3 there are 10 hundredths (i.e. for each tenth there are 10 hundredths).

The *for each* idea becomes increasingly important as students are exposed to problems involving event spaces and probability (e.g. what are your chances of winning Tattslotto?).

think + link

Issues involved in the teaching and learning of probability are considered in Chapter 28.

This idea is also involved in ratio, rate, and proportional reasoning problems. For example, while there are a number of different ways to find out how much concentrate and water is needed to make 12 litres of cordial given that the recipe calls for 2 parts concentrate to 6 parts of water, most would use the *for each* idea in one way or another as illustrated in the two solution strategies shown below.

Strategy A

2 : 6 is the same as 1 : 3

Need 1 litre of concentrate and 3 litres of water for each 4 litres

12 litres altogether so 3 × 1 : 3

So 3 litres of concentrate and 9 litres of water required

Strategy B

2 : 6 means 8 parts altogether

Find how many litres in one part: $\frac{12}{8}$ = 1.5 litres/part

2 parts concentrate = 2 × 1.5 litres = 3 litres of concentrate

6 parts water = 6 × 1.5 litres = 9 litres of water

Issues involved in working with ratios and rates are discussed further below.

consider and discuss

Relative **rate** problems have been around for a very long time, appearing on ancient Babylonian tablets and most major works on algebra. For example, consider what is involved in solving the following problem from 1559:

> An amphora of wine is placed before three mighty drinkers. The first can empty it in 24 hours, the second in 12 hours, and the third in 8 hours. How long will it take all three to empty the amphora? (reported in Mason, Pimm, Graham, & Gower, 1985, p. 81)

Chapter 24 Working with Multiplication, Division, and Proportional Reasoning

Division

There are two ideas for division, *quotition* (sometimes referred to as measurement division) and *partition* (or sharing). These have important implications for how fraction division is understood. The difference between the two forms depends upon the meaning attached to the **divisor**. For example, in the equation, 128 ÷ 8 = 16, the 8 can refer to either the number of groups (partitive division) or the number in each group (quotitive division). In the partitive case, the question is how many in each group/share, whereas in the quotitive case the question is how many 8s. These two meanings influence the sense that is made of '128 divided by 8' and the strategies adopted. For instance, the partitive interpretation leads to the 'think of multiplication' strategy (e.g. '8 what's are 128?'), whereas the quotitive interpretation leads to repeated subtraction/addition and a count of groups (e.g. 'how many 8s in 128?', '8 goes into 128 how many times?'). The quotitive interpretation becomes problematic when anything other than relatively small whole numbers or very simple common fractions is involved, and it is meaningless to think about how many xs in 10 for 10 ÷ x.

think + link

The quotition and partition ideas for division are discussed in more detail in Chapter 17.

Factor–factor–product idea

To work with fractions, algebraic texts, and more complex problems, students need to understand that for $a \times b = c$, a and b are both **factors** of c and that $\frac{c}{a} = b$ and $\frac{c}{b} = a$.

Ultimately, multiplication and division need to be understood as a single operator where dividing by b is recognised as equivalent to multiplying by $\frac{1}{b}$, or the *reciprocal* of b (e.g. that dividing by 8 is the same as multiplying by 0.125 or $\frac{1}{8}$). This is particularly useful when removing unwanted denominators to resolve fraction division situations, as we shall see below.

communicating mathematically

Multiple representations for multiplication

There are many ways of symbolically representing multiplication and division. For instance, while the multiplication sign is used in equations involving numbers (e.g. 456 × 27 or $4\frac{4}{5} \times 1\frac{1}{6}$), it is not used in expressions involving pronumerals (e.g. 3*ab*) but is included in expressions involving variables (e.g. A = *l* × *w*). In spreadsheet formulae, * is used to indicate multiplication and $a(b \pm c)$ is understood to mean $ab \pm ac$. These different forms can be confusing for students if not dealt with explicitly as they arise.

Working with an extended range of numbers

The option of choosing strategies appropriate to a problem-solving task is only available where students have developed a degree of procedural fluency based on conceptual understanding and have had plenty of opportunities to engage in mathematical problem solving and reasoning. That is, the four proficiencies included in the *Australian Curriculum: Mathematics* (ACARA, 2010) are interdependent; they cannot be treated in isolation. As a consequence, mathematics lessons should not be focused on the acquisition of a narrow set of particular procedures but on the knowledge and skills that students bring with them to the classroom. Exploring what can be done and why is not only enormously informative, it is the starting point for developing more efficient strategies. This requires systematic exposure to and discussion of the multiple ways in which problems can be represented and solved.

Unfortunately, school mathematics at this level is littered with well-intentioned shortcuts and 'rules', which are typically introduced after a few, carefully chosen examples and which students then are expected to apply and memorise (e.g. 'invert and multiply' for fraction division or 'multiply by 100 over 1 to change a fraction into a percentage'). This is hardly conducive to developing procedural fluency or conceptual understanding, and suggests to young learners that mathematics is all about learning and applying rules as opposed to thinking, reasoning, and justifying.

consider and discuss

What is involved in these everyday calculations?

1. You are considering renting a three-bedroom house with two friends. You find two suitable houses. The rent for the first one is $3460 per calendar month. The rent for the second one is $843 per week. Which house has the lower rent?
2. Driving in the country, you realise you have used more fuel than you expected. It appears that there is just under 1 eighth of a tank left and you estimate that you are at least 65 kilometres from the nearest town and petrol station. Will you make it?

Consider and discuss how you might go about solving these problems.

The first situation above requires an accurate analysis of the respective cost of the two houses, suggesting the use of digital tools is the most appropriate strategy. The second situation precludes an accurate calculation and demands some mental computation based on known facts about the capacity of the fuel tank, how the fuel gauge behaves at low levels, and the relative demands of the road ahead (steep hills use more fuel). Clearly, students need access to a range of strategies to operate effectively and confidently as numerate citizens.

In what follows we consider mental computation, estimation, and a range of written solution strategies, including algorithms. Digital tools are clearly an option but their use is either completely straightforward (e.g. performing any one or more of the four operations) or calculator-dependent, meaning that different brands of calculators function slightly differently when it comes to the use of registers, memory, and software to support fraction arithmetic. As a consequence we will not consider digital tools here in any detail. We will make the point, however, that when an answer is needed, use a calculator—when conceptual understanding, procedural fluency and/or mathematical reasoning is the objective, then it is wise to explore a range of alternative solution strategies.

Before proceeding, it is worth revisiting the general properties that apply across all number sets, namely commutativity, associativity, distributivity, and the notions of the multiplicative identity and inverse.

Useful properties

Understanding the invariant properties of operations can be extremely helpful, such as that the order in which two whole numbers are added or multiplied does not matter, whereas order does matter for subtraction and division. These properties are worth summarising here.

Commutativity and associativity

The commutative and associative properties of multiplication refer to the fact that the order in which numbers are multiplied does not matter: *commutativity* is restricted to two numbers (i.e. $a \times b = b \times a$), whereas *associativity* involves three or more numbers (e.g. $a \times b \times c = c \times a \times b$). The **associative property** is also represented as $a \times (b \times c) = (a \times b) \times c$.

Division is neither commutative nor associative, as the order in which the division is carried out does indeed make a difference to the outcome (try this for $56 \div 7 \div 2$).

Distributivity

The distributive property of multiplication over addition (and subtraction) refers to the fact that when multiplying two numbers, one number can be renamed as a sum or a difference and then each part multiplied separately and added (or subtracted) as required. Multiplication by parts is an extremely useful idea that we have already seen in relation to the array-based strategies for the multiplication facts (e.g. 6 sevens is 5 sevens and 1 more seven) and 2-digit multiplication, where each place-value part is multiplied by every other part. The distributive property is particularly useful in mental computation as we shall see below (other examples included in Table 10.1). It is written generally as:

$a(b + c) = ab + ac$ or $a(b - c) = ab - ac$ for any real numbers a, b, and c

Note that the multiplication sign is omitted in this case but included in the specific case:

$$6 \times (20 + 4) = (6 \times 20) + (6 \times 4)$$

Multiplicative identity and inverse

The *multiplicative identity* is the number that when multiplied by any non-zero number leaves the number unchanged. Obviously 1 satisfies this property for multiplication and division, just as 0, the additive identity, did for addition and subtraction. The *multiplicative inverse* of any number n is the number that when multiplied by n results in the multiplicative identity, 1. For example, 3 is the inverse of $\frac{1}{3}$ (and $\frac{1}{3}$ is the inverse of 3) as $\frac{1}{3} \times 3 = 1$ Another name for the multiplicative inverse of a number is the **reciprocal** (i.e. $\frac{1}{3}$ is the reciprocal of 3, $\frac{8}{5}$ is the reciprocal of $\frac{5}{8}$).

These properties are particularly useful when it comes to simplifying fractions and algebraic expressions, for example:

$$\frac{27}{48} = \frac{(3 \times 9)}{(3 \times 16)} = \frac{3}{3} \times \frac{9}{16} = \frac{9}{16}$$

This process, sometimes referred to as *cancelling*, is difficult for students who do not fully appreciate how numbers can be written in terms of their factors and the role of the multiplicative inverse.

consider and discuss

THOANs

Most of us at some time in our childhood would have been exposed to the playground classic, 'think of a number', referred to as THOANs by Mason et al. (1985). These have amused and amazed children and adults for many years, but few have ever considered why they work. Consider and discuss the following THOAN, then try to work out why it works.

THOAN. Triple it and take one-half the product. Triple this and take half the result. Now divide by nine. The quotient is one fourth of the original number (Mason et al., 1985, p. 80).

Properties of zero

While students have little difficulties with 0 eights, some experience difficulty with the notion of 8 zeros—it sounds like there are 8 'somethings'. Understanding why division by 0 is 'not allowed' or undefined is more complex. One way of demonstrating why this might be a useful convention is to take a number like 8 and progressively divide it by smaller and smaller decimal fractions on a calculator, noting what happens to the product as the divisor approaches 0. The same thing can be done from the 'other side' of 0 by dividing 8 by increasingly smaller negative decimal fractions. (Note that different calculators have different conventions about how to do this.) This usually generates a rich discussion, after which most students generally agree division by 0 is better left alone.

$8 \div 1 = 8$ $\qquad$ $8 \div -1 = -8$
$8 \div 0.1 = 80$ $\qquad$ $8 \div -0.1 = -80$
$8 \div 0.01 = 800$ $\qquad$ $8 \div -0.01 = -800$
$8 \div 0.001 = 8000$ $\qquad$ $8 \div -0.001 = -8000$
$8 \div 0.0001 = 80\,000$ $\qquad$ $8 \div -0.0001 = -80\,000$
$8 \div 0.000\,01 = 800\,000$ $\qquad$ $8 \div -0.000\,01 = -800\,000$
$8 \div 0.000\,001 = 8\,000\,000$ $\qquad$ $8 \div -0.000\,001 = -8\,000\,000$
$8 \div 0.000\,000\,1 = 80\,000\,000$ $\qquad$ $8 \div -0.000\,000\,1 = -80\,000\,000$

Order of operations

The order in which multiple operations are carried out used to be governed by rules with acronyms like BODMAS or BOMDAS. These were typically introduced as conventions to avoid errors after considering a few, carefully chosen examples. In general, the conventions governing the order of operations are only required in decontextualised situations such as $3 \times 4 + 5$, as problem context generally clarifies what is required; for example 'Janine bought 3 bags of fruit, each one containing 4 apples and 5 oranges. How many pieces of fruit did she buy?' In this case, the context dictates that 4 and 5 are added together then multiplied by 3 to get 27 pieces of fruit. However, in the decontextualised setting 3 would be multiplied by 4, then the 5 added to give 17.

This issue first arises in situations involving multiple applications of the same operation. For addition and multiplication, irrespective of the number of times the operations are used, the order of operating does not matter as these operations are associative (e.g. $6 + 8 + 13 + 4 = 13 + 4 + 6 + 8$ and $3 \times 7 \times 2 = 2 \times 3 \times 7$). But for subtraction and division, the order does matter (e.g. 16 − 9 − 5 ≠ 16 − 4 and 32 ÷ 8 ÷ 2 ≠ 32 ÷ 4). Situations involving multiple applications of either subtraction or division can only be completed accurately if they are dealt with from left to right.

Situations involving different operations can be ambiguous even when the problem situation points to what is required. For instance, consider the problem 'Skate hire was based on a flat fee of $8 and $3 per hour. What did Mary have to pay if she hired skates for 4 hours?' This situation could either be expressed as 8 + 3 × 4 or as 3 × 4 + 8. Working from left to right would give $44 in the first case and $20 in the second case. Clearly, an additional understanding is required, which is always to complete any multiplication or division before adding or subtracting. This is modified if sense demands, for example 'Ms Green bought 2 red pens and 5 blue pens for each of her 3 children. How many pens did she buy?' In this case, we need to know the number of pens per child before we multiply, so brackets are used to indicate that this calculation needs to be carried out first, that is, (2 + 5) × 3 or 3 × (2 + 5).

As these understandings progressively override one another the sequence is best described as follows:

1. Complete any calculations within brackets.
2. Do any multiplication or division before adding or subtracting.
3. Work from left to right.

for the classroom

Use the problems above and create some others that are similar to build an instructional sequence that explores the steps for determining the order of operations in more detail.

Explore the various options on a calculator working from left to right. What do you notice?

Whole numbers and decimal fractions

Mental strategies

Many of the strategies explored in Chapters 10, 16, and 17 can be used to support mental computation involving whole number multiplication and division at this level. For example, for 6 × 57 a number of strategies are possible. Note, these are written as *thinking strings* as the use of signs and symbols is suggestive of written strategies.

- Think: 5 and 1 more group, 570, 285, 292, 342
- Think: 3 groups, 150, 171, doubled, 342
- Think: place-value parts, 300, 342
- Think: rename, 360 less 18, 342

Mental computation at this level requires a sound knowledge of number facts and/or access to efficient mental strategies such as *doubling* and *making to 10*. One way of reinforcing number fact knowledge at this level is to use the strategies outlined in Chapter 17 with 2-digit numbers (e.g. 3 thirty-fours, Think: double and 1 more group, 68, 98, 102).

It is also worth 'unpacking' these mental strategies in symbolic form to ensure that the strategies are understood and as a means of developing alternative forms of written computation.

for the classroom

Invite students to annotate thinking strings as a means of making the various strategies transparent and establishing a common language for discussion. Some examples to consider for 8 × 42:

    42, 84, 168, 336 (double double double)
    320, 336 (by parts)
    420, 400, 336 (2 groups less than 10 groups)
    56, 112, 336 (factors)

This task can also be used as an assessment task once students are familiar with what is required (i.e. describe/label the thinking or strategy involved).

While short-term memory limits how many numbers can be managed at any one time, some individuals have been known to be able to mentally calculate the product of two 3-digit numbers (see Consider and discuss below).

consider and discuss

A prodigious calculator

George Bidder amazed people with his ability to multiply large numbers rapidly and accurately. There have been a number of others with apparent special gifts at computation. Investigation reveals that these people have strategies and techniques that they have perfected through practice. Find out what you can about George Bidder's method and discuss how this relates to the ideas for multiplication discussed above.

Adapted from Bolt and Hobbs (1993, p. 82).

The mental strategy for division is 'think of multiplication'. While this can be tricky, as it involves keeping track of the numbers involved, it can be used to support estimations. For example, 368 divided by 7 is going to be about fifty something, since 7 by 5 tens is 350; 18 remain so enough for 2 more per share, so 52 and 4 remainder.

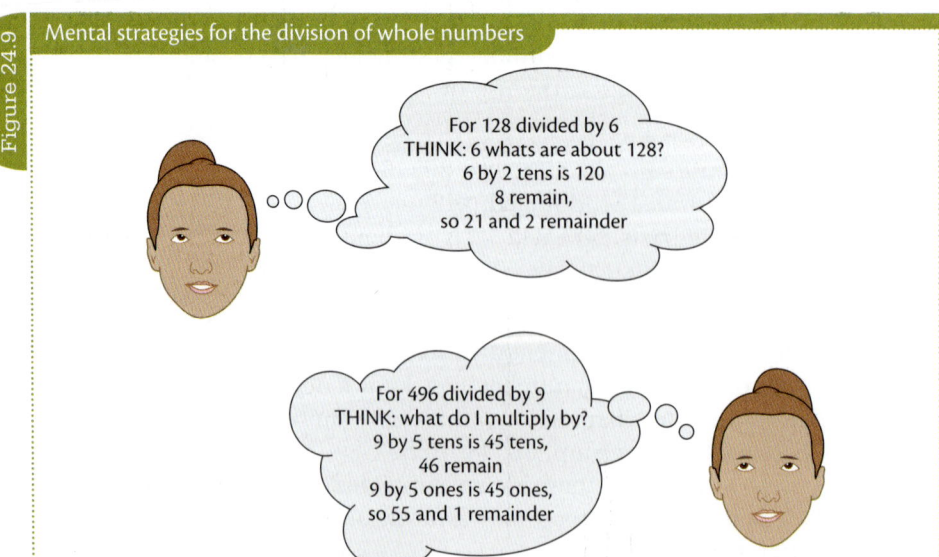

Figure 24.9 Mental strategies for the division of whole numbers

Situations requiring mental computation with decimal fractions are far less common but they do arise, for example in measurement problems such as deciding whether or not enough carpet remains to carpet an additional small room. In real situations these calculations are either important enough to be done with a calculator or an approximation is sufficient. It is important to recognise that, while money 'looks like' decimal fractions, in fact the thinking and the language is different. This is illustrated in Figure 24.10. It can cause problems with written computation involving decimal fractions if these differences are not noted.

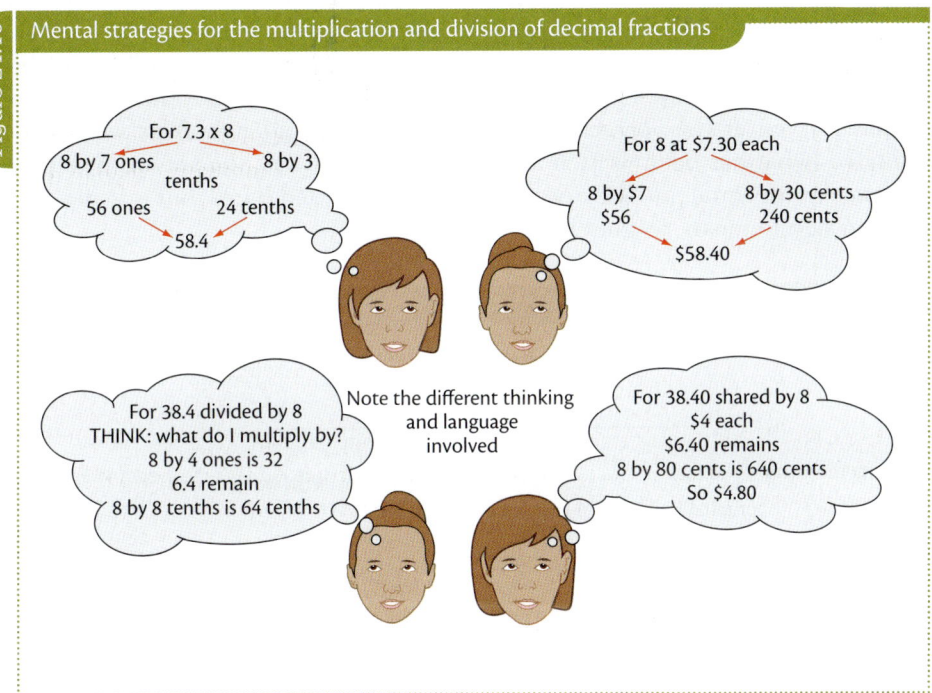

Figure 24.10 Mental strategies for the multiplication and division of decimal fractions

Estimation and approximation

The distinction between estimation and approximation was discussed in Chapter 23. Essentially, an approximation is made when decisions are made about the degree of accuracy required, whereas estimation involves more of an 'educated guess' based on common-sense assumptions. Estimates are usually made in the absence of any real data (e.g. estimate the number of counters in a jar) but approximations, such as the carpet situation above, are based on data that is often rounded to give an approximate solution. In a situation such as 2.4 × 6.2, one strategy is to rename this as about 2 and half times 6, that is, 15, which, if we consider the partial products 12, 0.4, 2.4, 0.08, is a fairly good approximation.

Written solution strategies

The vast majority of computational problems involving positive whole numbers or decimal fractions arise in contexts where it is both sensible and appropriate to use digital tools. As a consequence, the focus here will be on understanding the language and thinking involved in connecting the ideas for multiplication and division to written recording, equivalence, and the use of the number properties described above.

There are many different ways to record whole number calculations but one of the most fundamental is the use of equivalent number sentences or expressions. In the past the focus has been on developing number facts and introducing algorithms with little or no attention to equivalent forms of representation. This has meant that many students in the middle years have found it difficult to create their own mathematical texts, particularly for multiple-step problems such the 'medicine doses' problem (Beesey, Clarke, Clarke, Stephens & Sullivan, 1998), which was used in the Middle Years Numeracy Research Project (Siemon et al., 2001). The problem required students to use the rule: Child dose = Adult dose $\times \frac{\text{Age}}{(\text{Age} + 12)}$ to find (a) the dose for a 6-year-old child if the adult dose was 15 mL, and (b) the adult dose given that the dose for an 8-year-old boy was 6 mL. Figure 24.11 shows a Year 7 student's responses to each of these questions. What is interesting here is that although he has arrived at the correct solution for part (a), and it is clear what was intended, what has been written actually makes no sense: the second number sentence is not equal, and he does not mean '18 divided by 90' but is using the division sign to mean '18 goes into 90'.

Figure 24.11 Year 7 student's response to medicine dose problem

$$\text{Child dose} = \text{Adult dose} \times \frac{\text{Age}}{\text{Age} + 12}$$

(a) If the adult dose for a particular medication is 15 mL, what would be the appropriate dose for a 6-year-old child?

15 mL × 6 = 90 mL   6 + 12 = 18 ÷ 90 = 5 mLs

(b) A nurse used the formula to work out the dose for an 8-year-old boy. She correctly calculates it as 6 mL. What was the adult dose in this case?

15 mL × 8 = 120 mL   8 + 12 = 20 ÷ 120 = 6 mL

His response to part (b) assumes the adult dose from part (a) and that the calculation is exactly the same, when in fact it requires the rule to be manipulated (i.e. 6 = Adult dose × $\frac{8}{20}$). It is completely fortuitous that the adult dose in this case is 15 mL. Responses such as these are not atypical. They reflect the fact that too much emphasis has been placed on the use of formal algorithms (e.g. long multiplication and division) at the expense of working with equivalence and number properties.

Hopefully this situation will change with the inclusion of a content statement about using 'equivalent number sentences involving multiplication and division to find unknown quantities' in Year 5 of the *Australian Curriculum: Mathematics* (ACARA, 2010). As indicated above, mental strategies provide a fertile ground for 'unpacking' what is involved, and this should be encouraged from the middle primary years. For example, the mental strategies used on page 573 to calculate 6 by 57 can be 'unpacked' and justified as follows:

$6 \times 57 = (5 + 1) \times 57$ distributive property
$= (5 \times 57) + (1 \times 57)$
$= \frac{570}{2} + 57$ on the grounds that 5 of anything is half of 10 of it
$= 285 + 57$
$= 342$

$6 \times 57 = 2 \times (3 \times 57)$ associative property
$= 2 \times (171)$ doubling
$= 342$

$6 \times 57 = 6 \times (50 + 7)$ distributive property
$= (6 \times 50) + (6 \times 7)$
$= 300 + 42$
$= 342$

$6 \times 57 = 6 \times (60 - 3)$ distributive property
$= (6 \times 60) - (6 \times 3)$
$= 360 - 18$
$= 342$

While this may seem tedious, the point of this exercise is not to find answers but to model how equivalent number sentences can be used in conjunction with the properties of the real numbers under multiplication and addition to create texts that are understood by others and stand as justifications of particular solution strategies. This will also help to underpin students' confidence in working with algebraic texts at a later stage.

While these methods can also be applied to multi-digit situations such as 438×17, where it is helpful to recognise the **multiples** of 10 and partial products, this quickly becomes tedious and defeats the point of the exercise.

Use of factors

The use of the associative property justifies multiplication and division by factors, for example, 367×28 and $864 \div 9$.

```
    367          3 √864
  ×   7          3 √286
   2 569            96
  ×   4
  10 267
```

This feature is often not recognised, with the result that many students reach for the calculator when it might actually be simpler and easier to use factors, particularly if only an approximation is required.

Long multiplication

The algorithm referred to as 'long multiplication' is simply a systematic way of recording multi-digit multiplication problems in a way which ensures that every part is multiplied by every other part. As we have already considered this in relation to the *area* idea for multiplication, we review only the language here (Table 24.1).

Part 5: Extending Mathematics to the Middle Years

Table 24.1 Language and recording for 2-digit by 2-digit multiplication

Language	Recording
Ones by ones: 3 ones by 8 ones, 24 ones Record the ones with the ones and the tens to regroup	58 × ₂43 ——— 4
Ones by tens: 3 ones by 5 tens, 15 tens And 2 tens more, 17 tens, record with the tens	58 × ₂43 ——— 174
Tens by ones: 4 tens by 8 ones, 32 tens Record the tens with the tens—there are 0 ones—and the hundreds to regroup	58 × ₃₂43 ——— 174 20
Tens by tens: 4 tens by 5 tens, 20 hundreds And 3 hundreds more, 23 hundreds, record with the hundreds	58 × ₃₂43 ——— 174 2320
Sum the partial products:	58 × ₃₂43 ——— 174 2320 ——— 2494

did you know?

Long multiplication was routinely expected of Year 5 students attending school in the mid to late 1800s. Without calculating machines, there was a high priority on accuracy and neatness as shown in this excerpt from a fifth-grade exercise book in 1863, which illustrates the procedure for multiplying two recurring decimal fractions.

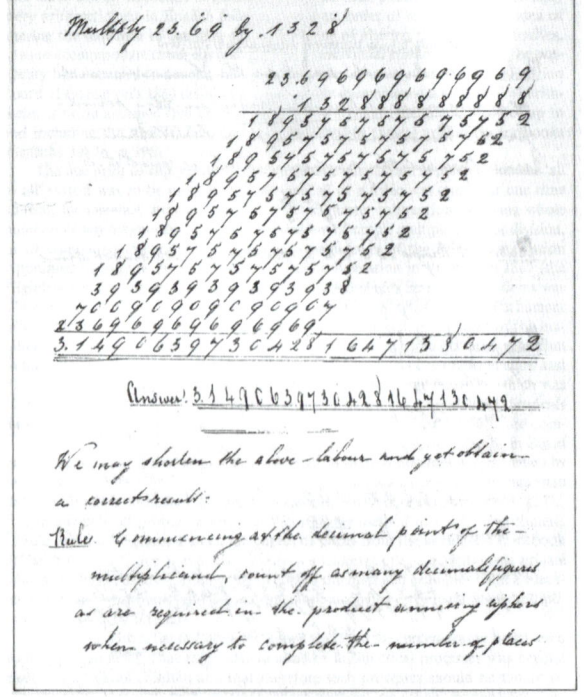

Figure 24.12 Long multiplication in 1863

As the language involved in multiplying decimal fractions becomes cumbersome, it is useful to rename these and treat as whole numbers. For example, 5.8 × 4.3 can be renamed as 58 tenths by 43 tenths and the product calculated as shown above. However, as tenths by tenths are hundredths, the product needs to be read as 2494 hundredths or 24.94. Exploring many examples will lead to the generalisation that the number of decimal places in the product is equal to the sum of the number of decimal places in the factors.

It is important to give students plenty of opportunities to estimate decimal **products** and **quotients** to help develop their sense of the relative magnitude of decimal fractions and how they behave when multiplied and divided.

Formal division

The two forms of division lead to two very different algorithms, at least in terms of the thinking and language involved. As quotition division is concerned with the number of groups in a given number, it leads to the language of 'goes into' and 'carry'. While this 'works' in terms of arriving at an answer, it comes at a cost in terms of meaning. For a start, asking how many sevens in 5971 can really only be answered meaningfully by a count of sevens, which is clearly tedious. The language of 'goes into' is also unhelpful, as it means nothing sensible in its own right and needs to be translated as 'how many sevens in …?'. This can lead to errors like the one seen in Figure 24.11 where '18 ÷ 90' is interpreted as '18 goes into 90'. The term 'carry' is also unhelpful in this context; while children can be taught that it means 'write what is left over beside the next number and read it as a 2-digit number', this ignores what is actually happening here in terms of place-value parts.

By contrast, the partitive division language is concerned with how many in each of 7 groups. Instead of thinking about how many sevens in 5971, this leads to the idea of '7 groups of what are 5971'. This immediately suggests something in the 800s, as 7 by 8 hundreds is 56 hundreds. The language associated with partition is the language of sharing, which relates directly to place-value parts. The processes of trading and renaming respect what is happening as the larger 'chunks' are shared.

Table 24.2 Contrasting the two forms of division

Quotition division		Partition division	
Language		Language	
Does 7 'go into' 5?	8 5 3	Can 5 thousands be shared among 7?	8 5 3
No, 'carry' 5	7 √5⁵9³7²1	No.	7 √5 9 7 1
Does 7 'go into' 59?		Trade for hundreds.	5 6
Yes, 8 and 3 left over, write 8 and 'carry' 3		Can 59 hundreds be shared among 7?	3 7 tens
		Yes, 8 each with 3 hundreds left to share. Trade for tens.	3 5
Does 7 'go into' 37?			2 1 ones
Yes, 5 and 2 left over, write 5 and 'carry' 2		Can 37 tens be shared among 7?	2 1
		Yes 5 tens each with 2 tens left to share. Trade for ones.	0
Does 7 'go into' 21?		21 ones shared among 7	
Yes, 3 times, 0 left over		3 ones each	

The two ideas also lead to different interpretations of the remainder. In a situation such as 326 divided by 5, the remainder in quotition division (how many fives in 326) is most naturally interpreted as what fraction of 5 remains—in this case 1 remains, so the quotient would be expressed as $65\frac{1}{5}$. For partition, the remainder can be further traded and 'shared', that is 10 tenths shared among 5 is 2, and the quotient would be expressed as 65.2.

issues in teaching

Long division

Many believe that long division is a thing of the past, but in fact it can be seen as a sensible question and answer story that supports division with decimal remainders and division more generally (e.g. $2x^2 + 5x + 3$ divided by $(x + 1)$). There is still an argument for working with long division even though in most cases it makes sense to use digital tools to carry out complex divisions. The main arguments raised against long division appear to be:

- It's too long and complicated.
- What's wrong with 'goes into'—it works?
- It's not necessary—easier and quicker on a calculator.

Use long division to solve 1613.24 divided by 31.

Rename the numbers involved to solve 57.4 divided by 5.6.

In both cases, consider the opportunities for teaching that arise as a result of working this way.

Where division needs to be carried out using an algorithm it makes sense to draw on the ideas that underpin partition division—while the language of sharing will eventually be replaced by 'what do I multiply by', number expanders and estimation are useful in supporting the language and thinking involved.

Table 24.3 Materials, language, and recording to support decimal division

Materials (number expander)	Language	Recording

4 hundreds 6 tens 4 ones 7 tenths 2 hundredths	464.72 divided by 37
	Can we share hundreds? No.
	Rename as 46 tens.
	THINK: 37 whats are 46 tens?
	37 by 1 ten, record in tens place.
	How many left to share?
	9 tens, trade for ones.
		.1
		37)464.72
		   37
		   ―
		   9 4 ones

4 6 tens 4 ones 7 tenths 2 hundredths		

9 4 ones 7 tenths 2 hundredths	Can we share 94 ones among 37?
	Yes, 2 ones each.
	Record 2 in the ones place.
	How many shared? 74
	How many left to share?
	20 ones, trade for tenths.
		1 2.
		37)464.72
		   37
		   ―
		   9 4 ones
		   7 4
		   ―
		  2 0 7 tenths

2 0 7 tenths 2 hundredths	Can we share 207 tenths? Yes.
	THINK: 37 whats are 207?
	37 by 5 tenths, record in the tenths place.
	How many shared? 185
	How many left to share?
	22 tenths, trade for hundredths.
		1 2.5
		37)464.72
		   37
		   ―
		   9 4 ones
		   7 4
		   ―
		  2 0 7 tenths
		  1 8 5
		  ―
		   2 2 2 hundredths
		   2 2 2
		   ―
		     0

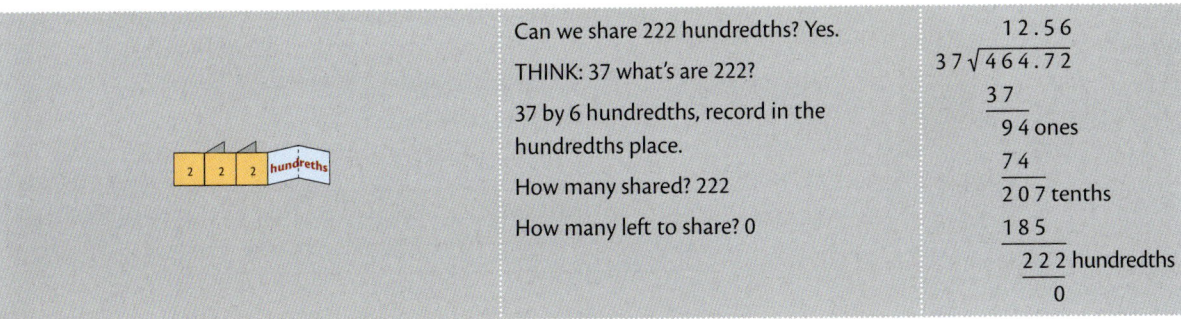

integrating technology/ICT

Spreadsheets

Spreadsheets are a wonderful tool for modelling complex situations such as the impact of a change in the price of oil on the price of household goods and services. Spreadsheets are used widely in finance and commerce as well as science to explore 'what if' scenarios and to collate and analyse data.

At the school level they can be used to support investigations and carry out a large number of calculations that would otherwise be tedious. From the teacher's perspective they are valuable in collating results of differently weighted assignments over the course of a semester.

consider and discuss

Using spreadsheets to track student results

At Angie's school, all feedback to students is given in terms of letter grades supported by rubrics, but it is left up to individual teachers to decide on the overall grade awarded at the end of each semester. Recognising that it would be unfair to simply count the number of As and Bs etc. across a range of very different tasks, some much easier than others, Angie wants to set up a spreadsheet that respects these differences to ensure that the overall result reflects the quality of students' work as accurately as possible. Her tasks are:

1. Task 1 (worth 10%), evaluated on a 4-point scale (A to D) where D means barely satisfactory/resubmit
2. Task 2 (worth 30%), evaluated on a 6-point scale (A to F) where F indicates well below satisfactory
3. Task 3 (worth 15%), evaluated on a 4-point scale (A to D) where D means barely satisfactory/resubmit
4. Task 4 (worth 20%), evaluated on a 6-point scale (A to F) where F indicates well below satisfactory
5. Task 5 (worth 25%), evaluated on a 6-point scale (A to F) where F indicates well below satisfactory.

Consider and discuss how Angie might set up her spreadsheet. What assumptions need to be made? How can the different weightings be incorporated into one formula to deliver a single overall result?

Fraction multiplication and division

As fractions are inherently multiplicative, multiplying and dividing fractions is in many respects more straightforward than adding and subtracting fractions. As we have already seen, the 'of' idea for multiplication is generally associated with multiplication of a number by a proper fraction, while the 'times as many' or 'by' idea tends to be associated with the multiplication of mixed numbers or improper fractions.

Area diagrams can be used effectively to show why fraction multiplication involves multiplying denominators by denominators and numerators by numerators (e.g. see Figure 24.13). As this observation can lead some students

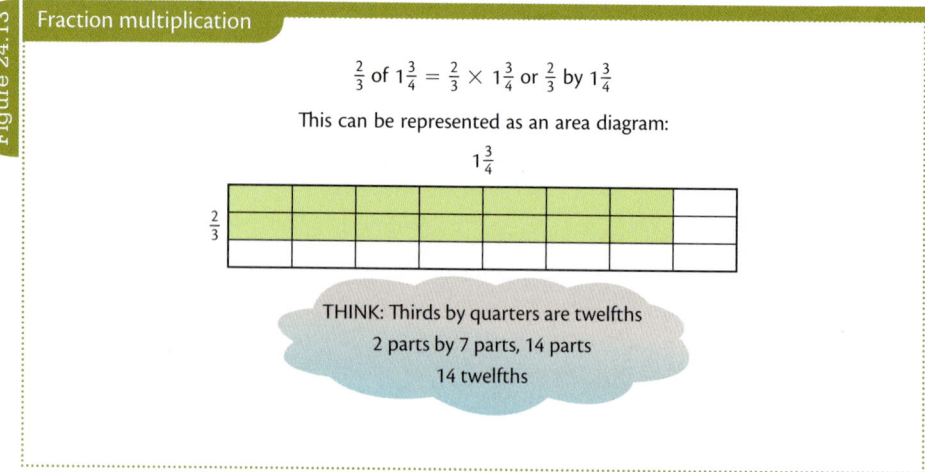

Figure 24.13 Fraction multiplication

to think that the same applies for addition and subtraction, considerable care needs to be taken to ensure students are familiar with the meanings and representations of the respective operations.

Fraction diagrams and line models (e.g. see Figure 24.6) can also be used to demonstrate that multiplication does not always 'make larger'. In particular, the area idea for multiplication and the operator idea for fractions (see Chapters 18 and 22) can be used to show that multiplying by a fraction such as a half, third, fifth, quarter etc. is equivalent to dividing by 2, 3, 5, and 4 respectively. This 'converts' multiplication of a number by a fraction into whole number operations. For example,

$$24 \times \tfrac{2}{3} = (24 \div 3) \times 2 = 8 \times 2 = 16$$

Mental computation

Apart from very simple common fractions (e.g. $\tfrac{1}{2}$ of $\tfrac{3}{4}$, $6 \div \tfrac{2}{3}$) there is not much call to multiply and divide fractions mentally. Unlike fraction addition and subtraction, which needs to be developed over time (e.g. see Chapters 18 and 23), fraction multiplication is supported by *partitioning* and the *area* idea for multiplication (e.g. fifths by thirds are fifteenths). In many ways there is an argument for dealing with fraction multiplication before addition and subtraction, as it is this that underpins the strategies for renaming fractions in equivalent forms.

Calculating with percentages

The most common demand for mental computation involving fractions relates to percentages. As mentioned in previous chapters, a sense of percentages needs to be developed based on benchmarks such as a half and halving.

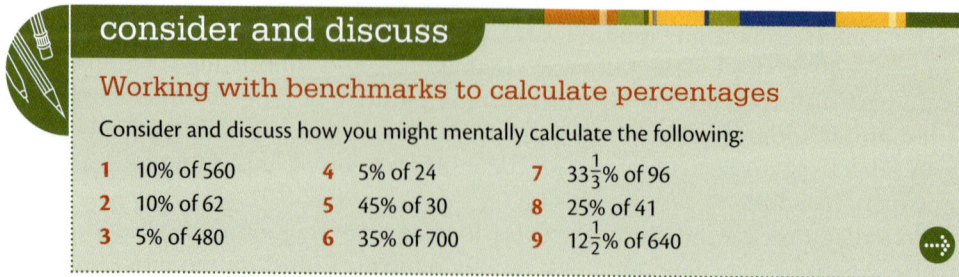

consider and discuss

Working with benchmarks to calculate percentages

Consider and discuss how you might mentally calculate the following:

1. 10% of 560
2. 10% of 62
3. 5% of 480
4. 5% of 24
5. 45% of 30
6. 35% of 700
7. $33\tfrac{1}{3}$% of 96
8. 25% of 41
9. $12\tfrac{1}{2}$% of 640

Percentages are also used to describe increases. Consider and discuss what is involved in the following.

10 $60 increased by 30%
11 125% of 42
12 300% of 70

What traps might there be here, and why?

One of the least necessary keys on a calculator is the per cent key. The misconception that you need to 'multiply a fraction by 100 over 1 and divide' to convert a fraction into a percentage is misleading, as it is makes it look as though we are dealing with whole numbers when in fact percentages are hundredths. It is much better to actually carry out the division, for example:

$\frac{5}{8}$ means 5 divided by 8 which is 0.625

Reading to the hundredths place and renaming in terms of hundredths, this is 62.5 hundredths or 62.5%.

This would lead to a better understanding of percentages as fractions (see Chapters 18 and 22) and a deeper appreciation of what this means in terms of calculation. For instance, to find the price of a garment that has been reduced by 45% it is sufficient to multiply the price by 0.55.

Written solution strategies

Fraction multiplication

Fraction multiplication, as we have already seen, is well supported by partitioning and area diagrams. While these lead to the generalisation that $\frac{a}{b} \times \frac{c}{d} = \frac{(a \times c)}{(b \times d)}$, it is also useful to recognise that, just as there are four partial products when a 2-digit number is multiplied by another 2-digit number, there are four partial products when two mixed numbers are multiplied together. This gives rise to the use of the distributive property in the same way that it was used above for 2-digit multiplication (see Figure 24.14). However, in this case, adding the partial products is not as straightforward as working with the improper fractions involved, that is, $\frac{7}{3} \times \frac{9}{5}$, which results in $\frac{63}{15}$ or 4 and $\frac{3}{15}$ more directly.

Figure 24.14 Using the distributive property

	1	$\frac{4}{5}$
2	$2 \times 1 = 2$	$2 \times \frac{4}{5} = \frac{8}{5}$
$\frac{1}{3}$	$\frac{1}{3} \times 1 = \frac{1}{3}$	$\frac{1}{3} \times \frac{4}{5} = \frac{4}{15}$

$$2\tfrac{1}{3} \times 1\tfrac{4}{5} = 2 + \tfrac{1}{3} + \tfrac{8}{5} + \tfrac{4}{15}$$
$$= 2 + \tfrac{4}{15} + \tfrac{24}{15} + \tfrac{4}{15}$$
$$= 2 + \tfrac{33}{15}$$
$$= 4\tfrac{3}{15}$$
$$= 4\tfrac{1}{15}$$

Fraction division

While 'invert and multiply' is arguably one of the best remembered rules in school mathematics, very few adults or students have a clear understanding of why this rule is used. This is because it is typically derived from a few very carefully chosen examples, generally with reference to only one of the two ideas for division, that is, quotition, and then applied and practised in a procedural way devoid of meaning. For example, most secondary texts will use examples such as $2\frac{1}{2} \div \frac{1}{2}$, $4 \div \frac{2}{3}$, and $\frac{3}{4} \div \frac{1}{8}$ and the notion of 'goes into', that is, how many halves in $2\frac{1}{2}$, how many $\frac{2}{3}$ in 4, and how many $\frac{1}{8}$ in $\frac{3}{4}$, to establish that dividing by a fraction is the same as multiplying by its reciprocal (in other words, the 'invert and multiply' rule). This is unsatisfactory in a climate of inquiry where explanations and justifications are expected.

Fraction division can and should be interpreted in terms of the two ideas for division. As we have seen, quotitive division interprets the divisor as the size of the group and asks how many of these 'groups' are there in the dividend or number to be divided. Another way to interpret this form of division is measurement, where the divisor is seen as the 'unit' and the question becomes what the measure of the **dividend** is in terms of this unit (i.e. how many units are needed to 'measure' this amount). In both cases, the solution strategy invariably involves counting 'groups' or 'units' (e.g. there are 5 halves in $2\frac{1}{2}$). Interestingly, the textbooks rarely include examples such as $\frac{1}{5} \div 3\frac{5}{6}$ in the carefully chosen, introductory examples.

By contrast, partitive division interprets the divisor as the number of shares and asks how many in each share. For example, from a partitive perspective, $24 \div 6$ means that 6 shares is 24 and the task is to find 1 share. By analogy, this means that for $\frac{3}{4} \div \frac{1}{8}$, a partitive interpretation would be that $\frac{1}{8}$ share is $\frac{3}{4}$, so what is 1 share? That is, 1 share is $8 \times \frac{3}{4} = 6$. But more importantly, partition division leads to the question, 'what do I have to multiply by?'. In this case, $\frac{1}{8} \times ? = \frac{3}{4}$.

Consider the following problems.

1. The recipe for pumpkin scones calls for $\frac{3}{4}$ cup of mashed pumpkin. As a result of cooking a whole pumpkin, Jo had 6 cups of mashed pumpkin. How many batches of pumpkin scones can she bake?
2. Adele likes to walk around the lake. It takes her $\frac{3}{4}$ of an hour to walk $2\frac{1}{2}$ times around the lake. Assuming she continues to walk at the same rate, how far around the lake will she walk in 1 hour?

The first problem requires that we find how many $\frac{3}{4}$ cups there are in 6 cups. A counting approach might be: 2 recipes from $1\frac{1}{2}$ cups, 4 recipes from 3 cups, so 8 recipes from 6 cups. Alternatively, the total number of quarters could be found by multiplying 6 by 4 (i.e. 24 quarters), then as 3 quarters of a cup is required for each recipe the problem becomes $24 \div 3 = 8$. Note that this is equivalent to multiplying 6 by the reciprocal of $\frac{3}{4}$.

The second problem requires that we find how far Adele would walk in 1 hour. A first step might be to find how far around the lake she walks in 1 quarter of an hour. This requires dividing $2\frac{1}{2}$ by 3, which is equivalent to finding $\frac{1}{3}$ of $\frac{5}{2}$ (think: thirds by halves are sixths, 1 part by 5 parts is 5 parts, so 5 sixths). Having found how far around the lake she can walk in 1 quarter of an hour (i.e. $\frac{5}{6}$ of a circuit), we can multiply y by 4 to find how many times around the lake she would walk in 1 hour. In this case, $\frac{10}{3}$ or $3\frac{1}{3}$ times around the lake. Note again, that this is equivalent to multiplying $2\frac{1}{2}$ by the reciprocal of $\frac{3}{4}$.

Chapter 24 Working with Multiplication, Division, and Proportional Reasoning

While fraction diagrams and line models can be used with carefully chosen examples to demonstrate why dividing by a fraction is the same as multiplying by its reciprocal, a more powerful explanation derives from the use of the multiplicative inverse as shown in Figure 24.15.

Figure 24.15 Two approaches to fraction division

$$\frac{1}{5} \div 3\frac{5}{6} = \frac{\frac{1}{5}}{\frac{23}{6}}$$
← Can simplify this by multiplying by the multiplicative inverse

$$= \frac{\frac{1}{5} \times \frac{6}{23}}{1 \frac{\cancel{23}}{\cancel{6}} \times \frac{\cancel{6}}{\cancel{23}}}$$
← But to preserve equality, the numerator also needs to be multiplied by this number

$$= \frac{1}{5} \times \frac{6}{23}$$

$$= \frac{6}{115}$$

Alternatively, $\frac{1}{2} \div 3\frac{5}{6}$

Implies that there is a number, m, such that

$$3\frac{5}{6} \times m = \frac{1}{5}$$

$$\frac{23}{6} \times m = \frac{1}{5}$$

Multiplying by the multiplicative inverse

$$1 \frac{\cancel{6}}{\cancel{23}} \times \frac{\cancel{23}}{\cancel{6}} \, m = \frac{1}{5} \times \frac{6}{23}$$

$$m = \frac{6}{115}$$

making connections

The processes involved in Figure 24.15 are essentially algebraic. To ensure you understand what is involved, work through both approaches for $\frac{a}{b} \div \frac{c}{d}$ to convince yourself that dividing by a number—any number—is the same as multiplying by its reciprocal.

Integers

Integer arithmetic is typically introduced in Year 8. We briefly review addition and subtraction before moving on to multiplication and division of integers.

One of the major sources of difficulty experienced by students is that the signs + and – are used to denote two separate notions: the familiar operations of addition and subtraction, and the less familiar status of the number in terms of positive and negative. The distinction between *operator* and *state* can be represented in many different ways for teaching purposes. For instance the operations of addition and subtraction can be represented respectively by walking backwards or forwards and the states by the direction faced—left or right. Coloured buttons (e.g. blue and red) or up and down arrows (↑ and ↓) can be used to distinguish between positive and negative numbers as shown in Figure 24.16. Activities with these representations lead to the generalisations:

- Adding a negative is the same as subtracting a positive.
- Subtracting a negative is the same as adding a positive.

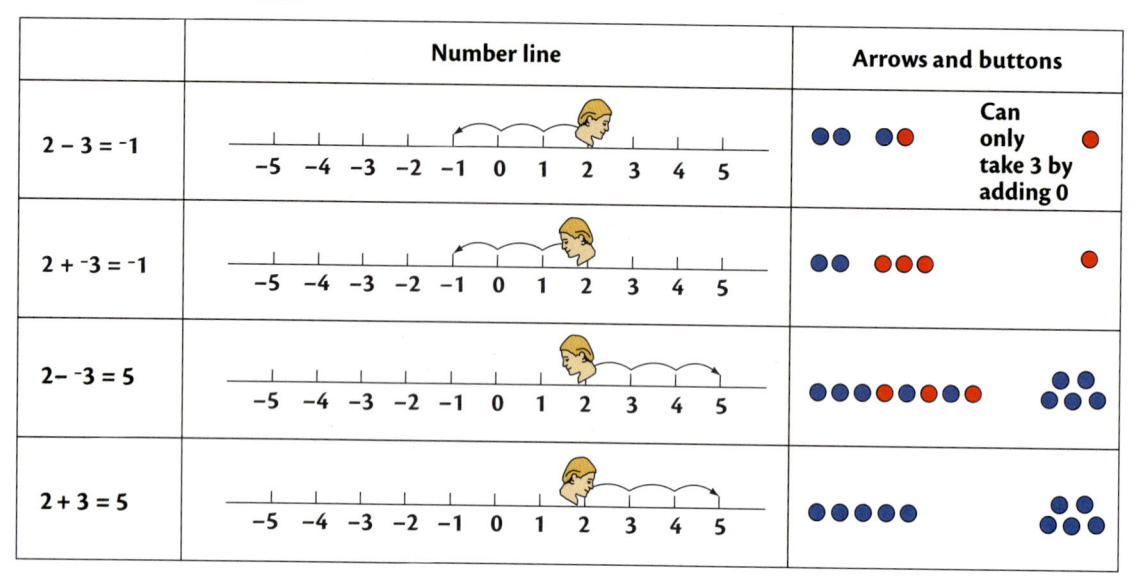

Figure 24.16 Integer addition and subtraction

The generalisations governing multiplication and division of integers can be derived in part from the generalisations governing addition and subtraction, in that multiplication can be interpreted as repeated addition for the situations where a positive number is multiplied by a negative number or vice versa. For example:

$$3 \times {}^-2 = {}^-2 + {}^-2 + {}^-2 = {}^-2 - 2 - 2 = {}^-6$$
$$^-3 \times 2 = {}^-3 + {}^-3 = {}^-3 - 3 = {}^-6$$

However, this does not support the division of integers. In this case the partitive concept is useful, in that division can be interpreted in terms of 'what do I multiply by?'. This gives rise to the argument that $6 \div {}^-2$ can be thought about as $^-2 \times ? = 6$. This can't be 3, as $^-2 \times 3 = {}^-6$, so it must be $^-3$. This reasoning demands that a negative multiplied by a negative is positive.

While individual examples are useful in suggesting patterns for multiplication and division of integers, such as 'unlike signs produce a negative, like signs produce a positive', they do not amount to a convincing argument.

Stacey and Vincent (2008) make a strong case for the use of patterns and number properties in helping students appreciate the generalisations governing integer multiplication and division. They suggest that students explore what happens as a number is progressively multiplied by a multiplicand that is 1 less than the one before, for example:

$$4 \times 4 = 16$$
$$4 \times 3 = 12$$
$$4 \times 2 = 8$$
$$4 \times 1 = 4$$
$$4 \times 0 = 0$$

In this case, students would observe that as the multiplicand decreases by 1 the product decreases by 4. Stacey and Vincent suggest using this observation to continue the pattern (column 1 below), then, applying the commutative property to $4 \times {}^-3 = {}^-12$, start another table (column 2) to recognise that as the multiplicand decreases by 1 the product increases by 3, leading to the conclusion on the basis of the patterns in columns 1 and 2 that factors with unlike signs produce a negative product. The third column extends the pattern in the second column to establish that two negative factors produce a positive product.

Column 1	Column 2	Column 3
4 × 2 = 8		
4 × 1 = 4		
4 × 0 = 0		
4 × ⁻1 = ⁻4		
4 × ⁻2 = ⁻8		
4 × ⁻3 = ⁻12 ⟶	⁻3 × 4 = ⁻12	
	⁻3 × 3 = ⁻9	
	⁻3 × 2 = ⁻6 ⟶	⁻3 × 2 = ⁻6
	⁻3 × 1 = ⁻3	⁻3 × 1 = ⁻3
	⁻3 × 0 = 0	⁻3 × 0 = 0
		⁻3 × ⁻1 = 3
		⁻3 × ⁻2 = 6
		⁻3 × ⁻3 = 9

Exponents

Writing numbers in exponent form is a particularly useful way of recording very large and very small numbers. For example, the recommended daily intake of vitamin B12 is 2×10^{-6} grams or 2 micrograms, and the average distance between the Earth and the Moon is approximately 3.84×10^5 kilometres.

for the classroom

Most food packaging contains information about the recommended daily intake of certain elements. Make a collection of this information and use it with middle year students to rename decimal fractions in other units and/or in exponent form. Explore how much of any one food type (e.g. a particular cereal) would need to be consumed to reach the recommended daily intake. (Most only provide a fraction of what is required.)

There are various ways of talking about exponents. An exponent can be referred to as a *power*, as in '10 raised to the *power* of 2' or as an *index* number (plural *indices*). Most adults will recall meeting the 'index laws' in school but may not remember what these are. Fortunately, they do not need to be remembered as they are easily constructed once it is recognised what we mean by numbers written in exponent form. For example, the base 10 system of numeration can be understood in terms of successive powers of 10 as shown in Table 24.4.

Base 10 system of numeration shown in exponent form							
Tens of thousands	Thousands	Hundreds	Tens	Ones	Tenths	Hundredths	Thousandths
10 000	1000	100	10	1	$\frac{1}{10}$	$\frac{1}{100}$	$\frac{1}{1000}$
10^4	10^3	10^2	10^1	10^0	10^{-1}	10^{-2}	10^{-3}

An index number indicates the number of times the base number is a factor of itself and 1. So $4 \times 4 \times 4 \times 4 \times 4 = 4^5$ as 4 is a factor of itself 5 times. Given this, it is easily shown that there is no direct way of working with index numbers if the bases are not the same (e.g. $2^5 + 3^4$ can only be evaluated by adding 32 and 27). Even if the bases are the same, it is a relatively straightforward task to check that numbers written in exponent form cannot be added or subtracted by adding or subtracting the indices (e.g. $4^5 - 4^2 \neq 4^3$ as $1024 - 16 \neq 64$). What can be established is that $a^m \times a^n = a^{m+n}$ and $a^m \div a^n = a^{m-n}$. For example:

$$3^5 \times 3^4 = (3 \times 3 \times 3 \times 3 \times 3) \times (3 \times 3 \times 3 \times 3) = 3^9$$

$$4^6 \div 4^3 = \frac{4 \times 4 \times 4 \times 4 \times 4 \times 4}{4 \times 4 \times 4} = 4 \times 4 \times 4 = 4^3$$

This explains the negative notation in the place-value chart above, in that $10^2 \div 10^3 = 10^{-1}$, which is another way of writing $\frac{1}{10}$ or 0.1.

Given $a^m \times a^n = a^{m+n}$ it can also be shown that if a^m is multiplied by itself n times, it is raised to the power of n, that is $(a^m)^n$, which is equal to $a^{m \times n}$. For example:

$$(2^5)^4 = 2^5 \times 2^5 \times 2^5 \times 2^5 = 2^{5+5+5+5} = 2^{5 \times 4} = 2^{20}$$

This has an interesting corollary in that fractional powers can be used to indicate square and other roots, for instance, we know that the square root of 100 is 10 but this can be shown as:

$$(10^2)^{\frac{1}{2}} = 10^{2 \times \frac{1}{2}} = 10^1 = 10$$

What is proportional reasoning?

Proportional reasoning refers to detecting, expressing, analysing, explaining, and providing evidence in support of assertions about proportional relationships. The word reasoning further suggests that one uses common sense, good judgement, and a thoughtful approach to problem solving, rather than plucking numbers from word problems and blindly applying rules and operations (Lamon, 2007, p. 647)

Proportional reasoning involves recognising and working with relationships between relationships (i.e. ratios) in different contexts. Proportional reasoning is important as it underpins the work done in other domains of mathematics (e.g. scale diagrams in measurement and/or geometry, the analysis of similar figures in geometry, and calculations involving percentages in financial mathematics), and provides a powerful basis for understanding functional relationships more generally.

At this level of schooling, there are essentially two types of problems: *comparison* problems, and *equivalence* or missing value problems. Comparison problems typically include two ratios that need to be evaluated and compared to see which represents the greater/lesser amount of some derived attribute (e.g. density, speed). Equivalence or missing value problems typically provide three values, two of which are related in some way, and the task involves finding the 'missing' value to ensure that this and the third value match the proportion of the first two. For example, consider the following:

1. Sean used 2.5 millilitres of cobalt blue tint in a litre of white paint. Brendan used 1.5 millilitres of the same tint in $\frac{3}{4}$ of a litre of white paint. Which mix was more blue?

2 To attend a family function, Kim travelled 85 kilometres in 1 hour and 15 minutes while it took Joanne 2 hours to travel 130 kilometres. Who travelled the faster?
3 The manager of the aviary at the zoo knows that 15 drops of nectar will feed 12 honey finches. How many drops of nectar will be needed to feed 28 honey finches?
4 If it takes 3 painters 24 hours (3 days) to paint sealant on the gym floor, how long will it take 2 painters working at the same rate to paint the gym floor?
5 Why is it that a baby left in a car on a summer's day is so much more at risk than an adult waiting in the same car?

The first two problems require a comparison of derived measures, in the first case 'blueness' and in the second case 'speed'. In the first problem, all the measures refer to the same attribute (volume). While comparisons of this sort are known to be easier than problems involving different attributes (Lamon, 2007), they can be rendered more or less difficult by the numbers and units involved (e.g. in this case, decimal fractions and fractions, millilitres and litres). In the end, problems such as this and the feral cat problem in Chapter 10 (in which 35 cats in a 146 hectare national park were compared to 27 cats in a 103 hectare national park, p. 210) come down to a *comparison* of fractions that requires a capacity to unitise, rename, and/or divide. For example, it is possible to compare the two girls' speeds by comparing how far they each travelled in 15 minutes (i.e. by *unitising*). This involves recognising that there are 5 fifteen-minute units in 85 km and 8 fifteen-minute units in 130 km. That is, Kim travelled $\frac{85}{5}$ = 17 km in 15 minutes whereas Joanne travelled $\frac{130}{8}$ = 16.25 km in 15 minutes, so Kim travelled faster overall.

consider and discuss

Renaming and dividing

Consider and discuss how renaming and dividing can be used to solve the tinting problem above.

The third and fourth problems above are not comparison problems as they each require a fourth value to be found, given a relationship between two values and a third value. These problems can be deceptive in that the nature of the relationship is not always transparent. For instance, while it makes sense that more nectar will be needed to feed more finches, the relationship is not so obvious in the painter situation where it needs to be recognised that fewer painters will take longer to paint the same area. In this case, recognising that the unit is the total amount of time taken to paint the floor, that is 9 'man-days', is crucial to the solution.

Recognising 'what to compare with what' is not trivial. For example, in considering why a baby is at much greater risk than an adult when left in a car on a hot summer's day, it is necessary to think about how one loses heat (through the skin and head particularly) relative to the body's capacity to withstand that loss. That this comparison involves the ratio between surface area and volume is not obvious, and students need to be exposed to problems such as this to recognise that *reasoning* in this context means exactly that—working through what one knows and making common-sense judgments about what is required.

The process of *unitising* is particularly pertinent to proportional reasoning, and to problems involving fractions, rate, ratio, and more generally. For example, the two solution strategies shown in Figure 24.17 to the beanie problem (Stephens, in press) use a form of unitising in that they are both working with fifths. The first might be fortuitous, but it is clear that a common relationship is being used in the ratio table.

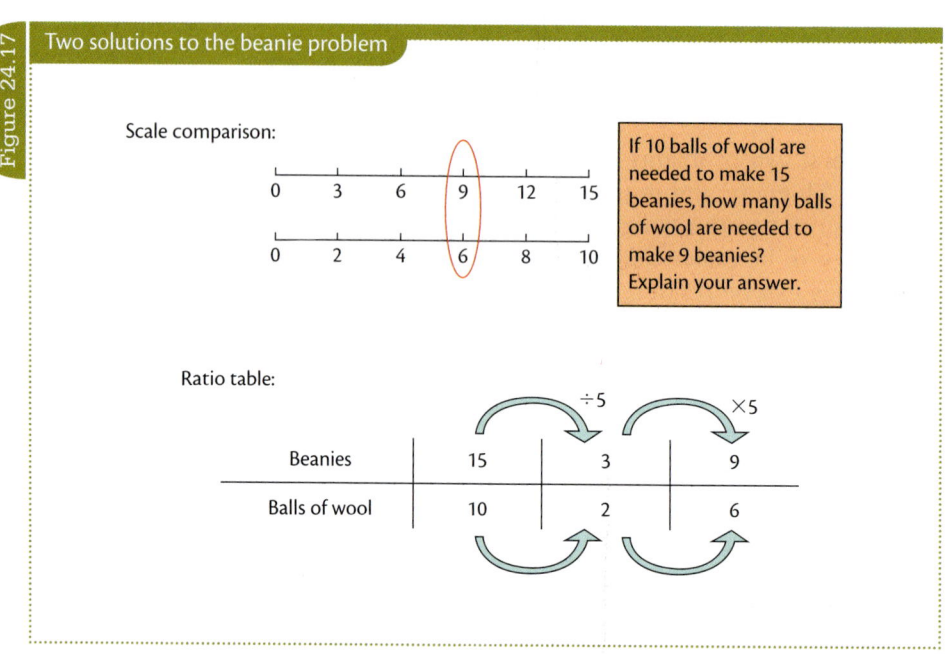

Figure 24.17 Two solutions to the beanie problem

Recognising relationships within and between ratios is very much dependent on the numbers involved and the individual's sense of number. For example, in deciding how much it would cost to buy 20 pens given that it costs $4.80 to buy 6 pens, it would seem sensible to find the cost of 1 pen as 6 is a divisor of $4.80. This is a 'within ratio' comparison. However, if asked to find the cost of 32 pens given that 8 cost $5.25, it appears to be more sensible to work with the 'between ratio' comparison, that is, 32 is 4 times 8, so 32 pens must be 4 times the cost.

Algebraic solutions can be set up in multiple ways. For example, for the beanie problem a *within ratio* comparison would be:

$$\frac{15 \text{ beanies}}{10 \text{ balls of wool}} = \frac{9 \text{ beanies}}{x \text{ balls}} \left(\frac{15}{10} = \frac{9}{x}\right) \text{ or}$$

$$\frac{10 \text{ balls of wool}}{15 \text{ beanies}} = \frac{x \text{ balls of wool}}{9 \text{ beanies}} \left(\frac{10}{15} = \frac{x}{9}\right)$$

A *between ratio* comparison would be

$$\frac{15 \text{ beanies}}{9 \text{ beanies}} = \frac{10 \text{ balls of wool}}{x \text{ balls of wool}} \left(\frac{15}{9} = \frac{10}{x}\right) \text{ or}$$

$$\frac{9 \text{ beanies}}{15 \text{ beanies}} = \frac{x \text{ balls of wool}}{10 \text{ balls of wool}} \left(\frac{9}{15} = \frac{x}{15}\right)$$

This suggests that teaching and learning about proportional reasoning involves much more than learning about how to apply techniques such as 'cross multiply'. It requires common sense, number sense, an awareness of the multiplicative relationships between numbers, and a capacity to recognise and keep track of the units involved.

Sources of difficulty

Proportional reasoning problems are a known source of error for a significant number of students in the middle years, with many students relying on additive rather than multiplicative strategies to solve problems involving multiplicative comparisons (e.g. Hart, 1984). Lamon (2007, p. 641) summarises these as follows:

- problem context: students may not be familiar with the implicit relationships or units involved
- nature of the numbers involved, discrete or continuous measures, integral or non-integral ratios, extensive (e.g. 3 metres) or intensive quantities (e.g. rates such as 65 km/hour), and how these are presented (i.e. as numbers, fractions or ratios)
- the location of the missing element in equivalence problems in relation to the other three numbers, and whether or not the number to be found is the largest
- whether perceptual cues are consistent or inconsistent.

In addition, many students have access to the necessary skills but find it difficult to work out exactly what is required. This is nicely illustrated in Con's response to the speedy snail problem from the Scaffolding Numeracy in the Middle Years project (Siemon et al., 2006) shown in Figure 24.18. Con appears to have little difficulty with the formal algorithm for multiplication, but his decision in part (b) simply to multiply the two numbers suggests he has assumed that this problem is the same as the first or he has not recognised the significance of the rate, 1.59 metres in 6 minutes. Although correct (for an incorrect reason), his response to the last part suggests that he does not understand the significance of the relationships involved as all he needed to do to compare the two snails was find out how far Harry's snail would travel in 24 minutes (15 × 24 = 360 centimetres or 3.6 metres).

Figure 24.18 Year 7 student response to speedy snail problem

a: Harry's snail can travel at 15 centimetres per minute. How far might Harry's snail travel in 34 minutes?

b: Samantha's snail covered 1.59 metres in 6 minutes. How far might Samantha's snail travel in 17 minutes. Record your answer in metres.

a)
$$\begin{array}{r} {}^{2}34 \text{ minutes} \\ \times\ 15 \text{ centimetres} \\ \hline 170 \\ 340 \\ \hline 510 \end{array}$$
It will travel 510 centimetres in 34 minutes.

b)
$$\begin{array}{r} 1.59 \text{ metres} \\ \times\ 17 \text{ min} \\ \hline 11.13 \\ +15.90 \\ \hline 27.03 \end{array}$$
It will cover 27.03 metres in 17 minutes.

c: Harry entered his snail in a race. Remember Harry's snail can travel at 15 centimetres per minute. Another snail entered in the same race, covered 3.71 metres in 24 minutes. Which is the faster snail?
Show all your working so we can understand your thinking.

c) The other snail was faster because it raced in metres and metres are longer than centimetres.

Planning for diversity

Large scale numeracy research projects at this level (e.g. Middle Years Numeracy Research Project (MYNRP) and Scaffolding Numeracy in the Middle Years (SNMY)) have identified that student capacity to think and work multiplicatively is the single most important reason for the enormous range in mathematics achievement in the middle years of schooling (Siemon et al., 2001; Siemon et al., 2006) These data suggest that textbooks aimed at a particular Year level in Years 5 to 9 are likely to support the learning needs of only 40 to 50 per cent of students. Approximately 10 to 15 per cent of students will already know most of what is considered in the text, and the remaining 35 to 50 per cent of students will find the text largely unsuited to their needs. Further questions about the legitimacy of relying too closely on any one resource are raised by a study that investigated the approach taken to three topics by nine Year 8 texts from four Australian states (Vincent & Stacey, 2008). The problems presented in each text were evaluated in terms of 'procedural complexity, type of solving processes, degree of repetition, proportion of "application" problems, and proportion of problems requiring deductive reasoning' (p. 82). While the authors found that there were differences both between and within textbooks, they noted that in 'some books, including the best-selling textbooks in several states, the balance is too far towards repetitive problems of low procedural complexity' (p. 82).

Streaming is counterproductive

While streaming is a fairly typical response to difference in mathematics achievement at this level, the literature suggests that this strategy is largely counterproductive unless the opportunity to work in like-ability groups is flexible and open to choice (see Chapter 8). For example, Boaler (2002) contrasted the impact of two different approaches on the mathematics achievement of junior secondary school students over the course of three years. Both schools were situated in 'low-income areas and the majority of students at both schools were White and working class' (p. 245). In one school, students were organised into ability groups (i.e. streamed) and followed a fairly procedural, skill-based curriculum. At the other school, the students worked in mixed ability groups and a more open-ended approach to the teaching and learning of mathematics was adopted. After three years, the students in the mixed-ability, reform-oriented classrooms outperformed their peers at the streamed school, despite the fact that there was no significant difference in their respective levels of mathematics attainment at the outset. That is, 'mixed ability teaching ... led to better results and better life chances than ... ability grouping practices [which] created in the words of one ex-pupil, "psychological prisons" that "break ambition" and "almost formally label kids as stupid"' (Boaler, 2005, p. 135).

It appears that the only students to benefit from streaming are exceptionally able students; however, this comes at the expense of lowering the results of average and below average attainers (Linchevski & Kutscher, 1998; Venkatakrishan & Wiliam, 2003), leading to the conclusion that 'heterogeneous groups appear to give the best opportunity to learn for both low-achieving pupils and average pupils' (Hootveen, van der Grift & Creemers, 2004, p. 345).

Taking the first step

Change the way it's explained, they need to think about how you understand, not how they explain (Vincent, Year 9, in Siemon et al., 2001).

Differentiated teaching can only occur where teachers have:

- access to accurate information about what the student knows (requires high-quality, reliable tools to assess students' mathematical knowledge and capacity to use that knowledge)
- a grounded knowledge of learning trajectories (i.e. the major 'growth points' in the development of key ideas and how to scaffold these with students)
- an expanded repertoire of teaching approaches that accommodates and nurtures discourse, helps uncover and explore students' ideas in a constructive way, and ensures all students can participate and contribute to the enterprise
- sufficient time with students to develop trust and supportive relationships
- flexibility to spend time with the students who need it most (Siemon et al., 2001).

In a large-scale study of effective school improvement in mathematics, Houtveen, van der Grift and Creemers (2004) found that diagnosing learning needs, implementing prescribed learning plans for students identified 'at risk', giving extended direct instruction, supporting self-confidence and creating an explorative learning environment, were all significant factors in improving student outcomes.

Assessment for learning and targeted teaching hold the key to success. Working with small groups of 'at risk' sixth graders over a period of 18 weeks, Breed (2011) found that a consistent focus on the 'big ideas' associated with the transition from additive to multiplicative thinking was highly effective in increasing students' knowledge and confidence in relation to multiplicative thinking. Breed used the student's results from the initial SNMY assessment round to identify learning needs, and the Learning Assessment Framework for Multiplicative Thinking (Siemon et al., 2006) as a guide in planning her targeted teaching approach.

Tools for assessing learning needs in this area that provide teaching advice regarding key ideas and learning trajectories are readily available. For example, the SNMY Assessment Materials (Siemon et al., 2006; Department of Education and Early Childhood Development, 2009) and the Assessment for Common Misunderstandings Tools (Siemon, 2006; DEECD, 2009).

Expanding the range of offerings

Rich tasks, open-ended questions, and investigations can be used in mixed-ability groups to expose all students to alternative representations and approaches to problem solving. Maths clubs and homework clubs can also be a useful means of providing valuable, additional support for students left behind, particularly where attendance is voluntary. *Maths300* (Educational Services Australia, 2010) offers an extensive range of interactive tasks that are suitable for independent, mixed-ability group work. Activities that are particularly valuable for revisiting essential knowledge in age-appropriate and engaging ways are 'Number Charts', 'Multo', 'Fraction Estimation', and 'This Goes With That', but there are many others that are worth exploring.

Fermi problems can also be used to good effect in mixed-ability groups to focus on key problem-solving strategies and skills. Enrico Fermi (1901–1954) was an Italian physicist who liked to demonstrate the power of using estimation to address seemingly unanswerable questions, such as, 'How many piano tuners in New York?'. Fermi type questions draw upon everyday experience, allow most students to make a start, encourage multiple approaches, and help develop number sense. They also help build a sense of community and mathematical confidence through discussion and justification of solutions strategies (Taggert, Adams, Elitze, Heinrichs, Hohman & Hickman, 2007). According to Helme and Clarke (2001), student–student interactions appear 'to offer more scope for manifesting high-level cognitive engagement than teacher–student interactions' (p. 151).

think + link

Examples of Fermi problems are included in Chapter 10.

Withdrawing individual students from their regular classroom activities to provide additional support is generally not conducive to supporting mathematics learning in the middle years, although where students have some choice and/or work with a partner this has been found to be productive in certain circumstances (e.g. Graham & Pegg, 2010).

Conclusion

In this chapter, we reviewed the key ideas for multiplication and division and the importance of being able to think and work multiplicatively at this level of work in order to understand and reason with an extended range of numbers. Students cannot be expected to develop the knowledge and confidence they need to work fluently with algebraic texts if their interpretation of multiplication and division is limited to *equal groups*. To interpret a much broader range of problem types involving multiplication and/or division, and numbers other than whole numbers, students need to be able to access a more generalised understanding of multiplication and division in terms of the *factor–factor–product* idea.

Proportional reasoning is fundamentally about identifying relationships between relationships. To interpret problems involving proportions and engage in proportional reasoning, students also need to be able to re-unitise and think in terms of the *for each* idea.

Given the enormous range in student achievement in this area across the middle years, we also considered some specific strategies to support the learning needs of all students, in particular, the importance of regularly assessing for learning and targeted teaching focused on key ideas and strategies.

key terms

Area idea for multiplication: an extension of the region idea, which represents the two numbers being muliplied in terms of length by width, the area idea supports the multiplication of multi-digit numbers in terms of their parts (e.g. for two 2-digit numbers, tens by tens, tens by ones, ones by tens, and ones by ones)

Associative property: the order in which three or more numbers are added or multiplied does not matter (e.g. 3 + 4 + 5 = 5 + 3 + 4 and 3 × 4 × 5 = 5 × 3 × 4)

Cartesian product or 'for each' idea for multiplication: multiplicative situations involving combinations (e.g. 4 pants, 3 tops, how many combinations?) or rates (e.g. $1.75/kilogram, how much for 3.5 kilograms?)

Dividend: the amount being divided

Divisor: the number by which another number is divided; in partitive division, it refers to the number of groups; in quotitive division it refers to the number in each group or the size of the group

Factor: one of two or more numbers being multiplied

Multiple: the result of multiplying one integer by another, a number than can be divided by another number without remainder (e.g. 8 is a multiple of 2 and 4)

Multiplicative thinking: capacity to work with an extended range of concepts, meanings, and representations for multiplication and division in a variety of contexts (see Chapter 17)

Multiplier: the amount by which a quantity is increased or decreased multiplicatively as opposed to additively

Product: the result of multiplying two or more numbers

Quotient: the result of a division

Rate: a type of ratio that involves the comparison of different attributes (e.g. speed, population density)

Ratio: multiplicative comparison of two quantities that may or not refer to the same attribute (e.g. a distance can be compared to another distance, as in 60 kilometres to 45 kilometres, or to time as in 60 kilometres/hour)

Reciprocal: a number is the reciprocal of another number if the product of the two is 1, that is, the reciprocal any number n is the multiplicative inverse of n, $\frac{1}{n}$

Review questions

1. What prerequisite knowledge and skills are needed to support meaningful solution strategies for fraction multiplication and division?
2. After years of working with whole number multiplication and division, many students believe that 'multiplication makes bigger and division makes smaller'. Describe how you might challenge this perception.
3. Describe and illustrate how the *area* idea for multiplication can be used to support multi-digit whole number multiplication, decimal fraction multiplication, and fraction multiplication.

4. Imagine you are on your last professional placement and you've been asked to (a) introduce fraction division to a group of exceptional Year 6 students (if you are in a primary school) or (b) review fraction division with a group of Year 8 students who do not seem to understand the process (if you are in a secondary school). Explain how you might go about this task. Include key questions you might ask as well as any models and representations you might use.
5. Write at least 6 proportional reasoning problems. Include *comparison* problems as well as *missing value* (i.e. equivalence problems) and a range of different numbers (e.g. measures such as 56 kg or 7.4 m and rates such as 80 km/h or $3.79/kg). Swap these with a friend and discuss how they might be used in a classroom.

Key references

Boaler, J. (2005). The 'psychological prisons' from which they never escaped: The role of ability grouping in reproducing social class inequalities. *Forum, 47*(2–3), 135–143.

Confrey, J. (1994). Splitting, similarity, and rate of change: A new approach to multiplication and exponential functions. In G. Harel & J. Confrey (Eds.), *The Development of Multiplicative Reasoning in the Learning of Mathematics* (pp. 293–332). New York: State University of New York Press.

Hart, K. (1984). *Ratio: Children's Strategies and Errors. A Report of the Strategies and Errors in Secondary Mathematics Project.* London: NFER–Nelson.

Helme, S., & Clarke, D. J. (2001). Identifying cognitive engagement in the mathematics classroom. *Mathematics Education Research Journal, 13*(2), 133–153.

Lamon, S. (2007). Rational numbers and proportional reasoning: Towards a theoretical framework for research. In F. Lester (Ed.), *Second Handbook of Research on Mathematics Teaching and Learning. A Project of the National Council of Teachers of Mathematics* (pp. 629–667). Charlotte, NC: Information Age.

Linchevski, L., & Kutscher, B. (1998). Tell me with whom you're learning and I'll tell you how much you've learned: Mixed ability versus same-ability grouping in mathematics. *Journal for Research in Mathematics Education, 29*(5), 533–554.

Siemon, D. (2006). *Assessment for Common Misunderstandings. Materials Prepared for the Victorian Department of Education and Early Childhood Development.* Melbourne: RMIT University.

Siemon, D., Breed, M., Dole, S., Izard, J., & Virgona, J. (2006). *Scaffolding Numeracy in the Middle Years – Project Findings, Materials, and Resources.* Final Report submitted to Victorian Department of Education and Training and the Tasmanian Department of Education, October. CD-rom subsequently published electronically: www.eduweb.vic.gov.au/edulibrary/public/teachlearn/student/snmy.ppt.

Stacey, K., & Vincent, J. (2008). Modes of reasoning in Year 8 textbooks. In M. Goos, R. Brown & K. Makur (Eds.), *Proceedings of the 31st Annual Conference of the Mathematics Research Group of Australasia* (pp. 475–481). Brisbane: MERGA.

Taggert, G., Adams, P., Elitze, E., Heinrichs, J., Hohman, J., & Hickman, K. (2007). Fermi questions. *Mathematics Teaching in the Middle School, 13*(3), 164–167.

Vincent, J., & Stacey, K. (2008). Do mathematical textbooks cultivate shallow teaching? Applying the TIMSS video study criteria to Australian eighth grade mathematics textbooks. *Mathematics Education Research Journal, 20*(1), 82–107.

Websites

www.education.vic.gov.au/studentlearning/teachingresources/maths/snmy/default.htm
www.simerr.educ.utas.edu.au/numeracy/critical_numeracy/critical_numeracy.htm
www.thenetwork.sa.edu.au/teachingandlearning
http://activated.act.edu.au/ectl
www.figurethis.org

25 Algebraic Thinking, Pattern, and Order

Contents

What is algebraic thinking?	587
Why is algebra important?	588
Arithmetic algebraic thinking, and problem structure	588
Letters, unknowns and variables	589
Functional thinking	592
Equivalance and equations	598
Model approach—using the length model	599
Conclusion	602

Chapter objectives

This chapter will enable the reader to:
- Recognise the difference between algebraic and arithmetic thinking
- Develop an understanding of the notion of a variable
- Explore linear functions in a variety of contexts and represent them in a range of ways
- Explore a variety of strategies that can be used to find unknown quantities.

Using variables to describe patterns

When we were exploring growing patterns with Year 6 students we asked them to predict what the pattern would look like for any position:

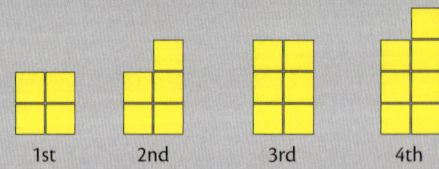

1st 2nd 3rd 4th

Teacher: How many tiles would you have in the 56th position?
Jim: There would be 56 add 3 (three more than the position number).
Teacher: What about the *n*th position? How many tiles?
Sally: That would be *q* tiles.
Teacher: How did you get *q* tiles?
Sally: You know like the alphabet ... *n o p q*.
Jim: No, it would be *nnn* (saying *nnn* as one long slow sound).
Jill: No, it would be *n* add 3, 3 more than the position number.

Big ideas

- The development of algebraic thinking and algebraic symbols is derived in a problem-solving context, employing practical problems and models to reach generalisations.
- The structure of our number system and the computational methods we use can be generalised and expressed algebraically. Algebraic thinking is not about manipulating symbols. It is about understanding mathematical structure and exploring generalisations.
- When looking for the relationship between two variables represented as tables of values, we can find a pattern as we examine one of the variables, but the more powerful thinking involves finding the relationship between the corresponding pairs of values.
- Functional relationships can be expressed in a range of representations. Each representation serves a different purpose, with each providing a deeper understanding of the mathematical relationship.
- In algebra, symbols stand for quantities that can vary. They are not abbreviations or shorthand for objects or concepts, such as m for metres, or p for perimeters.
- Variables are symbols that represent a range of numbers. If the same symbol appears more than once in an equation then it always represents the same number at the same time.

What is algebraic thinking?

Algebraic thinking is perceived as foundational to all areas of mathematics because it provides the tools (i.e. the language and structure) for representing and analysing quantitative relationships needed for modelling situations, solving problems, and proving **generalisations**. It has the capacity to assist in unifying concepts by allowing us to express similarities and differences in a way that helps us see the commonalities across the school curriculum, across Year levels, and across mathematical settings.

did you know?

Evidence of algebraic thinking exists from the year 250 CE in Europe. Symbolic algebra began to develop in Europe around the sixteenth century but wasn't used universally before the seventeenth century. Until then, algebra was expressed in words without the use of mathematical symbols. Describing an **equation** such as $(10 - x)(10 + x) = x^2 - 100$ could consist of a paragraph containing up to 15 lines. The need for symbols arose out of a need to express complex ideas in shorthand form. Thus the evolution to the use of symbols in arithmetic was somewhat slow and haphazard.

Englishman Robert Recorde (1510–1558) is considered to be the father of the equals sign. He explained his selection of a pair of equal parallel lines: 'I will settle on a pair of equal parallel or two lines of one length as no two things can be more equal.' It wasn't until nearly 100 years later that this symbol came into universal use. Until then = was used to mean parallel lines by some writers, and plus and minus by others.

Why is algebra important?

Generalising and mastering challenging mathematical problems, applying mathematics to real-world problems, and the ability to use technology as a tool for conjecturing and generalising, underpin economic success and innovation in a global knowledge economy (Australian Academy of Science [AAS], 2002; Federation of Australian Scientific and Technological Societies [FASTS], 2004; NCTM, 2000; Mullis, Martin, Gonzalez & Chrostowski, 2004). Not only is the shortfall in scientists and mathematicians of national concern (FASTS, 2004), but also many traditional industries are now calling for personnel with advanced skills in mathematics (Mullis et al., 2004). An understanding of rigorous mathematics increases one's chances of entering tertiary study, and makes a significant difference in opportunities for those who enter the workforce upon leaving school (NCTM, 2000; Mullis et al., 2004). Therefore, the mathematics taught in school is a critical factor affecting the future success of students in mathematics (NCTM, 2000) and many other disciplines (e.g. accounting and science).

Arithmetic, algebraic thinking, and problem structure

One must ask why many secondary students experience difficulties with algebra, when research has shown that young students can grasp algebraic concepts and notations. Is it to do with the way that the subject is taught in the secondary school, or is it because they enter secondary school with an understanding of arithmetic that impedes their successful participation in algebra? The results of both national and international research are beginning to suggest that the continual emphasis on finding computational answers to arithmetic problems impedes the development of algebraic thinking (Carraher & Schliemann, 2007; Warren, 2002). If students understand arithmetic at a level that enables them to explain and justify the operations they are using as they find solutions, they have reached a critical level that assists successful transition to algebra. Thus the intention of introducing algebraic thinking in the primary years is to focus students' attention on generalising the structure of arithmetic and justifying and explaining solutions to problems.

The distinction between arithmetic thinking and algebraic thinking can best be illustrated by how one attacks problems. In arithmetic the focus is on solving a problem, and in algebra the focus is on representing a problem.

Consider the problem: 'Jill bought herself and 4 friends tickets to a basketball game. At the game, she also bought herself a drink for $3. This cost her $33 in total. How much were the tickets?'

- Arithmetic thinking: She had $33. She spent $3 on a drink. That leaves $30 she spent on the tickets. There were 5 tickets. So she spent $6 on each [$(33 - 3) \div 5 = 6$].
- Algebraic thinking: Let n stand for the price of the tickets. Then $5 \times n$ is the cost of the tickets. $5n + 3$ was the amount she spent. The total amount was 33 [$5n + 3 = 33$].

The significant difference is that the first sequence is about solving the problem, and the second sequence is about representing the problem. Many primary aged students can express their algebraic thinking in language (e.g. she spent 5 times the cost of a ticket plus $3 for a drink. This amount came to $33), and many can write this with a ? for the unknown (e.g. 5 × ? + 3 = 33 or ? × 5 + 3 = 33). Both are important steps in the transition from arithmetic thinking to algebraic thinking.

consider and discuss

Comparing algebraic and arithmetic thinking

Consider the following problem:

> Thirty schools in a district compete in a basketball competition. Each team plays every other team twice. How many games are played?

Discuss how you would solve this problem using algebraic thinking, that is, representing the problem so that we can find a solution for any number of teams that enter the competition. Illustrate how this differs from arithmetic thinking.

Letters, unknowns, and variables

Letters in algebra are used as symbols to represent unknowns and variables, and as indicated by the introductory vignette many students find them problematic. Students commonly ignore the letters, replace them with numerical values, regard them as shorthand names, or regard them as letters of the alphabet (Kuchemann, 1981).

consider and discuss

The meaning of variables

You can exchange 1 euro for 2 dollars. If you have e euros and you exchange this for d dollars, write a relationship between the number of euros and the number of dollars. Justify your solution and explain why the answer $1e = 2d$ is incorrect.

The above problem is based on a famous problem:

> There are six times as many students as professors at this university. Use S for the number of students and P for the number of professors. Write the equation for this problem.

Research has shown that many adolescents proffer the incorrect equation $6S = P$. In this instance students perceive the letters standing for objects (a student, a professor, a euro, a dollar), rather than as a variable (the number of students, the number of professors, the number of euros, the number of dollars) (Clement, 1982). An extension of this misconception is what is commonly referred to in the literature as 'fruit salad algebra'.

issues in teaching

Fruit salad algebra

Avoid a fruit-salad approach to algebra, and saying statements such as '$3b + 2b$ is the same as $5b$' as 'three bananas and two bananas is five bananas', or anything similar that wrongly reinforces that a letter stands as shorthand for objects or specific numbers. The fruit-salad approach reinforces that b can stand for one object, where in algebra b can stand for *any number* of objects.

Use a range of letters and student-generated symbols (e.g. hearts, boxes). Emphasise that the letter chosen stands for *any number*, that is, it is a variable. Also ensure that the letter you choose cannot be misconceived as shorthand for the name of the object. In the above problem, letting y = the number of euros and x = the number of dollars would have assisted with representation of the problem.

The distinction between unknowns and variables is best seen in the context of a problem:

> Some frogs were swimming in a pond and four frogs were sitting on lily-pads. If there were 16 frogs altogether, how many frogs were swimming?

This is an example of a problem with an unknown. This problem could be represented as:

$n + 4 = 16$ (where n is the number of frogs). The unknown has a specific value.

> Some frogs were swimming in a pond and some frogs were sitting on lily-pads. If there were 16 frogs altogether, how many frogs were swimming and how many frogs were sitting?

This is an example of a problem with **variables**. This problem can be represented as $n + q = 16$ (where n is the number of frogs hopping and q is the number of frogs sitting). Neither variable has a specific value.

How to introduce variables to students

Many students grapple with the symbolic representations of problems using letters. Research suggests that this is because often symbols are presented to students in a very abstract way. Students commonly do not engage in the development of the sign system; nor are they introduced to it as a way of representing problems in context. Variables allow us to express generalisations. Thus students need to be introduced to variables in problem-solving situations. The following section present two different contexts, both applicable for exploration in the primary classroom (Warren, 2007).

Growing patterns

for the classroom

Growing patterns in real world contexts

The fence around John's yard is made from horizontal rails and vertical posts in the pattern opposite.

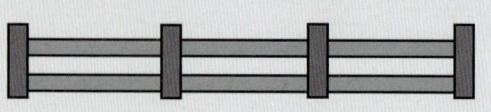

Ask students:

- If John has 10 posts, how many rails does he need?
- If John has 50 posts, how many rails does he need?
- If John has 50 rails, how many posts does he need?

Ask students to write a rule that would help John figure out how many posts he would need for any number of rails.

for the classroom

Repeating patterns as functions

Ask students to look at this pattern showing days of the week.

M	T	W	Th	F	Sa	Su	M	T	W	Th	F	Sa	Su

- What day will be the 70th tile?
- What day will be the 86th tile?

Ask students to write the rule you would use to figure out the day on a tile in any position.

In both the above examples students will begin to express their thinking in language. Ask them what symbol we could use to represent any number of rails or any position of the tiles. What if we called this n (meaning any number)? So what would we need to do to n to find out how many posts we need? Return to the problem and discuss how the number of rails is related to the number of posts. When there are 6 rails there are 4 posts. Using large numbers (e.g. What if I had 372 922 rails?) in classroom discussions assists students to move from arithmetic thinking (e.g. providing answers and saying you need 6 post for 10 rails) to algebraic thinking (e.g. you divide the number of rails by 2 and add one for the end post). Finally, represent this solution as 'dividing the number of rails by 2 and add 1', or 'n divided by 2, + 1'. In these contexts the letter is introduced to assist us to write the rule. Students will also see that everyday language can be cumbersome, and hence the variable has the power to assist us to write generalisations succinctly.

issues in teaching

Difficulties with language and symbols

Students experience three main difficulties when making the transition to using algebraic symbols (MacGregor & Stacey, 1995; Cooper & Warren, 2008).

The first difficulty relates to expressing a generality in language and then writing the generality in symbols. The language students use to describe the generality does not necessarily match the way we write the expression. For example, in the fence problem above, saying, 'to find out the number of rails you count the number of posts, subtract one and double that number' does not easily translate to $2(n - 1)$.

Another example is $5n + 7$. In language the instruction would be to multiply the number by 5 and then add 7, not 5 lots of the number plus 7.

Some young students find it easy to express the generality in language while others are more comfortable with symbols. With young students the focus should be on recognising and communicating the generality. This in itself is difficult for many students.

The second difficulty stems from the difference between the way we use symbols in algebra and the way we use symbols in number contexts. In algebra, $2n$ means multiply *n* by 2 (i.e. 2 × *n*), whereas in number the 2 indicates the number of tens (e.g. in 23 the 2 means 2 tens). In algebra we write the number followed by the letter rather than the letter followed by the number (e.g. 2*n* and not *n*2). When introducing the algebraic notation system it is important to demonstrate the similarities between the symbolic number system and the algebraic symbol system.

The third difficulty stems from the fact that algebraic thinking is often not closed. For example, 2*n* + 3 cannot be simplified any further. Unlike arithmetic, this is the answer. Many students experience difficulty with this notion, especially if most of their arithmetic experiences have involved finding specific answers to problems as opposed to representing generalisations. A common misconception that you see in many middle-year classrooms is students writing 2*n* + 3 as 6*n*. One way of addressing this issue is for teachers to pose unclosed problems in simple arithmetic contexts (write all the ways that we can make 7 (3 + 4, 1 + 6 and so on) instead of closed problems (3 + 4 = ☐). Unclosed problems can be asked at all levels of primary school and in all strands of mathematics.

As indicated by the above example, algebraic thinking emerges from contexts that can be generalised. From these contexts verbal descriptions are drawn from the students, gradually moving from descriptions that are very contextually based to using language that assists students to describe the generalisation in mathematical terms. The move to symbols is gradual, with using symbols as a shortened way of representing patterns or representing properties concisely.

consider and discuss

Generalisations in calendars

Calendars can be useful tools for exploring patterns and introducing symbols. For example:

1. How does the calendar change if you look across the week? How does it change as you look down the month? Look at a segment of a calendar:

Mon.	Tues.	Wed.
4	5	6
11	12	13
18	19	20

2. If the middle number 12 was *s*, how would you write the other numbers? What do you notice if you sum up all the numbers in the segment? Does this pattern work for other 3 × 3 segments from the calendar? Justify your generalisation.

3. If you take any four cells in the calendar arranged in a square (e.g. 5, 6, 12, and 13), and add them up, Simon can tell the numbers you chose. How does he work this out?

Pose some other unclosed problems for calendars.

Functional thinking

Functional thinking focuses on the relationship between two (or more) varying quantities. Many real world contexts can be modelled as functions. For example, if we are buying bananas in a supermarket, there is a relationship between the cost of the bananas, their mass, and the cost per kilogram.

Functions as growing patterns and symbols

In Chapter 13 we used growing patterns to introduce young students to number patterns. Growing patterns can be representations of functions if we introduce a second variable, the position of each term or shape in the growing pattern.

Chapter 25 Algebraic Thinking, Pattern, and Order

for the classroom

Growing patterns as functions

As the size of the swimming pool increases, the amount of decking required increases:

Pool 1

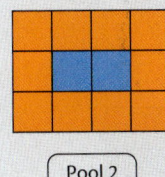
Pool 2

Pool 3

Pool 4

The two variables in this problem are the pool number and the number of decking blocks required to surround the pool.

Ask students:

- How many decking blocks would we need for Pool 5 (the next term)?
- How many decking blocks would we need for Pool 13 (a term close by that is countable)?
- How many decking blocks would we need for Pool 54 (an uncountable term)?

Ask students to describe how you would work out the number of decking tiles you would need for any sized pool (writing the generalisation).

Initially students will notice that for each additional pool you need 2 more tiles. This insight can be expressed as additive thinking. Pool 1 has 8 tiles, Pool 2 has 10 tiles, and Pool 3 has 12 tiles. Therefore, Pool 5 would have 16 tiles. They then work out Pool 13 by continually adding on 2 until they get to this Pool 13 (16 + 2 + 2 + 2 + 2 + 2 + 2 + 2 + 2 = 32). In mathematics we call this *recursive thinking*. This approach does not assist in finding the number of tiles required for large pools easily. Students' attention needs to shift to the relationship between the pool size and the number of decking tiles required (*relational thinking*) (see Chapter 6, p. 120).

issues in teaching

Using manipulatives to assist with finding the pattern rule

Students find it easier to generalise if they actively engage with the construction of the problem (Warren & Cooper, 2008). Give the students some blue and yellow tiles and cards with pool numbers (Pool 1 to Pool 4) on them, and ask them to construct the above pattern. Then give them a card with Pool 10 on it and ask them to construct this pool. This action begins to assist students to examine the relationship between the two variables (the pool number and the number of decking tiles required to surround it), that is, to make the shift from recursive thinking to relational thinking. Relying purely on worksheets and pen and paper examples from texts does not allow students access to this thinking. Some need to act it out to understand the construction of the problem.

The choice now is: do we introduce the table of values to help the students to reach the relationship between the pool number and the number of decking tiles, or do we stay with the visual? Our research indicates that while the students find the second approach cognitively easier, the first allows for rich discussions about mathematical thinking and equivalent expressions (Warren & Cooper, 2008). We conjecture that the initial difficulties students have with the first approach (relying solely on manipulating materials to generate the rule) arise from their inability to think visually. They have limited experience with visual thinking in many primary classroom contexts. For example the pool problem can be visually deconstructed in a number of ways.

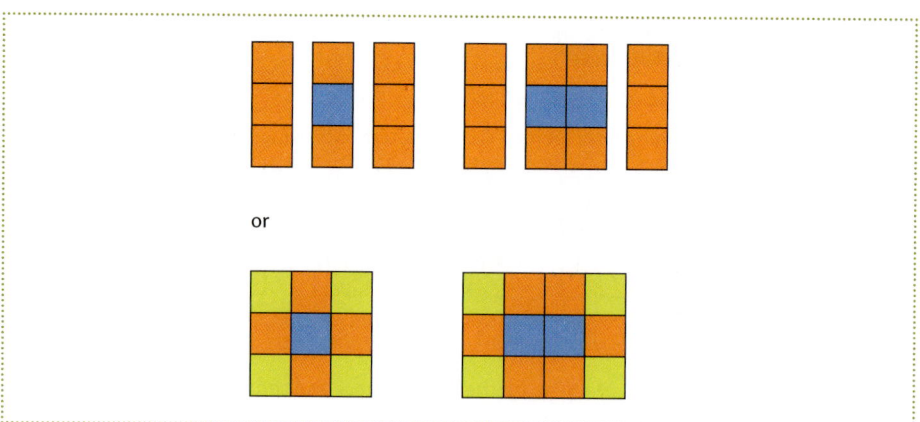

or

The first representation leads to the generalisation 'Multiply the length of the pool by 2 (for each side) and add 6 for the ends ($2n + 6$)' (or $2n + 3 + 3$ for 'add 3 for each end'). The second representation could lead to the generalisation 'Add the two lengths of the pool, add two for the end and four for the corners ($n + n + 2 + 4$)'. Discuss with your students whether these expressions are equivalent or not.

Maintaining the visual representation also assists students to justify their generalisation. What does the n represent? What do the numbers represent?

Functions as tables of values

think + link

Common problems students experience with tables of values are discussed in Chapter 6, including the tendency to engage in recursive thinking and prototypical thinking.

Some of the problems that students experience with reaching generalisations from tables of values mirror their propensity to engage in recursive thinking instead of relational thinking, as discussed above.

Introducing a horizontal representation for the table of values assists you to use language to link the visual pattern to the table of values and to talk about recursive thinking and relational thinking. For example, if we are searching *along* the pattern or *along* the rows of the table of values, then we are engaging with recursive thinking. If the table of values was represented vertically then the language would need to change from searching along for the visual pattern to searching down for the table of values, and students will be continually switching from a horizontal search to a vertical search throughout the discussion. When the table of values is represented horizontally, relational thinking requires searching for generalisation between the visual representation of the tiles and the pool number, or between the number of tiles and the pool number for the table of values. (One value is situated under the other.)

For the pool problem the horizontal table of values is:

Number of tiles	8	10	12	14	16			
Pool number	1	2	3	4	5	13	54	n

Horizontal tables of values should be used only in the initial stages of discussions. Once students have grasped the notion of relational thinking (searching for relationships between pairs of values in the table), vertical tables of values can be introduced.

The mathematical convention is that the **independent variable** (x value) is in the top row or first column, and the **dependent variable** (y value) is in the bottom row or second column. In this example, the pool number is the *x* and the number of tiles is the *y*. We need to allow students to engage with all the ways we can represent tables of values to avoid the development of 'prototypical thinking'.

Function machines also begin to assist the transition from recursive to relational thinking as they allow for entries in the table to be produced randomly, thus addressing the problem of having a table of values consisting of variables increasing by a uniform amount (e.g. increasing by 2 and increasing by 1 as in the above table). The next example illustrates this idea.

think + link

Suggestions for using function machines are explored in Chapter 6

for the classroom

Functions as relational thinking

An online bookstore charges $7 for each of its comics and a flat rate of $1.50 for shipping. Ask students to complete this table.

Number of comics	Cost of comics	Total
1		
5		
12		
20		

Ask students to write a rule for calculating the total and to write the matching equation.

Functions as mapping

Functions consist of beginning values (input values) that are subjected to a consistent change (a rule). The resultant values after the change has occurred are called output values. These three components constitute a mapping.

For the bookstore problem the mapping is:

This concept is all-pervading in algebra. Most situations we confront consist of input values, rules, and output values. When we work from the input to the output we commonly say 'we are following the rule'. At times we are not given the input number but have the output number and the rule. For example, in the bookstore problem, suppose we were told that online bookstores charge $7 for each comic and $1.50 for shipping, and were asked 'If your bill was $57.50, how many comics did you order?'. We now have rules and the output value and are required to find the corresponding input value.

A common approach for solving this type of problem involves trial and error. A more powerful approach is 'reversing the rule', or backtracking. For the bookstore problem this entails reversing your thinking (knowing that addition and subtraction, and multiplication and division, are inverse operations). For the reverse situation the mapping is:

```
Number of comics  ← ÷ 7 ←  Cost of comics  ← − $1.50 ←  Total cost
```

Thus to work out the number of comics we could buy for $57.50 we subtract $1.50 and divide by 7.

Students as young as 8 can engage with this type of thinking, but the use of physical function machines and kinaesthetics, walking forwards past the machine to follow the rule and walking backwards past the machine to reverse the rule, greatly assists students' understanding of 'following and reversing the change', and the inverse relationships between the operations. It also assists them to represent the function as a mapping and to see the inverse relationship between the operations explicitly.

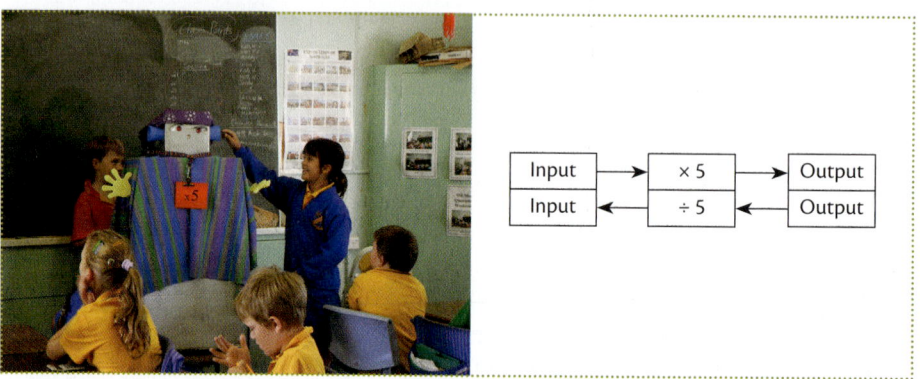

Backtracking has its limitations, and in some instances is an inapplicable strategy (MacGregor & Stacey, 1995). For example, for an equation such as $2x + 4 = x + 7$, backtracking will not work.

Our aim is to introduce students to a variety of ways of representing algebraic thinking and a variety of methods to solve problems, and to encourage them to move flexibly across representations and methods to reach solutions.

Physical machines can assist students to engage in the game of 'Guess my rule'. This game can be played in a variety of ways. The machine could be represented by a small box, shaped like a robot (see Chapter 13). One student places a rule in the function machine (e.g. multiply by 2 and add 1). The rule is known only to that student. A second student plays the role of recorder. As volunteers in the class call out an input number, the first student works out the corresponding output number. The second student records each input number with its output number in a table of values on the board. The game continues until a student correctly guesses the rule. The rule has to match what is in the box.

Younger students can use simple rules, for example 'add 2', and the function box could be a large box that they can stand in, with 'in' and 'out' windows. Concrete materials can be used to model the change rule, for example, one student could place three blocks or icy-pole sticks in the box and receive five in return through the out window.

A variation for older students is that the teacher draws a table of values with some of the values missing on the board.

Input	2	5	12	30		45	n
Output	5	14	35	89	119		

Before moving to writing the rule, ensure that students are searching for relationships between the pairs of input and output values. Encourage them to discuss in both words and numbers what the rule may be (e.g. add 3 to the input number). As they share their rule, test if their rule works for all pairs. Finally help them to try to generalise the relationship with symbols. They may say 'you add the number three times and then you take one from the answer'. Help them to see that adding the number three times is the same as $n + n + n$. Discuss how this is the same as multiplying the number by 3, and explore other ways they could write this. Ask if multiplying by three and taking off one is the same as taking off one and multiplying by three, and explain why $3n - 1$ and $3(n - 1)$ are not equal. This discussion allows you to revisit the order of operations and the need for brackets. Ensure that they realise that n takes the same value at the same time, for example, if the input is 236 then the output is $(236 + 236 + 236) - 1$.

Students need an array of experiences with these ideas as they progress through the primary school. All students enjoy acting out the machine rule. Ensure that there is a calculator at hand so that the 'rule followers' can check their calculations when the need arises. It is important to give the correct output number for each input number.

Functions as graphical representations

Most of the functions we explore in the middle years are linear functions, which are represented as straight line graphs. Revisiting the swimming pool decking problem, the relationship between the size of the pool and the number of decking tiles required is $2n + 6$.

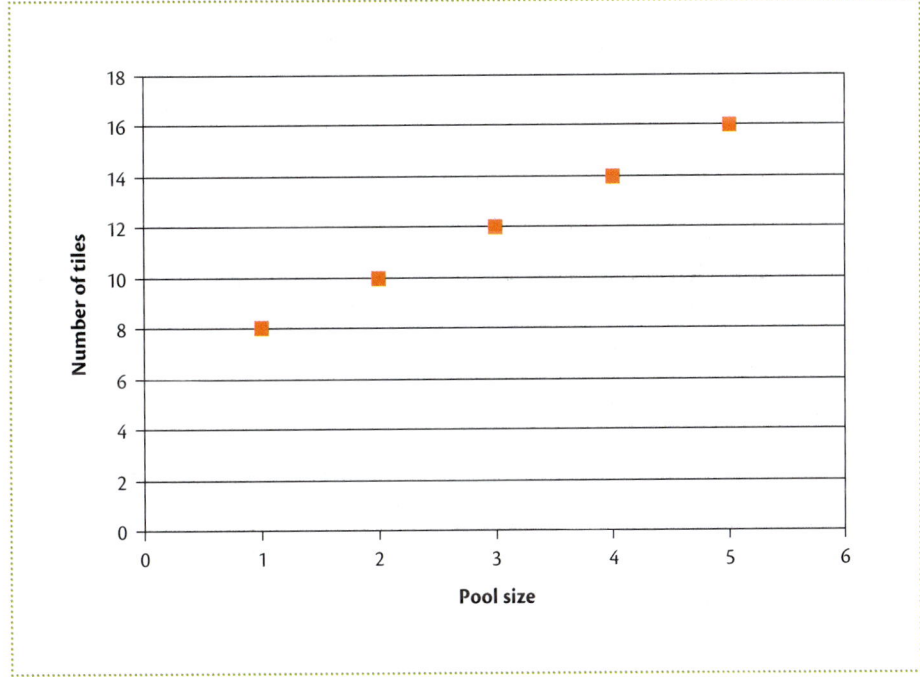

The graph shows that the relationship between the pool size and the number of decking tiles is linear. The points lie on a straight line that is increasing. The graph allows us to extrapolate our solutions to larger pool sizes.

consider and discuss

Structure of graphs

In the above graph, why haven't we joined all the points? How many decking tiles would you need for a size 30 pool? Which is the dependent variable, and which is the independent variable? Justify your answer.

When farmers harvest their hay, they choose from three packing methods. They pack it as small round bales, small rectangular bales, or large round bales. In choosing a method farmers consider the cost of the machinery, the amount of hay they need, and the weather patterns. The hay must not get wet during packing. The rates that the machines can pack are: small round 6 t per hour, small rectangular 15 t per hour, and large round 40 t per hour. Draw graphs for each and discuss the machine choice for a variety of conditions. Justify the reasons for your choices.

If a farmer works for 10 hours a day for 6 days with the small round bale machine, what mass of hay will be baled? What does the **slope** of each graph represent? How is rate of production related to the slope of the graph?

The focus of this problem is the construction of the graphs and interpreting the graphs to provide answers to contextual questions. We have found that to understand graphs fully students need to be involved in their construction, not just given graphs from which they read solutions.

Not all graphs are linear. For example, suppose we had a fixed 100 m length of fencing, and we wanted to make a rectangular paddock for our sheep. The area will vary according to the length we choose for our rectangle. What would the area graph look like?

Equivalence and equations

think + link

Chapter 13 explores ways to develop students' understanding of equality and balance.

Equivalence is another key concept of algebraic thinking, and must be grounded early and often. A common misconception is that equals means 'the answer is coming'. In the early grades we used a physical balance scale and strips of paper to represent different equations to help students develop an intuitive understanding of the connection between equality and balance. In this chapter we extend this understanding to investigate more complex problems, and explore the balance strategy for solving unknowns.

for the classroom

Solving problems using the balance strategy

A scale has three boxes of counters and four loose counters on one side, and a box and a bag with 20 counters on the other side. All boxes have the same number of counters.

Ask students to complete the steps to find the number of counters in one box (for 10–11-year-olds).

As students work through the problem the focus must be on maintaining the balance. When they take an amount from one side of the scale an equivalent amount must be taken from the other side of the scale.

The balance strategy for finding the number of counters in the box is not a guess and check strategy.

issues in teaching

Making connections between the operations in arithmetic and algebra

One of the most difficult processes in algebraic thinking is termed crossing the didactic cut, or crossing the cognitive gap. Put simply, this involves being able to solve equations with more than one unknown on each side, for example, $3n + 4 = n + 20$. Solving these types of problems requires a deep understanding of arithmetic and linking this understanding to algebra.

As a teacher, it is important to discuss how $3n$ is the same as $n + n + n$ (without using erroneous methods such as the fruit-salad algebra 'three bananas is banana plus banana plus banana'). A teaching approach that assists this discussion is to link back to arithmetic and use the mapping between repeated addition and multiplication.

$25 + 25 + 25$	$n + n + n$
3 groups of 25	3 groups of n
3×25	$3 \times n$
	$3n$

Students must also be aware of the inverse relationships between the operations. Addition and subtraction are inverse operations, and multiplication and division are inverse operations. Activities involving function machines greatly assist in establishing these connections.

$$3n + 4 = n + 20$$
$$n + n + n + 4 = n + 20 \text{ (ungrouping the } n\text{s)}$$
$$n + n + n = n + 16 \text{ (taking 4 from each side)}$$
$$n + n = 16 \text{ (taking } n \text{ from each side)}$$
$$2n = 16 \text{ (regrouping the } n\text{s)}$$
$$n = 8 \text{ (halving each side)}$$

Young students can engage with this thinking. Six–seven-year-olds can draw counters to balance a given number on scales, for example 'Draw counters to show different ways to balance the number 5'. and then write the appropriate mathematical equation ($5 = 3 + 2$, or $4 + 1 = 3 + 2$). It is important to ensure that equations are written horizontally and that students create equations with more than one number on both sides. Encourage students also to start with the symbolic equation and draw the appropriate balance. By age 7 or 8, students can write numbers on scales to illustrate simple inequalities and use these to complete sentences of the form '__ is greater than __' and its converse.

consider and discuss

Solving problems using the balance strategy

Phil's kitchen has 4 different sized measuring cups. He knows that Cup A holds as much as Cup B and Cup C; Cup C holds as much as Cup B and Cup D; 3 Cup Ds hold as much as 2 Cup As. What is the relationship between Cup B and Cup C? Represent your problem using a balance scale and discuss how you used the balance strategy to find your answer.

Model approach—using the length model

Another approach to representing algebraic situations has emerged from a large body of research from Singapore. This method uses diagrams to represent quantities and the relationships between and among quantities and unknowns (Ferrucci, Kaur, Carter & Yeap, 2008). It begins with identifying the variables related to the situation and creates a model that consists of different lengths to represent the knowns and unknowns as identified by the problem context. This can be a difficult process for students to learn (Kieran, 1992). Once the model is established, subsequent stages involve manipulating the model to derive results and then interpreting these results in terms of the initial model. The following two situations show how this approach can be used to solve complex problems.

Situation 1 (Equivalence problems)
Problem: There are 3 boxes of groceries lablelled A, B, and C.
Box A contains 3 times a many apples as Box B.
Box B contains half a many apples as Box C.
Box C contains 12 fewer apples than Box A.
Find the number of apples in each box.

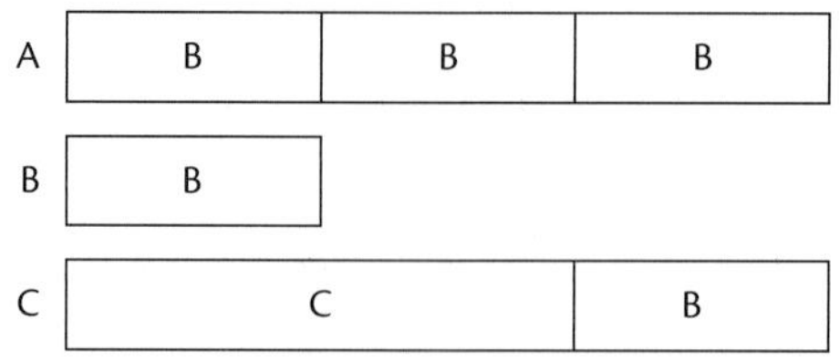

A	B	B	B

B	B

C	C	B

B has 12 apples, A has 36 and C has 24 apples.

Situation 2 (Change problems)
Problem: Charlotte has twice as much money as Billy has. If Charlotte spends $18 and Billy saves another $5, Billy will have $2 more than Charlotte. How much money did they each have at the beginning?

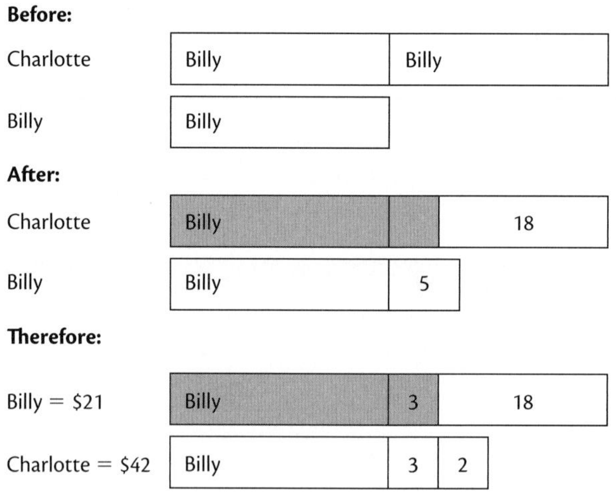

Before:

Charlotte | Billy | Billy

Billy | Billy

After:

Charlotte | Billy | 18

Billy | Billy | 5

Therefore:

Billy = $21 | Billy | 3 | 18

Charlotte = $42 | Billy | 3 | 2

The above examples serve as precursors for solving simultaneous problems with two unknowns. The advantage of this approach is that it allows students to create mathematical expressions represented by contextual diagrams. It also allows the focus to be on the structural aspects of the problem. Like formal algebra, it is only after the problem has been represented that it can be manipulated to reach solutions. As students work across different types of problems it also allows them to 'see' the structural similarities between problems. In Singapore this approach is often introduced to students as young as 8, where they apply it to simple problems such 'Jack has 345 marbles. Nancy has 265 marbles. How many more marbles has Jack than Nancy?'. As these students progress through school they begin to use this approach to solve multi-step problems, for example, 'Sam spent 20% of his money on model train. He then spent $\frac{2}{5}$ of the remainder on a book. He had $60 left. How much money did he start with?'

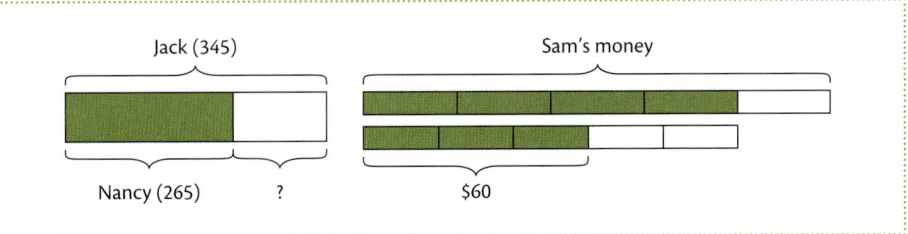

consider and discuss

Solving problems using a model approach

The ratio of the number of boys to the number of girls in the school is 3 : 8. There are 120 more girls than boys. If the number of boys increases by 3 and the number of girls decreases by 12, what will be the new ratio of the number of boys to the number of girls?

Discuss how you would solve this problem by two different approaches including the model approach described above. Identify the strengths and weaknesses of using the model approach to solve these problems. What prior knowledge would students need to have in order to engage in finding solutions?

integrating technology

Previously the functions that students explored tended to be simple and were predominantly linear functions. This was because of the tedium associated with computing and plotting function values, and making the link to real world contexts was almost impossible. With the introduction of spreadsheets and graphic calculators students are now able to investigate a wide range of functions.

for the classroom

Using technology

Let's return to the fencing problem.

Suppose we had a fixed length of fencing, 100 m, and we wanted to make a rectangular paddock for our sheep. The area will vary according to the length we choose for our rectangle. What would the area graph look like?

Discuss the relationship between the length, breadth, and area of a rectangle. What would happen to the breadth if we increased the length by 1 m? How would we work out the area? Can you write how the breadth and length are related?

Generate a number of answers to the problem. Organise them in tables of values, and look for the generalisations. Once students have recognised the generalisations, encourage them to use a spreadsheet to create a table of values and a graph of the function.

Extend the problem by asking: If we had a wall of the barn as one side of the paddock, what would the graph look like?

Conclusion

The introduction of algebraic thinking into primary schools is gaining momentum. This is best evidenced by the inclusion of a Number and Algebra strand in the Australian national curriculum for mathematics, with the algebra component delineating content descriptors from Foundation to Year 12. This has occurred for two main reasons. First, there is strong evidence that students have difficulties engaging with algebraic concepts in the secondary school, and that these difficulties stem from their understanding of arithmetic with its focus on computation and obtaining answers, whereas algebraic thinking is about representing problems and reaching generalisations. Second, research has demonstrated that young students can engage successfully with algebraic thinking in contextual situations. Algebraic thinking in the primary years is not about introducing formal methods (these are usually introduced in secondary schools). It is about engaging with a variety of problems in a structural way, using a variety of representations that assist students to think algebraically, to articulate generalisations, and to justify their solutions. This engagement supports the development of both algebraic and arithmetic thinking.

This chapter has illustrated a variety of ways to represent functional situations. The ability to construct and switch between representations is fundamental to learning. We have also examined ways to search for patterns and regularities that can then be expressed using mathematical models, such as diagrams, tables of values, language, equations, and graphs. These representations should never be considered in isolation. Each contributes to an understanding of the whole, a multi-representational approach to learning. As Kaput (1999) stated, 'the cognitive linking of the representations creates a whole that is more than the sum of its parts … it enables us to see complex ideas in a new way and apply these ideas more effectively.'

key terms

Dependent variable: the variable whose value depends on the value assigned to another variable, called the independent variable

Equation: a statement of equality existing between numbers and variables with the equalities being connected by an equals sign

Equivalence: a relation holding between two statements so that they both have to be simultaneously true or simultaneously false

Function: a function f of a variable x is a rule that assigns to each number x in the function's domain a single number $f(x)$

Generalisation: the process of formulating general concepts by abstracting common properties of instances

Independent variable: the variable whose value is independent of the value assigned to another variable

Slope: a synonym for gradient; the steepness, incline, or grade of a line

Variable: a value that may change within the scope of a given problem or set of operations

Review questions

1. What do we mean by the terms *variable* and *unknown*? How would you introduce students to the notion of a variable in the context of the classroom?
2. What is the correct meaning of the equals sign? What activities will assist students come to this understanding, especially in the early years of schooling?
3. Explain what is meant by *recursive thinking* and *relational thinking*. Illustrate your answer using both a growing pattern and a table of values.
4. Describe the differences between the backtracking and balance strategies for solving equations. Illustrate the difference by using both to solve the problem $3 \times \diamondsuit + 7 = 82$.
5. Make up a real-world example that defines a functional relationship. Useing your example, state the relationship in language, state the relationship in symbols, build a table of values that go with the relationship, and draw the graph of the relationship,

Key references

Carraher, D.W., & Schliemann, A. D. (2007), Early algebra and algebraic reasoning. In F. Lester (Ed.) *Second Handbook of Research on Mathematics Teaching and Learning: A Project of the National Council of Teachers of Mathematics* (Vol 2, pp. 669–705). Charlotte, NC: Information Age.

Kieran, C. (1992). The learning and teaching of school algebra. In D. A. Grouws (Ed.), *Handbook of Research in Mathematics Teaching and Learning* (pp. 390–419). New York: Macmillan.

Kuchemann, D. (1981). Algebra. In K. Hart (Ed.), *Children's Understanding of Mathematics: 11–16* (pp. 102–119). London: Murray.

Warren E. (2002). Children's understanding of turnarounds: A foundation for algebra. *Australian Primary Mathematics Classroom*, 7, 9–15.

26 Consolidating Measurement Concepts

Contents

Extending measurement concepts	605
Area	605
Developing area formulae	610
Volume and capacity	617
Mass	622
Money	623
Conclusion	624

Chapter objectives

This chapter will enable the reader to:
- Investigate approaches for extending measurement understandings to include the concepts of perimeter, area, volume, capacity, mass, and money
- Identify the challenges associated with extending student understandings into perimeter, area, volume, capacity, mass, and money.

Formula for success?

Some Year 7 students were asked to explain how they would use a formula to calculate the area of a triangle. Here are their responses:

Verity: I use $\frac{1}{2} \times b \times h$ because it always gives the right answer.
Kaleb: I know the formula is $\frac{1}{2} \times b \times h$ but I'm not sure why it works.
Lucy: Sometimes I forget what formula I need to use. I know that a triangle is half of a rectangle. So I know that I can use the rectangle formula ($l \times w$) and then find half.
Andrew: Triangles that are the same can always be joined together to make a parallelogram, so I draw the parallelogram and use $b \times h$ and then find half.

- Will Verity always get the right answer?
- Is it a cause for concern that Kaleb is using a formula that he does not understand?
- Will Lucy ever encounter any difficulties with her approach?
- Will Andrew always need to use his approach?

Big ideas

- The measurement of perimeter, area, and volume requires the measurement of length.
- Area and volume are rarely measured directly; rather they are calculated using formulae.

- The successful use of measurement formulae is underpinned by an understanding of how the formulae have been derived.
- Important relationships exist between various measures. These include: perimeter and area, area and volume, volume and capacity, and volume and mass. An understanding of these relationships is key to extending measurement concepts.

Extending measurement concepts

In the early primary years students begin to explore the meaning and process of measurement. They experience measuring length using non-standard units such as paper clips or hand spans. As a result, they develop an appreciation of the need for the use of standard units.

Expanding students' understanding of measurement concepts involves building upon earlier foundations to extend into investigations of perimeter and area, volume and capacity, and mass. Considering money as a measure of value is also essential when extending students' understandings of measurement concepts.

Area

Area teaching sequence

According to Battista (2007), a genuine appreciation of the measurement of area requires that students understand:

- what the area attribute is and how it behaves (conservation when figure is rearranged)
- how area is measured by iterating units of area
- how numerical processes can be used to determine area
- how these numerical processes are represented in words and algebraically.

Students in Year 4 and Year 8 have an incomplete understanding of area (Blume, Galindo & Walcott, 2007). This may be because area differs from length in that we do not usually measure area directly. On most occasions, we measure a combination of lengths and then use a formula to calculate area. Therefore, as with length, students need to first understand the attribute of area before measuring it and calculating it.

If an appropriate sequence of teaching and learning activities is adopted, such as the following, students will be provided with the opportunity to develop and build a sound conceptual understanding of the concept of area.

- Developing the concept of area begins by making direct physical comparisons of the areas of different objects (Years 2 and 3).
- This is followed by exploring the concept of **area** as a measure of covering. In this way the meaning of measurement as the number of units needed to cover the region is developed (Years 3 and 4).

think + link

A number of aspects in this area teaching sequence have parallels with the length learning sequence described in Chapter 19.

- Students use non-standard and standard units in covering activities to determine the area of regular and non-regular figures and regions (Years 4 and 5).
- Once students have successfully mastered these stages they are able to progress to developing and applying the various formulae that are used to calculate area (Years 6, 7, and 8).

As in the teaching of length, students also need to develop the ability to estimate areas using appropriate units of measurement, use appropriate language for the measurement of area, and relate the precision required to the magnitude of the area unit of measurement.

Comparing areas

Comparisons of area are more complex than comparisons of length. When comparing areas we must take into account length, width, and shape. If the area of these two figures were to be compared, most students would select figure B without any need to determine the area.

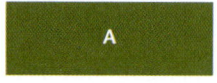
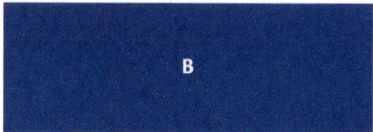

However, figures C and D make the task considerably more difficult. This is because one figure is wider and the other is longer. This requires the student to consider more than one dimension, and this is a particularly difficult concept for students to grasp.

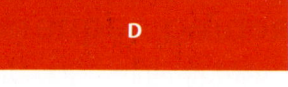

consider and discuss

How could a student successfully compare the areas of figures C and D by using a covering approach?

As shapes get more complex, the 'look and compare' strategy becomes increasingly difficult. The use of units of area is introduced at this stage in order to be able to compare areas, and the concept that area is a measure of covering is developed.

Measuring area using non-standard units

The concept of area as a measure of covering can be established through the use of manipulatives such as counters, coloured rods, or blocks. Care needs to be taken when using manipulatives that have three dimensions, such as coloured rods or blocks, as it is the surface area of just one face that is being used as the unit of measurement. Counters, on the other hand, are very useful as they approximate to having only two dimensions and they provide the opportunity to explore the importance of tiling.

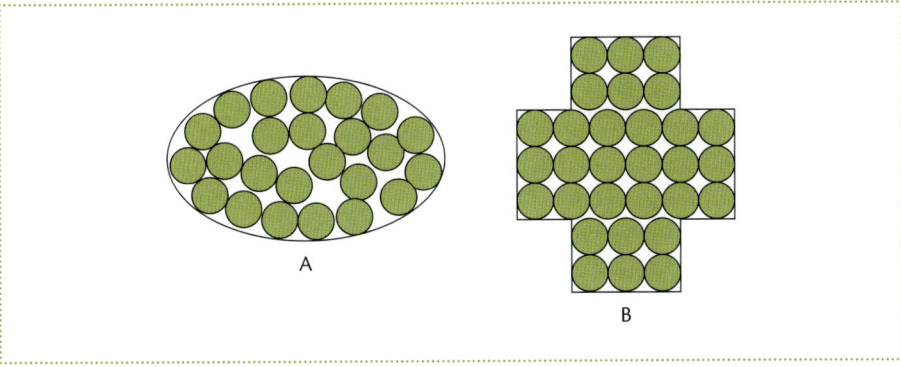

It is important to emphasise that the counters should not overlap or lie outside the boundary of the figure. We can see that it takes 24 counters to cover figure A and 30 counters to cover figure B. This will help students to decide that figure B has the greater area.

Now consider these two figures:

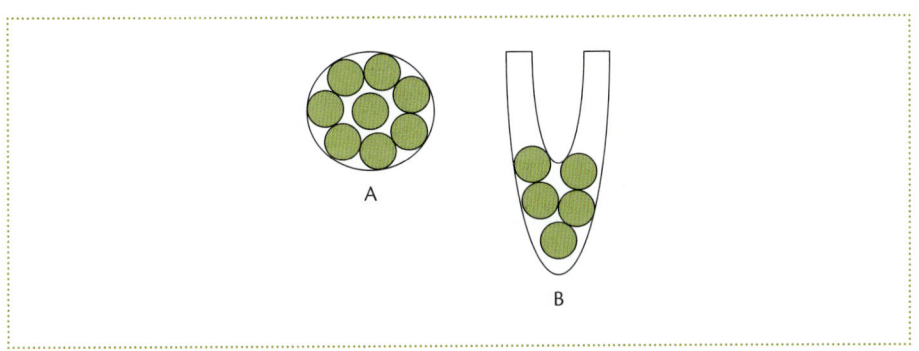

We can see that it takes eight counters to cover figure A but there are only five counters placed on figure B. However, does figure A actually have a greater area? Students will quickly observe that much of the inside of figure B has been left uncovered. This is because the counters do not fit together well when placed on this figure. Arising from this activity will be the recognition that a shape used as the unit of area must **tessellate**. This means that when the shapes are laid out they will match perfectly with no space between them, as in tiling.

A number of different tessellating shapes could be used as units of area, for example triangles, parallelograms, or hexagons (see Figure 26.1). However, students should mostly be using square units of area in their covering activities. Because square units of measurement are used when calculating area using formulae, the use of square units of area will emphasise that the area is the number of square units it takes to cover the figure internally (see Figure 26.2).

think + link

Have another look at Chapter 11 to review the concept of tiling.

Figure 26.1 Tessellating shapes that could be used as units of area

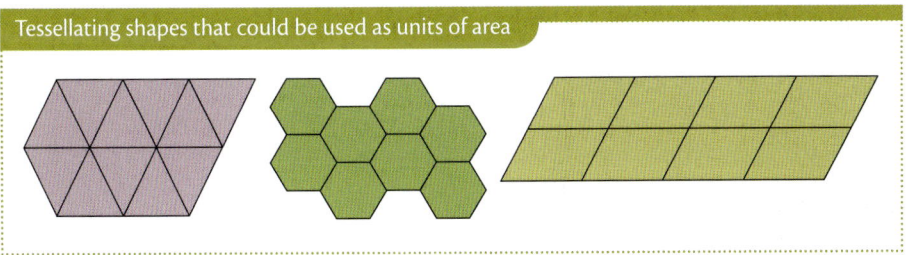

Figure 26.2 The area of this figure is 6 square units

Covering activities should progress to situations where some of the units only partially fit. Student will need to explore the concept of partial units and mentally put together two or more partial units to comprise one unit (see Figures 26.3 and 26.4).

Figure 26.3 To cover this figure we use 6 whole square units and 2 half square units. In total, the area is 7 square units.

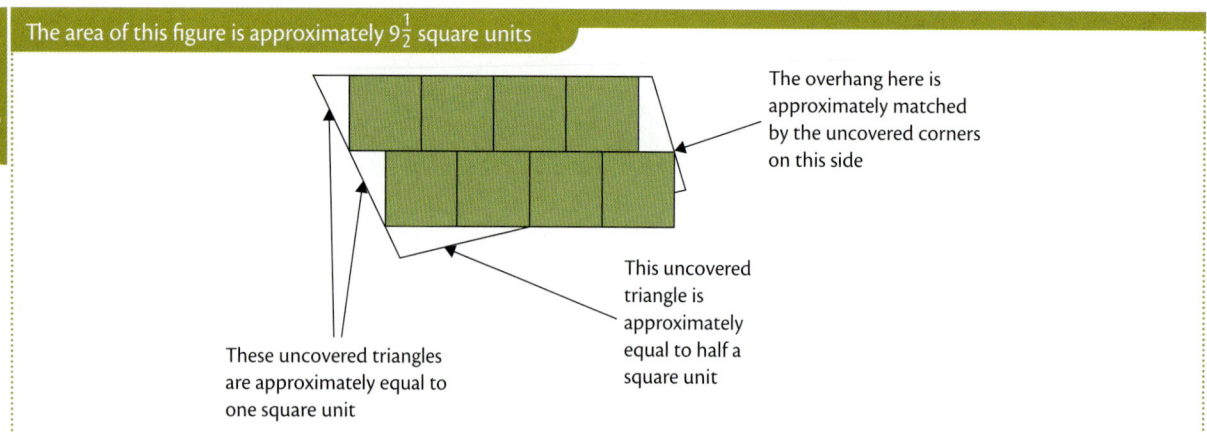

Figure 26.4 The area of this figure is approximately $9\frac{1}{2}$ square units

The overhang here is approximately matched by the uncovered corners on this side

This uncovered triangle is approximately equal to half a square unit

These uncovered triangles are approximately equal to one square unit

 ### for the classroom

Students can explore the concept of conservation of area by cutting an A4 sheet of paper in half diagonally and then rearranging into other shapes such as:

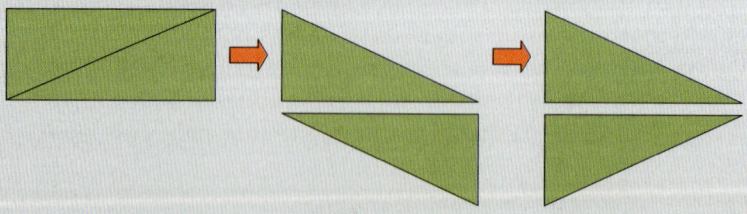

What other different shapes could be made using the two triangles?

Students can consider and discuss what might be an appropriate tessellating unit of area to investigate the area of each arrangement, including the original rectangle.

Encourage students to record what they have noticed and give reasons for why this may be so.

Measuring area using standard units

We have established that standard units of measurement are required to provide a consistent basis for comparison when measuring and for clear communication about measurement outcomes. The standard unit of area for small figures or objects is the square centimetre (cm²). The square metre (m²) is appropriate for determining, for instance, the area of rooms or walls. The hectare (ha) is the unit used for small areas of land, and square kilometres (km²) is used for measuring areas of land such as entire states or countries.

To move from non-standard units to standard units for measuring area, students commence with using 1 centimetre squares for covering activities. It is important to provide students with the chance to explore the area of irregular figures in this phase (as in Figure 26.4). In this way, students will begin to develop the understanding that it is possible to determine the area of both regular and irregular regions when using standard units.

for the classroom

Cut out 1 cm squares from paper or cardboard. Use these centimetre squares to cover rectangular and non-rectangular figures, estimating part units required as well. Practise using accurate language to describe the area of the figures. Alternatively, a transparent grid overlay could be used for this activity to avoid the need to cut out the squares.

Students could use centimetre square grid paper to trace an outline of their hand and then determine the area of their hand. Share and discuss strategies students use to count full and part squares on the grid.

Understanding the relationship between perimeter and area

Students can confuse the terms perimeter and area and misapply the respective formulae (Johnson & Norris, 2006). For this reason continual emphasis on the key difference between perimeter and area is necessary. **Perimeter** is a linear measurement that is the length around the boundary of a figure or a region. *Area* is a measurement of covering. Providing students with the opportunity to investigate the meaning of the word 'perimeter' will assist them in discriminating between the two measures. The word 'perimeter' has two parts: *peri*, which means around, and *meter*, from the Greek word *metron*, to measure. Therefore, perimeter means to measure around.

One significant source of confusion is that each measure involves a figure or region and that in applying formulae the same linear measurements—length, width, base, height—are used. If formulae are not understood conceptually, then students can easily become confused. A second source of confusion is the misconception that perimeter and area have a fixed relationship. Investigative activities that provide the students with the chance to explore the area of rectangles with fixed perimeters and the perimeters of rectangles with fixed areas reveal that two rectangles having the same area do not necessarily have the same perimeter. Similarly, two rectangles with the same perimeter do not always have the same area. Unsurprisingly, this concept is not restricted to rectangles.

for the classroom

Investigating fixed perimeters

Using centimetre grid paper, students draw rectangles with fixed perimeters of, for example, 18 or 24 units, and use the grid paper to calculate the area of each rectangle they have drawn.

Investigating fixed areas

Students are provided with a fixed number of square tiles, for example 24 or 36, and are required to form rectangles that use all of the tiles, ensuring that the region is completely covered. As new rectangles are created, the student records the results on grid paper by sketching the rectangle and labelling the dimensions. For each rectangle drawn, students determine and record the perimeter.

When using these activities, encourage students to explore the relationship between the length of the base and the height to notice that the closer these values are, the larger the area measured.

This type of activity can also be completed using a pre-populated spreadsheet. See the Integrating technology/ICT activity on page 612.

Developing area formulae

Area of rectangle

Students do not have a good understanding of the use of measurement formulae (Blume et al., 2007), possibly because of their rote use of formulae with little or no concept or appreciation of their origins. When students are given the chance to develop measurement formulae, they acquire a deeper conceptual understanding of the relationships involved in measuring and they engage with an authentic mathematical process.

The formula for the area of a rectangle is usually the first that students are able to develop. This formula has traditionally been written as $A = l \times w$, or area is equal to the length times the width. However, to provide greater consistency with other area and volume formulae, this formula might be better given as $A = b \times h$, or area is equal to the base times the height.

While filling in rectangles with square units may be useful for developing an understanding of the concept of area, this type of activity has almost no impact on understanding formulae. Battista (2003) observes that many students are unable to generalise that the area of a rectangle can be found by multiplying the number of square units lying along the base by the height. Rather, the students in his study filled in the missing square units to cover the rectangle and counted the result.

A return to the concept of multiplication as represented in an array can assist in developing an understanding of the formula for the area of a rectangle. Begin with an array of objects set out in rows and columns, and review how multiplication can give the total number of objects. That is, we count the number of objects in one row and then determine how many rows there are in all to find the total. This is the same concept that students need to use to calculate the area of a rectangle.

Battista (2003) found the students had not considered that a row of squares could be duplicated in multiple rows. He suggests that students could be given the chance to realise this by using diagrams that hide some of the square units covering the region (see Figure 26.5). This leads students to see that it is possible to calculate the area of a rectangle by multiplying the number of squares in each row by the number of rows.

Figure 26.5 In this rectangle the bottom row has 6 squares, so there must be 6 squares in all the other rows. There are 4 rows. So the area will be 6 × 4 = 24 square units

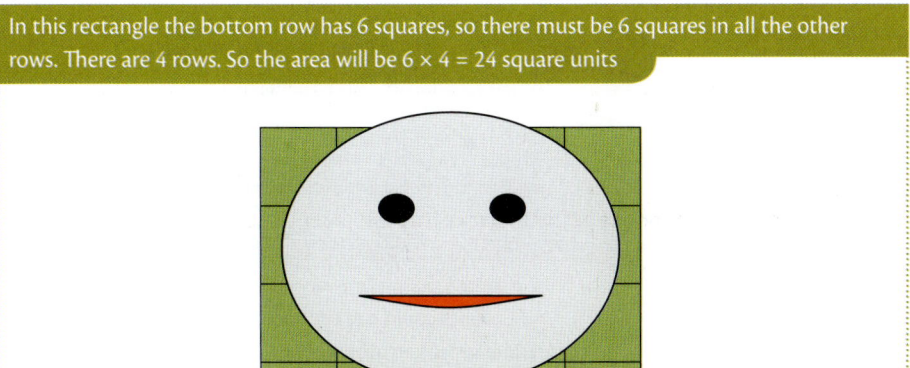

The final step in generating the formula is crucial to developing understanding. The focus is the concept that length of one row is equal to the number of squares that can fit exactly along that row, and the height is determined by the number of rows of squares that will fit into the rectangle. This concept is illustrated in Figure 26.6 with a 4 cm by 3 cm rectangle. Note that linear units are not being counted, but rather square units. This approach avoids the confusion that can result in linear units being mysteriously transformed into square units in the calculation of the area formula. When this concept has been well assimilated, the vocabulary of base and height can be introduced.

Figure 26.6 Three groups of 4 square centimetres or 3 × 4 square centimetres or 12 square centimetres

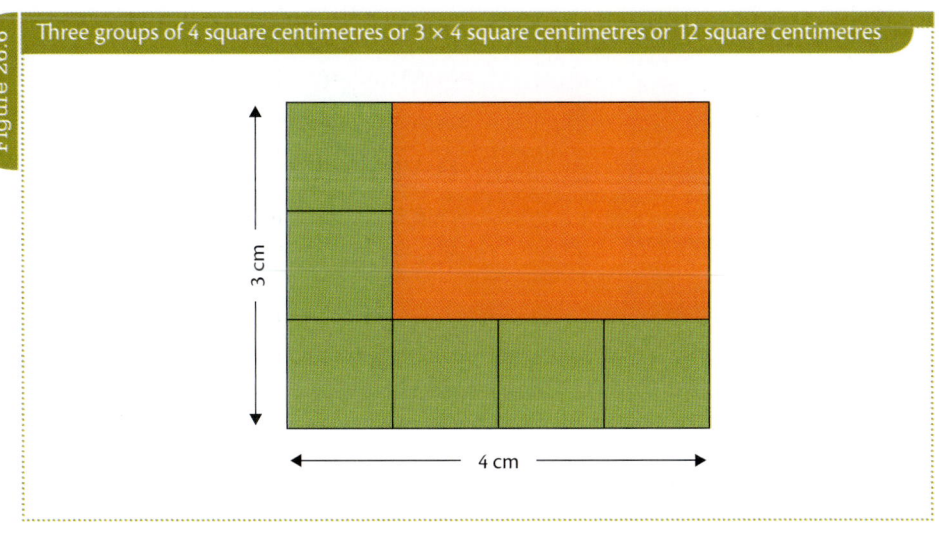

integrating technology/ICT

Using spreadsheets to investigate relationships between area and perimeter

Students could use spreadsheets with pre-populated formulae in an alternative approach to investigating the relationships between area and perimeter. For example, to explore the areas of rectangles with a fixed perimeter of 18 cm, the following spreadsheet could be used:

Base	Height	Perimeter	Area
	=9-A2	=2*(A2+B2)	=A2*B2
	=9-A3	=2*(A3+B3)	=A3*B3
	=9-A4	=2*(A4+B4)	=A4*B4
	=9-A5	=2*(A5+B5)	=A5*B5
	=9-A6	=2*(A6+B6)	=A6*B6
	=9-A7	=2*(A7+B7)	=A7*B7
	=9-A8	=2*(A8+B8)	=A8*B8
	=9-A9	=2*(A9+B9)	=A9*B9
	=9-A10	=2*(A10+B10)	=A10*B10
	=9-A11	=2*(A11+B11)	=A11*B11
	=9-A12	=2*(A12+B12)	=A12*B12
	=9-A13	=2*(A13+B13)	=A13*B13

Students can enter any values for the base length as shown, and the height, perimeter, and area will be generated automatically. Linked to a chart, the data in the spreadsheet would be visually represented for interpretation, as follows:

Base	Height	Perimeter	Area
0.5	8.5	18	4.25
1	8	18	8
1.5	7.5	18	11.25
2	7	18	14
3	6	18	18
4	5	18	20
5	4	18	20
5.5	3.5	18	19.25
6	3	18	18
6.5	2.5	18	16.25
7	2	18	14
7.5	1.5	18	11.25
8	1	18	8
8.9	0.1	18	0.89

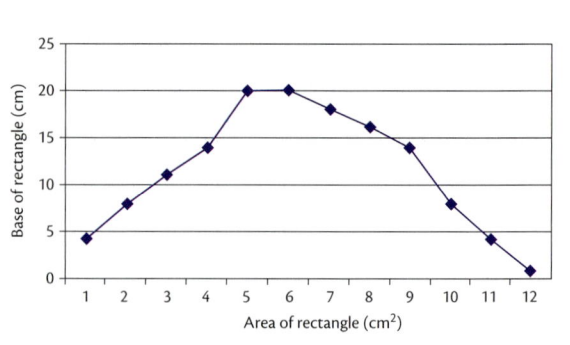

Students could use the spreadsheet to investigate whether or not an area of 20 is the maximum possible with a perimeter of 18. Explorations such as this are facilitated through spreadsheet use.

Similarly, a spreadsheet pre-populated with formulae can be used to investigate the perimeter of rectangles with fixed area. For example, to explore the perimeters of rectangles with a fixed area of 24, the following spreadsheet could be used:

Base	Height	Area	Perimeter
	=24/A2	=A2*B2	=2*(A2+B2)
	=24/A3	=A3*B3	=2*(A3+B3)
	=24/A4	=A4*B4	=2*(A4+B4)
	=24/A5	=A5*B5	=2*(A5+B5)
	=24/A6	=A6*B6	=2*(A6+B6)
	=24/A7	=A7*B7	=2*(A7+B7)
	=24/A8	=A8*B8	=2*(A8+B8)
	=24/A9	=A9*B9	=2*(A9+B9)
	=24/A10	=A10*B10	=2*(A10+B10)
	=24/A11	=A11*B11	=2*(A11+B11)
	=24/A12	=A12*B12	=2*(A12+B12)

As with the previous spreadsheet, students can enter any values for the base length and the height, perimeter and area will be generated automatically, and when linked to a chart, the data in the spreadsheet would be visually represented as follows:

Chapter 26 Consolidating Measurement Concepts

Base	Height	Area	Perimeter
1	24.0	24.0	50.0
2	12.0	24.0	28.0
3	8.0	24.0	22.0
4	6.0	24.0	20.0
6	4.0	24.0	20.0
8	3.0	24.0	22.0
10	2.4	24.0	24.8
12	2.0	24.0	28.0
16	1.5	24.0	35.0
20	1.2	24.0	42.4
24	1.0	24.0	50.0

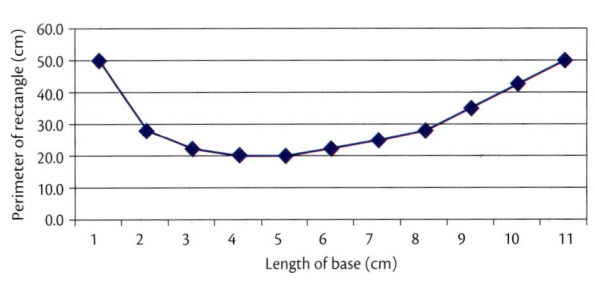

Using a spreadsheet students can investigate whether or not the minimum perimeter occurs when the figure is a square, and what the maximum perimeter possible might be.

Other area formulae

The key idea that underpins the development of most of the other area formulae is the concept of **conservation of area**: that the size of an area is not changed if the figure or region is rearranged. This means that we can generate area formulae for a number of other figures by rearranging their shapes to form a figure for which we do have an area formula, namely, the rectangle.

A logical first step is to move from the formula for a rectangle to the formula for other parallelograms. The successful development of this formula is underpinned by the use of the terms base and height in deriving $A = b \times h$ for the area of a rectangle, as suggested above. As illustrated in Figure 26.7, a parallelogram can always be rearranged into a rectangle with the same base and height, and hence with the same area. Therefore the area of a parallelogram is identical to that of a rectangle: $A = b \times h$.

Figure 26.7 Rearranging a parallelogram to form a rectangle: $A = b \times h$

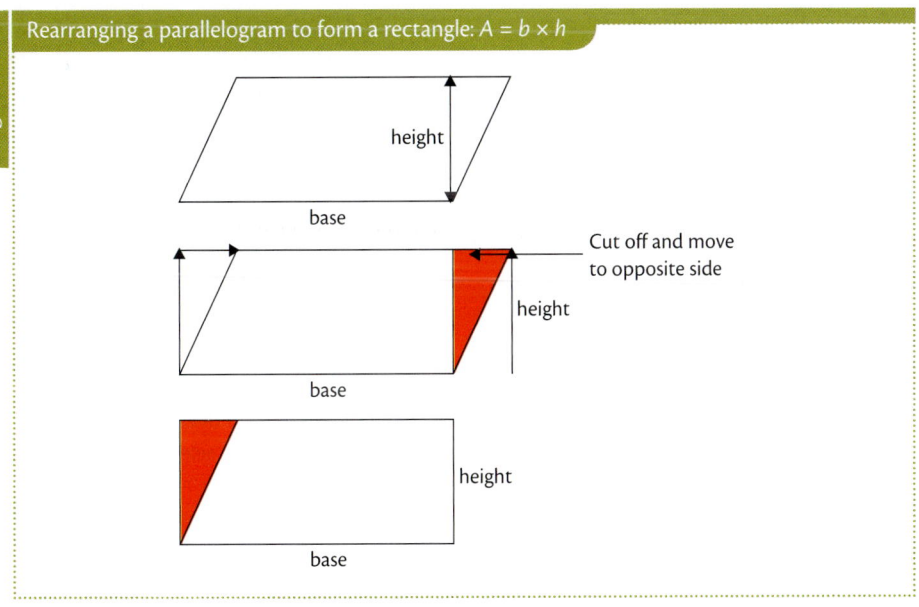

Moving from developing the formula for the area of parallelograms to deriving the formula for the area of a triangle is the next natural step. Underpinning this step is the concept that any two identical triangles can be arranged to form a parallelogram or a rectangle (Figure 26.8).

Figure 26.8 Arranging two identical triangles to form a parallelogram or a rectangle

This means that the total area of two identical triangles will be equal to the area of the parallelogram or rectangle: $A = b \times h$. Hence, the area of one triangle will be half the area of the parallelogram or rectangle, that is $A = \frac{1}{2} (b \times h)$.

consider and discuss

Developing the formula for the area of a trapezium

Explore how any two identical trapezia can be arranged to form a parallelogram. Use the arrangement to develop the formula for the area of a trapezium.

communicating mathematically

Some students have difficulty in conceptualising the meaning of the terms base and height in two- and three-dimensional figures. These figures have a slant side and a height as shown:

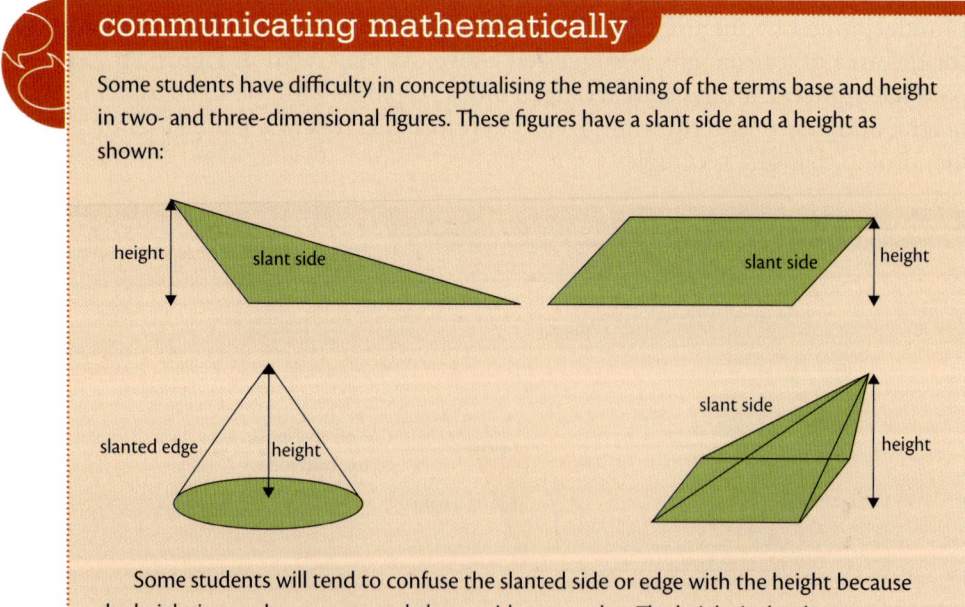

Some students will tend to confuse the slanted side or edge with the height because the height is not always measured along a side or an edge. The height is the shortest distance to the base. Encourage students to examine whether they have selected the shortest distance to the base as their height measurement.

Chapter 26 Consolidating Measurement Concepts

for the classroom

Fermi questions

Fermi questions associated with measurement often involve large numbers and the use of multiplicative thinking. Students may need to conduct some research to explore the required information. Here are some examples of Fermi questions that relate to measurement:

- How many people could we fit in the school gym when lying on the floor?
- What is the area our skin?
- How long would it take for our class to drink all of the water in the local swimming pool (if it were drinkable!)?
- If all the people in Australia stood side by side, how long would the line be?
- How many students would be needed to have the same mass as a blue whale?

think + link

Review the use of Fermi questions in Chapter 10.

Circumference and area of circles

Circles have many fascinating properties. One of these is the relationship between the *circumference* and and *diameter* of a circle. The **circumference** is the distance around its perimeter. The **diameter** of a circle is the straight line that passes through the centre of the circle joining two points on opposite sides of the circumference. The relationship between circumference and diameter is that, regardless of the size of the circle, when the length of the circumference is divided by the length of the diameter the result will be a constant value very close to 3.14. This value is represented by the Greek letter π (**pi**) and the relationship is summarised in the formula $\pi = \frac{C}{d}$, sometimes rearranged as $C = \pi d$. Since the radius of a circle is half the length of the diameter, another way to express the relationship is $C = \pi \times 2r$, or $C = 2\pi r$.

consider and discuss

How could students use a basketball to explore the special relationship between the circumference and the diameter of a circle?

think + link

Look back at Chapter 20 to review some of the other properties of circles.

Here is a circle. We want to find the area of this circle, but do not have a formula to do so. So we need to rearrange the circle to form a figure for which we have a formula, namely the rectangle. The following sequence develops the formula for the area of a circle.

The circle is divided into 8 equal parts.

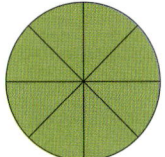

The 8 sectors are rearranged to form a shape that is very similar to a parallelogram. Notice that the height of this shape is the length of the radius, r, and that the base of this shape is half the length of the circumference, πr.

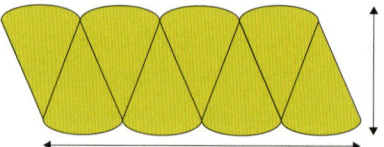

If the circle is divided into 16 sectors and rearranged the resulting shape is even more like a parallelogram.

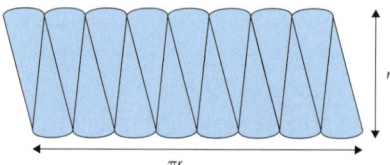

As the number of sectors increases further and is then rearranged, the resulting figure will be more and more like a rectangle. To find the area of this we multiply the base and the height.

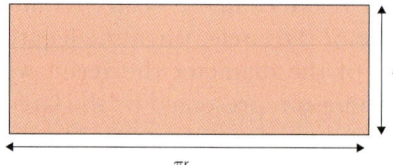

$A = \pi r \times r$ or $A = \pi r^2$

issues in teaching

Some students can easily confuse the formula for the circumference of a circle with the formula for area of a circle. This is because the formula for the circumference of a circle is often written as $C = 2\pi r$ and this too closely resembles the formula for the area of a circle $A = \pi r^2$. One suggestion is always to write the formula for the circumference of the circle as $C = \pi d$ to minimise the confusion and to more accurately represent the relationship between the circumference and the diameter. Writing the formula in this way also more meaningfully reinforces the development of the formula as the unique relationship between the diameter and the circumference of a circle.

communicating mathematically

Measurement similes

Chapter 11 discussed the value of students developing personal referents for a range of units in order to be able to estimate measurements effectively. Joram (2003) suggests that one way of encouraging students to develop personal measurement referents, or benchmarks, is to provide them with the chance to complete measurement similes, for example, the wave was 8 metres high, about as high as a/the ___ (school building, for instance). The measurement in the first part of the simile ought to be unfamiliar to the student, or difficult to represent because it is relatively large or small. The second part of the simile should be familiar. Working in groups for this activity, students are able to discuss and confirm that the objects being generated are within a reasonable estimation of the target measurement. Students could also sketch diagrams of the objects used in the similes in order to help them visualise the magnitude of the objects and their respective measurements.

making connections

It's light years away

A light year is a measure of distance, although the term contains the word 'year', which is a unit of time. We are used to measuring lengths or distances in centimetres, metres, or kilometres, and these are units of measurement appropriate for almost all practical situations that involve measuring length or distance. However, when astronomers observe stars, things are different. The distances are enormous. For example, the closest star to Earth (besides our Sun) is approximately 38 000 000 000 000 kilometres away, and there are stars that are billions of times further away than that. When we think about such colossal distances, a kilometre is not a practical unit to use because the numbers are too large.

To measure immense distances, astronomers use a unit called a light year. Light travels at approximately 300 000 kilometres per second. Therefore, in one second light travels 300 000 kilometres and a light second is 300 000 kilometres.

A light year is the distance that light travels in a year, or:

300 000 × 60 s/min × 60 min/h × 24 h/day × 365 day/year = 9 460 800 000 000 km/year!

How can you use this figure to calculate the distance in light years to the next closest star to Earth?

Light helps us look back in time. The light from a star travels at the speed of light to reach Earth. If a star is 1 million light years away, it has taken the star's light 1 million years to get here, and the light we are seeing was created 1 million years ago. So what we are seeing is really how the star looked a million years ago, not how it looks today. In the same way, the Sun is approximately 8 light minutes away. If the Sun were to suddenly explode right now, we would not know about it for 8 minutes because that is how long it would take for the light of the explosion to get here.

How far in kilometres is a light minute? How far away from the Earth is the Sun in kilometres?

Volume and capacity

Volume and *capacity* are both measures that describe the size of a three-dimensional figure. **Volume** is the three-dimensional space that a figure occupies; it could also be described as the internal size of an object. **Capacity** is a measure of how much a three-dimensional figure can hold. Volume could therefore be considered to be a solid measure, and capacity as a measure of how much a container can hold.

As with length and area, students need to develop an understanding of the concept of volume before they can measure and calculate it successfully Lehrer, Jaslow and Curtis (2003) suggest that investigations of volume can proceed in parallel with investigations of area measurement, and that students' growing conceptions of area connect to their emerging understandings of volume, although mentally mastering units in three dimensions is more challenging than working with a two-dimensional equivalent (Battista, 1999).

Extending measurement concepts into volume is best achieved through a sequence of teaching and learning activities that progresses from comparison activities, through using non-standard and standard units to make direct measurements of volume, and then developing and using volume formulae. The *Australian Curriculum: Mathematics* (ACARA, 2010) commences this teaching sequence at Year 4.

think + link

Review how very large numbers can be written using scientific notation (Chapter 22). Use this information to rewrite the distance in kilometres that light travels in a year using scientific notation.

Understanding the relationship between area and volume

Strong parallels exist between the concept of area and the concept of volume. Measuring area involves determining how many units it takes to cover the surface of a figure. Measuring volume involves finding how many units it takes to fill the interior of an object. We rarely measure area directly. Rather, we measure linear dimensions and calculate the area using an appropriate formula. Likewise, we measure the linear dimensions and calculate the volume of a solid using an appropriate formula. In developing area formulae, when we do not have a formula for a particular figure we rearrange the figure into a shape for which we do have a formula. The development of formulae for volume is the same. When we do not have a volume formula for a particular figure, we rearrange the object into a shape for which we do have a formula.

Comparing volumes

Initial comparison activities ought to focus on capacity. A simple comparison activity is to pour water or sand into one container and then pour that amount into a comparison container. This will lead to developing order language such as 'holds more' or 'holds less'. Children can have difficulty in conceiving that the quantity of the contents remains the same even though the shape of the container changes, although, according to Piaget, most children have grasped the conservation of capacity by about 11 years (Hatfield, Edwards, Bitter & Morrow, 2000).

The volume of two containers can be compared directly if the containers are similar in shape.

Direct comparison is more difficult if containers have different shapes. While it may be possible to compare the internal size of the two shapes below by measuring capacity, if they were solid objects the volume would need to be compared using solid units of measure.

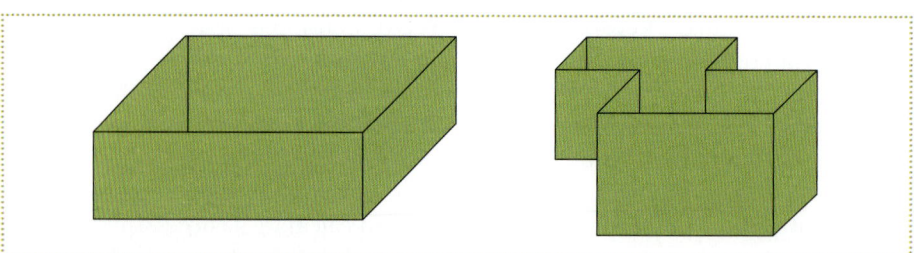

for the classroom

Use a pair of boxes where it is not possible to identify readily which has the larger volume. Have the students brainstorm as many ideas as possible for ways to determine the larger volume. Record every idea regardless of how sensible or practical it may be. Ask the students to decide which of the methods seems the most reasonable. Experiment with some of the suggested methods to decide how well they work.

Measuring volume using non-standard units

The concept of volume as a measure of filling with solid units can be established through the use of manipulatives such as marbles, small balls or blocks. For example, if each shape is filled with small balls, they can be counted to see which shape holds more.

As with measuring area using counters, there is space around each of the balls that is not being included in the measure. What is required is a solid unit of measurement that completely fills the three-dimensional space without any gaps, in other words a tessellating solid that can be used as a unit of measurement. Small cube blocks are the ideal tessellating manipulative to fill the internal space of boxes because in using cubes students will begin to grasp the understanding that the measure of volume is cubic units.

for the classroom

Pouring activities provide the opportunity for students to measure capacity using non-standard units of measurement. For example, students can measure how many of the small containers can be filled from a larger container like a sand bucket.

Measuring volume and capacity using standard units

The standard unit of volume for small three-dimensional objects, such as a shoebox, is cubic centimetres (cm^3). The volume of much larger three-dimensional spaces, for example a room, would be described using a standard unit of cubic metres (m^3). Millilitres (mL) is the standard unit applicable to small amounts of liquid, for instance a can of soft drink, and to the capacity of a small container. The standard unit adopted to measure the capacity of a larger object depends on the size of the object, for example litres (L), kilolitres (kL), and megalitres (ML). In a classroom, it would only be necessary to consider the capacity measurements of millilitres and litres.

Note that that one millilitre of water has a volume of one cubic centimetre and a mass of one gram.

consider and discuss

How could you demonstrate that a one cubic centimetre container has a capacity of one millilitre?

Developing volume formulae

Once students have grasped the development of area formulae, many parallels can be made when developing volume formula. Developing the formula for the volume of a rectangular prism is the most obvious starting point given the links that can be made with the formula for the area of a rectangle.

Just as a rectangle can be divided into unit squares to calculate its area, a rectangular prism can be divided into unit cubes. Encourage students to observe that each layer of cubes in a rectangular prism contains the same number of cubes as the base layer. If the number of layers is equal to the height of the rectangular prism, then the volume of the rectangular prism is the number of cubes in the base layer multiplied by the number of layers. Suppose the base layer contains 24 cubes and there are three layers, so the volume of this rectangular prism is $24 \times 3 = 72$ cubic units.

Since the number of cubes in the base layer is equal to the area of the base and the number of layers is equal to the height of the figure, the formula for the volume of a rectangular prism can be written as:

Volume = Area of base × Height or $V = A \times h$

The same formula can be used for any three-dimensional figure, provided each layer is exactly the same shape from base to top, in other words if the figure is a prism or cylinder.

issues in teaching

Square and cubic unit conversions

Some students may think that the conversion factor for metres to centimetres also applies for square metres to square centimetres, and cubic metres to cubic centimetres. Students need to be aware of double-checking square or cubic unit conversions as they become more familiar with them.

There are a number of ways that teachers can assist students with this. One way is to get students to think of square and cubic conversions as follows:

1 metre = 100 centimetres
1 square metre = 100^2 square centimetres
1 cubic metre = 100^3 cubic centimetres

Classroom models could be used to display the conversion factors as a visual mnemonic.

making connections

Administering drug doses

Medicines require careful measurement calculations.

Suppose a particular drug comes in vials that contain 50 mg of the drug in 2 mL of solution, and that the dose for children is 0.5 mg for each kilogram of body weight.

Two separate rate calculations are involved in this situation:

- calculating the amount of drug required, that is, the *mass* of the drug
- determining how much of the solution is needed, that is, the *volume* of the solution.

If this drug were to be administered to a child who weighs 25 kg, the two aspects to be calculated would be:

- How much of the drug would be prescribed for a 25 kg child if the dose is 0.5 mg per kilogram?
- The vials contain 50 mg in 2 mL of solution. How many millilitres would be needed to give the required dose?

In Australian hospitals, the first calculation is normally completed by the prescriber of the drug, that is, by the doctor.

The person who administers the drug, normally the nurse, carries out the second calculation. For patient safety nurses also check the reasonableness of the amount required.

Some nurses carry out their calculation using a mnemonic: **S**un **R**ise over **S**un **S**et.

Sun **R**ise describes **S**tock **R**equired, which in this case is 12.5 mg, or 25 kg × 0.5 mg.

Sun **S**et describes **S**tock **S**upplied, which in this case is the 50 mg in the vial.

The formula is Dose = $\frac{\text{Sun rise}}{\text{Sun set}}$ × volume

In other words, Dose = $\frac{\text{Stock required (12.5 mg)}}{\text{Stock supplied (50 mg)}}$ × volume (2 mL)

The dose for this child will be $\frac{12.5}{50}$ × 2 mL = 0.5 mL.

Consider another preparation that contains 60 mg of drug in 2.5 mL of solution. If the dose for an adult is 0.5 of drug for each kilogram of body weight, how much would be required for an adult weighing 80 kg?

did you know?

The National Measurement Institute (NMI) is Australia's peak measurement body responsible for the national measurement system and for maintaining Australia's units and standards of biological, chemical, legal, and physical measurement. The NMI is a division within the Commonwealth Department of Innovation, Industry, Science and Research.

The national measurement system, established in Australia in 1970, is a coherent formal system that ensures that measurements can be made on a consistent basis throughout the country. It ensures that practical measurements made by industry and the community are linked to the international system of units (**SI units**). SI units form the basis of Australia's hierarchy of measurement standards and are underpinned by seven base units that include metre, kilogram, and second.

All physical quantities may be measured in terms of the base units. Larger or smaller multiples of base units, as appropriate to the magnitude of the measurement required, are obtained by combining the base unit with a suitable prefix. For example, 'milli' is combined with 'metre' to form millimetre, a useful unit for small lengths.

integrating technology/ICT

Online resources designed to extend measurement concepts can be used for whole class or smaller group activities using an interactive whiteboard, or by individual students to consolidate their understandings. Check out the following websites.

Area tools

http://illuminations.nctm.org/ActivityDetail.aspx?ID=108

Students can use this tool to investigate how the length of the base and the height of a figure can be used to determine its area. This tool can also be used to explore the similarities and differences between the area formulae derived for trapezoids, parallelograms, and triangles.

http://illuminations.nctm.org/ActivityDetail.aspx?ID=21

This interactive geometry dictionary can be used to determine the areas of some common figures. Students can explore the relationships between the areas of triangles, parallelograms, and rectangles by finding the area of a triangle using the area of a parallelogram, which in turn can be found using the area of a rectangle.

Volume and capacity tools

http://illuminations.nctm.org/ActivityDetail.aspx?ID=6

Using this tool students fill a box with cubes, rows of cubes, or layers of cubes. The number of unit cubes needed to fill the entire box determines the volume of the box. This tool can also be used to investigate the relationship between width, depth, and height in deriving the formula for the volume of a rectangular prism.

http://www.abc.net.au/countusin/games/game15.htm

Students visually compare the volume of liquids poured into two containers. This tool would be ideally suited to students in the earlier primary years.

Perimeter explorer

http://www.shodor.org/interactivate/activities/PerimeterExplorer/

This tool automatically generates a random figure composed of a fixed number of square units. Using this tool, students can determine the perimeter of the figure and investigate the relationship between perimeter and area. There is also an area explorer that fixes the perimeter. Students can determine the area of the figure and further explore the relationship between perimeter and area. Using another associated tool, the shape explorer, students can investigate both the perimeter and the area of randomly generated figures.

Mass

What is mass?

The terms mass and weight are often used interchangeably but they have totally different definitions. **Mass** is the quantity of matter an object contains, and **weight** is the size of the force gravity exerts on an object. The weight of an object is determined by how much mass it has, and so tools to measure weight can be calibrated to measure mass. Because weight depends on the force of gravity it will be different on other planets, but the mass stays the same everywhere. In everyday language we usually disregard this extraordinary situation and make no distinction between the measures of mass and weight.

Measuring mass

Mass is never measured directly. Rather, it is measured using some type of spring-loaded scale. When the object being weighed is placed on the scale gravity pulls the object down causing the spring to stretch. The stretching spring triggers a display mechanism, either a dial or digital readout, that registers the mass as a number.

The *Australian Curriculum: Mathematics* introduces students to measuring mass in Year 2. These first approaches occur through making direct comparisons. Students can investigate heavy and light objects by manual comparison of objects. This type of activity naturally leads to ordering sets of objects according to their mass. Early experiences in measuring mass ought to also involve experimenting with beam balances to establish accurate interpretations of level and uneven beams.

Masses can also be compared indirectly using a beam balance. The mass of object A can be compared with another object B, and then the mass of another object C is also compared with object B. This investigation leads to generating comparative statements such as object A has greater or smaller mass than object C.

Eventually using standard units for the measurement of mass becomes necessary (Years 4, 5, and 6). Students should develop a feel for a one kilogram mass. A standard one litre bottle of water has a mass of one kilogram, and this is an object with which most students would be familiar. Comparisons should be made with other objects that have a one kilogram mass but differing volumes, for example a one kilogram bag of marbles, sawdust, or fabric scraps. Activities such as this develop an understanding of one of the relationships that exists between mass and volume, that objects with the same mass do not necessarily have the same volume.

making connections

The relationship between volume and mass is well known by bakers and cooks. Butter and margarine are normally sold in 500 g containers. However, many recipes call for a measure of butter in terms of volume units. Typically a recipe might require a $\frac{1}{2}$ cup of butter. An experienced cook knows that $\frac{1}{2}$ cup of butter is equivalent to 125 g. Because this conversion is not commonly taught in schools, cooks can only acquire the ability to carry out conversions such as this by building their experience in cookery.

What is the relationship between mass (grams) and volume (cups) for other ingredients such as oil, flour, or coconut?

Money

Money as a measure of value

Money is the unit used to measure the attribute known as value. This concept can provide a challenge for some students because what is of value to younger students will differ from what older students will value. For this reason, we need to distinguish between the concepts of value and worth. For example, a fine work of art will have greater worth to an art lover than to someone who is not, regardless of the price tag. Therefore, worth will always be relative.

for the classroom

Identifying and exploring the attribute of value

Discuss things that are most valuable to students and why they value them (worth).

Use retail catalogue pictures and have students rank items from cheapest to most expensive (value). Encourage the students to provide justifications for the way they have ranked particular items. Have the students share their rankings with each other to investigate any differences.

Activities such as this can help students to appreciate the concept that worth is relative rather than absolute.

Money learning sequence

The concrete learning experiences that facilitate an understanding of money as a unit of measurement involve developing money-handling skills. Concepts and skills in money are best approached through a coherent learning sequence, as described below.

Coin recognition and value

Early learning activities associated with coin recognition and value can be problematic for Australian students as the sizes of our coins are not proportional to their value. For example, the 50 cent coin is much larger than the two dollar coin. For many students the value of coins will be learnt only through repeated exposure to, and practice, in handling the various coins.

> **issues in teaching**
>
> Students whose number and measurement understandings remain linked to counting objects will be challenged by the value of coins, for example being given a single coin and then told this is '5'.

Counting money

Counting sets of coins involves first assigning a value to each coin, and then mentally adding up values. Therefore, some key number skills are essential to students being able to count sets of coins, most particularly in mentally adding one-digit and two-digit numbers. Students should encouraged to adopt whatever approach best suits them, such as starting with the coins with greater value or making combinations that comprise lots of 10. As money concepts are extended, skills in the use of decimal fractions will be required to manage money values that involve dollars and cents.

Once students are able to count sets of coins accurately they can compare the values of sets of coins and explore equivalent sets of coins that have the same value. An extension into selecting coins for a given amount provides a logical progression from counting sets of coins. The most valuable activities for students to develop money-handling skills that involve selecting coins for a given amount are those that extend into practical activities such as a class shop, or in authentic experiences such as making purchases in the school canteen.

Calculating change

Practical money-handling activities provide students with the chance to calculate the change required for a given transaction. Using the 'adding on' approach is preferable to using traditional subtraction. Calculating change, together with the other authentic money-handling experiences, contributes to the development of the proficient use of number necessary for a strong personal numeracy.

Conclusion

Measurement is a key component of the mathematics curriculum framework. In extending measurement concepts, students are provided with the opportunity to apply their understandings by using number processes and geometric reasoning. Measurement is also the most practical and hands-on application of mathematics in day-to-day life. Hence, extending measurement concepts in the mathematics classroom should involve extensive opportunities for practical activities, rather than just using textbook exercises. An extended understanding of measurement concepts provides the chance to integrate mathematics into other curriculum areas, thus boosting students' personal numeracy capacities.

An appreciation of the relationships that exist between measurement attributes such as length, area, volume, and mass, and the relationship between the various units of measurement relevant to each attribute, is key to fluently managing measurement tasks both in the classroom and more broadly. As emphasised in this chapter, students should be provided with the opportunity to develop measurement formulae as meaningful expressions of the measurement relationships. Taking an approach such as this is certain to be a formula for success!

key terms

Area: the measure that describes the extent or coverage of a two-dimensional figure
Capacity: the measure of the quantity that a three-dimensional shape can hold
Circumference: the distance around the perimeter of a circle
Conservation of area: the principle that the size of an area is not changed if the figure or region is rearranged
Diameter: the straight line that passes through the centre of the circle joining two points on opposite sides of the circumference
Mass: a measure of the amount of matter in an object
Money: the unit used to measure the attribute known as value
Perimeter: the linear measurement that is the length around the boundary of a figure or a region
Pi (π): the constant value that is generated when the length of the circumference is divided by the length of the diameter, regardless of the size of the circle
SI units: the international system of units; the basis of Australia's hierarchy of measurement standards
Tessellates: geometric property of a figure that when identical copies of the figure are laid out they will join perfectly with no space between them, as in tiling
Volume: the space occupied by a three-dimensional figure
Weight: the force that gravity exerts on an object

Review questions

1. Area and volume are rarely measured directly. Why?
2. Design a sequence of learning activities that could be used to develop the formula for the area of a triangle.
3. Design a sequence of learning activities that could be used to develop the formula for the area of a circle.
4. What relationships exist between perimeter and area, area and volume, volume and capacity, and volume and mass?
5. What are the significant challenges that students may have in learning to measure area, volume, and mass?
6. Explain the importance of the concept of conservation in developing measurement understandings.

Key references

Battista, M. (2003). Understanding students thinking about area and volume measurement. In D. Clements (Ed.), *Learning and Teaching Measurement*. Reston, VA: NCTM.

Battista, M. (2007). The development of geometric and spatial thinking. In F. Lester (Ed.), *Second Handbook of Research on Mathematics Teaching and Learning*. Reston, VA: NCTM.

Websites

www.measurement.gov.au/Pages/default.aspx

http://illuminations.nctm.org

www.abc.net.au/countusin/games.htm

www.shodor.org/interactivate/activities/

http://nlvm.usu.edu

Shape and Space: Geometric Thinking and Concepts in Years 5–9

27

Contents

Working with spatial objects	628
Transformational geometry	632
Non-Euclidean geometry	639
Location	641
Learning geometry in the middle years	643
Conclusion	644

Chapter objectives

This chapter will enable the reader to:
- Develop their personal knowledge and understanding of geometric concepts relevant for teaching Years 5–9
- Learn effective methods for teaching geometric thinking and concepts in Years 5–9, as identified from research.

consider and discuss

If you were to fly from Singapore to London, what countries would you fly over? Check a map.

Someone you know may have flown this route. Does their experience match what you predicted?

Now use a globe and a piece of string to find the shortest path between these cities. What do you notice?

Big ideas

- Learning geometry involves learning about our world and then extending ideas to abstract relationships and concepts.
- Geometry has expanded from Euclidean geometry to transformational geometry (particularly following the appreciation of mathematics from non-Western cultures) and non-Euclidean geometries.
- Geometric thinking involves considering what stays the same as changes are made.
- Teaching geometric thinking requires the provision of tasks that allow learners to engage in geometric processes.

Working with spatial objects

In Chapter 20, it was noted that an important aspect of geometry deals with spatial objects—children learn to classify shapes and look at relationships between them. As learners move into the middle years of schooling, their understanding of spatial objects continues to grow.

Properties of shapes

Young learners begin to organise their geometric concepts around prototypical shapes. They need to move to an understanding that properties are important in determining the classification of a shape. Learners become increasingly sophisticated in their recognition of properties and in the reasoning that can emerge in the process. We could consider a number of different spatial objects but we will focus on the properties of quadrilaterals, circles, and parallel lines. These have had a traditional place in secondary school mathematics curricula and continue to provide opportunities for thinking geometrically. You may wish to extend these ideas to studying the properties of other shapes.

Quadrilaterals

From the name, quadrilaterals are any plane (2D) shapes that have four sides. Quadrilaterals can be **convex** or **concave**: a shape is convex if a line segment joining any two points in the shape does not go outside the shape. You can explore convex and concave quadrilaterals further at <http://demonstrations.wolfram.com/ATestForTheConvexityOfAQuadrilateral/>.

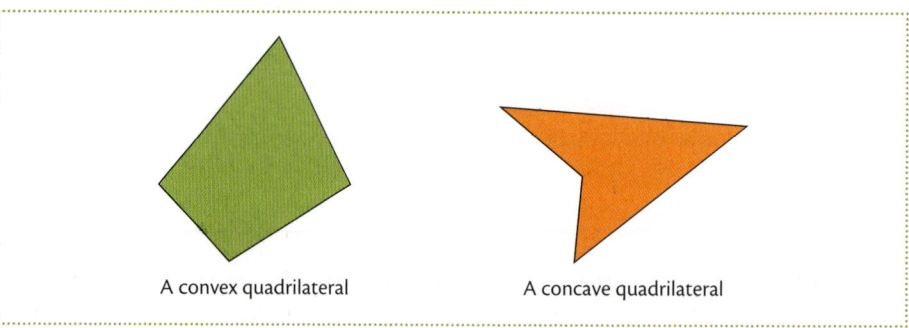

A convex quadrilateral   A concave quadrilateral

There are many types of quadrilaterals, named according to their properties. These include kite, square, rectangle, oblong, parallelogram, trapezium, and rhombus. Mathematics dictionaries can be used to note the properties of each type of quadrilateral.

>
> ### integrating technology/ICT
>
> #### Dynamic geometry environments (DGE)
> Use a DGE such as Geogebra to investigate types of quadrilaterals.
> - Measure sides and angles.
> - Check whether sides are parallel or perpendicular.
> - What features stay the same as you move points around? How does this change the classification of the quadrilateral?

Parallel lines

Parallel lines (and by extension, perpendicular lines) have interesting properties. Having experience with these properties allows us to explore other aspects of geometry.

integrating technology/ICT

Dynamic geometry environments (DGE)

Use a DGE such as Geogebra to investigate parallel lines.

Start with two parallel lines and draw a line across them (a **transversal**).

In geometrical drawing, parallel lines are indicated by drawing small arrows on the parallel pairs, for example:

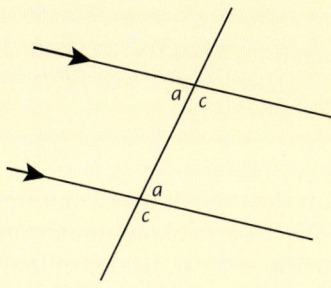

Investigate the angles that the transversal makes with the parallel lines. It will be important to try many different arrangements of the transversal. What stays the same (is invariant) no matter how the lines change?

Some middle school mathematics textbooks talk of rules about angles as 'F', 'Z', 'U', 'X' rules. What are these? Use your DGE to explain why these rules work.

Circles

> Circles are simple, elegant, and beautiful, exhibiting a genuine two-dimensional perfection. In the hands of the Greeks they were of interest not only in themselves but also as primary tools in the exploration of other geometric ideas. (Dunham, 1994, p. 23)

Compasses were one of the allowed types of drawing equipment of ancient geometers. They allow us to draw a shape where all the points are the same distance from a central point. Circles have remarkable properties and have inspired mathematicians for centuries. All circles are *similar*. Similarity has a particular mathematical meaning; two shapes are similar if they have the same shape but not necessarily the same size. Since circles are similar, we can enlarge or reduce a circle and it will exactly match any other circle.

communicating mathematically

Objects that are mathematically similar are the same shape but not necessarily the same size. Objects that are exactly the same size and shape are **congruent**. In geometry, angles, lines, and other shapes that are identical are described as being congruent, rather than equal. The measure of these attributes (i.e. a numerical amount) would be equal.

The symbol given for congruent is: ≅

The symbol for similar is: ≈

for the classroom

Finding a value for π

1. Carefully measure (to the nearest centimetre) the diameter (D) of the wheel of a bike, including the tyre. (Bike wheels are handy as they have an obvious centre.)
2. Place the wheel on a straight line in the school grounds and mark the tyre and the point of contact on the ground.
3. Now roll the wheel. More than one revolution will give greater distances and greater accuracy. Try four revolutions at first and then more or less to test this.
   Put a mark on the ground where the mark on the tyre once again comes in contact with the ground. For four revolutions, this distance will be four times the circumference (C).
4. Measure the distance for four revolutions to the nearest centimetre. Calculate the circumference.
5. Calculate $\frac{C}{D}$.
6. Repeat using tyres of other sizes.

Adapted from Paul Scott (2008, p. 3).

think + link

Chapter 22 has information on irrational numbers, including π.

Because circles are similar, the ratio of the circumference (C) to the diameter (D) is a constant. This ratio is a particular number and mathematicians have given this number the symbol π. That is, by definition, $\pi = \frac{C}{D}$.

You found an approximate value for π in the tyre activity.

did you know?

The existence of π has been known since the dawn of recorded mathematics (about 2000 BC). The Egyptians and the Babylonians not only knew of π, they had calculated an approximate value. Considering they had limited numeration systems, their calculations were remarkable feats.

Even though circles are simple, their fascination for mathematicians lies in the properties that can be explored. Here is one you can investigate.

consider and discuss

A property of circles

1. Using a DGE or compasses, draw a circle and label the centre.
2. Draw a chord (a line segment that cuts the circle in two places but does not go through the centre).
3. Draw the **perpendicular bisector** of this chord (a perpendicular line that goes through the centre of the chord). What do you notice?
5. Draw another chord, and its perpendicular bisector. What do you notice?
6. Convince yourself that this is not a coincidence. That is, prove that perpendicular bisectors of any chord must go through the centre of the circle.
7. Carefully record your thinking as you convince yourself and you convince a colleague that this property must be true.

Geometric proof

One of the defining features of the discipline of mathematics is its reliance on proof. As Simon Singh writes in his very readable book *Fermat's Last Theorem*:

> The idea of a classic mathematical proof is to begin with a series of axioms, statements which can be assumed to be true or which are self-evidently true. Then by arguing logically, step by step, it is possible to arrive at a conclusion. If the axioms are correct and the logic is flawless, then the conclusion will be undeniable. This conclusion is the theorem.
>
> Mathematical theorems rely on this logical process and once proven are true until the end of time. Mathematical proofs are absolute. (Singh, 1997, p. 21)

Geometric proof is a particular type of mathematical justification. We first looked at justification in Chapter 4 as one of the parts of mathematical thinking.

Geometric proof once had a large place in school geometry courses. Unfortunately, it was found to be extremely difficult to teach students to construct proofs, and many teachers and their students resorted to learning geometric proofs by heart for later recitation in examinations. The proofs that appeared in textbooks were finalised and so omitted the steps that led to the development of the original proof. This led many students to believe that 'true' mathematical thinkers were able to produce perfect proofs straight off.

Return to the investigation of the property of the circle that states that the perpendicular bisector of a chord passes through the centre of the circle (p. 630). If you recorded your thinking and your discussion with your colleagues carefully, you will have noticed yourself making conjectures based on ideas you already know to be correct. For example, you may have used the fact that the lengths of radii are equal. In Simon Singh's passage about proof, he notes that a proof follows step by step from initial axioms that are known to be true. Which axioms did you use in your justification? Which steps were important in your argument? At what point were you convinced? Rewrite the proof to include any other steps that are necessary. Remove ones that are redundant. Share your proof with another person. Ask them to challenge you to defend your statements.

Here is a published proof of the reverse theorem (Haese, Webber, Danielsen & Burch, 1983, p. 167): 'the perpendicular drawn from the centre of a circle to a chord bisects the chord'.

think + link

See Chapter 4 for a discussion of justification—the forerunner to mathematical proof.

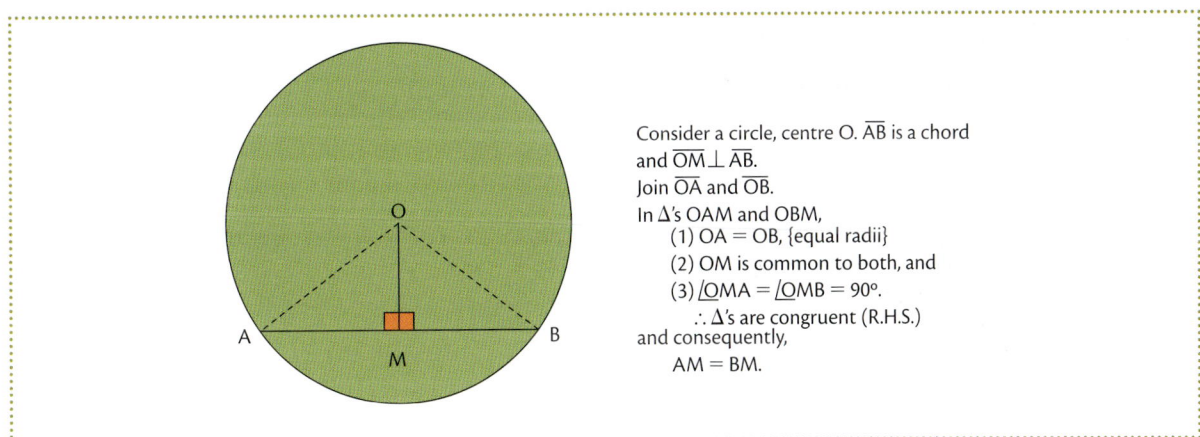

Consider a circle, centre O. $\overline{AB}$ is a chord and $\overline{OM} \perp \overline{AB}$.
Join $\overline{OA}$ and $\overline{OB}$.
In △'s OAM and OBM,
   (1) OA = OB, {equal radii}
   (2) OM is common to both, and
   (3) $\angle$OMA = $\angle$OMB = 90°.
   ∴ △'s are congruent (R.H.S.)
and consequently,
   AM = BM.

Work through the proof making sense of each line. How is your proof similar? How is it different? Reflect on the thinking you and your colleagues undertook to generate your proof. What thinking would be missing if you were merely to learn off a published proof?

communicating mathematically

Mathematical proof relies on communicating mathematics to others. Notice the succinct language of the mathematics in the published proof. Each step must still read as a sentence and make sense. If you are reading mathematics, you need to understand what each symbol means. You must also be prepared to read each line many times as well as read the whole proof many times. Often the first reading is needed to get a sense of where the argument is headed before you return to each individual line to ensure you understand each part.

Transformational geometry

The development of transformational geometry represented a different way of thinking about geometry (Johnston-Wilder & Mason, 2005). Rather than looking at properties of objects, transformational geometry focuses on what stays the same (is invariant) as a process happens to an object. In this section, we will look at transformations that do not change the shape or size of an object. These are called **rigid transformations** or isometries. We will also study **non-rigid transformations** where the process changes the object's shape or size.

did you know?

Transformational geometry includes a study of pattern and design. This has led to the appreciation of mathematics from other cultures where design is a feature. The field of ethnomathematics studies the development of mathematics in non-Western cultures, including Indigenous Australians, Papua New Guineans and Pacific Islanders.

See Chapter 20 for the introduction to rigid transformations.

Rigid transformations

Rigid transformations (also known as congruence transformations) preserve size and shape. In Chapter 20, we introduced the four rigid transformations: rotations, translations, reflections, and glide reflections.

We can record the movement of transformations using coordinates.

handy hint

Developing visualisation

Before using a dynamic geometry environment, models or diagrams, always try to *predict* what the effect of a transformation is likely to be. Record this prediction.

for the classroom

Investigating transformations

1. Plot the following points (see the section on coordinate systems on p. 641):
   (0, 2), (1, 0), (3, 1), (4, 2), (5, 1), (5, 3), (4, 2), (1, 3), (0, 2)
2. Join the points in order to make a 'fish'. Plot (1, 2) for the eye.
3. Predict what would happen if you doubled the x-coordinate for each point. Now draw it. Did your drawing match your prediction?
4. What changes would you need to make to make the fish swim:
   - upside down?
   - backwards?
   - vertically?
   - an angle?
5. Generalise your findings. Write a paragraph explaining how reflections, translations, rotations, and glide reflections can be generated from coordinates.
6. How can you generate enlargements?

Adapted from Fielker (1973, p. 67).

Tessellations

A fascinating and very beautiful area of mathematics involves **tessellations** or tilings. Tessellations are repeated shapes that cover a plane without gaps or overlaps. For there to be no gaps or overlaps, the sum of angles of shapes meeting at each vertex must be exactly 360°.

There are only three regular polygons that tessellate. Remember a regular **polygon** has congruent sides and angles; therefore, one regular polygon that tessellates is a square. As each angle is a right angle, at a vertex of a tiling there will be four right angles making a total of 360°. Convince yourself that an equilateral triangle and a regular hexagon will tessellate.

consider and discuss

Tessellations of polygons

Draw a large scalene triangle. Mark the angles in three different colours. Make copies of the triangle and cut them out. Arrange the triangles so they tessellate. Convince yourself that *any* triangle will tessellate.

Similarly, convince yourself and discuss with your table group that *any* quadrilateral will tessellate.

Explore other polygons.

Tilings would be very boring if we only had triangles, quadrilaterals, and regular hexagons to work with. Fortunately, we can use transformations to alter these three starting shapes to make other tile shapes that will tessellate.

did you know?

Escher art is a style of art first developed by the Dutch artist M.C. Escher. Blending mathematics with design and art, and drawing inspiration from the Islamic art found in Morocco, Escher produced works that have been reproduced in many books, posters, and murals. You can find examples by searching for 'Escher art' on the internet.

for the classroom

Making a tile

- Start with a regular polygon that tessellates (e.g. a square).
- Change one side in any way you like.
- Use tracing paper to make a copy of the side. Translate this to the opposite side of the square.
- Similarly, change one of the remaining sides and translate to the opposite side.
- Cut out your new tile and check that it tessellates. Convince yourself that it will tessellate in every direction.

An example:
- Start with a square. Change one side.

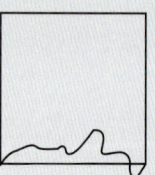

- Translate to the other side. Repeat.

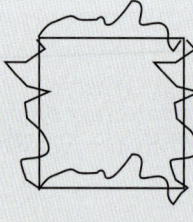

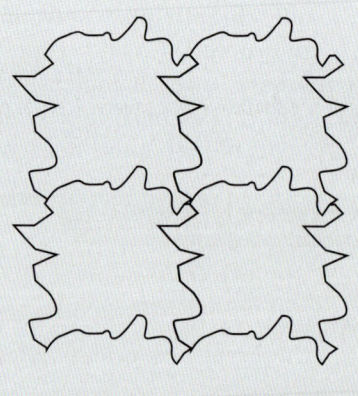

- Remove the original square and you have your new tile. Check that your tile tessellates. You can decorate your tile to make it look like an object, or use colours to bring out features of your design. The mathematics is in the transformation.

Non-rigid transformations

With rigid transformations, the size and shape of the object is preserved. We will now investigate two types of transformations where the object changes. Similar transformations keep the shape the same but the size changes. **Shear** transformations keep the area the same, but the shape changes.

Similarity

Shapes can be enlarged or reduced using scale factors. A scale factor of 1 makes the image congruent. A scale factor greater than 1 will make the image larger; a scale factor less than 1 will make the image smaller. Interestingly, images that are smaller are said to be 'enlargements' in mathematics!

Chapter 27 Shape and Space: Geometric Thinking and Concepts in Years 5–9

for the classroom

Even paper comes in metric sizes! 'A series' paper is metric and is used worldwide (except in North America) and includes paper from A0 to A10. We are most familiar with A4 and A3 sizes.

- Compare and contrast a sheet of A4 paper with a sheet of A3. Record your findings.
- Measure the sides of the A4 sheet to the nearest millimetre. You might have noticed that the length of A4 paper is the same as the width of A3 paper. Also, the length of A3 paper is twice the width of A4 paper. Use your findings to complete the following table:

Paper size	Length	Width	Area (length × width)	Aspect ratio (length/width)
A0				
A1				
A2				
A3				
A4				
A5				

- Convert the area of A0 to m^2. You should find that the area is very close to $1\ m^2$.

  Note that the shape is not a square. A series paper is a metric series so $1\ m^2$ makes sense. It is a little harder to explain the dimensions chosen. We need to look at the aspect ratio. **Aspect ratio** is a property of rectangles, and compares length with width. Aspect ratio is commonly quoted for computer and television screens. If the aspect ratio is different, the rectangles have different shapes. No amount of enlarging will allow a picture to be shown on a screen with a different aspect ratio. This is why black bands may appear at the top of a picture or the image may be squashed.

- Calculate the aspect ratio for each size of paper. You will need to decide how many decimal places you wish to record. Your results cannot be more accurate than your initial measurement.
- Write down your findings. Did you notice the following?
  - The aspect ratio is the same for each paper size. If the ratios are the same for each, this means they are in proportion. The paper is the same shape, just a different size. That is, the shapes are similar.
  - If you square the result, you get 2. This means that the aspect ratio is $\sqrt{2}$. You might have noticed photocopiers give a percentage enlargement of 141.4% when going from A4 to A3. This is $\sqrt{2} \times 100$. Going the other way, 70.7%, or $1/\sqrt{2} \times 100$.

These are very special properties and make the dimensions unique, allowing easy enlargements from one size to another. If you have tried to enlarge or reduce pages in US paper sizes, you will appreciate how difficult it is.

There are two common methods for enlarging a figure. Many children's activity books contain examples of using a grid to enlarge a simple cartoon. A grid is drawn over the shape. A second grid is then drawn with larger or smaller squares, depending on the chosen scale factor. Points where the drawing crosses grid lines are marked on the first and copied onto a similar location on the second. Lines are then joined to construct the enlarged image.

A second method uses a point of **enlargement**. This point can be inside or outside the original object. For example, in Figure 27.1 the image is twice the size of the object. The scale factor is 2. This means *DE* is twice the distance of *DA* and so on.

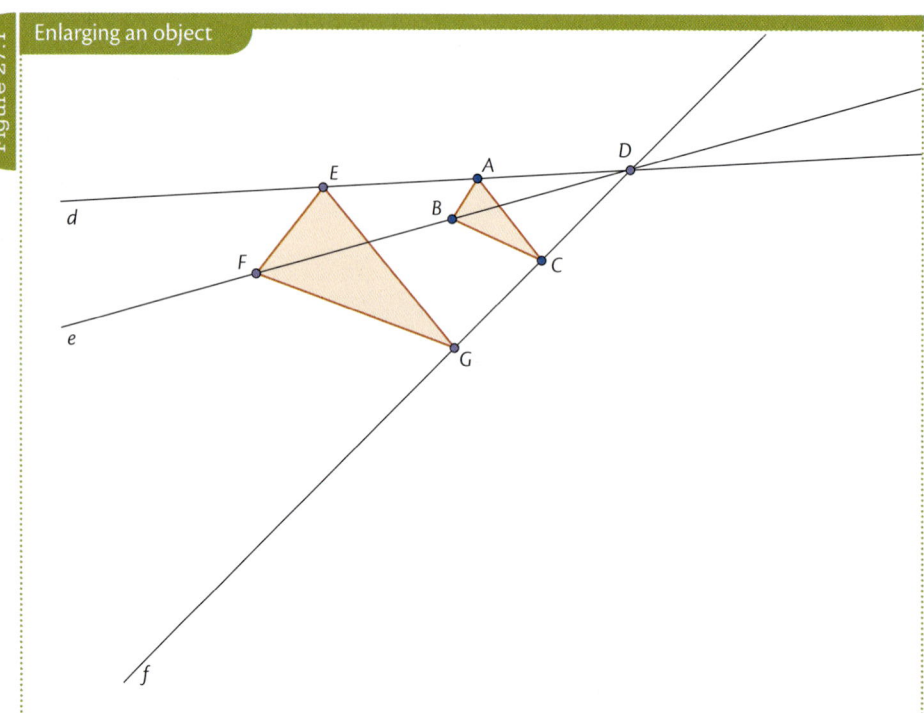

Figure 27.1 Enlarging an object

integrating technology/ICT

Enlargements

Use a DGE such as Geogebra to investigate enlarging objects. Draw an object and enlarge it with any scale factor (remember scale factors less than one reduce the size of the object). When you have constructed your object and image, use the DGE to measure sides, angles, and areas of the shapes. What do you notice?

Similar figures are important in measurement. Similar right-angled triangles have sides that are in proportion, which means the ratios of the lengths of corresponding sides are equivalent. These ratios have many uses and are given names: the sine ratio, the cosine ratio, and the tangent ratio.

Enlargements in three dimensions

When you used a DGE to explore enlargements of figures, you would have noticed that the angles of the image are the same size as the angles of the original object. The side lengths of the image can be found by multiplying the length of the corresponding sides on the original object by the scale factor. You would also have noticed that the area of the image is not found just by multiplying the original area by the scale factor—you need to multiply by the square of the scale factor, or (scale factor)^2. This is because there are two dimensions involved in area. Both the dimensions have been enlarged by the scale factor.

When we move to three dimensions, we have a similar problem.

Chapter 27 Shape and Space: Geometric Thinking and Concepts in Years 5–9

handy hint

Drawing 3D objects on 2D paper

Drawing diagrams of 3D objects on paper requires skill and technique. This is a specialist field and teachers of graphics or technical drawing can provide more information. In mathematics, we can make use of simplified techniques, such as the use of isometric dot paper.

- This paper has to be used in the correct orientation. Many websites provide pages of isometric dot paper ready for printing. Print some and practise drawing cubes arranged in different combinations.
- Start with a single cube. Put your finger on one vertex (corner). Choose a dot on the paper to correspond to this vertex. The vertex connects to three edges. Draw these in on the paper. Vertical lines on the cube are shown as vertical lines on the paper. The horizontal lines are drawn with lines on an angle.
- Move your finger on the cube to the next point (don't turn the cube). Draw in the lines on your paper that you can see. Continue until the block is drawn.
- Now try drawing other combinations of blocks.

integrating technology/ICT

Block builder

Technology can be used to help students link between 3D objects and their 2D representations. The Freudenthal Institute in the Netherlands has produced a website with many opportunities for students to explore mathematics concepts. Go to <www.fi.uu.nl/rekenweb/en/> and select 'Building Houses'. Explore this activity. Ensure you have a set of blocks, isometric dot paper and blank paper to record your thinking.

for the classroom

A mathematical model of a potato chip

There are a lot of differences between french fries and hot chips. French fries go cold faster, they have less potato inside, and they are thinner. We can use a model of a potato chip to see why french fries go colder faster.

1. Using five blocks, model a french fry. Draw a diagram of your model.
   Find the surface area and volume and write these in the table opposite. Take the side length of a cube to be one unit. The units for area will then be 'square units' and the units for volume will be 'cubic units'.
2. Now make a model of a shape that is twice as big. Does your model look the same shape but just a different size? If you have made the length twice as long but not changed the other dimensions, your model will now look long and skinny. You need to double each dimension to make it have the same shape—only twice as big. Your model will need 40 blocks.
   Draw a diagram of the enlarged shape and record the surface area and volume.
3. Repeat for a triple-scale shape (original shape is enlarged three times).

4. Complete the table and look for patterns in the results.

Scale factor	Diagram	Surface area	Volume
1		22	5
2			40
3			

Surface area (SA) is a two-dimensional quantity (and therefore requires square units). As we noticed before, the surface area increases by (scale factor)^2. That is, 22×2^2 giving a surface area of 88 units^2.

Volume (Vol) has three dimensions (and therefore requires cubic units). Confirm that the volume has increased by (scale factor)^3.

Calculate the surface area to volume ratio for each of your models.

Scale factor	SA : Vol	SA : Vol	Comparing the ratios is difficult unless compared to one.
1	22 : 5	4.4 : 1	
2	88 : 40	2.2 : 1	
3	198 : 135	1.46 : 1	

The ratio indicates why the fries (scale factor 1) go colder faster. They have more of their matter in contact with the air than the chips, with a lower SA:Vol ratio. Because of this, more of their matter is in contact with the hot fat and so they cook faster, which is important for fast-food chains.

The volume is increasing by the cube of the scale factor and the surface area is increasing by only the square, which means that the ratio of surface area to volume is changing. This is a very important ratio in many fields, including biology. It explains why babies and pets die if left in hot cars. They have a very high surface area to volume ratio, much higher than adults. They heat up and can reach points of distress far quicker than adults.

Shears

consider and discuss

Visualising a shear

Think of a shape drawn in a Cartesian plane, perhaps like this:

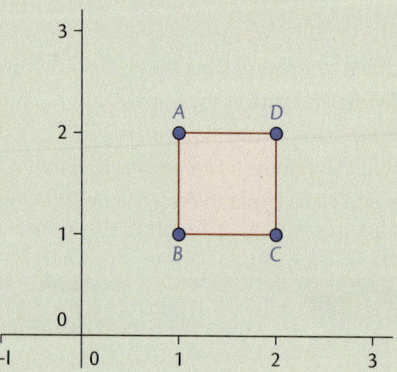

Predict what will happen if all points were transformed according to the following rules:

1. Points move to the right (parallel to the *x*-axis).
2. The distance a point moves is determined by how far the point is above the *x*-axis (the *y*-coordinate). The point moves half the distance of the value of the *y*-coordinate. Therefore, point C moves to the right 0.5 of a unit. The new coordinates for C would be (2.5, 1).
3. Before you draw a diagram, predict what will happen to each point. Imagine what you will see. Now plot the points carefully.
4. Try other shapes and transform them using the same rule.
5. Try transforming shapes where the rule in step 2 changes. For example, try 'The point moves twice the distance of the value of the *y*-coordinate'.

Adapted from Johnston-Wilder & Mason, 2005, p. 160.

Shears look as though slices of the original shape are sliding over each other, like a sliced loaf of bread pushed on an angle. Shears are transformations where the shape is not preserved. In shears, area stays the same but the perimeter changes. You may have noticed other features of the shears you drew, such as parallel lines staying parallel but angles changing. Shears are used in applications such as making italic shape letters from regular letters.

Non-Euclidean geometry

The effect of changing the parallel postulate

In Chapter 11, the existence of different types of geometries was foreshadowed. We will give a brief introduction to the widening field of geometry.

did you know?

For about 2000 years, Euclid's work on geometry, as recorded in *The Elements*, was largely unchallenged. Euclid listed five postulates that were considered 'self-evident'. That is, they could be accepted by all and did not require proof.

This is the list (adapted from COMAP, 1994, p. 629):

1. Two points determine a line.
2. A line segment can always be extended.
3. A circle can be drawn with any centre and any radius.
4. All right angles are congruent.
5. If l is any line and P is any point not on l, then there exists exactly one line m through P that does not meet l.

Notice how the fifth postulate is much more complicated? Mathematicians did too. Investigating this postulate led to the emergence of new fields of geometry, such as spherical and hyperbolic geometry. Non-Euclidean geometries have proved important in providing the mathematical basis to such fields as relativity.

When mathematicians began to question the 'self-evident' nature of the fifth or parallel postulate, they began to explore the effects of making changes to this assumption. If the postulate were changed from exactly one line to more than one line, hyperbolic geometry emerged. The mathematician Reimann adopted the postulate that every two lines intersect and discovered elliptic geometry. Earth geometry is an example of elliptic geometry, and we will study this briefly, as an example.

Earth geometry

The Earth is very nearly a sphere with slightly flattened poles. In Earth, or spherical, geometry, 'lines' take a new meaning. The shortest path between two points would go through the Earth, but this is not allowed. Lines are therefore arcs.

At the beginning of this chapter, you investigated the shortest flight path between Singapore and London. Initially this can be surprising, as many of us are very used to thinking about 2D representations of the world, rather than the spherical view. The Mercator projection is a very commonly reproduced map that attempts to draw the 3D world on a 2D surface. Many projections are possible, but each one will require a distortion.

did you know?

Mapping the Earth is a complex undertaking. Many projections are possible. You can learn more about the different types at: <http://erg.usgs.gov/isb/pubs/MapProjections/projections.html>.

An interesting projection is the Peter's projection. This view shows the continents with correct area but shape is altered. Notice how much bigger Africa and South America seem and how much smaller Europe seems in comparison to the Mercator projection where the directions are correct but the area is not. Some social scientists argue that the Peter's projection gives a more realistic view of the world. You can explore more about this projection at <http://ucatlas.ucsc.edu/>.

In Earth geometry, there are new terms to know:

- A **great circle** is any circle with its centre at the centre of the sphere. The shortest distance between two points is along a great circle. (Look back to the globe and the flight path between Singapore and London. This is an arc of a great circle.)

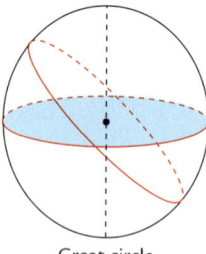
Great circle

- A **small circle** is any circle where the centre is not the centre of the sphere.

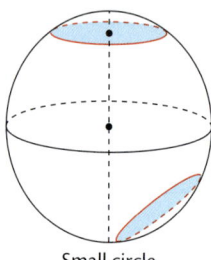
Small circle

- **Parallels of latitude** are circles with their centre on the **polar axis**. The equator is the only parallel of latitude that is also a great circle.

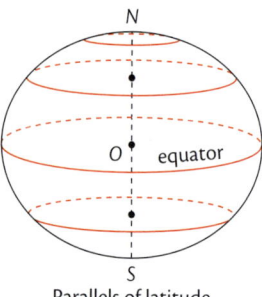
Parallels of latitude

- **Meridians of longitude** are semicircles running from pole to pole. These are all the same size—half a great circle.

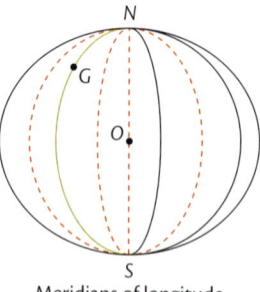
Meridians of longitude

Aspects of Euclidean geometry, such as the properties of triangles, can be explored in spherical geometry. Be prepared for surprises! For example, a triangle may have two or more right angles.

Location

Representing location

Knowing where we and other objects are, and being able to communicate that knowledge to others, is an important part of understanding our world. Aboriginal people living in tribal communities have a particular need for accurate spatial orientation. Pam Harris (1980), in her important contribution to understanding of Aboriginal mathematics, describes Aboriginal spatial ability, including the ability to maintain awareness of starting location, where a hunter 'after a circuitous kangaroo chase, always heads directly back to the waiting vehicle' (p. 12), citing possible explanations:

> It would appear then, that the essential psycho-physical mechanism was some kind of *dynamic image* or *mental 'map'* which was *continually updated* in terms of time, distance and bearing, and more radically *realigned at each change of direction*, so that the hunters remained *at all times* aware of the precise direction of their *base and/or objective*. (Lewis, 1976, p. 262, cited in Harris, 1980, p. 12. Italics in the original.)

Those of us who live in urban settings may not have developed spatial orientation to the same degree, but it is an important aspect of geometry and necessary for students in the middle years of schooling. We will look at the use of coordinate systems for two-dimensional maps and then at the use of a coordinate system for our three-dimensional globe.

think + link

In Chapter 11 there is a summary of research on the development of location.

Coordinate systems

If we wish to represent location of an object on a two-dimensional surface, we need to give a reference to both dimensions. In street directories, this is often given as a letter and a number. The object is then located in the square bounded by the letter and number.

We can also give a number for each direction, as long as it is clear which direction we are referring to. Cartesian coordinates is a system in which two axes are drawn on the **Cartesian plane**. The horizontal axis is known as the x-axis, and is a number line with real numbers ranging from negative infinity (on the left) to positive infinity. The vertical axis is known as the y-axis and has the same range. Points are located on the Cartesian plane using *ordered pairs*; for example the point (2, 3) would be located two units along the horizontal axis to the right of the origin and three units up.

The development of Cartesian **coordinates** was a major development in mathematics. It led to the connection between numbers, algebra, and geometry—the branch of coordinate geometry. Lines could be described by the relationship between values along the x-axis and corresponding values along the y-axis. For example, if we know a text message costs 25c per message, we could view this relationship in at least three ways: as a table of values, as a graph, and as an algebraic equation.

No. of texts	Cost (*c*)
0	0
1	25
2	50
3	75

The equation that expresses this relationship is Cost = 25 × Number of texts. The connection between algebra and coordinate geometry can be further explored in the *Access to Algebra* series of books and teachers guides (Lowe, Kissane & Willis, 1995).

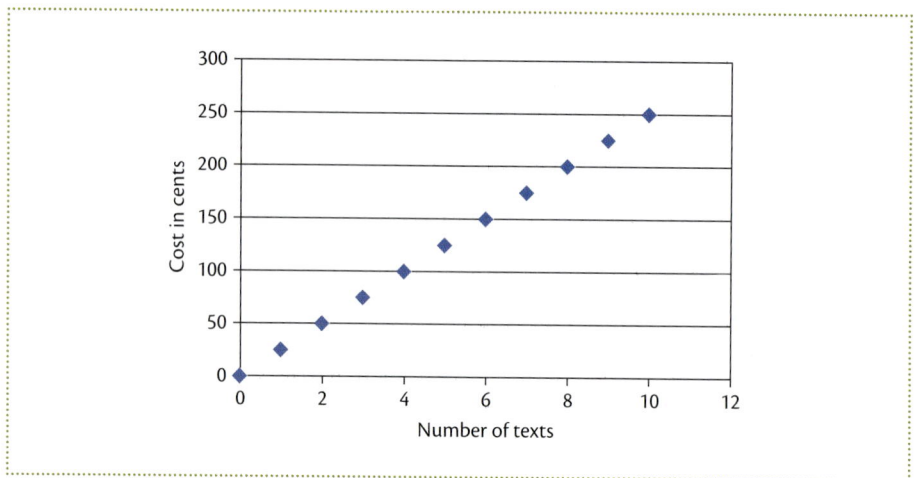

An alternative coordinate system on a 2D plane is the use of *polar* coordinates. Polar coordinates indicate the distance a point is from a central location (given the symbol, r, for radius) as well as the angular rotation (Θ). Polar coordinates are commonly used for radar, including for weather forecasting (Figure 27.2).

In mathematics, the starting point for the rotation is usually 'east', with anticlockwise rotations positive. Some applications place the origin of the rotation at the top of the circle.

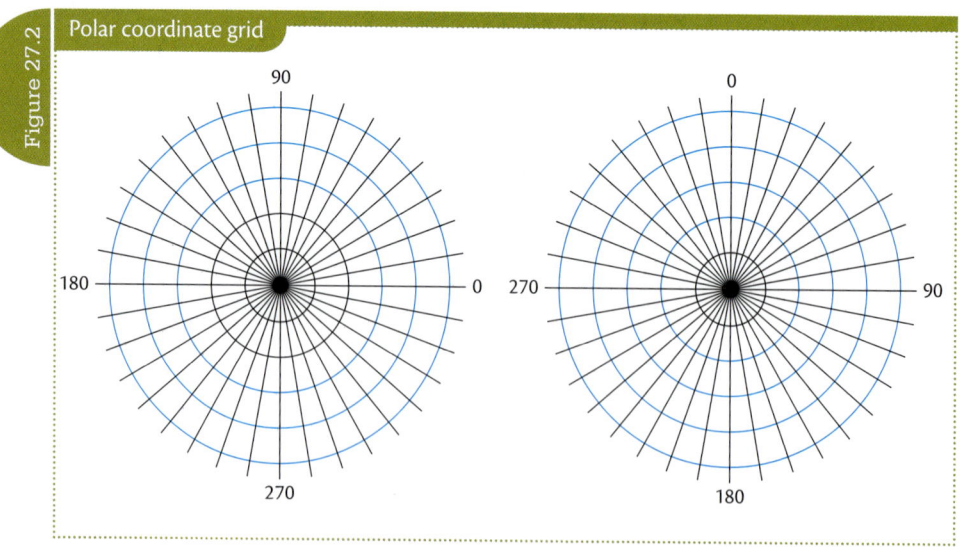

Figure 27.2 Polar coordinate grid

Source: http://whatis.techtarget.com/WhatIs/images/pol-coor.gif

Location on Earth

To find our location on Earth, we need two points of reference: our latitude, and our longitude. Latitude can be determined from the angle of the sun. If we are far from the equator, the sun appears very low in the sky at winter. If we are inside the Arctic or Antarctic circles, the sun does not rise above the horizon at all during winter! Look back to the diagram of parallels of latitude. Notice how the circles were different sizes. Cut an orange and look at the slices. The equator is the only great circle. It is given the value of 0°. The other parallels of latitude are indicated by the angle they make from the centre of the Earth. The poles are therefore 90°N or 90°S.

Longitude is not determined easily. If you cut an orange with slices from pole to pole, each segment is identical. A starting point had to be arbitrarily assigned. This was determined to be the line of longitude passing through Greenwich, UK, and is called the Prime Meridian. It is given the value of 0°. Other meridians are given as degrees east or west of the Prime Meridian.

did you know?

Finding longitude of ships at sea was a considerable problem for centuries. To determine longitude, it is necessary to be able to have an accurate reading of time. Until a clock was invented that could be taken to sea and keep accurate time over long voyages, sailors had very inaccurate ways of knowing where they were. You can read about the quest for a way to measure longitude in Dava Sobel's 1995 book, *Longitude*.

Learning geometry in the middle years

Throughout this chapter you have been encouraged to work through activities and also to reflect on your experiences. In watching yourself learn geometry, you are in a position to consider factors that are important for teaching geometry to learners in the middle years of schooling.

Geometry, as we have seen, is not merely about learning definitions and properties. Nor is it about learning off geometrical proofs. Certainly, there are aspects of knowledge and understanding that students need, but these are not useful without being able to think geometrically.

As Sue Johnston-Wilder and John Mason (2005, p.17) note:

> The most effective pedagogic strategies for promoting learning are based around provoking learners into using their natural powers to make sense of the world, listening to what learners have to say as they do this and engaging in discussion with them. In short, effective teaching involves being mathematical with, and in front of, learners.

Therefore, teachers need to provide opportunities for students to do geometrical tasks. As noted earlier, a vital step in developing visualisation is to predict or imagine what will happen before you draw a diagram or use technology to see. All students can learn to visualise, but this learning requires opportunities for considerable practice. Prediction is a habit that needs to be encouraged.

An essential part of geometrical investigation is the opportunity to explore what changes and what is invariant when processes happen to objects. In the past, hand-drawn diagrams were all that could be used. With the ready availability of dynamic geometry environments, this is no longer the case. Students should have access to DGEs and become confident in exploring geometrical environments.

Finally, in addition to having the opportunity to work on geometrical investigations, students need to reflect on their experiences. As you were encouraged in Chapter 4, documenting thinking aids in reflecting afterwards. This reflection may take the form of a formal report for assessment, or it could be a paragraph written in a student's learning journal. Recording findings in written form is an essential part of encouraging understanding and memory. Students are likely at this stage to identify areas that require further clarification.

Conclusion

Geometry places an emphasis on visualisation and spatial awareness, and this can be a delight for many students. Some students who struggle with the number aspects of school mathematics find renewed confidence in an area that requires different approaches to thinking.

key terms

Aspect ratio: a property of rectangles given by the ratio of length to width

Cartesian plane: a rectangular coordinate system based on two perpendicular axes—x (horizontal) and y (vertical)

Concave polygon: a plane shape in which there exists at least one line segment joining two interior points that goes outside the shape

Congruent: a geometric object of exactly the same size and shape as another

Convex polygon: a plane shape in which a line segment joining any two interior points does not go outside the shape

Coordinates: two letters or numbers that give location on coordinate axes

Enlargement: a similar figure made by increasing (or decreasing) an object by a given scale factor

Great circle: cross-section of a sphere where the centre of the circle is also the centre of the sphere

Meridians of longitude: semicircles running from pole to pole in a sphere

Non-rigid transformation: process that alters either a shape's size or or its shape

Parallels of latitude: cross-sections of a sphere where the centres of the circles are on the polar axis

Perpendicular bisector: a line at right angles to a line segment that cuts the line segment in two congruent parts

Polar axis: line through a sphere joining the poles

Polygon: two-dimensional closed shapes with straight sides

Rigid transformation: a process that maintains the transformed shape's size and shape

Shear: non-rigid transformation where the shape is not preserved, although area is

Similarity: an object is similar if it is the same shape, but not necessarily the same size, as another

Small circle: cross-section of a sphere where the centre of the circle is not the centre of the sphere

Tessellation: repeated shapes that cover a plane without gaps or overlaps

Transversal: a line drawn across a pair of parallel lines

Review questions

1. Sort quadrilaterals into categories based on their properties. Compare your sort with other students. Are there points of contention? Is more than one classification system possible?
2. Write a reflection on what you know about circles. Include reflections on your thinking while undertaking tasks in this chapter.
3. Compare and contrast Euclidean geometry with transformational geometry.
4. Name two non-Euclidean geometries. Undertake research on one of these.
5. What was the effect of questioning the parallel postulate?
6. What are the most important approaches to learning geometry for you? How would you encourage these approaches in your teaching? Which do you feel will be most difficult to include?

Key references

COMAP (1994). *For all Practical Purposes. Introduction to Comtemporary Mathematics* (3rd ed.). New York: Freeman.

Dunham, W. (1994). *The Mathematical Universe. An Alphabetical Journey through the Great Proofs, Problems, and Personalities*. New York: Wiley.

Harris, P. (1980). *Measurement in Tribal Aboriginal Communities*. Darwin: Northern Territory Department of Education.

Johnston-Wilder, S., & Mason, J. (Eds.) (2005). *Developing Thinking in Geometry*. London: The Open University, Paul Chapman Publishing.

Lowe, I., Kissane, B., & Willis, S. (1995). *Access to Algebra Book 4*. Melbourne: Curriculum Corporation.

Scott, P. (2008). π round and round. *Australian Mathematics Teacher*, 64(1), 3–5.

Singh, S. (1997). *Fermat's Last Theorem*. London: Fourth Estate.

Websites

www.geogebra.org

www.fi.uu.nl/rekenweb/en/

www.maths300.esa.edu.au

http://ucatlas.ucsc.edu/

http://enlvm.usu.edu/ma/nav/school.jsp?sid=nlvm

http://demonstrations.wolfram.com/ATestForTheConvexityOfAQuadrilateral/

28 Statistics and Probability in the Middle Years

Contents

Data investigation	647
Data representations	650
Data measures	654
Variation	655
Describing chance events	655
Conclusion	662

Chapter objectives

This chapter will enable the reader to:
- Build on knowledge of probability and statistics in the early years
- Develop understanding of the development of children's understanding of probability and statistics in the middle years
- Know key pedagogical strategies for teaching probability and statistics
- Recognise links between probability and statistics and other learning areas.

The importance of learning statistics and probability

This chapter expands on the big ideas associated with statistics and probability.

Probability and statistics have very clear connections to children's lives. Building a curriculum around children's interests and experiences provides excellent foundations for learning.

Visualise some typical experiences in your children's lives.
- Playing and watching sports:
  - the average number of goals per game for a team
  - a player's statistics such as possessions, interceptions, goals
- Playing games:
  - using dice or spinners to determine moves
  - dealing cards
- Collecting and organising:
  - Pokemon cards, beanie babies, stamps, rocks
- Deciding whether to go on a picnic or to a movie:
  - checking the weather forecast—70 per cent chance of rain
  - using 'scissors, paper, rock' to decide
- Being presented with statistics on *Behind the News* (a current affairs program designed for school children).

Ignoring the data
The *Challenger* disaster

The Space Shuttle *Challenger* disaster of 1986 shocked the world. The cause has been desribed as 'mounting probabilities' (Forrest, 2005). The shuttle program was threatened both politically and economically. Engineering and management decisions were made in light of strong external demands. The mission had suffered a previous cancellation and there was significant pressure for the next mission to go ahead. If a thorough risk analysis had been conducted, with safety given the highest priority, the launch might have been postponed. Shortly after the lauch the shuttle exploded, killing all crew.

Big ideas
- Data representations influence audience interpretation.
- Sets of data can be compared using measures of central tendency.
- Sample spaces define the parameters of chance events.
- Chance events can be described using fractions, decimals, and percentages.
- Children must develop a critical approach to reading statistics and probability.

did you know?

In the eighteen century, **statistics** referred to the collection of demographic and economic information by state.

Data investigation

Children in the middle years should be able to ask questions that require **data** collection outside the classroom and possibly beyond their personal experience. There are a number of more advanced concepts, such as sampling, associated with this kind of data investigation. As they grapple with increasingly complex concepts, children will begin to understand the connections between data collection, analysis, and representations. It is important to provide opportunities for children to justify their choices with regard to data collection and analysis.

issues in teaching

Unlike other areas of mathematics, statistics and probability requires children to accept uncertainty. The concepts may be uncomfortable for children to learn. Provide children with engaging activities that develop knowledge and confidence with regard to the uncertainty of these strands of mathematics.

According to Watson (2006), children need considerable practical experience to form a good understanding of sampling. Middle school children often wrongly consider using voluntary participation to be fair sampling because everyone has an opportunity to participate. The term **sample** is open to numerous interpretations. For example, children who watch criminal investigation programs will be familiar with DNA samples. Other children may think of samples given out at the Royal Show.

making connections

Statistics is used to persuade us to purchase products of all kinds. Empower your children to critique the statistics that they are presented with in advertisements.

consider and discuss

You are planning a social event for the Bachelor of Education students at your university.
1. What questions should you ask the students?
2. How many students should be included in your sample?
3. How should the students in the sample be selected?

Samples are used when it is impractical to collect data from the entire population being investigated. For example, in the discussion question above it is probably impractical for you to ask a few thousand students about their social event preferences. In this case, the population is all of the Bachelor of Education students at your university. A sample is chosen to be representative of a whole population. Is there an appropriate ratio of participants according to demographic characteristics such as gender, age, and course?

There are two parts to sampling. First is the idea of determining how large the sample needs to be, and second is randomness. Do all members of the population have an equal chance of being selected to participate in the data collection? While middle school children will not be expected to carry out complex statistical calculations to determine the exact nature of an appropriate sample, they can begin to consider the nature of good sampling.

The first step in developing an investigation is clearly to develop good questions that can be answered through data collection and analysis. The question usually arises from some issue or problem that the children have encountered. The next step involves collecting data from a sample of the population. Provide real examples of good and poor sampling to help your children to understand the importance of this step. Good understanding of this concept will develop over a number of years and must be supported by a range of real experiences.

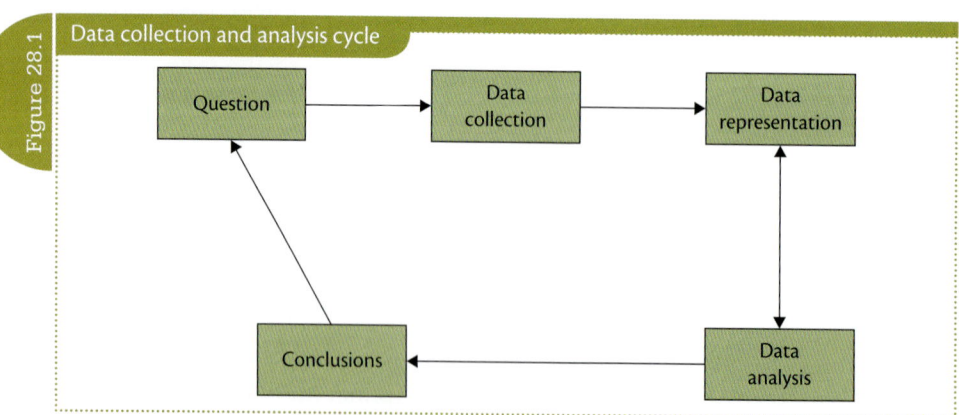

Figure 28.1 Data collection and analysis cycle

An important concept associated with sampling is randomness. Some of the issues children may have in understanding this concept were addressed in Chapter 21. According to Watson (2006), children think of random in terms of an unknown, or of selecting something by chance. They need specific instruction in order to grasp the concept of **random sampling** as it applies to 'all members of the population (or samples) having the same chance of being selected' (Watson, 2006, p. 47).

Children need to experience a wide range of sampling, such as measuring student's heights, asking what their favourite TV program is, and selecting and recording the colour of M&Ms from a packet. These three examples provide different insights into what samples are and all are important in developing a solid concept of random sampling.

The second part of sampling relates to size. Practical examples are probably the best way for children to gain understanding of the significance of having a sample that is large enough and representative of the whole population. You will be able to develop activities that allow children to collect samples of varying sizes to illustrate the impact on data. Clearly a sample size of 1 is insufficient to guarantee representativeness. Have children explore what happens to their results as they increase the size of samples.

for the classroom

Investigating sample size and repeated sampling

Work with a partner. One of you needs to put 10 counters of assorted colours in an envelope without your partner seeing. Your partner then takes a sample size of 2 from the envelope and records the colours of these counters, returns them, and repeats the process until a total of 10 samples of 2 counters have been recorded. Based on this information, he/she attempts to predict the number of each colour of counter in the envelope. Swap roles and repeat, but this time use 10 sample sizes of 4.

- Compare your results with those from other pairs in your classroom.
- How does sample size affect the accuracy of your estimate?
- How does the number of samples affect the accuracy of estimates?

As children develop more advanced understanding, you will be able to provide opportunities to incorporate bivariate data and to use secondary sources. For example, collect data on hours of training for an upcoming race and the finishing times. The data can be displayed graphically and analysed to determine any relationships between the two variables. Figure 28.2 is an example of a scatterplot.

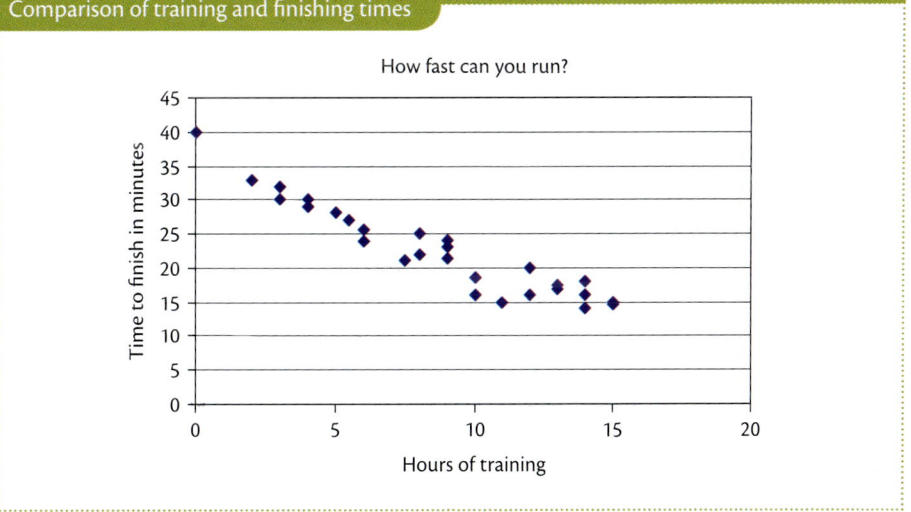

Figure 28.2 Comparison of training and finishing times

consider and discuss

Analyse and discuss the data in the scatterplot in Figure 28.2.

1. Is there a relationship between hours of training and finishing times?
2. What might explain the different finishing times?

The scatterplot indicates that there is a relationship or *correlation* between hours of training and finishing time. In general, faster finishing times appear to be associated with increased hours of training. This does not mean, however, that increased training hours directly cause faster finishing times. It is important for children to understand that often multiple variables have an impact on a situation. For example, diet, weight, height, and genetics will all play a role in determining an individual's ability to run in a race.

In addition, a scatterplot can only give a simple visual comparison. As children progress into senior high school they will learn about more precise calculations that quantify the level of correlation between variables. In the middle years, it is sufficient for children to understand that statistics can indicate possible relationships between data.

Data representations

Children must be provided with opportunities to use and interpret a range of data **representations** including tables, bar graphs, stem-and-leaf plots, scatterplots, and pie charts. While all of these examples can be easily produced using simple technology such as Excel, children should first hand-draw representations. As indicated in Chapter 21, children need to learn about data representations by working with data they themselves have collected.

Children in the middle years will build on the concrete examples presented in Chapter 21 and use more abstract representations. Selecting appropriate forms of representations provides opportunities to emphasise the purpose of statistics. Choice depends on the question, type of data collected, and intended audience. It is important to ask questions that require children to interpret the meaning conveyed by data representations in order for them to learn about the different purposes of the range of representation options.

communicating mathematically

Children need to understand that in communicating statistical information, they need to provide clear information to help people make sense of data. Choice of representation, such as tables, bar charts, pie charts, and stem-and-leaf plots, is important because of the way the form of representation influences data interpretation.

A Year 7 class collected traffic data on a main road located close to the school. Table 28.1 displays the data collected by the class. The children were concerned about crossing the busy road before and after school, and intended to write a letter to the local council to request that a school crossing be constructed. (Clearly this specific example is urban; it is important to be aware

Chapter 28 Statistics and Probability in the Middle Years

of appropriate opportunities for data collection in other contexts. In this case the safety concern was a real and relevant concern for the Year 7 students. Other students in an agricultural region may be interested in the local wildlife population. An ongoing survey of animals in a given area could be conducted by the students. For example, the numbers of feral and native animals can be compared over time.)

Table 28.1 Transportation survey

Type	Number
Cars	432
Motor bikes	111
Trucks	25
Taxis	10
Buses	6
Bikes	15
Scooters	13
Pedestrians	56

The children collected data during their mathematics lesson on Tuesday between 11:00 and 11:30 am. They constructed a bar graph (Figure 28.3) and a pie chart (Figure 28.4) to represent the data. It is important, for you as a teacher, to emphasise essential characteristics of any representations. The graph and axes must be appropriately labelled, correct scales used, and information presented as clearly as possible. If scales are not accurate the data will be open to misinterpretation. For example, readers may be misinformed by a graph that skews data representation.

Figure 28.3 Transportation survey: bar graph

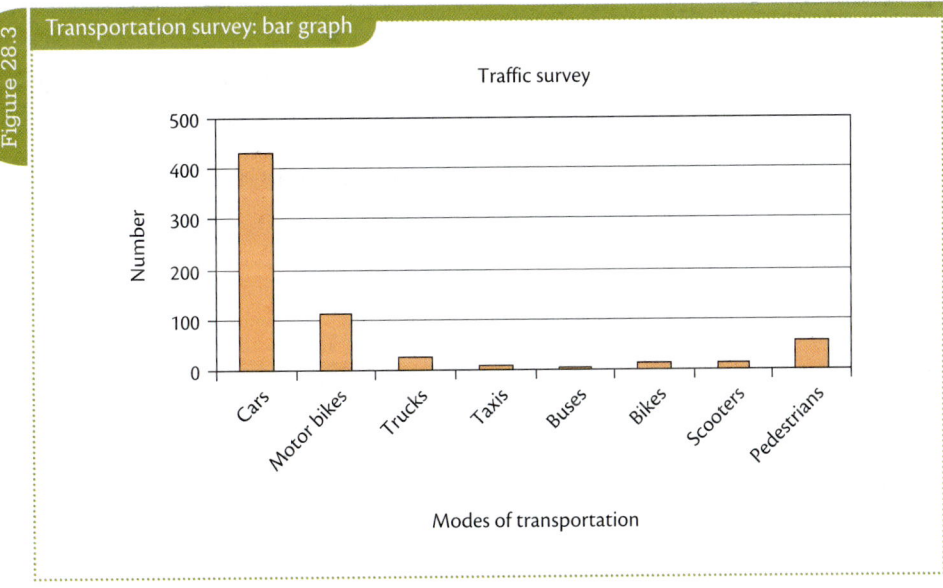

In order to construct the pie chart, the children calculated the percentage of the total for each mode of transportation. The percentage was then converted into degrees as shown below. Pie charts allow children to apply knowledge from other areas of mathematics such as number and geometry.

Cars:
$\frac{432}{668} \times 100 = 64.7\%$

$\frac{64.7}{100} \times 360 = 233°$

Calculate the percentage and degrees for the remaining types of transportation. Check your answers against Table 28.2.

Table 28.2

Pie chart calculations			
Type	Number	Percentage	Degrees
Cars	432	64.7	233
Motor bikes	111	16.6	60
Trucks	25	3.7	13
Taxis	10	1.5	5
Buses	6	1	3
Bikes	15	2.2	8
Scooters	13	1.9	7
Pedestrians	56	8.4	30
Total	668	100	360

In order to construct the pie chart some practical decisions must be made about the size of the circle, the rounding of percentages, and colour choice. This exercise gives the teacher good information about children's understanding of a number of different mathematics concepts.

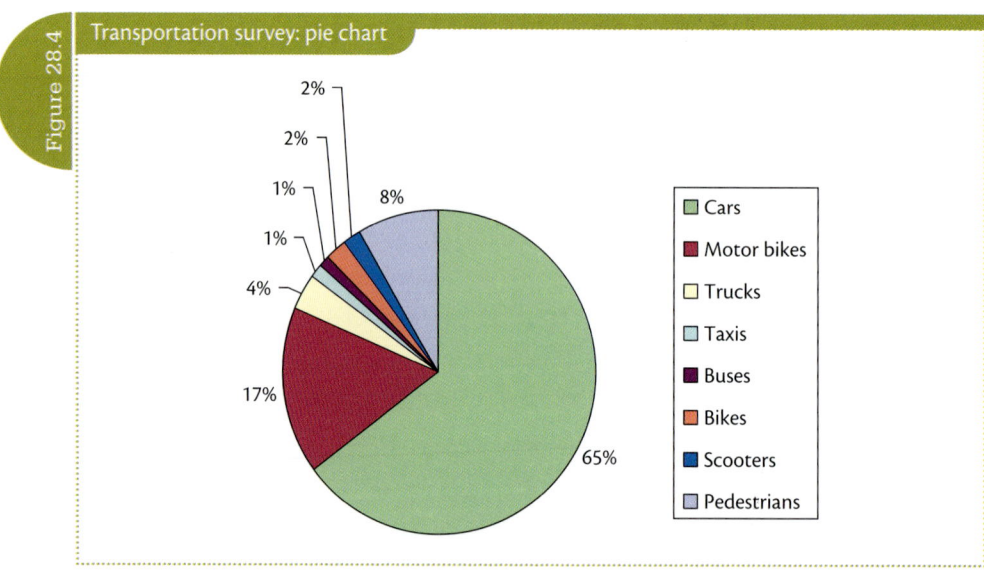

Figure 28.4 Transportation survey: pie chart

consider and discuss

1. What questions would you ask the children about the data?
2. Which representation do you think is most appropriate? Why?
3. Do these data provide children with support for their proposed school crossing?
4. Should more data be collected?

Some issues that may arise from class discussion include: time of day the data was collected; whether data should be collected for more than a single day; and criteria for determining safety issues for school children.

Another form of data representation used in the middle years is the stem-and-leaf plot. This is similar to a bar graph but provides more detailed information about the values of individual pieces of data. The data is arranged according to place value, in that the stem refers to the digits in the largest place and the leaves are the digits in the smallest place. Stem-and-leaf plots are particularly useful for organising large amounts of data.

You may even use a stem-and-leaf plot to analyse test data for your class. An example of a test on fractions is given in the following percentages:

50, 72, 62, 93, 81, 46, 47, 50, 94, 75, 83, 62, 47, 64, 76, 94, 51, 52, 65, 76, 78, 97, 66, 53, 66, 53, 79, 67, 57, 57, 62, 47

Data in this format is not very informative. Using the data to develop a stem-and-leaf plot (Figure 28.5) can provide you with a relatively simple tool for analysis.

Figure 28.5

Fraction tests scores

Test scores out of 100

Stem	Leaf
9	3 4 4 7
8	1 3
7	2 5 6 6 8 9
6	2 2 4 5 6 6 7 2
5	0 0 1 2 3 3 3 7 7
4	6 7 7

consider and discuss

1. What might the data indicate about children knowledge of fractions?
2. What action might you take as a teacher?

Back-to-back stem-and-leaf plots allow two sets of data to be compared. For example, points scored over a season by two opposing teams can be represented using back-to-back stem-and-leaf plots. In the example in Figure 28.6, the Galahs scored 31, 33, 35, and 36, while the Crows scored 39. The back-to-back stem-and-leaf plot displays data in a way that allows patterns to be identified easily.

Figure 28.6

Football scores

Scores

Leaf Galahs	Stem	Leaf Crows
1 3 5 6	3	9
2 2 6 6 8	4	3 5 5
1 3 7 9	5	8 8 8
5 7 8	6	1 5 5 6
1 2	7	0 2 2
1 7	8	8 9 9
0 0 6	9	1 2 4 8
	10	
	11	2 5 6

consider and discuss

1. What is the highest score for the Crows?
2. How do the teams' scores compare over the season? Explain your reasoning in terms of the relative distributions.

for the classroom

Construct your own stem-and-leaf plots

- Record or research the rainfall for towns in your state.
- Determine the stem for the data.
- Construct stem-and-leaf plots to display the rainfall data for individual towns.
- Select two towns for rainfall comparison and construct back-to-back stem-and-leaf plots according to the model shown in Figure 28.6.
- Use the stem-and-leaf plots to compare the data of different towns.

Data measures

think + link

You may wish to refer back to Chapter 12 to be reminded about the three types of averages—the mean, median and mode—and how to calculate them from raw data.

Measures of central tendency are used to summarise information about a set of data. The central tendency measures or **averages** are said to represent the data. While the three measures of central tendency can be problematic they are widely used, and they are useful to develop children's understanding of data measures.

The **mean** is the arithmetic average, the **median** is the middle or central value, and the **mode** is the most frequent value. Watson (2006) indicates that it takes many years for children to develop a deep understanding of average as being representative of a data set.

Calculate the mean, median, mode and range for the Crows and Galahs from the stem-and-leaf plot in Figure 28.6. Check your answers below.

- Crows average scores:

$$\text{Mean: } \frac{1661}{24} = 69.2; \text{ median: } \frac{70 + 72}{2} = 71; \text{ mode: } 58$$
$$\text{Range: } 116 - 39 = 77$$

- Galahs average scores

$$\text{Mean: } \frac{1365}{24} = 56.8, \text{ median: } \frac{53 + 57}{2} = 55, \text{ mode : } 42, 46$$
$$\text{Range: } 96 - 31 = 65$$

It is important for children to move beyond the computation of averages and to engage with the meaning. Analysis of this data reveals some interesting information about the two teams. Clearly the Crows scored more points, although additional information about number of matches won would be needed to determine which team was the most successful during the season. The three averages and range seem to indicate that while the Galahs scored a lower average on all measures they were more consistent. This kind of analysis can be used for many different kinds of data comparison.

Analysis may prompt further questions and collection of data. For example, why did the Crows have a larger range?

Averages are intended to be representative of the data. However, it is important to understand that individual pieces of data called *outliers* can significantly distort the representativeness of an average. Outliers are pieces of data that are numerically distant from the rest of the data. Refer back to the example given in Chapter 12. It is acceptable to remove an outlier from the calculation of averages if this is made explicit in the accompanying explanation.

Variation

'Data sets tell stories, and the heart of any statistical story is usually contained in the variability in the data' (Shaughnessey, 2007, p. 973). Variation can be a complex concept but it is also what makes statistics interesting. While measures of central tendency can provide some broad-brush pictures of data representation, it is often more important to examine the variation within the data.

Patterns outside of the mean, median, and mode may provide important information about a small but significant group or situation. While middle school children will not use formal variance analysis measures such as chi-square tests, they can start to examine unusual outliers or clumps of data. Such data can be significant and have often led to medical breakthroughs or scientific discoveries.

Box-and-whisker plots

Box-and-whisker plots are an excellent method for displaying the median, range, quartiles, and variance of data.

integrating technology/ICT

Microsoft Excel allows children to create graphs to illustrate data. Online tutorials and lesson materials are readily available. Children can easily explore the appropriateness of different representations.

Describing chance events

Jones, Langrall and Mooney (2007) state that the curriculum emphasis moves towards a focus on classical and frequentist approaches in the middle years. Children bring informal understandings of chance and random events from the early years and start to develop an understanding of both theoretical and experimental probability. Concepts are largely developed through the modelling and simulation of real-world situations. In addition, attention is given to the social contexts of probability such as medicine (genetics), weather, and insurance.

did you know?

Identical winning numbers occurred two weeks in a row in the Bulgarian lottery. The occurrence led to an investigation but it found no evidence of any corruption. Such events do happen, and will continue to happen. The probability of selecting the six winning numbers in any single lottery with 42 numbers is over 5 million to 1 (Biliak, 2009).

communicating mathematically

Encourage children to keep a dictionary of statistics and probability terms. They should write definitions in their own words and provide examples or illustrations to explain their ideas.

In the early primary years, children learn to use some of the vocabulary associated with probability. For example, they may classify the chance of an event occurring as likely or unlikely. In addition children learn about the concept of fairness—the chance of rolling any number, from 1–6, on a die is the same and therefore dice are understood to be fair. During Year 3 and 4 children encounter events with different probabilities such as spinners with unequal shading and therefore different chances of particular outcomes occurring.

Guided exploration is suggested as an appropriate method for students to learn probability concepts in the middle years. Hand-on activities are generally enjoyable and engaging for students. This method allows students to first develop an intuitive understanding of probability from data gathered in experiments. Students are also introduced to the concept of randomness and learn about the different expectations of outcomes in a few trials versus the outcomes of a large number of trials. This concept is referred to as the Law of Large Numbers. The larger the number of trials, the closer the experimental probability results to theoretical probability. As students approach the middle years of schooling they begin to quantify chance events with fractions, decimals, and percentages.

did you know?

In the eighteenth century there were more than 20 published dice games that allowed ordinary people to compose music in the form of minuets, marches, and waltzes. A chance roll of dice determined bars of music and note selection.

Children are expected to define the sample space for single-step experiments with equally likely outcomes. A **sample space** is defined as the set of possible outcomes from a probability experiment. Some examples are given below.

- Sample space for tossing a coin: {Head, Tail}
- Sample space for rolling a die: {1, 2, 3, 4, 5, 6}

handy hint

In order to muffle the sounds of 30 coins being tossed simultaneously 100 times, you may want to have the children toss the coins on a soft surface such as carpet!

issues in teaching

Children often have preconceived ideas about fairness and this can influence their ability to develop an understanding of probability concepts. Provide children with practical examples that challenge misunderstandings they may have about fairness and probability.

Children should be able to use the sample space to assign probability. **Probability** is defined as the chance that a particular outcome will occur, and is written as a ratio of the outcome of interest to all possible outcomes.

- Toss a coin: The probability of getting a head is 1 in 2 and can be written as $\frac{1}{2}$.
- Roll a die: The probability of getting a 6 is 1 in 6 and can be written as $\frac{1}{6}$.

Children should investigate the difference between theoretical and experimental probabilities by engaging in their own chance experiments. The relative frequencies can be compared over a series of trials. For example, how many heads are tossed for 10 trials, 20 trials, 100 trials, and 500 trials? The larger number can be gathered by grouping all of the class results together.

for the classroom

There are some wonderful children's books that can be used to support the teaching and learning of probability. One such book by Amy Axelrod is entitled *Pigs at Odds: Fun with Math and Games*. This book is one of a series of mathematical themed books featuring the Pig family. In this story Mr Pig seems to have the odds against him as he tries to win prizes at a fair.

There are many possible classroom activities associated with this book. For example, to win a prize in the Strength Game, Mr Pig must hit the bell three times in a row. He has five attempts to do this. What are the winning possibilities?

Additional associated activities can be found at <www.amyaxelrod.com>.

It is essential for children to understand the concepts of theoretical and experimental probability. Many people misunderstand the connection between these two concepts.

Theoretical probability is the chance of events happening under ideal circumstances:

$$\frac{\text{Number of outcomes in the event}}{\text{Number of possible outcomes}}$$

For example, the theoretical probability of rolling a 4 with one die is $\frac{1}{6}$, and ideally one out of every six rolls would be a 4.

Experimental probability is the chance of something happening based on repeated trials:

$$\frac{\text{Number of observed occurrences of the event}}{\text{Total trials}}$$

For example, when tossing a die 12 times the following results were observed:

6, 5, 6, 1, 3, 1, 6, 3, 5, 4, 6, 3

These trials highlight the differences between experimental and theoretical probability.

issues in teaching

While gambling provides a real-life example of probability, it is problematic for many people. Gambling can be addictive and detrimentally impact on the lives of individuals, families, and communities. Teachers must consider the specifc communities where they are teaching and determine whether gambling can be included in the curriculum. Clearly the issue, if explored, must be approached with sensititivity.

> **making connections**
>
> Probability is used to calculate insurance tables. For example, data collected concerning car accidents, including gender and age of driver and model of car, is used to determine the chance of accidents occurring.

In everyday life, people often expect theoretical probability to be reflected in a small number of trials. For example, if a family has three boys, many people believe that they have a high chance of having a girl if they have a fourth child. In reality the chance is $\frac{1}{2}$ for each child. *Experimental probability is only expected to approximate theoretical probability with a large number of trials.*

Shaughnessey (2003) describes the importance of having children experience the impact of sample size in experimental probability. Children must collect data from trials of varying sample sizes and compare outcomes systematically in order to develop understanding of the connection between theoretical and experimental probability.

> **for the classroom**
>
> An excellent probability activity entitled Crazy Animals is part of the maths300 series. Detailed information can be found at <www.maths300.esa.edu.au/index.php/free-sample-tour/1035-crazy-animals.html>. This activity can be used for a range of concepts including sample space and experimental probability, and is suitable for children in Years 3–12. Children construct different combinations of animals by randomly selecting a head, body, and tail (roll of die). Children form a sample space by naming each possible animal by the varied body parts. For example a *girorck* has the head of a giraffe, body of a horse, and tail of a duck. The activity is both fun and informative.

Complementary events

After children learn how to quantify simple chance events, they can be introduced to the concept of complementary events. The numerical probability of any event is between 0 and 1. Probabilities in a defined sample space always sum to 1. This knowledge can be used to calculate the probability of events. Some simple examples of this concept follow:

- When a coin is tossed it can land on either heads or tails. Because these two events are complementary, we know that:

$$P(\text{Head}) + P(\text{Tail}) = 1$$
$$\tfrac{1}{2} + \tfrac{1}{2} = 1$$

- Suppose three coloured marbles are in a jar: two are blue and one is red. Because the events are complementary we know that:

$$P(\text{Blue}) + P(\text{Red}) = 1$$
$$\tfrac{2}{3} + \tfrac{1}{3} = 1$$

The probability of not selecting a red marble in the above example is $1 - \tfrac{1}{3} = \tfrac{2}{3}$.

Using tree diagrams to calculate two-step examples

The tree diagram below illustrates all the possible outcomes from tossing a coin twice. Tracing each path allows children to determine the outcomes and to calculate the probability of each outcome.

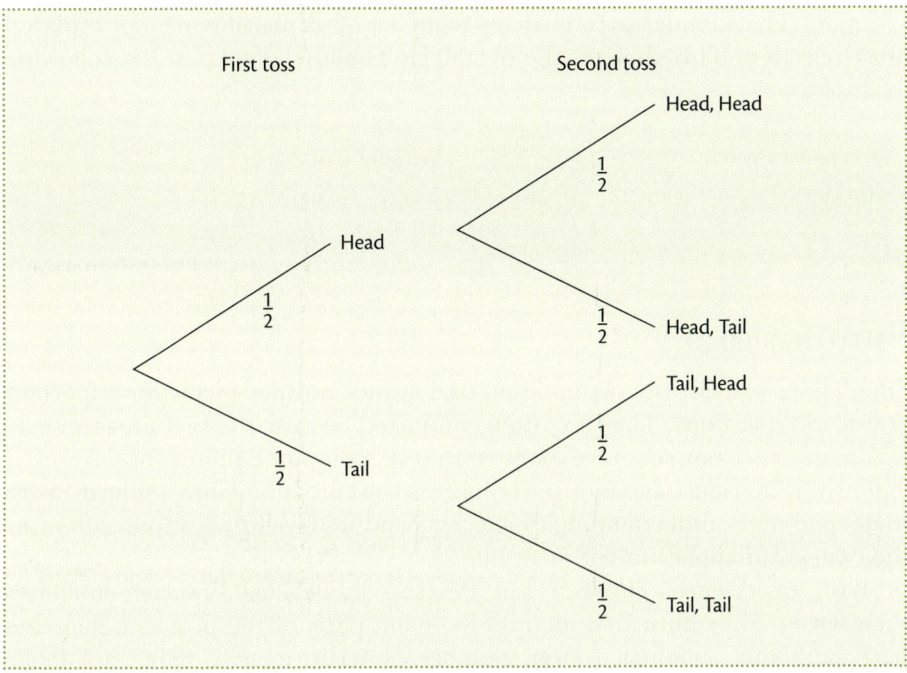

A typical question is 'Calculate the probability of tossing two heads when a coin is tossed twice'. An examination of the tree diagram reveals that there is one way among the four possible outcomes to toss two heads. This indicates that the probability is $\frac{1}{4}$.

Probability can be expressed using fractions, as seen in previous examples, or using decimals or percentages. In the case of the probability of tossing two heads the probability can also be expressed as 0.25 or 25%. This provides an opportunity to reinforce previous work concerning the connection between these three concepts. The choice of fraction, decimal, or percentage is usually made on the basis of context and audience.

consider and discuss

1. What is the probability of tossing a head and a tail in any order?
2. How can tree diagrams be used to help children learn about the fundamental probability concepts of *and* and *or*?

The issue of replacement

Replacement is another term children will know from everyday life. If batteries stop working, we replace them! You will need to be aware of student background knowledge of replacement as you create activities for them. Replacement in probability relates to the sample space in ongoing trials of an experiment.

When working with two-step examples we need to consider the impact of replacement. In the example with three coloured counters, additional consideration is required in two-step situations as to whether or not counters are replaced after the initial selection from the jar. If you need to calculate the probability of selecting 2 blue marbles from a jar that contains 2 blue and 1 red marble, you have two possible scenarios.

The sample space is initially 3, and remains 3 if marbles are replaced after selection. The sample space changes from 3 to 2 if marbles are not replaced after selection. This changes the overall probability, as seen in the following examples.

With replacement	Without replacement
P(Blue) × P(Blue)	P(Blue) × P(Blue)
$\frac{2}{3} \times \frac{2}{3} = \frac{4}{9}$	$\frac{2}{3} \times \frac{1}{2} = \frac{2}{6} = \frac{1}{3}$

Simulations

Simulations provide opportunities to trial events in order to answer important real-world questions. They are often conducted because the real situation may be dangerous, complex, or expensive to test. Computer simulations are used extensively in science and industry. Children can run simulations online in order to deepen their understanding of concepts and to develop an appreciation for the real-world application of probability.

With experience, children can develop models to simulate situations themselves. They must first identify the main parts of the problem, generate data randomly, conduct a large number of trials, analyse data, and make recommendations.

for the classroom

Capture–recapture simulation

An excellent and engaging activity that includes many of the concepts in this chapter is the capture–recapture (or catch and release) simulation. This activity simulates the real method developed by biologists for estimating the populations of mobile or elusive animals.

To simulate capture–recapture:

1 Provide a large envelope (imagine this is a lake) containing a number of counters (endangered fish whose population you want to monitor).
2 Take a sample (small handful) of 'fish'. Tag your fish by exchanging each for a counter of a colour not already in the lake.
3 Let the fish swim about (assist them by shaking the bag), then take another sample.
4 Consider how you can use the proportion of tagged fish in the second sample to estimate the wild population.

Figure 28.7 Student engaged with a capture–recapture simulation

5 Repeat steps 3 and 4 multiple times.
6 Once you have an estimate of the population in the lake you can 'drain it' and check the accuracy of your estimate (something we can't do with real animal populations!).
7 What other factors would need to be taken into account when using this method with a real population? How could the method be used to estimate the Flinders Ranges rock wallaby population, for example?
8 As an extension, have the children write a letter to a friend explaining how to use the capture–recapture method in a different situation. This is a great literacy and communication connection and is only limited by the students' imaginations.

In the example from the student notebook in Figure 28.8, seven separate samples were taken. An initial calculation using ratios was made after the first sample and the population was estimated to be 58. The children working together in the group questioned how accurate this estimate was and decided to recalculate the estimate using all of the sample data (Figure 28.9).

Work from a student's notebook

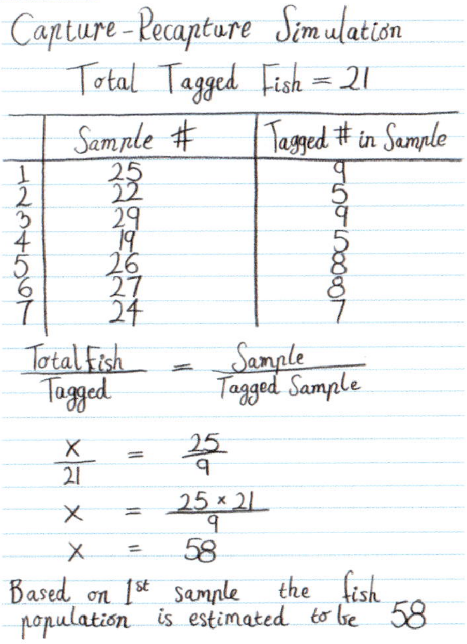

Capture-Recapture Simulation
Total Tagged Fish = 21

Sample #	Tagged # in Sample
1 25	9
2 22	5
3 29	9
4 19	5
5 26	8
6 27	8
7 24	7

$$\frac{\text{Total Fish Tagged}}{} = \frac{\text{Sample}}{\text{Tagged Sample}}$$

$$\frac{X}{21} = \frac{25}{9}$$

$$X = \frac{25 \times 21}{9}$$

$$X = 58$$

Based on 1st sample the fish population is estimated to be 58

Figure 28.8

Calculation using all of the data from all seven samples

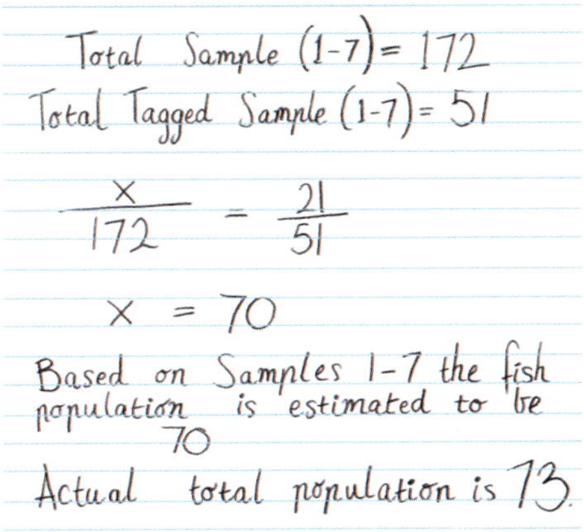

Total Sample (1-7) = 172
Total Tagged Sample (1-7) = 51

$$\frac{X}{172} = \frac{21}{51}$$

$$X = 70$$

Based on Samples 1-7 the fish population is estimated to be 70

Actual total population is 73.

Figure 28.9

The children found a different result when all seven samples were combined into the calculation. The estimated population was now calculated to be 70. The children eagerly emptied the bag of fish (counters) onto the desk and counted to find that the actual population was 73.

consider and discuss

1. Discuss the results of the capture–recapture simulation.
2. What could be asked by the teacher?
3. How could you, as a teacher, facilitate children learning through this activity?

integrating technology/ICT

The Learning Federation is a source of numerous probability learning objects to assist student's learning at all Year levels. Educators have free access to all of the learning objects. Information about the Learning Federation resources can be found at <www.thelearningfederation.edu.au/default.asp>.

One resource for probability is entitled Dice Duels: Bike Race, and is developed for Years 6–9. Children build a bike by the roll of two dice—they examine patterns of bike performance from the results of 100 races. This object is one of 11 objects in this series of probability objects.

Conclusion

In this chapter we have built on the concepts discussed in Chapter 21 where probability and statistics in the early years were explored. In the middle years, children learn to describe statistics and probability events in more formal mathematical terms. This knowledge empowers children to communicate findings to others using convincing data.

During these years, children become more equipped to critically examine statistics and probability used by others to support particular viewpoints. Among important concepts learned by children is knowledge of sampling, randomness, appropriate representation of data, and the difference between theoretical and experimental probability.

Although there is more emphasis on the use of formal mathematical representation and calculation of chance and data, children should continue to learn concepts through practical hands-on activities. This strand has natural connections to authentic situations and is best learnt through actual situations or simulations. In addition statistics and probability naturally integrate across all learning areas.

Chapter 28 Statistics and Probability in the Middle Years

key terms

Average: a number that best represents a set of data; this can be calculated as a mean, median, or mode

Data: information or facts you find out or are given; data can be words, numbers, or a mixture of both

Experimental probability: the estimated chance of something happening based on repeated trials

Mean: a kind of average determined by dividing the total quantities by the number of quantities

Median: a kind of average that is the middle value in a set of numerically ordered data

Mode: a kind of average that is the quantity or number that occurs most often

Probability: a number between 0 (impossible) and 1 (certain) that indicates the likelihood or chance that a particular outcome will occur or something will happen; can be written as a fraction or percentage

Random sample: a sample that is chosen purely by chance

Representations: ways of organising and communicating data

Sample space: the set of possible outcomes for a specific event

Statistics: the collection and analysis of data to describe the world

Theoretical probability: the calculated chance of events happening under ideal circumstances

Review questions

1. Describe how you can facilitate children's learning about random samples.
2. Develop examples for children to use different forms of data representations.
3. How can children best develop understanding of theoretical and experimental probability?
4. Design an activity to assess children's understanding of tree diagrams.
5. Describe a connection between statistics and another learning area in the Year 6 curriculum.

Key references

Axelrod, A. (2000). *Pigs at Odds: Fun with Math and Games*. Sydney: Scholastic.

Bialik, C. (2009). Lottery Math 101. Retrieved 31 January 2011 from http://blogs.wsj.com/numbersguy/lottery-math-101-801/.

Forrest, J. (2005). The space shuttle Challenger disaster: A failure in decision support system and human factors management. Retrieved 31 January 2011 from http://dssresources.com/cases/spaceshuttlechallenger/index.html.

Jones, G., Langrall, W., & Mooney, E. (2007). Research in probability. In F.J. Lester (Ed.), *Second Handbook of Research on Mathematics Teaching and Learning* (pp. 909–955). Charlotte, NC: Information Age

Shaughnessey, M. (2003). Research on students understanding of proability. In J. Kilpatrick, W. Martin, & D. Schifter (Eds.), *A Research Companion to Principles and Standards for School Mathematics* (pp 216–226). Reston, VA: NCTM.

Shaughnessey, M. (2007). Research on statistics and reasoning. In F.J. Lester (Ed.), *Second Handbook of Research on Mathematics Teaching and Learning* (pp. 957–1009). Charlotte, NC: Information Age.

Watson, J. (2006). *Statistical Literacy at School: Growth and Goals*. Marhwah, NJ: Erlbaum.

Websites

www.acara.edu.au/default.asp

www.abs.gov.au/websitedbs/cashome.nsf/home/home

www.amyaxelrod.com

www.free-training-tutorial.com/

www.maths300.esa.edu.au/index.php/free-sample-tour/1035-crazy-animals.html

29 Becoming a Professional Teacher of Mathematics

Contents

Looking forward	665
Standards for mathematics teaching	667
Final words of advice	676

Chapter objectives

This chapter will enable the reader to:
- Become familiar with the Australian Association of Mathematics Teachers standards for Excellence in Teaching Mathematics in Australian Schools
- Consider the professional knowledge, personal attributes, and professional practices of excellent teachers of mathematics
- Learn about ways that you can take responsibility for your own ongoing professional learning
- Consider some practical ideas related to planning, assessment and reporting in the context of mathematics teaching
- Reflect on the connection between your university studies and teaching career
- Consider the experiences of recent graduates who have made the transition from pre-service teacher to professional teacher

That was then, this is now

The following is a quotation from an interview with a primary teacher five years after graduating from university. Reflecting on the connection between her university studies and her work as a teacher she said:

> All you want to do when you are at university is go out and teach and you really are not so enthused about the theoretical aspect of it but then as you become a teacher you realise that you need all that theoretical stuff too actually, you know, it's got to be in the back of your mind when you're actually teaching and planning and assessing kids (Beswick & Dole, 2008, p. 73).

consider and discuss

- How useful do you think your university studies are?
- In what ways do you think they have prepared you for teaching?
- What will be of most value to you as you move into the next phase of your teaching career?

Big ideas

- Completion of your initial teaching qualification marks the first stage of an ongoing journey in the teaching profession.
- Excellent teachers learn continually: they seek out opportunities to develop their understandings and practice, and take responsibility for their development.
- Reflecting productively on your practice and your students' learning is a key means of professional learning.
- Being a professional teacher of mathematics involves engaging with and contributing to a community of professionals.

Looking forward

Graduating from university with a teaching qualification is a major milestone that recognises the learning that has occurred in the preceding years and acknowledges the graduates' readiness to join the teaching profession. It is both a celebration of achievement and the beginning of the next stage in the ongoing journey of becoming a teacher. Many beginning teachers find the first year(s) of teaching demanding, not only in terms of taking responsibility for a class but also in establishing themselves as professionals separate from the university context (Patkin & Gesser, 2009). Your university studies provide a starting point on which you can begin to build expertise. The following quote from a teacher who was interviewed five years after her graduation illustrates how she built upon these foundations:

> When I was beginning teaching, whenever I'd go to introducing a new topic, say space for example, I'd go back to the notes and remind myself of what the key concepts were that I should be focusing on developing with the kids, use some of the ideas from the tute notes that I thought were relevant to the group that I'm working with and then build on those.

In this chapter we consider what it means to be a teacher, and specifically a teacher of mathematics. This is framed in terms of professional standards and so we first need to consider what a profession is and what it means to be a professional.

Cheetham and Chivers (2005, cited in Beaton, 2010, p. 4) identified a list of characteristics of a **profession**. According to them a profession:

> confers status in society; organises itself into some sort of professional body; is learned i.e., requires prolonged and specialised training and education; is altruistic (oriented toward service rather than profit); offers autonomy within the job role; is informed by an ethical code of some kind; is non-commercial; has collective influence within society; is self-regulatory; is collegial; is client-focussed.

consider and discuss

Professions Australia (1997) defined a profession as:

> A profession is a disciplined group of individuals who adhere to ethical standards and hold themselves out as, and are accepted by the public as possessing special knowledge and skills in a widely recognised body of learning derived from research, education and training at a high level, and who are prepared to apply this knowledge and exercise these skills in the interest of others.
>
> It is inherent in the definition of a profession that a code of ethics governs the activities of each profession. Such codes require behaviour and practice beyond the personal moral obligations of an individual. They define and demand high standards of behaviour in respect to the services provided to the public and in dealing with professional colleagues. Further, these codes are enforced by the profession and are acknowledged and accepted by the community.

Discuss the implications of this definition for teaching mathematics.

1. To what ethical standards do teachers adhere?
2. What specialised knowledge/skills do teachers have?
3. How and to what extent is this knowledge and skill accepted by the public?
4. To what extent and in what ways do teachers use their knowledge and skills altruistically? How can this be reconciled with demands for improved pay and conditions?
5. What are the standards of behaviour to which teachers hold themselves?
6. In what ways does the teaching profession enforce standards of professional behaviour?

Concern about the professional status of teaching had been one of the drivers of the development of standards. These have attempted to set out the knowledge and skills that define the teaching profession and to articulate the ethical standards to which teachers aspire. Teacher registration authorities are intended to ensure that only those who meet the required standards are allowed entry to the profession, and in so doing provide public assurance of the quality of teachers.

issues in teaching

The status of teaching as a profession

Debates about whether or not teaching is a profession occasionally make it into newspapers and the issue is the subject of many online discussions (type 'Is teaching a profession?' into a search engine to see some of these). Those who question the professional status of teaching point to the relatively low social status of teaching, differences between the roles of unions in education compared with other professions, and constraints on teachers' autonomy. The following questions are worth considering:

- Why do teachers want to be considered members of a profession?
- How are union activities like calling strikes compatible with the characteristics of a profession?
- What evidence is there of relatively low social status of teaching? What contributes to this and how might it be influenced?

Chapter 29 Becoming a Professional Teacher of Mathematics

Standards for mathematics teaching

The Australian Institute for Teaching and School Leadership (AITSL) (2011) has developed national non-discipline specific professional **standards** for teachers that are based on a view of teachers' expertise as developing throughout their careers. The standards recognise four career stages from Graduate standards at entry to the profession. Standards at the Proficient stage are intended to provide the basis for nationally consistent teacher registration. The Highly accomplished and Lead standards attempt to define the further development of expertise throughout teachers' careers. At each stage the standards are organised according to three domains: Professional knowledge, Professional practice, and Professional engagement. At whatever stage of your career you may be, the standards are intended to provide a means for self-assessment and a framework for planning career development and professional learning. The higher stages can be regarded as standards to aspire to, while the Graduate standards recognise the considerable knowledge and skills with which beginning teachers are expected to enter the profession.

The Australian Association of Mathematics Teachers (AAMT) has, since 2002, promoted standards for excellence in teaching mathematics in Australian schools organised into the following domains: Professional Knowledge, Professional Attributes, and Professional Practice. Unlike the AITSL standards, the AAMT standards are concerned only with excellence and relate most closely to the Highly accomplished and Lead stages of the AITSL standards. They are also concerned only with mathematics, and hence they can provide more specific guidance for teachers wanting to develop their expertise in teaching that discipline. To this end the AAMT standards have been used in a number of professional learning projects involving teachers of Years F–12 (e.g. Bishop, Clarke & Morony, 2006). Because our concern is with mathematics teaching, the AAMT standards have been used to structure the remainder of this chapter.

Professional knowledge

In Chapter 3 we discussed the knowledge that is needed to teach mathematics using Shulman's (1987) seven knowledge types as a framework. The AAMT (2002) standards describe the knowledge required for excellence in mathematics teaching in terms of knowledge of students, of mathematics, and of students' learning mathematics. Between them these include aspects of Shulman's content knowledge, knowledge of students as learners, and pedagogical content knowledge for teaching mathematics.

Knowledge of students

Students have diverse social and cultural backgrounds and personal characteristics that necessarily inform how they interact with school and with mathematics. Excellent teachers of mathematics know about the contexts in which their students live, as well as the mathematics that they already know and use, how they feel about learning mathematics, and prefer to learn the subject (AAMT, 2002). Like Donna, quoted below, we all would like our students to enjoy their learning, but we cannot assume that experiences that are enjoyable for one student (or perhaps that you enjoyed) will be experienced in the same way by others.

> I prefer that they, they enjoy maths and that they, you know, um actually feel confident in their abilities rather than um you know, feel that they feel that it's a negative experience and that it's, you know, that they're not good at it. (Donna)

for the classroom

Ask students about their preferences in relation to learning mathematics. O'Shea (2009, p. 19) asked Year 5 students to complete the following task.

Write a story about your ideal maths class. Write about:

- the sorts of questions or problems you like to answer
- what you like to be doing
- what you like the teacher to be doing.

Knowledge of mathematics

Teachers of mathematics need a thorough understanding of the mathematics that they teach within the broader context of the mathematics curriculum (AAMT, 2002). That is, they need to know how the mathematics being taught at a particular Year level builds upon mathematics taught in earlier years and contributes to subsequent mathematics learning. They also need to know how to represent and communicate mathematical ideas and understand why it is taught. They can help students to make connections between mathematical topics and between mathematics and other school subjects and to society beyond school (AAMT, 2002). The AAMT (2002) also stressed that teachers must, themselves, be confident about the mathematics that they teach. Being confident about one's own ability to use mathematics in everyday contexts is, however, just a start and certainly not all that is needed. Beswick, Callingham and Watson (2011) found that for the 62 middle years teachers in their study, confidence to use mathematics in everyday contexts and to teach most middle school mathematics topics were in advance of specific knowledge of how to teach the key mathematical ideas. That is, it was possible to be confident about teaching mathematics without having the knowledge to do so effectively. Graven's (2004) conceptualisation of confidence as a component of learning, that is, being confident means being confident that one can learn what is needed. This is perhaps more helpful than regarding confidence as belief that one can do what is needed now.

It is our contention that teachers should have sufficiently deep understanding of mathematics and an appreciation of the discipline and of what it means to learn mathematics so that they can confidently continue to learn more mathematics and more about the mathematics they already, at some level, know.

The teachers who made the statements below were at the beginning of their teaching careers and appreciated the importance of deeply understanding even the most basic mathematics.

think + link

Re-read the section in Chapter 3 on Knowledge for teaching mathematics (p. xx). Create a table or diagram that shows how professional knowledge as described in the AAMT standards relates to the knowledge types described by Shulman (1987), and Ball and colleagues (1990).

> The best maths teaching is having a good understanding of what you're teaching ... when I came here I thought, 'Ah, Reception maths; it's basic'. But I had to revisit things like base ten understanding and [other] things that I hadn't necessarily thought about.

> I go through the concepts myself and make sure that I'm 100% happy with it. If I don't know exactly what I'm doing I get help before I go into the classroom to do it and make sure I am clear on that.

consider and discuss

Watson (2001) warned of the dangers of thinking that we know our students and that the ways in which judging mathematical ability based on a relatively small range of indicators can lead to unfair judgments.

Can you think of a time when you surprised a teacher by showing that you understood more than he/she expected? Can you think of someone else who surprised a teacher in this way? Recount your story and discuss what made the student's knowledge surprising. What had prevented the teacher from appreciating the student's ability?

Knowledge of students' learning of mathematics

Teachers need to know about contemporary theories about how students learn mathematics, including the representations, teaching sequences, and language that are most likely to be effective. Their repertoires of strategies needs to extend to strategies for facilitating the development of positive attitudes to mathematics, and engaging with parents to facilitate their involvement in their children's learning (AAMT, 2002).

The AAMT also included the use of information and communication technologies. It is important that the focus of such use is on enhancing mathematics teaching and not on the use of the technology for its own sake. Beauchamp (2004) illustrated this point in the context of interactive whiteboards (IWBs). He described a series of levels in teachers' use of the IWB from simply substituting it for a traditional whiteboard and using it to display information, through to integrating it fully into one's pedagogy and capitalising on its potential to enhance interactivity in lessons.

Professional attributes

The professional attributes of excellent teachers of mathematics identified by the AAMT (2002) are consistent with the altruistic character of professions and their emphasis on ethical behaviour and non-commercialism (Cheetham & Chivers 2005, cited in Beaton, 2010).

Personal attributes

Arguably the most important personal characteristic of an excellent teacher of mathematics is enthusiasm for the subject (AAMT, 2002). They enjoy playing with mathematics themselves (Beswick, 2007), and inspire their students to learn by setting high but realistic expectations, communicating a belief that all their students can learn mathematics, encouraging autonomy and enjoyment in learning, and displaying care and respect for their students (AAMT, 2002).

There is a considerable literature that points to a tendency for teachers to teach as they were taught (e.g. Ball, 1990). Klein (2006, p. 335) claimed that 'preservice teachers' ways of being a teacher of mathematics has less to do with theory and policy than their previous (and current) experiences of institutionalised teaching and learning'. This is in spite of the prevalence among pre-service teachers of negative recollections of learning mathematics at school (Beswick, 2006). A great deal of self-confidence and perseverance is needed for teachers, especially at the beginning of their careers, to take the risks inherent in trying approaches that might be different from those commonly being used around them.

Personal professional development

Maintaining professional knowledge requires a commitment to ongoing learning. This can take a range of forms, from informal collegial interactions, reading, trying new ideas and reflecting on their effectiveness in terms of students' learning, through to more formal professional learning opportunities and involvement in research and postgraduate study. The crucial feature of excellent teachers of mathematics is a commitment to ongoing learning and improvement (AAMT, 2002). Such teachers are committed to continually improving their own knowledge and understanding of mathematics, how students learn it, and how it can best be taught. As a result they have informed views of current developments (AAMT, 2002).

consider and discuss

How will you continue to develop as a teacher of mathematics? Consider the following list as a starting point for your thinking and planning.

- Join your local mathematics association—if it is an affiliate of AAMT you will automatically become a member of AAMT as well. Links to state-based affiliates of AAMT and information about the association's aims and benefits to members are available at <www.aamt.edu.au/>.
- Develop the habit of regularly reading articles of interest from professional and scholarly mathematics education journals. The reference lists at the ends of the chapters in this book cite some suitable journals. If you are a pre-service teacher your university library will have subscriptions to many suitable journals. If you are not enrolled at university, enquire about alumni membership of a university library.
- Initiate discussions with colleagues about mathematics teaching. You might do this through collaborative planning of mathematics units and lessons, developing a system for sharing and evaluating resources, including discussions of students' work in regular meetings, and suggesting that more than one teacher from your school attend a professional learning event or conference.
- Accept opportunities to be involved in research projects related to mathematics teaching and learning.
- Enroll in postgraduate study.
- Join and contribute to an online mathematics teacher community such as AAMT's email list (there is a link from their website).
- Subscribe to a resource list such as the CSIRO's Maths by email <www.csiro.au/resources/Maths-by-Email--ci_pageNo-3.html>.

Community responsibilities

The AAMT (2002) standards describe excellent teachers of mathematics as taking an interest in mathematics education beyond the day-to-day classroom teaching of the subject. In addition to this work excellent teachers make efforts to connect with families and the school community and to promote activities that support their students' mathematics learning beyond the classroom (e.g. mathematics competitions, including those with a focus on enjoyment and participation, and enrichment programs). They advocate for mathematics in their schools and encourage collaborative endeavour that improves mathematics teaching across the school. Beyond the school they contribute to professional associations for teachers of mathematics associations and engage with colleagues beyond their own schools through attending conferences and using web technologies (AAMT, 2002).

Many of the kinds of activities that excellent teachers of mathematics regard as part of their professional responsibilities are related to leadership. The three primary teachers, all in the early stages of their teaching careers, that Patkin and Gesser (2009) interviewed were all active in promoting and leading mathematics teaching, at least in their schools. They described being motivated by a desire to be excellent teachers, a love of mathematics, and a genuine concern that their students come to enjoy the discipline as much as they did. All had been promoted within the first several years of their careers and were influential in school decision-making about mathematics teaching. Roles involving numeracy coordination are common in primary and middle schools and often open to those with passion and enthusiasm for mathematics.

Writing about your practice for your peers and presenting at conferences is an important way to contribute to the profession and can also provide a catalyst for thinking more deeply about the underpinnings of your practice. There is no need to have a lot of experience in order to have something to offer that will be valued by other teachers. For example, Youdale (2010) wrote about her experiences of teaching a small group of children the number sequence 11–20 as part of her final mathematics curriculum unit, before she graduated.

consider and discuss

It is often difficult to persuade teachers to write and publish about their practice. Many say that they are not doing anything special, and others point to the long hours that they are already working as a reason for not engaging in this activity.

1. Why might even innovative teachers believe that they are not doing anything special? How could this perception be challenged?
2. How might teachers' reluctance to acknowledge their expertise relate to community perceptions of the teaching profession?
3. List as many reasons as you can why teachers should engage in writing about their practice.

Opportunities to be involved in mentoring or coaching activities around mathematics teaching are further ways that you can both extend your own leaning and contribute to the professional growth of others. Similarly, being involved in the supervision of pre-service teachers on practicum and the induction of new teachers is an important way to have a positive impact on your profession.

Professional practice

In Chapter 3 we discussed many of the elements that comprise this domain of the AAMT (2002) standards. Here the emphasis is on helping you to see how these everyday activities of teaching contribute to your professional journey, and providing you with some practical tools and advice.

The learning environment

Excellent teachers of mathematics establish learning environments designed to maximise learning. They are inclusive and cater for the diversity of students' needs, empowering them to take responsibility for their learning and to value engagement with mathematics, cooperation, and collaboration. Understanding is emphasised, and mathematical communication is developed and practised (AAMT, 2002).

An important part of creating the kinds of learning environments that the AAMT recommend is the establishment of social norms that emphasise mutual respect and the kinds of behaviours that evidence the mathematical proficiencies (understanding, fluency, reasoning, and problem solving) that are integral to the Australian curriculum (ACARA, 2011). These were described in Chapter 8.

for the classroom

Survey students about their perceptions of the learning environment in their maths lessons. Surveys and instructions for scoring them are available in the literature (e.g. Ryan & Patrick, 2001).

Planning for teaching

In Chapter 3 we focused on lesson planning, and stressed the importance of being clear about your objectives—the specific important mathematics that you want students to learn. The following quote is from a beginning teacher who understood this.

> I find it really hard, unless I have an aim, what do I want the kids to get from this lesson? ... I think you need to know where it's going as well because then it makes it easier to make the connections.

Planning units of work has many similarities with planning lessons. You need to be clear about the mathematical ideas with which you want the students to engage and then to consider the kinds of tasks and other learning experiences that are likely to facilitate the desired learning. Careful thinking about the sequence in which ideas are introduced and tasks offered is more complex than planning a single lesson. Careful consideration must be given to how the plan can be varied to cater for diverse learners and unanticipated difficulties that particular ideas present, as well as for when students understand something more quickly than expected. Opportunities and ways of making connections among ideas and helping students to appreciate the interconnectedness of mathematical ideas are also important considerations. Assessment strategies and tasks should be chosen or devised to provide information about the development of students' understanding both during and at the end of the unit.

Table 29.1 lists important features of a unit of work that can usefully be considered as your plan.

Table 29.1 Features of unit of work based on curriculum

Title	• Should be meaningful from the student's perspective
Rationale	• Should provide some motivation for students to do the unit
Objectives	• Should be expressed in student-friendly language, e.g. begin with a statement such as 'At the end of the unit of work I will be able to …' and start with verbs like solve, apply, demonstrate, draw, explain, estimate, experiment, decide, discuss, appreciate, construct, record, plan, represent, monitor. • Should be based on the content listed in the curriculum.
Plan of work	• Should provide opportunities to construct shared meanings for important concepts, skills, and strategies by linking new knowledge to prior knowledge and experience. • Should provide opportunities to apply what is known, collectively or individually, to solve problems that the group or an individual wants to solve. • Should incorporate a broad range of teaching and learning strategies, e.g. cooperative group work, problem solving, investigations, mental strategies, concrete materials, outdoor locations, calculators and/or computer applications. • Should connect students' language to appropriate mathematical language. • Should challenge and extend students' strategies. • Should provide opportunities for developing fluency, understanding, reasoning, and problem solving (the proficiency strands of the *Australian Curriculum: Mathematics*). • Should have a predictable structure, e.g. an introduction, a period of development, conjecture and evaluation, followed by a period of review, reflection, consolidation, and conclusions.
Assessment	• Should relate to all objectives and reflect the range of teaching and learning strategies used. • Should answer student questions like 'What do I know now that I did not know before?', 'What am I able to do now that I was not able to do before?' • Should answer teacher questions such as 'What do I need to consider next?', 'What do I report to parents, other teachers, and outside bodies?'
Evaluation	• Should answer the questions 'Did the unit of work succeed in terms of achieving the objectives?', 'What content and proficiency strands did the unit address?', 'How well do these relate to the objectives?', 'Do the objectives need to be re-defined?', 'Does the unit of work need to be modified?'

The final stage, evaluation, is a crucial part of continually improving your teaching. Even though the unit is finished, thoughtful evaluation allows you to make improvements to the unit the next time it is taught. It is important to develop a system for recording your evaluations and making notes about changes that would improve the unit in the future.

The following quotes are from teachers in the early stages of their careers. They encapsulate important lessons that they have learnt about planning for teaching and from which we can learn.

> There's more than one way to learn and to teach something and children learn differently at different levels at different stages. I now know that you just don't teach this to grade 3 students you teach it to the child itself, rather than you must know your three times tables in grade 3.

> I certainly don't do individual lesson plans to the detail that was required at university, however I still think through each of those steps when planning a lesson.
>
> ... making sure that I always know exactly what I'm teaching and why I'm teaching it, where it fits into the overall conceptual understanding that I'm trying to develop.

Teaching in action

The AAMT (2002) described the teaching of excellent teachers of mathematics as arousing curiosity, challenging students' thinking, and actively engaging them in learning mathematics. In Chapter 3 we considered several aspects that Muir (2008) suggested contribute to effective mathematics teaching (choice of tasks, choice of examples, capitalising on teachable moments, modelling, using representation, and questioning).

for the classroom

In case you are still wondering what a 'good' mathematics lesson looks like, the following is a list of things to look for. A good mathematics lesson will have one or more of these attributes (not all will be appropriate in every lesson).

- The use of concrete materials to facilitate the construction of meaning. Such materials will be perceptually strong, that is, they will appeal to children's perceptions of the world, not act against them or rely on abstract relationships.
- The lesson will be concerned with *meaning*, that is, the teacher will ask questions like:
  - What does it mean?
  - Can you draw a picture to show me what you mean?
  - Why have you written a 1 there?
  - Why are you measuring the distance around that shape?
  - Is a square a rectangle?
  - Can you make that number?
  - Can you make it/show me a different way?
  - What's the difference between ...?
  - How are these the same, how are they different?
- The lesson will be characterised by *discussion, dialogue,* and *debate*—children's language about experiences with materials and models will be valued and connected to conventional (mathematical) language.
- The lesson will carefully relate language and materials to symbols and written recording (not vice versa!).
- Opportunities will be provided *to apply what is known*, collectively or individually, to solve a problem that the group or child wants to solve.
- The teacher will value *reflective* discussion about what was done and why—and what was learnt.
- The lesson will be *varied*, that is, it will include a range of activities and response modes.
- A range of *assessment* strategies will be used where appropriate.

Assessment

Assessment is intimately linked with planning. Excellent teachers of mathematics assess not only cognitive outcomes but also affective outcomes, including confidence and attitude to mathematics. They use a range of inclusive assessment strategies and ensure that the judgments they make are fair (AAMT, 2002). Many of these points are articulated in the following quotes from beginning teachers:

> When it comes down to it a lot of it is your, you know, the day to day interactions you have and the more incidental conversations that you have with kids and um when you get them to try and articulate to you what they're thinking about and you know if they do have errors in their thinking you know what, what is it that's actually going on that's actually you know lead them to, to think this way.

> Taking photos, videos watching what they're doing their thinking because I think sometimes even though a child can do a one plus two equals three sum it's the way of going around it and actually the deeper thinking … So there's a lot more methods than just writing it down on paper.
>
> Self-assessment, peer assessment so that students are recognising their own understandings … I would try and um just provide anecdotal um feedback throughout lessons um and I guess limited, relatively limited written um feedback that was just provided by myself because I often feel that students don't um don't really use this as well as they do when they're given on the spot feedback.
>
> Fit the assessment to the child and make sure that the assessment is worthwhile, think about what you're actually assessing before you start, what, what are you looking for.

An important part of excellence in assessment is maintaining accurate and informative records of students' learning that can form the basis of future planning and of reports to a range of audiences that includes students, parents, school. and system authorities (AAMT, 2002). Evaluating your own effectiveness is also important, as is the ability to evaluate resources and alternative approaches.

for the classroom

Rich assessment tasks

Rich assessment tasks can provide useful insights into students' thinking. They can be used to assess students' understanding at the end of a unit of work but can also be extremely useful at the beginning. Their open nature can provide students with an opportunity to show what they know and perhaps surprise you. Clarke and Clarke (1998) provide the following list of features of rich tasks:

- connect naturally with what has been [or is about to be] taught
- allow all students to make a start
- engage the learner
- can be successfully undertaken using a range of methods or approaches
- provide a measure of choice or 'openness'
- encourage students to disclose their own understanding of what they have learnt
- allow students to show connections they are able to make between the concepts they have learnt
- are themselves worthwhile activities for students' learning
- provide a range of student responses, including a chance to show all that they know about the relevant content
- draw the attention of teachers and students to important aspects of mathematical activity
- help teachers to decide what specific help students may require in the relevant content areas.

issues in teaching

Assessment driving teaching

With increasing scrutiny of the effectiveness of schools and teaching in the form of national testing (NAPLAN), there is a temptation to narrow teaching to focus on the content and question types that students will encounter in these contexts. Some argue that it is the teacher's responsibility to do exactly this because the school's reputation as well as the success of students depends upon it. We would argue that if students are taught a full, rich curriculum in such a way that they develop a deep interconnected understanding of mathematics, and flexible strategies and confidence to tackle unfamiliar problems, the test results will take care of themselves.

- Discuss this issue and consider how you would respond to a colleague who advocated 'teaching to the test'.
- How would you explain your view of this issue to parents?

Final words of advice

In this section the authors offer you some final words of advice. We trust that they will be useful and perhaps inspire you to think about teaching differently.

Build on from known (Di)

Very early in my teaching career I came to appreciate the huge range of student learning needs in mathematics. I also realised I didn't know enough to address those needs and had to make a serious effort to find out. Scaffolding student learning is the primary task of teachers of mathematics but this cannot be achieved without accurate information about what each student knows already and what might be within the student's grasp with some support from the teacher and/or peers. Teacher knowledge is key and this requires, above all else, a life-long commitment to ongoing professional learning.

When are we going to use this? (Kim)

I struggled for years to answer this perennial question. I finally worked out that students who ask it don't really care about when they'll use the mathematics (any more than they care about when they'll use skills in analysing the plot of a novel or lino printing—things they tend not to ask their English or Art teachers about!). The question is an expression of frustration with the meaninglessness of the work they're doing and the best answer is 'Where did I lose you?'. This makes it a problem with my teaching rather than their intelligence and creates a safe place to talk about their struggles with the mathematics.

Hold on to your vision (Kathy)

As a graduating teacher you have a wealth of skills and knowledge that will help you to be an effective mathematics teacher. As a beginning teacher there will be plenty more to learn from your colleagues, but make sure to hold onto your vision. Be true to yourself, and to your beliefs, about how best to be a teacher of mathematics. Have the confidence to dare to do things differently, if that is what you feel might work. Finally, make sure you continue to engage reflectively with your practice; this is the key to successful mathematics teaching and, ultimately, your students' learning.

Believe in your students (Julie)

One of the most precious gifts you can give to your students is your absolute belief in their ability to succeed. Regardless of background experiences and learning difficulties, each student must know that someone believes in them. Mathematics is not something that only a few privileged students can learn—it is a universal language that is accessible to everyone. Learning mathematics should be challenging and interesting and above all understandable. Open up the wonders of mathematics in the world to your students. Mathematics is the language in which God has written the universe (Galileo Galilei).

Good beginnings (Rhonda)

Getting off to a good start is very important at each stage of learning: the beginning of the school year, the beginning of each unit, the beginning of each lesson. Plan these very carefully for maximum impact. Begin the year with interesting, challenging mathematics. Don't take this time testing children or revising previous work. Similarly, avoid starting a lesson with checking homework or administrative tasks. Finally, enjoy your new beginnings in a profession that provides one of the best opportunities for you to make a difference in the life of another person—a precious task indeed.

All children are capable of learning mathematics (Elizabeth)

A common trap for beginning teachers struggling to cater for students with diverse backgrounds is a lowering of expectations for children in low socioeconomic and rural areas. Even though children in these communities often have parents who themselves did not enjoy school, these children are very capable learners and their parents want them to succeed. Catering for diverse learners often entails reflecting on the pedagogical approaches being used to teach mathematics, not changing the content taught. The activities need to be engaging and hands-on, with a focus on oral communication and articulating thinking. Rather than having an array of different activities you can often use the same activity with a different array of numbers. Ensure that all children experience success with the activity—as the saying goes, 'success breeds success'.

making connections

Brooker and Mulford (2000, p. 50) reported on a study of teachers who were nominated by their students as influential in encouraging them to continue with their education. Three hundred and sixty-nine teachers were asked to nominate the six qualities that they believed characterised a good teacher. The most commonly mentioned words and the number of mentions that they received were:

- Knowledge (108)
- Fair (108)
- Humour (106)
- Enthusiasm (85)
- Caring (83)
- Understanding (67)
- Preparation (65)
- Organisation (63)
- Consistent (63)
- Interest (62)
- Patience (53)
- Respect (53)
- Honest (48)
- Flexible (48)
- Approachable (46)
- Commitment (46)

key terms

Profession: 'a disciplined group of individuals who adhere to ethical standards and hold themselves out as, and are accepted by the public as possessing special knowledge and skills in a widely recognised body of learning derived from research, education and training at a high level, and who are prepared to apply this knowledge and exercise these skills in the interest of others.' (Australian Council of Professions, 1997)

Standard: a benchmark against which performance and progress can be measured

Review questions

1. Write a paragraph explaining why teaching should be considered a profession or why it should not be considered a profession. Refer to the characteristics of a profession.
2. In what ways can standards such as those developed by AITSL and AAMT contribute to the professionalism of teaching?
3. The AAMT standards are specifically about teaching mathematics whereas the AITSL standards are generic. To what extent and why is there a need for discipline-specific standards? What purposes, if any, can discipline-specific standards serve that generic standards cannot?
4. Obtain a copy of the AAMT standards (available at <www.aamt.edu.au/Activities-and-projects/Standards/Standards-document>). Read them carefully and identify aspects that relate to pedagogical content knowledge for teaching mathematics.

Key references

Australian Association of Mathematics Teachers (AAMT) (2002). *Standards for Excellence in Teaching Mathematics in Australian Schools*. Adelaide: AAMT.

Australian Institute for Teaching and School Leadership. (2011). *National Professional Standards for Teachers*. Melbourne: Education Services Australia.

Beswick, K., & Dole, S. (2008). Recollections of mathematics education: Approaching graduation and 5 years later. In M. Goos, R. Brown & K. Makar (Eds.), *Navigating Currents and Charting Directions: Proceedings of the 31st Annual Conference of the Mathematics Education Research Group of Australasia* (Vol. 1, pp. 767–775). Brisbane: MERGA.

Callingham, R., (2011). Mathematics assessment: Everything old is new again. In J. Clark, B. Kissane, J. Mousley, T. Spencer & S. Thornton (Eds.) *Mathematics: Traditions and [New] Practices: Proceedings of the AAMT-MERGA Conference*. (Vol. 1, pp. 3–10). Adelaide: AAMT & MERGA.

Clarke, B., & Clarke, D. (1998). Developing and using rich assessment tasks: Some models, some lessons. In K. Baldwin & J. Roberts (Eds.) *Mathematics in the Next Millennium*, AAMT: Adelaide.

Muir, T. (2008). Principles of practice and teacher actions: Influences on effective teaching of numeracy. *Mathematics Education Research Journal*, 20(3), 78–101.

O'Shea, H. (2009). The ideal mathematics class for grades 5 and 6: what do the students think? *Australian Primary Mathematics Classroom*, 14(2), 18–23.

Shulman, L. S. (1987). Knowledge and teaching: Foundations of the new reform. *Harvard Educational Review*, 57(1), 1–22.

Watson, A. (2001). Making judgements about pupils' mathematics. In P. Gates (Ed.), *Issues in Mathematics Teaching* (pp. 217–231). New York: Routledge Falmer.

Youdale, L. (2010). Planning, teaching and assessing mathematics for real! *Australian Primary Mathematics Classroom*, 15(4), 29–32.

Websites

www.aamt.edu.au/

www.csiro.au/resources/Maths-by-Email--ci_pageNo-3.html

Glossary

Absolute magnitude (numbers): cardinality of a set (e.g. 5 eggs, 23 people)

Abstract thinking: thinking removed from the facts of the 'here and now', and from specific examples of the things or concepts being thought about

Addend: one of the numbers being added

Additive identity element: the additive identity element for a set of numbers is a number in the set that can be added to any number in the set without changing it; for rational numbers, and for real numbers, zero is the additive identity

Additive thinking: capacity to work with the ideas of aggregation and disaggregation with a range of number sets

Algebra: the branch of mathematics concerning the study of the rules of operations and relations, and the constructions and concepts arising from them

Algorithm: a set of clear steps that will lead to a solution

Approximation: an inexact result, sufficiently precise for the context and recorded as the outcome of an exact calculation

Area: the measure that describes the extent or coverage of a two-dimensional figure

Area idea for multiplication: an extension of the region idea, which represents the two numbers being multiplied in terms of length by width, the area idea supports the multiplication of multi-digit numbers in terms of their parts (e.g. for two 2-digit numbers, tens by tens, tens by ones, ones by tens, and ones by ones)

Array: situations where the number in each group and number of equal groups are aligned as discrete elements in rows and columns (e.g. strawberry patch with 6 rows and 9 plants in each row)

Aspect ratio: a property of rectangles given by the ratio of length to width

Assessment: judgment about the quality or quantity of learning

Assessment *for* learning: teachers and students gather evidence about student understanding to inform future learning; assessment for learning is formative in nature and this evidence is collected in diverse ways

Assessment *of* learning: teachers or school systems gather evidence about student learning to make judgments against goals and standards; this evidence often comes in the form of tests or examinations at the local school level as well as at the national and international levels, and is summative in nature

Associative property: the order in which three or more numbers are added or multiplied does not matter (e.g. $3 + 4 + 5 = 5 + 3 + 4$ and $3 \times 4 \times 5 = 5 \times 3 \times 4$)

Associativity: a property of an operation on a set of numbers (e.g. addition and multiplication of real numbers) that means that when three or more numbers are combined the result is the same no matter which two numbers are combined first

Attribute: the characteristic of an object that is to be measured, for example length or volume

Average: a number that best represents a set of data. This can be calculated as a mean, median or mode

Behaviourism: a view of learning as a result of the learner's responses to stimuli in the environment

Capacity: the measure of the quantity that a three-dimensional shape can hold

Cardinal number: specific number name for how many in a given collection of objects

Cartesian plane: a rectangular coordinate system based on two perpendicular axes—x (horizontal) and y (vertical)

Cartesian product or 'for each' idea for multiplication: situations involving combinations (e.g. 4 pants, 3 tops, how many combinations) or rates (e.g. $1.75/kilogram, how much for 3.5 kilograms?)

Cause: that which gives rise to an event

Chance: the likelihood of a particular outcome

Circumference: the distance around the perimeter of a circle

Closed questions: questions that can be answered with one word or a short phrase

Cognitive load: features of the learning situation or task that can affect attention and/or capacity to retain the information needed to undertake complex tasks

Commutative property: the order in two numbers are added or multiplied does not matter (e.g. $3 + 4 = 4 + 3$ and $3 \times 4 = 4 \times 3$)

Commutativity: a property of an operation on a set of numbers (e.g. addition and multiplication of real numbers) that means that the order in which numbers are combined does not affect the result

Comparing: determining whether objects, quantities, or measures are the same or different

Comparing attributes: determining the relationship between two objects with regard to a particular measurement attribute by comparing the extent of the attribute in each object

Composing and decomposing numbers: numbers can be constructed in many different ways using a combination of operations, or numbers can be broken down into their constituent parts in many different ways

Composite number: a number that is not prime

Composite unit: a unit made up of other units (e.g. when children understand 8 as 1 eight not as a collection of 8 ones; recognising 6 as 1 six not 6 ones)

Concave polygon: a plane shape in which there exists at least one line segment joining two interior points that goes outside the shape

Conceptual understanding: understanding indicated by the quality and quantity of connections that are made between new and existing ideas (e.g. a conceptual understanding of area enables students to solve unfamiliar problems such as determining the dimensions of a paddock given a certain length of fencing)

Concrete thinking: thinking characterised by a predominance of actual objects and events and the absence of concepts and generalisations

Congruent: a geometric object of exactly the same size and shape as another

Conjecture: a mathematical idea that seems reasonable but has not been proven

Connection: linking of signs and symbols that represent the same object or concept

Conservation of area: the principle that the size of an area is not changed if the figure or region is rearranged

Constructivism: a theory of learning as arising from learners' active interaction with their physical, social, and psychological environment

Content: subject matter (e.g. in mathematics this might refer to Pythagoras' Theorem or the formula for calculating the area of a rectangle

Content knowledge: knowledge of mathematical processes and understanding of the concepts that underpin them

Context: the circumstances or situation that requires the application of numeracy skills

Contexts for addition (parts known): join—items in the two sets are the same (e.g. 3 oranges and 4 more oranges is 7 oranges); combine—items in the two sets are different (e.g. 3 bananas and 4 oranges is 7 pieces of fruit)

Contexts for subtraction (whole – part known): take away—part of a single set is physically removed; missing addend—single set is increased to a given size; difference—comparison between two sets (e.g. Jake has 8 cards, Bill has 5: how many more cards does Jake have than Bill?)

Continuous fraction models: models based on attributes that, in principle, are infinitely divisible (e.g. length, area, volume, capacity, mass)

Convex polygon: a plane shape in which a line segment joining any two interior points does not go outside the shape

Coordinates: two letters or numbers that give location on coordinate axes

Coordinate geometry: the field of mathematics linking geometry with algebra

Count back: counting strategies for subtraction—solution found by counting backwards by ones; think of addition—solution found by counting up from subtrahend; count up from

Counting: ordered matching of number names to objects

Critical numeracy: the component of numeracy associated with a critical appreciation of how mathematics is used to describe and explain our world

Curriculum: document specifying content to be taught (often stated as outcomes), generally incorporating advice on how to teach (pedagogy) as well as assessment

Data: information or facts you find out or are given; observations or measurements collected as part of an investigation; data can be words, numbers, or a mixture of both

Decimal: a number written using the base 10 numeration system. Decimal numbers comprise an integer part and a fractional part; digits in the integer part indicate a multiple of a positive power of 10, digits in the fractional part indicate a multiple of a negative power of ten

Decimal marker: the symbol used to show where the ones begin; in Australia we use a point as the decimal marker, hence the term 'decimal point'

Denominator: in the fraction $\frac{a}{b}$, b is the denominator. 'It is the number of equal parts into which the whole is divided in order to obtain fractional parts' (ACARA, 2011)

Dependent variable: the variable whose value depends on the value assigned to another variable, called the independent variable

Deterministic: a view that all events have direct causes, in contrast to a probabilistic view that considers causation in terms of chance-raising or making an event more likely to occur

Development: change resulting from maturation

Diameter: the straight line that passes through the centre of the circle joining two points on opposite sides of the circumference

Difference: the result of subtracting the smaller of a pair of quantities from the larger

Digit: any of the 10 Hindu-Arabic numerals from 0 to 9

Direct comparison: physically comparing the objects being measured with each other

Disability: the functional consequence of an impairment; for example, because of the impairment of short-sightedness, the disability may be that a person is unable to see clearly

Discrete fraction models: collections that are not intended to be partitioned further than the items themselves (e.g. a packet of Smarties, a dozen eggs, a class of children)

Distribution: the overall 'shape' of a set of data

Dividend: the amount being divided

Divisor: the number by which another number is divided; in partitive division, it refers to the number of groups; in quotitive division it refers to the number in each group or the size of the group

Dynamic imagery: the ability to visualise changes to shapes as processes act on them

Dyscalculia: an inability to calculate as a result of brain injury; this term seems more commonly used in the United Kingdom

Effective teaching: teaching that is successful in achieving the intended learning objectives

Enabling prompts: planned support for learners that enables them to commence or continue work on a mathematical thinking task; provision of strategic assistance taking learners from where they are to a point from which they are able to proceed

Enlargement: a similar figure made by increasing (or decreasing) an object by a given scale factor

Enumerating: the process of determining how many in a given collection or set; this could be arrived at by matching (enumeration), counting (numeration), or visual recognition (subitising)

Enumeration: keeping track of the objects in a collection by a one-to-one matching of the objects with other objects used as checks or counters (Gundlach, 1989); this could include an ordered sequence of body parts or a collection of pebbles

Equal: having the same quantity, value, or measure of another

Equation: a statement of equality existing between numbers and variables with the equalities being connected by an equals sign

Equipartitioning: process of dividing (usually physically) a quantity or collection into equal parts with no remainder

Equivalence: a relation holding between two statements so that they both have to be simultaneously true or simultaneously false

Estimation: the process of arriving at an inexact result on the basis of general considerations of the numbers and operations involved rather than as a consequence of a precise mathematical procedure; the process of using mental and visual information to measure or make comparisons without the use of measuring devices

Exercise: a task for which the solution method is known

Expanded notation: the expression of a whole number in terms of the sum of its place-value parts written in symbolic form as ones (e.g. 456 = 400 + 50 + 6

Experimental probability: the estimated chance of something happening based on repeated trials

Extending prompts: supplementary tasks or questions that extend students' thinking and activity; planned support for learners to extend their mathematical thinking on a mathematical thinking task

External representation: an external sign or symbol that represents an object or concept

Factors: one of two or more numbers being multiplied; pairs of counting numbers that multiply to give another counting number

Feedback: information, written or oral, provided by the teacher to the student in relation to student progress and achievement; constructive feedback is comments framed in a way that allows for thinking to take place, which then enables students to take action to improve learning

Fifthing: the process of partitioning a continuous quantity into five equal parts using halving as a guide (i.e. by recognising that fifths are smaller than quarters, and in choosing where to locate 1 fifth, it needs to be possible to halve and halve again to create 2 more parts of the same size)

Figure–ground perception: the ability to identify and 'isolate' a specific figure out of a complex background polygon

Formative assessment: teachers use a range of assessment strategies in an ongoing manner to identify specific learning needs and target teaching accordingly

Fraction: a number written as $\frac{a}{b}$ (written alternatively as a/b) where a is a non-negative integer and b is a positive integer (i.e. $b \neq 0$), a is referred to as the numerator, and b is referred to as the denominator (ACARA, 2011b); a fraction is said to be *proper* if it is less than 1 (as in $\frac{2}{7}$) and *improper* when it is greater than 1 (as in $\frac{8}{5}$); the ratio of two numbers, usually a part to a whole, expressed with one number above a line and the other below

Function: a mathematical relation such that each element of a given set (the domain of the function) is associated with an element of another set (the range of the function); a function f of a variable x is a rule that assigns to each number x in the function's domain a single number $f(x)$

Fundamental Theorem of Arithmetic: any integer greater than one can be written as a unique product of prime factors

Generalisation: the process of formulating general concepts by abstracting common properties of instances

Generalising: a part of the process of mathematical thinking in which the underlying patterns in the mathematics are explored; a principle, statement, or idea having general application; capacity to devise general statements, symbolic expressions from patterns, form conclusions

Geometric reasoning: the type of thinking involved in the investigation of shape and space

Great circle: cross-section of a sphere where the centre of the circle is also the centre of the sphere

Groups of: situations where the number of equal groups (multiplier) and the size of each group (multiplicand) is known and the task involves finding the total number (product); generally involves integer values for the number in each group and the number of groups (e.g. 3 groups of 4)

Growing patterns: a pattern that grows or increases (or decreases) by a constant difference

Halving: the process of continually partitioning a continuous quantity into two equal parts to produce fractions in the halving family (i.e. halves, quarters or fourths, eighths, sixteenths)

Handicap: the social or environmental consequences of a disability, for example inability to follow television news because of short-sightedness

Identity: an equality that remains true regardless of any of the values for the variables that appear within it (e.g. $a \times 1 = a$; 1 is the identity)

Impairment: an abnormality in the way organs or systems function, usually of medical origin, for example short-sightedness, heart problems, cerebral palsy, Down syndrome, or deafness

Independent variable: the variable whose value is independent of the value assigned to another variable

Indirect comparison: using another item as a measurement referent to compare measurement attributes

Instrumentalist: a view of mathematics as a useful set of skills

Integers: the collective name for the positive whole numbers, zero, and negative whole numbers

Internal representation: a presentation to the mind in the form of an idea or image

Inverse: opposite in nature or effect or relation to another quantity

Investigation: a type of mathematical thinking in which the context is explored initially and no question has been posed

Justification: use of evidence to support an argument; a part of the process of mathematical thinking in which conjectures are proven for all cases

Knowledge: propositions that are widely accepted as true in the relevant context

Knowledge for teaching mathematics (KTM): synonymous with PCK but emphasises knowledge needed to teach particular content domain

Learning: lasting change that is a result of experience and not simply a consequence of maturation or development

Learning theory: a coherent set of principles that explains how learning occurs

Length: the measure that describes the extent of one dimension

Likelihood: the chance that a particular outcome will occur

Make-all-count-all: counting strategies for addition—solution found by physically modelling and counting all by ones; count on—solution found by counting on from one of the two numbers; count on from larger—solution found by count on from larger of the two numbers; use known relationships—solution derived from known facts

Mass: a measure of the amount of matter in an object

Mathematical communication: any mode of expression that supports an exchange of mathematical ideas or strategies; generally, spoken or written language, visual representations such as diagrams and graphs, or symbolic expressions

Mathematical fluency: capacity to use mathematical knowleddg and strategies in multiple ways (e.g. access to a variety of efficient ways to add 2 two-digit numbers mentally)

Mathematical model: A type of mathematical thinking in which mathematics is used to understand a context; it is cyclic, with solutions checked with the context and assumptions modified as required

Mathematical problem solving: processes involved in making sense of a mathematical problem, situation, or task, exploring and implementing possible strategies, and checking the reasonableness of results

Mathematical reasoning: capacity to think through mathematical problems logically and systematically and apply what is known; often involves inferring, proving, formulating, and testing conjectures

Mathematical symbol: a mathematical shorthand way of writing something e.g. %, =, π

Mathematical visualisation: a process of thinking leading to understanding based on use of images

Mathematics learning difficulties: those problems experienced by a large group of children who need extra assistance to learn mathematics

Mathematics learning disabilities (MLD): are experienced by a subset of students with mathematics learning difficulties who achieve at lower than the 25th percentile on mathematics achievement tests, often with low to average IQ results; between 5 and 8% of children have some form of MLD and both genetic and environmental factors may contribute

Mean: a kind of average determined by dividing the total of the quantities by the number of quantities

Measurement: the assignment of a numerical value to an attribute of an object

Measuring device: an item that is used to make indirect measurements of the extent or amount of a particular measurement attribute in terms of a consistent unit of measurement

Median: a kind of average that is the middle value in a set of numerically ordered data

Mental model: an internal representation of a concept or ideas indicating the relationships between its various parts

Mental object: images, words, and metaphors to describe or represent a particular experientially based phenomena (e.g. yellowness, square)

Mental objects for each of the numbers to 10: demonstrated by an ability to work flexibly with the numbers without having to make or represent the number

Mental rotation: the ability to produce dynamic mental images and to visualise a configuration in movement

Mental strategies for addition: count on 1, 2, or 3 (e.g. for 2 + 7, think: 7, 8, 9); doubles and near doubles (e.g. for 7 + 8, think: double 7 is 14 and 1 more, 15), make to 10 (e.g. for 6 + 8, think: 8, 10 and 4 more, 14)

Mental strategies for subtraction: think of addition (e.g. for 16 – 9, think: 9 and how many more to 16? 1 to 10, then 6 more, so 7); halving (e.g. for 16 – 9, think, half of 16 is 8, need to take 1 more, 7); make back to 10 (e.g. for 16 – 9, think: 16 back to 10 is 6, need to take 3 more, 7); use known relationships or place value (e.g. for 16 – 9, think: 16 take 10 is 6, need to add 1 back, 7)

Meridians of longitude: semicircles running from pole to pole in a sphere

Mixed fraction: a number made up of a positive integer and a proper fraction (e.g. $4\frac{5}{6}$)

Mode: a kind of average that is the quantity or number that occurs most often

Modelling: demonstrating a skill, process, or strategy

Money: the unit used to measure the attribute known as value

Multiple: the result of multiplying one integer by another, a number than can be divided by another number without remainder (e.g. 8 is a multiple of 2 and 4)

Multiplicative thinking: capacity to work with an extended range of concepts, meanings, and representations for multiplication and division in a variety of contexts

Multiplier: the amount by which a quantity is increased or decreased multiplicatively as opposed to additively

Multi-representational learning environment: using a variety of external representations simultaneously to explore an idea or concept

Nature of mathematics: what the discipline of mathematics actually is; what it concerns, and what distinguishes it from other disciplines

Non-rigid transformation: process that alters either a shape's size or its shape

Non-standard units: units of measurement that are created for a particular purpose that have no relevance outside the context in which they are used

Number: an idea about quantity

Number line: line marked with numbers

Glossary

Numeracy: the application of mathematical skills and knowledge to a broad range of authentic and practical contexts

Numeral: a symbol or group of symbols used to express a number (e.g. 3, 527, VI)

Numerate behaviour: the disposition to choose and use mathematics, with confidence, as appropriate to the context

Numeration: the use of an ordered sequence of number words to keep track of the number of objects

Numeration systems: the systematic use of number names and symbols to count independently of the nature of the objects or quantities being counted

Numerator: in the fraction $\frac{a}{b}$, a is the numerator; 'If an object is divided into b equal parts, then the fraction $\frac{a}{b}$ represents a of those parts taken together.' (ACARA, 2011)

Numerosity: the number in a given collection or set, equivalent to cardinal number

Open-ended questions/activities: questions or activities that generally involve some higher-order thinking (e.g. analysis, synthesis), present opportunities for learning, and have several plausible solutions (e.g. 'How might I have paid for an item costing $5.35?'; 'The answer is 24. What is the question?'); questions that prompt a respondent to think, allow multiple responses, and usually require a long answer

Operant conditioning: a behaviourist learning theory based on rewarding desired behaviours

Ordering: arranging objects, quantities, or measures according to some pattern or numerical sequence

Ordering attributes: describing the relationship between three or more objects with regard to a particular measurement attribute by ordering the objects in various ways, for example from longest to shortest

Ordinal number: a number word used to indicate position (e.g. first, second, third, ...)

Parallels of latitude: cross-sections of a sphere where the centres of the circles are on the polar axis

Partition (sharing) idea: situations where the total (dividend) and the number of groups or shares (divisor) is known, and the task involves finding the number in each group or share (quotient)

Partitioning: physically separating or renaming a collection in terms of its parts; this can be additive (as in 8 is 5 and 3, or 2 and 1 and 5), or multiplicative, where parts are equal (as in 8 is double 4 or 2 fours); the process of dividing (usually physically) a quantity or collection into equal parts with no remainder

Part–part–whole: recognising numbers to 10 in terms of their parts (e.g. 8 is 5 and 3, 6 and 2, double 4) and their relationship to larger numbers and 10 (e.g. 8 is 1 less than 9, 2 less than 10)

Pattern: a pattern constitutes a set of numbers or objects in which all the members are related with each other by a specific rule

Pedagogical content knowledge (PCK): accredited to Shulman (1986), PCK refers to the knowledge needed to teach a particular discipline; it involves content or subject-matter knowledge, pedagogical knowledge (how to teach in general), and knowledge about what makes the particular content easy/difficult to teach and learn (knowledge of students); an amalgam of content and general pedagogical knowledge that is more than the simple combination of the two

Pedagogy: the art and science of teaching; knowledge of the principles and practices of teaching and learning

Peer assessment: students assess each other's or a group's response against given criteria; self-assessment is similar and involves the student assessing their own responses

Perception of spatial positions: the ability to relate figures (object, picture, or mental image) to oneself

Perception of spatial relationships: the ability to relate several figures (as above) to each other, or simultaneously to oneself

Perceptual constancy: the ability to realise that some characteristics of an object are independent of size, colour, texture, or position

Perimeter: the linear measurement that is the length around the boundary of a figure or a region

Perpendicular bisector: a line at right angles to a line segment that cuts the line segment in two congruent parts

Personal referents: easily envisioned or enacted mental reference points used for estimating measurements

Pi (π): the constant value that is generated when the length of the circumference is divided by the length of the diameter, regardless of the size of the circle

Place value: system of assigning values to digits based on their position (e.g. in a base 10 system of numeration, positions represent successive powers of 10)

Planning: deciding on the learning you want to happen, designing activities likely to make it happen, and devising ways to know the extent to which the intended learning has occurred

Platonist: a view of mathematics as independently existing and comprised of interconnected and hierarchically structured ideas

Polar axis: line through a sphere joining the poles

Polygon: two-dimensional closed shapes with straight sides

Precision: the degree of accuracy required when making a measurement; greater precision results from small divisions of the unit of measurement

Prediction: an expectation of the outcome of an experiment

Prime number: a number that has *exactly* two factors: itself and one

Probability: a number between 0 (impossible) and 1 (certain) that indicates the likelihood or chance that a particular outcome will occur or something will happen; can be written as a fraction or percentage

Problem: a type of mathematical thinking in which there is a question to be answered but the path to the solution is initially unknown

Problem solving: a view of mathematics as a dynamic and creative human invention; a process rather than a product

Product: the result of multiplying two or more numbers

Profession: 'a disciplined group of individuals who adhere to ethical standards and hold themselves out as, and are accepted by the public as possessing special knowledge and skills in a widely recognised body of learning derived from research, education and training at a high level, and who are prepared to apply this knowledge and exercise these skills in the interest of others.' (Australian Council of Professions, 1997)

Proof: a set of logical arguments to demonstrate that a statement is always true

Proportional reasoning: capacity to recognise and work with relationships between relationships; thinking that involves accounting for the relative amounts of two or more multiplicatively related quantities

Questioning: asking for information with a view to understanding another's thinking more clearly and/or to stimulate their thinking in a particular direction

Quotient: the result of a division

Quotition (how many groups in): where the total and the size of the group is known and task involves finding the number of groups

Random sample: a sample that is chosen purely by chance

Rate: a type of ratio that involves the comparison of different attributes (e.g. speed, population density)

Ratio: a quotient or proportion of two numbers; a way of comparing one quantity with another quantity, ratios can be expressed as $m:n$ or as $\frac{m}{n}$ ($n \neq 0$); multiplicative comparison of two quantities that may or not refer to the same attribute (e.g. a distance can be compared to another distance, as in 60 kilometres to 45 kilometres, or to time as in 60 kilometres/hour)

Rational number: any number that can be expressed as $\frac{a}{b}$, where a and b are integers, and $b \neq 0$; rational numbers can be expressed as fractions, decimals or percentages

Glossary

Reciprocal: a number is the reciprocal of another number if the product of the two is 1, that is, the reciprocal any number *n* is the multiplicative inverse of n, $\frac{1}{n}$

Rectangular array: an arrangement or rows and columns in the shape of a rectangle

Region Area: as for arrays, but continuous rather than discrete, this accommodates ones by ones (regions) and multiplication by place-value parts (e.g. 4 tens 2 ones by 3 tens 5 ones) and non-integral measures (e.g. 3.5 by 2.7 or fraction multiplication)

Regrouping, Trading: ways of describing renaming when adding/multiplying or subtracting/ dividing respectively (e.g. 5 tens and 8 tens is 13 tens, it is regrouped for recording purposes as 1 hundred and 3 tens, but when subtracting 28 from 45, the 8 ones can only be taken if 1 of the 4 tens is traded for 10 ones)

Related denominators: the denominators of two fractions are related if one is a multiple of the other

Relative magnitude (numbers): measure (e.g. 8 centimetres versus 8 metres, 150 in 3000 compared to 150 in 300 chances)

Renaming: writing a number in an equivalent form, usually in terms of its place-value parts (e.g. 365 is 3 hundreds 6 tens and 5 ones, but it can be renamed as 36 tens and 5 ones, or 3 hundreds and 65 ones)

Repeating patterns: a pattern of a group of items that repeats over and over

Reporting: the communication of student achievement, progress, and improvement to students, parents, teachers, and the education system

Representations: forms of elaboration; a physical, visual, or symbolic model of a particular phenomenon (e.g. fractions can be represented using region diagrams or number lines, a set of ordered pairs can be represented in a table of values, as a graph, or a symbolic expression); models or images that assist with building understanding of mathematical ideas or communicating such understanding; ways of organising and communicating data

Representative: used to describe a sample that is the same as the population from which it is drawn in relation to attributes that are relevant to an investigation

Response: action resulting from a stimulus

Rich tasks: tasks similar to open-ended questions but generally more complex, involving investigation, data collection, analysis, and reporting (e.g. How much rubbish does our classroom produce in one year?)

Rigid transformation: a process that maintains the transformed shape's size and shape

Rubric: a scoring framework that provides teachers and students with established criteria for success, and clarifies and shares intentions of the given task; often different scores are allocated according to the varying levels of student response

Sample: a smaller set chosen from a population

Sample space: the set of possible outcomes for a specific event

Scientific notation: system of notation used for very large or small numbers

Shear: non-rigid transformation where the shape is not preserved, although area is

SI units: the international system of units; the basis of Australia's hierarchy of measurement standards

Similarity: an object is similar if it is the same shape, but not necessarily the same size, as another

Simulation: a chance process, the outcome of which mirrors that of a process of interest

Slope: a synonym for gradient; the steepness, incline or grade of a line

Small circle: cross-section of a sphere where the centre of the circle is not the centre of the sphere

Social constructivism: a constructivist theory of learning in which interactions with others play a crucial role in developing students' thinking

Spatial orientation: knowing where you are and how to move to another place

Spatial sense: the ability to 'see', inspect, and reflect on spatial objects, images, relationships and transformations

Specialising: a part of the process of mathematical thinking in which data is collected, specific examples are tried, and the person gains a feeling for the problem

Splitting: action of simultaneously creating multiple versions of a collection or whole or the fair sharing of collections or wholes to produce equal parts

Standard: a benchmark against which performance and progress can be measured

Standard units: universally employed units of measurement that are the same size regardless of who uses them

Statistics: the collection and analysis of data to describe the world; the discipline concerned with making inferences about chance processes; a single number that summarises a characteristic of a population

Stimulus: an environmental influence that provokes a response in a learner

Subitise: recognise the numerosity of a small collection without counting

Subitising: recognising the number in small collections without counting

Subtrahend: number being subtracted

Sum: the result of an addition

Summative assessment: those practices that locate and/or describe students' achievement in relation to defined goals and standards

Tasks: activities that students engage with in order to facilitate their learning

Teachable moments: Unplanned opportunities to make connections between the maths at hand and other mathematics or contexts

Teacher beliefs: propositions that a teacher accepts as true, which may or may not be more widely accepted

Teaching: processes that result in another's learning

Tessellates: geometric property of a figure that when identical copies of the figure are laid out they will join perfectly with no space between them, as in tiling

Tessellation: repeated shapes that cover a plane without gaps or overlaps

Theoretical probability: the calculated chance of events happening under ideal circumstances

Thirding: the process of partitioning a continuous quantity into three equal parts using halving as a guide (i.e. by recognising that thirds are smaller than halves and that in choosing where to locate 1 third it needs to be possible to halve the remaining part to create 2 more parts of the same size)

Time: the duration of an event from its beginning to its end

Transformational geometry: the study of the effects of various processes in transforming geometric objects

Transversal: a line drawn across a pair of parallel lines

Trusting the count: accessing mental objects for numbers to 10 without having to make, model, or record the number

Understanding: the extent and nature of connections between an idea and other ideas

Unitising: a cognitive process that involves 'thinking about a quantity in terms of different sized chunks' (Lamon, 1999, p. 83); for example, 24 can be thought about in terms of 3 eight-units, 4 six-units, or 8 three-units

Units of measurement: units that give a numerical value to an attribute that enable the measurement and comparison of quantities that are separated by time or space

van Hiele levels: a model for the development of geometric thinking

Variable: a value that may change within the scope of a given problem or set of operations

Variation: the extent to which the outcomes of a chance process differ from one another

Visual discrimination: the ability to compare several figures and to determine how they are similar and how they are different

Volume: the space occupied by a three-dimensional figure

Weight: the force that gravity exerts on an object

Bibliography

Aldrich, J. (2005). *Figure from the History of Probability and Statistics*. Retrieved 6 May 2010 from www.economics.soton.ac.uk/staff/aldrich/Figures.htm#kol.

Anghileri, J. (1989). An investigation of young children's understanding of multiplication. *Educational Studies in Mathematics*, 20(3), 367–385.

Anghilheri, J. (2006). *Teaching Number Sense* (2nd edn). London: Continuum.

Anghileri, J. (2007). *Developing Number Sense: Progression in the Middle Years*. London: Continuum International Publishing Group.

Anthony, G., & Walshaw, M. (2008). Characteristics of effective pedagogy for mathematics education. In H. Forgasz, A. Barkatsas, A. Bishop, B. Clarke, S. Keast, W Seah, & P. Sullivan (Eds.), *Research in Mathematics Education in Australasia 2004–2007*. (pp. 195–222). Rotterdam, The Netherlands: Sense Publishing.

Arditi, A., Holtzman, J. D., & Kosslyn, S. M. (1988). Mental imagery and sensory experience in congenital blindness. *Neuropsychologia*, 26, 1–12.

Arvedson, P. J. (2002). Young children with specific language impairment and their numerical cognition. *Journal of Speech, Language, and Hearing Research*, 45(5), 970–983.

Askew, M., Brown, M., Rhodes, V., Johnson, D., & Wiliam, D. (1997). *Effective Teachers of Numeracy*. London: School of Education, King's College.

Australian Association of Mathematics Teachers (1997). *Numeracy = Everyone's Business*. Adelaide, SA: Author.

Australian Association of Mathematics Teachers (2002). *Standards for Excellence in Teaching Mathematics in Australian schools*. Adelaide: Author.

Australian Association of Mathematics Teachers. (2006). *Standards for Excellence in Teaching Mathematics in Australian schools* (rev. ed.). Adelaide, SA: Author. Retrieved 12 January 2009 from www.aamt.edu.au/Standards/Standards-document/AAMT-Standards 2006 edition.

Australian Association of Mathematics Teachers, Inc. (2008). *Position Paper on the Practice of Assessing Mathematics Learning*. Adelaide: Author.

Australian Council for Educational Research (1998). *Developmental Assessment Resource for Teachers—Mathematics*. Camberwell: Author.

Australian Curriculum Assessment and Reporting Authority (2010). *The Australian Curriculum: Mathematics*. Sydney: ACARA.

Australian Curriculum Assessment and Reporting Authority (2010). *National Assessment Program: Literacy and Numeracy*. Sydney: ACARA. Retrieved 4 October 2010 from www.naplan.edu.au/verve/_resources/2009_NAPLAN_Summary_Report.pdf

Australian Curriculum, Assessment and Reporting Authority (2011). *The Australian Curriculum: Mathematics, Version 1.2*. Sydney: ACARA.

Australian Curriculum Assessment, and Reporting Authority (2011). *Australian Curriculum: Mathematics—Additional Information to Support the Glossary*. Sydney: ACARA. Retrieved 1 July 2011 from www.australiancurriculum.edu.au/Mathematics/Additional-glossary-information

Australian Education Council (1991). *A National Statement on Mathematics for Australian Schools*. Melbourne: Curriculum Corporation.

Australian Institute for Teaching and School Leadership (2011). *National Professional Standards for Teachers*. Carlton South, Vic: Education Servces Australia.

Axelrod, A. (2000). *Pigs at Odds: Fun with Math and Games*. Sydney: Scholastic.

Baddeley, A. D., & Hitch, G. (1974). Working memory. In G. H. Bower (Ed.), *The Psychology of Learning and Motivation: Advances in Research and Theory* (Vol. 8, pp. 47–89). New York: Academic Press.

Ball, D. (1990). Breaking with experience in learning to teach mathematics: The role of a preservice methods course. *For the Learning of Mathematics*, 10(2), 10–16.

Ball, D., Thames, M., & Phelps, G. (2008). Content knowledge for teaching: What makes it special? *Journal of Teacher Education*, 59(5), 389–407.

Bandura, A. (1977). *Social Learning Theory*. Englewood Cliffs, NJ: Prentice-Hall.

Barmby, P., Harries, T., Higgins, S., & Suggate, J. (2009). The array representation and primary children's understanding and reasoning in multiplication. *Educational Studies in Mathematics*, 70, 217–241.

Barry, B. Booker, G., Perry, B., & Siemon, D. (1983–91). *HBJ Mathematics: Beginning to Level 7. Pupil's, Teacher Resource and Activity Books*. Sydney: Harcourt Brace Jovanovich.

Bassarear, T. (1997). *Mathematics for Elementary School Teachers*. Boston: Houghton Mifflin.

Basson, A., Krantz, S., & Thorton, B., (2006). A new kind of instructional mathematics laboratory. *Primus*, 16(4), 332–328.

Battista, M. (2003). Understanding students thinking about area and volume measurement. In D. Clements (Ed.), *Learning and Teaching Measurement*. Reston, VA: NCTM.

Battista, M. T. (2007). The development of geometric and spatial thinking. In F. K. Lester (Ed.), *Second Handbook of Research on Mathematics Teaching and Learning* (pp. 843–908). Reston, VA: NCTM.

Bay-Williams, J. (2007). Is 'just good teaching' enough to support the learning of English language learners? Insights from sociocultural learning theory. In W. Martin, M.Struchen, & P. Elliot (Eds.), *The Learning of Mathematics: 69th Yearbook of National Council of Teachers of Mathematics*. Reston, VA: NCTM.

Beaton, G. (2010). *Why Professionalism is Still Relevant*. Retrieved 17 April 2011 from <www.professions.com.au/Files/Professionalism_Beaton.pdf>.

Beauchamp, G. (2004). Teacher use of the interactive whiteboard in primary schools: Towards an effective transition framework. *Technology, Pedagogy and Education*, 13(3), 327–348.

Becker, J., & Selter, C. (1996). Elementary school practices. In A. J. Bishop et al. (Eds.), *International Handbook of Mathematics Education* (pp. 511–564). Dordrecht, Netherlands: Kluwer.

Beckmann, P. (1971). *A History of Pi*. New York: St Martins Press.

Beesey, C., Clarke, B., Clarke, D., Stephens, M. & Sullivan, P. (1998) *Effective Assessment in Mathematics—Levels 4 to 6*. Melbourne: Board of Studies, Longman.

Beishuizen, M. (1999). The empty number line as a new model. In I. Thompson (Ed.), *Issues in Teaching Numeracy in Primary Schools*. Buckingham, UK: Open University Press.

Bell, G. (1990). Language and counting: Some recent results. *Mathematics Education Research Journal*, 2(1), 1–14.

Beswick, K. (2003). *The Impact of Secondary Mathematics Teachers' Beliefs on their Practices and the Classroom Environment*. Unpublished PhD thesis. Perth: Curtin University of Technology.

Beswick, K. (2004). *Developing Instruments to Assess the Number Sense of Young Children*. In P. Jeffery (Ed.), *Proceedings of the Annual Conference of the Australian Association for Research in Education*. Melbourne: AARE.

Beswick, K. (2005). The beliefs/practice connection in broadly defined contexts. *Mathematics Education Research Journal*, 17(2), 39–68.

Beswick, K. (2006). Changes in preservice teachers' attitudes and beliefs: The net impact of two mathematics education units and intervening experiences. *School Science and Mathematics*, 106(1), 36–47.

Beswick, K. (2007). Teachers' beliefs that matter in secondary mathematics classrooms. *Educational Studies in Mathematics*, 65(1), 95-120.

Beswick, K. (submitted). Positive experiences with negative numbers: Building on students in and out of school experiences.

Beswick, K., Callingham, R., & Watson, J. (2011). The nature and development of middle scholl mathematics teachers' knowledge. *Journal of Mathematics Teacher Education*. Published online first February, 2011, DOI 10.1007/s10857-011-9177-9. Available at <www.springerlink.com.ezproxy.utas.edu.au/content/th22781265818125/fulltext.pdf>

Beswick, K., & Dole, S. (2008). Recollections of mathematics education: Approaching graduation and 5 years later. In M. Goos, R. Brown & K. Makar (Eds.), *Navigating Currents and Charting directions* (Proceedings of the 31st annual conference of the Mathematics Education Research Group of Australasia, pp. 767–775). Brisbane: MERGA.

Beswick, K., Swabey, K., & Andrew, R. (2008). Looking for attributes of powerful teaching for numeracy in Tasmanian K–7 classrooms. *Mathematics Education Research Journal*, 20(1), 3–31.

Beswick, K., Watson, J., & Brown, N. (2006). Teachers' confidence and beliefs and their students' attitudes to mathematics. In P. Grootenboer, R. Zevenbergen, & M. Chinnappan (Eds), *Identities, Cultures and Learning Spaces* (Proceedings of the 29th annual conference of the Mathematics Education Research Group of Australasia, Canberra, pp. 68–75). Sydney: MERGA.

Bialik, C. (2009). *Lottery Math 101*. Retrieved 31 January 2011 from http://blogs.wsj.com/numbersguy/lottery-math-101-801/

Bigge, M. L., & Shermis, S. S. (1999). *Learning Theories for Teachers* (6th ed.). New York: Longman.

Biggs, J. B., & Telfer, R. (1981). *The Process of Learning*. Collingwood, Vic: Prentice-Hall.

Bishop, A. (Ed.) (1988). *Mathematics Education and Culture*. Dordrecht, Netherlands: Kluwer.

Bishop, A. (1991). *Mathematics Enculturation: A Cultural Perspective on Mathematics education*. Dordrecht, Netherlands: Kluwer.

Bishop, A., Clarke, B., & Morony, W. (2006). *Professional Learning Using the Mathematics Standards*. Canberra: Teaching Australia.

Bishop, A., & Forgasz, H. (2007). Issues in access and equity. In F. Lester (Ed.), *Second Handbook of Research on Mathematics Teaching and Learning* (Vol. 2, pp. 1145–1167). Charlotte, NC: Information Age Publishing, NCTM.

Black, P. & Wiliam, D. (1999). *Assessment for Learning: Beyond the Black Box*. Retrieved 11 December 2009 from www.mendeley.com/research/assessment-for-learning-beyond-the-black-box-1/.

Black, P., & Wiliam, D. (1998). Inside the black box. *Phi Delta Kappan*, 80(2), 139–148.

Bloom, B.S., Hastings, J.T., & Madaus, G.F. (1971). *Handbook on Formative and Summative Evaluation of Student Learning*. New York: McGraw-Hill.

Blume, G., Galindo, E., & Walcott, C. (2007). Performance in measurement and geometry for the viewpoint of Principles and Standards for School Mathematics. In P. Kloosterman & F. Lester, Jr. (Eds.), *Results and Interpretations of the 2003 Mathematics Assessment of the National Assessment of Educational Progress*. Reston, VA: NCTM.

Boaler, J. (1997). *Experiencing School Mathematics: Teaching Styles, Sex and Setting*. Buckingham: Open University Press.

Boaler, J. (2002a). *Experiencing School Mathematics: Traditional and Reform Approaches to Teaching and their Impact on Student Learning Outcomes*. Mahwah, NJ: Erlbaum.

Boaler, J. (2002b). Learning from teaching: Exploring the relationship between reform curriculum and equity. *Journal for Research in Mathematics Education*, 33(4), 239–258.

Boaler, J. (2005). The 'psychological prisons' from which they never escaped: The role of ability grouping in reproducing social class inequalities. *Forum*, 47(2–3), 135–143.

Boaler, J. (2006). How a detracked mathematics approach promoted respect, responsibility, and high achievement. *Theory into Practice*, 45(1), 40–46.

Board on Mathematical Sciences [and] Mathematical Sciences Education Board, National Research Council (1989). *Everybody Counts: A Report to the Nation on the Future of Mathematics Education*. Washington, DC: National Academy of Sciences.

Bobis, J. (2008). Early spatial thinking and the development of number sense. *Australian Primary Mathematics Classroom*, 13(3), 4–9.

Bodin, A., & Capponi, B. (1996). Junior secondary school practices. In A. J. Bishop, K. Clements, C. Keitel, J. Kilpatrick, & C. Laborde (Eds.), *International Handbook of Mathematics Education* (pp. 565–614). Dordrecht, Netherlands: Kluwer.

Bolt, B., & Hobbs, D. (1993). *101 Mathematical Projects: A Resource Book*. Cambridge: Cambridge University Press.

Booth, L. (1988). Children's difficulties in beginning algebra. In A. Coxford & A. Shulte (Eds.) *The Ideas of Algebra K–12: 1988 Yearbook of the National Council of Mathematics*. Reston, VA: NCTM.

Borgioli, G. (2008). Equity for English language learners in mathematics classrooms. *Teaching Children Mathematics*, 15(3), 185–191.

Bottge, B. A. (2001). Reconceptualizing mathematics problem solving for low-achieving students. *Remedial and Special Education*, 22(2), 102–112.

Boulton-Lewis, G. & Halford, G. (1992). The processing loads of young children's and teachers' representations of place-value and implications for teaching. *Mathematics Education Research Journal*, 4(1), 1–23.

Brady, K. (2007). Imagined classrooms: Primary teachers visualise their ideal mathematics classroom. In J. Watson & K. Beswick (Eds.), *Mathematics: Essential Research, Essential Practice* (Proceedings of the 30th Annual Conference of the Mathematics Education Research Group of Australasia pp. 143–150). Tasmania: MERGA.

Bransford, J. D., Brown, A. L., & Cocking, R. R. (Eds.). (2000). *How People Learn* (expanded ed.). Washington DC: National Academy Press.

Breed, M. (2011). *Constructing Paths to Multiplicative Thinking: Breaking Down the Barriers*. Unpublished PhD thesis. Melbourne: RMIT University.

Brodesky, A., Doherty, A., & Stoddard, J. (2008). *Digging into Data with TinkerPlots*. Emeryville, CA: Key Curriculum Press.

Brooker, P., & Mulford, B. (2000). Research and implications. In P. Brooker, P. Hughes and B. Mulford (Eds.), *Teachers Make a Difference*. Hobart: University of Tasmania.

Bryant, P. (1974). *Perception and Understanding in Young Children*. London: Methuen.

Bryson, B. (2003). *A Short History of Nearly Everything*. Toronto, Canada: Random House.

Burns, M. (1994). Arithmetic: The last holdout. *Phi Delta Kappan*, 75, 471–476.

Burton, L. (1995). Moving towards a feminist epistemology of mathematics. In P. Rogers & G. Kaiser (Eds.), *Equity in Mathematics Education: Influences of Feminism and Culture* (pp. 209–226). London: Falmer Press.

Buys, K. (2001). Preschool years: Emergent numeracy. In M. van den Heuvel-Panhuizen (Ed.), *Children Learn Mathematics* (pp. 23–30). Utrecht: Freudenthal Institute.

Buys, K., & de Moor, E. (2005). Domain description measurement. In M. van den Heuvel-Panhuizen & K. Buys (Eds.), *Young Children Learn Measurement and Geometry: A Learning-teaching Trajectory with Intermediate Attainment Targets for the Lower Grades in Primary School*. Utrecht, The Netherlands: Freudenthal Institute.

Buys, K., & Veltman, A. (2005). Measurement in kindergarten 1 and 2. In M. van den Heuvel-Panhuizen & K. Buys (Eds.), *Young Children Learn Measurement and Geometry: A Learning-teaching Trajectory with Intermediate Attainment Targets for the Lower Grades in Primary School*. Utrecht, The Netherlands: Freudenthal Institute.

Cairney, T. (2003). Literacy within family life. In N. Hall, J. Larson & J. Marsh (Eds.), *Handbook of Early Childhood Literacy* (pp. 85–98). London: Sage.

Callingham, R. (2008). Dialogue and feedback: Assessment in primary school mathematics. *Australian Primary Mathematics Classroom*, 13(3), 18–21.

Campbell, P. F., Rowan, T. E., & Suarez, A. R. (1998). What criteria for student-invented algorithms? In L. J. Morrow (Ed.). *The Teaching and Learning of Algorithms in School Mathematics*. Reston, VA: NCTM.

Caney, A. (2004). Perception of mental computation practice: Reports from middle school teachers and students. In I. Putt, R. Faragher & M. McLean (Eds.), *Mathematics Education for the Third Millennium: Towards 2010* (Proceedings of the 27th annual conference of the Mathematics Education Research Group of Australasia, pp. 159–166). Townsville: MERGA.

Carle, E. (1974). *The Very Hungry Caterpillar*. Blackburn, Vic: Dominion Press.

Carnine, D. (1997). Instructional design in mathematics for students with learning disabilities. *Journal of Learning Disabilities*, 30(2), 130–141.

Carpenter, P., Franke, M., & Levi, L. (2003). *Thinking Mathematically: Integrating Arithmetic and Algebra in the Elementary School*. Portsmouth, NH: Heinemann.

Carpenter, T., & Moser, J. (1983). The acquisition of addition and subtraction concepts. In R. Lesh & M. Landau (Eds.), *Acquisition of Mathematics Concepts and Processes* (pp. 7–44). New York: Academic Press.

Carpenter, T., & Moser, J. (1984). The acquisition of addition and subtraction concepts in grades one through three. *Journal for Research in Mathematics Education*, 15(3), 179–202.

Carraher, D.W. & Schliemann, A. D. (2007) Early algebra and algebraic reasoning. In F. Lester (Ed.) *Second Handbook of Research on Mathematics Teaching and Learning: A Project of the National Council of Teachers of Mathematics* (Vol 2, pp. 669–705). Charlotte, NC: Information Age.

Carraher, T., Carraher, D., & Schliemann, A. (1985). Mathematics in the streets and in the school. *British Journal of Developmental Psychology*, 3, 21–29.

Cazden, C., & Beck, S. (2003). Classroom discourse. In A. Graesser, M. Gernsbacher, & S. Goldman (Eds.), *Handbook of Discourse Processes* (pp. 165–197). Mahwah, NJ: Erlbaum.

Central Advisory Council for Education (England) (1959). *The Crowther Report 15–18*. London: Her Majesty's Stationery Office.

Charles, K. & Nason, R. (2000). Young children's partitioning strategies. *Educational Studies in Mathematics*, 43(2), 191–221.

Clark, J. (2007). Maths saves the day. *Australian Primary Mathematics Classroom*. 12(2), 21–24.

Clark, J. (2008). Year five students solving mental and written problems: What are they thinking? In M. Goos, R. Brown & K. Makar (Eds.), *Navigating Current and Charting Directions* (Proceedings of the 31st annual conference of the Mathematics Education Research Group of Australasia, pp. 131–137). Sydney: MERGA.

Clarke, B. & Clarke, D. (1998) Developing and using rich assessment tasks: Some models, some lessons. In K. Baldwin & J. Roberts (Eds.) *Mathematics the Next Millennium*, AAMT: Adelaide.

Clarke, B., & Faragher, R. (2004). Possibilities not limitations: Teaching special needs children. In B. Clarke, D. Clarke, G. Emanuelsson, B. Johansson, D. V. Lambdin, F. K. Lester, A. Wallby & K. Wallby (Eds.), *International Perspectives on Learning and Teaching Mathematics* (pp. 379–394). Goteborg: National Center for Mathematics Education.

Clarke, D. (1985). *The IMPACT Project: A User's Guide*. Clayton, Vic: Monash University Mathematics Education Centre.

Clarke, D. (1996). Assessment. In A. J. Bishop, K. Clements, C. Keitel, J. Kilpatrick, & C. Laborde (Eds.), *International Handbook of Mathematics Education* (pp. 327–370). Dordrecht: Klawer Acadmic Publishers.

Clarke, D. (2005a). Written algorithms in the primary years: Undoing the 'good work'? In M. Coupland, J. Anderson & T. Spencer (Eds.), *Making Mathematics Vital: Proceedings of the Twentieth Biennial Conference of the Australian Association of Mathematics Teachers* (pp. 93–98). Adelaide: AAMT.

Clarke, D. (2005b). Essential complementarities: Arguing for an integrative approach to research in mathematics classrooooms. In P. C. Clarkson, A. Downton, D. Gronn, M. Horne, A. McDonough, R. Pierce & A. Roche (Eds.), *Building Connections: Theory, Research, Practice*

(Proceedings of the 28th annual conference of the Mathematics Education Research Group of Australasia, pp. 3–17). Sydney: MERGA.

Clarke, D., Cheeseman, J., Gervasoni, A., Gronn, D., Horne, M., McDonough, A., Montgomery, P., Roche, A., & Sullivan, P., Clarke, B. & Rowley, G. (2002). *Early Numeracy Research Project final report*. Melbourne: Mathematics Teaching and Learning Centre, Australian Catholic University.

Clarke, D., & Clarke, B. (2004). Mathematics teaching in Grades K–2: Painting a picture of challenging, supportive, and effective classrooms. In R. N. Rubenstein & G. W. Bright (Eds.), *Perspectives on the Teaching of Mathematics: 66th Yearbook of National Council of Teachers of Mathematics* (pp. 67–81). Reston: NCTM.

Clarke, D. & Roche, A. (2010). The power of a single game to address a range of important ideas in fraction learning. *Australian Primary Mathematics Classroom*, 15(3), 18–23.

Clement, J. (1982). Algebra word problem solutions: thought processes underlying a common misconception. *Journal for Research in Mathematics Education*, 13(1), 16–30.

Clements, D. H. (1999a). Subitising: What is it? Why teach it? *Teaching Children Mathematics*, 5(7), 400–405.

Clements, D. H. (1999b). Geometric and spatial thinking in young children. In J. V. Copley (Ed.), *Mathematics in the Early Years* (pp. 66–79). Washington, DC: National Association for the Education of Young People.

Clements, D. H. (2000). *Geometric and spatial thinking in early childhood education*. Paper presented at the 78th Annual Meeting of the National Council of Teachers of Mathematics, San Fransisco, CA, April, 2000. Symposium: Linking research and the new early childhood mathematics standards.

Clements, D. H., & Battista, M. T. (1992). Geometry and spatial reasoning. In D. A. Grouws (Ed.), *Handbook of Research on Mathematics Teaching and Learning* (pp. 420–494). New York: Macmillan.

Clements, D. H., & Callahan, L. (1982). Number or pre-number foundational experiences for young children: Must we choose? *Arithmetic Teacher*, 30(3), 34–37.

Clements, D. H., & Sarama, J. (2007). Early childhood mathematics learning. In F. Lester (Ed.), *Second Handbook of Research on Mathematics Teaching and Learning* (Vol. 2, pp. 461–556). Charlotte NC: NCTM/Information Age Publishing.

Clements, D. H., Swaminathan, S., Hannibal, M. A. Z., & Sarama, J. (1999). Young children's concepts of shape. *Journal for Research in Mathematics Education*, 30(2), 192–212.

Clements, R. (1995). *Counting on Frank*. North Ryde, NSW: Collins/Angus & Robertson.

Cobb, P. (1994). Where is the mind? Constructivist and sociocultural perspectives on mathematical development. *Educational Researcher*, 23(7), 13–20.

Cobb, P. (1995). Cultural tools and mathematical learning: A case study. *Journal for Research in Mathematics Education*, 26(4), 362–385.

Cobb, P. (1999). Where is the mind? In P. Murphy (Ed.), *Learners, Learning and Assessment*. London: Paul Chapman

Cobb, P. (2007). Putting philosophy to work: Coping with multiple theoretical perspectives. In F. K. Lester Jr. (Ed.), *Second Handbook of Research on Mathematics Teaching and Learning* (Vol. 1, pp. 3–38). Charlotte, NC: Information Age Publishing.

Cobb, P., & Bauersfeld, H. (1995). *The Emergence of Mathematical Meaning: Interaction in Classroom Cultures*. Hillsdale, NJ: Erlbaum.

Cobb, P., & Yackel, E. (1996). Constructivist, emergent, and sociocultural perspectives in the context of developmental research. *Educational Psychologist*, 31(3), 175–190.

Coben, D. (2003). *Adult Numeracy: Review of Research and Related Literature*. London: National Research and Development Centre for Adult Literacy and Numeracy.

Committee of Inquiry into the Teaching of Mathematics in Schools (1982). *Mathematics Counts: Report of the Committee of Inquiry into the Teaching of Mathematics in Schools under the Chairmanship of W.H. Cockcroft*. London: Her Majesty's Stationery Office.

Commonwealth Department of Education and Youth Affairs (2000). *Numeracy: A Priority for All.* Canberra: Commonwealth of Australia.

Commonwealth Department of Education, Science and Training. (2004). *Researching Numeracy Teaching Approaches in Primary Schools.* Canberra: Commonwealth of Australia.

Confrey, J. (1994). Splitting, similarity, and rate of change: A new approach to multiplication and exponential functions. In G. Harel & J. Confrey (Eds.) *The Development of Multiplicative Reasoning in the Learning of Mathematics* (pp. 293–332). New York: State University of New York Press.

Confrey, J., Maloney, A., Nguyen, K., Mojica, G. & Myers, M. (2009). Equipartitioning/splitting as a foundation for rational number reasoning using learning trajectories. In M. Tzekaki, M. Kaldrimidrou & C. Sakondis (Eds.) *Proceedings of the 33rd Conference of the International Group for the Psychology of Mathematics Education*, (Vol. 2, pp. 345–352). Thessalonika, Greece: IGPME.

Consortium for Mathematics and its Applications (COMAP) (1994). *For All Practical Purposes: Introduction to Contemporary Mathematics* (3rd edn). New York: Freeman.

Conway, J.H., & Guy, R.K. (1998). *The Book of Numbers.* New York: Springer-Verlag.

Cooper, T. J., & Warren, E. (2008). The effect of different representations on Year 3 to 5 students' ability to generalise. *The International Journal of Mathematics Education*, 40(1), 23–38.

Cornoldi, C., & Vecchi, T. (2003). Congential blindness and spatial mental imagery. In Y. Hatwell, A. Streri & E. Gentaz (Eds.), *Touching for Knowing: Cognitive Psychology of Haptic Manual Perception* (pp. 173–187). Philadelphia, PA: John Benjamin.

Council of Australian Governments Human Capital Working Group (2008). *National Numeracy Review Report.* Canberra: Commonwealth of Australia.

Courant, R., & Robbins, H. (1941). *What is Mathematics? An Elementary Approach to Ideas and Methods.* New York: Oxford University Press.

Davis, W. (1875). *The Complete Book of Arithmetical Examples for Home and School Use.* London: Simpkin, Marshall and Company.

Davis, H. (1989). The history of computation. In J. Baumgart, D. Deal, B. Vogeli & A. Hallerberg (Eds.), *Historical Topics for the Mathematics Classroom* (2nd edn) (pp. 87–164), Reston, VA: NCTM.

Davydov, V. (1975). The psychological characteristics of the 'prenumeral' period of mathematics instruction. In L. P. Steffe (Ed.), *Children's Capacity for Learning Mathematics* (Vol VII, pp. 109–205). Chicago: University of Chicago Press.

Davydov, V., Gorbov, S., Mikulina, G., & Saveleva, O. (1999). *Class 1 Teacher's Book.* J. Schmittau (Ed.). Birmingham, NY: State University of New York.

Dehaene, S. (1997). *The Number Sense: How the Mind Creates Mathematics.* Oxford: Oxford University Press.

de Lange, J. (2003). Mathematics for literacy. In B. Madison & L. Steen (Eds.), *Quantitative Literacy: Why Numeracy Matters for Schools and Colleges.* Princeton, NJ: The National Council on Education and the Disciplines.

DeLoache, J. S., Miller, K. F., Rosengren, K., & Bryant, N. (1997). The credible shrinking room: Very young children's performance with symbolic and nonsymbolic relations. *Psychological Science*, 8, 308–313.

Department of Education and Early Childhood Development (2007). *Assessment for Common Misunderstandings.* Retrieved 2 February 2010 from www.education.vic.gov.au/studentlearning/teachingresources/maths/common/

Department of Education and Early Childhood Development (2009a). *Assessment and Reporting.* Retrieved 2 February 2010 from www.education.vic.gov.au/about/directions/blueprint1/fs1.htm#4

Department of Education and Early Childhood Development (2009b). *Scaffolding Numeracy in the Middle Years Assessment Materials.* Accessed 3 March 2009 from <www.education.vic.gov.au/studentlearning/teachingresources/maths/snmy/asstmaterials.htm>.

Department of Education & Early Childhood Development (2010). *Framework for Mathematical Learning—Early Numeracy Research Project Growth Points—Strategies for Multiplication and Division*. Retrieved 1 July 011 from: www.education.vic.gov.au/studentlearning/teachingresources/maths/enrp/enrplaf.htm#H3N100E7.

Department of Education and Training (2009). *Count Me in too*. Retrieved 2 February 2010 from www.curriculumsupport.education.nsw.gov.au/countmein/index.htm

Dickinson, D., McCabe, A., & Essex, M.. (2006). A window of opportunity we must open to all: the case for high-quality support for language and literacy. In D. K. Dickinson & S. B. Neuman (Eds.), *Handbook of Early Literacy Research* (pp. 11–28). New York: Guilford Press.

Dienes, Z. P. (1973). *Mathematics Through the Senses, Games, Dance and Art*. Windsor, UK: The National Foundation for Educational Research.

Diezmann, C., Faragher, R., Lowrie, T., Bicknell, B., & Putt, I. (2004). Exceptional students in mathematics. In R. Perry, G. Anthony & C. Diezmann (Eds.), *Research in Mathematics Education in Australasia 2000–2003*. Flaxton: Post Pressed.

Diezmann, C., & Watters, J. (2002). Summing up the education of mathematically gifted students. In B. Barton, K. C. Irwin, M. Pfannkuch & M. O. J. Thomas (Eds.), *Mathematics Education in the South Pacific* (Proceedings of the 25th Annual Conference of MERGA, pp. 219–226). Auckland: MERGA.

Diversity in Mathematics Education Center for Learning and Teaching (2007). Culture, race, power, and mathematics education. In F. K. Lester (Ed.), *Second Handbook of Research on Mathematics Teaching and Learning: A Project of the National Council of Teachers of Mathematics*. USA: Information Age Publishing.

Doig, B., McRae, B., & Rowe, K. J. (2003). *A Good Start to Numeracy*. Canberra: Commonwealth of Australia.

Dole, S. (2004). *Mental Computation: A Strategies Approach: Module 5: Fractions and Decimals*. Hobart: Department of Education, Tasmania.

Dole, S., & McIntosh A. (2004). *Mental Computation: A Strategies Approach*. Hobart: Department of Education Tasmania

Dossel, S. (1993). Maths anxiety. *Australian Mathematics Teacher*, 49(1), 4–8.

Dougherty, B. (2007). Measure up: A quantitative view of early algebra. In J. Kaput, D. Carraher, & M. Blanton (Eds.), *Algebra in the Early Grades*. Mahwah, NJ: Erlbaum.

Dowe, P., & Noordhof, P. (Eds.) (2004). *Cause and Chance: Causation in an Indeterministic World*. London: Routledge.

Dowling, P. (1998). *The Sociology of Mathematics Education: Mathematical Myths/Pedagogical Texts*. (Vol. 7). London: Falmer Press.

Downton, A. (2008). Links between children's understanding of multiplication and solution strategies for division. In M. Goos, R. Brown & K. Makar (Eds.), *Navigating Current and Charting Directions* (Proceedings of the 31st annual conference of the Mathematics Education Research Group of Australasia, pp. 171–178). Sydney: MERGA.

Downton, A., Knight, R., Clarke, D., & Lewis, G. (2006). *Mathematics Assessment for Learning: Rich Tasks and Work Samples*. Melbourne: Mathematics Teaching and Learning Centre, Australian Catholic University.

Dulin, D. (2007). Effects of the use of raised line drawings on blind people's cognition. *European Journal of Special Needs Education*, 22(3), 341–353.

Dunham, W. (1994). *The Mathematical Universe: An Alphabetical Journey Through the Great Proofs, Problems, and Personalities*. New York: Wiley.

Dweck, C. S. (2002). Messages that motivate: How praise moulds students' beliefs, motivation, and performance (in surprising ways). In J. Aronson (Ed.), *Improving Academic Achievement*. New York: Academic Press.

Educational Services Australia. (2010). *Maths 300 – Number Charts*. Retrieved 21 October 2010 from www.maths300.esa.edu.au

Ellemore-Collins, D., & Wright, R. (2008). Developing conceptual place value: instructional design for intensive intervention. In R. Hunter, B. Bicknell, & T. Burgess (Eds.), *Crossing Divides* (Proceedings of the 32nd annual conference of the Mathematics Education Research Group of Australasia, pp. 169–176). Palmerston, NZ: MERGA.

Ellerton, N., Clarkson, P., & Clements, M. (2000). Language factors in mathematics education. In K. Owens & J. Mousley (Eds.), *Research in Mathematics Education in Australasia 1996–1999* (pp. 25–95). Sydney: MERGA

Ellis, L. (2005). Balancing approaches: Revisiting the educational psychology research on teaching students with learning difficulties. *Australian Education Review*, 48, Melbourne: Australian Council for Educational Research.

Emerson, E., Graham, H., McCulloch, A., Blacher, J., Hatton, C., & Llewellyn, G. (2008). The social context of parenting 3-year-old children with developmental delay in the UK. *Child: Care, Health and Development*, 35(1), 63–70.

Empson, S., Junk, D., Dominguez, H. & Turner, E. (2006). Fractions as the coordination of multiplicatively related quantities: A cross-sectional study of children's thinking. *Educational Studies in Mathematics*, 63(1), 1–28.

Ernest, P. (1989). The impact of beliefs on the teaching of mathematics. In P. Ernest (Ed.), *Mathematics Teaching: The State of the Art* (pp. 249-253). New York: Falmer.

Ernest, P. (1991). *The Philosophy of Mathematics Education*. Basingstoke, UK: Falmer Press.

Ernest, P. (1998). *Social Constructivism as a Philosophy of Mathematics*. Albany, NY: State University of New York.

Eve, R. A., & Dunn, D. (1990). Psychic powers, astrology and creationism in the classroom? Evidence of pseudoscientific beliefs among high school biology and life sciences teachers. *The American Biology Teacher*, 52(1), 10–21.

Exley, B., & Abel, K. (2008). Ah! Now I see: the literacy demands of mathematics problems in the early years. *Curriculum Leadership*, 6(33). Retrieved on 1 July 2011 from www.curriculum.edu.au/leader/vol6_no33,25023.html?issueID=11616

Faragher, R. M. (2006). *Numeracy in the Context of Adulthood and Down Syndrome*. Unpublished PhD thesis, Adelaide: Flinders University of South Australia.

Faragher, R. M., & Brown, R. I. (2005). Numeracy for adults with Down syndrome: It's a matter of quality of life. *Journal of Intellectual Disability Research*, 49(10), 761–765.

Farkas, S., Johnson, J., & Foleno, T. (2000). *A Sense of Calling: Who Teaches and Why*. New York: Public Agenda

Fellowes, G., & Oakley, G. (2010). *Language, Literacy, and Early Childhood Development*. Melbourne: Oxford University Press.

Fennema, E., Carpenter, T., & Peterson, S. (1989). Teachers' decision making and cognitively guided instruction: A new paradigm for curriculum development. In N. Ellerton & M. A. Clements (Eds.), *School Mathematics: The Challenge to Change* (pp. 174–187). Geelong, Vic: Deakin University Press.

Ferrucci, B., Kaur, B., Carter, J., & Yeap, B. (2008). Using a model approach to enhance algebraic thinking in the elementary school mathematics classroom. In C. Greenes and R. Rubenstein (Eds.), *Algebra and Algebraic Thinking in School Mathematics: 70th Yearbook National Council of Teachers of Mathematics*. Reston, VA: NCTM.

Fielker, D.S. (1973). *Geometry for Enjoyment*. London: Schools Council Publications.

Filloy, E., & Sutherland, R. (1996). Designing curricula for teaching and learning algebra. In A. Bishop, McK. Clements, C. Keitel, J. Kilpatrick, & C. Laborde (Eds.) *International Handbook of Mathematics Education* (Part 1, pp. 139–160). Dordrecht: Kluwer.

FitzSimmons, G. E., Seah, W. T., Bishop, A. J., & Clarkson, P. C. (2000). *Conceptions of Values and Mathematics Education Held by Australian Primary Teachers: Preliminary Findings from VAMP*. Retrieved 23 November 2010 from www.education.monash.edu.au/research/groups/smte/projects/vamp/hpm2000c.pdf.

Forbringer, L. (2004). The thirteen days of Halloween: Using children's literature to differentiate instruction in the mathematics classroom. *Teaching Children Mathematics*, 11(2), 82–90.

Foreman, P. (Ed.). (1996). *Integration and Inclusion in Action*. Sydney: Harcourt Brace.

Forrest, J. (2005). The Space Shuttle Challenger Disaster: A failure in decision support system and human factors management. Retrieved 31 January 2011 from http://dssresources.com/cases/spaceshuttlechallenger/index.html

Forrest, M. (1997). *Four Roles of a Numerate Person*. Adelaide, SA: Department of Education and Children's Services.

Forgasz, H., Leder, G. C., & Vale, C. (2000). Gender and mathematics: Changing perspectives. In K. Owens & J. Mousley (Eds.), *Mathematics Education Research in Australasia: 1996-1999* (pp. 305–340). Turramurra, NSW: MERGA.

Franke, M., Kazemi, E., & Battey, D. (2007). Mathematics teaching and classroom practice. In F. Lester (Ed.), *Second Handbook of Research on Mathematics Teaching and Learning: A Project of the National Council of Teachers of Mathematics* (pp. 225–256). Charlotte, NC: Information Age Publishing.

Franke, M., Webb, N., Chan, A., Ing, M., Freund, D., & Battey, D. (2009). Teachers questioning to elicit students' mathematical thinking in elementary school classrooms. *Journal of Teacher Education*, 60(4), 380–392.

Freebody, P., & Luke, A. (1990). Literacies programs: Debates and demands in cultural context. *Propect: Australian Journal of TESOL*, 5(7), 7–16.

Freil, S., & Bright, G. (1998). Teach-Stat: A model professional development in data analysis and statistics teachers K–6. In S.P. Lajoie (Ed.), *Reflections on Statistics Learning, Teaching and Assessment in Grades K–12* (pp. 89–117). Mahwah, NJ: Erlbaum.

Freudenthal, H. (1991). *Revisiting Mathematics Education*. Dordrecht, The Netherlands: Kluwer.

Fuson, K. (1992). Research on whole number addition and subtraction. In. D. Grouws (Ed.), *Handbook of Research on Mathematics Teaching and Learning: A Project of the National Council of Teachers of Mathematics* (pp. 243–275). New York: Macmillan.

Fuson, K. (2009). Avoiding misinterpretations of Piaget and Vygotsky: Mathematical teaching without learning, learning without teaching, or helpful learning-path teaching? *Cognitive Development*, 24(4), 343–461.

Fuson, K. & Kwon, Y. (1992). Korean children's understanding of multi-digit addition and subtraction. *Child Development*, 63(2), 491–506.

Geary, D. C. (2004). Mathematics and learning disabilities. *Journal of Learning Disabilities*, 37(1), 4–15.

Gellert, U., & Jablonka, E. (2008). *The Demathematising of Technology: Calling for Critical Competence*. Paper presented to ICME 11 Discussion Group. Retrieved 10 October 2009 from http://dg.icme11.org/document/get/63

Giangreco, M. F., Edelman, S. W., Luiselli, T. E., & MacFarland, S. Z. C. (1997). Helping or hovering: Effects of instructional assistant proximity on students with disabilities. *Exceptional Children*, 64(1), 7–18.

Goldin, G. (2002). Representation in mathematical learning and problem solving. In L. D. English (Ed.), *Handbook of International Research in Mathematics Education* (pp. 197–218). Mahwah, NJ: Erlbaum.

Goldin, G., & Kaput, J. (1996). A joint perspective on the idea of representations in learning and doing mathematics. In S. P. Leslie and N. Pearla (Eds), *Theories of Mathematical Learning*. Mahwah NJ: Erlbaum.

Gould, P. (2003). Grasping space. *Australian Primary Mathematics Classroom*. 8(2), 4–7.

Graham, L. & Pegg, J. (2010). Hard data to support the effectiveness of QuickSmart numeracy. *Learning Difficulties of Australia Bulletin*, 42(1), 11–13.

Gravemeijer, K., Cobb, P., Bowers, J., & Whitenack, J. (2000). Symbolising, modeling and instructional design. In P. Cobb, E. Yackel, & K. McClain (Eds.), *Symbolizing and Communicating in Mathematics Classrooms* (pp. 225–273). Mahweh, NJ: Erlbaum.

Graven, M. (2004). Investigating mathematics teacher learning within an in-service community of practice: The centrality of confidence. *Educational Studies in Mathematics*, 57(2), 177–211.

Greeno, J. (1991). Number sense as situated knowing in a conceptual domain. *Journal for Research in Mathematics Education*, 22(3), 170–218.

Greer, B. (1992). Multiplication and division as models of situations. In D. Grouws (Ed.) *Handbook of Research on Mathematics Teaching and Learning* (pp. 276–295). Reston, VA: NCTM and Academic Press.

Griffith, K., & Kowalski, H. (2010). *Dictionary of Education Terms*. Melbourne: Oxford University Press.

Groza, V. (1968). *A Survey of Mathematics—Elementary Concepts and their Historical Development*. New York: Holt, Rinehart & Winston.

Gundlach, B. H. (1989). The history of number and numerals. In J. K. Baumgart, D. E. Neal, B. R. Vogeli,, & A. E. Hellerberg (Eds.). *Historical Topics for the Mathematics Classroom*. Reston, VA: NCTM.

Gutiérrez, A. (1996). Visualization in 3-dimensional geometry: in search of a framework. In L. Puig & A. Guttiérez (Eds.), *Proceedings of the 20th Conference of the International Group for the Psychology of Mathematics Education* (Vol. 1, pp. 3–19). Valencia: Universidad de Valencia.

Haese, R., Haese, S., Webber, B., Danielsen, F., & Burch, B. (1983). *Mathematics for Year 9*. Adelaide: Haese Publications.

Halliday, M. A. K. (1978). *Language as a Social Semiotic*. London: Edward Arnold.

Hardegree, G. (2001). *Numeration Systems*. Retrieved 3 January 2011 from www.people.umass.edu/gmhwww/382/pdf/05-numeration.pdf

Harris, P. (1980). *Measurement in Tribal Aboriginal Communities*. Darwin, NT: Northern Territory Department of Education.

Harris, P. (1991). *Mathematics in a Cultural Context: Aboriginal Perspectives on Space, Time and Money*. Geelong, Vic: Deakin University Press.

Handal, B., & Herrington, A. (2003). Mathematics teachers' beliefs and curriculum reform, *Mathematics Education Research Journal*, 15(1), pp. 59–69.

Harel, G., & Sowder, L. (2007). Toward comprehensive perspectives on the learning and teaching of proof. In F. Lester (Ed.), *Second Handbook of Research on Mathematics Teaching and Learning* (pp. 805–842). Charlotte, NC: Information Age Publishing.

Harries, A. V. (2001). Working through complexity: An experience of developing mathematical thinking through the use of Logo with low attaining pupils. *Support for Learning. British Journal of Learning Support*, 16(1), 23–27.

Harris, P. (1980). *Measurement in Tribal Aboriginal Communities*. Darwin, NT: Northern Territory Department of Education.

Hart, K. (Ed.) (1981). *Children's Understanding of Mathematics: 11–16*. London: John Murray.

Hart, K. (1984). *Ratio: Children's Strategies and Errors. A Report of the Strategies and Errors in Secondary Mathematics Project*. London: NFER–Nelson.

Hatano, G. (1982).Learning to add and subtract: A Japanese perspective. In T. Carpenter, J. Moser, & T. Romberg (Eds.), *Addition and Subtraction: A Cognitive Perspective* (pp. 211–223). Hillsdale, NJ: Erlbaum.

Hatfield, M., Edwards, N., Bitter, G. & Morrow, J. (2000). *Mathematics Methods for Elementary and Middle School Teachers*. New York: Wiley

Hattie, J. (1992). Measuring the effects of schooling. *Australian Journal of Education*, 36(1), 5–13.

Hattie, J. (2003a). *Distinguishing Expert Teachers from Novice and Experienced Teachers. Teachers Make a Difference. What is the Research Evidence?* [Electronic Version]. Retrieved 9 October 2009 from www.emr.vic.edu.au/Downloads/English%20and%20Maths%20Leader%20Professional%20Learning/Leaders%20and%20Data%20Collections/teachers_make_a_difference.pdf.

Hattie, J. (2003b). *Teachers Make a Difference: What is the Research Evidence?* Paper presented to the annual conference of the Australian Council for Educational Research, Melbourne, Australia.

Hegland, S. (1991). Kindergarten mathematics: Teaching or controlling. *Arithmetic Teacher*, 39(2), pp. 34–37.

Heinke, C. H. (1989). Origins of symbols for operations. In J. K. Baumgart, D. E. Neal, B. R. Vogeli, & A. E. Hellerberg (Eds.). *Historical Topics for the Mathematics Classroom*. Reston, VA: NCTM.

Heinze, A, Star, J. & Verschaffel, L. (2009). Flexible and adaptive use of strategies and representations in mathematics education. ZDM, 41(5), 535–540.

Heirdsfeld, A. (2003). Mental computation: Refining the cognitive frameworks. In L. Bragg, C. Campbell, G. Herbert & J Mousley (Eds.), *Mathematics Education Research: Innovation, Networking, Opportunity* (Proceedings of the 26th annual conference of the Mathematics Education Research Group of Australasia, pp. 618–625). Geelong, Vic: MERGA.

Helme, S. & Clarke, D. J. (2001). Identifying cognitive engagement in the mathematics classroom. *Mathematics Education Research Journal*, 13(2), 133–153.

Henningsen, M., & Stein, M. K. (1997). Mathematical tasks and student cognition: Classroom-based factors that support and inhibit high-level mathematical thinking and reasoning. *Journal for Research in Mathematics Education*, 28(5), 525–549.

Hiebert, J., & Carpenter, T. P. (1992). Learning and teaching with understanding. In D. A. Grouws (Ed.), *Handbook of Research on Mathematics Teaching and Learning* (pp. 65–97). New York: Macmillan.

Hiebert, J., & Grouws, D. A. (2007). The effects of classroom mathematics teaching on students' learning. In F. K. Lester Jr. (Ed.), *Second Handbook of Research on Mathematics Teaching and Learning* (Vol. 1, pp. 371–404). Charlotte, NC: Information Age Publishing.

Hill, L. T., Stremmel, A. J., & Fu, V. R. (2004). *Teaching as Inquiry: Rethinking Curriculum in Early Childhood Education*. New York: Allyn & Bacon.

Hogan, J. (2000). Numeracy—across the curriculum? *The Australian Mathematics Teacher*, 56(3), 17–20.

Hogan, J., Van Wyke, J., & Murcia, K. (2004). *Numeracy Across the Curriculum*. Canberra: Commonwealth of Australia

Horne, M. (2003). Properties of shape. *Australian Primary Mathematics Classroom*, 8(2), 8–13.

House of Representatives Standing Committee on Education and Training (2002). *Boys: Getting it Right. Report on the Inquiry into the Education of Boys*. [Electronic Version]. Retrieved 13 October 2009 from www.aph.gov.au/house/committee/edt/eofb/report/front.pdf.

Houssart, J. (2001). Counting difficulties at key stage two. *Support for Learning. British Journal of Learning Support*, 16(1), 11–16.

Houtveen, A., van der Grift, W. & Creemers, B. (2004). Effective school improvement in mathematics. *School Effectiveness and School Improvement*, 15(3–4), 337–376.

Howden, H. (1989). Teaching number sense. *Arithmetic Teacher*, 36(6), 12–16.

Huckstep, P., Rowland, T., & Thwaites, A. (2003). Observing subject knowledge in primary mathematics teaching. *Proceedings of the British Society for Research into Learning Mathematics*, 23(2), 85–90.

Hughes, M. (1986). *Children and Number: Difficulties in Learning Mathematics*. Oxford, UK: Blackwell.

Hughes-Hallett, D. (2001). Achieving numeracy: The challenge of implementation. In L. Steen (Ed.), *Mathematics and Democracy: The Case for Quantitative Literacy*. Princeton, NJ: The Woodrow Wilson National Fellowship Foundation.

Hughes-Hallett, D. (2003). The role of mathematics courses in the development of quantitative literacy. In B. Madison & L. Steen (Eds.), *Quantitative Literacy: Why Numeracy Matters for Schools and Colleges*. Princeton, NJ: The National Council on Education and the Disciplines.

Huinker, D. (1998). Letting fraction algorithms emerge through problem solving. In L. J. Morrow (Ed.), *The Teaching and Learning of Algorithms in School Mathematics* (pp. 170–182). Reston, VA: NCTM.

Irwin, K. (2001). Using everyday knowledge of decimals to enhance understanding. *Journal for Research in Mathematics Education*, 32(4), 399–421.

Jacob, L. & Willis, S. (2001). Recognising the difference between additive and multiplicative thinking in young children. In J. Bobis, B. Perry & M. Mitchelmore (Eds.) *Numeracy and Beyond* (Proceedings of the 24th Annual Conference of the mathematical Education Research Groups of Australasia, pp. 306–313). Sydney: MERGA.

Johnson, A., & Norris, K. (2006). *Teaching Today's Mathematics in the Middle Grades*. Boston, MA: Pearson.

Johnston-Wilder, S., & Mason, J. (2005). *Developing Thinking in Geometry*. London: Open University Press.

Jones, G. A., Langrall, C. W., & Mooney, E. S. (2007). Research in probability: Responding to classroom realities. In F. K. Lester Jr. (Ed.), *Second Handbook of Research on Mathematics Teaching and Learning* (Vol. 2, pp. 909–956). Charlotte, NC: Information Age.

Jones, K., Kershaw, L., & Sparrow, L. (1995). *Aboriginal Children Learning Mathematics*. Perth, WA: Mathematics, Science and Technology Education Centre, Edith Cowan University.

Joram, E. (2003). Benchmarks as tools for developing measurement sense. In D. Clements (Ed.), *Learning and Teaching Measurement: 65th Yearbook of National Council of Teachers of Mathematics*. Reston, VA: NCTM.

Jorgensen (Zevenbergen), R., & Niesche, R. (2008). Equity, mathematics and classroom practice: Developing rich mathematics experiences for disadvantaged students. *Australian Primary Mathematics Classroom*, 13(4), 21–27.

Joshua, A. (2001). Open-ended questions and investigations for Years 7 to 10. In B. Lee & T. Spencer (Eds.), *Mathematics Shaping Australia* (Proceedings of the 18th Biennial Conference of the Australian Association of Mathematics Teachers). Adelaide: AAMT.

Kamii, C., & Dominick, A. (1998). The harmful effects of algorithms in grades 1–4. In L. J. Morrow (Ed.), *The Teaching and Learning of Algorithms in School Mathematics* (pp. 130–140). Reston, VA: NCTM.

Kaput, J. (1998). Representations, inscriptions, descriptions and learning: A kaleidoscope of windows. *Journal of Mathematical Behaviour*, 17(2), 265–281.

Kaput, J. (1999). Teaching and learning a new algebra. In E. Fennema & T. Romberg (Eds.), *Mathematics Classrooms that Promote Understanding* (pp. 133–155). Mahwah, NJ: Erlbaum.

Kaput, J., & Blanton, M. (2001). Algebrafying the elementary mathematics experience. In H. Chick, K. Stacey, J. Vincent & J. Vincent (Eds.), *The Future of the Teaching and Learning of Algebra* (Proceedings of the 12th ICMI study conference, 344–352). Melbourne: University of Melbourne Press.

Kelly, S. M. (2009). Use of assistive technology by students with visual impairments: findings from a national survey. *Journal of Visual Impairment & Blindness*, 103(8), 470–480.

Kieran, C. (1992). The learning and teaching of school algebra. In D. A. Grouws (Ed.), *Handbook of Research in Mathematics Teaching and Learning* (pp. 390–419). New York: Macmillan.

Kieren, T. (1980). The rational number construct—Its elements and mechanisms. In T. Kieren (Ed.), *Recent Research on Number Learning* (pp. 125–149). Columbus: Ohio State University.

Kieren, T. (1988). Personal knowledge of rational numbers: Its intuitive and formal development. In J. Herbert & M. Behr (Eds.), *Number Concepts and Operations in the Middle Grades* (Vol. 2, pp. 162–181). Reston, VA: NCTM.

Kilpatrick, J., Swafford, J., & Findell, B. (Eds.). (2001). *Adding it up: Helping Children Learn Mathematics*. Washington, DC: National Academy Press.

Kilpatrick, J., & Wirszup. I. (Eds.) (1975). *Soviet Studies in the Psychology of Learning and Teaching Mathematics* (Vol. 5). Reston, VA: NCTM

Klein, A.S., Beishuizen, M, & Treffers, A. (1998). The empty number line in Dutch second grades: Realistic versus gradual program design. *Journal for Research in Mathematics Education*, 29, 443–464.

Klein, M. (2006). What to leave out when preservice mathematics education goes from four years to one: A poststructural account. In P. Grootenboer, R. Zevenbergen & M. Chinnappan (Eds.). *Identities, Cultures and Learning Spaces* (Proceedings of the 29th annual conference of the Mathematics Education Research Group of Australasia, pp. 328–335). Canberra, ACT: MERGA.

Konold, C. (1989). Informal conceptions of probability. *Cognition and Instruction*, 6, 59–98.

Konold, C., & Higgins, T. (2003). Reasoning about data. In J. Kilpatrick, W. Martin, & D. Schifter (Eds.), *A Research Companion to Principles and Standards for School Mathematics* (pp. 193–214). Reston, VA: NCTM.

Kramsch, C. (2003). *Language and Culture*. Melbourne, Vic: Oxford University Press.

Krause, K., Bochner, S., & Duchesne, S. (2003). *Educational Psychology for Learning and Teaching*. Southbank, Vic: Thomson.

Kruteskii, V. A. (1976). *The Psychology of Mathematical Abilities in School Children*. Chicago: University of Chicago Press.

Kuchemann, D. (1981). Algebra. In K. Hart (Ed.), *Children's Understanding of Mathematics*: 11–16 (pp. 102–119). London: Murray.

Labinowicz, E. (1985). *Learning from Children*. Menlo Park, CA: Addison-Wesley.

Lakoff, G., & Núñez, R. (1997). The metaphorical structure of mathematics: Sketching out cognitive foundations for a mind-based mathematics. In L. English (Ed.), *Mathematical Reasoning: Analogies, Metaphors, and Images* (pp. 21–89). Mahwah, NJ: Erlbaum.

Lambos, C., & Delfabbo, P. (2010). Numerical reasoning ability and irrational beliefs in problem gambling. *International Gambling Studies*, 7(2), 157–171.

Lamon, S. (1996). The development of unitising: Its role in children's partitioning strategies. *Journal for Research in Mathematics Education*, 27(2), 170–193.

Lamon, S. (1999). *Teaching Fractions and Ratios for Understanding: Essential Content Knowledge and Instructional Strategies for Teachers*. Mahwah, NJ: Erlbaum.

Lamon, S. (2001). Presenting and representing: From fractions to rational numbers. In A. Cuoco & F. Curcio (Eds.), *The Roles of Representation in School Mathematics. 2001 Yearbook* (pp. 146–165). Reston, VA: NCTM.

Lamon, S. (2007). Rational numbers and proportional reasoning: Towards a theoretical framework for research. In F. Lester (Ed.), *Second Handbook of Research on Mathematics Teaching and Learning. A Project of the National Council of Teachers of Mathematics* (pp. 629–667). Charlotte, NC: Information Age.

Lampert, M., & Cobb, P. (2003). Communication and language. In J. Kilpatrick, W. Martin, & D. Schifter (Eds.), *A Research Companion to Principles and Standards for School Mathematics* (pp. 237–249). Reston, VA: NCTM.

Lappan, G. & Bouck, M. K. (1998). In L. J. Morrow (Ed.), *The Teaching and Learning of Algorithms in School Mathematics* (pp. 183–197). Reston, VA: NCTM.

Leahy, S., Lyon, C., Thompson, M., & Wiliam, D. (2005). Classroom assessment minute by minute, day by day. *Educational Leadership*, 63, 18–24.

Lehrer, R. (2003). Developing understanding of measurement. In J. Kilpatrick, W. Martin, & D. Schifter (Eds.), *A Research Companion to Principles and Standards for School Mathematics*. Reston, VA: NCTM

Lehrer, R., Jaslow, L., & Curtis, C. (2003). Developing an understanding of measurement in the elementary grades. In D. Clements (Ed.), *Learning and Teaching Measurement: 65th Yearbook of National Council of Teachers of Mathematics*. Reston, VA: NCTM.

Lerman, S. (1989). Constructivism, mathematics and mathematics education. *Educational Studies in Mathematics*, 20, 211–213.

Lerman, S. (2002). Cultural, discursive psychology: A sociocultural approach to studying the teaching and learning of mathematics. *Educational Studies in Mathematics*, 46, 87–113.

Lewin, K. (1951). *Field Theory in Social Science: Selected Theoretical Papers*. (D. Cartwright, Ed.). New York: Harper & Row.

Lewis, D. (1976). Route finding by desert Aborigines in Australia. *The Journal of Navigation*. 29(1), 21–39.

Linchevski, L., & Kutscher, B. (1998). Tell me with whom you're learning, and I'll tell you how much you've learned: mixed-ability versus same-ability grouping in mathematics. *Journal for Research in Mathematics Education*, 29(5), 533–554.

Linchevski, L., & Williams, J. (1999). Using intuition in everyday life in 'filling' the gap in children's extension of their number concept to include negative numbers. *Educational Studies in Mathematics*, 39, 131–147.

Linn, M. C., & Eylon, B.-S. (2006). Science education: Integrating views of learning and instruction. In P. A. Alexander & P. H. Winne (Eds.), *Handbook of Educational Psychology* (2nd ed., pp. 511–544). Mahwah, NJ: Erlbaum.

Louden, W. (2000). Mapping the territory: Overview. In W. Louden, L. Chan, J. Elkins, D. Greaves, H. House, M. Milton, S. Nichols, J. Rivalland, M. Rohl & C. E. van Kraayenoord (Eds.), *Mapping the Territory* (Vol. 1, pp. 1–27). Canberra: Department of Education, Training and Youth Affairs, Commonwealth of Australia.

Lowe, I. (1991). *Geometry Everywhere: Examples, Worksheets and References for Teaching Geometry to Years 7–10*. Melbourne: The Education Shop, Ministry of Education and Training.

Lowe, I., Kissane, B. & Willis, S. (1995). *Access to Algebra Book 4*. Carlton, Vic.: Curriculum Corporation.

MacDonald, A. (2010). Heavy thinking: Young children's theorising about mass. *Australian Primary Mathematics Classroom*, 15(4), 4–8.

MacGregor, M. (1991). *Making Sense of Algebra: Cognitive Processes Influencing Comprehension*. Geelong, Vic: Deakin University Press.

MacGregor, M. and Stacey, K. (1995) Backtracking, Brackets, BODMAS and BOMDAS. *Australian Mathematics Teacher*, 51(3), pp 28–31.

Macmillan, A. (2009). *Numeracy in Early Childhood: Shared Contexts for Teaching and Learning*. Melbourne: Oxford University Press.

Malara, N., & Navarra, G. (2003). *ArAl Project: Arithmetic Pathways Towards Favouring Pre-algebraic Thinking*. Bologna, Italy: Pitagora Editrice.

Mankiewicz, R. (2000). *The Story of Mathematics*. London: Cassell.

Maor, E. (1994). *e: The Story of a Number*. Princeton NJ: Princeton University Press.

Martin, H. (2007). Mathematical literacy. *Principal Leadership*, 7(5), 28–31.

Mason, J. (1996). Expressing generality and roots of algebra. In N. Bednarz, C. Kieran & L. Lee (Eds.), *Approaches to Algebra: Perspectives for Research and Teaching*. Utrech: Kluwer.

Mason, J., Burton, L., & Stacey, K. (1985). *Thinking Mathematically*. (Revised ed.). Harlow, England: Prentice Hall.

Mason, J., Pimm, D., Graham, A., & Gower, N. (1985). *Routes to/Roots of Algebra*. Milton Keynes, UK: Open University Press.

Mathematical Sciences Education Board, National Research Council (1989). *Everybody Counts: A report to the Nation on the Future of Mathematics Education*. Washington, DC: National Academy of Sciences Press.

McCosker, N. & Diezmann, C. (2009). Scaffolding students' thinking in mathematical investigations. *Australian Primary Mathematics Classroom*, 14(3), 27–36.

McDuffe, A., & Young, T. (2003). Promoting mathematical discourse through children's literature. *Teaching Children Mathematics*, 9(7), 385–392.

McIntosh, A., DeNardi, E. & Swan, P. (1994). *Think Mathematically!* South Melbourne: Addison Wesley Longman.

McIntosh, A., & Dole, S. (2004). *Mental Computation: A Strategies Approach*. Hobart: Department of Education Tasmania.

McIntosh, A., Reys, B., & Reys, J. (1992). A proposed framework for examining basic number sense. *For the Learning of Mathematics*, 12(3), 2–8.

McIntosh, A. Reys, B., Reys, R., Bana, J., & Farrell, B. (1997). Number sense in school mathematics: Student performance in four countries. *Mathematics, Science and Technology Education, Monograph series No. 5*. Perth, WA: Edith Cowan University.

McLeod, D. B. (1992). Research on affect in mathematics education: A reconceptualization. In D. A. Grouws (Ed.), *Handbook of Research on Mathematics Teaching and Learning* (pp. 575–596). New York: Macmillan.

Metz, K. E. (1998). Emergent ideas of chance and probability in primary-grade children. In S. P. Lajoie (Ed.), *Reflections on Statistics Learning, Teaching and Assessment in Grades K–12* (pp. 149–173). Mahwah, NJ: Erlbaum.

Mighton, J. (2003). *The Myth of Ability*. Toronto: House of Anansi Press.

Miller, S. P., & Mercer, C. D. (1997). Educational aspects of mathematics disabilities. *Journal of Learning Disabilities*, 30(1), 47–56.

Ministerial Council on Education, Employment, Training and Youth Affairs (2008). *National Assessment Program—Literacy and Numeracy* (NAPLAN). Melbourne, Vic: MCEETYA.

Mitchell, A. & Horne, M. (2009). There are more than part-whole strategies at work in understanding non-equal parts fraction-area-models. In R. Hunter, B. Bicknell, & T. Burgess (Eds), *Crossing divides* (Proceedings of the 32nd annual conference of the Mathematics Education Research Group of Australasia, pp. 371–378). Palmerston North, NZ: MERGA.

Monari Martinez, E. (1998). Teenagers with Down syndrome study algebra in high school. *Down Syndrome Research and Practice*, 5(1), 34–38.

Moseley, B. (2005). Students' early mathematical representation knowledge: The effects of emphasising single or multiple perspectives of the rational number domain in problem solving. *Educational Studies in Mathematics*, 60(1), 37–69.

Moss, J. & Case, R. (1999). Developing children's understanding of the rational numbers: A new model and an experiemental curriculum. *Journal for Research in Mathematics Education*, 30(2), 122–147.

Moyer, P. (2000). Communicating mathematically: Children's literature as a natural connection. *The Reading Teacher*, 54(3), 246–255.

Moyer-Packenham, P.S., Salkind, G., & Bolyard, J.J. (2008). Virtual manipulatives used by K–8 teachers for mathematics instruction: considering mathematical, cognitive, and pedagogical fidelity. *Contemporary Issues in Technology and Teacher Education*, 8(3). Available: www.citejournal.org/vol8/iss3/mathematics/article1.cfm.

Mulligan, J. & Mitchelmore, M. (1997). Young children's intuitive models of multiplication and division. *Journal for Research in Mathematics Education*, 28(3), 309–330.

Mulligan, J., Mitchelmore, M., & Prescott, A. (2006). Integrating concepts and processes in early mathematics. In J. Novotna, H. Moraova, M. Kratka, & N. Stehlikova (Eds.), *Proceedings of the 30th Annual Conference of the International Group for the Psychology of Mathematics Education* (Vol. 4, pp. 209–216). Prague : PME.

Muir, T. (2008a). Principles of practice and teacher actions: Influences on effective teaching of numeracy. *Mathematics Education Research Journal*, 20(3), 78–101.

Muir, T. (2008b). 'Zero is not a number': Teachable moments and their role in effective teaching of numeracy. In M. Goos, R. Brown & K. Makar (Eds.), *Navigating Current and Charting Directions* (Proceedings of the 31st annual conference of the Mathematics Education Research Group of Australasia, pp. 361–367). Sydney: MERGA.

Mullis, I., Martin, M., Gonzalez, E., & Chrostowski, S. (2004). *TIMSS 2003 International Mathematics Report*. Amsterdam: International Association for the Evaluation of Educational Achievement [IEA].

Murphy, S. (1999). *Super Sandcastle Saturday*. New York: HarperCollins.

Murphy, S. (1999). *Room for Ripley*. New York: HarperCollins.

Myller, R. (1990). *How Big is a Foot?* New York: Random House Children's Books.

National Council of Teachers of Mathematics (1980). *An Agenda for Action*. Reston, VA: Author.

National Council of Teachers of Mathematics (2000). *Principles and Standards for School Mathematics*. Reston, VA: Author

National Curriculum Board (NCB) (2009). *Shape of the Australian Curriculum*: Mathematics. Canberra: Commonwealth of Australia. Retrieved 22 March 2010 from: www.acara.edu.au/verve/_resources/Australian_Curriculum_-_Maths.pdf.

National Numeracy Benchmarking Taskforce (1997). *The Numeracy Benchmarks*. Melbourne: Curriculum Corporation.

Neuschwander, C. (2001). *Sir Cumference and the Great Knight of Angleland*. Watertown MA: Charlesbridge.

Niss, (1996) Goals of mathematics teaching. In A. J. Bishop, K. Clements, C. Keitel, J. Kilpatrick, & C. Laborde (Eds.), *International Handbook of Mathematics Education* (pp. 11–48). Dordrecht, Netherlands: Kluwer.

Northcote, M. & McIntosh, M. (1999). What mathematics do adults really do in everyday life? *Australian Primary Mathematics Classroom*, 4(1), 19–21.

Northern Territory Department of Education (1987). *Mathematics in Aboriginal Schools—Stage 3*. Darwin: Author.

Nugent, H. (2006) *Germans are Brainiest (but at Least we're Smarter than the French)*. Rterieved 1 November 2007 from www.timesonline.co.uk/tol/news/uk/article697134.ece.

Nunes, T., & Bryant, P. (1996). *Children doing Mathematics*. Oxford, UK: Blackwell.

Nunes, T., & Moreno, C. (2002). An intervention program for promoting deaf pupils' achievement in mathematics. *Journal of Deaf Studies and Deaf Education*, 7(2), 120–133

O'Connor, J., & Robertson, E. (2002). Galileo Galilei. In: *The MacTutor History of Mathematics Archive*. Retrieved 10 October 2010 from www.gap-system.org/~history/Mathematicians/Galileo.html

Olive, J. (2001). Children's number sequences: An explanation of Steffe's constructs and an extrapoloation to rational numbers of arithmetic. *The Mathematics Educator*, 11(1), 4–9.

Olive, J. & Steffe, L. (2002). The construction of an iterative fractional scheme: The case of Jo. *Journal of Mathematical Behaviour*, 20, 413–437.

O'Shea, H. (2009). The ideal mathematics class for grades 5 and 6: What do the students think? *Australian Primary Mathematics Classroom*, 14(2), 18–23.

Outhred, L., Mitchelmore, M., McPhail, D., & Gould, P. (2003). Count me into measurement: A program for the early elementary school. In D. Clements (Ed.), *Learning and Teaching Measurement: 65th Yearbook of National Council of Teachers of Mathematics*. Reston, VA: NCTM.

Owens, K. (2010). Changing our perspective on space: place mathematics as a human endeavour. In L. Sparrow, B. Kissane, & C. Hurst (Eds.), *Shaping the Future of Mathematics Education* (Proceedings of the 33rd annual conference of the Mathematics Education Research Group of Australasia, pp. 454–461). Fremantle, WA: MERGA.

Panasuk, R., Stone, W., & Todd, J. (2002). Lesson planning strategy for effective mathematics teaching. *Education*, 122(4), 808–827.

Pape, S. J., Bell, C. V., & Yetkin, I. E. (2003). Developing mathematical thinking and self regulated learning: A teaching experiment in a seventh grade mathematics classroom. *Educational Studies in Mathematics*, 53(3), 179–202.

Papic, M. (2007). *Mathematics Patterning in Early Childhood: An intervention study*. Unpublished PhD Thesis. Sydney: Macquarie University.

Papert, S. (1993). *Mindstorms: Children, Computers, and Powerful Ideas*. (2nd ed.). New York: Harvester Wheatsheaf.

Parmar, R. S., & Cawley, J. F. (1991). Challenging the routines and passivity that characterize arithmetic instruction for children with mild handicaps. *Remedial and Special Education*, 12(5), 23–32, 43.

Parsons, S., & Bynner, J. (2005). *Does Numeracy Matter More?* London: National Research and Development Centre for Adult Literacy and Numeracy.

Patilla, P. (2003). *Oxford Primary Mathematics Dictionary*. Oxford, UK: Oxford University Press.

Patkin, D. & Gesser, D. (2009). The story of leading mathematics teachers from teacher-trainees to key positions. *International Journal of Qualitative Studies in Education*, 22(5), 527–548.

Pegg, J. (1997). Broadening the descriptors of van Hieles' levels 2 and 3. In F. Biddulph & K. Carr (Eds.), *People in Mathematics Education* (Proceedings of the 20th annual conference of the Mathematics Education Research Group of Australasia, pp. 391–396). Rotorua, NZ: MERGA.

Pegg, J., & Davey, G. (1998). Interpreting student understanding in geometry: A synthesis of two models. In R. Lehrer & D. Chazan (Eds.), *Designing Learning Environments for Developing Understanding of Geometry and Space* (pp. 109–133). Mahwah, NJ: Erlbaum.

Pereira-Mendoza, L. (1995). Graphing in the primary school: Algorithm versus comprehension. *Teaching Statistics*, 17, 2–6.

Perry, B., Young-Loveridge, J., Docket, S. & Doig, B. (2008). The development of young children's mathematical understanding. In H. Forgasz, A. Barkatsas, A. Bishop, B. Clarke, S. Keast, W-T. Seah, and P. Sullivan (Eds.), *Research in Mathematics Education in Australasia 2004–2007* (pp. 17–40). Rotterdam: Sense Publishers.

Perry, R., & Dockett, S. (2008). Young children's access to powerful mathematical ideas. In L. English & M. Bussi (Eds.), *Handbook of International Research in Mathematics Education* (2nd Edition) (pp. 75–108). New York: Routledge, Taylor & Francis.

Perso, T. (2003). *Improving Aboriginal Numeracy: Years K–9*. Adelaide, SA: Australian Association of Mathematics Teachers.

Piaget, J., & Inhelder, B. (1967). *The Child's Conception of Space* (F. J. Langdon & J. L. Lunzer, Trans.). New York: Norton.

Pinczes, E. (2001). *Inchworm and a half*. New York: Houghton Mifflin.

Pinker, S. (2003). Genetics: Are your genes to blame. *Time Magazine*, 20 January 2003. Retrieved 23 March 2010 from www.time.com/time/magazine/article/0,9171,1004084,00.html.

Pitino, D. (2005). *Too tall Tina*. New York: Kane Press.

Pothier, Y. & Sawada, D. (1990). Partitioning: An approach to fractions. *The Arithmetic Teacher*, 38(4), 12–16.

Presmeg, N. (2007). The role of culture in teaching and learning mathematics. In F. Lester (Ed.), *Second Handbook of Research on Mathematics Teaching and Learning: A Project of the National Council of Teachers of Mathematics* (pp. 435–460). Charlotte, NC: Information Age Publishing.

Professions Australia (1997). *About Professions Australia, Definition of a Profession: Adopted at Annual General Meeting, 26 May 1997*. Retrieved 18 April 2011 from http://professions.com.au/definitionprofession.html.

Reid, C. (1992). *From zero to infinity* (4th ed.). Washington DC: Mathematical Association of America.

Robinson, C. S., Menchetti, B. M., & Torgesen, J. K. (2002). Toward a two-factor theory of one type of mathematics disabilities. *Learning Disabilities Research and Practice*, 17(2), 81–89.

Roche, A. (2010). Decimats: Helping students to make sense of decimal place value. *Australian Primary Mathematics Classroom*, 15(2), 4–11.

Roennfeldt, R. (1984). *A Day on the Avenue*. New York: Viking.

Rogers, L. (no date). *The History of Negative Numbers*. Downloaded 10 March 2011 from http://nrich.maths.org/5961.

Rogers, W., & MacPherson, E. (2008). *Behaviour Management with Young Children: Crucial First Steps with Children 3–7 years*. London: SAGE.

Rosen, M. (1997) *We're Going on a Bear Hunt*. New York: Walker Books.

Rosenthal, R., & Jacobsen, L. (1969). *Pygmalion in the Classroom*. New York: Rinehart & Winston.

Ross, S. (1989). Parts, wholes and place-value: A developmental view. *Arithmetic Teacher*, 36(3), 47–51.

Rowe, K. (2006). *School Performance: Australian State/Territory Comparisons of Students' Achievements in National and International Studies*. Melbourne: ACER. Available online from: http://research_acer.edu.au/learning_processes/5.

Rowe, M. (1986). Wait time: Slowing down may be a way of speeding up! *Journal of Teacher Education*, 37(1), 43–50.

Russell, S. (2006). What does it mean that '5' has a lot? From the world to data and back. In G. Burrill & P. Elliott (Eds.), *Thinking and Reasoning with Data and Chance: 68th Yearbook of National Council of Teachers of Mathematics* (pp. 17–29). Reston, VA: NCTM.

Ryan, A., & Patrick, H. (2001). The classroom social environment and changes in adolescents' motivation and engagement during middle school. *American Educational Research Journal*, 38(2), 437–460.

Sagor, R., & Cox, J. (2004). *At-risk Students: Reaching and Teaching Them* (2nd ed.). New York: Eye on Education.

Sangster, M., & Cantrell, R. (2009). *Early Numeracy: Mathematical Activities for 3 to 5 year olds*. London: Continuum International.

Sankey, D. (2007). Minds, brains, and the difference in personal understandings. *Educational Philosophy and Theory*, 39(5), 543–558.

Saxe, G. (1995). From the field to the classroom: Studies in mathematical understanding. In L. Steffe & J. Gale (Eds.), *Constructivism in Education* (pp. 287–311). Hillsdale, NJ: Erlbaum.

Saxe, G., Taylor, E., McIntosh, C., & Gearhart, M. (2005). Representing fractions with standard notation: A developmental analysis. *Journal for Research in Mathematics Education*, 36(2), 137–157.

Sayre, A., & Sayre, J. (2003). *One is a Snail, Ten is a Crab: A Counting by Feet Book*. London: Walker Books.

Schaffer, J. (2000). Overlappings: Probability-raising without causation. *Australasian Journal of Philosophy*, 78(1), 40–46.

Schliemann, A., Araujo, C., Cassunde, M., Macedo, S. & Niceas, L. (1998). Use of multiplicative commutativity by school children and street sellers. *Journal for Research in Mathematics Education*, 29(4), 422–435.

Schmittau, J. (2003). Cultural historical theory and mathematics education. In A. Kozulin, B. Gindis, S. Miller, & V. Ageyev (Eds.). *Vygotsky's Educational Theory in a Cultural Context*. New York: Cambridge University Press.

Schmittau, J., & Morris, A. (2004). The development of algebra in the elementary mathematics curriculum of V. V. Davydov. *The Mathematics Educator*, 8(1), 60–87.

Schoenfeld, A. H. (1992). Learning to think mathematically: Problem solving, metacognition, and sense making in mathematics. In D. A. Grouws (Ed.), *Handbook of Research on Mathematics Teaching and Learning*. (pp. 334–370). New York: Macmillan.

Schuck, S. (1999). Teaching mathematics: A brightly wrapped but empty gift box. *Mathematics Education Research Journal*, 11(2), 109–123.

Schunk, D. H. (2004). *Learning Theories: An Educational Perspective*. Upper Saddle River, NJ: Pearson.

Schwartz, J. (2008). *Elementary Mathematics Pedagogical Content Knowledge: Powerful Ideas for Teachers*. Boston, MA: Pearson Education.

Scott, D. (1999). Essential ingredients for numeracy. *Australian Primary Mathematics Classroom*, 4(1), 4–8.

Scott, P. (2008). p round and round. *Australian Mathematics Teacher*, 64(1), 3–5.

Seah, R. & Booker, G. (2005). Lack of numeration and multiplication conceptual knowledge in middle school students: A barrier to the development of high school mathematics. In B. Bartlett, F. Bryer, & D. Roebuck (Eds.). *Stimulating the 'Action' as Participants in Participatory Research*, Vol. 3 (pp. 86–98). Nathan, Qld: Griffith University.

Selva, A., Falcao, J., & Nunes, T. (2005). Solving additive problems in pre-elementary school level with the support of graphical representations. In H. Chick & J. Vincent (Eds). *Proceedings* of the 29th Conference of the International Group for the Psychology of Mathematics Education (Vol. 4, pp. 161–168). Melbourne: PME.

Sfard, A. (2000). Symbolizing mathematical reality into being: How mathematical discourse and mathematical objects create each other. In P. Cobb, K. E. Yackel, & K. McClain (Eds), *Symbolizing and Communicating: Perspectives on Mathematical Discourse, Tools, and Instructional Design* (pp. 37–98). Mahwah, NJ: Erlbaum.

Sfard, A., & Prusak, A. (2005). Identity that makes a difference: substantial learning as closing the gap between actual and designated identities. In H. Chick and J. Vincent (Eds.). *Proceedings of the 29th Conference of the International Group for the Psychology of Mathematics Education*, Vol. 1 (pp. 37–52). Melbourne: PME.

Sharp, J., & Hoiberg, K. (2005). *Learning and Teaching K–8 Mathematics*. Boston, MA: Pearson Education.

Shaughnessey, M. (1998). Research on students' understandings of probability. In S. P. Lajoie (Ed.), *Reflections on Statistics Learning, Teaching and Assessment in Grades K–12.* (pp. 216–226). Mahwah, NJ: Erlbaum.

Shaughnessey, M. (2003). Research on students understanding of probability. In J. Kilpatrick, W. Martin, & D. Schifter (Eds.), *A Research Companion to Principles and Standards for School Mathematics.* (pp 216–226). Reston, VA: NCTM.

Shaughnessy, J. M. (2007). Research on statistics learning and reasoning. In F. K. Lester Jr. (Ed.), *Second Handbook of Research on Mathematics Teaching and Learning* (Vol. 2, pp. 957–1010). Charlotte, NC: Information Age.

Shaughnessy, J. M., Ciancetta, M., & Canada, D. (2004). Types of student reasoning on sampling tasks. In M. Johnsen Hoines & A. Berit Fuglestad (Eds.), *Proceeedings of the 28th Annual Conference of the International Group for the Psychology of Mathematics Education* (Vol. 4, pp. 177–184). Bergen, Norway: Bergen University College Press.

Shigematsu, K., & Sowder, J. (1994). Drawings for story problems: Practices in Japan and the United States. *Arithmetic Teacher*, 41(9), 544–547.

Shulman, L. S. (1986). Those who understand: Knowledge growth in teaching. *Educational Researcher*, 15(5), 4–14.

Shulman, L.S. (1987). Knowledge and teaching: Foundations of the new reform. *Harvard Educational Review*, 57(1), 1–22.

Siemon, D. (1988). Errors and the learning process. In D. Firth (Ed.), *Maths Counts–Who Cares?* (Proceedings of the 25th Annual Conference of the Mathematical Association of Victoria). Melbourne: MAV.

Siemon, D. (1989). Knowing and believing is seeing—a constructivist's perspective of change. In K. Clements & N. Ellerton (Eds.), *School Mathematics: The Challenge to Change* (pp. 250–268). Geelong, Vic: Deakin University Press.

Siemon, D. (1993). *The Role of Metacognition in Children's Mathematical Problem Solving*. Unpublished PhD thesis, Clayton, Vic.: Monash University.

Siemon, D. (1999). *A Marriage of Convenience—Pre-service Teacher's Ideas about Decimal Fractions*. Invited seminar presented to Twilight Decimals Conference, Department of Science and Mathematics Education, University of Melbourne, February.

Siemon, D. (2002). *Partitioning: The Missing Link in Building Fraction Knowledge and Confidence*. Department of Education, Victoria. Retrieved 10 March 2010 from www.eduweb.vic.gov.au/edulibrary/public/teachlearn/student/pppartitioning.pdf.

Siemon, D. (2003). Partitioning the missing link in building fraction knowledge and confidence. *Australian Mathematics Teacher*, 59(2), 22–24.

Siemon, D. (2006). *Assessment for Common Misunderstandings*. Materials prepared for and published electronically by the Victorian Department of Education and Early Childhood Development. Available from www.education.vic.gov.au/studentlearning/teachingresources/maths/common/default.htm.

Siemon, D., & Booker, G. (1990). Teaching and learning for, about and through problem solving. *Vinculum*, 27(2), 4–12.

Siemon, D. & Breed, M. (2005). From additive to multiplicative thinking: The big challenge in the middle years. In J. Mousley, L. Bragg, & Campbell, C. (Eds.) *Mathematics: Celebrating Achievement*. (Proceedings of the Annual Conference of the Mathematical Association of Victoria), Melbourne: MAV.

Siemon, D., Breed, M., Dole, S., Izard, J., & Virgona, J. (2006). *The Final Report of the Scaffolding Numeracy in the Middle Years Project* [CD-rom], Melbourne: RMIT University. Available online from: www.education.vic.gov.au/studentlearning/teachingresources/maths/snmy/default.htm

Siemon, D. E., Breed, M., Dole, S., Izard, J., & Virgona, J. (2006). *Scaffolding Numeracy in the Middle Years—Project Findings, Materials, and Resources*. Final report submitted to Victorian Department of Education and Training and the Tasmanian Department of Education, October. [CD-ROM] subsequently published electronically: www.eduweb.vic.gov.au/edulibrary/public/teachlearn/student/snmy.ppt

Siemon, D., Cathcart, J., Lasso, M., Parsons, V., & Virgona, J. (2004). Elaborating the teacher's role—towards a professional language. In M. Hoines & A. Fuglestad (Eds.), *Inclusion and Diversity* (Proceedings of the 28th conference of the International Group for the Psychology of Mathematics Education, pp. 193–200). Bergen, Norway: Bergen University.

Siemon, D., & Virgona, J. (2001). Roadmaps to numeracy: Reflections on the Middle Years Numeracy Research Project [CD-rom]. In P. Jeffery (Ed.), *Proceedings of the Annual Conference of the Australian Association for Research in Education*. Fremantle, WA: AARE.

Siemon, D., & Virgona, J. (2003). Identifying effective scaffolding practices through structured peer observation and review. In L. Bragg, C. Campbell, G. Herbert & J Mousley (Eds.), *Mathematics Education Research: Innovation, Networking, Opportunity* (Proceedings of the 26th annual conference of the Mathematics Education Research Group of Australasia, pp. 618–625). Geelong, Vic: MERGA.

Siemon, D., Virgona, J. and Corneille, K. (2001). *Final Report of the Middle Years Numeracy Research Project: 5–9*. Available from www.eduweb.vic.gov.au/edulibrary/public/curricman/middleyear/MYNumeracyResearchFullReport.pdf.

Simon, M. (1995). Reconstructing mathematics pedagogy from a constructivist perspective. *Journal for Research in Mathematics Education*, 26(2), 114–145.

Simon, M. (2000). Constructivism, mathematics teacher education, and research in mathematics teacher development. In L. P. Steffe & P. W. Thompson (Eds.), *Radical constructivism in action: Building on the Pioneering Work of Ernst von Glasersfeld* (pp. 213–230). London: Routledge Falmer.

Singh, S. (2005). *Fermat's Last Theorem*. London: Fourth Estate.

Skemp, R. R. (1976). Instrumental understanding and relational understanding. *Mathematics Teaching*, 77, 20–26.

Skemp, R. R. (1978). Relational understanding and instrumental understanding. *Arithmetic Teacher*, 26(3), 9-15.

Skoss, M. (n.d.) *Problem Solving Strategy Board*. Retrieved 30 July 2010 from http://maths-no-fear.wikispaces.com/Posters.

Skinner, B. F. (1974). *About Behaviourism*. London: Cape.

Smith, D. (2002). *If the World were a Village*. New York: Kids Can Press.

Smith, J. P. (2002). The development of students' knowledge of fractions and ratios. In B. Litwiller & G. Bright (Eds.), *Making Sense of Fractions, Ratios and Proportions: 2002 Yearbook of the National Council of Mathematics*. Reston, VA: NCTM.

Smith, S. (2009). Early childhood mathematics. Boston, MA: Pearson.

Smith, M. C., & Reio, T. G. (2006). Adult development, schooling and transition to work. In P. A. Alexander & P. H. Winne (Eds.), *Handbook of Educational Psychology* (2nd ed., pp. 115–138). Mahwah, NJ: Erlbaum.

Smith, T. J. (2003). Pedagogy as conversation: a metaphor for learning together. In B. Clarke, A. Bishop, R. Cameron, H. Forgasz, & W. T. Seah (Eds.), *Making Mathematicians* (Proceedings of the 40th annual conference of the Mathematical Association of Victoria, pp. 491–505). Brunswick, Vic: MAV.

Soanes, C., Stevenson, A., & Hawker, S. (Eds.) (2008). *Concise Oxford English Dictionary*. New York: Oxford University Press

Sobel, D. (1995). *Longitude*. London: Fourth Estate

Sousa, D. A. (2008). *How the Brain Learns Mathematics*. Thousand Oaks, CA: Corwin Press.

Sowder, J. (1992). Making sense of numbers in school mathematics. In G. Leinhardt, R. Putnam & R. Hattrup (Eds.), *Analysis of Arithmetic for Mathematics Teaching* (pp. 1–51). Hillsdale, NJ: Erlbaum

Sowder, J., & Schappelle, B. (1989). *Establishing Foundations for Research on Number Sense and Related Topics: Report of a Conference on Number Sense*. San Diego, CA: CRSME, San Diego State University.

Spencer, J. P., Blumberg, M. S., McMurray, B., Robinson, S. R., Samuelson, L. K., & Tomblin, J. B. (2009). Short arms and talking eggs: Why we should no longer abide the nativist–empiricist debate. *Child Development Perspectives*, 3(2), 79–87.

Stacey, K., Helme, S., Archer, S., & Condon, C. (2001). The effect of epistemic fidelity and accessibility on teaching with physical materials: A comparison of two models for teaching decimal numeration. *Educational Studies in Mathematics*, 47(2), 199–221.

Stacey, K., Helme, S. & Steinle, V. (2001). Confusions between decimals, fractions, and negative numbers: A consequence of the mirror as a conceptual metaphor in three different ways. In M. van den Heuvel-Panhuizen (Ed.), *Proceedings of the 25th Annual Conference of the International Group for the Psychology of Education*, Vol. 4. (pp. 217–224). Utrecht, The Netherlands: PME.

Stacey, K., Helme, S., Steinle, V., Baturo, A., Irwin, K. C., & Bana, J. (2001). Preservice teachers' knowledge of difficulties in decimal numeration. *Journal of Mathematics Teacher Education*, 4, 205–225.

Stacey, K. & Vincent, J. (2008). Modes of reasoning in Year 8 textbooks. In M. Goos, R. Brown & K. Makar (Eds.), *Navigating Current and Charting Directions* (Proceedings of the 31st annual conference of the Mathematics Education Research Group of Australasia, pp. 475-481). Sydney: MERGA.

Stafylidou, S. & Vosniadou, S. (2004). The development of students' understanding of the numerical value of fractions. In L. Veschaffel & S. Vosniadou (Eds), Extending the conceptual change to mathematics learning and teaching, *Learning and Instruction*, doi: 10.1016/j.learninstruct.2004.06.017

Steen, L. A. (1988). Literacy in mathematics. In R.J. Murnane & S. A. Raizen (Eds.), *Improving Indicators of Quality Science and Mathematics in Grades K–12* (pp. 20–22). Washington: National Academy Press.

Steen, L. (Ed.). (1997). *Why Numbers Count: Quantitative Literacy for Tomorrow's America*. New York: College Entrance Examination Board.

Steen, L. (2001). *Mathematics and democracy: The case for quantitative literacy*. Princeton, NJ: The Woodrow Wilson National Fellowship Foundation.

Steen, L. (2007a). Every teacher is a teacher of mathematics. *Principal Leadership*, 7(5), 16–20.

Steen, L. (2007b). How mathematics counts. *Educational Leadership*, November, pp. 9–14.

Steffe, L. (1992). Schemes of action and operation involving composite units. *Learning and Individual Differences*, 4(3), 259–309.

Steffe, L., Cobb, P., & von Glasersfeld, E. (1988). *Construction of Arithmetical Meanings and Strategies*. New York: Springer-Verlag.

Steffe, L., von Glasersfeld, E., Richards, J. & Cobb, P. (1983). *Children's Counting Types: Philosophy, Theory, and Applications*. New York: Praeger.

Steinke, D. (2001). *Part-whole Concept Understanding in a Population of 2nd and 3rd Graders*. Paper presented at the twenty-third annual meeting of the International Group for the Psychology of Mathematics Education – North American section. Snowbird, UT. 18–21 October. ERIC Number: SE 065164.

Steinle, V., & Stacey, K. (1998). The incidence of misconceptions of decimal notation amongst students in Grades 5 to 10. In C. Kanes, M. Goos & E. Warren (Eds.), *Teaching Mathematics in New Times* (Proceedings of the 21st annual conference of the Mathematics Education Research Group of Australasia. Gold Coast, pp. 548–555). Sydney: MERGA.

Stephens, M. (2003). Reforming arithmetic in the primary school years: The importance of quasi-variable expressions in arithmetic relations. In M. Goos & T. Spencer (Eds.). *Mathematics Making Waves* (Proceedings of the 19th Biennial Conference of the Australian Association of Mathematics Teachers, pp. 219–225). Brisbane:AAMT.

Stephens, M. (2006). Describing and exploring the power of relational thinking. In P. Grootenboer, R. Zevenbergen & M. Chinnappan (Eds.), *Identities, Cultures and Learning Spaces* (Proceedings of the 29th annual conference of the Mathematics Education Research Group of Australasia, pp. 496–503). Canberra: MERGA.

Stephens, M. (in press). *Rich Assessment Tasks in Mathematics: Years 5–8*. Melbourne: Catholic Education Office.

Stiggins, R. (2002). Assessment crisis: The absence of assessment for learning. *Phi Delta Kappan*, 83(10), 758–765.

Stigler, J., & Hiebert, J. (1999). *The Teaching Gap*. New York: The Free Press.

Stoessiger, R. (2002). An introduction to critical numeracy. *The Australian Mathematics Teacher*, 58(4), 17–20.

Sullivan, P. (2007). Teaching mixed ability mathematics classes. In S. Close, D. Corcoran & T. Dooley (Eds.), *Proceedings of Second National Conference on Research in Mathematics Education, Mathematics in Ireland* 2 (pp. 372–383). Dublin: St. Patrick's College.

Sullivan, P., Clarke, D., & Clarke, B. (2009). Converting mathematics tasks to learning opportunities: An important aspect of knowledge for mathematics teaching. *Mathematics Education Research Journal*, 21(1), 85–105.

Sullivan, P., & Lilburn, P. (1997). *Open-ended maths activities: Using 'good' Questions to Enhance Learning*. South Melbourne: Oxford University Press.

Sullivan, P., Mousley, J., & Zevenbergen, R. (2006a). Developing guidelines for teachers helping students experiencing difficulty in learning mathematics. In P. Grootenboer, R. Zevenbergen & M. Chinnappan (Eds.), *Identities, Cultures and Learning Spaces* (Proceedings of the 29th annual conference of the Mathematics Education Research Group of Australasia, pp. 496–503). Canberra: MERGA.

Sullivan, P., Mousley, J., & Zevenbergen, R. (2006b). Teacher actions to maximize mathematics learning opportunities in heterogeneous classrooms. International *Journal of Science and Mathematics Education*, 4, 117–143.

Swan, M. (1990). Becoming numerate: Developing conceptual structures. In S. Willis (Ed.) *Being Numerate—What Counts?* Hawthorn, Vic: Australian Council for Educational Research.

Swan, P. (1996). *Number Novelties: Practical Activities Designed to Motivate the Teaching and Learning of Number*. Perth, WA: A–Z Type.

Taggert, G., Adams, P., Elitze, E., Heinrichs, J., Hohman, J. & Hickman, K. (2007). Fermi Questions. *Mathematics Teaching in the Middle School*, 13(3), 164–167.

Tanner, H., Jones, S., Kennewell, S., & Beauchamp, G., (2005). Interactive whole class teaching and interactive white boards. In P. C. Clarkson, A. Downton, D. Gronn, M. Horne, A. McDonough, R. Pierce, U. Roche & A. Roche (Eds.), *Building Connections: Research, Theory and Practice* (Proceedings of the 28th annual conference of the Mathematics Education Research Group of Australasia, pp. 720–727). Sydney: MERGA.

Thomas, N. (2004). The development of structure in the number system. In M. Johnsen Hoines & A. Berit Fuglestad (Eds.), *Proceeedings of the 28th Annual Conference of the International Group for the Psychology of Mathematics Education*. Bergen, Norway: Bergen University College Press.

Thomson, S. & Buckley, S. (2009). *Informing Mathematics Pedagogy: TIMSS 2007 Australia and the world*. Melbourne: ACER.

Thompson, A. (1984). The relationship of teachers' conceptions of mathematics and mathematics teaching to instructional practice. *Educational Studies in Mathematics*, 15(2), 105–127.

Thompson, I. (1999). Written methods of computation. In I. Thompson (Ed.), *Issues in Teaching Numeracy in Primary Schools* (pp. 169–183). Buckingham, UK: Open University Press.

Thompson, P. (1994). Concrete materials and teaching for mathematical understanding. *Arithmetic Teacher*, 41(9), 556–558.

Thornton, S. (2009). The responses of one school to the 2008 Year 9 NAPLAN numeracy test. *Australian Primary Mathematics Classroom*, 65(4), 26–37.

Thornton, S., & Hogan, J. (2005). Numeracy across the curriculum: Demands and opportunities. *Curriculum Leadership*, 3(16), n.p.

Threlfall, J. (1999). Repeating patterns in the primary years. In A. Orton (Ed.), *Pattern in the Teaching and Learning of Mathematics* (pp. 18–30). London: Cassell.

Tickle, B. (2003). Handy hints for teaching number in the new syllabus. *Curriculum Support for Primary Teachers*, 8(4), 1–3. Sydney: NSW Department of Education and Training.

Torbeyns, J., Vanderveken, L., Verschaffel, L., & Ghesquière, P. (2006). Adaptive expertise in the number domain 20–100. In J. Novatna, H. Moraova, M Kratka & N. Stehlikova (Eds.), *Proceedings 30th Conference of the International Group for the Psychology of Mathematics Education* (Vol. 5, pp. 289–296). Prague: PME.

Treffers, A. & Buys, K. (2001). Grade 2 and 3 – Calculations up to 100. In M. van den Heuvel-Panhuizen (Ed.), *Children Learn Mathematics* (pp. 69–88). Utrecht, The Netherlands: Freudenthal Institute, Utrecht University.

Turner, P. (2007). Reflections of numeracy and streaming in mathematics education. *Australian Mathematics Teacher*, 62(2), 28–33.

Tzur, R., & Simon, M. (2004). Distinguishing two stages of mathematics conceptual learning. *International Journal of Science and Mathematics Education*, 2, 287–304.

Usiskin, Z. (1998). Paper-and-pencil algorithms in a calculator-and-computer age. In L. J. Morrow (Ed.). *The Teaching and Learning of Algorithms in School Mathematics*. Reston, VA: National Council of Teachers of Mathematics.

Vale, C. (2002). Girls back off mathematics again: The views and experiences of girls in computer based mathematics. *Mathematics Education Research Journal*, 14(3), 52–68.

Vale, C. (2003). Questions in primary mathematics classrooms. In L. Bragg, C. Campbell, G. Herbert & J. Mousley (Eds.), *Mathematics Education Research: Innovation, Networking, Opportunity*. (Proceedings of the 26th annual conference of the Mathematics Education Research Group of Australasia, pp. 688–695). Melbourne: Deakin University.

Vale, C., & Bartholomew, H. (2008). Gender and mathematics: Theoretical frameworks and findings. In H. Forgasz, A. Barkatsas, A. Bishop, B. Clarke, S. Keast, W. T. Seah & P. Sullivan (Eds.), *Research in Mathematics Education in Australasia 2004-2007* (pp. 271–290). Rotterdam: Sense Publishers.

van den Heuval-Panhuizen, M. (1999). *Children Learn Mathematics: A Learning-teaching Trajectory with Intermediate Attainment Targets for Calculation with Whole Numbers in Primary School*. Utrecht, The Netherlands: Freudenthal Institute.

van den Heuval-Panhuizen, M. (2001a). *Children Learn Mathematics – A Learning-teaching Trajectory with Intermediate Attainment Targets for Calculation with Whole Numbers in Primary School*. Utrecht, The Netherlands: Freudenthal Institute.

van den Heuvel-Panhuizen, M. (2001b) Realistic mathematics education in the Netherlands. In J. Anghileri (Ed.), *Principles and Practices in Arithmetic Teaching: Innovative Approaches for the Prima Classroom* (pp. 49–63). Buckingham/Philadelphia: Open University Press.

van Hiele, P.M. (1986). *Structure and Insight: A Theory of Mathematics Education*. Orlando, FL: Academic Press.

van Hiele-Geldof, D. (1984). The didactics of geometry in the lowest class of secondary school. In D. J. Fuys, D. Geddes, & R. Tischler (Eds.), *English Translation of Selected Writings of Dina Van Heile-Geldof and Pierre M. Van Hiele* (pp. 1–214). Brooklyn, NY: Brooklyn College, School of Education.

van Kraayenoord, C. E., & Elkins, J. (2004). Learning difficulties in numeracy in Australia. *Journal of Learning Disabilities*, 37(1), 32–41.

Van Zoest, L. R., Jones, G. A., & Thornton, C. A. (1994). Beliefs about mathematics teaching held by pre-service teachers involved in a first grade mentorship program. *Mathematics Education Research Journal*, 6(1), 37–55.

Venkatakrishnan, H. & Wiliam, D. (2003). Tracking and mixed-ability grouping in secondary school mathematics classrooms: A case study. *British Educational Research Journal*, 29(2), 189–204.

Verenikina, I. (2003). Understanding scaffolding and the ZPD in educational research. In P. Jeffrey (Ed.), *Proceedings of the Annual Conference of the Australian Association for Research in Education*. Auckland, NZ: AARE. Retrieved 13 November 2010 from www.aare.edu.au/03pap/ver03682.pdf.

Vergnaud, G. (1983). Multiplicative structures. In R. Lesh & M. Landau (Eds.), *Acquisition of Mathematics Concepts and Processes* (pp. 127–173). New York: Academic Press.

Verschaffel, L., & De Corte, E. (1996). Number and arithmetic. In A. Bishop, K. Clements, C. Keitel, J. Kilpatrick,, & C. Laborde (Eds.), *International Handbook of Mathematics Education* (pp. 1099–138). Dordrecht, Netherlands: Kluwer.

Verschaffel, L., Greer, B., & De Corte, E. (2007). Whole number concepts and operations. In F. Lester (Ed.), *Second Handbook of Research on Mathematics Teaching and Learning: A Project of the National Council of Teachers of Mathematics* (pp. 557–628). Charlotte, NC: Information Age.

Vincent, J., & Stacey, K. (2008). Do mathematical textbooks cultivate shallow teaching? Applying the TIMSS video study criteria to Australian eighth grade mathematics textbooks. *Mathematics Education Research Journal*, 20(1), 82–107.

Voigt, J. (1994). Negotiation of mathematical meaning and learning mathematics. *Educational Studies in Mathematics*, 26, 275–298.

von Glasersfeld, E. (1990). An exposition of constructivism: Why some like it radical. In R. B. Davis, C. A. Maher & N. Noddings (Eds.), *Constructivist Views on the Teaching and Learning of Mathematics* (pp. 19–29). Reston, VA: National Council of Teachers of Mathematics.

Vygotsky, L. (1978). Interaction between learning and development (pp. 79–91). In *Mind in Society*. (Trans. M. Cole). Cambridge, MA: Harvard University Press.

Walls, F. (2007). 'Doing maths': children talk about their classroom experiences. In J. M. Watson & K. Beswick (Eds.). *Mathematics: Essential Research, Essential Practice* (Proceedings of the 30th annual conference of the Mathematics Education Research Group of Australasia, pp. 755–764). Sydney: MERGA.

Warren E. (2002). Children's understanding of turnarounds: A foundation for algebra. *Australian Primary Mathematics Classroom*, 7, 9–15.

Warren, E. (2003). The role of arithmetical structure in the transition from arithmetic to algebra. *Mathematics Education Research journal of Australasia*, 15(2), 122–137

Warren E. (2006). Learning comparative mathematical language in the elementary school: a longitudinal study. *Education Studies in Mathematics*, 62(2), 169–189.

Warren, E. (2007). *Algebra for All: Blue Series*. Brisbane: Origo Education.

Warren, E., Benson, S., & Green S. (2007). Functional thinking in the Year 1 Classroom. *Australian Primary Mathematics Classroom*, 12(3), 14–17.

Warren, E., & Cooper T. J. (2008a). Patterns that support early algebraic thinking in the elementary school. In C. Greenes & R. Rubenstien (Eds.), *Algebra and Algebraic Thinking in School Mathematics: 70th Yearbook National Council of Teachers of Mathematics*. Reston, VA: NCTM.

Warren, E., & Cooper T. J. (2008b). Generalising the pattern rule for visual growth patterns: Actions that support 8 year olds thinking. *Education Studies in Mathematics*, 67(2). 171–185.

Warren E., & DeVries, E. (2009a). *Report on Rational Number Project*. ASISTM Project funded by the Australian Government Department of Education: http://www.acu.edu.au/160686

Warren, E, & DeVries, E. (2009b). Young Australian Indigenous students' engagement with numeracy: Actions that assist to bridge the gap. *Australian Journal of Education*, 53(2). 159–175.

Watson, A. (2001). Making judgements about pupils' mathematics. In P. Gates (Ed.), *Issues in Mathematics Teaching* (pp. 217–231). New York: Routledge Falmer.

Watson, A. (2004). Red herrings: Post-14 'best' mathematics teaching and curricula. *British Journal of Educational Studies*, 52(4), 359–376.

Watson, A., & De Geest, E. (2005). Principled teaching for deep progress: Improving mathematical learning beyond methods and materials. *Educational Studies in Mathematics*, 58(2), 209–234.

Watson, H. (1989). *Singing the Land, Signing the Land*. Geelong, Vic: Deakin University Press.

Watson, J. M. (1995). *Cautionary Tales: A Collection of Mathematical Essays for Teachers*. Adelaide: Australian Association of Mathematics Teachers.

Watson, J. M. (2005). Variation and expectation as foundations for the chance and data curriculum. In P. C. Clarkson, A. Downton, D. Gronn, M. Horne, A. McDonough, R. Pierce, U. Roche & A. Roche (Eds.), *Building Connections: Research, Theory and Practice* (Proceedings of the 28th annual conference of the Mathematics Education Research Group of Australasia, pp. 35–42). Adelaide: MERGA.

Watson, J. M. (2006). *Statistical Literacy at School: Growth and Goals*. Mahwah, NJ: Erlbaum.

Watson, J. M., Beswick, K., & Brown, N. (2006). Teachers' knowledge of their students as learners and how to intervene. In P. Grootenboer, R. Zevenbergen & M. Chinnappan (Eds.), *Identities, Cultures and Learning Spaces* (Proceedings of the 29th annual conference of the Mathematics Education Research Group of Australasia). Adelaide: MERGA.

Watson, J. M., & Moritz, J. B. (2000). Development of understanding of sampling for statistical literacy. *Journal of Mathematical Behavior*, 19, 109–136.

Watson, J. M., & Moritz, J. B. (2003). Fairness of dice: A longitudinal study of students' beliefs and strategies for making judgments. *Journal for Research in Mathematics Education*, 34(4), 270–304.

Watson, J. M., Stack, S., & Neal, D. (2009). *Developing Critical Numeracy Across the Curriculum*. Retrieved August 30, 2010 from www.simerr.educ.utas.edu.au/numeracy/default.html.

Weaver, C. S. (1977). Geoboard triangles with one interior point. *Mathematics Magazine*, 50(2), 92–94.

Weekley, E. (1921). *An Etymological Dictionary of Modern English*. London: John Murray.

Westwood, P. (2000). *Numeracy and Learning Difficulties: Approaches to Teaching and Assessment*. Melbourne: ACER.

Westwood, P. (2008). *What Teachers Need to Know about Numeracy*. Camberwell, Vic: ACER.

White, R. & Gunstone, R. (1992). *Probing Understanding*. London: Falmer.

Whitin, D. (2006). Learning to talk back to a statistic. In G. Burrill & P. Elliott (Eds.), *Thinking and Reasoning with Data and Chance: 68th Yearbook of National Council of Teachers of Mathematics* (pp. 31–39). Reston, VA: NCTM.

Wiliam, D. (2005). Keeping learning on track: Formative assessment and the regulation of learning. In M. Coupland, J. Anderson, & T. Spencer (Eds.), *Making Mathematics Vital* (Proceedings of the 20th biennial conference of the Australian Association of Mathematics Teachers, pp. 26–40). Adelaide: AAMT

Williams, E., Francis, L. J., & Robbins, M. (2007). Personality and paranormal belief: A study among adolescents. *Pastoral Psychology*, 56, 9–14.

Willis, S. (1990). *Being Numerate: What Counts?* Hawthorn, Vic: ACER.

Willis, S. (1998). Which numeracy? *Unicorn: Journal of the Australian College of Educators*, 24(2), 32–41

Willis, S. (2002). Crossing borders: Learning to count. *The Australian Education Researcher*, 29(2), 115–129.

Wilson, S., & Thornton, S. (2006). To heal and enthuse: Developmental bibliotherapy and pre-service primary teachers' reflections on learning and teaching mathematics. In P. Grootenboer, R. Zevenbergen & M. Chinnappan (Eds.), *Identities, Cultures and Learning Spaces* (Proceedings of the 29th annual conference of the Mathematics Education Research Group of Australasia, pp. 36–44). Canberra: MERGA.

Wong, M. & Evans, D. (2008). Fractions as measure. In M. Goos, R. Brown & K. Makar (Eds.), *Navigating Current and Charting Directions* (Proceedings of the 31st annual conference of the Mathematics Education Research Group of Australasia, pp. 597–603). Sydney: MERGA.

Wright, R., Stanger, G., Stafford, A., & Martlkand, J. (2006). *Teaching Number in the Classroom with 4 to 8 Year Olds*. London: Paul Chapman Publishing.

Wood, T. (1994). Patterns of interaction and the culture of mathematics classrooms. In S. Lerman (Ed.), *The Culture of the Mathematics Classroom* (pp.149–168). Dordrecht, Netherlands: Kluwer.

Yackel, E. (1995). Children's talk in inquiry mathematics classroom. In P. Cobb & H. Bauserfield (Eds.), *The Emergence of Mathematical Meaning: Interaction in Classroom Cultures* (pp. 131–161). Hillsdale, NJ: Erlbaum.

Yackel, E., & Cobb, P. (1996). Sociomathematical norms, argumentations, and autonomy in mathematics. *Journal for Research in Mathematics Education*, 27(4), 458–477.

Yates, S. (2005). Primary teachers' mathematical beliefs, teaching practices and curriculum reform experiences. In P. Jeffrey (Ed.), *Proceeding of the Annual Conference of Australian Association for Research in Education*. Parramatta, NSW: AARE. Retrieved 15 October 2009 from www.aare.edu.au/live/.

Youdale, L. (2010). Planning, teaching and assessing mathematics for real! *Australian Primary Mathematics Classroom*, 15(4), 29–32.

Zaslavsky, C. (1996). *The Multicultural Math Classroom: Bringing in the World*. Portsmouth, NH: Heinemann.

Zevenbergen, R. (2005). The construction of a mathematical habitus: Implications of ability grouping in the middle years. *Journal of Curriculum Studies*, 37(5), 607–619.

Zevenbergen, R., & Flavel, S. (2007). Undertaking an archaeological dig in search of pedagogical relay. *Montana Mathematics Enthusiast* (2007), 163–174.

Zimmermann, W., & Cunningham, S. (1991). Editors' introduction: What is mathematical visualization? In W. Zimmermann & S. Cunningham (Eds.), *Visualization in Teaching and Learning Mathematics* (Vol. MAA Notes Number 19, pp. 1–8): Mathematical Association of America.

Index

÷ sign 381
= sign 205, 206, 259–60, 291–2, 331, 335, 385
3D objects 637

a

ability, myth of 144
absolute magnitude (numbers) 188, 189, 272, 324
abstract composite unit 295, 338
abstract thinking 102–5
accommodation 272
addend 327, 328, 329, 333, 348
addition
    automatic recall of facts 334
    context for 324–9
    decimals 344–5, 537–9
    fractions 344–5, 527–31, 534–5
    integers 541–4
    language of 325
    meanings for 326–7
    mental strategies to 20 334–7
    non-binary forms 329
    order of introduction 329
    problem solving 345–7
    repeated 364
    tenths 345
    useful properties 519–20
    working with 518–20
additive identity element 520, 545
additive solution strategies 330–45
    initial counting strategies 331–4
    introducing formal recording 341–2
    mental strategies to 20 334–7
    for two-digit numbers 337–40
additive thinking 200, 321–48
    context for 324–9
    definition 321
    development of 324
    and numeration 323
    and place value 323
    problem solving 345–7
    solution strategies 330–45
    and trusting the count 323
affordances of mathematics 12–20
age-appropriate curriculum 148

algebra 205, 255, 513, 588, 599
algebraic irrationals 513
algebraic thinking 587
    early 256
    and problem structure 588–9
algorithms 520–4, 532–5, 539–40, 545
analysing (critical numeracy) 181
applying measurements 443
approximation 520, 537, 545, 563, 563
area(s) 415, 452, 605–10
    of circles 615–16
    comparing 606
    conservation of 613
    fixed 610
    formula, developing 610–17
    idea for multiplication 368, 371–3, 551–5
    measurement of 440, 452, 606–9
    measurement using non-standard units 606–8
    measurement using standard units 609
    and relationship between perimeter 609–10, 612
    of rectangle 610–13
    teaching sequence 605–6
argument (genre of mathematics) 84, 93, 191
arithmetic
    and algebra 599
    generalised 205
    operations 194–5
    and problem structure 588–9
array(s) 368–71, 374, 376, 392, 550
    rectangular 528, 546
array-based strategy 371, 549
aspect ratio 635
assessment 19, 51, 123–37
    formative 137, 139
    insights from research 125–6
    of learning 124, 126–8
    of mathematics learning 50–2, 674–6
    multi purposes of 125
    peer assessment 134–5
    rich assessment tasks 133–4
    self-assessment 134–5

    summative 128, 139
    today 124–5
assessment for learning 124, 128–37
    feedback 129–32
    interviews 132–3
    observation 136
    peer assessment 134–5
    rich assessment tasks 133–4
    self-assessment 134–5
assimilation 30, 272
associativity 519–20, 545, 559
attribute 213, 442
attributes, comparing 442, 444–5, 452
Australian Association of Mathematics Teachers (AAMT) 57, 58, 63, 126, 667–72, 674
Australian Curriculum: Mathematics 11, 13, 14, 71, 72, 148, 162, 211, 310, 353, 406, 426, 439, 441, 490, 545, 557, 564, 617, 622
Australian Institute for Teaching and School Leadership (AITSL) 667
average and statistics 237–8
averages 654

b

balance strategy 598
Bandura, A. 33–4
Bartholomew, H. 156–7
Battista, M.T. 223, 226, 605, 610–11
Beck, S. 90
Becker, J. 11
behaviour, learning as changing 32–3
behaviourism 32, 44
beliefs 26, 49
benchmarks 193
Beswick, Kim 26, 49, 541–2
Biggs, J.B. 32
binary numbers 271
Bishop, A. 7–8, 11
Black, P. 126
block builder 637
Body Mass Index (BMI) 180
box-and-whisker plots 655
brain development 31–2
brain structure, learning as changing 37

Index

Bransford, J.D. 32, 37
Breed, M. 581
Bruner, Jerome 29, 30–1, 34

C

calculating change (money) 624
calculations, everyday 558
calculators 75, 176, 386, 562
    and scientific notations 502
    and surds 514
Callingham, R. 50, 668
capacity 440, 452, 617–21
    definition 617
    measurement using standard units 619
capture–recapture simulations 660–1
cardinal numbers 266, 284
Carpenter, T.P. 40
Cartesian plane 638, 641, 644
Cartesian product 201, 228, 357, 360, 371, 392, 555–6, 583
causes 470, 488
Cawley, J.F. 151
Cazden, C. 90
Challenger disaster 646
chance 470, 488
chance events, describing 655–63
children's literature and mathematics 95–6, 277, 448
circles 629–30
    circumference and area of 615–16
    as a spacial object 455
circumference of area of circles 615–16
Clarke, D. 48, 58, 60, 61, 125, 148, 521
classification 326
    and geometry 226–7, 272, 457–8, 466, 628
    of shapes 459–60, 628
classroom
    communication, traditional and contemporary 89–93
    working with students with learning difficulties in diverse 149
    see also mathematics classrooms, communicating in the
Clements, D. 188, 223–4, 226, 273, 279, 280, 457, 466
coin recognition and value 624
clock face reading 450–1
closed questions 15, 60, 62, 89, 130–1
closer to 315, 316, 430
Cobb, P. 29, 43, 295, 338

cognitive load 305, 318
collections
    counting large 294–5, 358
    sampling small 476
commas as a separator 311
communication
    definition 15
    traditional and contemporary classroom 89–93
    written 84, 94
    see also mathematics classrooms, communicating in the
communicating mathematically 15, 77–8, 86, 102, 118
    in the classroom 89–96
commutative property 326, 348, 364, 370, 374, 375, 376, 574
commutativity 519, 545, 559
comparing 274, 313–14, 360, 442
    attributes 442, 444–5, 452
    lengths 445–6
comparison
    direct 445, 452
    indirect 446, 452
complex numbers 492, 493, 514, 515
complimentary events 658
composing numbers 193
composite numbers 497
composite units 280, 286, 294–5, 317, 336, 341, 353–4, 355, 358, 363, 376, 392
computation, mental 52, 188, 261, 279, 335–6, 338–9, 365, 383, 522, 523, 524–5, 526, 536, 558, 561–3, 570
computation strategies
    informal 337–40
    multiplication 380–9
computer drawing programs 465
concave 628
conceptions of scale 215
conceptions of units 215
concepts
    exploring 118
    understanding 99–102
conceptual foundations (measurement) 215–16
conceptual understanding 21
concrete thinking 100
congruent 629
conjectures 73
connection 61, 71, 95, 103, 105, 191–2
conservation of area 613
constraints of mathematics 12–20

constructivism 34–6, 272
constructivist theories 29
content knowledge (CK) 55
context 173
    for addition and subtraction 324–9, 348
continuous fraction models 402, 435
convex 628
coordinate geometry 222, 641–2
count-and-match misconception 403
count back 337
count back from, counting up to 333–4
count on 1, 2 or 3 (mental strategy) 334–5
counting 273, 274, 285–6
    count back from, counting up to 333–4
    cover and count on, count on from larger display 332–3
    definition 272
    forwards and backwards 307, 314
    fractions 509
    large collections 294–5, 358
    make-all-count-all 331, 347, 348, 359, 364, 380
    money 624
    role of 198
    skip 364–5
    strategies, initial 331–4
counting-based interpretations
    fractions 406, 407
    multiplicative thinking 358–61, 406
counting numbers 514, 515
cover and count on, count on from larger display 332–3
critical numeracy 179–83, 196
    incorporating across learning areas 182
cubic unit conversions 620
culture 86–9
Curcio, F. 478, 484
curriculum
    age-appropriate 148
    broad rich 148
    and diversity 147–52
    and mathematical thinking 14, 71–2
    measurement concepts in the 439–41
    and numeracy 176–8
    opportunities and challenges across the 177–8

Index

d

data
  definition 234, 475, 488
  investigation 647–50
  measures 654–5
  personal, using 485
  representations 239–40, 476–9, 480, 650–4
  and statistics 234, 237, 475
  summarising 477
  variation 237, 655
Davydov, Vasily 216–17, 274, 278
decimal fractions 410–11, 422–9, 554, 562–9
decimal marker 311
decimal misconceptions 506, 507
decimal place value 426–8
decimal recording 424
decimals 189, 411, 435, 504–5, 518, 536–40
  adding and subtracting 344–5, 537–9
  algorithms 539–40
  approximation 537
  definition 545
  mental strategies 536–7
  notation for recurring 506
de-coding 181
decomposing numbers 193
denominator(s) 404, 435
  related 526
density of the number line 514–15
dependent variables 594
deterministics 473, 488
development and learning 28–32
  brain development 31–2
  Bruner 30–1
  Piaget 29–30
diagrams
  fraction 202, 203, 399, 416–17
  and numeracy 179
Diezmann, C. 64, 158
difference 328, 329, 334, 519, 545
digit 279
digital clocks 450
direct comparison 445, 452
disabilities, learning 161–2
  mathematics (MLD) 145
disability 159
discrete fraction models 402, 435
discrete objects 542–4
distributions
  comparing 484–7
  definition 480, 488
  describing 480
  understanding 480–7
distributivity 559
diverse learners 143
diverse learners, supporting 153–64
  English as a second language 153–4
  gender differences 156–8
  hearing, vision and other sensory impairments 159–60
  Indigenous Australian 154–5
  learning disabilities 161–2
  learning styles 153
  talented learners 158–9
diversifying the curriculum 145–52
  being in the conversation 149
  broad rich curriculum 148
  working with students 146–7
diversity
  language of 143–5
  and learners 143, 153–63
  working with teacher assistants 163
diversity, planning for 580–2
  affective aspects of mathematics 151–2
  expanding the range of offering 581–2
  streaming is counterproductive 580
  taking the first step 581
  why not stream? 150–1
dividend 572
divisibility tests 497
division 557
  formal 567–8
  fraction 200, 569–73
  language of 353
  long 568
  meanings for 550–7
  recording 381, 388
  quotition 366–7, 379
  written solution strategies 386–8
  by zero 496
divisor 557
Dole, S. 525, 536
double-counting 403
doubles, near doubles (mental strategy) 335–6, 348, 376
doubling 361, 377, 561
dynamic geometry environments (DGE) 456, 628, 629, 636
dynamic imagery (geometric thinking) 464–5
dyscalculia 145

e

Early Numeracy Research Project (EYNRP) 57
Earth, location on 642–3
Earth geometry 222, 639–40
effective teaching 48, 57–64
enabling prompts 79, 146
English language learners (ELLs) 277
enlargement 636
enumeration 266
equal groups 363–5, 368
equals, meaning of 259–60
equals (=) sign 205, 206, 259–60, 291–2, 331, 335, 385
equations 588, 598–9
equipartitioning 355, 392
equivalence 259–60, 432–4, 598–9
equivalent expressions 258
Eratosthenes 497
estimation 388–9, 546, 561
  and fractions 520, 526, 537
  and measurement 219–20
ethnomathematics 86, 222, 632
events, chance
  describing 655–63
events, complimentary 658
exercise (mathematical thinking) 70
expanded notation 305
experimental probability 657
exponents 575–6
explanation (genre of mathematics) 15, 19, 36, 84, 91, 93–4
extending prompts 79
extended range of numbers
  exponents 575–6
  fraction multiplication and division 569–73
  integers 5735
  order of operations 560–1
  useful properties 559–60
  whole numbers and decimal factions 561–9
  working with an 557–75

f

factor–factor–product 550, 557
factors 496, 498–9
Faragher, R. 149
feedback 129–32
Fermi, Enrico 196
Fermi questions 615

Index

figure–ground perception 461, 467
fifthing 414, 419–20, 422, 435
flow charts 178
fluency 11, 71
'for each' idea 201–2, 359–61, 363, 367, 368, 370, 371, 392, 415, 417, 418, 419–20, 423, 433–4, 550, 555–6, 582, 583
formal recording 341–2
formative assessment 137, 139
Forrest, M. 173, 179
fraction diagrams 202, 203, 399, 416–17
fraction division 200
fraction models 402
fraction(s) 394–22, 429–34, 506–10, 518, 524–35
    adding and subtracting 344–5, 527–31, 534–5
    algorithms 532–5
    circles 510
    conventional wisdom 404–5
    counting 509
    counting-based interpretations 406, 407
    counting forward and backwards 431
    decimal 410–11, 422–9, 554, 562–9
    definition 435, 506, 546
    developing faction knowledge 411–22
    division 569–73
    equivalence 432–4
    and estimation 520, 526
    how many/how much 413
    knowledge and confidence 411–22
    line segment/number 510
    making sense of 397–411
    many faces of 406–11
    as measure 408, 421
    mental strategies 524–7
    mixed 405, 415, 435
    multiplication 569–73
    naming 429–30
    as operator 409, 421
    and partitioning 414
    as part-whole 403, 407–8, 421
    as quotient (number) 409, 421
    as ratio 410, 421
    rectangles 510
    renaming 430
    splitting-based interpretations 406, 407
    symbol 406, 420–1
    understanding 429–34
Freudenthal, H. 544
functional thinking 256–62, 592–8
functions 257, 394–5, 592–8
    as graphic representations 597–8
    as growing patterns and symbols 592–4
    as mapping 595–7
    as tables of values 594–5
Fundamental Theorem of Arithmetic 498

g

gender differences and learners 156–8
generalisations 545, 587, 592
generalised arithmetic 205
generalising
    definition 249
    mathematical thinking 73–5
    of the number system 260–2
    and sense of number 205–6
geometric measures 211–12, 440
geometric proof 631–2
geometric thinking 454–66
    and dynamic imagery 464–5
    and location 465–6, 641–3
    spatial objects, classifying 455–60
    spatial objects, relationship between 461–4
geometrical visualisation 221, 228, 461–4, 643, 644
geometry 221–2
    branches of 222
    coordinate 222, 641–2
    Earth 222, 639–40
    how it is learnt 225
    learning in the middle years 643–4
    and measurement 211–12, 240
    non-euclidean 639–40
    Piaget and Inhelder 225–6
    and spatial sense 223–8
    theories of learning 225–7
    transformational 222, 464, 632–8
    van Hiele levels 226–7, 229
Golden Ratio 262
graph sense 484
graphical representations 597–8
graphs 116, 179, 598
Graven, M. 668
grids 116
grocery label unit pricing 174–5
groups of 200–2, 203, 206, 301, 329, 363–4, 366, 368, 374, 377, 383, 392, 550
Grouws, D.A. 42
growing patterns 255–6, 263, 590–2
Gutiérrez, A. 223, 461, 462

h

halving 361, 377, 401, 414–17, 422, 435
handicap 159
Hattie, John 150
hearing impairment 159–60
Hiebert, J. 40, 42
Hogan, J. 173, 177, 178, 179
how many 413
how much 413
Huinker, D. 532
hundredths 404, 420, 422–3, 426–9, 510, 511, 536, 556, 571, 575
hunting for stars 159

i

impairment 159
index notation 162, 503
independent variables 594
indices 503–4
Indigenous Australians 87, 112, 154–5, 280, 283
indirect comparison 446, 452
informal computation strategies 337–40
Inhelder, B. 225–6
initial number fact knowledge (multiplication) 381
instrumentalist view 26
integers 501, 514, 515, 518, 540–5, 546, 573–5
    negative 501, 514, 515
interactive media 106–7
interviews 132–3
inverse 256, 257, 263
investigation (mathematical thinking) 70, 78
irrational numbers 8, 410, 506, 512–13

j

Joshua, A. 131
justifying (mathematical thinking) 76, 93–4

k

knowledge
- of content 13–14
- number fact 374–80
- professional (teachers) 667–9
- for teaching mathematics 12, 54–6, 667–9
- types 55

Kutscher, B. 150

l

labels for shapes 458
language
- of addition 325
- and culture 86–9
- of diversity 143–5
- effects on learning 161
- English as a second 153–4
- of mathematics 13–14, 84–9, 111–12
- of measurement 373
- of percentage 512
- person-first 144–5
- of ratio 509
- role of 276––7
- and spatial objects 457–8
- of subtraction 325
- and symbols 591–2

large numbers
- naming 502
- representing 500

learned difficulties 145
learners
- affective aspects of 152
- diverse, supporting 153–63
- and diversity 143, 153–63
- and English as a second language 153–4
- gender differences 156–8
- Indigenous Australian 154–5
- talented 158

learning
- assessing 50–2, 674–5
- as changing behaviour 32–3
- as changing brain structure 37
- as changing social participation 36–7
- as changing thinking 33–6
- definition 27
- and development 28–32
- difficulty/disability 145, 149
- and geometry 225–7
- language effects on 161–2
- and numeracy 182
- mathematics 26–43, 47, 49, 145
- planning 52–4
- rote vs meaningful 550–1
- sequence of measurement 441–3
- styles 153
- theoretical perspectives 47, 64
- and understanding mathematics 38–43

learning environments, multi-representational 117–18
learning mathematics 26–43, 49
learning sequence, measurement 441–3
learning theories 27, 43
Lehrer, R. 215, 617
length
- attribute 444–5
- comparing 445–6
- definition 452
- measurement of 440, 444–8, 452
- ordering 445–6
- understanding 444–8
- using non-standard units 446–7
- using standard units 447–8

length model 599–601
Lerman, S. 35, 36–7
letters 589–92
likelihood of events 471, 488
Lilburn, P. 60
Linchevski, L. 151, 543
line (spacial object) 455
line segment (spacial object) 455
location (geometric thinking) 465–6, 641–3
- coordinate systems 641–2
- on Earth 642–3
- representing 641

logos 461
long division 568
long multiplication 565–7
lowest cost multiple (LCM) 499

m

McIntosh, A. 53, 522
magic squares 544
make-a-whole game 433
make-all-count-all 331, 347, 348, 359, 364, 380
make to 10 and name (mental strategy) 336–7, 376, 561

many-to-one relationship 355
mapping 466, 595–8
maps 178
mass 440, 452, 622–3
materials
- choosing 107–10
- role of 106–7
- strengths and weaknesses 109–10

mathematical representations 15–18, 99–101, 113–16
mathematical thinking 69–80
- in the curriculum 14, 71–2
- generalising 73–5
- justifying 76
- and learners 78–80
- making a start 69–0
- specialising 72–3
- tasks, general processes for 72–8
- teaching 80
- types of 70

mathematical visualisation 160, 223, 229, 461–4, 466
mathematics
- affective aspects of 151–2
- affordances and constraints 12–20
- assessment 19, 50–2
- and children's literature 95–6, 277
- and communication 15, 77–8, 86, 89–96, 102, 118
- conceptual understanding 21
- connections between beliefs 49
- definition 6–8, 26–7
- developing your own theory 43
- describing the world with 88–9
- effective teaching 48, 57–64
- fluency 11, 71
- goals of school 9–12
- knowledge for teaching 54–6, 667–9
- language of 13–14, 84–9, 111–12
- learning 26–43, 47, 49, 50–4, 145
- meaningful contexts 18–19
- nature of 26
- need of 11
- and numeracy 172
- and pedagogy 14–19
- planning learning 52–4
- recording 111–12, 381
- social context 19–20
- student perspective 11
- teaching 13, 48, 49, 50–64, 216–17, 666–77
- teaching philosophy 64

understanding 38–43, 71
mathematics classrooms,
  communicating in the 15, 89–96
    and children's literature 95–6, 277, 448
    communication patterns 15
    traditional and contemporary 89–93
    explanation and justification 93–4
    role of materials and models 106
    written communication 94
mathematics learning difficulties 145
mathematics learning disabilities (MLD) 145
materials and models
  choosing 107–10
  role of 106
mean 328, 654
meaningful contexts 18–19
meaningful learning 550–1
meaning-making 181
measure as fraction 408, 421
measuring devices 442
measurement
  area 440
  apply 443
  capacity 440
  concepts, extending 605
  concepts in the curriculum 439–41
  conceptions of scale 215
  conceptions of units 215
  conceptual foundations 215–16
  definition 212–14
  devices 442
  and estimation 219–20
  geometric 211–12, 440
  language of 373
  learning sequence 441–3
  and length 440, 444–8, 452
  of mass 214, 440
  money 441
  pattern and structure 250
  physical attributes 440–1
  of purity 214
  sense, developing 214–20
  spatial 223–8, 440
  teaching 439
  and teaching mathematics 216–17
  and time 441, 449–51, 452
  understanding 210–11
  units of 213, 217–19
  using non-standard units 213, 217–18, 442, 446–7, 606–8, 618–19
  using standard units 443
  volume 440
  weight 440
media, interactive 106–7
median 238, 654
mental computation 52, 188, 261, 279, 335–6, 338–9, 365, 383, 522, 523, 524–5, 526, 536, 558, 561–3, 570
mental rotation 462–3, 467
mental strategies
  addition and subtraction to 20 334–7
  count on 1, 2 or 3 334–5
  decimals 536–7, 561–3
  doubles, near doubles 335–6
  flexible 195–6
  fractions 524–7
  make to 10 and name 336–7, 376
  multiple strategies for subtraction 337
  whole numbers 561–3
mental models/images 99
mental objects 197, 330
meridians of longitude 640
Middle Years Numeracy Research Project (MYNRP) 57, 191, 395, 580
missing addend 327, 328, 329, 348
mixed fractions 405, 415, 435
mode 238, 654
model (mathematical thinking) 70, 99
modelling 61
models
  choosing 107–10
  length 599–601
  role of 106–7
  strengths and weaknesses 109–10
money 316, 441, 452, 623–4
Moyer, P. 95
Muir, T. 59, 61, 674
multi-digit numbers, strategies for adding/subtracting 342–3
multiplication
  alternative methods of 553
  area idea for 368, 371–3, 551–5
  for division facts 379
  'for each' idea 201–2, 359–61, 363, 367, 368, 370, 371, 392, 415, 417, 418, 419–20, 423, 433–4, 550, 555–6, 582, 583
  fractions 569–73
  equal groups 363–5
  language of 353
  long 565–7
  meanings for 550–7
  number fact knowledge 374–80
  by powers of 10 391
  representations for 201, 372
  written solution strategies 384–5
multiplicative identity and inverse 559–60
multiplicative thinking 14, 351–92
  computation strategies 380–9
  counting and splitting 358–61, 406
  definition 202, 351–4, 549
  importance of 354–5
  initial ideas, representations and strategies 355–73
  number fact knowledge 374–80
  and sense of number 200–2
  problem solving 389–91
Multiplication Toss (game) 375
multiplier 550
multi-representational learning environments 117–18

n

naming convention 503
naming numbers 281–3, 294, 297–302, 309, 429–30, 502–3
Napier, John 504, 553
National Assessment Program–Literacy and Numeracy (NAPLAN) 50, 57, 58, 84, 123, 126–8, 154, 232, 234, 462
National Measurement Institute (NMI) 621
natural numbers 8, 204, 494, 514
negative integers 501, 514, 515
negative numbers 30, 251, 258, 261, 501, 514, 520, 535, 540, 541–2, 543, 544
Niss, 9, 10
non-euclidean geometry 639–40
non-rigid transformation 634–8, 644
non-standard units
  length 446–7
  and measurement 213, 217–18, 442, 446–7, 606–8, 618–19
  measuring area using 606–8
  measuring volume using 618–19
notation
  expanded 305
  index 162, 503
  for recurring decimals 506
  scientific 502–4
number(s)
  absolute magnitude 188, 189, 272, 324

binary 271
cardinal 266, 284
charts 295–6, 299, 302, 304, 315, 337, 380, 425, 427, 581
commas as a separator 311
composing/decomposing 193
composite 497
as composite units 280, 286, 294–5, 317, 336, 341, 353–4, 355, 358, 363, 376, 392
counting forwards and backwards 307, 314
definition 493
fact knowledge (multiplication) 374–80, 381
four-digit 307–9
of groups 550
irrational 8, 410, 506, 512–13
large, naming 502
large, representing 500
learning, research on early 272–5
mental objects for each number to 10 273
multi-digit 342–3
names 281–3, 284, 294, 297–302, 309, 429–30, 502–3
negative 30, 251, 258, 261, 501, 514, 520, 535, 540, 541–2, 543, 544
ordinal 284
origins of 266–71
in other bases 317
part–part–whole knowledge 198, 280–1, 321, 323
pattern and structure 250
patterns and properties 496–500
playing with 275–8
prime 497
properties 496–500
and quantitative reasoning 272–4
rational 404, 435, 504, 518, 546
renaming 309, 314, 323, 425, 430
rounding 315–16
scaffolding solution strategies 287
shapes 499–500
slides 300
and symbols 278, 281–3
and teaching mathematics 216–17
theoretical perspectives 272
theory 496
trusting the count 197–8, 275, 323
three-digit 304–7
two-digit 295, 302
types of 514
whole 310–11, 313–14, 494–501, 514, 515, 562–9
see also extended range of numbers
number line(s) 113–14, 300, 541–2
building the 493–4
density of the 514–15
extending 501
and negative numbers 261
numbers on a 515
number naming sequence 284
number sense
0 to 10 273, 279–86, 292
10 ones as 1 ten 296–7
10 tens is 1 hundred 304
1000 of these id 1 of those 310
beyond 10 286–7, 293
bridging 100 302
four-digit numeration 307–9
developing 197–206
generalising 2056
millions and beyond 310–17
multiplicative thinking 200–2
names for the multiples of 10 297–9
naming and recording four-digit numbers 307–9
naming and recording the numbers 20-99 299–300
naming and recording the teens 301–2
numbers in other bases 317
origins of 187–8
partitioning 202–3
place value 199–200
in practice 188–96
proportional reasoning 204–5
three-digit numeration 304–7
trusting the count 197–8
two-digit numeration 295, 302
understanding 187–8
understanding tens and ones 296–303
writing multiples of 10 306
number systems 101
generalisations 260–2
historical 267–71
numeracy
across the curriculum 176–8
and calculators 176
critical 179–83, 196
definition 169–75, 275
essence of 168
importance of 170–1
and mathematics 172
and socio-cultural contexts 171
numeral 279, 493
numerate
behaviour 170
being 173–4
numeration
and additive thinking 323
definition 268
four-digit 307–9
systems 267, 493–4
three-digit 304–7
two-digit 295, 302
numerator 404, 435
numerical composite unit 295

o

objects, 3D 637
observation 136
Olympic pools/stadiums 443
one-to-many relationship 355
operant conditioning 32–3
operator, fraction as 409, 421
operations
order of 560–1
with indices 503–4
ordering 272, 313, 442
attributes 442, 452
lengths 445–6
ordinal numbers 284

p

painted tyres 222
parallel lines 629
parallels of latitude 640
parallel postulate 639–40
Parmar, R.S. 151
part–part–whole knowledge 198, 280–1, 321, 323
part–whole interpretation (fractions) 403, 407–8, 421
partitioning 130, 188, 198, 202–3, 215, 219, 355, 361–2, 400, 413, 414, 416–17, 420, 423, 429, 432, 434, 435, 570
parts known 326–7, 347, 348
Patilla, P. 234, 237, 239, 241
pattern(s) 249–56
definition 249–50
growing 255–6, 263, 590–2
on the hundreds board 254
importance of 251–5
repeating 251–3

Index

pedagogical content knowledge (PCK) 12, 55, 56
pedagogy 14–19
peer assessment 134–5
percentages 423, 427–8, 510–12, 570–1
perception, role of 296
perception of spatial position 463, 467
perception of spatial relations 463, 467
perceptual constancy 462, 467
perceptual subitising 280
Pereira-Mendoza, L. 476, 479
perimeter 609–10, 612–13
perpendicular bisector 630
person-first language 144–5
personal referents 220
Pi ((π) 8, 279, 439, 512–13, 615, 625, 630
Piaget, Jean 29–30, 106, 225–6, 272–3, 471, 618
place value 290–1, 317, 376
    1 tenth of these is 1 of those 423
    10 ones as 1 ten 296–7
    and additive thinking 323
    charts 114
    counting forwards and backwards 307, 314
    decimal 426–8
    definition 199
    difficulty of teaching and learning 301–2
    four-digit numeration 307–9
    game 303
    millions and beyond 310–17
    names for the multiples of 10 297–9
    naming and recording the numbers 20-99 299–300
    naming and recording the teens 301–2
    numbers beyond 10 293
    numbers in other bases 317
    prerequisite ideas and strategies 291–6
    and sense of number 199–200
    tenths 423–5
    three-digit numeration 304–7
    two-digit numeration 302
    understanding tens and ones 296–303
    writing the numbers to 10 283
    writing multiples of 10 306
planning for mathematics learning 52–4
platonists 26
point (spacial object) 455
point of view 466

polar axis 640
polygon 633
polyhedrons 458
power keys 499
precision 213
predictions 476, 488
Primary Numeracy Research Project 332
prime factorisation 498
prime number 497
probability 232, 473–6, 657
    definition 241–3, 488, 663
    experimental 657
    teaching 242
    theoretical 657
problem (mathematical thinking) 70, 78
problem solving 18, 26, 72, 79, 389–91
    adding and subtracting 345–7
    in multiplication 389–1
problem structure
    arithmetic, algebraic thinking and 588–9
professional attributes (teachers) 669–71
professional knowledge (teachers) 667–9
professional practice (teachers) 672–5
professions 666
Program for International Student Assessment (PISA) 123
prompts
    enabling 79, 146
    extending 147
proof
    concept of 93
    geometric 631–2
    mathematical 76, 84, 93, 519
properties of 0 260
properties of shapes 459–60, 628–30
properties of zero 261
proportional reasoning 13, 113, 201, 204–5, 206, 307, 355, 360, 396, 432–3, 474, 549, 576–9, 582

q

quadrilaterals 628
quantitative information, interpreting and communicating 190–6
quantitative reasoning 272–4
questioning 62–3, 79, 91, 130–1, 150, 233, 472, 473
questions, closed 15, 60, 62, 89, 130–1

quotient (number), fraction as 409, 421
quotition 366–7, 379, 392, 557

r

random sampling 649
rates 549
ratio 549
    aspect 635
    fractions as 410, 421, 435
    language of 509
rational numbers 404, 435, 504, 518, 546
rationals 504–12, 514, 515
    decimals 505–6
    fractions 506–10
    percentages 510–12
ray (spacial object) 455
reals, the 512–15
    density of the number line 514–15
    irrational numbers 8, 410, 506, 512–13
    surds 279, 513–14
reasoning 11, 72
    proportional 13, 113, 201, 204–5, 206, 307, 355, 360, 396, 432–3, 474, 549, 576–9, 582
    quantitative 272–4
reciprocal 559
recording 111–12
    decimal 424
    difficulties 382–3
    division 381, 388
    formal 341–2
    four-digit numbers 307–9
    initial 381
    numbers 20-99 299–300
    symbolic 382
    the teens 301–2
rectangle, area of 610–13
rectangular arrays 528, 546
reflective abstraction 272
region idea 368–71, 374, 376, 415, 434, 550, 551
regrouping 341, 348
Reid, Constance 494
relate to tens 378
related denominators 526, 546
relative magnitude (numbers) 189, 190, 193, 272, 309, 312, 324, 327, 354, 567
renaming numbers 309, 314, 323, 425, 430
repeated addition 364
repeated subtraction 367

repeating patterns 251–3
replacement 659–60
reporting 138–9
representations
　data 239–40, 476–9, 480, 650–4
　definition 239
　difficulties 390
　external 99
　graphical 597–8
　importance of 101–2
　internal 99
　large numbers 500
　linking 258
　making connections between
　　different forms of 191–2
　mathematical 15–18, 99–101,
　　113–16
　for multiplication 201
　and multiplicative thinking 355–73
　multiple 300
　multi-representational learning
　　environments 117–18
　and statistics 239–40
　symbolic 192
　two-digit numbers 295
　and understanding concepts
　　99–102
　use of 61
representations, traditional 113–16
　graphs and grids 116
　number lines 113–14
　tables of values 115–16
representatives 475
research, insights from 125–6
rich assessment tasks 133–4
rigid transformation 464, 632–4, 644
rotational symmetry 464
rote learning 550–1
rounding 315–16
Rowe, K. 90
rubic 134

S

'same as' strategy 378
sample space 656
samples 475–6, 488, 647–8
sampling
　random 649
　small collections 476
Sarama, J. 188, 273, 279, 280, 466
scaffolding 64
Scaffolding Numeracy in the Middle
　Years (SNMY) Project 133, 580, 581
scaffolding solution strategies
　(numbers) 287
scale, conceptions of 215
Schunk, D.H. 32, 34, 37
Schwartz, J. 219, 449
scientific notation 502–4
Scott, P. 173, 174
self-assessment 134–5
Selter, C. 11
sensory impairment 159–60
sequence, number-naming 284
set notation 497
shapes
　classifying 459–60
　labels for 458
　number 499–500
　properties of 459–60, 628–30
　transformations 464
　within shapes 461
sharing equally 358–9
Shaughnessy, J.M. 475, 476, 478–9, 484
shear 634, 638
Shulman, S.L. 12, 22, 55, 667
SI units 621, 625
similarity 634–6
simulations 474, 488, 660
skip counting 364–5
slope 598, 602
social constructivists 36
social context of mathematics 19–20
social learning theory 33–4
social participation, learning as
　changing 36–7
social practice, understanding as a 42–3
socio-cultural contexts and
　numeracy 171
solution strategies, additive 330–45
spatial measures 440
spatial objects
　classifying 455–60
　geometric proof 631–2
　properties of shapes 459–60,
　　628–30
　relationship between 461–4
　spacial objects
　visualisation 461–4, 466, 644
　working with 628–32
spatial orientation 223
spacial position 463, 467
spatial reasoning 223
spatial relations 463, 467
spatial sense 223–8
space (pattern and structure) 250
specialising (mathematical
　thinking) 72–3
splitting-based interpretations
　fractions 406, 407
　multiplicative thinking 358–61, 406
spreadsheets 569
square and cubic unit conversions 620
standard units
　length 447–8
　measurement 213, 217–18, 443,
　　609, 619
　measuring area using 609
　measuring volume using 619
　SI units 621, 625
standards, professional 667
statistical literacy 232–4
statistics 232, 475
　average 237–8
　children's experiences 236–7
　and data 234, 237, 475
　definition 234–40, 488
　representations 239–40
　variation 237
streaming 150–1, 580
structure 249–56
　definition 249–50
　importance of 251–5
students
　with difficulty/disability 145, 149
　with impairments 159–60
　left behind 150
　working with 146–8
subitisation 198, 279, 280–2
subtraction
　automatic recall of facts 334
　context for 324–9
　decimals 344–5, 537–9
　fractions 344–5, 527–31, 534–5
　integers 541–4
　language of 325
　meanings for 327–8
　mental strategies to 20 334–7
　multi-digit numbers 342–3
　for two-digit numbers 337–40
　multiple strategies 337
　non-binary forms 329
　order of introduction 329
　problem solving 345–7
　repeated 367
　tenths 345
　useful properties 519–20
　working with 518–20

subtrahend 337, 348
Sullivan, P. 60, 79, 146
sum 518, 546
summative assessment 128, 139
surds 279, 513–14
symbolic recording 382
symbolic representations 192
symbols 88, 278, 281–3, 390, 406, 420–1, 591–2

t

tables and numeracy 178
tables of values 115–16, 594–5
talented learners 158
tasks
    choice of 60
    mathematical thinking 72–8
teachable moments 61
teacher assistants (TA) 163
teaching mathematics 48, 49, 50–64, 666–77
    affordances 12–20
    assessment 674–5
    community responsibilities 670–1
    constraints 12–20
    curriculum 14
    effectiveness 48, 57–64
    final words of advice 676–7
    knowledge for 54–6
    language of 13
    looking forward 665–6
    knowledge for 54–6
    measurement and number 216–17
    personal attributes 669–70
    personal professional development 670
    planning for teaching 672–4
    professional attributes 669–71
    professional knowledge 667–9
    professional practice 672–5
    standards 667–76
    starting point 216–17
    teaching philosophy 64
technology 11, 14, 21, 53, 160, 588, 601
Telfer, R. 32
tenthing 423, 426
tenths 423–5
tessellations 607, 633
Tetris 463
theoretical probability 657
thinking
    abstract 102–5

additive 200, 321–48
algebraic 256, 587, 588–9
concrete 100
in different ways 69
functional 256–62, 592–8
geometric 454–66
functional 256–62
multiplicative 200–2, 351–5
strings 561
valuing 51
see also mathematical thinking
thirding 414, 418–19, 435
THOANs 560
three-digit numeration 304–7
time
    clock face reading 450–1
    definition 452
    duration 449
    measurement of 441, 449–51, 452
    passing and sequencing 449–50
timelines and numeracy 179
times as many 368–70, 374, 376
times tables 365
trading 341
trading games 305, 329
transformational geometry 222, 464, 632–8
transformation 464
    investigating 633
    non-rigid 634–8, 644
    rigid 464, 632–4, 644
trapezium, area of a 614
tree diagrams 659
Trends in International and Science Study (TIMSS) 61, 123, 126
trusting the count 197–8, 275, 323, 376
turtle geometry 228
two-digit numbers 295, 302
    strategies for 338–40
two-step examples 659

u

uncertainty 469–72
    language of 471–2
understanding
    definition 38
    as an individual activity 40–1
    mathematics and learning 38–43, 71
    number sense 187–8
    as a social practice 42–3
unitising 355, 420, 434, 435, 577–8

units, conceptions of 215
units of measurement 213, 217–19
    non-standard 213, 217–18, 442, 446–7, 606–8, 618–19
    standard 213, 217–18, 443, 609, 619, 621, 625
unknowns 589–92
using (critical numeracy) 181

v

Vale, C. 62, 156–7
values, tables of 115–16
valuing thinking 51
van Hiele, Pierre and Dina 226–7, 457
van Hiele levels 226–7, 229
variables 589–92
    dependent/independent 594
variation 475, 488
    data 237, 655
    and statistics 237
visual discrimination 463–4, 467
visual impairment 159–60
visualisation 14, 147
    developing 228, 461–4, 632, 643
    geometrical 221, 228, 461–4, 643, 644
    language of 223
    mathematical 160, 223, 229, 461–4, 466
    spacial objects 461–4, 466, 644
volume(s) 440, 452, 617–21
    administering drug doses 620
    comparing 618
    definition 617
    formulae 619–20
    measurement using non-standard units 618–19
    measurement using standard units 619
    and relationship between area 617–18
    square and cubic unit conversions 620
von Glasersfeld, E. 34–5

w

wait time 90
walking school bus 183
Watson, A. 61
Watson, J. 182, 475, 476, 481–2, 647, 648, 654

Watters, J. 158, 237
weight 440, 452, 622
Whitin, D. 233
'whole', role of 531
whole numbers 310–11, 313–14, 494–501, 514, 515, 562–9
whole – part known 327–8, 348
Wiliam, D. 126, 132
Willis, S. 173, 197, 275
writing the numbers to 10 283
writing multiples of 10 306
written communication 84, 94
written solution strategies
    decimal fractions 563–9
    division 386–8
    fraction division 572–3
    fraction multiplication 571
    multiplication 384–5
    whole numbers 563–9

Z

zero
    division by 496
    playing with 494–5
    problem with 390–2
    properties of 261, 560